WELCOME TO THE CARIBBEAN

Yes, the Caribbean is famous for gorgeous beaches, but that's not all that lures travelers back year after year. The string of islands that arcs from Turks and Caicos to Aruba includes dozens of individual nations, each with a unique history, cuisine, and way of life. If you want to do more than soak up the sun on a white-sand beach, the Caribbean offers an abundance of sea and shore experiences, from snorkeling off remote cays to sipping cocktails under a palm tree. Whatever you choose, the tropical warmth and relaxed pace guarantee an enchanting vacation.

TOP REASONS TO GO

★ **Beaches:** Nearly every island has a beach that ranks among the world's best.

★ **Resorts:** There's everything from luxurious beachfront hideaways to simple inns.

★ **Water Sports:** Diving, sailing, snorkeling, and kayaking can be enjoyed year-round.

★ **Island Culture:** History and folklore give each island a unique identity.

★ **Nature:** Lush rain forests and mountains make for great hiking and bird-watching.

★ **Parties:** Beach bars, carnivals, and celebrations galore enliven the scene.

Fodor's ESSENTIAL CARIBBEAN

Design: Tina Malaney, *Associate Art Director*; Erica Cuoco, *Production Designer*

Photography: Jennifer Arnow, *Senior Photo Editor*; Mary Robnett, *Photo Researcher*

Maps: Rebecca Baer, *Senior Map Editor*; David Lindroth, Mark Stroud (Moon Street Cartography), *Cartographers*

Production: Angela L. McLean, *Senior Production Manager*; Jennifer DePrima, *Editorial Production Manager*

Sales: Jacqueline Lebow, *Sales Director*

Business & Operations: Chuck Hoover, *Chief Marketing Officer*; Joy Lai, *Vice President and General Manager*; Stephen Horowitz, *Head of Business Development and Partnerships*

Writers: Laura Adzich-Brander, Carol M. Bareuther, Carol Buchanan, Susan Campbell, Julie Schwietert Collazo, Jonique Gaynor, Elise Meyer, Vernon O'Reilly-Ramesar, Ann L. Phelan, Paulina Salach, Jordan Simon, Richard Sitler, Eileen Robinson Smith, Roberta Sotonoff, Jane E. Zarem

Editors: Douglas Stallings, Eric B. Wechter

Production Editor: Elyse Rozelle

1st Edition

ISBN 978–1–101–87999–3

ISSN 2471–9064

PRINTED IN THE UNITED STATES OF AMERICA

10 9 8 7 6 5 4 3 2 1

CONTENTS

CONTENTS

CONTENTS

ABOUT THIS GUIDE

Fodor's Recommendations

Everything in this guide is worth doing—we don't cover what isn't—but exceptional sights, hotels, and restaurants are recognized with additional accolades. **Fodor's**Choice★ indicates our top recommendations; and **Best Bets** call attention to notable hotels and restaurants in various categories. Care to nominate a new place? Visit Fodors.com/contact-us.

Trip Costs

We list prices wherever possible to help you budget well. Hotel and restaurant price categories from $ to $$$$ are noted alongside each recommendation. For hotels, we include the lowest cost of a standard double room in high season. For restaurants, we cite the average price of a main course at dinner or, if dinner isn't served, at lunch. For attractions, we always list adult admission fees; discounts are usually available for children, students, and senior citizens.

Hotels

Our local writers vet every hotel to recommend the best overnights in each price category, from budget to expensive. Unless otherwise specified, you can expect private bath, phone, and TV in your room. For expanded hotel reviews, visit Fodors.com.

Top Picks	Hotels &
★ **Fodor's**Choice	**Restaurants**
	☒ Hotel
Listings	↩ Number of
⊠ Address	rooms
⊠ Branch address	⦿ Meal plans
☎ Telephone	✕ Restaurant
🖷 Fax	⟲ Reservations
⊕ Website	⌂ Dress code
✉ E-mail	⊟ No credit cards
🎫 Admission fee	⑤ Price
⊙ Open/closed	
times	**Other**
Ⓜ Subway	⇨ See also
⊹ Directions or	☞ Take note
Map coordinates	⅄ Golf facilities

Restaurants

Unless we state otherwise, restaurants are open for lunch and dinner daily. We mention dress code only when there's a specific requirement and reservations only when they're essential or not accepted.

Credit Cards

The hotels and restaurants in this guide typically accept credit cards. If not, we'll say so.

EUGENE FODOR

Hungarian-born Eugene Fodor (1905–91) began his travel career as an interpreter on a French cruise ship. The experience inspired him to write *On the Continent* (1936), the first guidebook to receive annual updates and discuss a country's way of life as well as its sights. Fodor later joined the U.S. Army and worked for the OSS in World War II. After the war, he kept up his intelligence work while expanding his guidebook series. During the Cold War, many guides were written by fellow agents who understood the value of insider information. Today's guides continue Fodor's legacy by providing travelers with timely coverage, insider tips, and cultural context.

EXPERIENCE
THE CARIBBEAN

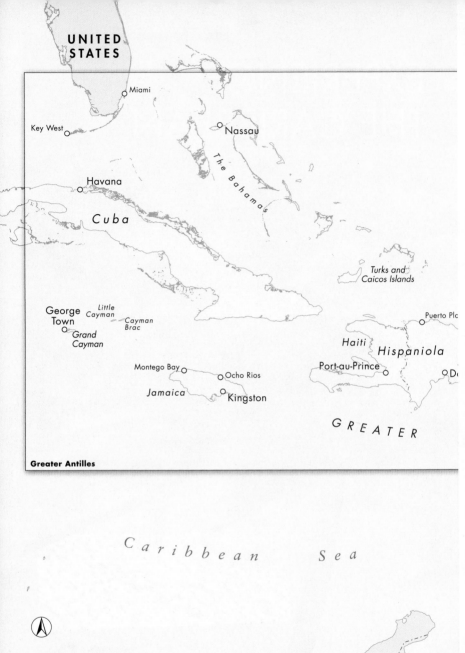

UNITED
STATES

○ Miami

Key West ○

Nassau ○

Havana ○

Cuba

T h e   B a h a m a s

Turks and
Caicos Islands

George
Town
*Little
Cayman*
○ *Grand
Cayman*
*Cayman
Brac*

Puerto Pl○

Haiti   *Hispaniola*

Port-au-Prince ○   ○ D○

Montego Bay ○   ○ Ocho Rios

Jamaica   ○ Kingston

G R E A T E R

Greater Antilles

C a r i b b e a n   S e a

0 _____ 200 mi
0 _____ 200 km

Cartagena ○   **COLOMBIA**   ○ Maracaibo

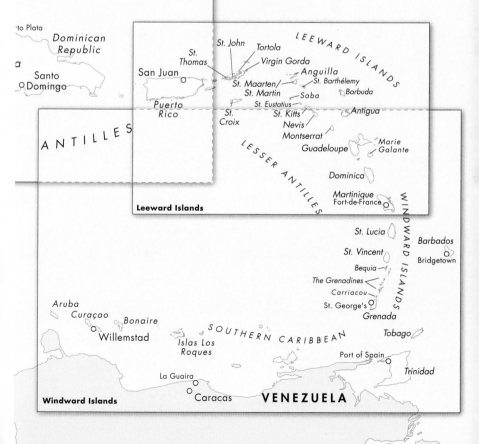

The Caribbean

A T L A N T I C   O C E A N

Puerto Plata
Dominican Republic
Santo Domingo

LEEWARD ISLANDS

St. Thomas
St. John
Tortola
Virgin Gorda
San Juan
St. Maarten/St. Martin
Anguilla
St. Barthélemy
Saba
Barbuda
Puerto Rico
St. Eustatius
St. Croix
St. Kitts
Antigua
Nevis
Montserrat
Guadeloupe
Marie Galante

ANTILLES

LESSER ANTILLES

Dominica

Martinique
Fort-de-France

Leeward Islands

WINDWARD ISLANDS

St. Lucia
Barbados
St. Vincent
Bridgetown
Bequia
The Grenadines
Carriacou
St. George's
Grenada

Aruba
Curaçao
Bonaire
Willemstad
Islas Los Roques
SOUTHERN CARIBBEAN
Tobago
Port of Spain
Trinidad

La Guaira
Windward Islands
Caracas
VENEZUELA

West Palm Beach

Little Abaco

Marsh Harbor

Grand Bahama

Abaco

Miami

Bimini Islands

U.S.A.

Eleuthera

Nassau

Florida Keys

Key West

Cat Island

San Salvaador

Andros

Cay Sal Bank

The Bahamas

Exuma Cays

Rum Cay

Havana

Lond Island

Cuba

Ragged Islands

Crooked Islands

Acklins

0   100 mi

0   100 km

Santiago de Cuba

Guantanamo

Little Cayman   Cayman Brac

Grand Cayman

George Town

Cayman Islands

Cayman Islands
⇨ Ch. 7

Vacationers appreciate the mellow civility of these islands, and Grand Cayman's exceptional Seven Mile Beach has plenty of fans. Divers come to explore the pristine reefs or perhaps to swim with sociable stingrays. Go if you want a safe, family-friendly vacation spot. Don't go if you're on a tight budget, because you'll find few bargains here.

Jamaica
⇨ Ch. 11

Easy to reach and with resorts in every price range, Jamaica is an easy choice for many travelers. Go to enjoy the music, food, beaches, and sense of hospitality that's made Jamaica one of the Caribbean's most popular destinations. Don't go if you can't deal with the idea that a Caribbean paradise still has problems of its own to solve.

Montego Bay

Jamaica

Negril

Ocho Rios

Black River

Kingston

G R E A T E R

C a r i b b e a n

THE GREATER ANTILLES

The four islands closest to the United States mainland—Cuba, Jamaica, Hispaniola (Haiti and the Dominican Republic), and Puerto Rico—are the largest in the chain that stretches in an arc from the Florida Keys to Venezuela. The Cayman Islands, just south of Cuba, are usually included in the Greater Antilles group. We also include Turks and Caicos Islands. Haiti and Cuba aren't covered in this book

Dominican Republic ⇨ Ch. 9

Dominicans have beautiful smiles and warm hearts and are proud of their island, which is blessed with pearl-white beaches and a vibrant Latin culture. Go for the best-priced resorts in the Caribbean and a wide range of activities that will keep you moving day and night. Don't go if you can't go with the flow. Things don't always work here, and not everyone speaks English.

Turks and Caicos Islands ⇨ Ch. 18

Miles of white-sand beaches surround this tiny island chain, only eight of which are inhabited. The smaller islands are reminiscent of some long-forgotten era of Caribbean life. Go for deserted beaches and excellent diving on one of the world's largest coral reefs. Don't go for nightlife and a fast pace. And don't forget your wallet. This isn't a budget destination.

ATLANTIC OCEAN

Mayaguana

Caicos Islands

Little Inagua

Providenciales

Turks & Caicos Islands

Grand Turk

Turks Islands

Great Inagua

Puerto Plata

Santiago

Dominican Republic

Samaná

San Juan

Haiti

Hispaniola

San Pedro de Macorís

Bayamon

Caguas

Port-au-Prince

San Cristóbal

Santo Domingo

Mayaguez

Ponce

Barahona

Isla Saona

Puerto Rico

ANTILLES

Sea

Puerto Rico ⇨ Ch. 13

San Juan is hopping day and night; beyond the city, you'll find a sunny escape and slower pace. Party in San Juan, relax on the beach, hike the rain forest, or play some of the Caribbean's best golf courses. You have the best of both worlds here, with natural and urban thrills alike. So go for both. Just don't expect to do it in utter seclusion.

WHAT'S WHERE

Anegada

St. Thomas
Tortola
Virgin Gorda
Road Town

San Juan
Isla de Culebra
British Virgin Islands

Puerto Rico
Charlotte Amalie
St. John
U.S. Virgin Islands

Mayaguez
Ponce
Isla de Vieques
St. Croix
Christiansted

LESSER ANTILLES AND THE LEEWARD ISLANDS

Smaller in size but larger in number than the Greater Antilles, the Lesser Antilles make up the bulk of the Caribbean arc. From the Virgin Islands in the north to Trinidad and Tobago in the south, these islands form a barrier between the Atlantic Ocean and the Caribbean Sea. The Lesser Antilles are further divided into the Leeward Islands, the northern islands in the chain; the Windward Islands, farther south in the chain; and the ABCs (Aruba/Bonaire/Curaçao), southwest of the Windwards and just off the coast of Venezuela. The Leewards and Windwards are also referred to as the Eastern Caribbean. On any of these islands, the best beaches are usually located on the Caribbean (leeward) side.

U.S. Virgin Islands ⇨ Ch. 19

A perfect combination of the familiar and the exotic, the U.S. Virgin Islands are a little bit of America surrounded by an azure sea. Go to St. Croix if you like history and interesting restaurants. Go to St. John if you crave a back-to-nature experience. Go to St. Thomas if you want a shop-'til-you-drop experience and a big selection of resorts, activities, and nightlife.

British Virgin Islands ⇨ Ch.6

The lure of the British Virgins is exclusivity and personal attention, not lavish luxury. Even the most expensive resorts offer a state of mind rather than state-of-the-art. So go with an open mind, and your stress may very likely disappear. Also go if you love sailing...and island hopping. Don't go if you expect glitz or stateside efficiency. These islands are about getting away, not getting it all.

Anguilla ⇨ Ch. 2

With miles of brilliant beaches and a range of luxurious resorts (even a few that mere mortals can afford), Anguilla is where the rich, powerful, and famous go to chill out. Go for the fine cuisine in elegant surroundings, great snorkeling, and funky late-night music scene. Don't go for shopping and sightseeing. This island is all about relaxing and reviving.

St. Maarten/ St. Martin ⇨ Ch. 17

Two nations (Dutch and French), many nationalities, one small island, and a lot of development—but there are also more white, sandy beaches than days in a month. Go for the awesome restaurants, excellent shopping, and wide range of activities. Don't go if you're not willing to get out and search for the really good stuff.

St. Barthélemy ⇨ Ch. 14

If you come to St. Barth for a taste of European village life, not for a conventional full-service resort experience, you will find yourself richly rewarded. Go for excellent dining and wine, great boutiques with the latest hip fashions, and an active, on-the-go vacation. Don't go for big resorts—and make sure your credit card is platinum.

St. Kitts and Nevis ⇨ Ch. 15

Things are unhurried on lush, hilly St. Kitts and Nevis. And the locals seem more cordial and courteous—eager to share their paradise with you—than on more touristy Caribbean islands. Go to discover Caribbean history, stay in a small plantation inn, or just relax. Don't go for nightlife or shopping. These islands are about laid-back "liming" and maybe buying some local crafts.

ATLANTIC OCEAN

LEEWARD ISLANDS

0   50 mi
0   50 km

Anguilla
West End Village
Marigot
Philipsburg
St. Maarten
St. Martin
Gustavia
St. Barthélemy

Saba
Oranjestad
St. Eustatius
St. Kitts
Basseterre
Nevis
Charlestown

Barbuda

St Johns
English Harbour
Antigua

Montserrat

Grande-Terre
Le Désirade
Guadeloupe
Abymes
Pointe-à-Pitre
Petite Terre
Basse-Terre
Basse-Terre
Les Saintes
Grande-Bourg
Marie Galante

Portsmouth
Dominica
Roseau

Martinique
St Pierre
Fort-de-France

Guadeloupe ⇨ Ch. 10

An exotic, tropical paradise, Guadeloupe is covered by lush rain forest and blessed with a rich Creole culture that influences everything from the dancing to the food. Go if you want to experience another culture—and still have your creature comforts and access to fine beaches. Don't go if you want five-star luxury, because it's rare here.

Antigua and Barbuda ⇨ Ch. 3

Beaches are bone-white and beckoning—there's one for every day of the year—and can be either secluded or hopping with activity. History buffs and nautical nuts will appreciate English Harbour, which sheltered Britain's Caribbean fleet in the 18th and 19th centuries. Go for those beaches but also for sailing. Don't go for local culture, because all-inclusives predominate. Lovely as they are, these islands are more for tourists than travelers.

WHAT'S WHERE

THE WINDWARD AND SOUTHERN ISLANDS

The Windward Islands—Dominica, Martinique, St. Lucia, St. Vincent and the Grenadines, Grenada, and Trinidad and Tobago—complete the Lesser Antilles arc. These dramatically scenic islands face the trade winds head-on. Barbados peeks out of the Atlantic Ocean 100 miles east of St. Lucia. And while not "officially" one of the Windward Islands, it is part of the Lesser Antilles. The Grenadines—more than 30 small islands between Grenada and St. Vincent—are a world-renowned sailing venue. The two-island nation of Trinidad and Tobago is just south of Grenada.

Aruba ⇨ Ch. 4
Some Caribbean travelers seek an undiscovered paradise; some seek the familiar and safe. Aruba is for the latter. On this, the smallest of the ABC islands, the waters are peacock blue and calm and the white sandy beaches are broad, beautiful, and powdery soft. For Americans, Aruba offers all of the comforts of home—including lots of casinos.

Curaçao ⇨ Ch. 8
Rich in heritage and history, Curaçao easily blends quaint island life and savvy city life, along with wonderful weather, spectacular diving, and charming beaches. Dutch and Caribbean influences are everywhere, but there's also an infusion of touches from around the world—particularly noteworthy in the great food. Willemstad is the picturesque capital and a treat for pedestrians, with shopping clustered in areas around the waterfront.

Martinique ⇨ Ch. 12
Excellent cuisine, fine service, highly touted rum, and lilting Franco-Caribbean music are the main draws in Martinique. Go if you're a Francophile drawn to fine food, wine, and sophisticated style. Don't go if you are looking for a bargain and have little patience. Getting here is a chore, but there are definitely rewards for the persistent.

St. Lucia ⇨ Ch. 16
One of the greenest and most beautiful islands in the Caribbean is, arguably, the most romantic. The scenic southwestern and central regions are mountainous and lush, with dense rain forest, endless banana plantations, and fascinating historic sites. In the north, some of the region's most appealing resorts are interspersed with dozens of delightful inns that welcome families as well as lovers and adventurers.

Caribbean

Sea

Aruba
○Oranjestad

Bonaire
○Kralendijk

Curaçao ○
Willemstad

Islas Los Roques

Isla La Tortuga

○**Caracas**

| 0 | 100 mi |
| 0 | 100 km |

VENEZUELA

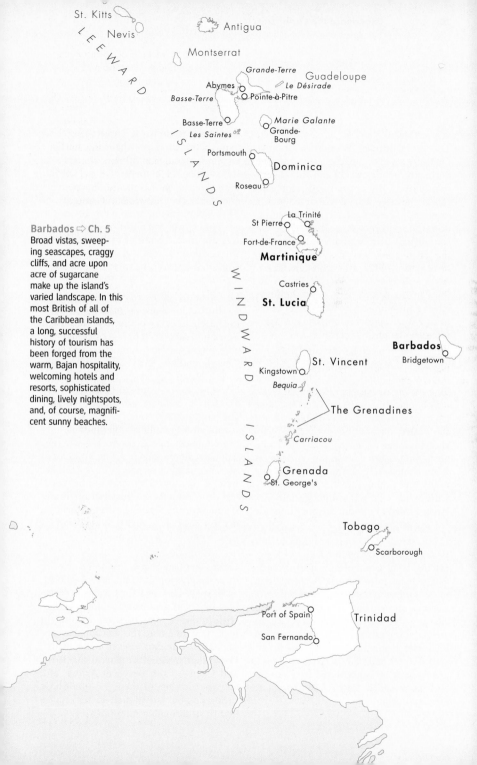

St. Kitts

Nevis

L E E W A R D

Antigua

Montserrat

Grande-Terre

Guadeloupe

Abymes

Le Désirade

Basse-Terre

Pointe-à-Pitre

I S L A N D S

Basse-Terre

Marie Galante

Les Saintes

Grande-Bourg

Portsmouth

Dominica

Roseau

Barbados ⇨ **Ch. 5**
Broad vistas, sweeping seascapes, craggy cliffs, and acre upon acre of sugarcane make up the island's varied landscape. In this most British of all of the Caribbean islands, a long, successful history of tourism has been forged from the warm, Bajan hospitality, welcoming hotels and resorts, sophisticated dining, lively nightspots, and, of course, magnificent sunny beaches.

La Trinité

St Pierre

Fort-de-France

Martinique

W I N D W A R D

Castries

St. Lucia

Barbados

Bridgetown

St. Vincent

Kingstown

Bequia

The Grenadines

I S L A N D S

Carriacou

Grenada

St. George's

Tobago

Scarborough

Port of Spain

Trinidad

San Fernando

CARIBBEAN LODGING

When to Reserve

The most popular properties book as much as a year in advance, particularly during the holiday weeks and school vacation periods, due to the high number of repeat guests—many of whom request the same room every year. Many high-end or popular chain resorts, such as Four Seasons, Ritz-Carlton, and Sandals properties, also book well in advance during peak periods. The most difficult time to find a well-priced room is typically around the Christmas and New Year's holidays, when minimum-stay requirements of one to two weeks may be common and room rates are the most expensive.

But for the typical Caribbean resort, two months is usually sufficient notice. In popular mass-market destinations such as Punta Cana or Negril, a couple of weeks may be enough advance notice. Of course, it's easiest to find an acceptable room in the busiest destinations by virtue of the sheer number of rooms available at any given time. Although waiting until the last minute doesn't always net bargains, flexibility and timing can sometimes pay off with either a deep discount (usually at a larger resort) or a room category upgrade.

Fees and Add-Ons

Every island charges an accommodations tax, whether you stay in a bed-and-breakfast inn, hotel, guesthouse, resort, or private villa, ranging from 7% to 15%. In addition, most Caribbean hotels and resorts tack on a service charge, usually 10%. The service charge isn't quite the same as a tip for service, so it is customary at most resorts (all-inclusives being an exception) to tip the staff. Expect taxes and services charges to add at least 20% above the base rate for a room. So-called "energy" surcharges are also not uncommon.

A growing trend is the "resort fee." You may encounter it anywhere but particularly at large resorts with lots of activities. Resort fees are almost universal in San Juan, Puerto Rico, but are less popular elsewhere. The fee, which can range from $5 to $50 per night, presumably covers the costs of services and resort facilities. Resort fees are more common at larger hotels. These add-ons aren't always mentioned when you book, so be sure to inquire.

Picking the Best Room

On virtually every island, especially at beachfront lodgings, the price increases as the beach access or ocean view improves. You could save $100 or more per night by choosing a garden-, mountain-, or town-view room. But regardless of view, be sure to ask about the property's layout. For example, if you want to be close to the "action" at many larger resorts, whether you have mobility concerns or just need to satisfy your gambling or gamboling itch, the trade-off might be noise—whether from screaming kids jumping in the pool or DJs pumping reggae in the bar. Likewise, saving that $100 may not be worth it if your room faces a busy thoroughfare. If you have any specific desires or dislikes, discuss them thoroughly and ahead of time with the reservations staff.

Types of Lodgings

Condos and Time-Shares Condo resorts are increasingly popular and can offer both extra space and superior savings for families or small groups traveling together, with kitchens, sofa beds, and more. In fact, they dominate the sensuous sweeps of Grand Cayman's Seven-Mile Beach, Provo's amazing Grace Bay in the Turks and Caicos, Palm Beach in Aruba, and elsewhere. Some of these are time-share properties, but not all time-shares require you to sit through a sales pitch.

Inns and B&Bs Historic inns come in all shapes and sizes. The old Spanish colonial capitals of Santo Domingo and San Juan have converted monasteries. Puerto Rico also offers affordable lodgings in its paradors; patterned after the Spanish system, most of them are historically and/or culturally significant buildings, such as old-time thermal baths or working coffee plantations. Longtime sailing and whaling destinations such as Antigua or Bequia in the Grenadines offer their own bits of history adapted to modern comfort, and Guadeloupe and Martinique feature converted sugar plantations. St. Kitts and Nevis, in particular, are prized by Caribbean connoisseurs for their restored great house plantation inns, often with a resident expat owner who enhances your experience with amusing anecdotes and insider insights.

Private Villas Another increasingly popular option for families or those seeking a good bargain are private villas. Self-catering means saving on dining out on more expensive islands such as St. Barth (where villas usually cost much less than hotels), though a car is often necessary. Many villas have private pools with stunning sea views and/or beachfront access.

Hotels and Resorts Most prevalent in the Caribbean are large resorts, including all-inclusives, that are usually positioned strategically on the beach or on a golf course or that may have a theme: couples, families, spa retreat, etc. You'll find familiar chain hotels in all price categories—from Ritz-Carlton to Comfort Suites.

All-Inclusive or Not?

The AI ("all-inclusive") concept is especially prominent in Jamaica, the Dominican Republic, Antigua, and St. Lucia. For those who have only a week for vacation, the allure is obvious: a hassle-free, prepaid vacation that includes accommodations, meals, unlimited drinks, entertainment, and most activities. And you tend to get what you pay for: AIs range from hedonistic, high-tech luxury to bare-bones, beachfront bang-for-the-buck, with prices to match. Some of these resorts are intimate romantic hideaways for couples, some emphasize sporting options, others cater to families, and still others cater to singles ready to mingle in a nonstop party atmosphere.

But there are caveats. Few AIs offer *everything* for free. That spa treatment, the scuba trip, the sunset cruise, or the tour of the nearby plantation may not be included. Moreover, there can be surcharges for dining in some restaurants.

AI resorts appeal mostly to travelers who just want to get away and bask in the sun, piña colada within easy reach. They're not for more adventuresome types who seek genuine interaction with the locals and immersion in their culture—nor are they good for people who want to eat local food, since most AI travelers rarely leave their resort boundaries.

CARIBBEAN PLANNER

Time

The Cayman Islands, Cuba, Haiti, Jamaica, and the Turks and Caicos Islands are all in the eastern standard time zone. All other Caribbean islands are in the Atlantic standard time zone, which is one hour later than eastern standard. Caribbean islands don't observe daylight saving time. During that period (March through October), when eastern standard time is turned back one hour, Atlantic standard time and eastern daylight time are the same.

Money

The U.S. dollar is the official currency in Puerto Rico, the U.S. Virgin Islands, the Turks & Caicos Islands, and the British Virgin Islands. The Eastern Caribbean Dollar is the official currency in Anguilla, Antigua & Barbuda, St. Kitts & Nevis, and St. Lucia. The euro is the official currency of Guadeloupe, Martinique, St. Barth, and St. Martin (French side only). Other countries (Aruba, Barbardos, Cayman Islands, Curaçao and St. Maarten [Dutch side only], the Dominican Republic, and Jamaica) have their own currencies.

On Grand Cayman you'll usually have a choice of Cayman or U.S. dollars when you take money out of an ATM and may even be able to get change in U.S. dollars. On most other islands (other than those that use the euro), U.S. paper currency (not coins) is usually accepted. When you pay in dollars, however, you'll almost always get change in local currency, so it's best to carry bills in small denominations. The exceptions are at airports, which will generally make every attempt to give you change in U.S. dollars, if you wish. Canadian dollars and British pounds are occasionally accepted, but don't count on this as the norm. If you do need local currency (say, for a day-trip to one of the French islands), take money out of a local ATM for the best rate. With regard to the EC dollar, Cayman dollar, Aruba guilder, Netherlands Antillean guilder, and Barbadian dollar, the exchange rate is fixed, so it makes little difference if you exchange your money in your hotel or at a bank (or, indeed, at all). The exchange rates for the Dominican peso and Jamaican dollar can change.

ATMs can be found on all islands, but because of persistent problems with fraud, many American debit and ATM cards may be blocked in Jamaica; on some islands, you'll be given the option of taking out local currency or U.S. dollars. Major credit cards are widely accepted at hotels, restaurants, shops, car-rental agencies, and other service providers throughout the Caribbean. The only places that might not accept them are open-air markets or tiny shops in out-of-the-way villages, but even they will often accept U.S. dollars, albeit at an unfavorable rate of exchange.

Driving

Your own valid driver's license works in some countries, but temporary local driving permits are required in several Caribbean destinations (Anguilla, Antigua, Barbados, the British Virgin Islands, Cayman Islands, Dominica, Grenada, Nevis, St. Kitts, St. Lucia, and St. Vincent and the Grenadines). You can secure the temporary permit at rental agencies or local police offices upon presentation of a valid license and small fee. St. Lucia and St. Vincent and the Grenadines require a temporary permit only if you don't have an International Driving Permit (available from AAA).

Flights

Many carriers fly nonstop or direct routes to the Caribbean from major international airports in the United States, including Atlanta, Boston, Charlotte, Chicago, Dallas, Fort Lauderdale, Houston, Miami, New York (JFK), Newark, Philadelphia, Phoenix, and Washington (Dulles). If you live elsewhere in the United States, you'll have to make a connection to get to your Caribbean destination. It's also not uncommon to make a connection in the Caribbean, most often in San Juan, Montego Bay, Barbados, or St. Maarten.

Some interisland flights will be on small planes operated by local or regional carriers, some of which may have code-share arrangements with major airlines from the United States. Or you can confidently book directly with the local carrier, using a major credit card, either online or by phone.

Some regional airlines may make multiple stops, accepting and discharging passengers and/or cargo at each small airport or airstrip along the way. This is not unusual—nor is the sometimes-unreliable schedule that these smaller airlines may follow. Flights can be late—or even depart early—without apology or explanation. Be sure to confirm your flights on interisland carriers, as you may be subject to their whims: for example, if no other passengers are booked on your flight, particularly if the carrier operates "scheduled charters," you'll be rescheduled on another flight or at a different departure time (earlier or later than your original reservation) that is more convenient for the airline. If you're connecting from an interisland flight to a major airline, be sure to include a substantial buffer of time for these kinds of delays.

TYPICAL NONSTOP TRAVEL TIMES BY AIR		
	New York	Miami
Puerto Rico	3¾ hours	2½ hours
Jamaica	4 hours	1¾ hours
St. Lucia	4½ hours	3¾ hours
Aruba	4¾ hours	2¾ hours

Airlines

Major Airlines: American Airlines (☎ 800/433–7300 ⊕ *www.aa.com*). **Caribbean Airlines** (☎ 800/920–4225 ⊕ *www.caribbean-airlines.com*). **Delta Airlines** (☎ 800/241–4141 ⊕ *www.delta.com*). **JetBlue** (☎ 800/538–2583 ⊕ *www.jetblue.com*). **Spirit Airlines** (☎ 801/401–2222 ⊕ *www.spirit.com*). **United Airlines** (☎ 800/864–8331 ⊕ *www.united.com*).

Smaller/Regional Airlines: Air Antilles Express (☎ 0890/648–648 *in Guadeloupe* ⊕ *www.airantilles.com*). **Air Caraïbes** (☎ 0820/835–835 *in Guyana www.aircaraibes.com*). **Air Sunshine** (☎ 800/327–9900, 800/435–8900 *in Florida www.airsunshine.com*). **Aruba Airlines** (☎ 297/583–8300 *in Aruba*, (599) 9/820–6000 *in Curaçao*, 855/527–8221 *in U.S.* ⊕ *www.arubaairlines.com*). **Bahamas Air** (☎ 242/702–4140 *in Nassau*, 800/222–4262 *in U.S.* ⊕ *bahamasair.com*). **Caicos Express** (☎ 649/941–5730 *in the Turks and Caicos*, 305/677–3116 *in U.S.* ⊕ *caicosexpressairways.com*). **Cape Air** (☎ 800/227–3247, 508/771–6944 *outside U.S. and USVI* ⊕ *www.capeair.com*). **Cayman Airways** (☎ 345/949–2311 *in the Cayman Islands*, 800/422–9626 *in U.S.* ⊕ *www.caymanairways.com*). **InselAir** (☎ 297/582–1200 *in Aruba*, (599) 9/737–0444 *in Curaçao*, 855/493–6004 *in U.S.* ⊕ *www.fly-inselair.com*). **InterCaribbean Airways** (☎ 888/957–3223 *in U.S.*, 649/946–4999 *in Turks and Caicos* ⊕ *intercaribbean.com*). **LIAT** (☎ 268/480–5582 in Antigua, 888/844–5428 within the Caribbean ⊕ www.liat.com). **Mustique Airways** (☎ 347/635–8332 in U.S., 784/458–4380 in St. Vincent ⊕ www.mustique.com). **Seaborne Airlines** (☎ 787/946–7800 in San Juan, PR, 809/563–7070 in Dominican Republic, 866/359–8784 in U.S. ⊕ www.seaborneairlines.com). **St. Barth Commuter** (☎ 590/27–54–54 in St. Barth ⊕ www.stbarthcommuter.com). **SVG Air** (☎ 246/247–3712 in Barbados, 784/457–5124 in St. Vincent ⊕ www.svgair.com). **Winair** (Windward Islands Airways ☎ 866/466–0410 ⊕ www.fly-winair.com).

Ferries

Interisland ferries are an interesting and often less expensive way to travel around certain areas of the Caribbean, but they are not offered everywhere. A few destinations are reached only by ferry (St. John, for example). In most cases, service is frequent (either daily or several times daily).

MAJOR FERRY ROUTES

Ferries connect Puerto Rico with the outlying islands of Vieques and Culebra; St. Thomas with Water Island, St. John, St. Croix, and the British Virgin Islands; the various islands of the British Virgin Islands with each other and with the U.S. Virgin Islands; St. Martin/St. Maarten with Anguilla, St. Barth, and Saba; St. Kitts with Nevis; Antigua with Barbuda and Montserrat; Guadeloupe with La Désirade, Marie-Galante, and Iles des Saintes (Les Saintes), as well as with Dominica, Martinique, and St. Lucia; St. Lucia with Guadeloupe, Martinique, and Dominica; St. Vincent with Bequia and the other islands of the Grenadines; Grenada with Carriacou and Petite Martinique; and Trinidad with Tobago; there's limited ferry service in the Turks and Caicos Islands (Provo and North Caicos,

Grand Turk and Salt Cay). In most cases, service is frequent—either daily or several times daily.

When to Go

The Caribbean high season is traditionally winter—from December 15 to April 14—when you're guaranteed the most entertainment at resorts and the most people with whom to enjoy it. It's also the most fashionable, the most expensive, and the most popular time to visit—and most hotels are heavily booked. You must make reservations at least two or three months in advance for the very best places (sometimes a year in advance for the most exclusive spots). Hotel prices can drop 20% to 50% after April 15; airfares and cruise prices also fall. Saving money isn't the only reason to visit the Caribbean during the off-season. Many islands now schedule their carnivals, music festivals, and other events during the off-season. Late August, September, October, and early November are the least crowded.

CLIMATE

The Caribbean climate is fairly constant. The average year-round temperatures for the region are 78°F to 88°F. The temperature extremes are 65°F low, 95°F high; but, as everyone knows, it's the humidity, not the heat, that makes you suffer—especially when the two go hand in hand. The off-season months, particularly August through November, are the most humid. As part of the late-fall rainy season, hurricanes occasionally sweep through the Caribbean. Check the news daily and keep abreast of brewing tropical storms. The southernmost Caribbean islands are generally spared the threat of hurricanes, although they may experience storm-surge flooding. The rainy season consists mostly of brief showers interspersed with sunshine. You can watch the clouds thicken, feel the rain, then have brilliant sunshine dry you off, all while remaining on your lounge chair. A spell of overcast days or heavy rainfall is unusual.

Hurricane Season
The Atlantic hurricane season lasts from June 1 through November 30, but it's fairly rare to see a large storm in either June or November. Most major hurricanes occur between August and October, with the peak season in September.

AVOIDING STORMS
Keep in mind that hurricanes are rarer the farther south you go. The ABC Islands (Aruba, Bonaire, and Curaçao), Trinidad and Tobago, and Grenada are the least likely to get a direct hit from a hurricane, although it's never a certainty that you'll avoid storms by going south. Grenada, for example, was severely affected by Hurricane Ivan in 2004—the island's first direct hit in nearly 50 years. Similarly, Barbados is less likely to be affected by hurricanes, because it lies out in the Atlantic, all by itself, 100 miles east of its nearest neighbor, St. Lucia. Barbados can sometimes experience heavy rain and flooding in September and October; accordingly, many hotels close during that period.

AIRLINES
Airports are usually closed during hurricanes and flights are canceled, which results in a disruption of the steady flow of tourists in and out of affected islands. If you are scheduled to fly into an area where a hurricane is expected, check with your airline regularly and often. If flights are disrupted, airlines will usually allow you to rebook for a later date. You will not get a refund if you have booked a nonrefundable ticket nor, in most cases, will you be allowed to change your ticket to a different destination; rather, you will be expected to reschedule your trip for a later date.

HOTELS AND RESORTS
If a hurricane warning is issued and flights to your destination are disrupted, virtually every Caribbean resort will waive cancellation and change penalties and allow you to rebook your trip for a later date. Some will allow you to cancel if a hurricane threatens to strike, even if flights aren't canceled. Some will give you a refund if you have prepaid for your stay, while others will expect you to rebook your trip for a later date. Some large resort companies—including Sandals and SuperClubs—have "hurricane guarantees," but they apply only when flights have been canceled or when a hurricane is sure to strike.

TRAVEL INSURANCE
If you plan to travel to the Caribbean during the hurricane season, it is wise to buy travel insurance that allows you to cancel for any reason. This kind of coverage can be expensive (up to 10% of the value of the trip), but if you have to prepay far in advance for an expensive vacation package, the peace of mind may be worth it. Just be sure to read the fine print; some policies don't kick in unless flights are canceled and the hurricane strikes, something you may not be assured of until the day you plan to travel. To get a complete cancellation policy, you must usually buy your insurance within a week of booking your trip. If you wait until after the hurricane warning is issued to purchase insurance, it will be too late.

RENTING A VILLA

In the Caribbean the term *villa* may describe anything from a traditional cottage to a luxurious architectural wonder but almost always means a stand-alone accommodation, often privately owned. Villa rentals provide some of the region's most desirable accommodations from both a comfort and an economic point of view. We recommend considering this option, especially if you're traveling with your family or a group of friends. A villa accommodation provides a lot more space, much more privacy, and a better sense of the island than you would get at a hotel—and usually at a fraction of the per-person cost. Factor in the ability to fix simple meals, snacks, and drinks, and the savings really add up.

What Does It Cost?

Rental rates vary widely by island and by season. In-season rates range from $1,200 for a simple one-bedroom cottage to more than $40,000 a week for a multiroom luxury home. Many full-service resorts also offer villas of varying sizes on their property; although pricey, that can be an excellent choice if you want the best of both worlds—full service and facilities but also space and privacy. In many cases, renting a villa at a resort will cost less than renting three or four individual rooms, and you can still have a waiter deliver your rum punch to a beach chair or enjoy access to a high-tech fitness room.

What's Included?

Villas are generally furnished nicely, have updated bathrooms and full kitchens, and are equipped with linens, kitchen utensils, DVD player, phone, TV, and, increasingly, Wi-Fi access. The sophistication of all of the above is factored into the price; the more luxurious the digs, the higher the price.

Upscale rental villas often have small, private plunge pools (few are beachfront); daily housekeeping service (except Sunday) is included in the quoted price. On some islands, including the Dominican Republic, Jamaica, and Barbados, two or even three staff members are common. Inquire about the villa's staff and specify particular needs or expectations right from the start, including start times and specific or additional duties such as laundry, cooking, or child care.

How Do You Rent?

Some owners rent their properties directly (e.g., ⊕ *www.vrbo.com*, ⊕ *www. homeaway.com*, ⊕ *www.ownerdirect. com*); but in general, we recommend renting a villa through a reputable local agency that both manages and maintains the properties and has an office with local staff to facilitate and troubleshoot on your behalf should something go wrong. Lavish catalogs or websites with detailed descriptions and photographs of each villa can help assuage any concerns about what to expect. The agent will meet you at the airport, bring you to the villa, explain and demonstrate the household systems, and (for a fee) stock the kitchen with starter groceries. Some agencies provide comprehensive concierge services, will arrange or recommend car rentals, and help you find additional staff such as chefs or babysitters or yoga instructors. Some of the larger companies even host a weekly cocktail party where renters can meet each other and form a community to share local information or socialize. Local villa-rental companies are listed and recommended throughout this guide.

1

Choosing a Villa

These days, your hunt will no doubt start on the Internet. A simple search for "villa rental [island name]" will get you started. The tourist board of each island can also provide a list of reputable local rental agents. It pays to seek out reputable companies, especially if you are a first-time renter.

Villa-rental websites allow you to see pictures of available villas; the websites often have a chat feature through which a knowledgeable representative can help you sort through the listings according to your requirements. But use caution: Sometimes the rental agent isn't personally familiar with the villas that the agency is renting. Rather, they consolidate listings from other sources.

Things to Consider When Searching for a Villa

How many people are in your family/group? How many bedrooms do you need? Must they be of equal size? Must all bedrooms be attached to the house? If you are two couples, you might want to specify that you'll need two master suites. If you are traveling with young children, you won't want them in a separate bedroom pavilion. Definitely confirm the types of beds in each room; couples may prefer queens or kings, whereas kids would be happy in single beds. Those looking for a bit more privacy might prefer bedrooms in a guesthouse or small cottage that's separate from the main house.

What location do you prefer? Do you want to be right on a beach? Do you want to walk to town? Will proximity to a particular activity, such as golf or scuba diving, enhance your vacation? Are you willing to rent a car to get around?

What are your requirements for electronics and appliances? Do you require a TV? Wi-Fi? Or would you be okay with something less connected? Do you want a dishwasher? A microwave? How about an outdoor gas grill, or is charcoal sufficient?

Is the villa child-friendly? Ask whether the rooms have direct access to the pool area, as that might not be a safe choice for younger kids who could open a sliding door and enter the pool area unsupervised. Are you comfortable having a pool at all? Most Caribbean villas don't have childproof security gates around pools or pool alarms. If the villa has two floors, are the rooms best suited for kids on the same floor as the master suite?

What specific issues about your destination will affect your villa choice? Personal security may be an issue in some areas of the Caribbean. Evaluate the location of potential rentals in relation to known problem areas—and ask if the villa has an alarm system. A surprisingly low rental rate on an otherwise expensive island could be a red flag.

Will you really be comfortable on your own? The final thing to consider is your relative travel hardiness and that of your traveling companions. Is this your first time in the destination? Do you relish or dread the idea of navigating local markets? Will you miss having a concierge to help arrange things for you? Do you really want to be faced with a sink full of dishes a few times a day? Will your kids be happy without a hotel full of peers? What about you?

CARIBBEAN TOP ATTRACTIONS

Sailing in the Virgin Islands

(A) Whether you set sail from the U.S. or British Virgin Islands, you can easily explore more than 100 islands and cays within a 50-nautical-mile radius. In the British Virgins, you'll find dozens of popular anchorages all along the Sir Francis Drake Channel. In the U.S. Virgins, sailing to and around St. John is the lure.

Hiking in Guadeloupe

(B) In Basse-Terre, the national park provides fascinating adventures. Ramble through lush rain forest, pass by countless rivers with cascading waterfalls, tramp past steaming hot springs, even trek to the peak of a volcano.

Snorkeling the Cayman Islands

(C) Shore diving and snorkeling excels throughout all three islands. At Stingray City sandbar, you can interact with gracefully balletic stingrays—so tame that you can feed them as they nuzzle you and beg for handouts.

Shopping St. Thomas

(D) While Curaçao's Willemstad and St. Maarten's Philipsburg are also known for duty-free shopping, Charlotte Amalie on St. Thomas is like an elegant bazaar. You'll find name-brand luxury boutiques tucked away in its charming historic arcades.

Chilling Out in Anguilla

(E) Whether you choose an ultragrand resort or simple inn, a casual café or a stylish restaurant, you'll always be at or near one of Anguilla's dazzling, often deserted, beaches—powdery white sand, brilliant blue sea, and a palm tree or two.

Whale-Watching in the DR

(F) Samaná in the northeastern Dominican Republic is revered for its shimmering water, champagne-hue strands, and superior sportfishing. But its signature aquatic activity is world-class whale-watching in

1

season (January through March), as pods of humpbacks mate and calve.

Dining in St. Martin

(G) Few places rival St. Martin for fine food. One small fishing village, Grand Case, has become the Caribbean's Restaurant Row. More than 40 eateries line the main beachfront drag, from humble *lolos* (shacks serving heaping helpings of cheap creole fare) to Michelin-worthy kitchens.

Discovering History on Nevis

(H) See the house where Alexander Hamilton was born, view the western hemisphere's largest collection of Lord Horatio Nelson memorabilia and visit (or stay at) the plantation house where he married Fanny Nisbet, bathe in the hot thermal springs where Samuel Taylor Coleridge "took the waters."

Feeling Irie in Jamaica

Reggae, Jamaica's own infectious beat, is everywhere—at festivals and nightspots, of course, but also on the beach, on tours, in taxis, on the street . . . always in the background. Hearing reggae music in the country of its birth will definitely have you feeling good—"feeling irie"—in no time.

Golfing in Barbados

Jamaica, Puerto Rico, and the Dominican Republic feature several splendid layouts, but Barbados arguably offers even more superb greens (albeit for more green) per capita, led by the fabled troika at Sandy Lane, including the Tom Fazio–designed Green Monkey.

History in Puerto Rico

(I) Old San Juan is a maze of cobblestone alleys that open onto broad tree-shaded plazas. Beautifully preserved 18th-century Spanish buildings range from stone mansions with wrought-iron balconies to the UNESCO World Heritage El Morro fortress that guards the bay.

CARIBBEAN TOP BEACHES

Maundays Bay, Anguilla
A dazzling, mile-long stretch of powdery soft sand on the island's southwest coast—great for swimming and long beach walks.

Shoal Bay, Anguilla
One of the world's prettiest beaches—family-friendly yet plenty of room for privacy.

Eagle Beach, Aruba
Bright sunshine, gleaming white sand, crystal-clear water—sunglasses essential.

Bottom Bay Beach, Barbados
The quintessential Caribbean beach—secluded and blessed with an endless ocean view.

Crane Beach, Barbados
A crescent of silky pink sand and ocean in varying shades of brilliant blue, accessible via 98 cliff-side steps—or a glass-walled elevator.

Pink Beach, Barbuda
Walk for miles on champagne-color, soft-as-silk sand with nary another footprint.

The Baths National Park, Virgin Gorda, British Virgin Islands
Swim among a pile of giant boulders, through placid ponds, and into remarkable grottoes at this celebrated site.

Seven Mile Beach, Grand Cayman, Cayman Islands
Dominating the island's west coast, free of litter and peddlers, a sight to behold.

Playa Grande, Dominican Republic
Dramatic, gorgeous, postcard-pretty . . . what more can we say?

Negril Beach, Jamaica
Miles of sand lined with beach bars, open-air restaurants, and resort hotels in westernmost Jamaica.

Playa Flamenco, Puerto Rico
Offshore on the isle of Culebra, the snow-white sand on this beautiful beach is pleasantly uncrowded during the week.

Anse de Grande Saline, St. Barth
Peaceful, secluded, and great for swimming—with a sandy ocean bottom—this is everyone's favorite beach.

Reduit Beach, St. Lucia
Bask in the sun on this long stretch of golden sand—play in the sea at the offshore water park.

Baie Orientale, St. Martin
Often crowded—actually, often crowded with "naturalists"—many consider this beach to be the island's most beautiful.

Half Moon Bay, Providenciales, Turks and Caicos Islands
A natural ribbon of ivory sand joins two tiny, uninhabited cays—explore limestone cliffs, snorkel over an offshore wreck, swim in the sparkling sea.

Buck Island, St. Croix, U.S. Virgin Islands
Truly a national treasure, this offshore island is a must-see—and snorkeling over the amazing reef here is a must-do.

Magen's Bay, St. Thomas, U.S. Virgin Islands
A heart-shape stretch of white sand on a beautiful bay—with a flat, sandy bottom—this beach is perfect (and popular) for sunning and swimming.

Trunk Bay Beach, St. John, U.S. Virgin Islands
A magnet for photographers attracted to its stunning beauty, and for swimmers attracted to the underwater snorkeling trail.

CARIBBEAN TOP
GOLF COURSES

CuisinArt Golf Resort, Anguilla

The Caribbean's answer to Pebble Beach—13 of the 18 holes on this Greg Norman course directly overlook the sea; an ecosystem of ponds and lagoons snake through the course.

Tierra del Sol, Aruba

The island's native beauty—cacti, rock formations, and stunning views—embellish the abundant bunkers and water hazards on this Robert Trent Jones Jr.–designed course at the northwestern tip of one very windy island.

Country Club at Sandy Lane, Barbados

Perhaps the most prestigious club in the Caribbean, golfers can play the Old Nine, with its small greens and narrow fairways, or one of two Tom Fazio–designed courses—the modern-style Country Club Course or the spectacular Green Monkey (reserved for hotel guests and club members).

Casa de Campo Resort, Dominican Republic

The Teeth of the Dog course, one of the resort's three extraordinary courses, is touted as the number-one course in the Caribbean and one of the top courses in the world.

La Cana Golf Club, Dominican Republic

Three 9s—Tortuga, Arrecife, and Hacienda—make up 27 holes of championship golf on this P.B. Dye–designed course at Puntacana Resort & Club—the first course in the Caribbean to use grass seed that can be watered with sea water.

Punta Espada Golf Course, Dominican Republic

There's a Caribbean view from all 18 holes, and 8 play right along the sea at this Jack Nicklaus–designed championship course at the Cap Cana resort in Punta Cana.

Tryall Club Golf Course, Jamaica
Combine first-class golf with the island's storied history at this Ralph Plummer–designed course, beautifully laid out on the site of a 19th-century sugar plantation 15 miles west of Montego Bay.

Four Seasons Golf Course, Nevis
The majestic scenery, unbelievably lush landscaping, and Robert Trent Jones Jr.'s wicked layout incorporating ravines and sugar mills make this experience well above par even among classic golf resorts.

The Golf Links at Royal Isabela, Puerto Rico
One of the most dramatic courses built in recent years, this challenging course features an incomparable setting along the dramatic bluffs at the northwest edge of the island.

Provo Golf and Country Club, Turks and Caicos
You'll find stunning scenery—rugged limestone outcroppings and freshwater lakes—along with immaculate greens and lush fairways at this top-ranked championship course in Providenciales.

Buccaneer Golf Course, St. Croix, U.S. Virgin Islands
You'll have a spectacular Caribbean view from 13 of the 18 holes at this challenging, yet very playable, course on the east end of the island and not far from Christiansted.

IF YOU LIKE

Boating and Sailing

Whether you charter a crewed boat or are experienced enough to captain the vessel yourself, the waters of the Caribbean are excellent for boating and sailing. The many secluded bays and inlets provide ideal spots to drop anchor and picnic or explore. Once deemed an exclusive domain of the rich and famous, chartering a boat is now an affordable and attractive vacation alternative. You'll delight in cruising to a different beautiful beach every day and visiting some of the Caribbean's great yacht harbors, such as:

Antigua. Sailors put in regularly at Nelson's Dockyard, which hosts a colorful annual regatta in late April or early May.

St. Lucia. Rodney Bay Marina, the destination of the annual transatlantic Atlantic Rally for Cruisers, is a premier yachting center that also provides easy access to neighboring islands such as St. Vincent and the Grenadines and Martinique.

St. Martin. Marigot's yacht harbor is a casting-off spot for trips to the nearby islands of Anguilla and St. Barth.

St. Thomas, U.S. Virgin Islands. Chartering a yacht in the Virgin Islands offers some of the best sailing opportunities in the world.

Tortola, British Virgin Islands. The opportunity to sail the length and breadth of Drake's Channel, stopping at intriguing islands en route, makes this, arguably, the best charter destination in the Caribbean.

Diving and Snorkeling

Many people would rather spend their days under the sea than on the beach. Generally, the best conditions for diving—clear water and lots of marine life—are also good for snorkelers, though you'll see less, particularly at wreck sites, simply looking down from the surface. If you aren't certified, take a resort course: You learn the basics in a pool, then do a short dive from shore. Here are some of the Caribbean's best dive destinations:

Anegada, British Virgin Islands. The reefs surrounding this flat coral-and-limestone atoll are a sailor's nightmare but a scuba diver's dream.

Barbados. More than two dozen dive sites lie along the west and southwestern coasts, including 9 sunken wrecks—and 10 more accessible only to experts.

Curaçao. At the Curaçao Underwater Marine Park, divers can explore more than 12½ miles of protected reefs and shores, wrecks, and caves.

Little Cayman, Cayman Islands. More than a dozen dive sites parallel the mile-long underwater ledge at Bloody Bay Wall, which drops from about 20 feet to several thousand feet.

St. Lucia. The underwater reef at Anse Chastanet, near the Pitons, drops from 20 feet to nearly 140 feet in a stunning coral wall; nearby, a spectacular wall called Superman's Flight, at the base of Petit Piton, drops to 200 feet.

Turks and Caicos Islands. The coral reef here is packed with exotic marine life, dramatic wall drop-offs, colorful fans, and pristine coral formations.

Shopping

Whether it's duty-free in St. Thomas, jewelry in St. Maarten, high-end designer fashions in St. Barth, or island crafts almost anywhere, you're likely to come home with a bag full of treasures.

Aruba. Find good prices on gold, silver, and jewelry; but the most interesting finds in gift shops everywhere are hand-embroidered linens, creams and balms made locally from aloe vera, and Dutch porcelains and figurines—even Dutch cheese.

Puerto Rico. From the boutiques of Old San Juan and ateliers of young designers elsewhere in metro San Juan to galleries scattered all over the island, there's plenty to see and buy. You may also consider picking up some hand-rolled cigars in Old San Juan, handmade *mundilllo* lace from Moca, Carnival masks from Loíza and Ponce, or *santos* (small carved figures of saints or religious scenes) created in the southwestern village of San Germán.

St. Barthélemy. Without a doubt, the shopping here for luxury goods and fashion is the best in the Caribbean. The prices here—all duty-free—are high but still less than what you'd pay in, say, Paris or St-Tropez.

St. Maarten/St. Martin. Hundreds of duty-free shops in Philipsburg make the Dutch side of the island the best in the Caribbean for bargain hunters, especially for high-quality jewelry and perfumes. Marigot, on the French side, has its fair share of boutiques with both locally made and French imported goods.

St. Thomas, U.S. Virgin Islands. The winding streets and alleys in Charlotte Amalie, the Caribbean's biggest cruise port, are lined with duty-free shops that sell everything from rum to designer fashions and gems.

Nightlife

Steel drums, limbo dancers, and jump-ups are ubiquitous in the Caribbean. Jump-ups? Simple. You hear music, jump up, and dance. Or just indulge in the art of "liming," which can mean anything from playing pool or dominoes to engaging in heated political debate or simply hanging out with friends.

Antigua. The fun begins at Shirley Heights Lookout on Sunday afternoons, when locals and tourists alike gather to barbecue, watch the sunset, and enjoy the music.

Aruba. Aruba has a vibrant nighttime scene, including a number of casinos that attract both high- and low-rollers. You definitely do not have to wait until spring to break free here.

Barbados. Oistins Fish Fry is the place to be on Friday evenings, when this little fishing village becomes a lively and convivial outdoor street party.

Dominican Republic. Merengue and salsa are part of the culture here. It's never a question of *whether* to go dancing but *where* to go. There's no better place to party than Santo Domingo.

Jamaica. Reggae Sumfest, held in July, is the island's big summer music festival. All year long, Montego Bay's so-called Hip Strip and Negril's Norman Manley Boulevard are lined with bars and clubs that keep things hopping until late.

Puerto Rico. With a full range of bars, nightclubs, and every form of entertainment, San Juan is a city that never sleeps.

St. Lucia. Family-friendly street parties are a main attraction here. The biggest one, the Gros Islet Jump-Up, is a Friday-night ritual in which locals and visitors alike enjoy music, street food, and drinks. Alternatively, Anse La Raye "Seafood Friday" focuses mainly on food, but there's a fair share of drink and music, too.

St. Maarten/St. Martin. There's lots of evening and late-night action in St. Maarten; the island's casinos—all 13 of them—are on the Dutch side of this two-nation island.

IF YOU WANT

To Take It Easy on Your Wallet

The Caribbean isn't all about five-star resorts. You may want to save some of your vacation cash to eat in an elegant restaurant or shop for the perfect gift. Saving money in the Caribbean doesn't have to mean sacrificing comfort. Sometimes it just means choosing a less-expensive island, such as the Dominican Republic, Saba, or Dominica. Most islands, though, have some inns and resorts where you can pay much less and still have a great time.

Bay Gardens Beach Resort, St. Lucia. One of three Bay Gardens properties in Rodney Bay known for their friendly hospitality, this family-friendly hotel has a prime location on beautiful Reduit Beach—with a huge "inflatable" water park just offshore.

Carringtons Inn, St. Croix, U.S. Virgin Islands. A stay at this spacious B&B harks back to a gentler time, when people spent the winter, rather than a week, in the Caribbean.

Coco Palm, St. Lucia. Rodney Bay is a beehive of activity, and this popular hotel is definitely the honey—comfortable rooms, amenities you'd expect at pricier resorts, a good restaurant, and nightly entertainment.

The Horny Toad, St. Maarten. Overlooking Simpson Bay, this marvelous little guesthouse with a funky name offers the island's best value for those who want to keep costs down.

Rockhouse Hotel, Jamaica. Perched on the cliffs of Negril's West End, unique bungalows blend comfort and rustic style. Regular rooms keep costs down; but if you want to spend a bit more, the dramatic villas are worth every penny.

Siboney Beach Club, Antigua. This beachfront oasis is nestled in a tranquil corner of Dickenson Bay. Service is warm and friendly, and the surroundings are natural and secluded.

To Have the Perfect Honeymoon

Swaying palms, moonlit strolls on the beach, candlelit dinners . . . no wonder the Caribbean is a favorite honeymoon destination. You can certainly find whatever you're looking for in a honeymoon—seclusion or active fun—and it will usually be on a perfect beach. Be pampered or left alone, stay up late or get up with the sun, get out and stay active or simply rest and relax, near the action or remote. Our favorites run the gamut; whatever your pleasure, we have the perfect spot.

Sandals Grande St. Lucian Spa & Beach Resort, St. Lucia. Big, busy, and all-inclusive, this resort is a favorite of young honeymooners—particularly for its complimentary weddings.

The Somerset, Providenciales, Turks and Caicos Islands. Provo's most beautiful resort is more focused on your comfort than on attracting a celebrity clientele, so "regular folks" always feel at home.

Sugar Beach, A Viceroy Resort, St. Lucia. You'll be hard put to find a more romantic spot. The resort's magnificent villas are tucked into dense tropical foliage that spills down a steep valley right between the Pitons. It's the most dramatic 192 acres in St. Lucia.

To Eat Well

Caribbean food is a complex blend of indigenous, African, and colonial influences. Native tubers such as yuca and dasheen, leafy vegetables like callaloo, herbs such as cilantro, and spices such as nutmeg and cinnamon recur in most island cuisines. Africans contributed plantains, yams, and pigeon peas. The Spanish introduced rice, and British seamen brought breadfruit from the South Pacific. Chefs in many of the Caribbean's finest restaurants—and there are many that are world-class—make local produce and spices the focal point of their dishes. Here are some of our favorite Caribbean restaurants:

Banana Tree Grille, St. Thomas, U.S. Virgin Islands. The eagle's-eye view of the Charlotte Amalie harbor from this breeze-cooled restaurant is as fantastic as the food.

Blue by Eric Ripert, Grand Cayman, Cayman Islands. Grand Cayman's best restaurant is brought to you by one of New York's finest chefs.

Boston Jerk Centre, Jamaica. To enjoy the best Jamaican jerk in the place where it was invented, the place to go is this collection of open-air jerk pits on Boston Beach in Port Antonio.

The Cliff, Barbados. Chef Paul Owens's mastery is the foundation of one of the finest dining experiences in the Caribbean, with prices to match.

Coral Grill, Nevis. The steak house at the Four Seasons Nevis is stunning and a memorable place to dine.

Coyaba Restaurant, Providenciales, Turks and Caicos Islands. This posh eatery is one of the island's most romantic and inviting places to dine—especially in the garden, under the stars.

Iguane Café, Guadeloupe. Unquestionably original cuisine with influences from around the world, the menu here is dramatic, always evolving, and delicious.

Le Tastevin, St. Martin. In the heart of Grand Case, Le Tastevin is on everyone's list of favorites.

Le Ti St. Barth, St. Barthélemy. Capture the funky, sexy spirit of the island at this wildly popular hilltop hot spot—especially when there's a cabaret show.

Marmalade, Puerto Rico. Old San Juan's hippest and finest restaurant, Marmalade's inventive menu is California-French.

Rainforest Hideaway, St. Lucia. A little ferry whisks you across pretty Marigot Bay to dine alfresco, on the waterfront, under a starry sky.

WEDDINGS

The Caribbean has become one of the most popular venues for destination weddings. Many resorts offer attractive packages for couples to create their ultimate island-paradise wedding. As an added bonus, many islands and resorts either provide or will recommend an experienced wedding planner. Some will even lend you a dress! So whether you picture an intimate beachfront ceremony for two or a full-blown affair, you can confidently leave the details to a professional and simply concentrate on exchanging your vows.

Finding a Wedding Planner

Hiring a wedding planner to handle all the logistics—from the preliminary paperwork right down to the final toast—allows you to relax and truly enjoy your big day. The best planners will advise you about legalities (residency requirements, fees, etc.), help organize the marriage license, and hire the officiant—plus arrange for venues, flowers, music, refreshments, or anything else your heart desires. Planners typically have established relationships with local vendors and can bundle packages with them, which can save you money. Many resorts have on-site wedding coordinators. But there are also many independents available, including those who specialize in certain types of ceremonies—by locale, size, religious affiliation, and so on. Island tourism boards often maintain an online list of names, and a simple "Caribbean weddings" Google search will yield scores more. What's important is that you feel *comfortable* with your coordinator. Ask for references—and call them. Share your budget. Ask how long they've been in business, how much they charge, how often you'll meet with them, and how they select vendors. Above all, request a detailed list—in writing—of what they'll provide. If your vision of the dream wedding doesn't match that vendor's services, try someone else.

Making It Legal

Your goal is to tie the knot, not get tied up in red tape. So it is important to be mindful of the legalities involved. Specifics vary widely, depending on the type of ceremony you want (civil ones are invariably less complicated than religious services) and the island where you choose to wed. In the Dominican Republic, for example, key documents must be submitted in Spanish: unless you enlist a translator, your wedding will be conducted in Spanish, too. On the French-speaking islands (Guadeloupe, Martinique, St. Barth, and St. Martin), language issues are further compounded by stringent residency requirements, which can make marrying there untenable.

There are, however, **standard rules** that apply throughout the islands:

Most places will expect you to produce valid passports and a certified copy of your birth certificates as proof of identification when applying for a marriage license (the exceptions being Puerto Rico and the U.S. Virgin Islands, where a government-issued picture ID will suffice for American citizens).

If either partner is under 18 years old, parental consent is generally required; in some cases (e.g., Puerto Rico), the parents of minors must be present.

If either partner is divorced, the original (or certified) divorce or annulment decree is required.

If either is a widow or widower, an original death certificate is required. (In certain locales, an *apostille* stamp confirming the authenticity of such documents must be attached.)

ISLAND	COSTS	WAITING PERIOD	GOOD TO KNOW
Anguilla ⊕ ivisit anguilla.com/ weddings	License and stamp fee, $284 ($40 if one partner resides in Anguilla for at least 15 days)	At least two business days to process license	Two witnesses are required in addition to the marriage officer.
Antigua ⊕ www. antigua-barbuda. org/agmarr01.htm	License, $150; marriage officer's fee, $50; registration, $40	None	Couples landing in Antigua after 3 pm won't have enough time to get a license from the Ministry of Justice and wed the same day. Also, planning a church ceremony will take extra time.
Aruba ⊕ www. aruba.com/ aruba-vacations/ weddings-honeymoons	License, $80 during office hours; $200 on Sat. or after hours	None, provided all documents are submitted at least one month in advance	A civil ceremony must first take place in Oranjestad's historic City Hall; a ceremony may then take place on the beach, church, or other venue of choice. Using a wedding coordinator is advised on Aruba.
Barbados ⊕ www. visitbarbados.org/ weddings	License, $50 plus $7 stamp fee. Separate magistrate and court fees for civil ceremonies at the court, $63; at alternative venues, $175	None	All fees must be paid in cash. Couples may wait at the Ministry of Home Affairs in Wildey, St. Michael, for the license to be processed, but both parties must be present to take the oath.
British Virgin Islands ⊕ www. bvitourism.com/ rules-requirements	Special license, $220; ordinary license, $120; marriage celebrated in the Registrar's Office in Tortola, $120; marriage celebrated outside the Registrar's Office or by a civil marriage officer, $220	One business day for a special license; 15 days or more for an ordinary license	You'll need two witnesses present when you sign your license application. They can be different from those in the ceremony. Don't be late for a wedding somewhere other than the Registrar's Office; there's a $75 late fee if you keep the Registrar General waiting!

ISLAND	COSTS	WAITING PERIOD	GOOD TO KNOW
Cayman Islands ⊕ www. caymanvows.ky	License, $250	None	When applying for a license, you must present a letter from the marriage officer who will officiate (obtain a list from the Passport and Corporate Services Office).
Curaçao ⊕ www. curacao.com/ en/directory/ plan/getting-married/license-requirements	License, $308	Couple must be on the island three days before applying for license.	Curaçao is a stickler for paperwork, so hiring a wedding consultant is advised. Documents, which must be original, recent, and apostille-stamped, must be submitted at least two months in advance.
Dominican Republic ⊕ www. godominican-republic.com	Combined fees, $450	Notice of the intended marriage must be published before ceremony.	Both partners must present their legal documents (translated into Spanish) at a Dominican consulate. All paperwork should be submitted at least six months in advance. Relatives may not be witnesses.
Jamaica ⊕ www. visitjamaica.com/ weddings-and-honeymoons	License, $50	24 hours	Accommodating laws and couples-only resorts make Jamaica a top pick. Some all-inclusives offer complimentary weddings, complete with officiant and license.
Nevis ⊕ www. nevisisland.com/ weddings	Application, $20; license, $80	None	Application forms must be completed before a justice of the peace. If you've never been married, present a notarized affidavit of single status or pay an extra $20 to have one prepared on Nevis.
Puerto Rico ⊕ www.see puertorico.com/ en/experiences/ lifestyle/weddings	License and stamp fees, $150	None	Nonresidents must submit an affidavit that the sole purpose of the visit to Puerto Rico is to get married. Also, each partner must submit to the Demographic Registry Office a medical certification indicating that you meet all the required tests for marriage back in your place of residence. The certification is valid for 10 days.

ISLAND	COSTS	WAITING PERIOD	GOOD TO KNOW
St. Kitts ⊕ stkitts tourism.kn/love-st-kitts-weddings-honeymoons.php	License, $75	None	Civil weddings are performed only from 8 to 6. Church weddings may be held 6 to 6.
St. Lucia ⊕ stlucia now.com/live/weddings	License, $125 for standard; $200 for special (same day); registrar and certificate fees, $60	None with a special license, three days with a standard license	St. Lucia, a leader in the destination wedding biz, has a streamlined process that makes marrying easy. Most lodgings have enticing packages and on-site planners.
St. Maarten ⊕ wwwsintmaarten gov.org	Combined cost of the license, civil ceremony, marriage book, certificate, and stamps ranges from $183 to $4,410, depending on the day and location of wedding.	Couples must submit a notice of intent to marry at least 14 days before the wedding date.	It is easier to marry in St. Maarten compared with St. Martin, although there's still a lot of detailed paperwork—and you'll need six witnesses for a ceremony performed other than in the Marriage Hall. French St. Martin requires translated documents, and requirements vary depending on the citizenships of the couple.
Turks and Caicos ⊕ www.turks andcaicostourism. com/ weddings/ marriage-license-requirements-turks-and-caicos	License, $250; special license for cruise-ship passengers, $50 additional	48 hours on island; cruise-ship passengers with a special license may be married the same day of arrival.	The marriage is registered here. To have it registered in your home country, you must make special arrangements.
U.S. Virgin Islands ⊕ www. visitusvi.com/plan_ events/weddings_ honeymoons/ stcroix	Marriage application and license fee $100; officiating fee, $200 if married by a judge.	Eight days from receipt of application	Applicants must appear personally before the Clerk of the Court to have the application notarized prior to picking up the license, also in person. Fees must be paid in cash, certified check, or money order. Marriages in court are performed Monday–Friday, except holidays. No shorts allowed in court!

KIDS AND FAMILIES

Choosing a Place to Stay

Many resorts, except those that are exclusively for adults or couples, offer kids-free promotions, special restaurant menus, and programs for tots on up to teens.

Let them entertain you. If you prefer to relax while the kids are entertained, choose a major resort with all-inclusive meal plan and kids' program. For example, **Beaches Resorts** in Providenciales, Turks and Caicos, and in Ocho Rios and Negril, Jamaica, offer kids' programs to match all ages from toddler to teen, outdoor playgrounds, gaming centers, field trips for ages 12 and up such as snorkeling and scuba diving, and *Sesame Street* character appearances. **Hyatt Regency Aruba Beach Resort & Casino** features Camp Hyatt, where kids ages 3 to 12 can participate in a variety of activities and adventures. **Club Med Punta Cana**, in the Dominican Republic, offers a baby gym, Crayola arts-and-crafts programs, hip-hop dance instruction, Petite Chef (ages 3 to 7) cooking classes, and the Ramp, an interactive club for 14- to 17-year-olds. The children's program at **Four Seasons Resort Nevis** offers cake baking, croquet, sea turtle–watch, beach walks, and a supervised lizard hunt—along with story time, a playground with a pirate ship and tree house, a children's menu, even kid-size bathrobes in the bedroom. And at **Coconut Bay Beach Resort & Spa** in St. Lucia, where half the 85-acre resort is reserved for families, Cocoland Kidz Club (infant–12 years) features a pirate ship, mini zip line, mini rock wall, a water park with a lazy river and exciting waterslides—but the whole family is involved in "fun nights," with music, dancing, movies, and more.

DIY. If you'd prefer more of a home base from which to explore the island on your own, choose a family-friendly hotel, condo, or villa near the attractions you'd most like to visit. Condos and villas provide an at-home atmosphere with full kitchens and separate bedrooms, and many include home entertainment systems.

Top Attractions

Museums. In Kingston, Jamaica, teenagers may enjoy the **Bob Marley Museum.** The former home of the late, great, king of reggae music—painted Rastafarian red, yellow, and green—is filled with Marley's personal memorabilia. A 15-minute video presents the singer's life story, along with familiar music clips. The **Barbados Museum** has a Children's Gallery with interactive exhibits on the island's Amerindian past, British colonialism, the development of the sugar industry, and island social life. The most fun: a "dress-up corner," where kids can don the garb of a Zouave soldier, an African prince, or a mulatto girl with full headgear.

Fortresses. A long grassy walk leads up to the 500-year-old **Castillo del Morro** (El Morro) Castle, an imposing structure in Puerto Rico's Old San Juan that looks like the Wicked Witch's scary fortress. Venture inside the thick walls and cruise the ramparts, tunnels, and dungeons. Wax mannequins model historic battle uniforms, and a video shows the history of building and defending this stronghold. Equally imposing is St. Kitts's **Brimstone Hill**, known as the Gibraltar of the West Indies. Ft. George, which sits atop the hill, is built of 7-foot-thick walls of black volcanic stone. Kids can woefully imagine being imprisoned here during a "time-out." From high atop the fort's cannon ways, kids can search the horizon for the islands of Nevis, Montserrat, Saba, St. Maarten/St. Martin, and St. Barth. It's also fun to try spotting the scampering green monkeys that play along the nature trails that wind around this 38-acre site.

Caves. An electric tram takes you into and through Barbados's **Harrison's Cave**, where specially lighted caverns illuminate the stalactites, stalagmites, and underground waterfalls so the caves don't seem too spooky (or confining!). The **Hato Caves** in Curaçao date back to the Ice Age; but today, instead of cavemen, the inhabitants are long-nose fruit bats. The Puerto Rico's **Rio Camuy Cave Park** tour begins with a short video and then a trolley ride right to the mouth of the cave. Though 200 feet high, the cave is only half a mile long. The walking tour is level and flat, allowing kids' eyes to roam all over without fear of stumbling.

Zoos. Roam freely with the animals at the **Barbados Wildlife Reserve.** This outdoor zoo keeps kids engaged as they walk along shady pathways and spot exotic animals, reptiles, and birds in their natural habitat. There are land turtles, fine-feathered peacocks, green monkeys, parrots, and even a caiman (who does not roam free!). After exploring outside, kids can check out the walk-in aviary and the many natural-history exhibits. On Grand Cayman, **Cayman Turtle Farm** is a marine theme park with tanks and ponds full of turtles; kids can touch and pick up the creatures, swim and snorkel among them, and learn about conservation, too. The **Emperor Valley Zoo,** named for Trinidad's native blue butterflies, is one of the best in the Caribbean. The island's president and prime minister both have houses on this site; but most intriguing for kids is the 8-acre zoo that is filled with birds and other wildlife from the region, ranging from blue-and-gold macaws and small red brocket deer to giant anacondas. Not exactly a zoo, but

Butterfly Farm—a beautiful garden filled with fluttering butterflies from around the world—has sites in Aruba, St. Martin, and St. Thomas. View, firsthand, the life cycle of these amazing insects from egg to caterpillar to butterfly—it's a fascinating experience for the whole family.

Aquariums. Coral World Ocean Park, on St. Thomas, is an interactive aquarium and water-sports center that has a 2-acre dolphin habitat, as well as several outdoor pools where you can pet baby sharks, feed stingrays, touch starfish, and view endangered sea turtles. You can also Snuba, swim with a sea lion, and view an 80,000-gallon coral reef exhibit. **Ocean World Adventure Park**, in Puerto Plata, Dominican Republic, has interactive marine and wildlife programs, including dolphin and sea lion shows, a tropical reef aquarium, stingrays, shark tanks, and more.

Fun parks. Kids will love **Kool Runnings Adventure Park** in Negril, Jamaica, which has 10 waterslides and a ¼-mile lazy-river float ride, as well as a go-kart track and kayaking. There are also outdoor laser combat games, bungee jumping, a "kool kanoe" adventure, a wave pool, and paintball. At Reduit Beach in St. Lucia, Splash Island Water Park is an open-water sports park with colorful, inflatable, modular features that include a trampoline, climbing wall, swing, slide, hurdles, and more. It's thrilling for kids and adults—but mostly kids—and a lifeguard is on duty.

FLAVORS OF THE CARIBBEAN

As an entry point to the New World, the Caribbean presents a rich and diverse culinary history. The blending of Spanish, African, East Indian, French, English, and Dutch influences has resulted in a cuisine that focuses on fresh, local ingredients and bold, spicy flavors and seasonings.

Local produce is varied and includes both familiar and unfamiliar vegetables (lima beans, pigeon peas, corn, yams, sweet potatoes, breadfruit, plantains, cassava, callaloo, christophene/chayote, and taro) and familiar and unfamiliar fruits (citrus, mangoes, bananas, melons, pineapple, guava, coconut, papaya, passion fruit, soursop, mammy apples, and tamarinds). Rice and beans are often seasoned with curry, cilantro, soy sauce, or ginger. The hot and spicy "jerk" style of preparing meat, fish, and fowl is prevalent. Barbecued chicken (legs, especially) is nearly everywhere. Fresh-caught seafood is ubiquitous. Modern menus don't stray far from tradition, opting instead for clever twists rather than reinvention—perhaps spiking black beans with tequila and olive oil or flavoring rice with coconut and ginger. No matter your culinary curiosities, plan on a well-seasoned eating adventure.

THE ISLANDS' GLOBAL FLAVOR

Island cuisine developed through waves of wars, immigration, and native innovations from the 15th century through the mid-19th century. Early Amerindian native peoples, the Arawaks and the Caribs, are said to have introduced chili peppers as a spice, a preparation that remains a hallmark of Caribbean cuisine. Pepper pot stew was a staple for the Caribs, who would make the dish with cassareep, a savory sauce made from cassava. The stew featured wild meats (possum, wild pig, or armadillo), squash, beans, and peanuts, which were added to the cassareep and simmered in a clay pot. The dish was traditionally served to guests as a gesture of hospitality. Today's recipes substitute meats like pig trotters, cow heel, or oxtail. After Columbus's discovery of the New World, European traders and settlers brought new fruits, vegetables, and meats to the islands—and, of course, African slaves and indentured servants with their own culinary traditions. Everyone, whether settler or trader, servant, or slave, brought something to expand the palette of flavors. Although Caribbean cooking varies from island to island, trademark techniques and spices unite the cuisine.

African Ingredients. The African slave trade that began in the early 1600s introduced foods from West Africa, including yams, okra, plantains, pigeon peas, and oxtail to the islands. Slave cooks often had to make do with root vegetables ("provisions") combined with plantation leftovers and scraps, yielding dishes like cow heel soup and pig-foot souse (a cool soup with pickled cucumber and meat), both of which are still popular today. One of the most significant African contributions to the Caribbean table is "jerking," the process of dry-rubbing meat with allspice, Scotch bonnet peppers, and other spices. Although the cooking technique originated with native Amerindians, the Jamaican Maroons—a population of runaway African slaves living in the island's mountains during the years of slavery—actually perfected it, resulting in the style of jerk meat familiar in restaurants today.

English Imports. British settlers brought pickles, preserves, and chutneys to the Caribbean, and current-day island chefs take advantage of indigenous fruits to produce these items. The British influence also is evidenced by the Indian and Chinese contributions to Caribbean cuisine. British (and Dutch) colonists brought indentured laborers from India and China to the Caribbean to work on sugar plantations, resulting in the introduction of popular dishes such as curry goat and roti, an Indian flatbread stuffed with curried vegetables or meat.

Dutch Ingenuity. Beginning in the 1620s, traders from the Dutch East India Company brought Southeast Asian ingredients such as soy sauce to the islands of Curaçao and St. Maarten. Dutch influence is also evident throughout Aruba and Bonaire (all have been under Dutch rule since the early 19th century), where dishes like *keshi yeni*, or "stuffed cheese," evolved from stuffing discarded rinds of Edam cheese with minced meat, olives, and capers. Another Dutch-influenced dish is *boka dushi* (Indonesian-style chicken satay), which translates to "sweet mouth" in the local Papiamento dialect.

French Technique. As tobacco and sugar crops flourished and the Caribbean became a center of European trade and colonization, the French settled Martinique and Guadeloupe in 1635 and later expanded to St. Barthélemy, St. Martin, Grenada, St. Lucia, and western Hispaniola. French culinary technique joined with the natural resources of the islands to create dishes such as whelk (sea snail) grilled in garlic butter, fresh fish *en papillote* (baked in parchment paper), and crabs *farcis* (land crab meat that is steamed, mixed with butter, bread crumbs, ham, chilies, and garlic, then stuffed back into the crab shells and grilled).

Spanish Influences. The Caribbean islands were discovered by Christopher Columbus in 1492, while he was sailing for the Spanish crown. When he returned to the islands a year later, his ships were laden with chickpeas, cilantro, eggplant, onions, and garlic. Along with the Bahamas and Hispaniola, Cuba was among Columbus's first landings; as a result, Cuba and nearby Puerto Rico have a tradition of distinctly Spanish-accented cuisine, including paella (a seafood-studded rice dish), arroz con pollo or *pelau* (chicken cooked with yellow rice), and white-bean stews.

CARIBBEAN'S NATURAL BOUNTY

Despite its spicy reputation, Caribbean food isn't always fiery; rather, the focus is on enhancing and intensifying flavors with local herbs and spices. Food plays a major role in island culture, family life, and traditions, and no holiday would be complete without traditional dishes prepared from the island's natural products.

Tantalizing Tropical Fruit
Breadfruit, a versatile starch with potato-like flavor, can be served solo—baked or grilled—or as a salad or added to soups and stews. With its rich, refreshing milk, **coconut** frequently appears in soups, stews, sauces, and drinks to help temper hot, spicy flavors. The bright pink **guava** is pleasantly sweet when mature and delicious when juiced or used in compotes, pastes, and jellies. The pungent smell of **jackfruit** may be off-putting for some, but its sweet fleshy meat is popular in milkshakes. **Papaya** is sweet and floral when ripe; unripe, it can be shredded and mixed with spices and citrus for a refreshing salad; it is also used in fruit salsas served with seafood. The brightly flavored

passion fruit is commonly pureed and used in sauces, drinks, and desserts. The dark-green skin, creamy-flesh **soursop** is known for its sweet-tart juice used in drinks, sorbets, and ice creams. The fibrous stalks of **sugarcane**, a giant grass native to India, are rich with sugar and consumed in several forms, including freshly extracted juice and processed sugar. **Tamarind** is the fruit of a large tree; the sticky pulp of its pod is used in chutneys and curries to impart a slightly sweet, refreshingly sour flavor.

Farm-Fresh Vegetables

Cassava (also called yuca) is used much like a potato in purees, dumplings, soups, and stews; the flour ground from its roots is used in breads and in tapioca. **Chayote**, also called christophene, is a versatile member of the squash and melon family and often used raw in salads or stuffed with cheese and tomatoes and baked. **Dasheen** (taro), much like a potato but creamier, can be sliced thinly and fried like a potato chip. **Fitweed** (or French thistle) is a tropical herb related to coriander (cilantro) and is a popular Caribbean seasoning. Podlike **okra** is commonly added along with crabmeat to callaloo, a leafy green soup and the national dish of Trinidad and Tobago. **Plantains**, which look like a big banana but are really a vegetable, are a staple across the Caribbean; whether sliced and fried for a side dish or sliced very thinly and deep fried as a chip, they're delicious. The bright fuschia-color sorrel flower, in season during the Christmas holidays, is typically boiled in water flavored with cinnamon, then cooled and served over ice as a refreshing drink.

Sweet and Savory Spices

Native **allspice**, also called Jamaican pepper, is the dried unripe berry of the evergreen pimento tree and is commonly added to Caribbean curries. Native Jamaicans used allspice to preserve meats, and it's an essential ingredient in jerk preparations. **Curries** are intensely seasoned sauces that originated in India and are most prevalent on the islands of Jamaica, Trinidad, and Tobago. Native Carib people pioneered the use of **chili peppers** as a hot, spicy flavoring, using primarily habaneros and Scotch bonnet peppers. **Ginger** is used raw or dried and ground into a powder to add both flavor and heat to ginger beer, sweet potatoes, or coconut milk-based sauces. It's also used to flavor a medicinal tea (great for a chest cold). The mix of ingredients in **jerk** seasoning vary, but typically include scallions, thyme, allspice, onions, and garlic. The tiny island of Grenada is the world's second-largest producer of **nutmeg**. Used to accent potatoes, vegetables, and meat dishes, nutmeg is also an important flavoring for fruit desserts, pies, ice cream, and other sweet dishes, as well as for an added kick in cocktails.

Island Fish and Seafood

Bonito is a medium-size fish in the mackerel family. Atlantic bonito—moderately fatty, with a firm texture and dark color—is served blackened, grilled (sometimes with fruit-based salsas), or Jamaican jerk style. On many islands, including the Bahamas, **conch**—a large shellfish—is used for conch salad and also for conch fritters, a mix of conch meat, cornmeal, and spices that are deep fried and make an excellent snack. **Cascadura** is a small fish found in the freshwater swamps of Trinidad and Tobago. It is typically served in a curry sauce, with a side of rice or dumplings. **Flying fish** have wing-like fins that enable the fish to glide or "fly" over water. Firm in texture, it is typically served steamed or fried. Flying fish is found in abundance off the coast of Barbados and, in fact, is the national fish. **Kingfish**, also called wahoo, is a delicate white fish commonly caught off the coasts of St. Croix and Barbados. It's also served escabeche style, marinated in a vinegar mixture then fried or poached. **Land crab** is found throughout the islands. Delicate in flavor, its common preparations include curried crab stewed in coconut milk, stuffed crab backs, and crab soup. **Mahimahi**, also called dorado or dolphin, is caught off the coast of several islands in the Caribbean. With a subtle, sweet flavor, its firm flesh lends itself to soy sauce glazes and Asian preparations. **Salt fish** is a dish made from dried cod, often seasoned with tomatoes, onions, and thyme; it's popular throughout the Caribbean. Stir-fried ackee (a tropical fruit with nutty-flavored flesh) and saltfish, for instance, is Jamaica's national dish. Green fig (banana) and saltfish is the national dish of St. Lucia.

THE RISE OF RUM

The Caribbean is the world center for rum production, with dozens of distillers throughout the islands producing their own brands and styles of rum. Although mainstream brands like Bacardi, Captain Morgan, and Mount Gay are available on every island, you may have to look harder for the smaller brands. The best-quality rums are dark, aged rums meant for sipping, priced from $30 to $700 a bottle. For excellent sipping rum at the lower end of the spectrum, try Appleton or Rhum Barbancourt. For mixed drinks, use clear or golden-colored rums that are less expensive and pair well with fruit juices or cola. Spiced and flavored rums are also popular in cocktails. Here are some of the best rums you'll encounter at an island bar:

Appleton Estate (Jamaica). The flagship VX brand is an amber-colored blend with a subtle brown-sugar aroma and a smooth, toasted-honey finish—an excellent mixer for classic cocktails.

Bacardí (Puerto Rico). Superior is a clear, mild rum with subtle hints of vanilla and fresh fruits. It is smooth and light on the palate. Best in mixed drinks.

Chairman's Reserve (St. Lucia). The island's finest rum also comes in a spiced version, a favorite during the holidays.

Clarke's Court (Grenada). Pure White is clear with a touch of sweetness—great for punches or straight with a dash of bitters.

Cruzan (St. Croix, U.S. Virgin Islands). Light, dark, or overproof, Cruzan rum is full-bodied, smooth, and fine for either mixing or sipping.

Havana Club (Cuba). The Añejo 3 Años is deceiving—light in color and body and delicate in flavor. It is a good rum to sip neat.

Mount Gay Rum (Barbados). Eclipse, the brand's flagship rum, has a golden color with a butterscotch caramel nose and sweet taste on the palate with mouth-warming flavor.

Pusser's Rum (British Virgin Islands). Self-described as "the single malt of rum," the aged 15-year variety boasts notes of cinnamon, woody spice, and citrus. A good sipping rum.

Rhum Barbancourt (Haiti). Aged 15 years, the Estate Reserve premium dark rum is distilled twice in copper pot stills and often called the "Cognac of rum." Sip it neat.

Ron Barceló (Dominican Republic). The Añejo is dark copper in color, with a rich flavor, while the aged Imperial boasts notes of toffee on the nose, and a buttery smooth finish.

Shillingford Estates (Dominica). Its most popular product, Macoucherie Spiced is a blend of rum made from local cane, the bark of the Bois Bande tree, and spices.

BEST BREWS

Beer in the Caribbean was largely home-made for centuries, a tradition inherited from British colonial rulers. The first commercial brewery in the islands was founded in Trinidad and Tobago in 1947. In the islands, do what the locals do: drink local beer. Whatever brand is brewed on-island is the one you'll find at every res-taurant and bar. And no matter where you go in the Caribbean, there's a local island brew worth trying. Another plus: local brands are almost always cheaper than imports like Corona or Heineken. Most island beers are pale lagers, though you'll find a smattering of Dutch-style pilsners and English-style pale ales. The beers listed below are our top picks for beachside sipping:

Banks Beer (Banks Breweries, Barbados). A straw-colored lager that is light tast-ing with a touch of maltiness on the nose and tongue.

Blackbeard Ale (Virgin Islands Brewing Co., St. Thomas, U.S. Virgin Islands). This English-style pale ale is bright amber in color with a creamy white head, well-crafted, with a hoppy bite at the finish.

Balashi Beer (Brouwerij Nacional Balashi N.V., Aruba). Refreshingly light, this Dutch pilsner boasts mild flavor, slight sweetness, and subtle hop bitterness.

Carib Lager Beer (Carib Brewery, Trini-dad and Tobago). This perfect beach thirst quencher is pale yellow in color with a foamy head. Fruity and malty, it may be considered the "Corona of the Caribbean."

Kalik Gold (Commonwealth Brewery LTD., New Providence, Bahamas). Clear straw color with gentle hoppy, herbal notes, this is an easy drinking, warm weather lager.

Medalla Light (Compañía Cervecería de Puerto Rico, Puerto Rico). This bright gold lager is substantial for a light beer. It's a local favorite.

Piton (Windward & Leeward Brewery Ltd., St. Lucia). Light and sparkly with subtle sweetness, this pale yellow pilsner lager is pleasant, crisp, and refreshing.

Presidente (Cervecería Nacional Domini-cana, Dominican Republic). Slight citrus aroma, light body, and fizziness, plus a clean finish make for easy drinking and a perfect pairing for barbecued meats.

Red Stripe (Desnoes & Geddes, Jamaica). A pale lager that pours golden yellow in color with lots of carbonation, it's light bodied, crisp, and smooth.

Wadadli (Antigua Brewery Ltd., Antigua and Barbuda) The brewery's flagship beer is a crisp, light-bodied, American-style lager.

ANGUILLA

WELCOME TO ANGUILLA

TRANQUIL AND UPSCALE

This dry limestone isle is the most northerly of the Leeward Islands, lying between the Caribbean Sea and the Atlantic. The low-lying island is only 16 miles (26 km) long and 3 miles (5 km) wide, and its highest spot is 213 feet above sea level. Since there are neither streams nor rivers—only saline ponds used for salt production—water comes from desalinization plants and cisterns that collect rainwater.

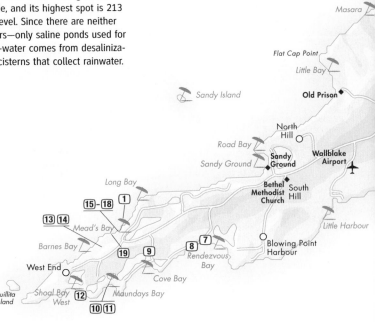

Ram's Head

Masara

Flat Cap Point

Little Bay

Sandy Island

Old Prison

North Hill

Road Bay

Sandy Ground

Sandy Ground

Wallblake Airport

Long Bay

Bethel Methodist Church

South Hill

15 - 18 1

13 14
Mead's Bay

Little Harbour

Barnes Bay

19 9

8 7

Rendezvous Bay

Blowing Point Harbour

West End

Cove Bay

Anguillita Island

Shoal Bay West 12

Maundays Bay

10 11

In tiny Anguilla, where fishermen have been heading out to sea for centuries in handmade boats, the beaches are some of the Caribbean's best and least crowded. Heavy development has not spoiled the island's atmospheric corners, and independent restaurants still thrive, as do a few low-key bungalow hotels, which share the island with some genuinely over-the-top palaces.

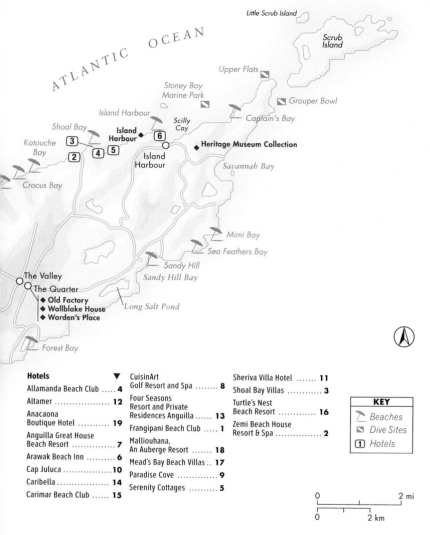

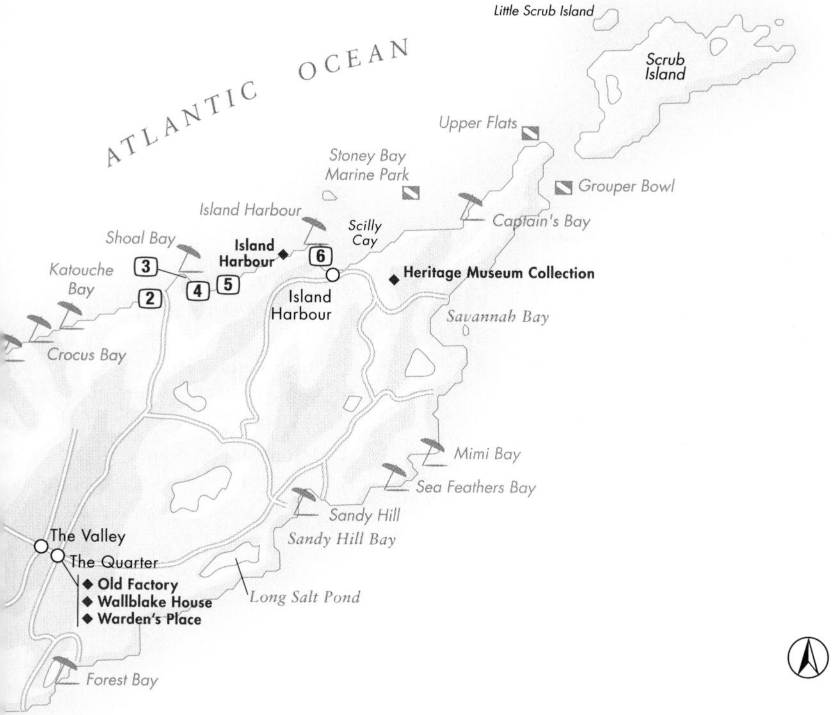
Little Scrub Island
Scrub Island
ATLANTIC OCEAN
Upper Flats
Stoney Bay Marine Park
Grouper Bowl
Island Harbour
Captain's Bay
Scilly Cay
Shoal Bay
Island Harbour
Katouche Bay
3
6
Heritage Museum Collection
2
4
5
Island Harbour
Savannah Bay
Crocus Bay
Mimi Bay
Sea Feathers Bay
Sandy Hill
Sandy Hill Bay
The Valley
The Quarter
Old Factory
Wallblake House
Warden's Place
Long Salt Pond
Forest Bay

Hotels ▼

Allamanda Beach Club **4**
Altamer **12**
Anacaona Boutique Hotel **19**
Anguilla Great House Beach Resort **7**
Arawak Beach Inn **6**
Cap Juluca **10**
Caribella **14**
Carimar Beach Club **15**
CuisinArt Golf Resort and Spa **8**
Four Seasons Resort and Private Residences Anguilla **13**
Frangipani Beach Club **1**
Malliouhana, An Auberge Resort **18**
Mead's Bay Beach Villas .. **17**
Paradise Cove **9**
Serenity Cottages **5**
Sheriva Villa Hotel **11**
Shoal Bay Villas **3**
Turtle's Nest Beach Resort **16**
Zemi Beach House Resort & Spa **2**

KEY
Beaches
Dive Sites
[1] Hotels

0 — 2 mi
0 — 2 km

TOP REASONS TO VISIT ANGUILLA

1 Beautiful Beaches: Miles of brilliant beach ensure you have a high-quality spot in which to lounge.

2 Great Restaurants: The dining scene offers both fine dining and delicious casual food on and off the beach.

3 Fun, Low-Key Nightlife: A funky late-night local music scene features reggae and string bands.

4 Upscale Accommodations: Excellent luxury resorts coddle you in comfort.

5 Hidden Bargains: You'll find a few relative bargains if you look hard enough.

NEED TO KNOW

Atlantic Ocean

ANGUILLA
The Valley

SAINT MARTIN

ST. KITTS AND NEVIS

Caribbean Sea

AT A GLANCE

Capital: The Valley

Population: 14,962

Currency: Eastern Caribbean dollar; pegged to U.S. dollar

Money: Some ATMs are closed Saturday and Sunday; credit cards accepted; U.S. dollar widely accepted.

Language: English

Country Code: ☎ 1 264

Emergencies: ☎ 911

Driving: On the left

Electricity: 110v/60 cycles; plugs are U.S. standard two-prong

Time: Same as New York during daylight savings time; one hour ahead otherwise

Documents: A valid passport and must have a return or ongoing ticket

Major Mobile Companies: LIME, Digicel

WEBSITES

Anguilla Tourist Office: ⊕ www.ivisitanguilla.com

GETTING AROUND

✈ **Air Travel:** Clayton J. Lloyd Airport is only airport in Anguilla; there are no nonstop flights from the U.S.

🚌 **Bus Travel:** Anguilla has no public bus system.

🚗 **Car Travel:** If you want to explore the island, a rental car is useful and recommended because taxis are very expensive. Note that some roads are poorly paved.

⛴ **Ferry Travel:** Regular ferry services connect Anguilla to St. Martin's Marigot harbor as well as to Simpson Bay near St. Maarten's Princess Juliana International Airport.

PLAN YOUR BUDGET

	HOTEL ROOM	MEAL	ATTRACTIONS
Low Budget	$275	$12	Sandy Island sea shuttle, $10
Mid Budget	$375	$30	Anguilla Culture Tour by Anguilla Access, $45
High Budget	$475	$50	Greens fees at Temenos Golf Course, $250

WAYS TO SAVE

Eat at roadside vendors. Head to "The Strip" in The Valley for local food trucks, or try one of the weekend pop-up BBQs.

Stay in a beach bungalow. Several local hotels have retained a true West Indian flair and lower prices.

Rent a car on-island. Local retailers and hotels are often cheaper than larger agencies.

Beach it up. All beaches on Anguilla are free and open to the public; the best include Meads Bay, Rendezvous Bay, and Shoal Bay.

Hassle Factor	Medium. Flights to St. Maarten are frequent, but a half-hour ferry or short flight connection is required to reach Anguilla.
3 days	Relax poolside or beachside at your resort; visit a second award-winning beach beyond your resort's, such as Shoal Bay (East) or Rendezvous Bay.
1 week	Combine resort-based relaxation with island exploration, visiting Anguilla's dozen-plus paradisiacal bays; take a day-trip to Scilly Cay or Prickly Pear Cay and another to tiny Sandy Island. Explore Anguilla's history on the self-guided 10-stop Anguilla Heritage Trail.
2 weeks	Island-hop in the Lesser Antilles, combining a trip to Anguilla with one or two other nearby islands: St. Martin, St. Barthelemy, Saba, or St. Eustatius.

WHEN TO GO

High Season: Mid-December through mid-April is the most fashionable and most expensive time to visit, when the weather is typically sunny and warm. Good hotels are often booked far in advance, and you're guaranteed the most entertainment at resorts and the most people with whom to enjoy it.

Low Season: From August to late October, temperatures can grow oppressively hot and the weather muggy, with high risks of tropical storms. Many upscale hotels close during these months for annual renovations. Those remaining open offer deep discounts.

Value Season: From late April to July and again November to mid-December, hotel prices drop 20% to 50% from high season prices. There are good chances of scattered showers, but expect sun-kissed days, too, with pleasant nighttime temperatures and fewer crowds.

BIG EVENTS

March: Visiting musicians join regional reggae superstar Bankie Banx for the annual Moonsplash music festival. ⊕ www.olaidebanks.wix.com/moonsplash

March–April: Celebrate Anguilla culture during Easter weekend's Festival del Mar. ⊕ www.ivisitanguilla.com/festival-del-mar

May: Join literary aficionados at the popular Anguilla Lit Fest. ⊕ www.ivisitanguilla.com/news/anguilla-lit-fest

May: The national love for boat racing peaks at the annual Anguilla Regatta. ⊕ www.anguillaregatta.com

READ THIS

■ *A Trip to the Beach,* Melinda and Robert Blanchard. An inspiring story of the island's most famous restaurateurs.

■ *Under an English Heaven,* Donald E. Westlake. Examines British rule over Anguilla.

■ *The Night of the Rambler,* Montague Kobbé. Fact-based yet fictional novel about Anguilla's revolution.

WATCH THIS

■ *Anguilla Rising.* Anguilla's history through the eyes of an American expat (still in production).

EAT THIS

■ *Crayfish:* daintier cousins of the lobster, grilled and brushed with butter or coconut curry.

■ *Spiny lobster bisque:* thick, hearty tomato- and cream-based soup with just-caught lobster.

■ *Anguilla barbecue:* ubiquitous roadside grills serving jerk or BBQ-basted chicken and ribs.

■ *Conch salad:* diced conch, chopped onions, tomato, fresh lime, and hot sauce.

■ *Johnny Cakes:* fried bread served with any meal.

■ *Goat:* Island-bred goat is delicious and not as gamy as you might think. Try it braised or curried.

Updated by
Elise Meyer

Peace, pampering, great food, and a wonderful local music scene are among the star attractions on Anguilla (pronounced ang-*gwill*-a). Beach lovers may become giddy when they first spot the island from the air; its blindingly white sand and lustrous blue-and-aquamarine waters are intoxicating. And if you like sophisticated cuisine served in casually elegant open-air settings, this may be your culinary Shangri-la.

The island's name, a reflection of its shape, is most likely a derivative of *anguille*, which is French for "eel." (French explorer Pierre Laudonnaire is credited with having given the island this name when he sailed past it in 1556.) In 1631 the Dutch built a fort here, but so far no one has been able to locate its site. English settlers from St. Kitts colonized the island in 1650, with plans to cultivate tobacco and, later, cotton and then sugar. But the thin soil and scarce water doomed these enterprises. Except for a brief period of independence, when it broke from its association with St. Kitts and Nevis in the 1960s, Anguilla has remained a British colony ever since.

From the early 1800s various island federations were formed and disbanded, with Anguilla all the while simmering over its subordinate status and forced union with St. Kitts. Anguillians twice petitioned for direct rule from Britain and twice were ignored. In 1967, when St. Kitts, Nevis, and Anguilla became an associated state, the mouse roared; citizens kicked out St. Kitts's policemen, held a self-rule referendum, and for two years conducted their own affairs. To what *Time* magazine called "a cascade of laughter around the world," a British "peacekeeping force" of 100 paratroopers from the Elite Red Devil unit parachuted onto the island, squelching Anguilla's designs for autonomy but helping a team of royal engineers stationed there to improve the port and build roads and schools. Today Anguilla elects a House of Assembly and its own leader to handle internal affairs, and a British governor is responsible for public service, the police, the judiciary, and external affairs.

The territory of Anguilla includes a few islets (or cays, pronounced "keys"), such as Scrub Island, Dog Island, Prickly Pear Cay, Sandy Island, and Sombrero Island. The 15,000 or so residents are predominantly of African descent, but there are also many of Irish background, whose ancestors came over from St. Kitts in the 1600s. Historically, because the limestone land was unfit for agriculture, attempts at enslavement never lasted long; consequently, Anguilla doesn't bear the scars of slavery found on so many other Caribbean islands. Instead, Anguillians became experts at making a living from the sea and are known for their boatbuilding and fishing skills. Tourism is the stable economy's growth industry, but the government carefully regulates expansion to protect the island's natural resources and beauty. New hotels are small, select, casino-free, and generally expensive; Anguilla emphasizes its high-quality service, serene surroundings, and friendly people.

PLANNING

GETTING HERE AND AROUND

AIR TRAVEL

There are no nonstop flights to Anguilla from the United States. Air Sunshine flies several times a day from St. Thomas and San Juan, and Anguilla Air Services flies from St. Maarten and St. Barth. Tradewind Aviation flies in from San Juan. TransAnguilla provides charter services throughout the Caribbean.

Local Airline Contacts Air Sunshine. ☎ 800/327–8900 ⊕ www.airsunshine. com. **Anguilla Air Services.** ☎ 264/498–5922 ⊕ www.anguillaairservices.com. **Tradewind Aviation.** ☎ 800/376–7922, 203/267–3305 ⊕ www.flytradewind. com. **TransAnguilla Airways.** ☎ 264/497–8690 ⊕ www.transanguilla.com.

Airport Clayton J. Lloyd International Airport. ☎ 264/497–2384 ⊕ www. anguillaairport.com.

BOAT AND FERRY TRAVEL

Public ferries run frequently between Anguilla and St. Martin. Boats leave from Blowing Point on Anguilla approximately every half hour from 7:30 am to 6:15 pm and from Marigot, St. Martin, every 45 minutes from 8 am to 7 pm. You pay a $23 departure tax before boarding ($5 for day-trippers coming through the Blowing Point terminal—but be sure to make this clear at the window where you pay), in addition to the $20 one-way fare. Children under 12 years of age are $10. On very windy days the 20-minute trip can be bouncy. The drive between the Marigot ferry terminal and the airport is vastly improved thanks to a new bridge across Simpson Bay. Some ferries operate between Blowing Point and Juliana Airport on the Dutch side of St. Maarten, with crossings four times daily. Fare is $55 one-way/$90 round-trip. Transfers by speedboat to Anguilla are available from a new terminal right at the airport at a cost of about $75 per person (arranged directly with a company or through your Anguilla hotel). Private ferry companies listed below run six or more round-trips a day, coinciding with major flights, between Blowing Point and the airport in St. Maarten. On the St. Maarten side they will bring you right to the terminal in a van, or

DID YOU KNOW?

Anguilla, about 150 miles east of Puerto Rico, has 33 beaches, each more beautiful than the last.

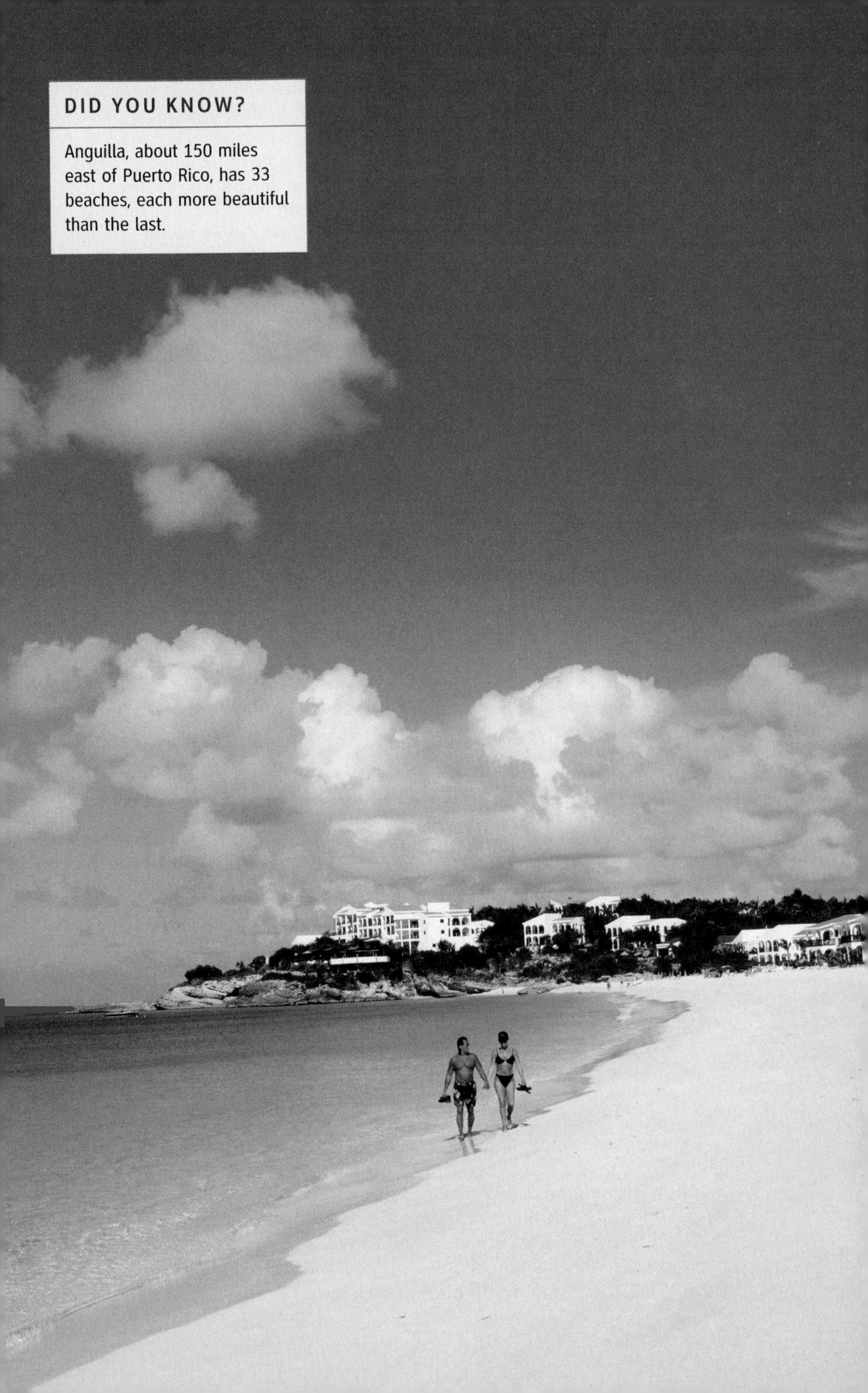

2

you can just walk across the parking lot. These trips are $65 one-way or $120 round-trip (cash only) and usually include departure taxes. There are also private charters available.

A late-night sea shuttle service leaves St. Maarten for Anguilla at 11:30 pm. This sea shuttle (leaving Blowing Point Terminal at 10:30 pm) meets the daily American flight from Miami, which arrives at 9:55 pm. It then takes you directly to Blowing Point in Anguilla. The trip costs $80 per adult and $40 per child. Another sea shuttle, which departs at 7 pm, also goes from St. Maarten to Anguilla. This connects with JetBlue and InselAir flights originating in San Juan; the cost is $65 per person.

Contacts Funtime Ferry. ☎ 264/476–1115 ⊕ www.funtimechartersanguilla. com. **GB Ferries.** ☎ 264/235–6205, 321/406–0414 in U.S. ⊕ www. anguillaferryandcharter.com. **Link Ferries.** ☎ 264/497–2231 ⊕ www.link.ai. **MV Shauna Ferries.** ☎ 264/476–6511.

CAR TRAVEL

Although many of the rental cars on-island have the driver's side on the left as in North America, Anguillian roads are like those in the United Kingdom—driving is on the left side of the road. It's easy to get the hang of, but the roads can be rough, so be cautious, and observe the 30 mph (48 kph) speed limit. Roundabouts are probably the biggest driving obstacle for most. As you approach, give way to the vehicle on your right; once you're in the rotary, you have the right of way.

Car Rentals: A temporary Anguilla driver's license is required to rent a car—you can get into real trouble if you're caught driving without one. You get it for $20 (good for three months) through any of the car-rental agencies at the time you pick up your car; you'll also need your valid driver's license from home. Rental rates start at about $45 to $55 per day, plus insurance.

Contacts Andy's Car Rental. ☎ 264/584–7010 ⊕ www.andyrentals.com. **Avis.** ✉ Airport Rd. ☎ 264/497–2642 ⊕ www.avisanguilla.com. **Bryans Car Rental.** ☎ 264/497–6407 ⊕ www.bryanscarrentals.com. **Triple K Car Rental/Hertz.** ✉ Airport Rd. ☎ 264/497–2934 ⊕ www.hertz.com/rentacar/location/axao60.

TAXI TRAVEL

Taxis are fairly expensive, so if you plan to explore many beaches and restaurants, it may be more cost-effective to rent a car. Taxi rates are regulated by the government, and there are fixed fares from point to point, listed in brochures the drivers should have handy and published in local guides. It's $26 from the airport or $22 from Blowing Point Ferry to West End hotels. Posted rates are for one or two people; each additional passenger adds $5, and there is a $1 charge for each piece of luggage beyond the allotted two. You can also hire a taxi for a flat rate of $28 an hour. A surcharges of $4 applies to trips between 6 pm and midnight. After midnight it's $10. You'll always find taxis at the Blowing Point Ferry landing and the airport, but you'll need to call for hotel and restaurant pickups and arrange ahead with the driver who took you if you need a late-night return from a nightclub or bar.

Contacts **Blowing Point Ferry Taxi Stand.** ☎ *264/497–6089* ⊕ *www.caribya. com/blowing.point/taxis.* **Maurice & Sons Exquisite Taxi Services.** ☎ *264/235– 2676* ⊕ *www.msexquisiteshuttle.com.*

HEALTH AND SAFETY

Dengue, chikungunya, and zika have all been reported throughout the Caribbean. We recommend that you protect yourself from these mosquito-borne illnesses by keeping your skin covered and/or wearing mosquito repellent. The mosquitoes that transmit these viruses are as active by day as they are by night.

HOTELS AND RESORTS

Anguilla is known for its luxurious resorts and villas, but there are also some places that mere mortals can afford (and a few that are downright bargains).

Resorts. Anguilla is known for luxurious, expensive resorts.

Villas and rentals. Private villa rentals are becoming more common and are improving in quality of design and upkeep every season as development on the island accelerates. Condos, with full kitchens and multiple bedrooms, are great for families or for longer stays.

Hotel reviews have been shortened. For full information, visit Fodors.com.

WHAT IT COSTS IN U.S. DOLLARS				
	$	$$	$$$	$$$$
RESTAURANTS	under $12	$12–$20	$21–$30	over $30
HOTELS	under $275	$275–$375	$376–$475	over $475

Restaurant prices are the average cost of a main course at dinner or, if dinner is not served, at lunch. Hotel prices are the lowest cost of a standard double room in high season.

VISITOR INFORMATION

CONTACTS

Anguilla Tourist Board. ⊠ *Coronation Ave., The Valley* ☎ *264/497–2759, 844/692–6484 from U.S.* ⊕ *www.ivisitanguilla.com.*

EXPLORING

Exploring on Anguilla is mostly about checking out the spectacular beaches and resorts. The island has only a few roads. Locals are happy to provide directions, but using the readily available tourist map is the best idea. Visit the Anguilla Tourist Board, centrally located on Coronation Avenue in The Valley.

You can take a free, self-guided tour of the Anguilla Heritage Trail, comprising 10 important historical sights that can be explored independently in any order. Wallblake House, in The Valley, is the main information center for the trail, or you can just look for the large boulders with descriptive plaques.

TOP ATTRACTIONS

Bethel Methodist Church. Not far from Sandy Ground, this charming little church, which celebrated its 135th anniversary in 2013, is an excellent example of skillful island stonework. It also has some colorful stained-glass windows. ⊠ *South Hill Village.*

Fountain National Park and Caverns. Although the prehistoric cavern, 50 feet below the surface, itself is not open to the public, there is an interesting exhibit with information and artifacts of the ancient Amerindian inhabitants of the island. Thousand-year-old carved fertility figures and petroglyphs in the rock surround the pool, which is believed to have been a pilgrimage site; it's the oldest known and longest used such ceremonial cave site in the Caribbean. ⊠ *Shoal Bay Village* ☎ *264/497–5297 Anguilla National Trust.*

FAMILY **Heritage Museum Collection.** A remarkable opportunity to learn about Anguilla, this tiny museum (complete with gift shop) is painstakingly curated by Colville Petty. Old photographs and local records and artifacts trace the island's history over four millennia, from the days of the Arawaks. High points include historical documents of the Anguilla Revolution and photo albums chronicling island life, from devastating hurricanes to a visit from Queen Elizabeth in 1964. You can see examples of ancient pottery shards and stone tools along with fascinating photographs of the island in the early 20th century—many depicting the heaping and exporting of salt and the christening of schooners—and a complete set of beautiful postage stamps issued by Anguilla since 1967. ⊠ *East End at Pond Ground* ☎ *264/235–7440* 🖃 *$5* ☉ *Weekdays 10–5.*

Sandy Ground. Almost everyone who comes to Anguilla stops by this central beach, home to several popular open-air bars and restaurants, as well as boat-rental operations. This is where you catch the ferry for tiny Sandy Island, 2 miles (3 km) offshore.

WORTH NOTING

Island Harbour. Anguillians have been fishing for centuries in the brightly painted, simple, handcrafted fishing boats that line the shore of the harbor. It's hard to believe, but skillful pilots take these little boats out to sea as far as 50 or 60 miles (80 or 100 km). Late afternoon is the best time to see the day's catch, and there are a couple of good, laid-back beach restaurants here. ■TIP→ **Hail the free boat to Gorgeous Scilly Cay, a classic little restaurant offering sublime lobster and Eudoxie Wallace's knockout rum punches on Wednesday and Sunday.** ⊠ *Island Harbor Rd.* ⊕ *www.scillycayanguilla.com.*

Old Factory. For many years the cotton grown on Anguilla and exported to England was processed in this beautiful historic building. Later it was a general store, and now it's the home of Sotheby's Real Estate. There is a small art gallery on the lower level in an old stone cellar featuring works by the Caribbean Impressionist artist, Sir Roland Richardson. ⊠ *Government Corner, The Valley* ☎ *264/498–0123* ⊕ *www. oldfactory-anguilla.ai* 🖃 *Free* ☉ *Weekdays 10–noon and 1–4.*

Wallblake House. Anguilla's only surviving plantation house, Wallblake House was built in 1787 by Will Blake (Wallblake is probably a corruption of his name). The place is associated with many a tale involving murder, high living, and the French invasion in 1796. On the grounds are an ancient vaulted stone cistern and an outbuilding called the Bakery, which wasn't used for making bread at all but for baking turkeys and hams. You can visit the thoroughly and thoughtfully restored house and grounds only on a guided tour, usually offered two days a week. It's also the information center for the Anguilla Heritage Trail. ⊠ *Wallblake Rd., The Valley* ☎ *264/497–6613* ⊕ *www.wallblake.ai* ☜ *Free* ⊗ *Tours Wed. and Fri. 10–noon.*

Warden's Place. This former sugar-plantation great house, on the Anguilla Heritage Trail, was built in the 1790s and is a fine example of island architecture. For many years it served as the residence of the island's chief administrator, who also doubled as the only medical practitioner. Across the street is the oldest dwelling on the island, originally built as slave housing. ⊠ *Coronation Ave., The Valley* ☎ *264/497–2930* ☜ *Free.*

BEACHES

Anguilla's beaches are among the best and most beautiful in the Caribbean. You can find long, deserted stretches suitable for sunset walks and beaches lined with lively bars and restaurants—all surrounded by crystal-clear warm waters in several shades of turquoise. The sea is calmest at 2½-mile-long (4-km-long) Rendezvous Bay, where gentle breezes tempt sailors. But Shoal Bay (East) is the quintessential Caribbean beach. The white sand is so soft and abundant that it pools around your ankles. Cove Bay and Maundays Bay must also rank among the island's best beaches. Maundays is the location of the island's famous resort Cap Juluca. Meads Bay's arc is dominated by the tony Four Seasons Resort, and smaller Cove Bay is just a walk away. In contrast to the French islands, Anguilla doesn't permit topless sunbathing.

NORTHEAST COAST

Captain's Bay. On the north coast just before the eastern tip of the island, this quarter-mile stretch of perfect white sand is bounded by a rocky shoreline where Atlantic waves crash. If you make the tough, four-wheel-drive-only trip along the dirt road that leads to the northeastern end of the island toward Junk's Hole, you'll be rewarded with peaceful isolation. The surf here slaps the sands with a vengeance, and the undertow is strong—so wading is the safest water sport. **Amenities:** none. **Best for:** solitude.

Island Harbour. For centuries Anguillians have ventured from these sands in colorful handmade fishing boats. Mostly calm waters are surrounded by a slender beach—good sightseeing, but not much for swimming or lounging. But there are a couple of good restaurants (Hibernia and Falcon's Nest). This is also the departure point for a three-minute boat ride to Scilly Cay, where a thatched beach bar serves seafood. Just hail the restaurant's free boat and plan to spend most of the day (the all-inclusive lunch—Wednesday and Sunday only—starts at $40 and is worth the price). **Amenities:** food and drink; toilets. **Best for:** partiers.

NORTHWEST COAST

Little Bay. On the north coast, not far from The Valley, this small gray-sand beach is a favored spot for snorkeling and night dives. It's essentially accessible only by water, as it's backed by sheer cliffs lined with agave and creeping vines. The easiest way to get here is a five-minute boat ride from Crocus Bay (about $10 round-trip). The only way to access the beach from the road is to clamber down the cliffs by rope to explore the caves and surrounding reef—for young, agile, and experienced climbers only. Do not leave personal items in cars parked here, because theft can be a problem. **Amenities:** none. **Best for:** snorkeling.

Road Bay (*Sandy Ground*). The big pier here is where the cargo ships dock, but so do some pretty sweet yachts, sailboats, and fishing boats. The brown-sugar sand is home to terrific restaurants that hop from day through dawn, including Veya, Roy's Bayside Grille, Dolce Vita, Sand Bar, the Pumphouse, and Elvis', the quintessential beach bar. There are all kinds of boat charters available here. The snorkeling isn't very good, but the sunset vistas are glorious, especially with a rum punch in your hand. **Amenities:** food and drink. **Best for:** sunset.

Sandy Island. A popular day trip, tiny Sandy Island shelters a pretty lagoon nestled in coral reefs about 2 miles (3 km) from Road Bay, with a restaurant that serves lunch and great islandy cocktails. Fans of TV's *The Bachelor* may recall the Valentine's Day picnic date here in 2011. From November through August you can take the *Happiness* sea shuttle from Sandy Ground ($10 round-trip). There is mooring for yachts and larger sailboats. Small boats can come right in the channel. ■TIP→ **The reef is great for snorkeling. Amenities:** food and drink. **Best for:** partiers; snorkeling; swimming. ⊕ *www.mysandyisland.com* ⊗ *Nov.–Aug., daily 10–4; Sept. and Oct. by reservation.*

FAMILY

Fodor's Choice ★

Shoal Bay. Anchored by sea grape and coconut trees, the 2-mile (3-km) powdered-sugar strand at Shoal Bay (not to be confused with Shoal Bay West, at the other end of the island) is one of the world's prettiest beaches. Two new beachfront resorts are near completion at this writing. You can park free at any of the restaurants, including Elodia's, Madeariman's, or Gwen's Reggae Grill, most of which either rent or provide chairs and umbrellas for patrons for about $20 a day per person. There is plenty of room to stretch out in relative privacy, or you can bar-hop or take a ride on Junior's Glass Bottom Boat. The relatively broad beach has shallow water that is usually gentle, making this a great family beach; a coral reef not far from the shore is a wonderful snorkeling spot. Sunsets over the water are spectacular. **Amenities:** food and drink. **Best for:** sunset; swimming; walking.

SOUTHEAST COAST

Sandy Hill. You can park anywhere along the dirt road to Sea Feathers Bay to visit this popular fishing center. What's good for the fishermen is also good for snorkelers, with a coral reef right near the shore. But the beach here is not much of a lounging spot. The sand is too narrow and rocky for that. However, it's a great place to buy lobsters and fish fresh out of the water in the afternoon. **Amenities:** food and drink. **Best for:** snorkeling; walking.

SOUTHWEST COAST

FodorsChoice ★   **Cove Bay.** Follow the signs to Smokey's at the end of Cove Road, and you will find water that is brilliantly blue and sand that's as soft as sifted flour. It's just as spectacular as its neighbors Rendezvous Bay and Maundays Bay. You can walk here from Cap Juluca for a change of pace, or you can arrange a horseback ride along the beach. Weekend barbecues with terrific local bands at Smokey's are an Anguillian must. **Amenities:** food and drink. **Best for:** partiers; swimming; walking.

FodorsChoice ★   **Maundays Bay.** The dazzling, platinum-white mile-long beach is especially great for swimming and long beach walks. It's no wonder that Cap Juluca, one of Anguilla's premier resorts, chose this as its location. Public parking is straight ahead at the end of the road near Cap Juluca's Pimms restaurant. You can have lunch or dinner here (be prepared for the cost) or, depending on the season, book a massage in one of the beachside tents. **Amenities:** food and drink; parking (no fee); toilets. **Best for:** partiers; swimming; walking.

FAMILY FodorsChoice ★   **Meads Bay.** Arguably Anguilla's premier beach, Meads Bay is home to many of the island's top resorts (Malliouhana, Four Seasons) and a dozen fine restaurants. Megayachts moor offshore. The powder-soft champagne sand is great for a long walk or swim. Park at any of the restaurants, and plan for lunch. Several of the restaurants offer chaises for patrons. **Amenities:** food and drink; parking (no fee); toilets. **Best for:** partiers; swimming; walking.

FAMILY   **Rendezvous Bay.** Follow the signs to Anguilla Great House for public parking at this broad swath of pearl-white sand that is some 1½ miles (2½ km) long. The beach is lapped by calm, bluer-than-blue water and a postcard-worthy view of St. Martin. The expansive crescent is home to three resorts; stop in for a drink or a meal at one, or rent a chair and umbrella at one of the kiosks. Don't miss the daylong party at the tree-house Dune Preserve, where Bankie Banx, Anguilla's most famous musician, presides. **Amenities:** food and drink; parking (no fee); toilets. **Best for:** partiers; swimming; walking.

Shoal Bay West. This glittering bay bordered by mangroves and sea grapes is a lovely place to spend the day. The 1-mile-long (1½-km-long) beach is home to Covecastles villas. The tranquility is sublime, with coral reefs for snorkeling not too far from shore. Punctuate your day with a meal at beachside Trattoria Tramonto and you can use their chairs and umbrellas. Reach the beach by taking the main road to the West End and bearing left at the fork, then continuing to the end. Note that similarly named Shoal Bay is a separate beach on a different part of the island. **Amenities:** food and drink; parking (no fee); toilets. **Best for:** solitude; swimming; walking.

WHERE TO EAT

Despite its small size, Anguilla has around 70 restaurants: stylish temples of haute cuisine; classic, barefoot beachfront grills; roadside barbecue stands; food vans; and casual cafés. Many have breeze-swept terraces for dining under the stars. Call ahead—in winter to make a reservation and in late summer and fall to confirm whether the place is open. Anguillian restaurant meals are leisurely events, and service often has a relaxed pace, so settle in and enjoy. Most restaurant owners are actively and conspicuously present, especially at dinner.

What to Wear: During the day, casual clothes are widely accepted: shorts will be fine, but don't wear bathing suits and cover-ups unless you're at a beach bar. In the evening, shorts are okay at the extremely casual eateries. Elsewhere, women wear sundresses or nice casual slacks; men will be fine in short-sleeve shirts and casual pants or nice shorts. Some hotel restaurants are slightly more formal, but that just means long pants for men.

$$$$
ECLECTIC
Fodor's Choice
★

✕ **Blanchards.** This delightful restaurant is one of the best in the Caribbean. Proprietors Bob and Melinda Blanchard moved to Anguilla from Vermont in 1994 to fulfill their culinary dreams. A festive atmosphere pervades the handsome, airy white room, accented with teal-blue, floor-to-ceiling shutters to let in the breezes, and colorful artwork by the Blanchards' son Jesse. Creative cuisine, an upscale atmosphere, attentive service, and an excellent wine cellar (including aged spirits) please the star-studded crowd. Ever changing but always good, the nuanced contemporary menu includes house classics like corn chowder, braised lamb shanks with potato gnocchi, and a Caribbean sampler, and vegetarians have good choices. You'll remember desserts like key lime "pie-in-a-glass" or the justly famous "cracked coconut" long after your suntan has faded. There is a also a three-course fixed-price menu ($48). $ *Average main: $43* ⊠ *Long Bay Village* ☎ *264/497–6100* ⊕ *www. blanchardsrestaurant.com* ✆ *No lunch* ⚐ *Reservations essential.*

$$
AMERICAN
FAMILY

✕ **Blanchards Beach Shack.** This spinoff on the sands of Meads Bay Beach is the perfect antidote to high restaurant prices. Right next to Blanchards, this chartreuse-and-turquoise cottage serves yummy lunches and dinners of lobster rolls, all-natural burgers, tacos, and terrific salads and sandwiches, and there are lots of choices for children and vegetarians. Frozen drinks like mango coladas and icy mojitos please grown-ups, while kids dig into fresh-made frozen-yogurt concoctions. Organic produce and happy smiles are always on offer. You can dine at picnic tables or rent a beach chair. ■TIP➔ **Diners are welcome to hang around on the beach.** $ *Average main: $12* ⊠ *Long Bay Village* ☎ *264/498–6100* ⊕ *www.blanchardsrestaurant.com* ✆ *Closed Sun.–Wed. Oct. 1–Nov. 1, and Aug. 22–Aug. 31* ⚐ *Reservations not accepted.*

$$$$ CARIBBEAN FAMILY 🍴 **da'Vida.** You could spend the whole day dining, drinking, snorkeling, kayaking, shopping, and lounging on the comfortable chairs at this beautifully designed resort, restaurant, and club on exquisite Crocus Bay. Picnic at the Beach Grill (burgers, hot dogs, wraps, salads) or head inside the main building for dumplings, soups, pastas, and pizzas. Lunch starts at 11, tapas and sunset drinks at about 5. At dinner, the stylish wood interior (built by craftsmen from St. Vincent) is accented by candlelight. Tasty dishes include seared snapper with gingered kale, coconut-crusted scallops, and Angus steaks. The owners, siblings David and Vida Lloyd, who also operate Lloyd's Guest House, grew up right here, and they have taken pains to get it all just right. **TIP→ Call for information about live music and nightly shuttle service.** [$] *Average main: $33* ✉ *Crocus Bay* ☎ *264/498–5433* 🌐 *www.davidaanguilla.com* 🕒 *Closed Mon.*

$$$$ ITALIAN 🍴 **Dolce Vita Italian Beach Restaurant & Bar.** Serious Italian cuisine and warm and attentive service are provided in a romantic beachside pavilion in Sandy Ground. Freshly made pasta stars in classic lasagna, Gorgonzola-napped gnocchi, pappardelle with duck sauce, and a meatless eggplant parmigiana. A carnivorous quartet can preorder suckling pig or sample first-quality chops and steaks. Pizza is offered only at lunch. Italian wine fans will discover new favorites. For dessert, how about Nutella cheesecake? [$] *Average main: $31* ✉ *Sandy Ground Village* ☎ *264/497–8668* 🕒 *Closed Sun. and Sept.–mid-Oct. No lunch Sat. and May–Aug.* ✍ *Reservations essential.*

$$ CARIBBEAN 🍴 **English Rose Bar and Restaurant.** Lunchtime finds this neighborhood hangout packed with locals: cops flirting with sassy waitresses, entrepreneurs brokering deals with politicos, schoolgirls in lime-green outfits doing their homework. The decor is nothing to speak of, but this is a great place to eavesdrop or people-watch while enjoying island-tinged specialties like beer-battered shrimp, fish-and-chips, jerk-chicken Caesar salad, snapper creole, and buffalo wings. [$] *Average main: $12* ✉ *Carter Rey Blvd., The Valley* ☎ *264/497–5353* 🕒 *Closed Sun.*

$$$ CARIBBEAN FAMILY 🍴 **Firefly Restaurant.** Set on a breezy poolside patio, the restaurant at Anacaona Boutique Hotel turns out huge portions of tasty Caribbean fare by a longtime Anguillian chef. The pumpkin-coconut soup is a winner, as are the local snapper, mahimahi, and crayfish. Breakfast, lunch, and dinner are served, as well as tasty drinks, bar snacks like buffalo wings and crispy calamari, and pizza to eat in or take away. Lunch and drinks can be delivered to the beach. For great value and fun, book a table at the Thursday night buffet, with a lively performance by the folkloric theater company Mayoumba. [$] *Average main: $30* ✉ *Anacaona Boutique Hotel, Long Bay Village* ☎ *264/497–6827* 🌐 *www.anacaonahotel.com.*

$$ FRENCH FAMILY 🍴 **Geraud's Patisserie.** A stunning array of delicious French pastries and breads—and universal favorites like cookies, brownies, and muffins—are produced by Le Cordon Bleu dynamo Geraud Lavest in this well-located shop. Come in the early morning for cappuccino and croissants or healthy fresh juices and smoothies, and pick up fixings for a wonderful and thrifty lunch, including the blackboard's daily specials. The little shop carries a small selection of condiments, teas, and gourmet goodies. December

through May, a terrific Sunday brunch is available. Geraud also does off-site catering, from intimate villa and yacht dinners to weddings; his wedding cakes are an island wonder. $ *Average main: $13 ⊠ South Hill Plaza, South Hill Village* ☎ 264/497–5559 ⊕ *www.anguillacakesandcatering. com* ⊗ *Closed Mon. and weekend afternoons. No dinner.*

$$$$ ╳**Hibernia Restaurant and Art Gallery.** Creative dishes are served in this
ECLECTIC wood-beam cottage restaurant overlooking the water at Anguilla's east-
Fodor'sChoice ern end. The lovely Zen garden has been redesigned with a small water-
★· fall and stone artifacts from Bali, and the intimate dining room (only nine tables) has been updated, also. Unorthodox yet delectable culinary pairings—inspired by chef-owners Raoul Rodriguez and Mary Pat's annual travels to Asia—bring new tastes and energy to the tables. Local organic products are used whenever possible. Long-line fish is served with a gratin of local pumpkin, shiitake mushrooms, and an essence of bitter oranges grown by the front gate. The owners' passion for life is expressed through the vibrant combination of setting, art, food, unique tableware, and thoughtful hospitality. A $12.50 per person shuttle service lets you enjoy the stellar wine collection at dinner. New in 2016 is a lovely three-bedroom villa for hard-core fans. Hours vary seasonally. ■TIP➔ Mary Pat stocks the tiny art gallery here with amazing, and reasonable, finds from her travels. $ *Average main: $36 ⊠ Harbor Ridge Dr., Island Harbour* ☎ 264/497–4290 ⊕ *www.hiberniarestaurant.com* ⊗ *Closed Mon. and mid-July–Nov.* ⌔ *Reservations essential.*

$$$ ╳**Jacala Beach Restaurant.** On beautiful Meads Bay, this restaurant
FRENCH continues to receive raves, with Martha Stewart dubbing it her "new
Fodor'sChoice favorite Caribbean restaurant." Chef Alain (named one of the Carib-
★ bean's top 25 chefs in 2014) and maître d' Jacques (from the "old" Malliouhana) have created a lovely open-air restaurant that turns out carefully prepared and nicely presented French food accompanied by good wines and personal attention. A delicious starter terrine of feta and grilled vegetables is infused with pesto. Hand-chopped steak tartare and olive oil–poached mahimahi with curry-lemongrass sauce are entrée standouts. Lighter lunchtime options include a tart cucumber-yogurt soup garnished with piquant tomato sorbet. After lunch you can digest on the beach in a Fatboy lounger, but save room for the chocolate *pot de crème.* $ *Average main: $30 ⊠ Long Bay Village* ☎ 264/498–5888 ⊗ *Closed Mon. and Tues. and Aug. and Sept.* ⌔ *Reservations essential.*

$$$$ ╳**Mango's Seaside Grill.** Sparkling-fresh fish specialties have starring
SEAFOOD roles here. Light and healthy choices include spicy grilled whole snap-
FAMILY per and Cruzan rum–barbecued chicken, while the warm apple tart and coconut cheesecake are worth a splurge. Adding to the luxury are an extensive wine list and a Cuban cigar humidor. Lunch features sandwiches, pizza, salads, and burgers. $ *Average main: $36 ⊠ Barnes Bay* ☎ 264/497–6479 ⊕ *www.mangosseasidegrill.com* ⊗ *Closed Tues. and Aug. and Sept.* ⌔ *Reservations essential.*

$$$$ ╳**Ocean Echo.** It's nonstop every day from lunch until late at this relaxed
CARIBBEAN and friendly restaurant, great for salads, burgers, grills, pasta, and fresh
FAMILY fish. Heartier appetites will enjoy the ribs and steaks. A couple of times a week there is live music as well as the possibility of dancing with an

excellent islandy cocktail in hand. $ *Average main: $35* ✉ *Long Bay Village* ☎ *264/498–5454* ⊕ *www.oceanechoanguilla.com.*

$$$ ✕ **Picante.** This casual, wildly popular bright-red roadside Caribbean
MEXICAN *taquería*, opened by a young California couple, serves huge, tasty bur-
FAMILY ritos with a choice of fillings, fresh warm tortilla chips with first-rate guacamole, huge (and fresh) taco salads, seafood enchiladas, chipotle ribs, and tequila-lime chicken grilled under a brick. Passion-fruit margaritas are a must, and there are some serious tequila options. The creamy Mexican chocolate pudding and a bananas Foster chimichanga make great choices for dessert. Seating is at picnic tables; the friendly proprietors cheerfully supply pillows on request. Reservations are recommended. $ *Average main: $21* ✉ *West End Rd., West End Village* ☎ *264/498–1616* ⊕ *www.picante-restaurant-anguilla.com* ⊗ *Closed Tues. and mid-Aug.–Nov. 1. No lunch.*

$$$$ ✕ **The Restaurant at Malliouhana.** The romantic setting of Auberge Resort's
ECLECTIC revamped Malliouihana, on a promontory overlooking Meads Bay,
Fodor'sChoice sets the stage for a memorable meal. Chef Ortiz Cupertino's California
★ influence is apparent in the farm-to-table approach; local farms provide fresh ingredients. Start with a creative rum cocktail, like a Chili Passion, infused with ginger and a touch of heat, while you study the menu and nibble hot house-made rolls. Starters feature light salads with local greens (the shaved artichoke is delicious). Dishes are creative, and vegetarians will find a larger than usual selection. Try the super-grain pasta with white truffles for a special treat. Locally bred goat is wonderful in a sausage, and a tasty braise, making the most of the tender, not-too-gamy meat. A deep fudge chocolate tart is served with a refreshing mango mousse, the perfect taste of the tropics. Keep this restaurant in mind for a special occasion; it won't disappoint. $ *Average main: $34.50* ✉ *Meads Bay, Long Bay Village* ☎ *264/497–6111* ⊕ *www.malliouhana.aubergeresorts.com* ⊗ *Closed Aug. 28–Oct. 28* ⌂ *Reservations essential* ▬ *No credit cards.*

$$$ ✕ **Roy's Bayside Grill.** Come any time of day for good cooking and a
CARIBBEAN friendly vibe. Try chocolate chip pancakes or an Anguillian breakfast
FAMILY of johnnycakes. At lunch enjoy the beachfront and grills, salads, and sandwiches. Some of the island's best grilled lobster is served here, along with tasty burgers, fish-and-chips, and home-style cooking. Every day but Sunday there's a happy hour with bar snacks, and Sunday brings roast beef and Yorkshire pudding. A prix-fixe menu ($35) has lots of choices, and kids and people with food allergies are accommodated. There's free Wi-Fi, too. $ *Average main: $27* ✉ *Road Bay, Sandy Ground Village* ☎ *264/497–2470* ⊕ *www.roysbaysidegrill.com.*

$$ ✕ **SandBar.** Tasty and shareable small plates, a friendly beach vibe, and
ECLECTIC gorgeous sunsets are on offer here, as are cool music, gentle prices, a hammock on the beach, and potent tropical cocktails. The menu changes seasonally, but favorites include spicy fries, zucchini carpaccio, Carib beer–battered fish bites with lemon-caper aioli, pulled-pork sliders, and a refreshing dish of watermelon, feta, and olives. Try the banana rum. $ *Average main: $13* ✉ *Sandy Ground Village* ☎ *264/476–5301.*

$$$ ✕ **Sarjai's Eclectic Cuisine.** Sarjai's chef Darren Connor honed his cook-
CARIBBEAN ing chops at the former Viceroy and garnered a top award at the 2015
FAMILY Taste of the Caribbean Competition. His small restaurant (named for
his daughter) is a bit away from the Meads Bay action, but is walk-
able from Malliouhana. Tasty and ample dishes are tinged with island
flavor, and local favorites like the delicious johnnycakes that precede
the meal are standouts. The big salads are sparkling fresh, as are fish
choices like local tuna with mango salsa served on a bed of creamy
mustard-seed-flecked mashed potatoes. Try the Anguillian stewed goat
or jerk chicken bursting with savory spice. Don't miss dessert: the warm
coconut tart with ginger caramel glaze and passion-fruit cheesecake are
winners. For lunch try fish-and-chips, burgers, quesadillas, or salads.
You're sure to receive a warm welcome and perhaps an update of island
gossip with your meal. Prices are gentle by island standards. $ *Aver-
age main: $25* ✉ *Long Bay Village* ☎ *264/497–6755* ⊕ *www.sarjais-
anguilla.com* ⊘ *Closed Mon.*

$$$ ✕ **Smokey's.** This quintessential Anguillian beach barbecue is on the
CARIBBEAN sands of pretty Cove Bay. Lounges with umbrellas await on the beach.
FAMILY Hot wings, honey-coated smoked ribs, curried goat, smoked chicken
salad, and grilled lobsters are paired with local-staple side dishes such
as spiced-mayonnaise coleslaw, hand-cut sweet-potato strings, and
crunchy onion rings. If your idea of the perfect summer lunch is a
roadside lobster roll, try the one here, served on a home-baked roll
with a kick of hot sauce. Dinner includes lobster fritters, grilled tuna
with lemon-caper butter, and rum chicken. On Saturday afternoon, a
popular local band enlivens the laid-back atmosphere, and on Sunday
this is party central; there is entertainment every day but Thursday.
$ *Average main: $22* ✉ *Cove Rd., Cove Bay* ☎ *264/497–6582* ⊕ *www.*
smokeysatthecove.com.

$$$$ ✕ **Straw Hat.** Charming owners, a gorgeous oceanfront location, sophis-
ECLECTIC ticated and original food, and friendly service are why this stylish restau-
FAMILY rant has been in business since the mid-1990s. Whether for breakfast,
Fodor's Choice lunch, or dinner, you will find appealing, tasty, and fresh choices to
★ mix up or share. Try Anguilla's only "real" bagel, tuna flatbread, jerk-
braised pork belly, lobster spring rolls, or curried goat. Fish of the day
is truly caught that day, and vegetarians and kids find many options,
too. Big flat-screens with satellite TV make the bar a fine place to catch
the game or make new friends. $ *Average main: $32* ✉ *Frangipani*
Beach Club, Long Bay Village ☎ *264/497–8300* ⊕ *www.strawhat.com*
⊘ *Closed Sept. and Oct.* ⌕ *Reservations essential.*

$$$ ✕ **Tasty's.** Once your eyes adjust to the quirky kiwi, lilac, and coral color
CARIBBEAN scheme, you'll find that breakfast, lunch, tapas, or dinner at Tasty's is,
FAMILY well, very tasty. It's open all day, so if you land mid-afternoon starving,
head here—it's near the airport and ferry terminal. Chef-owner Dale
Carty trained at Malliouhana, and his careful, confident preparation
bears the mark of French culinary training, but the menu is classic
Caribbean with a creole edge. It's worth leaving the beach at lunch for
the lobster salad. A velvety pumpkin soup garnished with roasted coco-
nut shards is superb, as are the seared jerk tuna and the garlic-infused
marinated conch salad. Don't be stuffy—try the goat stew. Yummy

2

Straw Hat's outdoor patio on Forest Bay

desserts end meals on a high note. This is one of few nonsmoking restaurants, so take your Cubans elsewhere. The popular Sunday brunch buffet features island specialties like saltfish cakes, and there is live music on Tuesday night. $ *Average main: $26* ✉ *Main Rd., South Hill Village* ☎ *264/497–2737* ⊕ *www.tastysrestaurant.com* ⊙ *Closed Thurs.* ⌃ *Reservations essential.*

$$$$
SUSHI
FAMILY
× **Tokyo Bay.** This sophisticated sushi and teppanyaki restaurant, dramatically lit and perched at the top of CuisinArt's spa building, owes its raves to its Japanese chef. Chances are you will find local chefs and other restaurant people here on their night out. The sake bar features terrific cocktails with names like Eager Ninja and Saketini, and chefs slice up ocean-fresh fish for sushi both traditional and otherwise. Fresh vegetables come from CuisinArt's on-site hydroponic farm. Hot pots, rice dishes, Wagyu beef, and yakitori skewers round out the menu. "Chocolate sushi" is an amusing finale. $ *Average main: $42* ✉ *CuisinArt Golf Resort and Spa, Rendezvous Bay* ☎ *264/498–2000* ⊕ *www.cuisinartresort.com* ⊙ *Closed Tues. No lunch.*

$$$
ITALIAN
FAMILY
× **Trattoria Tramonto and Oasis Beach Bar.** The island's beloved beachfront Italian restaurant features a dual (or dueling) serenade of soft jazz on the sound system and gently lapping waves a few feet away. Pastas are homemade and served in a dozen ways. Try the delicate lobster ravioli in truffle-cream sauce, or a spicy *arrabiata* pizza. For dessert, don't miss the tiramisu. If you wander in after a swim for lunch, when casual dress is okay, you'll still be treated to the same impressive menu. You can also choose from a luscious selection of champagne fruit drinks, a small and fairly priced Italian wine list, and homemade grappa at the

beach bar. Come after 5 for sundowners and tasty bar snacks like truffle fries and prosciutto carrot zucchini bundles. Hang out on chairs on the spectacular beach before or after your meal. $ *Average main: $27* ✉ *Shoal Bay Village* ☎ *264/497–8819* ⊕ *www.trattoriatramonto.com* ⊗ *Closed Mon. and Aug.–Oct.* ⚠ *Reservations essential.*

$$$$ ✕ **Veya and Meze at Veya.** On the suavely minimalist four-sided veranda,
ECLECTIC stylishly appointed tables glow with flickering candlelight from sea
Fodor's Choice urchin–shape porcelain votive holders. Chic patrons mingle and sip
★ mojitos to the purr of soft jazz in a lively lounge. Carrie Bogar's "cuisine of the sun" features ingenious preparations, first-rate provisions, and ample portions that are shareable works of art. Sample Moroccan-spiced shrimp "cigars" with roast tomato–apricot chutney or Vietnamese-spiced calamari. Jerk-spiced tuna is served with a rum-coffee glaze on a juicy slab of grilled pineapple, and butter-poached lobster is divine, as is warm chocolate cake with chili-roasted banana ice cream and caramelized bananas. Consider splurging on the $95 five-course tasting menu. For a relaxing casual evening, head downstairs to Meze at Veya to lounge in an open-air Moroccan tent while you share small tapas-style Mediterranean plates. Omari Banks, one of the island's best musicians, plays on Monday and Thursday. $ *Average main: $44* ✉ *Sandy Ground Village* ☎ *264/498–8392* ⊕ *www.veya-axa.com* ⊗ *Closed Sun., Sat. June–Aug. and late Oct., and Sept.–mid-Oct. No lunch* ⚠ *Reservations essential.*

WHERE TO STAY

Tourism on Anguilla is a relatively recent phenomenon—most development didn't begin until the early 1980s. The lack of native topography and, indeed, vegetation, and the blindingly white expanses of beach have inspired building designs of some interest; architecture buffs might have fun trying to name some of the most surprising examples. Inspiration largely comes from the Mediterranean: the Greek Islands, Morocco, and Spain, with some Miami-style art deco thrown into the mixture.

Anguilla accommodations basically fall into two categories: grand resorts and luxury resort-villas, or low-key, simple, locally owned apartments and small beachfront complexes. The former can be surprisingly expensive, the latter surprisingly reasonable. In the middle are some condo-type options, with full kitchens and multiple bedrooms, which are great for families or for longer stays. Private villa rentals are becoming more common and are increasing in number and quality of design and upkeep every season as development on the island accelerates.

A good phone chat or email exchange with the management of any property is a good idea, as units within the same complex can vary greatly in layout, accessibility, distance to the beach, and view. When calling to reserve a room, ask about special discount packages, especially in spring and summer. Most hotels include Continental breakfast in the price, and many have meal-plan options. But keep in mind that Anguilla is home to dozens of excellent restaurants before you lock yourself into an expensive meal plan that you may not be able to

CuisinArt Golf Resort and Spa, Rendezvous Bay

change. All hotels charge a 10% tax, a $1 per room/per day tourism marketing levy, and—in most cases—an additional 10% service charge. A few properties include these charges in the published rates, so check carefully when you are evaluating prices.

PRIVATE VILLAS AND CONDOS

The tourist office publishes an annual *Anguilla Travel Planner* with informative listings of available vacation apartment rentals.

RENTAL CONTACTS

Anguilla Luxury Collection. The Ricketts, longtime Anguilla residents, manage lovely luxury properties as well as the Anguilla Affordable Collection, a selection of less expensive villas. ☎ *264/497–6049* ⊕ *www. anguillaluxurycollection.com.*

Ani Villas. Two stunning cliff-side villas for up to 24 guests offer breathtaking views and total luxury to families or groups looking for pampering. Included in the rental are private boat transfers from St. Martin, rental car, a full-service team (concierge, butler, chef, housekeepers), breakfast, and all beverages. A tennis court, bikes, fitness room, pool, cliff-side hot tubs, and playrooms mean you don't have to leave except for the beach. (Tennis pros, spa services, trainers, and guides are available on demand.) There is room for 100 guests for a party or wedding on the dramatic and romantic promontory. Promotions can include unlimited golf at the CuisinArt course. ⊠ *Little Bay* ☎ *264/497–7888* ⊕ *www.anivillas.com.*

FAMILY **Kishti Villas.** This group of stunning new four- and five-bedroom villas fuses Eastern and Western aesthetics. The name, from the Urdu for "canoe," expresses a mystic sense of being in tune with nature and the lords of creation. Appointed with lovely Asian artifacts, villas have huge windows and gorgeous views, giving the sense of actually being at sea. While rates are high, attention is paid to every detail, and everything from a full staff, house manager, chef, and sports equipment is included. This is a terrific choice for destination weddings and other large family gatherings. ✉ *Long Bay Village* ☎ *264/497–6049* 🌐 *www.kishtivillacollection.com.*

RECOMMENDED HOTELS AND RESORTS

$ RENTAL FAMILY 🏨 **Allamanda Beach Club.** Youthful, active couples from around the globe happily fill this quiet, casual, three-story, white-stucco building hidden in a palm grove a short walk from the beach, opting for location and price over luxury. **Pros:** easy on the pocketbook; young crowd. **Cons:** location requires a car; rooms are pleasant but not fancy; this part of Shoal Bay has suffered recent beach erosion. [$] *Rooms from: $169* ✉ *The Valley* ☎ *264/497–5217, 305/396–4472* 🌐 *www.allamanda.ai* ⏲ *Closed Sept.* 🛏 *20 units* 🍴 *No meals.*

$$$$ RENTAL FAMILY 🏨 **Altamer.** Architect Myron Goldfinger's geometric symphony of floor-to-ceiling windows, cantilevered walls, and curvaceous floating staircases set on a white-sand private beach is fit for any celebrity (or CEO)—as is the price tag. **Pros:** stunning decor and beautiful architectural design; outstanding luxury and service; great for big groups. **Cons:** a bit out of the way; you'll very likely need a big group to split the price tag. [$] *Rooms from: $30,000/week* ✉ *Rte. 1, Shoal Bay Village* ☎ *264/498–4000* 🌐 *www.altamer.com* 🛏 *3 5-bedroom villas* 🍴 *Some meals.*

$$ RESORT FAMILY 🏨 **Anacaona Boutique Hotel.** Imbued with island culture and traditions, this resort (its name is pronounced "an-nah-cah-*oh*-na") makes a low-key yet comfortable hideaway where guests feel like treasured friends. **Pros:** friendly clientele, sensitive to local culture; modern and good value; high-tech amenities. **Cons:** bit of a walk to beach; smallish rooms. [$] *Rooms from: $280* ✉ *Meads Bay, West End Village* ☎ *264/497–6827, 877/647–4736* 🌐 *www.anacaonahotel.com* ⏲ *Closed mid-Aug.–Oct.* 🛏 *27 rooms and suites* 🍴 *Some meals.*

$ RESORT FAMILY 🏨 **Anguilla Great House Beach Resort.** These traditional West Indian–style bungalows are strung along one of Anguilla's longest beaches. **Pros:** real, old-school Caribbean; right on the gorgeous beach; young crowd; good prices. **Cons:** very simple rooms; spotty Internet. [$] *Rooms from: $210* ✉ *Rendezvous Bay* ☎ *264/497–6061, 800/583–9247* 🌐 *www.anguillagreathouse.com* 🛏 *31 rooms* 🍴 *Some meals.*

$$ B&B/INN 🏨 **Arawak Beach Inn.** These hexagonal two-story villas are a good choice for a funky, budget-friendly, low-key guesthouse experience. **Pros:** funky, casual crowd; friendly owners; very competitive rates, especially for monthlong stays. **Cons:** not on the beach; air-conditioning only in premium rooms; isolated location makes a car a must. [$] *Rooms from:*

$375 ✉ Island Harbour ☎ 264/497–4888, 877/427–2925 reservations 🌐 www.arawakbeach.com 🛏 17 rooms 🍴 No meals.

$$$$ RESORT FAMILY Fodor's Choice ★ 🏨 **Cap Juluca.** Strung along 179 acres of breathtaking Maundays Bay, these romantic, domed, Moorish-style villas are an Anguilla favorite, thanks to caring staff, great sports facilities, and plenty of privacy and comfort. **Pros:** miles of talcum-soft sand; warm service; romantic. **Cons:** ongoing renovations; comparatively high rates; some units currently closed. [$] *Rooms from: $1395 ✉ Maunday's Bay ☎ 264/497–6779, 888/858–5822 in U.S. 🌐 www.capjuluca.com 🛏 69 rooms, 7 patio suites, 6 pool villas 🍴 Some meals.*

$$$$ RENTAL 🏨 **Caribella.** These spacious Mediterranean-style villas on the broad sands of Barnes Bay are a good deal at the much-discounted weekly rate. **Pros:** huge amount of space for the cost; beautiful views from huge balconies. **Cons:** basic decor; minimum stays in high season and December and February; some bedrooms do not have air-conditioning. [$] *Rooms from: $495 ✉ Barnes Bay ☎ 264/497–6045 🌐 www.lambertventures.com 🛏 6 units 🍴 No meals.*

$$$ RENTAL FAMILY 🏨 **Carimar Beach Club.** This horseshoe of bougainvillea-draped Mediterranean-style buildings on beautiful Meads Bay has the look of a Sun Belt condo. **Pros:** tennis courts; easy walk to restaurants and spa; great beach location; laundry facilities. **Cons:** no pool or restaurant; air-conditioning only in bedrooms. [$] *Rooms from: $435 ✉ Meads Bay, West End Village ☎ 264/497–6881, 866/270–3764 🌐 www.carimar.com ⏲ Closed Sept.–mid-Oct. 🛏 24 apartments 🍴 Some meals.*

$$$$ RESORT FAMILY Fodor's Choice ★ 🏨 **CuisinArt Golf Resort and Spa.** Anguilla's best family-friendly full-service resort has it all: miles of stunning beach, world-class golf, a gorgeous spa and health club, top dining, and sports galore. **Pros:** family-friendly; great spa and sports; gorgeous beach and gardens. **Cons:** food service can be slow; pool area is noisy. [$] *Rooms from: $995 ✉ Rendezvous Bay ☎ 264/498–2000, 800/943–3210 🌐 www.cuisinartresort.com ⏲ Closed Sept. and Oct. 🛏 100 rooms, 2 penthouses, 6 villas 🍴 Some meals.*

$$$$ RESORT FAMILY Fodor's Choice ★ 🏨 **Four Seasons Resort and Private Residences Anguilla.** On a promontory over 3,200 feet of pearly sand on Barnes Bay, the newly reflagged showpiece (formerly the Viceroy) wows international sophisticates. **Pros:** state-of-the-art luxury; cutting-edge contemporary design; spacious rooms. **Cons:** international rather than Caribbean feel; very large resort; see-and-be-seen scene; really expensive. [$] *Rooms from: $800 ✉ Barnes Bay, West End Village ☎ 800/819–5053 in U.S. 🌐 www.fourseasons.com ⏲ Closed Sept. 🛏 163 suites, 3 villas 🍴 Breakfast.*

$$$ RESORT FAMILY 🏨 **Frangipani Beach Club.** This flamingo-pink Mediterranean-style property perches on the beautiful champagne sands of Meads Bay. **Pros:** great beach; good location for restaurants and resort-hopping; first-rate on-site restaurant; helpful staff. **Cons:** some rooms lack a view, so be sure to ask if you care. [$] *Rooms from: $450 ✉ Meads Bay, West End Village ☎ 264/497–6442, 877/593–8988 🌐 www.frangipaniresort.com ⏲ Closed Sept. and Oct. 🛏 19 rooms 🍴 Breakfast.*

$$$$ RESORT Fodor's Choice ★ 🏨 **Malliouhana, An Auberge Resort.** This classic luxury hotel perched cliffside over beautiful Meads Bay beach has been transformed by Auberge Resorts into a fancifully modern beach paradise. **Pros:** great location on Meads Bay; friendly and attentive service; huge comfortable rooms

and spacious bathrooms. **Cons:** lots of stairs to climb and no elevator. [$] *Rooms from: $975* ✉ *Meads Bay* ☎ *844/284–2682* 🌐 *malliouhana.aubergeresorts.com* 🕒 *Closed Aug. 28–Oct. 27* 🛏 *46 rooms, 8 suites* 🍴 *Breakfast* 💳 *No credit cards.*

$$$$ RENTAL FAMILY 🏨 **Meads Bay Beach Villas.** These gorgeous one-, two-, and three-bedroom villas right on Meads Bay have a cult following, so it can be hard to book them. **Pros:** big private apartments; beautiful beach; private plunge pools; free phone calls to U.S. **Cons:** more condo than hotel in terms of service. [$] *Rooms from: $650* ✉ *Meads Bay Rd., West End Village* ☎ *264/497–0271* 🌐 *www.meadsbaybeachvillas.com* 🛏 *4 villas* 🍴 *No meals.*

$$ RENTAL FAMILY 🏨 **Paradise Cove.** Located 500 yards away from Cove Beach, this simple complex of huge, reasonably priced studios and one- and two-bedroom apartments has two whirlpools, a large pool, and tranquil tropical gardens where you can pluck fresh guavas for breakfast. **Pros:** reasonable rates for a lot of space; great pool; lovely gardens. **Cons:** a bit far from the beach; bland decor. [$] *Rooms from: $375* ✉ *Cove Bay* ☎ *264/497–6959, 264/497–6603* 🌐 *www.paradisecoveanguilla.com* 🛏 *12 studios, 17 1- and 2-bedroom apartments* 🍴 *No meals.*

$$ RENTAL FAMILY 🏨 **Serenity Cottages.** Despite the name, these aren't cottages but large, fully equipped, and relatively affordable one- and two-bedroom apartments (and studios created from them) in a small complex set in a lush garden at the far end of glorious Shoal Bay Beach. **Pros:** big apartments; quiet end of beach; snorkeling outside the door; weeklong packages. **Cons:** no pool; more condo than hotel in terms of staff; location requires a car and extra time to drive to the West End. [$] *Rooms from: $325* ✉ *Shoal Bay Village* ☎ *264/497–3328* 🌐 *www.serenity.ai* 🕒 *Closed Sept.* 🛏 *2 1-bedroom suites, 8 2-bedroom apartments* 🍴 *No meals.*

$$$$ RENTAL FAMILY 🏨 **Sheriva Villa Hotel.** This intimate, luxury-villa hotel is made up of three cavernous villas with a total of 20 guest rooms and seven private swimming pools overlooking a broad swath of turquoise sea. **Pros:** incredible staff; all the comforts of home; good value for groups. **Cons:** not on the beach; you risk being spoiled for life by the staff's attentions; expensive. [$] *Rooms from: $1500* ✉ *Maundays Bay Rd., West End Village* ☎ *264/498–9898* 🌐 *www.sheriva.com* 🛏 *20 rooms* 🍴 *Some meals.*

$$$ RENTAL FAMILY 🏨 **Shoal Bay Villas.** In this old-style property on Shoal Bay's incredible 2-mile (3-km) beach, studios and one- and two-bedroom apartments all have balconies over the water. **Pros:** friendly and casual; full kitchens; beachfront. **Cons:** rather basic; you'll want a car; there's construction in the area, so check before booking. [$] *Rooms from: $385* ✉ *Shoal Bay Village* ☎ *264/497–2051* 🌐 *www.sbvillas.ai* 🕒 *Closed Aug. 30–Oct. 24* 🛏 *12 units* 🍴 *No meals.*

$$ RENTAL FAMILY 🏨 **Turtle's Nest Beach Resort.** This complex of studios and one- to three-bedroom oceanfront condos is right on Meads Bay Beach, with some of the island's best restaurants a sandy stroll away. **Pros:** beachfront; huge apartments; well-kept grounds and pool. **Cons:** no elevator, so fourth-floor units are a climb (but have great views); seven-night minimum stay in high season. [$] *Rooms from: $374* ✉ *Meads Bay, West End Village* ☎ *264/462–6378* 🌐 *www.turtlesnestbeachresort.com* 🛏 *29 units* 🍴 *No meals.*

$$$$ $\square$ **Zemi Beach House Resort & Spa.** This new luxury resort is on a gor-
RESORT geous, 400-foot stretch of Shoal Bay East's white-sand beach. **Pros:**
fabulous beach location; desirable amenities such as a lap pool, spa,
and a rum and cigar room; beautiful boutique property. **Cons:** need a
car to get around the island. $ *Rooms from: $699* $\boxtimes$ *Shoal Bay Village* $\square$ *264/584–0001* $\oplus$ *www.zemibeach.com* $\square$ *69 rooms and suites*
$\lozenge$ *No meals.*

NIGHTLIFE

In late February or early March, on the first full moon before Easter,
reggae star and impresario Bankie Banx stages Moonsplash, a three-day
music festival that showcases local and imported talent. Anguilla Day's
boat races, in May, are the most important sporting event of the year.
At the end of July, the Anguilla Summer Festival has boat races by day
and Carnival parades, calypso competitions, and parties at night. Some
years bring a jazz festival.

Nightlife action doesn't really start until 11 and runs late into the night.
Be aware that taxis are not readily available then. If you plan to take a
cab back to your lodging at the end of the night, make arrangements in
advance with the driver who brings you or with your hotel concierge.

Dune Preserve. There is music most nights at the funky driftwood-fab-
ricated home of reggae star Bankie Banx, who often performs here
weekends and during the full moon. By day its the quintessential beach
bar with BBQ ribs and grilled fresh seafood. At night there's a dance
floor, beach bar, small menu, and potent rum cocktails, of course. In
high season there's a $15 cover. $\boxtimes$ *Rendezvous Bay* $\square$ *264/497–6219*
$\oplus$ *www.bankiebanx.net.*

Fodor's Choice **Elvis' Beach Bar.** Actually a boat, this is a great place to hear music and
★ sip the best rum punch on Earth. You can also snack on Mexican
food (try the goat tacos), play beach volleyball, or watch football on
the big TV. The bar is closed Tuesday, and there's live music Wednesday through Sunday nights in high season—plus food until 1 am. The
full-moon LunaSea party doesn't disappoint. $\boxtimes$ *Sandy Ground Village*
$\square$ *264/772–0637.*

Johnno's Beach Stop. There's live music and alfresco dancing every night
and on Sunday afternoon, when just about everybody drops by (on
Sunday night, there's live jazz). This is *the* classic Caribbean beach bar,
attracting a funky eclectic mix, from locals to movie stars. It's open
Tuesday–Sunday from 11 to 9. Johnno's has a daytime lunch outpost on
Prickly Pear Cay, with excellent snorkeling—it's a short boat trip from
Sandy Ground. $\boxtimes$ *Sandy Ground Village* $\square$ *264/497–2728* $\oplus$ *http://
johnnosbeachstop.com.*

Fodor's Choice **The Pumphouse.** In an old rock-salt factory, you can dance to live music
★ most nights, drink craft beers, and snack on pub food. A mini museum
has artifacts and equipment from 19th-century salt factories. Tuesday
is ladies' night, and Monday is trivia. Dancing doesn't kick into high
gear till after 10 pm. $\boxtimes$ *Sandy Ground Village* $\square$ *264/497–5154* $\oplus$ *www.
pumphouse-anguilla.com.*

SHOPPING

Anguilla is by no means a shopping destination, but a couple of boutiques stock cute beachwear and accessories. Hard-core shopping enthusiasts might like a day trip to nearby St. Martin.

The island's tourist publication, *What We Do in Anguilla,* has shopping tips and is available free at the airport and in shops. For upscale designer sportswear, check out small boutiques in the larger resorts like the Four Seasons and CuisinArt. Outstanding local artists sell their work in galleries, which often arrange studio tours (or check with the Anguilla Tourist Board).

ART AND CRAFTS

Anguilla Arts and Crafts Center. This gallery carries island crafts, including textiles and ceramics. ⊠ *The Valley* ⌖ *Across the parking lot from English Rose restaurant* ☎ *264/497–2200.*

Cheddie's Carving Studio. Cheddie's showcases Cheddie Richardson's fanciful wood carvings, coral and stone sculptures, and bronzes cast from nature. It's closed Sunday. ⊠ *Driftwood Haven, Cove Bay* ☎ *264/497–6027* ⊕ *http://www.cheddieonline.com* ⊗ *Closed Sun.*

Devonish Art Gallery. This gallery purveys the wood, stone, and clay creations of Courtney Devonish, an internationally known potter and sculptor, plus creations by his wife, Carolle, a bead artist. Works by other Caribbean artists and regional antique maps are also available. ⊠ *West End Rd., George Hill* ☎ *264/497–2949* ⊕ *www.devonishart.com.*

The Galleria at World Art and Antiques. The peripatetic proprietor, Christy Douglas, displays a veritable United Nations of antiquities: exquisite Indonesian ikat hangings to Thai teak furnishings, Aboriginal didgeridoos to Dogon tribal masks, Yuan Dynasty jade pottery to Uzbeki rugs. There is also handcrafted jewelry and handbags, and Anguilla souvenirs. ⊠ *West End Rd., West End Village* ☎ *264/497–5950, 264/497–2767.*

Hibernia Restaurant and Art Gallery. Striking pieces are culled from the owners' travels, from contemporary Eastern European art to traditional Indo-Chinese crafts. ⊠ *Harbor Ridge Dr., Island Harbour* ☎ *264/497–4290* ⊕ *www.hiberniarestaurant.com* ⊗ *Closed Mon. and mid-July–Nov. No lunch Sun.*

L. Bernbaum Art Gallery. Originally from Texas, Lynne Bernbaum has been working and living in Anguilla for more than a decade and exhibits around the world. Her paintings and prints are inspired by the island's natural beauty but have unusual perspectives and a hint of surrealism. The gallery is open Monday–Saturday 4–8 pm. ⊠ *Sandy Ground Village* ☎ *264/497–5211* ⊕ *www.lynnebernbaum.com.*

Savannah Gallery. Adjacent historic houses contain high-quality works by Anguillian artists; other contemporary Caribbean and Central American art, including oil paintings by Marge Morani; works from the renowned Haitian St. Soleil school; Guatemalan textiles; Mexican pottery; and Haitian metal sculpture, some made from recycled oil drums. ⊠ *Coronation St., Crocus Bay* ☎ *264/497–2263* ⊕ *www.savannahgallery.com* ⊗ *Closed Sun.*

CLOTHING

Caribbean Silkscreen. Caribbean Silkscreen creates designs and prints island-theme golf shirts, hats, sweatshirts, and jackets. ⊠ *South Hill Village* ☏ *264/497–2272.*

Irie Life. This popular boutique sells vividly hued beach and resort wear and flip-flops, as well as attractive handcrafts, jewelry, and collectibles from all over the Caribbean, many with a Rasta theme. ⊠ *South Hill Village* ☏ *264/497–6526* ⊕ *www.irielife.com.*

Limin' Boutique. Visit this attractive boutique for sensational repurposed jewelry and handicrafts such as iPad cases and wristlets made of old sails from Anguilla's famous racing boats, bracelets made from island musicians' discarded guitar strings, "Dune Jewelry" made from the sand from local beaches, and sea-salt body scrubs. There is also a good selection of stylish beach cover-ups. ⊠ *West End Main Rd., West End Village* ☏ *264/583–3733.*

Petals Boutique. This lovely boutique has attractive beachwear, jewelry, and accessories, as well as an assortment of local products. ⊠ *Frangipani Beach Resort, Rte. 1, Long Bay Village* ☏ *264/497–6442.*

SeaSpray Gifts and Smoothies. Enjoy a rum punch or a fruit smoothie while you shop for Anguillian arts and crafts, handcrafted jewelry, and charming handmade Christmas ornaments. They stock delicious locally made preserves from Anguilla's Jammin and other souvenirs. ⊠ *South Hill Roundabout, The Valley* ☏ *264/235–1650.*

ZaZaa. Sue Ricketts, the first lady of Anguilla marketing, owns three boutiques; on the Main Road in South Hill, near the entrance of Anacaona Boutique Hotel, on Meads Bay, and at the Shoal Bay Beach entrance. They carry Anguillian crafts; wonderful ethnic jewelry and beachwear, such as sexy Brazilian bikinis and chic St. Barth goodies; and beach hats, sundries, and souvenirs. ⊠ *Lower South Hill, South Hill Village* ☏ *264/497–6049* ⊕ *www.anguillaluxurycollection.com/zazaa-boutique.*

SPORTS AND THE OUTDOORS

Anguilla's expanding sports options include an excellent golf course (at the CuisinArt Golf Resort), designed by Greg Norman to accentuate the natural terrain and maximize the stunning ocean views over Rendezvous Bay. Players say the par-72 course is reminiscent of Pebble Beach. Personal experience says bring a lot of golf balls! The Anguilla Tennis Academy, designed by noted architect Myron Goldfinger, operates in the Blowing Point area. The 1,000-seat stadium, equipped with pro shop and seven lighted courts, was created to attract major international matches and to provide a first-class playing option for tourists and locals.

DIVING

Anguilla boasts seven marine park;. sunken wrecks; a long barrier reef; walls, canyons, and hulking boulders; varied marine life, including greenback turtles and nurse sharks; and exceptionally clear water. All make for excellent diving. **Prickly Pear Cay** is a favorite spot. **Stoney Bay Marine Park,** off the northeast end, showcases the *El Buen Consejo,* a 960-ton Spanish galleon that sank in 1772. Divers love finding all 29 cannons. Other good dive sites include **Grouper Bowl,** with exceptional hard-coral formations; **Ram's Head,** with caves, chutes, and tunnels; and **Upper Flats,** where you are sure to see stingrays.

FAMILY **Dophin Discovery.** Swim, hug, or dance with dolphins, or just learn about them and their habitat, at this new attraction located right across from the Blowing Point Ferry. Tours are offered four times a day, except Saturday. Be sure to investigate the different options that offer more or less contact with the dolphins. Kids must be at least eight years old and must swim with an adult. ✉ *Blowing Point Beach, Blowing Point Village* ☎ *264/497–7946* 🌐 *www.dolphindiscovery.com/anguilla* 🎟 *$179.*

FAMILY Fodor's Choice ★ **Shoal Bay Scuba and Watersports.** This highly rated PADI dive center runs up to six dives a day (closed Sundays) from two locations: at Roy's at Sandy Ground, and in West End. Single-tank dives start at $80, two-tank dives at $100. There is a discount for multiday dives, and advanced courses are available. Snorkeling trips (1 pm) are $25. Numerous kids' programs include a scuba intro in a pool and PADI Jr. certification. The shop sells masks, snorkels, fins, T-shirts, hats, shorts, and SPF-50 water shirts. Private dives, snorkeling and sightseeing charters, private fishing charters, and sunset cruises are also offered. ✉ *Sandy Ground Village* ☎ *264/235–1482* 🌐 *www.shoalbayscuba.com.*

GOLF

FAMILY **Anchor Miniature Golf.** This new, tropical-themed 18-hole miniature golf course is fun for the whole family. There's an ice-cream parlor next door. ✉ *Walter Hodge Rd., Island Harbour* ☎ *264/498–7258* 🌐 *www.anchorminiaturegolf.com* 🎟 *$5/day, $7 after 5 pm.*

Fodor's Choice ★ **CuisinArt Golf Resort.** This Greg Norman course, a $50 million wonder, qualifies as one of the best golf courses in the Caribbean. Thirteen of its 18 holes are directly on the water, and it features sweeping sea vistas, elevation changes, and an ecologically responsible watering system of ponds and lagoons that snake through the grounds. Players including President Bill Clinton have thrilled to the spectacular vistas of St. Maarten and blue sea at the tee box of the 390-yard starting hole—the Caribbean's answer to Pebble Beach. An attractive Italian restaurant serves lunch. The course typically closes the second half of October for maintenance. Dress requirements include long shorts or slacks and a collared shirt. ✉ *Rendezvous Bay* ☎ *264/498–5602* 🌐 *www.cuisinartresort.com* 🎟 *$270 for 18 holes ($225 guests), $170 for 9 holes ($145 guests)* 🏌 *18 holes, 7200 yards, par 72.*

A Day at the Boat Races

If you want a different kind of trip to Anguilla, try for a visit during Carnival, which starts on the first Monday in August and continues for about 10 days. Colorful parades, beauty pageants, music, delicious food, arts-and-crafts shows, fireworks, and nonstop partying are just the beginning. The music starts with sunrise jam sessions—as early as 4 am—and continues well into the night. The high point? The boat races. They are the national passion and the official national sport of Anguilla.

Anguillians from around the world return home to race old-fashioned, made-on-the-island wooden boats that have been in use on the island since the early 1800s. Similar to some of today's fastest sailboats, these are 15 to 28 feet in length and sport only a mainsail and jib on a single 25-foot mast. The sailboats have no deck, so heavy bags of sand, boulders, and sometimes even people are used as ballast. As the boats reach the finish line, the ballast—including some of the sailors—gets thrown into the water in a furious effort to win the race. Spectators line the beaches and follow the boats on foot, by car, and from even more boats. You'll have almost as much fun watching the fans as you will the races.

GUIDED TOURS

A round-the-island tour by taxi takes about 2½ hours and costs about $55 for one or two people, $5 for each additional passenger. Special-interest nature and culture tours are available.

FAMILY **Anguilla Access Tours.** A three-hour tour gives an introduction to island heritage, culture, food, nightlife, arts and crafts, or just beaches. Tours are three times a day, including the nightlife tour at 9 pm. You can get picked up from your lodging for the half-day tour ($45 per person). ⊠ *Government Center, The Valley* ☎ *267/772–9827* ⊕ *www. anguillaaccess.com* 🖃 *$45 adults, $35 under 12, nightlife $15.*

Anguilla Tourist Board. Tuesdays at 10, by appointment, Sir Emile Gumbs, the island's former chief minister, leads tours of the Sandy Ground area that highlight historic and ecological sites. Its $20 fee benefits the Anguilla Archeological and Historical Society. Gumbs also organizes bird-watching expeditions that spy everything from frigate birds to turtledoves. Tours tailored to almost any interest—sea turtle nesting sites, historic buildings, birding sites, gardens, and art galleries—can also be booked through the office. ⊠ *Coronation Ave., The Valley* ☎ *264/497–2759, 800/553–4939* ⊕ *www.ivisitanguilla.com.*

Bennie's Travel & Tours. One of the island's more reliable tour operators also arranges private boat charters, event planning, real-estate tours, and personal security services. ⊠ *Blowing Point Village* ☎ *264/497–4559* ⊕ *www.benniestravel.com.*

FAMILY **Nature Explorers Anguilla.** Ecotourists, photographers, families, and bird-watchers can enjoy a variety of tours of Anguilla's wildlife and wetlands. Tours can be customized by age of the group and interests, and range in time and price. Pickup is at your hotel or villa. Tours include use of binoculars, guidebooks, and bottled water. They also offer a seven-day/six-night tour package. ☎ *264/584–0346* ⊕ *http:// natureexplorersanguilla.com* 🖃 *From $50.*

HORSEBACK RIDING

FAMILY **Seaside Stables.** Ever dreamed of a sunset gallop (or slow clomp) on the beach? A bareback ocean romp is $125, private rides any time of day are $90 per hour, and morning and afternoon group rides are $75. Prior riding experience is not required, as the horses are very gentle. Choose from English, Western, or Australian saddles. ✉ *Paradise Dr., Cove Bay* ☎ *264/235–3667* ⊕ *www.seaside-stables.com* 🖃 *$90 private ride, $75 group ride.*

SEA EXCURSIONS

A number of boating options are available for airport transfers, day trips to offshore cays or neighboring islands, night trips to St. Martin, or just whipping through the waves en route to a picnic spot.

Calypso Charters. Book a private or semiprivate charter with Calypso on one of their five powerboats for a trip around Anguilla, a fishing trip, or a sea excursion to St. Barth, St. Maarten, or the surrounding islands. They offer a lovely two-hour sunset cruise leaving from Cole Bay every Tuesday and Thursday. They also provide airport transfers. ✉ *Sandy Ground Village* ☎ *264/584–8504* ⊕ *www.calypsochartersanguilla.com.*

Funtime Charters. With five powerboats from 32 to 38 feet, this charter and shuttle service arranges private and scheduled boat transport to the airport, including luggage services ($70 per person); day trips to St. Barth; and other powerboat excursions. The air-conditioned 42-seat *Sunshine Express* runs to SXM in the late night and early morning, as well as interisland excursions. ✉ *Cove Bay* ☎ *264/497–6511, 866/334–0047* ⊕ *www.funtime-charters.com.*

FAMILY **Junior's Glass Bottom Boat.** For an underwater peek at sea turtles and stingrays without getting wet, catch a ride ($20 per person) on this boat. Guided snorkeling trips and instruction are available, too. Junior is great with kids and very knowledgeable. Best to book in advance, especially during holidays. Hotel transport is available. ✉ *Shoal Bay Village* ☎ *264/497–4456* ⊕ *www.junior.ai.*

No Fear Sea Tours. In addition to private airport transportation, day snorkeling trips, sunset cruises, and fishing trips on three 32-foot speedboats and a 19-foot ski boat, this charter service offers water-sports rentals (tubing, skiing, knee-boarding). ✉ *Cove Bay* ☎ *264/235–8406* ⊕ *www. nofearcharters.com/.*

Sail Chocolat. This 35-foot EDEL catamaran, with four private cabins, is available for private charter or scheduled excursions to nearby cays. Captain Rollins is a knowledgeable, affable, safety-conscious guide. Trips visit Prickly Pear Cay for snorkeling, then on to Sandy Island for lunch. ✉ *Sandy Ground Village* ☎ *264/497–3394* ⊕ *www. sailinganguilla.com.*

Sandy Island Enterprises. Picnic, swimming, and diving excursions to Prickly Pear Cay, Sandy Island, and Scilly Cay are available through this outfit, which also rents Sunfish and windsurfers and arranges fishing charters. The Sandy Island sea shuttle *Happiness* leaves from the small pier in Sandy Ground daily November–August and by reservation September and October. ✉ *Sandy Ground Village* ☎ *264/476–6534* ⊕ *www. mysandyisland.com* ☞ *Open by reservation only Sept. 1–Oct. 31.*

Sea Pro Boat Charters. Whether it's kayaking, windsurfing, stand-up paddleboarding, or waterskiing, head to Sea Pro's center at Sandy Ground. They also run a sunset cruise, a sightseeing tour around the island, a shopping trip to St. Barth, a night in St, Maarten, or a chance to snorkel at some of the less accessible reefs and shoals. They have a beach bar in Sandy Ground with a water trampoline and live music on Sundays, too. ✉ *Sandy Ground Village* ☎ *264/584–0074* ⊕ *www.seaprocharters.com.*

Surf AXA. Surf AXA offers everything for beginner or experienced surfers and paddleboarders, including instruction and rentals. They offer guided surf tours, too. ✉ *South Hill Village* ☎ *264/582–7425* ⊕ *surfaxa. com* ✉ *$60 half-day surfboard rental.*

ANTIGUA AND BARBUDA

3

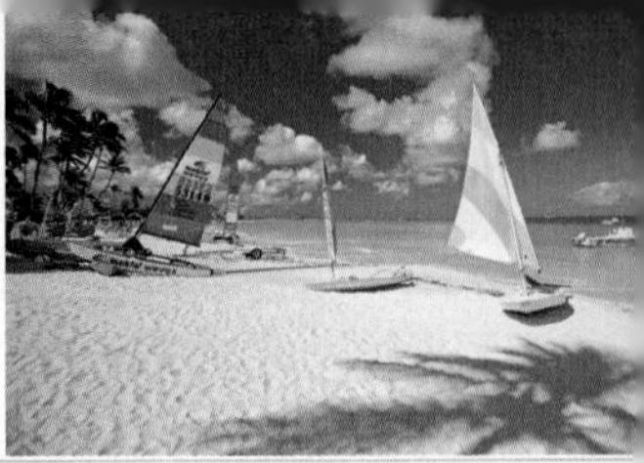

WELCOME TO ANTIGUA AND BARBUDA

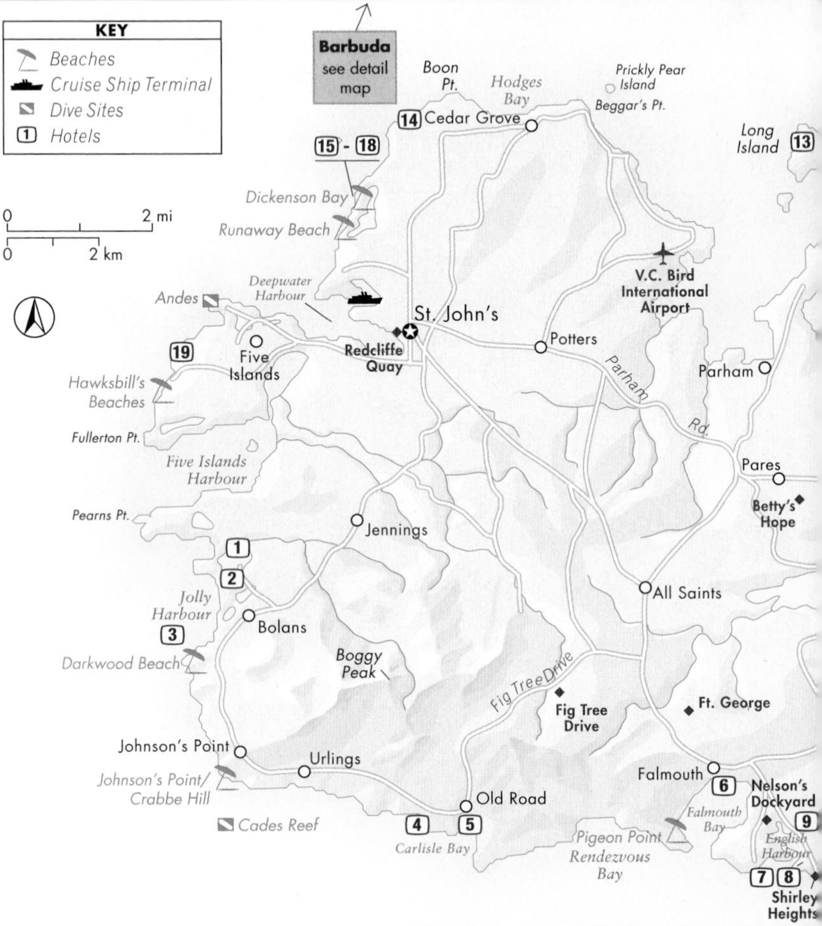
KEY
Beaches
Cruise Ship Terminal
Dive Sites
[1] Hotels
0
2 mi
0
2 km
Barbuda see detail map
Boon Pt.
Hodges Bay
Prickly Pear Island
Beggar's Pt.
[14] Cedar Grove
Long Island [13]
[15] - [18]
Dickenson Bay
Runaway Beach
V.C. Bird International Airport
Deepwater Harbour
Andes
St. John's
Redcliffe Quay
Potters
[19]
Five Islands
Hawksbill's Beaches
Parham Rd.
Parham
Fullerton Pt.
Five Islands Harbour
Pares
Betty's Hope
Pearns Pt.
Jennings
[1]
[2]
All Saints
Jolly Harbour
Bolans
[3]
Darkwood Beach
Boggy Peak
Fig Tree Drive
Fig Tree Drive
Ft. George
Johnson's Point
Urlings
Johnson's Point/ Crabbe Hill
Falmouth
[6]
Nelson's Dockyard
Old Road
Cades Reef
[4]
[5]
Carlisle Bay
Falmouth Bay
[9]
English Harbour
Pigeon Point
Rendezvous Bay
[7] [8]
Shirley Heights

Excellent beaches—365 of them—might make you think that the island has never busied itself with anything more pressing than the pursuit of pleasure. But for much of the 18th and 19th centuries, English Harbour sheltered Britain's Caribbean fleet. These days, pleasure yachts bob where galleons once anchored.

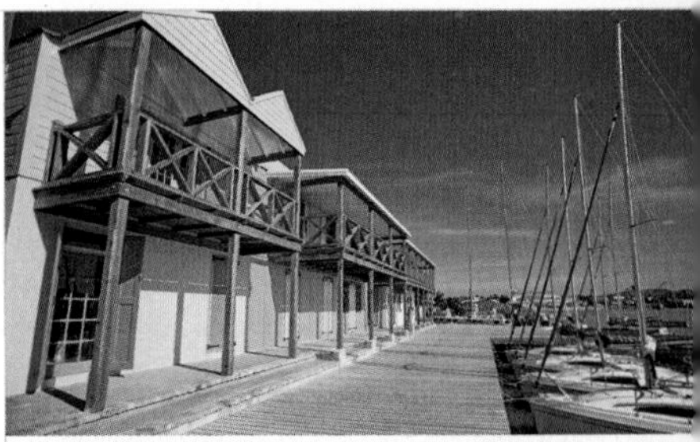

A BEACH FOR EVERY DAY

At 108 square miles (280 square km), Antigua is the largest of the British Leeward Islands. Its much smaller sister island, Barbuda, is 26 miles (42 km) to the north. Together, they are an independent nation and part of the British Commonwealth. The islands were under British control from 1667 until it achieved independence in 1981.

ANTIGUA AND BARBUDA

3

TOP REASONS TO VISIT ANTIGUA AND BARBUDA

1 **Beaches Galore:** So many paradisiacal beaches of every size provide a tremendous selection for an island its size.

2 **Nelson's Dockyard:** One of the Caribbean's best examples of historic preservation.

3 **Sailing Away:** With several natural anchorages and tiny islets to explore, Antigua is a major sailing center.

4 **Activities Galore:** Land and water sports, sights to see, and nightlife.

5 **Shopping Options:** A nice selection of shopping options, from duty-free goods to local artists and craftspeople (especially distinctive ceramics).

NEED TO KNOW

Atlantic Ocean

BARBUDA

ANTIGUA
AND
BARBUDA

Saint John's

ANTIGUA

Caribbean Sea

AT A GLANCE

Capital: Saint John's

Population: 90,000

Currency: Eastern Caribbean dollar; pegged to the U.S. dollar

Money: ATMs dispense EC$; credit cards and U.S. dollars widely accepted

Language: English

Country Code: ☎ 1 268

Emergencies: ☎ 999

Driving: On the left

Electricity: 230v/60 cycles; plugs are U.S. standard two- and three-prong. Power converter needed

Time: Same as New York during daylight savings time; one hour ahead otherwise

Documents: A valid passport and a return or ongoing ticket

Major Mobile Companies: Digicel, LIME

WEBSITES

Antigua & Barbuda Department of Tourism: ⊕ www.antigua-barbuda.org

GETTING AROUND

✈ **Air Travel:** Fly from the U.S. to Antigua's V.C. Bird International Airport; connect to reach Barbuda's Codrington Airport.

🚌 **Bus Travel:** Buses leave St. John's from Market Street or Independence Avenue. Service is unreliable and not recommended.

🚗 **Car Travel:** If island exploring is on the agenda, a car rental is useful. Main roads are mostly in good condition, with some bumpy dirt stretches and potholes. Four-wheel-drive vehicles are recommended.

⛴ **Ferry Travel:** Barbuda Express ferries run five times per week between Antigua and Barbuda.

PLAN YOUR BUDGET

	HOTEL ROOM	MEAL	ATTRACTIONS
Low Budget	$275	$12	Museum of Antigua & Barbuda, $3
Mid Budget	$375	$30	Half-day windsurfer rental, $70
High Budget	$475	$45	Two-tank dive package, $285

WAYS TO SAVE

Go all-inclusive. Many of Antigua's best resorts have all-inclusive rates including both food and drinks.

Visit between mid-November and mid-December. Nearly the same weather as high season but considered shoulder season, this time period offers tremendous value and few crowds.

Travel to Barbuda by boat. The seven-seat plane ride to Barbuda is nearly the same price as the ferry.

Sightsee. Most of Antigua's attractions, from beaches to nature trails to naval dockyards and museums, are free.

Hassle Factor	Medium. Flights to Antigua are frequent, but Barbuda usually requires an overnight stay in Antigua.
3 days	Relax poolside or beachside at your resort. Dabble in a few of Antigua's 365 beaches (one for every day of the year).
1 week	Relax, sightsee, and shop your away across Antigua. Charter a sailboat to visit tiny islets. Spend a few days escaping the 21st century in pristine and remote Barbuda.
2 weeks	Stay at two different Antigua resorts on opposite ends of the island to appreciate the diversity in landscapes. Visit Barbuda for several days, then go to nearby Montserrat, a 20-minute flight away.

WHEN TO GO

High Season: Mid-December through mid-April. The most fashionable and expensive time to visit, when the weather is typically sunny and warm. Hotels are booked far in advance, and everything is open.

Low Season: From August to late October, temperatures can grow oppressively hot and the weather muggy, with high risks of tropical storms. Upscale hotels may close for annual renovations; others offer deep discounts.

Value Season: From late April to July and again November to mid-December, hotel prices drop 20% to 50% from high season prices. There are chances of scattered showers, but expect sun-kissed days and comfortable nighttime temperatures, along with fewer crowds.

BIG EVENTS

April: Mid-April sees the Antigua Classic Yacht Regatta, a five-day event that includes a tall-ships race. ⊕ www.antiguaclassics.com

April–May: The year's big event is Antigua Sailing Week, one of the top regattas in the world. The Back II Life Music Festival usually overlaps. ⊕ www.sailingweek.com

July–August: Summer Carnival runs 10 days and is elaborate, with eye-catching costumes and fierce music competitions. ⊕ www.antiguacarnival.com

December: The first week of December ushers in the annual Charter Yacht Show, the world's largest. ⊕ www.antiguayachtshow.com

READ THIS

■ *A Small Place,* Jamaica Kincaid. Autobiographical novel from the Antigua-born writer.

■ *Oh Gad! A Novel,* Joanne C. Hillhouse. An Antiguan woman returns home after being raised in the U.S.

■ *Moonwitch,* Nicole Jordan. A best-selling historical romance.

WATCH THIS

■ *Working Girl.* A promising student becomes a prostitute.

■ *The People vs. Larry Flynt.* The life of one of Antigua's most infamous part-time residents.

EAT THIS

■ *Dukuna*: steamed dumpling made from sweet potatoes and coconut.

■ *Barbudan snapper*: day-catch served either deep-fried or steamed.

■ *Fungi*: like polenta, made of cornmeal and water and served as a side dish.

■ *Black pudding*: sausage made with blood, rice, meat, and seasonings.

■ *Pepper pot*: local version, with pigeon peas, smoked ham, corned beef, eggplant, and spinach.

■ *Antiguan pineapple*: small, juicy, sweet, and dark.

Updated by
Jordan Simon

Antigua is famous for its 365 sensuous beaches, "one for every day of the year," as locals love saying—though when the island was first developed for tourism, the unofficial count was 52 ("one for every weekend"). Either way, even longtime residents haven't combed every stretch of sand.

The island's extensive archipelago of cays and islets is what attracted the original Amerindian settlers—the Ciboney—at least 4,000 years ago. The natural environment, which is rich in marine life, flora, and fauna, has been likened to a "natural supermarket." Antigua's superior anchorages and strategic location naturally caught the attention of the colonial powers. The Dutch, French, and English waged numerous bloody battles throughout the 17th century (eradicating the remaining Arawaks and Caribs in the process), with England finally prevailing in 1667. Antigua remained under English control until achieving full independence on November 1, 1981, along with Barbuda, 26 miles (42 km) to the north.

Boats and beaches go hand in hand with hotel development, and Antigua's tourist infrastructure has mushroomed since the 1950s. Though many of its grandes dames such as Curtain Bluff remain anchors, today all types of resorts line the sand, and the island offers something for everyone, from gamboling on the sand to gambling in casinos. Environmental activists have become increasingly vocal about preservation and limiting development, and not just because green travel rakes in the green. Antigua's allure is precisely that precarious balance and subliminal tension between its unspoiled, natural beauty and its sun-sand-surf megadevelopment. And the British heritage persists, from teatime (and tee times) to fiercely contested cricket matches.

PLANNING

GETTING HERE AND AROUND
AIR TRAVEL
Nonstop flights are available from Atlanta (Delta, twice weekly in season), Charlotte (American, once weekly in season), Miami (American, Caribbean Airlines, United), New York–JFK (American, Caribbean, JetBlue thrice weekly), and Newark (United, twice weekly off-season, four to five times in season).

Airport Contact V. C. Bird International Airport (*ANU*). ☎ *268/462–4672, 268/462–0358, 268/562–6798, 268/484–2300* ⊕ *www.vcbia.com.*

Airline Contacts American Airlines. ☎ *268/462–0950, 268/481–4699* ⊕ *www.aa.com.* **Antigua Barbuda Montserrat Air.** ☎ *268/562–8033, 268/562–7183* ⊕ *www.abm-air.com, www.antigua-flights.com, www.montserrat-flights. com.* **Caribbean Airlines.** ☎ *268/480–2900, 800/744–2225* ⊕ *www.caribbean-airlines.com.* **Delta Airlines.** ☎ *800/532–4777, 268/562–5951 for customer support from Antigua* ⊕ *www.delta.com.* **JetBlue.** ☎ *800/538–2583* ⊕ *www. jetblue.com.* **LIAT.** ☎ *268/480–5600* ⊕ *www.liatairline.com.* **Seaborne Airlines.** ☎ *866/359–8784* ⊕ *www.seaborneairlines.com.* **United Airlines.** ☎ *268/462–5355* ⊕ *www.united.com.*

BOAT AND FERRY TRAVEL
Ferries between Antigua and Barbuda run five days a week (generally Tuesday and Thursday–Sunday, but call for the changing schedule), departing St. John's Harbour at the bottom of High Street by the Heritage Quay Ferry Dock.

Contacts Barbuda Express. ⊠ *High St., St. John's* ☎ *268/560–7989* ⊕ *www. antiguaferries.com, www.barbudaexpress.com.*

CAR TRAVEL
The main roads are mostly in good condition, with some bumpy dirt stretches at remote locations and a few hilly areas that flood easily and become impassable for a day. Driving is on the left. To rent a car, you need a valid license and a temporary permit ($20), available through the rental agent. Costs start at about $50 per day in season, with unlimited mileage, though multiday discounts are standard. Most agencies offer automatic or stick shift and right- and left-hand drive. Four-wheel-drive vehicles (from $55 per day) will get you more places and are useful because so many roads are full of potholes.

Contacts Avis. ☎ *268/462–2840.* **Budget.** ☎ *268/561–6399, 268/736–6400* ⊕ *www.budget.com.* **Dollar.** ☎ *268/462–0362* ⊕ *www.dollarantigua.com.* **Hertz.** ☎ *268/481–4440 St. John's, 268/481–4455 airport branch.* **Thrifty.** ☎ *268/462–9532 St. John's, 268/462–8803 airport.*

TAXI TRAVEL
Some cabbies may take you from St. John's to English Harbour and wait for about a half hour while you look around, for about $50.

Contact St. John's taxi stand. ☎ *268/462–5190, 268/460–5353 for 24-hr service.*

DID YOU KNOW?

During the plantation days, particularly in Barbados and Antigua, it was necessary for working-class people to build tiny chattel houses. Their homes needed to be small and portable (*chattel* is movable property) because workers were often fired without notice and ordered off the land where they lived and worked.

HEALTH AND SAFETY

Dengue, chikungunya, and zika have all been reported throughout the Caribbean. We recommend that you protect yourself from these mosquito-borne illnesses by keeping your skin covered and/or wearing mosquito repellent. The mosquitoes that transmit these viruses are as active by day as they are by night.

HOTELS AND RESORTS

In Antigua you're almost certain to have an excellent beach regardless of where you stay. Dickenson Bay and Five Islands Peninsula suit beachcombers who want proximity to St. John's, and Jolly Harbour offers affordable options and activities galore. English Harbour and the southwest coast have the best inns and several excellent restaurants—although many close from August well into October; it's also the yachting crowd's hangout. Resorts elsewhere on the island are ideal for those seeking seclusion; some are so remote that all-inclusive packages or rental cars are mandatory. Barbuda has one posh resort, one fairly upscale hotel, and several guesthouses. The new Labour government has aggressively pursued investment. There have been rumors of a $2-billion multi-property project on the east coast from Chinese developers. A memorandum of intent was signed with a UAE developer to invest $150 million in an upscale resort. And more is in the wings according to government sources. None of this is likely to impact travelers until 2017 at the earliest.

All-Inclusive Resorts: Most of the all-inclusives aim for a mainstream, package-tour kind of crowd—with varying degrees of success—though offerings such as Jumby Bay, Galley Bay, and Curtain Bluff are more upscale.

Luxury Resorts: A fair number of luxury resorts cater to the well-heeled in varying degrees of formality on both Antigua and Barbuda.

Small Inns: A few small inns, some historic, can be found around Antigua, mostly concentrated in or near English Harbour.

Hotel reviews have been shortened. For full information, visit Fodors.com.

WHAT IT COSTS IN U.S. DOLLARS				
	$	$$	$$$	$$$$
RESTAURANTS	under $12	$12–$20	$21–$30	over $30
HOTELS	under $275	$275–$375	$376–$475	over $475

Restaurant prices are the average cost of a main course at dinner or, if dinner is not served, at lunch. Hotel prices are the lowest cost of a standard double room in high season.

VISITOR INFORMATION

Contacts Antigua & Barbuda Tourist Offices. 212/541–4117 in New York City, 305/381–6762 in Miami, 888/268–4227 www.antigua-barbuda.org. **Barbudaful.net.** www.barbudaful.net.

ANTIGUA

Some say Antigua has so many beaches that you could visit a different one every day for a year. Most have snow-white sand, and many are backed by lavish resorts that offer sailing, diving, windsurfing, and snorkeling. The largest of the British Leeward Islands, Antigua was the headquarters from which Lord Horatio Nelson (then a mere captain) made his forays against the French and pirates in the late 18th century. You may wish to explore English Harbour and its carefully restored Nelson's Dockyard, as well as tour old forts, historic churches, and tiny villages. Appealing aspects of the island's interior include a small tropical rain forest ideal for hiking and zip-lining, ancient Native American archaeological digs, and restored sugar mills.

EXPLORING

Most Antigua hotels provide free island maps, and you should get your bearings before heading out on the road. Street names aren't listed (except in St. John's), though *some* easy-to-spot signs lead the way to major restaurants and resorts. Locals generally give directions in terms of landmarks (turn left at the yellow house, or right at the big tree). Wear a swimsuit under your clothes—one of the sights to strike your fancy might be a secluded beach.

ST. JOHN'S

Antigua's capital, with some 45,000 inhabitants (approximately half the island's population), lies at sea level at the inland end of a sheltered northwestern bay. Although it has seen better days, a couple of notable historic sights and some good waterfront shopping areas make it worth a visit.

At the far south end of town, where Market Street forks into Valley and All Saints roads, haggling goes on every Friday and Saturday, when locals jam the **Public Market** to buy and sell fruits, vegetables, fish, and spices. Ask before you aim a camera; your subject may expect a tip. This is old-time Caribbean shopping, a jambalaya of sights, sounds, and smells.

TOP ATTRACTIONS

Fodor'sChoice ★ **Redcliffe Quay.** Redcliffe Quay, at the water's edge just south of Heritage Quay, is the most appealing part of St. John's. Attractively restored (and superbly re-created) 19th-century buildings in a riot of cotton-candy colors house shops, restaurants, galleries, and boutiques and are linked by courtyards and landscaped walkways. ⊠ *Redcliffe St., St. John's* ⊕ *www.historicredcliffequay.com.*

WORTH NOTING

Anglican Cathedral of St. John the Divine. At the south gate of the Anglican Cathedral of St. John the Divine are figures of St. John the Baptist and St. John the Divine, said to have been taken from one of Napoléon's ships and brought to Antigua. The original church was built in 1681, replaced by a stone building in 1745, and destroyed by an earthquake in 1843. The present neo-baroque building dates from 1845; the parishioners had the interior completely encased in pitch pine, hoping to forestall future earthquake damage. Tombstones bear eerily eloquent testament to the colonial days. ⊠ *Between Long and Newgate Sts., St. John's* ☎ *268/461–0082.*

Heritage Quay. Shopaholics head directly for Heritage Quay, an ugly multimillion-dollar complex. The two-story buildings contain stores that sell duty-free goods, sportswear, down-island imports (paintings, T-shirts, straw baskets), and local crafts. There are also restaurants, a bandstand, and a casino. Cruise-ship passengers disembark here from the 500-foot-long pier. Expect heavy shilling. ⊠ *High and Thames Sts., St. John's* ⊕ *www.heritagequayantigua.com.*

Museum of Antigua and Barbuda. Signs at the Museum of Antigua and Barbuda say "Please touch," encouraging you to explore Antigua's past. Try your hand at the educational video games or squeeze a cassava through a *matapi* (grass sieve). Exhibits interpret the nation's history, from its geological birth to its political independence in 1981. There are fossil and coral remains from some 34 million years ago; models of a sugar plantation and a wattle-and-daub house; an Arawak canoe; and a wildly eclectic assortment of objects from cannonballs to 1920s telephone exchanges. The museum occupies the former courthouse, which dates from 1750. The superlative museum gift shop carries such unusual items as calabash purses, seed earrings, warri boards (warri being an African game brought to the Caribbean), and lignum vitae pipes, as well as historic maps and local books (including engrossing monographs on varied subjects by the late Desmond Nicholson, a longtime resident). ⊠ *Long and Market Sts., St. John's* ☎ *268/462–1469, 268/462–4930* ⊕ *www.antiguamuseums.net* ☞ *$3; children under 12 free* ☽ *Weekdays 8:30–4, Sat. 10–2. Closed Sun.*

ELSEWHERE ON ANTIGUA
TOP ATTRACTIONS

Fodor'sChoice **Nelson's Dockyard.** Antigua's most famous attraction is the world's only
★ Georgian-era dockyard still in use, a treasure trove for history buffs and nautical nuts alike. In 1671 the governor of the Leeward Islands wrote to the Council for Foreign Plantations in London, pointing out the advantages of this landlocked harbor. By 1704 English Harbour was in regular use as a garrisoned station.

In 1784, 26-year-old Horatio Nelson sailed in on the HMS *Boreas* to serve as captain and second-in-command of the Leeward Island Station. Under him was the captain of the HMS *Pegasus,* Prince William Henry, duke of Clarence, who was later crowned King William IV. The prince acted as best man when Nelson married Fannie Nisbet on Nevis in 1787.

When the Royal Navy abandoned the station at English Harbour in 1889, it fell into a state of decay, though adventuresome yachties still lived there in near-primitive conditions. The Society of the Friends of English Harbour began restoring it in 1951; it reopened with great fanfare as Nelson's Dockyard on November 14, 1961. Within the compound are crafts shops, restaurants, and two splendidly restored 18th-century hotels, the Admiral's Inn and the Copper & Lumber Store Hotel, worth peeking into. (The latter, occupying a supply store for

Nelson's Dockyard at English Harbour

Nelson's Caribbean fleet, is a particularly fine example of Georgian architecture, its interior courtyard evoking Old England.) The Dockyard is a hub for oceangoing yachts and serves as headquarters for the annual Boat Show in early December and the Sailing Week Regatta in late April and early May. Water taxis will ferry you between points for EC$5. The Dockyard National Park also includes serene nature trails accessing beaches, rock pools, and crumbling plantation ruins and hilltop forts.

The **Dockyard Museum,** in the original Naval Officer's House, presents ship models, mock-ups of English Harbour, displays on the people who worked there and typical ships that docked, silver regatta trophies, maps, prints, antique navigational instruments, and Nelson's very own telescope and tea caddy. ⊠ *Dockyard Dr., English Harbour Town* ☎ *268/481–5027, 268/460–1379 both for Dockyard Museum, 268/481–5021 for National Parks Authority* ⊕ *www. nationalparksantigua.com* ✉ *$2 suggested donation* ⊙ *Daily 9–5.*

Shirley Heights. This bluff affords a spectacular view of English Harbour and Falmouth Harbour. The heights are named for Sir Thomas Shirley, the governor who fortified the harbor in 1781. At the top is Shirley Heights Lookout, a restaurant built into the remnants of the 18th-century fortifications. Most notable for its boisterous Sunday barbecues that continue into the night with live music and dancing, it serves dependable burgers, pumpkin soup, grilled meats, and rum punches.

Not far from Shirley Heights is the **Dows Hill Interpretation Centre,** where observation platforms provide still more sensational vistas of the English Harbour area. A multimedia sound-and-light presentation on island history and culture, spotlighting lifelike figures and colorful tableaux accompanied by running commentary and music, results in a cheery, if bland, portrait of Antiguan life from Amerindian times to the present. ⊠ *Dockyard Dr., Shirley Heights* ☎ *268/481–5045, 268/481–5021* ⊕ *www.nationalparksantigua.com* 🖃*EC$15* ⊙ *Weekdays 9–5.*

WORTH NOTING

Betty's Hope. Just outside the village of Pares, a marked dirt road leads to Antigua's first sugar plantation, founded in the 1670s. You can tour the twin windmills, various ruins, still-functional crushing machinery, and the visitor center's exhibits (often closed) on the island's sugar era. The private trust overseeing the restoration has yet to realize its ambitious, environmentally aware plans to replant indigenous crops destroyed by the extensive sugarcane plantings. Indeed, the site is somewhat neglected, with goats grazing the grounds. ⊠ *Pares Village Main Rd., Pares* ☎ *268/462–1469* ⊕ *www.antiguamuseums.net* 🖃 *$2* ⊙ *Tues.–Sat. 10–4.*

Devil's Bridge. This limestone arch formation, sculpted by the crashing breakers of the Atlantic at Indian Town, is a national park. Blowholes have been carved by the hissing, spitting surf. The park also encompasses some archaeological excavations of Carib artifacts. ⊠ *Dockyard Dr., Long Bay* ⊕ *www.nationalparksantigua.com.*

Falmouth. This town sits on a lovely bay backed by former sugar plantations and sugar mills. The most important historic site here is St. Paul's Church, which was rebuilt on the site of a church once used by troops during the Horatio Nelson period.

Fig Tree Drive. This often muddy, rutted, steep road takes you through the rain forest, which is rich in mangoes, pineapples, and banana trees (*fig* is the Antiguan word for "banana"). The rain forest is the island's hilliest area—1,319-foot Boggy Peak (renamed Mt. Obama), to the west, is the highest point. At its crest, Elaine Francis sells seasonal local fruit juices—ginger, guava, sorrel, passion fruit—and homemade jams at a stall she dubs the Culture Shop. A few houses down (look for the orange windows) is the atelier of noted island artist Sallie Harker (⊕ *www.sallieharker.com*) whose work displays shimmering seascapes and vividly hued fish incorporating gold leaf. You'll also pass several tranquil villages with charming churches and Antigua Rainforest Canopy Tours here. ⊠ *Fig Tree Dr.*

Ft. George. East of Liberta—one of the first settlements founded by freed slaves—on Monk's Hill, this fort was built between 1689 and 1720. Among the ruins are the sites for 32 cannons, water cisterns, the base of the old flagstaff, and some of the original buildings. ⊠ *Great Fort George Monk's Hill Trail, St. Paul.*

Harmony Hall. Northeast of Freetown (follow the signs), this art gallery/restaurant is built on the foundation of a 17th-century sugar-plantation great house. No longer affiliated with the original Jamaican outpost, the Antigua facility is run by enterprising Italians who operate a fine restaurant and six spare but chic cottage suites (with a villa development planned). Its remote location is a headache, but you can allot the whole afternoon to enjoy lunch (Tuesday through Sunday; dinner

Wednesday through Saturday), soak in the historic ambience and panoramic ocean views, browse through the exhibits, comb the beach, and perhaps even snorkel at nearby Green Island via the property's dragon boat, *Luna*. ✉ *Brown's Bay Mill, Dockyard Dr., Freetown* ☎ *268/460–4120* ⊕ *www.harmonyhallantigua.com* ☼ *Mid-Nov.–May, daily 10–6, later Wed., Fri., and Sat.*

Parham. This sleepy village is a splendid example of a traditional colonial settlement. St. Peter's Church, built in 1840 by English architect Thomas Weekes, is an octagonal Italianate building with unusual ribbed wooden ceiling, whose facade is richly decorated with stucco and keystone work, though it suffered considerable damage during an 1843 earthquake.

BEACHES

Antigua's beaches are public, and many are lined with resorts that have water-sports outfitters and beach bars. The government does a fairly good job of cleaning up seaweed and garbage. Most restaurants and bars on beaches won't charge for beach-chair rentals if you buy lunch or drinks; otherwise the going rate is $3 to $5. Access to some of the finest stretches, such as those at the Five Islands Peninsula resorts, is restricted to hotel guests (though, often, if you're polite, the guards will let you through). Sunbathing topless is strictly illegal except on one small beach at Hawksbill by Rex Resorts. When cruise ships dock in St. John's, buses drop off loads of passengers on most of the west-coast beaches. Choose such a time to visit one of the more remote east-end beaches or take a day trip to Barbuda.

Darkwood Beach. This ½-mile (1-km) beige ribbon on the southwest coast has stunning views of Montserrat. Although popular with locals and cruise-ship passengers on weekends, it's virtually deserted during the week. Waters are generally calm, but there's scant shade, little maintenance, no development other than Darkwood Beach Bar (and Admiral's Bar across the coastal road), and little to do other than bask in solitude. **Amenities:** food and drink. **Best for:** solitude; swimming. ✉ *2 miles (3 km) south of Jolly Harbour and roughly ½ mile (1 km) southwest of Valley Church, off Valley Rd.*

Dickenson Bay. Along a lengthy stretch of well-kept powder-soft white sand and exceptionally calm water, you can find small and large hotels (including Siboney Beach Club, Sandals, and Rex Halcyon Cove), water sports, concessions, and beachfront restaurants (Coconut Grove and Ana's on the Beach are recommended). There's decent snorkeling at either point. **Amenities:** food and drink; water sports. **Best for:** partiers; snorkeling; swimming; walking. ✉ *2 miles (3 km) northeast of St. John's, along main coast road.*

Half Moon Bay. This ½-mile (1-km) ivory crescent is a prime snorkeling and windsurfing area. On the Atlantic side, the water can be rough at times, attracting intrepid hard-core surfers and wakeboarders. The northeastern end, where a protective reef offers spectacular snorkeling, is much calmer. A tiny bar called Tibby's has restrooms, snacks, and beach chairs. Half Moon is a real trek, but one of Antigua's showcase beaches. **Amenities:** food and drink. **Best for:** snorkeling; sunrise; surfing; windsurfing. ⊠ *On southeast coast, 1½ mile (2½ km) from Freetown, Dockyard Dr.*

Johnson's Point/Crabbe Hill. This series of connected, deserted beaches on the southwest coast looks out toward Montserrat, Guadeloupe, and St. Kitts. Notable beach bar–restaurants include OJ's, Jacqui O's Beach-House, and Turner's. The water is generally placid, though not good for snorkeling. **Amenities:** food and drink. **Best for:** sunset; swimming; walking. ⊠ *3 miles (5 km) south of Jolly Harbour complex, on main west-coast road.*

Pigeon Point. Near Falmouth Harbour lie two fine white-sand beaches reasonably free of seaweed and driftwood. The leeward side is calmer, the windward side is rockier, and there are sensational views and snorkeling around the point. Several restaurants and bars are nearby, though Bumpkin's (and its potent banana coladas) and the more upscale bustling Catherine's Cafe Plage satisfy most on-site needs. **Amenities:** food and drink. **Best for:** snorkeling; swimming; walking. ⊠ *Off main south-coast road, southwest of Falmouth.*

Runaway Beach. An often unoccupied stretch of bone-white sand, this beach is still rebuilding after years of hurricane erosion, with just enough palms left for shelter. Both the water and the scene are relatively calm, the sand is reasonably well maintained, and beach restaurants such as Sandhaven and La Bussola offer cool shade and cold beer. Hug the lagoon past the entrance to Siboney Beach Club to get here; the Buccaneer Beach Club is the unofficial demarcation point between Dickenson and Runaway bays. **Amenities:** food and drink. **Best for:** snorkeling; swimming; walking. ⊠ *Approximately 2 miles (3 km) northwest of St. John's, down main north-coast road from Dickenson Bay, St. John's.*

WHERE TO EAT

Antigua's restaurants are almost a dying breed since the advent of all-inclusives. But several worthwhile hotel dining rooms and nightspots remain, especially in the English/Falmouth Harbour and Dickenson Bay areas. Virtually every chef incorporates local ingredients and elements of West Indian cuisine.

Most menus list prices in both EC and U.S. dollars; if not, ask which currency the menu is using. Always double-check whether credit cards are accepted and service is included. Dinner reservations are needed during high season.

What to Wear: Perhaps because of the island's British heritage, Antiguans tend to dress more formally for dinner than dwellers on many other Caribbean islands. Wraps and shorts (no beach attire) are de rigueur for lunch, except at local hangouts.

$$$ ✕ **The Bay @ Nonsuch.** This restaurant's tiered wooden decks, swaddled
ECLECTIC   in billowing white curtains, wrap around the bluff fronting Nonsuch Bay. Chef Mitchell Husbands deftly marries local ingredients to international techniques. His presentation alone is appetizing, the plates painted with swirls of red-pepper coulis or basil reduction. The stellar

starters are sometimes superior to the fine entrées. For lunch order several, tapas-style: perhaps the chunky yet silken crab cakes perfectly counterpointed by arugula aioli. Or try such creative wraps and panini as pulled pork and jerk mahimahi. For dinner, enjoy cocktails in the refined lounge with the lively mix of yachties and expats, then order soft-shell crab with pink peppercorn marmalade over sweet corn–flavored blini, segueing into blackened mahimahi with coconut- and saffron-infused risotto and *pico de gallo*. U.K.-based wine director Liam Stevenson's small, savvy list is admirably suited to the menu and climate, with selections like Eden Valley Rieslings and Albariños. Or look for the frequent four-course pairing menus and wine events. Finish with the dense, decadent banoffee (banana toffee) pie drowning in warm brandy sauce. $ *Average main: $28* ⊠ *Nonsuch Bay Resort, Hughes Point, Nonsuch Bay* ☎ *268/562–8000, 888/844–2480* ⊕ *www. nonsuchbayresort.com* ⊗ *Closed Sept.* ⌕ *Reservations essential.*

$$ ✕ **Big Banana—Pizzas in Paradise.** This tiny, often crowded spot is tucked
PIZZA into one side of a restored 18th-century rum warehouse with broad
FAMILY plank floors, wood-beam ceiling, and stone archways. Cool, Benetton-style photos of locals and musicians jamming adorn the brick walls. Big Banana serves some of the island's best pizza—try the lobster or the seafood variety—as well as fresh fruit crushes, classic pastas, wraps, burgers, and sub sandwiches bursting at the seams. There's live entertainment some nights, and a large-screen TV for sports fans. $ *Average main: $18* ⊠ *Redcliffe Quay, Redcliffe St., St. John's* ☎ *268/480–6985* ⊕ *www.bigbanana-antigua.com* ⊗ *Closed Sun.*

$$$ ✕ **Cecilia's High Point Café.** The eponymous owner, a vivacious, striking
ECLECTIC Swedish ex-model, floats (and once in a while flirts) about the tables in this cozy beachfront creole cottage plastered with vivid paintings of sailing and island scenes. An equally animated cross section of Antiguan life usually packs the coveted patio tables (it's a terrific spot to eavesdrop on island gossip), as well as the lounges on the point. The day's selections, including wine specials, are written on a blackboard. Stellar standbys run from goat cheese and caramelized apples in puff pastry to homemade gravlax on potato pancake to mushroom ravioli nestled in spinach with a gossamer creamy pesto, but the high points are the setting and Cecilia herself. As a bonus, Wi-Fi access is free. $ *Average main: $27* ⊠ *Dutchman's Bay, Texaco Dock Rd.* ☎ *268/562–7070* ⊕ *www.highpointantigua.com* ⊗ *Closed Tues. and Wed. No dinner Fri.–Sun.* ⌕ *Reservations essential.*

$$$ ✕ **Coconut Grove.** Coconut palms grow through the roof of this open-
ECLECTIC air thatched restaurant, flickering candlelight illuminates colorful local murals, waves lap the white sand, and the waitstaff provides just the right level of service. Jean-François Bellanger's dishes artfully fuse French culinary preparations with island ingredients. Top choices include pan-seared mahimahi served over cauliflower puree with fingerling potatoes and mango-pineapple chutney, and sautéed shrimp with roasted plantain and hickory bacon finished with champagne-Parmesan sauce. The signature coconut shrimp is the best lunch option. The kitchen can be uneven, the wine list is unimaginative and overpriced, and the buzzing happy-hour bar crowd lingering well into dinnertime can detract

from the otherwise romantic atmosphere. Nonetheless, Coconut Grove straddles the line between casual beachfront boîte and elegant eatery with aplomb. [$] *Average main: $30* ✉ *Siboney Beach Club, Marina Bay Rd., Dickenson Bay* ☎ *268/462–1538* 🌐 *www.coconutgroveantigua.com* ✍ *Reservations essential.*

$$$$ ASIAN FUSION 🍴 **East.** Imposing Indonesian carved doors usher you into this bold and sexy Asian fusion spot. Flames flicker in the outdoor lily pond while candles illuminate lacquered dark-wood tables with blood-red napery and oversize fuchsia-color chairs. Exquisite pan-Pacific fare (with delicious detours to the Indian subcontinent) courts perfection through simplicity and precision: prawn spring rolls with hoisin–sweet chili sauce, superlative sashimi, entrées from Thai lobster curry to tandoori chicken, and green tea crème brûlée. The small main courses mandate tapas-style dining; the comprehensive wine list is pricey but offers values from intriguing lesser-known regions. Families appreciate the extensive, comparatively inexpensive children's menu. [$] *Average main: $32* ✉ *Carlisle Bay, Old Road* ☎ *268/484–0000* 🕓 *No lunch* ✍ *Reservations essential.*

$$$$ ECLECTIC 🍴 **Jacqui O's BeachHouse at Love Beach.** A bevy of Bouviers would no doubt adore this stylish beachfront boîte, which conjures a St. Tropez–gone–tropical vibe. Brit owner Lance Leonhardt visited six islands and 65 properties before settling on this spot. The turquoise throw pillows, fuchsia upholstery, and vivid abstract artworks are a sexy contrast with the giant white canopied beach chairs. The sound track, ranging from Pavarotti to Papagayo Club, duets harmoniously with the soothing surf; the almost ritualistic dancing between 6 and 8 is purely optional. Lance claims that his kitchen offers the Caribbean's only sous vide molecular cooking. The results are stunning, from tiger prawn ravioli in gossamer lobster sauce kissed with lemongrass and ginger to decadent foie gras burger with veal-truffle dipping sauce to velvety chocolate-crusted *panna cotta*. Pair your selections with the excellent if occasionally pricey wines, including superb rosés. Add stellar service and you might walk out feeling like a Kennedy. [$] *Average main: $35* ✉ *Off Valley Rd., Crab Hill* ☎ *268/562–2218* 🕓 *Closed Mon. and 4 nights weekly; call ahead.*

$$$ ITALIAN Fodor's Choice ★ 🍴 **La Bussola.** Blend a genuinely simpatico welcome with lapping waves, the murmur of jazz, and expert Italian fare and you have Omar Tagliaventi and family's recipe for the perfect beachfront bistro. Bleached-wood ceilings, old island photos of Antigua, boating paraphernalia, and brightly painted plates enhance the relaxed, romantic mood. The presentation is invariably pretty and Omar has a particularly facile touch with seafood; try the artichoke-shrimp pie in satiny garlic sauce, lobster-asparagus risotto, shark tartare with grapefruit nestling on a bed of arugula, mahimahi with olive "pâté" in filo, or the "fishermen's" spaghetti. Or savor the "true Italian-style" thin-crust pizzas. The carefully considered, affordable wine list showcases lesser-known Italian regions. Your evening ends with a complimentary grappa, Frangelico, or *limoncello* (lemon liqueur), representing northern, central, and southern Italy. La Bussola means "the compass" in Italian, and it certainly takes the right gastronomic direction. [$] *Average main: $26* ✉ *Rush Night Club Rd., Runaway Bay* ☎ *268/562–1545* 🌐 *www.labussolarestaurant.net* 🕓 *Closed Tues.* ✍ *Reservations essential.*

$$$$ FRENCH 🍴 **Le Bistro.** This Antiguan institution's peach, periwinkle, and pistachio accents subtly match the tile work, jade chairs, mint china, and painted lighting fixtures. Trellises divide the large space into intimate sections. Chef Patrick Gauducheau delights in blending classic regional fare with indigenous ingredients, displaying an especially deft hand with delicate sauces. The kitchen now runs smoothly after bouts of inconsistency. Opt for daily specials, such as smoked marlin carpaccio with pink peppercorns, prawns in a gossamer ginger white wine sauce laced with leeks, lobster medallions in roasted red bell pepper–lime sauce flamed with grappa, and almost anything swaddled in puff pastry. The fine wine list hits all the right spots, geographically and varietally, without outrageous markups. Co-owner Phillipa Esposito doubles as hostess and pastry chef; her passion-fruit mousse and chocolate confections are sublime. [$] *Average main: $34* ✉ *Hodges Bay Rd., Hodges Bay* ☎ *268/462–3881* 🌐 *www.antigualebistro.com* 🕒 *Closed Mon. No lunch* ✍ *Reservations essential.*

$$$$ FRENCH 🍴 **Le Cap Horn.** As Piaf and Aznavour compete with croaking tree frogs in a trellised, plant-filled room lighted by straw lamps, it's easy to imagine yourself in a tropical St. Tropez. Begin with escargots in tomato, onion, and pepper sauce (sop it up with the marvelous home-baked bread) or the ultimate in hedonism (and expense), lobster–foie gras mille-feuille; then segue into tiger shrimp swimming in gossamer vanilla-lobster sauce or duck breast wrapped with mango in rice sheet floating in rum-tamarind sauce. Or cook your own seafood and/or beef on a hot volcanic stone at your table. Gustavo Belaunde (he's Peruvian of Catalan extraction) elicits delicate, almost ethereal flavors from his ingredients; his versatility is displayed in the restaurant's other half, a pizzeria replete with wood-burning oven (with much lower prices and rowdier ambience). Finish with wife Hélène's divine desserts or a cognac and cigar. [$] *Average main: $39* ✉ *English Harbour Town* ☎ *268/460–1194* 🕒 *Closed Aug., Sept., and Thurs. Closed Wed. in low season (May–July, Oct. and Nov.). No lunch.*

$$$ CARIBBEAN 🍴 **Papa Zouk.** Who would have thought that two jovial globe-trotting German gents could create a classic Caribbean hangout? But the madras tablecloths, straw lamps, fishnets festooned with Christmas lights, painted bottles of homemade hot sauces, art naïf, colorful island clientele, and lilting rhythms on the sound system justify the name (*zouk* is a sultry musical stew of soul and calypso). Seafood is king, from butterfish to Barbudan snapper, served either deep-fried or steamed with a choice of such sauces as guava-pepper teriyaki or tomato-basil-coriander. Tangy Caribbean bouillabaisse with garlicky Parmesan mayonnaise and the tapas platter are specialties, as are the knockout rum ti' punches. Finish dinner with a snifter of aged rum: the tiny, Pollock-style hand-painted bar once held 250 varieties, many of which were lost in a 2014 fire. But rum fan(atic)s contributed over 100 bottles for its reopening, and co-owner Bert Kirchner salvaged what he could from the ashes and created a very special house blend in a barrel. [$] *Average main: $24* ✉ *Hilda Davis Dr., Gambles Terrace, St. John's* ☎ *268/464–0795, 268/464–6044* 💳 *No credit cards* 🕒 *Closed May–Oct. and Sun. No lunch sometimes; call ahead for hrs.*

$$$$
ECLECTIC
✕ **Pillars Restaurant & Bar.** This restaurant at the Admiral's Inn is a must for Anglophiles and mariners. Soak up the centuries at the inside bar, where 18th-century sailors reputedly carved their ships' names on the dark timbers. Most diners sit on the flagstone terrace under shady Australian gums to enjoy the views of the harbor complex (framed by the namesake pillars) and trendy exhibition kitchen; yachts seem close enough to eavesdrop. The menu is limited but expertly prepared; consider ordering two or three appetizers tapas-style. Specialties include ceviche, lobster toast, and the pulled-pork open sandwich with chipotle mayo and red onion marmalade. Ⓢ *Average main: $35 ⊠ Dockyard Dr., Nelson's Dockyard, English Harbour Town ☎ 268/460–1027 ⊕ www. admiralsantigua.com ⌕ Reservations essential.*

$$
CARIBBEAN
✕ **Russell's.** By restoring part of Ft. James, with its glorious views of the bay and headlands, and converting it into a semi-alfresco eatery, Russell's delivers a delightful dining experience. Jazz and reggae on the sound system (live music Friday and Sunday, with open mike Monday), beamed ceilings, cool canvases of musical instruments in fevered Fauvist hues, and red or black hurricane lamps lend a romantic aura to the stone-and-wood terrace. The limited menu—local specialties emphasizing seafood—includes fabulous chunky conch fritters and whelks in garlic butter. Danielle Russell maintains the tradition her father established at this restaurant. Russell's sister Faye co-owns Papa Zouk, and sister Valerie runs Shirley Heights Lookout; the Hodges might well be Antigua's first family of food. Ⓢ *Average main: $20 ⊠ Fort James ☎ 268/462–5479 ⊗ Closed Tues. No lunch Sun.*

$$$
ECLECTIC
Fodor's Choice
★
✕ **Sheer Rocks.** This sensuous eatery, a series of tiered wood decks carved into a sheer cliff side, showcases the setting sun from the staggered thatched dining nooks, many separated by billowing white-gauze curtains. White four-poster beds surround infinity pools, making it equally sybaritic for daytime lounging. The menu encompasses a tapestry of creative tapas, many of which can be served in larger portions. Chef Alex Grimley's philosophy emphasizes simplicity, detail, and only the freshest ingredients to create a symphonic counterpoint of flavors and textures—subtle to lusty, crispy to creamy. He's ably abetted by his chef de cuisine, Simon Christey-French, who offers his own spin. Witness foie gras parfait with onion puree, lentil vinaigrette, and seven-grain toast; decadent truffle mac-and-cheese infused with porcini stock; or slow-cooked mahimahi with bok choy, black olives, and saffron sauce. Add a dash of sultry music, season with smashing views, complement with an admirable wine list (not to mention inventive cocktails), and you have the recipe for a tropical St. Tropez experience. It closes more often in low season; call ahead. Ⓢ *Average main: $28 ⊠ CocoBay Resort, Valley Rd. ☎ 268/562–4510, 268/464–5283 ⊕ www.sheer-rocks.com ⊗ Closed Tues. No dinner Sun. ⌕ Reservations essential.*

WHERE TO STAY

Scattered along Antigua's beaches and hillsides are exclusive, elegant hideaways; romantic restored inns; and all-inclusive hot spots for couples. Check individual lodgings for restrictions (many have minimum stays during certain high-season periods). Look also for specials on the

Web or from tour packagers, since hotels' quoted rack rates are often negotiable (up to 45% off in season). There are several new condo and villa developments: Keyonna Beach and South Point Resort opened successfully in 2015 (the latter with an already wildly popular seafood eatery), while Tamarind Hills and Hodges Bay Club are among several other major developments slated to open in late 2016.

$

B&B/INN

Fodor's Choice

★

Admiral's Inn. This Georgian brick edifice, originally the shipwright's offices in what is now Nelson's Dockyard, has withstood acts of God and war since 1788. **Pros:** historic ambience yet contemporary boutique style; central English Harbour location; fine value; free Wi-Fi; charming restaurant setting. **Cons:** occasionally noisy when yachties take over the bar; recently remodeled bathrooms are still cramped; no beach; no air-conditioning in some units. $ *Rooms from: $205* ⌧ *Dockyard Dr., English Harbour Town* ☎ *268/460–1027, 268/460–1153* ⊕ *www. admiralsantigua.com* ⇋ *18 rooms, 4 suites* ⦿ *No meals.*

$$$

RESORT

Blue Waters Hotel. A well-heeled Brit crowd goes barefoot at this swank yet understated seaside retreat. **Pros:** pomp without pretension; exquisite setting; huge savings on weeklong packages; free Wi-Fi. **Cons:** small beachfront; little steps along the hillside make it less accessible for the physically challenged; difficult to obtain reservations at Bartley's at peak times. $ *Rooms from: $466* ⌧ *Boon Point, Atlantic Ave., Soldier's Bay, Weatherills* ☎ *268/462–0290, 800/557–6536 reservations only* ⊕ *www.bluewaters.net* ☾ *Closed Sept.* ⇋ *67 rooms, 32 suites, 3 villas, 4 penthouses* ⦿ *Some meals.*

$

RENTAL

Buccaneer Beach Club. This stylish compound opens onto the quieter part of Dickenson Bay, yet it's merely steps from the rollicking restaurants and nightlife. **Pros:** free Wi-Fi; quieter part of beach; well-equipped units with flat-screen TVs in the living room and every bedroom; complimentary laundry facilities (individual washer/dryers in the cottages). **Cons:** few facilities on-site; hotel's section of beach sometimes eroded. $ *Rooms from: $245* ⌧ *Marina Bay Rd., Dickenson Bay* ☎ *268/562–6785* ⊕ *www.buccaneerbeach.com* ⇋ *15 1-bedroom suites, 2 2-bedroom cottages* ⦿ *No meals.*

$$$$

RESORT

Fodor's Choice

★

Carlisle Bay. This cosmopolitan, boutique sister property of London's trendy One Aldwych hotel daringly eschews everything faux colonial and creole. **Pros:** luxury resort; attentive service; family-friendly. **Cons:** aggressively hip; lovely beach but often murky water; pricey restaurants; no elevators. $ *Rooms from: $1020* ⌧ *Old Rd., Carlisle Bay* ☎ *268/484–0000, 866/502–2855 reservations only* ⊕ *www.carlisle-bay. com* ☾ *Closed late Aug.–early Oct.* ⇋ *82 suites* ⦿ *Breakfast.*

$

HOTEL

Catamaran Hotel. The main building at the congenial cozy harbor front "Cat Club" evokes a plantation great house with verandas, white columns, and hand-carved doors. **Pros:** intimacy; central location; friendly staff; children under 12 stay free; free sailing lessons. **Cons:** small beach (swimming not advised); smallish rooms; surrounding area has limited dining and nightlife options during off-season (May–November). $ *Rooms from: $170* ⌧ *Great Fort George Monks Hill Trail, Falmouth Harbour* ☎ *268/460–1036* ⊕ *www.catamaran-antigua. com* ⇋ *12 rooms, 2 suites* ⦿ *No meals.*

One of the beaches at Curtain Bluff resort

$$$$
RESORT
 **CocoBay.** This healing, hillside hideaway aims to "eliminate all potential worries" by emphasizing simple, natural beauty and West Indian warmth. **Pros:** emphasis on local nature and culture, including no room TVs; beautiful views; free Wi-Fi; nice main pool and bar; generally pleasant staff. **Cons:** mediocre food; stifling on breezeless days; difficult climb for those with mobility problems; bar closes early; poor bedroom lighting. $ *Rooms from: $540* ✉ *Valley Rd., Valley Church, Jolly Harbour* ☎ *268/562–2400, 508/506–1006 toll-free in U.S.* ⊕ *www.cocobayresort.com* ⇄ *49 rooms, 4 2-bedroom houses* ⊙ *All-inclusive.*

$$$$
RESORT
Fodor's Choice
★
Curtain Bluff. An incomparable beachfront setting, impeccable service, superb extras (free scuba diving), effortless elegance: Curtain Bluff is that rare retreat that stays modern while exuding a magical timelessness. **Pros:** luxury lodging; sublime food, including the new Italian eatery on the beach; beautiful beaches; incredible extras. **Cons:** some find clientele standoffish; lodgings atop bluff not ideal for those with mobility problems; despite offering value, pricey by most standards. $ *Rooms from: $1265* ✉ *Old Rd., Morris Bay* ☎ *268/462–8400, 888/289–9898 for reservations* ⊕ *www.curtainbluff.com* ⊗ *Closed late Aug.–late Oct.* ⇄ *18 rooms, 54 suites* ⊙ *All-inclusive.*

$
RENTAL
Dickenson Bay Cottages. Lush landscaping snakes around the two-story buildings and pool at this small hillside complex, which offers excellent value for families. **Pros:** relatively upscale comfort at down-home prices; walking distance to Dickenson Bay dining and activities. **Cons:** hike from beach; lacks cross-breeze in many units. $ *Rooms from: $160* ✉ *Anchorage Rd., Marble Hill* ☎ *268/462–4940* ⊕ *www.dickensonbaycottages.com* ⇄ *11 units* ⊙ *No meals.*

$$$$
RESORT
Fodor's Choice
★

Galley Bay. This posh, adult-only all-inclusive channels the fictional Bali H'ai (with colonial architectural flourishes) on 40 lush acres. **Pros:** luxury lodging; gorgeous beach and grounds; impeccable maintenance; fine food by all-inclusive standards. **Cons:** some lodgings are small and lack a view; outdoor spa can get hot; surf is often too strong for weaker swimmers; only suites have tubs. $ *Rooms from: $1020 ⊠ Grays Farm Rd., Five Islands Village* ☎ 268/462–0302, 866/237–1644, 800/771–4711 reservations only ⊕ www.galleybayresort.com ☉ Closed mid-Aug.–early Sept. ↪ 98 rooms ⦿ All-inclusive.

$$$$
RESORT

Inn at English Harbour. This genteel resort, long a favorite with Brits and the boating set, is ideal for those seeking beachfront accommodations near English Harbour's attractions, yet it suffers from a split personality. **Pros:** spectacular views; central English Harbour location; stylish rooms; complimentary water sports; appealing spa. **Cons:** tiny beach; uneven food and service; insufficient ventilation in most rooms; high prices. $ *Rooms from: $756 ⊠ Freeman's Bay, Dockyard Dr., English Harbour Town* ☎ 268/460–1014 ⊕ www.theinnantigua.com ☉ Closed Sept. and Oct. ↪ 28 units ⦿ Some meals.

$$$
RESORT

Jolly Beach Resort. If you're looking for basic sun-sand-surf fun, this active resort—Antigua's largest—fits the bill luring a gregarious blend of honeymooners, families, and singles. **Pros:** great range of activities for the price; nice beach; good food for a cheaper all-inclusive; incredible online specials. **Cons:** many cramped, ugly rooms; overrun by tour groups; often impersonal service; lack of elevators and rambling layout make it difficult for the physically challenged. $ *Rooms from: $408 ⊠ Valley Rd., Jolly Harbour* ☎ 268/462–0061, 866/905–6559 ⊕ www.jollybeachresort.com ↪ 461 units, 2 2-bedroom cottages, 1 1-bedroom cottage ⦿ Some meals ☞ Room rates without all-inclusive packages are substantially less.

$
RENTAL

Jolly Harbour Villas. These duplex, two-bedroom villas ring the marina of a sprawling, 500-acre compound offering every conceivable facility from restaurants and shops to a golf course. **Pros:** nice beach; good value; plentiful recreational, dining, and nightlife choices nearby. **Cons:** mosquito problems; reports of hidden surcharges; inability to charge most restaurants and activities to your villa; some units have 220-volt outlets requiring adapters. $ *Rooms from: $200 ⊠ Jolly Harbour* ☎ 268/462–6166, 268/484–6100 ⊕ www.hbkvillas.com ↪ 150 villas ⦿ No meals.

$$$$
RESORT
FAMILY
Fodor's Choice
★

Jumby Bay Island. This refined resort proffers all the makings of a classic Caribbean private island hideaway, right from the stylish airport private car pickup, private launch, dockside greeting, and registration at your leisure. **Pros:** isolated private island location; free bicycles; inventive, complimentary children's programs; thoughtful extras upon request such as cooking classes and wireless baby monitors; the lovely Sense by Rosewood spa. **Cons:** isolated private island location; jet noise occasionally disturbs the main beach. $ *Rooms from: $1675 ⊠ Burma Rd., Long Island* ☎ 268/462–6000, 888/767–3966 ⊕ www.jumbybayresort.com ↪ 28 suites, 12 rooms, 14 villas ⦿ All-inclusive.

$$$$ RESORT FAMILY Fodor's Choice ★ **Nonsuch Bay Resort.** This exclusive 40-acre compound's handsome, gabled Georgian-style buildings cascade down the lushly landscaped hillside to the eponymous bay, flecked with sails. **Pros:** contemporary luxury; fully equipped units; standout cuisine; lovely beach and setting; free Wi-Fi. **Cons:** remote setting mandates a car; pretty but poky beach; hilly layout presents mobility challenges. [$] *Rooms from: $595* ✉ *Hughes Point, Nonsuch Bay* ☎ *268/562–8000, 888/844–2480* 🌐 *www.nonsuchbayresort.com* 🕒 *Closed Sept.* 🛏 *13 1-bedroom apartments, 16 2-bedroom apartments, 8 3-bedroom apartments, 7 2-bedroom cottages, 7 3-bedroom residences, 4 villas* 🍴 *Some meals.*

$ B&B/INN **Ocean Inn.** Views of English Harbour, affable management, and affordability distinguish this homey inn. **Pros:** fabulous views; affable staff; inexpensive. **Cons:** rickety paths down a steep hill linking cottages; worn rooms need updating; Wi-Fi dodgy; gym is very basic and public. [$] *Rooms from: $110* ✉ *English Harbour Town* ☎ *268/463–7950* 🌐 *www.theoceaninn.com* 🛏 *6 rooms, 4 with bath; 4 cottages* 🍴 *Breakfast.*

$$$$ RESORT FAMILY **St. James's Club.** Management has diligently smartened the public spaces and exquisite landscaping here, taking full advantage of the peerless location straddling 100 acres on Mamora Bay. **Pros:** splendid remote location; beautiful beaches and landscaping; complimentary Wi-Fi in public areas and Royal Suites; plentiful activities; additional adult pools offer more privacy. **Cons:** remote location makes a car a necessity for non-all-inclusive guests; tour groups can overrun the resort; uneven food and service; sprawling hilly layout not ideal for physically challenged. [$] *Rooms from: $760* ✉ *Dockyard Dr., Mamora Bay* ☎ *268/460–5000, 800/771–4711 reservations only, 866/237–2071* 🌐 *www.stjamesclubantigua.com* 🛏 *230 rooms, 72 villas (usually 15–20 in rental pool)* 🍴 *All-inclusive.*

$$$$ RESORT **Sandals Grande Antigua Resort & Spa.** The sumptuous public spaces, lovely beach, glorious gardens, and plethora of facilities almost mask this resort's impersonal atmosphere. **Pros:** lively atmosphere; excellent spa; good dining options; huge online advance booking savings. **Cons:** sprawling layout; too bustling; uneven service. [$] *Rooms from: $648* ✉ *Dickenson Bay* ☎ *888/726–3257 reservations only, 268/484–0100* 🌐 *www.sandals.com* 🛏 *100 rooms, 257 suites, 16 rondavels* 🍴 *All-inclusive* ☞ *3-night minimum.*

$$ HOTEL Fodor's Choice ★ **Siboney Beach Club.** This affordable beachfront oasis nestled in a tranquil corner of Dickenson Bay delights with intimacy and warmth, and knowledgeable Aussie owner Tony Johnson gladly acts as a de facto tourist board. **Pros:** friendly service; superb location; great value; well maintained with rooms smartly refurbished regularly. **Cons:** no TV in bedrooms; patios lack screens, thus forcing a choice between sweltering and swatting pests on rare still days; no elevator; inconsistent Wi-Fi signal. [$] *Rooms from: $315* ✉ *Dickenson Bay* ☎ *268/462–0806, 800/533–0234, 620/420–0334 Vonage in U.S.* 🌐 *www.siboneybeachclub.com* 🛏 *12 suites* 🍴 *No meals.*

$$$$ RESORT FAMILY **Verandah Resort & Spa.** Verandah's splendid hillside setting overlooks calm, reef-protected Dian Bay, and hiking trails snake around the property to Devil's Bridge National Park. **Pros:** gorgeous remote location;

sprawling but cleverly centralized; good kids' club and facilities with own pool; frequent discounted packages. **Cons:** smallish beaches; noise carries between adjoining units; inconsistent service; though shuttles ply the resort, its hilly layout is problematic for the physically challenged. [$] *Rooms from: $710* ✉ *Long Bay* ☎ *268/562–6848, 800/771–4711, 866/237–1785 reservations only* 🌐 *www.verandahresortandspa.com* 🛏 *180 suites, 12 2-bedroom villas* 🍴 *All-inclusive.*

NIGHTLIFE

Most of Antigua's evening entertainment takes place at the resorts, which occasionally present calypso singers, steel bands, limbo dancers, and folkloric groups. Check with the tourist office for up-to-date information. In addition, a cluster of clubs and bars pulsate into the night in season around English and Falmouth harbors.

BARS

Abracadabra. It's always a party at busy, bright trattoria Abracadabra. Late nights often turn into a disco with live music from jazz to soca or DJs spinning reggae and 1980s dance music, while special events run from art exhibits to masquerades to fashion shows to fire-eating performances. There's even a fine late-night Italian snack menu and a fun, funky boutique. ✉ *Nelson's Dockyard, English Harbour Town* ☎ *268/460–2701* 🌐 *www.theabracadabra.com.*

Ana's on the Beach. This enormous, multitier, mostly alfresco beach bar–cum–art gallery styles itself a restaurant-lounge. Although the ramrod chrome-finished chairs make for rigid seating, the loud music begs for earplugs, and the globe-trotting menu is too ambitious, this is nonetheless a hip, happening spot and prime Grade A meet market. The friendly staff is garbed in black pants and bubblegum-pink shirts (stenciled "love is in the air"), the cocktails are fairly inventive, and the rotating art on the walls, including an epoxy-painted surfboard dangling from the white-beamed ceiling, displays a savvy selection of the hottest up-and-coming local artists in various media. ✉ *Dickenson Bay* ☎ *268/562–8562* 🌐 *www.anas.ag.*

Carmichael's. Carmichael's is the fine-dining hilltop aerie at the Sugar Ridge residential complex. Nestle into a banquette or lounge in the infinity pool while sipping luscious libations that match the setting sun's colorful display. It's also a splendid spot for a postprandial cigar and port or single malt. You can always head downhill to sister night spot, the bustling, buzzing **Sugar Club** (by the resort entrance) for live music (jazz to funk) and DJ disco evenings. ✉ *Tottenham Park, Jolly Harbour* ☎ *268/562–7700* 🌐 *www.sugarridgeantigua.com.*

Indigo on the Beach. Indigo on the Beach is a soigné spot, yet it's relaxed and great any time of day for creative tapas, salads, grills, and burgers. But the beautiful people turn out in force come evening to pose at the fiber-optically lighted bar, or on white lounges scattered with throw pillows. ✉ *Carlisle Bay, Old Road* ☎ *268/480–0000.*

Inn at English Harbour Bar. The Inn at English Harbour Bar—with its green leather, wood beams, fieldstone walls, 19th-century maps, steering-wheel chandeliers, petit point upholstery, and maritime prints—is uncommonly refined. ⊠ *English Harbour Town* ☎ *268/460–1014.*

Mainbrace Pub. The Mainbrace Pub has a historic ambience, right down to its warm brick walls and hardwood accents, and is known as a beer, darts, and fish-and-chips kind of hangout for the boating set. ⊠ *Copper & Lumber Store Hotel, English Harbour Town* ☎ *268/460–1058.*

Fodor's Choice ★ **Shirley Heights Lookout.** Sunday-afternoon barbecues continue into the night with reggae, soca, and steel-band music and dancing that sizzles like the ribs on the grill. Residents and visitors gather for boisterous fun, the latest gossip, and great sunsets. Most tourist groups vanish by 7 pm, when the real partying begins. Admission is EC$20. There's occasionally another, less frenetic party Thursday evenings called Made in Pride in Antigua, which, in addition to barbecue, serves up traditional food, drink, crafts, and music. ⊠ *Shirley Heights* ☎ *268/460–1785, 268/728–0636, 268/764–0389* ⊕ *www.shirleyheightslookout.com* ☾ *Closed Mon.*

Trappas. Trappas is a hipster hangout set in a bamboo-walled courtyard hung with huge hibiscus paintings. It serves delectable, sizable tapas (tuna sashimi, deep-fried Brie with blackcurrant jelly, Thai mango chicken curry, beer-batter shrimp with garlic dip) for reasonable prices (EC$26–EC$52) into the wee hours. Live music is often on the menu. ⊠ *Main Rd., English Harbour Town* ☎ *268/562–3534.*

CASINOS

King's Casino. You can find abundant slots and gaming tables at the somewhat dilapidated, unintentionally retro (icicle chandeliers, Naugahyde seats, and 1970s soul crooners on the sound system) King's Casino. The best time to go is Friday and Saturday nights, which jump with energetic karaoke competitions, live bands, and dancing. ⊠ *Heritage Quay, St. John's* ☎ *268/462–1727* ⊕ *www.kingscasino.com.*

SHOPPING

Antigua's duty-free shops are at Heritage Quay, one reason so many cruise ships call here. Bargains can be found on perfumes, liqueurs, and liquor (including English Harbour Antiguan rum), jewelry, china, and crystal. As for other local items, check out straw hats, baskets, batik, pottery, Susie's Hot Sauce, and hand-printed cotton clothing. Fine artists to look for include Gilly Gobinet (neo-postimpressionist island-scapes), Heather Doram (exquisite, intricately woven collage wall hangings), Jan Farara, Jennifer Meranto (incomparable hand-painted black-and-white photos of Caribbean scenes), and Heike Petersen (delightful dolls and quilts). Several artists and craftspeople have banded together to form ⊕ *www.antiguanartists.com*, which lists their information, including whether they accept atelier visits by appointment. ■TIP➔ **Many businesses in the English/Falmouth harbors area close from June to October. Call ahead to confirm hours of operation.**

SHOPPING AREAS

Fodor's Choice
★

Heritage Quay, in St. John's, has 35 shops—including many that are duty-free—that cater to the cruise-ship crowd, which docks almost at its doorstep. Outlets here include Benetton, the Body Shop, Sunglass Hut, Dolce & Gabbana, and Oshkosh B'Gosh. There are also shops along **St. John's, St. Mary's, High,** and **Long Streets.** The tangerine-and-lilac-hue four-story **Vendor's Mall** at the intersection of Redcliffe and Thames streets gathers the pushy, pesky vendors who once clogged the narrow streets. It's jammed with stalls; air-conditioned indoor shops sell some higher-price, if not higher-quality, merchandise. On the west coast the Mediterranean-style, arcaded **Jolly Harbour Marina** holds some interesting galleries and shops, as do the marinas and the main road snaking around English and Falmouth harbors.

Redcliffe Quay, on the waterfront at the south edge of St. John's, is by far the most appealing shopping area. Several restaurants and more than 30 boutiques, many with one-of-a-kind wares, are set around landscaped courtyards shaded by colorful trees.

ALCOHOL AND TOBACCO

Quin Farara. You'll find terrific deals on both liquor and wines, as well as cigars at Quin Farara. ⊠ *Long St. and Corn Alley, St. John's* ☎ *268/462–3869* ⊠ *Jolly Harbour* ☎ *268/462–6245, 268/462–6245* ⊠ *Heritage Quay, St. John's* ☎ *268/462–1737, 268/462–3197.*

ART

Fodor's Choice
★

Harmony Hall. This is Antigua's top exhibition venue. A large space is used for one-person shows; other rooms display works in various media, from Aussie aboriginal carvings to Antillean pottery. The sublime historic ambience, sweeping vistas, and fine Italian fare compensate for the remote location. ⊠ *Brown's Mill Bay, Freetown* ☎ *268/460–4120* ⊕ *www.harmonyhallantigua.com.*

BOOKS AND MAGAZINES

Best of Books. This bookstore is an excellent, extensive source for everything from local cookbooks and nature guides to international newspapers. Check out the works of Jamaica Kincaid, whose writing about her native Antigua has won international acclaim. You'll also find an intriguing selection of crafts and artworks. ⊠ *Lower St. Mary's St., St. John's* ☎ *268/562–3198.*

CLOTHING

Exotic Antigua. This shop sells everything from antique Indonesian ikat throws to crepe de chine caftans to Tommy Bahama resort wear. ⊠ *Redcliffe Quay, St. John's* ☎ *268/562–1288.*

Galley Boutique. At Galley Boutique, Janey Easton personally seeks out exclusive creations from both international (Calvin Klein, Adrienne Vittadini) and local Caribbean designers, ranging from swimwear to evening garb. She also sells handicrafts and lovely hammocks. There's also a small outpost at Pigeon Point beach. ⊠ *Nelson's Dockyard, English Harbour Town* ☎ *268/460–1525.*

New Gates. For duty-free threads, head to New Gates, an authorized dealer for such name brands as Ralph Lauren, Calvin Klein, and Tommy Hilfiger. ⊠ *Heritage Quay, St. John's* ☎ *268/562–1626.*

Noreen Phillips. Glitzy appliquéd and beaded evening wear—inspired by the colors of the sea and sunset—in sensuous fabrics ranging from chiffon and silk to Italian lace and Indian brocade are created at Noreen Phillips. ⊠ *Redcliffe Quay, St. John's* ☎ *268/462–3127.*

Sunseakers. At Sunseakers, you'll find every conceivable bathing suit and cover-up—from bikini thongs to sarongs—by top designers. ⊠ *Heritage Quay, St. John's* ☎ *268/462–3618.*

DUTY-FREE GOODS

Abbott's. You'll find luxury items from Breitling watches to Belleek china to Kosta Boda art glass in a luxurious, air-conditioned showroom at Abbott's. ⊠ *Heritage Quay, St. John's* ☎ *268/462–3107* ⊕ *www.abbottsjewellery.com.*

Lipstick. You'll find high-priced imported scents and cosmetics—from Clarins to Clinique and Gucci to Guerlain—at Lipstick. ⊠ *Heritage Quay, St. John's* ☎ *268/562–1133.*

HANDICRAFTS

Cedars Pottery. The airy studio of Michael and Imogen Hunt is Cedars Pottery. Michael produces a vivid line of domestic ware and Zen-simple teapots, vases, and water fountains featuring rich earth hues and sensuous lines. Imogen fashions ethereal paper-clay fish sculptures, and mask-shaped, intricately laced light fixtures and candelabras. Take time to savor their lush gardens where found objects and sculptural installations emerge like restless sprites from the ground. ⊠ *St. Clare Estate, Buckleys Rd., Buckleys* ☎ *268/460–5293* ⊕ *www.cedarspottery.com.*

Eureka. The offerings at Eureka span the globe, from Azerbaijani hand-blown glass to Zambian weavings and carvings. ⊠ *Thames St., St. John's* ☎ *268/560–3654.*

Isis. Island and international baubles and bric-a-brac, such as antique jewelry, hand-carved walking sticks, elaborate chess sets, and glazed pottery, are available at Isis. ⊠ *Redcliffe Quay, St. John's* ☎ *268/462–4602.*

Pottery Shop. This shop sells the work of gifted potter Sarah Fuller, whose hand-painted tiles, wind chimes, plates, and cobalt-blue glazes are striking (as are her driftwood hangings mixed with clay and copper). You can also visit her studio-gallery on Dutchman's Bay. ⊠ *Redcliffe Quay, St. John's* ☎ *268/562–1264 studio-gallery, 268/462–5503 shop* ⊕ *www.sarahfullerpottery.com.*

Rhythm of Blue Gallery. Nancy Nicholson co-owns Rhythm of Blue Gallery; she's renowned for her exquisite glazed and matte-finish ceramics, featuring Caribbean-pure shades, as well as her black-and-white yachting photos and flowing batik creations. You'll also find exhibitions showcasing leading regional artists working in media from batik to copper, as well as handcrafted salt scrubs and jewelry. ⊠ *Dockyard Dr., English Harbour Town* ☎ *268/562–2230* ⊕ *www.rhythmofblue.com.*

JEWELRY

Colombian Emeralds. The Antiguan branch of the largest retailer of Colombian emeralds in the world also carries a wide variety of other gems. There's a smaller airport store as well. ⊠ *Heritage Quay, St. John's* ☎ *268/462–3462* ⊕ *www.colombianemeralds.com/ourstores/antigua.*

Diamonds International. You'll find a huge selection of loose diamonds as well as a variety of watches, rings, brooches, bracelets, and pendants at Diamonds International. Several resorts have branches. ⊠ *Heritage Quay, St. John's* ☎ *268/481–1880* ⊕ *www.diamondsinternational.com.*

Goldsmitty. Hans Smit is the Goldsmitty, an expert goldsmith who turns gold, black coral, petrified coral (which he dubs Antiguanite), and precious and semiprecious stones into one-of-a-kind works of art. ⊠ *Redcliffe Quay, St. John's* ☎ *268/462–4601* ⊕ *www.goldsmitty.com.*

SPORTS AND THE OUTDOORS

Several all-inclusives offer day passes that permit use of all sporting facilities, from tennis courts to water-sports concessions, as well as free drinks and meals. The cost begins at $50 for singles (but can be as much as $200 for couples at Sandals), and hours generally run from 8 am to 6 pm, with extensions available until 2 am. Antigua has long been famed for its cricketers (such as Viv Richards and Richie Richardson); aficionados will find one of the Caribbean's finest cricket grounds right by the airport, with major test matches running January through June.

ADVENTURE TOURS

Antigua is developing its ecotourist opportunities, and several memorable offshore experiences involve more than just snorkeling. The archipelago of islets coupled with a full mangrove swamp off the northeast coast is unique in the Caribbean.

Adventure Antigua. The enthusiastic Eli Fuller, who is knowledgeable not only about the ecosystem and geography of Antigua but also about its history and politics (his grandfather was the American consul), runs Adventure Antigua. His thorough seven-hour excursion (Eli dubs it "recreating my childhood explorations") includes stops at Guiana Island (for lunch and guided snorkeling; turtles, barracuda, and stingrays are common sightings), Pelican Island (more snorkeling), Bird Island (hiking to vantage points to admire the soaring ospreys and frigate and red-billed tropic birds), and Hell's Gate (a striking limestone rock formation where the more intrepid may hike and swim through sunken caves and tide pools painted with pink and maroon algae). The company also offers a fun "Xtreme Circumnavigation" variation on a racing boat catering to adrenaline junkies who "feel the need for speed" that also visits Stingray City and Nelson's Dockyard, as well as a more sedate Antigua Classic Yacht sail-and-snorkel experience that explains the rich West Indian history of boatbuilding. ☎ *268/727–3261, 268/726–6355* ⊕ *www.adventureantigua.com.*

"Paddles" Kayak Eco Adventure. Paddles takes you on a 3½-hour tour of serene mangroves and inlets with informative narrative about the fragile ecosystem of the swamp and reefs and the rich diversity of flora and fauna. The tour ends with a hike to sunken caves and snorkeling in the North Sound Marine Park, capped by a rum punch at the fun creole-style clubhouse nestled amid botanic gardens. Experienced guides double as kayaking and snorkeling instructors, making this an excellent opportunity for novices. Conrad and Jennie's brainchild is one of Antigua's better bargains. ⊠ *Seaton's Village* ☎ *268/463–1944, 268/720–4322* ⊕ *www.antiguapaddles.com.*

FAMILY **Stingray City Antigua.** Stingray City Antigua is a carefully reproduced "natural" environment nicknamed by staffers the "retirement home," though the 30-plus stingrays, ranging from infants to seniors, are frisky. You can stroke, feed, even hold the striking gliders ("they're like puppy dogs," one guide swears), as well as snorkel in deeper, protected waters. The tour guides do a marvelous job of explaining the animals' habits, from feeding to breeding, and their predators (including man). ⊠ *Seaton's Village* ☎ *268/562–7297* ⊕ *www.stingraycityantigua.com.*

BOATING

Antigua's circular geographic configuration makes boating easy, and its many lovely harbors and coves provide splendid anchorages. Experienced boaters will particularly enjoy Antigua's east coast, which is far more rugged and has several islets; be sure to get a good nautical map, as there are numerous minireefs that can be treacherous. If you're just looking for a couple of hours of wave-hopping, stick to the Dickenson Bay or Jolly Harbour area.

Nicholson Yacht Charters. Nicholson Yacht Charters are real professionals, true pioneers in Caribbean sailing, with three generations spanning 60 years of experience. A long-established island family, they can offer you anything from a 20-foot ketch to a giant schooner. ⊠ *English Harbour Town* ☎ *268/460–1530, 305/433–5533* ⊕ *www.nicholsoncharters.com.*

Ondeck. Ondeck runs skippered charters on the likes of Farr and Beneteau out of the Antigua Yacht Club Marina in Falmouth Harbour, terrific one- and two-day sailing workshops, and ecoadventure trips to Montserrat on a racing yacht. You can even participate in official regattas. Instructors and crew are all seasoned racers. Bareboating options and sunset cruises are also available. ☎ *268/562–6696* ⊕ *www. ondeckoceanracing.com.*

Sunsail. Sunsail has an extensive modern fleet of dinghies and 32-foot day-sailers starting at $25 per half day, $50 for a full day (always call in advance as the Nelson's Dockyard office is open sporadically). But its primary focus is bareboat yachting, often in conjunction with hotel stays; a week starts at $4,849. ☎ *268/460–2615, 888/350–3568, 877/651–4710* ⊕ *www.sunsail.com.*

DIVING

Antigua is an unsung diving destination, with plentiful undersea sights to explore, from coral canyons to sea caves. Barbuda alone features roughly 200 wrecks on its treacherous reefs. The most accessible wreck is the 1890s bark *Andes*, not far out in Deep Bay, off Five Islands Peninsula. Among the favorite sites are **Green Island, Cades Reef,** and **Bird Island** (a national park). Memorable sightings include turtles, stingrays, and barracuda darting amid basalt walls, hulking boulders, and stray

17th-century anchors and cannon. One advantage is accessibility in many spots for shore divers and snorkelers. Double-tank dives run about $90.

Dockyard Divers. Owned by British ex-merchant seaman Captain A.G. "Tony" Fincham, Dockyard Divers is one of the island's most established outfits and offers diving and snorkeling trips, PADI courses, and dive packages with accommodations. They're geared to seasoned divers (two-tank dives are a quite reasonable $89), but staff work patiently with novices. Tony is a wonderful source of information on the island; ask him about the "Fincham's Follies" musical extravaganza he produces for charity. ⊠ *Nelson's Dockyard, English Harbour Town* ☎ *268/460–1178* ⊕ *www.dockyard-divers.com.*

FISHING

Antigua's waters teem with game fish such as marlin, wahoo, and tuna. Most boat trips include equipment, lunch, and drinks. Figure at least $495 for a half day, $790 for a full day, for up to six people.

Obsession. The 45-foot Hatteras Convertible Sportfisherman *Obsession* has top-of-the-line equipment, including an international-standard fighting chair, Rupp outriggers, and handcrafted rods. Also available is the new 55-foot Hatteras Sportfisherman, the *Double Header.* Beer and soft drinks are included in the rates. Captain Derek Biel is a seasoned sea salt, a certified I.G.F.A. Ambassador who has competed in many tournaments over the past quarter century. ☎ *268/462–3174, 954/636–4862* ⊕ *www.charternet.com/charters/obsession* ⊠ *$600 per half day, $1,000 for 8 hrs.*

Overdraft. Frankie Hart, a professional fisherman who knows the waters intimately and regales clients with stories of his trade, operates *Overdraft,* a spacious, fiberglass 40-footer outfitted with the latest techno-gadgetry. He also rents the 26-foot *H2O,* a ProKat versatile enough to accommodate fly-fishing and deeper-water bay bait fishing. ⊠ *English Harbour Town* ☎ *268/464–4954, 268/463–3112* ⊕ *www. antiguafishing.com* ⊠ *From $495.*

GOLF

Though Antigua hardly qualifies as a duffer's delight, its two 18-hole courses offer varied layouts.

Cedar Valley Golf Club. Finished as Antigua's first 18-hole golf course in 1977, Cedar Valley is not particularly well maintained terrain, but nonetheless offers some attractive vistas and challenges with narrow hilly fairways and numerous doglegs (hole 7 is a perfect example). The 5th hole has exceptional ocean vistas from the top of the tee, and the par-5 9th offers the trickiest design with steep slopes and swales. Carts are $42 ($22 for nine holes). And unlimited weekly golf pass costs $220. The Spinach! Cafe offers free Wi-Fi. ⊠ *Friar's Hill, St. John's* ☎ *268/462–0161* ⊕ *www.cvgolfantigua.com* ⊠ *$60 ($31 for 9 holes)* ⚐ *18 holes, 6157 yards, par 70.*

Jolly Harbour Golf Course. The flat Florida-style layout of Jolly Harbour was designed by Karl Litten. It's lushly tropical with the trade winds a challenge. Seven lakes add to the challenge, but the facility struggles with conditioning. The 15th is the signature hole, with a sharp dog-leg and long carry over two hazards. Unfortunately, despite improved maintenance, fairways are often dry and patchy, drainage is poor, and the pro shop and "19th hole" are barely adequate. Visitors can participate in regular tournaments and "meet-and-greet" events. ⊠ *Jolly Harbour* ☎ *268/462–7771* ⊕ *www.jollyharbourantigua.com/golf* ⌦ *$57.50 ($97.75 including cart); $34.50 for 9 holes, $23 for cart* ⚐ *18 holes, 5587 yards, par 71.*

GUIDED TOURS

Almost all taxi drivers double as guides; an island tour with one costs about $25 an hour. Every major hotel has a cabbie on call and may be able to negotiate a discount, particularly off-season. Several operators specialize in off-road, four-wheel-drive adventures that provide a taste of island history and topography.

Island Safaris. Four-wheel off-road adventures by Island Safaris, which also runs other land- and water-based excursions, enables you to fully appreciate the island's natural beauty, history, folklore, and cultural heritage as you zoom about the southwest part of Antigua. Hiking is involved, though it's not strenuous. Lunch and snorkeling are also included. Active adventurers will particularly enjoy the combo Land Rover–kayak outback ecotour. ☎ *268/480–1225* ⊕ *www.tropicaladventures-antigua.com* ⌦ *From $99 per adult, $60 per child 7–12.*

Scenic Tours. Scenic Tours gives affordable half- and full-day island tours, geared toward cruise passengers, that focus on such highlights as Devil's Bridge, Shirley Heights, and English Harbour, as well as soft adventure hikes. ⊠ *Woods Mall, St. John's* ☎ *268/764–3060, 888/271–4004* ⊕ *www.scenictoursantigua.com.*

HORSEBACK RIDING

Comparatively dry Antigua is best for beach rides, though you won't find anything wildly romantic and deserted à la *Black Stallion.*

Antigua Equestrian Center. The former Spring Hill Riding Club specializes in equestrian lessons in show jumping and dressage but also offers $65 hour-long trail rides on the beach or through the bush past ruined forts, $125 for two hours (bareback riding in the ocean is an additional $45); half-hour private lessons from a British Horse Society instructor are $35. ⊠ *Falmouth Harbour* ☎ *268/460–7787, 268/773–3139* ⊕ *www.antiguaequestrian.com.*

SAILING AND SNORKELING

Not a sailor yourself? Consider signing up for one of the following boat tours. Each tour provides a great opportunity to enjoy the seafaring life while someone else captains the ship.

Miguel's Holiday Adventures. Miguel's Holiday Adventures leaves every Tuesday, Thursday, and Saturday morning at 10 from the Hodges Bay jetty for snorkeling, rum punches, and lunch at Prickly Pear Island, which offers both shallow and deepwater snorkeling, as well as hiking. In this comfortable family operation, Miguel's wife, Josephine, prepares an authentic, lavish West Indian buffet including lobster, and

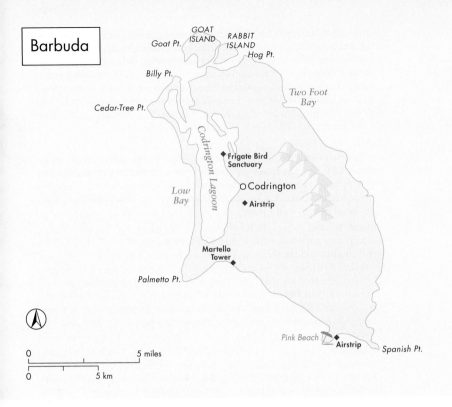

Barbuda

GOAT ISLAND
Goat Pt.
RABBIT ISLAND
Hog Pt.
Billy Pt.
Two Foot Bay
Cedar-Tree Pt.
Codrington Lagoon
Frigate Bird Sanctuary
Low Bay
Codrington
Airstrip
Martello Tower
Palmetto Pt.
Pink Beach
Airstrip
Spanish Pt.

0   5 miles
0   5 km

Miguel and his son Terrence are caring instructors. ☎ 268/460–9978, 268/772–3213, 268/723–7418 mobile ⊕ www.pricklypearisland.com.

Tropical Adventures. Barbuda day trips on the catamaran *Excellence* overflow with rum and high spirits, as do circumnavigations of Antigua. Tropical Adventures also operates ecokayaking tours and slightly more sedate, intimate catamaran cruises from sunset to snorkeling on the *Mystic*. ☎ 268/480–1225 ⊕ www.tropicaladventures-antigua.com ✉ From $85.

Wadadli Cats. Wadadli Cats offers several cruises, including a circumnavigation of the island and snorkeling at Bird Island or Cades Reef, on its five sleek catamarans, including the handsome, fully outfitted *Spirit of Antigua*. Prices are fair, and advance direct bookers get a free T-shirt. ☎ 268/462–4792 ⊕ www.wadadlicats.com ✉ From $95.

WINDSURFING AND KITEBOARDING

Most major hotels offer windsurfing equipment. The best areas are Nonsuch Bay and the east coast (notably Half Moon and Willoughby bays), which is slightly less protected and has a challenging juxtaposition of sudden calms and gusts.

KiteAntigua. KiteAntigua offers kiteboarding lessons; kiteboard rentals (for the certified) are also available at $30 per hour, $50 half day, and $70 full day. The varied multiday lesson packages are expensive but thorough. KiteAntigua closes from September through November, when winds aren't optimal. The center is on a stretch near the airport, but road trips to secret spots are arranged for experienced kitesurfers seeking that sometimes harrowing "high." ⊠ *Jabberwock Beach* ☎ *268/720–5483, 268/727–3983* ⊕ *www.kitesurfantigua.com* ✉ *$280, 4-hr private beginner's course.*

3

Windsurfing Antigua. Patrick Scales of Windsurfing Antigua has long been one of Antigua's, if not the Caribbean's, finest instructors; he now offers a mobile service in high season. He provides top-flight equipment for $30 per hour (first hour; $25 subsequent hours, $70 per half day, and $80 per day), two-hour beginner lessons for $90, and specialty tours to Half Moon Bay and other favorite spots for experienced surfers. ⊠ *Jabberwock Beach* ☎ *268/461–9463, 268/773–9463* ⊕ *www.windsurfantigua.net.*

ZIP-LINING

Antigua Rainforest Canopy Tours. Release your inner Tarzan at Antigua Rainforest Canopy Tours. You should be in fairly good condition for the ropes challenges, which require upper-body strength and stamina; there are height and weight restrictions. But anyone (vertigo or acrophobia sufferers, beware) can navigate the intentionally rickety "Indiana Jones–inspired" suspension bridges, then fly (in secure harnesses) 200 to 300 feet above a rain forest–filled valley from one towering turpentine tree to the next on lines with names like "Screamer" and "Leap of Faith." There are 23 stations, as well as a bar–café and interpretive signage. First-timers, fear not: the "rangers" are affable, amusing, and accomplished. It's open Monday–Saturday from 8 to 6, with three scheduled tours at 9:15, 10:15, and 11:15 (other times by appointment). ⊠ *Fig Tree Dr., Wallings* ☎ *268/562–6363* ⊕ *www.antiguarainforest.com* ✉ *From $85.*

BARBUDA

Barbuda is a flat, 62-square-mile (161-square-km) coral atoll—with 17 miles (27 km) of gleaming white-sand beaches (sand is the island's main export)—that is 26 miles (42 km) north of Antigua. Most of Barbuda's 1,200 people live in Codrington. Nesting terns, turtles, and frigate birds outnumber residents at least 10 to 1. Goats, guinea fowl, deer, and wild boar roam the roads, all fair game for local kitchens. There are a few very basic efficiencies and guesthouses, but most visitors stay overnight at the deluxe Coco Point Lodge or Lighthouse Bay (two other glam properties have closed). Pink Beach lures beachcombers, a bird sanctuary attracts ornithologists, caves and sinkholes filled with rain forest or underground pools (containing rare, even unique crustacean species) attract spelunkers, and reefs and roughly 200 offshore wrecks draw divers and snorkelers. Barbuda's sole historic ruin is the 18th-century, cylindrical, 56-foot-tall **Martello Tower**, which was probably a lighthouse built by the Spaniards before English occupation. The **Frigate Bird Sanctuary,** a wide mangrove-filled lagoon, is home to an estimated 400 species of birds, including frigate birds with 8-foot wingspans. Your hotel can make arrangements.

GETTING HERE

Barbuda is reachable by plane on ABM Air (⊕ *www.abm-air.com*)and by boat via the *Barbuda Express* (⊕ *www.antiguaferries.com*), although the 95-minute ride is extremely bumpy ("a chiropractor's nightmare— or fantasy," quipped one passenger).

BEACHES

Fodor's Choice **Pink Beach.** You can sometimes walk miles of this classic strand without ★ encountering another footprint. It has a champagne hue, with sand soft as silk; crushed coral often imparts a rosy glint in the sun, hence its unofficial name (officially the part in front of the exclusive former K Club has been renamed Princess Diana Beach). The water can be rough with a strongish undertow in spots, though it's mainly protected by the reefs that make the island a diving mecca. Hire a taxi to take you here, since none of the roads are well marked. **Amenities:** none. **Best for:** snorkeling; solitude; walking. ✛ *1 mile (2 km) from ferry and airstrip along unmarked roads.*

4

ARUBA

WELCOME TO ARUBA

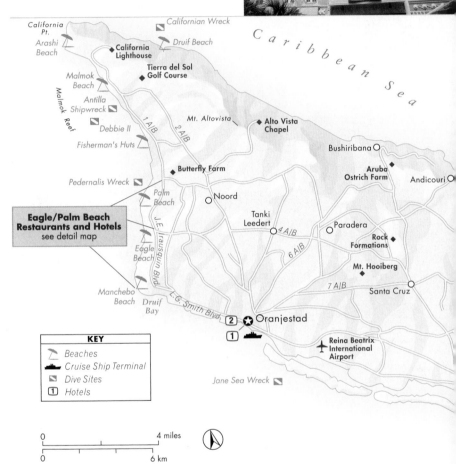

KEY
- Beaches
- Cruise Ship Terminal
- Dive Sites
- [1] Hotels

California Pt.
Arashi Beach
California Lighthouse
Malmok Beach
Antilla Shipwreck
Debbie II
Fisherman's Huts
Pedernalis Wreck
Eagle/Palm Beach Restaurants and Hotels see detail map
Palm Beach
Eagle Beach
Manchebo Beach
Druif Bay

Californian Wreck
Druif Beach
Tierra del Sol Golf Course
Mt. Altovista
Alto Vista Chapel
Bushiribana
Aruba Ostrich Farm
Andicouri
Butterfly Farm
Noord
Tanki Leedert
Paradera
Rock Formations
Mt. Hooiberg
Santa Cruz
Oranjestad
Reina Beatrix International Airport
Jane Sea Wreck

Caribbean Sea

1 A/B
2 A/B
4 A/B
6 A/B
7 A/B
J.E. Irausquin Blvd.
L.G. Smith Blvd.
Malmok Reef

0 ___ 4 miles
0 ___ 6 km

The pastel-color houses of Dutch settlers still grace the waterfront in the capital city of Oranjestad. Winds are fierce, even savage, on the north coast, where you'll find a landscape of cacti, rocky desert, and wind-bent divi-divi trees. On the west coast the steady breezes attract windsurfers to the shallow, richly colored waters.

THE A IN THE ABC ISLANDS

The A in the ABC Islands (followed by Bonaire and Curaçao), Aruba is small—only 19½ miles (31½ km) long and 6 miles (9½ km) across at its widest point. It became an independent entity (Status Aparte) within the Netherlands in 1986. The official language is Dutch, but the local language is Papiamento, though almost every native speaks English and Spanish as well. The island's population is 108,000.

4

ARUBA

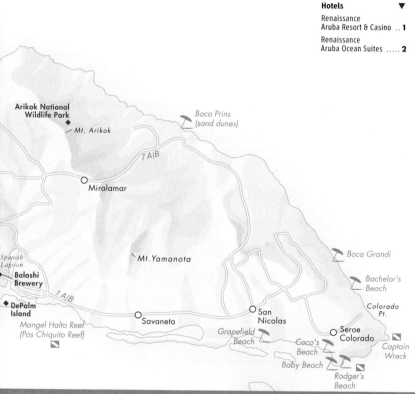

Hotels	▼
Renaissance Aruba Resort & Casino ..	**1**
Renaissance Aruba Ocean Suites	**2**

Arikok National Wildlife Park
◆ Mt. Arikok
Boca Prins (sand dunes)
7 A|B
○ Miralamar
Mt. Yamanota
Boca Grandi
Spanish Lagoon
◆ Balashi Brewery
Bachelor's Beach
Colorado Pt.
1 A|B
◆ DePalm Island
Savaneta
San Nicolas
Seroe Colorado
Mangel Halto Reef (Pos Chiquito Reef)
Grapefield Beach
Captain Wreck
Coco's Beach
Baby Beach
Rodger's Beach

TOP REASONS TO VISIT ARUBA

1 **The Beaches:** Powder-soft beaches and turquoise waters or wild waves crashing rocky cliffs.

2 **The Nightlife:** An after-dark vibe for everyone and dance-till-you-drop spots, plus party buses like the Kukoo Kunuku, which rolls the revelry right into the streets, make this island really move after sunset.

3 **The Restaurants:** Restaurants with fare from the around the world and local snack hideaways offer foodies much to discover.

4 **The Casinos:** Aruba's modern casinos will please both casual and serious gamblers.

5 **The Welcome:** A friendly multilingual population devoted to tourism guarantees smiles everywhere you go. "Bon bini" means "Welcome," and you'll always feel as if you are.

NEED TO KNOW

Caribbean Sea

ARUBA

⭐ Oranjestad

AT A GLANCE

Capital: Oranjestad

Population: 112,062

Currency: Aruban florin

Money: ATMs common; credit cards and U.S. dollars widely accepted.

Language: Dutch, Papiamento, English

Country Code: ☎ 297

Emergencies: ☎ 911

Driving: On the right

Electricity: 127v/60 cycles; plugs are U.S. standard two- and three-prong

Time: Same as New York during daylight savings time; one hour ahead otherwise

Documents: 30 days with valid passport; immigration pre-clearance returning to U.S.

Mobile Phones: GSM (900, 1800, and 1900 bands)

Major Mobile Companies: SETAR, Digicel. MIO

WEBSITES

Aruba Tourism Authority: ⊕ www.aruba.com

GETTING AROUND

✈ **Air Travel:** All flights arrive and depart from Reina Beatrix International Airport.

🚌 **Bus Travel:** Buses are reliable and clean and are an easy and affordable way to travel around the island.

🚗 **Car Travel:** Excellent, well-marked roads make navigating the island by rental car easy. But for just getting to and around town, taxis are preferable; rent a four-wheel-drive vehicle if you plan to explore the island's natural sights.

🚕 **Taxi Travel:** You can flag down a taxi or call one. Rates are fixed, but settle on the cost with the driver before your ride.

PLAN YOUR BUDGET

	HOTEL ROOM	MEAL	ATTRACTIONS
Low Budget	$200	$12	Aruba Aloe Museum tour, Free
Mid Budget	$300	$25	Open-bar "Sunset Sail" with Jolly Pirates, $32
High Budget	$400	$40	Half-day snorkel trip incl. lunch, $60

WAYS TO SAVE

Dine at local eateries. Dozens of places—including many a fish and seafood shack—cater to locals.

Book a condo. For more room (and a kitchen), rent a furnished condo—a great option for longer stays. Many time-share resorts are full-service.

"One Happy Family." This long-running promo offers myriad freebies for kids, from free snorkeling trips to free breakfasts.

Take public transit. Modern, clean, economical buses travel to the main resorts and beaches.

Hassle Factor	Low. Flights to Aruba are frequent, and the island is easy to navigate.
3 days	Relax beachside or poolside at your resort. Do a bit of sightseeing by day and later experience Aruba's renowned nightlife.
1 week	Enjoy the amenities of your resort, explore various beaches, sightsee, and party; but also rent a 4x4 to explore the island's more remote, untouched reaches.
2 weeks	After exploring every nook of Aruba (both on land and under the sea), hop on a 20-minute flight over to neighboring Bonaire or Curaçao (or both).

WHEN TO GO

High Season: January to June, the most popular and most expensive time to visit, when the weather is typically sunny and warm. Hotels are booked far in advance, and everything is open.

Low Season: Officially the rainy season from October to December, temperatures can grow hot and the weather muggy. Resorts remain open for business and offer deep discounts.

Value Season: During peak hurricane season, from July to September, hotel prices drop 20% or more. However, with Aruba outside of the main hurricane belt, resorts remain open for business and offer deep discounts. There are chances of scattered showers, but expect sun-kissed days and comfortable nighttime temperatures with fewer crowds.

BIG EVENTS

January–March: Carnival is a two-month-plus affair, packed with parties, cultural events, and street parades. ⊕ www.visitaruba.com/things-to-do/carnival

May: Memorial Day Weekend's Aruba Soul Beach Music Festival features international artists. ⊕ www.soulbeach.net

June–July: The Aruba Hi-Winds wind- and kite-surf competitions unfold over six days. ⊕ www.hiwindsaruba.com

August: Aruba Regatta is three days of nonstop boat racing and parties. ⊕ www.aruba-regatta.com

READ THIS

■ *An Island Away,* Daniel Putkowski. A best-selling novel set in the shady Aruba oil industry.

■ *Tropical Kiss,* Jan Coffey. Romance unfolds on the beaches of Aruba.

■ *CRUDE!: A Story of Passion in Aruba,* Laura Carabello. A daughter looks into her mom's past in 1960s Aruba.

WATCH THIS

■ *Timecop.* Van Damme is to Aruba what the Hoff is to Germany.

■ *Heb Het Lief.* First feature film shot in Aruba.

EAT THIS

■ *Pastechi*: fried pastry, filled with traditional spiced meat or cheese.

■ *Keshi yena*: baked cheese stuffed with chicken, spices, and raisins.

■ *Pan bati*: a fried corn-meal pancake, commonly eaten as a side.

■ *Bitterballen*: crispy, breaded and fried bite-size meatballs.

■ *Maripampoen*: a vegetable often stewed with meat and potatoes.

■ *Pika*: a condiment of fiery hot peppers and onions in vinegar.

Updated
by Susan
Campbell

Cruise ships gleam in Oranjestad Harbour, and thousands of eager tourists spill out into downtown Oranjestad. The mile-long stretch of L.G. Smith Boulevard (aka "The Strip") is lined with cafés, designer stores, restaurants, and Palm Beach Plaza, a modern shopping mall. The countryside is dotted with colorful *cunucu* (country-style houses) and stretches out into a cacti-studded rocky desert landscape that becomes Arikok National Park—a protected preserve covering 20% of the island's landmass.

Aruba not only has beautiful beaches and world-class resorts, but also near-perfect weather: It's outside the hurricane belt and receives just 20 inches of rainfall per year and has constant cooling trade winds. On the south coast, the action is nonstop both day and night; whereas the rugged north coast boasts a desolate beauty that calls to those who seek solitude in nature.

As with Bonaire and Curaçao, the island was originally populated by the Caquetio, an Amerindian people related to the Arawak. After the Spanish conquered the island in 1499, Aruba was basically left alone, since it held little in the way of agricultural or mineral wealth. The Dutch took charge of the island in 1636, and things remained relatively quiet until gold was discovered in the 1800s.

Like the trademark *watapana* (divi-divi) trees that have been forced to bow to odd angles by the constant trade winds, Aruba has always adjusted to changes in the economic climate. Mining dominated the economy until the early part of the 20th century, when the mines became unprofitable. Shortly thereafter, Aruba became home to a major oil-refining operation, which was the economic mainstay until the early 1990s, when its contribution to the local economy was eclipsed by tourism. Today, after being so resolutely dedicated to attracting visitors for so many years, Aruba's national culture and tourism industry are inextricably intertwined.

There is good reason why Aruba has more repeat visitors than any other island in the Caribbean. It offers something for everyone: a pleasant climate, excellent facilities, nightlife, nature, and warm and friendly locals. The hospitality industry here is of the highest order. The U.S. dollar is accepted everywhere, and English is spoken universally.

PLANNING

GETTING HERE AND AROUND

AIR TRAVEL

Many airlines fly nonstop to Aruba's modern **Reina Beatrix International Airport** (AUA) from several cities in North America; connections will usually be at a U.S. airport.

NONSTOP FLIGHTS
There are nonstop flights from Atlanta (Delta), Boston (American, Jet-Blue, American), Charlotte (American), Chicago (United), Fort Lauderdale (Spirit), Houston (United), Miami (American), Newark (United), New York–JFK (American, Delta, JetBlue), Philadelphia (American), and Washington, D.C.–Dulles (United). Southwest Airlines has begun flying to Aruba from Baltimore, Orlando, and Houston as well.

Airline Contacts American Airlines. ☎ 297/582-2700 on Aruba, 800/433-7300 ⊕ www.aa.com. **Delta Airlines.** ☎ 297/800-1555 on Aruba, 297/ 582-1200 for U.S. reservations, 800/241-4141 for international reservations ⊕ www.delta. com. **JetBlue.** ☎ 297/588-5388 ⊕ www.jetblue.com. **KLM.** ☎ 297/582-4536 on Aruba ⊕ www.klm.com. **Southwest Airlines.** ☎ 800/435-9792. **Spirit Airlines.** ☎ 800/772-7117 ⊕ www.spiritair.com. **United Airlines.** ☎ 297/582-9592 on Aruba, 800/864-8331 in North America ⊕ www.united.com.

BUS TRAVEL

Public transportation with Arubus is excellent; it's a great way to explore the different resorts and beaches along the main tourist areas or get groceries to bring back to your hotel. A modern, air-conditioned fleet of clean, well-scheduled buses travels from the downtown Oranjestad terminal and stops at every major resort all the way to the end of Palm Beach. Fare is less than $5. Schedules are online.

Contacts Arubus. ⊕ www.arubus.com.

CAR TRAVEL

To explore the countryside and try different beaches, you should rent a car. Try to make reservations before arriving, and rent a four-wheel drive if you plan to explore the island's natural sights. For just getting to and around town, taxis are preferable, and you can use tour companies to arrange your activities.

To rent a car, a deposit of $500 (or a signed credit-card slip) is often required. Rates vary but can be between $47 and $75 a day (local agencies generally have lower rates).

International traffic signs and Dutch-style traffic signals (with an extra light for a turning lane) can be misleading if you're not used to them; use extreme caution, especially at intersections, until you grasp the rules of the road. Speed limits are rarely posted but are usually 50 mph (80 kph) in the countryside. Aside from the major highways, the island's winding roads are poorly marked. Gas prices average about $1 per liter (about $6 per gallon), which is reasonable by Caribbean standards. But this changes often.

Contacts Avis. ✉ *Barcadera 4 Balashi, Oranjestad* ☎ *297/585–0041, 800/532–1527* ⊕ *www.avis.aw/main.* **Budget.** ✉ *J.E. Irasquin Blvd. 370, Oranjestad* ☎ *297/582–8600, 800/472–3325* ⊕ *www.budgetaruba.com.* **Dollar.** ✉ *Reina Beatrix Airport, Oranjestad* ☎ *297/583–0101* ⊕ *www.dollar.com.* **Economy.** ✉ *Bushiri 27, Oranjestad* ☎ *297/582–0009* ⊕ *www.economyaruba.com.* **Hertz.** ✉ *Sabana Blanco 35, near airport, Oranjestad* ☎ *297/582–1845* ⊕ *www.arubarentcar.com.* **Thrifty.** ✉ *Wayaca 33-F, Oranjestad* ☎ *297/583–4042* ⊕ *www.thriftycarrentalaruba.com.*

TAXI TRAVEL

There's a dispatch office at the airport; you can also flag down taxis on the street (look for license plates with a "TX" tag). Alternatively, ask at the front desk of any resort to call you a cab. Rates are fixed (i.e., there are no meters; the rates are set by the government and displayed on a chart), though you and the driver should agree on the fare before your ride begins. Add $2 to the fare after midnight and $3 on Sunday and holidays. An hour-long island tour should cost about $45 with up to four people, but agree on a fare before heading out.

Contact Arubas Transfer Tour & Taxi C.A. ✉ *Airport* ☎ *297/582–2116, 297/582–2010* ⊕ *www.airportaruba.com.*

HEALTH AND SAFETY

Dengue, chikungunya, and zika have all been reported throughout the Caribbean. We recommend that you protect yourself from these mosquito-borne illnesses by keeping your skin covered and/or wearing mosquito repellent. The mosquitoes that transmit these viruses are as active by day as they are at night.

HOTELS AND RESORTS

Almost all the resorts are along the island's southwest coast, along L.G. Smith and J.E. Irausquin boulevards, with the larger high-rise properties being farther away from Oranjestad. A few budget places are in Oranjestad itself. Since most hotel beaches are equally fabulous, it's the resort, rather than its location, that's going to be a bigger factor in how you enjoy your vacation.

Boutique Resorts: You'll find a few small resorts that offer more personal service, though not always the same level of luxury as the larger places. But smaller resorts are better suited to the natural sense of Aruban hospitality you'll find all over the island.

Large Resorts: These all-encompassing vacation destinations offer myriad dining options, casinos, shops, water-sports centers, health clubs, and car-rental desks. Many large resorts are also adding all-inclusive options or are already all-inclusive now.

Time-shares: Large time-share properties offer visitors everything needed to prepare their own meals (except for food) and have a bit more living space than in a typical resort hotel room; some also have in-room laundry equipment.

Hotel reviews have been shortened. For full information, visit Fodors.com.

WHAT IT COSTS IN U.S. DOLLARS				
	$	**$$**	**$$$**	**$$$$**
RESTAURANTS	under $12	$12–$20	$21–$30	over $30
HOTELS	under $275	$275–$375	$376–$475	over $475

Restaurant prices are the average cost of a main course at dinner or, if dinner is not served, at lunch. Hotel prices are the lowest cost of a standard double room in high season.

VISITOR INFORMATION
Contact Aruba Tourism Authority. ⊠ *L.G. Smith Blvd. 8, Eagle Beach* ☎ *800/862–7822 in the U.S./international, 297/582–3777 in Aruba* ⊕ *www. aruba.com.*

EXPLORING

Aruba's wildly sculpted landscape is replete with rocky deserts, cactus clusters, secluded coves, blue vistas, and the trademark divi-divi tree. To see the island's wild, untamed beauty, you can rent a car, take a sightseeing tour by bus, van, jeep, and even motorcycle tours, or hire a cab for approximately $45 an hour (for up to four people). The main highways are well paved, but on the windward side (the north- and east-facing side) some roads are still a mixture of compacted dirt and stones. A four-wheel-drive vehicle is recommended to really explore the outback.

Traffic can get dense near Oranjestad and L.G. Smith Boulevard, especially at rush hour, but once out of the city it is sparse. Route 1A travels southbound along the western coast, and 1B is simply northbound along the same road. If you lose your way, just look to the divi-divi trees, which always lean southwest. Most rental cars have GPS now.

ORANJESTAD AND ENVIRONS

Aruba's capital is best explored by the free ecotrolley—hop on/hop off affair—and on foot. Major improvements downtown have opened up the back roads of Main Street and have created many resting spaces and pedestrian-only lanes. New small malls, restaurants, attractions, and museums can be explored there. Also worth exploring is the new linear park and boardwalk and the new outdoor art spaces along the waterfront.

TOP ATTRACTIONS
Aruba Aloe Museum & Factory. Aruba has the ideal conditions to grow the aloe vera plant. It's an important export, and there are aloe stores all over the island. The museum and factory tour reveal the process of extracting the serum to make many products used for beauty, health, and healing; and guided or self-guided tours are available in English, Dutch, Spanish, and Papiamento. There's also a store to purchase their products

on-site. Products are also available online. ⊠ *Pitastraat 115, Oranjestad* ☏ *800/952–7822* ⊕ *www.arubaaloe.com* ☉ *Weekdays 8–5, Sat. 9–5.*

Balashi Brewery & Beer Garden. Aruba is the only nation in the world to make beer out of desalinated sea water, and it's really good beer! They also now make a version called "Chill" with added lemon flavor. See how it's done at their factory and sample some afterward. There is also a lovely outdoor beer garden for lunch, and sometimes they offer live music at their happy hour, too. Closed-toe shoes required for factory tour. ⊠ *Balashi 75, Balashi* ☏ *297/ 523–6544* ⊕ *www.balashi.com* 🎫 *$10, includes one free beer.*

Fodor's Choice ★ **Bon Bini Festival.** This year-round folklore event (the name means "welcome" in Papiamento), is held every Tuesday from 6:30 pm to 8:30 pm at Ft. Zoutman in Oranjestad. In the inner courtyard, you can check out the Antillean dancers in resplendent costumes, feel the rhythms of the steel drums, browse among the stands displaying local artwork, and sample local food and drink. ⊠ *Fort Zoutman, Oranjestad* ⊕ *www. aruba.com* 🎫 *$5.*

FAMILY Fodor's Choice ★ **DePalm Island.** A must-do for a full- or half-day trip is a visit to this terrific little private island outpost full of incredible adventures for the entire family. Their all-inclusive offerings include snorkeling with giant neon blue parrot fish, a giant water park, banana boat rides, salsa lessons, beach volleyball, zip-lining, air jumpers, and a massive all-you-can-eat buffet plus open bar and snack shack. For additional cost, you can also try Snuba®—deep snorkeling with an oxygen raft—and children ages four to seven can join their parents with their unique SNUBA Doo® setup. Motorized Power Snorkel is another fun undersea option. They also have Seatrek®—underwater walking tours with air-supplied helmets. And there's a small seaside spa on-site. Complimentary bus transportation from all major hotels includes access to the island by water taxi. ⊠ *De Palm Island Way Z/N, Balashi* ☏ *297/522–4400* ⊕ *www.depalmtours.com* 🎫 *Adults full day $99; half-day $89. Children $69 either.*

FAMILY Fodor's Choice ★ **National Archaeological Museum of Aruba.** Located in a multi-building complex that once housed the Ecury Family Estate, this modern, air-conditioned museum showcases the island's beginnings right back to the indigenous Arawak people, including a vast collection of farm and domestic utensils dating back hundreds of years. Among the highlights are the re-created Arawak Village, multimedia and interactive presentations, and rotating exhibits of art, history, and cultural shows. ⊠ *42 Schelpstraat, Oranjestad* ☏ *297/582–8979* ⊕ *namaruba.org* 🎫 *Free* ☉ *Tues.–Fri. 10–5, weekends 10–2.*

WORTH NOTING

Ft. Zoutman. One of the island's oldest edifices, Aruba's historic fort was built in 1796 and played an important role in skirmishes between British and Curaçao troops in 1803. The Willem III Tower, named for the Dutch monarch of that time, was added in 1868 to serve as a lighthouse. Over time the fort has been a government office building, a police station, and a prison; now its historical museum displays Aruban artifacts in an 18th-century house. This is also the site of the weekly

Tuesday night welcome party called the Bon Bini festival, with local music, food, and dance. ⊠ *Zoutmanstraat, Oranjestad* ☎ *297/582–5199* 🎫 *$5* ⊗ *Weekdays 8:30–4.*

MANCHEBO AND DRUIF BEACHES

One beach seamlessly merges with another, resulting in a miles-long stretch of powdery sand peppered with a few low-rise resorts. This part of the island is much less crowded than Palm Beach and great for a morning or evening stroll.

EAGLE BEACH

Eagle Beach is often referred to as Aruba's low-rise hotel area. It's lined with smaller boutique and time-share resorts. Eagle Beach is considered one of the best beaches in the Caribbean; the white-sand carpet here seems to stretch on forever. The water is great for swimming, and there are numerous refreshment spots along the beach. Although it can get busy during the day, there's never a problem finding a spot. But if you're looking for shade, it's best to stick near one of the hotel bar huts along the beach. Note: All beaches are open to the public, but the lounges and shade palapas are reserved for hotel guests.

PALM BEACH AND NOORD

The district of Noord is home to the strip of high-rise hotels and casinos that line Palm Beach. The hotels and restaurants, ranging from haute cuisine to fast food, are densely packed into a few miles running along the beachfront. When other areas of Aruba are shutting down for the night, this area is guaranteed to still be buzzing with activity. Here you can also find the beautiful **St. Ann's Church,** known for its ornate 19th-century altar. In this area, Aruban-style homes are scattered amid clusters of cacti.

TOP ATTRACTIONS

FAMILY
Fodor's Choice
★

Butterfly Farm. Hundreds of butterflies and moths from around the world flutter about this spectacular garden. Guided tours (included in the price of admission) provide an entertaining look into the life cycle of these insects, from egg to caterpillar to chrysalis to butterfly or moth. After your initial visit, you can return as often as you like for free during your vacation. ■ TIP→ Go early in the morning when the butterflies are most active; wear bright colors if you want them to land on you. Early morning is also when you are most likely to see the caterpillars emerge from their cocoons and transform into butterflies or moths. ⊠ *J.E. Irausquin Blvd., Palm Beach* ✛ *Across from Divi Phoenix Aruba Beach Resort* ☎ *297/586–3656* ⊕ *www.thebutterflyfarm.com* 🎫 *$15* ⊗ *Mon.–Sun. 8:30–4:30 (last tour at 4).*

WESTERN TIP (CALIFORNIA DUNES)

No trip to Aruba is complete without a visit to the California Lighthouse, and it's also worth exploring the rugged area of the island's western tip. This is the transition point between Aruba's calmer and rougher coasts. Malmok Beach and Arashi Beach are popular for windsurfing and are excellent for dramatic sunset photos. The California Lighthouse was designated a national monument in 2015 and at this writing is in the process of receiving a major restoration.

TOP ATTRACTIONS

California Lighthouse. Declared a national monument in 2015, the landmark lighthouse on the island's eastern tip is being restored to its original glory. It was named after a merchant ship that sunk nearby called the *Californian*, a tragedy that spawned its construction. Built in 1910, the lighthouse has been a famous Aruba attraction for decades and a typical stop on most island tours. ⊠ *Arashi, Noord.*

WORTH NOTING

Alto Vista Chapel. Meaning "high view," Alto Vista was built in 1750 as the island's first Roman Catholic Church. The simple yellow and orange structure stands out in bright contrast to its stark desertlike surroundings, and its elevated location affords a wonderful panoramic view of the northwest coast. Restored in 1953, it's still in operation today with regular services and also serves as the culmination point of the annual walk of the cross at Easter. You will see small signposts guiding the faithful to the Stations of the Cross all along the winding road to its entrance. This landmark is a typical stop on most island tours. ⊠ *Alto Vista Rd., Oranjestad* ✛ *Follow the rough, winding dirt road that loops around the island's northern tip, or from the hotel strip, take Palm Beach Road through 3 intersections and watch for the asphalt road to the left just past the Alto Vista Rum Shop.*

SANTA CRUZ

Though not a tourist hot spot (by Aruba standards), this town in the center of the island offers a good taste of how the locals live. It's not architecturally interesting, but there are many restaurants and local shops offering something a bit different from the usual tourist fare (and at reasonable prices).

Mt. Hooiberg. Named for its shape (*hooiberg* means "haystack" in Dutch), this 541-foot peak lies inland just past the airport. If you have the energy, you can climb the 562 steps to the top for an impressive view of Oranjestad (and Venezuela on clear days). ⊠ *Oranjestad.*

SAVANETA

The Dutch settled here after retaking the island in 1816, and it served as Aruba's first capital. Today it's a bustling fishing village with a 150-year-old *cas di torto* (mud hut), the oldest dwelling still standing on the island. Here you can watch local fisherman bring in the fresh catch of the day. They will fillet and cook it for you on the spot if you like at a small hut with cold beer and soft drinks. Many of the restaurants get their daily fish from these fishermen. Savaneta is also home to two gorgeous seaside-dining spots—the Old Man and the Sea and the Flying Fishbone, which are side by side.

SAN NICOLAS

During the oil refinery heyday, San Nicolas, Aruba's oldest village, was a bustling port; now its primary purpose is tourism. The major institution in town is Charlie's Restaurant & Bar. Stop in for a drink and advice on what to see and do in this little town.

The new Carnival Village in San Nicolas has a workshop where you can see costumes made and a new Carnival Museum lets you retrace its history. That's also where the sunrise jump-up at 4 am called "The Pajama Party" begins.

SEROE COLORADO

Originally established as a community for oil workers, Seroe Colorado is also known for its intriguing 1939 chapel. Here, organ-pipe cacti form the backdrop for sedate whitewashed cottages. The best reason to come here is the natural bridge. Keep bearing east past the community, continuing uphill until you run out of road. You can then hike down to the cathedral-like formation. It's not too strenuous, but watch your footing as you descend. Be sure to follow the white arrows painted on the rocks, as there are no other directional signs. Although this bridge isn't as spectacular as its more celebrated sibling (which collapsed in 2005), the raw elemental power of the sea that created it, replete with hissing blowholes, certainly is.

ARIKOK NATIONAL PARK AND ENVIRONS

The large, modern visitor center is the ideal place to begin exploring Arikok, a national park preserve that spans 18% of the island across the eastern interior and the northeast coast. Guided ranger hikes, exhibits, films, and maps will get you well started.

The park is the keystone of the government's long-term ecotourism plan to preserve Aruba's resources, and it showcases the island's flora and fauna as well as ancient Arawak petroglyphs, the ruins of a gold-mining operation at Miralmar, and the remnants of Dutch peasant settlements at Masiduri. Within the confines of the park are Mt. Arikok and the 620-foot Mt. Yamanota, Aruba's highest peak.

TOP ATTRACTIONS

FAMILY **Arikok National Park.** There are more than 20 miles (34 km) of trails concentrated in the island's eastern interior and along its northeastern coast. Arikok Park is crowned by Aruba's second-highest mountain, the 577-foot Mt. Arikok, so you can also go climbing here.

Hiking in the park, whether alone or in a group led by guides, is generally not too strenuous. You'll need sturdy shoes to grip the granular surfaces and climb the occasionally steep terrain. You should also exercise caution with the strong sun—bring along plenty of water and wear sunscreen and a hat. At the park's main entrance, the Arikok Visitor Center houses exhibits, restrooms, and food facilities and provides maps and marked trail information, park rules, and features. Free guided mini-tours are the best way to get oriented at the park entrance. ☎ *297/585–1234* ⊕ *www.arubanationalpark.org* ✉ *$11 per person. Children under 17 free. Yearly passes available* ⊙ *Park closes at 4 pm.*

WORTH NOTING

FAMILY **Aruba Ostrich Farm.** Everything you ever wanted to know about the world's largest living birds can be found at this farm and ranch. There are emus, too! A large *palapa* (palm-thatched roof) houses a gift shop and restaurant that draws large bus tours, and tours of the farm are available every half hour. Feeding the ostriches is fun, and you can also hold an egg in your hands. ✉ *Makividiri Rd., Paradera* ☎ *297/585–9630* ⊕ *www.arubaostrichfarm.com* ✉ *Adults $12, children (under 12) $6* ⊙ *Daily 9–4.*

Rock Formations. The massive boulders at Ayo and Casibari are a mystery, as they don't match the island's geological makeup. You can climb to the top for fine views of the arid countryside. The main path to Casibari has steps and handrails, and you must move through tunnels and along narrow steps and ledges to reach the top. At Ayo you can find ancient pictographs in a small cave (the entrance has iron bars to protect the drawings from vandalism). At the base there is a new café/bar/restaurant open for lunch, and their dinner at night when lit up with colored lights around the rocks is surreal. Some party bus tours stop there for dinner before continuing on their bar-hop journey. ✛ *Access to the rock formations at Casibari is via Tanki Hwy. 4A; you can reach Ayo via Rte. 6A. Watch carefully for the turnoff signs near the center of the island on the way to the windward side* ⊕ *www.aruba.com.*

BEACHES

Virtually every popular Aruba beach has resorts attached, but because nearly all beaches are public, there is never a problem with access. However, lounges, showers, and shade palapas are reserved for hotel guests.

The major beaches, which back up to the hotels along the southwestern strip, are usually crowded but you can usually keep walking to find a secluded spot. Make sure you're well protected from the sun. Burning happens fast; you feel the intensity of the rays less because of the cool trade winds. Luckily, there are many covered bars and refreshment stands at every hotel and many piers with shade and bars as well. On the island's northeastern side, stronger winds make the waters too choppy for swimming, but the vistas are great, and the terrain is wonderful for exploring. You'll often find expert kitesurfers, bodyboarders, and windsurfers enjoying the wild surf there though.

Arashi Beach. This is the local favorite, a ½-mile (1-km) stretch of gleaming white sand with a rolling surf and good snorkeling. It can get busy on weekends, especially Sunday with local families bringing their own picnics, but during the week it is typically quiet, though Tierra del Sol

Resort now provides transporation to it for their guests. **Amenities:** some shade palapas. **Best for:** swimming; walking. ⊠ *West of Malmok Beach, on west end.*

FAMILY
Fodor'sChoice
★

Baby Beach. On the island's eastern tip (near the now-closed refinery), this semicircular beach borders a placid bay of turquoise water that's just about as shallow as a wading pool—perfect for families with little ones. A small coral reef basin at the sea's edge offers superb snorkeling, but do not pass the barrier as the current is extremely strong outside of the rocks. The JADS dive shop offers snorkel and dive rentals, and their full-service bar and restaurant also offers a shower and washrooms, a small children's playground, and a new infinity pool. **Amenities:** food and drink; clamshell shade rentals. **Best for:** snorkeling; swimming; walking. ⊠ *Near Seroe Colorado, on east end, Seroe Colorado.*

Boca Grandi. This is *the* choice for the island's best kiteboarders and expert windsurfers, even more so than Fisherman's Huts. But the currents are strong so it's not safe for casual swimming. It's very picturesque though and a perfect spot for a picnic. It's a few minutes from San Nicolas; look for the big red anchor or the kites in the air. **Amenities:** none. **Best for:** kiteboarding; walking; windsurfing. ⊠ *Near Seagrape Grove, on east end, San Nicolas.*

Druif Beach. Fine white sand and calm water make this beach a fine choice for sunbathing and swimming. It's the base beach for the Divi collections of all-inclusive resorts, so amenities are reserved for guests. But the locals like it, too, and often camp out here as well with their own chairs and coolers. The beach is accessible by bus, rental car, or taxi, and it's in walking distance to stores. **Amenities:** parking. **Best for:** swimming; sunbathing. ⊠ *Parallel to J.E. Irausquin Blvd., near Divi resorts, south of Punta Brabo.*

Fodor'sChoice
★

Eagle Beach. Aruba's most photographed beach and the widest by far, especially in front of the Manchebo resort, Eagle Beach is not only a favorite with visitors and locals, but also of sea turtles. More sea turtles nest here than anywhere else on the island. This pristine stretch of blinding white sand and aqua surf frequently ranks among the best beaches in the world. Many of the hotels have facilities on or near the beach, and refreshments are never far away, but chairs and shade palapas are reserved for guests only. **Amenities:** food and drink; toilets. **Best for:** sunset; swimming; walking. ⊠ *J.E. Irausquin Blvd., north of Manchebo Beach.*

Fisherman's Huts (*Hadicurari*). Beside the Ritz-Carlton, Fisherman's Huts is a windsurfer's and kiteboarder's haven. Swimmers might have a hard time avoiding all the boards going by, as this is the nexus of where the lessons take place for both sports, and it's always awash in students and experts and board hobbyists. It's a gorgeous spot to just sit and watch the sails on the sea. Only drinks and small snacks are available at the operator's shacks. No washrooms, but the Ritz lobby is nearby in a pinch. **Amenities:** food. **Best for:** kiteboarding; windsurfing. ⊠ *North of Aruba Marriott Resort, Palm Beach.*

Malmok Beach (*Boca Catalina*). On the northwestern shore, this small, nondescript beach borders shallow waters that stretch 300 yards from shore. There are no snack or refreshment stands here, but shade is available under the thatched umbrellas. Right off the coast here is a favorite haunt for divers and snorkelers—the wreck of the German ship *Antilla*, scuttled in 1940. All the snorkel boat tours stop here for a dip as well. **Amenities:** none. **Best for:** solitude; snorkeling. ⊠ *At end of J.E. Irausquin Blvd., Malmokweg.*

Fodor'sChoice **Manchebo Beach** (*Punta Brabo*). Impressively wide, the white-sand shore-
★ line in front of the Manchebo Beach Resort is the backdrop for the numerous yoga classes now taking place under the giant palapa since the resort began offering health and wellness retreats. This sand stretch is the broadest on the island; in fact you can even get a workout just getting to the water! Waves can be rough and wild there though, so mind the current and undertow when swimming. **Amenities:** food and drink; toilets. **Best for:** bodyboarding; swimming. ⊠ *J.E. Irausquin Blvd., at Manchebo Beach Resort.*

Fodor'sChoice **Palm Beach.** This is the island's most populated and popular beach run-
★ ning along the high-rise resorts, and it's crammed with every kind of water sports activity and food and drink emporium imaginable. It's always crowded no matter the season, but it's a great place for people-watching, sunbathing, swimming, and partying, and there are always activities happening, such as the increasingly popular beach tennis. The water is pond calm and the sand is powder fine. **Amenities:** food and drink; shade; toilets; water sports. **Best for:** partying; people-watching; sunbathing; swimming; water sports. ⊠ *J.E. Irausquin Blvd., between Westin Aruba Resort and Marriott's Aruba Ocean Club.*

FAMILY **Rodger's Beach.** Near Baby Beach on the island's eastern tip, this beautiful curving stretch of sand is only slightly marred by its proximity to the tanks and towers of the now defunct oil refinery at the bay's far side. Swimming conditions are excellent here. Full facilities next door at Jad's dive center strip on Baby Beach. **Amenities:** food and drink. **Best for:** swimming; water sports. ⊠ *Next to Baby Beach, on east end, San Nicolas.*

WHERE TO EAT

Be sure to seek out spots where you can try Aruban specialties such as *pan bati* (a mildly sweet bread that resembles a pancake) and *keshi yena* (a baked concoction of Gouda or Edam cheese, spices, and meat or seafood in a rich brown sauce). Most restaurants are more international in style. Reservations are essential for dinner in high season. The larger restaurants don't typically close any day of the week, but if they do, Monday is usually the day of choice.

What to Wear. Cover-ups, shorts, and flip-flops should be reserved for casual beach bars. But formal dress is rarely required. The finest restaurants require at most a jacket for men and a sundress for women. If you plan to eat in the open air, bring along insect repellent—the mosquitoes can come out when the wind dies down.

Aruba Gastronomic Association: Dine-Around Program & Culinary Tours (*AGA*). To give visitors an affordable way to sample the island's eclectic

CLOSE UP

Cunucu Houses

Pastel houses surrounded by cacti fences adorn Aruba's flat, rugged *cunucu* ("country" in Papiamento). The features of these traditional houses were developed in response to the environment. Early settlers discovered that slanting roofs allowed the heat to rise, and small windows helped to keep in the cool air. Among the earliest building materials was caliche, a durable calcium carbonate substance found in the island's southeastern hills. Many houses were also built using interlocking coral rocks that didn't require mortar (this technique is no longer used, thanks to concrete). Contemporary design combines some of the basic principles of the earlier homes with touches of modernization: windows, though still narrow, have been elongated; roofs are constructed of bright tiles; pretty patios have been added; and doorways and balconies present an ornamental face to the world beyond. Cacti fences are still used to keep meandering wild goats out of gardens.

cuisine, the Aruba Gastronomic Association has created a Dine-Around program involving more than 30 island restaurants. Savings abound with all kinds of different packages. Other programs, such as gift certificates and coupons for dinners at the association's VIP member restaurants, are also available. You can buy Dine-Around tickets using the association's online order form, through travel agents, or at the De Palm Tours sales desk in many hotels. Participating restaurants and conditions change frequently; the AGA website has the latest information. They have also added a selection of culinary tours to their offerings—minimum eight people for guided tastings at the island's top restaurants. ✉ *Rooi Santo 21, Noord* ☎ *297/586–1266, 914/595–4788 in U.S.* 🌐 *www.arubadining.com.*

$$$ CONTEMPORARY Fodor's Choice ★

🍴 **Amuse Bistro.** The chef-owner at Amuse Bistro provides creative French-inspired fusion cuisine, sometimes available in full and small portions, while his sommelier wife will help pair perfect choices of wine from their extensive selection. Pretension, however, is not on the menu here; it's a friendly spot where you can dine outside along Aruba's busiest tourist boulevard or inside in a warm and inviting enclave. The main menu offers mostly classic French dishes with surprising twists, but you're really better served to let the chef delight you with his daily three-course or five-course carte blanche surprise menu that can also be paired with the sommelier's choice of wines. The carte blanche menu can only be ordered for the whole table, not individually. [$] *Average main: $28* ✉ *J.E. Irausquin Blvd. 87, Palm Beach* ☎ *297/596–9949* ✍ *Reservations essential.*

$$ INTERNATIONAL Fodor's Choice ★

🍴 **Arubaville.** Arubaville is a fun, laid-back, beach bar that makes a great place to gather for drinks and, come evening, food as well. The make-your-own-salad has a nice selection of ingredients, and the rack of lamb and seafood platters are served with big appetites in mind. There are a few vegetarian choices on the menu as well. Live music most weekends keeps things hopping, and board games and hammocks make this a favorite for day-trippers. Come at sunset for wonderful views. $ *Average main: $20* ✉ *Bucutiweg 50* ☎ *297/582–0157* ⊕ *arubaville.aw* ☽ *No lunch* ⊟ *No credit cards.*

$$$$
INTERNATIONAL
Fodor'sChoice
★

✕ **Atardi.** Formerly Simply Fish, Atardi offers an expanded menu, extending its offerings beyond fish. Meat dishes such as local keshi yena are excellent, and the fresh fish is still prepared to perfection. It's one of the most romantic spots for toes-in-the-sand dining—tiki torches and specacular sunsets frame the Palm Beach experience—and the superb signature cocktails and attentive service also make it well worth the price. $ *Average main: $40* ✉ *Aruba Marriott Resort, L. G. Smith Blvd. 101, Noord* ☎ *297/520–6537* ⊕ *www.marriott.com* ◿ *Reservations essential.*

$$$
CONTEMPORARY
Fodor'sChoice
★

✕ **Barefoot.** In keeping with an "elegant dining in flip-flops" concept, Barefoot is a palapa restaurant with sand on the floor inside and tables on the sand outside. Chef Gerco Aan het Rot and maitre d' and sommelier Luc Beerepoot excel at pairing food and wine or cocktails. Their menu of creative international fusion cuisine is complemented by superb signature cocktails and an impressive selection of wines, yet the atmosphere is never stuffy. This duo truly takes it up a notch above your basic toes-in-the-sand dining spot, and the sunset views are always spectacular. $ *Average main: $26* ✉ *L.G. Smith Blvd. 1, across the street from the Talk of the Town Hotel on Surfside Beach, Oranjestad* ☎ *297/588–9824* ⊕ *www.barefootaruba.com* ☽ *No lunch.* ◿ *Reservations essential.*

$$$
CUBAN
Fodor'sChoice
★

✕ **Cuba's Cookin'.** Old Havana meets the Caribbean here with authentic music and food from what locals call The Big Island. The signature dish is the *ropa vieja*, a sautéed flank steak served with a rich sauce, and it's perfectly spiced and melts in your mouth. Vegetarian and gluten-free offerings are served as well. And their boast of the best mojitos in town is a fair claim. There's hot live music every night, as well as interesting offerings like Poetry Night, when locals get up and express themselves through spoken word. The atmosphere is fun and friendly, and the location ideal for people-watching along the seaport marina. And it's the only place in town to get a famous Cuban sandwich for lunch. $ *Average main: $28* ✉ *Renaissance Marketplace, L.G. Smith Blvd. 82, Oranjestad* ☎ *297/588–0627* ⊕ *www.cubascookin.com.*

$$$$
STEAKHOUSE
FAMILY

✕ **El Gaucho Argentine Grill.** Faux-leather-bound books, tulip-top lamps, wooden chairs, and tile floors decorate this Argentina-style steak house, which has been in business since 1977. The key here is meat served in mammoth portions (think 16-ounce steaks), and the "biggest shish kebab ever served" is also their specialty. But it's not all about meat; their seafood platters are something to consider as well. It's a boisterous and fun atmosphere with strolling musicians, and the kids will enjoy the separate children's playroom. Appropriate attire is appreciated. $ *Average main: $40* ✉ *Wilhelminastraat 80, Oranjestad* ☎ *297/582–3677* ⊕ *www.elgaucho-aruba.com.*

$$$$
SEAFOOD

✕ **Flying Fishbone.** This friendly, relaxed beach restaurant is well off the beaten path in Savaneta, a small fishing town, so you know the fish is seriously fresh, often caught that day. You can dine with your toes in the sand (they have hooks for your shoes), or enjoy your meal on the wooden deck. The emphasis here is on fresh seafood—beautifully presented on colorful beds of vegetables—but there are good choices for landlubbers, too, like grilled maple leaf duck breast. The shrimp, shiitake, and blue-cheese casserole is a tried-and-true favorite kept on the menu to keep the regulars happy. For dessert, the chocolate ravioli with poached pear and ice cream is not to be missed. **TIP→ Arrive early for dinner to get a good table closer to the water.** [$] *Average main: $34* ✉ *Savaneta 344, Savaneta* ☎ *297/584–2506* 🌐 *www.flyingfishbone.com* ✍ *Reservations essential.*

$$$ STEAKHOUSE 🍴 **French Steakhouse & Omakase Sushi Bar.** A classic French restaurant with a modern sushi bar under the same roof in a landmark Aruba hotel might sound like a spot with something of an identity crisis, but it actually works. Well known as a place for high-end steak served with European flare, the addition of the Asian offerings brings the entire dining room into this century. The Omakase name of the sushi bar means "I will leave it to you," and you are expected to leave it to the sushi chef to delight you with the selection of dishes beginning with the lightest to the heaviest. Seating is limited so reservations at the sushi bar are essential. The French Steakhouse also offers an early-bird menu. Live piano music often adds to the ambience. [$] *Average main: $30* ✉ *Manchebo Beach Resort, J.E. Irausquin Blvd. 55, Druif* ☎ *297/582–3444* 🕓 *No lunch. Sushi bar closed Mon.* ✍ *Reservations essential.*

$$$ CARIBBEAN 🍴 **Gasparito Restaurant & Art Gallery.** You can find this enchanting hideaway in a beautifully restored 200-year-old *cunucu* (country) house in Noord. Dine indoors, where works by local artists are showcased on softly lit walls, or on the outdoor patio. Either way, the service is excellent. The Aruban specialties like pan bati and keshi yena come from centuries of tradition, and the standout dish is the Gasparito chicken; the sauce recipe was passed down from the owner's ancestors and features seven special ingredients, including brandy, white wine, and pineapple juice. (The rest, they say, are secret.) Vegetarian entrées and American-style ribs round out the menu of local dishes that include fresh fish and seafood. Only 20 guests per evening—choice of seatings at 6, 7, or 8 pm. [$] *Average main: $25* ✉ *Gasparito 3, Noord* ☎ *297/594–2550* 🌐 *www.gasparito.com* 🕓 *Closed Sun. No lunch* ✍ *Reservations essential.*

$$$$ STEAKHOUSE 🍴 **L.G. Smith's Steak & Chop House.** A study in teak, cream, and black, this fine steak house offers some of the best beef on the island. Subdued lighting and cascading water create a pleasant atmosphere, and the view over L.G. Smith Boulevard to the harbor makes for an exceptional dining experience. Their comprehensive wine list has won a Wine Spectator Award of Excellence. The menu features high-quality cuts of meat, all superbly prepared. The casino is steps away if you fancy some slots after dinner. Nightcaps can be had at the trendy bar Blu just below. [$] *Average main: $37* ✉ *Renaissance Aruba Beach Resort & Casino, L.G. Smith Blvd. 82, Oranjestad* ☎ *297/523–6195* 🌐 *www.lgsmiths.com* 🕓 *No lunch.*

$$$$ EUROPEAN Fodor's Choice ★ 🍴 **Madame Janette.** The food at this restaurant, named after the Scotch bonnet pepper called Madame Janette in Aruba, is surprisingly not Caribbean spicy but French-inspired from the classic haute cuisine–trained chef. Though they do fuse Caribbean flavors when they see

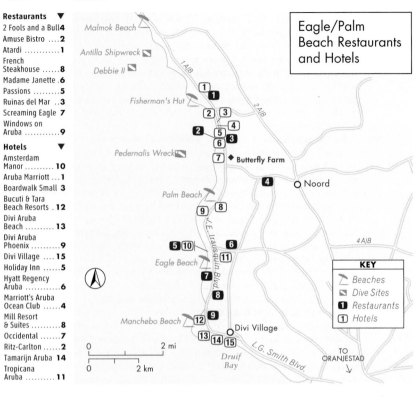

Eagle/Palm
Beach Restaurants
and Hotels

fit, especially in the fish and seafood dishes, you'll find a lot of classic heavy butter-and-cream-sauce offerings for the meats like peppercorn cognac, béarnaise, and hollandaise. They have Aruba's largest selection of specialty beers due to one co-owner's avid interest in craft brewing. They also have a surprising number of specialty schnitzels. The commitment of the owners to serve only top quality in all of their offerings has won Madame Janette many prestigious culinary awards. You can be sure that a night at this spot will never disappoint when it comes to an over-the-top taste experience. $ *Average main: $33* ⊠ *Cunucu Abao 37, Cunucu Abao* ☎ *297/587–0184* ⊕ *www.madamejanette.info* ☺ *Closed Sun. No lunch* ⌖ *Reservations essential.*

$$$$ ✕**Papiamento.** The Ellis family converted its 126-year-old manor into a
ECLECTIC   bistro with an atmosphere that is elegant, intimate, and always romantic. You can feast in the dining room, which is filled with antiques, or outdoors on the terrace by the pool (sitting on plastic patio chairs covered in fabric). The chef mixes Continental and Caribbean cuisines to produce sumptuous seafood and meat dishes and goes out of his way to source locally for fresh ingredients. Those seeking a bit of novelty can order one of the hot-stone dishes, which come to the table sizzling. Service is unhurried and the atmosphere laid-back. Papiamento is one of the best spots on the island to try the famous local specialty keshi yena. $ *Average main:*

$32 ⊠ Washington 61, Noord ☎ 297/586–4544 ⊕ papiamentoaruba.com ⊘ Closed Mon. No lunch ⚒ Reservations essential.

$$$$
CARIBBEAN

✕ **Passions on the Beach.** Every night the Amsterdam Manor Beach Resort transforms the area of Eagle Beach in front of the hotel into a magical and romantic beach dining room. Tiki torches illuminate the white sand, and the linen-covered tables are within inches of the lapping water. Dine on imaginative dishes that are as beautiful as they are delicious. The huge tropical watermelon salad presented in a watermelon half is refreshing and whets the appetite with a slight chili heat. In this "reef cuisine," the main courses lean toward seafood, though meat lovers also are indulged. After dinner, relax with your toes in the sand and enjoy the best show that nature has to offer over signature cocktails. $ *Average main: $32 ⊠ Amsterdam Manor Beach Resort, J.E. Irausquin Blvd. 252, Eagle Beach ☎ 297/527–1100 ⊕ www.passions-restaurant-aruba.com ⚒ Reservations essential.*

$$$
ECLECTIC
Fodor'sChoice
★

✕ **Pinchos Grill & Bar.** Built on a pier, this casual spot with only 16 tables has one of the most romantic settings on the island. At night the restaurant glimmers from a distance as hundreds of lights reflect off the water. The restaurant's name comes from the Spanish word for a skewered snack, so there are always a few of those on the menu. Guests can watch as the chef prepares delectable meals on the grill in his tiny kitchen while owners, Anabela and Robby, keeps diners comfortable and happy. The fish-cakes appetizer with a pineapple-mayonnaise dressing is a marriage made in heaven. The bar area is great for enjoying ocean breezes over one of their excellent signature cocktails or artisanal sangrias, and sometimes there's live entertainment. Magical at night is the lit-up water below the tables where you can see the colorful fish swimming by. Romance is always on tap here, especially with the lover's swing by the bar. $ *Average main: $24 ⊠ L.G. Smith Blvd. 7, Oranjestad ☎ 297/583–2666 ⊘ No lunch.*

$$$
DUTCH
Fodor'sChoice
★

✕ **Quinta del Carmen.** Quinta del Carmen is set in a beautifully restored 100-year-old mansion with stunning manicured lawns and a lovely outdoor courtyard. The cuisine here is best defined as modern Caribbean-Dutch with a few traditional Dutch favorites, like cheese croquettes and mushrooms and cream, appearing on the menu as "Grandma's favorites." The watermelon salad is sweet, salty, and perfectly refreshing, and the *sucade-lappen* (flank steak stewed in red wine and herbs) has a depth of flavor that comes from hours in the pot. End the meal with a stroopwafel parfait and something from the generous cocktail menu. Seating in the courtyard is sometimes taken over by wedding parties, so it's good to call ahead. $ *Average main: $30 ⊠ BUBALI 119, Oranjestad ☎ 297/587–7200 ⊕ www.quintadelcarmen.com ⊘ No lunch ⚒ Reservations essential.*

$$$$
CARIBBEAN

✕ **Ruinas del Mar.** Meaning "ruins by the sea," this scenic spot is the focal point of the grand dame Hyatt Regency hotel, famous for its gorgeous tropical grounds and water circuit of falls and pools leading to the sea. The trademark black swans swimming around the koi pond cresting the tiki-torch-lit terrace of the dining room make for a very romantic setting, and the interior is elegant and refined. Specialties include stone-hearth-cooked items and basic international fare that changes at the chef's fancy and with the seasons. Not to be missed is the local pumpkin soup with coconut milk and cilantro. The Sunday champagne brunch buffet is also very popular, and the setting is unparalleled for breakfast weekdays as well. [$] *Average main: $39* ✉ *Hyatt Regency Aruba Beach Resort & Casino, J.E. Irausquin Blvd. 85, Palm Beach* ☎ *297/586–1234* 🌐 *www.aruba.hyatt.com* ⏲ *No lunch. No dinner Sun.* ✍ *Reservations essential.*

$$$$ INTERNATIONAL Fodor's Choice ★ 🍴 **Screaming Eagle.** The perfect spot for a romantic evening, this elegant French eatery serves creative combinations of fusion cuisine, innovative cocktails, and selections from its generous wine list. The decor is both sophisticated and relaxing, with dramatic triangular sails shading the patio, and soft lighting and billowing draperies inside. Menu items are decidedly French, and each plate is prepared like a mini work of art. For an indulgent experience, ask to dine on one of the canopy beds and lounge like an emperor. The Dover sole is prepared table-side (or bed-side) *à la meunière* (lightly floured and sautéed) and makes for a great photo op. Crêpes suzette are also prepared table-side. Explore some of the signature or specialty cocktails, like the apple cinnamon mojitos. They're some of the best on the island. [$] *Average main: $35* ✉ *J. E. Irausquin Blvd. 228, Eagle Beach* ☎ *297/587–8021* 🌐 *www.screaming-eagle.net* ⏲ *No lunch.* ✍ *Reservations essential.*

$$$$ INTERNATIONAL 🍴 **2 Fools and a Bull.** Friends Paul and Bas have teamed up to offer an evening of culinary entertainment that's more like a fun dinner party than a mere dining experience. Guests are assembled and introduced to one another. Then the evening's meal is explained before everyone sits down at the U-shaped communal dinner table for a five-course culinary adventure. The menu changes daily, and there's a selection of suggested wine pairings available by the glass. This isn't a cheap eating-out experience, but it'll certainly be a cherished memory of Aruba. Reservations are advisable at least a few weeks in advance. ■ **TIP→ Be sure to state any dietary restrictions in advance.** [$] *Average main: $90* ✉ *Palm Beach 17, Noord* ☎ *297/586–7177* 🌐 *www.2foolsandabull.com* ⏲ *Closed weekends* ✍ *Reservations essential.*

$$$$ INTERNATIONAL Fodor's Choice ★ 🍴 **Windows on Aruba.** Always famous for its stunning views over the golf course and impeccable service, now the Divi Resorts' new executive chef Matt Boland has also introduced a new menu at Windows. Highlights focus on farm-and-sea to fork offerings whenever possible. Exotic flavor twists are often introduced to dishes, such as tamarind and miso glaze for sea bass and portobello cocoa sauce for filet mignon. The new brunch menu has also been voted the best on the island with creative dishes like eggs Benedict with caviar hollandaise sauce. Brunch also features unlimited champagne. Live soft music most nights as well. [$] *Average main: $36* ✉ *Divi Village Golf Resort, J.E. Irausquin Blvd. 41, Druif* ☎ *297/730–5017* 🌐 *www.windowsonaruba.com* ⏲ *No lunch Sat.* ✍ *Reservations essential.*

Amsterdam Manor Beach Resort

WHERE TO STAY

Hotels on the island are categorized as low-rise or high-rise and are grouped in two distinct areas along L.G. Smith and J.E. Irausquin boulevards north of Oranjestad. The low-rise properties are closer to the capital, the high-rises in a swath a little farther north. Hotel rates, with the exception of those at a few all-inclusives, generally do not include meals or even breakfast. The larger resorts are destinations unto themselves, with shopping, entertainment, and casinos.

$
HOTEL
FAMILY

Amsterdam Manor Beach Resort. Amsterdam Manor is an intimate, family-run hotel with a genuinely friendly staff, offering excellent value without too many frills. **Pros:** feels like a European village; friendly and helpful staff; mini-grocery on-site; public bus stop in front of hotel for easy access to downtown and the high-rise area. **Cons:** across the road from the beach; lacks the boutiques and attractions of a larger hotel; small pool; Jet Skis at beach can be noisy. $ *Rooms from: $225* ✉ *J.E. Irausquin Blvd. 252, Eagle Beach* ☎ *297/527–1100, 800/932–2310* ⊕ *www.amsterdammanor.com* ⤳ *68 rooms, 4 suites* ⦿ *All-inclusive.*

$$$
RESORT
Fodor's Choice
★

Aruba Marriott Resort & Stellaris Casino. One of the first landmark resorts on the high-rise beach strip, the Aruba Marriott combines family-fun offerings with romance and business by offering an entirely separate luxury floor. **Pros:** every kind of amenity including full-service spa and beauty salon, large conference center/ballroom; shopping. **Cons:** charge for Wi-Fi beyond lobby; can be boisterous around the pool area; beach can become crowded in high season. $ *Rooms from: $411*

✉ *L.G. Smith Blvd. 101, Palm Beach* ☎ *297/586–9000, 800/223–6388* 🌐 *www.marriott.com* ⇨ *388 rooms, 23 suites* 🍴 *No meals.*

$ HOTEL Fodor's Choice ★ 🏨 **Boardwalk Small Hotel Aruba.** A gorgeous luxury boutique oasis in an ex-coconut plantation, this family run gem is decorated in bright tropical hues with unique accents supplied by local artists. **Pros:** beautiful grounds and decor; intimate and romantic; highly personal service; eco-aware operation; free Wi-Fi. **Cons:** not right on the beach; limited views; fair walk from shopping. [$] *Rooms from: $250* ✉ *Bakval 20, Palm Beach* ☎ *297/586–6654* 🌐 *www.boardwalkaruba.com* ⇨ *11 1-bedroom suites, 2 2-bedroom suites* 🍴 *No meals.*

$$$ HOTEL Fodor's Choice ★ 🏨 **Bucuti & Tara Beach Resort.** An extraordinary beach setting, impeccable personal service, and attention to detail help this elegant Green Globe resort easily outclass anything else on the island. **Pros:** sophisticated atmosphere; impeccable service; free self-service laundry; free Wi-Fi and local calls; free use of netbooks during stay. **Cons:** beach can get busy because other hotels share it; no room service; no longer doing beach weddings. [$] *Rooms from: $451* ✉ *L.G. Smith Blvd. 55B, Eagle Beach* ☎ *297/583–1100* 🌐 *www.bucuti.com* ⇨ *63 rooms, 38 suites, 3 bungalows* 🍴 *Some meals* ☞ *Completely non-smoking except for 2 outdoor designated areas.*

$$$$ RESORT FAMILY Fodor's Choice ★ 🏨 **Divi Aruba Beach Resort All Inclusive.** The free food and drinks here and the ability to use the facilities of the adjoining sister Tamarijn Resort mean you have very little reason to wander far from the idyllic beach location. **Pros:** on wonderful stretch of beach; common areas feel light and airy; great staff; free Wi-Fi. **Cons:** buffet could use more variety; the all-inclusive bracelets; public access lane beside resort beach. [$] *Rooms from: $638* ✉ *L.G. Smith Blvd. 93, Druif* ☎ *297/525-5200, 800/554–2008* 🌐 *www.diviaruba.com* ⇨ *265 rooms, 4 suites* 🍴 *All-inclusive* ☞ *5-night minimum.*

$$$ RESORT Fodor's Choice ★ 🏨 **Divi Aruba Phoenix Beach Resort.** With incredible views from its high-rise tower, stunning rooms awash in tropical colors and state-of–the-art amenities, and comfortable, homey accommodations, Divi Aruba Phoenix rises above the rest of big box hotels on Palm Beach. **Pros:** beautifully appointed rooms; great beach; privacy from main Palm Beach frenzy; great vibe. **Cons:** children don't always stick to their appointed areas; wave runners from nearby operator can be noisy. [$] *Rooms from: $414* ✉ *J.E. Irausquin Blvd. 75, Palm Beach* ☎ *297/586–1170* 🌐 *www.diviarubaphoenix.com* ⇨ *140 luxury suites, 101 rooms* 🍴 *No meals.*

$$ RESORT FAMILY 🏨 **Divi Village Golf & Beach Resort.** Although it's just across the road from its sister Divi properties, this all-suites version is quieter and more refined. **Pros:** excellent golf course; spacious rooms; lush grounds; free shuttles to sister Divi resorts on the beach. **Cons:** bit of a hike from some rooms to the lobby; it might be a bit too quiet for some; no ocean views. [$] *Rooms from: $309* ✉ *J.E. Irausquin Blvd. 93, Oranjestad* ☎ *297/583–5000, 297/583–5000* 🌐 *www.divivillage.com* ⛳ *Divi Links Course on-site* ⇨ *250 suites* 🍴 *All-inclusive* ☞ *3-night minimum.*

$$ RESORT FAMILY 🏨 **Holiday Inn Resort Aruba.** Three new distinct zones for different types of travelers make this Holiday Inn appealing to different tastes. **Pros:** thematic zones provide distinct amenities; gorgeous pool area with sea views; lively vibe; free Wi-Fi. **Cons:** frequently fully booked; busy

pool area; busy reception area. $ *Rooms from: $315* ⊠ *J.E. Irausquin Blvd. 230, Palm Beach* ☎ *297/586–3600, 800/465–4329* ⊕ *www. holidayarubaresort.com* ⤴ *597 rooms, 7 suites* |◎| *Some meals.*

$$$$
RESORT
FAMILY
Fodor's Choice
★

Hyatt Regency Aruba Beach Resort & Casino. This 12-acre property is one the most lavishly landscaped resorts on the island, with a glorious array of bright tropical blooms and lush foliage surrounding a circuit of waterfalls culminating in a koi pond where black swans glide gracefully by. **Pros:** beautiful grounds; great for kids; excellent restaurants. **Cons:** small balconies for a luxury hotel; some rooms are quite a stretch from the beach. $ *Rooms from: $650* ⊠ *J.E. Irausquin Blvd. 85, Palm Beach* ☎ *297/586–1234, 800/554–9288* ⊕ *aruba.hyatt.com* ⤴ *342 rooms, 24 suites, 29 regency club rooms* |◎| *Breakfast.*

$$$$
RENTAL
FAMILY

Marriott's Aruba Ocean Club. First-rate amenities and lavishly decorated villas have made this time-share the island favorite. **Pros:** relaxed atmosphere; feels more like a home than a hotel room; excellent beach. **Cons:** beach can get crowded; attracts large families, so lots of kids are about. $ *Rooms from: $700* ⊠ *L.G. Smith Blvd. 99, Palm Beach* ☎ *297/586–2641* ⊕ *www.marriott.com* ⤴ *93 rooms, 213 suites* |◎| *No meals.*

$
RESORT
FAMILY

Mill Resort & Suites. Quaint yet colorful interiors, a small pool, and a quick shuttle or stroll to one of Aruba's best beaches make Mill Resort a good choice for families on a budget. **Pros:** good value; intimate setting; family-friendly; free Wi-Fi. **Cons:** rooms have limited views and spare amenities; pool can be crowded with children; not on beach. $ *Rooms from: $228* ⊠ *J.E. Irausquin Blvd. 330, Palm Beach* ☎ *297/526–7700* ⊕ *www.millresort.com* ⤴ *64 studios, 121 suites* |◎| *Breakfast.*

$$$$
RESORT

Occidental Grand Aruba Resort & Casino. On a stellar expanse of beachfront, the Occidental Grand (now a Barcelo hotel) offers something for everyone with great nightly entertainment and an eclectic choice of dining. **Pros:** great beach location; lots of water sports in front; friendly; not spring-break style. **Cons:** nonstop action; few quiet escape spots; size can make it seem somewhat impersonal at times. $ *Rooms from: $640* ⊠ *J.E. Irausquin Blvd. 83, Palm Beach* ☎ *297/586–4500, 800/448–8355* ⊕ *www.barcelo.com* ⤴ *368 rooms* |◎| *All-inclusive.*

$$
RESORT
FAMILY
Fodor's Choice
★

Renaissance Aruba Ocean Suites. Spacious suites attract families and groups to this downtown resort that offers its own man-made beach on the sea and free water taxi to its lovely private island minutes away. **Pros:** private island access; spacious water circuit and stellar sea views; steps from downtown. **Cons:** limited dining on-site; limited water sports; airplane landing and takeoffs can be noisy. $ *Rooms from: $300* ⊠ *Renaissance Beach, L.G. Smith Blvd., Oranjestad* ☎ *297/583–6000* ⊕ *www.arubaresortandspa.com* ⤴ *258 suites* |◎| *Breakfast.*

$$$
RESORT
Fodor's Choice
★

Renaissance Aruba Resort & Casino. A landmark property right on the marina in the heart of the Oranjestad, Renaissance Aruba offers guests the best of many worlds, including adult-only accommodations, stellar upscale shopping, and a free water taxi from the lobby to an idyllic private island minutes away. **Pros:** in the heart of the downtown shopping district; lobby and shopping areas are always lively; pool area offers an unmatched view of the port; free access to private island. **Cons:** rooms overlooking the atrium can be a bit claustrophobic; beach is off-site; no hotel grounds; no balconies in downtown section, nights can be noisy. Ⓢ *Rooms from: $400* ✉ *L.G. Smith Blvd. 82, Oranjestad* ☎ *297/583–6000, 800/421–8188* ⊕ *www.renaissancearuba.com* ⤳ *300 rooms* ⍩ *Some meals.*

$$$$ ⌆ **Ritz-Carlton Aruba.** The high standards of Ritz-Carlton properties
RESORT   are well represented at the Aruba property with rooms that have private balconies, and ocean-view rooms that offer sweeping vistas of the Caribbean. **Pros:** absolute luxury; two pools so they never feel crowded; 24-hour room service; excellent restaurants on-site. **Cons:** far from downtown shopping at the end of Palm Beach; beach is off-site; lacks the intimate feel of smaller properties. Ⓢ *Rooms from: $650* ✉ *L.G. Smith Blvd. 107, Palm Beach* ☎ *297/527–2222* ⊕ *www.ritzcarlton.com/ en/properties/aruba* ⤳ *265 rooms, 55 suites* ⍩ *No meals.*

$$$$ ⌆ **Tamarijn Aruba All-Inclusive Beach Resort.** Sister property of the Divi
RESORT   Aruba All-Inclusive, this property is decidedly more laid-back, and all rooms are oceanfront on a spectacular beach that is within walking distance from town. **Pros:** stunning beach; access to the Divi Aruba All-Inclusive next door; nightly entertainment. **Cons:** Wi-Fi is an additional charge; daytime might be too quiet for some. Ⓢ *Rooms from: $614* ✉ *J.E. Irausquin Blvd. 41, Punta Brabo* ☎ *297/594–7888, 800/554– 2008* ⊕ *www.tamarijnaruba.com* ⤳ *216 rooms, 20 suites* ⍩ *All-inclusive* ☞ *3-night minimum.*

$ ⌆ **Tropicana Aruba Resort & Casino.** An excellent waterslide, fast-food
RESORT   options, and a nearby supermarket make this complex of self-contained
FAMILY   time-share units right across from Eagle Beach a popular choice for families. **Pros:** nice pools and waterfall; supermarket right across the street; price is hard to beat for a hotel so close to the beach. **Cons:** feels like an apartment complex; public areas are noisy and crowded; despite the attractions for children, there are no kids' programs available. Ⓢ *Rooms from: $200* ✉ *J.E. Irausquin Blvd. 250, Eagle Beach* ☎ *297/587–9000, 800/835–7193* ⊕ *www.troparuba.com* ⤳ *362 condo style suites* ⍩ *No meals.*

NIGHTLIFE

Unlike many islands, Aruba's nightlife isn't confined to the touristy folkloric shows at hotels. Arubans like to party. They usually start celebrating late, and the action doesn't pick up until around midnight.

BARS AND CLUBS

Fodor'sChoice   **Bugaloe Bar & Grill.** This colorful beach bar at the tip of De Palm Pier
★   on busy Palm Beach is hopping night and day with visitors and locals alike. Paint-spattered wooden tables and chairs on a plank floor under a massive palapa draw barefoot beachcombers in for frozen cocktails, cold beer, and casual fare where live music is king. The revelry starts as early as happy hour and continues well into the night. Karaoke nights, salsa nights, and even a crazy fish night on Monday mean there's always something wild and fun going on here. It's also an optimal spot to catch a magical sunset over the waves. ✉ *De Palm Pier, Noord* ✛ *In between Riu and Hilton on Palm Beach* ☎ *297/586–2233* ⊕ *www.bugaloe.com.*

Gusto. Definitely Aruba's most cosmopolitan high-octane dance club, Gusto is where master bartenders show off excellent flair skills while serving up fabulous cocktails and pretty people party late into the night. The island's hottest DJs and dazzling light show keep the dancing going nonstop. Late-night happy hour is from 9 pm to 11 pm. All kinds of special events and theme nights add to Gusto's allure as a highly popular party spot. ✉ *J.E. Irausquin Blvd. 348-A, Palm Beach* ☎ *297/592–8772* ☾ *Closed Mon.*

Iguana Joe's. The reptilian-themed decor is as colorful and creative as the specialty cocktails served here, a favorite hangout for those who want to enjoy the view of the port from the second-floor balcony. The crowd is primarily tourists during the early evening, and many locals enjoy the laid-back vibe on Friday and Saturday nights. Though famous for their potent drinks, especially their signature Pink Iguana, the food deserves a shout-out as well, especially the jerk chicken and coconut shrimp. ✉ *Royal Plaza Mall, L.G. Smith Blvd. 94, Oranjestad* ☎ *297/583–9373* ⊕ *www.iguanajoesaruba.com* ☾ *Closed Sun.*

MooMba Beach Bar. As the central party spot on the busiest part of Palm Beach, this open-air bar is famous for its Sunday night blowouts with big crowds of locals gathering to dance in the sand to live bands or DJs. The barkeeps are flair and mixology masters, and happy hours are very hot. Its sister dining establishment is also a wonderful surf-side spot for breakfast, lunch, and dinner. ✉ *Between Holiday Inn and Marriott Surf Club, J.E. Irausquin Blvd. 230, Palm Beach* ☎ *297/586–5365* ⊕ *www. moombabeach.com.*

Reflexions. Aruba's answer to South Beach is just steps from downtown Oranjestad on Surfside Beach. This upscale hot spot is party central on weekends with the island's hottest DJs and crowds of dancers under techno lights inside and right on the beach. By day it's a whole different scene—sleek and sophisticated—with VIP bottle service, an international bites menu, and fancy frozen cocktails. You'll often spot the beautiful people lounging in for-rent cabanas and daybeds or in the massage loungers in the seaside pool. Reflexions offers luggage storage and free transportation to the airport once you've checked out of your hotel if you want a few more hours of beach time before you return home. It's also a very popular spot for private parties, so call ahead to make sure they're open to the public. ✉ *L. G. Smith Blvd. 2, Oranjestad* ☎ *297/582–0153* ⊕ *beach-aruba.com.*

CASINOS

Alhambra Casino. Refurbished and refreshed as part of the new Alhambra Mall reconstruction, this is a lively, popular casino with a big selection of modern slots, blackjack, craps, poker, roulette, and more. Be sure to join their Player's Club—it's free and offers free slot credits, and you earn points with your card as well. Their restaurant, called The Cove, serves light meals and drinks, and you'll also receive free drinks on the floor when you're playing the games. Special themes nights and promotions all week, and on Saturday afternoons they have

Super Bingo. It is owned by the Divi family of resorts. ⊠ *L.G. Smith Blvd. 47, Oranjestad* ☎ *297/583–5000* ⊕ *www.casinoalhambra.com.*

Crystal Casino. Adorned with Austrian crystal chandeliers and gold-leaf columns, the Renaissance Aruba's glittering casino evokes Monaco's grand establishments. The Salon Privé offers serious gamblers a private room for baccarat, roulette, and high-stakes blackjack. This casino is popular among cruise-ship passengers, who stroll over from the port to watch and play in slot tournaments and bet on sporting events. Luxury car giveaways are also a big draw there. Open 11 am to 6 am daily. ⊠ *Renaissance Aruba Resort & Casino, L.G. Smith Blvd. 82, Oranjestad* ☎ *297/583–6000.*

Hyatt Regency Casino. Ablaze with neon, with a Carnival-in-Rio theme, the most popular games here are slots, blackjack, craps, and baccarat. In the heart of the main tourist strip in one of the nicest hotels along Palm Beach, this gambling emporium is also known for its live music Thursday through Sunday and lively party atmosphere. Don't forget to ask for your $10 free play card (ID equired). Open until 4 am. ⊠ *Hyatt Regency Aruba Beach Resort & Casino, J.E. Irausquin Blvd. 85, Palm Beach* ☎ *297/586–1234* ⊕ *www.aruba.hyatt.com.*

Fodor'sChoice ★ **Stellaris Casino.** This is the largest casino on the island and boasts 500 modern interactive slots and 28 tables with games like craps, roulette, poker, and blackjack. They also have a state-of-the-art race and sports betting operation. Don't forget to join their VIP Club program, where you can earn points, comps, and prizes. Free cocktails for gamers, and there are many special theme and entertainment nights. ⊠ *Aruba Marriott Resort, L.G. Smith Blvd. 101, Palm Beach* ☎ *297/520–6428.*

NIGHTLIFE TOURS AND FESTIVALS

Carubbian Festival. Every Thursday night in San Nicolas, the main streets of Aruba's old refinery town that locals called Sunrise City come to life in a spectacular fashion with a mini-carnival called the Carubbian Festival. It's a culture and heritage extravaganza featuring live music concerts, dancing shows, and even a big colorful parade finale where visitors are encouraged to fully participate. There are also arts and crafts stalls and food and drink kiosks that include local specialties set up for the occasion. There are activities planned for children as well. Festival runs from 6 pm to 10 pm. Sometimes it takes a break the last weeks of December for the holidays and resumes mid-January. ■TIP→ A hotel bus package is a good idea as the roads at night are not lit, and navigation can be challenging. ⊠ *Main St., San Nicolas* 🖾 *Free.*

FAMILY
Fodor'sChoice ★ **Kukoo Kunuku Party Bus & Day Tours.** Aruba's premier wild and crazy party bus outfit has been operating for almost two decades now, and they've added a new twist. Evenings, it's all about shaking your maracas and bar-hopping through the town via their famous "Pub Krawl" tour or doing a dinner and bar-hop night that stops at the cool Casibari Grill in the outback for great BBQ, and then motors on for a wild tour to local party spots. But during the day, the bus morphs into one big happy family-friendly vehicle that offers a trip to the Casibari rock formations and Baby Beach in San Nicolas, or an "Animal Lover's" outing that goes

to the Aruba Donkey Sanctuary, Phillips Animal Garden, and the Butterfly Farm. Either way, their guides are fabulous entertainers night and day. Hotel pickup and drop-off included. No tours on Sunday. Private charters also available. ■ TIP→ **Book direct by phone for a discount, or book a night tour at the same time as a day tour and receive $10 off.** ⊠ *Noord 128 P, Noord* ☎ *297/586–2010* ⊕ *www.kukookunuku.com.*

SHOPS AND SPAS

SHOPS

The only real duty-free shopping is in the departure area of the airport. (Passengers bound for the United States should be sure to shop before proceeding through U.S. customs in Aruba.) Downtown stores do have very low sales tax though and some excellent bargains on high-end luxury items like gold, silver, and jewelry. Major credit cards are welcome everywhere, as are U.S. dollars. Aruba's souvenir and crafts stores are full of Dutch porcelains and figurines, as befits the island's heritage. Dutch cheese is a good buy, as are hand-embroidered linens and any products made from the native aloe vera plant. Local arts and crafts run toward wood carvings and earthenware emblazoned with "Aruba: One Happy Island" and the like, but there are many shops with unique Aruban items like designer wear and artwork. Don't try to bargain unless you are at a flea market. Arubans consider it rude to haggle.

AREAS AND MALLS

Fodor's Choice ★ **Alhambra Mall.** There's an eclectic array of shops and dining in the Alhambra Mall with the casino as its focal point. Dotted with designer retail stores like the Lazy Lizard and the Aruba Aloe outlet, and a full-service market and deli, the alfresco mall also has fast-food outlets like Juan Valdez Coffee Shop, Baskin-Robbins, and Subway. Fusions Wine & Tapas Bar and popular new eateries Hollywood Smokehouse and Twist of Flavors restaurant round out the dining options. There's also a small full-service spa. Stores are open late. ⊠ *L.G. Smith Blvd. 47, Druif* ⊕ *www.casinoalhambra.com.*

Fodor's Choice ★ **Caribbean Queen.** A unique boutique dedicated to the spirit of West Indian women, Caribbean Queen has jewelry, adornments, and fashionable accessories that are mostly handcrafted, and they are often beautiful works of art in their own right. As a way to promote locally made products, a creator/crafter is chosen to be the Caribbean Queen of the Month to conduct workshops in the store and demonstrate how items are made. A portion of all purchases goes to local charities and nonprofit foundations. They also sell handbags, belts, hats, and shoes. ⊠ *Palm Beach Plaza, L. G. Smith Blvd. 95, #123, Noord* ☎ *297/586–8737* ⊕ *www.caribbean-queen.com.*

Caya G.F. Betico Croes (Main St.). Oranjestad's original "Main Street" (behind the Renaissance Marina Resort) had been neglected since most cruise passengers preferred to stick to the front street near the marina where the high-end shops and open-market souvenir stalls are. However, a recent massive renovation of the entire downtown region has breathed new life into the backstreets with pedestrian-only stretches, compact malls, and open resting areas. A free ecotrolley now loops all through downtown, allowing you to hop on and off to shop at all kinds of stores. Fashions, souvenirs, specialty items, sporting goods, cosmetics . . . you name it, you'll find them all on this renewed street. ⊠ *Oranjestad.*

Colombian Emeralds. A trusted international jewelry dealer specializing in emeralds, this outlet also has a top-notch selection of diamonds, sapphire, tanzanite, rubies, ammolite, pearls, gold, semiprecious gems, luxury watches, and more at very competitive prices. A highly professional and knowledgeable staff adds to their credibility. ⊠ *Renaissance Mall, L.G. Smith Blvd. 82, Oranjestad* ☎ *297/583–6238* ⊕ *www. colombianemeralds.com.*

Fodor'sChoice **Diamonds International.** One of the pioneer diamond retailers in the
★ Caribbean with over 130 stores throughout the chain, the Aruba outlet has been operating in the same spot since 1997. They are well known for their expertise, selection, quality, and competitive prices on diamonds, and they also sell high-end timepieces. The founders of Diamonds International are both graduates of the Gemological Institute of America. ⊠ *Port of Call Marketplace, L.G. Smith Blvd. 17, Oranjestad* ☎ *800/515–3935* ⊕ *www.diamondsinternational.com.*

J.L. Penha & Sons. Originating in Curaçao in 1865, Penha has branched out throughout the Caribbean and has seven stores on Aruba. The largest is right next to the Renaissance Hotel. Known for good prices on high-end perfumes, cosmetics, skin-care products, and more recently, eyewear and fashions. Brand and designer names include MAC, Lancôme, Estée Lauder, Clinique, Chanel, Dior, Montblanc, and Victoria's Secrets to name just a few. They also have a store in Plaza Daniel Leo in downtown Oranjestad. ⊠ *Caya G.F. Betico Croes 11/13, Oranjestad* ☎ *297/582–4160, 297/582–4161* ⊕ *www.jlpenha.com.*

Fodor'sChoice **Little Switzerland.** With five stores on the island—mostly in high-rise
★ resorts and the original location in downtown Royal Plaza Mall—these well-known outlets specialize in designer jewelry and upscale timepieces by big-name designers like TAGHeuer, David Yurman, Breitling, Roberto Coin, Chopard, Pandora, Tiffany & Co., and Cartier Movado, Omega, and John Hardy. ⊠ *Royal Plaza Mall, L.G. Smith Blvd. 94, Oranjestad* ☎ *284/809–5560* ⊕ *www.littleswitzerland.com.*

Fodor'sChoice **The Mask-Mopa Mopa Art.** These shops specialize in original masks and
★ crafty items called Mopa-Mopa Art. Originating with the Quillacingas Indians of Ecuador and Colombia, the art is made from the bud of the mopa-mopa tree, boiled down into a resin, colored with dyes, and applied to carved mahogany and other woods like cedar. Masks, jewelry boxes, coasters, whimsical animal figurines, and more make wonderfully unique gifts and souvenirs. The masks are also believed to ward off evil spirits. Find them in Paseo Herencia Mall, Royal Plaza Mall, and Renaissance Marketplace. ⊠ *Paseo Herencia, J.E. Irausquin Blvd. 382-A, Local C017, Palm Beach* ☎ *297/586–2900* ⊕ *www.mopamopa.com.*

Fodor'sChoice **Palm Beach Plaza.** Aruba's most modern multistory mall has three floors
★ of shops offering fashion, tech, electronics, jewelry, souvenirs, and

more. Entertainment includes, glow-in-the-dark bowling, a modern video arcade, a sports bar, and the main floor indoor courtyard is often used for local festivals and events like fashion shows. Dining includes a food court and stand-alone restaurants and bars, and there are also modern air-conditioned cinemas and a spa within. ⊠ *Palm Beach Plaza, L.G. Smith Blvd. 95, Palm Beach* ☎ *297/586–0045* ⊕ *www. palmbeachplaza.com.*

FAMILY

Fodor's Choice
★

Paseo Herencia. A gorgeous, old-fashioned colonial-style courtyard and clock tower encases souvenir and specialty shops, cinemas, dining spots, cafés, and bars in this low-rise alfresco mall just off Palm Beach. Famous for its "liquid fireworks" shows when three times a night neon-lit water fountains waltz to music in a choreographed dance. Visitors can enjoy it for free from an outdoor amphitheater where many cultural events take place, and there's an Aruban walk of fame there. There's also a fancy carousel for children. A must visit—if not for the shopping—then for the water show. ⊠ *J.E. Irausquin Blvd. 382, Palm Beach* ☎ *297/586–6533* ⊕ *paseoherencia.com.*

Fodor's Choice
★

Renaissance Mall. Upscale, name-brand fashion and luxury brands of perfume, cosmetics, leather goods are what you'll find in the array of 60 stores spanning two floors in this mall located within and underneath the Renaissance Marina Resort. You'll also find specialty items like cigars and designer shoes plus high-end gold, silver, diamonds, and quality jewelry at low-duty and no-tax prices. Cafés and high-end dining, plus a casino and spa round out the offerings. Late-night shopping until 8 pm daily. ⊠ *Renaissance Marina Resort, L.G. Smith Blvd. 82, Oranjestad* ☎ *297/582–4622* ⊕ *www.shoprenaissancearuba.com.*

FAMILY

Renaissance Marketplace. The Renaissance Marketplace is more of a dining and gathering spot along the marina than a market. It's a lively spot with a few souvenir shops and specialty stores. There is also a modern cinema. But mostly it's full of eclectic dining emporiums and trendy cafés, and they have live music some weekends in their alfresco square. The Seaport casino is also there, and it's steps from the cruise terminal on the marina. ⊠ *L.G. Smith Blvd. 82, Oranjestad* ⊕ *www. shoprenaissancearuba.com.*

Royal Plaza Mall. It's impossible to miss this gorgeous colonial-style, cotton-candy-colored building with the big gold dome gracing the front street along the marina. It's one of the most photographed in Oranjestad. Three levels of shops—indoor and outdoor—make up this artsy arcade full of small boutiques, cigar shops, designer clothing outlets, gift and jewelery stores, and souvenir kiosks. Great dining and bars within as well. ⊠ *L.G. Smith Blvd. 94, Oranjestad* ☎ *297/588–0351.*

SPAS

Okeanos. The ocean provides the backdrop for this spa in the Renaissance, which has its own massage cove that seems a world apart from the rest of the resort. Outdoor massages and showers help to bring the calming effects of nature into the treatments. In addition to the usual assortment of massages and wraps, the spa also offers both anti-cellulite and anti-aging treatments. There are a huge number of packages available, including one that combines Swedish massage with a meal served by your own butler. Pampering doesn't get much better than this. There are also optional packages to use the spa services at the Cove Spa located on the resort's private island. ⊠ *Renaissance Aruba Resort & Casino, L.G. Smith Blvd. 82, Palm Beach* ☎ *297/583–6000* ⊕ *www. renaissancearubaspa.com.*

Fodor's Choice ★ **Pure Indulgence Spa.** The new Pure spa at Divi Aruba Phoenix Resort is in keeping with the Pure Beach and Pure Ocean Divi branding. With gorgeous new rooms and couple's suites, they offer Microsilk Hydrotherapy baths and premium Hansgrohe Raindance rain showers, and the facility features top-of-the-line treatments and many extras, including beach massages. A new mani-pedi loft boasts spectacular sea views as well, and they are well equipped to accommodate bridal parties. ⊠ *Divi Aruba Phoenix Resort, J.E. Irausquin Blvd. 75* ☎ *297/586–6066* ⊕ *www.purespaaruba.com.*

ZoiA Spa. It's all about indulgence at the Hyatt's upscale spa, named after the Papiamento word for balance. Gentle music and the scent of botanicals make the world back home fade into the background. Newly arrived visitors to the island can opt for the jet lag massage that combines reflexology and aromatherapy, and those with the budget and time for a full day of relaxation can opt for the Serene package. There's even a mother-to-be package available. Island brides can avail themselves of a full menu of beauty services ranging from botanical facials (using local ingredients) to a full makeup job for the big day. The Pure High Tea package offers a delicious assortment of snacks and teas along with an hour of treatments. ⊠ *Hyatt Regency Aruba Beach Resort & Casino, J.E. Irausquin Blvd. 85, Palm Beach* ☎ *297/586–1234* ⊕ *www. aruba.hyatt.com.*

SPORTS AND THE OUTDOORS

Aruba has recently become the beach tennis capital of the world and now hosts many international tournaments on its beaches. As for water sports, there is little you cannot do on Aruba, including modern thrill activities such as Jetlev®, an over-water jet pack flight; the hoverboard, an air-propelled skateboard over the waves; and jet blades, ski boots on a board that lifts you over the water. Parasailing, banana boats, wave runners, kayaking, paddleboarding, yoga on paddleboard . . . Aruba has it all, even a real submarine.

DAY SAILS

There is a large variety of snorkeling, dinner, sunset, and party cruises to choose from. The larger operators offer the best experience, though the smaller ones might offer the best price.

FAMILY **Mi Dushi.** *Mi Dushi* means "my sweetheart" in the local lingo, and this operator has been offering guests snorkeling and sailing trips on Aruban waters for more than three decades. Having recently scuttled their older ship to make a man-made reef, they have a brand-new vessel: a huge, colorful four-deck catamaran than can hold up to 70 people.

Tours include music, an open bar, snorkel gear, instruction, and a pirate rope swing. Snorkel tours cover Aruba's three most popular reefs, and romantic sunset sails are also available. You can also charter them for private parties. Excursions depart from the DePalm Pier on Palm Beach. ⊠ *DePalm Pier, Palm Beach* ☎ *297/640–3000* ⊕ *www.midushi.com.*

Tranquilo Charters Aruba. Captain Mike Hagedoorn, a legendary Aruban sailor, has recently handed the helm over to his son Captain Anthony after 20 years of running the family business. Today, *The Tranquilo*— a 43-foot sailing yacht—still takes small groups of passengers to a secluded spot at a Spanish lagoon named "Mike's Reef" after his father, where no other snorkel trips venture. The lunch cruise to the south side always includes "Mom's famous Dutch pea soup," and they also do private charters for dinner sails and sailing trips around Aruba's lesser-explored coasts. Look for the red boat docked at the Renaissance Marina beside the Atlantis Submarine launch. ⊠ *Renaissance Marina, Oranjestad* ☎ *297/586–1418* ⊕ *www.tranquiloaruba.com.*

DIVING AND SNORKELING

With visibility of up to 90 feet, the waters around Aruba are excellent for snorkeling and diving. Advanced and novice divers alike will find plenty to occupy their time, as many of the most popular sites—including some interesting shipwrecks—are found in shallow waters ranging from 30 to 60 feet. Coral reefs covered with sensuously waving sea fans and eerie giant sponge tubes attract a colorful menagerie of sea life, including gliding manta rays, curious sea turtles, shy octopuses, and grunts, groupers, and other fish. Marine preservation is a priority on Aruba, and regulations by the Conference on International Trade in Endangered Species make it unlawful to remove coral, conch, and other marine life from the water, and the new Marine Park Foundation is ensuring the protection of the reefs. There are many snorkeling trips for all ages with large operators and DePalm Island also has excellent snorkeling.

Scuba diving operator prices vary depending on the trip. If you want to go all the way, complete open-water certification takes at least four days worth of instruction.

Aruba Pro Dive. The fact that this is a small outfit that only caters to small groups (six max) helps make each dive more personal, flexible, and unique. They also do night dives and all levels of PADI certification. ⊠ *Ponton 90, Noord* ☎ *297/582–5520* ⊕ *www.arubaprodive.com.*

FAMILY

Fodor's Choice ★

DePalm Pleasure Sail & Snorkeling. The luxury catamaran *DePalm Pleasure* offers three-stop snorkel trips to the island's most popular fish-filled spots daily including the *Antilla* shipwreck. They also offer the option to try Snuba. Their romantic sunset sails are popular excursions. Buffet and open bar are included. Hotel pickup and drop-off are included unless they are within easy walking distance of their pier on Palm Beach. ⊠ *DePalm Pier, Palm Beach, Noord* ✛ *Between the Hilton and the Riu resorts on Palm Beach.* ☎ *297/522–4400* ⊕ *www.depalmtours.com.*

A bouquet of colorful reefs can be explored in the waters of Aruba.

Native Divers Aruba. A small, personal operation, Native Divers Aruba specializes in PADI open-water courses. Ten different certification options include specialties like Multilevel Diver, Search & Recovery Diver, and Underwater Naturalist. Their boat schedule is also flexible, and it's easy to tailor instruction to your specific needs. ⊠ *Marriott Surf Club, Palm Beach* ☏ *297/586–4763* ⊕ *www.nativedivers.com.*

GOLF

The Links at Divi Aruba. This 9-hole course was designed by Karl Litten and Lorie Viola. The par-36 flat layout stretches to 2952 yards and features paspalum grass (best for seaside courses) and takes you past beautiful lagoons. It's a testy little course with water abounding, making accuracy more important than distance. Amenities include a golf school with professional instruction, a swing-analysis station, a driving range, and a two-story golf clubhouse with a pro shop. Two restaurants are available: Windows on Aruba for fine dining and Mulligan's for a casual and quick lunch. ⊠ *Divi Village Golf & Beach Resort, J.E. Irausquin Blvd. 93, Oranjestad* ☏ *297/581–4653* ⊕ *www.divilinks.com* 🏌 *9 holes, 2952 yards, par 36.*

Fodor'sChoice
★

Tierra del Sol. Stretching out to 6811 yards, this stunning course is situated on the northwest coast near the California Lighthouse and is Aruba's only 18-hole course. Designed by Robert Trent Jones Jr., Tierra del Sol combines Aruba's native beauty—cacti and rock formations, stunning views—with good greens and beautiful landscaping. Wind can also be a factor here on the rolling terrain, as are the abundant bunkers and water hazards. Greens fees include a golf cart equipped with GPS and a communications system that allows you to order drinks for your return to the clubhouse. The fully stocked golf shop is one of the Caribbean's most elegant, with an extremely attentive staff. ⊠ *Caya di Solo 10, Malmokweg* ☎ *297/586–7800* ⊕ *www.tierradelsol.com* ⚑ *18 holes, 6811 yards, par 71.*

GUIDED TOURS AND MULTISPORT OUTFITTERS

FAMILY
Fodor's Choice
★

De Palm Tours. Aruba's premier tour company covers every inch of the island on land and under sea, and they even have their own submarine (*Atlantis*) and semi-submarine (*Seaworld Explorer*) and their own all-inclusive private island destination (De Palm Island). Land exploration options include air-conditioned bus sightseeing tours and rough and rugged outback jaunts by jeep safari to popular attractions like the natural pool. You can also do off-road tours in a UTV (two-seater utility task vehicle) via their guided caravan trips. On the waves, their luxury catamaran DePalm Pleasure offers romantic sunset sails and snorkel trips that include an option to try Snuba—deeper snorkeling with an air-supplied raft at Aruba's most famous shipwreck. DePalm also offers airport transfers. ⊠ *L.G. Smith Blvd. 142, Oranjestad* ☎ *297/582–4400* ⊕ *www.depalmtours.com.*

Rancho Notorious. One of Aruba's oldest tour operators, Rancho Notorious offers horseback riding for all levels and many different guided tours, including ATV outback adventures and mountain biking. All adventures are a great way to experience the island's rugged arid outback and scenic rocky seasides where cars cannot venture. ⊠ *Boroncana, Noord* ☎ *297/586–0508* ⊕ *www.ranchonotorious.com.*

Fodor's Choice
★

Red Sail Sports Aruba. A dynamic company established almost two decades ago and experts in the field of water-sports recreation, Red Sail offers excellent diving excursions, snorkel sails, sunset, sails, and full dinner sails. They even have their own sports equipment shop. They are also the original operator to introduce the cool new sport of Jetlev®—a personal jet pack over the water—and jet blades—like roller blades on the waves and hoverboards. They also have the island's only certified instructors for these activities, and have recently opened their own beach tennis club with expert instruction as well. ⊠ *Palm Beach, Noord* ☎ *297/586–1603* ⊕ *www.aruba-redsail.com.*

HIKING

Aruba's arid and rugged countryside is full of flora and fauna. Arikok National Wildlife Park is an excellent place to glimpse the real Aruba; start at the visitor center to get guidance and maps, or see their website for online trails maps (⊕ *www.arubanationalpark.org*). The heat can be oppressive, so be sure to take it easy, wear a hat, wear plenty of sunscreen, and have lots of water handy. A guided hike will show you where to find the island's elusive but interesting wildlife in the arid outback.

FAMILY **Nature Sensitive Tours.** Eddy Croes, a former park ranger whose passion for nature is infectious, runs this outfitter with care. Groups are never larger than eight people, so you'll see as much detail as you can handle. The hikes are done at an easy pace and are suitable for just about anyone. Moonlight tours also available. If you'd rather not hike, Eddy also has a 4x4 monster jeep–guided tour of the arid outback for up to 20 people as well. ⊠ *Pos Chiquito 13E, Savaneta* ☎ *297/585–1594* ⊕ *www.naturesensitivetours.com* ☞ *Jeep tours also available.*

HORSEBACK RIDING

FAMILY **Rancho Daimari.** Rancho Daimari offers treks to the incredible natural pool in the heart of Arikok National Park, or to a scenic and secret surfer's beach. Tours are very family-friendly and accommodate all levels of riding skills. Complimentary return transportation from hotels. Reservations mandatory. ⊠ *Palm Beach 33B, Noord* ☎ *297/586–6284* ⊕ *www.arubaranchodaimari.net.*

FAMILY **Rancho La Ponderosa.** Run by one of Aruba's best-known horsemen, and
Fodor's Choice using steeds from his private stock, Rancho La Ponderosa offers quality
★ rides of two or two-and-a-half hours. Choose from rides along the wild coast to gold mill ruins and fallen land bridge or the famous ostrich farm. It's noteworthy that their tours never encounter vehicular traffic. ⊠ *Arikok National Park* ☎ *297/587–1142* ⊕ *rancholaponderosaaruba.com.*

KAYAKING

FAMILY **Aruba Watersports Center.** This family-run, full-service water activity
Fodor's Choice center is right on Palm Beach. They offer a comprehensive variety of
★ adventures including diving, snorkeling, parasailing, Jet Skis, wave runners, tubing, Hobie Cat sailing, stand-up paddleboarding, kayaking, wakeboard, and waterskiing. Speedboat and bike rentals as well. Lovely lounging area on the beach, and the Breadbasket café on-site with free Wi-Fi has excellent coffees and unique snacks. ⊠ *Between Occidental and Hilton on Palm Beach, L.G. Smith Blvd. 81B, Noord* ☎ *297/586–6613* ⊕ *arubawatersportscenter.com.*

WINDSURFING

The southwestern coast's tranquil waters at Fishermen's Huts make windsurfing conditions ideal for both beginners and intermediates alike, and expert instruction and modern equipment rental will have you up on the waves in no time. Aruba has some of the best windsurfers in the world, and the annual Hi-Winds Competition also attracts the world's best each year and brings out big crowds to party on the beach.

Fodor's Choice **Aruba Active Vacations.** Aruba Active Vacations is a major outdoor activ-
★ ity center on the island that includes kiteboarding, windsurfing, mountain bike tours and rentals, stand-up paddleboarding, and landsailing. Instruction and rentals for all included. Located on one of Aruba's most ideal beaches for windsurfing and kiteboarding at Fisherman's Huts. ⊠ *Near Fisherman's Huts beside Ritz-Carlton Aruba, Malmokweg* ☎ *297/586–0989* ⊕ *www.aruba-active-vacations.com.*

BARBADOS

WELCOME TO BARBADOS

Broad vistas, sweeping seascapes, craggy cliffs, and acre upon acre of sugarcane—that's Barbados. Beyond that, visitors are drawn to the island by the Bajan hospitality, the welcoming hotels and resorts, the sophisticated dining, the never-ending things to see and do, the exciting nightspots, and, of course, the sunny beaches.

TOP REASONS TO VISIT BARBADOS

1 Great Resorts: They run the gamut—from unpretentious to sublime.

2 Great Golf: Tee off at some of the best championship courses in the Caribbean.

3 Restaurants Galore: Great food ranges from street-party barbecue to world-class dining.

4 Wide Range of Activities: Land and water sports, historic sites, tropical gardens, and night-life ... there's always plenty to do.

5 Welcoming Locals: Bajans are friendly, welcoming, helpful, and hospitable. You'll like them; they'll like you.

North Pt.

Animal ◆
Flower Cave

Crabhill

1B

ST. LUCY

Fairfield

Maycock's Bay 🏖 19
Shermans

Six Men's Bay
Pamir 🏖 20 St. James Rd. 1
Speightstown Rose Hill
ST. PETER

Mullins Beach 🏖

Mullins Bay

ST. JAMES

Folkestone
Underwater Park
& Marine Reserve ◆

Holetown & Vicinity
see detail map Holetown

Dottins Reef 🏖

Paynes Bay Beach 🏖 1

Cockspur Beach Club

Stavronikita 🏖 *Brighton Beach*
Deep Water Harbour
Bell Buoy 🏖
Silver Bank 🏖

Bridgetown
see detail map *Carlisle Bay*

Pebbles Beac

1 - 3

BARBADOS BASICS

Barbados stands apart—both geographically and geologically—from its Caribbean neighbors. It's a full 100 miles (161 km) east of the Lesser Antilles chain. The top of a single submerged mountain of coral and limestone, Barbados is 21 miles (34 km) long, 14 miles (22½ km) wide, and relatively flat. The population is nearly 300,000, and the capital city is Bridgetown.

KEY

- Beaches
- Cruise Ship Terminal
- Dive Sites
- ① Hotels

Cuckold Pt.

Gay's Cove

Id

St. Nicholas Abbey
Cherry Tree Hill
Barbados Wildlife Reserve
Morgan Lewis Sugar Mill
Farley Hill National Park ①
Belleplaine
Chalky Mount ◆

ST. ANDREW

Mt. Hillaby

Barclays Park Beach

Cattlewash Beach
Bathsheba Beach
Cattlewash
Tent Bay
Bathsheba
18
Soup Bowl

Flower Forest
Hunte's Gardens
ST. JOSEPH

Welchman Hall Gully

Harrison's Cave

Blackmans

Andromeda Botanic Gardens 17

Conset Bay

Codrington Theological College

ST. THOMAS
Groves

Four Crossroads

ST. JOHN

Marley Vale

Ragged Pt.

Orchid World & Tropical Flower Garden

4

4B

ST. PHILIP

Bottom Bay Beach

Warrens 2
ST. GEORGE

Gun Hill
Gun Hill Signal Station

ST. MICHAEL

3

Edgecumbe

Sunbury Plantation House and Museum

Mount Gay Rum Visitors Centre

Tyrol Cot Heritage Village 4

Emancipation Statue

CHRIST CHURCH

Crane Bay

16 Crane Beach
Crane

George Washington House
7 ◆ Harry Bayley Observatory
5
4 6 ◆ Barbados Museum

Hastings
Worthing
7
Dover Turtle Casuarina
Beach Beach Beach
St. Lawrence
Gap
Oistins

Accra Beach

Sandy Beach

Oistins Bay

8 9
10-13
Miami Beach
14
South Point Light 15

South Pt.

Barbados Concorde Experience
✈ Grantley Adams International Airport

Long Bay

Silver Sands·
Silver Rock Beach

COBBLER'S REEF

0   2 mi

0   2 km

NEED TO KNOW

Atlantic Ocean

BARBADOS

Bridgetown

Capital: Bridgetown

Population: 287,400

Currency: Barbados dollar; pegged to the U.S. dollar at Bds$1.98 to US$1

Money: ATMs common; credit cards and U.S. dollar are widely accepted

Language: English

Country Code: ☎ 1 246

Emergencies: ☎ 211

Driving: On the left

Electricity: 110v/50 cycles; plugs are U.S. standard two- and three-prong

Time: Same as New York during daylight savings time; one hour ahead otherwise

Documents: Up to six months with valid passport

Mobile Phones: GSM (900, 1800 and 1900 bands)

Major Mobile Companies: Digicel, Flow (formerly LIME)

WEBSITES

Barbados Travel Guide: ⊕ www.barbados.org

GETTING AROUND

✈ **Air Travel:** Grantley Adams International Airport is Barbados' only airport.

🚌 **Bus Travel:** Bus service is an efficient and inexpensive way to get around the island.

🚗 **Car Travel:** Barbados has good roads, but traffic can be heavy around Bridgetown. Be sure to keep a map handy, as the road system in the countryside can be very confusing.

🚕 **Taxi Travel:** Rates are fixed, albeit expensive.

PLAN YOUR BUDGET

	HOTEL ROOM	MEAL	ATTRACTIONS
Low Budget	$275	$12	Sunbury Plantation House and Museum, $7.50
Mid Budget	$375	$30	Cavern tour at Harrison's Cave, $30
High Budget	$475	$45	All-day catamaran cruise with Tiami or Cool Runnings, $90

WAYS TO SAVE

Head south. Compared to the west coast, the south coast (south of Bridgetown) tends to have more affordable options for lodging, restaurants, and nightlife.

Take buses. Buses are an inexpensive way to explore Barbados, especially between Bridgetown and stops along the west and south coasts.

Hit the beach. All of the island's beaches are free and open to the public.

Hassle Factor	Low. Direct flights to Barbados are frequent, and travel around the island is fairly easy (friendly and helpful locals are a big plus).
3 days	Relax beachside or poolside at your resort. Take a day to sightsee and explore the island.
1 week	Base yourself at a resort on a sandy beach on either the west or south coast, but do day trips to visit attractions in the interior, explore the island's stunning east (Atlantic) coast, and get out on the water on a catamaran day sail.
2 weeks	Rent a car to explore the island's every nook and cranny, including: historic Bridgetown and The Garrison, Holetown and the "Platinum" Coast, Speightstown and the far north, the rugged east coast, peaceful tropical gardens in the interior, remote beaches in the southeast, and nightlife in towns along the busy south coast.

WHEN TO GO

High Season: Mid-December through mid-April is the most fashionable and most expensive time to visit; the weather is typically sunny and warm with low humidity. Good hotels are often booked far in advance, and you're guaranteed the most entertainment at resorts and the most people with whom to enjoy it. Some hotels require a meal plan during high season.

Low Season: From August to late October, temperatures can become oppressively hot and the weather muggy, with a risk of tropical storms. Many upscale hotels close during September and October for annual renovations. Those remaining open offer deep discounts and do not usually require a meal plan.

Value Season: From late April to July and again from November to mid-December, hotel prices drop 20% to 50% from high-season prices. There are chances of scattered showers, but expect sun-kissed days and comfortable nighttime temperatures with fewer crowds.

BIG EVENTS

February: The weeklong Holetown Festival commemorates when the first European settlers arrived in Barbados in 1627. ⊕ www.holetownfestivalbarbados.org

April: Barbados Reggae Festival is the island's biggest musical festival. ⊕ www.thebarbadosreggaefestival.com

July: Crop Over, a monthlong festival similar to Carnival, begins in July and ends on Kadooment Day (a national holiday). ⊕ www.barbadoscropoverfestival.com

November: In mid-November, the annual Food, Wine & Rum Festival attracts international chefs, wine experts, and local rum ambassadors. ⊕ www.foodwinerum.com

READ THIS

- **Captain Blood,** Rafael Sabatini. A classic novel of high-seas adventure.

- **The Polished Hoe: A Novel,** Austin Clark. Award-winning story of a personal confession that reflects national history.

- **Star-Crossed,** Linda Collison. A British woman comes to claim her family estate.

WATCH THIS

- **Island in the Sun.** Interracial romance, starring Harry Belafonte and Dorothy Dandridge.

- **The Story of Adele H.** French historical drama by Truffaut.

- **The Tamarind Seed.** Love story about expats on Barbados during the Cold War.

EAT THIS

- **Pumpkin fritters:** sweet, deep-fried goodness.

- **Buljol:** marinated, seasoned cod.

- **Cou-cou:** a mush, similar to polenta, of cornmeal and okra.

- **Flying fish:** the official national fish, often served fried.

- **Stewed lambi:** stewed conch.

- **Breadfruit mash:** the island fruit is boiled, mashed, and seasoned.

Updated by
Jane E. Zarem

Isolated in the Atlantic Ocean, 100 miles (161 km) due east of St. Lucia, Barbados stands apart from its neighbors in the Lesser Antilles archipelago, the chain of islands that stretches in a graceful arc from the Virgin Islands to Trinidad. It's a sophisticated tropical island with a rich history, lodgings to suit every taste and pocketbook, and plenty to pique your interest both day and night.

Geologically, most of the Lesser Antilles are the peaks of a volcanic mountain range, whereas Barbados is the top of a single, relatively flat protuberance of coral and limestone—historically, the source of building blocks for many a plantation manor. Some of those "great houses," in fact, have been carefully restored. Two are open to visitors.

Bridgetown, both capital city and commercial center, is on the southwest coast of pear-shape Barbados. Most of the nearly 300,000 Bajans (*Bay*-juns, derived from the British pronunciation of *Barbadian*) live and work in and around Bridgetown, elsewhere in St. Michael Parish, or along the idyllic west coast or busy south coast. Others reside in tiny villages that dot the interior landscape. Broad sandy beaches, craggy cliffs, and numerous coves make up the coastline; the interior is consumed by forested hills and gullies and acre upon acre of sugarcane.

Without question, Barbados is the "most British" island in the Caribbean. In contrast to the turbulent colonial past experienced by neighboring islands, including repeated conflicts between France and Britain for dominance and control, British rule in Barbados carried on uninterrupted for 340 years—from the first established British settlement in 1627 until independence was granted in 1966. That's not to say, of course, that there weren't significant struggles in Barbados, as elsewhere in the Caribbean, between 17th- and 18th-century British landowners and their African-born slaves and other indentured servants.

With that unfortunate period of slavery relegated to the history books, the British influence on Barbados remains strong today in local manners, attitudes, customs, and politics—tempered, of course, by the characteristically warm nature and Caribbean style of the Bajan people. In keeping with British-born traditions, many Bajans worship at the Anglican church, afternoon tea is a ritual, cricket is the national pastime (a passion, most admit), dressing for dinner is a firmly entrenched tradition, and patrons at some bars are as likely to order a Pimm's Cup or a shandy as a rum and Coke. And yet, Barbados is hardly stuffy—this is still the Caribbean, after all.

Tourist facilities are concentrated on the west coast in St. James and St. Peter parishes (appropriately dubbed the "Platinum Coast") and on the south coast in Christ Church Parish. Traveling north along the west coast from Bridgetown, the capital city, to historic Holetown, the site of the first British settlement, and continuing to the city of Speightstown, you can find posh beachfront resorts, luxurious private villas, and fine restaurants enveloped by tropical gardens and lush foliage. The trendier, more commercial south coast offers competitively priced hotels and beach resorts, and the St. Lawrence Gap area is known for its restaurants and nightlife. The relatively wide-open spaces along the southeast coast are proving ripe for development, and some wonderful inns and hotels already take advantage of those intoxicatingly beautiful ocean vistas. For their own vacations, though, Bajans escape to the rugged east coast, where the Atlantic surf pounds the dramatic shoreline with unrelenting force.

Barbadians (Bajans) are a warm, friendly, and hospitable people who are genuinely proud of their country and culture. Although tourism is the island's number one industry, the island has a sophisticated business community and stable government; so life here doesn't skip a beat once passengers return to the ship. Barbados is the most "British" island in the Caribbean. Afternoon tea is a ritual, and cricket is the national sport. The atmosphere, though, is hardly stuffy. This is still the Caribbean, after all. Beaches along the island's south and west coasts are picture-perfect, and all are available to cruise passengers. On the rugged east coast, the Atlantic Ocean attracts world-class surfers. Rolling hills and valleys dominate the northeast, while the interior of the island is covered by acres of sugarcane and dotted with small villages. Historic plantations, a stalactite-studded cave, a wildlife preserve, rum distilleries, and tropical gardens are among the island's attractions. Bridgetown is the capital city, and its downtown shops and historic sites are a short walk or taxi ride from the pier.

PLANNING

GETTING HERE AND AROUND
AIR TRAVEL

You can fly nonstop to Barbados from Atlanta (Delta), Boston (JetBlue), Fort Lauderdale (JetBlue), Miami (American), and New York–JFK (JetBlue). Caribbean Airlines offers connecting service from Miami and New York via Port of Spain, Trinidad, but this adds at least two hours to your flight time even in the best of circumstances and may not be the best option for most Americans. Barbados is also well connected to other Caribbean islands via LIAT. Mustique Airways and SVG Air connect Barbados to St. Vincent and the Grenadines. Many passengers use Barbados as a transit hub, sometimes spending the night each way.

Not all airlines flying into Barbados have local numbers. If your airline doesn't have a local contact number on the island, you will have to pay for the call.

Airline Contacts American Airlines. ☎ 800/744–0006 in Barbados, 246/428–4170 ⊕ www.aa.com. **Caribbean Airlines.** ☎ 246/429–5929, 800/744–2225 in the Caribbean ⊕ www.caribbean-airlines.com. **Delta Air Lines.** ☎ 800/221–1212 in the Caribbean ⊕ www.delta.com. **JetBlue.** ☎ 877/596–2413 in Barbados, landline only, 800/538–2583 in U.S. ⊕ www.jetblue.com. **LIAT.** ☎ 246/434–5428 in Barbados, 888/844–5428 in the Caribbean ⊕ www.liat.com. **Mustique Airways.** ☎ 246/428–1638 ⊕ www.mustique.com. **SVG Air.** ☎ 246/247–3712 ⊕ www.svgair.com.

Airport Grantley Adams International Airport (BGI). ☎ 246/418–4242 ⊕ www.gaia.bb.

BUS TRAVEL

Bus service is efficient and inexpensive. Public buses are blue with a yellow stripe; yellow buses with a blue stripe are privately owned and operated; and "ZR" vans (so called for their ZR license plate designation) are white with a maroon stripe and also privately owned and operated. All buses travel frequently along Highway 1 (St. James Road) and Highway 7 (South Coast Main Road), as well as inland routes. The fare is Bds$2 for any one destination; exact change in either local or U.S. currency ($1) is appreciated. Buses run about every 20 minutes. Small signs on roadside poles that say "To City" or "Out of City," meaning the direction relative to Bridgetown, mark the bus stops. Flag down the bus with your hand, even if you're standing at the stop. Bridgetown terminals are at Fairchild Street for buses to the south and east and at Lower Green for buses to Speightstown via the west coast.

CAR TRAVEL

Barbados has good roads, but traffic can be heavy on main highways, particularly around Bridgetown. Be sure to keep a map handy, as the road system in the countryside can be very confusing—although the friendly Bajans are always happy to help you find your way. Drive on the left, British-style. Seat belts are compulsory, and children under five must use a child seat. Use of a cell phone while driving is prohibited. When someone flashes headlights at you at an intersection, it means "after you." Be especially careful negotiating roundabouts (traffic circles). The speed limit is 50 mph (80 kph) on highways, 37 mph (60 kph) in the countryside, and 20 mph (30 kph) in cities. Bridgetown actually has rush hours: 7 to 9 am and 4 to 6 pm. Park only in approved parking lots or in parking spots marked with a P sign.

Car Rentals: Most car-rental agencies require renters to be at least 21; some agencies have an age limit between 70 and 80 without a medical certificate. Dozens of agencies rent cars, jeeps, or minimokes (small, open-sided vehicles). Rates range from about $70 per day for a minimoke to $80 per day for a four-wheel-drive vehicle and $100 or more for a luxury car (or $225 to $400 or more per week) in high season.

Most firms also offer discounted three-day or seven-day rates, and some require at least a two-day rental in high season. You'll need either an international driver's license or a temporary driving permit, available through the rental agency for Bds$10.

Car-Rental Contacts Coconut Car Rentals. ⊠ *Bayside, Bay St., Bridgetown* ☎ *246/437–0297* ⊕ *www.coconutcars.com.* **Courtesy Rent-A-Car.** ⊠ *Grantley Adams International Airport* ☎ *246/431–4160* ⊕ *www.courtesyrentacar.com.* **Drive-a-Matic Car Rental.** ⊠ *CWTS Complex, Lower Estate* ☎ *246/422–3000, 800/581–8773* ⊕ *www.carhire.tv.*

TAXI TRAVEL

Taxis operate 24 hours a day. They aren't metered but rates are fixed by the government. Taxis carry up to three passengers, and the fare may be shared. Sample one-way fares from Bridgetown are $22 to Holetown, $30 to Speightstown, $18 to St. Lawrence Gap, and $38 to Bathsheba. Drivers can also be hired for an hourly rate of about $35–$40 for up to three people.

HEALTH AND SAFETY

Dengue, chikungunya, and zika have all been reported throughout the Caribbean. We recommend that you protect yourself from these mosquito-borne illnesses by keeping your skin covered and/or wearing mosquito repellent. The mosquitoes that transmit these viruses are as active by day as they are by night.

HOTELS AND RESORTS

Most people stay either in luxurious enclaves on the fashionable west coast—north of Bridgetown—or on the action-packed south coast with easy access to small, independent restaurants, bars, and nightclubs. A few inns on the remote southeast and east coasts offer ocean views and tranquillity, but those on the east coast don't have good swimming beaches nearby. Prices in Barbados are sometimes twice as high in season as during the quieter months. Most hotels include no meals in their rates. Some include breakfast, many offer a meal plan, some require you to purchase the meal plan in the high season, and a few offer all-inclusive packages.

Resorts: Great resorts run the gamut—from unpretentious to knock-your-socks-off—in terms of size, intimacy, amenities, and price. Many are well suited to families.

Small Inns: A few small, cozy inns are located in the east and southeast regions of the island.

Villas and Condos: Families and long-term visitors may choose from a wide variety of condos (everything from busy time-share resorts to more sedate vacation complexes). Villas and villa complexes can be luxurious, simple, or something in between.

Hotel reviews have been shortened. For full information, visit Fodors.com.

WHAT IT COSTS IN U.S. DOLLARS				
	$	**$$**	**$$$**	**$$$$**
RESTAURANTS	under $12	$12–$20	$21–$30	over $30
HOTELS	under $275	$275–$375	$376–$475	over $475

Restaurant prices are the average cost of a main course at dinner or, if dinner is not served, at lunch. Hotel prices are the lowest cost of a standard double room in high season.

VISITOR INFORMATION

Contacts Barbados Tourism Marketing, Inc. ⊠ *Warrens Office Complex, Lodge Rd., 1st fl., West Wing, Warrens* ☎ *246/427–2623, 800/221–9831* ⊕ *www.visitbarbados.org* ⊠ *Grantley Adams International Airport, Arrivals Lounge* ☎ *246/428–5570* ⊠ *Cruise-ship terminal, Deep Water Harbour, Bridgetown* ☎ *246/426–1718.*

EXPLORING

The terrain changes dramatically from each of the island's 11 parishes to the next, and so does the pace. Bridgetown, the capital, is a busy and fairly sophisticated city. West-coast resorts and private estates ooze luxury, whereas the small villages and vast sugar plantations found throughout central Barbados reflect the island's history. The relentless Atlantic surf shaped the cliffs of the dramatic east coast, and the northeast is called Scotland because of its hilly landscape and broad vistas. Along the lively south coast, the daytime hustle and bustle produce a palpable energy that continues well into the night at restaurants and nightspots.

BRIDGETOWN

This bustling capital city, inscribed in 2011—along with The Garrison—onto the UNESCO World Heritage List, is a duty-free port with a compact shopping area. The principal thoroughfare is Broad Street, which leads west from National Heroes Square. A shuttle service (☎ 246/227–2200) operates between hotels and downtown during business hours.

TOP ATTRACTIONS

The Careenage. In the early days, Bridgetown's natural harbor was where schooners were turned on their sides (careened) to be scraped of barnacles and repainted. Today, The Careenage serves as a marina for pleasure yachts and excursion boats, as well as a gathering place for locals and tourists alike. A boardwalk skirts the north side of the Careenage; on the south side, a lovely esplanade has pathways and benches for pedestrians and a statue of Errol Barrow, the first prime minister of Barbados. The Chamberlain Bridge and the Charles Duncan O'Neal Bridge span The Careenage. ⊠ *Bridgetown.*

Nidhe Israel Synagogue. Providing for the spiritual needs of one of the oldest Jewish congregations in the Western Hemisphere, this synagogue was formed by Jews who arrived in 1628 from Brazil and introduced sugarcane to Barbados. The adjoining cemetery has tombstones dating from the 1630s. The original house of worship, built in 1654, was destroyed in an 1831 hurricane, rebuilt in 1833, and restored in 1987 with the assistance of the Barbados National Trust. The museum, housed in a restored coral-stone building from 1750, documents the story of the Barbados Jewish community. Friday-night services are held during the winter months, but the building is open to the public year-round. Shorts are not acceptable during services but may be worn at other times. ⌧ *Synagogue La., Bridgetown* ☎ *246/436–6869* ⊕ *www.nidheisrael.com* ✉ *Synagogue free; museum $12.50* ⊘ *Weekdays 9–4; weekends by appointment.*

Queen's Park. Northeast of Bridgetown, this national park is the site of one of the island's two immense baobab trees. Brought to Barbados from Guinea, West Africa, around 1738, this tree has a girth of more than 60 feet. Queen's Park Art Gallery, managed by the National Culture Foundation, is the island's largest gallery; exhibits change monthly. Queen's Park House, built in 1783 and the historic home of the British troop commander, has been converted into a theater, with an exhibition room on the lower floor and a restaurant. Originally called King's House, the name was changed upon Queen Victoria's succession to the throne. ⌧ *Constitution Rd., Bridgetown* ☎ *246/427–2345 gallery* ✉ *Free* ⊘ *Weekdays 9–5, Sat. 9–2.*

WORTH NOTING

National Heroes Square. Across Broad Street from Parliament and bordered by High and Trafalgar streets, this triangular plaza marks the center of town. Its monument to Lord Horatio Nelson, who visited Barbados only briefly in 1777 as a 19-year-old navy lieutenant, predates Nelson's Column in London's Trafalgar Square by 30 years (1813 vs. 1843). There's also a war memorial and a fountain commemorating the advent of running water on Barbados in 1865. ⌧ *Broad St., across from Parliament, Bridgetown.*

FAMILY **Parliament Buildings.** Overlooking National Heroes Square in the center of town, these Victorian buildings were constructed around 1870 to house the British Commonwealth's third-oldest parliament (after Britain itself and Bermuda). A series of stained-glass windows in the East Wing depicts British monarchs from James I to Victoria. The National Heroes Gallery & Museum is in the West Wing. ⌧ *National Heroes Sq., Trafalgar St., Bridgetown* ☎ *246/427–2019* ⊕ *www.barbadosparliament.com* ✉ *Museum $5* ⊘ *Museum Mon. and Wed.–Fri. 10–4, Sat. 10–3.*

St. Michael's Cathedral. Although no one has proven it, George Washington is said to have worshipped here in 1751 during his only trip outside the United States. By then, the original structure was already nearly a century old. Destroyed twice by hurricanes, the cathedral was rebuilt in 1789 and again in 1831. It currently seats 1,600 persons and boasts the largest pipe organ in the Caribbean. ⌧ *St. Michael's Row, east of National Heroes Sq., Bridgetown* ☎ *246/427–0790* ⊕ *www.saintmichaelscathedral.bb.*

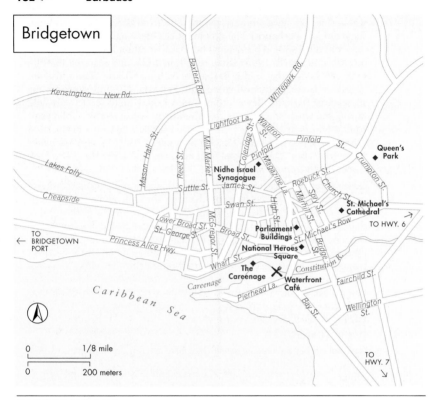

Bridgetown

SOUTH COAST

Christ Church Parish, which is far busier and more developed than the west coast, is chockablock with condos, high- and low-rise hotels, and beach parks. It is also the location of St. Lawrence Gap, with its many places to eat, drink, shop, and party. As you move southeast, the broad, flat terrain comprises acre upon acre of cane fields, interrupted only by a few tiny villages. Along the byways are colorful chattel houses, which were the traditional homes of tenant farmers. Historically, these typically Barbadian, ever-expandable small buildings were built so they could be dismantled and moved, as required.

TOP ATTRACTIONS

FAMILY **Barbados Concorde Experience.** The Concorde Experience focuses on the British Airways Concorde G-BOAE (Alpha Echo, for short) that for many years flew between London and Barbados. The retired supersonic jet has made its permanent home here. Besides boarding the sleek aircraft itself, you learn about how the technology was developed and how this plane differed from other jets. It's just a two-minute walk from the terminal and a perfect place to spend about an hour if you have a long layover between flights. ⊠ *Grantley Adams International Airport, adjacent to the terminal building* ☎ *246/420–7738* ⊕ *www.barbadosconcorde.com* ⊡ *$20* ☉ *Tues.–Sat. 9–4.*

FAMILY
Fodor'sChoice
★

Barbados Museum. Established in 1933 in the former British Military Prison (1815) in the historic Garrison area, this intriguing museum has artifacts from Arawak days (around 400 BC) and galleries that depict 19th-century military history and everyday social history. You can see cane-harvesting tools, wedding dresses, ancient (and frightening) dental instruments, and slave sale accounts in spidery copperplate handwriting. The Harewood Gallery showcases the island's natural environment, the Cunard Gallery has a permanent collection of West Indian prints bequeathed by Sir Edward Cunard, and the Warmington Gallery contains decorative arts depicting the planter's lifestyle. One gallery has exhibits for children. The Shilstone Memorial Library houses rare West Indian materials—archival documents, genealogical records, photos, books, and maps—dating to the 17th century. There is also a gift shop and café. ⊠ *The Garrison, Hwy. 7, Garrison* ☎ 246/427–0201 ⊕ *www. barbmuse.org.bb* ☜ *$7.50* ⊙ *Mon.–Sat. 9–5, Sun. 2–6.*

FAMILY
Fodor'sChoice
★

George Washington House. George Washington slept here! This carefully restored and refurbished 18th-century plantation house in Bush Hill was the only place where the future first president of the United States actually slept outside North America. Teenage George and his older half-brother Lawrence, who was suffering from tuberculosis and seeking treatment on the island, rented this house overlooking Carlisle Bay for two months in 1751. Opened to the public in 2007, the lower floor of the house and the kitchen have period furnishings; the upper floor is a museum with both permanent and temporary exhibits that display artifacts of 18th-century Barbadian life. The site includes an original 1719 windmill and bathhouse, along with a stable added to the property in the 1800s. Kids enjoy the network of secret tunnels. Guided tours begin with an informative 15-minute film, appropriately called *George Washington in Barbados.* ⊠ *Bush Hill, Garrison* ☎ 246/228–5461 ⊕ *www. georgewashingtonbarbados.org* ☜ *$10* ⊙ *Oct.–Aug., weekdays 9–4:30.*

5

Fodor'sChoice
★

Sunbury Plantation House and Museum. Lovingly rebuilt after a 1995 fire destroyed everything but the thick flint-and-stone walls of this 300-year-old great house, Sunbury offers an elegant glimpse of the 18th and 19th centuries on a Barbadian sugar estate. Period furniture, old prints, and a collection of horse-drawn carriages lend an air of authenticity. A buffet luncheon ($22.50 per person, $34 on Sunday) and high tea ($14) are served daily in the Courtyard Restaurant. A five-course candlelight dinner ($100 per person, including drinks, minimum 12 people, reservations required) is served at the 200-year-old mahogany table in the dining room. ⊠ *Off Hwy. 5* ⊹ *Look for the sign at Six Cross Roads Roundabout* ☎ 246/423–6270 ⊕ *www.barbadosgreathouse.com* ☜ *$7.50* ⊙ *Daily 9–5; last tour at 4:30.*

WORTH NOTING

Codrington Theological College. An impressive stand of cabbage palm trees lines the road leading to the coral-stone buildings and serene grounds of Codrington College, the oldest Anglican theological seminary in the Western Hemisphere, opened in 1745 on a cliff overlooking Conset Bay. The college's benefactor was Christopher Codrington III (1668–1710), a former governor-general of the Leeward Islands, whose antislavery views were unpopular in the plantocracy of the times. In an effort to "Christianize" the slaves and provide them with a general education, Codrington specified in his will that "300 negroes at least" would always be allowed to study at the institution; the planters who acted as trustees, however, were loath to teach slaves to read and write. You may visit the chapel, stroll the grounds, even have a picnic—but remember that beachwear is not appropriate here. ⊠ *Sargeant St., Codrington College* ☎ *246/423–1140* ⊕ *www.codrington.org* ✉ *Donations welcome* ⊙ *Daily 10–4.*

Emancipation Statue. This powerful statue of a slave—whose raised hands, broken chains hanging from each wrist, evoke both contempt and victory—is commonly referred to as the Bussa Statue. Bussa was the man who, in 1816, led the first slave rebellion on Barbados. The work of Barbadian sculptor Karl Brodhagen, the statue was erected in 1985 to commemorate the emancipation of the slaves in 1834. ⊠ *St. Barnabas Roundabout, intersection of ABC Hwy. and Hwy. 5, Haggatt Hall.*

FAMILY **Harry Bayley Observatory.** Reopened in January 2014 with a fresh interior, high-tech fittings, and a new dome—and reequipped with a 16-inch Meade telescope with the latest robotic controls and digital cameras and a new Lunt 80mm solar telescope—the observatory lets you view the moon, stars, planets, and other astronomical objects that may not be visible from mainland North America or Europe. The evening program, which starts with an informative presentation, is run by volunteers; call ahead to make sure it's open. The observatory has been the headquarters of the Barbados Astronomical Society since 1963. ⊠ *Observatory Rd., Clapham* ✛ *Off Hwy. 6* ☎ *246/622–2000, 246/422–2394* ⊕ *www. hbo.bb* ✉ *$10* ⊙ *Fri. 8–10 pm.*

Ragged Point. This is the location of East Coast Light, one of four strategically placed lighthouses on the island. Although civilization in the form of new homes is encroaching on this once-remote spot, the view of the entire Atlantic coastline is still spectacular—and the cool ocean breeze is refreshing on a hot day. ⊠ *Marley Vale.*

South Point Light. This is the oldest of four lighthouses on Barbados. Assembled on the island in 1852, after being displayed at London's Great Exhibition the previous year, the landmark lighthouse is just east of Miami (Enterprise) Beach near the southernmost point of land on Barbados. The 89-foot tower, with its distinguishing red and white horizontal stripes, is closed to the public; but visitors may freely walk about the site, take photos, and enjoy the view. ⊠ *South Point, Lighthouse Dr., Atlantic Shores.*

Tyrol Cot Heritage Village. This coral-stone cottage just south of Bridgetown, constructed in 1854, is preserved as an example of period architecture. In 1929, it became the home of Sir Grantley Adams, the first premier of Barbados and the namesake of the island's international airport. Part of the Barbados National Trust, the cottage is filled with antiques and memorabilia that belonged to the late Sir Grantley and Lady Adams. It's also the centerpiece of the Heritage Village, a living museum where artisans and craftspeople have workshops in a cluster of traditional chattel houses. Workshops are open, crafts are for sale, and refreshments are available at the "rum shop" primarily during

Sunbury Plantation House

the winter season and when cruise ships are in port. ⊠ *Codrington Hill, Bridgetown* ☎ *246/424–2074* ⊕ *www.barbadosnationaltrust.org* ✉ *$11.50* ⊗ *Weekdays 8–4:30; last tour at 4.*

CENTRAL BARBADOS

On the central west coast, in St. James Parish, Holetown marks the center of the Platinum Coast—so called for the vast number of luxurious resorts and mansions that face the sea. Holetown is also where Captain John Powell and the crew of the British ship *Olive Blossom* landed on May 14, 1625, to claim the island for King James I (who had actually died of a stroke seven weeks earlier). On the central east coast, the crashing Atlantic surf has eroded the shoreline, forming steep cliffs and exposing prehistoric rocks that look like giant mushrooms. Bathsheba and Cattlewash are favorite seacoast destinations for local folks on weekends and holidays. In the interior, narrow roads weave through tiny villages and along and between the ridges. The landscape is covered with tropical vegetation and rife with fascinating caves and gullies.

TOP ATTRACTIONS

Fodor's Choice
★

Andromeda Botanic Gardens. More than 600 beautiful and unusual plant specimens from around the world are cultivated in 6 acres of gardens nestled among streams, ponds, and rocky outcroppings overlooking the sea above the Bathsheba coastline near Tent Bay. The gardens were created in 1954 with flowering plants collected by the late horticulturist Iris Bannochie (1914–1988). They're now administered by the Barbados National Trust. The Gallery Shop features local art, photography, and crafts. The Garden Café serves sandwiches, salads from the gardens, desserts, and drinks. ⊠ *Bathsheba* ☎ *246/433–9384* ⊕ *www. andromedabarbados.com* 🖃 *$12.50* ⊗ *Daily 9–5.*

Fodor's Choice ★   **Flower Forest.** It's a treat to meander among fragrant flowering bushes, canna and ginger lilies, puffball trees, and more than 100 other species of tropical flora in a cool, tranquil forest of flowers and other plants. A ½-mile (1-km) path winds through the 53.6-acre grounds, a former sugar plantation; it takes about 30 to 45 minutes to follow the path, or you can wander freely for as long as you wish. Benches throughout provide places to pause and reflect. There's also a snack bar, a gift shop, and a beautiful view of Mt. Hillaby, at 1,100 feet the island's highest point. ⊠ *Hwy. 2, Richmond* ☎ *246/433–8152* ⊕ *www.flowerforestbarbados. com* 🖃 *$12.50* ⊗ *Daily 8–4.*

FAMILY **Fodor's Choice** ★   **Gun Hill Signal Station.** The 360-degree view from Gun Hill, at 700 feet, was of strategic importance to the 18th-century British army. Using lanterns and semaphore, soldiers here could communicate with their counterparts at the south coast's Garrison and the north's Grenade Hill about approaching ships, civil disorders, storms, or other emergencies. Time moved slowly in 1868, and Captain Henry Wilkinson whiled away his off-duty hours by carving a huge lion from a single rock—on the hillside below the tower. Come for a short history lesson but mainly for the view; it's so gorgeous that military invalids were sent here to convalesce. There's a small café for refreshments. ⊠ *Fusilier Rd., Gun Hill* ☎ *246/429–1358* ⊕ *www.barbadosnationaltrust.org* 🖃 *$5* ⊗ *Mon.–Sat. 9–5.*

FAMILY **Fodor's Choice** ★   **Harrison's Cave.** This limestone cavern, complete with stalactites, stalagmites, subterranean streams, and a 40-foot underground waterfall, is a rare find in the Caribbean—and one of Barbados's most popular attractions. Tours include a nine-minute video and an hour-long underground journey via electric tram. The visitor center has interactive displays, life-size models and sculptures, a souvenir shop, restaurant, and elevator access to the tram for people with disabilities. Tram tours fill up fast, so book ahead. More intrepid visitors may like the 1½-hour walking tour or 4-hour ecoadventure tour, exploring nature trails and some of the cave's natural passages. ⊠ *Hwy. 2, Welchman Hall* ☎ *246/417–3700* ⊕ *www.harrisonscave.com* 🖃 *Tram tour $30, walk-in $20, ecoadventure $101* ⊗ *Tram tours, daily 8:45–3:45, walk-in Sat. 4 and 4:30; ecoadventure, daily 9 and noon.*

Fodor's Choice ★   **Hunte's Gardens.** Horticulturist Anthony Hunte spent two years converting an overgrown sinkhole (caused by the collapse of a limestone cave) into an extraordinary garden environment. Trails lead up, down, and around 10 acres of dense foliage—everything from pots of flowering plants and great swaths of thick ground cover to robust vines, exotic tropical flowers, and majestic 100-year-old cabbage palms reaching for the sun. Benches and chairs, strategically placed among the greenery, afford perfect (and fairly private) vantage points, while classical music plays overhead. Hunte lives on the property and welcomes visitors to his veranda for a glass of juice or rum punch. Just ask, and he'll be happy to tell you the fascinating story of how the gardens evolved. ⊠ *Hwy. 3A, Castle Grant* ☎ *246/433–3333* ⊕ *www.huntesgardensbarbados. com* 🖃 *$15* ⊗ *Daily 9–4.*

Mount Gay Rum Visitors Centre. On this popular tour, you learn the colorful story behind the world's oldest rum, made in Barbados since 1703. Although the modern distillery is in the far north in St. Lucy Parish, tour guides here explain the rum-making process. Equipment, both historic and modern, is on display, and rows and rows of barrels are stored in this location. Tours conclude with a tasting and an opportunity to buy duty-free rum and gifts—and even have lunch or cocktails (no children on cocktail tour), depending on the time of day. ⊠ *Exmouth Gap, Brandons, Spring Garden Hwy., Bridgetown* ☎ *246/425–8757* ⊕ *www.mountgayrum.com* 💷 *$10, $50–$62 with cocktails or lunch and transportation* ◷ *Weekdays 9:30–2:30, Sat. 10:30–2:30; lunch tour, Tues. and Thurs. noon; cocktail tour, Mon., Wed., Fri. 1:30.*

WORTH NOTING

Chalky Mount. This tiny east-coast village is perched high in the clay-yielding hills that have supplied local potters for about 300 years. A few working potteries are open daily to visitors, who can watch as artisans create bowls, vases, candleholders, and decorative objects—which are, of course, for sale. ⊠ *Coggins Hill, Chalky Mount.*

FAMILY **Cockspur Beach Club.** Just north of Bridgetown, the fun-loving folks at West Indies Rum Distillery, makers of Cockspur and Malibu rums, invite visitors to enjoy a day at the beach, a variety of water sports, and a complimentary rum punch. Changing rooms with lockers and showers are available, along with beach umbrellas and chairs. Snorkeling equipment may be rented for the day ($5). The beachside grill serves lunch and drinks. Since this is a popular outing for cruise-ship passengers, the beach gets crowded when ships are in port. ⊠ *Brighton Beach, Black Rock* ☎ *246/425–9393* 💷 *$10* ◷ *Daily 9–5.*

FAMILY **Folkestone Underwater Park & Marine Reserve.** The mission of this family-oriented marine park, located just north of Holetown, is to provide high-quality recreational activities in a sustainable way to educate and entertain Barbadians and visitors alike. Facilities include a playground, basketball court, picnic area, beach with lifeguards, and a museum (two rooms with artifacts and photos of how the sea is used for various purposes) that illuminates island marine life. For firsthand viewing, there's an underwater snorkeling trail (equipment rental, $10 for the day) around Dottins Reef, just off the beach in the 2.2-mile (3.5-km) protected marine reserve; nonswimmers can opt for a glass-bottom boat tour. The ship *Stavronikita*, deliberately sunk in 120 feet of water about a half-mile from shore, is home to myriad fish and a popular dive site. A canteen serves snacks and drinks. ⊠ *Hwy. 1, Church Point, Holetown* ☎ *246/422–2314* 💷 *Free, exhibits $1* ◷ *Daily 9–5.*

Orchid World & Tropical Flower Garden. Meandering pathways thread gardens filled with more than 30,000 colorful orchids and other tropical plants. You'll see Vandaceous orchids attached to fences or wire frames, Schomburgkia and Oncidiums stuck on mahogany trees, Aranda and Spathoglottis orchids growing in a grotto, and Ascocendas suspended from netting in shady enclosures as well as seasonal orchids, scented orchids, and multicolor Vanda orchids. Benches are well placed to rest, admire the flowers, or take in the expansive view of the surrounding cane fields and distant hills of Sweet Vale. Snacks, cold beverages, and other refreshments are served in the café. ⊠ *Hwy. 3B, Sweet Vale* ☎ *246/433–0306* ⊕ *www.orchidworldbarbados.com* 🎫 *$12.50* ⊙ *Daily 9–4.*

Welchman Hall Gully. This 1½-mile-long (2-km-long) natural gully is really a collapsed limestone cavern, once part of the same underground network as Harrison's Cave. The Barbados National Trust protects the peace and quiet here, making it a beautiful place to hike past acres of labeled flowers and stands of trees. You can see and hear some interesting birds—and, with luck, a native green monkey. There are limited scheduled free guided tours, and a guide can be arranged with 24 hours' notice. Otherwise, the 30- to 45-minute walk is self-guided. ⊠ *Welchman Hall* ☎ *246/438–6671* ⊕ *www.welchmanhallgullybarbados.com* 🎫 *$12* ⊙ *Daily 9–4, last tour at 3:30.*

NORTHERN BARBADOS

Speightstown, the north's commercial center and once a thriving port city, now boasts appealing local shops and informal restaurants. Many of Speightstown's 19th-century buildings, with traditional overhanging balconies, have been restored. The island's northernmost reaches, St. Peter and St. Lucy parishes, have a varied topography and are lovely to explore. Between the tiny fishing towns along the northwestern coast and the sweeping views out over the Atlantic to the east are forest and farm, moor and mountain. Most guides include a loop through this area on a daylong island tour—it's a beautiful drive.

TOP ATTRACTIONS

FAMILY **Animal Flower Cave.** Small sea anemones, or sea worms, resemble flowers when they open their tiny tentacles. They live in small pools in this sea cave at the island's very northern tip. The cave itself, discovered in 1780, has a coral floor that ranges from 126,000 to 500,000 years old, according to geological estimates. Coral steps lead through an opening in the "roof" into the cave. Bring your bathing suit. Depending on that day's sea swells, you can swim in the naturally formed pool, and the view of breaking waves from inside the cave is magnificent. Steep stairs, uneven surfaces, and rocks make this an unwise choice for anyone with walking difficulties. ⊠ *North Point* ☎ *246/439–8797* ⊕ *www. animalflowercave.com* 🎫 *$10* ⊙ *Daily 9–4:30.*

FAMILY **Barbados Wildlife Reserve.** This reserve at the top of Farley Hill is the habitat of herons, innumerable land turtles, screeching peacocks, shy deer, elusive green monkeys, brilliantly colored parrots (in a large walk-in aviary), snakes, and a caiman. Except for the snakes and the caiman, the animals run or fly freely—so step carefully and keep your hands to yourself. Late afternoon is your best chance to catch a glimpse of a green monkey. ⊠ *Hwy. 2* ⊹ *Across from Farley Hill National Park* ☎ *246/422–8826* 🎫 *$12.50* ⊙ *Daily 10–5.*

Fodor'sChoice **St. Nicholas Abbey.** The island's oldest great house (circa 1650) was ★ named after the original British owner's hometown, St. Nicholas Parish near Bristol, and Bath Abbey nearby. Its stone-and-wood architecture makes it one of only three original Jacobean-style houses still standing in the Western Hemisphere. It has Dutch gables, finials of coral stone, and beautiful grounds that include an "avenue" of mahogany trees, a "gully" filled with tropical trees and plantings, formal gardens, and an old sugar mill. The first floor, fully furnished with period furniture and portraits of family members, is open to the public. A fascinating home movie, shot by a previous owner's father, records Bajan life in the 1930s. Behind the great house is a rum distillery with a 19th-century steam press; cane grinding occurs Wednesdays and Thursdays, February through mid-May. Visitors can purchase artisanal plantation rum, browse the gift shop's traditional Barbadian products, and enjoy light refreshments at the Terrace Café. ⊠ *Cherry Tree Hill Rd., Moore Hill* ☎ *246/422–5357* ⊕ *www.stnicholasabbey.com* ☜ *$20* ☉ *Sun.–Fri. 10–3:30.*

WORTH NOTING

Cherry Tree Hill. Stop at the crest of this hill, just east of St. Nicholas Abbey, for a stunning panoramic view of the entire eastern coast and the Atlantic surf. ⊠ *Cherry Tree Hill Rd., Moore Hill.*

Farley Hill National Park. At this national park in northern St. Peter, across from the Barbados Wildlife Reserve, gardens and lawns—along with an avenue of towering palms and gigantic mahogany, whitewood, and casuarina trees—surround the imposing ruins of a plantation great house built by Sir Graham Briggs in 1861 to entertain royal visitors from England. Partially rebuilt for the filming of *Island in the Sun,* the classic 1957 film starring Harry Belafonte and Dorothy Dandridge, the structure was destroyed by fire in 1965. Behind the estate is a sweeping view of the region called Scotland for its rugged landscape. The park is also the site of festivals and musical events. ⊠ *Hwy. 2* ☜ *$2 per car, pedestrians free* ☉ *Daily 8:30–5:30.*

FAMILY **Morgan Lewis Sugar Mill.** Built in 1727, the mill was operational until 1945. Today it's the only remaining windmill in Barbados with its wheelhouse and sails intact. No longer used to grind sugarcane, except for occasional demonstrations during crop season, the mill was donated to the Barbados National Trust in 1962 and eventually restored to original working specifications in 1998 by millwrights from the United Kingdom. Surrounding acres are used for dairy farming. ✛ *Southeast of Cherry Tree Hill* ☎ *246/426–2421* ⊕ *www.barbadosnationaltrust.org.*

BEACHES

Geologically, Barbados is a coral-and-limestone island (not volcanic) with few rivers and, as a result, beautiful beaches, particularly along the island's southern and southeastern coastlines.

The west coast has some lovely beaches as well, but they're more susceptible to erosion after major autumn storms, if any, have taken their toll.

When the surf is too high and swimming becomes dangerous, a red flag will be hoisted on the beach. A yellow flag—or a red flag at half-staff—means swim with caution. Topless sunbathing—on the beach or at the pool—is not allowed anywhere in Barbados.

St. Nicholas Abbey

SOUTH COAST

A young, energetic crowd favors the south-coast beaches, which are broad and breezy, blessed with powdery white sand, and dotted with tall palms. The reef-protected areas with crystal clear water are safe for swimming and snorkeling. The surf becomes medium to high and the waves get bigger and the winds stronger (windsurfers, take note) the farther southeast you go.

FAMILY **Accra Beach** (*Rockley Beach*). This popular beach, adjacent to the Accra Beach Hotel, has a broad swath of white sand with gentle surf and a lifeguard, plenty of nearby restaurants for refreshments, a playground, and beach stalls for renting chairs and equipment for snorkeling and other water sports. The Barbados Boardwalk, great for walking or running, begins here and follows the waterfront west—past private homes, restaurants, and bars—for about a mile (1.6 km) to Needham's Point. **Amenities:** food and drink; lifeguards; parking (no fee); water sports. **Best for:** snorkeling; swimming; walking. ⊠ *Hwy. 7, Rockley.*

Fodor'sChoice **Bottom Bay Beach.** Popular for fashion and travel-industry photo shoots, ★ Bottom Bay is the quintessential Caribbean beach. Secluded, surrounded by a coral cliff, studded with a stand of palms, and blessed with an endless ocean view, this dreamy enclave is near the southeasternmost point of the island. The Atlantic Ocean waves can be too strong for swimming, but it's the picture-perfect place for a day at the beach and a picnic lunch. Park at the top of the cliff and follow the steps down to the beach. **Amenities:** none. **Best for:** solitude; swimming; walking. ⊠ *Hwy. 5, Apple Hall.*

Fodor's Choice ★ **Crane Beach.** This exquisite crescent of pink sand on the southeast coast was named not for the elegant, long-legged wading bird but for the crane used to haul and load cargo when this area served as a busy port. Crane Beach usually has a steady breeze and lightly rolling surf that varies in color from aqua to turquoise to lapis and is great for body-surfing. Access to the beach is either down 98 steps or via a cliff-side, glass-walled elevator on The Crane resort property. **Amenities:** food and drink; lifeguards; parking (no fee); toilets. **Best for:** swimming; walking. ⊠ *Crane.*

FAMILY **Dover Beach.** All along the St. Lawrence Gap waterfront, Dover Beach is one of the most popular beaches on the south coast. The sea is fairly calm, with small to medium waves, and the white-sand beach is broad and brilliant. Divi Southwinds and Ocean Two resorts, as well as several restaurants, are nearby. There's a small boardwalk, a promenade with a food court, water sports and beach chair rentals, and a playground. **Amenities:** food and drink; parking (no fee); toilets; water sports. **Best for:** snorkeling; swimming. ⊠ *St. Lawrence Gap, Dover.*

Fodor's Choice ★ **Miami Beach** (*Enterprise Beach*). This lovely spot on the coast road, just east of Oistins, is a slice of pure white sand with shallow and calm water on one side, deeper water with small waves on the other, and cliffs on either side. In a mainly upscale residential area, the beach is mostly deserted except for weekends, when folks who live nearby come for a swim. You'll find a palm-shaded parking area, snack carts, and chair rentals. It's also a hop, skip, and jump from Little Arches Hotel. **Amenities:** food and drink; parking (no fee). **Best for:** solitude; swimming. ⊠ *Enterprise Beach Rd., Enterprise.*

FAMILY **Fodor's Choice** ★ **Pebbles Beach.** On the southern side of Carlisle Bay, just south of Bridgetown, this broad half circle of white sand is one of the island's best beaches—and it can become crowded on weekends and holidays. The southern end of the beach wraps around the Hilton Barbados; the northern end is adjacent to the Radisson Aquatica Resort Barbados and a block away from Island Inn. Park at Harbour Lights or at the Boatyard Bar and Bayshore Complex, both on Bay Street, where you can also rent umbrellas and beach chairs and buy refreshments. **Amenities:** food and drink. **Best for:** snorkeling; swimming; walking. ⊠ *Off Bay St., south of Bridgetown, Garrison.*

FAMILY **Sandy Beach** (*Worthing Beach*). This beach has calm waters and a picturesque lagoon, making it an ideal location for families with small kids. It also has several artificial bays separated by rocks, with a shallow reef close to shore. Park right on the main road. You can rent beach chairs and umbrellas, and plenty of places nearby sell food and drinks. **Amenities:** food and drink. **Best for:** swimming; walking. ⊠ *Hwy. 7, Worthing.*

FAMILY **Silver Sands–Silver Rock Beach.** Nestled between South Point, the southernmost tip of the island, and Inch Marlow Point, Silver Point Hotel overlooks this long, broad strand of beautiful white sand that always has a strong breeze. That makes this beach the best in Barbados for intermediate and advanced windsurfers and, more recently, kiteboarders. There's a small playground and shaded picnic tables. **Amenities:**

5

parking (no fee); water sports. **Best for:** solitude; swimming; walking; windsurfing. ⊠ *Off Hwy. 7.*

Turtle Beach. Stretched from Turtle Beach Resort and Sandals Barbados at the eastern end of St. Lawrence Gap to Bougainvillea Beach Resort on Maxwell Coast Road, this broad strand of powdery white sand is great for sunbathing, strolling, and—with low to medium surf—swimming and boogie boarding. This beach is a favorite nesting place for turtles, hence its name; if you're lucky, you may see hundreds of tiny hatchlings emerge from the sand and make their way to the sea. Find public access and parking on Maxwell Coast Road, near the Bougainvillea Beach Resort. **Amenities:** food and drink; parking (no fee). **Best for:** swimming; walking. ⊠ *Maxwell Coast Rd., Dover.*

EAST COAST

Be cautioned: While you might see surfers at Bathsheba Soup Bowl, swimming at east-coast beaches is treacherous, even for strong swimmers, and is *not* recommended. Waves are high, the bottom tends to be rocky, the currents are unpredictable, and the undertow is dangerously strong.

Bathsheba Beach. Although unsafe for swimming, the miles of untouched sand along the East Coast Road in St. Joseph Parish are great for beachcombing and wading. As you approach Bathsheba Soup Bowl, the southernmost stretch just north of Tent Bay, you'll see enormous mushroom-shape boulders and impressive rolling surf. Expert surfers from around the world converge on the Soup Bowl each November for the Barbados Independence Pro competition. **Amenities:** none. **Best for:** solitude; sunrise; surfing; walking. ⊠ *East Coast Rd., Bathsheba.*

Cattlewash Beach. Swimming is unwise at this windswept beach with pounding surf, which follows the Atlantic Ocean coastline in St. Andrew, but you can take a dip, wade, and play in the tidal pools. Barclays Park, a 50-acre public park across the road, has a shaded picnic area. **Amenities:** none. **Best for:** solitude; sunrise; walking. ⊠ *Ermy Bourne Hwy., Cattlewash.*

WEST COAST

Gentle Caribbean waves lap the west coast, and leafy mahogany trees shade its stunning coves and sandy beaches. The water is perfect for swimming and water sports. An almost unbroken chain of beaches stretches between Bridgetown and Speightstown. Elegant homes and luxury hotels face much of the beachfront property in this area, dubbed Barbados's "Platinum Coast," although all beaches are open to the public.

West-coast beaches are considerably smaller and narrower than those on the south coast. Also, prolonged stormy weather in September and October may cause sand erosion, temporarily making the beaches even narrower. Even so, west-coast beaches are seldom crowded. Vendors stroll by with handmade baskets, hats, dolls, jewelry, even original watercolors; owners of private boats offer waterskiing, parasailing, and snorkeling excursions. Hotels and beachside restaurants welcome nonguests for terrace lunches (wear a cover-up), and you can buy picnic items at supermarkets in Holetown.

FAMILY **Brighton Beach.** Calm as a lake, this is where you can find locals taking a quick dip on hot days—particularly weekends. Just north of Bridgetown, Brighton Beach is also home to the Cockspur Beach Club. **Amenities:** food and drink; parking (no fee). **Best for:** swimming; walking. ⊠ *Spring Garden Hwy., Bridgetown.*

FAMILY **Mullins Beach.** At this lovely beach just south of Speightstown, the water
Fodor's Choice is safe for swimming and snorkeling. There's easy parking on the main
★ road, and Mullins Restaurant serves snacks, meals, and drinks—and rents chairs and umbrellas. **Amenities:** food and drink; toilets. **Best for:** sunset; swimming; walking. ⊠ *Hwy. 1B, Mullins.*

Paynes Bay Beach. The stretch of beach just south of Sandy Lane is lined with luxury hotels—Tamarind, The House, and Treasure Beach among them. It's a very pretty area, with plenty of beach to go around, calm water, and good snorkeling. Public access is available at several locations along Highway 1, though parking is limited. **Amenities:** food and drink. **Best for:** snorkeling; sunset; swimming; walking. ⊠ *Hwy. 1, Sunset Crest.*

5

WHERE TO EAT

First-class restaurants and hotel dining rooms serve quite sophisticated cuisine—often prepared by chefs with international experience and rivaling the dishes served in the world's best restaurants. Most menus include seafood: dolphin (mahimahi), kingfish, snapper, and flying fish prepared every way imaginable. Flying fish is so popular that it has become an official national symbol. Shellfish also abounds, as do steak, pork, and local black-belly lamb.

Specialty dishes include *buljol* (a cold salad of pickled codfish, tomatoes, onions, sweet peppers, and celery) and *conkies* (cornmeal, coconut, pumpkin, raisins, sweet potatoes, and spices, mixed together, wrapped in a banana leaf, and steamed). *Cou-cou,* often served with steamed flying fish, is a mixture of cornmeal and okra and usually topped with a spicy creole sauce made from tomatoes, onions, and sweet peppers. Bajan-style pepper pot is a hearty stew of oxtail, beef, and other meats in a rich, spicy gravy, simmered overnight.

For lunch, restaurants often offer a traditional Bajan buffet of fried fish, baked chicken, salads, macaroni pie (macaroni and cheese), and a selection of steamed or stewed provisions (local roots and vegetables). Be cautious with the West Indian condiments—like the sun, they're hotter than you think. Typical Bajan drinks—in addition to Banks Beer and Mount Gay, Cockspur, or Malibu rum—are *falernum* (a liqueur concocted of rum, sugar, lime juice, and almond essence); *mauby* (a nonalcoholic drink made by boiling bitter bark and spices, straining the mixture, and sweetening it); and Ponche Kuba, a creamy spiced rum liqueur (Caribbean eggnog) that's especially popular around the holidays. You're sure to enjoy the fresh fruit or rum punch, as well.

What to Wear: The dress code for dinner in Barbados is conservative, casually elegant, and, occasionally, formal—a jacket and tie for gentlemen and a cocktail dress for ladies in the fanciest restaurants and hotel dining rooms, particularly during the winter holiday season. Jeans, shorts, and T-shirts (either sleeveless or with slogans) are always frowned upon at dinner. Beach attire is appropriate only at the beach.

BRIDGETOWN

$$$ ✗ **Waterfront Café.** This busy bistro on the walkway facing the south side
CARIBBEAN   of The Careenage is the perfect place to enjoy a drink, snack, or meal—
FAMILY   and to people-watch. Locals and tourists alike gather for alfresco, all-day dining on sandwiches, salads, fish, pasta, pepper-pot stew, and tasty Bajan snacks such as buljol, fish cakes, or plantation pork (plantains stuffed with spicy minced pork). The panfried flying-fish sandwich is an especially popular lunchtime treat. Dinner is accompanied by live jazz. Ⓢ *Average main: $26* ✉ *The Careenage, Bridgetown* ☎ *246/427–0093* ⊕ *www.waterfrontcafe.com.bb* � *Closed Sun. No dinner Mon.–Wed.*

SOUTH COAST

$$$$ ✗ **Beach One.** Whether you dine beachside or on the balcony, you're
SEAFOOD   just steps from the smashing waves at the eastern end of Dover Beach. Add twinkling stars in the dark of night, and you have a stunning atmosphere: elegant, inviting, sophisticated, romantic, and tropical. The menu is almost entirely seafood. For a main course, choose blackened scallops, seafood penne, grilled salmon with raisin rice, jumbo garlic shrimp, or Bajan flying fish, battered and deep-fried in olive oil. Ⓢ *Average main: $33* ✉ *St. Lawrence Gap, Worthing* ☎ *246/838–7337* ⊕ *beachonebarbados.com* ☼ *No lunch* ⌂ *Reservations essential.*

$$$ ✗ **Brown Sugar.** Set back from the road in a traditional Bajan home, the
CARIBBEAN   lattice-trimmed dining patios here are filled with ferns, flowers, and
FAMILY   water features. Brown Sugar is a popular lunch spot for local business-
Fodor's Choice   people, who come for the nearly 30 delicious local and creole dishes
★   spread out at the all-you-can-eat, four-course Planter's Buffet lunch ($29.50). Here's your chance to try local specialties such as flying fish, cou-cou, buljol, *souse* (pickled pork, stewed for hours in broth), fish cakes, and pepper pot. In the evening, the à la carte menu has dishes such as fried flying fish, coconut shrimp, plantain-crusted mahimahi, curried lamb, filet mignon, broiled pepper chicken, and seafood or pesto pasta. Bring the kids—there's a special children's menu with fried chicken, fried flying-fish fingers, and pasta dishes. Save room for the warm pawpaw (papaya) pie or Bajan rum pudding with rum sauce. Ⓢ *Average main: $27* ✉ *Aquatic Gap, Garrison* ⊹ *Off Bay St.* ☎ *246/426–7684* ⊕ *www.brownsugarbarbados.net* ☼ *No lunch Sat.*

$$$$ ✗ **Café Luna.** With a sweeping view of pretty Miami (Enterprise) Beach,
ECLECTIC   the alfresco dining deck on top of the Mediterranean-style Little Arches Hotel is spectacular at lunchtime and magical in the moonlight. Breakfast and lunch are available only for hotel guests. At dinner, the expertise of executive chef and owner Mark de Gruchy is displayed through contemporary dishes that include oven-roasted New Zealand rack of

lamb with sweet-potato crust and balsamic syrup, grilled U.S. beef tenderloin with blue-cheese butter and tempura onion rings, fresh seafood bouillabaisse simmered in tomato Pernod broth, and sesame-crusted yellow-fin tuna with peppercorn sauce. The special three-course Bajan menu ($40) is a good deal; sushi is a specialty on Thursday and Friday nights. $ *Average main: $33* ⊠ *Little Arches Hotel, Enterprise Beach Rd., Oistins* ☎ *246/428–6172* ⊕ *www.cafelunabarbados.com* ⌁ *Reservations essential.*

$$
MEXICAN
FAMILY

✕ **Café Sol.** Have a hankerin' for good Tex-Mex food? Enjoy nachos, tacos, burritos, empanadas, fajitas, and tostadas in this Mexican bar and grill at the western entrance to busy St. Lawrence Gap. Or choose a burger, honey-barbecue chicken, or flame-grilled steak from the gringo menu. Helpings of rice and beans, a Corona, and plenty of jalapeño peppers, guacamole, and salsa give everything a Mexican touch. Some people come just for the margaritas—15 fruity varieties rimmed with Bajan sugar instead of salt. With two happy hours every night, this place gets really busy; reservations are accepted only for parties of five or more. $ *Average main: $20* ⊠ *St. Lawrence Gap, Dover* ☎ *246/420–7655* ⊕ *www.cafesolbarbados.com* ⊗ *No lunch Mon.* ⌁ *Reservations not accepted.*

$$$$
ECLECTIC
FAMILY
Fodor'sChoice
★

✕ **Champers.** Chiryl Newman's snazzy seaside restaurant is in an old Bajan home just off the main road in Rockley. Luncheon guests—about 75% local businesspeople—enjoy repasts such as char-grilled beef salad, Champers fish pie, or fried flying fish with caper dressing. Dinner guests swoon over dishes such as the herb-crusted rack of lamb with mint and port wine jus, seared Atlantic salmon with linguine primavera, and the sautéed prawns with red Thai curry and coconut sauce. The portions are hearty and the food is well seasoned with Caribbean flavors, "just the way the locals like it," according to Newman. Dining out with the family? There's a kid's menu, too. The cliff-top setting overlooking the eastern end of Accra Beach offers diners a panoramic view of the sea and a relaxing atmosphere for daytime dining. Nearly all the artwork gracing the walls is by Barbadian artists and may be purchased through the on-site gallery. $ *Average main: $35* ⊠ *Skeetes Hill, off Hwy. 7, Rockley* ☎ *246/434–3463* ⊕ *www.champersbarbados.com* ⊗ *No lunch Sat.* ⌁ *Reservations essential.*

$$$$
SEAFOOD
Fodor'sChoice
★

✕ **L'Azure at the Crane.** Perched on an oceanfront cliff overlooking Crane Beach, L'Azure is an informal breakfast and luncheon spot by day that becomes elegant after dark. Enjoy seafood chowder or a light salad or sandwich while absorbing the breathtaking panoramic view of the beach and sea beyond. At dinner, candlelight and soft guitar music enhance tamarind-glazed snapper or a fabulous Caribbean lobster seasoned with herbs, lime juice, and garlic butter and served in its shell. If you're not in the mood for seafood, try the crusted rack of lamb or herb-infused pork tenderloin. Sunday is really special, with a gospel brunch ($30) at 9 or 10 am and a Bajan buffet lunch ($40) at 12:30 pm. $ *Average main: $32* ⊠ *The Crane Resort, Crane* ☎ *246/423–6220* ⊕ *www.thecrane.com* ⊗ *No dinner Wed.* ⌁ *Reservations essential.*

$$
CARIBBEAN

✕ **Shaker's.** Locals and visitors alike gather at this no-frills hangout for drinks—perhaps a Banks beer or two, a margarita, a pitcher of sangria, or whatever wets their whistle—and the delicious local food. Simple dishes like beer-battered flying fish, grilled catch of the day, barbecued chicken, grilled steak, or a solid cheeseburger deliver the goods, but the barbecued ribs are the main event. All main dishes include crisp green salad, coleslaw, and either grilled or french-fried potatoes. It's a colorful, convivial place, full of laughter and chatter—partly because the tables are so close together and partly because of the rum shop atmosphere. Arrive early or make a reservation if you want an outside table, as it fills up quickly; and be prepared to pay in cash. $ *Average main: $15* ✉ *Browne's Gap, Rockley* ☎ *246/228–8855* ⊕ *www.shakersbarbados. com* ▭ *No credit cards* ⊘ *Closed Sun. and Mon. and mid-Aug.–mid-Sept. No lunch* ⚐ *Reservations essential.*

$$$
BISTRO
FAMILY

✕ **Sharkey's Tropical Café.** Although it's primarily a bar, you can also enjoy a top-of-the-line meal here at Sharkey's. Extraordinary dishes include lobster thermidor, honey-crusted rack of lamb with sautéed potatoes, catch of the day served with warm berry vinaigrette, jerk pork tenderloin, and a "gourmet" Angus beefburger with all the trimmings. This is a casual place for lunch or dinner—but also for the Big Boy breakfast—and popular among tourists and locals alike. $ *Average main: $28* ✉ *St. Lawrence Gap* ☎ *246/234–6527* ⊕ *sharkeysbarbados. com* ⊘ *Closed Thurs.*

$$$$
ASIAN

✕ **Zen at the Crane.** Thai and Japanese specialties reign supreme in a magnificent setting overlooking Crane Beach. The centerpiece of the sophisticated, Asian-inspired decor is a 12-seat sushi bar, where chefs prepare exotic fare before your eyes. Try sizzling lobster kabayaki served in a cast-iron grill pan, teriyaki beef or chicken, tempura prawns, stir-fried meats and vegetables in oyster sauce, or a deluxe bento box. An extensive menu of Thai appetizers, soups, noodles, fried rice, and chef's specials and main courses from the wok are noted as being spicy, spicier, and spiciest. Choose to dine in the tatami room for a traditional Japanese dining experience (no shoes). $ *Average main: $32* ✉ *The Crane Resort, Crane* ☎ *246/423–6220* ⊕ *www.thecrane.com* ⊘ *Closed Tues. No lunch* ⚐ *Reservations essential.*

EAST COAST

$$$
CARIBBEAN
FAMILY
Fodor's Choice
★

✕ **The Atlantis.** For decades, an alfresco lunch on the Atlantis deck overlooking the ocean has been a favorite of both visitors and Bajans. Pleasant atmosphere and good food have always been the draw, with an elegant dining room and a top-notch menu that focuses on local produce, seafood, and meats. The Wednesday and Sunday Bajan buffet lunch—with pepper pot, saltfish, chicken stew, peas and rice, cou-cou, yam pie, and breadfruit mash—is particularly popular. Lunch and dinner entrées include fresh fish, lobster (seasonal), curried goat or chicken, fricassee of rabbit, pepper-crusted flat iron steak, and several main-course salads, pasta dishes, and paninis. There's a kids' menu, too. $ *Average main: $27* ✉ *The Atlantis Hotel, Tent Bay* ☎ *246/433–9445* ⊕ *www.atlantishotelbarbados.com* ⊘ *Closed Sept. No dinner Sun.* ⚐ *Reservations essential.*

$$ CARIBBEAN 🍴 **Naniki Restaurant.** Rich wooden beams and stone tiles, clay pottery, straw mats, and colorful dinnerware set the style at Naniki (an Arawak word meaning "full of life" or, in this case, "lush life"). Huge picture windows and outdoor porch seating allow you to enjoy the exhilarating view of surrounding hills and gardens along with your lunch of well-prepared Caribbean standards. Seared flying fish, grilled dorado, stewed lambi (conch), and jerk chicken or pork are accompanied by cou-cou, peas and rice, or salad. For dinner (by special request only), start with conch fritters or Caribbean fish soup; then try roasted Bajan black-belly lamb or shrimp garnished with tarragon. Sunday brunch is a Caribbean buffet often featuring great jazz music by some of the Caribbean's best musicians. Vegetarian dishes are always available. [$] *Average main: $20* ✉ *Lush Life Nature Resort, off Hwy. 3, Surinam* ☎ *246/433–1351* 🌐 *www.lushlife.bb/Lushlife/naniki* 🕘 *No dinner. No lunch Mon.* ✍ *Reservations essential.*

$$$ SEAFOOD FAMILY 🍴 **Round House.** Owners Robert and Gail Manley oversee the menu for guests staying in their inn, tourists enjoying the east coast, and Bajans dining out. The lunch menu—served on the deck overlooking the Atlantic Ocean—includes homemade soups and quiches, sandwiches, salads, and pasta. Dinner choices—served in the moonlight—extend from shrimp scampi, oven-baked dolphin steak, or grilled flying-fish fillet to baked ham, sirloin steak, or homemade pasta specials. Some people come just for the flying-fish pâté. Rolls and breads (whether for sandwiches or dessert), along with apple and coconut pies, are personally made by the owners. The Round House is an ocean-facing manse-turned-inn built in 1832. From the outdoor dining deck, the view of ocean waves smashing on the rugged coastline is mesmerizing. In the off-season, the restaurant closes at 4 pm. [$] *Average main: $26* ✉ *Bathsheba* ☎ *246/433–9678* 🌐 *www.roundhousebarbados.com* 🕘 *Closed Sept. No dinner May–Oct. or Fri. Nov.–Apr.* ✍ *Reservations essential.*

5

WEST COAST

$$$$ ECLECTIC Fodor's Choice ★ 🍴 **The Cliff.** Chef Paul Owens's mastery creates one of the finest dining experiences in the Caribbean, with prices to match. Steep steps hug the cliff on which the restaurant sits to accommodate those arriving by yacht, and every candlelit table has a sea view. The first course may include spicy Thai-style beef salad, snow crab cake, or savory snails in puff pastry. For the main course, try swordfish with yellow curry sauce and jasmine rice, seared tuna with saffron caper sauce and tomato coulis, or a prime beef tenderloin with wild mushroom fumé and truffle Parmesan fries. Dessert falls into the sinful category, and service is impeccable. The prix-fixe menu will set you back $132.50 per person for a two-course meal or $155 per person for a three-course meal. Reserve days or even weeks in advance to snag a table at the front of the terrace for the best view. [$] *Average main: $132.50* ✉ *Hwy. 1, Derricks* ☎ *246/432–1922* 🌐 *www.thecliffbarbados.com* 🕘 *Closed Sun. Apr. 15–Dec. 15. No lunch* ✍ *Reservations essential.*

$$$$ ✕ **Daphne's.** Executive chef Marco Festini Cromer whips up contempo-
ITALIAN rary Italian cuisine at The House's beachfront restaurant, a chic outpost
Fodor'sChoice of the London eatery of the same name. Grilled yellow-fin tuna becomes
★ "modern Italian" when combined with spicy chickpeas and *pepero-
nata* (stewed peppers, tomatoes, onions, and garlic). Perfectly prepared
melanzane (eggplant) and zucchini *alla parmigiana* is a delicious starter;
a half portion of risotto with porcini mushrooms, green beans, and
Parma ham is fabulously rich; and branzino (sea bass) in salt crust with
buttered potatoes and tartare sauce is a sublime main course. There's
even a gluten-free dinner menu and a "summer special" prix-fixe menu
($50, $60 with dessert). The extensive wine list features both regional
Italian and fine French selections. $ *Average main: $37 ⊠ The House,
Hwy. 1, Paynes Bay* ☎ 246/432–2731 ⊕ *www.daphnesbarbados.com*
⊙ *Closed Mon. June–Nov. No lunch* ⌂ *Reservations essential.*

$ ✕ **Fisherman's Pub.** As local as local gets, this open-air, waterfront beach
CARIBBEAN bar (a former rum shop) is built on stilts a stone's throw from the Spei-
FAMILY ghtstown fish market. For years, fishermen and other locals have come
here for the inexpensive, authentic Bajan lunch buffet. For $10 or so
you can soak up the atmosphere and fill your plate with fried flying fish,
stewed chicken or pork, curried goat or lamb, pepper pot, macaroni
pie, fried plantain, peas and rice, sweet potatoes, cou-cou, and crisp
green salad. Eat inside or on the deck. And on Wednesday night, you
can also dance—or simply listen—to catchy steel pan or calypso music.
(Whether dinner is served varies from season to season, so call ahead.)
$ *Average main: $10 ⊠ Queen St., Speightstown* ☎ 246/422–2703
⌂ *Reservations not accepted.*

$$$$ ✕ **Fish Pot.** Just north of the little fishing village of Six Men's Bay, on
MEDITERRANEAN the northwestern coast of Barbados, this attractive seaside restaurant
Fodor'sChoice serves excellent Mediterranean cuisine and some of the island's freshest
★ fish. Gaze seaward through windows framed with pale-green louvered
shutters while lunching on a seafood crêpe, a grilled panini, snow-
crab salad, or perhaps pasta with seafood or roasted-pepper-and-chili
tomato sauce. In the evening, the menu may include cumin-seared
scallops, herb-crusted tuna with green peppercorn sauce, mushroom
and green pea risotto, or braised lamb shank with oven-fried tomatoes
and mint sauce. Bright and cheery by day and relaxed and cozy by
night, the Fish Pot offers a tasty dining experience in a setting that's
classier than its name might suggest. $ *Average main: $35 ⊠ Little
Good Harbour Hotel, Shermans, Colleton* ☎ 246/439–3000 ⊕ *www.
littlegoodharbourbarbados.com* ⌂ *Reservations essential.*

$$$$ ✕ **Lone Star.** At the tiny but chic Lone Star Hotel, top chefs turn the fin-
EUROPEAN est local ingredients into gastronomic delights. At lunch, tasty salads,
sandwiches, and wood-fired pizzas are served in the oceanfront bar.
After sunset, the casual daytime atmosphere turns trendy. Start with
open wild-mushroom and butternut-squash ravioli or crispy coconut
prawns with mango chili sauce, followed by seared yellowfin tuna with
warm potato-and-grain-mustard salad, pistachio-crusted halibut with
sweet potato wonton, roasted rack of lamb, wild mushroom risotto,
or dozens of other land, sea, and vegetarian dishes. $ *Average main:
$42 ⊠ Lone Star Hotel, Hwy. 1, Mount Standfast* ☎ 246/629–0599
⊕ *www.thelonestar.com.*

$$$
EUROPEAN

✕ **The Mews.** Dining at the Mews is like being invited to a friend's chic home for dinner. Once a private home, the front room is now an inviting bar, and an interior courtyard is an intimate, open-air dining area. The second floor is a maze of small dining rooms and balconies, but it's the food—classic, bistro, or tapas—that draws the visitors. A plump chicken breast, for example, may be stuffed with cream cheese, smoked salmon, and herb pâté and served on a garlic-and-chive sauce, while a braised lamb shank is presented on a bed of cabbage with a port-thyme jus and creamed potatoes. Some call the atmosphere avant-garde; others call it quaint. Everyone calls the food delicious. $ *Average main: $28* ✉ *2nd St., Holetown* ☎ *246/432–1122* ⊕ *www.themewsbarbados.com* ⊘ *Closed Sun. mid-Apr.–mid-Dec. No lunch.* ⌧ *Reservations essential.*

$$$
CARIBBEAN

✕ **Ragamuffins.** Tiny, funky, lively, and informal, this is the only Barbados restaurant in an authentic chattel house. Dine inside or out on seafood, perfectly broiled T-bone steaks, West Indian curries, and vegetarian dishes such as Bajan stir-fried vegetables with noodles. The kitchen is within sight of the bar, a popular meeting spot most evenings. Sunday night's Drag Show becomes a huge party that spills into the street. $ *Average main: $22* ✉ *1st St., Holetown* ☎ *246/432–1295* ⊕ *www. ragamuffinsbarbados.com* ⊘ *No lunch* ⌧ *Reservations essential.*

$$$
ECLECTIC

✕ **Scarlet.** Movers and groovers come to this bright-red building on the side of the road to chill over a martini and share nibbles, such as a plate of Bajan fish cakes with "calypso" dip, or to settle in after cocktails for a burger with sophisticated toppings, grilled lamb cutlets, lemongrass salmon skewers, or perhaps Baxter's Road chicken. Enjoy your meal sitting at the large bar—the centerpiece of this casual but stylish watering hole—or at a nearby table. The specialty of the house is Scarlet Rocks: vodka, raspberry schnapps, strawberries, cranberry juice, basil, and black pepper. $ *Average main: $28* ✉ *Hwy. 1, Payne's Bay* ☎ *246/432–3663* ⊕ *www.scarletbarbados.com* ⊘ *Closed Sun. and Mon. No lunch* ⌧ *Reservations essential.*

$$$$
EUROPEAN
Fodor's Choice
★

✕ **The Tides.** After entering the courtyard of what was once a private mansion, have a cocktail at the cozy bar or visit the on-site art gallery before proceeding to your seaside table. Perhaps the most intriguing feature of this stunning setting—besides the sound of waves crashing onto the shore just feet away—is the row of huge tree trunks growing right through the dining room. The food is equally dramatic. Executive chef and co-owner Guy Beasley and his team give a contemporary twist to fresh seafood, filet of beef, rack of lamb, and other top-of-the-line main courses by adding inspired sauces and delicate vegetables and garnishes. A full vegetarian menu is also available. Save room for the sticky toffee pudding—definitely worth the calories. $ *Average main: $50* ✉ *Balmore House, Hwy. 1, Holetown* ☎ *246/432–8356* ⊕ *www. tidesbarbados.com* ⊘ *No lunch Sat. No lunch Sun. May–Nov.* ⌧ *Reservations essential.*

5

WHERE TO STAY

Most visitors stay either on the fashionable west coast north of Bridgetown or on the action-packed south coast. On the west coast, the beachfront resorts in St. Peter and St. James parishes are mostly luxurious, self-contained enclaves. Highway 1, a two-lane road with considerable traffic, runs past these resorts; strolling to a nearby bar or restaurant can be a bit difficult. Along the south coast in Christ Church Parish, several hotels are close to the busy strip known as St. Lawrence Gap, convenient to a number of small restaurants, bars, and nightclubs. On the much more remote east coast, a few small inns offer oceanfront views and get-away-from-it-all tranquility.

In keeping with the smoke-free policy enforced throughout Barbados, smoking is restricted to open outdoor areas such as the beach. It is not permitted in hotels (neither rooms nor public areas) or in restaurants.

Room rates in Barbados may be twice as high in season (December 15–April 15) compared with rates in the quieter months; however, special promotions and vacation packages are available throughout the year. Most hotels include no meals in their rates, but some include breakfast and many offer a meal plan. Some require you to purchase a meal plan in the high season, and a few offer all-inclusive packages.

Resorts run the gamut from unpretentious to exceedingly formal, and in terms of size, intimacy, amenities, and price. Families and long-term visitors may choose from a wide variety of villas and condos. A few small, cozy inns are found along the east and southeast coasts, as well as in the northwest, and these can be ultraluxurious, fairly simple, or something in between.

Villa and condo complexes, which continue to crop up along the south and west coasts, may be the most economical option for families, groups, or couples vacationing together. Nonowner vacationers rent units from property managers, the same as reserving hotel accommodations. Apartments are also available for vacation rentals in buildings or complexes with from 3 or 4 units to 30, 40, or even more.

PRIVATE VILLAS AND CONDOS

Local real-estate agencies arrange vacation rentals of privately owned villas and condos along the west coast in St. James and St. Peter. All villas and condo units are fully furnished and equipped—including appropriate staff depending on the size of the villa or unit, which can range from one to eight bedrooms. The staff usually works six days a week. Most villas have TVs and other entertainment devices, all properties have telephones, and some have Internet access. International telephone calls are usually blocked; plan on using your cell phone, a phone card, or calling card. Vehicles generally are not included in the rates, but rental cars can be arranged for and delivered to the villa upon request. Linens and basic supplies (such as bath soap, toilet tissue, and dishwashing detergent) are normally included.

Villas or condos with one to eight bedrooms and as many baths run $250 to $1,500 per night in summer and at least double that in winter.

Rates include utilities and government taxes. The only additional cost is for groceries and staff gratuities. A security deposit is required upon booking and refunded seven days after departure less any damages or unpaid miscellaneous charges.

VILLA RENTAL CONTACTS

Altman Real Estate. ✉ *Hwy. 1, Derricks, Durants* ☎ *246/432–0840, 866/360–5292 in U.S.* 🌐 *www.altmanbarbados.com.*

Blue Sky Luxury. ✉ *Newton House, Hwy. 1B, Little Battaleys* ☎ *246/622–4466, 866/404–9600 in U.S.* 🌐 *www.blueskyluxury.com.*

Island Villas. ✉ *Trents Bldg., Holetown* ☎ *246/432–4627, 866/978–8499 in U.S.* 🌐 *www.island-villas.com.*

APARTMENT RENTAL CONTACTS

Barbados Tourism Marketing, Inc. This office has a list of apartments in prime resort areas on the south and west coasts, complete with facilities offered and current rates. ✉ *Warrens Office Complex, 1st fl., West Wing, Warrens* ☎ *246/427–2623, 800/221–9831 in U.S.* 🌐 *www.visitbarbados.org.*

5

SOUTH COAST

$ RESORT 🏨 **Accra Beach Hotel and Spa.** A full-service resort in the middle of the busy south coast, Accra is large, modern, competitively priced, and faces a great beach. **Pros:** can't beat that beach; walk to shopping, restaurants, and nightspots; helpful, friendly staff. **Cons:**"island view" rooms facing the street have an unattractive view and can be noisy; rooms could use some TLC. [$] *Rooms from: $237* ✉ *Hwy. 7, Rockley* ☎ *246/435–8920, 888/579–8879 in U.S.* 🌐 *www.accrabeachhotel.com* 🛏 *190 rooms, 34 suites* 🍴 *No meals.*

$$ RESORT FAMILY 🏨 **Bougainvillea Beach Resort.** Attractive seaside town houses, each with a separate entrance, wrap around the pool or face the beachfront; the suites are huge compared with hotel suites elsewhere in this price range, are decorated in appealing Caribbean pastels, and have full kitchens. **Pros:** great for families but also appeals to couples and honeymooners; easy stroll to St. Lawrence Gap and Oistins; three pools, one with a swim-up bar. **Cons:** rooms are on four levels with no elevator; sea can be a little rough for swimming. [$] *Rooms from: $340* ✉ *Maxwell Coast Rd., Maxwell* ☎ *246/628–0990, 800/495–1858 in U.S.* 🌐 *www.bougainvillearesort.com* 🛏 *138 suites* 🍴 *No meals.*

$$ RESORT 🏨 **The Crane.** Hugging a seaside bluff on the southeast coast, The Crane incorporates the island's oldest hotel in continuous operation; the original coral-stone hotel building (1887) is the centerpiece of a luxurious, 40-acre villa complex. **Pros:** enchanting view; lovely beach; fabulous suites; great restaurants. **Cons:** remote location; rental car recommended; villas are considerably more expensive and more modern than historic hotel rooms. [$] *Rooms from: $318* ✉ *Crane* ☎ *246/423–6220, 866/978–5942 in U.S.* 🌐 *www.thecrane.com* 🛏 *4 rooms, 14 suites, 412 villas* 🍴 *No meals.*

$ RESORT FAMILY 🏨 **Divi Southwinds Beach Resort.** This all-suites resort is situated on 20 acres of lawn and gardens bisected by action-packed St. Lawrence Gap. **Pros:** beautiful beach; four pools; close to shopping, restaurants, and

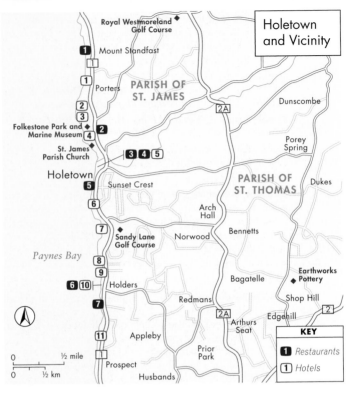

Holetown and Vicinity

nightspots; kids' club. **Cons:** water sports cost extra; some rooms aching for renovations. $ *Rooms from: $264* ✉ *St. Lawrence Main Rd., Dover* ☎ *246/428–7181, 800/367–3484* ⊕ *www.divisouthwinds.com* ⤵ *121 1-bedroom suites, 12 2-bedroom suites* ¶⊙¶ *No meals.*

$$
HOTEL
FAMILY
Fodor's Choice
★
🏨 **Hilton Barbados.** Beautifully situated on the sandy Needham's Point peninsula, all 350 units in this high-rise resort hotel have private balconies overlooking either the ocean or Carlisle Bay; 77 rooms on executive floors offer a private lounge and concierge services. **Pros:** great location near town and on a beautiful beach; lots of services and amenities; accessible rooms available; frequent promotional deals. **Cons:** service could be better; huge group/convention hotel; lacks island ambience. $ *Rooms from: $370* ✉ *Aquatic Gap, Needham's Point, Garrison* ☎ *246/426–0200* ⊕ *www.hiltonbarbadosresort.com* ⤵ *317 rooms, 33 suites* ¶⊙¶ *No meals.*

$$$
HOTEL
🏨 **Island Inn Hotel.** Constructed in 1804 as a rum storage facility for the British Regiment, this quaint, all-inclusive boutique hotel—less than a mile from Bridgetown and steps away from beautiful Pebbles Beach on Carlisle Bay—appeals to singles, couples, and families. **Pros:** friendly, accommodating atmosphere; smartly decorated rooms; excellent value. **Cons:** small pool; rooms near the front may be noisier and don't have a patio. $ *Rooms from: $440* ✉ *Aquatic Gap, Garrison* ☎ *246/436–6393* ⊕ *www.islandinnbarbados.com* ⤵ *20 rooms, 4 suites* ¶⊙¶ *All-inclusive.*

$$
HOTEL
🛏 **Little Arches Hotel.** Just east of the fishing village of Oistins, this classy boutique hotel has a distinctly Mediterranean ambience and a perfect vantage point overlooking the sea. **Pros:** stylish accommodations; good restaurant; across from fabulous Miami Beach. **Cons:** fairly remote; rental car advised. [$] *Rooms from: $325* ✉ *Enterprise Beach Rd., Oistins* ☎ *246/420–4689* ⊕ *www.littlearches.com* 🛏 *8 rooms, 2 suites* 🍴*No meals.*

$$
RESORT
FAMILY
Fodor's Choice
★
🛏 **Ocean Two.** Couples and families are drawn to this sophisticated beachfront resort in the midst of lively St. Lawrence Gap. **Pros:** large, luxurious accommodations; beautiful beach; planned children's activities in summer and holiday season. **Cons:** showers only, no tubs; Taste restaurant could be more tasty—and it's expensive—but plenty of dining options nearby. [$] *Rooms from: $358* ✉ *St. Lawrence Gap, Dover* ☎ *246/418–1800* ⊕ *www.oceantwobarbados.com* 🛏 *18 rooms, 68 1- and 2-bedroom suites* 🍴*No meals.*

$$
HOTEL
🛏 **Radisson Aquatica Resort Barbados.** Rooms in this high-rise hotel overlooking pretty Carlisle Bay, just south of Bridgetown are modern and sleek with espresso-color furniture, sparkling white linens, desk with ergonomic chair, comfortable sitting chair and ottoman, 42-inch flat-screen TV, and the latest in-room technology. **Pros:** lovely beach; beautiful sunsets from ocean-facing rooms; convenient location. **Cons:** pool area could use more umbrellas; noisy air-conditioning, no room fridge; skip the Aquatic Club restaurant and opt for neighboring Brown Sugar or the Hilton. [$] *Rooms from: $279* ✉ *Garrison* ☎ *246/426–6000* ⊕ *www.radisson.com/barbados* 🛏 *124 rooms* 🍴*Breakfast.*

$$$$
RESORT
Fodor's Choice
★
🛏 **Sandals Barbados.** Romance is definitely in the air at this truly magnificent (couples-only) Sandals property, which surrounds an 8-acre garden and lagoon—the longest and largest in Barbados. **Pros:** great beach and beautiful garden; myriad activities, including unlimited scuba diving, windsurfing, and sailing; a great place for weddings, honeymoons, and vow renewals; oceanfront and swim-up lagoon rooms are top choices. **Cons:** fabulously expensive, so look for frequent promotional offers; with so much to do, it's easy to forget there's a whole island to explore; too few pool chaises to meet demand. [$] *Rooms from: $1900* ✉ *St. Lawrence Gap, at Maxwell Coast Rd., Maxwell* ☎ *246/620–3600, 888/726–3257* ⊕ *www.sandals.com/barbados* 🛏 *280 rooms* 🍴*All-inclusive.*

$
HOTEL
🛏 **Savannah Beach Hotel.** Appealing to those who don't require organized entertainment, the Savannah is convenient for walks to the Garrison Historic Area, the Barbados Museum, and the racetrack—and minutes from Bridgetown by car or taxi. **Pros:** inviting pool; convenient to Bridgetown and sites; friendly, accommodating staff. **Cons:** beach is somewhat rocky; rather dreary interior hallways; some rooms need a little TLC. [$] *Rooms from: $255* ✉ *Hastings Main Rd., Hastings* ☎ *246/434–3800* ⊕ *www.savannahbarbados.com* 🛏 *84 rooms, 8 suites* 🍴*Breakfast.*

$$
HOTEL
🛏 **Silver Point Hotel.** This remote, gated community of modern condos at Silver Sands–Silver Rock Beach is operated as a trendy boutique hotel that appeals to singles, couples, and families—but especially to windsurfers and kitesurfers. **Pros:** stylish suites; perfect location for

Fairmont Royal Pavilion

windsurfers and kitesurfers; gated community. **Cons:** far from anything but the beach, so a rental car is recommended; sea can be rough for swimming. [$] *Rooms from: $280* ⊠ *Silver Rock Beach, Silver Sands, Silver Sands* ☎ *246/420–4416* ⊕ *www.silverpointhotel.com* ⇨ *58 suites* ¶⊙ *No meals.*

$$$$ **The SoCo Hotel.** Sophisticated travelers, particularly couples, love
HOTEL this ultramodern boutique hotel strategically poised on the beachfront in Hastings. **Pros:** stylish rooms; personalized service; excellent restaurant; lovely beach with long boardwalk. **Cons:** showers only, no tubs; very expensive. [$] *Rooms from: $800* ⊠ *Hastings Main Rd., Hastings* ☎ *246/228–6955* ⊕ *www.thesocohotel.com* ⇨ *24 rooms* ¶⊙ *All-inclusive.*

$$ **Southern Palms Beach Club & Resort Hotel.** This resort is pretty in pink,
RESORT you might say, with its (pink) plantation-style main building opening
FAMILY onto an inviting pool area and 1,000 feet of white sandy beach. **Pros:** friendly and accommodating staff; hotel food and entertainment are very good, and other options are nearby; nice beach. **Cons:** rooms are large and clean but dated; beach vendors can be a nuisance (not the hotel's fault). [$] *Rooms from: $275* ⊠ *St. Lawrence Gap, Dover* ☎ *246/428–7171* ⊕ *www.southernpalms.net* ⇨ *70 rooms, 20 suites* ¶⊙ *No meals.*

$$$ **Sweetfield Manor.** Perched on a ridge about a mile from Bridgetown,
B&B/INN this lovely and romantic restored plantation house (circa 1900) was
Fodor's Choice once the residence of the Dutch ambassador and is now the island's
★ most delightful bed-and-breakfast. **Pros:** peaceful enclave, primarily for adults; inviting pool and gardens; delicious gourmet breakfast;

perfect wedding venue. **Cons:** long walk (or short car ride) to beach; rental car advised; not appropriate for kids or those with physical disabilities. [$] *Rooms from: $396* ✉ *Brittons New Rd., Brittons Hill* ☎ *246/429–8356* 🌐 *www.sweetfieldmanor.net* 🛏 *6 rooms, 4 with bath; 1 suite* 🍴 *Breakfast.*

$$$$ RESORT FAMILY 🏨 **Turtle Beach Resort.** Families flock to this resort because it offers large, bright suites and enough all-included activities for everyone. **Pros:** attractive spot for a family vacation; nice pools; roomy suites. **Cons:** beach is relatively narrow due to storm erosion; time for the rooms to be refurbished. [$] *Rooms from: $663* ✉ *St. Lawrence Gap, at Maxwell Coast Rd., Dover* ☎ *246/428–7131* 🌐 *www.turtlebeachresortbarbados.com* 🛏 *161 suites* 🍴 *All-inclusive.*

EASTERN BARBADOS

$$ B&B/INN Fodor's Choice ★ 🏨 **The Atlantis Hotel.** Renowned for its spectacular oceanfront location, this hotel has been a fixture on the rugged east coast for more than a century. **Pros:** historical and modern blend beautifully; spectacular oceanfront location; excellent restaurant. **Cons:** from oceanfront rooms, smashing waves can be noisy at night; showers only, no tubs; remote location, so rental car is advised; no beach for swimming. [$] *Rooms from: $367* ✉ *Tent Bay* ☎ *246/433–9445* 🌐 *www.atlantishotelbarbados.com* 🕒 *Closed Sept.* 🛏 *5 rooms, 3 suites, 2 apartments* 🍴 *Breakfast.*

$ B&B/INN 🏨 **Sea-U Guest House.** Uschi Wetzels, a German travel writer in an earlier life, became smitten with the wild and woolly east coast of Barbados while on assignment and returned in 1999 to build this delightful guesthouse. **Pros:** peaceful and relaxing; couldn't be friendlier. **Cons:** remote location; few on-site activities; no TV or in-room telephone (but complimentary Wi-Fi is available). [$] *Rooms from: $179* ✉ *Tent Bay* ☎ *246/433–9450* 🌐 *www.seaubarbados.com* 🛏 *8 rooms* 🍴 *Breakfast.*

WEST COAST

$$$$ RESORT 🏨 **The Club Barbados Resort & Spa.** This is one of the island's few adults-only (age 16 and up) all-inclusive resorts and the only one on the west coast; only spa and salon services and room service cost extra. **Pros:** intimate atmosphere; walk to Holetown and Sandy Lane Beach; waterskiing and boat trip included. **Cons:** beach erodes to almost nothing sometimes—usually after fall storms—but the sandy beach deck is a good substitute. [$] *Rooms from: $790* ✉ *Hwy. 1, Vauxhall, Holetown* ☎ *246/432–7840, 866/317–8009* 🌐 *www.theclubbarbados.com* 🛏 *96 rooms, 65 suites* 🍴 *All-inclusive.*

$$$$ RESORT Fodor's Choice ★ 🏨 **Cobblers Cove Hotel.** Flanked by tropical gardens on one side and the sea on the other, this English country-style resort has elegant suites, each with a comfy sitting room with sofa bed, a small library, and a wall of louvered shutters that open wide to a patio. **Pros:** very classy; lovely grounds; amazing penthouse suites; peaceful and quiet. **Cons:** small beach; too quiet for some; only bedrooms have air-conditioning; adults only January–March. [$] *Rooms from: $770* ✉ *Road View, Hwy. 1B, Speightstown* ☎ *246/422–2291* 🌐 *www.cobblerscove.com* 🕒 *Closed Sept.–mid-Oct.* 🛏 *40 suites* 🍴 *Some meals.*

Coral Reef Club luxury cottage

$$$$
RESORT
Fodor'sChoice
★
🛏 **Colony Club Hotel.** The signature hotel of five Elegant Hotel properties on Barbados is certainly elegant, but with a quiet, friendly, understated style primarily targeted to adults. **Pros:** swim-up rooms; complimentary organic garden tour and cooking demo, historic Holetown walk, snorkel safari, and fishing with the chef; some ADA-compliant rooms; complimentary Wi-Fi. **Cons:** pricey; kid-friendly activities only summer and holidays; beach comes and goes, depending on storms. $ *Rooms from: $901* ⊠ *Hwy. 1, Porters* 🕾 *246/422–2335, 888/996–9948* ⊕ *www.colonyclubhotel.com* ⊙ *Closed Sept.* 🛏 *62 rooms, 34 junior suites* ⦿I *Some meals.*

$$$$
RESORT
Fodor'sChoice
★
🍽 **Coral Reef Club.** This upscale resort, with pristine coral-stone cottages scattered over 12 acres of flower-filled gardens, offers elegance in a welcoming, informal atmosphere. **Pros:** delightful appearance and atmosphere; beautiful suites with huge verandas; delicious dining. **Cons:** few room TVs; narrow beach sometimes disappears, depending on weather; no kids mid-January through February; seven-night minimum stay during winter and spring holidays. $ *Rooms from: $895* ⊠ *Hwy. 1, Porters* 🕾 *246/422–2372* ⊕ *www.coralreefbarbados.com* ⊙ *Closed mid-May–mid-July and Sept.* 🛏 *29 rooms, 57 suites, 2 villas* ⦿I *Some meals.*

$$$$
RESORT
FAMILY
🍽 **Crystal Cove Hotel.** This seaside colony of attached duplex cottages, whitewashed and trimmed in perky pastels, appeals to both couples and families. **Pros:** kids' club with activities all day and nanny service at night; exchange dining program with sister resorts on the west coast; all water sports, including waterskiing and banana boat or tube rides, are complimentary; Green Globe–certified. **Cons:** few activities immediately outside the resort, although it's not far from Bridgetown. $ *Rooms from: $889*

✉ *Hwy. 1, Appleby* ☎ *246/432–2683, 888/996–9948 in U.S.* ⊕ *www. crystalcovehotelbarbados.com* ➦ *62 rooms, 26 suites* ❙⊙❙ *All-inclusive.*

$$$$
RESORT
Fodor'sChoice
★

Fairmont Royal Pavilion. Every unit in this luxurious adults-oriented resort (kids welcome mid-March through October) has immediate access to 11 acres of lovely tropical gardens and an uninterrupted sea view from a broad balcony or patio. **Pros:** top-notch service—everyone remembers your name; excellent dining. **Cons:** dining—and everything else—is expensive. $ *Rooms from: $1179* ✉ *Hwy. 1, Porters* ☎ *246/422–5555, 866/540–4485* ⊕ *www.fairmont.com/barbados* ➦ *48 rooms, 24 suites, 1 3-bedroom villa* ❙⊙❙ *Some meals.*

$$$$
HOTEL
Fodor'sChoice
★

The House. Privacy, luxury, and service are hallmarks of this intimate adults-only sanctuary adjacent to sister resort Tamarind. **Pros:** trendy and stylish; privacy assured; pure relaxation; complimentary half-hour massage. **Cons:** atmosphere can be stuffy. $ *Rooms from: $1052* ✉ *Hwy. 1, Paynes Bay* ☎ *246/432–5525, 888/996–9948 in U.S.* ⊕ *www.thehousebarbados.com* ➦ *34 suites* ❙⊙❙ *Breakfast.*

$$$
RENTAL
FAMILY

Little Good Harbour. A cluster of modern, spacious, self-catering cottages, built in updated chattel-house style with gingerbread balconies, overlooks a narrow strip of beach in far north Barbados—just beyond the fishing community of Six Men's Bay. **Pros:** spacious, beautifully decorated suites; laid-back atmosphere; good choice for families. **Cons:** busy road, tiny beach; air-conditioning in bedrooms only; remote location. $ *Rooms from: $425* ✉ *Hwy. 1B, Shermans* ☎ *246/439–3000* ⊕ *www.littlegoodharbourbarbados.com* ⊘ *Closed Sept.* ➦ *21 suites* ❙⊙❙ *No meals.*

$$$$
RESORT

Mango Bay. This boutique beachfront resort in the heart of Holetown is within walking distance of shops, restaurants, nightspots, historic sites, and the public bus to Bridgetown and Speightstown. **Pros:** pleasant accommodations; great food; friendly staff. **Cons:** small pool; fairly narrow beach. $ *Rooms from: $495* ✉ *2nd St., Holetown* ☎ *246/432–1384* ⊕ *www.mangobaybarbados.com* ➦ *64 rooms, 10 suites, 2 penthouse suites* ❙⊙❙ *All-inclusive.*

$$$$
RESORT
FAMILY
Fodor'sChoice
★

The Sandpiper. An intimate vibe and (practically) private beach keep guests coming back to this family-oriented hideaway, with accommodations spread throughout 7 acres of gardens. **Pros:** private and sophisticated; dining, spa, and tennis privileges at nearby Coral Reef Club; Tree Top suites are fabulous—but pricey; concoct your own signature cocktail for the Harold's Bar menu. **Cons:** beach is small, typical of west-coast beaches; hotel is small and popular (75% repeat guests), so book far in advance. $ *Rooms from: $895* ✉ *Hwy. 1, Holetown* ☎ *246/422–2251* ⊕ *www.sandpiperbarbados.com* ⊘ *Closed Sept.* ➦ *22 rooms, 25 suites, 3 Tree Top suites* ❙⊙❙ *Some meals.*

$$$$
RESORT
FAMILY
Fodor'sChoice
★

Sandy Lane Hotel and Golf Club. Few places in the Caribbean can compare to Sandy Lane's luxurious facilities and ultrapampering service—or to its astronomical prices. **Pros:** cream of the crop; excellent dining; lovely beach; amazing spa; great golf. **Cons:** over the top for most mortals; while you don't need to dress up to walk through the lobby, you'll feel like you should. $ *Rooms from: $1700* ✉ *Hwy. 1* ☎ *246/444–2000* ⊕ *www.sandylane.com* ➦ *96 rooms, 16 suites, 1 5-bedroom villa* ❙⊙❙ *Breakfast.*

5

$$$$ RESORT FAMILY ▣ **Tamarind.** This sleek Mediterranean-style resort, which sprawls along 750 feet of prime west-coast beachfront, is large enough to cater to active families and sophisticated couples, including honeymooners. **Pros:** very big resort, yet layout affords privacy; right on Paynes Bay Beach; lots of complimentary water sports, including motorized. **Cons:** some rooms could use a little TLC; uninspired buffet breakfast. $ *Rooms from: $830* ⊠ *Hwy. 1, Paynes Bay* ☎ *246/432–1332, 888/917–9948 in U.S.* ⊕ *www.tamarindbarbados.com* ⟿ *57 rooms, 47 suites* ⦿ *Some meals.*

$$$$ HOTEL ▣ **Treasure Beach.** Quiet, upscale, and intimate, this boutique hotel has a residential quality. **Pros:** cozy retreat; congenial crowd; swimming with the turtles just offshore. **Cons:** narrow beach; offshore turtle swimming often attracts boatloads of tourists. $ *Rooms from: $856* ⊠ *Hwy. 1, Paynes Bay* ☎ *246/419–4200, 800/355–6161 in U.S.* ⊕ *www.treasurebeachhotel.com* ⊗ *Closed Sept. and Oct.* ⟿ *35 suites* ⦿ *Some meals.*

NIGHTLIFE

When the sun goes down, Bajans "lime"—which can mean anything from getting together for a drink and casual chat to enjoying a full-blown "jump-up" or street party. Most resorts have nightly entertainment in season, and nightclubs often have live bands for listening and dancing. The busiest bars and dance clubs rage until 3 am. On Saturday nights, some clubs—especially those with live music—charge a cover of $20 or more. Many bars and nightspots feature happy hours.

Barbados supports the rum industry with more than 1,600 "rum shops," simple bars where (mostly) men congregate to discuss the world or life in general, drink rum, and eat a cutter (sandwich). In more sophisticated establishments, you can find upscale rum cocktails made with the island's renowned Mount Gay and Cockspur brands—and no shortage of Barbados's own Banks Beer.

BRIDGETOWN AREA

The Boatyard. There's never a dull moment at this popular beachside bar—day or night. From happy hour until the wee hours, the patrons at Sharkey's Bar enjoy refreshing cocktails, beautiful sunsets, and lively music. ⊠ *Bay St., south of town, Carlisle Bay, Bridgetown* ☎ *246/436–2622* ⊕ *www.theboatyard.com.*

Harbour Lights. This open-air, beachfront club claims to be the "home of the party animal." Wednesday and Friday nights are the hottest, with dancing under the stars to reggae and soca music. ⊠ *Marine Villa, Bay St., south of town, Carlisle Bay, Bridgetown* ☎ *246/436–7225* ⊕ *www.harbourlightsbarbados.com.*

Waterfront Café. From November through April, there's live jazz Thursday, Friday, and Saturday evenings. The location alongside the wharf and small dance floor are also draws. ⊠ *The Careenage, Bridgetown* ☎ *246/427–0093* ⊕ *www.waterfrontcafe.com.bb* ⊗ *Closed Sun.–Wed.*

A local chef cooks up a tasty meal at the Oistins Fish Fry.

SOUTH COAST

Bubba's Sports Bar. Merrymakers and sports lovers find live action on three 10-foot video screens and a dozen TVs, along with bar food and drinks. ✉ *Rockley Main Rd., Worthing* ☎ *246/435–8731* ⊕ *www.bubbassportsbar.net.*

FAMILY

Fodor's Choice

★

Oistins Fish Fry. This is the place to be on Friday evening, when this south-coast fishing village becomes a lively and convivial outdoor street party suitable for the whole family. Barbecued chicken and a variety of fish, along with all the traditional sides, are served fresh from the grill and consumed at roadside picnic tables. Servings are huge, and prices are inexpensive—about $10 per plate. Drinks, music, and dancing add to the fun. ✉ *Oistins Main Rd., Oistins.*

Sugar Ultra Lounge. This chic, upscale, techno nightspot—complete with light show wall—attracts international talent in addition to the usual DJ and occasional local band. Groove to dance hall, soca, hip hop, and Top 40 music from 10 pm to 3 or 4 am on Thursday and Saturday. Dress "club chic": no shorts, sleeveless shirts, or hats allowed. ✉ *St. Lawrence Gap, Dover* ☎ *246/420–7662* ⊕ *www.sugarbarbados.com* 🎟 *$12.50 (sometimes more) on Thurs. and Sat. nights.*

SHOPPING

WHAT TO BUY

One of the most long-lasting souvenirs to bring home from Barbados is a piece of authentic Caribbean art. The colorful flowers, quaint villages, mesmerizing seascapes, and fascinating cultural experiences and activities that are endemic to the region and familiar to visitors have been translated by local artists onto canvas and into photographs, sculpture, and other media. Gift shops and even some restaurants display local artwork for sale, but the broadest array of artwork will be found in a gallery. Typical Bajan crafts include pottery and ceramics, shell and glass art, wood carvings, handmade dolls, watercolors, and other artwork (both originals and prints).

Although many of the private homes, great houses, and museums in Barbados are filled with priceless antiques, you'll find few for sale—mainly British antiques and some local pieces, particularly mahogany furniture. Look instead for old prints and paintings.

DUTY-FREE SHOPPING

Duty-free luxury goods—china, crystal, cameras, porcelain, leather items, electronics, jewelry, perfume, and clothing—are found at Bridgetown's Broad Street department stores and their branches, shops in the high-end Limegrove Lifestyle Centre in Holetown, the Bridgetown Cruise Terminal (for passengers only), and the departure lounge at Grantley Adams International Airport. Prices are often 30% to 40% less than full retail. To buy goods at duty-free prices, you must produce your passport, immigration form, or driver's license, along with departure information (such as flight number and date) at the time of purchase—or you can have your purchases delivered free to the airport or harbor for pickup; duty-free alcohol, tobacco products, and some electronic equipment *must* be delivered to you at the airport or harbor.

GROCERIES

If you've chosen self-catering lodgings, want some snacks, or just like to explore local grocery stores, you'll find large, modern supermarkets at Sunset Crest in Holetown on the west coast; in Oistins, at Sargeants Village (Sheraton Mall), and in Worthing on the south coast; and at Warrens (Highway 2, north of Bridgetown) in St. Michael.

BRIDGETOWN

Bridgetown's **Broad Street** is the primary downtown shopping area. **DaCosta Manning Mall,** in the historic Colonnade Building on Broad Street, has more than 25 shops that sell everything from Piaget watches to postcards; across the street, **Mall 34** has 22 shops where you can buy duty-free goods, souvenirs, and snacks. At the **cruise-ship terminal** shopping arcade, passengers can buy both duty-free goods and Barbadian-made crafts at more than 30 boutiques and a dozen vendor carts and stalls. And the **airport departure lounge** is a veritable shopping mall.

Where de Rum Come From

For more than 300 years (from 1655 through "Black Tot Day," July 31, 1970), a daily "tot" of rum (2 ounces) was duly administered to each sailor in the British navy—as a health ration. At times, rum has also played a less appetizing—but equally important—role. When Admiral Horatio Nelson died in 1805 aboard ship during the Battle of Trafalgar, his body was preserved in a cask of his favorite rum until he could be properly buried.

Hardly a Caribbean island doesn't have its own locally made rum, but Barbados is truly "where de rum come from." Mount Gay, the world's oldest rum distillery, has continuously operated on Barbados since 1703, according to the original deed for the Mount Gay Estate, which itemized two stone windmills, a boiling house, seven copper pots, and a still house. The presence of rum-making equipment on the plantation at the time suggests that the previous owners were actually producing rum in Barbados long before 1703.

Today, much of the island's interior is still planted with sugarcane—where the rum really does come from—and several great houses on historic sugar plantations have been restored with period furniture and are open to the public.

To really fathom rum, however, you need to delve a little deeper than the bottom of a glass of rum punch. Mount Gay offers an interesting 45-minute tour of its main plant, followed by a tasting. You can learn about the rum-making process from cane to cocktail, hear more rum-inspired anecdotes, and have an opportunity to buy bottles of its famous Eclipse or Extra Old rum at duty-free prices. Bottoms up!

CLOTHING

Dingolay. This shop sells tropical clothing designed and made in Barbados for women and girls, as well as shoes, handbags, and accessories from around the world. ⊠ *Sheraton Mall, Hwy. 6, Sargeant* ☎ *246/435–6482.*

DEPARTMENT STORES

Cave Shepherd. The main store on Broad Street sells an array of clothing and luxury goods. Branches are at Holetown's Sunset Crest and West Coast malls and Worthing's Vista shopping complex; the airport departure lounge has a boutique. ⊠ *10-14 Broad St., Bridgetown* ☎ *246/431–2121* ⊕ *www.caveshepherd.com.*

Harrison's. There's a large store on Broad Street and a branch at the Sheraton Mall on the south coast. ⊠ *1 Broad St., Bridgetown* ☎ *246/431–5500.*

DUTY-FREE GOODS

Little Switzerland. This mini-chain's anchor shop is at DaCosta Manning Mall, with branches at the West Coast and Sunset Crest malls in Holetown. Here you can find perfume, jewelry, cameras, audio equipment, Swarovski and Waterford crystal, and Wedgwood china. ⊠ *DaCosta Manning Mall, Broad St., Bridgetown* ☎ *246/431–0030* ⊕ *www.littleswitzerland.com.*

The Royal Shop. The Royal Shop carries fine watches and jewelry fashioned in Italian gold, Caribbean silver, diamonds, and other gems in its main shop on Broad Street and branch shop at the Cruise Terminal. ⊠ *32 Broad St., Bridgetown* ☎ *246/429–7072* ⊕ *www.theroyalshop-barbados.com.*

SOUTH COAST

At **Chattel House Village,** a cluster of boutiques in St. Lawrence Gap, you can buy locally made crafts and other souvenirs. In Rockley, Christ Church, **Quayside Centre** has a small number of boutiques.

Best of Barbados. Architect Jimmy Walker founded these shops to showcase the works of his artist wife. Products range from her framable prints, housewares, and textiles to arts and crafts in both native style and modern designs. Everything is made or designed on Barbados. Branch shops are at Chattel Village in Holetown, at Southern Palms Resort in St. Lawrence Gap, at the cruise-ship terminal, and in the airport departure lounge. ⊠ *Quayside Centre, Main Rd., Rockley* ☎ *246/622–1761* ⊕ *www.best-of-barbados.com.*

WEST COAST

Holetown has the upscale **Limegrove Lifestyle Centre,** a stylish shopping mall with high-end designer boutiques, as well as **Chattel House Village,** small shops in colorful cottages with local products, fashions, beachwear, and souvenirs. Also in Holetown, **Sunset Crest Mall** has two branches of the Cave Shepherd department store, a bank, a pharmacy, and several small shops; at **West Coast Mall** you can buy duty-free goods, island wear, and groceries.

ART GALLERIES

Fodor's Choice
★
Earthworks Pottery. At his family-owned and -operated pottery workshop, items range from dishes and knickknacks to complete dinner services and one-of-a-kind art pieces. The characteristically blue or green—and, more recently, peach and brown—pottery decorates hotel rooms and is sold in gift shops throughout the island, but the biggest selection (including "seconds") is here, where you also can watch the potters at work. ⊠ *2 Edgehill Heights, Edgehill* ☎ *246/425–0223* ⊕ *www.earthworks-pottery.com* ☾ *Closed Sun.*

Gallery of Caribbean Art. This gallery is committed to promoting Caribbean art from Haiti and Cuba in the north to Curaçao and Guyana in the south—and, particularly, the works of Barbadian artists. ⊠ *Northern Business Centre, Queen St., Speightstown* ☎ *246/419–0858* ⊕ *www.artgallerycaribbean.com* ☾ *Closed Sun.*

On the Wall Art Gallery. Artist and gallery owner Vanita Comissiong offers an array of original paintings by Barbadian artists, along with handmade arts and crafts and jewelry products. An additional gallery is located in a dedicated space at Champers restaurant in Rockley on the south coast. ⊠ *Earthworks Pottery, 2 Edgehill Heights* ☎ *246/234–9145* ⊕ *www.onthewallartgallery.com* ☾ *Closed Sun.*

SPORTS AND THE OUTDOORS

Cricket, football (soccer), polo, and rugby are extremely popular sports in Barbados for participants and spectators alike, with local, regional, and international matches held throughout the year. Contact Barbados Tourism Marketing, Inc., or check newspapers for information.

DIVING AND SNORKELING

More than two-dozen dive sites lie along the west coast between May-cocks Bay and Bridgetown and off the south coast as far as the St. Lawrence Gap. Certified divers can explore flat coral reefs and see dramatic sea fans, huge barrel sponges, and more than 50 varieties of fish. Divers regularly explore 9 sunken wrecks, and at least 10 more are accessible to experts. Underwater visibility is generally 80 to 90 feet. The calm waters along the west coast are also ideal for snorkeling. The marine reserve, a stretch of protected reef between Sandy Lane and the Colony Club, contains beautiful coral formations accessible from the beach.

On the west coast, **Bell Buoy** is a large, dome-shape reef where huge brown coral tree forests and schools of fish delight all categories of divers at depths of 20 to 60 feet. At **Dottins Reef**, off Holetown, you can see schooling fish, barracudas, and turtles at depths of 40 to 60 feet. **Maycocks Bay,** on the northwest coast, is particularly enticing; large coral reefs are separated by corridors of white sand, and visibility is often 100 feet or more. The 165-foot freighter *Pamir* lies in 60 feet of water off Six Men's Bay; it's still intact, and you can peer through its portholes at dozens of varieties of tropical fish. **Silver Bank** is a healthy coral reef with beautiful fish and sea fans; you may get a glimpse of the *Atlantis* submarine at 60 to 80 feet. Not to be missed, the *Stavronikita* is a scuttled Greek freighter at about 135 feet; hundreds of butterfly fish hang out around its mast, and the thin rays of sunlight filtering down through the water make exploring the huge ship a wonderfully eerie experience.

Farther south, **Carlisle Bay** is a natural harbor and marine park just below Bridgetown. Here you can retrieve empty bottles thrown overboard by generations of sailors and see cannons and cannonballs, anchors, and six shipwrecks (*Berwyn, Fox, CTrek, Eilon,* the barge *Cornwallis,* and *Bajan Queen*) lying in 25 to 60 feet of water, all close enough to visit on the same dive. The *Bajan Queen,* a cruise vessel that sank in 2002, is the island's newest wreck.

Dive shops provide a two-hour beginner's "resort" course (about $100) followed by a shallow dive, or a weeklong certification course (about $450). Once you're certified, a one-tank dive costs about $70 to $80; a two-tank dive runs $120 to $125. All equipment is supplied, and you can purchase multidive packages. Gear for snorkeling is available (free or for a small rental fee) from most hotels. Snorkelers can usually accompany dive trips for $30 for a one- or two-hour trip. Most dive shops have relationships with hotels and offer dive packages to hotel guests, including round-trip transfers.

Dive Shop, Ltd. Next to the marine park on Carlisle Bay, just south of Bridgetown, the island's oldest dive shop offers daily reef and wreck dives, plus beginner classes, certification courses, and underwater photography instruction. Underwater cameras are available for rent. Free transfers are provided between your hotel and the dive shop. ⊠ *Amey's Alley, Upper Bay St., next to Nautilus Beach Apts.* ☎ *246/426–9947* ⊕ *www.thediveshopbarbados.com.*

Hightide Watersports. On the west coast, Hightide Watersports offers three dive trips daily—one- and two-tank dives and night reef–wreck–drift dives—for up to eight divers, along with PADI instruction, equipment rental, and free transportation. ⊠ *Coral Reef Club, Hwy. 1, Holetown* ☎ *246/432–0931, 800/970–0016, 800/513–5763* ⊕ *www. divehightide.com.*

FISHING

Fishing is a year-round activity in Barbados, but prime time is January through April when game fish are in season. Whether you're a serious deep-sea fisher looking for marlin, sailfish, tuna, and other billfish or prefer angling in calm coastal waters where wahoo, barracuda, and other fish reside, you can choose from a variety of half- or full-day charters departing from The Careenage in Bridgetown. Expect to pay $195 per person for a shared half-day charter; for a private charter (up to six people), expect to pay $500 to $700 per boat for a four- to six-hour half-day charter or $900 to $1,000 for an eight-hour full-day charter. Spectators who don't fish are welcome for $50 per person.

Billfisher Deepsea Fishing. *Billfisher III*, a 40-foot Viking Sport Fisherman, accommodates up to six passengers with three fishing chairs and five rods. Captain Winston ("The Colonel") White has been fishing these waters since 1975. His full-day charters include a full lunch; all trips include drinks and transportation to and from the boat. ⊠ *Bridge House Wharf, The Careenage, Bridgetown* ☎ *246/431–0741.*

Cannon Charters. *Cannon II*, a 42-foot Hatteras Sport Fisherman, has three chairs and five rods and accommodates six passengers. Drinks and snacks are complimentary, and lunch is served on full-day charters. ⊠ *The Careenage, Bridgetown* ☎ *246/424–6107* ⊕ *www. fishingbarbados.com.*

High Seas Charters. *Ocean Hunter*, a 42-foot custom-built sportfishing boat, has an extended cockpit that easily accommodates six people. Choose a four-, six-, or eight-hour charter. All tackle and bait are supplied, as well as drinks and snacks. Charter rates include hotel transfers. ⊠ *The Careenage* ☎ *246/233–2598* ⊕ *www.sportfishingbarbados.com.*

GOLF

Barbadians love golf, and golfers love Barbados. Courses open to visitors are listed below.

Barbados Golf Club. The first public golf course on Barbados, an 18-hole championship course, was redesigned in 2000 by golf course architect Ron Kirby. The course has hosted numerous competitions, including the European Senior tour in 2003. Several hotels offer preferential tee-time reservations and reduced rates. Cart, trolley, club, and shoe rentals are all available. ⊠ *Hwy. 7, Durants* ☎ *246/428–8463* ⊕ *www.barbadosgolfclub. com* ⊠ *$105 for 18 holes; $55 for 9 holes; 3-, 5-, and 7-day passes $255, $400, $525, respectively* ⅄ *18 holes, 6805 yards, par 72.*

Fodor's Choice ★ **Country Club at Sandy Lane.** At this prestigious club, golfers can play the Old Nine or either of two 18-hole championship courses: the Tom Fazio–designed Country Club Course and the spectacular Green Monkey Course, which is reserved for hotel guests and club members. The layouts offer a limestone quarry setting (Green Monkey), a modern style with lakes (Country Club), and traditional small greens and narrow fairways (Old Nine). Golfers can use the driving range for free. The Country Club Restaurant and Bar, overlooking the 18th hole, is open to the public. Caddies, trolleys, clubs, and shoes are available for rent, as are GPS-equipped carts, which alert you to upcoming hazards, give tips on how to play holes, and even let you order refreshments. ⊠ *Sandy Lane, Hwy. 1, Sunset Crest* ☎ *246/444–2500* ⊕ *www.sandylane.com/ golf* ⊠ *$240 for 18 holes ($200 hotel guests); $150 for 9 holes ($130 guests); 7-day pass $1,350 ($1,250 guests)* ⅄ *Green Monkey: 18 holes, 7343 yards, par 72; Country Club: 18 holes, 7060 yards, par 72; Old Nine: 9 holes, 3345 yards, par 36.*

Royal Westmoreland Golf Club. This well-regarded Robert Trent Jones Jr.–designed, 18-hole championship course meanders through 500 tropically landscaped acres. Highlights include challenging greens, a great set of par threes, and ocean views from every hole. The course is primarily for members and villa renters, with 10 to 11 am tee times for visitors, subject to availability (no Saturdays). Greens fees include an electric cart (required); club and shoe rentals are available. ⊠ *Royal Westmoreland Resort, Westmoreland* ☎ *246/419–7242* ⊕ *www.royal-westmoreland.com* ⊠ *$250 for 18 holes (day rate for nonresidents)* ⅄ *18 holes, 7045 yards, par 72.*

GUIDED TOURS

Taxi drivers give personalized tours for about $35 to $40 per hour for up to three people. Or you can choose an overland mountain-bike journey, a 4x4 safari expedition, or a full-day bus excursion. Prices vary by mode of travel and attractions included. Ask guest services at your hotel to help with arrangements.

Island Safari. Discover all the popular attractions and scenic locations via a 4x4 jeep—including some gullies, forests, and remote areas that are inaccessible by conventional cars and buses. A full-day tour (5½ hours) includes snacks or lunch. You can also arrange your own private safari (three to six hours). ⊠ *CWTS Complex, Salters Rd., Lower Estate* ☎ *246/429–5337* ⊕ *www.islandsafari.bb* ⊠ *From $92.50.*

SunTours Barbados. Whether you want to take a full-day island tour, concentrate on historic sites, focus on photography, or go as you please, SunTours is happy to accommodate your interests. Options range from a half-day tour of Bridgetown and The Garrison to a full-day island tour (including lunch and entrance fees)—or you can pay by the hour for a personalized adventure for up to four people. Vehicles vary depending on the group; the fleet includes comfortable passenger cars and SUVs, luxury cars and limos, minivans (with or without a wheelchair lift), and large tour buses. ⊠ *CWTS Complex, Lower Estate* ☎ *246/434–8430* 💷 *From $55.*

HIKING

Hilly but not mountainous, the northern interior and the east coast are ideal for hiking.

Arbib Heritage and Nature Trail. Maintained by the Barbados National Trust, these are actually two trails. The Whim Adventure trail offers a rigorous hike (3½ hours) through gullies and plantations to old ruins and remote north-country areas; the shorter, easier Round-de-Town Stroll (2 hours) goes through Speightstown's side streets and past an ancient church and chattel houses. Guided hikes run from 9 to 2 on Wednesday, Thursday, and Saturday (with a minimum of four people); group rates are available. Book ahead, preferably four days in advance. Not recommended for children under five. ⊠ *Speightstown* ☎ *246/426–2421* ⊕ *www.barbadosnationaltrust.org* 💷 *From $25.*

Hike Barbados. Free walks sponsored by the Barbados National Trust are led year-round on Sunday from 6 to 9 am and from 3:30 to 6:30 pm; once a month, a moonlight hike at 5:30 pm substitutes for the afternoon hike (bring a flashlight). Experienced guides group you with others of similar ability on Stop and Stare, 5 to 6 miles (8 to 10 km); Here and There, 8 to 10 miles (13 to 16 km); or Grin and Bear, 12 to 14 miles (19 to 23 km). Wear loose clothes, sensible shoes, sunscreen, and a hat, and bring a camera and water. Routes and locations change, but each hike is a loop, finishing where it began. Check newspapers, call the Trust, or check online for schedules and meeting places. ⊠ *Wildey House, Errol Barrow Hwy., Wildey* ☎ *246/436–9033, 246/426–2421* ⊕ *www.barbadosnationaltrust.org.*

SEA EXCURSIONS

Mini-submarine voyages are enormously popular with families and those who enjoy watching fish but don't wish to get wet. Party boats depart from Bridgetown's Deep Water Harbour for sightseeing and snorkeling or romantic sunset cruises. Prices are $45 to $125 per person for four- or five-hour daytime cruises and $60 to $85 for three- or four-hour sunset cruises, depending on the type of refreshments and entertainment included; transportation to and from the dock is provided. For an excursion that may be less splashy in terms of a party atmosphere—but is definitely splashier in terms of the actual experience—turtle tours allow participants to feed and swim with a resident group of hawksbill and leatherback sea turtles.

FAMILY **Atlantis Submarine.** This 50-foot, 48-passenger submarine turns the Caribbean into a giant aquarium. The 45-minute voyage (including hotel transfer) takes in wrecks and reefs as deep as 150 feet. Children love the adventure, but they must be at least 3 feet tall. ⊠ *Shallow Draught,*

Bridgetown ☎ *246/436–8929* ⊕ *www.barbados.atlantissubmarines. com* ✉ *From $104.*

FAMILY **Black Pearl Party Cruises.** The whole family will get a kick out of a "pirate" ship adventure on *Jolly Roger 1.* The four-hour day and sunset (Thursday only) cruises along the island's west coast include a barbecue lunch or dinner, free-flowing drinks, lively music, swimming with turtles, and pirate activities such as walking the plank and rope swinging. ⊠ *Carlisle House, The Careenage, Bridgetown* ☎ *246/436–2885, 246/826–7245* ⊕ *www.barbadosblackpearl-jollyroger1.com* ✉ *From $87.50.*

FAMILY *Cool Runnings* **Catamaran Cruises.** Owner Captain Robert Povey skippers a five-hour lunch cruise with stops to swim with the fishes, snorkel with sea turtles, and explore a shallow shipwreck. A four-hour sunset cruise includes swimming, snorkeling, and exploring underwater as the sun sinks. Delicious meals with wine, along with an open bar, are part of all cruises. ⊠ *Carlisle House, Carlisle Wharf, Hincks St., Bridgetown* ☎ *246/436–0911* ⊕ *www.coolrunningsbarbados.com* ✉ *From $80.*

FAMILY **Tiami Catamaran Cruises.** Tiami operates five catamaran party boats for luncheon cruises to a secluded bay for swimming with turtles or for romantic sunset and moonlight cruises with catering and live music. ⊠ *Shallow Draught, Bridgetown* ☎ *246/430–0900* ⊕ *www. tiamicatamarancruises.com.*

SURFING

The best surfing is at the east coast's Bathsheba Soup Bowl, where the Barbados Independence Pro competition is held each November, but note that the island's windward (Atlantic) side is safe only for the most experienced surfers. Surfers also congregate at Surfer's Point, at the southern tip of Barbados near Inch Marlow, where the Atlantic Ocean meets the Caribbean Sea.

Dread or Dead Surf Shop. This surf shop promises to get beginners from "zero to standing up and surfing" in one afternoon. The three-hour course—"or until you stand up or give up"—includes a board, wax, rash guard (if necessary), a ride to and from the surf break, and instruction; additional 2½-hour lessons can be purchased after the 3-hour course. More experienced surfers can simply rent boards. ⊠ *Hastings Main Rd., Hastings* ☎ *246/228–4785* ⊕ *www.dreadordead.com* ✉ *From $75.*

Zed's Surfing Adventures. This outfit rents surfboards, provides lessons, and offers surf tours including equipment, guide, and transportation to surf breaks appropriate for your experience. Two-hour group lessons are held regularly, but six hours of surfing (three lessons) is cheaper by the lesson. Surfboard rentals are also available. ⊠ *Surfer's Point, Inch Marlowe* ☎ *246/428–7873* ⊕ *www.zedssurftravel.com* ✉ *From $80.*

5

WINDSURFING AND KITEBOARDING

Barbados is part of windsurfing's World Cup circuit. Winds are strongest November through April at Silver Sands–Silver Rock Beach, on the southern tip of the island, where the Barbados Windsurfing Championships are held in mid-January. Windsurfing boards and equipment, as well as instruction, are often available at larger hotels and sometimes can be rented by nonguests. Kiteboarding is more difficult, requiring several hours of instruction to reach proficiency; Silver Sands is about the only location in Barbados with kiteboarding equipment and instruction.

deAction Surf Shop. Directly on Silver Sands–Silver Rock Beach, Brian "Irie Man" Talma's shop stocks a range of rental surfing equipment and offers beginner windsurfing, kiteboarding, surfing, and stand-up paddling lessons. Conditions are ideal, with waves off the outer reef and flat water in the inner lagoon. Kiteboarding, which isn't easy, generally involves six hours of instruction broken up into two or three sessions: from flying a small kite to getting the body dragged with a big kite to finally getting up on the board. All equipment is provided. ✉ *Silver Sands–Silver Rock Beach, Silver Sands* ☎ *246/428–2027* ⊕ *www.briantalma.com.*

BRITISH VIRGIN ISLANDS

WELCOME TO THE BRITISH VIRGIN ISLANDS

NATURE'S LITTLE SECRETS

Most of the 60-some islands, islets, and cays that make up the British Virgin Islands (BVI) are remarkably hilly and volcanic in origin, having exploded from the depths of the sea some 25 million years ago. The exception is Anegada, which is a flat coral-limestone atoll. Tortola (about 10 square miles [26 square km]) is the largest member of the chain.

The British Virgin Islands are mostly quiet and casual, so don't expect to party until dawn, and definitely leave the tux at home. Luxury here means getting away from it all rather than getting the trendiest state-of-the-art amenities. And the jackpot is the chance to explore the many islets and cays by sailboat.

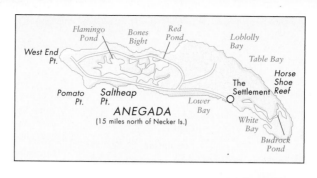

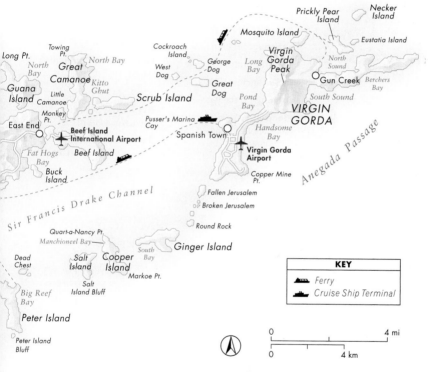

KEY

🛳 Ferry
⛴ Cruise Ship Terminal

TOP REASONS TO VISIT THE BRITISH VIRGIN ISLANDS

1 **The Perfect Place to Sail:** With more than 60 islands in the chain, sailors can drop anchor at a different, perfect beach every day.

2 **Low-Key Resorts:** Laid-back (but luxurious) resorts offer a full-scale retreat from your everyday life.

3 **Diving and Snorkeling:** Both are great, and vibrant reefs are often just feet from the shore.

4 **Jost Van Dyke:** Your trip isn't complete until you've chilled at the casual beach bars here.

5 **Few Crowds:** There's no mass tourism; the farther you get from Tortola, the quieter things become.

NEED TO KNOW

Road Town

AT A GLANCE

Capital: Road Town

Population: 28,300

Currency: U.S. Dollar

Money: No ATMs on smaller islands; bring cash. Credit cards accepted at resorts.

Language: English

Country Code: ☎ 1 284

Emergencies: ☎ 999

Driving: On the left

Electricity: 110v/60 cycles; plugs are U.S. standard two- and three-prong

Time: Same as New York during daylight savings; one hour ahead otherwise

Documents: Up to 30 days with valid passport with requirements (ASEAN, Schengen)

Mobile Phones: GSM (850, 900, 1800, and 1900 bands)

Major Mobile Companies: Digicel, LIME

WEBSITES

BVI Tourist Board:
⊕ www.bvitourism.com

BVI Welcome Guide:
⊕ www.bviwelcome.com

GETTING AROUND

✈ **Air Travel:** Terrance B. Lettsome International Airport on Tortola is the main airport, followed by Virgin Gorda Airport.

🚌 **Bus Travel:** Shared vans called "safaris" traverse some of the larger islands.

🚗 **Car Travel:** A rental car is a fun way to explore the larger islands of Tortola and Virgin Gorda but not for the faint-hearted. Beware of unpaved roads and lack of streetlights.

⛴ **Ferry Travel:** Regular ferries connect St. Thomas and St. John to Tortola and Virgin Gorda; Tortola is the ferry hub for service within the BVI.

PLAN YOUR BUDGET

	HOTEL ROOM	MEAL	ATTRACTIONS
Low Budget	$275	$15	Cane Garden Bay, free
Mid Budget	$375	$30	Island taxi tour, $75 for two passengers
High Budget	$475	$50	Half-day private charter of 50-foot catamaran, $650

WAYS TO SAVE

Go all-inclusive. Some resorts offer an AI option when booking. Given the prices of food and drink in the BVI, it can be a money-saver.

Camp in the BVI. Rough it for a night or two at Ivan's on Jost Van Dyke, with a bar, restaurant, primitive cabins, and plenty of space for tents.

Island-hop by ferry. Reliable ferries connect the USVI with the BVI; and then other ferries connect the various islands of the BVI.

Hit the beach. All beaches on the BVI are free and open to the public.

Hassle Factor	Medium. There are currently no direct flights to the BVI from the U.S. Connections must be made from Puerto Rico or the USVI.
3 days	Visit either Tortola or Virgin Gorda, the largest and most visited of the British Virgin Islands. Relax at your resort and explore the island, making sure to visit The Baths.
1 week	Base yourself on either Tortola or Virgin Gorda but visit a few of the BVI's other must-see islands on day trips. Spend a day diving or beaching it up on Anegada, and another day on Jost Van Dyke.
2 weeks	Explore both Virgin Gorda and Tortola with day trips to Anegada, Jost Van Dyke, and Norman Island. Charter a yacht to see the other 50-some islands and cays that comprise the BVI.

WHEN TO GO

High Season: Mid-December through mid-April is the most fashionable and most expensive time to visit, when the weather is typically sunny and warm and winter weather is at its worst in the U.S. and Europe. Good hotels are often booked far in advance, and you're guaranteed the most entertainment at resorts and the most people with whom to enjoy it.

Low Season: From August to late October, temperatures can grow very hot and the weather muggy, with high risks of tropical storms. Some upscale hotels close during these months for annual renovations. However, things perk up as boat racing season kicks into gear in October.

Value Season: From late April to July and again November to mid-December, hotel prices drop 20% to 50% from high-season prices. There are chances of scattered showers, but expect sun-kissed days. The water is clearest for snorkeling and smoothest for sailing in May, June, and July.

BIG EVENTS

July–August: The two-week British Virgin Islands Emancipation Festival includes a vast schedule of parades, pageants, and street parties.

October: Kick off boat racing season with the Moorings Interline Regatta in the Caribbean's sailing capital.

October–November: Enjoy the boat races at the annual Pro-AM Regatta, taking place on Virgin Gorda.

November: Compete in the Necker Cup, a five-day Pro-Am Tennis Event on Sir Richard Branson's posh Necker Island.

READ THIS

■ *Losing My Virginity,* Sir Richard Branson. Memoir of the Virgin and Necker Island owner.

■ *Down Island,* Mark Hill. Adventure thriller set in the BVI.

■ *Really Dead: A Ria Butler Mystery,* J.E. Forman. Murder mystery set in the BVI.

WATCH THIS

■ *Muppet Treasure Island.* The classic tale with Kermit and crew.

■ *Our Virgin Island.* True story of Marina Cay's first residents, with Sidney Poitier.

■ *The Deep.* The film of Peter Benchley's novel was filmed in the BVI.

EAT THIS

■ *Callaloo*: thick soup with the namesake green, okra, peppers, and meat

■ *Whelk*: escargot of the sea, prepared with garlic butter

■ *Fish Creole*: Grilled fish topped with tomato- and onion-based sauce

■ *Painkiller*: the famed rum-based cocktail from Jost Van Dyke

■ *Goat water*: curried goat stew

■ *Tamarind Balls*: candy made of brown sugar and tamarind pulp

Updated
by Carol
Bareuther

Once a collection of about 60 sleepy islands and cays, the British Virgin Islands now see huge cruise ships. Shoppers clog the downtown area, and traffic occasionally comes to a standstill. Even the second-largest island, Virgin Gorda, gets its share of smaller ships anchored off the main village of Spanish Town. Despite this explosive growth in the territory's tourism industry, it's still easy to escape the hubbub. Hotels outside Road Town usually provide a quiet oasis, and those on the other islands can be downright serene.

Each island has a different flavor. Want access to lots of restaurants and shopping? Make Tortola your choice. The largest of the BVI, it covers 10 square miles (26 square km) and sits only a mile from St. John in the United States Virgin Islands (USVI). If you want to kick back at a small hotel or posh resort, try Virgin Gorda. Sitting nearly at the end of the chain, the 8-square-mile (21-square-km) island offers stellar beaches and a laid-back atmosphere. If you really want to get away from it all, the outermost islands, including Anegada and Jost Van Dyke, will fill the bill. Some of the smallest—Norman, Peter, Cooper, and Necker— are home to just one resort or restaurant. Others remain uninhabited specks on the horizon.

Visitors have long visited the BVI, starting with Christopher Columbus in 1493. He called the islands Las Once Mil Virgines—the 11,000 Virgins—in honor of the 11,000 virgin companions of St. Ursula, martyred in the 4th century AD. Pirates and buccaneers followed, and then came the British, who farmed the islands until slavery was abolished in 1834. The BVI are still politically tied to Britain, so the queen appoints a royal governor, but residents elect a local Legislative Council. Offshore banking and tourism share top billing in the territory's economy, but the majority of the islands' jobs are tourism-related. Despite the growth, you can usually find a welcoming smile.

PLANNING

GETTING HERE AND AROUND

AIR TRAVEL

Several airlines have regularly scheduled service to either Tortola or Virgin Gorda. Although it may be cheaper to fly via Puerto Rico, the connections are better through St. Thomas. If you have seven or more people in your party, you can also charter a plane from St. Thomas or San Juan.

AIRPORTS Tortola (EIS), Virgin Gorda (VIJ), and Anegada (NGD).

Airline Contacts Air Sunshine. ☎ 800/327–8900, 800/435–8900 in Florida, 888/879–8900 in USVI, 284/495–8900 in BVI ⊕ www.airsunshine.com. **American Airlines.** ☎ 800/433–7300 in Tortola, 340/776–2560 in St. Thomas, 340/778–2000 in St. Croix, ⊕ www.aa.com. **Cape Air.** ☎ 866/227–3247, 508/771–6944 outside the U.S./USVI ⊕ www.capeair.com. **Fly BVI.** ☎ 284/495–1747 in BVI, 866/819–3146 in U.S. ⊕ www.bviaircharters.com. **LIAT.** ☎ 888/844–5428, 866/549–5428 in USVI, 284/495–1693 in Tortola ⊕ www.liatairline.com.

Airport Transfers Mahogany Car Rentals. ☎ 284/495–5469 ⊕ www.mahoganycarrentalsbvi.com.

BOAT AND FERRY TRAVEL

Frequent daily ferries connect Tortola with St. Thomas (both Charlotte Amalie and Red Hook) and St. John. Ferries also link Tortola with Jost Van Dyke, Peter Island, and Virgin Gorda. Tortola has three ferry terminals—one at West End, one on Beef Island (at the airport), and one in Road Town. Schedules vary, and not all companies make daily trips. All Red Hook–bound ferries stop in Cruz Bay to clear customs and immigration.

Ferries also connect Virgin Gorda with St. Thomas (both Charlotte Amalie and Red Hook) and St. John, but not daily. All Red Hook–bound ferries stop in Cruz Bay to clear customs and immigration. Ferries to Virgin Gorda land in Spanish Town. Schedules vary by day, and not all companies make daily trips.

The BVI Tourist Board website ⊕ *www.bvitourism.com/inter-island-ferries* has links to all the ferry companies, and these sites are the best sources for ever-changing routes and schedules.

Boat and Ferry Contacts Dohm's Water Taxi. ☎ 340/775–6501 in St. Thomas ⊕ www.virginislandswatertaxi.com. **Inter-Island Boat Service.** ☎ 340/776–6597 in St. John, 284/495–4166 in Tortola, 340/473–8567 St. John cell ⊕ www.interislandboatservices.com. **Native Son.** ☎ 340/774–8685 in St. Thomas (Charlotte Amalie), 284/495–4617 in Tortola (West End), 284/494–5674 in Tortola (Road Town), 340/775–3111 in St Thomas (Red Hook) ⊕ www.nativesonferry.com. **New Horizon Ferry Service.** ☎ 284/495–9278 in Tortola ⊕ www.newhorizonferry.com. **North Sound Express.** ☎ 284/495–2138 in Tortola. **Peter Island Ferry.** ☎ 284/495–2000 in Tortola, 800/346–4451 ⊕ www.peterisland.com. **Road Town Fast Ferry.** ☎ 284/494–2323 in Tortola, 340/777–2800 in St. Thomas ⊕ www.tortolafastferry.com. **Smith's Ferry.** ☎ 340/775–7292 in St. Thomas, 284/494–4454 in Tortola ⊕ www.bviferryservices.com.

6

Speedy's Ferries. ☎ 284/495–5235 in Tortola ⊕ www.speedysbvi.com. **Varlack Ventures.** ☎ 340/776–6412 in St. John ⊕ www.varlack-ventures.com.

CAR TRAVEL

Driving in the BVI is on the left, British-style, but your car will always have its steering wheel on the left, as in the United States. Your valid U.S. license will also do for driving in the BVI. The minimum age to rent a car is 25. Most agencies offer both four-wheel-drive vehicles and cars (often compacts). Both Tortola and Virgin Gorda have a number of car-rental agencies.

Tortola Car-Rental Contacts Avis. ⊠ *Opposite police station, Road Town* ☎ *284/494–3322, 284/495–4973 Frenchman's Cay branch, 284/495–0110 airport branch* ⊕ *www.avisbvi.com.* **D&D Car Rentals.** ⊠ *West End Rd.* ☎ *284/495–4765.* **Itgo Car Rental.** ⊠ *Wickham's Cay I, Road Town* ☎ *284/494–2639* ⊕ *www.itgobvi.com.* **National.** ⊠ *Long Bay* ☎ *284/494–3197, 284/495–4877 Frenchman's Cay branch, 284/494–3197 Road Town branch* ⊕ *www.nationalcarbvi.com.*

Virgin Gorda Car-Rental Contacts L&S Jeep Rental. ☎ *284/495–5297* ⊕ *www.landsjeeprental.com.* **Mahogany Rentals & Taxi Service.** ☎ *284/495–5469* ⊕ *www.mahoganycarrentalsbvi.com.* **Speedy's Car Rentals.** ☎ *284/495–5240, 284/495–5235* ⊕ *www.bviferries.com/rentals.html.*

TAXI TRAVEL

Taxi rates aren't set in the BVI, so you should negotiate the fare with your driver before you start your trip. Fares are per destination, not per person here, so it's cheaper to travel in groups. The taxi number is always on the license plate.

Tortola Taxi Contacts BVI Taxi Association. ☎ *284/494–2322.* **Waterfront Taxi Association.** ☎ *284/494–4959.* **West End Taxi Association.** ☎ *284/495–4934.*

Virgin Gorda Taxi Contacts Andy's Rentals & Tours. ☎ *284/495–5252* ⊕ *www.virgingordatours.com.*

HEALTH AND SAFETY

Dengue, chikungunya, and zika have all been reported throughout the Caribbean. We recommend that you protect yourself from these mosquito-borne illnesses by keeping your skin covered and/or wearing mosquito repellent. The mosquitoes that transmit these viruses are as active by day as they are by night.

HOTELS AND RESORTS

Pick your island carefully, because each is different, as are the logistics of getting there. **Tortola** gives you a wider choice of restaurants, shopping, and resorts. **Virgin Gorda** has fewer off-resort places to eat and shop, but the resorts themselves are often better, and the beaches are wonderful. **Anegada** is remote and better suited for divers. **Jost Van Dyke** has some classic Caribbean beach bars, along with fairly basic accommodations.

Private-island resorts. When you want to be pampered and pampered some more, consider a private-island resort, reached only by ferry, or even one of the appealing outer-island resorts that are still somewhat affordable for mere mortals.

Resorts. The largest resort in the British Virgin Islands has 120-some rooms, and most have considerably fewer. Luxury here is more about personal service than over-the-top amenities.

Sailboat charter. To enjoy everything the BVI have to offer, drop anchor where and when you want.

Villas and condos. A good option for families, you'll find these accommodations in abundance.

Hotel reviews have been shortened. For full information, visit Fodors.com.

WHAT IT COSTS IN U.S. DOLLARS				
	$	$$	$$$	$$$$
RESTAURANTS	under $12	$12–$20	$21–$30	over $30
HOTELS	under $275	$275–$375	$376–$475	over $475

Restaurant prices are the average cost of a main course at dinner or, if dinner is not served, at lunch. Hotel prices are the lowest cost of a standard double room in high season.

VISITOR INFORMATION

Contacts BVI Tourist Board. ☎ *212/563–3117, 800/835–8530 in the U.S.* ⊕ *www.bvitourism.com.*

6

TORTOLA

Once a sleepy backwater, Tortola is definitely busy these days, particularly when several cruise ships tie up at the Road Town dock. Passengers crowd the streets and shops, and open-air jitneys filled with cruise-ship passengers create bottlenecks on the island's byways. That said, most folks visit Tortola to relax on its deserted sands or linger over lunch at one of its many delightful restaurants. Beaches are never more than a few miles away, and the steep green hills that form Tortola's spine are fanned by gentle trade winds. The neighboring islands glimmer like emeralds in a sea of sapphire. It can be a world far removed from the hustle of modern life, but it simply doesn't compare to Virgin Gorda in terms of beautiful beaches—or even luxury resorts, for that matter.

Initially settled by Taíno Indians, Tortola saw a string of visitors over the years. Christopher Columbus sailed by in 1493 on his second voyage to the New World, and ships from Spain, Holland, and France made periodic visits about a century later. Sir Francis Drake arrived in 1595, leaving his name on the passage between Tortola and St. John. Pirates and buccaneers followed, with the British finally laying claim to the island in the late 1600s. In 1741 John Pickering became the first lieutenant governor of Tortola, and the seat of the British government moved from Virgin Gorda to Tortola. As the agrarian economy continued to grow, slaves were imported from Africa. The slave trade was abolished in 1807, but slaves in Tortola and the rest of the BVI did not gain their freedom until August 1, 1834, when the Emancipation Proclamation was read at Sunday Morning Well in Road Town. That date is celebrated every year with the island's annual Carnival.

Visitors have a choice of accommodations, but most fall into the small and smaller-still categories. Only Long Bay Resort on Tortola's North Shore qualifies as a resort, but even some of the smaller properties add an amenity or two. A couple of new hotel projects are in the works, so look for more growth in the island's hotel industry over the next decade.

EXPLORING

Tortola doesn't have many historic sights, but it does have lots of beautiful natural scenery. Although you could explore the island's 10 square miles (26 square km) in a few hours, opting for such a whirlwind tour would be a mistake. There's no need to live in the fast lane when you're surrounded by some of the Caribbean's most breathtaking panoramas. Also, the roads are extraordinarily steep and twisting, making driving demanding. The best strategy is to explore a bit of the island at a time. For example, you might try Road Town (the island's tiny metropolis) one morning and a drive to Cane Garden Bay and the little town of West End the next afternoon. Or consider a visit to East End, a *very* tiny town exactly where its name suggests. The North Shore is where all the best beaches are found. Sights are best seen when you stumble on them on your round-the-island drive.

AROUND ROAD TOWN

The bustling capital of the BVI looks out over Road Harbour. It takes only an hour or so to stroll down Main Street and along the waterfront, checking out the traditional West Indian buildings painted in pastel colors and with corrugated-tin roofs, bright shutters, and delicate fretwork trim. For sightseeing brochures and the latest information on everything from taxi rates to ferry schedules, stop in at the BVI Tourist Board office. Or just choose a seat on one of the benches in Sir Olva Georges Square, on Waterfront Drive, and watch the people come and go from the ferry dock and customs office across the street.

TOP ATTRACTIONS

Fodor's Choice
★

Old Government House Museum. The official government residence until 1997, this gracious building now displays a nice collection of artifacts from Tortola's past. The rooms are filled with period furniture, hand-painted china, books signed by Queen Elizabeth II on her 1966 and 1977 visits, and numerous items reflecting Tortola's seafaring legacy. ⊠ *Waterfront Dr., Road Town* ☎ *284/494–4091* ⊕ *www.oghm.org* 🎟 *$5* ☉ *Weekdays 9–3.*

WORTH NOTING

Dolphin Discovery. Get up close and personal with dolphins as they swim in a spacious seaside pen. There are three different programs. In the Royal Swim, dolphins tow participants around the pen. The less expensive Adventure and Discovery programs allow you to touch the dolphins. ⊠ *Waterfront Dr., Road Town* ✛ *Located at Prospect Reef* ☎ *284/494–7675, 888/393–5158* ⊕ *www.dolphindiscovery.com* 🎟 *Royal Swim $149, Adventure $99, Discovery $79* ☉ *Royal Swim daily at 10, noon, 2, and 4. Adventure and Discovery daily at 11 and 1.*

Fort Burt. The most intact historic ruin on Tortola was built by the Dutch in the early 17th century to safeguard Road Harbour. It sits on a hill at the western edge of Road Town and is now the site of a small hotel and restaurant. The foundations and magazine remain, and the structure offers a commanding view of the harbor. ⊠ *Waterfront Dr., Road Town* ⊠ *Free* ☉ *Daily dawn–dusk.*

J.R. O'Neal Botanic Gardens. Take a walk through this 4-acre showcase of lush plant life. There are sections devoted to prickly cacti and succulents, hothouses for ferns and orchids, gardens of medicinal herbs, and plants and trees indigenous to the seashore. From the tourist office in Road Town, cross Waterfront Drive and walk one block over to Main Street and turn right. Keep walking until you see the high school. The gardens are on your left. ⊠ *Botanic Station, Road Town* ☎ *284/494–2069* ⊕ *www.bvinationalparkstrust.org* ⊠ *$3* ☉ *Mon.–Sat. 8:30–4:30.*

WEST END

TOP ATTRACTIONS

Soper's Hole. On this little island connected by a causeway to Tortola's western end, you can find a marina and a captivating complex of pastel West Indian–style buildings with shady balconies, shuttered windows, and gingerbread trim that house art galleries, boutiques, and restaurants. Pusser's Landing is a lively place to stop for a cold drink (many are made with Pusser's famous rum) and a sandwich, and to watch the boats in the harbor. ⊠ *Soper's Hole.*

WORTH NOTING

Fort Recovery. The unrestored ruins of a 17th-century Dutch fort sit amid a profusion of tropical greenery on the grounds of Fort Recovery Beachfront Villas and Suites. There's not much to see here, and there are no guided tours, but you're welcome to stop by and poke around. ⊠ *Waterfront Dr., Pockwood Pond, Road Town* ☎ *284/541–0955* ⊠ *Free.*

NORTH SHORE

TOP ATTRACTIONS

Fodor's Choice
★
Cane Garden Bay. Once a sleepy village, Cane Garden Bay has become one of Tortola's most important destinations. Stay at a small hotel or guesthouse here, or stop by for lunch, dinner, or drinks at a seaside restaurant. You can find a few small stores selling clothing and basics such as suntan lotion, and one of Tortola's most popular beaches is at your feet. Myett's offers hotel rooms almost directly on the beach. The roads in and out of this area are dauntingly steep, so use caution when driving. ⊠ *Cane Garden Bay.*

MID-ISLAND

WORTH NOTING

Mount Healthy National Park. The remains of an 18th-century sugar plantation can be seen here. The windmill structure has been restored, and you can see the ruins of a mill, a factory with boiling houses, storage areas, stables, a hospital, and many dwellings. It's a nice place to picnic. ⊠ *Ridge Rd., Todman Peak* ⊕ *www.bvinpt.org* ⊠ *Free* ☉ *Daily dawn–dusk.*

Sage Mountain National Park. At 1,716 feet, Sage Mountain is the highest peak in the BVI. From the parking area, a trail leads you in a loop not only to the peak itself (and extraordinary views) but also to a small rain forest that is sometimes shrouded in mist. Most of the forest was cut

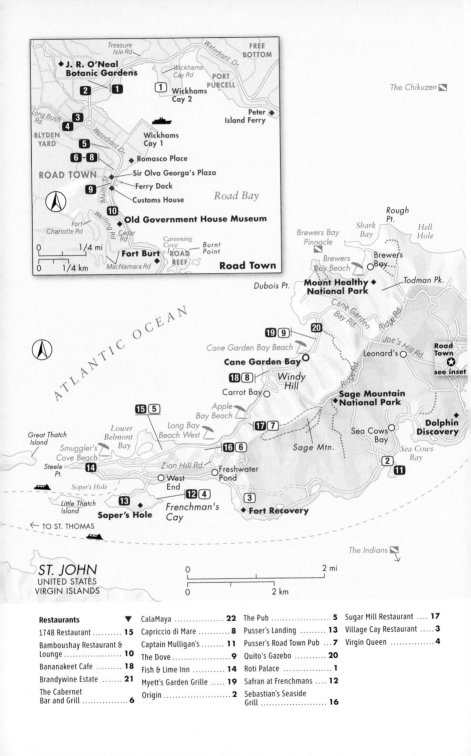

Road Town

FREE BOTTOM

Treasure Isle Rd
Waterfront Dr
Wickhams Cay Rd
PORT PURCELL

♦ J. R. O'Neal Botanic Gardens

2 **1**

1 Wickhams Cay 2

Long Bush Rd

3
4

BLYDEN YARD

Waterfront Dr

Peter Island Ferry

Wickhams Cay 1

5

6 - **8** ♦ Romasco Place

ROAD TOWN

Sir Olva Georga's Plaza

9 Ferry Dock

Road Bay

Customs House

10 Old Government House Museum

Fort Charlotte Rd

Wailling Rd

Main St

Cedar Rd

Careening Cove

Burnt Point

Fort Burt ROAD REEF

0   1/4 mi

0   1/4 km

MacNamara Rd

Road Town

The Chikuzen 🏴

Rough Pt.

Shark Bay

Hell Hole

Brewers Bay Pinnacle

Brewers Bay Beach

Brewer's Bay

Todman Pk.

Dubois Pt.

Mount Healthy ♦ National Park

Cane Garden Bay Rd

Ridge Rd

ATLANTIC OCEAN

19 **9**

20

Cane Garden Bay Beach

Cane Garden Bay

Joe's Hill Rd.

Leonard's

Road Town see inset

18 **8**

Windy Hill

Carrot Bay

Ridge Rd

Sage Mountain National Park

Apple Bay Beach

17 **7**

Sea Cows Bay

Dolphin Discovery

Great Thatch Island

Lower Belmont Bay

Long Bay Beach West

15 **5**

16 **6**

Sage Mtn.

Sea Cows Bay

Smuggler's Cove Beach

Zion Hill Rd.

Freshwater Pond

2

11

Steele Pt.

14

○ West End

Soper's Hole

12 **4**

Little Thatch Island

13

Soper's Hole

Frenchman's Cay

3

♦ **Fort Recovery**

← TO ST. THOMAS

The Indians 🏴

ST. JOHN
UNITED STATES
VIRGIN ISLANDS

0   2 mi

0   2 km

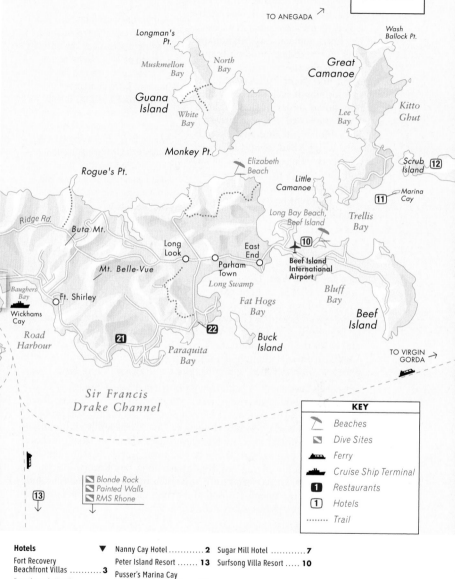

Tortola

TO ANEGADA

Longman's Pt.

Wash Ballock Pt.

Muskmellon Bay

North Bay

Great Camanoe

Guana Island

White Bay

Lee Bay

Kitto Ghut

Monkey Pt.

Elizabeth Beach

Little Camanoe

Scrub Island **12**

Rogue's Pt.

Long Bay Beach, Beef Island

Marina Cay

11

Trellis Bay

Ridge Rd.

Buta Mt.

Long Look

East End

10

Mt. Belle-Vue

Parham Town

Beef Island International Airport

Bluff Bay

Baughers Bay

Ft. Shirley

Long Swamp

Beef Island

Wickhams Cay

Road Harbour

21

Paraquita Bay

22

Fat Hogs Bay

Buck Island

TO VIRGIN GORDA

Sir Francis Drake Channel

KEY

- Beaches
- Dive Sites
- Ferry
- Cruise Ship Terminal
- **1** Restaurants
- **1** Hotels
- .... Trail

Blonde Rock
Painted Walls
RMS Rhone

13

down over the centuries for timber, to create pastureland, or for growing sugarcane, cotton, and other crops. In 1964 this park was established to preserve what remained. Up here you can see mahogany trees, white cedars, mountain guavas, elephant-ear vines, mamey trees, and giant bullet woods, to say nothing of such birds as mountain doves and thrushes. Take a taxi from Road Town or drive up Joe's Hill Road and make a left onto Ridge Road toward Chalwell and Doty villages. The road dead-ends at the park. ⊠ *Ridge Rd., Sage Mountain* ☎ *284/852–3650* ⊕ *www.bvinpt.org* ⊠ *$3* ⊙ *Daily dawn–dusk.*

DRIVING ON TORTOLA

Tortola's main roads are well paved for the most part, but there are exceptionally steep hills and sharp curves. Road Town's traffic and parking can be horrific. Try to avoid driving along the Waterfront Drive at morning and afternoon rush hours. It's longer, but often quicker, to take a route through the hills above Road Town. Parking can be very difficult in Road Town, particularly during the busy winter season. There's parking along the waterfront and on the inland side on the eastern end of downtown.

BEACHES

WEST END

Long Bay Beach West. This beach is a stunning, mile-long stretch of white sand; have your camera ready to snap the breathtaking approach. Although Long Bay Resort sprawls along part of it, the entire beach is open to the public. The water isn't as calm here as at Cane Garden or Brewers Bay, but it's still swimmable. Rent water-sports equipment and enjoy the beachfront restaurant at the resort. Turn left at Zion Hill Road; then travel about half a mile. **Amenities:** food and drink; toilets; water sports. **Best for:** swimming. ⊠ *Long Bay Rd., Long Bay.*

Smuggler's Cove Beach. A beautiful, palm-fringed beach, Smuggler's Cove is down a pothole-filled dirt road. After bouncing your way down, you'll feel as if you've found a hidden piece of the island. You probably won't be alone on weekends, though, when the beach fills with snorkelers and sunbathers. There's a fine view of Jost Van Dyke from the shore. The beach is popular with Long Bay Resort guests who want a change of scenery. Follow Long Bay Road past Long Bay Resort, keeping to the roads nearest the water until you reach the beach. It's about a mile past the resort. **Amenities:** food and drink; parking. **Best for:** snorkeling; swimming. ⊠ *Long Bay Rd., Long Bay.*

NORTH SHORE

Apple Bay Beach. Along with nearby Little Apple Bay and Capoon's Bay, this is your spot if you want to surf—although the white, sandy beach itself is narrow. Sebastian's, a casual hotel, caters to those in search of the perfect wave. The legendary Bomba's Surfside Shack—a landmark festooned with all manner of flotsam and jetsam—serves drinks and casual food. Otherwise, there's nothing else in the way of amenities. Good waves are never a sure thing, but you're more apt to find them in January and February. If you're swimming and the waves are up,

Old Government House Museum, Road Town

take care not to get dashed on the rocks. **Amenities:** food and drink; toilets. **Best for:** surfing; swimming. ⊠ *North Shore Rd. at Zion Hill Rd., Apple Bay.*

Brewers Bay Beach. This beach is easy to find, but the steep, twisting paved roads leading down the hill to it can be a bit daunting. An old sugar mill and ruins of a rum distillery are off the beach along the road. You can actually reach the beach from either Brewers Bay Road East or Brewers Bay Road West. **Amenities:** none. **Best for:** snorkeling; swimming. ⊠ *Brewers Bay Rd. E, off Cane Garden Bay Rd., Brewers Bay.*

Fodor'sChoice **Cane Garden Bay Beach.** A silky stretch of sand, Cane Garden Bay has
★ exceptionally calm, crystalline waters—except when storms at sea turn the water murky. Snorkeling is good along the edges. Casual guesthouses, restaurants, bars, and shops are steps from the beach in the growing village of the same name. The beach is a laid-back, even somewhat funky place to put down your towel. It's the closest beach to Road Town—one steep uphill and downhill drive—and one of the BVI's best-known anchorages (unfortunately, it can be very crowded). Watersports shops rent equipment. **Amenities:** food and drink; toilets; water sports. **Best for:** snorkeling; swimming. ⊠ *Cane Garden Bay Rd., off Ridge Rd., Cane Garden Bay.*

EAST END

Elizabeth Beach. Home to a small resort, Elizabeth Beach is a palm-lined, wide, sandy beach with parking along its steep downhill access road. Other than at the hotel and its restaurant, which welcomes nonguests, there are no amenities aside from peace and quiet. Turn at the sign for Lambert Beach Resort. If you miss it, you wind up at Her Majesty's

Prison. **Amenities:** food and drink; parking; toilets. **Best for:** solitude; swimming. ⊠ *Lambert Rd., off Ridge Rd., East End.*

Long Bay Beach, Beef Island. Long Bay on Beef Island has superlative scenery: the beach stretches seemingly forever, and you can catch a glimpse of Little Camanoe and Great Camanoe islands. If you walk around the bend to the right, you can see little Marina Cay and Scrub Island. Long Bay is also a good place to search for seashells. Swim out to wherever you see a dark patch for some nice snorkeling. There are no amenities, so come prepared with your own drinks and snacks. Turn left shortly after crossing the bridge to Beef Island. **Amenities:** none. **Best for:** birdwatching; snorkeling; swimming. ⊠ *Beef Island Rd.*

WHERE TO EAT

Local seafood is plentiful on Tortola, and although other fresh ingredients are scarce, the island's chefs are a creative lot who apply their skills to whatever the boat delivers. Contemporary American dishes with Caribbean influences are very popular, but you can find French and Italian fare as well. The more expensive restaurants have dress codes: long pants and collared shirts for men and elegant but casual resort wear for women. Prices are often a bit higher than they are back home, and the service can be a tad on the slow side, but enjoy the chance to linger over the view.

AROUND ROAD TOWN

$$ ╳ **Bamboushay Restaurant & Lounge.** Attached to the Bamboushay pottery boutique on Main Street, Bamboushay Lounge on adjacent Waterfront Drive serves weekday lunch options such as salads, pastas, rotis, and stuffed potatoes in an idyllic open-air gardenlike setting. The free Wi-Fi seems to attract a lively mix of young local professionals, resident expats, visiting yachties, and tourists who have eagerly returned to lounge "after hours" on Thursdays and Fridays, helping Bamboushay Lounge gain itself a reputation as the new "it" spot. Call for dinner reservations. Ⓢ *Average main: $16* ⊠ *Waterfront Dr., Road Town* ☎ *284/342–0303* ⊘ *Closed weekends.*

CAFÉ

$$$$ ╳ **Brandywine Estate.** At this Brandywine Bay restaurant, candlelit outdoor tables have sweeping views of nearby islands. The menu has a Mediterranean flair but changes often; you might find a three-cheese tortellini with garlic-and-truffle sauce or scallops in a saffron sauce. Finish your meal with a delightful cheese platter. Ⓢ *Average main: $41* ⊠ *Sir Francis Drake Hwy., east of Road Town, Brandywine Bay* ☎ *284/495–2301* ⊕ *www.brandywinerestaurant.com* ⊘ *Closed Tues.*

MEDITERRANEAN
Fodor'sChoice
★

$$$ ╳ **The Cabernet Bar and Grill.** Birds and bougainvillea brighten the patio of this breezy restaurant and bar, a popular gathering spot for locals and visitors alike. The menu boasts everything from meaty burgers to prime rib, plus entrées such as Caribbean-style grouper in an onion-butter sauce, smoked pork shoulder, rack of lamb, and beer-can chicken (a method of grilling chicken that keeps it moist and tender). Save room for such tasty desserts as chocolate cake and crème brûlée. There's a great craft beer selection. Ⓢ *Average main: $23* ⊠ *Waterfront Dr., Road Town* ☎ *284/494–8660* ⊘ *Closed Sun.*

FRENCH

$$ ITALIAN Fodor's Choice ★ 🍴 **Capriccio di Mare.** Stop by this casual, authentic Italian outdoor café for an espresso, a fresh pastry, a bowl of perfectly cooked penne, or a crispy tomato-and-mozzarella pizza. Drink specialties include a mango Bellini, an adaptation of the famous cocktail served at Harry's Bar in Venice. [$] *Average main: $19* ✉ *Waterfront Dr., Road Town* ☎ *284/494–5369* ⏲ *Closed Sun.* ✍ *Reservations not accepted.*

$$ AMERICAN FAMILY 🍴 **Captain Mulligan's.** Located at the entrance to Nanny Cay, this sports bar attracts expats, locals, and sailors with its promise to have "the second-best burger on the island," underlining the eatery's irreverent tone (we never found out who has the best!). Hot wings, pizza, ribs, and burgers are on the menu, and most people come to watch the game on the big screen. A mini-golf course has also been established and provides an activity for children of all ages, along with a children's recreation area. [$] *Average main: $16* ✉ *Nanny Cay* ☎ *284/494–0602* 🌐 *www.captainmulligans.com.*

$$$$ ECLECTIC 🍴 **The Dove.** The food matches the romantic feeling at this Road Town restaurant. Start with jumbo prawns sautéed with vanilla bean and almonds before moving on to the mushroom-and-Parmesan-crusted rib-eye steak. Desserts are often new twists on old standards, as with the soursop (the fruit of a Caribbean evergreen tree) crème brûlée. [$] *Average main: $32* ✉ *Waterfront Dr., Road Town* ☎ *284/494–0313* 🌐 *www.thedovebvi.com* ⏲ *Closed Sun. and Mon. No lunch.*

$$ SUSHI 🍴 **Origin.** Located in the heart of Road Town across from the Ferry Terminal, this lively sushi restaurant and cocktail bar offers high-quality, affordable sushi. The place jumps on Friday nights and can be a noisy dining experience; request a table on the rooftop for a more relaxed setting. [$] *Average main: $12* ✉ *Road Town* ☎ *284/494–8295* 🌐 *www.originbvi.com* ⏲ *Closed Sun. and Mon.*

$$$ ECLECTIC 🍴 **The Pub.** At this waterfront spot, tables are arranged along a terrace facing a small marina and the harbor in Road Town. Hamburgers, salads, and sandwiches are typical lunch offerings, along with classic British fare such as shepherd's pie and liver and onions. In the evening you can also choose grilled fish, sautéed conch, sizzling steaks, or barbecued ribs. There's live entertainment Thursday and Friday, and locals gather here nightly for spirited games at the pool table. [$] *Average main: $26* ✉ *Waterfront Dr., Road Town* ☎ *284/494–2608* ⏲ *No lunch Sun.* ✍ *Reservations not accepted.*

$$ ECLECTIC FAMILY 🍴 **Pusser's Road Town Pub.** Almost everyone who visits Tortola stops here at least once to have a bite to eat and to sample the famous Pusser's Rum Painkiller (fruit juice and rum). The nonthreatening menu includes cheesy pizza, shepherd's pie, fish-and-chips, and hamburgers. Dine inside in air-conditioned comfort or outside on the veranda, which looks out on the harbor. [$] *Average main: $15* ✉ *Waterfront Dr., Road Town* ☎ *284/494–3897* 🌐 *www.pussers.com.*

$$ CARIBBEAN 🍴 **Roti Palace.** You might be tempted to pass this tiny spot on Road Town's Main Street when you see the plastic tablecloths and fake flowers, but the restaurant's reputation for dishing up fantastic roti is known far and wide. Flatbread is filled with curried potatoes, onions, and either chicken, beef, conch, goat, or vegetables. Ask for the bones out if you order the chicken, to save yourself the trouble of fishing them out of

6

your mouth. [$] *Average main: $15* ✉ *Main St., Road Town* ☎ *284/494–4196* 💳 *No credit cards* 🕒 *Closed Sun. No dinner.*

$$$$ ECLECTIC 🍴 **Village Cay Restaurant.** Docked sailboats stretch nearly as far as the eye can see at this busy Road Town restaurant. Its alfresco dining and convivial atmosphere make it popular with both locals and visitors. For lunch, try the grouper club sandwich with an ancho chili mayonnaise, or their extensive lunch buffet which is popular with local professionals and yachties alike. Dinner offerings run to fish served a variety of ways, including West Indian–style with okra, onions, and peppers, as well as a seafood jambalaya with lobster, crayfish, shrimp, mussels, crab, and fish in a mango–passion fruit sauce. [$] *Average main: $32* ✉ *Wickhams Cay I, Road Town* ☎ *284/494–2771.*

$$$ ECLECTIC 🍴 **Virgin Queen.** The sailing and rugby crowds head here to play darts, drink beer, and eat Queen's Pizza—a crusty, cheesy pie topped with sausage, onions, green peppers, and mushrooms. Also on the menu is excellent West Indian and English fare: barbecued ribs with beans and rice, bangers and mash, shepherd's pie, and grilled sirloin steak. [$] *Average main: $21* ✉ *Flemming St., Road Town* ☎ *284/494–2310* 🌐 *www.virginqueenbvi.com* 🕒 *Closed Sun. No lunch Sat.*

WEST END

$$$ SEAFOOD 🍴 **Fish and Lime Inn.** In walking distance of the West End Ferry terminal, this pleasantly breezy, waterside restaurant delights daytime visitors with burger, salad, and sandwich offerings that are accompanied by hand-cut french fries. After sunset, candles illuminate the picnic tables on the waterside deck and visiting yachties arrive by dinghy to enjoy menu items that include grilled lobster, Cornish game hen, Asian-marinated barbecue ribs, and a savory hot spinach-and-avocado cheesecake that will delight vegetarians. Occasional live music and happy hour specials also keep the bar lively, which fills will local expats on weekends. [$] *Average main: $23* ✉ *Soper's Hole* ☎ *284/495–4276* 🌐 *www.fishnlime.com.*

$$$ AMERICAN 🍴 **Pusser's Landing.** Yachties navigate their way to this waterfront restaurant. Downstairs, from late morning to well into the evening, you can belly up to the outdoor mahogany bar or sit downstairs for sandwiches, fish-and-chips, and pizzas. At dinnertime head upstairs for a harbor view and a quiet alfresco meal of grilled steak or fresh fish. [$] *Average main: $26* ✉ *Soper's Hole* ☎ *284/495–4554* 🌐 *www.pussers.com.*

$$$ FRENCH FUSION 🍴 **Safran at Frenchmans.** This idyllic, off-the-beaten-path restaurant nestled within the well-manicured grounds of Frenchmans' Hotel offers exceptional food. Chef Roberto Brea, from Spain, works diligently to incorporate fresh, local Caribbean ingredients and spices into traditional Spanish-inspired meals. On Sundays, the restaurant offers a three-course fixed-price brunch that is one of the best values on island and includes eggs Benedict, rum-and-coconut battered French toast, yellowfin tuna, and sirloin steaks. Brunch guests dine leisurely both indoors and by the small pool. Dinner items include the signature shrimp and mango ceviche appetizer, grilled beefsteak, fresh fish, and daily specials like *gambas al ajillo* (Spanish-style shrimp flavored with garlic, olive oil, and paprika). [$] *Average main: $30* ☎ *284/494–8811* 🌐 *www.frenchmansbvi.com* 🕒 *Closed Mon.*

NORTH SHORE

$$$
ECLECTIC
Fodor's Choice
★
✕**Bananakeet Café.** The sunset sea-and-mountain views are stunning, so arrive early for the predinner happy hour. "Caribbean fusion" best describes the fare, with an emphasis on seafood, including local Anegada conch swimming in an herb-butter broth. Those without a taste for seafood won't go hungry—the menu also includes lamb, beef, and chicken dishes. Locals and tourists alike come to enjoy the spectacular sunset, and enjoy a complimentary "sundowner" shot. $ *Average main: $24 ☒ North Coast Rd., Great Carrot Bay ☎ 284/494–5842 ☽ No lunch.*

$$$$
ECLECTIC
✕**Myett's Garden & Grille.** Partly because it's right on the beach, this bilevel restaurant and bar is hopping day and night for breakfast, lunch, and dinner. Chowder made with fresh conch is the specialty here, and the menu includes vegetarian dishes as well as grilled shrimp, steak, and tuna. There's live entertainment every night in winter. $ *Average main: $32 ☒ Cane Garden Bay ☎ 284/495–9649 ⊕ www.myetts.com.*

$$$
CARIBBEAN
✕**Quito's Gazebo.** This rustic beachside bar and restaurant is owned and operated by island native Quito Rymer, a multitalented recording star who plays and sings solo on Tuesday and Thursday and performs with his reggae band on Friday. The menu is Caribbean, with an emphasis on fresh fish; try the conch fritters or the barbecue chicken. $ *Average main: $26 ☒ Cane Garden Bay ☎ 284/495–4837 ⊕ www.quitosltd.com.*

$$$
ECLECTIC
✕**Sebastian's Seaside Grill.** The waves practically lap at your feet at this beachfront restaurant on Tortola's North Shore. The menu emphasizes seafood—especially lobster, conch, and local fish—but you can also find dishes such as ginger chicken and filet mignon. It's a perfect spot to stop for lunch on your around-the-island tour. Try the grilled dolphinfish (mahimahi) sandwich, served on a soft roll with an onion tartar sauce. Finish off with a cup of Sebastian's coffee, spiked with home-brewed rum. $ *Average main: $29 ☒ Sebastian's on the Beach, North Coast Rd., Apple Bay ☎ 284/495–4212 ⊕ www.sebastiansbvi.com.*

$$$
INTERNATIONAL
✕**1748 Restaurant.** Relax over dinner in this open-air eatery at Long Bay Beach Club. Tables are well spaced, offering enough privacy for intimate conversations. The menu changes daily, but several dishes show up regularly. Start your meal with a seafood cocktail, creamy carrot soup, or a mixed green salad. Entrées include grilled London broil served with a rosemary mushroom sauce, roasted potatoes and vegetables, grilled tuna steak in a spicy cilantro-coconut sauce, and a pesto-marinated grilled vegetable plate. There are always at least five desserts, and they might include Belgian chocolate mousse, strawberry cheesecake, or a fluffy lemon-and-coconut cake. $ *Average main: $28 ☒ Long Bay Beach Club, Long Bay Rd., Long Bay ☎ 284/495–4252 ⊕ www.longbay.com.*

$$$$
ECLECTIC
Fodor's Choice
★
✕**Sugar Mill Restaurant.** Candles gleam and the background music is peaceful in this romantic restaurant inside a 17th-century sugar mill. Well-prepared selections on the à la carte menu, which changes nightly, include some pasta and vegetarian entrées. Lobster bisque with basil croutons and a creamy conch chowder are good starters. Favorite entrées include scallops in champagne sauce, coconut-crusted chicken

6

breast, and Caribbean specialties like Jamaican pulled pork belly. Save room for the Rum Baba for dessert, a doughnut lighter than air served with rum and ice cream. [$] *Average main: $32* ✉ *Sugar Mill Hotel, North Coast Rd., Apple Bay* ☎ *284/495–4355* 🌐 *www.sugarmillhotel.com* 🕑 *No lunch.*

EAST END

$$ ECLECTIC 🍴 **CalaMaya.** Casual fare is what you can find at this waterfront restaurant. You can always order a burger or Caesar salad; the chicken wrap with sweet-and-sour sauce is a tasty alternative. For dinner, try the mahimahi with sautéed vegetables and rice. [$] *Average main: $17* ✉ *Hodge's Creek Marina, Blackburn Hwy., East End* ☎ *284/495–2126.*

WHERE TO STAY

Luxury on Tortola is more about a certain state of mind—serenity, seclusion, gentility, and a bit of Britain in the Caribbean—than about state-of-the-art amenities and fabulous facilities. Some properties, especially the vacation villas, are catching up with current trends, but others seem stuck in the 1980s. But don't let a bit of rust on the screen door or a chip in the paint on the balcony railing mar your appreciation of the ambience. You will likely spend most of your time outside, so the location, size, or price of a hotel should be more of a factor to you than the decor.

Hotels in Road Town don't have beaches, but they do have pools and are within walking distance of restaurants, bars, and shops. Accommodations outside Road Town are relatively isolated, but most face the ocean. Tortola resorts are intimate—only a handful have more than 50 rooms. Guests are treated as more than just room numbers, and many return year after year. This can make booking a room at popular resorts difficult, even off-season, despite the fact that more than half of the island's visitors stay aboard their own or chartered boats.

A few hotels lack air-conditioning, relying instead on ceiling fans to capture the almost constant trade winds. Nights are cool and breezy, even in midsummer, and never reach the temperatures or humidity levels that are common in much of the United States. Note that all accommodations listed here have air-conditioning unless we mention otherwise. Remember that some places may be closed during the peak of hurricane season—August through October—to give their owners a much-needed break.

PRIVATE VILLAS

Renting a villa is growing in popularity. Vacationers like the privacy, the space to spread out, and the opportunity to cook meals. As is true everywhere, the most important thing is location. If you want to be close to the beach, opt for a villa on the North Shore. If you want to dine out in Road Town every night, a villa closer to town may be a better bet. Prices per week during the winter season run from around $2,000 for a one- or two-bedroom villa up to $10,000 for a five-room beachfront villa. Rates in summer are substantially less. Most, but not all, villas accept credit cards.

CLOSE UP

American or British?

Yes, the Union Jack flutters overhead in the tropical breeze, schools operate on the British system, place-names have British spellings, Queen Elizabeth II appoints the governor—and the Queen's picture hangs on many walls. Indeed, residents celebrate the Queen's birthday every June with a public ceremony. You can overhear that charming English accent from a good handful of expats when you're lunching at Road Town restaurants, and you can buy "biscuits"—what Americans call cookies—in the supermarkets.

But you can pay for your lunch and the biscuits with American money, because the U.S. dollar is legal tender here. The unusual circumstance is a matter of geography. The practice started in the mid-20th century, when BVI residents went to work in the nearby USVI. On trips home, they brought their U.S. dollars with them. Soon they abandoned the barter system, and in 1959 the U.S. dollar became the official form of money. Interestingly, the government sells stamps (for use only in the BVI) that often carry pictures of Queen Elizabeth II and other royalty with the monetary value in U.S. dollars and cents.

The American influence continued to grow when Americans began to open businesses in the BVI because they preferred its quiet to the hustle and bustle of St. Thomas. Inevitably, cable and satellite TV's U.S.-based programming, along with Hollywood-made movies, further influenced life in the BVI. And most goods are shipped from St. Thomas in the USVI, meaning you can find more American products than British ones on the supermarket shelves.

VILLA RENTAL CONTACTS

McLaughlin-Anderson Luxury Villas. The St. Thomas–based McLaughlin-Anderson Luxury Villas manages nearly two dozen properties around Tortola. Villas range from one to six bedrooms and come with full kitchens and stellar views. Most have pools. The company can hire a chef and stock your kitchen with groceries. ☎ *340/776–0635, 800/537–6246* 🌐 *www.mclaughlinanderson.com.*

Smiths Gore. Although Smiths Gore has properties all over the island, many are in the Smuggler's Cove area. They range from two to five to bedrooms: all have stellar views, lovely furnishings, and lush landscaping. ☎ *284/494–2446* 🌐 *www.smithsgore.com.*

AROUND ROAD TOWN

$ HOTEL 🏨 **Moorings-Mariner Inn.** If you enjoy the camaraderie of a busy marina, this inn on the edge of Road Town may appeal to you. **Pros:** good dining options; friendly guests; excellent spot to charter boats. **Cons:** busy location; long walk to Road Town; need car to get around. [$] *Rooms from: $250* ✉ *Waterfront Dr., Road Town* ☎ *284/494–2333, 800/535–7289* 🌐 *www.bvimarinerinnhotel.com* 🛏 *32 rooms, 7 suites* 🍴 *No meals.*

$ HOTEL 🏨 **Nanny Cay Hotel.** This quiet oasis is far enough from Road Town to give it a secluded feel but close enough to make shops and restaurants convenient. **Pros:** nearby shops and restaurant; pleasant rooms; marina atmosphere. **Cons:** busy location; need car to get around. [$] *Rooms from: $175* ✉ *Waterfront Dr., Nanny Cay* ☎ *284/494–2512* 🌐 *www.nannycay.com* 🛏 *40 rooms* 🍴 *No meals.*

WEST END

$$ RESORT FAMILY 🏨 **Fort Recovery Beachfront Villas.** This is one of those small but special properties that stands out because of its friendly service and the chance to get to know your fellow guests rather than the poshness of the rooms and the upscale amenities. **Pros:** beautiful beach; spacious units; historic site. **Cons:** need car to get around; isolated location. [$] *Rooms from: $345* ✉ *Waterfront Dr.* ☎ *284/495–4354, 855/349–3355* 🌐 *www.fortrecoverytortola.com* 🛏 *30 suites* 🍴 *No meals.*

NORTH SHORE

$$ RESORT 🏨 **Frenchmans Hotel.** Small and tucked on a beautiful but often overlooked corner of Tortola (technically it's a separate island), Frenchman's Hotel is a quiet, intimate resort with stunning scenic vistas and beautifully landscaped, lush grounds. **Pros:** a tranquil spot. **Cons:** you need a car to get around. [$] *Rooms from: $365* ☎ *284/494–8811* 🌐 *www.frenchmansbvi.com* 🛏 *8 villas* 🍴 *Breakfast.*

$ B&B/INN 🏨 **Heritage Inn.** The gorgeous sea and mountain views are the stars at this small hotel perched on the edge of a cliff. **Pros:** stunning views; fun vibe; room has kitchenette. **Cons:** need car to get around; close to road. [$] *Rooms from: $225* ✉ *North Coast Rd., Great Carrot Bay* ☎ *284/494–5842* 🌐 *heritageinnbvi.com* 🛏 *6 rooms* 🍴 *No meals.*

$$$ RESORT 🏨 **Long Bay Beach Club.** If you want all the amenities like a beach, pool, spa, and tennis courts, in an intimate setting, then this is just for you. **Pros:** beach-club atmosphere; good restaurant on-site; many activities. **Cons:** need car to get around; sometimes curt staff; uphill hike to some rooms. [$] *Rooms from: $395* ✉ *Long Bay Rd., Long Bay* ☎ *284/495–4252, 800/858–4618* 🌐 *www.longbay.com* 🛏 *20 villas, 10 suites, 10 cabanas* 🍴 *Some meals.*

$ HOTEL 🏨 **Myett's.** Tucked away in a beachfront garden, this tiny hotel puts you right in the middle of Cane Garden Bay's busy hustle and bustle. **Pros:** beautiful beach; good restaurant; shops nearby. **Cons:** busy location. [$] *Rooms from: $200* ✉ *Cane Garden Bay* ☎ *284/495–9649* 🌐 *www.myetts.com* 🛏 *6 rooms, 4 cottages, 1 villa* 🍴 *No meals.*

$ HOTEL 🏨 **Sebastian's Seaside Villas.** Sitting on the island's north coast, Sebastian's definitely has a beachy feel, and that's its primary charm. **Pros:** nice beach; good restaurants; beachfront rooms. **Cons:** on busy road; some rooms nicer than others; need car to get around. [$] *Rooms from: $150* ✉ *North Coast Rd., Apple Bay* ☎ *284/495–4212, 800/336–4870* 🌐 *www.sebastiansbvi.com* 🛏 *26 rooms, 9 villas* 🍴 *No meals.*

$$ RESORT Fodor's Choice ★ 🏨 **Sugar Mill Hotel.** Though it's not a sprawling resort, the Sugar Mill Hotel has a Caribbean cachet that's hard to beat, and it's a favorite place to stay on Tortola. **Pros:** lovely rooms; excellent restaurants on-site; nice views. **Cons:** on busy road; small beach; need car to get around. [$] *Rooms from: $350* ✉ *North Coast Rd., Apple Bay* ☎ *284/495–4355, 800/462–8834* 🌐 *www.sugarmillhotel.com* 🛏 *19 rooms, 2 suites, 1 villa, 1 cottage* 🍴 *No meals.*

Surfsong Villa Resort

EAST END

$$$$ **Surfsong Villa Resort.** Nested in lush foliage right at the water's edge,
RESORT   this small resort on Beef Island provides a pleasant respite for vacation-
Fodor's Choice   ers who want a villa atmosphere with some hotel amenities. **Pros:** lovely
★   rooms; beautiful beach; chef on call. **Cons:** need car to get around;
no restaurants nearby. $ *Rooms from: $600* ⊠ *Off Beef Island Rd.*
☎ *284/495–1864* ⊕ *www.surfsong.net* ✇ *1 suite, 7 villas* ❍❘ *No meals;
Some meals* ↰ *No children under 8.*

NIGHTLIFE AND PERFORMING ARTS

NIGHTLIFE

Like any other good sailing destination, Tortola has watering holes that
are popular with salty and not-so-salty dogs. Many offer entertainment; check the weekly *Limin' Times* (⊕ *www.limin-times.com*) for
schedules and up-to-date information. Bands change like the weather,
and what's hot today can be old news tomorrow. The local beverage is
the Painkiller, an innocent-tasting mixture of fruit juices and rums. It
goes down smoothly but packs quite a punch, so give yourself time to
recover before you order another.

Bomba's Surfside Shack. By day, you can see that Bomba's, which is covered with everything from crepe-paper leis to ancient license plates to
spicy graffiti, looks like a pile of junk; by night it's one of Tortola's
liveliest spots. There's a fish fry and a live band every Wednesday and
Sunday. People flock here from all over on the full moon, when bands
play all night long. ⊠ *North Coast Rd., Apple Bay* ☎ *284/495–4148.*

Myett's. Local bands play at this popular spot, which has live music during happy hour. There's usually a lively dance crowd. ⊠ *Cane Garden Bay* ☎ *284/495–9649* ⊕ *www.myetts.com.*

The Pub. At this popular watering hole, there's a happy hour from 5 to 7 every day and live music on Thursday and Friday. ⊠ *Waterfront St., Road Town* ☎ *284/494–2608.*

Pusser's Road Town Pub. Courage is what people are seeking here—John Courage beer by the pint. Or try Pusser's famous mixed drink, called the Painkiller, and snack on the excellent pizza. ⊠ *Waterfront St., Road Town* ☎ *284/494–3897* ⊕ *www.pussers.com.*

Quito's Gazebo. BVI recording star Quito Rhymer sings island ballads and love songs at his rustic beachside bar–restaurant. Solo shows are on Tuesday and Thursday at 8:30; on Friday at 9:30 Quito performs with his band. ⊠ *Cane Garden Bay* ☎ *284/495–4837* ⊕ *www.quitosltd.com.*

PERFORMING ARTS

Performing Arts Series. Musicians from around the world take to the stage during the island's Performing Arts Series, held annually October through May. Past artists have included Latin jazz artist Tito Puente Jr., gospel singer Kim Burrell, and pianist Richard Ormond. ⊠ *H. Lavity Stoutt Community College, Blackburn Hwy., Paraquita Bay* ☎ *284/494–4994* ⊕ *www.hlscc.edu.vg.*

SHOPPING

AREAS AND MARKETS

Many shops and boutiques are clustered along and just off Road Town's **Main Street.** You can shop in Road Town's **Wickham's Cay I** adjacent to the marina. The **Crafts Alive Market** on the Road Town waterfront is a collection of colorful West Indian–style buildings with shops that carry items made in the BVI. You might find pretty baskets or interesting pottery or perhaps a bottle of home-brewed hot sauce. A growing number of art and clothing stores are opening at **Soper's Hole** in West End.

ART

Allamanda Gallery. Photography by the gallery's owner, Amanda Baker, as well as books, gifts, and cards are on display and available to purchase. ⊠ *124 Main St., Road Town* ☎ *284/494–6680* ⊕ *www.virgin portraits.com.*

CLOTHES AND TEXTILES

Arawak. This boutique carries batik sundresses, sportswear, and resort wear for men and women. There's also a selection of children's clothing. ⊠ *Nanny Cay Marina, Nanny Cay* ☎ *284/494–3983* ⊕ *www.arawakvi.com.*

Latitude 18°. This store sells Maui Jim, Ray-Ban, and Oakley sunglasses; Freestyle watches; and a fine collection of beach towels, sandals, Crocs, sundresses, and sarongs. ⊠ *Main St., Road Town* ☎ *284/494–6196* ⊕ *www.latitude18.com.*

Pusser's Company Store. The Road Town Pusser's sells nautical memorabilia, ship models, and marine paintings. There's also an entire line

Most of Tortola's shops are in Road Town.

of clothing for both men and women, handsome decorator bottles of Pusser's rum, and gift items bearing the Pusser's logo. ✉ *Main St. at Waterfront Rd., Road Town* ☏ *284/494–2467* ⊕ *www.pussers.com.*

Zenaida's of West End. Vivian Jenik Helm travels through South America, Africa, and India in search of batiks, hand-painted and hand-blocked fabrics, and interesting weaves that can be made into *pareus* (women's wraps) or wall hangings. The shop also sells unusual bags, belts, sarongs, scarves, and ethnic jewelry. ✉ *Soper's Hole Marina* ☏ *284/495–4867.*

FOOD

Ample Hamper. Head here to stock your yacht or rental villa—or have the staff do it for you. It carries an outstanding collection of cheeses, wines, fresh fruits, and canned goods from the United Kingdom and the United States. ✉ *Inner Harbour Marina, Road Town* ☏ *284/494–2494* ⊕ *www.amplehamper.com.*

Best of British. This boutique has lots of nifty British food you won't find elsewhere. Shop here for Marmite, Vegemite, shortbread, frozen meat pies, and delightful Christmas "crackers" filled with surprises. ✉ *Wickham's Cay I, Road Town* ☏ *284/494–3462.*

RiteWay. This store is akin to a mainland market with fresh produce, deli, prepared foods, meats, bakery, and all the grocery items you'll need. RiteWay will stock villas and yachts. The Flemington Street location is convenience store–like in size and selection. ✉ *Waterfront Dr. at Pasea Estate, Road Town* ☏ *284/494–2263* ⊕ *www.rtwbvi.com.*

GIFTS

Sunny Caribbee. In a brightly painted West Indian house, this store packages its own herbs, teas, coffees, vinegars, hot sauces, soaps, skin and suntan lotions, and exotic concoctions—Arawak Love Potion and Island Hangover Cure, for example. There's another location at Soper's Hole Marina. ⊠ *119 Main St., Road Town* ☎ *284/494–2178* ⊕ *www. sunnycaribbee.com.*

JEWELRY

Samarkand. The charming jewelry sold here includes gold-and-silver pendants, earrings, bracelets, and pins, many with island themes such as seashells, lizards, pelicans, and palm trees. There are also reproduction Spanish pieces of eight (old Spanish coins) similar to those found on sunken galleons, and those including local Virgin Islands green jasper. ⊠ *Main St., Road Town* ☎ *284/494–6415* ⊗ *Closed Sun.*

SPORTS AND THE OUTDOORS

DIVING AND SNORKELING

Clear waters and numerous reefs afford some wonderful opportunities for underwater exploration. In some spots visibility reaches 100 feet, but colorful reefs teeming with fish are often just a few feet below the sea surface. The BVI's system of marine parks means the underwater life visible through your mask will stay protected.

There are several popular dive spots around the islands. **Alice in Wonderland** is a deep dive south of Ginger Island with a wall that slopes gently from 15 feet to 100 feet. It's an area overrun with huge mushroom-shape coral, hence its name. Crabs, lobsters, and shimmering fan corals make their homes in the tunnels, ledges, and overhangs of **Blonde Rock,** a pinnacle that goes from 15 feet below the surface to 60 feet deep. It's between Dead Chest and Salt Island. When the currents aren't too strong, **Brewers Bay Pinnacle** (20 to 90 feet down) teems with sea life. At the **Indians,** near Pelican Island, colorful coral decorates canyons and grottoes created by four large, jagged pinnacles that rise 50 feet from the ocean floor. The **Painted Walls** is a shallow dive site where coral and sponges create a kaleidoscope of colors on the walls of four long gullies. It's northeast of Dead Chest.

The *Chikuzen,* sunk northwest of Brewers Bay in 1981, is a 246-foot vessel in 75 feet of water; it's home to thousands of fish, colorful corals, and big rays. In 1867 the **RMS *Rhone,*** a 310-foot royal mail steamer, split in two when it sank in a devastating hurricane. It's so well preserved that it was used as an underwater prop in the 1977 movie *The Deep.* You can see the crow's nest and bowsprit, the cargo hold in the bow, and the engine and enormous propeller shaft in the stern. Its four parts are at various depths, from 30 to 80 feet. Get yourself some snorkeling gear and hop aboard a dive boat to this wreck near Salt Island (across the channel from Road Town). Every dive outfit in the BVI runs scuba and snorkel tours to this part of the BVI National Parks Trust; if you have time for only one trip, make it this one. Rates start at around $85 for a one-tank dive and $130 for a two-tank dive.

Your hotel probably has a dive company right on the premises. If not, the staff can recommend one nearby. Using your hotel's dive company makes a trip to the offshore dive and snorkel sites a breeze. Just stroll down to the dock and hop aboard. All dive companies are certified by PADI, the Professional Association of Diving Instructors, which ensures that your instructors are qualified to safely take vacationers diving. The boats are also inspected to make sure they're seaworthy. If you've never dived, try a short introductory dive, often called a resort course, which teaches you enough to get you underwater. In the unlikely event you get a case of the bends, a condition that can happen when you rise to the surface too fast, your dive team will take you to the decompression chamber at Roy L. Schneider Regional Medical Center in nearby St. Thomas.

Blue Water Divers. If you're chartering a sailboat, Blue Waters Divers will meet yours at Peter, Salt, Norman, or Cooper Island for a rendezvous dive. The company teaches resort, open-water, rescue, and advanced diving courses, and also makes daily dive trips. Rates include all equipment as well as instruction. Reserve two days in advance. ⊠ *Nanny Cay Marina, Nanny Cay* ☎ *284/494–2847* ⊕ *www.bluewaterdiversbvi. com* ⊠ *Soper's Hole Marina, Soper's Hole* ☎ *284/495–1200* ⊕ *www. bluewaterdiversbvi.com.*

FISHING

Most of the boats that take you deep-sea fishing for blue marlin, white marlin, wahoo, tuna, and dolphinfish (mahimahi) leave from nearby St. Thomas, but local anglers like to fish the shallower water for bonefish. A half day for two people runs about $480, a full day around $890. Wading trips are $345.

Caribbean Fly Fishing. ⊠ *Nanny Cay Marina, Nanny Cay* ☎ *284/494– 4797, 284/499–1590* ⊕ *www.caribflyfishing.com.*

SAILING

Fodor's Choice
★

The BVI are among the world's most popular sailing destinations. They're clustered together and surrounded by calm waters, so it's fairly easy to sail from one anchorage to the next. Most of the Caribbean's biggest sailboat charter companies have operations in Tortola. If you know how to sail, you can charter a bareboat (perhaps for your entire vacation); if you're unschooled, you can hire a boat with a captain. Prices vary depending on the type and size of the boat you wish to charter. In season, a weekly charter runs from $2,500 to $35,000 or more. Book early to make sure you get the boat that fits you best. Most of Tortola's marinas have hotels, which give you a convenient place to spend the nights before and after your charter.

If a day sail to some secluded anchorage is more your cup of tea, the BVI have numerous boats of various sizes and styles that leave from many points around Tortola. Prices start at around $90 per person for a full-day sail, including lunch and snorkeling equipment.

Aristocat Charters. This company's 48-foot catamarans, *Aristocat* and *Lionheart*, set sail daily to Jost Van Dyke, Norman Island, and other small islands. *Aristocat* sails out of Soper's Hole (Frenchman's Cay),

West End, and *Lionheart* sails out of Village Cay Marina in Road Town. ☎ 284/499–1249 ⊕ *www.aristocatcharters.com.*

BVI Yacht Charters. The 31- to 52-foot sailboats for charter here come with or without a captain and crew. ⊠ *Port Purcell, Road Town* ☎ 284/494–4289, 888/615–4006 ⊕ *www.bviyachtcharters.com.*

The Catamaran Company. The catamarans here come with or without a captain. ⊠ *Maya Cove Marina, Fat Hog's Bay* ☎ 284/494–6661, 800/262–0308 ⊕ *www.catamarans.com.*

The Moorings. One of the world's best bareboat operations, the Moorings has a large fleet of both monohulls and catamarans. Hire a captain or sail the boat yourself. ⊠ *Wickham's Cay II, Road Town* ☎ 800/535–7289 ⊕ *www.moorings.com.*

Regency Yacht Vacations. If you prefer a powerboat, call Regency Yacht Vacations. It handles captain and full-crew sail and powerboat charters. ⊠ *Wickham's Cay I, Road Town* ☎ 284/495–1970, 800/524–7676 ⊕ *www.regencyvacations.com.*

Sunsail. A full fleet of boats to charter with or without a captain is available here. ⊠ *Wickham's Cay II, Road Town* ☎ 888/350–3568, 800/327–2276 ⊕ *www.sunsail.com.*

Voyage Charters. Voyage has a variety of sailboats for charter, with or without a captain and crew. ⊠ *Soper's Hole Marina* ☎ 284/494–0740, 888/869–2436 ⊕ *www.voyagecharters.com.*

SURFING

Surfing is big on Tortola's north shore, particularly when the winter swells come into Josiah's and Apple bays. Rent surfboards starting at $65 for a full day.

HIHO. Lots of good surfboards and stand-up paddleboards are available for rent as well as for sale. The staff will give you advice on the best spots to put in your board. ⊠ *Trellis Bay, Trellis Bay* ☎ 284/494–7694 ⊕ *www.go-hiho.com.*

WINDSURFING

Steady trade winds make windsurfing a breeze. Three of the best spots for sailboarding are Nanny Cay, Slaney Point, and Trellis Bay on Beef Island. Rates for sailboards start at about $40 an hour or $120 for a two-hour lesson.

Island Surf and Sail. This company rents equipment and offers private and group lessons. ⊠ *Frenchman's Cay* ☎ 284/494–0123 ⊕ *www. bviwatertoys.com.*

SIDE TRIPS FROM TORTOLA

There are several islands that make great side trips from Tortola, including lovely Marina Cay and tony Peter Island. Both have great accommodations, so you might want to spend the night.

MARINA CAY

Beautiful little Marina Cay is in Trellis Bay, not far from Beef Island. Sometimes you can see it and its large J-shape coral reefs—a most dramatic sight—from the air soon after takeoff from the airport on Beef Island. Covering 8 acres, this islet is considered small even by BVI standards. On it there's a restaurant, Pusser's Store, and a six-unit hotel. Ferry service is free from the dock on Beef Island.

WHERE TO STAY

$ HOTEL **Pusser's Marina Cay Hotel and Restaurant.** If getting away from it all is your priority, this may be the place for you, because there's nothing to do on this beach-rimmed island other than swim, snorkel, and soak up the sun—there's not even a TV to distract you. **Pros:** lots of character; beautiful beaches; interesting guests. **Cons:** older property; ferry needed to get here. *Rooms from: $175 West side of Marina Cay 284/494–2174 www.pussers.com 4 rooms, 2 2-bedroom villas Breakfast.*

$$$$ RESORT Fodor's Choice ★ **Scrub Island Resort, Spa and Marina.** Part of Marriott's Autograph Collection, this swanky resort is located on a 250-acre island near Tortola's Beef Island Airport. **Pros:** new property; lots of activities. **Cons:** need ferry to get there; expensive. *Rooms from: $760 877/890–7444, 284/394–3440 www.scrubisland.com 52 rooms, 7 villas No meals.*

PETER ISLAND

Although Peter Island is home to the resort of the same name, it's also a popular anchorage for charter boaters and a destination for Tortola vacationers. The scheduled ferry trip from Peter Island's shore-side base outside Road Town runs $15 round-trip for nonguests. The island is lush, with forested hillsides sloping seaward to meet white sandy beaches. There are no roads other than those at the resort, and there's nothing to do but relax at the lovely beach set aside for day-trippers. You're welcome to dine at the resort's restaurants.

WHERE TO STAY

$$$$ RESORT Fodor's Choice ★ **Peter Island Resort & Spa.** Total pampering and prices to match are the ticket at this luxury resort. **Pros:** lovely rooms; nice beach. **Cons:** need ferry to get here; pricey rates. *Rooms from: $900 284/495–2000, 800/346–4451 www.peterisland.com 52 rooms, 3 villas Some meals.*

VIRGIN GORDA

Virgin Gorda, or "Fat Virgin," received its name from Christopher Columbus. The explorer envisioned the island as a pregnant woman in a languid recline, with Gorda Peak being her big belly and the boulders of The Baths her toes. Different in topography from Tortola, with its arid landscape covered with scrub brush and cactus, Virgin Gorda has a slower pace of life, too. Goats and cattle own the right-of-way, and the unpretentious friendliness of the people is winning.

The Baths

EXPLORING

One of the most efficient ways to see Virgin Gorda is by sailboat. There are few roads, and most byways don't follow the scalloped shoreline. The main route sticks resolutely to the center of the island, linking The Baths on the southern tip with Gun Creek and Leverick Bay at North Sound. The craggy coast, cut through with grottoes and fringed by palms and boulders, has a primitive beauty. If you drive, you can hit all the sights in one day. The best plan is to explore the area near your hotel (either Spanish Town or North Sound) first, then take a day to drive to the other end. Stop to climb Gorda Peak, which is in the island's center. There are few signs, so come prepared with a map.

THE VALLEY

TOP ATTRACTIONS

FAMILY
Fodor's Choice
★

The Baths National Park. At Virgin Gorda's most celebrated sight, giant boulders are scattered about the beach and in the water. Some are almost as large as houses and form remarkable grottoes. Climb between these rocks to swim in the many placid pools. Early morning and late afternoon are the best times to visit if you want to avoid crowds. If it's privacy you crave, follow the shore northward to quieter bays— Spring Bay, the Crawl, Little Trunk, and Valley Trunk—or head south to Devil's Bay. ⊠ *Off Tower Rd., Spanish Town* ☎ *284/852–3650* ⊕ *www. bvinationalparkstrust.org* ✉ *$3* ☉ *Daily dawn–dusk.*

WORTH NOTING

Copper Mine Point. A tall stone shaft silhouetted against the sky and a small stone structure that overlooks the sea are part of what was once a copper mine, now in ruins. Established 400 years ago, it was worked first by the Spanish, then by the English, until the early 20th century. The route is not well marked, so turn inland near LSL Restaurant and look for the hard-to-see sign pointing the way. ⊠ *Copper Mine Rd., Spanish Town* ⊕ *www.bvinpt.org* ▧ *Free.*

Spanish Town. Virgin Gorda's peaceful main settlement, on the island's southern wing, is so tiny that it barely qualifies as a town at all. Also known as The Valley, Spanish Town has a marina, some shops, and a couple of car-rental agencies. Just north of town is the ferry slip. At the Virgin Gorda Yacht Harbour you can stroll along the dock and do a little shopping. ⊠ *Spanish Town.*

NORTHWEST SHORE

Virgin Gorda Peak National Park. There are two trails at this 265-acre park, which contains the island's highest point, at 1,359 feet. Signs on North Sound Road mark both entrances. It's about a 15-minute hike from either entrance up to a small clearing, where you can climb a ladder to the platform of a wooden observation tower to see a spectacular 360-degree view. ⊠ *North Sound Rd., Gorda Peak* ⊕ *www.bvinpt.org* ▧ *Free.*

BEACHES

THE VALLEY

The Baths Beach. This stunning maze of huge granite boulders extending into the sea is usually crowded midday with day-trippers. The snorkeling is good, and you're likely to see a wide variety of fish, but watch out for dinghies coming ashore from the numerous sailboats anchored offshore. Public bathrooms and a handful of bars and shops are close to the water and at the start of the path that leads to the beach. Lockers are available to keep belongings safe. **Amenities:** food and drink; parking; toilets. **Best for:** snorkeling; swimming. ⊠ *Tower Rd., about 1 mile (1½ km) west of Spanish Town ferry dock, Spanish Town* ☎ *284/852–3650* ⊕ *www.bvinpt.org* ▧ *$3* ☉ *Daily dawn–dusk.*

Spring Bay Beach. This national-park beach gets much less traffic than the nearby Baths, and has the similarly large, imposing boulders that create interesting grottoes for swimming. It also has no admission fee, unlike the more popular Baths. The snorkeling is excellent, and the grounds include swings and picnic tables. Guavaberry Spring Bay Vacation has villas and cottages right near the beach. **Amenities:** none. **Best for:** snorkeling; swimming. ⊠ *Spanish Town* ☎ *284/852–3650* ⊕ *www.bvinpt.org* ▧ *Free* ☉ *Daily dawn–dusk.*

NORTHWEST SHORE

Fallen Jerusalem Island and Dog Islands. You can easily reach these quaintly named islands by boat, which you can rent in either Tortola or Virgin Gorda. They're all part of the National Parks Trust of the Virgin Islands, and their seductive beaches and unparalleled snorkeling display the

Virgin Gorda

Cockroach Island

George Dog

Dog Islands

West Dog

Great Dog

Sir Francis Drake Channel

← TO TORTOLA

Mountain Pt.

Nail Bay Beach **6**

Virgin Gorda Peak National Park

Mango Bay

Mahoe Bay **5**

Pond Bay

Savannah Bay Beach

Little Dix Bay

Colison Pt. **3 9**

Handsome Bay **4 8**

St. Thomas Bay

Virgin Gorda Airport

Spanish Town **7**

Fort Pt.

2 4 **5**

6

The Valley

Copper Mine Bay

1

Spring Bay Beach **1**

Devil's Bay **The Baths Beach** **2**

Crook's Bay

◆ **Copper Mine Point** **3**

The Baths National Park

Stoney Bay

Fallen Jerusalem

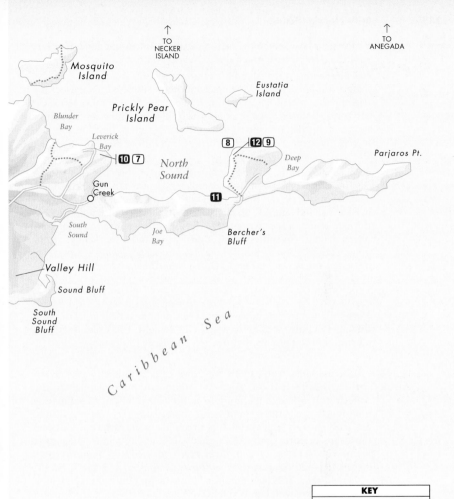

↑
TO
NECKER
ISLAND

↑
TO
ANEGADA

Mosquito Island

Prickly Pear Island

Eustatia Island

Blunder Bay

Leverick Bay

[10] [7]

North Sound

[8] [12] [9]

Deep Bay

Parjaros Pt.

Gun Creek

[11]

South Sound

Joe Bay

Bercher's Bluff

Valley Hill

Sound Bluff

South Sound Bluff

C a r i b b e a n   S e a

KEY	
⚓	*Beaches*
🚢	*Ferry*
🚢	*Cruise Ship Terminal*
1	*Restaurants*
[1]	*Hotels*
......	*Trail*

0 ————————— 1 mi

0 ————————— 1 km

BVI at their beachcombing, hedonistic best. **Amenities:** none. **Best for:** exploring; solitude; snorkeling. 🌐 *www.bvinpt.org* 🎟 *Free.*

Nail Bay Beach. At the island's north tip, the three beaches at Nail Bay Resort are ideal for snorkeling. Mountain Trunk Bay is perfect for beginners, and Nail Bay and Long Bay beaches have coral caverns just offshore. The resort has a restaurant, which is an uphill walk but perfect for beach breaks. **Amenities:** food and drink; toilets. **Best for:** snorkeling; swimming. ✉ *Nail Bay Resort, off Plum Tree Bay Rd., Nail Bay* 🎟 *Free* 🕓 *Daily dawn–dusk.*

Savannah Bay Beach. This is a wonderfully private beach close to Spanish Town. It may not always be completely deserted, but you can find a spot to yourself on this long stretch of soft, white sand. Bring your own mask, fins, and snorkel, as there are no facilities. Villas are available through rental property agencies. The view from above is a photographer's delight. **Amenities:** none. **Best for:** solitude; snorkeling; swimming. ✉ *Off N. Sound Rd., ¾ mile (1¼ km) east of Spanish Town ferry dock, Savannah Bay* 🎟 *Free* 🕓 *Daily dawn–dusk.*

WHERE TO EAT

Most folks opt to have dinner somewhere at or near their hotel to avoid driving on Virgin Gorda's twisting roads at night. The Valley does have a handful of restaurants if you're sleeping close to town.

THE VALLEY

$$ ECLECTIC 🍴 **Bath and Turtle.** You can sit back and relax at this informal tavern with a friendly staff (or enjoy the outdoor Rendezvous Bar on the waterfront), although the noise from the television can sometimes be a bit much. Well-stuffed sandwiches, homemade pizzas, pasta dishes, and daily specials such as conch soup round out the casual menu. Local musicians perform many Wednesday and Sunday nights. [$] *Average main: $19* ✉ *Virgin Gorda Yacht Harbour, Lee Rd., Spanish Town* ☎ *284/495–5239* 🌐 *www.bathandturtle.com.*

$$$$ ECLECTIC 🍴 **Chez Bamboo.** This pleasant little hideaway isn't difficult to find; look for the building with bamboo fencing. Candles in the dining room and on the patio help make this a mellow place where you can enjoy a bowl of lobster bisque, something from the tapas menu, or one of the specialties such as lobster curry. For dessert, try the chocolate cake or crème brûlée. Stop by Friday night for live music. [$] *Average main: $32* ✉ *Lee Rd., Spanish Town* ☎ *284/495–5752* 🌐 *www.chezbamboo.com.*

$$$$ ECLECTIC 🍴 **Fischer's Cove Restaurant.** Dine seaside at this alfresco restaurant that's open to the breezes. If pumpkin soup is on the menu, give it a try for a true taste of the Caribbean. Although you can get burgers and salads at lunch, local fish (whatever is available) and *fungi* (a cornmeal-based side dish) are tasty alternatives. For dinner, try the Caribbean lobster or grilled mahimahi with lemon and garlic. [$] *Average main: $36* ✉ *Lee Rd., Spanish Town* ☎ *284/495–5252* 🌐 *www.fischerscove.com.*

$$$$ INTERNATIONAL 🍴 **Little Dix Bay Pavilion.** For an elegant evening, you can't do better than this—the candlelight in the open-air pavilion is enchanting, the always-changing menu sophisticated, the service attentive. Superbly prepared seafood, meat, and vegetarian entrées draw locals and visitors

alike. Favorites include a Cajun pork loin with mango salsa and scallion potatoes, and mahimahi with warm chorizo and chickpea salad served with a zucchini-and-tomato chutney. The Monday evening buffet shines. $ *Average main: $38* ⊠ *Little Dix Bay Resort, Off Little Rd., Spanish Town* ☎ *284/495–5555* ⊕ *www.littledixbay.com* ⚓ *Reservations essential.*

$$
ECLECTIC
✕ **LSL Bake Shop & Restaurant.** Along the road to The Baths, this small restaurant with pedestrian decor is a local favorite. You can always find fresh fish on the menu, but folks with a taste for other dishes won't be disappointed. Try the pork tenderloin pesto with herb potatoes and a peppercorn sauce, or the banana curry shrimp with a coconut milk sauce. $ *Average main: $16* ⊠ *Tower Rd., Spanish Town* ☎ *284/495–5151.*

$$
ECLECTIC
✕ **Mine Shaft Café.** Perched on a hilltop that offers a view of spectacular sunsets, this restaurant near Copper Mine Point serves simple, well-prepared food, including grilled fish, steaks, and baby back ribs. Tuesday night features an all-you-can-eat Caribbean-style barbecue. The monthly full-moon parties draw a big local crowd. $ *Average main: $20* ⊠ *Near Copper Mine Point, Spanish Town* ☎ *284/495–5260.*

$$$$
ITALIAN
✕ **The Rock Café.** Good Italian cuisine and seafood is served among the waterfalls and giant boulders that form the famous Baths. For dinner at this open-air eatery, feast on saffron lobster pasta or fresh red snapper with a creamy risotto. For dessert, don't miss the chocolate mousse. $ *Average main: $39* ⊠ *Tower Rd., Spanish Town* ☎ *284/495–5482* ⊕ *www.therockcafebvi.com* ⊘ *No lunch.*

$$$
ECLECTIC
FAMILY
✕ **Top of the Baths.** At the entrance to The Baths, this popular restaurant has tables on an outdoor terrace or in an open-air pavilion; all have stunning views of the Sir Francis Drake Channel. The restaurant starts serving at 8 am for breakfast; for lunch, hamburgers, coconut chicken sandwiches, and fish-and-chips are among the offerings. Sushi is served 11 am to 3 pm every day except Sunday. For dessert, the key lime pie is excellent. The Sunday barbecue, served from noon until 3 pm, is an island event. $ *Average main: $23* ⊠ *Spanish Town* ☎ *284/495–5497* ⊕ *www.topofthebaths.com.*

$$$
ECLECTIC
✕ **The Village Cafe & Restaurant.** Meals are served poolside under the shade of umbrellas at this casual eatery. The lunch menu includes salads, wraps, and burgers, but the lobster-and-crab salad (yes, it contains both!) is a must-have. Friday and Saturday the flavors of jerk seasonings rule with a special menu featuring jerk chicken, fish, and pork. $ *Average main: $27* ⊠ *Virgin Gorda Village, North Sound Rd., Spanish Town* ☎ *284/495–5350* ⊕ *www.virgingordavillage.com* ⊘ *Closed Mon.*

NORTH SOUND

$$$$
ECLECTIC
✕ **The Clubhouse.** The Bitter End Yacht Club's open-air waterfront restaurant is a favorite rendezvous for sailors and their guests, so it's busy day and night. You can find lavish buffets for breakfast, lunch, and dinner, as well as an à la carte menu. Dinner selections include grilled mahimahi or tuna, local lobster, and porterhouse steak, as well as vegetarian dishes. $ *Average main: $32* ⊠ *Bitter End Yacht Club, North Sound* ☎ *284/494–2745* ⊕ *www.beyc.com* ⚓ *Reservations essential.*

6

$$$
ECLECTIC
FAMILY
✕ **Fat Virgin's Café.** This casual beachfront eatery offers a straightforward menu of baby back ribs, chicken roti, vegetable pasta, grouper sandwiches, and fresh fish specials for lunch and dinner. You can also find a good selection of Caribbean beer. $ *Average main: $23* ⊠ *Biras Creek, North Sound* ☎ *284/495–7052* ⊕ *www.fatvirgin.com.*

$$$
ECLECTIC
✕ **Restaurant at Leverick Bay.** The laid-back menu at this beach restaurant draws cruise ship passengers on tour as well as hotel guests and locals. The menu includes burgers, pizza, roti, chili, and fish-and-chips for lunch. Upstairs, there's an upscale restaurant that serves dinner with dishes that feature wild salmon and Anegada lobster. $ *Average main: $25* ⊠ *Leverick Bay Resort & Marina, Leverick Bay Rd., Leverick Bay* ☎ *284/340–3005* ⊕ *www.leverickrestaurant.com.*

WHERE TO STAY

Villas are scattered all over Virgin Gorda, but hotels are centered in and around The Valley, Nail Bay, and in the North Sound area. Except for Leverick Bay Resort, which is around the point from North Sound, all hotels in North Sound are reached only by ferry.

PRIVATE VILLAS

Those craving seclusion would do well at a villa. Most have full kitchens and maid service. Prices per week in winter run from around $2,000 for a one- or two-bedroom villa up to $10,000 for a five-room beachfront villa. Rates in summer are substantially less. On Virgin Gorda a villa in the North Sound area means you can pretty much stay put at night unless you want to make the drive on its narrow roads. If you opt for a spot near The Baths, it's an easier drive to town.

VILLA RENTAL AGENTS

McLaughlin-Anderson Luxury Villas. The St. Thomas–based McLaughlin-Anderson Luxury Villas represents about 15 properties all over Virgin Gorda. Villas range in size from one bedrooms to five bedrooms, and come with full kitchens, pools, stellar views, and other amenities. The company can hire a chef and stock your kitchen with groceries. A seven-night minimum is required during the winter season. ☎ *340/776–0635, 800/537–6246* ⊕ *www.mclaughlinanderson.com.*

Villas Virgin Gorda. This management company's seven properties stretch from The Baths to the Nail Bay area. Several budget properties are included among the pricier offerings. Most houses have private pools, and a few are right on the beach. A sister company at the same number, Tropical Nannies, provides babysitting services. ☎ *284/495–6493* ⊕ *www.villasvirgingorda.com.*

Virgin Gorda Villa Rentals. This company's 30 properties are all near Leverick Bay Resort and Mahoe Bay, so they are perfect for those who want to be close to activities. Many of the accommodations—from studios to six or more bedrooms—have private swimming pools and air-conditioning, at least in the bedrooms. All have full kitchens, are well maintained, and have spectacular views. ⊠ *Mahoe Bay* ☎ *284/495–7421, 800/848–7081* ⊕ *www.virgingordabvi.com.*

THE VALLEY

$
RESORT

Fischer's Cove Beach Hotel. The rooms are modest, the furniture is discount-store-style, and the walls are thin, but you can't beat the location right on the beach and within walking distance of Spanish Town's shops and restaurants. **Pros:** beachfront location; budget price; good restaurant. **Cons:** very basic units; thin walls; no air-conditioning in some rooms. $ *Rooms from: $165* ✉ *Lee Rd., Spanish Town* ☎ *284/495–5252* ⊕ *www.fischerscove.com* ↗ *12 rooms, 8 cottages* ᠐| *No meals.*

$$
RENTAL

Guavaberry Spring Bay Vacation Homes. Rambling back from the beach, these hexagonal one- and two-bedroom villas give you all the comforts of home—and that striking boulder-fringed beach is just minutes away. **Pros:** short walk to The Baths (and excellent snorkeling); easy drive to town; great beaches nearby. **Cons:** few amenities; older property; basic decor. $ *Rooms from: $280* ✉ *Tower Rd., Spanish Town* ☎ *284/495–5227* ⊕ *www.guavaberryspringbay.com* ▭ *No credit cards* ↗ *12 1-bedroom units, 6 2-bedroom units, 1 3-bedroom unit, 16 villas* ᠐| *No meals.*

$$$$
RESORT
FAMILY
Fodor'sChoice
★

Rosewood Little Dix Bay. This laid-back luxury resort offers a gorgeous crescent of sand, plenty of activities, and good restaurants. **Pros:** convenient location; lovely grounds; near many restaurants. **Cons:** expensive; very spread out; insular though not isolated. $ *Rooms from: $780* ✉ *Off Little Rd., Spanish Town* ☎ *284/495–5555* ⊕ *www.littledixbay. com* ↗ *78 rooms, 20 suites, 7 villas* ᠐| *No meals.*

$$
RENTAL

Virgin Gorda Village. All the condos in this upscale complex a few minutes' drive from Spanish Town have at least partial ocean views. **Pros:** close to Spanish Town; lovely pool; recently built units. **Cons:** no beach; on a busy street; some noisy roosters nearby. $ *Rooms from: $280* ✉ *North Sound Rd.* ☎ *284/495–5544* ⊕ *www.virgingordavillage. com* ↗ *30 condos* ᠐| *No meals.*

NORTHWEST SHORE

$$$
RENTAL

Mango Bay Resort. Sitting seaside on Virgin Gorda's north coast, this collection of contemporary condos and villas will make you feel right at home. **Pros:** nice beach; lively location; easy drive to restaurants. **Cons:** drab decor; some units have lackluster views; need car to get around. $ *Rooms from: $445* ✉ *Plum Tree Bay Rd., Pond Bay* ☎ *284/495–5672* ⊕ *www.mangobayresort.com* ↗ *17 condos, 5 villas* ᠐| *No meals.*

$$
RESORT

Nail Bay Resort. On a hill above the coast, this beachfront resort offers a wide selection of rooms and suites. **Pros:** full kitchens; lovely beach; close to town. **Cons:** busy neighborhood; bit of a drive from main road; uphill walk from beach. $ *Rooms from: $375* ✉ *Off Nail Bay Rd., Nail Bay* ☎ *284/494–8000, 800/871–3551* ⊕ *www.nailbay.com* ↗ *4 rooms, 4 suites, 2 apartments, 7 villas* ᠐| *No meals.*

NORTH SOUND

$$$$
RESORT
FAMILY
Fodor'sChoice
★

Bitter End Yacht Club. Sailing's the thing at this busy hotel and marina in the nautically inclined North Sound, and the use of everything from small sailboats to kayaks to windsurfers is included in the price. **Pros:** lots of water sports; good diving opportunities; friendly guests. **Cons:** expensive rates; isolated; lots of stairs. $ *Rooms from: $675*

6

✉ *North Sound* ☎ *284/494–2746, 800/872–2392* ⊕ *www.beyc.com* ⇴ *85 rooms* ♚ *All-inclusive.*

$ ⊞ **Leverick Bay Resort and Marina.**
RESORT With its colorful buildings and bustling marina, Leverick Bay is a good choice for visitors who want easy access to water-sports activities. **Pros:** fun location; good restaurant; small grocery store. **Cons:** small beach; no laundry in units; 15-minute drive to town. $ *Rooms from: $149* ✉ *Off Leverick Bay Rd., Leverick Bay* ☎ *284/495–7421, 800/848–7081* ⊕ *www.leverickbay. com* ⇴ *13 rooms, 4 apartments* ♚ *No meals.*

$$ ⊞ **Saba Rock Resort.** Reachable only by a free ferry or by private yacht,
RESORT this resort on its own tiny cay is perfect for folks who want to mix and mingle with the sailors who drop anchor for the night. **Pros:** party atmosphere; convenient transportation; good diving nearby. **Cons:** tiny beach; isolated location; on a very small island. $ *Rooms from: $310* ✉ *North Sound* ☎ *284/495–7711, 284/495–9966* ⊕ *www.sabarock. com* ⇴ *7 1-bedroom suites, 1 2-bedroom suites* ♚ *Breakfast.*

NIGHTLIFE

Pick up a free copy of the *Limin' Times* (⊕ *www.limin-times.com*)—available at most resorts and restaurants—for the most current local entertainment schedule.

Bath and Turtle. During high season, the Bath and Turtle is one of the liveliest spots on Virgin Gorda, hosting island bands Wednesday and Sunday from 8 pm until midnight. ✉ *Virgin Gorda Yacht Harbour, Lee Rd., Spanish Town* ☎ *284/495–5239* ⊕ *www.bathandturtle.com.*

Chez Bamboo. This is the place for calypso and reggae on Tuesday and Friday nights. ✉ *Lee Rd., Spanish Town* ☎ *284/495–5752* ⊕ *www. chezbamboo.com.*

Mine Shaft Café. The café has music on Tuesday and Friday. ✉ *Near Copper Mine Point, Spanish Town* ☎ *284/495–5260* ⊕ *www.mineshaftbvi. com.*

Restaurant at Leverick Bay. This resort's main restaurant hosts music on Tuesday and Friday in season. ✉ *Leverick Bay Resort & Marina, Leverick Bay Rd., Leverick Bay* ☎ *284/340–3005* ⊕ *www. therestaurantatleverickbay.com.*

Rock Café. There's live piano music nearly every night (except Sundays) during the Rock Café's winter season. ✉ *Lee Rd., Spanish Town* ☎ *284/495–5482* ⊕ *www.bvidining.com.*

SHOPPING

FOOD

Bitter End Emporium. This store at the Bitter End is the place for local fruits, cheeses, fresh baked goods, and gourmet prepared food. ⊠ *Bitter End Yacht Club, North Sound* ☏ *284/494–2746* ⊕ *www.beyc.com.*

Buck's Food Market. This market is the closest the island offers to a full-service supermarket, with an in-store bakery and deli as well as fresh fish and produce departments. ⊠ *Virgin Gorda Yacht Harbour, Lee Rd., Spanish Town* ☏ *284/495–5423* ⊕ *bucksfoodmarket.homestead.com.*

Chef's Pantry. This store has the fixings for an impromptu party in your villa or on your boat—fresh seafood, specialty meats, imported cheeses, daily baked breads and pastries, and an impressive wine and spirit selection. ⊠ *Leverick Bay Marina, Leverick Bay Rd., Leverick Bay* ☏ *284/340–3005.*

Rosy's Supermarket. This store carries the basics plus an interesting selection of ready-to-cook meals, such as a whole seasoned chicken. ⊠ *Rhymer Rd., Spanish Town* ☏ *284/495–6765* ⊕ *www.rosysenterprisesvg.com* ⊗ *Closed Sun.*

Virgin Gorda Cash & Carry. The store isn't much to look at, inside or out, but it has the best wine prices on Virgin Gorda, along with the usual basic supermarket items. ⊠ *Lee Rd., Spanish Town* ☏ *284/347–1200* ⊕ *https://www.rtwbvi.com/store-locations* ⊗ *Closed Sun.*

GIFTS

Allamanda Gallery. This shop showcases owner Amanda Baker's tropical photography, but it's also a good place to browse for cards, magnets, and other take-home gifts. ⊠ *The Baths, Tower Rd., Spanish Town* ☏ *284/495–5935* ⊕ *www.virginportraits.com.*

Caribbean Flavor. While this cozy store sells T-shirts and other vacation necessities, it's also a great place to shop for tropical wear in linen and other comfortable fabrics. ⊠ *The Baths, Tower Rd., Spanish Town* ☏ *284/495–5914.*

Reeftique. This store carries island crafts and jewelry, clothing, and nautical odds and ends with the Bitter End logo. ⊠ *Bitter End Yacht Club, North Sound* ☏ *284/494–2746* ⊕ *www.beyc.com.*

Thee Artistic Gallery. This boutique sells attractive handcrafted jewelry, paintings, and one-of-a-kind gift items, as well as books about the Caribbean. ⊠ *Virgin Gorda Yacht Harbor, Spanish Town* ☏ *284/495–5104.*

SPORTS AND THE OUTDOORS

DIVING AND SNORKELING

Where you go snorkeling and what company you pick depends on where you're staying. Many hotels have on-site dive outfitters, but if they don't, one won't be far away. If your hotel does have a dive operation, just stroll down to the dock and hop aboard—no need to drive anywhere. The dive companies are all certified by PADI. Costs vary, but count on paying about $85 for a one-tank dive and $130 for a two-tank dive. All dive operators offer introductory courses as well

6

You can learn to sail at the Bitter End Yacht Club.

as certification and advanced courses. Should you get an attack of the bends, which can happen when you ascend too rapidly, the nearest decompression chamber is at Roy L. Schneider Regional Medical Center in St. Thomas.

There are some terrific snorkel and dive sites off Virgin Gorda, including areas around The Baths, the North Sound, and the Dogs. The Chimney at Great Dog Island has a coral archway and canyon covered with a wide variety of sponges. At Joe's Cave, an underwater cavern on West Dog Island, huge groupers, eagle rays, and other colorful fish accompany divers as they swim. At some sites you can see 100 feet down, but divers who don't want to go that deep and snorkelers will find plenty to look at just below the surface.

FAMILY **Bitter End Yacht Club.** The BEYC schedules two snorkeling trips a day. ⌧ *North Sound* ☎ *284/494–2746* ⊕ *www.beyc.com* ✉ *From $15 for resort guests.*

Dive BVI. In addition to day trips, Dive BVI also offers expert instruction and certification. ⌧ *Virgin Gorda Yacht Harbour, Lee Rd., Spanish Town* ☎ *284/495–5513, 800/848–7078* ⊕ *www.divebvi.com* ⌧ *Leverick Bay Marina, Leverick Bay Rd., Leverick Bay* ☎ *284/495–7328, 800/848–7078* ⊕ *www.divebvi.com.*

Sunchaser Scuba. Resort, advanced, and rescue courses are all available here. ⌧ *Bitter End Yacht Club, North Sound* ☎ *284/495–9638, 800/932–4286* ⊕ *www.sunchaserscuba.com.*

SAILING AND BOATING

FAMILY **Bitter End Sailing School.** Classroom, dockside, and on-the-water lessons are available for sailors of all levels. Private lessons are $75 per hour. Beginners' and children's sailing lessons are free for guests. ⊠ *Bitter End Yacht Club, North Sound* ☎ *284/494–2746* ⊕ *www.beyc.com.*

Double "D" Charters. If you just want to sit back, relax, and let the captain take the helm, choose a sailing or power yacht from Double "D" Charters. Rates run from $110 for a day trip. Private full-day cruises or sails for up to eight people run from $1,100. ⊠ *Virgin Gorda Yacht Harbour, Lee Rd., Spanish Town* ☎ *284/499–2479* ⊕ *www.doubledbvi.com.*

JOST VAN DYKE

Named after an early Dutch settler, Jost Van Dyke is a small island northwest of Tortola. It's also a place to *truly* get away from it all. Mountainous and lush, the 4-mile-long (6½-km-long) island—with fewer than 200 full-time residents—has one tiny resort, some rental houses and villas, a campground, a few shops, a handful of cars, and a single road. There are no banks or ATMs on the island, and many restaurants and shops accept only cash. It's a good idea to buy groceries on St. Thomas or Tortola before arriving if you're staying for a few days. Life definitely rolls along on "island time," especially during the off-season from August to November, when finding a restaurant open for dinner can be a challenge. Water conservation is encouraged, as the source is rainwater collected in basement-like cisterns. Many lodgings will ask you to follow the Caribbean golden rule: "In the land of sun and fun, we never flush for number one." Jost is one of the Caribbean's most popular anchorages, and there are a disproportionately large number of informal bars and restaurants, which have helped earn Jost its reputation as the "party island" of the BVI.

BEACHES

FAMILY **Great Harbour Beach.** Great Harbour has an authentic Caribbean feel
Fodor's Choice that's not just for tourists. Small bars and restaurants line the sandy
★ strip of beach that serves as the community's main street. While the island's main settlement may not have the unspoiled natural beauty of some popular beaches, it holds a quaint charm. Activity picks up after dark, but many of the restaurants also serve excellent lunches without huge crowds. There are a few areas suited to swimming, with calm, shallow water perfect for children; however the attraction here is more about the facilities than the actual beach. Ali Baba and SeaCrest Inn have rooms on the bay. Bring your bug spray for sand flies in the early evenings. **Amenities:** food and drink; toilets. **Best for:** walking; swimming. ⊠ *Great Harbour.*

Sandy Cay Beach. Just offshore, the little islet known as Sandy Cay is a gleaming sliver of white sand with marvelous snorkeling and an inland nature trail. Previously part of the private estate of the late philanthropist and conservationist Laurance Rockefeller, the Cay recently became a protected area. You can hire any boatman on Jost Van Dyke to take

6

you out; just be sure to agree on a price and a time to be picked up again. As this is a national park, visitors are asked to "take only photos and leave only footprints." Nevertheless, it's become an increasingly popular location for weddings, which require approval from the BVI National Parks Trust. Experienced boaters can rent a boat or dinghy to go here, but be aware that winter swells can make beach landings treacherous. **Amenities:** none. **Best for:** snorkeling; swimming; walking.

FAMILY

Fodor'sChoice

★

White Bay Beach. On the south shore, this long stretch of picturesque white sand is especially popular with boaters who come ashore for a libation at one of the many beach bars that offer refuge from the sun. Despite the sometimes rowdy bar scene, the beach is large enough to find a quiet spot, particularly late in the day when most of the day-trippers disappear and the beach becomes serene. Accommodations directly on or just steps from the sand include the Sandcastle Hotel, White Bay Villas, Perfect Pineapple, and the Pink House Villas. Swimmers and snorkelers should be cautious of boat traffic in the anchorage. **Amenities:** food and drink; toilets. **Best for:** partiers; swimming; walking. ⊠ *White Bay.*

WHERE TO EAT

Restaurants on Jost Van Dyke are informal (some serve meals family-style at long tables) and often charming. The island is a favorite charter-boat stop, and you're bound to hear people exchanging stories about the previous night's anchoring adventures. Most restaurants don't take reservations (but for those that do, they are usually required). In all cases, dress is casual.

$$$

ECLECTIC

✕ **Abe's by the Sea.** Many sailors who cruise into this quiet bay come so they can dock right at this open-air eatery to enjoy the seafood, conch, lobster, and other fresh catches. Chicken and ribs round out the menu, and affable owners Abe Coakley and his wife, Eunicy, add a pinch and dash of hospitality that makes a meal into a memorable evening. Casual lunches are also served, and an adjoining market sells ice, canned goods, and other necessities. Dinner reservations are required by 5 pm. $ *Average main: $29* ⊠ *Little Harbour* ☎ *284/495–9329* ⚓ *Reservations essential.*

$$$

SEAFOOD

✕ **Ali Baba's.** Lobster is the main attraction at this beach bar with a sandy floor, which is just some 20 feet from the sea. Grilled local fish, including swordfish, kingfish, and wahoo, are specialties and caught fresh daily. There's also a pig roast on Monday nights in season. Beware: Ali Baba's special rum punch is as potent as it is delicious. Reservations aren't mandatory for dinner, but you'll probably find yourself waiting a long time without them. $ *Average main: $30* ⊠ *Great Harbour* ☎ *284/495–9280* ⊕ *www.alibabasrestaurantandbarbvi.com* ▭ *No credit cards.*

$$$

BARBECUE

✕ **Cool Breeze Bar & Restaurant.** This brightly colored eatery is often frequented by island locals. The establishment offers full dinner options, serving fresh grilled lobster, barbecue, and baby back ribs. $ *Average main: $29* ⊠ *Great Harbour* ☎ *284/496–0855* ▭ *No credit cards.*

$$$$

ECLECTIC

✕ **Corsairs Beach Bar and Restaurant.** On an island known for seafood, it's the pizza that draws raves at this friendly beach bar considered by some

Boaters docking at Jost Van Dyke

to be Jost's version of *Cheers*. If pizza doesn't appeal, the lunch and dinner menus have a wide variety of selections with an eclectic, Continental flare. Bring an appetite to breakfast, when the choices include hearty omelets and breakfast burritos. The bar is easily recognized by its signature pirate paraphernalia and a restored U.S. military M37 Dodge truck parked next to the steps-from-the-sea dining room. $ *Average main: $32* ✉ *Great Harbour* ☎ *284/495–9294* ⊕ *www.corsairsbvi.com.*

$$$$ ╳ **Foxy's Taboo.** It's well worth the winding hilly drive or sometimes
ECLECTIC   rough sail to get to Taboo, where there's a sophisticated menu and
FAMILY   friendly staff with a welcoming attitude. Located on Jost's mostly undeveloped East End, Taboo is less of a party bar than Foxy's in Great Harbour but has scenic views and usually a great breeze. You'll find specialties with a Mediterranean twist like eggplant cheesecake, kebabs, and hot-from-the-oven pizza. The lunch menu differs from the standard island fare. Even the burgers are a step up from average, and the salads are the best on the island. Coupled with a walk to the nearby Bubbly Pool (ask for a map at the bar), a visit to Taboo is a good way to while away a few hours. Dinner reservations are required by 4 pm. $ *Average main: $35* ✉ *East End* ☎ *284/340–9258* ⊕ *foxysbar.com/foxystaboo.*

$$$ ╳ **Foxy's Tamarind Bar and Restaurant.** The big draw here is the owner,
ECLECTIC   Foxy Callwood, a famed calypso singer who will serenade you with
FAMILY   lewd and laugh-worthy songs as you fork into burgers, grilled chicken, barbecue ribs, and lobster. Check out the pennants, postcards, and weathered T-shirts that adorn every inch of the walls and ceiling of this large, two-story beach shack; they've been left by previous visitors. On Friday and Saturday nights in season, Foxy hosts a Caribbean-style

barbecue with grilled fresh fish, chicken and ribs, peas and rice, salad, and more, followed by live music. Other nights choose from steak, fresh lobster, pork, or pasta; at lunch Foxy serves sandwiches and salads. Whether because of the sheer volume of diners or the experience of the management, Foxy's is one of the most reliable eating establishments on Jost. And it's also home to the only locally brewed beer in the BVI. You're unlikely to find Foxy performing at night, but he takes the mike many afternoons and makes time to mingle with guests—this a popular happy-hour pit stop. $ *Average main: $29* ⊠ *Great Harbour* ☎ *284/495–9258* ⊕ *www.foxysbar.com.*

$$$ × **Gertrude's Beach Bar.** A casual bar right on White Bay Beach, Ger-
BURGER trude's will make you feel at home with burgers, conch fritters, and rotis. It's open for lunch and dinner, but it's a good idea to call ahead for dinner reservations. Sometimes Gertrude, and helpful staffer Olga, will let you pour your own drinks. $ *Average main: $21* ⊠ *White Bay* ☎ *284/495–9104.*

$$$$ × **Harris' Place.** Owner Cynthia Harris is as famous for her friendli-
ECLECTIC ness as she is for her food. Lobster in a garlic butter sauce, and other
FAMILY freshly caught seafood, as well as pork, chicken, and ribs, are on the menu. Homemade key lime pie and expertly blended Bushwackers are "to live for," as Cynthia would say, but diners also praise the fresh fish and lobster. Call for schedule of live music, which varies from season to season. Breakfast and lunch are served, too. Call ahead for reservations. $ *Average main: $34* ⊠ *Little Harbour* ☎ *284/495–9302.*

$$$ × **One Love Bar and Grill.** The Food Network's Alton Brown sought out
ECLECTIC this beachfront eatery and featured its stewed conch on a 2008 flavor-finding trip. Menu items include freshly caught seafood, quesadillas, sandwiches, and salads. Try their specialty drink, a Bushwacker. Seddy built the bar himself and decorated it with the flotsam and jetsam he collected during his years as a fisherman. $ *Average main: $28* ⊠ *White Bay* ⊕ *www.onelovebar.com.*

$$$$ × **Soggy Dollar Bar.** Candles illuminate this tiny, beachfront, palm-
ECLECTIC lined dining room during the evening meal, making it one of the most
Fodor's Choice romantic dinner settings on the island. Native-born Jost Van Dyke chef
★ Dwayne Donovan keeps things interesting with five to seven entrée and appetizer choices that change weekly and feature local flourishes like a passion-fruit demi-glaze. Don't miss the Painkiller ice cream, inspired by the Painkiller cocktail created here. For lunch, if you can find your way through the throngs ordering Painkillers at the bar, choices include mahimahi sandwiches, hamburgers, chicken roti, and conch fritters. Management has recently relaxed its reservations-only dinner policy, but it's still wise to call ahead. $ *Average main: $33* ⊠ *Sandcastle, White Bay* ☎ *284/495–9888* ⊕ *www.soggydollar.com.*

$$$$ × **Sydney's Peace and Love.** Here you can find great local lobster and
ECLECTIC fish, as well as barbecue chicken and ribs with all the fixings, including peas and rice, corn, coleslaw, and potato salad. Book early for all-you-can-eat lobster on Monday and Thursday nights. Meals are served on an open-air terrace or in an air-conditioned dining room at the water's edge. The find here is a sensational (by BVI standards) jukebox. The cognoscenti sail here for dinner, since there's no beach—and therefore

no annoying sand fleas. Breakfast and lunch are served, too, and guests help themselves at the honor bar. [$] *Average main: $35* ✉ *Little Harbour* ☎ *284/495–9271.*

WHERE TO STAY

$ B&B/INN 🏨 **Ali Baba's Heavenly Rooms.** Just above Ali Baba's restaurant, owner Wayson "Baba" Hatchett has added three simple but attractive rooms, each equipped with air-conditioning and a private bath. **Pros:** convenient location. **Cons:** noisy area of Great Harbour. [$] *Rooms from: $140* ✉ *Great Harbour* ☎ *284/495–9280* 🛏 *3 rooms* 🍴 *No meals.*

$ B&B/INN 🏨 **Perfect Pineapple Guest Houses.** One-bedroom suites, as well as one- and two-bedroom guesthouses, all come equipped with private bath, air-conditioning, stove, satellite TV, and refrigerator. **Pros:** located just steps from the popular White Bay beach. **Cons:** rooms have only basic furnishings; in need of updating. [$] *Rooms from: $160* ✉ *White Bay* ☎ *284/495–9401* 🌐 *www.perfectpineapple.com* 🛏 *6 rooms* 🍴 *No meals.*

$$ HOTEL 🏨 **Sandcastle.** Sleep steps from beautiful White Bay beach at this tiny beachfront hideaway, an island favorite for more than 40 years. **Pros:** beachfront rooms; near restaurants and bars; comfy hammocks. **Cons:** some rooms lack air-conditioning; beach sometimes clogged with day-trippers; no children allowed. [$] *Rooms from: $310* ✉ *White Bay* ☎ *284/495–9888* 🌐 *www.soggydollar.com* 🛏 *2 rooms, 4 1-bedroom cottages* 🍴 *Some meals.*

$ RENTAL FAMILY 🏨 **White Bay Villas and Seaside Cottages.** Beautiful views and friendly staff keep guests coming back to these hilltop one- to three-bedroom villas and cottages. **Pros:** incredible views; full kitchens; friendly staff. **Cons:** 10- to 15-minute walk to White Bay and Great Harbour's restaurants and beaches; rental car recommended. [$] *Rooms from: $260* ✉ *White Bay* ☎ *410/571–6692, 800/778–8066* 🌐 *www.jostvandyke.com* 🛏 *7 villas, 3 cottages* 🍴 *No meals.*

NIGHTLIFE

Jost Van Dyke is the most happening place to go bar-hopping in the BVI, so much so that it is an all-day enterprise for some. In fact, yachties will sail over just to have a few drinks. All the spots are easy to find, clustered in three general locations: Great Harbour, White Bay, and Little Harbour *(see Where to Eat, above)*. On the Great Harbour side you can find Foxy's, Corsairs, and Ali Baba's; on the White Bay side are the One Love Bar and Grill and the Soggy Dollar Bar, where legend has it the famous Painkiller was first concocted; and in Little Harbour are Harris' Place, Sydney's Peace and Love, and Abe's by the Sea. If you can't make it to Jost Van Dyke, you can have a Painkiller at almost any bar in the BVI.

SPORTS AND THE OUTDOORS

Abe and Eunicy Rentals. This company's two-door Suzukis ($65 a day), four-door Suzukis ($75 a day), and four-door Monteros ($80 a day) will help you explore by land. There's pickup and drop-off service from anywhere on the island. ⊠ *Little Harbour* ☎ *284/495–9329.*

Endeavour II Sailing. Built entirely from scratch on island with local high school students, this 32-foot traditional sailing vessel was part of a maritime heritage project initiated by the Jost Van Dyke's Preservation Society. Day sails aboard help fund dive and sail training for young Jost Van Dyke islanders. ⊠ *Great Harbour* ☎ *284/540–0861* ⊕ *www. jvdps.org.*

JVD Scuba and BVI Eco-Tours. Check out the undersea world around the island with dive master Colin Aldridge. One of the most impressive dives in the area is off the north coast of Little Jost Van Dyke. Here you can find the Twin Towers: a pair of rock formations rising an impressive 90 feet. A one-tank dive costs $110, a two-tank dive $135, and a four-hour beginner course is $140 plus the cost of equipment. Colin also offers day-trips to Sandy Cay and Sandy Spit, Norman Island, Virgin Gorda (The Baths), and custom outings. You can also rent snorkel equipment, dive gear, standup paddleboards, dinghies, and outboard boats here. ⊠ *Great Harbour* ☎ *284/495–0271* ⊕ *www.bvi-ecotours. com* ⊙ *Closed Sat.*

Paradise Jeep Rentals. Paradise Jeep Rentals offers the ideal vehicles to tackle Jost Van Dyke's steep, winding roads. Even though Jost is a relatively small island, you really need to be in shape to walk from one bay to the next. This outfit rents two-door Suzukis for $70 per day and four-door Grand Vitaras and Sportages for $80. Discounts are available for rentals of six or more days. It's next to the Fire Station in Great Harbour. Reservations are a must. ⊠ *Great Harbour* ☎ *284/495–9477.*

ANEGADA

Anegada lies low on the horizon about 14 miles (22½ km) north of Virgin Gorda. Unlike the hilly volcanic islands in the chain, this is a flat coral-and-limestone atoll. Nine miles (14 km) long and 2 miles (3 km) wide, the island rises no more than 28 feet above sea level. In fact, by the time you're able to see it, you may have run your boat onto a reef. (More than 300 captains unfamiliar with the waters have done so since exploration days; note that bareboat charters don't allow their vessels to head here without a trained skipper.) Although the reefs are a sailor's nightmare, they (and the shipwrecks they've caused) are a scuba diver's dream. Snorkeling, especially in the waters around Loblolly Bay on the North Shore, is a transcendent experience. You can float in shallow, calm water just a few feet from shore and see one coral formation after another, each shimmering with a rainbow of colorful fish. Many local captains are happy to take visitors out fishing for bonefish. Such watery pleasures are complemented by ever-so-fine, ever-so-white sand (the northern and western shores have long stretches of the stuff) and the occasional beach bar (stop in for burgers, local lobster, or a frosty beer). The island's population of about 180 lives primarily in a small south-side village called the Settlement, which has two grocery stores, a bakery, and a general store. In 2009 Anegada got its first bank, but it's open only one day a week, and there's still no ATM. Many restaurants and shops take only cash.

WHERE TO EAT

$$$$ SEAFOOD Fodor's Choice ★ 🍴 **Anegada Reef Hotel Restaurant.** Seasoned yachties gather here nightly to share tales of the high seas; the open-air bar is the busiest on the island. Dinner is by candlelight under the stars and always includes famous Anegada lobster, steaks, and succulent baby back ribs—all prepared on the large grill by the little open-air bar. The ferry dock is right next door, so expect a crowd shortly after it arrives. Dinner reservations are required by 4 pm. Breakfast favorites include lobster omelets and rum-soaked French toast; at lunch the Reef serves salads and sandwiches. [$] *Average main: $37* ✉ *Setting Point* ☎ *284/495–8002* 🌐 *www.anegadareef.com* ✍ *Reservations essential.*

$$$$ SEAFOOD FAMILY 🍴 **Big Bamboo.** This beachfront bar and restaurant tucked among sea grape trees at famous Loblolly Bay is the island's most popular destination for lunch. After you've polished off a plate of succulent Anegada lobster, barbecue chicken, or fresh fish, you can spend the afternoon on the beach, where the snorkeling is excellent and the view close to perfection. Fruity drinks from the cabana bar and ice cream from the freezer will round out your day. Dinner is by request only. If your heart is set on lobster, it's a good idea to call in the morning or day before to put in your request. [$] *Average main: $32* ✉ *Loblolly Bay* ☎ *284/495–2019* 🌐 *www.bigbambooanegada.com.*

$$$$ SEAFOOD 🍴 **Cow Wreck Bar and Grill.** Named for the cow bones that once washed up on shore, this wiggle-your-toes-in-the-sand beachside eatery on the northern shore is a fun place to watch the antics of surfers and kiteboarders skidding across the bay. Tuck into conch ceviche, lobster fritters, or the popular hot wings for lunch. The homemade coconut pie is a winner. Pack your snorkel gear and explore the pristine reef just a few strokes from the shore before you eat, or browse the on-site gift shop. Dinner is served by request; reservations required by 4 pm. [$] *Average main: $36* ✉ *Cow Wreck Bay* ☎ *284/495–8047* 🌐 *www.cowwreckbeach.com* ✍ *Reservations essential.*

$$$$ SEAFOOD FAMILY Fodor's Choice ★ 🍴 **Neptune's Treasure.** The owners, the Soares family, have lived on the island for more than half a century, and the Soares men catch, cook, and serve the seafood at this homey bar and restaurant a short distance from Setting Point. The fresh lobster, swordfish, tuna, and mahimahi are all delicious. Pam's Kitchen, a small bakery to the exterior of the property, was incorporated into the restaurant and rounds out offerings with freshly baked breads; sweet treats including made-from-scratch desserts (including key lime pie, chocolate brownies, and apple pie); and pizzas. Dinner is by candlelight at the water's edge, often with classic jazz playing softly in the background. If you've tired of seafood, Neptune's has a nice variety of alternatives, including vegetarian pasta, pork loin, and orange chicken. The view is spectacular at sunset. Breakfast and lunch are also served. Dinner reservations are essential by 4 pm. [$] *Average*

6

Anegada has miles of beautiful white-sand beaches.

main: $32 ✉ *Pomato Point* ☏ *284/495–9439* ⊕ *www.neptunestreasure.com* ♿ *Reservations essential.*

$$$$
SEAFOOD

✕ **Pomato Point Restaurant.** This relaxed restaurant and bar sits on one of the best beaches on the island and enjoys Anegada's most dramatic sunset views. Entrées include lobster, stewed conch, and freshly caught seafood. It's open for lunch daily; call by 4 pm for dinner reservations. Be sure to take a look at owner Wilfred Creque's displays of island artifacts, including shards of Arawak pottery and 17th-century coins, cannonballs, and bottles. These are housed in a little one-room museum adjacent to the dining room. ⓢ *Average main: $38* ✉ *Pomato Point* ☏ *284/495–9466* ☾ *Closed Sept.* ♿ *Reservations essential.*

$$$$
SEAFOOD

✕ **Potter's By the Sea.** Owner Liston Potter, a great staff, and a lively atmosphere just a few steps from the dock complement freshly grilled lobster and other seafood selections such as snapper and grouper. Potter's also offers a beach shuttle, free Wi-Fi, pool tables, and live music (ask about the schedule when you call ahead for dinner reservations). ⓢ *Average main: $37* ✉ *Setting Point* ☏ *284/495–9182* ⊕ *www.pottersbythesea.com* ♿ *Reservations essential.*

WHERE TO STAY

$
RESORT

🏨 **Anegada Beach Club.** This is a laid-back beach club setting where beach enthusiasts can enjoy beach volleyball and badminton. **Pros:** option to adjoin king and junior suites makes this a great spot for families; bar and restaurant on-site; plenty of outdoor activities. **Cons:** some find the resort too remote. ⓢ *Rooms from: $265* ✉ *Keel Point*

☎ *800/871–3551, 284/852–4500* 🌐 *www.anegadabeachclub.com* 🛏 *16 rooms, 7 luxury tents* 🍴 *No meals.*

$ HOTEL 🏨 **Anegada Reef Hotel.** Head here if you want to bunk in comfortable lodging near Anegada's most popular anchorage. **Pros:** everything you need is nearby; nice sunsets. **Cons:** basic rooms; no beach; often a party atmosphere at the bar. [$] *Rooms from: $210* ✉ *Setting Point* ☎ *284/495–8002* 🌐 *www.anegadareef.com* 🛏 *16 rooms* 🍴 *Some meals.*

$$ RENTAL 🏨 **Cow Wreck Beach Resort.** The resort's best attribute is its location at Cow Wreck Beach. **Pros:** secluded location; great snorkeling. **Cons:** the island's infamous, free-roaming livestock sometimes leave "presents" behind; location too remote for some. [$] *Rooms from: $300* ✉ *Cow Wreck Bay* ☎ *284/495–8047* 🌐 *www.cowwreckbeach.com* 🛏 *3 units* 🍴 *No meals.*

$ B&B/INN FAMILY 🏨 **Neptune's Treasure.** Basic waterfront rooms with simple furnishings and lovely views of the ocean are the hallmark of this family-owned guesthouse. **Pros:** waterfront property; run by a family full of tales of the island; nice sunset views. **Cons:** simple rooms; no kitchens; no beach. [$] *Rooms from: $150* ✉ *Pomato Point* ☎ *284/495–9439* 🌐 *www.neptunestreasure.com* 🛏 *9 rooms, 2 cottages* 🍴 *No meals.*

6

SPORTS AND THE OUTDOORS

Anegada Reef Hotel. Call the hotel to arrange bonefishing and sportfishing outings with seasoned local guides. ✉ *Setting Point* ☎ *284/495–8002* 🌐 *www.anegadareef.com.*

Danny Vanterpool. Danny offers half-, three-quarter-, and full-day bonefishing excursions around Anegada. The cost ranges from $400 for a half day to $600 for a full day. ☎ *284/441–6334* 🌐 *www.dannysbonefishing.com.*

OTHER BRITISH VIRGIN ISLANDS

COOPER ISLAND

Updated by Carol Bareuther

This small, hilly island on the south side of the Sir Francis Drake Channel, about 8 miles (13 km) from Road Town, Tortola, is popular with the charter-boat crowd. There are no paved roads (which doesn't really matter, as there aren't any cars), but you can find a beach restaurant, a casual hotel, a few houses (some are available for rent), and great snorkeling at the south end of Manchioneel Bay.

WHERE TO STAY

$$ RESORT Fodor's Choice ★ 🏨 **Cooper Island Beach Club.** Diving is the focus at this small resort, but folks who want to simply swim, snorkel, or relax can also feel right at home. **Pros:** lots of quiet; the Caribbean as it used to be. **Cons:** small rooms; island accessible only by ferry; there is no nightlife. [$] *Rooms from: $280* ✉ *Manchioneel Bay* ☎ *284/495–9084, 800/542–4624* 🌐 *www.cooperislandbeachclub.com* 🛏 *9 rooms* 🍴 *Breakfast.*

GUANA ISLAND

Guana Island sits off Tortola's northeast coast. Sailors often drop anchor at one of the island's bays for a day of snorkeling and sunning. The island is a designated wildlife sanctuary, and scientists often come here to study its flora and fauna. It's home to a back-to-nature resort that offers few activities other than relaxation. Unless you're a hotel guest or a sailor, there's no easy way to get here.

WHERE TO STAY

$$$$
RESORT
Fodor'sChoice
★

Guana Island Resort. Here's a good resort if you want to stroll the hillsides, snorkel around the reefs, swim at its seven beaches, and still enjoy some degree of comfort. **Pros:** secluded feel; lovely grounds. **Cons:** very expensive; need boat to get here. $ *Rooms from: $1300* 284/494–2354, 800/544–8262 *www.guana.com* 15 rooms, 1 1-bedroom villa, 1 2-bedroom villa, 1 3-bedroom villa *All meals.*

NORMAN ISLAND

This uninhabited island is the supposed setting for Robert Louis Stevenson's *Treasure Island.* The famed caves at Treasure Point are popular with day sailors and powerboaters. If you land ashore at the island's main anchorage in the Bight, you can find a small beach bar and behind it a trail that winds up the hillside and reaches a peak with a fantastic view of the Sir Francis Drake Channel to the north. The island boasts nearly 12 miles (20 km) of hiking trails. Call Pirate's Bight for information on ferry service to accommodate day-trippers.

GETTING HERE AND AROUND

The only way to reach this island is by private boat or on a charter boat that puts you aboard the *Willy T.* for a meal and drinks.

WHERE TO EAT

$$$$
ECLECTIC

Pirate's Bight. This breezy, open-air dining establishment boasts quirky beach bar eccentricities (a cannon is fired at sunset and bar-goers play games like "Giant Jenga"), all while maintaining a slightly refined feeling. Sail Caribbean operates a dive shop on the property and owners offer ferry service, giving the restaurant the feel of a casual day resort. Dinner offerings include a variety of seafood and poultry dishes, and appetizers and bar food include choices such as tuna tartar and coconut shrimp. The restaurant hosts live entertainment several nights a week. Call ahead for music schedule and for dinner reservations. $ *Average main: $32* The Bight 284/443–1405 *www.piratesbight.com.*

$$
ECLECTIC

Willy T. *Willy T* is a floating bar and restaurant that's anchored to the north of the Bight. Lunch and dinner are served in a party-hearty atmosphere. Try the conch fritters for starters. For lunch and dinner, British-style fish-and-chips, West Indian roti sandwiches, and the baby back ribs are winners. Call ahead for dinner reservations. $ *Average main: $17* The Bight 284/496–8603 *willy-t.com* *Reservations essential.*

CAYMAN
ISLANDS

WELCOME TO THE CAYMAN ISLANDS

KEY	
⌇	Beaches
◪	Dive Sites

C a r i b b e a n   S e a

LITTLE CAYMAN

Jacksons Pt.

Bloody Bay Wall ◪

Anchorage Bay

Gov. Gore Bird Sanctuary

South Town

South Hole Sound

West End Point

Edward Bodden Airfield

Owen Island

Tarpoon Alley ◪

◪ Eagle Ray Pass

Head of Barkers

MARINE PARK

Rum Point

◪ Stingray City

Water Cay

A4

Old Man Bay

A3

Cayman Kai

West Bay

A1

North Sound

Booby Cay

HUTLAND

Malportas Pond

OLD MAN BAY

GRAND CAYMAN

A4

HALF MOON BAY

BREAKERS

PEASE BAY

A3

A2

NORTH SOUND ESTATES

BELFORD ESTATES

A3

Pease Bay

Ironshore Point

NEWLANDS

SAVANNAH

A2

Bodden Bay

Southweat Point

A5

Grand Cayman may be the world's largest offshore finance hub, but other offshore activities have put the Cayman Islands on the map. Pristine waters, breathtaking coral formations, and plentiful and exotic marine creatures beckon divers from around the world. Other vacationers are drawn by the islands' mellow civility.

FUN ON AND OFF SHORE

Grand Cayman, which is 22 miles (36 km) long
and 8 miles (13 km) wide, is the largest of the
three low-lying islands that make up this British
colony. Its sister islands (Little Cayman and
Cayman Brac) are almost 90 miles (149 km)
north and east. The Cayman Trough between
the Cayman Islands and Jamaica is the deepest
part of the Caribbean.

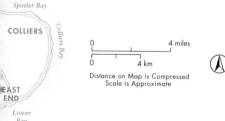

0 — 4 miles
0 — 4 km
Distance on Map is Compressed
Scale is Approximate

7

CAYMAN ISLANDS

TOP REASONS TO VISIT THE CAYMAN ISLANDS

1 Diving: Underwater visibility is among the best in the Caribbean, and nearby reefs are healthy.

2 Safety and Comfort: With no panhandlers, little crime, and top-notch accommodations, it's an easy place to vacation.

3 Dining Scene: The cosmopolitan population extends to the varied dining scene, from Italian to Indian.

4 Fabulous Snorkeling: A snorkeling trip to Stingray City is an experience you'll always remember.

5 Beaches: Grand Cayman's Seven Mile Beach is one of the Caribbean's best sandy beaches.

NEED TO KNOW

CAYMAN ISLANDS

LITTLE CAYMAN

CAYMAN BRAC

George Town
GRAND CAYMAN

Caribbean Sea

AT A GLANCE

Capital: George Town

Population: 58,400

Currency: Cayman Islands dollar

Money: ATMs common; credit cards accepted in most places on Grand Cayman.

Language: English

Country Code: ☎ 1 345

Emergencies: ☎ 911

Driving: On the left

Electricity: 120v/60 cycles; plugs are U.S. standard two- and three-prong

Time: One hour earlier than New York during daylight savings; same time as New York otherwise

Documents: A valid passport and a return or ongoing ticket.

Major Mobile Companies: Digicel, LIME

WEBSITES

Cayman Islands Department of Tourism: ⊕ www.caymanislands.ky

Cayman Islands Destination Magazine: ⊕ www.destination.ky

GETTING AROUND

✈ **Air Travel:** Fly direct from the U.S. to Grand Cayman; connect from there to Brac and Little Cayman.

🚌 **Bus Travel:** On Grand Cayman, bus service is efficient, inexpensive, and frequent. All routes branch from the George Town terminal adjacent to the library on Edward Street.

🚗 **Car Travel:** You can get by without a car on Grand Cayman if you are staying in the Seven Mile Beach area, but if you stay or want to explore further you'll need a car. Though less necessary on Cayman Brac or Little Cayman, cars are available.

PLAN YOUR BUDGET

	HOTEL ROOM	MEAL	ATTRACTIONS
Low Budget	$275	$15	Cayman Islands National Museum, $8
Mid Budget	$375	$30	Mastic Trail Tour, $20
High Budget	$475	$50	Stingray City Trip, $45

WAYS TO SAVE

Clarify menu prices. Ask if menu prices are in U.S. dollars or Cayman Islands dollar before you order. That's a 25% difference on the check.

Group travel. Many resort units and condo rentals are two and three bedrooms; traveling as a group helps split the overall accommodation cost.

Travel by Omni Bus. Inexpensive minivans marked "Omni Bus" run from 6 am to midnight from West Bay to Rum Point and the East End.

Change currency. Withdraw Cayman Island dollars from one of the many ATMs; some establishments offer a poor exchange if you use U.S. dollars.

WHEN TO GO

High Season: Mid-December through mid-April is the most fashionable and most expensive time to visit, when the weather is typically sunny and warm. Good hotels are often booked far in advance, and you're guaranteed the most entertainment at resorts and the most people with whom to enjoy it.

Low Season: From August to late October, temperatures can grow oppressively hot and the weather muggy, with high risks of tropical storms. Many upscale hotels close during these months for annual renovations. Those remaining open offer deep discounts.

Value Season: From late April to July and again November to mid-December, hotel prices drop 20% to 50% from high season prices. There are chances of scattered showers, but expect sun-kissed days and fewer crowds.

BIG EVENTS

January: January gets the Cayman calendar literally cooking with the celebrity-heavy Cayman Cookout co-organized by top toque Eric Ripert.

April—May: Cayman explodes with color every April with its take on Carnival called Batabano ⊕ www.caymancarnival.com, and Cayman Islands International Fishing Tournament lures anglers from around the world ⊕ www.fishcayman.com.

November: Pirates Week Festival is a massive 11-day party, featuring parades, costume competitions, street dances, fireworks, and more. ⊕ www.piratesweekfestival.com

READ THIS

■ **The Firm,** John Grishman. A young lawyer becomes embroiled in his new firm's shady dealings, some in Grand Cayman.

■ **Letters in Blood,** Gerald Arthur Winter. Mystery thriller set in Cayman.

■ **Nurse on Assignment,** Dorothy Brenner Francis. Romantic tale of a young nurse in Grand Cayman.

WATCH THIS

■ **The Firm.** Blockbuster legal thriller partly filmed here.

■ **National Lampoon's Last Resort.** 1990s slapstick comedy with scenes filmed on location in Cayman.

■ **Haven.** Romantic thriller directed by Caymanian Frank E. Flowers.

EAT THIS

■ **Fish 'n' fritters**: seasoned fried fish served alongside fried dough

■ **Heavy cake**: thick and sweet cassava-based cake

■ **Green turtle stew**: from farmed turtles

■ **Coconut dinner**: steamy Caymanian fish or beef stew in coconut milk

■ **Cayman-style fish**: local fish, fried and topped with a creole sauce

■ **Fish rundown**: fish stewed in coconut milk with breadfruit, yams, and more

Updated by
Jordan Simon

This British Overseas Territory, which consists of Grand Cayman, smaller Cayman Brac, and Little Cayman, is one of the Caribbean's most popular destinations, particularly among Americans, who have become homeowners and constant visitors. The island's extensive array of banks also draws travelers.

Columbus is said to have sighted the islands in 1503 and dubbed them *"Las Tortugas"* after seeing so many turtles in the sea. The name was later changed to Cayman, referring to the caiman crocodiles that once roamed the islands. The Cayman Islands remained largely uninhabited until the late 1600s, when England seized them and Jamaica from Spain. Emigrants from England, Holland, Spain, and France arrived, as did refugees from the Spanish Inquisition and deserters from Oliver Cromwell's army in Jamaica; many brought slaves with them as well. The Cayman Islands' caves and coves were also perfect hideouts for the likes of Blackbeard, Sir Henry Morgan, and other pirates out to plunder Spanish galleons. Many ships fell afoul of the reefs surrounding the islands, often with the help of Caymanians, who lured vessels to shore with beacon fires.

Today's Cayman Islands are seasoned with suburban prosperity (particularly Grand Cayman, where residents joke that the national flower is the satellite dish) and stuffed with crowds (the hotels that line the famed Seven Mile Beach are often full, even in the slow summer season). Most of the 52,000 Cayman Islanders live on Grand Cayman, where the cost of living is at least 20% higher than in the United States, but you won't be hassled by panhandlers or fear walking around on a dark evening (the crime rate is very low). Add political and economic stability to the mix, and you have a fine island recipe indeed.

PLANNING

GETTING HERE AND AROUND
AIR TRAVEL

You can fly nonstop to Grand Cayman from Atlanta (Delta), Boston (US Airways, once weekly; JetBlue), Charlotte (US Airways), Chicago (Cayman Airways, twice weekly), Detroit (Delta, once weekly), Fort Lauderdale (Cayman Airways), Houston (United, twice weekly), Miami (American, Cayman Airways), Minneapolis (Delta, once weekly), New York–JFK (Cayman Airways, Delta, JetBlue), New York–Newark (United, once weekly), Philadelphia (US Airways, once weekly), Tampa (Cayman Airways), and Washington, D.C. (United).

Almost all nonstop air service is to Grand Cayman, with connecting flights on Cayman Airways Express to Cayman Brac and Little Cayman on a small propeller plane; there's also interisland charter-only service on Island Air. Once-weekly nonstops on Cayman Airways link Miami and Orlando with Cayman Brac.

Airline Contacts American Airlines. ☎ 345/949–0666 ⊕ www.aa.com. **Cayman Airways.** ☎ 345/949–2311. **Delta.** ☎ 345/945–8430. **Island Air.** ☎ 345/949–5252 ⊕ www.islandair.ky. **JetBlue.** ☎ 800/538–2583, 855/710–2951 ⊕ www.jetblue.com. **United.** ☎ 345/916–5545.

Airports Edward Bodden Airstrip (LYB). ☎ 345/948–0021. **Gerrard Smith International Airport** (CYB). ☎ 345/948–1222. **Owen Roberts International Airport** (GCM). ☎ 345/943–7070.

BIKE AND SCOOTER TRAVEL

When renting a motor scooter or bicycle, remember to drive on the left and wear sunblock and a helmet. Bicycles ($15 a day) and scooters ($35 to $40 a day) can be rented in George Town. On Cayman Brac or Little Cayman your hotel can make arrangements (most offer complimentary bicycles for local sightseeing).

BUS TRAVEL

On Grand Cayman, bus service—consisting of minivans marked "Omni Bus"—is efficient, inexpensive, and plentiful, running from 6 am to midnight (depending on route) roughly every 15 minutes in the Seven Mile Beach area and George Town, with fares from CI$1.50 to CI$3.

CAR TRAVEL

Driving is easy on Grand Cayman, but there can be considerable traffic, especially during rush hour. One major road circumnavigates most of the island. Driving is on the left, British-style, and there are roundabouts. Speed limits are 30 mph (50 kph) in the country, 20 mph (30 kph) in town. There's much less traffic on Cayman Brac and even less on Little Cayman. Gas is expensive.

Car Rentals: You'll need a valid driver's license and a credit card to rent a car. Most agencies require renters to be between 21 and 70, though some require you to be 25. If you are over 75, you must have a certified doctor's note attesting to your ability. A local driver's permit, which costs $20, is obtained through the rental agencies, many of which offer complimentary pickup and drop-off along Seven Mile Beach. Rates can be expensive (from $45 to $95 per day), but usually include insurance.

Car-Rental Contacts (Grand Cayman) Ace Hertz. ☎ *345/949–2280, 800/654–3131, 855/212–1713 toll free, 345/943–4378* ⊕ *www.hertzcayman. com.* **Andy's Rent a Car.** ☎ *345/949–8111, 855/691–3991 toll free* ⊕ *www. andys.ky.* **Avis.** ☎ *345/949–2468* ⊕ *www.aviscayman.com.* **Budget.** ☎ *345/949–5605* ⊕ *www.budgetcayman.com.* **Dollar.** ☎ *345/949–4790* ⊕ *www.dollarlac. com.* **Economy.** ☎ *345/949–9550* ⊕ *www.economycarrental.com.ky.* **Thrifty.** ☎ *345/949–6640, 800/367–2277* ⊕ *www.thrifty.com.*

Car-Rental Contacts (Cayman Brac) B&S Motor Ventures. ☎ *345/948–1646* ⊕ *www.bandsmv.com.* **CB Rent-a-Car.** ☎ *345/948–2424, 345/948–2847* ⊕ *www.cbrentacar.com.* **Four D's Car Rental.** ☎ *345/948–1599, 345/948–0459.*

Car-Rental Contacts (Little Cayman) McLaughlin Rentals. ☎ *345/948–1000* ✍ *littlcay@candw.ky.*

TAXI TRAVEL

On Grand Cayman, taxis operate 24 hours a day; if you anticipate a late night, however, make pickup arrangements in advance. You generally cannot hail a taxi on the street except occasionally in George Town. Fares are metered, and are not cheap, but basic fares include as many as three passengers. Taxis are scarcer on the Sister Islands; rates are fixed and fairly prohibitive. Your hotel can recommend drivers.

HEALTH AND SAFETY

Dengue, chikungunya, and zika have all been reported throughout the Caribbean. We recommend that you protect yourself from these mosquito-borne illnesses by keeping your skin covered and/or wearing mosquito repellent. The mosquitoes that transmit these viruses are as active by day as they are by night.

HOTELS AND RESORTS

Grand Cayman draws the bulk of Cayman Island visitors. It's expensive during the high season but offers the widest range of resorts, restaurants, and activities both in and out of the water. Most resorts are on or near Seven Mile Beach, but a few are north in the West Bay Area, near Rum Point, or on the quiet East End. Both Little Cayman and Cayman Brac are more geared toward serving the needs of divers, who make up the majority of visitors. Beaches on the Sister Islands, as they are called, don't measure up (literally) to Grand Cayman's Seven Mile Beach. The smaller islands are cheaper than Grand Cayman, but with the extra cost of transportation, the overall savings are minimized.

Resorts: Grand Cayman has plenty of medium-size resorts as well as the Ritz-Carlton, a large seven-story resort on Seven Mile Beach. Little Cayman has a mix of small resorts and condos, most appealing to divers.

Condos and Villas: Grand Cayman has a wide range of condos and villas, many in resortlike compounds on or near Seven Mile Beach and the Cayman Kai area. There are even a few small guesthouses for budget-minded visitors. Cayman Brac has mostly intimate resorts and family-run inns.

Hotel reviews have been shortened. For full information, visit Fodors.com.

WHAT IT COSTS IN U.S. DOLLARS				
	$	**$$**	**$$$**	**$$$$**
RESTAURANTS	under $12	$12–$20	$21–$30	over $30
HOTELS	under $275	$275–$375	$376–$475	over $475

Restaurant prices are the average cost of a main course at dinner or, if dinner is not served, at lunch. Hotel prices are the lowest cost of a standard double room in high season.

VISITOR INFORMATION

Contacts Cayman Islands Department of Tourism. ☎ *305/599–9033 in Miami, 847/678–6446 in Chicago, 212/889–9009 in New York City, 713/461–1317 in Houston, 877/422–9626 in U.S., 345/949–0623 in Caymans* ⊕ *www.caymanislands.ky.*

GRAND CAYMAN

Grand Cayman has long been known for two offshore activities: banking (the new piracy, as locals joke) and scuba diving. With 296 banks, the capital, George Town, is relatively modern and usually bustles with activity, but never more so than when two to seven cruise ships are docked in the harbor, an increasingly common occurrence. Accountants in business clothes join thousands of vacationers in their tropical togs, jostling for tables at lunch. When they're not mingling in the myriad shops or getting pampered and pummeled in spas, vacationers delve into sparkling waters to snorkel and dive; increasingly, couples come to be married, or at least to enjoy their honeymoon.

The effects of recent devastating hurricanes such as Omar and Paloma, both in 2008, are visible only in the mangrove swamps and interior savanna. There is a lot of new construction and plenty of traffic, so check with a local to plan driving time. It can take 45 minutes during rush hours to go 8 miles (13 km).

EXPLORING

The historic capital of George Town, on the southwest corner of Grand Cayman, is easy to explore on foot. If you're a shopper, you can spend days here; otherwise, an hour will suffice for a tour of the downtown area. To see the rest of the island, rent a car or scooter or take a guided tour. The portion of the island called West Bay is noted for its jumble of neighborhoods and a few attractions. When traffic is heavy, it's about a half hour to West Bay from George Town, but the bypass road that runs parallel to West Bay Road has made the journey easier. The less-developed East End has natural attractions from blowholes to botanical gardens, as well as the remains of the island's original settlements. Plan at least 45 minutes for the drive out from George Town (more during rush hours). You need a day to explore the entire island—including a stop at a beach for a picnic or swim.

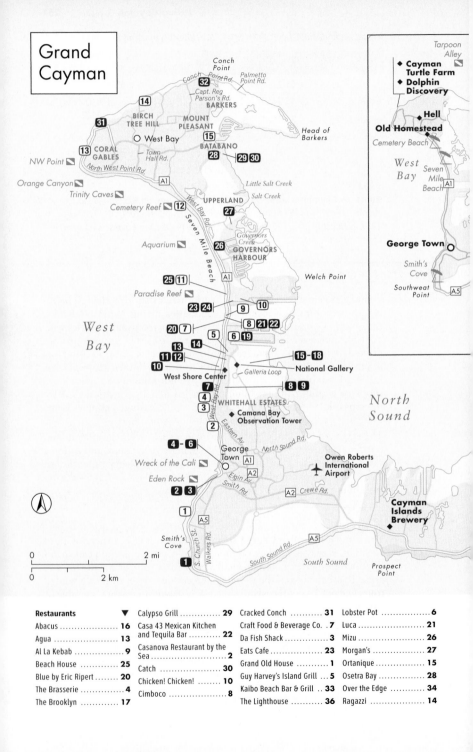

Grand Cayman

Conch Point

Conch Point Rd.

Palmetto Point Rd.

32

Capt. Reg Parson's Rd.

BARKERS

14

MOUNT PLEASANT

31

BIRCH TREE HILL

○ West Bay

15

Head of Barkers

13 CORAL GABLES

Town Hall Rd.

BATABANO

28

29 **30**

NW Point ◣

North West Point Rd.

A1

Little Salt Creek

Orange Canyon ◣

Salt Creek

Trinity Caves ◣

Cemetery Reef ◣ **12**

West Bay Rd.

UPPERLAND

27

Aquarium ◣

Governors Creek

26

GOVERNORS HARBOUR

Welch Point

Seven Mile Beach

A1

25 **11**

Paradise Reef ◣

10

23 **24**

9

West Bay

20 **7**

8 **21** **22**

5

6 **19**

13 **14**

15 - **18**

11 **12**

10

West Shore Center

Galleria Loop

National Gallery

North Sound

7

8 **9**

4

WHITEHALL ESTATES

3

West Bay Rd.

Camana Bay Observation Tower

2

Eastern Av.

4 - **6**

George Town

North Sound Rd.

Wreck of the Cali ◣

A1

Owen Roberts International Airport

Eden Rock ◣

A2

2 **3**

Elgin Av.

Smith Rd.

A2

Crewe Rd.

Cayman Islands Brewery

1

A5

Smith's Cove

S. Church St.

Walkers Rd.

South Sound Rd.

South Sound

Prospect Point

1

| 0 | | 2 mi |
| 0 | 2 km | |

Tarpoon Alley

◆ **Cayman Turtle Farm**
◆ **Dolphin Discovery**

◆ **Hell**

Old Homestead

Cemetery Beach ◣

West Bay

Seven Mile Beach

A1

George Town ○

Smith's Cove

Southweat Point

A5

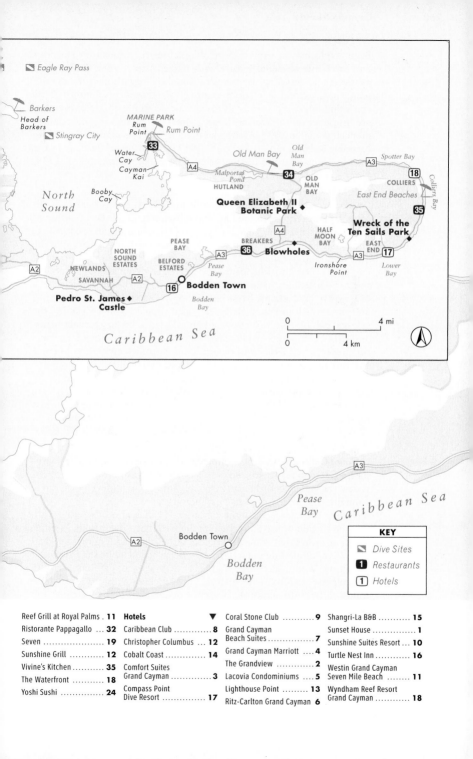

Eagle Ray Pass

Barkers
Head of
Barkers
Stingray City

MARINE PARK
Rum
Point
Rum Point

Water
Cay
Cayman
Kai

33

Old Man Bay

Old
Man
Bay

Spotter Bay

A4

34

A3

18

COLLIERS

East End Beaches

Colliers Bay

*North
Sound*

Booby
Cay

Malportas
Pond

HUTLAND

OLD
MAN
BAY

**Queen Elizabeth II
Botanic Park** ◆

**Wreck of the
Ten Sails Park**

35

PEASE
BAY

NORTH
SOUND
ESTATES

BELFORD
ESTATES

NEWLANDS

SAVANNAH

A2

A2

BREAKERS

A4

36 **Blowholes**

*Pease
Bay*

A3

HALF
MOON
BAY

*Ironshore
Point*

EAST
END

A3

17

*Lower
Bay*

16

Bodden Town

*Bodden
Bay*

Pedro St. James ◆
Castle

C a r i b b e a n   S e a

| 0 | | 4 mi |
| 0 | | 4 km |

*Pease
Bay*

C a r i b b e a n   S e a

A3

A2

Bodden Town

*Bodden
Bay*

KEY

◣	*Dive Sites*
1	*Restaurants*
⬜1	*Hotels*

GEORGE TOWN

Begin exploring the capital by strolling along the waterfront Harbour Drive to **Elmslie Memorial United Church,** named after the first Presbyterian missionary to serve in Cayman. Its vaulted ceiling, wooden arches, and sedate nave reflect the religious nature of island residents. In front of the court building, in the center of town, names of influential Caymanians are inscribed on the **Wall of History,** which commemorates the islands' quincentennial in 2003. Across the street is the **Cayman Islands Legislative Assembly Building,** next door to the **1919 Peace Memorial Building.** In the middle of the financial district is the **General Post Office,** built in 1939. Let the kids pet the big blue iguana statues.

TOP ATTRACTIONS

FAMILY **Cayman Islands National Museum.** Built in 1833, the historically signifi-
Fodor's Choice cant clapboard home of the national museum has had several different
★ incarnations over the years, serving as courthouse, jail, post office, and dance hall. It features an ongoing archaeological excavation of the Old Gaol and excellent 3-D bathymetric displays, murals, dioramas, and videos that illustrate local geology, flora and fauna, and island history. The first floor focuses on natural history, including a microcosm of Cayman ecosystems, from beaches to dry woodlands and swamps, and offers such interactive elements as a simulated sub. Upstairs, the cultural exhibit features renovated murals, video history reenactments, and 3-D back panels in display cases holding thousands of artifacts ranging from a 14-foot catboat with animatronic captain to old coins and rare documents. These paint a portrait of daily life and past industries, such as shipbuilding and turtling, and stress Caymanians' resilience when they had little contact with the outside world. There are also temporary exhibits focusing on aspects of Caymanian culture, a local art collection, and interactive displays for kids. ⊠ *Harbour Dr., George Town* 🕾 *345/949–8368* ⊕ *www.museum.ky* 🖃 *$8* ⊙ *Weekdays 9–5, Sat. 10–2.*

Fodor's Choice **National Gallery.** A worthy nonprofit, this museum displays and pro-
★ motes Caymanian artists and craftspeople, both established and grassroots. The gallery coordinates first-rate outreach programs for everyone from infants to inmates. It usually mounts six major exhibitions a year, including three large-scale retrospectives or thematic shows and multimedia installations. Director Natalie Urquhart also brings in international shows that somehow relate to the island, often inviting local artists for stimulating dialogue. The gallery hosts public slide shows, a lunchtime lecture series in conjunction with current exhibits, Art Flix (video presentations on art history, introduced with a short lecture and followed by a discussion led by curators or artists), and a CineClub (movie night). The gallery has also developed an Artist Trail Map with the Department of Tourism and can facilitate studio tours. There's an excellent shop and an Art Café. ⊠ *Esterly Tibbetts Hwy. at Harquail Bypass, Seven Mile Beach* 🕾 *345/945–8111* ⊕ *www.nationalgallery. ky* 🖃 *Free* ⊙ *Weekdays 10–5, Sat. 10–3.*

NEED A
BREAK?

Full of Beans Cafe. On the surprisingly large, eclectic, Asian-tinged menu using ultrafresh ingredients, standouts include homemade carrot cake, mango smoothies, cranberry-Brie-pecan salad, and rosemary-roasted portobello and pesto chicken panini. The espresso martini will perk up anyone wanting a pick-me-up. Owner Cindy Butler fashions a feast for weary eyes as well, with rotating artworks (many for sale) and stylish mosaic mirrors contrasting with faux-brick walls and vintage hardwood tables. ⊠ *Pasadora Pl., Smith Rd., George Town* ☎ *345/943–2326, 345/814–0157* ⊕ *www.fullofbeans.ky.*

WORTH NOTING

Cayman Spirits/Seven Fathoms Rum. Surprisingly, this growing company, established in 2008, is Cayman's first distillery. It's already garnered medals in prestigious international competitions for its artisanal small-batch rums (and is now making a splash for its smooth Gun Bay vodka as well). You can stop by for a tasting and self-guided tour (a more intensive, extensive guided tour costs $15) to learn how the rum is aged at 7 fathoms (42 feet) deep; supposedly the natural motion of the currents maximizes the rum's contact with the oak, extracting its rich flavors and enhancing complexity. Based on the results, it's not just yo-ho-hokum. ⊠ *65 Bronze Rd., George Town* ☎ *345/925–5379, 345/926–8186* ⊕ *www.caymanspirits.com, www.sevenfathomsrum.com.*

National Trust. This office provides a wonderful map of historic and natural attractions, books and guides to Cayman, and, on its website, more than 50 information sheets on cultural and natural topics from iguanas to schoolhouses. Regularly scheduled activities range from boat tours through the forests of the Central Mangrove Wetlands to cooking classes with local chefs to morning walking tours of historic George Town. Stop in, but be forewarned: though the office is walkable from George Town, it's an often-hot 20-minute hike from downtown. ⊠ *Dart Park, 558 S. Church St., George Town* ☎ *345/749–1121* ⊕ *www.nationaltrust.org.ky* ⊗ *Weekdays 9–5.*

SEVEN MILE BEACH

WORTH NOTING

FAMILY **Camana Bay Observation Tower.** This 75-foot structure provides striking 360-degree panoramas of otherwise flat Grand Cayman, sweeping from George Town and Seven Mile Beach to the North Sound. The double-helix staircase is impressive in its own right. Running alongside the steps (an elevator is also available), a floor-to-ceiling mosaic replicates the look and feel of a dive from seabed to surface. Constructed of tiles in 114 different colors, it's one of the world's largest marine-themed mosaics. Benches and lookout points let you take in the views as you ascend. Afterward you can enjoy 500-acre Camana Bay's gardens, waterfront boardwalk, and pedestrian paths lined with shops and restaurants, or frequent live entertainment. ⊠ *Between Seven Mile Beach and North Sound, 2 miles (3 km) north of George Town, Camana Bay* ☎ *345/640–3500* ⊕ *www.camanabay.com* ⊠ *Free* ⊗ *Daily sunrise–10 pm.*

WEST BAY
WORTH NOTING

FAMILY **Cayman Turtle Farm.** Cayman's premier attraction has been transformed into a marine theme park with souvenir shops and restaurants. Still, the turtles remain a central attraction, and you can tour ponds in the original research–breeding facility with thousands in various stages of growth, some up to 600 pounds and more than 70 years old. Four areas—three aquatic and one dry—cover 23 acres; different-color bracelets determine access (the steep full-pass admission includes snorkeling gear and waterslides). The park helps promote conservation, encouraging interaction (a tidal pool houses invertebrates such as starfish and crabs) and observation. When turtles are picked up from the tanks, the little creatures flap their fins and splash the water. Animal Program events include Keeper Talks, where you might feed birds or iguanas, and biologists' conservation programs. The freshwater **Breaker's Lagoon,** replete with cascades plunging over moss-carpeted rocks, evokes Cayman Brac. The saltwater **Boatswain's Lagoon,** replicating all the Cayman Islands and the Trench, teems with 14,000 denizens of the deep milling about a cannily designed synthetic reef. You can snorkel here (lessons and guided tours are available). Both lagoons have underwater 4-inch-thick acrylic panels that look directly into **Predator Reef,** home to six brown sharks, four nurse sharks, and other predatory fish such as tarpons, eels, and jacks, which can also be viewed from terra (or terror, as one guide jokes) firma. Look for feeding times. The free-flight **Aviary,** designed by consultants from Disney's Animal Kingdom, is a riot of color and noise with feathered friends representing the entire Caribbean basin; it doubles as a rehabilitation center for Cayman Wildlife and Rescue. A winding interpretive **nature trail** culminates in the Blue Hole, a collapsed cave once filled with water. Audio tours are available with different focuses, from butterflies to bush medicine. The last stop is the living museum, **Cayman Street,** with facades duplicating vernacular architecture; an herb and fruit garden; model catboats; and interactive craft demonstrations from painting mahogany to thatch weaving. ✉ *786 Northwest Point Rd., Box 812, West Bay* ☎ *345/949–3894* ⊕ *www.turtle.ky* ✉ *Comprehensive, $45; Turtle Farm only, $18* ⏱ *Mon.–Sat. 8–5, Sun. 10–5; lagoons close ½ hr–2 hrs earlier.*

FAMILY **Dolphin Discovery.** If you ever dreamed of frolicking with Flipper, here's your (photo) opportunity, as the organizers of this global business promise a "touching experience." The well-maintained facility, certified by the Alliance of Marine Mammal Parks and Aquariums, offers three main options ($119–$189, less for kids, who must swim with an adult), depending on time spent splashing in the enormous pool with the dolphins and stingrays. The premium Royal Swim includes a dorsal tow and foot push, showcasing the amazing strength, speed, and agility of these majestic marine mammals. Other options offer a handshake, kiss, belly ride, and a new underwater dive experience dubbed Dolphin Trek. All participants receive free entrance to Stingray City or the Turtle Farm across the street, taking some of the sting out of the high prices. ✉ *Northwest Point Rd., West Bay* ☎ *345/769–7946, 866/393–5158 toll-free in U.S., 345/949–7946* ⊕ *www.dolphindiscovery.com/grand-cayman.*

Cayman Turtle Farm, Grand Cayman

Hell. Quite literally the tourist trap from Hell, especially when overrun by cruise-ship passengers, this attraction does offer free admission, fun photo ops, and sublime surrealism. Its name refers to the quarter-acre of menacing shards of charred brimstone thrusting up like vengeful spirits (actually blackened and "sculpted" by acid-secreting algae and fungi over millennia). The eerie lunarscape is now cordoned off, but you can prove you had a helluva time by taking a photo from the observation deck. The attractions are the small post office and a gift shop where you can get cards and letters postmarked from Hell, not to mention wonderfully silly postcards titled "When Hell Freezes Over" (depicting bathing beauties on the beach), "The Devil Made Me Do It" bumper stickers, Scotch bonnet–based Hell sauce, and "The coolest shop in Hell" T-shirts. Ivan Farrington, the owner of the Devil's Hang-Out store, cavorts in a devil's costume (horn, cape, and tails), regaling you with demonically bad jokes. ⊠ *Hell Rd., West Bay* ☎ *345/949-3358* 🖫 *Free* ⊙ *Daily 9–6.*

NORTH SIDE
TOP ATTRACTIONS

Fodor'sChoice
★

Queen Elizabeth II Botanic Park. This 65-acre wilderness preserve showcases a wide range of indigenous and nonindigenous tropical vegetation, approximately 2,000 species in total. Splendid sections include numerous water features from limpid lily ponds to cascades; a Heritage Garden with a traditional cottage and "caboose" (outside kitchen) that includes crops that might have been planted on Cayman a century ago;

and a Floral Colour Garden arranged by color, the walkway wandering through sections of pink, red, orange, yellow, white, blue, mauve, lavender, and purple. A 2-acre lake and adjacent wetlands include three islets that provide a habitat and breeding ground for native birds just as showy as the floral displays: green herons, black-necked stilts, American coots, blue-winged teal, cattle egrets, and rare West Indian whistling ducks. The nearly mile-long Woodland Trail encompasses every Cayman ecosystem from wetland to cactus thicket, buttonwood swamp to lofty woodland with imposing mahogany trees. You'll encounter birds, lizards, turtles, and agoutis, but the park's star residents are the protected endemic blue iguanas, found only in Grand Cayman. The world's most endangered iguana, they're the focus of the National Trust's Blue Iguana Recovery Program, a captive breeding and reintroduction facility. This section of the park is usually closed to the public, though released "blue dragons" hang out in the vicinity. The Trust conducts 90-minute behind-the-scenes safaris Monday–Saturday at 11 am for $30. ⊠ *367 Botanic Rd., North Side* ☏ *345/947–9462* ⊕ *www.botanic-park.ky* 🖅 *$10, children under 12 free with adult* ⊘ *Daily 9–5:30; last admission 1 hr before closing.*

BODDEN TOWN

In the island's original south-shore capital you can find an old **cemetery** on the shore side of the road. Graves with A-frame structures are said to contain the remains of pirates. There are also the ruins of a fort and a wall erected by slaves in the 19th century. The National Trust runs tours of the restored 1840s **Mission House.**

Pedro St. James Castle. Built in 1780, the great house is Cayman's oldest stone structure and the island's only remaining late-18th-century residence. In its capacity as courthouse and jail, it was the birthplace of Caymanian democracy, where in December 1831 the first elected parliament was organized and in 1835 the Slavery Abolition Act signed. The structure still has original or historically accurate replicas of sweeping verandas, mahogany floors, rough-hewn wide-beam ceilings, outside louvers, stone and oxblood- or mustard-color lime-wash-painted walls, brass fixtures, and Georgian furnishings (from tea caddies to canopy beds to commodes). Paying obsessive attention to detail, the curators even fill glasses with faux wine. The mini-museum also includes a hodgepodge of displays from slave emancipation to old stamps. The buildings are surrounded by 8 acres of natural parks and woodlands. You can stroll through landscaping of native Caymanian flora and experience one of the most spectacular views on the island from atop the dramatic Great Pedro Bluff. First watch the impressive multimedia show, on the hour, complete with smoking pots, misting rains, and two screens. The poignant Hurricane Ivan Memorial outside uses text, images, and symbols to represent important aspects of the 2004 disaster. ⊠ *Pedro Castle Rd., Savannah* ☏ *345/947–3329* ⊕ *www.pedrostjames. ky* 🖅 *$10* ⊘ *Daily 9–5.*

EAST END
WORTH NOTING

FAMILY **Blowholes.** When the easterly trade winds blow hard, crashing waves force water into caverns and send impressive geysers shooting up as much as 20 feet through the ironshore. The blowholes were partially filled during Hurricane Ivan in 2004, so the water must be rough to recapture their former elemental drama. ⊠ *Frank Sound Rd., roughly 10 miles (16 km) east of Bodden Town, near East End.*

Cayman Islands Brewery. In this brewery occupying the former Stingray facility, tour guides explain the iconic imagery of bottle and label as well as the nearly three-week brewing process: 7 days' fermentation, 10 days' lagering (storage), and 1 day in the bottling tank. The brewery's eco-friendly features are also championed: local farmers receive the spent grains to feed their cattle at no charge, while waste liquid is channeled into one of the Caribbean's most advanced water-treatment systems. Then enjoy your complimentary tasting knowing that you're helping the local environment and economy. ⊠ *366 Shamrock Rd., Red Bay Estate* ☎ *345/947–6699* ⊕ *caybrew.com* ⌷ *$6* ☉ *Weekdays 9–5, tours 9–4 on the hr by appointment.*

Wreck of the Ten Sails Park. This lonely, lovely park on Grand Cayman's windswept eastern tip commemorates the island's most (in)famous shipwreck. On February 8, 1794, the *Cordelia,* heading a convoy of 58 square-rigged merchant vessels en route from Jamaica to England, foundered on one of the treacherous East End reefs. Its warning cannon fire was tragically misconstrued as a call to band more closely together due to imminent pirate attack, and nine more ships ran aground. Local sailors, who knew the rough seas, demonstrated great bravery in rescuing all 400-odd seamen. Popular legend claims (romantically but inaccurately) that King George III granted the islands an eternal tax exemption. Queen Elizabeth II dedicated the park's plaque in 1994. Interpretive signs document the historic details. The ironically peaceful headland provides magnificent views of the reef (including more recent shipwrecks); bird-watching is superb from here half a mile south along the coast to the Lighthouse Park, perched on a craggy bluff. ⊠ *Gun Bay, East End* ☎ *345/949–0121 National Trust* ⌷ *Free* ☉ *Daily.*

7

BEACHES

Limestone, coral, shells, water, and wind collaborated to fashion the Cayman Islands beaches. It's a classic example of the interaction between geology and marine biology. Most of the beaches in Cayman, especially on Grand and Little Cayman, resemble powdered ivory. A few, including those on Cayman Brac, are more dramatic, a mix of fine beige sand and rugged rocky "ironshore," which often signals the healthiest reefs and best snorkeling.

Barkers. Secluded, spectacular beaches are accessed via a dirt road just past Papagallo restaurant. There are no facilities (that's the point!), but some palms offer shade. Unfortunately, the shallow water and rocky bottom discourage swimming, and it can be cluttered at times with seaweed and debris. Kitesurfers occasionally come here for the gusts.

Amenities: none. **Best for:** solitude; walking; windsurfing. ⊠ *Conch Point Rd., Barkers, West Bay.*

Cemetery Beach. A narrow, sandy driveway takes you past the small cemetery to a perfect strand just past the northern end of Seven Mile Beach. The dock here is primarily used by dive boats during winter storms. You can walk in either direction. The sand is talcum-soft and clean, the water calm and clear (though local surfers take advantage of occasional small reef breaks), and the bottom somewhat rocky and dotted with sea urchins, so wear reef shoes if wading. You'll definitely find fewer crowds. **Amenities:** none. **Best for:** snorkeling; solitude; surfing. ⊠ *West Bay Rd., Seven Mile Beach.*

East End Beaches. Just drive along and look for any sandy beach, park your car, and enjoy a stroll. The vanilla-hue stretch at Colliers Bay, by the Reef and Morritt's resorts (which offer water sports), is a good, clean one with superior snorkeling. **Amenities:** food and drink; water sports. **Best for:** snorkeling; solitude; sunrise; walking. ⊠ *Queen's Hwy., East End.*

Old Man Bay. The North Side features plenty of hidden coves and pristine stretches of perfect sand, where you'll be disturbed only by seabirds dive-bombing for lunch and the occasional lone fishers casting nets for sprats, then dumping them into buckets. Over the Edge restaurant is less than 1 mile (1½ km) west. Otherwise, it's fairly undeveloped for miles, save for the occasional private home. Snorkeling is spectacular when waters are calm. **Amenities:** food and drink. **Best for:** snorkeling; solitude; walking. ⊠ *Queen's Hwy., just off Frank Sound Rd., North Side.*

Rum Point. This North Sound beach has hammocks slung in towering casuarina trees, picnic tables, casual and "fancier" dining options, a well-stocked shop for seaworthy sundries, and Red Sail Sports, which offers various water sports and boats to explore Stingray City. The barrier reef ensures safe snorkeling and soft sand. The bottom remains shallow for a long way from shore, but it's littered with small coral heads, so be careful. The Wreck is an ultracasual hangout serving outstanding pub grub from fish-and-chips to wings, as well as lethal Mudslide cocktails. Just around the bend, another quintessential beach hangout, Kaibo, rocks during the day. **Amenities:** food and drink; parking (no fee); showers; toilets; water sports. **Best for:** partiers; snorkeling. ⊠ *Rum Point, North Side.*

Fodor'sChoice **Seven Mile Beach.** Grand Cayman's west coast is dominated by this
     ★   famous beach—actually a 6½-mile (10-km) expanse of powdery white sand overseeing lapis water stippled with a rainbow of parasails and kayaks. Free of litter and pesky peddlers, it's an unspoiled (though often crowded) environment. Most of the island's resorts, restaurants, and shopping centers sit along this strip. The public beach toward the north end offers chairs for rent ($10 for the day, including a beverage), a playground, water toys aplenty, beach bars, restrooms, and showers. The best snorkeling is at either end, by the Marriott and Treasure Island or off Cemetery Beach, to the north. **Amenities:** food and drink; showers; toilets; water sports. **Best for:** partiers; snorkeling. ⊠ *West Bay Rd., Seven Mile Beach.*

Smith's Cove. South of the Grand Old House, this tiny but popular protected swimming and snorkeling spot makes a wonderful beach wedding location. The bottom drops off quickly enough to allow you to swim and play close to shore. Although slightly rocky (its pitted limestone boulders resemble Moore sculptures), there's little debris and few coral heads, plenty of shade, picnic tables, restrooms, and parking. Surfers will find decent swells just to the south. Note the curious obelisk cenotaph "In memory of James Samuel Webster and his wife Arabella Antoinette (née Eden)," with assorted quotes from Confucius to John Donne. **Amenities:** parking (no fee); toilets. **Best for:** snorkeling; sunset; swimming. ⊠ *Off S. Church St., George Town.*

WHERE TO EAT

Despite its small size, comparative geographic isolation, and British colonial trappings, Grand Cayman offers a smorgasbord of gastronomic goodies. With more than 100 eateries, something should suit and sate every palate and pocketbook (factoring in the fast-food franchises sweeping the islandscape like tumbleweed, and stands dispensing local specialties). The term *melting pot* describes both the majority of menus and the multicultural population. The sheer range of dining options from Middle Eastern to Mexican reflects the island's cosmopolitan clientele. Imported ingredients make up their own United Nations, with chefs sourcing salmon from Norway, foie gras from Périgord, and lamb from New Zealand. Wine lists can be equally global in scope. And don't be surprised to find both Czech and Chilean staffers at a remote East End restaurant. As one restaurateur quipped, "Cayman is the ultimate culture-shock absorber."

Prices are about 25% more than those in a major U.S. city. Many restaurants add a 10% to 15% service charge to the bill; be sure to check before leaving a tip. Alcohol with your meal can send the tab skyrocketing. Buy liquor duty-free before you leave the airport and enjoy a cocktail or nightcap from the comfort of your room or balcony. Cayman customs limits you to two bottles per person. You should make reservations at all but the most casual places, particularly during the high season. Note that many bars offer fine fare (and many eateries have hip, hopping bar scenes).

What to Wear: Grand Cayman dining is casual (shorts are okay, but *not* beachwear and tank tops). Mosquitoes can be pesky when you're dining outdoors, especially at sunset, so plan ahead or ask for repellent. Winter can be chilly enough to warrant a light sweater.

AROUND GEORGE TOWN

$$$$
ECLECTIC
Fodor'sChoice
★

✕ **The Brasserie.** Actuaries, bankers, and CEOs frequent this contemporary throwback to a colonial country club for lunch and "attitude adjustment" happy hours for creative cocktails and complimentary canapés. Inviting fusion sea-to-table cuisine, emphasizing local ingredients whenever possible (the restaurant has its own boat and garden), includes terrific bar tapas. Several evenings, you can get a five-course market-driven Random Acts of Cooking blind tasting. Dishes deftly balance flavors and textures without sensory overload: this is serious food with a sense of playfulness. Save room for dessert, from an artisanal cheese plate to an ice-cream-and-sorbet tasting menu to elaborate architectural confections. Lunch is more reasonably priced but equally creative; the adjacent Market excels at takeout, and the wine list is well considered. $ *Average main: $31* ⊠ *171 Elgin Ave., Cricket Sq., George Town* ☎ *345/945–1815* ⊕ *www.brasseriecayman.com* ⊘ *Closed weekends* ⚞ *Reservations essential.*

$$$ ╳ **Casanova Restaurant by the Sea.** Owner Tony Crescente and younger
ITALIAN brother–maitre d' Carlo offer a simpatico dining experience, practically exhorting you to *mangia* and sending you off with a chorus of ciaos. There's some decorative *formaggio* (cheese): murals of grape clusters and cavorting cherubs, paintings of the Amalfi Coast, and *"una finestra sul mare"* ("window to the sea") stenciled redundantly over arches opening onto the harbor. The kitsch doesn't extend to the kitchen. Sterling Italian favorites include salmon marinated in citrus, olive oil, and basil; lemony veal piccata; gnocchetti in velvety four-cheese sauce with a blush of tomato; and seafood grill in parsley-garlic-lemon sauce. Enjoy grappa at the marble bar of Il Bacio lounge amid its wooden wine racks (the impressive selection isn't overly Italian-centric). The patio juts over the harbor, and moonlight, abetted by a sound track of Bocelli to Bennett, can transform an amorous coward into a Casanova. $ *Average main: $30* ⊠ *65 N. Church St., George Town* ☎ *345/949–7633* ⊕ *www.casanova.ky* ⚞ *Reservations essential.*

$$$ ╳ **Da Fish Shack.** This classic clapboard seaside shanty couldn't be hom-
SEAFOOD ier: constructed from an old fishing vessel, the structure is an authentic representation of original Caymanian architecture. The deck couldn't be better placed to savor the breezes and water views, and the chill Caribbean vibe makes it feel like you're dining at a friend's home. The owners source fresh, local ingredients wherever possible and developed relationships with Caymanian fishermen, who often cruise up to the dock with their catch. Savor jerk fish tacos, saltfish fritters, coconut shrimp with pineapple tomato salsa, and golden crunchy breadfruit fries. A wide array of non-seafood dishes is offered, from chicken schnitzel to a rib eye with sauce chasseur. The place hops on Sundown Saturdays with a CI$20 waterfront barbecue. Free Wi-Fi and occasional DJs are bonuses. $ *Average main: $25* ⊠ *127 N. Church St., George Town* ☎ *345/947–8126* ⊕ *www.dafishshack.com.*

$$$$ ╳ **Grand Old House.** Built in 1908 as the Petra Plantation House and
EUROPEAN transformed into the island's first upscale establishment decades ago,
Fodor'sChoice this grande dame evokes bygone grandeur sans pretension. The interior
★ rooms, awash in crystal, recall its plantation-house origins. Outside, hundreds of sparkling lights adorning the gazebos compete with the starry sky. Live nightly music and rumors of a charming blond ghost trailing white chiffon complete the picture. Expertly executed classics include panfried foie gras with berries, plantain, duck roulade, cranberry vinaigrette, and orange jus; butter-poached lobster; and coriander-crusted rack of lamb. The subtle yet complex flavor interactions, stellar service, and encyclopedic if stratospherically priced wine list ensure legendary status. Nightly happy hours with discounted tapas are a substantial bargain. $ *Average main: $45* ⊠ *648 S. Church St., George*

Town ☎ *345/949–9333* 🌐 *www.grandoldhouse.com* ⏱ *Closed Sept. and Sun. in low season. No lunch weekends* ✍ *Reservations essential.*

$$$$ SEAFOOD 🍴 **Guy Harvey's Island Grill.** Guy Harvey's is a stylish upstairs bistro, with a mahogany furnishings, ship's lanterns, porthole windows, fishing rods, and Harvey's action-packed marine art. The cool blues echo the sea and sky on display from the balcony. Seafood is carefully chosen to exclude overexploited and threatened species. Seasonally changing dishes are peppered with Caribbean influences but pureed through the original French chef's formal training. Hence, silken lobster bisque is served with puff pastry, scallops Rockefeller with spinach and béarnaise sauce, and the signature crab cakes with roasted-red-pepper aioli. You can select your fish baked, pan-sautéed, or grilled with any of eight sauces. Many specialties are cheaper at lunch. [$] *Average main: $38* ✉ *Aquaworld Duty-Free Mall, 55 S. Church St., George Town* ☎ *345/946–9000* 🌐 *www.guyharveysgrill.com.*

$$$$ SEAFOOD 🍴 **Lobster Pot.** The nondescript building belies the lovely marine-motif decor and luscious seafood at this intimate, second-story restaurant overlooking the harbor. Enjoy lobster prepared several ways (market price, it can be as much as $60) along with reasonably priced wine, which you can sample by the glass in the cozy bar. The two musts are the Cayman Trio (lobster tail, grilled mahimahi, and garlic shrimp) and the Pot (lobster, giant prawns, and crab). The kitchen happily provides reduced-oil and -fat alternatives to most dishes; vegetarians love the flavorful chili-lime polenta with grilled artichoke in mango cream, and tofu, zucchini, and yellow-squash spaghetti. The balcony offers a breathtaking view of the sunset tarpon feeding. [$] *Average main: $45* ✉ *245 N. Church St., George Town* ☎ *345/949–2736* 🌐 *www.lobsterpot.ky* ⏱ *No lunch weekends.*

SEVEN MILE BEACH

$$$$ ECLECTIC Fodor's Choice ★ 🍴 **Abacus.** This handsome Camana Bay hangout, once more notable for its stunning decor (witness the smoked glass-and-cast-iron chandeliers) has been transformed into a foodie mecca by Executive Chef Will O'Hara. Credit his farm-to-table "contemporary Caribbean cuisine" and the solid relationships he's developed with local purveyors, farmers, and fishermen. Start your evening with fresh in-season fruits in O'Hara's take on the classic Bellini (guava, mango). Segue into sashimi of the day or pork belly in Asian BBQ glaze beautifully counterpointed in taste and texture by pickled red cabbage. Daily market-inspired catch might be mahimahi over roasted local pumpkin drizzled with Cayman honey, allspice, and thyme. You can also make a fine meal from a couple of appetizers and/or such tasty tapas as oxtail spring rolls with island spiced coleslaw and chili dip or chickpea fritters accompanied by vibrantly hued local sun-dried cherry tomatoes, beetroot puree, and spinach. [$] *Average main: $35* ✉ *45 Market St., Camana Bay* ☎ *345/623–8282* 🌐 *www.deckers.ky* ⏱ *Closed Sun.* ✍ *Reservations essential.*

$$$$ ITALIAN Fodor's Choice ★ 🍴 **Agua.** This quietly hip spot plays up an aquatic theme with indigo glass fixtures, black-and-white photos of bridges and waterfalls, and cobalt-and-white walls subtly recalling foamy waves. Its young, international chefs emphasize seafood, preparing regional dishes from around the globe with a Caymanian slant, albeit emphasizing Peruvian and

Italian specialties from *tiraditos* to *tiramisu*. The Thai ceviche and the tender *entraña* (skirt steak Argentinean-style with *chimichurri*) burst with flavor. Presentation is painterly throughout, and authentic gelatos cap off the meal. Wine selections from lesser-known regions often represent good value, with 20 offered by the glass; the bartenders also creatively pair cocktails and food. Free tapas at happy hour and the three-course lunch menu are steals. [$] *Average main: $39* ✉ *Galleria Plaza, Seven Mile Beach* ☎ *345/949–2482* 🌐 *www.agua.ky* ✍ *Reservations essential.*

$$
MIDDLE EASTERN

🍴 **Al La Kebab.** The Silvermans started by serving late-night kebabs and gyros. Today their eatery works miracles out of two makeshift lean-tos splashed in vibrant colors and is still open until 4 am weeknights, 2 am weekends. Alan calls it a building-block menu; you can modify the bread and sauce—a dozen varieties, including several curries, peanut satay, jerk mayo, mango *raita* (yogurt, tomatoes, chutney), tahini, teriyaki, garlic cream, even gravy like Mom used to make. Food romps from Malaysia through the Mediterranean to Mexico: spicy chicken tikka, Thai chicken-lemongrass soup, and tzatziki as well as unusual salads (the Lebanese *fattoush*—toasted bread, mint, and parsley—is fabulous) and creative sides (addictive jalapeño-cheddar salsa for fries). [$] *Average main: $12* ✉ *Marquee Plaza, West Bay Rd., Seven Mile Beach* ☎ *345/943–4343* 🌐 *www.kebab.ky* ✍ *Reservations not accepted.*

$$$$
SEAFOOD

🍴 **Beach House** (*Casa Havana*). This refined eatery glamorously channels South Beach and Santa Monica, with a sexy black bar, an earthy color scheme, and sparkly ecru curtains dividing dining spaces. Executive chef Sandy Tuason apprenticed with such masters as the Roux brothers, Daniel Boulud, and David Burke. He masterfully adapts Mediterranean and Asian influences to local traditions and ingredients. The "coastal cuisine" menu offers mostly small plates and large plates to be shared family-style. Seafood is the star, unsurprisingly. But the mouthwatering sous vide beef tenderloin is a winner, too. Pairings are suggested for each dish, and the wine list features several fine $40 options and some surprising high-end bargains. Wine Master dinners pair several courses with wines (Marchese di Barolo to Gosset champagne), often introduced by guest winemakers or owners from as far afield as Tuscany, Australia, Napa, and Chile. [$] *Average main: $40* ✉ *Westin Grand Cayman Seven Mile Beach Resort & Spa, West Bay Rd., Seven Mile Beach* ☎ *345/945–3800* 🌐 *www.westingrandcayman.com* ⏲ *No lunch* ✍ *Reservations essential.*

$$$$
SEAFOOD
Fodor's Choice ★

🍴 **Blue by Eric Ripert.** *Top Chef* judge Eric Ripert's trademark ethereal seafood (executed by his handpicked brigade), flawless but not fawning service, swish setting, and soothing, unpretentious sophistication make this one of the Caribbean's finest restaurants. Choose from hedonistic six- and seven-course tasting menus (with or without wine pairing); there are also trendy "almost raw" and "barely touched" options. Many dishes are clever riffs on the mother restaurant (New York's celebrated Le Bernardin), using the island's natural bounty. Sensuous options might include lobster with purple cauliflower and macadamia nuts in truffle butter, or seared turbot with braised endive in a clam–foie gras emulsion. The vast wine list showcases heavy hitters, hot new regions, and lesser-known varietals. $ *Average main: $150* ✉ *Ritz-Carlton Grand Cayman, West Bay Rd., Seven Mile Beach* ☎ *345/943–9000* ⊘ *Closed Sun. and Mon. and Sept.–mid-Nov. No lunch* ⚐ *Reservations essential.*

$$$
ECLECTIC

✕ **The Brooklyn.** The industrial chic setting of this wildly popular new pizza and pasta joint cleverly recalls similar Brooklyn eateries in DUMBO and Williamsburg with natural wood tables for family-style dining, exposed piping, oversize metal lighting fixtures, distressed floors, and silkscreen paintings of musicians like Ray Charles and Diana Ross in Fauvist tones. The food proves equally trendy and appealing. You might start with the bountiful butcher's board of artisanal cheeses and charcuterie or a definitive fried calamari tossed with blistered tomatoes, artichokes, olives, and aioli. Pastas are all Mamma Mia garlic and attitude (marvelous meatballs), while the creative pizzas (the jerk chicken is dynamite in more ways than one, and the Nutella S'mores 'za makes a divine dessert) display Wolfgang Puck–ish flair. The attention to detail shows in everything from the garnishes on the craft cocktails to the marvelously presented flowerpot brimming with homemade sourdough. $ *Average main: $25* ✉ *The Crescent, Camana Bay* ☎ *345/640–0005* ⊕ *www.thebrooklyncayman.com* ▬ *No credit cards.*

$$
MEXICAN
Fodor'sChoice
★

✕ **Casa 43 Mexican Kitchen and Tequila Bar.** Mariachi music, sombreros, and intricate Talavera tile work set the tone at this authentic and innovative Mexican eatery tucked away off West Bay Road. Start with the savory ceviches (winners include Caribbean shrimp, Peruvian-style red snapper, and tuna Chino-Latino in soy with sesame, chile, mint, and cilantro). Or try such terrific tacos as the Tecate-battered rock shrimp, chicharrón, or fish. Sterling main courses range from salmon quesadilla to a pork chop in tamarind-orange-chipotle reduction. But the two musts are the delectable duck confit *chilaquiles* and fabulous *torta de cochinita pibil* (suckling pig sandwich) brimming with avocado, refried beans, pickled onions, and roasted tomato aioli, served with a heaping helping of the signature chili fries. Wash it down with magnificent margaritas. $ *Average main: $16* ✉ *Canal Point Dr., West Bay Rd., Seven Mile Beach* ⊹ *Behind Copper Falls Steakhouse* ☎ *345/949–4343* ⊕ *www.casa43.ky* ⊘ *Closed Sun.* ▬ *No credit cards.*

$$$$
SEAFOOD
Fodor'sChoice
★

✕ **Catch.** With the fishermen practically cruising up to your table with glistening seafood, this restaurant right on the harbor lives up to its name. Even the decor is appetizing, with walls daubed in edible hues like mustard, tomato, and mint, setting off bleached distressed wood. The prime seating is on the two patios, one of which has a retractable roof. The same appetizers are served at lunch and dinner, making a fine tapas-style option. You might savor the coriander-toasted crispy octopus; the tuna-wahoo carpaccio duo, both exquisite; tenderized thin slices of panko-fried conch; or the house answer to surf and turf: pork belly porchetta and seared scallop with apple and celery *all'amatriciana*. The standout among the stunners: oxtail ravioli, with sprouts adding just the right crunchiness while local pepper jelly contributes just enough heat. Like parent restaurant Agua there's a fabulous cocktail list, emphasizing modern twists on the classics, while Peter Bedocs, a member of the Court of Master Sommeliers oversees the excellent wine

7

list. **$** *Average main: $36* ✉ *Batabano Rd., Morgan's Harbour, West Bay* ☎ *345/949–4321* ⊕ *www.catch.ky* ▭ *No credit cards.*

$$ ✕ **Chicken! Chicken!** Devotees would probably award four exclamation
CARIBBEAN points to the marvelously moist chicken, slow-roasted on a hardwood
FAMILY open-hearth rotisserie. Most customers grab takeout, but the decor is appealing for a fast-food joint; the clever interior replicates an old-time Cayman cottage. Bright smiles and home cooking from scratch enhance the authentic vibe. Hearty but (mostly) healthful heaping helpings of sides include scrumptious Cayman-style corn bread, honey-rum beans, jicama coleslaw, and spinach-pesto pasta. Prices are even cheaper at lunch. **$** *Average main: $12* ✉ *West Shore Centre, West Bay Rd., Seven Mile Beach* ☎ *345/945–2290* ⊕ *www.chicken2.com.*

$$ ✕ **Cimboco.** This animated space celebrates all things fun and Carib-
ECLECTIC bean with walls saturated in orange, lemon, and lavender; cobalt glass fixtures; and flames dancing up the exhibition kitchen's huge wood-burning oven. The *Cimboco* was the first motorized sailing ship built in Cayman (in 1927) and for 20 years the lifeline to the outside world; National Archive photographs and old newspapers invest the space with still more character. Everything from breads (superlative brus-chetta and jalapeño corn bread) to ice creams is made from scratch. Artisanal pizzas come topped with balsamic-roasted eggplant, pesto, and feta or with jerk chicken with Bermuda onions. Signature items include banana-leaf-roasted snapper and fire-roasted bacon-wrapped shrimp. Amazingly good desserts include a sinfully rich brownie. The popular breakfast and brunch are equally creative. **$** *Average main: $19* ✉ *Marquee Plaza, West Bay Rd. at Harquail Bypass, Seven Mile Beach* ☎ *345/947–2782* ⊕ *www.cimboco.com.*

$$$ ✕ **Craft Food & Beverage Co.** Arguably Cayman's first true gastropub,
ECLECTIC Craft impresses with gorgeous post-industrial decor (contrasting warm
Fodor's Choice white exposed brick with gray piping) and contemporary rustic cui-
★ sine that defies labels. Executive Chef Dylan Benoit calls it "famil-iar food with a twist." The globe-trotting menu changes monthly and Dylan himself takes sabbaticals, traveling the world for inspiration. Stellar starters include jerk pork poutine, giant kale-cheddar piero-gies with house-made bacon, and addictive beer-battered cheese curds with spicy ranch dip. They even make their own condiments. Every day features a special: There's "Melting Pot" Wednesday (fondue), a raw bar on Thursday, featuring sublime ceviches and truly wild game such as ostrich chili or wild boar rack appears on Tuesday. They take pride in their remarkable beer selection, including gluten-free options, organizing tastings and flights, as well as food pairings. Bourbon and rum lovers have a fabulous selection, and mixology mavens can dive into the house infusions. **$** *Average main: $23* ✉ *Marquee Plaza, 489 West Bay Rd., Seven Mile Beach* ☎ *345/640–0004* ⊕ *www.craftcayman. com* ▭ *No credit cards.*

$$ ✕ **Eats Cafe.** This happy, hopping hangout is more eclectic and styl-
ECLECTIC ish than any diner, with dramatic decor (crimson booths and walls,
FAMILY flat-screen TVs lining the counter, steel pendant lamps, an exhibition kitchen, gigantic flower paintings, and Andy Warhol reproductions) and vast menu (Cajun to Chinese), including smashing breakfasts. The

10-plus burgers alone (Sauteed 'Shroomer to Smokey Mountain BBQ, as well as fish and veggie versions) could satisfy almost any craving, but you could also get a Caesar salad or samosas, Philly cheesesteak or chicken fajitas. It's noisy, busy, buzzing, and hip—but not aggressively so. $ *Average main: $16* ⊠ *Falls Plaza, West Bay Rd., Seven Mile Beach* ☏ *345/943–3287* ⊕ *www.eats.ky.*

$$$$

ITALIAN

Fodor's Choice

★

✕ **Luca.** Owners Paolo Polloni and Andi Marcher spared no expense in creating a smart beachfront trattoria that wouldn't be out of place in L.A. Everything was handpicked, from the wine wall of more than 3,000 international bottles to Murano glass fixtures, arty blown-up photographs, leather banquettes, and a curving onyx-top bar. Chef Frederico Destro delights in unorthodox pairings, all gorgeous. Tuna is served with pea pesto, wild rice, and Scotch bonnet aioli. Hudson Valley foie gras knits poached apple with sherry reduction and onion fondue. Homemade pastas like pumpkin ravioli in drawn thyme butter also shine, but the standout is a whole Mediterranean striped bass baked in salt crust. $ *Average main: $42* ⊠ *Caribbean Club, 871 West Bay Rd., Seven Mile Beach* ☏ *345/623–4550* ⊕ *luca.ky* ⊙ *Closed Mon. in Sept. and Oct. No lunch Sat.* ⌂ *Reservations essential.*

$$

ASIAN

Fodor's Choice

★

✕ **Mizu.** It's a toss-up as to which is sexier at this pan-Pacific bistro: the sleek decor, the model-worthy waitstaff, or the glistening, artfully presented food. The first, courtesy of Hong Kong designer Kitty Chan, is as sensuous as a 21st-century opium den with a back-lit dragon, contemporary Buddhas, glowing granite bar, wildly hued throw pillows, and enormous mirrors. The bartenders have developed a loyal local following for their flair in more ways than one. The last trots effortlessly all over Asia for culinary inspiration: terrific tuna tartare, decadent duck gyoza, killer kung pao chicken, smashing Singapore fried noodles, heavenly honey-glazed ribs, beautifully crispy Okinawan-style pork belly, and two dozen ultrafresh maki (try the signature roll). An extensive tea selection and a sake and wine list are also offered. $ *Average main: $20* ⊠ *Camana Bay* ☏ *345/640–0001* ⊕ *www.mizucayman.com.*

$$$

ECLECTIC

Fodor's Choice

★

✕ **Morgan's.** Energetic, effervescent Janie Schweiger patrols the front while husband Richard rules the kitchen at this simpatico marina spot with smashing Governor's Creek views. Locals and fishermen literally cruise into the adjacent dock for refueling of all sorts. You can sit in the large but homey room decorated with Depression-era fish-themed chandeliers and vivid aquatic artworks or admire the dexterous marine maneuverings from the expansive tiered deck. Richard's menu dances just as deftly from Asia to his Austrian home. Nimbly prepared nibbles include the wildly popular 10-ounce Brie-topped jerk burger and ceviche, but everything from chicken schnitzel to Thai seafood curry is expertly cooked to order. Lunch offers several of the restaurant's greatest hits at more palatable prices. $ *Average main: $29* ⊠ *Governor's Creek, Cayman Islands Yacht Club, Seven Mile Beach* ☏ *345/946–7049* ⊕ *www. morganscayman.com* ⊙ *Closed Tues. and Oct.* ⌂ *Reservations essential.*

$$$$

ECLECTIC

Fodor's Choice

★

✕ **Ortanique.** The vibrant food here lives up to its nickname: "cuisine of the sun." It's an outpost of chef Cindy Hutson and Delius Shirley's Miami Ortanique, which helped revolutionize Floribbean fusion fare. The interior gleams in rich yellows and oranges that subtly recall

7

plantation living, though prize seating is on the patio, shaded by sea grape trees overlooking an islet. There is an emphasis on Caribbean and South American cuisine infused with Asian inspirations. The kitchen reinvents classics with an island twist: jerk-rubbed foie gras with burnt-orange marmalade, and the signature jerked double pork chop, fire-tamed by passion-fruit-mango *chimichurri*. Save room for such decadent desserts as a deceptively airy Cloud of Coconut Joy or rum-soaked banana fritters. Best of all are almost nightly happy hour specials from Mojito Madness Mondays to Throwback Thursdays. [$] *Average main: $36* ✉ *47 Forum La., The Crescent, Camana Bay* ☎ *345/640–7710* 🌐 *www.ortaniquerestaurants.com* 🕓 *Closed Sun. June–Oct.*

$$$ ITALIAN Fodor's Choice ★ 🍴 **Ragazzi.** The name means "good buddies," and this strip-mall jewel percolates with conversation and good strong espresso. The airy space is convivial: blond woods, periwinkle walls and columns, and handsome artworks of beach scenes, sailboats, and palm trees. Chef Adriano Usini meticulously prepares standards; the antipasto alone is worth a visit, as are homemade breadsticks and focaccia, carpaccio, and insalata Caprese. The shellfish linguine in a light, silken tomato sauce, with cherry-tomato skins pulled back and crisped, and gnocchi in four-cheese sauce with brandy and pistachios please pasta perfectionists. Two dozen first-rate pizzas emerge from the wood-burning oven, and meat and seafood mains are beautifully done, never overcooked. The wine list is notable (400-odd choices) for a casual eatery, offering affordability even on heavy hitters such as Biondi Santi Brunello, Jermann Pinot Grigio, and Giacosa Barbaresco; the knowledgeable staff will gladly suggest pairings. [$] *Average main: $24* ✉ *Buckingham Square, West Bay Rd., Seven Mile Beach* ☎ *345/945–3484* 🌐 *www.ragazzi.ky.*

$$$$ ECLECTIC 🍴 **Reef Grill at Royal Palms.** This class act appeals to a casual, suave crowd, many of them regulars, who appreciate its consistent quality, efficient service, soothing seaside setting, top-notch entertainment, and surprisingly reasonable prices. The space is cannily divided into four areas, each with its own look and feel, including private beach cabanas (no extra charge). Co-owner-chef George Dahlstrom gives his perfectly prepared, familiar items just enough twist to satisfy jaded palates: calamari is fried in arborio rice batter with jalapeño aioli while Chilean sea bass swims amid Thai salad and homemade wontons. The Royal Palms menu offers more casual, inexpensive fare. Dance the calories off to the estimable reggae, calypso, and soca sounds of Coco Red or really sweat it out during Chill Wednesdays, and then adjourn to the cozy lounge for an aged rum or single malt. It's equally enticing at lunch, when it exudes a soigné beach bar ambience. [$] *Average main: $33* ✉ *537 West Bay Rd., Seven Mile Beach* ☎ *345/945–6358* 🌐 *www.reefgrill.com* 🕓 *No dinner Sun. May–Nov.*

$$$$ STEAKHOUSE 🍴 **Seven.** The Ritz-Carlton's all-purpose dining room transforms from a bustling breakfast buffet to an elegant evening eatery. Tall potted palms, soaring ceilings, a black-and-beige color scheme, twin wine walls bracketing a trendy family-style table, and the tiered pool outside are lighted to stylish effect. Sinatra and Ella keep a sultry beat while the kitchen jazzes standard meat-and-potatoes dishes with inventive seasonings and eye-catching presentations. Splendid aged Niman Ranch steaks come

with five sauces and rubs, from five-peppercorn to béarnaise. Even such sides as truffled mac-and-cheese redefine decadence. The calorie- and cholesterol-conscious can savor the likes of melt-in-your-mouth ahi tuna poke. Then surrender to the chocolate and sea-salt caramel candy bar. Nightly happy hour (5–7) offers superb bar snacks like tempura Brie with local pepper jelly and jerk maple-glazed pork belly. $ *Average main: $51* ⊠ *Ritz-Carlton Grand Cayman, West Bay Rd., Seven Mile Beach* ☎ *345/943–9000* ⊕ *www.ritzcarlton.com.*

$$$ ✕ **Sunshine Grill.** This cheerful, cherished locals' secret serves haute com-
CARIBBEAN fort food at bargain prices. Even the chattel-style poolside building,
FAMILY painted a delectable lemon with lime shutters and orange and blue-
berry accents, whets the appetite. Sunshine ranks high in the island's greatest burger debate, while the chicken egg rolls with mango chutney and jerk mayo and the fabulous fish tacos elevate pub grub to an art. Wash your food down with a signature libation like the Painkiller, and take advantage of affordable nightly dinner specials such as red snap-per amandine in lemon butter caper sauce, and Cuban roast chicken marinated with sour orange, garlic, lime, and olive oil. $ *Average main: $23* ⊠ *Sunshine Suites Resort, 1465 Esterley Tibbetts Hwy., Seven Mile Beach* ☎ *345/949–3000, 345/946–5848* ⊕ *www.sunshinesuites.com.*

$$ ✕ **The Waterfront.** Ultracontemporary design with industrial elements
AMERICAN (exposed piping, raw timber, tugboat salvage) is a counterpoint to the
FAMILY down-home fare at this bustling glorified diner, whose choice seats
are on the patio. Comfort food aficionados can launch into the splen-did chicken and waffles, meat loaf, pizzas, and poutine. The kitchen is also adept at sexier dishes, such as polenta-portobello burger with goat cheese and pork belly flatbread with cilantro and spicy kimchi sauce. Finish off your meal with the enormous cinnamon bun, though it might finish you off. $ *Average main: $19* ⊠ *The Crescent, Camana Bay* ☎ *345/640–0002* ⊕ *www.waterfrontcayman.com.*

$$$ ✕ **Yoshi Sushi.** This modish locals' lair serves superlative sushi. The main
JAPANESE room's scarlet cushions, cherry blown-glass pendant lamps, leather-and-
bamboo accents, orchids, and maroon walls create a sensuous, charged vibe. At the backlighted bar, carefree customers try to work their chop-sticks after a few kamikaze sake bomber missions (hot cups of sake plunged into frosty Kirin beer). Savvy diners literally leave themselves in Yoshi's hands (the rolls and nightly sushi "pizzas" are particularly creative), while the raw-phobic can choose from fine cooked items, from tuna tataki to tempura to teriyaki. The congenial staff recommends sake and beer pairings, but the wine and martini selections are also admirable for an Asian eatery. $ *Average main: $23* ⊠ *Falls Plaza, West Bay Rd., Seven Mile Beach* ☎ *345/943–9674* ⊕ *www.eats.ky/yoshisushi* ✍ *Reservations essential.*

WEST BAY

$$$$ ✕ **Calypso Grill.** Shack chic describes this inviting split-level space
ECLECTIC splashed in Dr. Seuss primary colors that contrast with brick walls,
hardwood furnishings, terra-cotta floors, trompe l'oeil shutters, and (real) French doors opening onto sweeping North Sound vistas. If the interior is like a Caribbean painting, the outdoor deck, with a view of frigate birds circling fishing boats, is a Winslow Homer. George Fowler's

menu emphasizes fish hauled in at the adjacent dock, fresh and rarely overcooked. You won't go wrong with the unvarnished catch of the day grilled, blackened, or sautéed. Though this is seafood turf, landlubbers can savor escargot bourguignonne, beef carpaccio, or a proper rack of lamb. End with the sticky toffee pudding. $ *Average main: $43* ⊠ *Morgan's Harbour, West Bay* ☎ *345/949–3948* ⊕ *www.calypsogrillcayman.com* ⊘ *Closed Mon.* ⚱ *Reservations essential.*

$$$$ ✕ **Cracked Conch.** This island institution effortlessly blends upscale and
ECLECTIC   down-home. The interior gleams from the elaborate light-and-water sculpture at the gorgeous mosaic-and-mahogany entrance bar to the plush booths with subtly embedded lighting. Take in the remarkable water views through large shutters, but for maximum impact, dine on the multitiered patio. The capable chefs reinvent familiar dishes to create such delectables as honey-jerk-glazed tuna tartare with tomato sorbet and crispy calamari with cardamom-marinated carrots and chipotle sauce. Stellar signature items include the conch chowder or ceviche, silken short rib ravioli with truffles and Parmesan foam, crispy soft shell crab and braised pork belly with mint-pea puree and guava gastrique, and sous vide lobster over mango-orange demiglace. Locals flock to Sunday brunch and hang out at the dockside Macabuca tiki bar (fab sunsets, sunset-hued libations), which lives up to its mellow name, indigenous Taíno for "What does it matter?" $ *Average main: $45* ⊠ *Northwest Point Rd., West Bay* ☎ *345/945–5217* ⊕ *www.crackedconch.com.ky* ⊘ *Closed Sept.–mid-Oct. No lunch June–Aug.*

$$$$ ✕ **Osetra Bay.** At sunset (when brightly colored fishing boats bob in
ECLECTIC   the tourmaline North Sound) and at night (when Cayman Kai's lights twinkle and the moon dapples the water with gold doubloons), the view alone guarantees a memorable meal. The design is almost as appetizing—glowing columns strategically placed to flatter diners; intimate, billowingly draped dining cabanas; stark Starck-ish white-on-white ultralounges—infusing casual Caribbean underpinnings with a chic South Beach sensibility, literally bringing caviar to Cayman. The seasonal menu (sourced locally when possible) emphasizes seafood: seared coffee-crusted yellowfin tuna with wasabi mash and roasted red pepper sauce and wahoo with pea and smoked-potato purees, pickled beets, and lemon butter sauce. Carnivores can stake out crispy pork belly with pineapple-corn relish and sorrel chutney, oxtail ravioli with red-wine veal jus and Parmesan foam, or dry-aged rib eye. $ *Average main: $52* ⊠ *Morgan's Harbour, West Bay* ☎ *345/325–5000, 345/623–5100* ⊕ *www.osetrabay.com* ⊘ *Closed Sun. No lunch* ⚱ *Reservations essential.*

$$$$ ✕ **Ristorante Pappagallo.** Pappagallo, Italian for "parrot," hauntingly
ITALIAN   perches on the edge of a lagoon in a 14-acre bird sanctuary. Inside, riotously colored macaws, cockatoos, and parrots perch on swings behind plate glass, primping, preening, and practically commenting on the billing and cooing clientele. You feel like hacking through the luxuriant vegetation inside and out; the lost-in-the-jungle exoticism is enhanced by locally hewn stones, bamboo, homemade rope, and thatched palapas for outdoor seating. Yet the sleek deco-inspired black marble and polished brass accents bespeak the underlying seriousness. Italian-born

Chef Marco Signori's food is definitely not for the birds, especially his sublime risotti, pastas, local suckling pulled pig with apple-sorrel puree and licorice sauce, and seafood such as mahimahi, the kick of its smoked chipotle emulsion balanced by the sweet and tart mango-papaya salsa. Be sure to thank Bogie, the African gray parrot, who really rules the roost. $ *Average main: $39* ⊠ *Barkers, 444B Conch Point Rd., West Bay* ☎ *345/949–1119* ⊕ *www.pappagallo.ky* ☾ *No lunch* ✍ *Reservations essential.*

EAST END

$$$
SEAFOOD

✕ **The Lighthouse.** This lighthouse surrounded by fluttering flags serves as a beacon for hungry East End explorers. The interior replicates a yacht: polished hardwood floors, ship's lanterns, mosaic hurricane lamps, steering wheels, portholes, and waiters in crew's garb with chevrons. Most tables afford sweeping sea vistas, but prized romantic seating is on a little deck. Starters include Miss Nell's red conch chowder and flash-fried calamari with sweet chili dip. Entrées include a platter of seafood floating on linguine Alfredo and a mustard/herb-crusted rack of lamb with Marsala-mint sauce. Vegetarian options include curries, tofu stir-fries, and pastas. Desserts include the Illy espresso crème brûlée. The comprehensive wine list extends to a superb postprandial selection of liqueurs, aged rums, ports, and grappas. Inexpensive prix-fixe lunch and dinner pasta specials are CI$9.95 and CI$15, respectively. $ *Average main: $30* ⊠ *2114 Bodden Town Rd., Oceanside, Breakers, East End* ☎ *345/947–2047* ⊕ *www.lighthouse.ky.*

$$
CARIBBEAN

✕ **Vivine's Kitchen.** Cars practically block the road at this unprepossessing hot spot for classic Caymanian food—literally Vivine and Ray Watler's home. Prime seating is in the waterfront courtyard, serenaded by rustling sea grape leaves, crashing surf, and screeching gulls. The day's menu, sourced locally for freshness, is scrawled on a blackboard: perhaps stewed turtle, curried goat, barbecued chicken, and snapper, with cassava and sweet-potato cake sides. Burgers, dogs, and chicken-and-chips make a concession to more timid taste buds. Alcohol isn't served, but fresh tamarind, mango, and sorrel juices pack a flavorful punch. Vivine's generally closes early (and occasionally on Monday), but stays open if there's demand—and any food left. $ *Average main: $17* ⊠ *Austin Dr., Gun Bay, East End* ☎ *345/947–7435* ▭ *No credit cards.*

NORTH SIDE

$$$
CARIBBEAN

✕ **Kaibo Beach Bar and Grill.** Overlooking the North Sound, this beach hangout rocks days (fantastic lunches that cost half the price of dinner, festive atmosphere including impromptu volleyball tourneys, and free Wi-Fi) and serves murderous margaritas and mudslides well into the evening to boisterous yachties, locals, sports buffs, and expats. Enjoy New England–style conch chowder with a hint of heat, smoked mahimahi pâté, hefty burgers, and wondrous wraps, either on the multitiered deck garlanded with ships' rope and Christmas lights or in hammocks and thatched cabanas amid the palms. Swaddled in white muslin, the nautically themed Upstairs dining room (noted for its rare rum selection) is open Thursday through Sunday nights (reservations essential) and serves more creative fare at higher prices. Specialties include baked

7

grouper with Kaffir lime–leaf crust in sweet corn velouté. The ultimate in romance is the catered Luna del Mar on the Friday evening closest to the full moon. Tuesday beach barbecues are popular (including limbo dancing, live music, half-price drinks, and discounted water taxi service to the "mainland"). [$] *Average main: $30* ✉ *585 Water Cay Rd., Rum Point* ☎ *345/947–9975* 🌐 *www.kaibo.ky.*

$$$ CARIBBEAN 🍴 **Over the Edge.** This fun, funky seaside spot brims with character and characters. (A soused regular might welcome you by reciting "the daily lunch special: chilled barley soup . . . That's beer.") The nutty nautical decor—brass ships' lanterns dangle from the ceiling, and steering wheels, lacquered turtle shells, and fishing photos adorn the walls—contrasts with cool mirrored ads for Gitanes and Mumm Cordon Rouge and the trendily semi-open kitchen with fresh fish prominently displayed. The jukebox jumps (country music rules the roost), and the tiki-lighted terrace offers stunning views and fresh breezes. Expertly prepared local fare (Cajun chicken to conch steak to Cayman rock lobster escoveitch, served with rice and beans, plantains, and fried festival bread) is a bargain, especially at lunch, though the chef also surprises with such gussied-up fare as shrimp in Pernod sauce and turtle steak in port. [$] *Average main: $21* ✉ *312 North Side Rd., Old Man Bay* ☎ *345/947–9568* 🌐 *www.overtheedgecayman.com.*

WHERE TO STAY

Brace yourself for resort prices—there are few accommodations in the lower price ranges. You'll find no big all-inclusive resorts on Grand Cayman (though the Reef Resort offers an optional AI plan to its guests), and very few offer a meal plan other than breakfast. Parking is always free at island hotels and resorts. Although the island has several resorts (mostly along Seven Mile Beach), the majority of accommodations are vacation rentals, and these are scattered throughout the island. Some of the condo complexes even offer resort-style amenities. The big news is Kimpton Hotels' eagerly awaited unveiling of the mixed-use Seafire Resort & Spa on a prime stretch of Seven Mile Beach. It's slated for completion by the end of 2016, featuring 265 rooms and 61 condos in two 10-story towers.

They may be some distance from the beach and short on style and facilities, but the island's guesthouses offer rock-bottom prices, a friendly atmosphere, and your best shot at getting to know the locals. Rooms are clean and simple, and most have private baths.

PRIVATE VILLAS AND CONDOS

Most condo complexes are very similar, with telephones, satellite TV, air-conditioning, living and dining areas, patios, and parking. Differences are amenities, proximity to town and beach, and the views. As with resorts, rates are higher in winter, and there may be a three- or seven-night minimum. There are dozens of large private villas available on the beach, especially on the North Side near Cayman Kai. A growing trend: "green" condos. We no longer recommend individual private villas, especially since they frequently change agents. However, among the properties we've inspected, worth looking for are Coral Reef, Venezia,

Villa Habana, Great Escapes, Fishbones, and Pease Bay House. Several of the condo and villa rental companies have websites where you can see pictures of the privately owned units and villas they represent.

RENTAL CONTACTS

Cayman Island Vacations. Longtime Cayman homeowners Don and Linda Martin represent more than 50 villas and condos (including their own). Extremely helpful with island suggestions, they can make arrangements for a rental car, diving discounts, and extras, and Linda is a leading wedding coordinator. ☎ *813/854–1201, 888/208–8935* 🌐 *www.caymanvacation.com.*

Cayman Villas. This locally owned agent represents top-notch villas and condos on Grand and Little Cayman, offering concierge service before and during your stay. ✉ *177 Owen Roberts Dr., George Town* ☎ *800/235–5888, 345/945–4144* 🌐 *www.caymanvillas.com.*

Grand Cayman Villas. Virginia resident Jim Leavitt carries listings for dozens of fine properties island-wide. He and his staff visit the island regularly to ensure quality and remain up-to-date. ☎ *866/358–8455* 🌐 *www.grandcaymanvillas.net.*

Wimco. The West Indies Management Company is synonymous with quality, especially in the Caribbean. ☎ *866/850–6140, 800/449–1553* 🌐 *www.wimco.com.*

7

AROUND GEORGE TOWN

$$ HOTEL 🏨 **Sunset House.** This amiable seaside dive-oriented resort is on the ironshore south of George Town, close enough for a short trip to stores and restaurants yet far enough to feel secluded. **Pros:** great shore diving and dive shop; lively bar scene; fun international clientele; great package rates. **Cons:** often indifferent service; somewhat run-down; no real swimming beach; spotty Wi-Fi signal; five-night minimum stay required in high season. [$] *Rooms from: $281* ✉ *390 S. Church St., George Town* ☎ *345/949–7111, 800/854–4767* 🌐 *www.sunsethouse.com* 🛏 *58 rooms, 2 suites* 🍴 *Breakfast.*

SEVEN MILE BEACH

$$$$ RENTAL Fodor's Choice ★ 🏨 **Caribbean Club.** This gleaming boutique facility has a striking lobby with aquariums, infinity pool, and contemporary trattoria, Luca. **Pros:** luxurious, high-tech facilities beyond the typical apartment complex; trendy Italian restaurant; service on the beach. **Cons:** stratospheric prices; poor bedroom reading lights; though families are welcome, they may find it imposing; smaller top-floor balconies (albeit amazing views). [$] *Rooms from: $1256* ✉ *871 West Bay Rd., Seven Mile Beach* ☎ *345/623–4500, 800/941–1126* 🌐 *www.caribclub.com* 🛏 *37 3-bedroom condos* 🍴 *No meals.*

$$ RENTAL FAMILY 🏨 **Christopher Columbus.** This enduring favorite on the peaceful northern end of Seven Mile Beach is a discovery for families. **Pros:** excellent snorkeling; fine beach; great value; complimentary Wi-Fi. **Cons:** car needed; often overrun by families during holidays and summer; top floors have difficult access for physically challenged. [$] *Rooms from: $375* ✉ *2013 West Bay Rd., Seven Mile Beach* ☎ *345/945–4354, 866/311–5231* 🌐 *www.christophercolumbuscondos.com* 🛏 *30 2- and 3-bedroom condos* 🍴 *No meals.*

$ 🏨 **Comfort Suites Grand Cayman.** This no-frills, all-suites hotel has an
HOTEL ideal location, next to the Marriott and near numerous shops, restaurants, and bars. **Pros:** affordable; complimentary buffet breakfast
and Wi-Fi; fun, young-ish crowd. **Cons:** rooms nearly a block from
the beach; new condo blocks sea views; no balconies; bar closes early.
$ *Rooms from: $241* ⊠ *West Bay Rd., George Town* ☎ *345/945–7300,
800/517–4000* ⊕ *www.caymancomfort.com* ⮞ *108 suites* ⦿ *Breakfast.*

$$$$ 🏨 **Coral Stone Club.** In the shadow of the Ritz-Carlton, this exclusive
RENTAL enclave still shines by offering understated barefoot luxury, stellar
service, and huge condos. **Pros:** large ratio of beach and pool space
to guests; walking distance to restaurants and shops; free airport
transfers; excellent off-season deals. **Cons:** expensive in high season;
Ritz-Carlton guests sometimes wander over to poach beach space.
$ *Rooms from: $800* ⊠ *West Bay Rd., Seven Mile Beach* ☎ *345/945–
5820, 888/927–2322* ⊕ *www.coralstoneclub.com* ⮞ *30 3-bedroom
condos* ⦿ *No meals.*

$$$$ 🏨 **Grand Cayman Beach Suites.** The former Hyatt all-suites section, now
RESORT locally run, offers a terrific beachfront location and trendy eateries.
Pros: fine beach; superior dining and water-sports facilities; free use of
gym (unusual on Grand Cayman); supermarkets and restaurants within
walking distance; significant online discounts. **Cons:** most entrances
face the street, making it noisy on weekends; small parking lot; several units need refurbishment; music often blaring around the pool.
$ *Rooms from: $965* ⊠ *West Bay Rd., Seven Mile Beach* ☎ *345/949–
1234* ⊕ *www.grand-cayman-beach-suites.com, www.gcbs.ky* ⮞ *53
suites* ⦿ *No meals.*

$$$ 🏨 **Grand Cayman Marriott Beach Resort.** The soaring, stylish marble
RESORT lobby (with exquisite art glass, spectacular blown-up underwater
FAMILY photos, marine paraphernalia, and fun elements such as red British-
Fodor'sChoice style telephone boxes and apothecary cart dispensing "holistic hand-
★ crafted infusions") sets the tone for this bustling beachfront property,
which received a $16-million renovation in 2015. **Pros:** lively bars and
restaurants; good snorkeling and water sports; free bike and kayak
rentals; convenient to both George Town and Seven Mile Beach; air-
port connectivity lets you print your boarding pass. **Cons:** often over-
run by tour groups and conventioneers; narrowest section of Seven
Mile Beach; pool and bar often noisy late; $45 resort fee. $ *Rooms
from: $399* ⊠ *389 West Bay Rd., Seven Mile Beach* ☎ *345/949–0088,
800/223–6388* ⊕ *www.marriottgrandcayman.com* ⮞ *273 rooms, 22
suites* ⦿ *No meals.*

$$$ 🏨 **The Grandview.** Grand view, indeed: all 69 two- and three-bedroom
RENTAL units (sadly only 15 are generally in the rental pool) look smack onto
FAMILY the Caribbean and the beach past splendidly maintained gardens. **Pros:**
restaurants and shops within walking distance; wine concierge dispenses
advice; free Wi-Fi (when it's available); nice pool and hot tub. **Cons:** the
long beach can be rocky; some units a tad worn though meticulously
maintained; not all units have access to the free Wi-Fi signal. $ *Rooms
from: $475* ⊠ *95 Snooze La., Seven Mile Beach* ☎ *345/945–4511,
866/977–6766* ⊕ *www.grandviewcondos.com* ⮞ *69 2- and 3-bedroom
condos* ⦿ *No meals.*

$$$
RENTAL

Lacovia Condominiums. The carefully manicured courtyard of this handsome arcaded Mediterranean Revival property could easily be mistaken for a peaceful park. **Pros:** central location; exquisite gardens; extensive beach. **Cons:** rear courtyard rooms can be noisy from traffic and partying from West Bay Road; pool fairly small (though most people prefer the beach). $ *Rooms from: $415* ⊠ *697 West Bay Rd., Seven Mile Beach* ☎ *345/949–7599* ⊕ *www.lacovia.com* ⇨ *35 1-, 2-, and 3-bedroom condos* ⦿ *No meals.*

$$$$
RESORT
FAMILY
Fodor's Choice
★

Ritz-Carlton Grand Cayman. This 144-acre resort, as exquisitely manicured as its clientele, offers unparalleled luxury and service infused with a sense of place, with works by local artists and craftspeople. **Pros:** exemplary service; exceptional facilities with complimentary extras. **Cons:** annoyingly high resort fee; sprawling with a confusing layout; long walk to beach (over an interior bridge) from most rooms. $ *Rooms from: $799* ⊠ *West Bay Rd., Seven Mile Beach* ☎ *345/943–9000* ⊕ *www.ritzcarlton. com* ⇨ *353 rooms, 12 suites, 24 condos* ⦿ *Breakfast.*

$
HOTEL

Sunshine Suites Resort. This friendly, all-suites hotel is an impeccably clean money saver. **Pros:** good value and Internet deals; cheerful staff; rocking little restaurant; thoughtful free extras including business center and access to nearby World Gym. **Cons:** poor views; not on the beach. $ *Rooms from: $265* ⊠ *1465 Esterley Tibbetts Hwy., off West Bay Rd., Seven Mile Beach* ☎ *345/949–3000, 877/786–1110* ⊕ *www. sunshinesuites.com* ⇨ *130 suites* ⦿ *Breakfast.*

$$$$
RESORT
FAMILY
Fodor's Choice
★

Westin Grand Cayman Seven Mile Beach Resort & Spa. The Westin offers something for everyone, from conventioneers to honeymooners to families, not to mention what the hospitality industry calls "location location location." **Pros:** terrific children's programs; superb beach (the largest resort stretch at 800 feet); better-than-advertised ocean views; heavy online discounts. **Cons:** occasionally bustling and impersonal when large groups book; daily $45 resort fee. $ *Rooms from: $505* ⊠ *West Bay Rd., Seven Mile Beach* ☎ *345/945–3800, 800/937–8461* ⊕ *www.westingrandcayman.com* ⇨ *339 rooms, 8 suites* ⦿ *No meals.*

WEST BAY

$$
RESORT

Cobalt Coast Resort and Suites. This small eco-friendly hotel is perfect for divers who want a moderately priced spacious room or suite right on the ironshore far from the madding crowds. **Pros:** superb dive outfit; friendly service and clientele; free Wi-Fi; environmentally aware. **Cons:** poky golden-sand beach; unattractive concrete pool area; remote location, so a car (included in some packages) is necessary. $ *Rooms from: $290* ⊠ *18-A Sea Fan Dr., West Bay* ☎ *345/946–5656, 877/673–8820* ⊕ *www.cobaltcoast.com* ⇨ *7 rooms, 15 suites* ⦿ *Some meals.*

$$$
RESORT
Fodor's Choice
★

Lighthouse Point. Scuba operator DiveTech's stunning ecodevelopment (motto "living lightly on the planet") features sustainable wood interiors and recycled concrete, a gray-water system, energy-saving appliances and lights, and Cayman's first wind turbine generator. **Pros:** eco-friendly; fantastic shore diving (and state-of-the-art dive shop); creative and often recycled upscale look; superb eatery. **Cons:** no real beach; car necessary; bit difficult for physically challenged to navigate. $ *Rooms from: $450* ⊠ *571 Northwest Point Rd., West Bay* ☎ *345/949–1700* ⊕ *www.lighthouse-point-cayman.com* ⇨ *9 2-bedroom apartments* ⦿ *No meals.*

7

Shaded beach loungers at the Ritz-Carlton, Grand Cayman

$
B&B/INN
Shangri-La B&B. Accomplished pianist George Davidson and wife Eileen built this lavish lakeside retreat; their daughter Gillian truly makes guests feel at home. **Pros:** use of kitchen; elegant decor; DVD players and Wi-Fi included. **Cons:** rental car necessary; not on the beach. *Rooms from: $149* ✉ *1 Sticky Toffee La., West Bay* ☎ *345/526–1170* ⊕ *www.shangrilabandb.com* ⤴ *6 rooms, 1 apartment* ¶○¶ *Breakfast.*

EAST END

$$
RESORT
Compass Point Dive Resort. This tranquil, congenial getaway run by the admirable Ocean Frontiers scuba operation would steer even nondivers in the right direction. **Pros:** top-notch dive operation; free bike/kayak use; good value, especially packages; affable international staff and clientele; environmentally friendly, Green Globe–certified. **Cons:** isolated location requires a car; conservation is admirable but air-conditioning can't go too low; poky beaches with poor swim access. *Rooms from: $295* ✉ *Austin Conolly Dr., East End* ☎ *345/947–7500, 800/348–6096,, 345/947–0000* ⊕ *www.compasspoint.ky* ⤴ *17 1-bedroom, 9 2-bedroom, and 3 3-bedroom condos* ¶○¶ *No meals.*

$
RENTAL
Turtle Nest Inn and Condos. This affordable, intimate, Mediterranean-style seaside inn has roomy one-bedroom apartments and a pool overlooking a narrow beach with good snorkeling. **Pros:** wonderful snorkeling; thoughtful extras; caring staff; free Wi-Fi. **Cons:** car necessary; occasional rocks and debris on beach; ground-floor room views slightly obscured by palms; road noise in back rooms. *Rooms from: $149* ✉ *166 Bodden Town Rd., Bodden Town* ☎ *345/947–8665* ⊕ *www.turtlenestinn.com, www.turtlenestcondos.com* ⤴ *8 apartments, 10 2-bedroom condos* ¶○¶ *No meals.*

$$ 🖼 **Wyndham Reef Resort Grand Cayman.** This exceedingly well-run time-
RESORT share property seductively straddles a 600-foot beach on the less hec-
tic East End. **Pros:** romantically remote; glorious beach; enthusiastic
staff (including a crackerjack wedding coordinator); great packages
and online discounts. **Cons:** remote; few dining options nearby; sprawl-
ing. 💲 *Rooms from: $279* ✉ *Queen's Hwy., Colliers* ☎ *345/947–3100,*
888/232–0541 ⊕ *www.thereef.com* ↘ *152 suites* ❘○❘ *Some meals.*

NIGHTLIFE

Grand Cayman nightlife is surprisingly good for such a quiet-seeming
island. Check the Friday edition of the *Caymanian Compass* for list-
ings of music, movies, theater, and other entertainment. Bars are open
during evening hours until 1 am, and clubs are generally open from 10
pm until 3 am, but none may serve liquor after midnight on Saturday
and none can offer dancing on Sunday. Competition is fierce between
Grand Cayman's many bars and restaurants. In addition to entertain-
ment (fish feeding to fire eating), even upscale joints host happy hours
offering free hors d'oeuvres and/or drinks.

AROUND GEORGE TOWN
BARS AND MUSIC CLUBS

Cayman Cabana. The popular restaurant and bar (formerly Hammer-
heads), adorned with wild murals, fab old-timer photos, and surfboards
doubling as signs, offers a classic Cayman sight: fishers anchor their
boats right offshore and display their catch right outside (condo and
villa renters, head here if you're in the market for fresh fish!). The
capable kitchen specializes in classic Caymanian cuisine. This is also a
prime pyrotechnic sunset- and cruise ship–watching spot, where locals
laze in locally carved chairs, slowly getting hammered from the house
microbrews, on the vast thatch-shaded, tiered deck. Stop by the Swanky
Shack by the entrance for cool T-shirts and island gossip. ✉ *N. Church
St., George Town* ☎ *345/949–3080.*

Hard Rock Café. Grand Cayman's Hard Rock replicates its 137-odd
brethren around the world, only with more specialty drinks (try the
Orangelicious margarita with Monin pomegranate and blood-orange
juices) to complement its extensive burger selection (the Red White
and Blue—crumbled blue cheese, Cajun seasoning, and Buffalo sauce—
is surprisingly tasty). The usual T-shirts, plasma-screen TVs stream-
ing videos, a 1960 pink Cadillac, a Madonna bullet bra, and rotating
memorabilia (including gold records, glasses, costumes, guitars, and
autographed photos from the likes of Elton John, Korn, John Lennon,
U2, and *NSYNC before Justin broke out and Lance came out) are
the decor. In truth, it rocks hard only on weekends, when the bar can
be a prime Grade A meet market. ✉ *43 S. Church St., George Town*
☎ *345/947–2020* ⊕ *www.hardrock.com.*

Fodor'sChoice **Minus 5° Ice Bar.** Everything about the Minus 5° Experience Ice Bar
★ is, well, cool in more ways than one. You don gloves and a white
or black faux fur coat, then step into a futuristic space completely

fashioned from ice: the intricately carved walls, the bar, the tables, the banquettes (draped in fur throws), even the shot and highball glasses. An LED light show plays off the ice sculptures, from pirates to palm trees, which the talented artists change every 8 to 10 weeks. The very chill bartenders serve you a shot, then you choose from one of eight cocktails (with names like Chilly Willy, natch), both included in the entry fee. For a nice contrast, warm up in the adjacent Smuggler's Bar (same building and ownership) serving 100 different rums, and decked with Union Jacks, glass buoys, rigging, fish nets, and old apothecary cabinets. ⊠ *Flagship Bldg., Harbor Dr., George Town* ☎ *345/925–4002* ⊕ *www.minus5experience.com* ✉ *CI$10.*

My Bar. Perched on the water's edge, this bar has great sunset views. The leviathan open-sided cabana is drenched in Rasta colors and crowned by an intricate South Seas–style thatch roof with about 36,000 palm fronds. Christmas lights and the occasional customer dangle from the rafters. Great grub and a mischievous mix of locals, expats, and tourists prove that eco-centric Cayman offers wild life alongside wildlife. ⊠ *Sunset House, S. Church St., George Town* ☎ *345/949–7111* ⊕ *www. sunsethouse.com.*

Rackam's Waterfront Pub and Restaurant. Fishermen to Who's-the-Hugo-Boss financiers savor sensational sunsets and joyous happy hours followed by exuberantly pirouetting tarpon feeding at this open-air, marine-theme happenin' bar on a jetty jutting into the harbor. Boaters—even snorkelers—cruise up the ladder for drinks, while anglers leave their catch on ice. There's complimentary snacks on Friday and pub fare at fair prices until midnight. ⊠ *93 N. Church St., George Town* ☎ *345/945–3860* ⊕ *www.rackams.com.*

Fodor'sChoice
★

South West Collective. A celebration of all things mixology, South West Collective occupies a prime second-floor spot with a patio and enormous picture windows overlooking the harbor. The convivial hangout offers board games, live music on Fridays (and DJs spinning genuine vinyl), a trendily loungy but unpretentious ambience. The pub fare comes at fair prices, whether lunch or such bar bites as smoked oyster dip goosed with lemon and capers or spiced beef patties with rum barbecue sauce. But the drinks are the thing, from loose-leaf teas to global artisan beers, homemade sangria or kombucha smoothies to craft cocktails (as well as the house moonshine). ⊠ *Harbour Place, S. Church St., Level 2, George Town* ☎ *345/946–3004* ⊕ *www.southwestcollectivecayman.com.*

SEVEN MILE BEACH
BARS AND MUSIC CLUBS

The Attic. This chic sports bar has three billiard tables, classic arcade games (Space Invaders, Donkey Kong), air hockey, and large-screen TVs (nab a private booth with its own flat-panel job). Events are daily happy hours, trivia nights, and the Caribbean's reputedly largest Bloody Mary bar on Sunday. Along with downstairs sister "O" Bar, it's ground zero for the Wednesday Night Drinking Club. For a $25 initiation (with T-shirt and personalized leather wristband, toga optional) and $10 weekly activity fee, you're shuttled by bus to three different bars, with free shots and drinks specials. ⊠ *Queen's Court, 2nd fl., West Bay Rd., Seven Mile Beach* ☏ *345/949–7665* ⊕ *www.obar.attic.ky.*

Calico Jack's. This friendly outdoor beach bar at the public beach's north end has a DJ on Saturday, open mike on Tuesday, bands many Fridays, and riotous parties during the full moon, when even Ritz-Carlton guests let their hair down. ⊠ *West Bay Rd., Seven Mile Beach* ☏ *345/945–7850.*

Deckers. Always bustling and bubbly, Deckers takes its name from the red English double-decker bus that forms the focal point of the main outdoor bar. You can luxuriate indoors on cushy sofas over a chess game and signature blood-orange mojito; hack your way through the 18-hole safari miniature-golf course; find a secluded nook in the garden terrace framed by towering palms, old-fashioned, ornate street lamps, and colonial columns; or groove Thursday through Saturday nights to the easy-listening potpourri of pop, reggae, blues, and country courtesy of the Hi-Tide duo. Worthy Carib-Mediterranean fusion cuisine is a bonus (try the Caribbean lobster mac-and-cheese or the coconut shrimp with citrus marmalade and green papaya salad). ⊠ *West Bay Rd., Seven Mile Beach* ☏ *345/945–6600* ⊕ *www.deckers.ky.*

Duke's Seafood & Rib Shack. This is the ultimate in beach shack chic (albeit a half-block from the sand): awesome surfing photos, reclaimed driftwood patio bar, and a statue of the big kahuna with shades and board atop a manta ray. Locals and visitors belly up to the raw and real bars, especially at nightly happy hours, for "Cayman's endless summer." ⊠ *West Bay Rd., across from public beach, Seven Mile Beach* ☏ *345/640–0000* ⊕ *www.dukescayman.com.*

Fidel Murphy's Irish Pub. Thanks to the unusual logo (a stogie-smoking Castro surrounded by shamrocks) and congenial Irish wit and whimsy, you half expect to find Fidel and Gerry Adams harping on U.S. and U.K. policy over a Harp. The Edwardian decor of etched glass, hardwood, and brass is prefabricated (constructed in Ireland, disassembled, and shipped), but everything else is genuine, from the warm welcome to the ales and cider on tap to the proper Irish stew (the kitchen also turns out conch fritters and chicken tikka curry). Sundays host all-you-can-eat extravaganzas (fish-and-chips, carvery) at rock-bottom prices. Trivia nights, happy hours, and live music lure regulars through the week. Weekends welcome live, televised Gaelic soccer, rugby, and hurling, followed by karaoke and *craic* (if you go, you'll learn the definition). ⊠ *Queen's Court, West Bay Rd., Seven Mile Beach* ☏ *345/949–5189* ⊕ *www.fidelscayman.com.*

Legendz. This sports bar with a clubby, retro feel (Marilyn Monroe and Frank Sinatra photos channel glamour days, while scarlet booths and bubble chandeliers add oomph) is a testosterone test drive with plentiful scoring of both types. Good luck wrestling a spot at the bar for pay-per-view and major sporting events, but 10 TVs, including two 6-by-8-foot screens, broadcast to every corner. Also an entertainment venue, Legendz books local bands, stand-up comics, and island DJs and serves grilled fare at fair prices. ⊠ *Falls Centre, West Bay Rd., Seven Mile Beach* ☏ *345/943–3287* ⊕ *www.legendz.ky.*

Lone Star Bar and Grill. Calling itself Cayman's top dive (dive masters to dentists get down and occasionally dirty over kick-ass margaritas), the noisy bar glorifies sports, Texas, T&A, and the boob tube, from an amazing sports memorabilia collection (with items signed by both Bushes) to 17 big-screen TVs tuned to different events. Trivia and Rock 'n' Roll Bingo nights lasso locals. ⊠ *686 West Bay Rd., Seven Mile Beach* ☎ *345/945–5175* ⊕ *www.lonestarcayman.com.*

Stingers Resort and Pool Bar. Tasty, affordable food is served in an appealing setting (check out the stupendous "stinger" mosaic), with cover-free live music and dancing Thursday and Friday. Wednesday nights there's an all-you-can-eat Caribbean luau. The band Heat, a local institution, sizzles with energetic, emotional calypso, reggae, soca, salsa, and oldies; limbo dancers and fire-eaters keep the temperature rising. If you recoil from audience participation, stay far away. Exhibitionistic "spring break" sorts may find their photo on the Wall of Shame, but another blue-green Stingers punch is a worse fate. ⊠ *Comfort Suites Grand Cayman, West Bay Rd., Seven Mile Beach* ☎ *345/945–3000.*

The Wharf. Dance near the water to mellow music on Saturday evenings; when there's a wedding reception in the pavilion, the crashing surf and twinkling candles bathe the proceedings in an almost Gatsby-esque glow. For something less sedate, try salsa lessons and dancing on Tuesday after dinner; most Fridays morph into a wild 1970s disco night (after free hors d'oeuvres during happy hour). The legendary Barefoot Man (think Jimmy Buffett–style expat) performs Saturdays. The stunning seaside setting on tiered decks compensates for often undistinguished food and service. The Ports of Call bar is a splendid place for sunset, and tarpon feeding off the deck is a nightly 9 o'clock spectacle. ⊠ *43 West Bay Rd., George Town* ☎ *345/949–2231* ⊕ *www.wharf.ky.*

CIGAR AND WINE LOUNGES

Nectar. Don't let the location, in the back of a strip mall, fool you. This is a chic New York–style martini lounge/sushi bar with a tapestry of tapas on tap and more than 30 drinks—including 'tinis with 'tude. Choose from bar, tall tables, or sofas in the sleek, slick, mostly monochrome space with chrome accents, blue seats, and red lighting. There's new art on the walls every month, special *shisha* (hookah) evenings, and DJs spinning Sexy Fridays and Tropical Saturdays, when it becomes a hard-body club that delivers a Latin dancing high for Jessica Alba wannabes in spandex and Gap poster-boy slackers (potential hell for those over 30 years old or 20% body fat). ⊠ *Seven Mile Shops, Seven Mile Beach* ☎ *345/949–1802.*

Silver Palm Lounge. The Silver Palm drips with cash and cachet, with a model waitstaff and chic clientele. One section replicates a classic English country library (perfect for civilized, proper afternoon tea or a pre- or post-dinner champagne or single malt). The other forms Taikun, a sensuous sushi spot clad mostly in black, with a popular public table. Also on tap: fab cocktails, including specialty martinis (the Silver Palm cosmopolitan is a winner—Ketel One citron, triple sec, a squeeze of fresh lime juice, and a splash of cranberry topped off with Moët champagne); pages of wines by the glass; and an impressive list of cigars, cognacs, and aged drums. ⊠ *Ritz-Carlton Grand Cayman, West Bay Rd., Seven Mile Beach* ☎ *345/943–9000.*

Fodor's Choice **West Indies Wine Company.** At this ultracontemporary wine store, you
★ purchase tasting cards, allowing you to sample any of the 80-odd wines
and even spirits available by the sip or half or full glass via the argon-
enhanced "intelligent dispensing system." Selections traverse a vast
canny range of prices, regions, styles, and terroirs. The enterprising
owners struck a deal with neighboring restaurants and gourmet shops
to provide appetizers or cheese and charcuterie plates, best savored
alfresco at the tables in front of the handsome space. Small wonder
savvy locals congregate here after work or movies at the nearby cin-
eplex. ⊠ *Corner of Market St. and the Paseo, Camana Bay* ☎ *345/640–
9492* ⊕ *www.wiwc.ky.*

DANCE CLUBS

"O" Bar. This trendy black-and-crimson, industrial-style dance club has
mixed music (live on Saturdays), while juggling, flame-throwing bartenders—practically local celebs—flip cocktails every night. It's as close
to a stand-and-pose milieu as you'll find on Cayman, with the occasional fashion fascist parading in Prada. An upper-level private loft is
available by reservation. ⊠ *Queen's Court, West Bay Rd., Seven Mile
Beach* ☎ *345/943–6227* ⊕ *www.obar.attic.ky.*

WEST BAY

BARS AND LOUNGES

Macabuca Oceanside Tiki Bar. This classic hip-hopping happening beach
bar has a huge deck over the water, thatched roof, amazing Asian-
inspired mosaic murals of waves, spectacular sunsets (and sunset-col-
ored libations), and tiki torches illuminating the reef fish come evening.
Macabuca means "What does it matter?" in the indigenous Antillean
Taíno language, perfectly encapsulating the mellow vibe. Big-screen
TVs, live bands and DJs on weekends, excellent pub grub, and daily
specials (CI$9 jerk dishes weekends; Monday all-night happy hour, DJ,
and CI$17 all-you-can-eat barbecue) lure everyone from well-heeled
loafers to barefoot bodysurfers animatedly discussing current events
and dive currents in a Babel of tongues. ⊠ *Northwest Point Rd., West
Bay* ☎ *345/945–5217* ⊕ *www.crackedconch.com.ky.*

EAST END

BARS AND MUSIC CLUBS

Rusty Pelican. This spot draws an eclectic group of dive masters, expats,
honeymooners, and mingling singles. The knockout, colorful cocktails
pack quite a punch, making the sunset last for hours. The bar dialogue is
entertainment enough, but don't miss local legend, country-calypsonian
Barefoot Man, when he plays "upstairs" at Pelican's Reef—he's to Cayman what Jimmy Buffett is to Key West. ⊠ *Reef Resort, Queen's Hwy.,
Colliers* ☎ *345/947–3100* ⊕ *www.thereef.com.*

South Coast Bar and Grill. This delightful seaside slice of old Cayman
(grizzled regulars slamming down dominoes, fabulous sea views, old
model cars, Friday-night dances to local legend Lammie, karaoke Saturdays with Elvis impersonator Errol Dunbar, and reasonably priced red
conch chowder and jerk chicken sausage) is also a big politico hangout.

7

("That big shark mural ain't just about nature," one bartender cackled.) Fascinating photos, some historical, show local scenes and personalities. The juke jives, from Creedence Clearwater Revival to Mighty Sparrow. ✉ *Breakers, East End* ☎ *345/947–2517* ⊕ *www.southcoastbar.com.*

SHOPPING

On Grand Cayman the good news is that there's no sales tax *and* there's plenty of duty-free merchandise. Locally made items to watch for include woven mats, baskets, jewelry made of a marblelike stone called Caymanite (from the cliffs of Cayman Brac), and authentic sunken treasure, though the latter is never cheap. In addition, there are several noteworthy local artists, some of whose atelier–homes double as galleries, such as Al Ebanks, Horacio Esteban, and Luelan Bodden. Unique items include Cayman sea salt and luxury bath salts (solar harvested in an ecologically sensitive manner) and Tortuga rum and rum cakes. Seven Fathoms is the first working distillery actually in Cayman itself, its award-winning rums aged underwater (hence the name). Cigar lovers, take note: some shops carry famed Cuban brands, but you must enjoy them on the island; bringing them back to the United States is illegal.

Although you can find black-coral products in Grand Cayman, they're controversial. Most of the coral sold here comes from Belize and Honduras; Cayman Islands' marine law prohibits the removal of live coral from its own sea, so most of it has been taken illegally. Black coral grows at a very slow rate (3 inches every 10 years) and is an endangered species. Buy other products instead.

There are seven modern, U.S.-style supermarkets for groceries (three of them have full-service pharmacies) on Grand Cayman. Together, they will spoil you for choices of fresh fruit and vegetables and a wide variety of groceries, as well as a good selection of meats, poultry, and fish. All have deli counters serving hot meals, salads, sandwiches, cold cuts, and cheeses. Kirk Supermarket carries a wide range of international foods from the Caribbean, Europe, and Asia. The biggest difference you'll find between these and supermarkets on the mainland is in the prices, which are about 25% to 30% more than at home.

GEORGE TOWN

ART GALLERIES

Al Ebanks Studio Gallery. This gallery shows the eponymous artist's versatile, always provocative work in various media. Since you're walking into his home as well as atelier, everything is on display. Clever movable panels maximize space "like Art Murphy beds." His work, while inspired by his home, could never be labeled traditional Caribbean art, exhibiting vigorous movement through abstract swirls of color and textural contrasts. Though nonrepresentational (save for his equally intriguing sculpture and ceramics), the focal subject from carnivals to iguanas is always subtly apparent. Ask him about the Native Sons art movement he cofounded. ✉ *186B Shedden Rd., George Town* ☎ *345/927–5365, 345/949–0693.*

Cathy Church's Underwater Photo Centre and Gallery. The store has a collection of the acclaimed underwater shutterbug's spectacular color and limited-edition black-and-white underwater photos as well as the latest marine camera equipment. Cathy will autograph her latest coffee-table book, talk about her globe-trotting adventures, and schedule private underwater photography instruction on her dive boat, with graphics-oriented computers to critique your work. She also does wedding photography, above and underwater. If you can't stop in, check out the world's largest underwater photo installation (9 by 145 feet) at the Owen Roberts Airport baggage claim, curated by Cathy and her team. ⊠ *390 S. Church St., George Town* ☎ *345/949–7415* ⊕ *www. cathychurch.com.*

Guy Harvey's Gallery and Shoppe. World-renowned marine biologist, conservationist, and artist Guy Harvey showcases his aquatic-inspired, action-packed art in every conceivable medium, from tableware to sportswear (even logo soccer balls and Zippos). The soaring, two-story 4,000-square-foot space is almost more theme park than store, with monitors playing sport-fishing videos, wood floors inlaid with tile duplicating rippling water, dangling catboats "attacked" by shark models, and life-size murals honoring such classics as Hemingway's *Old Man and the Sea*. Original paintings, sculpture, and drawings are expensive, but there's something (tile art, prints, lithographs, and photos) in most price ranges. ⊠ *49 S. Church St., George Town* ☎ *345/943–4891* ⊕ *www.guyharvey.com.*

Pure Art. About 1½ miles (2½ km) south of George Town, Pure Art purveys wit, warmth, and whimsy from the wildly colored front steps. Its warren of rooms resembles a garage sale run amok or a quirky grandmother's attic spilling over with unexpected finds, from foodstuffs to functional and wearable art. ⊠ *S. Church St. and Denham-Thompson Way, George Town* ☎ *345/949–9133* ⊕ *www.pureart.ky.*

CLOTHING

Blue Wave. Your adrenaline starts pumping as soon as you enter this so-called lifestyle wear-surf shop. All the accoutrements you need to play the Big Kahuna are handsomely displayed, from sandals to sunglasses, Billabong plaid shirts to Quicksilver shorts, surfboards to eco-sensitive Olukai footwear (talk to the clerks and you're ready to sign up for Greenpeace). ⊠ *10 Shedden Rd., George Town* ☎ *345/949–8166.*

FOODSTUFFS

Foster's Food Fair-IGA. The island's biggest chain has five supermarkets. The Airport Centre and Strand stores, with full-service pharmacies, are open Monday–Saturday 7 am–11 pm. ⊠ *Airport Centre, 63 Dorcy Dr., George Town* ☎ *345/949–5155, 345/945–3663* ⊕ *www.fosters-iga.com.*

Tortuga Rum Company. This company bakes, then vacuum-seals more than 10,000 of its world-famous rum cakes daily, adhering to the original, "secret" century-old recipe. There are eight flavors, from banana to Blue Mountain coffee (the new taffy also comes in eight varieties). The 12-year-old rum, blended from private stock though actually distilled in Guyana, is a connoisseur's delight for after-dinner sipping. You can buy a fresh rum cake at the airport on the way home at the same prices as at the factory store. ⊠ *Industrial Park, N. Sound Rd., George Town* ☎ *345/943–7663* ⊕ *www.tortugarumcakes.com.*

MALLS AND SHOPPING CENTERS

Kirk Freeport Plaza. This downtown shopping center, home to the Kirk Freeport flagship department store, is ground zero for couture; it's also known for its boutiques selling fine watches and jewelry, china, crystal, leather, perfumes, and cosmetics, from Baccarat to Bulgari, Raymond Weil to Waterford and Wedgwood (the last two share their own autonomous boutique). Just keep walking—there's plenty of eye-catching, mind-boggling consumerism in all directions: Boucheron, Cartier (with its own mini-boutique), Chanel, Clinique, Christian Dior, Clarins, Estée Lauder, Fendi, Guerlain, Lancôme, Yves Saint Laurent, Issey Miyake, Jean Paul Gaultier, Nina Ricci, Rolex, Roberto Coin, Rosenthal and Royal Doulton china, and more. ⊠ *Cardinal Ave., George Town.*

SEVEN MILE BEACH

JEWELRY

24K-Mon Jewelers. This store sells works of art from many jewelers, including Wyland, Merry-Lee Rae, and Stephen Douglas, as well as designs courtesy of owner-goldsmith Gale Tibbetts and her friends, incorporating everything from Swarovski crystals to Spanish doubloons. Most pieces are inspired by the sea. The adjacent gallery is one of the few commercial outlets for local artists such as Miguel Powery. ⊠ *Buckingham Sq., Seven Mile Beach* ☎ *345/949–1499* ⊕ *www.24k-mon.com.*

SPORTS AND THE OUTDOORS

DIVING

One of the world's leading dive destinations, Grand Cayman's dramatic underwater topography features plunging walls, soaring skyscraper pinnacles, grottoes, arches, swim-throughs adorned with vibrant sponges, coral-encrusted caverns, and canyons patrolled by Lilliputian grunts to gargantuan groupers, hammerheads to hawksbill turtles.

There are more than 200 pristine dive sites, many less than half a mile from land and easily accessible, including wreck, wall, and shore options. Add exceptional visibility from 80 to 150 feet and calm, current-free water at a constant bathlike 80°F. Cayman is serious about conservation, with Marine Park, Replenishment, and Environmental Park zones and stringently enforced laws to protect the fragile, endangered marine environment (fines of up to $500,000 and a year in prison are the price for damaging living coral, which can take years to regrow). Most boats use biodegradable cleansers and environmentally friendly drinking cups; moorings at popular sites prevent coral and sponge damage caused by continual anchoring, and diving with gloves is prohibited to reduce the temptation to touch.

Pristine clear water, breathtaking coral formations, and plentiful marine life mark the **North Wall**—a world-renowned dive area along the North Side of Grand Cayman. **Trinity Caves**, in West Bay, is a deep dive with

CAYMAN DIVE DEVELOPMENTS

The Cayman Islands government acquired the 251-foot, decommissioned U.S. Navy ship USS *Kittiwake*. Sunk in 2011, it has already become an exciting new dive attraction (⊕ *www.kittiwakecayman.com*) while providing necessary relief for some of the most frequently visited dive sites. The top of the bridge is just 15 feet down, making it accessible to snorkelers. There's a single-use entry fee of $10 ($5 for snorkelers).

The **Cayman Dive 365** (⊕ *www. dive365cayman.com*) initiative is part of a commitment to protect reefs from environmental overuse. New dive sites will be introduced while certain existing sites are "retired" to be rested and refreshed. Visitors are encouraged to sponsor and name a new dive site from the list of selected coordinates.

numerous canyons starting at about 60 feet and sloping to the wall at 130 feet. The South Side is the deepest, its wall starting 80 feet deep before plummeting, though its shallows offer a lovely labyrinth of caverns and tunnels in such sites as Japanese Gardens. The less visited, virgin East End is less varied geographically beyond the magnificent Ironshore Caves and Babylon Hanging Gardens ("trees" of black coral plunging 100 feet) but teems with "Swiss cheese" swim-throughs and exotic life in such renowned gathering spots as the Maze.

Shore-entry snorkeling spots include **Cemetery Reef**, north of Seven Mile Beach, and the reef-protected shallows of the **north and south coasts**. Ask for directions to the shallow wreck of the *Cali* in the George Town harbor area; there are several places to enter the water, including a ladder at Rackam's Pub. Among the wreckage you'll find the winch and lots of friendly fish.

Fodor'sChoice ★ **Devil's Grotto.** This site resembles an abstract painting of anemones, tangs, parrot fish, and bright purple Pederson cleaner shrimp (nicknamed the dentists of the reef, as they gorge on whatever they scrape off fish teeth and gills). Extensive coral heads and fingers teem with blue wrasse, horse-eyed jacks, butterfly fish, and Indigo hamlets. The cathedral-like caves are phenomenal, but tunnel entries aren't clearly marked, so you're best off with a dive master. ⊠ *George Town.*

Fodor'sChoice ★ **Eden Rock.** If someone tells you that the silverside minnows are in at Eden Rock, drop everything and dive here. The schools swarm around you as you glide through the grottoes, forming quivering curtains of liquid silver as shafts of sunlight pierce the sandy bottom. The grottoes themselves are safe—not complex caves—and the entries and exits are clearly visible at all times. Snorkelers can enjoy the outside of the grottoes as the reef rises and falls from 10 to 30 feet deep. Avoid carrying fish food unless you know how not to get bitten by eager yellowtail snappers. ⊠ *S. Church St., across from Harbour Place Mall by Paradise Restaurant, George Town.*

Fodor'sChoice ★ **Stingray City.** Most dive operators offer scuba trips to Stingray City in the North Sound. Widely considered the best 12-foot dive in the world, it's a must-see for adventurous souls. Here dozens of stingrays congregate—tame enough to suction squid from your outstretched palm. You can stand in 3 feet of water at **Stingray City Sandbar** as the gentle stingrays glide around your legs looking for a handout. Don't worry—these stingrays are so acclimated to tourist encounters that they pose no danger; the experience is often a highlight of a Grand Cayman trip. ⊠ *Near West Bay, North Sound.*

Turtle Reef. The reef begins 20 feet out and gradually descends to a 60-foot mini-wall pulsing with sea life and corals of every variety. From there it's just another 15 feet to the dramatic main wall. Ladders provide easy entrance to a shallow cover perfect for pre-dive checks, and since the area isn't buoyed for boats, it's quite pristine. ⊠ *West Bay.*

DIVE OPERATORS

As one of the Caribbean's top diving destinations, Grand Cayman is blessed with many top-notch dive operations offering diving, instruction, and equipment for sale and rent. A single-tank boat dive averages $80, a two-tank dive about $105 (discounts for multidive packages). Snorkel-equipment rental is about $15 a day. Divers are required to be certified and possess a C-card. If you're getting certified, save time by starting the book and pool work at home and finishing the open-water portion in warm, clear Cayman waters. Certifying agencies offer a referral service.

Strict marine-protection laws prohibit taking marine life from many areas.

Ambassador Divers. This on-call (around the clock), guided scuba-diving operation offers trips for two–eight persons. Co-owner Jason Washington's favorite spots include sites on the West Side and South and North Wall. Ambassador offers three boats: a 28-foot custom Parker (maximum six divers), a 46-foot completely custom overhauled boat, and a 26-footer primarily for snorkeling. Divers can be picked up from their lodgings. A two-tank boat dive is $105 ($90 for four or more days). ⊠ *Comfort Suites, 22 Piper Way, West Bay Rd., Seven Mile Beach* ☎ *345/743–5513, 345/949–4530, 844/507–0441 toll-free* ⊕ *www.ambassadordivers.com.*

Cayman Aggressor IV. This 110-foot live-aboard dive boat offers one-week cruises for divers who want to get serious bottom time, as many as five dives daily. Nine staterooms with en suite bathrooms sleep 18. The fresh food is basic but bountiful (three meals, two in-between snacks), and the crew offers a great mix of diving, especially when weather allows the crossing to Little Cayman. Digital photography and video courses are also offered (there's an E-6 film-processing lab aboard) as well as nitrox certification. The price is $2,695 to $3,295 double occupancy for the week. ☎ *345/949–5551, 800/348–2628* ⊕ *www. aggressor.com.*

Fodor'sChoice **DiveTech.** With comfortable boats and quick access to West Bay, ★ DiveTech offers shore diving at its northwest-coast location, providing loads of interesting creatures, a mini-wall, and the North Wall. Technical training (a specialty of owner Nancy Easterbrook) is unparalleled, and the company offers good, personable service as well as the latest gadgetry such as underwater DPV scooters and rebreathing equipment. They even mix their own gases. Options include extended cross-training

Ranger packages, Dive and Art workshop weeks, photography-video seminars with Courtney Platt, deep diving, less disruptive free diving, search and recovery, stingray interaction, reef awareness, and underwater naturalist. Snorkel and diving programs are available for children eight and up, SASY (supplied-air snorkeling, with the unit on a personal flotation device) for five and up. Multiday discounts are a bonus. ⊠ *Lighthouse Point, near Boatswain's Beach, 571 Northwest Point Rd., West Bay* ☏ *345/949–1700* ⊕ *www.divetech.com.*

Don Foster's Dive Cayman Islands. This operation offers a pool with shower, an underwater photo center, and snorkeling along the ironshore at Casuarina Point, easily accessed starting at 20 feet and extending to 55 feet. Night dives and Stingray City trips take divers and snorkelers in the same boat (good for families). Specialties include Nitrox, Wreck, and Peak Performance Buoyancy courses. Rates are competitive, and there's free shuttle pickup–drop-off along Seven Mile Beach. If you go out with Don, he might recount stories of his wild times as a drummer, but all crews are personable and efficient. The drawback is larger boats and groups. ⊠ *218 S. Church St., George Town* ☏ *345/949–5679, 345/945–5132* ⊕ *www.donfosters.com.*

Indigo Divers. This full-service, mobile PADI teaching facility specializes in exclusive guided dives from its 28-foot Sea Ray Bow Rider or 32-foot Donzi Express Cruiser, the *Cats Meow* and the *Cats Pyjamas.* Comfort and safety are paramount. Luxury transfers are included, and the boat is stocked with goodies like fresh fruit and homemade cookies. Captain Chris Alpers has impeccable credentials: a licensed U.S. Coast Guard captain, PADI master scuba diver trainer, and Cayman Islands Marine Park officer. Katie Alpers specializes in wreck, DPV, dry suit, boat, and deep diving, but her primary role is videographer. She edits superlative DVDs of the adventures with music and titles. They guarantee a maximum of six divers. The individual attention is pricier, but the larger the group, the more you save. ⊠ *Seven Mile Beach* ☏ *345/946–7279, 345/525–3932* ⊕ *www.indigodivers.com.*

Neptune's Divers. Offering competitive package rates and free shuttle service along Seven Mile Beach, this is one of the best companies for physically challenged divers. Captain Keith Keller and his staff try to customize trips as best they can, taking no more than eight divers on their 30-foot custom Island Hopper and 36-foot Crusader. A wide range of PADI courses is available. Instructors are patient and knowledgeable about reef life, and Casey Keller can offer helpful tips on underwater photography. The operation is computer-friendly to permit longer bottom time. ⊠ *West Bay Rd., Seven Mile Beach* ☏ *345/945–3990* ⊕ *www. neptunesdivers.com.*

Fodor'sChoice **Ocean Frontiers.** This excellent ecocentric operation offers friendly ★ small-group diving and a technical training facility, exploring the less trammeled, trafficked East End. The company provides valet service, personalized attention, a complimentary courtesy shuttle, and an emphasis on green initiatives and specialized diving, including unguided computer, technical, nitrox instructor, underwater naturalist, and cave diving for advanced participants. You can even participate in lionfish

Diving at one of the Cayman Islands' famous coral reefs

culls. But even beginners and rusty divers (there's a wonderful Skills Review and Tune-Up course) won't feel over their heads. Special touches include hot chocolate and homemade muffins on night dives; the owner, Steve, will arrange for a minister to conduct weddings in full face masks. ⊠ *Compass Point, 346 Austin Connelly Dr., East End* ☏ *345/640–7500, 800/348–6096, 345/947–0000, 954/727–5312 Vonage toll-free in U.S.* ⊕ *www.oceanfrontiers.com.*

FAMILY **Red Sail Sports.** Daily trips leave from most major hotels, and dives are often run as guided tours, good for beginners. If you're experienced and your air lasts long, ask the captain if you must come up with the group (when the first person runs low on air). Kids' options, ages 5 to 15, include SASY and Bubblemakers. The company also operates Stingray City tours, dinner and sunset sails, and water sports from Wave Runners to windsurfing. ☏ *345/949–8745, 345/623–5965, 877/506–6368* ⊕ *www.redsailcayman.com.*

Sunset Divers. At a hostelry that caters to the scuba set, this full-service PADI teaching facility has great shore diving and six dive boats that hit all sides of the island. Divers can be independent on boats as long as they abide by maximum time and depth standards. Instruction and packages are comparatively inexpensive. Though the company is not directly affiliated with acclaimed underwater shutterbug Cathy Church (whose shop is also at the hotel), she often works with the instructors on special courses. ⊠ *Sunset House, 390 S. Church St., George Town* ☏ *345/949–7111, 800/854–4767* ⊕ *www.sunsethouse.com.*

FISHING

If you enjoy action fishing, Cayman waters have plenty to offer. Experienced, knowledgeable local captains charter boats with top-of-the-line equipment, bait, ice, and often lunch included in the price (usually $700 to $950 per half day, $1,200 to $1,600 for a full day). Options include deep-sea, reef, bone, tarpon, light-tackle, and fly-fishing. June and July are good all-around months for blue marlin, yellow- and blackfin tuna, dolphinfish, and bonefish. Bonefish have a second season in the winter months, along with wahoo and skipjack tuna.

Black Princess Charters. Captain Chuckie Ebanks leads deep-sea and reef fishing as well as snorkel trips on his fully equipped and supplied eponymous 40-foot *Sea Ray*. Rates are reasonable, and he can arrange clean, inexpensive accommodations. ☎ *345/916–6319, 345/949–0400* ⊕ *www.fishgrandcayman.com.*

Oh Boy Charters. Charters include a 60-foot yacht with complete amenities (for day and overnight trips, sunset and dinner cruises) and a 34-foot Crusader. Charles and Alvin Ebanks—sons of Caymanian marine royalty, the indomitable Captain Marvin Ebanks—jokingly claim they've been playing in and plying the waters for a century and tell tales (tall and otherwise) of their father reeling them in for fishing expeditions. No more than eight passengers on the deep-sea boats ensures the personal touch (snorkeling on the 60-footer accommodates more people). Guests always receive a good selection of their catch; if you prefer others to do the cooking, go night fishing (including catch-and-release shark safaris), which includes dinner. ☎ *345/949–6341, 345/926–0898* ⊕ *www.ohboycharters.com.*

R&M Fly Shop and Charters. Captain Ronald Ebanks is arguably the island's most knowledgeable fly-fishing guide, with more than 10 years' experience in Cayman and Scotland. He also runs light-tackle trips on a 24-foot Robalo. Everyone from beginners—even children—to experienced casters enjoy and learn, whether wading or poling from a 17-foot Stratos Flats boat. Free transfers are included. Captain Ronald even ties his own flies (he'll show you how). ☎ *345/947–3146, 345/946–0214* ⊕ *www.flyfishgrandcayman.com.*

GOLF

Britannia. Next to the Grand Cayman Beach Suites and designed by Jack Nicklaus, the course is really a 9-hole routing with two sets of tees so as to provide an 18-hole experience. The courses feature artificial abrupt mounding and lots of water, similar to what Nicklaus did early on in Florida. Tough holes include 3 and 10; beware tricky winds on 7 through 11. Amenities include a full pro shop and the split-level Britannia Golf Grille (with particularly good breakfasts and local fare, as well as killer views of the prominent water hazards). ✉ *West Bay Rd., Seven Mile Beach* ☎ *345/745–4653* ⊕ *www.britannia-golf.com* 🏷 *$123.75 for 18 holes, $81.25 for 9 holes; twilight discounts* ⚐ *9-hole course with 2 tees, 5829 yards, par 70.*

North Sound Golf Club. Formerly the Links at Safehaven, this is Cayman's only 18-hole golf course and infamous among duffers for its strong wind gusts. Roy Case factored the wind into his design, which incorporates lots of looming water and sand bunkers. The handsome setting features many mature mahogany and silver thatch trees where iguana lurk. Wear shorts at least 14 inches long (15 inches for women) and collared shirts. Greens fees change seasonally, and there are twilight and walking discounts (though carts are recommended), a fine pro shop, and an open-air bar with large-screen TVs. ⊠ *Off West Bay Rd., Seven Mile Beach* ☎ *345/947–4653* ⊕ *www.northsoundclub.com* 🖼 *$175 for 18 holes, $110 for 9 holes, including cart; twilight rates* 🏌 *18 holes, 6605 yards, par 71.*

GUIDED TOURS

Taxi drivers give personalized tours of Grand Cayman for about $25 per hour for up to three people. Hotels also arrange helicopter rides, horseback or mountain-bike journeys, 4x4 safari expeditions, and full-day bus excursions.

Costs and itineraries are about the same regardless of the tour operator. Half-day tours average $40 to $50 a person and generally include a visit to Hell and the Turtle Farm at Boatswain's Beach aquatic park in West Bay, as well as shopping downtown. Full-day tours ($75 to $100 per person) add lunch, a visit to Bodden Town (the first settlement), and the East End, with stops at the Queen Elizabeth II Botanic Park, blowholes (if the waves are high) on the ironshore, and the site of the wreck of the *Ten Sails* (not the wreck itself—just the site). The pirate graves in Bodden Town were destroyed during Hurricane Ivan in 2004, and the blowholes were partially filled. As you can tell, land tours here are low-key. Children under 12 often receive discounts.

A.A. Transportation Services. For taxis and tour buses, ask for Burton Ebanks. ☎ *345/949–6598, 345/926–8294, 345/949–7222.*

Cayman Safari. This hits the usual sights but emphasizes interaction with locals, so you learn about craft traditions, folklore, and herbal medicines; careening along in Land Rovers is incidental fun. Rates range from $79 to $99 ($69 to $79 for children under 12). ☎ *345/925–3001, 866/211–4677* ⊕ *www.caymansafari.com.*

Majestic Tours. The company caters mostly to cruise-ship and incentive groups but offers similar options to individuals and can customize tours, starting at $45 per person; it's particularly good for West Bay, including the Cayman Turtle Farm and Hell. ⊠ *Industrial Park, 322 N. Sound Rd.* ☎ *345/949–7773* ⊕ *www.majestic-tours.com.*

McCurley Tours. This outfit is owned by B.A. McCurley, a free-spirited, freewheeling Midwesterner who's lived in Cayman since the mid-1980s and knows everything and everyone on the East End. Not only is she encyclopedic and flexible, but she also offers car rentals and transfers for travelers staying on the North Side or East End; don't be surprised if she tells you what to order at lunch, especially if it's off the menu. ☎ *345/947–9626, 345/916–0925.*

Tropicana Tours. With several excellent itineraries on large buses, tours include Stingray City stops as well as reef runner adventures across the North Sound through the mangrove swamps. ☎ *345/949–0944* ⊕ *www. tropicana-tours.com.*

Webster's Tours. This family-run outfit, with many drivers who have been with the company for years, gladly customizes tours according to your interests, with a variety of vehicles at their disposal. The staffers are unfailingly cordial, punctual, and knowledgeable. ☎ *345/945–1433* ⊕ *www.websters.ky.*

HIKING

Mastic Trail. This significant trail, used in the 1800s as the only direct path to the North Side, is a rugged 2-mile (3-km) slash through 776 dense acres of woodlands, black mangrove swamps, savanna, agricultural remnants, and ancient rock formations. It embraces more than 700 species, including Cayman's largest remaining contiguous ancient forest (one of the heavily deforested Caribbean's last examples). A comfortable walk depends on weather—winter is better because it's drier, though flowering plants such as the banana orchid blaze in summer. Call the National Trust to determine suitability and to book a guide ($30); tours run daily 9 to 5 by appointment and Thursdays and Fridays at 9 (sometimes earlier in summer). Or walk on the wild side with a $5 guidebook covering the ecosystems, endemic wildlife, seasonal changes, poisonous plants, and folkloric uses of flora. The trip takes about three hours. ⊠ *Frank Sound Rd., entrance by fire station at botanic park, Breakers, East End* ☎ *345/749–1121, 345/749–1124 for guide reservations* ⊕ *www.nationaltrust.org.ky.*

HORSEBACK RIDING

Coral Stone Stables. Leisurely 90-minute horseback rides take in the white-sand beaches at Barkers and inland trails at Savannah; photos are included. Your guide is Nolan Stewart, whose ranch contains 20 horses, chickens, and "randy" roosters. Nolan offers a nonstop narrative on flora, fauna, and history. He's an entertaining, endless font of local information, some of it unprintable. Rides are $80; swim rides cost $120. ⊠ *Conch Point Rd., next to Restaurante Papagallo on the left, West Bay* ☎ *345/916–4799* ⊕ *www.csstables.com.*

FAMILY **Pampered Ponies.** Offering "the ultimate tanning machine"—horses walking, trotting, and cantering along the beach—the stable leads private tours and guided trips, including sunset, moonlight, and bareback swim rides along the uninhabited beach from Conch Point to Morgan's Harbour on the north tip beyond West Bay. ⊠ *355 Conch Point Rd., West Bay* ☎ *345/945–2262, 345/916–2540* ⊕ *www.ponies.ky.*

KAYAKING

FAMILY **Cayman Kayaks.** This outfitter explores Grand Cayman's protected mangrove wetlands, providing an absorbing discussion of indigenous animals (including a mesmerizing stop at a gently pulsing, nonstinging Cassiopeia jellyfish pond) and plants, the effects of hurricanes, and conservation efforts. Even beginners find the tours easy (the guides dub it low-impact aerobics), and the sit-on-top tandem kayaks are stable and comfortable. The Bio Bay tour involves more strenuous paddling, but the underwater light show is magical as millions of bioluminescent microorganisms called dinoflagellates glow like fireflies when disturbed. It runs only on moonless nights and books well in advance. Tours ($39–$59 with some kids' and group discounts) depart from different locations, most from the public

7

access jetty to the left of Rum Point. ⊠ *Rum Point* ☎ *345/746–3249, 345/926–4467* ⊕ *www.caymankayaks.com.*

SEA EXCURSIONS

The most impressive sights in the Cayman Islands are on and underwater, and several submarines, semisubmersibles, glass-bottom boats, and Jules Verne–like contraptions allow you to see these wonders without getting your feet wet. Sunset sails, dinner cruises, and other theme (dance, booze, pirate) cruises are available from $30 to $90 per person.

FAMILY **Atlantis Submarines.** This submarine takes 48 passengers safely and comfortably along the Cayman Wall down to 100 feet. Peep through panoramic portholes as good-natured guides keep up a humorous but informative patter. A guide dons scuba gear to feed fish, who form a whirling frenzy of color rivaling anything by Picasso. At night, the 10,000-watt lights show the kaleidoscopic underwater colors and nocturnal stealth predators more brilliantly than during the day. Try to sit toward the front so you can watch the pilot's nimble maneuverings and the depth gauge. If that literally in-depth tour seems daunting, get up close and personal on the *Seaworld Observatory* semisubmersible (glorified glass-bottom boat), which just cruises the harbor (including glimpses of the *Cali* and *Balboa* shipwrecks). The cost is $89–$104 (children $49–$64) for the submarine, $39 (children $24) for the semisubmersible. There are frequent online booking discounts. ⊠ *30 S. Church St., George Town* ☎ *345/949–7700, 800/887–8571* ⊕ *www. caymanislandssubmarines.com.*

FAMILY **Jolly Roger.** This is a two-thirds-size replica of Christopher Columbus's 17th-century Spanish galleon *Niña*. (The company also owns the *Anne Bonny*, a wooden Norwegian brig built in 1934 that holds more than 100 passengers.) On the afternoon snorkel cruise, play Captain Jack Sparrow while experiencing swashbuckling pirate antics, including a trial, sword fight, and walking the plank; kids can fire the cannon, help hoist the main sail, and scrub the decks (they will love it even if they loathe doing chores at home). Evening options (sunset and dinner sails) are more standard booze cruises, less appropriate for the kiddies. Food is more appropriate to the brig, and it's more yo-ho-hokum than remotely authentic, but it's fun. Prices are $25–$65 (children's discounts available). ⊠ *South Terminal, next to Atlantis Submarines, George Town* ☎ *345/945–7245* ⊕ *www.jollyrogercayman.com, www. piratesofthecaymans.com.*

FAMILY **Sea Trek.** Helmet diving lets you walk and breathe 26 feet underwater for an hour—without getting your hair wet. No training or even swimming ability is required (ages eight and up), and you can wear glasses. Guides give a thorough safety briefing, and a sophisticated system of compressors and cylinders provides triple the amount of air necessary for normal breathing while a safety diver program ensures four levels of backup. The result at near-zero gravity resembles an exhilarating moonwalk ($89, $99 for Ultimate Stingray City excursion). ⊠ *Cayman Cabana, 53 N. Church St., George Town* ☎ *345/949–0008* ⊕ *www. seatrekcayman.com, www.snubacayman.com.*

A group of stingrays patrols the grassy shallows of Grand Cayman.

SNORKELING

SNORKELING SITES

Fodor's Choice
★

Stingray City Sandbar. This site (as opposed to Stingray City, a popular 12-foot dive) is the island's stellar snorkeling attraction. Dozens of boats head here several times daily. It's less crowded on days with fewer cruise ships in port. ⊠ *North Sound.*

Wreck of the *Cali*. You can still identify the engines and winches of this old sailing freighter, which settled about 20 feet down. The sponges are particularly vivid, and tropical fish, shrimp, and lobster abound. Many operators based in George Town and Seven Mile Beach come here. ⊠ *About 50 yards out from Rackam's Waterfront Pub, 93 N. Church St., George Town.*

SNORKELING OPERATORS

Bayside Watersports. Offering half-day snorkel trips, North Sound beach lunch excursions, Stingray City and dinner cruises, and full-day deep-sea fishing, this company operates several popular boats out of West Bay's Morgan's Harbour. Full-day trips include lunch and conch diving November–April. ⊠ *Morgan's Harbour, West Bay* 🕾 *345/949–3200* ⊕ *www.baysidewatersports.com.*

FAMILY **Captain Crosby's Watersports.** Offering favorably priced snorkeling ($40–$73 including refreshments) and dive excursions on well-equipped 47- and 40-foot trimarans, Captain Crosby is one of the more colorful captains in a group of genuine characters. He's actively involved in preserving Cayman's maritime heritage as a founder of the Catboat Association. As a bonus, trips usually run a little long and often include a sing-along with the "singing captain." He also leads deep-sea fishing charters. ⊠ *Cayman*

Islands Yacht Club, Dock C-29, Seven Mile Beach ☎ *345/945–4049, 345/916–1725* ⊕ *www.captaincrosbywatersports.com.*

FAMILY **Fantasea Tours.** Captain Dexter Ebanks runs tours on his 38-foot trimaran, *Don't Even Ask,* usually departing from the Cayman Islands Yacht Club ($40 including transfers). He doesn't pack you in like sardines (20 people max) and is particularly helpful with first-timers. Like many captains, he has pet names for the rays (ask him to find Lucy, whom he "adopted") and rattles off factoids during an entertaining, nonstop narration. It's a laid-back trip, with Bob Marley and Norah Jones playing, fresh fruit and rum punch on tap. ⊠ *West Bay Rd., Seven Mile Beach* ☎ *345/916–0754* ⊕ *www.dexters-fantaseatours.com.*

FAMILY **Red Sail Sports.** Luxurious 62- and 65-foot catamarans (the *Spirits of Cayman, Poseidon, Calypso,* and *Ppalu)* often carry large groups on Stingray City, sunset, and evening sails ($45–$85, $22.50–$42.50 children under 12) including dinner in winter. Although the service may not be personal, it's efficient. A glass-bottom boat takes passengers to Stingray City/Sandbar and nearby coral reefs. Trips run from several hotels, including the Westin and Morritt's, in addition to the Rum Point headquarters. ☎ *345/949–8745, 345/623–5965, 877/506–6368* ⊕ *www.redsailcayman.com.*

CAYMAN BRAC

Cayman Brac is named for its most distinctive feature, a rugged limestone bluff (*brac* in Gaelic) that runs up the center of the 12-mile (19-km) island, pocked with caves and culminating in a sheer 140-foot cliff at its eastern end. The Brac, 89 miles (143 km) northeast of Grand Cayman, is a splendidly serene destination for ecoenthusiasts, offering world-class birding, scuba diving, bonefishing in the shallows or light-tackle and deep-sea angling, hiking, spelunking, and rock climbing. With only 1,800 residents—they call themselves Brackers—the island has the feel and easy pace of a small town. Brackers are known for their friendly attitude toward visitors, so it's easy to strike up a conversation. Locals wave on passing and might invite you home for a traditional rundown (a thick, sultry fish stew) and storytelling, usually about the sea, turtle schooners, and the great hurricane of 1932 (when the caves offered shelter).

EXPLORING

TOP ATTRACTIONS

Cayman Brac Museum. A diverse, well-displayed collection of historic Bracker implements ranges from dental pliers to pistols to pottery. A meticulously crafted scale model of the Caymanian catboat *Alsons* has pride of place. The front room reconstructs the Customs, Treasury, bank, and post office as they looked decades ago. Permanent exhibits include those on the 1932 hurricane, turtling, shipbuilding, and old-time home life. The back room hosts rotating exhibits such as one on herbal folk medicine. ⊠ *Old Government Administration Bldg., Stake Bay* ☎ *345/948–2622, 345/244–4446* ▣ *Free* ☉ *Weekdays 9–4, Sat. 9–noon.*

Parrot Preserve. The likeliest place to spot the endangered Cayman Brac parrot—and other indigenous and migratory birds—is along this National Trust hiking trail off Major Donald Drive, aka Lighthouse Road. Prime time is early morning or late afternoon; most of the day they're camouflaged by trees, earning them the moniker "stealth parrot." The loop trail incorporates part of a path the Brackers used in olden days to cross the bluff to reach their provision grounds on the south shore or to gather coconuts, once a major export crop. It passes through several types of terrain: old farmland under grass and native trees from mango to mahogany unusually mixed with orchids and cacti. Wear sturdy shoes, as the terrain is rocky, uneven, and occasionally rough. The 6-mile (10-km) gravel road continues to the lighthouse at the bluff's eastern end, where there's an astonishing view from atop the cliff to the open ocean—the best place to watch the sunrise. ⊠ *Lighthouse Rd., ½ mi (1 km) south of town, Tibbetts Turn* ☎ *345/948–0319* 🖷 *Free* ☉ *Daily sunrise–sunset.*

BEACHES

Much of the Brac's coastline is ironshore, though there are several pretty sand beaches, mostly along the southwest coast (where swimmers also find extensive beds of turtle grass, which creates less than ideal conditions for snorkeling). In addition to the hotel beaches, where everyone is welcome, there is a public beach with good access to the reef; it's well marked on tourist maps. The north-coast beaches, predominantly rocky ironshore, offer excellent snorkeling.

Pollard Bay. The beach by Cayman Breakers is fairly wide for this eastern stretch of the island. Start clambering east underneath the imposing bluff, past the end of the paved road, to strikingly beautiful deserted stretches accessible only on foot. The water here starts churning like a washing machine and becomes progressively rockier, littered with driftwood. Locals search for whelks here. Steps by the Breakers lead to shore dive sites. Flocks of seabirds darken the sun for seconds at a time, while blowholes spout as if answering migrant humpback whales. Don't go beyond the gargantuan rock called First Cay—the sudden swells can be hazardous—unless you're a serious rock climber. **Amenities:** none. **Best for:** solitude; walking. ⊠ *South Side Rd. E, East End.*

Public Beach. Roughly 2 miles (3 km) east of the Brac Reef and Carib Sands/Brac Caribbean resorts, just past the wetlands (the unsightly gate is visible from the road; if you hit the Bat Cave you've passed it), lie a series of strands culminating in this beach, relatively deserted despite its name. The surf is calm and the crystalline water fairly protected for swimming. There are picnic tables and showers in uncertain condition. Snorkeling is quite good. **Amenities:** showers. **Best for:** snorkeling. ⊠ *South Side Rd. W.*

Sea Feather Bay. The central section of the south coast features several lengthy ribbons of soft ecru sand, only occasionally maintained, with little shade aside from the odd coconut palm, no facilities, and blissful privacy (aside from some villas). **Amenities:** none. **Best for:** solitude; swimming, walking. ⊠ *South Side Rd., just west of Ashton Reid Dr., Sea Feather Bay.*

7

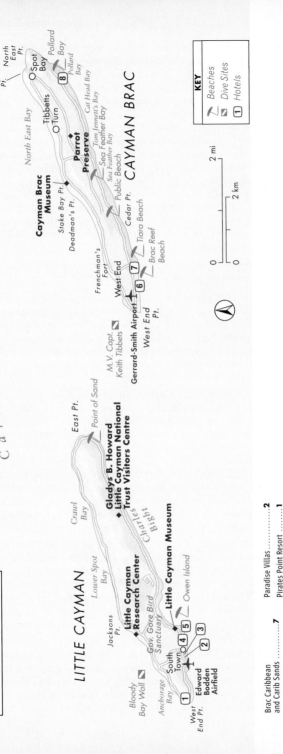

Cayman Brac and Little Cayman

Caribbean Sea

LITTLE CAYMAN

Bloody Bay Wall
Jacksons Pt.
Lower Spot Bay
Anchorage Bay
West End Pt.
Gov. Gore Bird Sanctuary
South Town
Edward Bodden Airfield
Little Cayman Research Center
Charles Bight
Owen Island
Little Cayman Museum
Crawl Bay
Gladys B. Howard
Little Cayman National Trust Visitors Centre
East Pt.
Point of Sand

CAYMAN BRAC

Gerrard-Smith Airport
West End Pt.
West End
Frenchman's Fort
M.V. Capt. Keith Tibbets
Deadman's Pt.
Stake Bay Pt.
Cayman Brac Museum
Cedar Pt.
Tiara Beach
Brac Reef Beach
Public Beach
Sea Feather Bay
Tom Jennett's Bay
Car Head Bay
Parrot Preserve
North East Bay
Tibbetts Turn
Booby Pt.
North East Pt.
Spot Bay
Pollard Bay
Pollard Bay

KEY
- Beaches
- Dive Sites
- 1 Hotels

0   2 mi
0   2 km

Brac Caribbean and Carib Sands 7
Cayman Brac Beach Resort 6
Cayman Breakers 8
The Club 4
Little Cayman Beach Resort 3
Paradise Villas 2
Pirates Point Resort 1
Southern Cross Club 5

WHERE TO EAT

$$ CARIBBEAN 🍴 **Coral Isle Club.** This seaside eatery daubed in a virtual rainbow of blues from turquoise to teal serves up fine local food, emphasizing fresh seafood and, on weekends, mouth- and eye-watering barbecue. The lusciously painted outdoor bar offers equally colorful sunsets, cocktails, and characters (one regular swears, "If I were any better, I'd be dangerous," before buying another round). At night, spotlights illuminate the reef sharks and lobsters lurking in the turtle grass below the patio. The congenial owner, Carlton Ebanks, offers regular entertainment from DJs to fashion shows to domino tournaments, whenever possible on weekends in season. [$] *Average main: $15* ✉ *Off South Side Rd., West End* ☎ *345/925–4848.*

WHERE TO STAY

Cayman Brac has several hotels, resorts, and apartments. Several private villas on Cayman Brac can also be rented, most of them basic but well maintained, ranging from one to four bedrooms. Most resorts offer optional meal plans, but there are several restaurants, some of which provide free transport from your hotel. Most restaurants serve island fare (local seafood, chicken, and curries). On Friday and Saturday nights the spicy scent of jerk chicken fills the air; several roadside stands sell takeout.

7

PRIVATE VILLAS AND CONDOS

Fodor's Choice ★ **Golden Sun/Le Soleil d'Or.** Mirjana Mirjanic's company rents some of the Brac's newest, most luxurious homes, as well as some individual suites, but sets itself apart with the little extras (for a price): in-house spa treatments, personal training, gourmet chefs, even cooking classes. The rental office also doubles as a delightful shop, selling Mirjana's organic foodstuffs (sorrel flower jam, Meyer lemon marmalade), goat cheese soaps, and candles, all sourced from Golden Sun's own garden farm. (You can arrange a farm-to-table tour of the sustainable facility, too.) The main house now incorporates a sun-filled restaurant for guests (though it may open on a limited basis to other visitors). ✉ *2147 South Side Rd.* ☎ *345/948–0555, 888/988–0521* 🌐 *www.goldensuncayman.com.*

HOTELS AND RESORTS

$ RESORT 🏨 **Brac Caribbean and Carib Sands.** These neighboring, beachfront sister complexes offer condos with one to four bedrooms, all individually owned and decorated. **Pros:** lively restaurant-bar; weekly discounts excellent value for families. **Cons:** pretty but narrow, often unmaintained beach; limited staff; Wi-Fi dodgy. [$] *Rooms from: $190* ✉ *Bert Marson Dr.* ☎ *345/948–2265, 866/843–2722* 🌐 *www.caribsands.com, www.866thebrac.com* 🛏 *65 condos* 🍽 *No meals.*

$$ RESORT 🏨 **Cayman Brac Beach Resort.** Popular with divers, this well-run eco-friendly resort, completely renovated in 2015, features a beautiful sandy beach shaded by sea grape trees slung with hammocks. **Pros:** great dive outfit; friendly vibe; free Wi-Fi; good online packages; coin-operated laundry. **Cons:** noise from planes; view often obscured from ground-floor units; mandatory airport transfer of $20 per person. [$] *Rooms*

from: $317 ✉ *West End* ☎ *345/948–1323, 727/323–8727 for reservations in Florida,, 855/484–0808* 🌐 *www.caymanbracbeachresort.com* 🛏 *40 rooms* 🍴 *Some meals.*

$ RENTAL 🏢 **Cayman Breakers.** This attractive, pink-brick, colonnaded condo development sitting between the bluff and the southeast coastal ironshore caters to climbers, who scale the bluff's sheer face, as well as divers, who appreciate the good shore diving right off the property. **Pros:** spectacular views; thoughtful extras like complimentary bikes, jigsaw puzzles, and climbing-route guides; very attentive managers who live on-site. **Cons:** nearest grocery is a 15-minute drive; gorgeous beach is rocky with rough surf; some units slightly musty and faded. [$] *Rooms from: $155* ✉ *1902 South Side Rd. E, near East End* ☎ *345/948–1463* 🌐 *www.caybreakers.com* 🛏 *26 2-bedroom condos* 🍴 *No meals.*

NIGHTLIFE

Divers are notoriously early risers, but a few bars keep things hopping if not quite happening, especially on weekends, when local bands (or "imports" from Grand Cayman) often perform. Quaintly reminiscent of *Footloose* (without the hellfire and brimstone), watering holes are required to obtain music and dancing permits. Various community events including talent shows, recitals, concerts, and other stage presentations at the Aston Rutty Centre provide the rest of the island's nightlife.

Barracuda's Bar. New Yorker Terry Chesnard built his dream bar from scratch, endowing it with an almost 1960s Rat Pack ambience. Nearly everything is handcrafted, from the elegant bar itself to the blown-glass light fixtures to the shot specials (try the Barracuda "if you dare") and cocktails with *cojones* (though Terry takes greatest pride in his top-of-the-line espresso machine). The kitchen elevates pub grub to an art form, with pizzas, Reubens, and French melts. Locals flock here for free pasta Fridays, karaoke Wednesdays, and live music on Thursdays. You might walk in on a hotly contested darts or dominoes tournament, but the vibe is otherwise mellow at this charming time-warp hangout. ✉ *West End* ☎ *345/948–8511* 🌐 *www.barracudas.ky.*

SPORTS AND THE OUTDOORS

DIVING AND SNORKELING

Cayman Brac's waters are celebrated for their rich diversity of sea life, from hammerhead and reef sharks to stingrays to sea horses. Divers and snorkelers alike will find towering coral heads, impressive walls, and fascinating wrecks. The snorkeling off the **north coast** is spectacular, particularly at West End, where coral formations close to shore attract all kinds of critters. The walls feature remarkable topography with natural gullies, caves, and fissures blanketed with Technicolor sponges, black coral, gorgonians, and sea fans. Some of the famed sites are the West Chute, Cemetery Wall, Airport Wall, and Garden Eel Wall. The South Wall is a wonderland of sheer drop-offs carved with a maze of vertical swim-throughs, tunnels, arches, and grottoes that divers nickname Cayman's Grand Canyon. Notable sites include Anchor Wall,

Rock Monster Chimney, and the Wilderness. Many fish have colonized the 330-foot MV *Capt. Keith Tibbetts,* a Russian frigate—now broken in two—that was deliberately scuttled within swimming distance of the northwest shore. An artist named Foots has created an amazing underwater Atlantis off Radar Reef. The island's two dive operators offer scuba and snorkel training and PADI certification.

Brac Scuba Shack. Partners Martin van der Touw, wife Liesel, and Steve Reese form a tremendous troika at this PADI outfit, whose selling points include small groups (10 divers max on the custom Newton 36), flexible departures, valet service, and computer profiles. The 30-foot central console *Big Blue* takes no more than five divers and does double-duty for deep-sea fishing. Courses range from Discover Scuba through Divemaster Training, as well as such specialties as wreck, nitrox, and night diving. Rates are par for the course ($110 for two-tank dives), but multiday discounts are available. ⊠ *West End* ☎ *345/948–8472* ⊕ *www. bracscubashack.com.*

Reef Divers. Pluses here include five Newton boats from 42 to 46 feet, valet service, and enthusiastic, experienced staff. Certified divers can purchase à la carte dive packages even if they aren't hotel guests. They also arrange snorkeling tours. ⊠ *Brac Reef Beach Resort, West End* ☎ *345/948–1642, 345/948–1323* ⊕ *www.reefdiverscaymanbrac.com, www.bracreef.com.*

HIKING

Brac Tourism Office. Free printed guides to the Brac's many heritage and nature trails can be obtained here (and from the airport and hotels). Traditional routes across the bluff have been marked, as are trailheads along the road. It's safe to hike on your own, though some trails are fairly hard going (wear light hiking boots) and others could be better maintained. ⊠ *West End Community Park, west of airport* ☎ *345/948– 1649* ⊕ *www.itsyourstoexplore.com.*

Christopher Columbus Gardens. For those who prefer less-strenuous walking, these gardens have easy trails and boardwalks. The park showcases the unique natural flora and features of the bluff, including two cave mouths. This is a peaceful spot dotted with gazebos and wooden bridges comprising several ecosystems from cacti to mahogany trees. ⊠ *Ashton Reid Dr. (Bluff Rd.), just north of Ashton Rutty Centre.*

Sister Islands District Administration. The administration arranges free, government-sponsored, guided nature and cultural tours with trained local guides. Options include the Parrot Reserve, nature trails, wetlands, Lighthouse/Bluff View, caving, birding, and heritage sites. You just supply the wheels and spirit of adventure. ☎ *345/948–2222.*

SPELUNKING

If you plan to explore Cayman Brac's caves, wear good sneakers or hiking shoes, as some paths are steep and rocky and some cave entrances are reachable only by ladders. **Peter's Cave** offers a stunning aerial view of the northeastern community of Spot Bay. **Great Cave,** at the island's southeast end, has numerous chambers and photogenic ocean views. In **Bat Cave** you may see bats hanging from the ceiling (try not to disturb them). **Rebecca's Cave** houses the grave site of a 17-month-old child who died during the horrific hurricane of 1932.

LITTLE CAYMAN

The smallest, most tranquil of the Cayman Islands, Little Cayman has a full-time population of only 170, most of whom work in tourism. This 12-square-mile (31-square-km) island is still unspoiled and has only a sand-sealed airstrip, no official terminal building, and few vehicles. The speed limit remains 25 mph (40 kph), as no one is in a hurry. In fact, the island's iguanas use roads more than residents; signs created by local artists read "Iguanas Have the Right of Way." With little commercial development, the island beckons ecotourists who seek wildlife encounters, not urban wildlife. It's probably best known for its spectacular diving on Bloody Bay Wall and adjacent Jackson Marine Park. The ravishing reefs and plummeting walls encircling the island teem with more than 500 species of fish and more than 150 kinds of coral. Fly-, lake-, and deep-sea fishing are also popular, as are snorkeling, kayaking, cycling, and hiking. And the island's certainly for the birds. The National Trust Booby Pond Nature Reserve is a designated wetland, protecting around 20,000 red-footed boobies, the Western Hemisphere's largest colony. It's just one of many spots for avian aerial acrobatics. Pristine wetlands, secluded beaches, unspoiled tropical wilderness, mangrove swamps, lagoons, bejeweled coral reefs: Little Cayman practically redefines *escape*. Yet aficionados appreciate that the low-key lifestyle doesn't mean sacrificing high-tech amenities, and some resorts cater to a wealthy yet unpretentious crowd.

EXPLORING

TOP ATTRACTIONS

Fodor'sChoice **Gladys B. Howard Little Cayman National Trust Visitors Centre.** This tradi-
★ tional Caymanian cottage overlooks the Booby Pond Nature Reserve; telescopes on the breezy second-floor deck permit close-up views of their markings and nests, as well as other feathered friends. Inside are shell collections; panels and dioramas discussing endemic reptiles; models "in flight"; and diagrams on the growth and life span of red-footed boobies, frigate birds, egrets, and other island "residents." The shop sells exquisite jewelry made from Caymanite and spider-crab shells, extraordinary duck decoys and driftwood carvings, and great books on history, ornithology, and geology. Mike Vallee holds an iguana information session and tour every Friday at 4. The cheeky movie *Calendar Girls* inspired a local equivalent: Little Cayman women, mostly in full, ripe maturity, going topless for an important cause—raising awareness of the red-footed booby and funds to purchase the sanctuary's land. Nicknamed, appropriately, "Support the Boobies," the calendar is tasteful, not titillating: the lasses strategically hold conch shells, brochures, flippers, tree branches, etc. ⊠ *Blossom Village* ⊕ *www.nationaltrust. org.ky* ⊙ *Weekdays 3–5.*

WORTH NOTING

Little Cayman Museum. This newly renovated, gorgeously laid out and curated museum displays relics and artifacts, including one wing devoted to maritime memorabilia and another to superlative avian and marine photographs, that provide a good overview of this tiny island's history and heritage. ⊠ *Across from Booby Pond Nature Reserve, Blossom Village* ☎ *345/948–1033 for Little Cayman Beach Resort* ⌨ *Free* ☙ *Mon.–Thurs. 4:30–6, Fri. 2–5, Sat. 10–11:30.*

Little Cayman Research Center. Near the Jackson Point Bloody Bay Marine Park reserve, this vital research center supports visiting students and researchers, with a long list of projects studying the biodiversity, human impact, reef health, and ocean ecosystem of Little Cayman. Its situation is unique in that reefs this unspoiled are usually far less accessible; the National Oceanic and Atmospheric Administration awarded it one of 16 monitoring stations worldwide. The center also solicits funding through the parent U.S. nonprofit organization Central Caribbean Marine Institute; if you value the health of our reefs, show your support on the website. Chairman Peter Hillenbrand proudly calls it the "Ritz-Carlton of marine research facilities, which often are little more than pitched tents on a beach." Tours explain the center's mission and eco-sensitive design (including Peter's Potty, an off-the-grid bathroom facility using compostable toilets that recycle fertilizer into gray water for the gardens); sometimes you'll get a peek at the upstairs functional wet labs and dormitories. To make it layperson-friendlier, scientists occasionally give talks and presentations. The Dive with a Researcher program (where you actually help survey and assess environmental impact and ecosystem health, depending on that week's focus) is hugely popular. ⊠ *North Side* ☎ *345/948–1094* ⊕ *www.reefresearch.org* ☙ *By appointment only.*

BEACHES

The southwest part of the island seems like one giant beach; this is where virtually all the resorts sit, serenely facing Preston Bay and South Hole Sound. But there are several other unspoiled, usually deserted strands that beckon beachcombers, all the sand having the same delicate hue of Cristal champagne and just as apt to make you feel giddy.

Fodor'sChoice ★ **Owen Island.** This private, forested island can be reached by rowboat, kayak, or an ambitious 200-yard swim. Anyone is welcome to come across and enjoy the deserted beaches and excellent snorkeling. Nudity is forbidden as "idle and disorderly" in the Cayman Islands, though that doesn't always stop skinny-dippers (who may not realize they can be seen quite easily from shore). **Amenities:** none. **Best for:** snorkeling; solitude; swimming.

Fodor'sChoice ★ **Point of Sand.** Stretching over a mile on the island's easternmost point, this secluded beach is great for wading, shell collecting, and snorkeling. On a clear day you can see 7 miles (11 km) to Cayman Brac. The beach serves as a green- and loggerhead turtle nesting site in spring, and a mosaic of coral gardens blooms just offshore. It's magical, especially at moonrise, when it earns its nickname, Lovers' Beach. There's a palapa for shade but no facilities. The current can be strong, so watch the kids carefully. **Amenities:** none. **Best for:** snorkeling; solitude; sunset; walking.

WHERE TO EAT

$$$ ECLECTIC 🍴 **Hungry Iguana.** The closest thing to a genuine sports bar and nightclub on Little Cayman, the Iggy caters to the aquatically minded set with a marine mural, wood-plank floors, mounted trophy sailfish, lots of fishing caps, and yummy fresh seafood. Conch fritters are near definitive, while lionfish fingers with jerk mayo are mouth- and eye-watering. It's a great hangout for (relatively) cheap eats; prix-fixe theme nights between CI$20 and CI$40 offer fine value: pizza, fajitas, curry, and more. Drink in the smashing sunset views on the delightful patio overlooking the water, and also drink the house specialty Iguana Punch (rum, rum, more rum, and coconut rum with orange and pineapple juices). [$] *Average main: $26* ✉ *Paradise Villas, Blossom Village* ☎ *345/948–0001* 🌐 *www.hungryiguana.com* 🕓 *No dinner Sun.*

WHERE TO STAY

Accommodations are mostly in small lodges, many of which offer meal and dive packages. The meal packages are a good idea; the chefs in most places create wonderful dishes with often limited resources.

$$ RENTAL 🏨 **The Club.** These ultramodern, luxurious, three-bedroom condos are Little Cayman's nicest units, though only five are usually included in the rental pool. **Pros:** luxurious digs; lovely beach; hot tub. **Cons:** housekeeping not included; rear guest bedrooms dark and somewhat cramped; handsome but heavy old-fashioned decor. [$] *Rooms from: $311* ✉ *South Hole Sound* ☎ *345/948–1033, 727/323–8727, 800/327–3835* 🌐 *www.theclubatlittlecayman.com* 🛏 *8 condos* 🍽 *No meals.*

$$$ RESORT FAMILY 🏨 **Little Cayman Beach Resort.** This two-story hotel, the island's largest, offers modern facilities in a boutique setting. **Pros:** extensive facilities; fun crowd; glorious LED-lit pool; great bone- and deep-sea fishing. **Cons:** less intimate than other resorts; tiny patios; bike rental fee. [$] *Rooms from: $434* ✉ *Blossom Village* ☎ *345/948–1033, 800/327–3835* 🌐 *www.littlecayman.com* 🛏 *40 rooms* 🍽 *Some meals.*

$ RENTAL 🏨 **Paradise Villas.** Cozy, sunny, one-bedroom units with beachfront terraces and hammocks are simply but immaculately appointed with rattan furnishings, marine artwork, painted driftwood, and bright abstract fabrics. **Pros:** friendly staff; good value, especially online deals and dive packages. **Cons:** noisy some weekend nights in season; poky beach; small bike rental fee; off-site dive shop. [$] *Rooms from: $225* ✉ *South Hole Sound* ☎ *345/948–0001, 877/322–9626* 🌐 *www.paradisevillas.com* 🕓 *Closed mid-Sept.–late Oct.* 🛏 *12 1-bedroom villas* 🍽 *No meals.*

$$$$ RESORT Fodor's Choice ★ 🏨 **Pirates Point Resort.** Comfortable rooms and fine cuisine make this hideaway nestled between sea grape and casuarina pines on a sweep of sand one of Little Cayman's best properties. **Pros:** fabulous food; fantastic beach; dynamic dive program; fun-loving staff and owner. **Cons:** everyone respects honeymooners' privacy, but this isn't a resort for antisocial types; tasteful rooms are fairly spare; occasional Internet problems. [$] *Rooms from: $500* ✉ *Pirates Point* ☎ *345/948–1010* 🌐 *www.piratespointresort.com* 🕓 *Closed Sept.–mid-Oct.* 🛏 *11 rooms* 🍽 *All-inclusive.*

$$$$ RESORT Fodor's Choice ★ 🏨 **Southern Cross Club.** Little Cayman's first resort was founded in the 1950s as a private fishing club by the CEO of Sears-Roebuck and CFO of General Motors, and its focus is still on fishing and diving. **Pros:** barefoot luxury; free use of kayaks and snorkel gear; splendiferous beach; international staff tells of globe-trotting exploits. **Cons:** not child-friendly (though families can rent a cottage); Wi-Fi not available in some rooms and spotty elsewhere. [$] *Rooms from: $738* ✉ *South Hole Sound* ☎ *345/948–1099, 800/899–2582* 🌐 *www.southerncrossclub.com* ⏲ *Closed mid-Sept.–mid-Oct.* 🛏 *12 suites, 1 2-bedroom cottage* 🍴 *All meals.*

SPORTS AND THE OUTDOORS

BIRD-WATCHING

Little Cayman offers bountiful bird-watching, with more than 200 indigenous and migrant species on vibrant display, including red-footed boobies, frigate birds, and West Indian whistling ducks. Unspoiled wetland blankets more than 40% of the island, and elevated viewing platforms (carefully crafted from local wood to blend harmoniously with the environment) permit undisturbed observation—but then, it's hard to find an area that doesn't host flocks of warblers and waterfowl. Brochures with maps are available at the hotels for self-guided bird-watching tours.

Fodor's Choice ★ **Booby Pond Nature Reserve.** The reserve is home to 20,000 red-footed boobies (the Western Hemisphere's largest colony) and Cayman's only breeding colony of magnificent frigate (man-of-war) birds. Other sightings include the near-threatened West Indian whistling duck and vitelline warbler. The RAMSAR Convention, an international treaty for wetland conservation, designated the reserve a wetland of global significance. Near the airport, the sanctuary also has a gift shop and reading library. ✉ *Next to National Trust, Blossom Village.*

DIVING AND SNORKELING

A gaudy, voluptuous tumble of marine life—lumbering grouper to fleet guppies, massive manta rays to miniature wrasse, sharks to stingrays, blue chromis to Bermuda chubs, puffers to parrot fish—parades its finery through the pyrotechnic coral reefs like a watery Main Street on Saturday night. Gaping gorges, vaulting pinnacles, plunging walls, chutes, arches, and vertical chimneys create a virtual underwater city, festooned with fiery sponges and sensuously waving gorgonians draped like come-hither courtesans over limestone settees.

Expect to pay around $105–$110 for a two-tank boat dive and $25–$30 for a snorkeling trip. The island is small and susceptible to wind, so itineraries can change like a sudden gust.

RECOMMENDED DIVE OPERATORS

Pirates Point Dive Resort. This popular resort has fully outfitted 42-foot Newtons with dive masters who excel at finding odd and rare creatures, and encourage computer diving so you can stay down longer. ✉ *Pirates Point Resort* ☎ *345/948–1010* 🌐 *www.piratespointresort.com.*

Reef Divers. Little Cayman Beach Resort's outfitter offers valet service and a full complement of courses, with nitrox a specialty. The custom boats include AEDs (defibrillators). ⊠ *Little Cayman Beach Resort, Blossom Village* ☎ *345/948–1033* ⊕ *www.littlecayman.com.*

Southern Cross Club. Each boat has its own dock and takes 12 divers max. The outfit has good specialty courses and mandates computer diving. ⊠ *Southern Cross Club, 73 Guy Banks Rd., South Hole Sound* ☎ *345/948–1099, 800/899–2582* ⊕ *www.southerncrossclub.com.*

FISHING

Bloody Bay is celebrated equally for fishing and diving, and the flats and shallows including South Hole Sound Lagoon across from Owen Island, Tarpon Lake, and the Charles Bight Rosetta Flats offer phenomenal light-tackle and fly-fishing action: large tarpon, small bonefish, and permit (related to pompano) up to 35 pounds. Superior deep-sea fishing, right offshore, yields game fish such as blue marlin, dolphinfish, wahoo, tuna, and barracuda.

Southern Cross Club. The resort offers light-tackle and deep-sea fishing trips. ⊠ *Southern Cross Club, 73 Guy Banks Dr., South Hole Sound* ☎ *345/948–1099, 800/899–2582* ⊕ *www.southerncrossclub.com.*

8

CURAÇAO

Visit Fodors.com for advice, updates, and bookings

WELCOME TO CURAÇAO

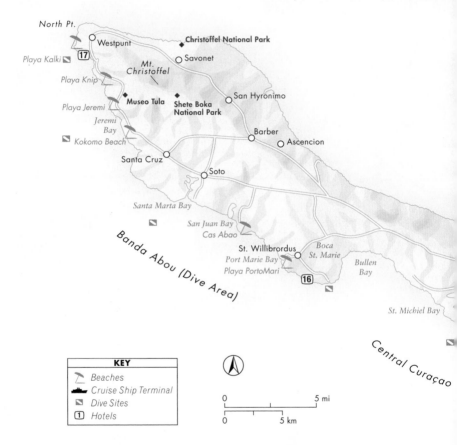

North Pt.

Westpunt

Playa Kalki ⌂ [17]

Christoffel National Park

Savonet ○

Mt. Christoffel

Playa Knip

Museo Tula ◆ **Shete Boka National Park**

San Hyronimo ○

Playa Jeremi

Jeremi Bay

Kokomo Beach ⌂

Santa Cruz ○

Soto ○

Barber ○

Ascencion ○

Santa Marta Bay

San Juan Bay
Cas Abao

St. Willibrordus ○
Port Marie Bay
Playa PortoMari [16]

Boca St. Marie

Bullen Bay

Banda Abou (Dive Area)

St. Michiel Bay

Central Curaçao

KEY
⌐ Beaches
⛴ Cruise Ship Terminal
⌂ Dive Sites
① Hotels

0   5 mi

0   5 km

Willemstad's fancifully hued, strikingly gabled town houses glimmer across Santa Anna Bay, and vendors at the Floating Market sell tropical fruit from their schooners. Curaçao's diverse population mixes Latin, European, and African ancestries. Religious tolerance is a hallmark here. All people are welcome in Curaçao, and even tourists feel the warmth.

AN ISLAND REBORN AND REDISCOVERED

The largest and most populous of the Netherlands Antilles is 38 miles (61 km) long and no more than 7½ miles (12 km) wide. Its capital, Willemstad, has been restored and revived over the past few years and is a recognized UNESCO World Heritage Site. The colorful waterfront town houses are unique to the island.

CURAÇAO

8

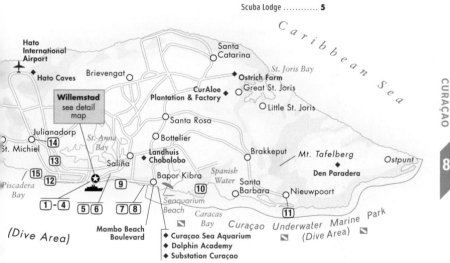

TOP REASONS TO VISIT CURAÇAO

1 Below the Belt: Curaçao sits below the hurricane belt, so the weather is almost always alluring, even during the off-season.

2 Carnival: Curaçao's biggest party draws an increasingly large crowd.

3 Culture: The island's cultural diversity is reflected in the good food from many different cultures.

4 History You Can See: Striking architecture and fascinating historic sites give you something to see when you're not shopping or sunning on the charming beaches.

NEED TO KNOW

AT A GLANCE

Capital: Willemstad

Population: 153,000

Currency: Netherlands Antillean florin or guilder; pegged to the U.S. dollar

Money: Most ATMs are in Willemstad; credit cards and U.S. dollars widely accepted.

Language: Dutch, Papiamento, English

Country Code: ☎ 599 9

Emergencies: ☎ 911

Driving: On the right

Electricity: 127v/50 cycles; plugs are U.S. standard two- and three-prong

Time: Same as New York during daylight savings; one hour ahead otherwise

Documents: Up to 90 days with valid passport

Mobile Phones: GSM (900, 1800 and 1900 bands)

Major Mobile Companies: Digicel, CHIPPIE

WEBSITES

Curaçao Tourist Board: ⊕ www.curacao.com

Caribbean Sea

CURACAO

Willemstad

GETTING AROUND

✈ **Air Travel:** Hato International Airport is the sole airport on Curaçao.

🚌 **Bus Travel:** Bus service exists but is rather limited on Curaçao. There are two major bus terminals: one in Punda, outside the postal office, the other in Otrobanda, next to the underpass.

🚗 **Car Travel:** Well-marked roads make navigating the island by rental car easy. Rent a four-wheel-drive vehicle if you plan to explore the island's natural sights.

🚕 **Taxi Travel:** For just getting around town, taxis are preferable. Rates are set by the government.

PLAN YOUR BUDGET

	HOTEL ROOM	MEAL	ATTRACTIONS
Low Budget	$150	$12	Curaçao Liqueur Factory, free
Mid Budget	$225	$20	Entry fee Christoffel National Park, $12
High Budget	$300	$30	Sunset sail with open bar, $45

WAYS TO SAVE

Don't add a 20% tip. Most restaurants already add a 10% service charge to the bill; another 10% is more than generous.

Book a rental. For more spacious accommodations and a kitchen, rent a furnished apartment or time-share condo.

Free shuttles. Many of the larger hotels have free shuttles into Willemstad; hotels in Willemstad usually provide a free beach shuttle.

Welcome Card Curaçao. Buy a Welcome Card Curaçao online for $10, entitling you to a wealth of deep discounts across the island.

PLAN YOUR TIME

Hassle Factor	Medium. Most flights to Curaçao require a connection in Miami.
3 days	Relax poolside at your hotel and hit the reef for sublime diving and snorkeling. Hit the soft, white beaches of the west coast. Do a bit of sightseeing one day.
1 week	Enjoy the amenities of your hotel, dive, sightsee, and relax; but also rent a 4x4 to explore the island's more remote, untouched reaches. Enjoy a few day sails to circumvent the island.
2 weeks	After exploring every nook of Curaçao (both on land and under the sea), hop on a 20-minute flight over to neighboring Bonaire or Aruba (or both).

WHEN TO GO

High Season: January to June is the most fashionable and most expensive time to visit, when the weather is typically sunny and warm (though expect some rain in January). Good hotels are often booked far in advance, and everything is open.

Low Season: The rainy season lasts from October to December, and the weather is hot and muggy. Resorts remain open but offer deep discounts.

Value Season: During peak hurricane season, from July to September, hotel prices drop 20% or more. But Curaçao is outside of the main hurricane belt. There are chances of scattered showers, but expect sun-kissed days and fewer crowds.

BIG EVENTS

January–March: Curaçao Carnival starts on New Year's Day and concludes on Ash Wednesday. ⊕ *www. curacaocarnival.info*

June: The Heineken Regatta Curaçao features exciting boat races and musical events. ⊕ *www. heinekenregattacuracao.com*

August–September: The Curaçao North Sea Jazz Festival features big-name stars of jazz and pop. ⊕ *www. curacaonorthseajazz.com*

November: The Amstel Curaçao Race offers intense cycling. ⊕ *www.amstelcuracaorace.com*

READ THIS

■ *The Cay,* Theodore Taylor. A child and his mom attempt to escape Curaçao during WWII.

■ *The Curaçao Connection: A Jan Kokk Mystery,* R. F. Sullivan. Mystery thriller set in Curaçao.

■ *Tumbleweed,* Janwillem Van De Wetering. Dutch mystery leads to the Curaçao black magic underworld.

WATCH THIS

■ *Curaçao.* Action thriller about two shady expats living on the island.

■ *Tula: The Revolt.* The story of Curaçao's slave uprising.

■ *Filmpje!* Out-of-the box, over-the-top Dutch comedy.

EAT THIS

■ *Keshi yena*: seasoned meat wrapped in cheese and then baked.

■ *Kònkòmber*: cucumbers stewed with papaya and meat.

■ *Sate*: grilled chicken or pork grilled served with spicy peanut sauce.

■ *Nasigoreng*: Asian-inspired stir-fry with bean sprouts and meat.

■ *Panseiku*: national version of peanut brittle.

■ *Curaçao liqueur*: blue liqueur made from the peels of the Laraha orange.

Updated
by Susan
Campbell

Curaçao is the most colorful and culture-rich of the Dutch Caribbean triumvirate of tropical islands called the ABCs (Aruba, Bonaire, and Curaçao). Fringed with 38 beaches and ringed with coral walls full of resplendent marine life, Curaçao is a haven for snorkelers and divers with first-rate facilities for both and a wide range of cosmopolitan hotels that welcome all. From the UNESCO World Heritage harbor city to the arid interior dotted with plantation houses to the surf-pounded cliffs overlooking endless seas, there is something to satisfy every kind of traveler.

The UNESCO World Heritage city of Willemstad is divided by a deep natural harbor making it a perfect crossroads for trade, and a valuable destination for maritime powers that once ruled the high seas. It has changed hands many times over the centuries in a constant tug-of-war between the Dutch, the French, and the Spanish, and even the Americans once had a brief foothold there. Today, it still attracts voyagers from all over the globe, but their designs on the historic city are purely recreational, as tourism is slated to become an increasingly important driver of the economy.

Curaçao is continually awash in colorful celebrations; from the long-lasting Carnival to a multitude of live music events like the Curaçao North Sea Jazz Festival, there is always something additionally special to enjoy beyond the unique architecture and beautiful beaches.

The Handelskade—the long row of candy-colored buildings lining Santa Anna Bay—is the signature postcard shot one will see in reference to this island. Local lore has it that in the 1800s, the governor claimed he suffered from migraines and blamed the glare from the sun's reflection off the then-white structures. To alleviate the problem, he ordered the facades painted in colors. (It's also rumored he might have had an interest in the local paint company!) But there's so much more to Willemstad for history buffs and culture seekers than brightly colored buildings. The ancient neighborhoods are alive with history and interesting stories, with many of the colonial structures that house museums and heritage sites like the Maritime Museum. Restored forts now house entertainment complexes and resorts, and recently transformed neighborhoods like Pietermaai also invite visitors to take a walk through then-and-now contrasts sitting side by side in real time.

Though first inhabited by Arawak Indians, Curaçao was "discovered" by Alonzo de Ojeda (a lieutenant of Columbus) in 1499. The first Spanish settlers arrived in 1527. In 1634 the Dutch came via the Netherlands West Indies Company. Eight years later Peter Stuyvesant began his rule as governor (in 1647, Stuyvesant became governor of New Amsterdam, which later became New York). Twelve Jewish families arrived in Curaçao from Amsterdam in 1651, and by 1732 a synagogue had been built; the present structure is the oldest synagogue in continuous use in the Western Hemisphere. Over the years the city built fortresses to defend against French and British invasions—the standing ramparts now house restaurants and hotels. The Dutch claim to Curaçao was recognized in 1815 by the Treaty of Paris. From 1954 through 2006, Curaçao was the seat of government of the Netherlands Antilles, a group of islands under the umbrella of the Kingdom of the Netherlands. In 2010, after discussions with the Netherlands, Curaçao's island council granted the territory autonomy (the same status Aruba attained in 1986).

Today Curaçao's population derives from nearly 60 nationalities—an exuberant mix of Latin, European, and African roots speaking a Babel of tongues—resulting in superb restaurants and a flourishing cultural scene. Although Dutch is the official language, Papiamento is the preferred choice for communication among the locals. English and Spanish are also widely spoken. The island, like its Dutch settlers, is known for its religious tolerance, and Curaçao is one of the most LGBT-friendly islands in the Caribbean.

PLANNING

GETTING HERE AND AROUND
AIR TRAVEL

Curaçao is becoming easier to get to by air as major North American airlines, including JetBlue and Air Canada, are adding more direct or one-stop connection flights.

Airline Contacts American Airlines. ☎ 5999/869–5707 ⊕ www.aa.com. **Avianca.** ☎ 5999/820–2020 ⊕ www.avianca.com. **JetBlue.** ☎ 800/538–2583 ⊕ www.jetblue.com. **KLM.** ☎ 5999/ 736–1422 ⊕ www.klm.com.

Airport Curaçao International Airport. ⊠ CUR ☎ 5999/839–1000 ⊕ www.curacao-airport.com.

NONSTOP FLIGHTS Atlanta (Delta, seasonal), Miami (American, Insel), and New York (JetBlue). American Airlines also offers service from San Juan, Puerto Rico. Air Canada Rouge offers seasonal nonstop from Toronto.

CAR TRAVEL

Some of the larger hotels have free shuttles into Willemstad, or you can take a quick, cheap taxi ride; some hotels in Willemstad usually provide a free beach shuttle, so it's possible to get by without a car. But if you want to really see the island contrasts, a rental car is necessary. If you're planning to do country driving or rough it through Christoffel National Park, a four-wheel-drive vehicle is best. All you need is a valid driver's license. Driving in Curaçao is on the right-hand side of the road; right turns on red are prohibited. Seat belts are required, and motorcyclists must wear helmets. Children under age four must be in child safety seats.

Car Rental: You can rent a car from any of the major car agencies at the airport or have one delivered free to your hotel. Rates range from $30 to $80 a day depending on the vehicle. Add 5% tax and optional daily insurance.

Contacts Avis. ☎ 5999/461–1255, 800/331–1084 ⊕ www.aviscuracao.com. **Budget.** ☎ 5999/868–3466, 800/472–3325 ⊕ www.curacao-budgetcar.com. **Hertz.** ⊠ Curaçao International Airport ☎ 5999/888–0088 ⊕ www.hertz.com. **National Car Rental.** ☎ 5999/869–4433 ⊕ www.nationalcuracao.com.

TAXI TRAVEL

Fares from the airport to Willemstad and the nearby beach hotels run about $20 to $35, and those to hotels at the island's western end about $40 to $47 (be sure to agree on the rate before setting off). The government-approved rates, which do not include waiting time, can be found in a brochure called "Taxi Tariff Guide," available at the airport, hotels, cruise-ship terminals, and the tourist board. Rates are for up to four passengers. There's a 25% surcharge after 11 pm. Note: If you call a taxi and then decide you do not want it, you will still have to pay a fee, typically $10.

Central Dispatch. Taxis are readily available at hotels and at taxi stands at the airport, in Punda, and in Otrobanda; in other cases, call Central Dispatch. ⊠ F.D. Rooseveltweg 32U ☎ 5999/869–0747.

HEALTH AND SAFETY

Dengue, chikungunya, and zika have all been reported throughout the Caribbean. We recommend that you protect yourself from these mosquito-borne illnesses by keeping your skin covered and/or wearing mosquito repellent. The mosquitoes that transmit these viruses are as active by day as they are by night.

HOTELS AND RESORTS

Resort development is concentrated around the capital, Willemstad, so most resorts are within easy reach of town, by shuttle or on foot. As the island becomes more developed, visitors have more options, and there are a few resorts farther removed as well, but it's the amenities that should drive your decision more than location. Choose the type of lodging that best appeals to your interests and style. Those spending a bit more time gravitate to villas and bungalows.

Resorts: Most of Curaçao's larger hotels are midsize resorts of 200 to 300 rooms, and many of them are within easy striking distance of town,

but some are secreted away in their own neighborhoods like Santa Barbara or Jan Thiel and Pietermaai. The island offers a full range of resorts from the intimate and luxurious to historic properties—few other destinations offer a downtown hotel with a saltwater infinity pool complete with palm-lined beach.

Dive Resorts: Most of the resorts catering to divers are smaller operations of fewer than 100 rooms (often much smaller). Although some of these are in and around Willemstad, there are also a few on the secluded west end of the island, and that's where shore diving is best.

Villas and Bungalows: Though they are marketed primarily to European travelers who have more time to spend on the island, self-catering accommodations are an option for anyone who has at least a week to spend in Curaçao. Coral Estates has gorgeous villa homes to rent.

Hotel reviews have been shortened. For full information, visit Fodors.com.

WHAT IT COSTS IN U.S. DOLLARS				
	$	$$	$$$	$$$$
RESTAURANTS	under $12	$12–$20	$21–$30	over $30
HOTELS	under $275	$275–$375	$376–$475	over $475

Restaurant prices are the average cost of a main course at dinner or, if dinner is not served, at lunch. Hotel prices are the lowest cost of a standard double room in high season.

VISITOR INFORMATION
Contacts Curaçao Tourist Board. ✉ *Pietermaai 19, Pietermaai* ☎ *5999/434–8200* ⊕ *www.curacao.com.*

EXPLORING

WILLEMSTAD

Dutch settlers came here in the 1630s, about the same time they sailed through the Verrazano Narrows to Manhattan, bringing with them original red-tile roofs, first used on the trade ships as ballast and later incorporated into the architecture of Willemstad. Much of the original colonial structures remain, but this historic city is constantly reinventing itself and the government monument foundation is always busy restoring buildings in one urban neighborhood or another. The salty air causes what is called "wall cancer," resulting in the ancient abodes continually crumbling over time. The city is cut in two by Santa Anna Bay. On one side is Punda (the point)—crammed with shops, restaurants, monuments, and markets and a new museum retracing its colorful history. And on the other side is Otrobanda (literally meaning the "other side"), with lots of narrow, winding streets and alleyways (called "steekjes" in Dutch), full of private homes notable for their picturesque gables and Dutch-influenced designs. In recent years the ongoing regeneration of Otrobanda has been apparent, marked by a surge in development of

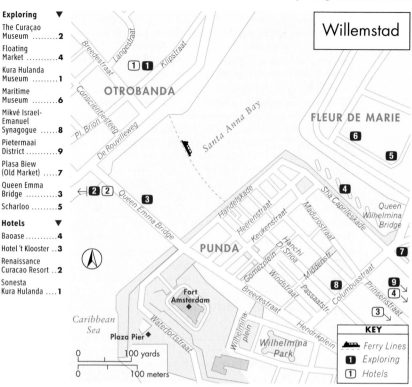

new hotels, restaurants, and shops; the rebirth, concentrated near the waterfront, was spearheaded by the creation of the elaborate Kura Hulanda complex. The old districts of Pietermaai and Scharloo are also being revitalized with restored mansions and new dining, lodging, and entertainment options.

There are three ways to cross the bay: by car over the Juliana Bridge; by foot over the Queen Emma pontoon bridge (locally called "the Swinging Old Lady"); or by free ferry, which runs when the pontoon bridge is swung open for passing ships. All the major hotels outside town offer free shuttle service to town once or twice daily. Shuttles coming from the Otrobanda side leave you at Riffort. From here it's a short walk north to the foot of the pontoon bridge. Shuttles coming from the Punda side leave you near the main entrance to Ft. Amsterdam.

TOP ATTRACTIONS

Fodor'sChoice **Kura Hulanda Museum.** Pet project of Dutch billionaire philanthropist
★ Jacob Gelt-Dekker who brought the Otrabanda neighborhood back to life in the '90s, this fascinating anthropological museum reveals the island's diverse roots. Housed in a restored 18th-century village, the museum is built around a former mercantile square (Kura Hulanda means "Holland courtyard"), where the Dutch once housed slaves mostly before they were sold and exported. Somber exhibits of the

transatlantic slave trade are tempered by sections that highlight the origins of the diaspora, including relics from West African empires, examples of pre-Columbian gold, and Antillean art. Call ahead for guided tours or rent an audio guide. ⊠ *Klipstraat 9, Otrobanda* ☎ *5999/434–7765* ⊕ *www.kurahulanda.com/en/museumx* ⊟ *$10* ☉ *Mon.–Sat. 9:30–4:30.*

Mikvé Israel-Emanuel Synagogue. The temple—the oldest in continuous use in the Western Hemisphere—is one of Curaçao's most important sights and draws thousands of visitors per year. The synagogue was dedicated in 1732 by the Jewish community, which had already grown from the original 12 families who came from Amsterdam in 1651. They were later joined by Jews from Portugal and Spain fleeing persecution from the Inquisition. White sand covers the synagogue floor for two symbolic reasons: a remembrance of the 40 years Jews spent wandering the desert, and a re-creation of the sand used by secret Jews, or *conversos,* to muffle sounds from their houses of worship during the Inquisition.

The Jewish Cultural Museum, in back of the synagogue, displays antiques and artifacts from around the world. Many of the objects are used in the synagogue, making it a "living" museum. ⊠ *Hanchi Snoa 29, Punda* ☎ *5999/461–1067* ⊕ *www.snoa.com* ⊟ *$10; donations also accepted* ☉ *Weekdays 9–4:30.*

WORTH NOTING

The Curaçao Museum. Housed in an 1853 restored plantation house that later served as a military hospital, this small museum is filled with artifacts, paintings, and antiques that trace the island's history. An outdoor sculpture garden features local artists, and this is also a venue for local and international art exhibitions. ⊠ *V. Leeuwenhoekstraat z/n, Otrobanda* ☎ *5999/462–3873* ⊕ *www.thecuracaomuseum.com* ⊟ *Free* ☉ *Tues.–Fri. 8:30–4:30, Sat. 10–4.*

Floating Market. Curaçao is such an arid island that most of the fruit and vegetables need to be imported. The floating market consists of dozens of Venezuelan schooners laden with tropical fruits and vegetables that dock to sell their wares on the Punda side of the city. Mangoes, papayas, and exotic vegetables vie for space with freshly caught fish and herbs and spices. The buying is best at 6:30 am—too early for many people on vacation—but there's plenty of action throughout the afternoon. Vendors will stay on island for months away from their families—forming their own little community—awaiting fresh supplies each day. ⊠ *Sha Caprileskade, Punda.*

Maritime Museum. The museum—designed to resemble the interior of a ship—gives you a sense of Curaçao's maritime history that spans some 500 years, using model ships, historic maps, nautical charts, navigational equipment, and audiovisual displays. Topics explored in the exhibits include the development of Willemstad as a trading city, Curaçao's role as a contraband hub, the remains of *De Alphen* (a Dutch marine freighter that exploded and sank in St. Anna Bay in 1778 and was excavated in 1984), the slave trade, the development of steam navigation, and the role of the Dutch navy on the island. The museum

A daring, mast-eye view of the Handelskade in Punda

also offers a two-hour guided tour (Wednesday and Saturday, 1 pm) on its "water bus" through Curaçao's harbor—a route familiar to traders, smugglers, and pirates. The museum is wheelchair accessible. Bar/restaurant *Sails* on-site open for lunch. ✉ *Van der Brandhofstraat 7, Scharloo* ☎ *5999/65–2327* ⊕ *www.curacaomaritime.com* ✉ *Museum $6.50* ☼ *Tues.–Sat. 9–4 (also Sun. and Mon. during cruise season Nov.–Apr.).*

Fodor's Choice ★ **Pietermaai District.** An incredible transformation has taken place in this historic district over the past few years; it has morphed from a decrepit neighborhood to a colorful seat of culture and happenings. New boutique hotels, fine dining, and trendy cafés have taken hold in restored mansions and new enclaves. It has its own security force and designated community organization, which hosts many special events and artistic projects. Hosted photo walks are also offered with a side of history. ✉ *District Pietermaai, Pietermaai* ⊕ *http://pietermaaidistrict.com.*

Plasa Bieuw (Old Market) (*Marsche Bieuw*). Also known as the Marsche Bieuw, the Old Market is a popular lunch stop for locals working downtown. Visitors will appreciate the hearty, simple authentic fare and good prices. Enjoy such Curaçaoan specialties as *funchi* (polenta), goat stew, fried fish, stewed okra, fried plantains, and rice and peas prepared right in front of your eyes in open kitchens by local cooks. ✉ *De Ruyterkade, Punda.*

Fodor's Choice ★ **Queen Emma Bridge.** Affectionately called the "Swinging Old Lady" by locals, this bridge connects the two sides of Willemstad—Punda and Otrobanda—across the Santa Anna Bay. The bridge swings open at least 30 times a day to allow passage of ships to and from the sea. The original bridge, built in 1888, was the brainchild of the American consul

Leonard Burlington Smith, who made a mint off the tolls he charged for using it: 2¢ per person for those wearing shoes, free to those crossing barefoot. But though that toll distinction was meant to help the poor, the rich often saved money by crossing barefoot, and the poor would often borrow shoes to cross because they were too proud to admit they could not afford the toll! Today it's free to everyone. The bridge was dismantled and completely repaired and restored in 2005 and also restored further in 2015. ⊠ *Willemstad* ⊕ *www.curacao.com.*

Scharloo. The Wilhelmina Drawbridge connects Punda with the once-flourishing district of Scharloo where the early Jewish merchants built stately homes. It was a tight-knit community and the architecture along Scharlooweg (much of it from the 17th century) is magnificent. Some of the neighborhood has been restored as part of the UNESCO heritage site and the Curaçao Monuments Foundation will be restoring more old mansions in the future. This neighborhood is also home to the island's most photographed building, a light-green mansion dubbed the "Wedding Cake House" since it looks like it's been frosted with white icing. Kleine Werf—the little wharf cresting Scharloo—has now become a venue for large-scale outdoor concerts. New nightlife corners such as District 1850 are popping up there as well. ⊠ *Scharloo, Scharloo* ⊕ *www.curacao.com.*

ELSEWHERE ON CURAÇAO

As you drive out of town the arid, cacti-studded outback becomes rougher the farther you travel inland, and you might feel as if you have been transported into a stretch of Arizona desert. Wild donkeys and goats might step off onto the road, so use caution on curvy stretches, and be sure to bring plenty of water.

Many of Curaçao's secret attractions and tiny towns are pocketed within plain sight if you know where to go. One simple turnoff might lead to a spectacular beach like Cas Abao, or a beautiful plantation house like the Tula Museum at Kenepa or the art gallery at Jan Kok. Or maybe it will lead to a natural wonder like the salt pool full of flamingoes at Salina St. Marie or the thunderous blowhole at Boca Pistol. Make sure to get a good map and clear directions to unearth all the unique adventures scattered throughout the *kunuku* (countryside) as few are easily sighted from the main roads, but often not very far from them. Christoffel National Park and Shete Boka Park are protected preserves well worth exploring as well. And you'll find plenty of information and assistance at their new Savonet Museum there.

TOP ATTRACTIONS

Fodor's Choice ★ **Aquafari.** You don't have to snorkel or dive to discover Curaçao's spectacular underwater world of coral reefs and tropical fish if you ride with Aquafari. Go 30 feet deep on Aquafari's unique eco-friendly, one-piece underwater scooter with an air-supplied helmet from which you breathe just as normally as you would on land. The instructors are also divers, and after a safety briefing, they accompany you down to one of the coolest underwater adventures on the island. Your underwater guide also takes photos of your journey for purchase. The journey including topside briefing takes approximately 1½ hours with 45 minutes underwater. There's full facilities—food, drink, and changing rooms right next door at Pirate's Bay Beach. ✉ *Piscaderaweg, Pirate Bay Beach, Willemstad* ☎ *5999/513–2625* ⊕ *aquafari.net* 🖃 *$125* ☞ *Minimum age 10, minimun height 4 feet, maximum weight 275 pounds.*

Fodor'sChoice
★
Christoffel National Park. The 1,239-foot Mt. Christoffel, Curaçao's highest peak, is at the center of this 4,450-acre garden and wildlife preserve now under the protection of CARMABI (Caribbean Research and Management of Biodiversity). They offer many forms of touring the natural preserve, including guided hikes, jeep safaris, mountain biking, deerwatching (the island's elusive white-tailed deer are very shy), animal presentations, cave explorations, and special activities like full-moon nature walks. Visitors can also hike the mountain on their own. The exhilarating climb takes about two hours for a reasonably fit person. On a clear day, the panoramic view from the peak stretches to the mountain ranges of Venezuela. CARMABI recommends an early start as it gets very hot later in the day. Throughout the park are eight hiking trails and a 20-mile (32-km) network of driving trails (use heavy-treaded tires if you wish to explore the unpaved stretches). The old Savonet plantation house there (one of the island's first plantations) has been restored and now serves as a modern museum with exhibits retracing the region's history as far back as the original Indian inhabitants. ■TIP→ **There's a separate entrance fee to the museum but you can also get a combo-entrance pass that includes park and museum for less.** ✉ *Christoffel Park, Savonet* ☎ *5999/462–4242 for information and tour reservations,* ⊕ *www.christoffelpark.org* 🖃 *$12* ⊙ *Mon.–Sat. 7:30–4, Sun. 6–3; last admission 90 mins before closing.*

FAMILY
Fodor'sChoice
★
Curaçao Sea Aquarium. The Sea Aquarium is an original installation that became the island's largest marine life attraction. Though it's in the same physical location as the Dolphin Academy and Animal Encounters—all part of the Sea Aquarium Park—it operates independently. Admission allows visitors to view dolphin shows and sea lion shows, and to view marine life in the Animal Encounter lagoon from an underwater observatory. A new Sea Lion Encounter program enables visitors to get up close under the supervision of a trainer as well (additional cost). The aquarium hall has over 40 saltwater tanks full of marine life and offers visitors the opportunity to feed sharks, interact with stingrays, sea turtles, flamingos—and lots more. Extremely educational for all ages. Snack bar and souvenir shop also on-site. ✉ *Seaquarium Beach, Bapor Kibra* ☎ *5999/461–6666* ⊕ *www.curacao-sea-aquarium.com/en* 🖃 *$20 adults* ⊙ *Daily 8–5.*

CurAloe Plantation & Factory. Visit the home of the island's thriving aloe product sold in shops and stores all over Curaçao where you'll see the 100,000 specimens of plants used in CurAloe's hundreds of cosmetic and medicinal applications. No reservations required and no admission fee. Information is provided by video, and staff are happy to answer questions. You can sample and purchase many products. ✉ *Kaminda Mitologia, Groot St. Joris, Willemstad* ☎ *5999/767–5577* ⊕ *www. ecocityprojects.com.*

8

Plantation house in Christoffel National Park with Mt. Christoffel in the distance

FAMILY
Fodor'sChoice
★
Dolphin Academy. The Dolphin Academy—run independently from the sea aquarium—specializes in up-close interactions with these friendly, ever-smiling mammals. There are many different kinds of encounters available, including swimming, free diving, snorkeling, scuba, and simple interactions in shallow water. There are also open-water dive opportunities. You can also become an assistant trainer for a day, or do an extremely in-depth dolphin course that takes two or three half-days. The trainers are extremely professional and knowledgeable and the dolphins are very well cared for and thrive in a spacious, natural saltwater lagoon. (The scuba and dive encounters are offered in conjunction with Ocean Encounters dive operators.) ⊠ *Seaquarium Beach, Bapor Kibra* ☎ *5999/465–8900* ⊕ *www.dolphin-academy.com* ✉ *From $99 depending on program* ⊙ *Daily 8–5.*

Hato Caves. Stalactites and stalagmites form striking shapes in these 200,000-year-old caves. Hidden lighting adds to the dramatic effect. Indians who used the caves for shelter left petroglyphs about 1,500 years ago. More recently, slaves who escaped from nearby plantations used the caves as a hideaway. Hour-long guided tours wind down to the pools in various chambers. Keep in mind that there are 49 steps to climb up to the entrance and the occasional bat might not be to everyone's taste. A new Indian Trail walking path and cactus garden enlighten visitors about local vegetation. The space is also available for special events. Located just two minutes from Hato International Airport. ⊠ *Rooseveltweg z/n, Hato* ☎ *5999/868–0379* ✉ *$8* ⊙ *Daily 9–4.*

FAMILY

Fodor'sChoice

★

Mambo Beach Boulevard. This is the liveliest, most full-service beach and entertainment spot on the island. There is something for all ages at the Mambo Beach Boulevard complex beside the Sea Aquarium Beach and Park. Shoppers, sunbathers, swimmers, families, teens, couples, partiers, and even foodies will find their groove with upscale eateries like Fuoco Italian Chophouse sandwiched beside dozens of bars and cool boutiques like the Flip Flop Shop. And there are dive and activity operators, beauty salons, spa, a children's playground, small casino, and even an amusement park–style ride. There is a small fee to use the beach for just swimming and sunbathing, and the water is calm due to a man-made breakwater. There is always some kind of special event going on here, and there's also a special tourism police force to keep it safe and secure. ⊠ *Bapor Kibra* ⊕ *www.blvdcuracao.com* ☕ *$3.50 for beach use.*

FAMILY

Ostrich Farm. Though ostriches are not native to Curaçao, this is one of the largest ostrich farms outside of Africa. Guided safari tours depart every hour. You'll learn about the bird's development from egg to maturity. Kids and adults alike will enjoy the chance to hold an egg, stroke a day-old chick, and sit atop an ostrich for a memorable photo. At the Restaurant Zambezi you can sample ostrich meat specialties and other African dishes. A combo safari and tour of the farm, which includes lunch or dinner, is also available. Quad tours that cover more of the countryside are also offered. There's also a Special African Nights package, which includes a visit to the aloe farm, ostrich facility tour, and three-course dinner with pickup and drop-off at your hotel. The souvenir shop sells crafts made by local artisans. ⊠ *Groot St. Joris* ☏ *5999/747–2777* ⊕ *http://curacaoostrichfarm.com/* ☕ *Adults $16, children $13* ☉ *Weekdays 9–5, Weekends 9 am–10 pm.*

Fodor'sChoice

★

Substation Curaçao. Substation Curaçao takes you on an incredible undersea odyssey 1,000 feet below the waves. The four-person submarine is the same kind used by director James Cameron to film many of the underwater scenes in *Titanic*. It's called *Curasub*, and it dives from 500 to 1,000 feet to view colorful fish, coral walls, and shipwrecks. Souvenir photos are taken by professionals. There is no change of pressure, so anyone can enjoy going to depths that even divers cannot imagine. They also offer fascinating night dives where different species of fish come out to glow in the dark. The sub is also used for very important marine life research with major world ocean organizations. A truly unique experience, and only on Curaçao. ⊠ *Curacao Sea Aquarium, Bapor Kibra, Bapor Kibra* ☏ *5999/465–2051* ⊕ *www. substation-curacao.com.*

WORTH NOTING

Den Paradera. Dazzle your senses at this organic herb garden, where traditional folk medicines used to treat everything from stomach ulcers to diabetes are grown. Owner Dinah Veeris is a renowned expert and author in the field of herbs and plants. The kitchen is a factory of sorts used to turn homegrown plants like cactus, aloe vera, and calabash into homemade body- and skin-care products like shampoos, ointments, and oils—all for sale at the gift shop. Reservations are essential for guided tours in English, Monday through Friday at 9:30 and 10:30 am, but you can take a self-guided tour with a brochure any time of day. (Santa

8

Barbara Resort's spa uses ingredients made at Den Paradera.) ✉ *Seru Grandi 105A, Morgenster* ☎ *5999/767–5608* ⊕ *www.dinahveeris.com* ✉ *$8 self-guided tour; $9 guided* ⊙ *Mon.–Sat. 9–6.*

Fodor's Choice **Landhuis Chobolobo.** This is the distillery where the famed Curaçao
★ liqueur, which is made from the peels of the bitter Laraha oranges, is made. The family-run distillery is in a heritage mansion that dates to the 1800s. Self-guided factory tours include samples, and they also have a new terrace café that serves all kinds of delights including dishes and cocktails using the liqueurs. Though best known for its neon blue-colored spirit, the original liqueur was clear; it was colored later and also comes in green, red, and orange, and in different flavors including rum raisin, coffee, and chocolate. ✉ *Landhuis Chobolobo, Saliña* ☎ *5999/461–3526* ⊕ *www.curacaoliqueur.com* ✉ *Free* ⊙ *Weekdays 8– noon and 1–5. Café weekdays 8–5.*

Fodor's Choice **Museo Tula.** Landhouse Kenepa was an ancient plantation house that
★ became the site of the slavery revolt led by Tula in 1795. (In 2013, an English feature movie was made about Tula and the revolt.) Today the house has been restored to become the Tula Museum, dedicated to the life and times of Dutch colonial days before and leading up to the revolt. It rotates many cultural exhibits. They also have nature-walking tours of the area, a restaurant in a restored cottage offering local dishes, and a souvenir shop with local crafts. ✉ *Weg Naar Santa Cruz, Knip* ☎ *5999/888–6396* ⊕ *www.museotula.com* ⊙ *Weekdays 9–4, weekends 10–4.*

National Park Shete Boka. Shete Boka means "seven inlets" in Papiamento, and this national park by the sea is well worth exploring. The rugged coastline with scenic inlets is dramatic and wild—the incessantly crashing waves have sculptured the coral rock into fascinating natural works art. The most impressive is Boka Tabla, where you can descend a natural rock stairway (take care, it's very slippery) to view an arched opening that looks out on the sea like a giant eye. Boka Pistol is also spectacular—jetting up into towering plumes of spray, often leaving rainbows lingering in the mist. And if you look closely as you walk upon the volcanic rock landscape, you will see coral fossil formations below your feet that are thousands of years old. This is also a popular nesting region for sea turtles. ✉ *Westpunt Hwy., just past village center, Dorp Soto* ⊕ *www.shetebokapark.org* ✉ *$3.50* ⊙ *Daily 9–5.*

BEACHES

Curaçao's some 38 beautiful beaches run the gamut from isolated scenic small-cove escapes to party-hearty, full-service entertainment venues, and include family-friendly gentle surf spots and wild and rugged cliff-ringed white-sand pockets. Klein Curaçao—the uninhabited satellite sister island only accessible by boat—also has some stellar stretches of sand. Beaches along the southeast coast tend to be rocky in the shallow water (wear reef shoes—some resorts lend them out for free), but they are typically the best spots to snorkel or dive—for where there are rocks, there are usually fish! The west side has more stretches of smooth sand

Curaçao Liqueur: The Bitter Smell of Success

Some say the famed Curaçao liqueur is what put this spirited island on the map. Oddly, the bitter oranges used to flavor the liqueur weren't recognized for their value until hundreds of years after they were introduced locally. The liqueur is made from the peels of the Laraha orange. In the 16th century, the Spaniards brought over and planted Valencia oranges, but arid conditions rendered the fruit bitter, and the crops were left to grow in the wild. The plant became known as the Laraha, the so-called Golden Orange of Curaçao.

It was not until the mid-19th century that Edouard Cointreau of France came to appreciate the fragrance of the bitter fruit's dried peels, and he combined them with sweet oranges to make an aperitif. Eventually, the Senior family created a recipe of its own using the Laraha and began producing Curaçao liqueur commercially in 1896. Today, only Senior's Curaçao is allowed to use the "authentic" label, signifying it is made from the indigenous citrus fruit.

Laraha oranges are harvested twice a year, when the fruit is still green. The peels are sun-dried, then put in a copper still (the original!) with alcohol and water for several days, and finally mixed with Senior's "secret" ingredients and distilled some more. The final product is clear. Colorings (including the famous blue) are added but do not change the flavor. Bartenders, however, use the colorful varieties with great flourish to create fanciful drinks.

at the shoreline. Exploring the beaches away from the hotels is a perfect way to soak up the island's character, and some have become attractions in their own right, famous for special events, like Kokomo Beach and its crazy full moon blowout parties. There are snack bars and restrooms on most beaches, and some will have entrance fees or charge for loungers, while others are open to the public with few facilities but are popular with locals who bring their own picnics and outdoor grills on weekends. Some tour companies are now offering half- or full-day beach tours, so you can set foot on a lot of them to discover where you might like to return to spend more time. Note entrance fees are subject to change.

WEST END

FAMILY **Cas Abao.** This white-sand gem has the brightest blue water in Curaçao, a treat for swimmers, snorkelers, and sunbathers alike. Full services include a beach bar and restaurant, lockers, changing rooms on-site, and even full massages surf-side are available. It can become crowded on weekends, especially Sunday, when local families descend in droves. You can rent beach chairs, paddle boats, and snorkeling and diving gear. The entry fee is $5–$6 per car, more on weekends, and the beach is open from 8 am to 6 pm. **Amenities:** food and drink; lifeguards; parking; showers; toilets; water sports. **Best for:** partiers; snorkeling; swimming. ⊠ *West of St. Willibrordus, about 3 miles (5 km) off Weg Naar Santa Cruz ✛ Turn off Westpunt Hwy. at the junction onto Weg Naar Santa Cruz; follow until* *the turnoff for Cas Abao, and then drive along the winding country road for about 10 mins to the beach ⊕ www.casabaobeach.com.*

FAMILY **Kokomo Beach.** The beach at Vaersenbaai, now better known as "Kokomo" after the restaurant/bar by the same name there, is famous for massive full-moon-party blowouts with live music and thousands of partiers. Daytime it's a quiet, family-friendly public with lots of free lounges, shade, and full facilities. At night it kicks it up a notch with a young-adult party scene. Sunday happy hours are famous for DJ dance parties, and it's the only night Kokomo serves dinner. There is also a dive center on-site. **Amenities:** food and drink; parking (free); toilets. **Best for:** partiers; snorkeling; swimming. ⊠ *Vaersenbaai* ⊕ *www. kokomo-beach.com.*

Playa Jeremi. No snack bar, no dive shop, no facilities, no fee—in fact, there's nothing but sheer natural beauty. Though the beach is sandy, there are rocky patches, so barefoot visitors should exercise care. The parking area is offset from the beach, and vehicle break-ins are common. Quite a bit of development is planned for this beach, so have a look before it's too late. **Amenities:** none. **Best for:** picnics, snorkeling; solitude; swimming. ⊠ *Off Weg Naar Santa Cruz, west of Lagun.*

Playa Kalki. This beach is at the western tip of the island right under Kura Hulanda Lodge. Sunbathers may find the narrow and rocky beach less than ideal and there is a long steep staircase down to the sand, but go to GoWest Diving there for snorkel and dive trips to the Blue Room, a cool underwater cave. **Amenities:** food and drink; parking; toilets; water sports. **Best for:** snorkeling; solitude; swimming. ⊠ *Near Jaanchi's, Westpunt.*

FAMILY **Playa Knip.** Two protected coves offer crystal-clear turquoise waters. Big (Groot) Knip, also known as Playa Kenepa, is an expanse of alluring white sand, perfect for swimming and snorkeling. You can rent beach chairs and hang out under the *palapas* (thatch-roof shelters) or cool off with ice cream at the snack bar. There are restrooms here but no showers. It's particularly crowded on Sunday and school holidays. Just up the road, also in a protected cove, sister beach Little (Klein) Knip is a charmer, too, with picnic tables and palapas. There's no fee for these beaches. **Amenities:** food and drink; lifeguards; parking; toilets; water sports. **Best for:** snorkeling; sunrise; sunset; swimming. ⊠ *Just east of Westpunt, Banda Abou.*

FAMILY
Fodor's Choice
★
Playa PortoMari. Set beneath an historic plantation site, you'll find calm, clear water and a long stretch of white sand and full facilities on this beach. A decent bar and restaurant, well-kept showers, changing facilities, and restrooms are all on-site; a nature trail is nearby. The double coral reef—explore one, swim past it, explore another—is a special feature that makes this spot popular with snorkelers and divers. The entrance fee is $3, children under 12 free. **Amenities:** food and drink; lifeguards; parking; showers; toilets. **Best for:** partiers; snorkeling; swimming; walking. ⊠ *Off Willibrordus Rd.* ✛ *From Willemstad, drive west on Westpunt Hwy. for 4 miles (7 km); turn left onto Willibrordus Rd. at the PortoMari billboard, and then drive 3 miles (5 km) until you see a large church; follow signs on the winding dirt road to the beach* ⊕ *http://www.playaportomari.com.*

WHERE TO EAT

Curaçao's culinary scene has become seriously cosmopolitan in the past few years. Though you can still find places to get traditional, local dishes like iguana soup, *keshi yena* (seasoned meat wrapped in cheese and baked), and goat stew, the emerging generation of chefs has really raised the bar. Caribbean meets international with a side of nouvelle cuisine or farm-to-fork organic offerings. All combine for a cornucopia of tastes and flavors that meet world-class standards. And the range of locations where you can enjoy these creations is as eclectic as the fare. You'll find romantic toes-in-the-sand surf-side spots, family-friendly air-conditioned emporiums, lush countryside gardens, and unique historic sites like forts and plantation houses all hosting diners. For authentic local-style lunches drop by the Old Market in Punda; or after the night-clubs, seek out one of the late-night snack trucks (*truki pan*) for cheap, yet satisfying, eats. Many beach bars also have fabulous fare for less than you'd expect to pay. But for the most part, fine dining will cost you what it's typically worth, especially since almost every kind of food on this island needs to be imported from elsewhere.

What to Wear. Dress in restaurants is almost always casual (though beachwear isn't acceptable). Some of the resort dining rooms and more elegant restaurants require that men wear jackets, especially in high season; ask when you make reservations.

$$$$ EUROPEAN

🍴 **Bistro Le Clochard.** Built into a 19th-century fort, this romantic gem anchors the entrance to the 21st-century Rif Fort complex, and the waterside terrace offers an enchanting view of the harbor. They present French cuisine with a Caribbean twist, but there are many international specialities as well as Swiss fondue, raclette, and Wiener schnitzel. The menu differs depending on where you sit—for example, you can only order their bouillabaisse on the terrace. But both inside and out, you can order their most famous decadent dessert, Swiss Toblerone chocolate mousse with strawberry foam. [$] *Average main: $40* ✉ *Rif Fort Unit 1, Otrobanda* ☎ *5999/462–5666* 🌐 *www.bistroleclochard.com* ✍ *Reservations essential.*

$$ CONTEMPORARY Fodor's Choice ★

🍴 **Blues Bar & Restaurant.** Jutting out onto a pier over the ocean at the Avila Beach Hotel, this legendary perch is famous for their live jazz and blues nights on Thursdays, and the fact that the band is also perched over the bar. Now featuring *pinchos* (skewers), the cuisine is also beginning to steal the show with a tasty selection of fish, seafood, and meat specialties, and the ribs are first-rate as well. The vibe is always convivial, and it's a popular place for locals to gather, especially on Thursday at happy hour. [$] *Average main: $20* ✉ *Avila Beach Hotel, Penstraat 130, Punda* ☎ *5999/461–4377* 🌐 *www.avilahotel.com* 🕒 *Closed Mon. No lunch.*

$$$$ EUROPEAN Fodor's Choice ★

🍴 **Fort Nassau Restaurant.** On a hill above Willemstad, this elegant restaurant is built into an 18th-century fort with a 360-degree view. Among the highlights of the diverse menu is the medley of Caribbean seafood, but the best bets come from their special menu—three courses with a fixed price—your choice of appetizer, main course, and dessert. Entrées include a chicken and a beef dish, but most interesting is the caramelized salmon with sugared bacon. The watermelon soup with honey, rum,

8

basil, and mint is certainly a unique creation for dessert. Vegetarian mains are also available. Superb views of the sunset over the port can be enjoyed from the terrace. [$] *Average main: $31* ✉ *Schottegatweg 82, near Juliana Bridge, Otrobanda* ☎ *5999/461–3450, 5999/461–3086* 🌐 *www.fortnassau.com* 🕒 *No lunch weekends* ✍ *Reservations essential.*

$$$ ECLECTIC Fodor's Choice ★

🍴 **Gouverneur de Rouville Restaurant & Café.** Dine on the veranda of a restored 19th-century Dutch mansion overlooking the Santa Anna Bay and the resplendent Punda skyline. Though often busy and popular with tourists, the ambience makes it worth a visit. Intriguing soup options include Cuban banana soup and Curaçao-style fish soup. *Keshi yena* and spareribs are among the savory entrées. After dinner, you can stick around for live music at the bar, which stays open until 1 am. The restaurant is also popular for lunch and attracts crowds when cruise ships dock. Reserve ahead if you would like a balcony table. A wine tasting room is available for special events. [$] *Average main: $22* ✉ *De Rouvilleweg 9, Otrobanda* ☎ *5999/462–5999* 🌐 *www.de-gouverneur.com.*

$$$ CARIBBEAN

🍴 **Jaanchies Restaurant.** Over the years this has become something of a road marker on Curaçao's beaten tourist path, with prices to match. You'll be greeted by the owner, Jaanchi himself, a self-described "walking, talking menu," who will recite your choices of authentic local dishes for lunch. Jaanchi's iguana soup, touted in folklore as an aphrodisiac, is one of their specialities. Although predominantly a lunch spot, the restaurant will accommodate groups of four or more for dinner by prior arrangement. [$] *Average main: $23* ✉ *Westpunt 15, Westpunt* ☎ *5999/864–0126.*

$$ INTERNATIONAL

🍴 **Karakter.** Karakter is a popular beachfront restaurant for the Coral Estate villas crowd, and it also caters for them. It's the nexus of surfside revelry with live music weekends and tapas and drinks. Lounges and patio tables set the scene, and friendly barkeeps make you feel right at home. Coral Estates is a gated community, so you must present ID to enter when you visit Karakter. [$] *Average main: $20* ✉ *Rif Marie Coral Estates, Coral Estate Rif St. Marie* ☎ *5999/864–2233* 🌐 *www.karaktercuracao.com.*

$$$$ CONTEMPORARY Fodor's Choice ★

🍴 **Kome.** Ask any local foodie where to get creative fusion fare with a Curaçao twist, and Kome will be the first spot they mention. It's not super fancy, in fact it's no-nonsense rustic with basic wooden tables and chairs, but it's the food that attracts. They are always changing specialties due to constant efforts to source locally, and the results are often surprising. The menu is divided into small plates and big plates, and the dishes can range from pork belly confit and tamarind-glazed pork tenderloin to smoked beef brisket to seafood paella. And don't forget to leave room for dessert because one of the owners is a talented pastry chef! They are also known for their tapas nights on Wednesday with creative small bites to go with superb signature cocktails and excellent sangrias. [$] *Average main: $40* ✉ *Johan van Walbeeckplein 6, Pietermaai* ☎ *5999/465–0413* 🕒 *Closed Sun.*

$$$$ STEAKHOUSE

🍴 **L'aldea Steakhouse/ Rainforest Mystery.** A unique installation on such an arid island, L'aldea is in a small rain-forest reserve, replete with lizards, animals, fish, and birds that you would find typically in lusher climes. But what is most impressive here is the handcrafted design of absolutely everything including faux Mayan and other ancient culture recreations, caves and tropical atmospheres by local craftsmen (some of whom are the owners) using wood and cement to recreate a "lost world" in the middle of nowhere. They have also recently added a few small rooms as ecoaccommodation stays there. The easiest way to visit is to take a tour that includes a facility visit and then stay for their Latin American-themed dinner. The fare is incredible—the largest salad bar on the island—plus a carnivore's heaven with grilled meats served Brazilian grill-style until you burst. Live music also adds to the full-on experience. For day-trippers though, it would be great if they served some kind of lunch. [$] *Average main: $58 ⊠ Sta. Catharina 66, Willemstad ☎ 5999/767–6777 ⊕ laldeacur.com ⊙ Closed Mon. No lunch ⚖ Reservations essential.*

$$$ ✕ **Madero Ocean Club.** The new anchor of the entire Mambo Beach Bou-
INTERNATIONAL levard complex Madero Ocean Club offers dining, entertainment, a
Fodor's Choice great beach bar, a massive pool and surf-side lounge, and daybed rent-
★ als. Pool parties, bottle service, and special events on their own stage with hot DJs and live bands, especially on Sundays, give the entire scene a South Beach vibe. The eclectic dinner menu includes seafood and meats and great tapas. Breakfast and lunch also served. [$] *Average main: $25 ⊠ Mambo Beach Blvd., Bapor Kibra ☎ 5999/465–0053 ⊕ http://maderooceanclub.com.*

$$ ✕ **Primas.** In a restored plantation mansion called Landhuis Vredenberg
ECLECTIC on a lush estate, Primas is a family-run restaurant that offers authentic
Fodor's Choice homemade lunch fare in a superb setting. The menu is up to the chef,
★ but typically hearty savory meat stews, fresh fish dishes, and Curaçaon specialties like keshi yena will pop up. You can view their daily menu on their Facebook page. They're usually not open for dinner (private parties abound), but on Thursday nights Primas is one of the few places left on the island where you can sample real *rijsttafel* (rice table), an Indonesian-influenced extravaganza of dozens of small dishes served community-style. It's also worth the trip just to see the magnificent restored mansion full of exquisite antiques. Groups of 15 or more can make special dinner arrangements. [$] *Average main: $14 ⊠ Bramendiweg 200, Willemstad ☎ 5999/461–2901 ⊙ Closed Sun. No dinner except Thurs. ⚖ Reservations essential.*

$$ ✕ **Royal Dutch Cheesery.** Tucked away in the corner of the historic Rif
DUTCH Fort Village courtyard, Royal Dutch Cheesery is much more than a cheese shop. Of course they do sell cheese and are the only suppliers of Reypenaer cheese on the island, but it's more of a dining spot and tasting emporium replete with a large wine list and even artisanal spirits. A wine pairing along with various types of cheese (on a wooden plank shaped like Curaçao) is a must, as are their gourmet grilled cheese sandwiches, fondues, and raclette. Weekend nights, this is a perfect spot to enjoy outdoor live music on the courtyard while sipping some of their unique small-batch limoncello. [$] *Average main: $15 ⊠ Rif Fort Village, Otrobanda ☎ 5999/788–5599.*

$$$ ✕ **Scampi's Restaurant.** Part of the Waterfort Terrace complex, this open-
SEAFOOD air dining spot serves an interesting selection of international fare, steak, seafood, and some dishes with Asian twists or Latin American heat.

8

Daily specialties like freshly caught lobster are a best bet. Their evening setting can be very romantic with a stellar view of the sunset and the port at night and their signature cocktails like Coastal Kiss and Fancy Scampis will get you in the mood. Families aren't left out as there is also a children's menu. $ *Average main: $22* ⊠ *Waterfortstraat 41-42, Punda* ☎ *5999/465–0769.*

$$$
CONTEMPORARY
Fodor'sChoice
★

✕ **Shore.** The main dining room of Santa Barbara Beach & Golf Resort is set upon a hill beside the golf course with stunning sea views. A gourmet burger–and–sandwich emporium by day, it morphs into a causal yet romantic dining enclave by night with cool tropical breezes wafting in from the open design, and incredible aromas coming from the open-air kitchen. Chef Hortencia surprises daily with fabulous fusions of local and international flavors. His specials are top-notch and often involve fresh fish and seafood. Try the short ribs: seasoned to perfection and falling off the bone, they melt in your mouth. Top it off with a decadent chocolate trio of delights for dessert. New fly-and-dine packages are available with BlueSkies Helicopter. $ *Average main: $30* ⊠ *Santa Barbara Beach & Golf Resort, Nieuwpoort* ☎ *5999/840–1234* ⊕ *www. santabararesortcuracao.com.*

WHERE TO STAY

Simple beachside relaxation, culture and history, snorkel and dive-centered, adult-only romantic solitude, or fun family-friendly activity spots: On Curaçao you'll find it all, including small boutique-style stays and all-inclusive full-service complexes. You'll generally find that hotels at all price levels provide friendly, prompt, detail-oriented service and clean, well-maintained accommodations, and English is spoken by staff just about everywhere. Many of the large-scale resorts east and west of Willemstad proper have lovely beaches and provide a free shuttle to the city, 5 to 10 minutes away, but there are also fine hotels right in the city center should you want to be in the heart of the action. There are also resorts in their own self-maintained neighborhoods just out of town in Santa Barbara and Jan Thiel.

Villas and Rentals. Villa and bungalow rentals are especially popular with divers and European visitors and are generally good options for large groups or longer stays. Coral Estates (⊕ *www.coralestatevillas. com*) has gorgeous villa homes to rent. The Curaçao Tourist Board (⊕ *www.curacao.com*) has a complete list of rental apartments, villas, and bungalows on its website.

$$
HOTEL
Fodor'sChoice
★

🏨 **Avila Beach Hotel.** Even though it's been around for over six decades, beautifully restored Dutch colonial architecture and a lively contemporary vibe keep this legendary complex from ever feeling dated. **Pros:** superb on-site dining and entertainment; calm protected waters; gorgeous location; free Wi-Fi. **Cons:** main beach overcrowds easily due to insufficient lounges on second beach; not all rooms are ocean view. $ *Rooms from: $310* ⊠ *130 Penstraat, Punda* ☎ *5999/461–4377* ⊕ *www.avilahotel.com* ⇄ *154 rooms, 11 suites* ⦿*Breakfast.*

$$$ RESORT Fodor's Choice ★ 🏨 **Baoase.** No other resort on Curaçao can match this Balinese-inspired gem for understated elegance and attention to detail. **Pros:** beautiful landscaping; complete privacy; unsurpassed luxury. **Cons:** lacks some of the distractions of a larger resort; exclusivity can sometimes become isolating. [$] *Rooms from: $425* ✉ *Winterswijkstraat 2, Willemstad* ☎ *8884/409–3506* 🌐 *www.baoase.com* 🛏 *9 villas, 3 1-bedroom suites, 10 beachfront suites* 🍴 *Breakfast.*

$ HOTEL FAMILY 🏨 **Blue Bay Curaçao.** Set in a storied plantation estate and on a beautiful beach, Blue Bay's accommodations range from luxury apartment–style rooms to stand-alone villas and bungalows—hillside or beachfront. **Pros:** spacious units; ideal location for golfers, divers, and families. **Cons:** a bit isolated, so a car is absolutely necessary; little nightlife. [$] *Rooms from: $200* ✉ *Landhuis Blauw z/n, Willemstad* ☎ *5999/888–8800* 🌐 *www.bluebay-curacao.com* 🛏 *48 apartments, 36 3-bedroom villas* 🍴 *No meals.*

$ RESORT FAMILY Fodor's Choice ★ 🏨 **Curaçao Marriott Beach Resort & Emerald Casino.** The cream of the crop of Curaçao's resorts beckons you to live it up from the moment you arrive. **Pros:** no need to leave the compound for anything but sightseeing; excellent beach location; first-class fitness center; five-star PADI dive shop. **Cons:** feels big and impersonal; pool area can get very busy. [$] *Rooms from: $219* ✉ *John F. Kennedy Boulevard, Piscadera Bay* ☎ *5999/736–8800* 🌐 *www.curacaomarriott.com* 🛏 *237 rooms, 10 suites* 🍴 *Breakfast.*

$ HOTEL 🏨 **Floris Suite Hotel.** Dutch interior designer Jan des Bouvrie has used warm mahogany shades offset by cool, sleek stainless-steel adornments in the suites of this modernist hotel, all of which have a balcony or porch and a full kitchen. **Pros:** great for a quiet escape; beautifully designed rooms and public spaces. **Cons:** decor lacks romantic feel; bit of a hike to decent shopping and restaurants. [$] *Rooms from: $195* ✉ *Piscaderaweg, Piscadera Bay* ☎ *5999/462–6111* 🌐 *www.florissuitehotel.com* 🛏 *72 suites* 🍴 *No meals.*

$ RESORT FAMILY 🏨 **Hilton Curaçao.** Two beautiful beaches of pillowy white sand beyond the open-air lobby make this resort a jewel in its price range. **Pros:** gorgeous beachfront; lots of on-site facilities; friendly staff. **Cons:** lacks the intimacy of smaller resorts; not all rooms are ocean view. [$] *Rooms from: $200* ✉ *Piscadera* ☎ *5999/462–5000* 🌐 *www.hiltoncuracaoresort.com* 🛏 *196 rooms, 12 suites* 🍴 *Some meals.*

$ HOTEL 🏨 **Hotel 't Klooster.** Located in a former monastery (*klooster* means cloister), this bright yellow structure looks impressive from the outside, but it's a more spartan hotel within. **Pros:** historical charm; reasonable price. **Cons:** small rooms; can be noisy. [$] *Rooms from: $110* ✉ *Veerstraat 12, Punda* ☎ *5999/461–2650* 🌐 *www.hotelklooster.com* 🛏 *24 rooms* 🍴 *Breakfast.*

$ RESORT FAMILY 🏨 **Lions Dive & Beach Resort.** Divers are lured by the first-rate program here, but this low-key resort has a lot to offer nondivers as well. **Pros:** ideal for diving; beautiful private beach and access to Seaquarium Beach; family-friendly, Olympic-length pool. **Cons:** beach can get busy; kids everywhere; noisy weekends. [$] *Rooms from: $199* ✉ *Seaquarium Beach, Bapor Kibra* ☎ *5999/434–8888* 🌐 *www.lionsdive.com* 🛏 *102 rooms, 10 suites, 1 penthouse* 🍴 *No meals.*

$ **Lodge Kura Hulanda & Beach Club-GHL Hotel.** On the island's remote
RESORT   western tip, this sprawling resort with tranquil gardens will make you
Fodor's Choice   feel far removed from the daily grind. **Pros:** perfect for a complete
★   escape; unparalleled ocean views; great value; beautifully appointed
rooms; free Wi-Fi. **Cons:** a bit quiet for some tastes; miles away from
everything; although there's a shuttle, a rental car is necessary if you
want to explore the island. $ *Rooms from: $179 ⊠ Playa Kalki 1,
Westpunt* 🕾 *5999/839–3600* ⊕ *www.kurahulanda.com* ➴ *30 rooms,
69 suites* ❖ *All-inclusive* ☞ *Additional meal plan options include
breakfast only or no meals.*

$ **Papagayo Beach Hotel.** Set upon its own private beach with a massive
RESORT   infinity pool overlooking the sea, the sleek white and steel structure is
no-nonsense modern with a South Beach feel and popular with European visitors seeking a classy escape in an upscale neighborhood. **Pros:**
great spa on-site; spacious pool; modern amenities; fine dining. **Cons:**
though adults-only, lots of children/families go to the public beach right
next door on weekends; far from Willemstad; traffic can be an issue.
$ *Rooms from: $220 ⊠ Jan Thiel* 🕾 *5999/747–4333* ⊕ *www.papagayo-
designhotel.com/nl/home.html* ➴ *75 bungalows* ❖ *No meals.*

$ **PM78 Urban Oasis Curacao.** Set within a stunning three-story cobalt-
B&B/INN   blue mansion right in the heart of trendy Pietermaai, this small family-
Fodor's Choice   run luxury boutique property offers some special stay options. **Pros:**
★   sleek modern design; homey and inviting with friendly family owners
on-site. **Cons:** occasional noise from restaurant next door at night; sea is
too rough for swimming. $ *Rooms from: $125 ⊠ Punda* 🕾 *5999/528–
6118* ⊕ *www.pietermaai78.com* ➴ *4 rooms* ❖ *No meals.*

$$ **Renaissance Curaçao Resort & Casino.** The four gabled buildings of
RESORT   this downtown resort are painted in colors that seem to mirror those
Fodor's Choice   of Punda across the harbor and fit in perfectly with the historic sur-
★   roundings. **Pros:** coolest (and only) pool-beach in town; every amenity
imaginable; walking distance to all the attractions of both Otrobanda
and Punda; exceptionally helpful staff. **Cons:** Rif Fort area is a major
tourist draw and can get busy; common-area color scheme is not
exactly calming. $ *Rooms from: $280 ⊠ Pater Euwensweg, Otrobanda*
🕾 *5999/435–5000* ⊕ *www.renaissancecuracao.com* ➴ *223 rooms, 14
suites* ❖ *Breakfast.*

$ **Santa Barbara Beach & Golf Resort.** The sprawling hacienda-style com-
RESORT   plex is set along a beautiful stretch of ocean, and their first-class Pete
FAMILY   Dye–designed golf course has spectacular views of the sea and country-
Fodor's Choice   side. **Pros:** gorgeous location; elegant public areas; top-flight dining; first-
★   rate spa. **Cons:** long distance from town; rental car required to explore
island. $ *Rooms from: $200 ⊠ Nieuwpoort* 🕾 *5999/840–1234* ⊕ *www.
santabararesortcuracao.com* ➴ *335 rooms, 15 suites* ❖ *Some meals.*

$ **Scuba Lodge and Suites.** An interesting surprise in the residential
HOTEL   neighborhood of Pietermaai, spanning five brightly painted renovated
heritage homes, this friendly and casual seaside resort and full PADI div-
ing center combines casual chic with bohemian boutique. **Pros:** homey
vibe; great staff; expert dive instruction. **Cons:** far from shopping;
beach isn't swimmable; few amenities. $ *Rooms from: $155 ⊠ Punda*
🕾 *5999/465–2575* ⊕ *www.scubalodge.com* ➴ *31 rooms* ❖ *No meals.*

$ **Sonesta Kura Hulanda Village & Spa.** Sonesta's luxury boutique accom-
HOTEL modations include modern amenities surrounded by unique antiques
Fodor'sChoice and bespoke decor—different in every room and suite—gleaned from
★ owner Jacob Gelt-Dekker's personal collection. **Pros:** UNESCO heritage
site; walking distance to all downtown attractions; unique museum also
on-site. **Cons:** not near a beach; narrow alleyways and small rooms can
become somewhat confining. $ *Rooms from: $200* ⊠ *Langestraat 8,
Otrobanda* ☎ *5999/434–7700* ⊕ *www.sonesta.com/kurahulanda* ⊅ *68
rooms, 14 suites* ⦿*Breakfast.*

$$$ **Sunscape Curaçao Resort, Spa & Casino.** This family-friendly all-inclusive
RESORT resort has its own house reef and great snorkeling steps from your room.
FAMILY **Pros:** ample distractions for the whole family; renovated rooms are beauti-
Fodor'sChoice fully appointed and airy; nice laid-back atmosphere. **Cons:** beach gets very
★ busy; no-reservations dining can also mean long waits for tables at prime
times. $ *Rooms from: $425* ⊠ *Martin Luther King Blvd. 78, Willems-
tad* ☎ *5999/736–7888, 866/SUNSCAPE* ⊕ *www.sunscaperesorts.com/
curacao* ⊅ *285 rooms, 56 suites* ⦿*All-inclusive* ☞ *3-night minimum.*

$$$ **Villa Seashell.** Perfect for families or small groups looking for value
RENTAL and amenities, Villa Seashell is a gorgeous four-bedroom villa on the
FAMILY wild coast of Rif Marie with incredible sea views and plenty of space
Fodor'sChoice for cooking and lounging. **Pros:** spectacular scenery; luxury amenities;
★ free Wi-Fi. **Cons:** far from city, so a rental car is needed to visit; no
shopping nearby. $ *Rooms from: $385* ⊠ *Coral Estates Bandabou,
Banda Abou* ☎ *297/740–5130* ⊕ *www.villaseashell.com* ⊅ *4 villas*
⦿*No meals* ☞ *Actual price is for 1–4 people; $25 extra per person.*

NIGHTLIFE

8

There are quite a few bars and nightlife hot spots scattered about the
island in different neighborhoods, and something different going on
every night of the week. But there is no one "nightlife" district per
say. Your best bet it to seek out the Curaçao Party Guide (⊕ *www.
curacaopartyguide.com*) for complete up-to-date events and music and
theme nights to find your style and where it's happening. There are a
few pockets, however, that are always nightlife-lively, like Maambo
Beach Boulevard, Jan Thiel, and more recently, the newly transformed
neighborhood of Pietermaai and Scharloo, where you can bar-hop in
one spot without having to drive anywhere. And most resorts have some
kind of nightly entertainment on-site on weekends.

BARS AND CLUBS

Fodor'sChoice **District 1850.** An entire pocket of the historic neighborhood of Scharloo
★ has turned into a trendy party block called District 1850. An alfresco
stage and a collection of cool bars and restaurants with live and DJ
bands keep the streets hopping till the wee hours. Beautifully restored
heritage buildings and cool new colorful cafés set the scene for lots of
lively nocturnal happenings. ⊠ *Scharloo, Scharlooweg 72-76, Scharloo*
☎ *5999/766–7101.*

Grand Café de Heeren. This is a great spot to grab a locally brewed Amstel Bright and meet a happy blend of tourists and transplanted Dutch locals. Live music DJs keep it hopping. ⊠ *Zuikertuintjeweg, Willemstad* ☎ *5999/736–0491.*

Miles Jazz Cafe. Curaçao is addicted to jazz, and there are many live jazz festivals throughout the year, but if you really want to get into the swing of it any night of the week, head to Miles Jazz Vinyl and Cigars Cafe. Named after the legendary musician Miles Davis, it's a cool little getaway in the heart of Pietermaai where you can hear jazz played on vinyl, play board games, and have a cigar and a drink. Local musicians occasionally stop by to jam as well. ⊠ *Nieuwestraat 42, Pietermaai* ☎ *5999/520–5200* ⊕ *www.milescuracao.com.*

Fodor's Choice   **Mundo Bizarro.** As the name suggests, the decor here is definitely
★   bizarre—a hodgepodge of paraphernalia with no rhyme or reason but a lot of creativity. Locals and visitors alike flock here weekends for super signature cocktails, live music, great snacks, and an unparalleled offbeat atmosphere. ⊠ *Nieuwestraat 12, Pietermaai* ☎ *5999/461–6767* ⊕ *www.mundobizarrocuracao.com.*

Fodor's Choice   **Riffort Village.** The entire courtyard interior of the old fort and Renais-
★   sance Mall has restaurants and bars stacked side by side all around the open space. The local business owners hire live bands to entertain guests alfresco on weekends. It's always a lively spot with dancing and music, and many special events take place here throughout the year as well. ⊠ *Rif Fort, Otrobanda* ⊹ *Steps away from the cruise ship terminal.*

Rif Fort Bar & Terrace. Located within the stone walls of Rif Fort, there's usually a lively crowd on weekends. A good place to sit outside and enjoy the evening breezes with one of their signature cocktails like the Rifortini or killer shooters like the Devil's Breath. Live entertainment in the courtyard weekends give the historic scene a vibrant party atmosphere. ⊠ *Rif Fort, Otrobanda* ☎ *5999/462–5666.*

Saint Tropez Ocean Club. Part of the Saint Tropez Suites resort in Pietermaai, this unique day club is where French Riviera–style meets Dutch Caribbean cool. A gorgeous infinity pool crests a rocky coast with crashing waves and is surrounded by plush daybeds, private cabanas, and loungers. A trendy bar and open-air dining spot serves small bites and full lunch, and there's also surf-side bottle service and tapas by the pool. Access is free to resort guests, and some neighboring hotels also have complimentary access; others must buy a pass. At night, it morphs into a cool open-air lounge and dinner spot often featuring hot DJs and special events. ⊠ *Pietermaai 152, Pietermaai* ☎ *5999/461–7727* ⊕ *www.sainttropezcuracao.com.*

Waterfort Terrace (*Waterfort Arches*). This collection of bars and dining spots gathered in the historic stone bastion affords glorious views of the harbor and sea by day and morphs into a magical strip by night with twinkling lights and live music emanating from the many different venues. ⊠ *Waterfortstraat Boog 1, Punda* ☎ *5999/465–0769.*

Wet & Wild Beach Club. One of the anchor party spots below Mambo Beach Boulevard, there's never a dull moment at Wet & Wild Beach Club, where the name speaks for itself. Friday happy hour features free barbecue snacks; on Saturday a DJ or live band jams until it's too late to care about the time. Sundays are also wild, starting with happy hour at 6 pm and another one at 10 pm. ⊠ *Seaquarium Beach, Bapor Kibra* ☎ *5999/561–2477.*

CASINOS

The following hotels have casinos that are open daily: Sunscape Curaçao, the Curaçao Marriott Beach Resort & Emerald Casino, the Hilton Curaçao, Holiday Beach Hotel & Casino, Plaza Hotel & Casino, Otrobanda Hotel & Casino, Trupial Inn Hotel & Casino, and Papagayo Beach Hotel. And Veneto Casino at the Holiday Beach Resort is newly renovated and also the largest on the island. Slot machines open earlier than table games, between 10 am and 1 pm, and most of the rooms have penny and nickel slots in addition to the higher-priced machines. Tables generally open at 3 pm or 4 pm. Casinos close about 1 am or 2 am weekdays; some stay open until 4 am on weekend nights. Some have sports betting.

SHOPPING

From Dutch classics like embroidered linens, Delft earthenware, and cheeses to local artwork and handicrafts, shopping in Willemstad can turn up some fun finds. But don't expect major bargains on watches, jewelry, or electronics; Willemstad is not a duty-free port (the few establishments that claim to be "duty-free" are simply absorbing the cost of some or all of the tax rather than passing it on to consumers). However, if you come prepared with some comparison prices, you might still dig up some good deals. But there are new complexes out of downtown now for ultimate retail therapy—Mambo Beach Boulevard has an eclectic collection of trendy shops at the Sea Aquarium Park and the brand-new Sambil megamall is a massive multilevel shopping and entertainment complex in Veeris Commercial Park with hundreds of modern stores and trendy boutiques.

AREAS AND MALLS

Willemstad's **Punda** is a treat for pedestrians, with most shops concentrated within a bustling area of about six blocks. Closed to traffic, Heerenstraat and Gomezplein are pedestrian malls covered with pink inlaid bricks. Other major shopping streets are Breedestraat and Madurostraat. Here you can find jewelry, cosmetics, perfumes, luggage, and linens—and no shortage of trinkets and souvenirs. Savvy shoppers don't skip town without a stop across the bay to Otrobanda, where the Riffort Village Shopping Mall houses a variety of retailers. It's worth noting that many of the bargain-price designer labels found in smaller clothing shops are just knockoffs from Latin America. The Renaissance Mall right next to Rif Fort has retailers such as Guess and Tiffany & Co. next to local shops offering a range of jewelry and fashion. Mambo Beach Boulevard is a new, popular shopping spot, as is the Sambil megamall in Veeris.

Fodors Choice
★ **Mambo Beach Blvd.** Lots of trendy shops, cool boutiques, and a ton of restaurants and bars line the boulevard on Mambo Beach. Also look for swimwear, souvenirs, fashions, flip-flops, beauty care, and more. ⊠ *Mambo Beach, Bapor Kibra* ☎ *5999/461–0616* ⊕ *www. blvdcuracao.com.*

Fodors Choice
★ **Sambil Mall.** Sambil Mall is a massive multilevel indoor complex of shops and entertainment venues in Veeris. There are hundreds of stores, a food court, and both upscale and casual dining enclaves, plus the most modern, high-tech cinemas in the Caribbean. For more indoor fun, there are state-of-the-art bowling alleys. Free parking special events, and family-friendly lounging and activity areas add to the allure. ⊠ *Verris Commercial Park, Nst Block No. 5, Willemstad* ☎ *5999/735–3131* ⊕ *www.sambil.cw.*

ART GALLERIES

Gallery Alma Blou. The oldest established gallery on the island, located in Landhouse Habaai, showcases works by top local artists in rotating exhibits. You can find shimmering landscapes, dazzling photographs, ceramics, even African-inspired carnival masks here, and there is also a separate gift shop with artsy souvenirs. ⊠ *Frater Radulphusweg 4, Otrobanda* ☎ *5999/462–8896* ⊕ *www.galleryalmablou.com* ☉ *Closed Sun.*

Fodors Choice
★ **Nena Sanchez Gallery.** At the Nena Sanchez Gallery, you can find this local artist's cheerful paintings in characteristically bright yellows, reds, greens, pinks, and blues. Her work depicting marine life and island scenes is available in various forms, including posters, mouse pads, and picture frames. She often gives art classes at her workshop and gallery at restored historic plantation Landhuis Jan Kok. ⊠ *Bloempot Shopping Mall, Windstraat 15, Punda* ☎ *5999/461–2882* ⊕ *www. nenasanchez.com.*

Fodors Choice
★ **Serena's Art Factory.** You might have noticed brightly painted sculptures of colorful Caribbean women with highly exaggerated physical features in many public places around the island and miniature versions of them for sale as souvenirs in many shops. These are Chichis®—creations by artist Serena Janet Israel that are unique to Curaçao. "Chi Chi" means big sister in the local lingo, and the figures are meant to exude the warmth of matronly Caribbean women. Many different local female artists have been trained by Serena to custom-paint them, but visitors are welcome to create their own for a one-of-a-kind souvenir at Serena's Art Factory near the Ostrich Farm. Group workshops and walk-in workshops for nontour visitors are available on a regular basis. A workshop is about two hours. ⊠ *Jan Louis 87a* ☎ *5999/738–0648* ⊕ *www.chichi-curacao.com* ▱ *Free tour of factory.*

CIGARS

Cigar Emporium. A sweet aroma permeates Cigar Emporium, where you can find the largest selection of Cuban cigars on the island, including H. Upmann, Romeo y Julieta, and Montecristo. Visit the climate-controlled cedar cigar room. ⊠ *Gomezplein 4, Punda* ☎ *5999/465–3955.*

CLOTHING

Tommy Hilfiger. This label's Curaçao outposts carry the full designer line for men, women, and children. Stores located in Punda and Zuikertuin Mall. Hilfiger Denim is a specialty store in the Rif Fort. ⊠ *Willemstad* ☎ *5999/461–2266.*

FOOD

Centrum Supermarket. Centrally located with a good selection of wares. A bakery is also on the premises. ⊠ *Dr Caprillesweg 2, Willemstad* ☎ *5999/767–7337.*

GIFTS

FodorśChoice ★ **Boolchand's.** The best-known brand for electronics in the Caribbean, Boolchand's is a legendary family-run chain, and their main store is in Punda, though they have many other outlets around Curaçao. Beyond electronics and tech, they also sell fine jewelry, Swarovski crystal, Swiss watches, cameras, and more with a good reputation for fair price and good quality. ⊠ *Breedstraat 50, Punda* ☎ *5999/461–6233* ⊕ *www.boolchand.com/locations.*

Little Switzerland. A well-established, high-end chain offering designer jewelry, watches, crystal, china, and leather goods with outlets throughout the Caribbean, Little Switzerland's three Curaçao outlets are located in the Renaissance complex and at Rif Fort. Top-quality brands include Tiffany, Cartier, Movado, Tag Heuer, and more, at prices much lower than on the mainland. ⊠ *Renaissance and Rif Fort, Punda* ☎ *877/800–9988* ⊕ *www.littleswitzerland.com.*

Penha Curaçao. Founded in 1865 and still run by the Penha family, this landmark store is housed in one of Punda's most iconic structures and specializes in offering a wide range of duty-free items, including French perfumes, cosmetics, clothing, eyewear, watches, and high-end lingerie and accessories. It's also a UNESCO property and one of the most photographed on the island, another reason it draws tourists in droves. ⊠ *Heerenstraat 1, Punda* ☎ *5999/461–2266* ⊕ *www.jlpenha.com.*

HANDICRAFTS

Landhuis Groot Santa Martha. Run by the Tayor Soshal Foundation, this ex-plantation houses a project designed to help people with disabilities train and receive education and paid employment in a beneficial environment. The program takes place in a 17th-century land house that has been converted into an artisan's factory and museum, where visitors can purchase creative handmade crafts and souvenirs made by the residents. ⊠ *Soto, Santa Martha Bay* ☎ *5999/864–1323, 5999/864–2969* ⊕ *www.tayersoshal.com* ⌨ *$10.*

JEWELRY

Freeport Jewelers. The Freeport Jeweler's Group consists of six stores around the island featuring high-end brands of fine jewelry, watches, and collectibles. They have four stores in Willemstad (two on the Handelsakde), one in Punda, and one in Otrabanda at the Renaissance Mall. The other two are located in the Zuikertuin Mall. Their newest outlet there, Fashion Zone by Freeport, offers good prices on trendy watches by names like Calvin Klein, Swatch, Armani, Diesel, and more. ⊠ *Punda* ☎ *800/617–0766* ⊕ *www.freeportjewelers.com.*

PERFUMES AND COSMETICS

The Yellow House and Zylo. Also known as La Casa Amarilla, the Yellow House specializes in high-end duty-free perfumes and cosmetics with exclusive rights to big names like Guerlain. They have recently teamed up with Zylo (another retail chain) under the same roof to expand their range of wares. Now with their new partner, shoppers can also purchase high-end fashion watches, jewelry, handbags, and sunglasses there. They have outlets in Salina as well as the airport. ⊠ *Breedestraat 46, Punda* ☎ *5999/461–3222* ⊕ *www.theyellowhouse-zylo.com.*

SPORTS AND THE OUTDOORS

ATVS AND SCOOTERS

FAMILY **Curaçao Buggy Adventures (Scooby Tours).** Strap on a helmet for an adventurous, guided excursion called a "Scooby Tour" around the island's most popular sites. Visit caves and forts, stop for a swim or snorkel; you can even design your own tour if you're a group of four or more. Daily tours average 2½ hours. No experience required, but drivers must be 18 or older with a valid driver's license. Children over five can ride as passengers. Hotel pickup is available. They also do boat tours and open bus land tours. ⊠ *Seaquarium Beach and Zanzibar Beach–Jan Thiel, Willemstad* ☎ *5999/461–1076* ⊕ *www.scoobytours.com.*

Eric's ATV Adventures. Hit the road in rugged style behind the wheel of an all-terrain vehicle with Eric's ATV Adventures. All you need for a guided tour of the countryside is a regular driver's license. If you're 10 or older, you can ride as a passenger in the back seat. Helmets and goggles are provided. ⊠ *Babor Kibra z/n, Jan Thiel* ☎ *5999/461–0071* ⊕ *http://www.curacao-atv.com.*

BIKING

FAMILY **Wanna Bike Curaçao.** The island's premier biking outfit, Wanna Bike offers tours all over Curaçao with professional guides and top equipment. They are also the founders of the Mountain Bike Kids Club and organize many mountain bike clinics throughout the year. Their sister company "Wanna Go Outdoors" organizes corporate retreats and team-building events centered around biking and ecoadventures. ⊠ *Jan Thiel Beach z/n, Jan Thiel, Willemstad* ☎ *5999/527–3720* ⊕ *www. wannabike.com.*

DIVING AND SNORKELING

The **Curaçao Underwater Marine Park** includes almost a third of the island's southern diving waters. Scuba divers and snorkelers can enjoy more than 12½ miles (20 km) of protected reefs and shores, with normal visibility from 60 to 150 feet. With water temperatures ranging from 75°F to 82°F (24°C to 28°C), wet suits are generally unnecessary. No coral collecting, spearfishing, or littering is allowed. Some of the most popular dive sites are the Mushroom Forest, the wreck of the *Superior Producer*, and the Blue Room secret cave at Westpunt. Snorkelers and divers also enjoy the little sunken tugboat at Spanish Water. Wall diving is good around the Sea Aquarium Park and they also offer open-water dives with dolphins. The north coast—where conditions are dangerously rough—is not recommended for diving.

Introductory scuba resort courses are often done in resort pools and prices vary. To become fully PADI certified, carve out at least four or five days of your holiday for instruction and practice and at least one open-water dive. Prices vary depending on operation.

FAMILY **Divers Republic.** Divers Republic provides a highly personalized experience with professional PADI dive masters. They offer instruction and a large range of dives at the island's best spots, as well as a Bubblemaker program for children. Sunset boat trips and boat rental are also offered. ⊠ *Coral Estates Rif Marie* ☎ *5999/864–3344* ⊕ *http://divers republic.org.*

Fodor's Choice **Ocean Encounters.** This is the largest dive operator on Curaçao, and ★ they offer a vast menu of scheduled shore and boat dives and packages as well as certified PADI instruction. They cover the island's most popular dive sites including the *Superior Producer* wreck—where barracudas hang out—an adorable little tugboat wreck, the renowned Mushroom Forest, and much more. In July, the dive center sponsors a children's sea camp in conjunction with the Sea Aquarium, and they now run the unique Animal Encounters experience in the Sea Aquarium lagoon. They also offer Sleep & Dive packages at Lion's Dive and Sunscape Resorts. ⊠ *Sea Aquarium Park, Bapor Kibra* ☎ *5999/461–8131* ⊕ *www.oceanencounters.com.*

8

FISHING

Miss Ann Boat Trips. a wide range of seaborne adventures including day trips with barbecue lunch and diving and snorkeling ops at sister satellite island, uninhabited Klein Curaçao. Fishing trips, private charters, and more are available with their modern fleet of motor yachts. Guided kayaking tours are now offered on Spanish Waters. ✉ *Jan Sofat 232, Van Engelen* ☎ *5999/767–1579* ⊕ *www.missannboattrips.com.*

GOLF

Blue Bay Golf. Part of the Blue Bay Hotel, an ex-plantation house turned resort, the golf course is famous for its incredible sea views. Designed by Rocky Roquemore, it measures 6,735 yards from the tips and beckons experts and novices alike. You will be sure to enjoy the par-three 5th, which plays across and is guarded by the sea the entire left-hand side. Facilities include a golf shop, locker rooms, and a snack bar. You can rent carts, clubs, and shoes though don't expect too much with any of them or the facilities. If you'd like to drive your game to a new level, take a lesson from the house pro. With Pay & Play, no membership is required. Rates vary depending on time of day and high or low season. ✉ *Blue Bay Hotel, St. Michiel* ☎ *5999/868–1755* ⊕ *www.bluebay-curacao.com* ⅃ *18 holes, 6735 yards, par 72.*

Old Quarry Golf Course. This lush course designed by Pete Dye has incredible vistas on the sheltered bay known as Spanish Water. The course features a breathtaking mixture of ocean views and various forms of desert cactus, along with Dye's dramatic bunkering. The 6,920-yard layout is the best and toughest on the island and includes an 8,000-square-foot clubhouse. There is a full range of facilities, and with the Santa Barbara Resort nearby, drinks and fine dining are mere steps away. Greens fees feature multiple play packages as well as resort discounts. You can rent carts, clubs, and shoes. A new fly-and-golf package with Blue Skies Helicopters lands you right on the course with everything you need for a game ready and waiting for you. ✉ *Santa Barbara Plantation, Porta Blancu, Nieuwpoort* ☎ *5999/840–6886* ⊕ *www.oldquarrygolfcuracao. com* ⅃ *18 holes, 6920 yards, par 72.*

GUIDED TOURS

Most tour operators have pickups at the major hotels and offer tours in several languages including English. Tour offerings have expanded beyond simple island tours in air-conditioned motor coaches to include themes such as beach-hopping, nightlife, culture, culinary, or history—some in combinations covering more than one theme.

FAMILY **Atlantis Adventures Trolley Tour.** A novel way to explore the historic city of Willemstad is via the Trolley Train, which is as brightly colored in pastel hues as the Handelskade buildings. It begins and ends at Fort Amsterdam and winds through the neighborhoods of Punda, Scharloo, and Pietermaai with many points of local color and interest throughout. ✉ *Punda* ☎ *5999/461–0011* ⊕ *www.curacao-atlantisadventures.com.*

Fodor's Choice ★ **Blue Skies Helicopters.** Blue Skies is a first-rate helicopter operation that offers all kinds of exhilarating aerial tours and adventures—city tours, beach tours, nature tours, and a hop out to the small, deserted island Klein Curaçao among them. They offer Fly & Dine and Fly & Golf packages and airport transfers to top-end resorts. A new program is their Top Gun flight—for daredevils wishing to simulate the experience of secret military flight missions. They also offer island hops to Aruba and Bonaire. ⊠ *Motetwerf Wharf, Willemstad* ☎ *5999/461–2088* ⊕ *www.blueskieshelicopters.com.*

FAMILY **PeterTrips Curacao.** Small and large air-conditioned buses transport visitors for full-day or half-day outings to beaches, natural wonders, historical sights, and points of interest like the Ostrich Farm or Landhuis Chobolobo for Curaçao liqueur tastings. Special group adventures are also possible. They offer pickup at most major hotels. ☎ *5999/465–2703, 5999/465–2703* ⊕ *www.petertrips.com.*

Touraçao Tourism Services. Fabulous attractions on Curaçao are secreted all around the island, so tours are highly recommended. Touraçao offers a wide range of choices from city tours and beach tours to off-road adventures and fun nights on the town. Their equipment is top-notch, and their guides are highly professional, multilingual, and well-informed. They can also customize private tours to your interests, and they specialize in VIP airport transfers, which means skipping the customs line so you have more time for fun in the sun! ⊠ *Fokkerweg 5D, Willemstad* ☎ *5999/465–4611* ⊕ *www.touracao.com.*

Yellow Tourism Solutions. Part of the Yellow Group company that offers a full range of tourism services on the island, this operator offers a wide range of tours by motor coach and boat that include many of Curaçao's best attractions and activities. Choose half- and full-day tours to beaches or historical sites, or horseback riding, diving, or snorkeling opportunities. Or discover the rugged interior by Yellow Jeep Safari that takes you throughout Christoffel National Park and its many hidden scenic wonders. ⊠ *Curaçao Marriott Beach Resort, Piscadera Bay* ☎ *5999/462–6262* ⊕ *www.tourism-curacao.com.*

WALKING TOURS

When making reservations for any tour, mention that you speak English.

Gigi Scheper Tours. Gigi Scheper leads historical walking tours of Willemstad and also does a car tour focusing on Jewish heritage and architecture, including an insider's look at the synagogue. ⊠ *Punda* ☎ *5999/697–0290.*

Fodor's Choice ★ **Photo Walking Tours.** Professional photographer Caroline Castendijk will show you around the historic and colorful sections of Willemstad and give you great pointers on photographing the scenes. She'll take you through Scharloo and Pietermaai, old quarters undergoing major transformations, offering incredible photo ops. You'll learn plenty of the island's history to give context to your images. Caroline will lead you through all the secret alleys and nooks in the old districts and can take you through Otrobanda and Punda, too. ⊠ *Willemstad* ☎ *5999/515–8971* ⊕ *http://carolinecastendijk.com.*

8

VIP Tours Curacao. Create your own tour with VIP's list of must-see attractions, and they will do the rest. They personalize every service and customize flexible itineraries, which may include full days of Westpunt or the national park or Willemstad or a combo of all, including land and sea adventures. They also offer a special geocaching tour. ☎ *5999/673–4567* ⊕ *www.viptourscuracao.com.*

Walking Tours Otrabanda and Punda. Walking tours of historic Otrobanda focusing on the unique architecture and history are led by architects Anko van der Woude and Micheal Newton, and Punda tours by Gerda Gehlen. ☎ *5999/461–3554 Otrobanda, 5999/668–8579 Punda* ⊕ *www. otrobanda-pundatour.com.*

SEA EXCURSIONS

Many sailboats, motorboats, and catamarans offer sunset cruises and daylong snorkeling and picnic trips to Klein Curaçao, the uninhabited island between Curaçao and Bonaire, and other destinations.

Bounty Adventures. Two custom-built, high-speed catamarans and a luxury motor yacht take guests for snorkel sails, sunset trips, day trips to Klein Curaçao, and deep-sea fishing adventures that include an open bar and barbecue lunch. Charters also available. ✉ *Jan Thiel Beach* ☎ *5999/767–9998* ⊕ *www.bountyadventures.com.*

Insulinde. The majestic 120-foot Dutch sailing ketch is very popular for weddings and special event charters but also offers many snorkeling/swimming/scenic-tour combos and romantic sunset sails. They also now offer three-day trips to neighboring island Bonaire. ✉ *Handelskade z/n* ☎ *5999/560–1340* ⊕ *www.insulinde.com.*

Mermaid. The *Mermaid* is a 66-foot motor yacht that carries up to 60 people to deserted island Klein Curaçao four times a week. A buffet lunch, beer, and soft drinks are provided at the boat's exclusive beach house, they are the only tour operator that goes there with their own picnic tables, shade huts, and facilities. ☎ *5999/560–1530* ⊕ *www. mermaidboattrips.com.*

Seaworld Explorer. A semi-submersible sub run by Atlantis Adventures takes you down under the waves without getting wet to view colorful marine life. Informative narrative while you go helps you understand what you are seeing, and a diver tags alongside to feed the fish to ensure you see lots on your journey. Tour is approximately one hour. ✉ *Hilton Curaçao Hotel, Piscadera Bay* ☎ *5999/461–0011* ⊕ *www. curacao-atlantisadventures.com* 🎫 *$39.*

DOMINICAN
REPUBLIC

WELCOME TO THE DOMINICAN REPUBLIC

Ocean World Adventure Park
Playa Dorada
Cofresí Beach
17 - 20
Playa Sosúa
Luperón Beach
Montecristi
16
15
Playa Cabarete
Puerto Plata
Museo de Ambar Dominicano
Sosúa Cabarete
10 - 14
Cabo Francés Viejo
Guayubin
Cibao Valley
Mt. Isabel de Torres
Gregorie Luperón International Airport
9
Laguna Grí-Grí
HAITI
Cabrera
Playa Grande
Santiago
Moca
Bahía Escocesa
Las Terrenas
Pico Duarte
La Vega Vieja
San Francisco de Macorís
Playa Cosón
8 7
Nagua
Los Haitises National Park
Taino Park
Bahía de Samaná
HISPANIOLA
Jarabacoa
← TO HAITI
Sabana de la Mar
San Juan
Monte Plata
Lago Enriquillo
Neiba
Las Américas International Airport
Azua
Duvergé
San Cristóbal
Boca Chica
Juan Dolio
Bahía de Ocoa
Bani
Santo Domingo see detail map
Barahona
Playa Bahoruco
Pto. Palenque
Caribbean Sea
21
Oviedo
Cabo Beata

Like the merengue seen on all the dance floors in Santo Domingo, the Dominican Republic is charismatic yet sensuous, energetic yet elegant. The charm of the people adds special warmth: a gracious wave of greeting here, a hand-rolled cigar tapped with a flourish there. Dazzling smiles just about everywhere will quickly beguile you.

LA ISLA ESPAÑOLA

The Dominican Republic covers the eastern two-thirds of the island of Hispaniola (Haiti covers the other third). At 18,765 square miles (48,730 square km), it's the second-largest Caribbean country (only Cuba is larger), and with more than 8.8 million people, the second-most-populous country, too. It was explored by Columbus on his 1492 voyage to the New World.

KEY
⌐ Beaches
◥ Dive Sites
1 Hotels

TOP REASONS TO VISIT THE DOMINICAN REPUBLIC

1 Great Beaches. There are some 1,000 miles of excellent beaches, many of which are white and powdery.

2 Great Value. You'll find the best-value all-inclusive resorts in the Caribbean here.

3 Myriad Water Sports. Every imaginable activity—world-class golf, horseback riding,

white-water rafting, surfing, diving, windsurfing—is available here.

4 Friendly People. The genuine hospitality of the people and their love of *norteamericanos*.

5 Happening Nightlife. The Dominicans love to party, dance, drink, and have a good time at happening bars and clubs.

NEED TO KNOW

DOMINICAN REPUBLIC

★ Santo Domingo

AT A GLANCE

Capital: Santo Domingo

Population: 10,404,000

Currency: Dominican Peso

Money: ATMs in major towns; major credit cards and U.S. dollars often accepted at resorts. Need pesos outside resort areas.

Language: Spanish

Country Code: ☎ 1 809/829/849

Emergencies: ☎ 911

Driving: On the right

Electricity: 120v/60 cycles; plugs are U.S. standard two- and three-prong

Time: Same as New York during daylight savings; one hour ahead otherwise

Documents: Up to 60 days with valid passport

Mobile Phones: GSM (850, 900, 1800 and 1900 bands)

Major Mobile Companies: Claro, Orange, Tricom, Viva

WEBSITES

Dominican Republic Tourist Office: ⊕ www.godominicanrepublic.com

Dominican Republic: ⊕ www.dominicanrepublic.com

DR1: ⊕ www.dr1.com/travel

GETTING AROUND

✈ **Air Travel:** Punta Cana is the island's busiest, followed by Las Américas, Gregorio Luperón, and La Romana.

🚌 **Bus Travel:** Privately owned air-conditioned buses are an inexpensive way to get between major points like Santiago, Puerto Plata, Punta Cana, and Santo Domingo. *Guaguas* (local buses) are not recommended.

🚗 **Car Travel:** Driving in the Dominican Republic can be harrowing and expensive; don't rent a car unless you are staying in a villa.

🚗 **Taxi Travel:** Taxis are available everywhere but can be expensive

PLAN YOUR BUDGET

	HOTEL ROOM	MEAL	ATTRACTIONS
Low Budget	$200	$12	Columbus Lighthouse, $1.50
Mid Budget	$300	$25	Altos de Chavon, $25
High Budget	$475	$40	18-hole round of golf on "Teeth of the Dog," $195

WAYS TO SAVE

Book an all-inclusive package. AI resorts offer the best value at many different levels and are the norm rather than the exception in the D.R.

Flight and hotel packages. With most hotels already all-inclusive, grander packages that include hotel and flight to the D.R. are usually money-saving options.

Take the bus. The buses of Metro and Caribe Tours offer cheap, regular routes all around the country.

Haggle. In open-air markets, you're expected to haggle if you want to get a decent price.

PLAN YOUR TIME

Hassle Factor	Medium. Flights to the D.R. are frequent, but travel within the country can be challenging.
3 days	Relax poolside or beachside at your resort in Puerto Plata, Punta Cana, or La Romana. Take a side trip to Altos de Chavon.
1 week	Split your time between the beaches of Puerto Plata and Punta Cana or La Romana. Spend a day and night feeling the pulse of the D.R. capital, Santo Domingo.
2 weeks	Rent a car and base yourself at various points across the island for explorations. Besides the typical Punta Cana and La Romana, visit Isla Saona, spend a few nights in Santo Domingo, and spend time in Cabarete before or after exploring Puerto Plata.

WHEN TO GO

High Season: December through May is the most fashionable and most expensive time to visit, when the weather is typically sunny and warm. Good hotels are often booked far in advance, and you're guaranteed the most entertainment at resorts and the most people with whom to enjoy it.

Low Season: From August to early November, temperatures can grow oppressively hot and the weather muggy, with high risks of tropical storms. Some smaller hotels close in the off-season, but larger resorts offer discounted rates (20% or more).

Value Season: During what is considered value season in the rest of the Caribbean, there's a spike in travel by Europeans to the D.R. This means that the island's resorts have no real value season during the late spring and summer months.

BIG EVENTS

February - March: Carnival celebrations rage for weeks; the most famous carnival celebration is in La Vega, followed by the one in Santiago.

August: Celebrate independence from Spain on August 16 in Santiago and Santo Domingo.

October: Dance and sing in Puerto Plata at the annual Merengue music festival.

READ THIS

■ *The Brief Wondrous Life of Oscar Wao,* Junot Díaz. His Pulitzer Prize winning novel.

■ *The Feast of the Goat,* Mario Vargas Llosa. Reflections on the assassination of D.R. dictator Rafael Trujillo.

■ *In the Time of Butterflies.* Julia Alvarez. A novelized portrayal of the very real revolutionary Mirabal sisters.

WATCH THIS

■ *The Godfather II.* Scenes from this 1970s classic were filmed here.

■ *Fast & Furious 4.* This one takes place in the D.R.

■ *Sugar.* Film about baseball player Miguel Santos.

EAT THIS

■ *Mofongo*: mashed green plantains with shredded pork (or chicken).

■ *Moro*: a combination of rice and beans (or peas).

■ *Sancocho*: thick stew of five meats and poultry, served with white rice and avocado.

■ *Queso frito*: white, pan-fried cheese.

■ *Chicharrón de pollo*: deep-fried, boneless chunks of chicken.

■ *Arroz con leche*: sweet and creamy rice pudding

PIRATES IN THE CARIBBEAN

Peg legs, parrots, and an easy-to-imitate "ahoy matey" lexicon: these are requisite elements in any pirate tale, but so are avarice and episodes of unspeakable violence. The combination is clearly compelling. Our fascination with pirates knows no bounds.

The true history of piracy has largely been obscured by competing pop-culture images. On one hand, there is the archetypal opportunist—fearsome, filthy, and foul-mouthed. On the other is the lovable scallywag epitomized by Captain Jack Sparrow in Disney's *Pirates of the Caribbean* franchise. Actual pirates, however, usually fell somewhere between these two extremes.

They could be uneducated men with limited life choices or crewmen from legitimate commercial and exploratory vessels left unemployed in the wake of changing political agendas. In either case, the piratical career path offered tempting benefits. Making a fast doubloon was only the beginning. Piracy also promised adventure plus egalitarian camaraderie—a kind of social equality unlikely to be found elsewhere during that class-conscious period.

Life aboard ship was governed by majority, as opposed to autocratic, rule. Pirates, moreover, adhered to the Pirate's Code (a sort of "honor among thieves" arrangement). On the ships, at least, the common good took precedence.

"X" MARKS THE SPOT

The Caribbean offered easy pickings for pirates because Spanish imperialists had already done the heavy lifting, extracting gems and precious metals from their South American colonies. Pirates from competing powers (namely England and

France) could simply grab the spoils as Spanish ships island-hopped homeward.

Jamaica: Calico Jack Rackham, his lover Anne Bonny, and Mary Read were ultimately captured in Bloody Bay near Negril. Reportedly the male crew members were too busy drinking rum to mount a proper defense.

Dominican Republic: The centuries-old Spanish architecture in Santo Domingo's Zona Colonial is so well-preserved you can almost picture the area populated with tankard-toting buccaneers and corset-clad wenches.

Puerto Rico: Massive fortifications, like Castillo San Felipe del Morro in Old San Juan, show just how far the Spanish were prepared to go to protect their assets from seagoing attackers, whether authorized or otherwise.

British Virgin Islands: Sir Francis Drake Channel, Jost Van Dyke, and Great Thatch Island were named for pirates or privateers. Ditto for Norman Island, which reputedly inspired the setting for R.L. Stevenson's *Treasure Island*.

St. Thomas: A strategic location, protected anchorages, plus easy-to-hide-in inlets made the U.S. Virgin Islands an ideal habitat for plunderers. High points like Drake's Seat and Blackbeard's Castle were used to survey the terrain.

Anguilla: Underwater heritage preserves let divers explore vessels that sailed during piracy's Golden Age. Stoney Ground

Marine Park contains a Spanish galleon wrecked in 1772, plus cannons, anchors, and other artifacts.

St. Barthélémy: Logically enough, Frenchman Daniel Montbars used this French island as his home base. Legend has it some of his treasure remains hidden in the beachfront caves around Anse du Gouverneur.

St. Lucia: Now a peaceful national park, Pigeon Island (on St. Lucia's northern tip) was once the hideout of François Le Clerc. This peg-legged pirate orchestrated attacks from his hilly vantage point in the late 16th century.

FAMOUS PIRATES

Sir Francis Drake: Drake was a busy fellow. The first Englishman to circumnavigate the globe, he popularized tobacco, led slave-trading expeditions, helped destroy the Spanish Armada, and still had time to terrorize treasure-laden ships with Queen Elizabeth's blessing.

Henry Morgan: Captain Morgan led a colorful life before lending his name to a ubiquitous brand of rum. Leaving Wales for the West Indies as a young man, he successfully segued from debauched buccaneer to semi-respectable privateer and, after dodging piracy charges in England, ended up as the Lieutenant Governor of Jamaica.

(left) A replica ship near Punta Cana; *(lower right)* Castillo San Felipe del Morro; *(upper right)* Sir Francis Drake

9

Exploring at Stoney Ground Marine Park

Blackbeard: Born Edward Teach, Blackbeard was notable for his business savvy (which included making profit-sharing deals with politicos) as well as his fiendish looks. His signature beard was braided and often laced with lit fuses to terrify enemies. Alas, in 1718 Blackbeard's head was severed in a dramatic showdown with Lt. Robert Maynard of the Royal Navy.

William Kidd: Life was a roller-coaster ride for the legendary Captain Kidd. Kidd was a retired privateer living in New York when he accepted a commission to hunt pirates and then became one himself with the encouragement of a mutinous crew. He was executed in London in 1701, but hopefuls still hunt for the treasure he supposedly left buried.

Black Bart Roberts: Though not the most famous pirate, he is often considered the most successful. He racked up impressive credits, plundering some 400 ships between 1719 and 1722. A snappy dresser who was fashionably attired even in battle, he was also a strict disciplinarian.

Daniel Montbars: Montbars proved Brits didn't hold a monopoly on bad behavior. French lineage aside, he differed from his 17th-century peers in that he was affluent and educated. His manners needed polishing, though. Violent outbursts (disemboweling Spaniards was a favorite sport) earned Montbars the nickname "The Exterminator."

Calico Jack Rackham: An Englishman who ascended from mate to captain, Rackham secured his legend by adding women to his crew. Workwise, his favorite tactic was attacking small vessels close to shore. Such boldness led to an inglorious end. Rackham was hung then tarred, feathered, and displayed in a cage in Port Royal, Jamaica.

Anne Bonny and Mary Read: Thought to be unlucky, female pirates were rare. Yet the comely Bonny and cross-dressing Read were respected by their shipmates and feared by their victims. Captured together in 1720, they were sentenced to death. Both, however, escaped the noose by claiming to be pregnant.

Updated by Eileen Robinson Smith

Dominicans will extend a gracious welcome, saying, "This is your home!" and indeed are happy to share their beautiful island bathed by the Atlantic Ocean to the north and the Caribbean Sea to the south. Among its most precious assets are 1,000 miles (1,600 km) of gorgeous beaches studded with coconut palms and sands ranging from pearl-white to golden brown to volcanic black. The Caribbean sun kisses this exotic land, which averages 82°F year-round. In recent years, the D.R. has grown up, as the all-inclusive resorts have become more upscale, and small, stellar boutique properties have opened in all of the most popular tourist areas. The level of service staff and middle management has also improved.

A land of contrasts, the Dominican Republic has mountain landscapes, brown rivers with white-water rapids, rain forests full of wild orchids, and fences of multicolor bougainvillea. Indigenous species from crocodiles to the green cockatoo, symbol of the island, live in these habitats. Bird-watchers, take note: there are 29 endemic species flying around here.

The contrasts don't stop with nature. You can see signs of wealth, for the upper strata of society lives well indeed. In the capital, the movers and shakers ride in chauffeur-driven silver Mercedes. On the country roads you'll be amazed that four people with sacks of groceries and a stalk of bananas can fit on a smoky old *motoconcho* (motorbike–taxi). This is a land of mestizos who are a centuries-old mix of native Indians, Spanish colonists, and African slaves, plus every other nationality that has settled here, from Italian to Arabic.

9

Accommodations offer a remarkable range—including surfers' camps, exclusive boutique hotels, and amazing megaresorts that have brought the all-inclusive hotel to the next level of luxury. Trendy restaurants, art galleries, boutique hotels, and late-night clubs help make Santo Domingo a superb urban vacation destination. Regrettably, most Dominican towns and cities are neither quaint nor pretty, and poverty still prevails. However, the standard of living has come up along with the growth of North American tourism. Prices at all-inclusive resorts have been slowly increasing since the early aughts; however, a vacation in the D.R. can still be a relative bargain. Even the new boutique hotels are still well priced for the Caribbean. Nevertheless, government taxes on hotels and restaurants are 18%, and most non-AI hotels charge an additional 10% service charge This 28% is obviously a major budget item. Also, when making a reservation, inquire if the rates quoted include this 28%; sometimes they do, especially with the smaller properties.

The vibrant lifestyle of this sun-drenched Latin-Caribbean country, where Spanish is the national language and where people are hospitable, makes the Dominican Republic a different cultural experience. If you pick up the rhythm of life here, as freewheeling as the trademark merengue, this can be a beguiling destination.

PLANNING

GETTING HERE AND AROUND
AIR TRAVEL
You can fly nonstop to the Dominican Republic from Atlanta (Delta, Southwest), Baltimore (Southwest), Boston (JetBlue), Charlotte (American), Chicago–Midway (Southwest), Chicago–O'Hare (American, United), Dallas–Ft. Worth (American), Detroit (Delta), Fort Lauderdale (Spirit), Miami (American), Minneapolis (Delta), New York–JFK (Delta, JetBlue), New York–Newark (United), Orlando (JetBlue), Philadelphia (American), and Washington Dulles (United). However, not all airlines fly to all the destinations in the D.R., and some flights connect in San Juan or airports throughout the United States. Many visitors fly nonstop on charter flights direct from the U.S. East Coast and Midwest, particularly into Punta Cana; these charters are part of a package and can be booked only through a travel agent.

LIAT also flies between Antigua and Santo Domingo, and Air Antilles Express flies to Santo Domingo and Punta Cana from several Caribbean destinations. Air Caraïbes flies to Santo Domingo from the French Antilles. Alas, there are no regularly scheduled domestic flights, just charters.

Airport Transfers: If you book a package through a travel agent or vacation provider, your airport transfer will almost certainly be included. If you book independently, you will have to take a taxi, rent a car, or hire a private driver-guide. ⊕ *DominicanShuttles.com* offers drivers and private transfers in addition to scheduling domestic airline flights and excursions.

Airports Cibao International Airport (*STI*). ⊕ *www.aeropuertocibao.com. do*. **El Catey International Airport** (*AZS*). **Gregorio Luperón International Airport** (*POP*). ⊕ *www.puerto-plata-airport.com*. **La Isabella International Airport** (*JBQ*). ⊠ *Higuero, Santo Domingo*. **La Romana/Casa de Campo International Airport** (*LRM*). ⊕ *romanaairport.com*. **Las Américas International Airport** (*SDQ*). **Punta Cana International Airport** (*PUJ*). ⊕ *www. puntacanainternationalairport.com*.

International Airlines Air Antilles Express. ☎ *809/688–6661 air ticket agency, 809/560–0168 call center/agency* ⊕ *www.flyairantilles.com*. **Air Caraïbes.** ☎ *809/621–8888 general services, 0590/82–47–00 in Guadeloupe, 0820/83–58–35* ⊕ *www.aircaraibes.com*. **American Airlines.** ☎ *809/959–2420 in Punta Cana, 800/433–7300 in U.S., 800/222–2377 Web help, 809/200–5151 toll-free, 809/542–5151 in Santo Domingo* ⊕ *www.aa.com*. **Delta.** ☎ *809/955–1500 in D.R., 800/221–1212 in U.S.* ⊕ *www.delta.com*. **JetBlue.** ☎ *809/200–9898 in D.R. (SDQ), 800/538–2583 in U.S.* ⊕ *www.jetblue.com*. **LIAT.** ☎ *809/621–8888 general services, 888/844–5428 in the D.R., 809/549–2036 in Santo Domingo* ⊕ *www.liatairline.com*. **Southwest.** ☎ *800/435–9792* ⊕ *www.southwest.com*. **Spirit Airlines.** ☎ *829/946–5957 in Santo Domingo, 849/937–0808 in Santiago, 801/401–2222 in the U.S.* ⊕ *www.spirit.com*. **United.** ☎ *809/262–1060 in the D.R., 800/864–8331 in the U.S.* ⊕ *www.united.com*.

Domestic Charter Airlines Air Century. ⊠ *La Isabella International Dr. Joaquin Balaguer, Av. Presidente Antonio Guzmán Fernández, Santo Domingo* ☎ *809/826–4333 charters, 305/677–9641 in U.S.* ⊕ *www.aircentury.com*. **DominicanShuttles.com.** ⊠ *Torre Empresarial Forum, Av. 27 de Febrero at Av. Privada, Santo Domingo* ☎ *809/931–4073, 829/410–3326* ⊕ *www. dominicanshuttles.com*. **Helidosa Helicopters.** ⊠ *Punta Cana International Airport, Punta Cana* ☎ *809/552–6069* ⊕ *www.helidosa.com*.

CAR TRAVEL

Driving in the D.R. can be a harrowing and expensive experience; we don't recommend that the typical vacationer rent a car. It's best if you don't drive outside the major cities at night. If you must, use extreme caution, especially on narrow, unlighted mountain roads.

Local agencies exist, but it is highly advisable to rent only from internationally known companies. U.S. citizens should really consider only U.S.–based chains, so that if you have a problem you have easier recourse. Major agencies are in most of the island's airports. At Las Americas International Airport, most agencies are open 7 am–11 pm.

Car-Rental Contacts Avis. ☎ *809/549–0468 at Las Americas International Airport, 800/331–1212 in the U.S.* **Budget.** ⊠ *Punta Cana International Airport* ☎ *800/472–3325 for reservations outside the U.S., 800/214–6094 customer service, 809/466–2028 at Punta Cana International Airport, 809/586–0413 at Gregorio Luperón International Airport, 809/549–0351 at Las Américas International Airport* ⊕ *www.budget.com*. **Europcar.** ☎ *809/549–0942 at Las Américas Airport, 809/686–2861 at Punta Cana International Airport* ⊕ *www.europcar. com*. **Hertz.** ☎ *809/586–0200 at Gregory Luperon Airport* **National.** ⊠ *Casa de Campo* ☎ *809/523–8191 at Casa de Campo* ⊕ *www.nationalcar.com*.

9

TAXI TRAVEL

Wherever you are, hotel taxis are generally the best and safest option, although they can be expensive. Carry small bills; drivers rarely have change; some destinations have rather high minimum fares. Always let your hotel or restaurant call a taxi for you. Don't use "street" or gypsy taxis, which are often in poor repair and can be a security risk. Recommendable radio-taxi companies in Santo Domingo are Tecni-Taxi (which also operates in Puerto Plata) and Apolo. Most taxis will also carry you out of town and will have rate charts for major destinations; just be aware that these private taxi transfers can be expensive (well over US$100) for a destination that's less than hour away and more for destinations further afield.

DominicanShuttles provides safe and reliable long-distance private taxi service, but trips must be arranged in advance online (as little as 24 hours or as much as weeks in advance in the case of a long-distance airport transfer).

Contacts Apolo Taxi. ☎ 809/537–0000, 809/537–1245 for high-end cars or SUVs ⊕ www.apolotaxi.com. **DominicanShuttles.** ⊕ www.dominicanshuttles. com. **Taxi-Cabarete.** ☎ 809/571–0767 in Cabarete. **Taxi-Queen Santiago.** ☎ 809/570–0000 in Santiago. **Taxi-Sosúa.** ☎ 809/571–3097 in Sosúa. **Tecni-Taxi.** ☎ 809/567–2010 in Santo Domingo, 809/320–7621 in Puerto Plata.

HEALTH AND SAFETY

Never drink tap water in the D.R. (look for a hotel or restaurant that has earned an *H* for food-service hygiene or that has a Crystal America certification). Don't buy food or even juice from the street vendors.

Dengue, chikungunya, and zika have all been reported in Martinique. We recommend that you protect yourself from these mosquito-borne illnesses by keeping your skin covered and/or wearing mosquito repellant. The mosquitoes that transmit these viruses are as active by day as they are at night.

Although crime rates in the D.R. can be high, violent crime is rare against tourists. Nevertheless, poverty is everywhere in the D.R., and petty theft, pickpocketing, and purse snatching are an increasing concern, particularly in Santo Domingo. Pay attention, especially when leaving a bank or casino. Take hotel-recommended taxis at night.

HOTELS AND RESORTS

All-inclusives: All-inclusive resorts predominate in Punta Cana and some other areas, and some of them are quite luxurious.

Condos: In places like Playa Dorada, apart-hotels and classy condos are now popular.

Small Hotels: Sosúa and Cabarete still have a few charming independent inns and small resorts

Hotel reviews have been shortened. For full information, visit Fodors.com.

WHAT IT COSTS IN U.S. DOLLARS				
	$	**$$**	**$$$**	**$$$$**
RESTAURANTS	under $12	$12–$20	$21–$30	over $30
HOTELS	under $275	$275–$375	$376–$475	over $475

Restaurant prices are the average cost of a main course at dinner or, if dinner is not served, at lunch. Hotel prices are the lowest cost of a standard double room in high season.

VISITOR INFORMATION

Contacts Dominican Republic One. ⊕ *www.dr1.com.* **Dominican Republic Tourist Office.** ☎ *212/588–1012 in New York City, 888/358–9594 in Miami* ⊕ *www.godominicanrepublic.com.*

EXPLORING

SANTO DOMINGO

Since many visitors to Santo Domingo base themselves in the historic Zona Colonia (and because this is where the vast majority of the interesting sights are located), most exploration in the city is done on foot. At night, however, you'll always want to take a taxi, particularly to outlying areas. Some hotels are now being built in the newer parts of Santo Domingo, such as Piantini, which can't be navigated on foot.

Parque Independencia separates the old city from modern Santo Domingo, a sprawling, noisy city with a population of close to 2 million. The 12 cobblestone blocks of Santo Domingo's **Zona Colonial** contain most of the major sights in town. It's one of the most appealing historic districts in the Caribbean and is best explored on foot. The Zona ends at the seafront, called the Malecón.

ZONA COLONIAL

Spanish civilization in the New World began in Santo Domingo's 12-block Zona Colonial. As you stroll its narrow streets, it's easy to imagine this old city as it was when the likes of Columbus, Cortés, and Ponce de León walked the cobblestones, pirates sailed in and out, and colonists started settling. Tourist brochures claim that "history comes alive here"—a surprisingly truthful statement. Almost every Thursday to Sunday night at 8:30 a typical "folkloric show" is staged at Parque Colón and Plaza de España. During the Christmas holidays there is an artisans' fair and live-music concerts take place.

Fun horse-and-carriage ride throughout the Zona are available year-round, though the commentary will likely be in Spanish; the steeds are no thoroughbreds, but they clip right along. You can also negotiate to use them as a taxi, say, to go down to the Malecón. The drivers usually hang out in front of the Hostal Nicolas de Ovando. You can get a free walking-tour map and brochures in English at the Secretaria de Estado

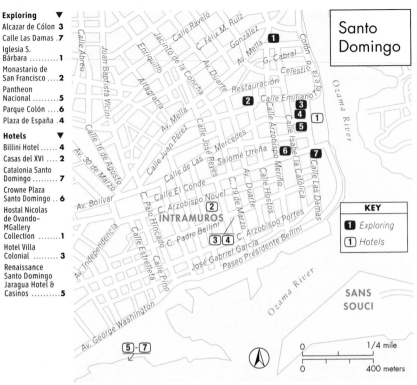

de Turismo office at Parque Colón (Columbus Park), where you may be approached by freelance, English-speaking guides who will want to make it all come alive for you. They'll work enthusiastically for $25 an hour for four people.

Most major reconstruction projects in the Zona Colonial have finally come to an end. Shopkeepers and visitors alike are once again loving the joy of this charmed neighborhood. Unfortunately, the Zona is not as safe as it once was—particularly at night and during festivals. Don't walk on the streets with little pedestrian traffic and low lighting. Do not carry a lot of cash or your passport (leave them in the hotel safe).

TOP ATTRACTIONS

Alcázar de Colón. The castle of Don Diego Colón, built in 1517, was the home to generations of the Christopher Columbus family. The Renaissance-style structure, with its balustrade and double row of arches, has strong Moorish, Gothic, and Isabelline influences. The 22 rooms are furnished in a style to which the viceroy of the island would have been accustomed—right down to the dishes and the vice regal shaving mug. The mansion's 40-inch-thick coral-limestone walls make air-conditioning impossible. Bilingual guides are on hand for tours peppered with fascinating anecdotes, like weddings once-upon-a time. Audio tours (about 25 minutes) are available in English. ⊠ *Plaza de España,* *off Calle Emiliano Tejera, Zona Colonial* ☎ *809/682–4750* ⊕ *www. museoalcazardecolon.com* ✉ *RD$100* ⊘ *Tues.–Sun. 9–5.*

Calle Las Damas. "The Ladies Street" was named after the elegant ladies of the court: in the Spanish tradition, they promenaded in the evening. Here you can see a sundial dating from 1753 and the Casa de los Jesuitas, which houses a fine research library for colonial history as well as the **Institute for Hispanic Culture**; admission is free, and it's open weekdays from 8 to 4:30. The boutique Hostal Nicolas de Ovando is on this street, across from the French Embassy. If you follow the street going toward the Malecón, you will pass a picturesque alley, fronted by a wrought-iron gate, where there are perfectly maintained colonial structures owned by the Catholic Church. ⊠ *Calle las Damas, Zona Colonial.*

WORTH NOTING

Iglesia Santa Bárbara. This combination church and fortress, the only one of its kind in Santo Domingo, was completed in 1562. It is a fine example of colonial Spanish architecture, and not as touristic as the cathedrals. ∎TIP➔ **For Mass times, be sure to check the day before you want to attend.** ⊠ *Av. Mella, between Calle Isabel la Católica and Calle Arzobispo Meriño, Zona Colonial* ☎ *809/682–3307* ✉ *Free* ⊘ *Mon.– Sat. 9 am–4:43 pm; daily Mass is weekdays at 5 pm. Sun. Mass is just at noon.*

Monasterio de San Francisco. Constructed between 1512 and 1544, the St. Francis Monastery contained the church, convent, and hospital of the Franciscan order. Sir Francis Drake's demolition squad significantly damaged the building in 1586, and in 1673 an earthquake nearly finished the job, but when it's floodlit at night, the eerie ruins are dramatic indeed. The Spanish government has donated money to turn this into a beautiful cultural center, but we are still waiting. In the meantime, there's music many nights at 7 pm (often live) and on Sunday night from 5 to 10 pm. These performances are by bands with different music genres—merengue, jazz, etc. The scene is like an old-fashioned block party. Zone residents mingle with expats and tourists, who snap pictures of the octogenarians dancing the merengue and the bachata. Others who come are content to just sit in white plastic chairs, swaying and clapping. It's nice. ⊠ *Calle Hostos at Calle Emiliano, Zona Colonial.*

Pantheon Nacional. The National Pantheon (circa 1714) was once a Jesuit monastery and later a theater. The real curiosity here is the military guard, who stays as still as the statues, despite the schoolchildren who try to make him flinch. ⊠ *Calle Las Damas, near Calle de Las Mercedes, Zona Colonial* ☎ *809/689–6010* ✉ *Free* ⊘ *Mon.–Sat. 8 am–9 pm.*

Parque Colón. The huge statue of Christopher Columbus in the park named after him dates from 1897 and is the work of sculptor Ernesto Gilbert. At the far end, the Catedral Primada de América is a landmark and most worthy of a visit. Like all the parks in the Zona Colonial, this one is quite a social gathering place, as is the sidewalk café across from it. ⊠ *El Conde at Calle Arzobispo Meriño, Zona Colonial.*

Plaza de España. This wide esplanade, which goes past the Casas de Reales in front of Don Diego Columbus's former palace, El Alcazar de

Colón, is the area in the Zona Colonial where national holidays are celebrated. The annual Coca-Cola–sponsored Christmas tree is here. It's bordered by what once were the ramparts of the original walled city. People enjoy the views of the Ozama River from here, and watch the cruise-ship activity below at the terminal. Lovers stroll by night, sharing a kiss under the gas lamps. When many people talk about the Plaza de España, they are often referring to the half-dozen restaurants in a row, which are on the upper level of these 16th- and 17th-century warehouses. The popular tables are on their outdoor decks. Cultural performances are held on a stage across from the Plaza on certain weekends. ■TIP→ Make dinner reservations on those nights and you'll have a special Santo Domingo experience. ⊠ *Calle La Atarazana, Zona Colonial.*

PIANTINI

A surprising number of luxury hotels and trendy restaurants have opened in the city's main business district. While it's a great place to dine and stay, it's not within walking distance of any sights, so you'll need taxis to get around.

GAZCUE

Santo Domingo's seafront Malecón is lined with large convention hotels that are popular for business travelers and groups. While it's a popular place to stay, it's not within easy walking distance of the Zona Colonial, where most of the city's historic sights are located. Always take a taxi at night; it's not safe to walk here after dark.

SOUTHEAST COAST

Las Américas Highway runs east along the coast from Santo Domingo to La Romana. Midway are well-established beach resorts such as Juan Dolio, and inland, Sammy Sosa's hometown, San Pedro de Macorís. Much farther east are Punta Cana and Bávaro, glorious beaches on the sunrise side of the island. At the end of the highway lies the luxurious Casa de Campo resort (along with its marina and shopping village, Altos de Chavón) and its airport, both in La Romana. There are some gems among the small number of resorts in Bayahibe and Dominicus Americus. But Bayahibe Bay, all juxtaposed with fishing villages, is idyllic and truly memorable.

LA ROMANA

48 miles (78 km) east of Juan Dolio.

Neither pretty nor quaint, La Romana has a central park, an interesting market, a couple of good restaurants, banks and small businesses, a public beach, and Jumbo, a major supermarket. ■TIP→ If you are staying for a week or more you may want to buy a Dominican cell phone at Jumbo. It's a mere $20 for a basic one, plus minutes. It can save you untold money if you'll be making local calls from your hotel/resort. It is, at least, a real slice of Dominican life. Casa de Campo is just outside La Romana, and other resorts are found in the vicinity of nearby Bayahibe. Although there are now more resorts in the area, this 7,000-acre luxury enclave put the town on the map. Casa de Campo Marina, with its Mediterranean design and impressive yacht club and villa complex,

The architecture in the town of Altos de Chavón re-creates a 16th-century Mediterranean village.

is as fine a marina facility as can be found anywhere; the shops and restaurants at the marina are a big draw for all tourists to the area.

Fodor's Choice
★

Altos de Chavón. This replica 16th-century Mediterranean village sits on a bluff overlooking the Río Chavón, on the grounds of Casa de Campo but about 3 miles (5 km) east of the main facilities. There are cobblestone streets lined with lanterns, wrought-iron balconies, wooden shutters, courtyards swathed with bougainvillea, and **Iglesia St. Stanislaus,** the romantic setting for many a Casa de Campo wedding. More than a museum piece, this village is a place where artists live, work, and play. Emilio Robba, a famous European designer, is now directing the art studios. You can visit the ateliers and see the talented artisans making pottery, tapestry, and serigraphic art. The artists sell their finished wares at the Art Studios Boutique. The village also has an amber museum, an archaeological museum, a handful of restaurants, and a number of unique shops. Strolling musicians enliven the rustic ambience of ceramic tiles and cobblestone terrace, but there are now more bars and nightclubs geared to Casa de Campo's guests. Big names, including Elton John, perform at the amphitheater. Christmastime is sheer magic, what with the lights, music concerts, giant Christmas tree, and Santa making a cameo appearance. ⊠ *Casa de Campo, La Romana* ⊕ *www. casadecampo.com.do.*

Amphitheater at Altos de Chavón. A 5,000-seat, Grecian-style amphitheater features *Kandela,* a spectacular musical extravaganza showcasing the island's sensuous Afro-Caribbean dance moves, music, and culture (December–April only). The production is continually enhanced by new music and choreography. Concerts and celebrity performances by

9

such singers as Elton John, Julio Iglesias, his son Enrique, Sting, and the Pet Shop Boys share the amphitheater's schedule of events. Show dates vary to coincide with cruise-ship arrivals, usually Sunday and Monday nights. You can combine the show with dinner at one of the village's restaurants. ✉ *Casa de Campo, La Romana* ☎ *809/523–2424 Kandela tickets* ⊕ *www.kandela.com.do* ✍ *$35 for Kandela; other concert prices vary.*

PUNTA CANA

As the sun rises in the Dominican Republic, Punta Cana awakens to the lapping ocean—clear, unspoiled blue brushing up against the pristine stretches of sugar-white sand, with swaying coco palms in the backdrop. A thriving tourism industry fuels the region, and with such plentiful ingredients as sun, sand, and sea, it's no wonder.

The larger area known as Punta Cana encompasses Juanillo (home of the Cap Cana development), Bávaro, and continues all the way around the peninsula to Uvero Alto. Development continues in Galerias Punta-Cana Village, a shopping center that is a draw for visitors from around the area. A Four Points by Sheraton has opened across from the area and is the only "airport" hotel in the region. Five minutes from the village on a gorgeous stretch of beach within the Punta Cana Group's domain is the Westin Punta Cana Resort & Club. Characteristic of this American chain, it is an upscale, non–all inclusive property.

This stretch between Club Med, the Westin, and the Puntacana Resort & Club is one of the most beautiful. Farther up the coast to the Playa El Cortecito section of Bávaro is more how life used to be, with fishermen bringing in their catch, and it is where the wild and crazy restaurant Capitán Cook's is located. Farther north along the coast is a stretch of beach known as Arena Gorda, literally "fat sand," and Playa Bávaro itself. About 20 miles (32 km) from Punta Cana International Airport, it's an area brimming with coconut groves and the location of many resorts. Each has its own strip of sand with rows of chaises longues, and most of these hotels will grant outsiders day passes for a fee. Macao is a pastoral village, but its public beach is no longer a good option, having first been taken over by four-wheeler excursions and now dominated by the huge Hard Rock Hotel & Casino Punta Cana. At the northern end of the peninsula is Uvero Alto.

JUANILLO

FAMILY **Scape Park at Cap Cana.** Like Xcaret near Cancún, this complex in Cap Cana combines beautiful natural scenery with plenty of fun activities for a full day; it can only be visited as part of a daylong tour. The Hoyo Azul combines a tour of the bush with a refreshing swim in a natural cave pool. Another option is the Cenote Indigena Las Ondes, which ends in a swim in a natural sinkhole. The park also has a zip line, a mountain bike trail, horseback riding, and a cruise; zip-line ecoadventure; mountain bike ecotrail; Scape Ranch for horseback riding; and the Sunshine Cruise (a booze and snorkeling cruise). Packages can be as short as a half day or as long as a full day, and you have your pick of tours and fun. Lunch, which is a good barbecue meal, can be added but can be a bit busy. Nevertheless, everything is well organized and fun. ■TIP➔ **For the best prices, book through the Park, and you'll be picked up from your Punta Cana, Bávaro, or Uvero Alto resort.** ✉ *Cap Cana, Santo Domingo* ☎ *809/469–7484* ⊕ *www.scapepark.com* ✈ *From $109* ⊙ *Daily 9–6.*

MACAO
20 miles (32 km) north of Punta Cana.

Macao is a pastoral village amid farms and ranches. Its striking beach, with dramatic headlands, inspired one of the most ambitious resort development projects on the East Coast. The giant Hard Rock Hotel & Casino (the company's first all-inclusive property) dominates the area.

UVERO ALTO
7 miles (12 km) north of Macao, 24 miles (39 km) north of Punta Cana.

Ranches and rustic living characterize this beach village, which has coconut groves and a stunning beach where development continues to press north of Macao. It's home to several high-end all-inclusive resorts.

NORTH COAST

The Autopista Duarte ultimately leads (via a three- to four-hour drive) from Santo Domingo to the North Coast, sometimes called the Amber Coast because of its large, rich amber deposits. The coastal area around Puerto Plata, notably Playa Dorada, is a region of well-established, all-inclusive resorts and developments; the North Coast has more than 70 miles (110 km) of beaches, with condominiums and villas going up fast.

The farther east you go from Puerto Plata and Sosúa, the prettier and less spoiled the scenery becomes. The autopista runs past Cabarete, a town that's a popular windsurfing haunt, and Playa Grande, which has a miraculously unspoiled white-sand beach with a new Aman resort, which opened in December 2015 and accompanies the famous Playa Grande Golf Course, open only to Aman guests and members of the golf club. Surrounded by high cliffs, this incredibly beautiful Playa Grande beach once had food shacks and cheapie souvenir stands that marred its beauty. Vendors now have brightly painted, Victorian-style huts that have been relocated to the end of the beach. There is now a proper parking area, and vehicles can no longer drive on the beach. The Playa Grande Beach Club has a new collection of high-end bungalows available for rent.

PUERTO PLATA
Although it has been sleeping for decades, this was a dynamic city in its heyday. You can get a feeling for this past in the magnificent Victorian gazebo in the central **Parque Independencia.** Painted a crisp white, the park looks postcard pretty, with gleaming statuary. On the Malecón, which had had a multimillion-dollar refurbishment, the **Fortaleza de San Felipe** protected the city from many a pirate attack and was later used as a political prison. Nearby, a new amphitheater is in the planning stages. The nearby **lighthouse** has been restored. Much is happening in Puerto Plata and its original hotel zone, Playa Dorada. New nonstop flights are contributing to the area's revival.

9

The Office of Cultural Patrimony is working with private business owners and investors on a long-term plan to beautify the city, which has hundreds of classic wooden gingerbread buildings. Mansions, including Casa Olivores and the Tapounet family home, are being restored; at the same time new resorts are under development both on and off Playa Dorada's beautiful beachfront.

At Puerto Plata's Port, the new 30-acre, Amber Cove Cruise Center enjoyed its inaugural season in 2016 as the first cruise ships docked here since the 1980s. The $65-million project, which includes restaurants, bars, retail shops, and an elaborate pool complex with waterslides, will welcome several ships a week.

Casa Museo General Gregorio Luperón. A long time in the making, this modest, wood-frame house is where Puerto Plata's famous son, General Gregorio Luperón, spent his last years. Known for his courage and patriotic love of his homeland, he led the Dominican revolution against Spain, ending the island's foreign occupation in 1865. The museum's mission is to expose the life and ideals of this national hero to visitors both foreign and domestic. It has been accomplished with quality cultural displays depicting the various stages of Luperón's life, enhanced with signage in both Spanish and English. The home is both a slice of 19th-century life and an emblem of the city's rich history. ⊠ *12 de Julio No. 54, Puerto Plata* ☎ *809/261–8661, 809/261–9028* ⊠ *$5* ⊗ *Tues.–Sun. 9–5.*

Mt. Isabel de Torres. Southwest of Puerto Plata, this mountain soars 2,600 feet above sea level and is notable for its huge statue of Christ. Up there also are botanical gardens that, despite efforts, still are not memorable. If you go independently, you can choose to hire a knowledgeable English-speaking guide. A cable car takes you to the top for a spectacular view. The cars usually wait until filled to capacity before going up—which can make them crowded. You should visit in the morning, preferably by 9 am; by afternoon, the cloud cover rolls in, and you can see practically nothing. That said, some visitors consider this the highlight of a city tour and take dozens of aerial photos from the tram. It goes continuously until 4:45 pm. ■TIP→ **The vendors are particularly tenacious here.** ⊠ *Manolo Tavarez Justo, off Autopista Duarte, follow signs, Puerto Plata* ☎ *809/970–0501* ⊕ *telefericopuertoplata.com* ⊠ *Cable car RD$350* ⊗ *Mon.–Sun. 8:30–5.*

Museo de Ambar Dominicano (*Dominican Amber Museum*). In an opulent, galleried mansion, restored to its former Victorian glamour, the museum displays and sells the Dominican Republic's national stone: semiprecious, translucent amber. Amber is essentially prehistoric hardened tree sap, and Dominican amber is considered the best in the world. Many pieces are fascinating for what they have trapped inside, and the small, second-floor museum contains a piece with a lizard reported to be 50 million years old, give or take a few millennia. The museum's English text is informative. Shops on the museum's first floor sell authentic, albeit rather expensive, amber, souvenirs, and ceramics. ⊠ *Calle Duarte 61, Puerto Plata* ☎ *809/586–2848 museum, 809/320–2215 gift shop* ⊕ *www.ambermuseum.com* ⊠ *RD$50* ⊗ *Mon.–Sat. 9–6 multilingual guided tours.*

FAMILY **Ocean World Adventure Park.** This multimillion-dollar aquatic park in Cofresí has marine and wildlife interactive programs, including dolphin and sea lion shows and encounters, a double-dolphin swim, a tropical reef aquarium, stingrays, shark tanks, an aviary, a rain forest, and a new pirates pool for kids. You must make advance reservations if you want to participate in one of the swims or encounters; children must be at least six and accompanied by an adult. The exhilarating (though expensive) double-dolphin swim will produce lifelong memories. If you are brave enough for the (nurse) shark encounter, you will feed them and touch them in the shark cove; the stingray encounter is also included. A photo lab and video service can capture the moment, but there is a charge. If you're staying at nearby Lifestyle resorts, or hotels in Puerto Plata, transfers are free. If in Sosúa or Cabarete, transfers are $5 per person; hotels should have the tour schedules. ■ TIP➜ There's a private beach, showers, and a locker room on-site. ✉ *Calle Principal 3, 3 miles (5 km) west of Puerto Plata, Cofresi* ☎ *809/291–1000* ⊕ *www. oceanworld.net* 🎟 *From $69* ☉ *Mon.–Sun. 9–6.*

PLAYA DORADA
5 miles (8 km) east of Puerto Plata

One of the Dominican Republic's longest established resort areas, Playa Dorada has benefited both from good reefs, which are right off-shore, and a major beach restoration project. Large condo complexes and resorts line the beach, each with its own private slice of beachfront. The Atlantic waters here are great for windsurfing, waterskiing, and fishing.

SOSÚA
15 miles (24 km) east of Puerto Plata.

This small community was settled during World War II by 600 Austrian and German Jews. After the war many of them returned to Europe or went to the United States, and most who remained married Dominicans. Only a few Jewish families reside in the community today, and there's the original one-room wooden synagogue and Museo Judio Sosua (Jewish Museum). Also, a small park has been built on the waterfront to commemorate the Jewish colony.

Sosúa is called Puerto Plata's little sister, and consists of two communities—El Batey, the more modern hotel development, and Los Charamicos, the old quarter—separated by a cove and one of the island's prettiest beaches. The sand is soft and nearly white, the water crystal clear and calm. The walkway above the beach is packed with tents filled with souvenirs, pizzas, and even clothing for sale. The town had developed a reputation for prostitution, but much is being done to eliminate that and to clean up the more garish elements. Conversely, there are many fine, cultured types here, both Dominican and expats, and the recent opening of a cultural center, Casa del Arte de Sosua, was a major coup for them.

Casa del Arte de Sosúa. The new cultural center of Sosúa, inaugurated with much celebration by Mayor Llana in 2013, continues to "grow up." Open to the public and free of charge, the ground-floor gallery has rotating exhibitions that primarily feature work by Sosúa and Dominican artists, such as Teddy Tejada. Music and dance lessons, from violin to ballet, are offered to local children on the second floor, as are other culturally minded activities, including photography workshops. ☒ *Pedro Clisante, across from the casino, Sosúa* ☎ *Free* ☉ *Weekdays 9–5.*

Museo Judío Sosúa. Sosúa is not a destination known for its sights. However, this museum stands as one of the exceptions, chronicling the immigration and settlement of the Jewish refugees in the 1940s. The adjacent small wooden synagogue is the wedding spot for many Jewish couples from abroad. Hours can be irregular, but chances are good that someone will be at the museum to let you in if you get there early in the day. ■TIP→ You can try phoning Sosúa Villas or the accommodating Hotel Casa Valeria nearby to confirm if the museum is open. ☒ *Calle Dr. Rosen at David Stern, near Banco Popular, Sosúa* ☎ *809/377–2038 Sosúa Villas, 809/477–2038 Sosúa Villas, 809/571–3565 Hotel Casa Valeria* ⊕ *www.sosua-villas.com/jewish-museum* ☒ *RD$75* ☉ *Sun.–Fri. 10–1 (but hrs are irregular).*

CIBAO VALLEY

The heavily trafficked four-lane highway north from Santo Domingo, known as the Autopista Duarte, cuts through the banana plantations, rice and tobacco fields, and royal poinciana trees of the Cibao Valley. Along the road are stands where a few pesos buy pineapples, mangoes, avocados, *chicharrones* (fried pork rinds), and fresh-fruit drinks.

SANTIAGO

The second city of the D.R., where many past presidents were born, sits about 90 miles (145 km) northwest of Santo Domingo and is about an hour's drive from Puerto Plata and 90 minutes from Cabarete via the scenic mountain road. An original route from centuries past, the four-lane highway between Santiago and Puerto Plata is dotted with sugar mills. The Office of Cultural Patrimony is overseeing their restoration. Although an industrial center, Santiago has a surprisingly charming, provincial feel; the women of Santiago are considered among the country's most beautiful. High on a plateau is an impressive monument honoring the restoration of the republic. Traditional yet progressive, Santiago is still relatively new to the tourist scene but already has several thriving restaurants and hotels. It's definitely worth setting aside some time to explore the city. Colonial-style buildings— with wrought-iron details and tiled porticoes—date from as far back as the 1500s. Others are from the Victorian era, with the requisite gingerbread latticework and fanciful colors, and recent construction is nouveau Victorian. Santiago is the D.R.'s cigar-making center; the Fuente factory is here, though its cigars can be bought on the island only in special designated cigar stores and clubs. (If you see them for sale on the streets, they are counterfeit.)

Fodor'sChoice ★ **Centro León.** Without question, this is a world-class cultural center for Dominican arts and culture. A postmodern building full of light from a crystal dome, the center includes several attractions, galleries for special exhibits, a sculpture garden, and an aviary. It has a replica of La Aurora's first cigar factory, too. Tobacco money coupled with the Jimenes family's generosity built this wonder. Many visitors are most

Hand-rolling cigars in the Cibao Valley

enthralled with the permanent collection of photography and Dominican art, but temporary art exhibits can also be a draw. There's a first-rate cafeteria and a museum shop, where you can buy high-quality, artsy souvenirs, books, and jewelry. On Friday night there is a free soiree, with live music or a music video (from Spanish pop to R&B), and the café stays open, serving beer, wine, and light fare. It can be a fine way to meet sophisticated Santiagueros who have a high level of fluency in English. ■ TIP→ It's best to give advance notice if you want a guided tour in English. ✉ *Av. 27 de Febrero 146, Villa Progreso, Santiago* ☎ *809/582–2315* ⊕ *www.centroleon.org.do* ✉ *RD$150, guides in English from RD$300; audio guide in English RD$100* ☾ *Exhibitions Tues.–Sun. 10–7.*

SAMANÁ PENINSULA

Samaná (pronounced sah-mah-NAH) is a dramatically beautiful peninsula, like an island unto itself, of coconut trees stretching into the sea. It's something of a microcosm of the Dominican Republic: here you'll see poverty and fancy resorts, brand-new highways as well as bad roads, verdant mountainsides, tropical forests, tiny villages lined with street-side fruit vendors, secluded beaches, and the radiant warmth of the Dominican people. Samaná is the name of both the peninsula and its biggest town, as well as the bay to the south. It's worth noting that to locals, Samaná denotes only the largest town, Santa Bárbara de Samaná, which makes a great departure point for whale-watching or an excursion to Los Haitises Park across the bay. The bay is home to some of the world's best whale-watching from mid-January to late

March. It is now the site of Puerto Bahía Marina & Residences and the Bannister Hotel, contemporary, luxurious, yet moderately priced. This complex has brought an entirely new level of tourism to this area, and given yachts a full-service facility in what has always been a desirable cruising destination. A visit here is really about two things: exploring the preserved natural wonders and relaxing at a beachfront hotel. The latter is most readily accomplished in **Las Terrenas,** the peninsula's original tourist center, where you can find beachfront restaurants, accommodations of all types (from small hotels to full-service resorts to luxury condos), and great beaches. At Las Terrenas you can enjoy peaceful playas, take advantage of the vibrant nightlife, and make all your plans for expeditions on the peninsula. The other pleasures are solitary—quiet beaches, the massive national park Los Haitises, and water sports and hiking. A relatively new toll road connects Santo Domingo to the peninsula; it's now less than a two-hour drive. Small El Catey International Airport is near Las Terrenas and is now being served by twice-weekly JetBlue flights.

SANTA BÁRBARA DE SAMANÁ
22 miles (35 km) southeast of Las Terrenas.

The official name of the city is Santa Bárbara de Samaná; but these days it's just called "Samaná." An authentic port town, it's getting its bearings as a tourist zone, and still is not a magnet like Las Galeras and Las Terrenas. It has a typical *malecón* (seaside promenade) that's ideal for strolling and watching the boats in the harbor. Lookout "towers" have been built; ascend the stairs and see the whales in season or just look out to the horizon. Strong night lighting has been added, too, so you will see Dominicans and tourists alike taking walks after dinner. A small but bustling town, Samaná is filled with friendly residents, skilled local craftsmen selling their wares, and a handful of outdoor, sea-view, and courtyard restaurants.

A big all-inclusive resort, the Bahía Príncipe Cayacoa, is on one end of the bay road up on a hill. Day passes are available (and the resort has the only beach in town). The hotel also operates a block of colorful gift shops and a small casino. This group was the town's first attempt to capture cruise-ship-passenger money. It's the string of buildings called Pueblo Príncipe, which replicates small Victorian buildings painted in Caribbean colors and trimmed in white gingerbread. Along Avenida del Malecón, across from the waterside, is the office of Whale Samaná, ground zero for boat excursions shoving off to see whales from January until late March.

Fodor'sChoice   **Los Haitises National Park.** A highlight of any visit to the Samaná Penin-
★   sula is Los Haitises National Park (pronounced High-tee-sis), which is across Samaná Bay. The park is famous for its karst limestone formations, caves, and grottoes filled with pictographs and petroglyphs left by the indigenous Taínos. The park is accessible only by boat, and a professionally guided kayaking tour is highly recommended (a licensed guide from a tour company or the government is mandatory for any visitor). You'll paddle around dozens of dramatic rock islands and spectacular cliff faces, while beautiful coastal birds—magnificent frigate

birds, brown pelicans, brown booby, egrets, and herons—swirl around overhead. A good tour will also include the caverns, where your flashlight will illuminate Taíno petroglyphs. It's a continual sensory experience, and you'll feel tiny, like a human speck surrounded by geological grandeur. DominicanShuttles (⊕ *DominicanShuttles.com*) can arrange a park tour and a stay at the adjacent, and rustic Paraiso Caño Hondo Ecolodge, which has authentic creole cuisine and multiple waterfalls. ⊠ *Samaná Bay, Samaná* ☎ *809/472–4204* ⌂ *$4, not including mandatory use of licensed guide* ⊗ *Daily dawn–dusk.*

BEACHES

SOUTHEAST COAST

BAYAHIBE

Playa Bayahibe. Playa Bayahibe, where several seafood restaurants are situated, is somewhat thin, with hard-packed taupe sand and no lounge chairs. However, as you move away from the village, a 10-minute walk along the shoreline, you'll reach the glorious, half-moon cove where you'll find the Dreams resort. Although you'll be able to get to the cove and the soft sand, bring a towel (the resort's security won't let you use the facilities). At night, when no one is on the playa and the silver moon illuminates the phosphorescence, it's the stuff that Caribbean dreams are made of. **Amenities:** food and drink; toilets. **Best for:** partiers; sunset; swimming; walking; windsurfing. ⊠ *Starts in the center of town, near the Dreams resort, Bayahibe.*

PUNTA CANA

PUNTA CANA

Playa Punta Cana. This long stretch of sandy coastline on the Caribbean side of the peninsula is where tourism first began in Punta Cana. This undulating beach with powdery white sand is shaded by lilting coconut palms. Much of it still looks like virgin beach, since there is not the proliferation of all-inclusive hotels you find farther north in Bávaro. The beach extends south to Playa Juanillo, which is similarly incredible and now the site of the Cap Cana development. The waters are generally calm, with more wave action in the winter and during hurricane season. Seaweed has become more of a problem in recent years, and resorts have crews that gather it and rake their stretch of sand. Coral rock can make areas difficult to walk in the water, which is often shallow close to shore; however, the reefs are super for snorkeling and one can walk or swim from shore. The Westin Punta Cana has fresh contemporary food offerings at their beachside restaurant, Playa Blanca, a delightful seafood restaurant adjacent to the Kite-Club and Club Med. **Amenities:** food and drink; toilets; water sports. **Best for:** kitesurfing; snorkeling; swimming; walking; windsurfing. ⊠ *Playa Punta Cana, Punta Cana.*

9

BÁVARO

Playa Bávaro. Bávaro is the most developed stretch of the 35 miles (56 km) of white-sand beach in the Punta Cana area, which is lined with both midsized and mega-sized all-inclusive resorts. Although it encompasses many smaller towns, the main area, which is past Cabeza de Toro, is thought to begin with the massive Barcelo Bávaro Beach Resort and extend to the funky, fun fishermen's beach, Playa El Cortecito, known for the landmark restaurant Capitán Cook's. The water is characteristically warm and fairly shallow, with seaweed kept in check by hotels. Each resort has its own designated area with its chaise longues lined up in neat rows. Although there are stretches that are idyllically quiet, for the most part it is nonstop action. Boats and water sports provide the entertainment, wandering beach vendors the aggravation. In several areas there are designated, makeshift markets. **Amenities:** food and drink; toilets; water sports. **Best for:** walking; swimming; windsurfing. ⊠ *Playa Bávaro, Bávaro.*

NORTH COAST

PLAYA DORADA

Playa Dorada. Playa Dorada is one of the island's most established resort areas. Each hotel has its own slice of the beach, which is covered with soft sand, nearly white now thanks to its participation in a $6 million beach rejuvenation. Reefs for snorkeling are right offshore. Gran Ventana Beach Resort, which is on a point, marks the easternmost end of the beach, followed by Casa Colonial and Blue Bay Villa Doradas. If you're not staying at one of the resorts in the Playa Dorada complex, then it's best to enter the beach before this point. Zealous hotel security guards try to keep you off "their" stretch of beach, but by law they cannot if you walk along the water's edge. They can, however, keep you off the chaise longues and the resort's property. This is a good swimming beach with mild wave action. **Amenities:** none (though resorts on the beach offer full service). **Best for:** fishing; swimming; walking; water skiing; windsurfing. ⊠ *Off Autopista Luperón, at the entrance to the Playa Dorada Complex, approximately 10-min drive east of town, Playa Dorada* ⊕ *www.playadorada.com.do.*

SOSÚA

Playa Sosúa. This long stretch of beach on Sosúa Bay, renowned for its coral reefs and dive sites, is a 20-minute drive east of Puerto Plata. Here, calm waters gently lap at a shore of soft, golden sand. Swimming is delightful—except after a heavy rain, when litter floats in. But beware of sea urchins in the shallow water—beach shoes are definitely recommended—and bring your own mask and snorkel if possible. You can see mountains in the background, the cliffs that surround the bay, and seemingly miles of coastline. Snorkeling from the beach can be good, but the best spots are offshore, closer to the reefs. The beach is backed by a string of tents where hawkers push souvenirs, snacks, drinks, and water-sports equipment rentals. The weekend scene here is incredible— local families pack the beach, and the roar of Dominican fun fills the air. Alas, with the closing of the Sosúa Bay Resort, the tourist presence has diminished. Don't bring valuables or leave your belongings unattended. There is a small parking area on the beach's north end at the south end of La Puntilla Street. **Amenities:** food and drink; parking (free). **Best for:** snorkeling; swimming; walking. ⊠ *Carretera Puerto Plata–Sosúa, El Batey.*

CABARETE

Playa Cabarete. This is the main business district of Cabarete. If you follow the coastal road east from Playa Dorada, you can't miss it. The beach, which has strong waves after a calm entrance, and ideal, steady wind (from 15 to 20 knots), is an integral part of the international windsurfing circuit. Segments of this long beach are strips of sand punctuated only by palm trees. The regeneration of Cabarete Beach was a massive engineering project that made the beach some 115 feet wider, adding an infusion of white sand. In the most commercial area, restaurants and bars are back-to-back, spilling onto the sand. The informal scene is young and fun, with expats and tourists from everywhere. **Amenities:** food and drink; lifeguards; toilets; water sports. **Best for:** partiers; surfing; swimming; windsurfing; kitesurfing. ⊠ *Sosúa–Cabarete Rd., Cabarete.*

CABRERA

Fodor's Choice **Playa Grande.** This dramatic, mile-long stretch is widely considered to
★ be one of the top beaches in the world. Many a photo shoot was made at this picture-perfect beach with off-white sands and turquoise water. Just east of the famous golf course of the same name, Playa Grande's drama comes from craggy cliffs dropping into the crystalline sea. Shade can be found in the palm trees that thicken into Parque Nacional Cabo Frances Viejo, a jungle preserve south of the beach.

This simply gorgeous stretch of sand had food shacks and cheapie souvenir stands that marred its beauty, but the vendors now have brightly painted, cutesy, Victorian-style huts that have been relocated to the end of the beach where a large parking area was constructed, and some sell food and drink. Security is present, and there are clean restrooms. Surfboards, paddleboards, and boogie boards are for rent; although the surf can swell, it can also be smooth. Just behind the beach, screened by a palm-frond fence, is the Playa Grande Beach Club, a luxury resort, and nearby is another, the new Amanera. **Amenitites:** food and drink; toilets. **Best for:** surfing; swimming; walking. ⊠ *Carretera Río San Juan–Cabrera, Km 12, Río San Juan* ⊕ *www.playagrande.com* ⊠ *Free* 🏌 *Playa Grande Golf & Reserve.*

SAMANÁ PENINSULA

On the north coast of the Samaná Peninsula, tall palms list toward the sea, and the beaches are extensive and postcard perfect, with crystalline waters and soft, golden sand. There's plenty of color—vivid blues, greens, and yellows—as well as colorful characters. To the west is Playa El Cosón, opposite Cayo Ballena, a great whale-watching spot (from January to April). Samaná has some of the country's best beaches and drop-dead scenery, the rough roads notwithstanding.

LAS TERRENAS

Fodor'sChoice   **Playa Cosón.** This is a long, wonderful stretch of nearly white sand and
★   the best beach close to the town of Las Terrenas. Previously undeveloped, it's now reachable by a new highway, Carretera Cosón, and there
are a number of condo developments under construction (so the current sense of solitude probably won't last). One excellent restaurant,
The Beach, serves the entire 15-mile (24-km) shore, and there's the
European-owned boutique hotel Casa Cosón and its restaurant and
bar. If beachgoers buy lunch and/or drinks at either, then they can use
the restrooms. **Amenities:** food and drink; parking; toilets. **Best for:**
swimming; sunset; walking; windsurfing. ⊠ *Las Terrenas.*

WHERE TO EAT

The island's culinary repertoire includes Spanish, Italian, Middle Eastern, Indian, Japanese, and *nueva cocina Dominicana* (contemporary
Dominican cuisine). If Caribbean seafood is on the menu, it's bound to
be fresh. The dining scene in Santo Domingo is the best in the country
and probably offers as fine a selection of restaurants as you will find in
most Caribbean destinations. Keep in mind that the touristy restaurants,
such as those in the Zona Colonial, with mediocre fare and just-okay
service, are becoming more and more costly, while the few fine-dining
options here have lowered some of their prices. For example, La Residence now offers a daily prix-fixe chef's menu with three courses. Or
you can order two generous appetizers for even less. You will have caring service and be sequestered in luxe surroundings away from the tourist hustle. Know that *capitaleños* (residents of Santo Domingo) dress for
dinner and dine late. The crowds pick up after 9:30 pm.

What to Wear: In resort areas, shorts and bathing suits under beach
wraps are usually (but not always) acceptable at breakfast and lunch.
For dinner, long pants, skirts, and collared shirts are the norm. Restaurants tend to be more formal in Santo Domingo, both at lunch and
at dinner, with trousers (vs. shorts), required for men and dresses, or
casual, chic attire suggested for women. Ties aren't required anywhere
and now jackets are seldom mandatory in even the finer establishments.

SANTO DOMINGO

ZONA COLONIAL

$$$ ✕**La Residence.** This fine-dining enclave has an unparalleled setting—
FRENCH   Spanish-colonial architecture, with pillars and archways overlooking
a courtyard—and remains a haven from the hustle of the tourist trips
even as it no longer hits the same high points it once did. Alas, the
veteran French chef has left, though the French menu remains. A three-
course prix-fixe is reasonably priced and available for both lunch and
dinner; the best days are still Wednesday and Friday nights. À la carte
prices will make the bill higher, but they are still reasonable, though
portions are not large. A guitarist romantically serenades diners Friday
through Sunday nights. The breakfast buffet continues to be superlative.
Ⓢ *Average main: $24* ⊠ *Hostal Nicolas de Ovando, Calle Las Damas,*

Zona Colonial ✣ Across from the French embassy ☎ 809/685–9955 🌐 www.hostal-nicolas-de-ovando-santo-domingo.com ✍ Reservations essential.

ON THE MENU

Among the best Dominican specialties are *queso frito* (fried cheese), *sancocho* (a thick stew of meats and chicken, served with rice and avocado slices), *arroz con pollo* (rice with beans and chicken), *pescado al coco* (fish in coconut sauce), *plátanos* (plantains), and *tostones* (fried green plantains). Presidente is the best local beer. Brugal rum is popular with the Dominicans, but Barceló *añejo* (aged) rum is as smooth as cognac, and Barceló Imperial is so special that it was sold only around Christmastime. But now, due to demand, it is on the shelves all year-round.

$$ FUSION Fodor's Choice ★ 🍴 **Lulu Tasting Bar.** This modern tapas bar is housed in a centuries-old edifice with an enchanting brick courtyard adorned with greenery. Skilled mixologists craft everything from spot-on margaritas and mojitos to more exotic concoctions. The evolving menu consists of well-presented, global appetizers, typically rich and filling, created by a most imaginative Italian chef. The tapas concept allows you to graze as you wish, but if you are looking for a bargain, come on Tuesday night, when it's all you can eat for a very reasonable set price. Nearly every night is a scene with live jazz, DJ sessions, or wine tasting at the wineshop next door. The multigenerational crowd spills out onto the terrace till the wee small hours. *[$] Average main: $18 ✉ Plazoleta Padre Billini, Calle Padre Billini 151, Zona Colonial ✣ Across from La Briciola ☎ 809/687–8360 🌐 www.lulu.do ⏲ No lunch.*

$$ CARIBBEAN 🍴 **Mesón D' Bari.** For some 30 years, this popular restaurant, where baseball is inevitably on the TV at the bar, has been feeding the local Zoners what their grandmothers used to make. This simple Dominican restaurant is still a hangout for artists, baseball players, politicians, businessmen, tourists, and even unaccompanied gringas, who feel comfortable here. Really flavorful dishes include creole-style eggplant, empanadas of crab and conch, grilled crabs and chivo (goat), with stewed, sweet orange peels to finish. Prices are up even though the culinary ambition is not. You'll hear bachata and American music from decades past (think "Moonglow"). If you want a quieter atmosphere, go upstairs. *[$] Average main: $16 ✉ Calle Hostos 302, corner of Salomé Ureña, Zona Colonial ☎ 809/687–4091.*

$$ INTERNATIONAL FAMILY 🍴 **MIX.** Mix, match, and *compartir* (share) is the thought behind this trendy restaurant in an apartment tower that is still packing in the well-heeled capitaleños. It's a place best enjoyed with a group with a fun atmosphere, though you might want your very own tamarind-grilled chicken salad. Italian-Dominican influences often prevail in the main courses; vegetarians will be pleased to know they have options, too. The cultivated wine list offers many fine Italian and Spanish bottles and there's a signature sangria. To finish, go grappa. Family-friendly, with a convivial bar and a late-night scene, this is a crowd-pleaser and always packed. **■ TIP→ Check out the new casual sister restaurant, Market.**

9

$ *Average main: $18* ⊠ *Torre Washington, Gustavo Mejia Ricart 69, Local 102, Ensanche Serralles* ☎ *809/472–0100* ⊕ *www.mix.com.do.*

$$
FRENCH
✕ **Paco Cabana Bistro.** If you are craving classic French cuisine, you'll find it here, in generous portions, and with few contemporary flourishes. The charismatic French owner and his capable maître d' are both exceptionally knowledgeable about the cuisine and wine, adding to the authenticity of this neighborhood bistro. In a quiet corner is the retail wineshop, and you can choose a French vintage here and pay just a 400 peso corkage fee. Classic desserts like crème brûlée and tarte tatin are a small addition. French music plays, and live jazz is often scheduled. Mature and wealthy Piantini residents fill the room and the outdoor terrace on Edith Piaf and Beaujolais nouveau nights. You may not have a life-changing meal here, but if you have fond memories of France, it will be a very pleasant walk down that lane. $ *Average main: $18* ⊠ *Federico Geraldino 14, corner Paseo Roberto, Ensanche Piantini* ☎ *809/565–3569.*

$$$
INTERNATIONAL
✕ **Pat'e Palo European Brasserie.** Ideally located on Plaza de España across from the Alcazar de Colón, this restaurant has good claim to being the first tavern in the New World (the building itself is 500 years old) and capitalizes on its historic heritage. The alfresco dining terrace makes it perfect for watching the free cultural performances that happen across from the plaza. The innovative chef prepares a contemporary, gastro-fusion menu, offering tasting menus and cuisine-related events. Although the waiters are still dressed like pirates (with bandanas askew), the restaurant's culinary profile has only grown. The wine carte is impressive but pricey, and you can enjoy an after-dinner cigar from the humidor if you're so inclined. $ *Average main: $26* ⊠ *Calle Atarazana 25, Plaza de Espana, Zona Colonial* ☎ *809/687–8089* ⊕ *www.patepalo.com.*

PIANTINI

$$
ECLECTIC
✕ **La Dolcerie Café Bistro.** This cutesy, kid-friendly restaurant/bakery looks like a French café where chic ladies do lunch. It's buzzing for all three meals (it's the "in" brunch place for residents of this fashionable Piantini neighborhood). Happily, it's still moderately priced, even for apps the size of mains, and generous dishes such as one of the croque madames (perhaps with pulled pork added) or eggs Benedict. At breakfast, they squeeze your juice and tempt you with house-made croissants and beignets. For lunch there's grilled sausages and such sides as homemade waffle-cut fries in silver baskets. Dinner includes delicious *mofongquitos* (plantain cups filled with veal osso bucco). Signature desserts are luscious. If only the service was so good. Try to snag a seat on the less noisy terrace. $ *Average main: $17* ⊠ *Rafael Augusto Sanchez 20, Ensanche Piantini* ☎ *809/338–0814.*

$$$
ECLECTIC
Fodor's Choice
★
✕ **Sophia's Bar & Grill.** This formerly old-fashioned and elegant restaurant has morphed into something much more contemporary, but still retained many of its old-world touches. But the kitchen is now open and the music is loud; you'll also find a sushi bar to complement the grill menu offering both fish and foie gras. The young, passionate chef wants each bite to be a sensory explosion, and so it is. Prices are surprisingly reasonable for such a classy environment—there are even gourmet

burgers. End your meal with a slice of warm guava cheesecake and an aged port. If you want to smoke, you'll have to take a seat on the outdoor terrace. You can join the young and beautiful at the granite bar until 3 am on Friday and Saturday (1 am the rest of the week). Signature cocktails are as attractive as they are heady. ■ TIP➔ **Look for a sign that says simply "SBG".** $ *Average main: $25* ⊠ *Paseo de los Locutores 9, Ensanche Piantini* ☎ *809/620–1001* ⊕ *www.sbg.com.do.*

SOUTHEAST COAST

LA ROMANA

$$$ ✕ **Peperoni.** Although the name may sound as Italian as *amore,* this
ECLECTIC restaurant's menu is more eclectic than Italian. It has a classy, contemporary, white-dominated decor in a dreamy, marina setting. Strolling musicians perpetuate the mood, the moored yachts provide people-watching. Astounding appetizers are found under the Asian section, like the sweet plantain roll or the Peperoni roll. Pasta dishes and risottos with rock shrimp or porcini taste authentic, and the more inventive items such as house-made pear-and-goat-cheese ravioli with pine nuts are delectable. *Pulpo* (octopus) with fava beans stewed in limoncello vinaigrette is highly recommended. You can also opt for stylishly simple charcoal-grilled steaks (sauce or no), burgers, gourmet wood-oven pizzas, sandwiches, or even sushi and sashimi. Desserts are worthy here. There have been some complaints that food quality is not what it once was. $ *Average main: $21* ⊠ *Casa de Campo, Plaza Portafino 16, Casa de Campo Marina, La Romana* ☎ *809/523–2227, 809/523–3333.*

PUNTA CANA

JUANILLO

$$$ ✕ **Blue Marlin.** The fresh catch of the day is always the best choice at
SEAFOOD this restaurant on a palapa-shaded pier overlooking the gentle Caribbean. As a new chef has taken over, more Dominican specialties are offered, and the plate presentation has become relatively simple. The menu offers everything from mixed seafood ceviche to Caribbean lobster cakes to burgers, but the wonderfully flavorful soups like pumpkin and sancocho, or even a classic gazpacho, are also worthwhile. Service is caring and attentive. A blue-tiled fireplace at the bar adds an unexpected, decorative element; it's a great place to chill with an authentic piña colada. Nonhotel guests are welcome but now must purchase a day or night pass, which also includes use of the other resort facilities. ■ TIP➔ **Lobster and other high-ticket seafood items do come with a supplement if you have the Sanctuary Cap Cana AI plan.** $ *Average main: $24* ⊠ *Sanctuary Cap Cana, Blvd. Zona Hotelera, Juanillo* ☎ *809/562–9191* ⊕ *www.sanctuarycapcana.com* ⌘ *Reservations essential.*

$$$ ✕ **Il Cappuccino.** Enchanting views of the Cap Cana Marina enhance
MEDITERRANEAN your meal at this Mediterranean-style eatery with an alfresco deck well suited for a romantic waterfront dinner or lively conversation with friends. When it opened years ago it was *the* place to be, but it then went into a downhill spiral. Happily, Il Cappuccino is on the way up

9

again, with far more compliments than complaints. Wine aplenty (with knowledgeable guidance from the maître d') can accompany the savory, hearty plates of house-made pasta (like the delectable black fettuccine with lobster and shrimp) or meat and seafood entrées. What really gets raves is the pizza. Coffees and desserts, like the authentic tiramisu, emanate from the adjacent café. Convenient hours mean the restaurant is open daily from breakfast until dinner. $ *Average main: $27* ✉ *Marina Cap Cana, Juanillo* ☎ *809/469–7095* ⚠ *Reservations essential.*

$$$
CONTEMPORARY

✕ **La Mona.** This beach restaurant is much better than the typical beachside spot, drawing both visitors and locals with a savvy menu and laidback, fun vibe. It's popular by both day and night, with a charming host and a master chef at the helm. Sushi is a healthful, refreshing choice on a hot day, but there are also delicious Mexican dishes. Peruvian-style ceviche is a great starter, perhaps as a prelude to Kobe beef or delicious grilled lobster. If you want to attend Sunday's bubbly brunch, when a jazz band adds sizzle to the special menu, make a reservation. $ *Average main: $23* ✉ *Playa Juanillo, Blvd. Zona Hotelera, Cap Cana, adjacent to the Fortress at Sanctuary Cap Cana By ALSOL, Juanillo* ☎ *809/469–7191.*

$$$
SEAFOOD

✕ **La Palapa by Eden Roc.** If you crave waterfront dining, this palapa-roof restaurant is a great option, exuding Caribbean charisma with an Italian accent. The aromas promise exceptional seafood specialties, even hard finds like baby octopus, which is deftly prepared. The quality of the ingredients is immediately apparent from the delectable gnocchi to the authentic Parmigiano Reggiano that can be found in many dishes and the wines by the glass from the international list. New are some Dominican specialities, including mofongo. The manager and waiters are professionals, yet the atmosphere remains as casual as the *pareos* on the beachgoers who drop in for lunch. $ *Average main: $24* ✉ *Eden Roc Beach Club, Cap Cana, Juanillo* ☎ *809/469–7593, 809/695–5555* ⊕ *www.edenroccapcana.com.*

PUNTA CANA

$$
SEAFOOD
Fodor's Choice
★

✕ **Playa Blanca.** On a white-sand beach shaded by coco palms, this understatedly cool seafood restaurant is efficient, friendly, and fun. Start with a perfectly executed cocktail—like a lime or mango daiquiri—then dig into the savvy menu, where fresh fish is a staple and are shrimp done three ways. The prices are an excellent value for the amount of creativity and skill, which seems to increase each season. Refreshing salads and cooked appetizers never disappoint. And there are paellas, pasta, risotto, ravioli, and grilled lobster and meat. Sides are usually extra but worth it. The best dessert is the coffee rum trifle. Live music weekly is just one aspect of the beachfront entertainment; another is watching the kitesurfers—poetry in motion—just next door. $ *Average main: $20* ✉ *Puntacana Resort & Club, Playa Blanca, Punta Cana* ☎ *809/959–2262* ⊕ *www.puntacana.com.*

BÁVARO

$$$
MEDITERRANEAN

✕ **Pearl Beach Club.** This contemporary, eye-popping newbie may be the epitome of beach bars, offering Mediterranean-Caribbean fusion cuisine as well as upscale burgers. It's trendy both day and night. The open-air restaurant is joined with three handsome wood bars and savvy management, making it a destination worth paying for. Tropical cocktails with fresh ingredients are worthy of center stage. And when you're sated, there are Balinese sunbeds surrounding an infinity pool, Jacuzzis, and even basic hammocks. Kayaks and stand-up paddleboards are available on the beach if you want some activity after your siesta. There are daytime parties with DJs from Wednesday to Sunday. [$] *Average main: $22* ✉ *Cabeza de Toro, Bávaro* ✥ *Adjacent to the Catalonia Bávaro Beach Casino & Golf Resort* ☎ *809/933–3171* 🌐 *www.pearlbeachclub.com.*

MACAO

$$$
CONTEMPORARY
Fodor's Choice ★

🍴 **Simon Mansion Restaurant.** This contemporary fusion restaurant, which was developed by the late chef Kerry Simon, is the only full-service restaurant at the Hard Rock open to outside guests. Cleverly designed as the mansion of a mythical rock star, the various dining rooms are lavishly furnished as if they were rooms in his house. Your dining experience will be a sensory rush from the innovative rum cocktails to Peruvian ceviche or main courses like rack of lamb. For lighter fare, you can sit in the bar (or rather the library) and order from the menu of small plates to share. All meat served is natural, the steaks dry-aged, and the produce organic, so feel no guilt when you order one of the luscious desserts. Follow the wine and other suggestions of the savvy manager, and prepare to be pampered. [$] *Average main: $29* ✉ *Hard Rock Hotel & Casino Punta Cana, Blvd. Turistico del Este 74, Km 28, Macao* ☎ *809/731–0094 restaurant, 809/687–0000 hotel* 🌐 *www.hardrockhotels.com* ⌚ *No lunch.*

UVERO ALTO

$$$$
FUSION
Fodor's Choice ★

🍴 **C/X Culinary Experience.** Reservations at this intimate, 12-seat restaurant within the new Chic Resort in Uvero Alto are highly coveted since it welcomes nonresort guests and is not on the resort's all-inclusive plan. The chef's table offers a nightly six-course tasting menu, including wine pairings and choreographed musical accompaniments. The talented chef prepares all courses in an open show kitchen. The cuisine is food art, the presentation contemporary, the menu ever-evolving and never disclosed beforehand. This meal is well worth the long ride to Uvero Alto. In fact, it may be the best meal you have in the country. [$] *Average main: $120* ✉ *Chic All Exclusive Resorts by Royalton, Los Cambrones, Uvero Alto* ☎ *809/468–0404 (ask for the club concierge)* 🌐 *www.chicpuntacana.com* ⌚ *Closed Sun. or Mon. (days vary)* ✍ *Reservations essential.*

NORTH COAST

The Cabarete area in particular—where all-inclusive resorts don't yet totally dominate the scene—has some fun, original restaurants, but these are often small places, so it's important that you make reservations in advance. Expat residents complain that the prices in this town have moved past the good-value-for-money mark. Also, more and more restaurants are insisting on cash only, be it pesos, dollars, or euros. The area has lovely fine-dining options *listed below*.

PUERTO PLATA

$$$
CARIBBEAN
Fodor's Choice
★

✕ **Lucía.** With a setting as artistic as a gallery—befitting its location within Casa Colonial, a refined boutique hotel—and an ambitious Caribbean-fusion menu, Lucía is successful on all fronts. In a room with orchids galore, crisp white linens, and waiters in white guayabera shirts giving impeccable service, guests love the delicious appetizers, which include perfectly seared foie gras with mango sauce, or seared tuna. Remarkable main courses include rack of lamb and Caribbean lobster. The molten chocolate volcano is a signature dessert. When the digestif cart is rolled over, be daring with a Brunello grappa or the local Brugal Unico rum. $ *Average main: $27* ⊠ *Casa Colonial, Playa Dorada* ☎ *809/320–3232* ⊕ *www.casacolonialhotel.com* ☾ *No lunch.*

$$$
CONTEMPORARY
Fodor's Choice
★

✕ **Mares Restaurant & Pool Lounge.** This residence-cum-restaurant is the home of the D.R.'s most acclaimed chef, Rafael Vasquez. The indoor dining room is a sophisticated white-on-white room, accented with contemporary paintings by Rafael's father (you'll also find an art gallery and museum in the garden). The outdoor seating is arranged between the bar and the swimming pool; the twinkle lights of the former play on the latter, and at night candles make a romantic setting. The chef's Dominican heritage always is represented in his global repertoire. His island version of sushi, for example, is a sweet plantain roll with tempura shrimp. The main courses are more international, including everything from baby lobsters to braised goat. The staff is mature, discreet, and professional. At the end of your meal, simply get a dessert sampler. $ *Average main: $25* ⊠ *Francisco J. Peynado 6A, Puerto Plata* ☎ *809/261–3330, 809/224–1998* ⊕ *www.maresrestaurant.com* ☾ *Closed Mon. No lunch* ⌕ *Reservations essential.*

SOSÚA

$$$
CONTEMPORARY
Fodor's Choice
★

✕ **Aguazul.** A new culinary experience awaits diners at this restaurant perched above Sosúa Bay, with a superlative setting, a classy but casual ambience, and delicious Japanese-Peruvian cuisine. Within the stellar Gansevoort Resort, this love child of Peru and Japan offers contemporized versions of Peruvian comfort food with strong Asian influences, all prepared under the artful direction of a talented chef imported from Peru. The freshest seafood (with Peruvian ingredients) is given center stage; a range of dishes, from Peruvian ceviche to teppanyaki grill specialties, is offered in a chic, white-on-white setting, with indoor and outdoor dining. The resort's other restaurant, Baia Restaurant & Lounge, is also open to the general public—both by reservation only. $ *Average main: $30* ⊠ *Gansevoort Dominican Republic, Playa Imbert, Calle Bruno Phillip 5, El Batey* ☎ *849/816–2434* ⊕ *www. gansevoorthotelgroup.com* ⌕ *Reservations essential.*

$$
EUROPEAN

✕ **B.Y.O.W. Restaurant.** This cozy restaurant's name stands for "Bring Your Own Wine," a concept that has evolved into a popular spot offering a moderately priced, internationally inspired menu. A palm tree snakes its way through the thatched roof that rises above the salmon-colored adobe walls. From the kitchen come such classics as Wiener schnitzel (even fish schnitzel), as well as a good avocado salad. Finish your meal with a creditable tiramisu for dessert. The daily breakfast is also very popular here, notably the yogurt parfaits and frittatas. Guests at the restaurant's host hotel, Casa Valeria, have it for free. $ *Average main: $12* ⊠ *Casa Valeria Boutique Hotel, Calle Dr. Rosen 28, El Batey* ☎ *809/571–3565, 809/949–3845* ⊕ *www.hotelcasavaleria.com* ⊗ *No lunch or dinner Wed.*

CABARETE

$$$
INTERNATIONAL

✕ **The Beach Club at Sea Horse Ranch.** Overlooking a craggy shoreline with unobstructed ocean vistas, this restaurant with a global menu is hitting all the high points, offering both delicious food and a fun atmosphere. The menu runs the gamut from pizza to fragrant Tandoori chicken from deliciously light gnocchi to hearty Ethiopian *zilzil* (a dish of braised beef and peppers). Ingredients are high quality, from the pancetta to the house-made gelato. The music nights are sceney. ■ TIP➔ **Reservations are essential when there's live music, the best time to be there; otherwise just tell the security gate that you are going to the Beach Club.** $ *Average main: $21* ⊠ *Sea Horse Ranch, Carretera Principal Sosua-Cabarete, Cabarete* ☎ *809/571–4995* ⊕ *www.sea-horse-ranch. com* ⊗ *Closed Wed. in low season.*

$$$
MEDITERRANEAN

✕ **Bliss.** The tables at this tranquil Italian restaurant flank a night-lit pool, offering the kind of intimate, romantic setting tailor-made for a wedding proposal. The young Italian owners have embraced slow food, offering delicious antipastos, carpaccios, and tartares to start and excellent house-made pastas, including feather-light gnocchi and tender half-moons in a sage-and-butter sauce. Paired with a vibrant Tuscan red, this is the perfect meal. Perfect panna cotta is the kind of dessert you hope to find. End your evening with a mild grappa or Sambuca. The chic set come to dinner and may leave with a new painting under their arm—an adjacent room is an unexpected gallery. $ *Average main: $21* ⊠ *Callejón de la Loma 1, Cabarete* ✛ *This home is at the entrance of a residential neighborhood off Sosua-Cabareta Hwy. 5. The side street is directly across from the Ocean Dreams complex on the other side of the highway* ☎ *809/571–9721* ⊕ *www.activecabarete.com/bliss* ⊗ *Closed Wed. No lunch.*

$$
ECLECTIC
Fodor's Choice
★

✕ **Eze Beach Bar & Restaurant.** This chic, upscale Italian oasis has evolved from what was a simple beach bar. By day, it's a haven for wallet-watching windsurfers, who come for well-priced burgers and salads. By night, wealthy capitaleño families enjoy the romantic ambience, house-made pastas, seafood, and grilled meats, all prepared with Mediterranean flair. Ingredients, including fresh burrata, are always top quality. A wide variety of events, including jazz nights and theme parties with DJs, is sceney. The restaurant is both family- and dog-friendly by day; there's an extensive children's menu and beach toys to entertain. $ *Average main: $18* ⊠ *Cabarete Beach, Plaza Carib Wind, Cabarete* ✛ *Adjacent to Carib Wind* ☎ *829/601–8892* ⊕ *www.ezerestaurant.com* ▭ *No credit cards.*

$$
ECLECTIC

✕ **Miró's on the Beach.** Miró's is constantly evolving, keeping current with food trends and offering a varied international menu for its savvy, well-traveled clientele. Mediterranean and healthful options dominate, and much effort has been put into the expanded vegan and vegetarian options. Plate presentations are eye-popping. As you might expect, fresh fish is always making its way to the kitchen. Owner Lydia Wazana has

9

Moroccan roots, and the menu has strong Middle Eastern influences. For groups she will make her aromatic tagines and kebabs. It's become a beachside landmark, so take a table on the sand and listen to the gentle jazz. $ *Average main: $18* ⊠ *Cabarete Beach, Cabarete* ☎ 809/853–6848, 809/571–9709 ⊙ *No lunch on some days in low season.*

$$$ ✕ **Natura Restaurant at Natura Cabana Boutique Hotel.** If you're staying at
SEAFOOD this beachfront ecoparadise, you'll likely take most of your meals here; if not, it's worth the trip, not only for the freshest seafood but also for the soothing ambience. The menu changes seasonally but holds tight to some perennial favorites. Most vegetables and herbs are grown in Natura's own organic garden or are procured locally. If you aren't into seafood, Natura offers one of the area's best filet mignons. But don't miss the rich, flavorful soups and vegetarian (and vegan) dishes that round out the menu. The house-made pastas are delectable, and almost everything—including the gluten-free bread, burger buns, pastries, etc.—is made from scratch. Desserts are seasonal, but anything chocolate is a judicious choice. The wines are French, Spanish, and Chilean. Service is warm, caring, and efficient, the international music atmospheric. $ *Average main: $23* ⊠ *Natura Cabana Boutique Hotel, Paseo del Sol 5, Perla Marina, Cabarete* ☎ 809/571–1507 ⊕ *www.naturacabana.com* ⌲ *Reservations essential.*

SANTIAGO

$$ ✕ **Il Pasticcio.** Everyone from college students to cigar kings, presidents
ITALIAN to politicos, photographers to movie stars pack this eccentrically deco-
Fodor's Choice rated culinary landmark. Tourists take photos of the bathrooms, with
★   their ornate mirrors and Romanesque plaster sinks. Chef-owner Paolo's mouthwatering creations are authentic and fresh. Ask about the tasting menu, or try the great antipasto selections; commence with the Pasticcio salad. Even the bread service comes with three sauces (the best is a creamy anchovy). Finish with a shot of limoncello and cheesecake. And if it's too dim to read the menu, just look up—it's also written on the ceiling. The outdoor terrace seating is new, along with a wall of black-and-white photos of former film stars. The value here is remarkable. $ *Average main: $15* ⊠ *Av. El Lano, corner Calle 3, Gurabo al Medio* ☎ 809/806–1277 ⊕ *www.ilpasticciord.com* ⊙ *Closed Mon.*

SAMANÁ PENINSULA

LAS TERRENAS

$$$ ✕ **The Beach.** Some of the best food in Samaná is served up for lunch (and
SEAFOOD lunch only) in a wooden, Victorian-style bungalow with an alfresco ter-
Fodor's Choice race restaurant facing beautiful Playa Cosón—decidedly not the usual
★   beach shack. Hidden past a long stretch of lawn and behind a grove of coconut trees, it's on a 12-mile (19-km) stretch of virgin beach. You'll find the same refined ambience as its big sister, The Peninsula House. The daily menu is concise and changes based on what fresh ingredients, fish, and lobster are available. Lunch here on fine china makes for a cherished travel memory. $ *Average main: $23* ⊠ *Playa Cosón, Antiqua*

carretera de Playa Coson (Old Beach Rd.), Las Terrenas ☎ *809/962–7447* 💳 *No credit cards* 🕒 *Closed Mon. No dinner.*

$$ INTERNATIONAL 🍴 **El Lugar Coctel Bar-Restaurante.** This gastropub is the go-to place for both local expats and tourists with taste. Why the popularity? It's simply this: owner Bruno lends this modest establishment a personality, offering warm welcomes and quality food. The international menu ranges from Thai beef salad to great burgers with authentic Belgian frites. While meats dominate the menu, fish is not neglected, and you won't be disappointed if you go surf instead of turf. The Caribbean rum cocktails that are served up in frosty, metal mugs are creativity personified. The only drawbacks are a lack of water views and sometimes haphazard service, but that doesn't seem to keep anyone from coming back. [$] *Average main: $17* ✉ *Calle 27 de Febrero, Las Terrenas* ✥ *Between Alba Chiara and Pizza Coco* ☎ *849/248–2580, 809/240–5950* 🕒 *Closed Tues.*

$$ FRENCH 🍴 **Paco Cabana.** Smack in the middle of Las Terrenas town but on the quiet beach, this social restaurant has French savoir faire, from its contemporary bar with its stainless shine to the cushy couches and Asian beds. Classical French cuisine is coupled with Caribbean flair. The fish all but swim onto your white geometric plate, and the artistry that comes out of this kitchen is quite contemporary. The catch of the day, local sardines, or wiggly fresh lobster are all good choices. And if you adore profiteroles, this is one of the few places where you will find them. When the bill comes, you'll still be smiling since the prices are pleasing. [$] *Average main: $17* ✉ *Calle Libertad 1, Las Terrenas* ☎ *809/240–5301, 809/602–0406* 🕒 *Closed Mon.*

$$ SEAFOOD 🍴 **Porto.** This jaw-dropping, beachfront beauty is one of the better players in the ever-evolving, European-accented restaurant scene in Las Terrenas. The nautically themed dining room is by the well-known Dominican designer Patricia Reid. Smart servers take pride in providing the kind of service that normally is found only in Santo Domingo's finest restaurants. Though beautiful, the setting is decidedly casual; in between courses, guests who come in their cover-ups can dive into the crystalline waters just past the sea grape trees. The Peruvian-influenced cuisine has roots in Italian cooking, with Asian undertones and focuses primarily on fresh seafood, including delightful Peruvian-style ceviche. The wine cave is impressive as well. There are fire pits and oftentimes live entertainment, usually a jazz trio. Sadly, new management is not keeping standards as high as they once were. ■ **TIP→ In low season the hours are cut back some.** [$] *Average main: $18* ✉ *Xeliter Balcones del Atlántico, Playa Las Terrenas, Las Terrenas* ✥ *Directly across the street from the hotel* ☎ *809/682–0954* 🌐 *www.xeliter.com.*

WHERE TO STAY

The Dominican Republic has the largest hotel inventory (at this writing some 70,000 rooms) in the Caribbean and draws large numbers of stateside visitors. Surfers can still find digs for $25 a night in Cabarete, and the new generation of luxurious all-inclusives in Punta Cana and Uvero Alto is simply incredible.

Santo Domingo properties generally base their tariffs on the European Plan (no meals)—though many include breakfast—and maintain the same room rates year-round. Beach resorts have high winter rates, with prices reduced for the shoulder seasons of late spring and early fall (summer has become another strong season). All-inclusives dominate in Punta Cana. Cabarete was a stronghold of the small inn, but it does have all-inclusives. Villa rentals are gaining in popularity all over the island, particularly in Cabarete and the Cabrera area.

During your stay your patience may be tested at times, particularly at all-inclusives. Even in the busiest tourist areas, the D.R. still has vestiges of a third-world country. The nodding in and out of the electricity is one annoyance, and sometimes the *plantas* (generators) either don't kick in or wheeze and hiss from age. Service lapses and the language barrier can also be frustrating. But when an employee sincerely says, "How can I serve you, missus?" followed by, "It's a pleasure to help you. Have a happy day!" you're pleasantly reminded of the genuine hospitality of the locals. You gotta love it!

SANTO DOMINGO

The seaside capital of the country is in the middle of the island's south coast. In Santo Domingo, most of the better hotels have always been on or near the Malecón, with several small, desirable properties in the trendy Zona Colonial, allowing you to feel part of that magical environment. In recent years, stunning new properties have opened in the business district and in the fashionable neighborhood Piantini. They belong to both European and U.S. hotel chains and leisure travelers (especially on weekends) as well as business travelers are gravitating toward these contemporary, urban "resorts." The capital is also where you'll find some of the country's most sophisticated dining and nightlife, too. However, such an urban vacation is best coupled with a beach stay elsewhere on the island.

ZONA COLONIAL

$

HOTEL

Fodor's Choice

★

Billini Hotel. A wonderful addition to this charmed neighborhood, this boutique hotel, which was created from a collection of buildings that date back to the 1700s, debuted in spring 2014. **Pros:** special promotions and discounts found on the website; blackout drapes, monogrammed linens and towels; location in one of the best neighborhoods in the Colonial Zone. **Cons:** local residents can sometimes overwhelm the pool area; some aspects of the hotel are cramped; rooms are beautiful but strictly modern in design. $ *Rooms from: $250* ⊠ *Calle Padre Billini 258, Santo Domingo* ☎ *809/338–4040* ⊕ *www.billinihotel.com* ⊅ *24 suites* ⦿| *Breakfast.*

$$$

B&B/INN

Fodor's Choice

★

Casas del XVI. This unique hotel concept comprises three former colonial residences that date back to the 16th century (hence the name) that have been restored and modernized by celebrity designer Patricia Reid. **Pros:** designs are magnificent; pampering service; excellent deals help mitigate the high price tag. **Cons:** you must generally call for service; guests don't intermingle much; no in-room phone and hotel's cell phones can be problematic. $ *Rooms from: $399* ⊠ *Calle Padre Billini*

252, corner 19 de Marzo, Zona Colonial ☎ *809/688–4061, 855/849–6396* ⊕ *www.casasdelxvi.com* ⤳ *11 rooms* ⦿ *Breakfast.*

$ 🛏 **Hostal Nicolas de Ovando–MGallery Collection.** This historic boutique
HOTEL   hotel owned by the French Accor group was sculpted from the residence
Fodor'sChoice   of the first governor of the Americas, and it just might be the best thing
★   to happen in the Zone since Diego Columbus's palace was finished in
1517. **Pros:** lavish breakfast buffet; beautifully restored historic section;
a safe haven with tight security. **Cons:** breakfast is no longer included
in rates; some rooms could be larger; the restaurant is no longer the
gastronomic experience it once was. $ *Rooms from: $175* ⊠ *Calle Las
Damas, Zona Colonial* ⊹ *Across the street from the French Embassy*
☎ *809/685–9955, 800/763–4835, 809/682–9612 direct line for reservations* ⊕ *www.mgallery.com/2975* ⤳ *97 rooms* ⦿ *No meals.*

$ 🛏 **Hotel Villa Colonial.** Owner Lionel Biseau turned this circa-1920s town
B&B/INN   house into a lovely boutique hotel, keeping as much of the original structure as possible, including a second-floor veranda and old-timey, patterned
tile floors. **Pros:** stylish breakfast room and bar overlooking the petite
pool; low rates make this an exceptional value; near the tourist area but
on quiet street with rooms facing an inner courtyard. **Cons:** the small street
sign is easy to miss and reads only "Villa Colonial"; not haute luxury;
Wi-Fi can be intermittent—best in first-floor rooms—which are the better
ones. $ *Rooms from: $85* ⊠ *Calle Sanchez 157, between Calles Padre Billini and Arzobispo Noel, Zona Colonial* ☎ *809/221–1049, 809/849–3104
mobile* ⊕ *www.villacolonial.net* ⤳ *11 rooms* ⦿ *Breakfast.*

GAZCUE

$ 🛏 **Catalonia Santo Domingo.** On the Malecón, the former Hilton Santo
HOTEL   Domingo has been reflagged by Catalonia Hotels & Resorts, who plan
to invest in a major renovation to be conducted over the course of
2016. **Pros:** the lobby is both colorful and tasteful; totally soundproof
rooms; the executive-level lounge and corner executive rooms. **Cons:**
little about the property is authentically Dominican; Malecón neighborhood is sketchy by night; unrenovated rooms are tired. $ *Rooms from:
$129* ⊠ *Av. George Washington 500, Gazcue* ☎ *809/685–0000* ⊕ *www.
hoteles-catalonia.es* ⤳ *260 rooms* ⦿ *No meals.*

$ 🛏 **Crowne Plaza Santo Domingo.** Leisure-minded guests may find little reason to leave this stylish 15-story hotel, especially with the second-story
HOTEL   outdoor pool and Jacuzzi that overlook the Caribbean. **Pros:** excellent
service throughout, particularly at the front desk; on-site convenience
store and beauty salon; Malecón address is one of closest to Colonial Zone. **Cons:** this busy hotel can get noisy late into the evening;
geared for large convention groups; maintenance is lax and rooms are
tired-looking. $ *Rooms from: $160* ⊠ *Av. George Washington 218,
Gazcue* ☎ *809/221–0000, 877/859–5095 toll-free* ⊕ *www.ihg.com/
crowneplaza* ⤳ *196 rooms* ⦿ *No meals.*

$ 🛏 **Renaissance Santo Domingo Jaragua Hotel & Casino.** It's remarkable what
HOTEL   a major renovation can do to revive an iconic, albeit tired, landmark; the
newly transformed Jaragua is jaw-dropping. **Pros:** security is tight and
solo female travelers feel safe; large, well-appointed fitness center and
spa; room service is surprisingly good. **Cons:** can be a bit noisy at times
with conventions and large meetings; service in restaurants can be slow,

9

especially with language barriers; more of a business hotel than a leisure hotel. [$] *Rooms from: $162* ✉ *Av. George Washington 367, Gazcue* ☎ *809/221–2222* 🌐 *www.marriott.com* 🛏 *300 rooms* 🍴 *No meals.*

THE SOUTHWEST

$ B&B/INN FAMILY 🏨 **Casa Bonita Tropical Lodge.** This boutique property southwest of Santo Domingo, formerly a family estate, has style normally associated with urban hotels. **Pros:** concierge can arrange private transfers from the capital; suite brings many extra amenities; a truly relaxing retreat. **Cons:** only one restaurant with few nearby choices; it's much cooler here than in Santo Domingo; service is caring but not slick or always efficient. [$] *Rooms from: $245* ✉ *Km. 17 Carretera de La Costa, Bahoruco* ☎ *809/476–5059, 809/540–5908 reservations, 800/961–5133* 🌐 *casabonitadr.com* 🛏 *28 rooms, 1 suite* 🍴 *No meals.*

SOUTHEAST COAST

La Romana is on the southeast coast, about an hour and a half drive from Santo Domingo and 45 minutes southwest of Punta Cana, now that the road has been improved. An international airport here has nonstop service from the United States. Casa de Campo's Marina Chavón, with its Mediterranean design, impressive yacht club, and villa complex, is as fine a marina facility as can be found anywhere. The shops and restaurants are a big draw for all tourists to the area, as is Altos de Chavón, the re-created 16th-century Mediterranean town on the grounds of Casa de Campo. The resorts in nearby Bayahibe Bay, which has an idyllic, horseshoe-shape beach and a real fishing village, have always been popular with *capitaleños* and Europeans. But North Americans are also checking in here and leaving satisfied. Often, when guests want to party down, they buy an inexpensive night pass to the Viva Wyndham, allowing them entry to the resort's discos along with dinner and drinks. The actual town of La Romana is not pretty or quaint, although it has a lovely central park and a couple of recommendable restaurants, and is a real slice of Dominican life. ■ TIP→ **One way to sample the wares at Casa de Campo, if you can't afford to stay there, is to buy the resort's day pass ($75 for adults, $45 for children 4–12 years). It will give you a place in the sun at Minitas Beach, towels, nonmotorized water sports, lunch at the Beach Club by Le Cirque, and entrance to Altos de Chavon.**

LA ROMANA

$$$$ RESORT FAMILY Fodor's Choice ★ 🏨 **Casa de Campo.** One of the country's oldest and most famous resorts, which set the benchmark for luxury travel in the Caribbean when it was built in the mid-1970s, has had a dramatic renovation of its public spaces, rooms, and suites, bringing it back into the top tier of luxury properties. **Pros:** excellent golf and tennis; fine restaurant choices, even for those with meal plans; beautiful, modern design. **Cons:** not the largest beach; the standard accommodations have not enjoyed the same attention as the higher room categories; a bit too sprawling although the golf carts do help. [$] *Rooms from: $880* ✉ *La Romana* ☎ *809/523–3333, 305/856–5405, 800/877–3643* 🌐 *www.casadecampo.com.do* 🛏 *173 rooms, 12 suites, 50 villas* 🍴 *All-inclusive.*

BAYAHIBE

$$$

RESORT

FAMILY

Fodor'sChoice

★

Dreams La Romana. This outstanding all-inclusive resort sits on an exceptional palm-fringed ribbon of white sand protected by a coral reef that offers great snorkeling from the (Blue Flag) beach, and a professional PADI dive school. **Pros:** good location within an hour of all the major airports in the area; the wedding gazebos and pier-wedding, honeymoon, and anniversary packages; free Wi-Fi throughout and free calls within the D.R., U.S., and Canada. **Cons:** large and busy property can feel overly full; constant entertainment can be noisy until about 11 pm; lots of local groups book August–October and can be overwhelming. $ Rooms from: $400 ⊠ Playa Bayahibe, Bayahibe ☎ 809/221–8880 ⊕ www.dreamsresorts.com/la-romana ➔ 788 rooms ⦿ All-inclusive.

PUNTA CANA

The easternmost coast of the island has 35 miles (56 km) of incredible beach punctuated by coconut palms; add to that a host of all-inclusive resorts, an atmospheric thatch-roof airport that's the busiest in the Dominican Republic (the second busiest in the Caribbean basin), and it's easy to see why this region—despite having more than 50,000 hotel rooms (more than on most other Caribbean islands)—can regularly sell out. It has become the Cancún of the D.R. Most hotels in the region are clustered around Punta Cana and Bávaro beaches, where more than 90% of the existing properties are all-inclusive. The Westin Puntacana Resort & Club, an upscale American chain hotel, is one of the few that is not all-inclusive. Development continues to press north to the more remote locations of Macao and Uvero Alto, and south to the nearby Juanillo—and several of the newer offerings, such as the Eden Roc Cap Cana, are luxurious and not all-inclusive.

The region commonly referred to as Punta Cana actually encompasses the beaches and villages of Juanillo, Punta Cana, Bávaro, Cabeza de Toro, El Cortecito, Arena Gorda, Macao, and Uvero Alto, which hug an unbroken stretch of the eastern coastline; however, Uvero Alto, the farthest developed resort area to the north, lies some 45 minutes from the Punta Cana International Airport on a significantly improved road.

In November 2014, a second terminal opened at Punta Cana International Airport (PUJ). With this expansion, PUJ is expected to become the Caribbean's largest airport hub. Designated Terminal B, it can accommodate 6,500 passengers daily, or more than 2 million passengers annually. The Passenger Departure Area has 50 check-in counters, an air-conditioned concourse equipped with seven jet bridges, associated parking, and nine departure gates. Passengers will find a food court, a VIP lounge, duty-free stores, champagne bar, kids' playground, a designated smoking area, access to Wi-Fi, and a recharging area for electronic equipment. But the main improvement for passengers has been decreased wait times both for check-in and, more important, to clear customs and immigration on arrival.

9

JUANILLO

$$
RESORT
FAMILY
☒ **ALSOL Tiara Collection.** The fourth of Cap Cana's ALSOL resorts, which debuted in mid-2015, brings the classy sophistication of a boutique hotel yet is a smaller all-inclusive that continues to be remarkably affordable. **Pros:** swim-out rooms, which are in high demand; a safe, familial haven now that the Sanctuary Cap Cana has gone adults-only; quality construction means rooms are quiet. **Cons:** some staffers are still inexperienced and not good with English; aside from the fine breakfast buffet, restaurants still need some work; quieter resort than the Sanctuary Cap Cana, especially at night. $ *Rooms from: $375* ☒ *Cap Cana, Fishing Lodge Blvd., Juanillo* ☏ *809/469–7560, 844 /413–2658* ⊕ *alsoltiaracapcana.com* ↝ *115 rooms* ⏚ *All-inclusive.*

$$$$
HOTEL
Fodor's Choice
★
☒ **Eden Roc at Cap Cana.** Within Cap Cana, the most luxurious resort is unquestionably this all-suite boutique hotel with interior decor straight from the mid-century French Riviera. **Pros:** pampering, discreet service; a golf cart is included with rooms; the charismatic Riva Bar is a great spot for a drink and some piano music. **Cons:** suites don't have sea views; limited number of one-bedrooms, which are in demand; expensive, though promotions are often offered. $ *Rooms from: $1182* ☒ *Cap Cana, Juanillo* ☏ *809/469–7469* ⊕ *www.edenroccapcana.com* ↝ *34 suites* ⏚ *Breakfast.*

$$$$
RESORT
Fodor's Choice
★
☒ **Sanctuary Cap Cana By ALSOL.** The stellar keystone of Cap Cana is now for adults only and has never been in better shape since a major renovation in 2014. **Pros:** new deck off the spa makes famous, white-sand Playa Juanillo more accessible; professional management and many exceptional staffers; world-class golf is just a swing away at Punta Espada. **Cons:** the standard junior suites are long but narrow; beach by main pool has coral and shallow, milky water; at peak season only the AI plan may be offered. $ *Rooms from: $508* ☒ *Cap Cana, Blvd. Zona Hotelera, Playa Juanillo, Juanillo* ☏ *809/562–9191* ⊕ *www.sanctuarycapcana.com* ↝ *125 junior suites, 33 suites, 19 villas* ⏚ *All-inclusive.*

PUNTA CANA

$$$$
RESORT
FAMILY
Fodor's Choice
★
☒ **Club Med Punta Cana.** Whimsy and camaraderie are characteristic of this family-friendly resort—Punta Cana's original all-inclusive—situated on 75 tropical acres, with a coastline of incredibly white sandy shores and a separate luxury Reserve for adults only. **Pros:** two-bedroom Tiara suites and Zen Oasis rooms are the best; animated, fun, and interesting global staff; many theme weeks and events. **Cons:** Wi-Fi is expensive both in-room and in public spaces; peak holiday times can be particularly busy and stressful; standard rooms are aging and have maintenance issues. $ *Rooms from: $544* ☒ *Playa Punta Cana, Punta Cana* ☏ *809/686–5500, 800/258–2633* ⊕ *www.clubmed.com* ↝ *631 rooms* ⏚ *All-inclusive.*

$$$$
RENTAL
Fodor's Choice
★
☒ **Tortuga Bay.** Shuttered French windows that open to grand vistas of the sea and a cotton-white private beach are hallmarks of this luxury-villa enclave within the grounds of Puntacana Resort & Club that was originally designed by the late Oscar de la Renta, whose elegant style includes four-poster beds clad in Frette linens and breathtaking stone bathrooms. **Pros:** sprawling grounds with virgin beaches; VIP check-in

at airport; breakfast poolside with fresh-squeezed OJ. **Cons:** little night-life; Bamboo restaurant is pricey, as is the resort; too isolating for singles. $ *Rooms from: $905* ✉ *Puntacana Resort & Club, Playa Punta Cana, Punta Cana* ☎ *809/959–8229, 888/442–2262* ⊕ *tortugabayhotel. com* ↩ *30 suites* ◯| *Breakfast.*

$$$$ 🖫 **The Westin Puntacana Resort & Club.** The Punta Cana Group has
RESORT eschewed the all-inclusive in favor of a beautiful Westin property on a glorious stretch of beach with ocean views from floor-to-ceiling windows and private balconies in every guest room. **Pros:** well-trained staff, especially receptionists; the pool segues to the idyllic white-sand beach; bartenders put the happy in the happy hour. **Cons:** regular rates very high for what you get; hotel shuttle has few runs to Punta Cana Village during dinner hours; not much to do after dinner. $ *Rooms from: $626* ✉ *Puntacana Resort & Club, Playa Blanca, Punta Cana* ☎ *809/959–2222* ⊕ *www.westinpuntacana.com* ↩ *206 rooms, 7 suites* ◯| *No meals.*

BÁVARO

$$$ 🖫 **Barceló Bávaro Beach Resort.** Barceló deserves loud applause for trans-
RESORT forming an aging, middle-of-the-road has-been to a glamorous complex
FAMILY of two resorts worthy of gushing praise, which is popular with both tourists and locals. **Pros:** enormous range of entertainment and activity options; no other kids' club is this contemporary; clean, gorgeous beach. **Cons:** huge resort draws large conventions and big crowds on both sides; club level not a worthwhile upgrade; Wi-Fi expensive and irregular. $ *Rooms from: $435* ✉ *Carretera Bávaro, Km 1, Bávaro* ☎ *809/686–5797* ⊕ *www.barcelo.com* ↩ *2,887 rooms* ◯| *All-inclusive.*

$$ 🖫 **Catalonia Bavaro Beach, Golf & Casino Resort.** This sprawling resort,
RESORT always thought of as a moderately priced playground for families, golf-
FAMILY ers, and convention attendees, has improved its offering while keeping prices affordably low. **Pros:** extreme value with all of the new upgrades and additions; club-level with waiter service and premium bar service; golf deeply discounted for guests. **Cons:** remains awfully busy and sometimes crowded; domestic drinks are the norm; time-share salespeople too aggressive. $ *Rooms from: $345* ✉ *Cabeza de Toro, Bávaro* ☎ *809/ 412–0000* ⊕ *cataloniacaribbean.com* ↩ *874 rooms* ◯| *All-inclusive.*

$$ 🖫 **Catalonia Royal Bavaro.** This adults-only haven with meticulously
RESORT kept grounds and a sparkling pool is a perfect example of how an
Fodor's Choice all-inclusive resort can offer top-tier hospitality without a herd men-
★ tality. **Pros:** all rooms have hammocks on terraces; 11 dining options (3 at Royal, 8 at the Bávaro); less expensive than other deluxe AIs. **Cons:** even the bi-level suites need some maintenance and better lighting; busier than a comparable boutique hotel would be; quality of food even in Royal restaurants going down. $ *Rooms from: $375* ✉ *Playa Bávaro, Bávaro* ☎ *809/412–0011* ⊕ *www.cataloniacaribbean.com; www.hoteles-catalonia.com* ↩ *255 rooms* ◯| *All-inclusive.*

$$$ 🖫 **Dreams Palm Beach Punta Cana.** Both family- and American-friendly,
RESORT the fine Dreams resort is perched on a gorgeous stretch of beach with
FAMILY white-sugar sand and is looking fabulous, offering a wrist-band–free all-inclusive experience. **Pros:** close to the airport; management is especially conscientious; now free Wi-Fi throughout and free calls to U.S.

9

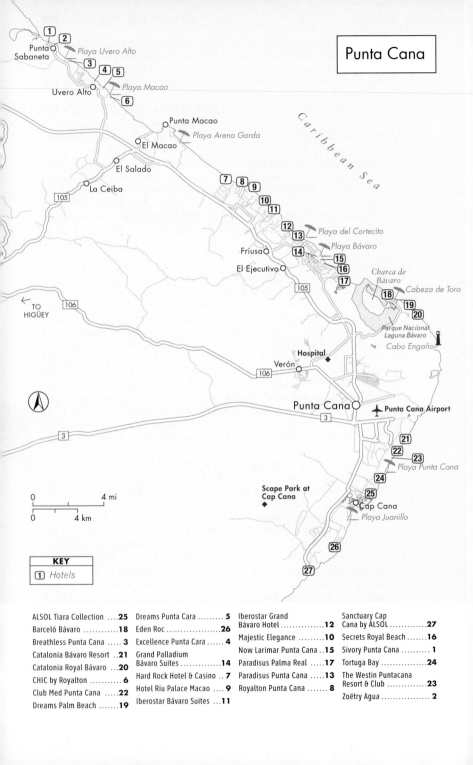

Punta Cana

Playa Uvero Alto
Punta Sabaneta
Uvero Alto
Playa Macao
Punta Macao
Playa Arena Gorda
El Macao
El Salado
La Ceiba
105

Caribbean Sea

Playa del Cortecito
Fríusa
Playa Bávaro
El Ejecutivo
Charca de Bávaro
Cabeza de Toro
105
Parque Nacional
Laguna Bávaro
Cabo Engaño

TO HIGÜEY
106

106
Verón
Hospital

Punta Cana
Punta Cana Airport
3

3

Scape Park at
Cap Cana

Playa Punta Cana

Cap Cana
Playa Juanillo

0   4 mi
0   4 km

KEY
1 Hotels

and Canada. **Cons:** the pool can be very busy, crowded, and loud; time-share sales staff are aggressive; service and maintenance can be inconsistent. $\boxed{\$}$ *Rooms from: $450* ✉ *Cabeza de Toro, Bávaro* ☎ *809/552–6000* ⊕ *www.dreamsresorts.com/palmbeach* ✈ *500 rooms* ⦿| *All-inclusive.*

$$ ⊞ **Grand Palladium Bávaro Suites Resort & Spa.** Four sprawling, contiguous resorts (with a shuttle service until 2 am) share these well-kept grounds and feel like a beachside village, and three of these—Grand Palladium Bávaro, Grand Palladium Punta Cana, and Grand Palladium Palace—share one another's facilities, including a top-notch spa and health club. **Pros:** excellent offshore snorkeling (though at an extra charge); guest rooms are exceptionally spacious and quiet; front desk staff is professional, bilingual, and smart. **Cons:** few rooms have sea views; it's a huge resort that can feel busy at times; Royal Suites area may be too quiet for some. $\boxed{\$}$ *Rooms from: $345* ✉ *Carretera El Cortecito, El Cortecito, Bávaro* ☎ *809/221–8149 Grand Palladium Bávaro, 809/221–0719 Grand Palladium Palace, 800/961–7661 in the U.S.* ⊕ *www.palladiumhotelgroup.com* ✈ *1,823 rooms* ⦿| *All-inclusive.*

RESORT
FAMILY

$$$ ⊞ **Iberostar Bávaro Suites Resort.** Like its two sister resorts, this Spanish entry has panache—evidenced in its lobby, an artistic showpiece, and contemporary guest rooms with plush bedding—making it competitive with Punta Cana's newer properties. **Pros:** great kids' water playground; good specialty restaurants; extra-special management keeps the staff in fine spirits. **Cons:** buffet not quite as good as it once was; the property is showing its age; unrenovated rooms should be avoided. $\boxed{\$}$ *Rooms from: $379* ✉ *Playa Bávaro, Bávaro* ☎ *809/221–6500, 888/923–2722* ⊕ *www.iberostar.com* ✈ *596 rooms* ⦿| *All-inclusive.*

RESORT
FAMILY

$$$$ ⊞ **Iberostar Grand Bávaro Hotel.** Iberostar's adults-only resort—an architectural gem—is a knockout from the moment you walk into the glamorous lobby and is one resort where the term "no expense was spared" is actually true. **Pros:** impressive selection of designer restaurants with contemporary cuisine; excellent lunch buffet at beach; idyllic beach weddings and honeymoons. **Cons:** although improving, there are still service lapses from lack of English-language skills; some inconsistent service in restaurants; the hotel is pricey for an AI in this area. $\boxed{\$}$ *Rooms from: $708* ✉ *Playa Bávaro, Bávaro* ☎ *809/221–6500, 888/923–2722* ⊕ *iberostar.com* ✈ *260 suites, 13 grand suites, 1 presidential* ⦿| *All-inclusive.*

RESORT
Fodor's Choice
★

$$$$ ⊞ **Majestic Elegance.** The younger of Punta Cana's two Majestic resorts, which is an all-suites property, is the more sophisticated sister—and a busy one. **Pros:** fun and welcoming staff is eager to please; premium liquors served at all bars and à la carte restaurants; free Wi-Fi in rooms and public areas. **Cons:** guests not in the VIP Club may feel second-class; high occupancy makes it feel crowded; some rooms are not soundproof. $\boxed{\$}$ *Rooms from: $495* ✉ *Majestic St., Arena Gorda* ☎ *809/221–9898* ⊕ *www.majestic-resorts.com* ✈ *596 rooms* ⦿| *All-inclusive.*

RESORT

$$ ⊞ **Now Larimar Punta Cana.** This relatively new, moderately priced branch of the AMResorts family has style as well as a gorgeous 700-yard beachfront. **Pros:** within walking distance of shops and off-site cafés; close to the airport; large housekeeping and entertainment team. **Cons:** some complaints about maintenance and repairs and uncomfortable beds;

RESORT
FAMILY

9

in-room Wi-Fi is expensive; music can be very loud and time-share staff annoying. $ *Rooms from: $375* ⊠ *El Cortecito, Av. Alemania s/n, Bávaro* ☎ *809/221–4646* ⊕ *www.nowresorts.com* ⇱ *720 rooms* ⦿ *All-inclusive.*

$$$$
RESORT
FAMILY
Fodor'sChoice
★

▩ **Paradisus Palma Real Resort.** This luxury all-inclusive is a visual show-stopper and has one of the country's best spas and also one of Punta Cana's best restaurants in Passion by Martin Berasategui. **Pros:** adjacent to the Palma Real Shopping Center; guests enjoy unlimited golf at Cocotal Golf & Country Club; special promos on website offers discounted rates. **Cons:** restaurants and nightlife are far from some rooms; rooms at the Reserve do not have sea views, and guests must shuttle to main beach; a very large resort with little personal service unless you are in one of the special areas. $ *Rooms from: $486* ⊠ *Bávaro Beach, Bávaro* ☎ *809/688–5000* ⊕ *www.paradisuspalmareal.com* ⇱ *554 rooms* ⦿ *All-inclusive.*

$$$
RESORT
FAMILY
Fodor'sChoice
★

▩ **Paradisus Punta Cana.** Paradisus has many innovative amenities while also exuding a charismatic quality—like vintage wine—that produces the warm feeling that makes for loyal, repeat guests. **Pros:** some impressive architecture, decor, mature landscaping and gardens; professional and caring management strives for good service; unlimited greens fees are a draw for golfers. **Cons:** no elevators; some rooms have yet to be renovated and should be avoided; Wi-Fi is sporadic. $ *Rooms from: $379* ⊠ *Bávaro Beach, Bávaro* ☎ *809/687–9923, 888/741–5600 reservations* ⊕ *www.melia.com/Paradisus-Punta-Cana* ⇱ *686 rooms* ⦿ *All-inclusive.*

$$$
RESORT
FAMILY

▩ **Royalton Punta Cana Resort & Casino.** Although there are adults-only sections at this resort, including the upper-strata Blue Diamond Club, couples and adults without kids are better served elsewhere; the right demographic for this stunning hotel is young families and groups. **Pros:** the level of service is quite high, friendly, fun and helpful; free Wi-Fi throughout; just 30 minutes from the airport—important for traveling families. **Cons:** no elevators; overbooking during high season is a problem; guests have been shunted to less luxurious sister properties; butlers at the Blue Diamond Club do not always get high marks. $ *Rooms from: $440* ⊠ *Playa Arena Gorda, Carretera Macao, Bávaro* ☎ *809/468–0404* ⊕ *www.bluediamondresorts.com* ⇱ *475 rooms, 10 suites* ⦿ *All-inclusive.*

$$$
RESORT
Fodor'sChoice
★

▩ **Secrets Royal Beach.** The lobby at this sceney, adults-only all-suites resort is like a modern art gallery, but the Caribbean-accented guest rooms do not quite match these high expectations, though the white-sand beach is glorious. **Pros:** nightly entertainment and dancing at the main plaza; fun activities like cooking competitions on the beach; exceptional 17,000-square-foot Spa by Pevonia. **Cons:** beach vendors and overzealous entertainment crew can be annoying; all rooms can be loud, but tropical/garden-view rooms especially don't compare; Wi-Fi is slow and costly. $ *Rooms from: $475* ⊠ *El Cortecito, Av. Alemania s/n, Bávaro* ☎ *809/221–4646* ⊕ *www.secretsresorts.com* ⇱ *475 rooms* ⦿ *All-inclusive.*

Excellence Punta Cana

MACAO

$$$$
RESORT
Fodor's Choice
★

⊞ **Hard Rock Hotel & Casino Punta Cana.** Hard Rock's first all-inclusive property has its own unique identity, different from any other Dominican resort, and it's a great choice if you want nightlife and a busy, fun atmosphere. **Pros:** the resort is a lot of fun; mostly good service, particularly waitstaff at the buffet; music is everywhere. **Cons:** resort can be too crowded during the busiest times of the year; some maintenance and room refurbishment needed due to high occupancy; doesn't have a Caribbean feel except at the beach. $ *Rooms from: $505* ⊠ *Blvd. Turístico del Este 74, Km 28, Macao* ☎ *809/687-0000* ⊕ *www. hardrockhotels.com* ⤶ *1,787 rooms* ⊙ *All-inclusive.*

$$$
RESORT
Fodor's Choice
★

⊞ **Hotel Riu Palace Macao.** After a major, much-needed renovation, this adults-only resort has gone from dowdy to stellar, and it's now the star of the five Riu resorts in Macao. **Pros:** great entertainment staff who try to get guests to have fun (in a good way); good food; helpful front desk staff, who work well under high-volume pressure. **Cons:** excellent value, but still not really luxurious; its new popularity equals high occupancy; free Wi-Fi is erratic. $ *Rooms from: $408* ⊠ *Playa Arena Gorda, Bávaro* ☎ *809/221-7171* ⊕ *www.riu.com* ⤶ *328 rooms, 36 suites* ⊙ *All-inclusive.*

UVERO ALTO

$$$$
RESORT
Fodor's Choice
★

⊞ **Breathless Punta Cana Resort & Spa.** For adults only, this edgy resort with a sexy yet whimsical vibe, is particularly good for singles, filling a void that's been lacking in Punta Cana. **Pros:** premium liquors are served in the lobby bar Wink and the Xhale club lounge; Xhale level is a worthy upgrade; the entertainment teams works hard to keep the party going. **Cons:** standard rooms are nicely decorated but basic and smallish; no reservations needed for à la cartes can mean longish waits; some staffers lack sufficient English. $ *Rooms from: $550* ⊠ *Playa Uvero Alto, Km 275, Uvero Alto* ☎ *809/551–0000* ⊕ *breathlessresorts. com* ⤵ *750 rooms* ⦿ *All-inclusive.*

$$$ **CHIC Punta Cana by Royalton.** The adults-only CHIC Punta Cana has
ALL-INCLUSIVE   been designed with active, younger (twenty- to thirtysomething) partiers
Fodor's Choice   in mind, so there is entertainment all day and night, Las Vegas style.
★   **Pros:** Wi-Fi and calls to the U.S. are free; friendly and fun, accommodating staff; food in restaurants generally very good. **Cons:** windy beach with lots of wave action; house wine is barely potable, so plan on buying better, albeit expensive, bottles; time-share salespeople are annoying. $ *Rooms from: $450* ⊠ *Carretera Uvero Alta-Punta Cana, Uvero Alto* ☎ *809 /468–0404* ⊕ *royaltonresorts.com* ⤵ *234 rooms, 79 club rooms and suites* ⦿ *All-inclusive.*

$$$$ **Dreams Punta Cana Resort & Spa.** Massive improvements in appearance
RESORT   and all areas of service have made this fun resort in a remote, pastoral
FAMILY   setting super for families, young couples, wedding entourages, honeymooners, ladies getaways—yes, even singles. **Pros:** staff are friendly and personable; food offerings and nightly entertainment are a cut above; lovely guest rooms. **Cons:** some rooms still need updating as do some of older public spaces; expensive Wi-Fi (free at the Club level); a popular resort that runs at high occupancy. $ *Rooms from: $480* ⊠ *Playa Uvero Alto, Km 269.5, Uvero Alto* ☎ *809/682–0404, 866/237–3267 in the U.S.* ⊕ *www.dreamsresorts.com/punta-cana* ⤵ *620 rooms* ⦿ *All-inclusive.*

$$$$ **Excellence Punta Cana.** Originally known to be a sumptuous lovers'
RESORT   lair, this adults-only, all-inclusive is particularly appealing to couples
Fodor's Choice   (honeymooners, for sure) and wedding parties, but it now attracts a
★   younger, fun clientele. **Pros:** no reservations are required at any of the restaurants; super-sized, renovated Excellence Club suites are an expensive but worthy upgrade; lots of inclusions. **Cons:** far from shopping, other restaurants, and nightlife; isolating for singles; the interior decor of the accommodations is a bit dated. $ *Rooms from: $570* ⊠ *Playa Uvero Alto, Uvero Alto* ☎ *809/685–9880* ⊕ *www.excellenceresorts.com* ⤵ *456 rooms* ⦿ *All-inclusive.*

$$$$ **Sivory Punta Cana Boutique Hotel.** The best things really do come in
RESORT   small packages at this romantic boutique hotel, which delivers on its promise of expressly personal service and utter tranquility. **Pros:** caring and accommodating staff (mostly); free, strong Wi-Fi throughout; near virgin Atlantic beach, albeit not on the calmer Caribbean. **Cons:** no nightlife, and few activities; food and waitstaff are frequently cited as disappointing; mosquitoes can be a problem. $ *Rooms from: $500* ⊠ *Playa Sivory, Uvero Alto Rd., Uvero Alto* ☎ *809/333–0500* ⊕ *www. sivorypuntacana.com* ⤵ *55 rooms* ⦿ *No meals.*

$$$$ **Zoëtry Agua Punta Cana.** At this serene oceanfront resort, rustic, natural
RESORT   beauty and high architectural style blend seamlessly. **Pros:** all guests get a complimentary 20-minute spa treatment; top-shelf liquor and good wines; excellent service. **Cons:** open bathrooms mean bugs; some low-key entertainment but limited nightlife; original rooms need renovations. $ *Rooms from: $705* ⊠ *Playa Uvero Alto, Uvero Alto* ☎ *809/468–0000* ⊕ *www.zoetryresorts.com/agua* ⤵ *89 rooms, 5 villas* ⦿ *All-inclusive.*

NORTH COAST

The northern coast of the island, with mountains on one side, is also called the Amber Coast because of the large quantities of amber found in the area. The sands on its 75 miles (121 km) of beach are also golden. Major resort areas are Playa Dorada, Cabarete, and Sosúa. Plan to fly into Puerto Plata's Gregorio Luperón International Airport. Much has changed in Playa Dorada with new companies coming in, old companies departing, and apart-hotels taking their place.

PUERTO PLATA

$$ RENTAL FAMILY

Blue Jack Tar Condos. This new condominium complex that debuted in 2015 shares the grounds of the Hotel Blue Jack Tar, adding an upscale option to generally moderately priced Playa Dorada. **Pros:** condo dwellers can utilize the hotel's facilities; restaurants nearby; beautiful, spacious condos with solid security. **Cons:** only one restaurant at the hotel; hotel guests are not as upscale as condo renters; first-floor condos do not have views, so you have to go up and pay for that. [$] *Rooms from: $300* ✉ *Playa Dorada* ☎ *809/320–3800* 🌐 *www.bluejacktar.com* 🛏 *30 condominiums (15 in the rental pool)* 🍴 *No meals.*

$$ HOTEL Fodor's Choice ★

Casa Colonial Beach & Spa. Designed by architect Sara Garcia, sophisticated Casa Colonial, a boutique property exuding refinement and relaxation on the quiet end of the long beach, is a surprise among the all-inclusives of Playa Dorada. **Pros:** architectural gem offering the full luxury, boutique experience; glorious spa; exceptional gourmet dining in Lucia. **Cons:** can feel empty during the low season; large suites could use a splash of color; service is attentive but sometimes a bit off. [$] *Rooms from: $340* ✉ *Playa Dorada* ☎ *809/320–3232, 866/376–7831* 🌐 *www.casacolonialhotel.com* 🛏 *50 rooms* 🍴 *No meals.*

$ RESORT FAMILY Fodor's Choice ★

Gran Ventana Beach Resort. This longtime all-inclusive has had a rebirth, maintaining its moderate price point but now offering more luxury upgrade options. **Pros:** consistently good food and service for this price point; particularly efficient and caring front-desk staff; animated staff are a bit more laid-back than at other resorts. **Cons:** a few aspects are still dated; charge for safes and Wi-Fi (though the latter offers good service); limited access to à la carte restaurants. [$] *Rooms from: $220* ✉ *Playa Dorada* ☎ *809/320–2111, 809/320–3232* 🌐 *www.granventanahotel.com* 🛏 *506 rooms* 🍴 *All-inclusive.*

$$$ RESORT

Presidential Suites—Puerto Plata Lifestyle. This hilltop enclave consists mainly of apartment-style, two-bedroom suites decorated in a modern, masculine style with black leather chairs, cherry wood, and bedroom Jacuzzis. **Pros:** pool with cascading waterfall and fabric-draped lounging beds; caring employees and management try hard to please; VIP beach club. **Cons:** a fast shuttle from the beach; heavily occupied so can feel overly crowded, and restaurants can jam up; relentless time-share sellers. [$] *Rooms from: $450* ✉ *1 Paradise Dr., Cofresi* ☎ *809/970–7777* 🌐 *www.lhvcresorts.com* 🛏 *60 suites* 🍴 *All-inclusive.*

9

SOSÚA

$$$$
RENTAL
Fodor's Choice
★

🖫 **Gansevoort Playa Imbert.** An opulent oasis, the edgy, innovative Gansevoort resort provides full one- to four-bedroom apartments overlooking a magnificent bay. **Pros:** large, beautiful apartments have full kitchens; incomparable views; free resort-wide Wi-Fi. **Cons:** service can be inconsistent; the surrounding neighborhood is not wonderful; quiet at night. $\mathbb{S}$ *Rooms from: $555* ✉ *Playa Imbert, Calle Bruno Philip 5, Sosúa* ☎ *809/571–3000, 877/248–9850* ⊕ *gansevoortdpi.com* ⇨ *40 apartments* ⫟◯⫟ *Breakfast* Ⓜ .

$$$$
RENTAL
FAMILY

🖫 **Sea Horse Ranch.** This enclave of private homes, each with large front- and backyards and private pool, is an elite bastion set within a vast country club–like setting near Cabarete. **Pros:** one of the country's most organized, well-managed groups of villas; potent security makes your vacation worry-free; all villas have free, unlimited Wi-Fi. **Cons:** guests usually feel the need to rent a car or hire a driver; it's a walk or short drive to reach two petite, communal beaches; complex doesn't have a resort feel. $\mathbb{S}$ *Rooms from: $700* ✉ *Coastal Hwy., Cabarete* ☎ *809/571–3880, 800/635–0991* ⊕ *www.sea-horse-ranch.com* ⇨ *20 villas* ⫟◯⫟ *No meals.*

CABARETE

$
HOTEL

🖫 **Hotel El Magnifico.** You will find a healthy dose of unexpected pleasure at this stellar, boutique hotel made up primarily of one- to three-bedroom condominiums and a few regular hotel rooms tucked in a serene oasis away from the noisy main town. **Pros:** never feels crowded; the interior decor is très chic in many (but not all) units; children under 15 stay free. **Cons:** steep spiral staircases and no elevators; no restaurant or bar, though there's a place to get breakfast next door; no in-room phones. $\mathbb{S}$ *Rooms from: $94* ✉ *Calle del Cementario, Cabarete* ☎ *809/571–0868* ⊕ *www.hotelmagnifico.com* ⇨ *30 units* ⫟◯⫟ *No meals.*

$
RENTAL
FAMILY
Fodor's Choice
★

🖫 **Le Reef Beach Condos.** This small condominium complex is made up of primarily two-bedroom units with full kitchens that are spacious and stylish, reflecting Cabarete's surfing craze (kite, wind, and otherwise). **Pros:** condos are spacious and stylish; beautiful beachfront and convenient location; good selection of American TV channels. **Cons:** open-concept bathrooms offer very little privacy; some water views are restricted; no phones, no microwaves. $\mathbb{S}$ *Rooms from: $230* ✉ *Cabarete Beach, next to The Palms condos, Cabarete* ☎ *809/571–0848, 809/858–2589* ⊕ *www.le-reef.com* ⇨ *6 condos* ⫟◯⫟ *Breakfast.*

$
RENTAL
FAMILY
Fodor's Choice
★

🖫 **Millennium Resort & Spa.** If a reasonably priced contemporary and spacious apartment with remarkable ocean vistas is your tropical dream, this small condo resort delivers. **Pros:** good, free Wi-Fi throughout; comfortable and inviting environment; two elevators. **Cons:** 15-minute walk along the beach to bars and restaurants; ocean breezes are often strong here; junior and ocean suites have only a small kitchenette. $\mathbb{S}$ *Rooms from: $120* ✉ *Ocean Dream 101, Autopista/Sosua Cabarete Km 1, Cabarete* ⊹ *Coming from Sosua, turn left at signage, which is right before Ocean Dream Plaza* ☎ *809/571–0402* ⊕ *www. cabaretemillennium.com* ⇨ *53 condominiums* ⫟◯⫟ *No meals.*

$ 🏠 **Natura Cabana Boutique Hotel & Spa.** If your idea of perfection is thatch-
B&B/INN   roof cabanas and a quiet, private beach, then this may be your ocean-
FAMILY   front nirvana. **Pros:** natural, peaceful beachfront stay; good restaurant;
free Wi-Fi throughout. **Cons:** no TVs, phones, or air-conditioning, but
sea breezes; car is an asset, but taxis to town are safer; no ocean views
from many cabanas. $ *Rooms from: $180* ⊠ *Playa Perla Marina, Paseo
del Sol 5, Cabarete* 🕾 *809/571–1507* ⊕ *www.naturacabana.com* ⤳ *12
suites* ⦿ *Breakfast.*

$ 🏠 **Velero Beach Resort.** You'll appreciate the location of this well-man-
HOTEL   aged hotel and residential enclave with its own beachfront and gardens,
just a few minutes' walk east of the noise of town yet also just minutes
from the happening bars and restaurants. **Pros:** blenders, microwaves,
and DVD players in the junior suites and above; draped Balinese sun
beds at the pool are dreamy; high-speed Wi-Fi throughout. **Cons:** no
elevators—it's a climb up the spiral staircases to the third floor; standard
rooms are not spacious; showing some signs of age. $ *Rooms from: $80*
⊠ *Calle la Punta 1, Cabarete* 🕾 *809/571–9727, 888/770–9886* ⊕ *www.*
velerobeach.com ⤳ *29 units* ⦿ *No meals.*

CABRERA

$ 🏠 **Villa Castellamonte.** When not rented in its entirety, this elegant villa in
B&B/INN   Orchid Bay Estates operates as a high-end B&B. **Pros:** for all its gran-
FAMILY   deur, it's as laid-back as the garden hammock; 24-hour security; three
Fodor'sChoice   rooms have been updated with Italian-themed murals. **Cons:** beach is
★   rocky and best visited with reef shoes; the staff of eight can be too much
service; Cabrera as a destination is not for everyone. $ *Rooms from:*
$195 ⊠ *Orchid Bay Estates, Casa 10, Cabrera* 🕾 *829/629–1012 cell,*
888/589–8455 toll-free in U.S. and Canada, 702/900–3121 U.S. direct
⊕ *www.villa-castellamonte.com* ⤳ *8 rooms* ⦿ *Breakfast.*

SAMANÁ

Samaná is the name of both the peninsula that curves around the eponymous bay and of the largest town. Conveniently, El Catey Airport (AZS)
is served regularly (twice a week) by JetBlue from New York–JFK;
otherwise, you can usually arrange flights from Punta Cana and small
charters from several D.R. airports.

LAS TERRENAS

$ 🏠 **Hotel Alisei & Spa.** An excellent location across from Las Terrenas
RENTAL   Beach—within walking distance to town—gives this apart-hotel an
FAMILY   edge for those looking for a few resort services to go along with more
spacious accommodations. **Pros:** windows are double-paned and keep
apartments quiet; quiet music is played at the pool; good discounts
available in the off-season. **Cons:** mostly international TV; not terribly
luxurious; some of the decor and art are dated. $ *Rooms from: $235*
⊠ *Calle F. Caamaño, Las Terrenas* 🕾 *809/240–5555, 829/383–2655*
⊕ *www.aliseihotelspa.com* ⤳ *48 units* ⦿ *Breakfast.*

$$$$ 🏠 **The Peninsula House.** The gorgeous Victorian-style plantation house
B&B/INN   with wraparound verandas overlooks acres of coconut palms down to
Fodor'sChoice   the ocean and is one of the best B&Bs in the Caribbean. **Pros:** quiet
★   and remote; many English TV channels plus DVDs; seamless service,

Peninsula House, Las Terrenas

but waitstaff doesn't speak English. **Cons:** very pricey; owner's dogs detract somewhat from the formal atmosphere; not much to do on-site at night. $ *Rooms from: $650* ⊠ *Camino Cosón, Las Terrenas* ☎ *809/962–7447, 809/847–7540* ⊕ *www.thepeninsulahouse.com* ➷ *6 rooms* ❖ *Breakfast.*

$$$
HOTEL
Fodor's Choice
★
Sublime Samaná. With dramatic, contemporary architecture that allows each suite water views, this resort offers large two- and three-bedroom condo accommodations with designer kitchens and living rooms, two flat-screen TVs, and a balcony that looks down upon the inviting labyrinth of swimming pools lined with draped sun beds. **Pros:** the beach bar offers a great lunch, tropical cocktails, and fresh juices; chic interior furnishings are designed with taste and Caribbean spirit; the high-quality mattresses and linens promote sleep. **Cons:** relatively isolated, so a car is likely necessary; restaurant options are limited, and main dining room has no water views; not a lot of on-site activities. $ *Rooms from: $445* ⊠ *Bahía de Cosón, Ramal Viva, Las Terrenas* ☎ *809/240–5050* ⊕ *www.sublimesamana.com* ➷ *15 suites* ❖ *Breakfast.*

$$$
RENTAL
FAMILY
Xeliter Balcones del Atlantico. This condotel on a large tract of virgin land offers beautifully designed, spacious apartments with dreamy bedding and private Jacuzzis on terraces that are basically outdoor rooms. **Pros:** intelligent and caring concierge staff; ideal for longer stays; beds are commodious with luxe linens. **Cons:** not on the beach (it's across the road); isolated location that requires a rental car; phone and maintenance problems continue. $ *Rooms from: $450* ⊠ *Carretera Las Terrenas/El Limon Km. 2, across from Porto on Playa Las Terrenas, Las Terrenas* ☎ *809/240–5011* ⊕ *www.balconesdelatlantico.com.do* ➷ *35 units* ❖ *No meals.*

SANTA BÁBARA DE SAMANÁ

$ HOTEL Fodor's Choice ★ **The Bannister Hotel.** This stylish marina complex smack on the Bay of Samaná has changed the face of tourism in this area and become the social center for the upscale residents, a safe harbor for visiting yachtsmen, and a deluxe, yet reasonably priced option for international visitors. **Pros:** wonderful ambience; natural beauty everywhere. **Cons:** the bedrooms in the one-bedroom accommodations could be more spacious; too far from town to walk; service staff is caring but not professional. [$] *Rooms from: $170* ✉ *Puerto Bahía, Carretera Sánchez, Km 5, Samaná* ☎ *809/503–6363* 🌐 *www.thebannisterhotel.com* 🛏 *24 one-bedrooms, 5 two-bedrooms* 🍴 *No meals.*

LAS GALERAS

$ HOTEL **Villa Serena.** Decidedly one of the better hotels in the eastern corner of the peninsula, Villa Serena makes for a wonderful, stress-free Samaná vacation. **Pros:** small, private beachfront without vendors or loud music; reliable in-room Wi-Fi; accommodating, English-speaking front-desk staff and management. **Cons:** main section is dated; most rooms have air-conditioning but no TVs or phones; no blackout drapes. [$] *Rooms from: $150* ✉ *Las Galeras Beach, Las Galeras* ☎ *809/538–0000* 🌐 *www.villaserena.com* 🛏 *21 rooms* 🍴 *Breakfast.*

NIGHTLIFE

Santo Domingo's nightlife is vast and ever changing. Check with the concierges and hip capitaleños. However clubs and bars must close at midnight during the week, and 2 am on Friday and Saturday nights. There are some exceptions to the latter, primarily those clubs and casinos in hotels. Sadly, the curfew has put some clubs out of business, but it has cut down on the crime and late-night noise, particularly in the Zona Colonial. Some clubs are now pushing the envelope and staying open until 3, but they do get in trouble with the authorities when caught, and you probably don't want to be there then.

Dancing is as much a part of the culture here as eating and drinking. As in other Latin countries, after dinner it's not a question of *whether* people will go dancing but *where* they'll go. Move with the rhythm of the merengue and the pulsing beat of salsa (adopted from neighboring Puerto Rico). Among the young, the word is that there's no better place to party in the Caribbean than Santo Domingo. Almost every resort in Puerto Plata and Punta Cana has live entertainment, dancing, or both.

The action can heat up—and the island does have casinos—but gambling in the Dominican Republic is more a sideline than a raison d'être. Most casinos are in the larger hotels of Santo Domingo, with a couple on the North Coast, plus many more in Punta Cana. All offer slot machines, blackjack, craps, and roulette and are generally open daily from 3 pm to 4 am, the exception being those in Santo Domingo, which, for now, must close at midnight (2 am on Friday and Saturday). You must be 18 to enter.

SANTO DOMINGO

BARS AND CLUBS

Arturo Fuente Cigar Club. This is the cigar club that other cigar bars look up to, a classy, sceney bar and salon elegant enough that you don't need to be a smoker to enjoy it. A high-tech ventilation system keeps the room from being unpleasantly smoky. And, of course, Fuente cigars are among the best, pairing well with the finest aged rums or cognacs from the bar. This club is populated by well-heeled capitaleños, so dress the part, or you may be turned away. ⊠ *27 de Febrero Av. 211, Santo Domingo* ☎ *809/683–2771.*

Cock's Tail. This hideaway off the typical tourist radar is a safe haven, where the local owners and residents will welcome you to their fun. The bar's provocative name is as titillating as the creative cocktails themselves, all made with premium liquor, fresh herbs and juices, and house-made syrups. Another intriguing element is the new-generation jukebox: no quarters needed. The playlist includes rock, a lot of Latin music, and even Bruce Springsteen. Seating is indoors and out. Should you need to graze, simple tapas range from hummus to olives on ice, all for very little. ⊠ *Gustavo Mejia Ricart Av. 144, Ensanche Piantini* ✛ *At Freddy Prestol Castillo, in the U-shaped plaza behind Blue Mall* ☎ *809/768–7185.*

SUD Supperclub. In addition to a place to get a simple, casual meal, this mellow, youth-oriented hot spot is primarily a bar. However, live music performances are a fairly regular presence when there isn't a DJ working the room. A large wooden deck is the preferred place to hang out. Sangria is the house specialty, red, white, and rose—even ginger and spicy mango. ⊠ *Av. Roberto Pastoriza 401, Santo Domingo* ☎ *809/807–1138, 809/299–9784.*

Wine Tasting Room at El Catador. This avant-garde wine bar and wine store was created by the major wine distributor El Catador. Cushy leather armchairs and hardwood floors help create a clubby atmosphere. If you want to eat, there's a good menu of tapas. You will want to buy one of the 500 bottles of wine from around the wine-making world. Generally there are a dozen wines for tasting, but there are no samplings during the busy Christmas holidays. ⊠ *Calle Jose Brea Péna 43, Corner Avaristo Morales, Ensanche Piantini* ☎ *809/540–1644* ⊕ *www.elcatador.com.do.*

CASINOS

Diamante Casino. Diamante knows how to make casinos popular, and so it is with this latest effort. The action includes some 50 slot machines and 16 gaming tables. You can also play a couple of hands of black-jack, shoot craps, or take a spin at the roulette wheel. There's action here 24/7. Diamante's disco, Trio, is a hot ticket, too. Security runs a safe ship. ⊠ *Sheraton Santo Domingo, Av. George Washington 365, Gascue* ✛ *Adjacent to the Sheraton Santo Domingo* ☎ *809/221–6666.*

Renaissance Santo Domingo Jaragua Casino. After a recent renovation, this Malecón casino is the largest in the capital with some 50 slot machines, baccarat, roulette, craps, blackjack, and Pai Gow poker tables. Ladies dress for this casino, men likewise. ⊠ *Renaissance Santo Domingo Jaragua Hotel & Casino, Av. George Washington 367, Gascue* ☎ *809/221–2222* ⊕ *www.marriott.com.*

PUNTA CANA

BARS AND CLUBS

CocoBongo Club. This popular Mexican club has opened a branch in Punta Cana. Latin Club music is interspersed with shows (such as celebrity impersonators or samba demos) lasting some 20 minutes, long enough for the dancers to cool off and drink. The atmosphere is loud, hot, and crowded. Paying extra for VIP service may be a good idea if you don't want to compete with the throngs on the main floor, and this includes transportation; however, buses don't leave until close to closing at 3 am. ⊠ *Downtown Mall, Carretera Barcelo-Vernon, corner El Boulevard, Bávaro* ☎ *809/466–1111* ⊕ *www.cocobongoclub.com.*

Fodor'sChoice ★

Imagine. Imagine you were dancing the night away in a natural cave, with earth-rocking acoustics. You can bounce back and forth between the various "cave" rooms with their stalactites and stalagmites, with equally hot dance floors, featuring house/club jams, merengue/salsa/world beats, current Top 40, and more. Theme nights change, like Crazy Thursday might switch to Brazil's Carnaval. Come late and stay early: things start getting steamy well after midnight, when many club crawlers descend via shuttle (round-trip) from the local resorts. (The free bus is great, but know that it stops at every resort in the area, beginning around 11 pm. Service from Uvero Alto resorts is extra. Taxis wait outside for those who can't hang.) Special rates are offered for a weekly, multiple-entrance pass, with one night including an open bar. Although most disco goers are in awe, others say that it's a lot of hype. ⊠ *Carretera Cocoloco–Riu, Coco Loco/Friusa, Bávaro* ☎ *809/466–1049, 809/466–1049* ⊕ *www.imaginepuntacana.com.*

La Mona. At this new high-end beach bar, the mellow lineup of entertainment will satisfy the twenty- or thirtysomethings without causing the baby boomers to bolt. Ideally positioned on glorious Juanillo Beach, adjacent to the Fortress section of the Sanctuary Cap Cana, it is chic and offers fine dining by night. Mixologists create brilliant cocktails with top-shelf liquor. The entertainment changes nightly. ⊠ *Cap Cana, Blvd. Zona Hotelera, adjacent to the Fortress section of Sanctuary Cap Cana By ALSOL, Juanillo* ☎ *809/469–7191.*

Pacha. A favorite among locals and still one of the best resort-based dance spots, Pacha plays more merengue and bachata than most of the other clubs, but still is geared to young, contemporary music. The later it gets, typically the louder it gets. The place is not that large, but it's attractive, and drink prices are cheaper than other clubs in the area. Cover charges apply when live bands perform; otherwise it's free to enter, and nonresort guests are welcome. ■TIP➜ **If you're staying at the Riu Macao complex, it's an easy, safe enough walk.** ⊠ *Riu Naiboa Resort, Av. Estados Unidos, on Caribbean St., Bávaro* ☎ *809/221–7575 Riu Naiboa Resort.*

Pearl Beach Club. If you love the night life *and* partying on the beach, you should get yourself to this new club posthaste. An upscale beach bar and restaurant by day, it transforms into a hopping spot after 8. But even by day, a DJ rocks the place from Wednesday through Sunday afternoon, which is a traditional party day. If there's no special event,

9

children are allowed; otherwise, it's 18 and over only. ✉ *Cabeza de Toro, adjacent to the Catalonia Bávaro Beach Casino & Golf Resort, Bávaro* ☎ *809/933–3171* ⊕ *www.pearlbeachclub.com.*

NORTH COAST

BARS AND CLUBS

LAX Ojo Cabarete. At this perennially popular bar that really comes alive by night, you can sit in the sand in lounge chairs or jump into the action on the outdoor deck, where a DJ will be spinning madly or a live band might be playing. It's one of the few dance clubs in the area without a cover charge. The inexpensive food is good, and there are special theme nights and drink specials. ✉ *Cabarete Beach, Cabarete* ☎ *829/745–8811* ⊕ *www.laxojo.com.*

Onno's Bar Cabarete. This remains a serious party place, and it's usually wall-to-wall and back-to-back as the young and fit pack the dance floor and groove to techno sounds. There's a daily happy hour as well as theme nights. DJs spin on weekends, when there's no cover; however, in high season the scene can get rowdy. It's also easier to get served at the beach bar than on the dance floor. Cabarete's Onno's now has sister establishments in Bávaro and Altos de Chavón. ✉ *Cabarete Beach, Calle Principal, Cabarete* ☎ *809/571–0461* ⊕ *www.onnosbar.com.*

SHOPS AND SPAS

Cigars continue to be the hottest commodity coming out of the D.R. Many exquisite, hand-wrapped smokes come from the island's rich Cibao Valley, and Fuente Cigars—handmade in Santiago—are highly prized. Only reputable cigar shops sell the real thing, and many you will see sold on the street are fakes. You can also buy and enjoy Cuban cigars here, but they still can't be brought back to the United States unless you purchase them in Cuba. Dominican rum and coffee are also good buys. *Mamajuana* is a popular herbal liqueur sold almost everywhere. The D.R. is the homeland of late designer Oscar de la Renta, and you may want to stop at the chic shops that carry his label's creations. La Vega is famous for its *diablos cajuelos* (devil masks), which are worn during Carnival. Look also for the delicate, faceless ceramic figurines that symbolize Dominican culture.

Though locally crafted products are often of a high caliber (and very affordable), expect to pay hundreds of dollars for designer jewelry made of amber and larimar. Larimar—a semiprecious stone the color of the Caribbean Sea—is found on the D.R.'s south coast in the hills above the city of Barahona. Prices vary according to the stone's hue and category, AAA being the highest. Amber has been mined extensively between Puerto Plata and Santiago. A fossilization of resin from a prehistoric pine tree, it sometimes encases ancient animal and plant life, from leaves to spiders to tiny lizards. Beware of fakes, which are especially prevalent in street stalls. A reputable dealer can show you how to tell the difference between real larimar and amber and imitations.

Bargaining is both a game and a social activity in the D.R., especially with street vendors and at the stalls in El Mercado Modelo. Vendors are disappointed and perplexed if you don't haggle. They're also tenacious so unless you really plan to buy, don't even stop to look.

SANTO DOMINGO

SHOPPING AREAS AND MALLS

Acropolis Mall, between Avenida Winston Churchill and Calle Rafael Augusto Sanchez, has become a favorite shopping arena for the young and/or hip capitaleños. Stores like Zara and Mango (both from Spain) have today's look without breaking your budget.

One of the main shopping streets in the Zona is **Calle El Conde,** a pedestrian thoroughfare. With the advent of so many restorations, the dull and dusty stores with dated merchandise are giving way to some hip new shops. However, many of the offerings, including local designer shops, are still of a caliber and cost that the Dominicans can afford. Some of the best shops are on **Calle Duarte,** north of the Zona Colonial, between Calle Mella and Avenida de Las Américas. **El Mercado Modelo,** a covered market, borders Calle Mella in the Zona Colonial; vendors here sell a dizzying selection of Dominican crafts.

Piantini is a swanky residential neighborhood that has an increasing number of fashionable shops and clothing boutiques, often housed in contemporary shopping malls. Its borders run from Avenida Winston Churchill to Avenida Lope de Vega and from Calle Jose Amado Soler to Avenida 27 de Febrero.

RECOMMENDED STORES

Casa Virginia. One of the Dominican Republic's leading department stores, Casa Virginia was founded in 1945. The store is stocked mostly with high-end designer clothing (including a Jenny Polanco department) and fashion finds, but also has Italian jewelry and some moderately priced gift items. ⊠ *Av. Roberto Pastoriza 255, Ensanche Naco* ☎ *809/566–4000* ⊕ *casavirginia.com* ☾ *Closed Sun.*

Galería de Arte Nader. Top Dominican artists in various mediums are on display here. The gallery staff are well known in Miami and New York, and they work with Sotheby's. ⊠ *Calle Rafael Augusto Sánchez 22, Ensanche Piantini* ☎ *809/544–0878* ☾ *Closed Sun.*

Galeria Toledo. A fascinating array of artwork, including Haitian voodoo banners and metal sculpture, and souvenirs, chandeliers, and estate jewelry, are sold here. The gallery's second room is dedicated to Dominican fine art. Tamika, the daughter of American expat owner Bettye Marshall, oversees the business. You can also rent a basic, affordable room with breakfast upstairs in Hostal Plaza Toledo. ⊠ *Isabel la Católica 163, Zona Colonial* ☎ *809/688–7649* ⊕ *www.galeriatoledo.com.*

La Leyenda del Cigarro, S.R.L. This shop along El Conde in the Zona Colonial makes and sells its own branded premium cigars to clients worldwide and anyone who happens to walk into the cozy store. Enjoy the leather couch in the seating area, and let owner Julio Vilchez Rosso or a member of his personable staff regale you with the history of cigar

9

making in the Dominican Republic and learn what makes a good cigar a good cigar. This store is perfect for the experienced connoisseur or those who'd like to become one. ⊠ *Calle El Conde 161, Zona Colonial* ☎ *809/686–5489, 809/445–3728.*

L'ile Au Tresor. After many years on Conde Street, across from the Hotel Mercure, the shop has moved to a historic house in the Zona Colonial. The owner, Patrick Le Clercq, has some of the most attractive and creative designer pieces in native larimar and amber. If you have never bought any of these lovely stones because of cheesy settings or high prices, take a look here. His innovative custom work, in sterling or gold, can be done in 48 hours. Some staff do not speak English but can call Patrick if he's not there. ⊠ *Arzobispo Meriño 209, Zona Colonial ✢ In front of the Colonial Tour Agency* ☎ *829/688–8751, 809/688–8751.*

Lyle O. Reitzel Art Contemporaneo. This gallery showcases mainly Latin artists from Mexico, South America, and Spain, and some of the most controversial Dominican visionaries. Specializing in contemporary art, it's been in business since 1995. Their rotating collection can include the new, the strange, and the daring. ⊠ *Gustavo Mejia Ricart, Torre Piantini Suites 1 and 2 A, Ensanche Piantini* ☎ *809/227–8361, 809/519–9214 cell for L.O.R., 305/510–2833 in the U.S.* ⊕ *www.lyleoreitzelgallery. com* ☉ *Closed Sun.*

SOUTHEAST COAST

SHOPPING AREAS AND MALLS

Altos de Chavón. Altos de Chavón is a re-creation of a 16th-century Mediterranean village on the grounds of the Casa de Campo resort, where you can find a church, art galleries, boutiques, restaurants, nightspots, and souvenir shops, and a 5,000-seat amphitheater for concerts grouped around a cobbled square. At the Altos de Chavón Art Studios you can find ceramics, weaving, and screen prints made by local and resident artists. Extra special is the Jenny Polanco Project. A top Dominican fashion designer, she has made an outlet for Dominican, Haitian, and Caribbean craftsmen to sell their wares, from Carnival masks to baskets and carved plates. Tienda Batey sells fine linens handcrafted by woman from the sugar plantation *bateys* (poor villages). ⊠ *Casa de Campo, La Romana.*

Casa de Campo Marina. Casa de Campo's top-ranked marina is home to shops and international boutiques, galleries, and jewelers scattered amid restaurants, banks, and other services. The chic shopping scene includes Luxury Shops Carmen Sol and Kiwi St. Tropez for French bathing suits. Polanco-Leon with Dominican designer Jenny Polanco's has resort wear, purses, and jewelry as well as Bibi Leon's tropical-themed home accessories. There's also a marvelous Italian antiques shop, Nuovo Rinascimento, and Club Del Cigarro (Fumo). The *supermercado* Nacional has not only groceries but sundries, postcards, and snacks. ⊠ *Casa de Campo Marina, Calle Barlovento, La Romana* ⊕ *www. marinacasadecampo.com.do.*

PUNTA CANA

SHOPPING AREAS AND MALLS

Fodor's Choice ★ **Galerias at Puntacana Village.** The Galerias at Puntacana Village lie within a still-blossoming shopping, dining, and residential complex built on the road to the Punta Cana International Airport. Originally the village was built to house employees of the Puntacana Group, but now the shops and restaurants are also a tourist draw. The village is comprised of churches, an international school, and this commercial area with its restaurants, shops, a supermarket, banks (with ATMs), a beauty salon, pharmacy, and doctors' offices. Family-oriented, there is an ice cream parlor, a playground, and a children's clothing boutique as well as those for ladies. The restaurants are less expensive than those at most resorts and very popular. The Sheraton Four Points Puntacana Village is across the street, just a two-minute drive from the airport. ⊠ *Blvd. Primero de Noviembre, Punta Cana* ⊕ *www.puntacanavillage.com.*

Fodor's Choice ★ **Palma Real Shopping Village.** A standout among the region's shopping centers, Palma Real Shopping Village is a swanky, partially enclosed mall (similar to something you would see in Southern California), that is also overall the most expensive. Fountains and tropical plants infuse life into the bright and airy interiors beneath the blue-tile roof. Music pipes through the stone-floor plaza in the center, where seating is available and security is tight. Upscale retail shops, which sell beachwear, clothing, skin-care products, and jewelry, line the walls. Several restaurants give visitors welcome dining alternatives beyond the gates of their resorts, and the shopping center holds Punta Cana's first movie theater. There are two banks, ATMs, and a money exchange outlet. Stores are open 10–10, but the restaurants stay open later. It has the best pharmacy in the area. Shuttle buses run to and from many of the hotels, with pickups every two hours. ⊠ *Av. Alemania 57, Bávaro* ☎ *809/552–8725* ⊕ *www.palmarealshoppingvillage.com.*

Plaza Uvero Alto. You won't find brand-name shops at Plaza Uvero Alto, but it's a convenient shopping center for the hotels in the remote Uvero Alto area of Punta Cana. Especially useful are a bank, outdoor ATM, and a money exchange, followed by Internet access, a small pharmacy, gift shops, and two minimarkets (one in the front, the other in the back row of booths). Here you can get sundries like sunscreen and deodorant at prices much cheaper than in the hotels. Behind the first row of enclosed stores, visit the colorful kiosks full of handicrafts, paintings, ceramics, and other gift items. Most shopkeepers here, although very friendly, don't speak much English, so be prepared to practice your Spanish. For beautifully designed jewelry with larimar and amber as well as other locally made novelties, visit **Tesoro Caribeño** (Suite 5, front row of stores), where the owner speaks fluent English. There's also a branch of the tourist police in the plaza. ⊠ *Carretera Uvero Alto, Uvero Alto.*

RECOMMENDED STORES

Harrison's Fine Jewelry. It's hard to walk by the windows of Harrison's Fine Jewelry without stepping in to admire the collection of jewelry, including a large selection of larimar and amber pieces in striking settings, as well as diamonds and other classic gems. Outlets of this renowned chain are also in several resorts of Punta Cana, like the Palma Real Shopping Village itself. ⊠ *Palma Real Shopping Village, Bávaro* ☎ *809/552–8721* ⊕ *www.harrisons.com.*

SPORTS AND THE OUTDOORS

BASEBALL

Baseball is a national passion, the cultural icon of the D.R., and yes, Sammy Sosa is still a legend in his own time. But he is just one of many celebrated Dominican baseball heroes, including pitcher Odalis Revela. Triple-A Dominican and Puerto Rican players and some American major leaguers hone their skills in the D.R.'s professional Winter League, which plays from October through January. Some games are held in the Tetelo Vargas Stadium, in the town of San Pedro de Macorís, east of Boca Chica.

Estadio Francisco A. Michelli. Estadio Francisco A. Michelli is La Romana's baseball stadium. Know that *la temporada* (the season) is short; your window of opportunity is just October through December, with an occasional game in January. ⊠ *Av. Padre Abreu, near monument, La Romana* ☎ *809/556–6188* 🎫 *$8.*

Liga de Béisbol Stadiums. Liga de Béisbol Stadiums can be a helpful information source if you're planning an independent trip to a baseball game. ⊠ *Santo Domingo* ⊕ *lidom.com.*

BIKING AND HIKING

Pedaling is easy on pancake-flat beaches, but there are also some steep hills in the D.R. Several resorts rent bikes to guests and nonguests alike.

NORTH COAST

FAMILY
Fodor'sChoice
★

Iguana Mama. This well-established, safety-oriented company's offerings include mountain bike tours that will take you along the coastal flats or test your mettle on steeper climbs in the national parks. Downhill bike rides include a taxi up to 3,000 feet, breakfast, and lunch and can be a full- or half-day. Advanced rides on- and off-road are also offered, as are guided day-hikes. Other half- and full-day trips include swimming, climbing up and jumping off various waterfalls, rappelling, and natural waterslides, white-water rafting, horseback riding, ecotours, and other adventures sports. The company also organizes longer, multiday excursions that include outdoor activities. ⊠ *Calle Principal 74, across from Scotia Bank, Cabarete* ☎ *809/571–0908, 809/571–0734, 809/654–2325* ⊕ *www.iguanamama.com* 🎫 *From $55.*

BOATING

Sailing conditions are ideal, with constant trade winds. Favorite excursions include day trips to Catalina and Saona islands—both in La Romana area—and sunset cruises on the Caribbean. Prices for crewed sailboats of 26 feet and longer, with a capacity of 4 to 12 people, are fixed according to size and duration, from a low of $200 a day to the norm of $700 a day. Charters of powerboats are much more expensive. For example, prices for the fleet at the upscale Cap Cana Marina are as follows: sportfishermen from 47 to 51 feet accommodating up to eight people (crewed with all equipment, snacks, and beverages with sandwiches on all-day trips), $1,800 for four hours, $2,500 for eight hours; a 62-foot custom, luxury power-sail catamaran, $1,650 for two hours (everything included for Cap Cana guests); a 56-foot Sea Ray Sedan Bridge motor yacht, $2,000 for two hours, $2,500 for four hours, $3,500 for eight hours (everything included); and a luxury 90-foot custom motor yacht, ideal for an incentive group, $3,500 for two hours, $5,000 for four hours, $8,500 for eight hours.

SOUTHEAST COAST

Fodor'sChoice ★ **Casa de Campo Marina.** Casa de Campo Marina has much going on, from sailing to motor yacht charters to socializing at the Casa de Campo Yacht Club. At the sailing school, students learn to conquer the Caribbean Sea from knowledgeable instructors. With everything from a laundry to ship chandlery and shipyard, as well as video surveillance that guarantees security, this is a safe haven for yachtsmen with 350 slips. Those who dock here have access to not only the marina but the amenities of Casa de Campo resort. ⊠ *Casa de Campo, Calle Barlovento 3, La Romana* ☎ *809/523–3333, 809/523–3333* ⊕ *www. marinacasadecampo.com.do.*

NORTH COAST

Carib Wind Cabarete. A renowned windsurfing center (known for decades as BIC Center) Carib Wind Cabarete has been operating since 1988. Since its founding, it's been transformed into a high-performance Olympic training center for Laser sailors from around the world. Here you can rent Lasers, 17-foot catamarans, bodyboards, ocean kayaks, and paddleboards. ⊠ *Cabarete* ☎ *809/571–0640* ⊕ *www.caribwind.com.*

SAMANÁ PENINSULA

Puerto Bahía Marina. This stunning marina on the north end of pristine Samaná Bay is a relatively new entity and is a first-class, full-service facility with slips from 40 to 150 feet. This marina not only has the necessary amenities, including fuel, restrooms with showers, 24-hour security, garbage pickup, Internet access, water taxis, and car rentals, but all the services and facilities of the Bannister Hotel. ⊠ *Carretera Sánchez–Samaná, Km 5, Samaná* ☎ *809/503–6363, 855/503–6363* ⊕ *www.puertobahiasamana.com.*

DIVING

Ancient sunken galleons, undersea gardens, and offshore reefs are among the lures here. Most divers head to the north shore. In the waters off Sosúa alone you can find a dozen dive sites (for all levels of ability) with such catchy names as Three Rocks (a deep, 163-foot dive), Airport Wall (98 feet), and Pyramids (50 feet). Some dive schools are represented on or near Sosúa Beach, in the town of Bayahibe, and in

Las Terrenas and Las Galeras on the Samaná Peninsula resorts have dive shops on-site or can arrange trips for you.

NORTH COAST

Northern Coast Aquasports. Located on the main street of Sosúa, this PADI 5-Star dive center with a well-stocked retail store offers all levels of PADI courses from Discover Scuba Diving to Instructor, with diving and snorkeling seven days a week. Professionalism is apparent in the initial classroom and pool training. Moreover, the company offers trips to a selection of outstanding sites in the calm, protected waters of Sosúa Bay. This location is not too far from the new Amber Cove cruise ship port in Maímon. All activities are guided by (multilingual) PADI professionals. ⊠ *Calle Pedro Clisante, 8, Sosúa* ☎ *809/571–1028* ⊕ *www.northerncoastdiving.com.*

SAMANÁ

Las Galeras Divers. This is a professional, safety-conscious operation. Owner Serge is a PADI, OWSI, and nitrox instructor, and every level of PADI course is offered. Diving lessons and trips are offered in English, French, and Spanish, and diving equipment rentals are also available. Discounts are given to groups, families, and divers who want a package deal. ⊠ *Calle Principal, Las Galeras* ☎ *809/538–0220, 809/715-4111* ⊕ *www.las-galeras-divers.com* ◎ *From $45.*

FISHING

Big-game fishing is big in Punta Cana, with blue and white marlin, wahoo, sailfish, and dorado among the most common catches in these waters. Several fishing tournaments are held every summer. The Punta Cana Resort & Club hosted the ESPN Xtreme Billfishing Tournament for many years. Blue-marlin tournaments are held at La Mona Channel in Cabeza de Toro. Several tour operators offer organized deep-sea fishing excursions.

LA ROMANA

Casa de Campo Marina. Casa de Campo Marina is the best charter option in the La Romana area. Yachts (22- to 60-footers) are available for deep-sea fishing charters for half or full days. Prices go from $824 for a half day on *Scorpio* to $3,555 for a full day on *Gabriella.* They can come equipped with rods, bait, dinghies, drinks, and experienced guides. Going out for the big billfish that swim the depths of the Caribbean is a major adrenaline rush. The marina hosts the annual Casa de Campo International Blue Marlin Classic Tournament in late March, which is celebrated with a round of parties. ⊠ *Casa de Campo, Calle Barlovento 3, La Romana* ☎ *809/523–3333, 809/523–3333* ⊕ *www.marinacasadecampo.com.do* ◎ *Charters from $824.*

PUNTA CANA

Marina Cap Cana. On the Mona Passage, this is a superb port for sport fishing during the summer season, when the grounds are renowned for an abundance of blue marlin and white marlin. Anglers participating in seasonal fishing tournaments receive favorable dockage rates. For sport fishing, chartered vessels are available for four or eight-hour excursions for marlin, wahoo, tuna, snapper, grouper, etc. (best organized through a Cap Cana hotel). There's also a designated fishing area for snook, tarpon, barracuda, and jack, with guides and equipment for hire. It's a catch-and-release marina. ⊠ *Cap Cana, Juanillo* ☎ *809/695–5539* ⊕ *www.marinacapcana.com.*

Puntacana Marina. The marine is on the southern end of the resort, where the restaurant La Yola is located. Big-game fishing is what this destination is famous for, and the marina hosts numerous summer tournaments such as ESPN2s Billfishing Xtreme Tournament. All water-sports rentals are handled through the new Punta Cana Aquatic Center, situated between the Westin and Playa Blanca. ⊠ *Puntacana Resort & Club, Punta Cana* ☎ *809/959–2262 Punta Cana Aquatic Center* ⊕ *www. puntacana.com.*

GOLF

Fodor's Choice ★ The D.R. has some of the best courses in the Caribbean, designed by top golf architects; among these leading designers are Pete Dye, P.B. Dye, Jack Nicklaus, Robert Trent Jones, Gary Player, Tom Fazio, and Nick Faldo. The country's courses have won awards for customer satisfaction, quality of courses and accommodations, value for money, support from suppliers and tourist boards, and professional conduct. Most courses charge higher rates during the winter high season; some, but not all, reduce their rates between April and October, so be sure to ask. Also, some have cheaper rates in the afternoon (mornings are cooler). And guests of certain hotels get better prices.

SOUTHEAST COAST

Fodor's Choice ★ **Casa de Campo Resort.** The Resort is considered by most to be the premier multiple golf resort in the Caribbean. The famed 18-hole Teeth of the Dog course at Casa de Campo, with seven holes on the sea, is usually ranked as the number-one course in the Caribbean and is among the top courses in the world. Pete Dye regards Teeth of the Dog as one of his best designs and has long enjoyed living at Casa part-time. The Teeth of the Dog requires a caddy for each round (for an additional fee). Pete Dye has designed this and two other globally acclaimed courses here. Dye Fore, now with a total of 27 holes, is close to Altos de Chavón, hugging a cliff that features commanding vistas of the sea, a river, Dominican mountains, and the marina. The Links is a gamey 18-hole inland course. Resort guests must reserve tee times for all courses at least one day in advance; nonguests should make reservations earlier. ⊠ *Casa de Campo, La Romana* ☎ *809/523–3333 resort, 809/523–8115 golf director* ⊕ *www.casadecampo.com.do* ▭ *Teeth of the Dog: $320 per round per golfer for nonhotel guests, $250 per round per player for guests; Dye Fore: $250 for nonguests, $225 for guests; The Links: $150 for nonguests, $135 for guests* ⚐ *Teeth of the Dog: 18 holes, 6989 yards, par 72; Dye Fore: 18 holes, 7740 yards, par 72; The Links: 18 holes, 6664 yards, par 71.*

9

PUNTA CANA

Barceló Bávaro Golf. Integrated within the Barceló Bávaro Beach Golf & Casino Resort complex in the Punta Cana region, this course is open to both resort and nonresort guests. The course traverses a lush inland mangrove forest and features 22 inland lakes and 122 bunkers, and totals 6,655 yards. It was actually the first course in the area and was designed by Juan Manuel Gordillo. Complete renovations, executed by designer P.B. Dye in 2010, breathed new life to the layout. The best rates are available for guests of the more upscale Barceló hotels, such as the Barceló Palace Deluxe. Walking is not permitted. ⊠ *Barceló Bávaro Beach Golf & Casino Resort, Bávaro* ☎ *809/686–5797* ⊕ *www. barcelobavarogolf.net* ⊠ *$70 for 18 holes for Barceló guests; $145 for nonguests* ⚐ *18 holes, 6655 yards, par 72.*

Catalonia Caribe Golf Club. Challenging and reasonably priced, Catalonia Caribe Golf Club is spread out on greens surrounded by five lakes and an abundance of shady palms. It's a relatively short course and features an island green. The architect, Alberto Sola, designed it to be challenging for both experienced and novice golfers. Rates include a cart. Outside guests may not be able to get tee times during peak season; always call ahead. ⊠ *Catalonia Bávaro Resort, Cabeza de Toro, Bávaro* ☎ *809/321–7058, 809/412–0000* ⊕ *www.cataloniabavaro.com* ⊠ *$45 for 18 holes for Catalonia Resort guests; $90 for nonresort guests* ⚐ *18 holes, 6950 yards, par 72.*

Cocotal Golf Course. Named for the coconut plantation on which it was built, Cocotal Golf Course, designed by Spaniard José "Pepe" Gancedo, has an 18-hole championship layout. It's a challenging par-72 course dotted with palm trees and serene lakes within the residential community Palma Real. There's also a driving range, clubhouse, pro shop, and golf academy. Fees include a golf cart. Advance booking is mandatory. Lessons and club rentals are available. ⊠ *Palma Real Villas, Bávaro* ☎ *809/ 221–1290 resort operator, 809/687–4653* ⊕ *www.cocotalgolf. com* ⊠ *$65–$75 for resort guests; $112 for 18 holes for nonguests* ⚐ *18 holes, 7285 yards, par 72.*

Corales Golf Club. "The Augusta National of the Caribbean" has expansive, finely landscaped grounds. Designed by Tom Fazio, it's a dramatic 18-hole course with six Caribbean seaside holes with a finishing hole that encourages players to cut off as much of the Caribbean off the tee as they dare. Laid out along the natural cliffs and coves of the sea and inland lakes and Coralina quarries, the 700 acres here are part of the extensive Puntacana Resort & Club. The club is open to its members and their guests, guests of Tortuga Bay, and Puntacana Resort guests who purchase the resort's Golf Experience packages, but a limited number of nonguests are allowed to play in both high and low season; enquiries and tee-time requests should be made by email. Caddies are mandatory at Corales. ⊠ *Puntacana Resort & Club, Punta Cana* ☎ *809/959–4653* ✉ *golfcorales@puntacana.com* ⊕ *www.puntacana. com* ⊠ *$195–$295 for resort guests; $295–$395 (including lunch) for nonguests* ⚐ *18 holes, 7555 yards, par 72.*

Hard Rock Golf Club at Cana Bay. This Jack Nicklaus–designed course is just a golf cart ride down from the resort on Macao Beach. It's a challenging and well-maintained course with ocean views and regularly hosts tournaments and other events. Hard Rock guests can use their resort credits to play. The Emerald driving range is close to the golf clubhouse (which rents Calloway clubs). Emblazoned Hard Rock golf cars are included. ⊠ *Hard Rock Hotel & Casino Punta Cana, Blvd. Turistico del Este, Km 28, Macao* ☎ *809/687-0000* ⊕ *www.hrhcpuntacana.com* 🖃 *$200 ($130 for "Twilight Play")* ⚐ *18 holes, 7253 yards, par 72.*

Fodor's Choice
★

La Cana Golf Club. You will enjoy the ocean views on 14 of the La Cana Golf Club's 27 holes of championship golf designed by P. B. Dye. The three 9s—Tortuga, Hacienda, and Arrecife—make for a very popular offering, particularly the oceanside finish on the La Cana Nine. The latest 9, Hacienda, opened in 2012 not as a full course but rather a set of 9 individual holes; it's punctuated with many lakes amid an unspoiled tropical landscape, a challenging addition to the existing, spectacular courses. All fees include a golf cart, taxes, and use of the expansive practice facility. Caddies are optional. Lessons and golf schools are offered by PGA professional staff. Rental clubs are available and should be reserved two weeks in advance from November through April. Guests of the resort's Westin or Tortuga Bay get discounted rates; nonguests who book with the resort can get transportation included. ⊠ *Puntacana Resort & Club, Punta Cana* ☎ *809/959-4653* ⊕ *www.puntacana.com* 🖃 *$105–$135 for resort guests; $140–$175 for nonguests* ⚐ *27 holes; Tortuga Nine: 9 holes, 3483 yards, par 36; Arrecife Nine: 9 holes, 3676 yards, par 36; Hacienda Nine: 9 holes, 3768 yards, par 36.*

Fodor's Choice
★

Punta Espada Golf Course. Jack Nicklaus cast his mark in the Caribbean with the magnificent Punta Espada Golf Course. You will discover a par-72 challenge with striking bluffs, lush foliage, and many gently tumbling fairways with spectacular water vistas. Incidentally, the water often does come into play. Having hosted the PGA Champions Tour, the course is even better in person than it looks on TV, and you won't find smoother putting surfaces! Yes, there's a Caribbean view from all the holes, and eight of them play right along the sea. The course's length can be extended to nearly 7,400 yards, but it's advisable to play a more forward tee. This exceptional golf club has concierge services, a restaurant, the Hole 19 bar, a pro shop, a members' trophy gallery, a library, lockers, an equipment repair shop, and a meeting room. Rates are discounted for guests in any of Cap Cana's accommodations and include golf cart, caddy, tees, water, and practice on the driving range. In high season, reservations are required, and it's best to make them two weeks in advance for tee times. ⊠ *Cap Cana, Carretera Juanillo, Juanillo* ☎ *809/469-7767* ⊕ *www.capcana.com* 🖃 *$225–$295 for resort guests; $295–$395 for nonguests* ⚐ *18 holes, 7396 yards, par 72.*

NORTH COAST

Playa Dorada Golf Club. *Golf Digest* has named Playa Dorada Golf Club one of the top 100 courses outside the United States. It's open to guests of all the hotels in the area. Caddies are mandatory for foursomes (and carry an extra fee); carts are optional. The attractive clubhouse has lockers, a pro shop, a bar, and the Fairways Restaurant. Reservations

9

during high season should be made as far in advance as possible. Guests at certain hotels in the Playa Dorada complex get discounts and check out the packages for multiple plays. ✉ *Playa Dorada* ☎ *809/320–4262* ⊕ *www.playadoradagolf.com* ✉ *$50 for 9 holes, $75 for 18 holes ⓘ 18 holes, 6730 yards., par 72.*

GUIDED TOURS

Visitors to the Dominican Republic will have a plethora of excursions to choose from, but many options are not wonderful and are wildly overpriced. Wait until you arrive before booking anything. As for group excursions, "interview" fellow guests to find out if their tour was worth the money and effort, or do research before you arrive. Often the full-day excursions are too long and leave too early. Best are half-day trips—particularly boat excursions. Horseback riding can sound appealing, as the trails usually include some stretches of beach, but horses, equipment, and instruction are often not optimal, and guides often don't speak sufficient English. Clients traveling on a tour-company package tend to book excursions with that company, or through the tour company affiliated with their resort.

SOUTHEAST COAST

FAMILY **Tropical Tours.** The primary and best tour operator on the Southeast Coast is Tropical Tours (based at Casa de Campo), whose prices are even less than some non-pros and cruise-ship excursions. Their vans are new or nearly new and well maintained. Also, most of their staff speaks English as well as other languages. They can take you on a tour of Santo Domingo, to fascinating caves, and to baseball games in La Romana's baseball stadium. Although most water-based excursions (outback safaris and zip-lining, too) now go through the concierges at Casa, Tropical does still offer some trips. The company also provides transfers to Las Americas and Punta Cana International Airports. ✉ *Casa de Campo, La Romana* ☎ *809/523–2029, 809/523–2028* ⊕ *tropicaltoursromana. com.do* ✉ *From $35.*

PUNTA CANA

Fodor'sChoice ★ **Amstar DMC–Apple Vacations.** Amstar is well managed and reliable, and it is associated with Apple Vacations, a major player that packages all-inclusive vacations in the D.R., particularly in Punta Cana. Once in the area, they can take you on a variety of half- or full-day tours, like to Bávaro Splash, Zipline, and the new Scape Park. They also offer airport transfers, particularly executive and VIP transfers in late-model vehicles with uniformed drivers. ✉ *Carretera Bávaro, Bávaro* ☎ *809/221–6626* ⊕ *www.amstardmc.com.*

Fodor'sChoice ★ **Go Golf Tours (GGT).** Go Golf has services tailored to clients seeking to make golf part of their getaway—whether it's the primary focus or just a one-time outing; the company will help arrange tee times, golf instruction, and transport to courses in Punta Cana or Casa de Campo by private driver at costs that are usually considerably less than those in a private taxi. They can also provide airport transfers. ✉ *Cocotal Golf & Country Club, Bávaro* ☎ *855/374–4653 toll-free in the U.S.,*

809/200–4653 toll-free in the D.R., 809/200–9556 toll-free in the D.R., 829/251–4653 ⊕ www.golfreservationcenter.com.

NORTH COAST

Alf's Tours. In Sosúa, Alf's Tours has been a mainstay for years. Why? It has only multilingual, licensed tour guides, and it's open daily. Plus, it has excursions all over the island for moderate prices, offering complimentary pickup service at any hotel in Sosúa, Puerto Plata, and Cabarete. Vehicles are closer to new than old, and guests are insured whether they are going to the famous waterfall El Limón in Las Terrenas or hopping aboard a Funny Buggy. ⊠ *Eugenio Kunhardt 68, El Batey* ☎ *809/571–1461.*

HORSEBACK RIDING

SOUTHEAST COAST

Equestrian Center at Casa de Campo. The 250-acre Equestrian Center at Casa de Campo has something for both Western and English riders—a dude ranch, a rodeo arena (where Casa's trademark "Donkey Polo" is played), three polo fields, guided trail rides, riding, jumping, and polo lessons. There are early-morning and sunset trail rides, too. Unlimited horseback riding is included in some Casa de Campo packages. Trail rides are offered through the property's private cattle ranch, through a herd of water buffalo and passing by lakes populated with ducks and the on-site horse-breeding operation. ⊠ *Casa de Campo, La Romana* ☎ *809/523–3333* ⊕ *www.casadecampo.com.do* ▢ *From $57.*

PUNTA CANA

Adventure Land Punta Cana. Long-established, the former Southfork Ranch (Rancho Pat), which has been the stable of choice in Punta Cana, is now a part of the Barceló resort complex (owners are still the same). Trail rides are along Barceló's "private" beach and on open-country roads. Morning rides start out at 9 and include a mojito break at a typical bar. Another includes an exploratory mission to Taíno caves and culminates in a lobster beach cookout. Then there is the memorable sunset beach ride, which can end with a beach bonfire barbecue. The company also offers other activities, including ATV tours. ⊠ *Barceló Resort Complex, Bávaro* ☎ *809/223–8896* ⊕ *adventures-puntacana. com* ▢ *From $55.*

El Rancho in Punta Cana. El Rancho in Punta Cana is across from the main entrance of the Puntacana Resort & Club. A one-hour trail ride winds along the beach, the golf course, and through tropical forests. The two-hour jungle trail ride has a stopover at a lagoon fed by a natural spring, so wear your swimsuit under your long pants. You can also do a one-hour sunset excursion (weekly) or take riding lessons. The Equestrian Center offers adult riding classes for beginners that include basic horse care. ⊠ *Puntacana Resort & Club, Punta Cana* ☎ *829/470–1367, 829/470–1350, 829/763–7474, 809/959–9221 resort main number* ⊕ *www.puntacana.com* ▢ *From $65.*

9

NORTH COAST

Sea Horse Ranch Equestrian Center. This equestrian center is a professional, well-staffed operation. The competition ring is built to international regulations, and there is a large schooling ring. Private lessons for experienced riders, including dressage or jumping instruction, are offered by the half-hour; "laissez faire" rides last from 90 minutes to three hours and include drinks and snacks—but make reservations. The most popular ride includes stretches of beach and a bridle path across a neighboring farm's pasture that's full of wildflowers and butterflies. Feel free to tie your horse to a palm tree and jump into the waves. ⊠ *Sea Horse Ranch, Sosua/Cabarete Hwy., Km. 2.5, Cabarete ✛ Between Sosua and Cabarete* ☎ *809/571–3880, 809/571–4462* ⊕ *www.sea-horse-ranch.com* ✉ *From $35.*

WHALE-WATCHING

SAMANÁ PENINSULA

Humpback whales come to Samaná Bay to mate and give birth each year for a relatively limited period, from approximately January 15 through March 30. Samaná Bay is considered one of the top 10 destinations in the world to watch humpbacks. If you're here during the brief season, this can be the experience of a lifetime. You can listen to the male humpback's solitary courting song and witness incredible displays as the whales flip their tails and breach (humpbacks are the most active species of whales in the Atlantic).

Fodor'sChoice
★

Whale Samaná. Owned by Kim Beddall, a Canadian who is incredibly knowledgeable about whales and Samaná in general, having lived here for decades, this operation is far and away the region's best, most professional, and environmentally sensitive. On board *Pura Mia*, a 55-foot motor vessel, a marine mammal specialist narrates and answers questions in several languages. Kim herself conducts almost all the English-speaking trips. Normal departure times are 9 for the morning trip and 1:30 for the afternoon trip; she is flexible whenever possible for cruise-ship passengers but does require advance reservations. ⊠ *Across street from town dock, beside park, Calle Sra. Morellia Kelly, Samaná* ☎ *809/538–2494* ⊕ *www.whalesamana.com* ✉ *From $59.*

GUADELOUPE

WELCOME TO GUADELOUPE

Guadeloupe Passage

La Pointe de la Grande Vigie

Plage de la Chapelle à Anse-Bertrand

Anse Bertrand
Campêche
Port Louis
Beauport
Les Mangles
Gros-Cap
Petit-Canal

Anse du Vieux Fort
Pte. Allègre

Ilet à Fajou
Anse du Canal

GRANDE

Plage de La Grande-Anse
Vieux-Bourg
Morne-à-l'Eau

[11] [12] [10]
Ste-Rose
[13]
[14]

Grand Cul-de-Sac Marin
Jabrun du Sud
Jabrun du Nord

Deshaies
Abymes

Domaine de Séverin Distillery
Lamentin
Destrelan
Airport [9]

Musée Camélia Costumes Traditions

Pointe-Noire

BASSE

Pointe-à-Pitre
Fort Fleur d'Epée
LeGosier

Anse Caraïbe
Cascade aux Ecrevisses
Bas-du-Fort
[1] [2]

Mahaut
La Traversée
Vernou
Petit-Bourg
Aquarium de la Guadeloupe

Plag Caravelle

Ilet de Pigeon
Les Mamelles

Pigeon Island
Plage de Malendure
Pigeon
Parc National de la Guadeloupe
Goyave

Bouillante

TERRE

Marigot
Domaine de Vanibel
Ste-Marie

Caribbean Sea

[15]
La Soufrière

Vieux-Habitants
Le Musée Volcanologique
Capesterre-Belle-Eau

Plage de Rocroy
Matouba
St-Claude
Chutes du Carbet
Anse Chapelle
St-Sauveur

Gourbeyre
Bananier
Trois-Rivières
[16]

Basse-Terre ★
Anse Turlet
Vieux Fort

KEY

⤴	Beaches
🚢	Cruise Ship Terminal
⛴	Ferry
◿	Dive Sites
[1]	Hotels

Iles des Saintes (Les Saintes)
Pompierre Bay
[17] – [23]
Fort Napoléon
Terre-de-Haut
Anse Crawen
Terre-de-Bas
La Coche
Grand Ilet

A heady blend of Afro-Caribbean customs, French style, and tropical delights, butterfly-shape Guadeloupe is actually two islands divided by a narrow channel: smaller, flatter, and drier Grande-Terre (Large Land) and wetter and more mountainous Basse-Terre (Low Land). Sheltered by palms, the beaches are beguiling, and the waterfront sidewalk cafés are a bit like the Riviera.

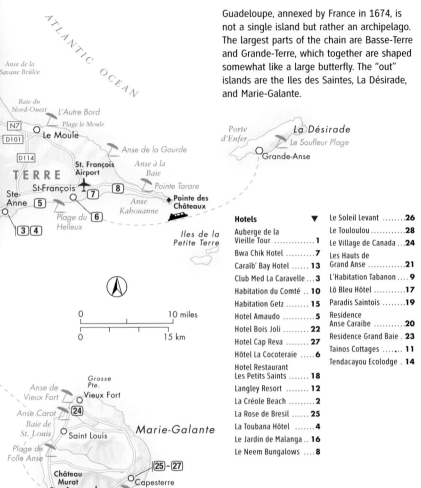

THE BUTTERFLY ISLAND

Guadeloupe, annexed by France in 1674, is not a single island but rather an archipelago. The largest parts of the chain are Basse-Terre and Grande-Terre, which together are shaped somewhat like a large butterfly. The "out" islands are the Iles des Saintes, La Désirade, and Marie-Galante.

Hotels ▼

Auberge de la Vieille Tour 1

Bwa Chik Hotel 7

Caraïb' Bay Hotel 13

Club Med La Caravelle ... 3

Habitation du Comté .. 10

Habitation Getz 15

Hotel Amaudo 5

Hotel Bois Joli 22

Hotel Cap Reva 27

Hôtel La Cocoteraie 6

Hotel Restaurant Les Petits Saints 18

Langley Resort 12

La Créole Beach 2

La Rose de Bresil 25

La Toubana Hôtel 4

Le Jardin de Malanga .. 16

Le Neem Bungalows 8

Le Soleil Levant 26

Le Touloulou 28

Le Village de Canada ... 24

Les Hauts de Grand Anse 21

L'Habitation Tabanon 9

Lô Bleu Hôtel 17

Paradis Saintois 19

Residence Anse Caraibe 20

Residence Grand Baie . 23

Tainos Cottages 11

Tendacayou Ecolodge . 14

TOP REASONS TO VISIT GUADELOUPE

1 Creole Flavors: Guadeloupe's restaurants and hotel dining rooms highlight the island's fine creole cuisine.

2 Small Inns: Also called *relais* and *gites* (apartments) these intimate accommodations give you a genuine island experience.

3 Adventure Sports: Parc National has plenty of activities to keep the adrenaline pumping.

4 La Désirade: Remote and affordable, this friendly island provides an escape-from-it-all experience.

NEED TO KNOW

AT A GLANCE

Capital: Basse-Terre

Population: 406,000

Currency: Euro

Money: ATMs common; few places accept U.S. dollars, so plan on exchanging them for euros

Language: French, Creole

Country Code: ☎ 590

Emergencies: ☎ 17

Driving: On the right

Electricity: 230v/50 cycles; plugs are European standard with two round prongs

Time: Same as New York during daylight savings; one hour ahead otherwise

Documents: Up to 90 days with valid passport

Mobile Phones: GSM (900 and 1800 bands)

Major Mobile Companies: Digicel, Orange

WEBSITES

Comité du Tourisme des Iles de Guadeloupe: ⊕ www.lesilesdeguadeloupe. com

GUADELOUPE

GRANDE-TERRE

Basse-terre

BASSE-TERRE

MARIE-GALANTE

Caribbean Sea

GETTING AROUND

✈ **Air Travel:** Aéroport International Pôle Caraïbes near Pointe-à-Pitre, is the sole airport in Guadeloupe.

🚌 **Bus Travel:** Buses connect all points on the island to Pointe-à-Pitre—except for the airport. Smaller islands do not have buses.

🚗 **Car Travel:** Most visitors can get by with a rental car for a day or two. There are no car rentals on Guadeloupe's smaller islands.

⛴ **Ferry Travel:** Ferries operate between the main island, Terre-de-Haut, and Marie-Galante. Another ferry connects Guadeloupe to Martinique and Dominica.

PLAN YOUR BUDGET

	HOTEL ROOM	MEAL	ATTRACTIONS
Low Budget	$150	$12	Fort Napoleon, $6
Mid Budget	$300	$30	Aquarium, $15
High Budget	$475	$50	Diving trip, $85

WAYS TO SAVE

Get the fixed-price menu. Most restaurants on Guadeloupe offer a multicourse, fixed-price menu that saves a significant amount of money.

Rent a villa. Unlike other islands where you might want to rent a condo or time-share, multibedroom villas are very affordable on Guadeloupe.

Time your taxi rides. Taxi prices on Guadeloupe are 40% higher from late evening to early morning.

Note exchange rates. Withdraw euros from the ATM if possible. If you must exchange cash do it in a *bureau de change*, which has a better exchange rate than you'll get at the hotels.

Hassle Factor	Medium. Flights to Guadeloupe require a transfer in Miami or somewhere in the Caribbean.
3 days	Relax poolside or beachside at your resort. Rent a car for a day to check out Guadeloupe's outstanding beaches—few resorts are near the ones that are the islands' best.
1 week	Explore Guadeloupe in detail, paying close attention to the southern shore of Grande-Terre, Basse-Terre's wild national park, and dive in the surrounding waters. Take a day trip to one of the Iles des Saintes.
2 weeks	Explore Guadeloupe, coast to coast. Spend a few days checking out the eight-island group known as Iles des Saintes. Also take the ferry to neighboring islands Marie-Galante and La Désirade.

WHEN TO GO

High Season: Mid-December through mid-April is the most fashionable and most expensive time to visit, when the weather is typically sunny and warm. Good hotels are often booked far in advance, and you're guaranteed the most entertainment at resorts and the most people with whom to enjoy it.

Low Season: From August to late October, temperatures can grow oppressively hot and the weather muggy, with high risks of tropical storms. Some upscale hotels close during these months for annual renovations. Those remaining open offer discounts.

Value Season: From late April to July and again November to mid-December, hotel prices drop 20% to 50% from high-season prices. There are chances of scattered showers, but expect sun-kissed days, too, and fewer crowds.

BIG EVENTS

February–March: Carnival is an annual highlight, starting in February and continuing until Ash Wednesday, finishing with a parade and a huge street party.

June: The Creole Blues Festival on Marie-Galante is popular with music lovers. ⊕ www.terredeblues.com

August: The Tour Cycliste de la Guadeloupe, which runs over 800 miles of both Grande-Terre and Basse-Terre, is the Caribbean's answer to the Tour de France. ⊕ www.guadeloupecyclisme.com

November: Le Route du Rhum is the largest solitary, transatlantic sailboat race, which starts in France and finishes in Pointe-à-Pitre. ⊕ www.routedurhum.com

READ THIS

■ *Crossing the Mangrove,* Maryse Condé. Insight into Guadeloupean culture through a man's wake.

■ *The Drifting of Spirits,* Gisèle Pineau. Thought-provoking, spiritual drama.

■ *Anabasis,* Saint-John Perse. Poetic work by the Nobel Prize winner.

WATCH THIS

■ *Bitter Sugar.* Examines the controversial actions of Joseph Ignace.

■ *Tèt Grenné.* French drama directed by Christian Grandman.

■ *La La Soufrière.* German documentary on volcanic eruptions on Guadeloupe.

EAT THIS

■ *Colombo*: a stew with *poudre de Colombo* (Colombo powder) and meat, similar to an Indian curry.

■ *Accras de morue*: salt fish fritters made with cassava flour.

■ *Boudin creole*: a dark and spicy blood sausage.

■ *Matété*: spicy land-crab meat curry, also known as matoutou.

■ *Ouassous*: freshwater crayfish prepared similar to the French bouillabaisse.

■ *Breadfruit migan*: mashed breadfruit with salted pork and cod.

EATING AND DRINKING WELL IN THE FRENCH WEST INDIES

Creole cuisine, a sultry mélange of African, European, Arawak, even Asian traditions, reflects the islands' turbulent territorial tugs-of-war.

Deceptively simple yet robustly flavored, authentic "kweyol" cuisine demands patience to make: continual macerating and marinating, then seasoning as the food simmers. Many dishes developed in response to economic necessities, recycling leftovers and incorporating ingredients such as starches (both hardy and impervious to spoilage). The indigenous Arawaks provided tubers such as tannia and yuca; lemongrass and capsicum for seasoning; arrowroot for thickening; and *roucou* (annatto, a yellowish-reddish seed) for coloring. The Africans imported plantains, pigeon peas, potatoes, and peppers. The French and British introduced tomatoes, onions, and less perishable salt cod. East Indian indentured servants brought cumin, cardamom, and coriander, notably used in *colombo*, a meat (try *cabri*, goat), poultry, or seafood

dish that detonates the palate. Wash it down with fresh local juices from pulpy papaya to puckering passion fruit or the fine rums. Bon appétit!

Blaff. This typical method of preparation is usually used for firm, flaky, white fish such as mahimahi or grouper. The fish is poached in a seasoned broth, often a classic court-bouillon (a quick stock perfumed with fresh herbs). The incendiary condiment *sauce chien* is served with accras, grilled fish, chicken, and "whatever." The components are vegetable oil, chopped chives, crushed garlic, hot pepper, lemon juice, salt, and pepper. Consensus has it that the derivation of the name came from the brand name of the knife, Chien, which is used to cut the ingredients. However, as its etymology is obscure, it may indeed have been named "dog's sauce" because it would render even canines edible.

Cod. France contributed many basic ingredients over time to economize, notably dried salt cod, which required no refrigeration and became a staple in creole cooking. *Accras de morue*, fluffy cod fritters, grace every menu. Other popular traditional dishes include *chiquetaille*, shredded cod usually served with a spicy vinaigrette, and *feroce* (saltfish mixed with avocado and peppers, deep-fried in manioc flour). *Tinnain morue*, grilled cod and bananas believed to energize, still jump-starts many locals' days.

Crayfish. This spiky freshwater crustacean, both wild and, increasingly, farmed, is usually served whole with a variety of sauces. It goes by many names in the French West Indies, including the more Gallic *écrevisse*, patois *z'habitant* or *crebiche*, and *ouassou* (generally larger). A favorite preparation is stewed with *dombrés* (manioc dumplings served pancake-style); you may also see it *étouffée* (stewed with vegetables, served over rice), underscoring the similarity to Cajun cuisine (alongside such dishes as *boudin*, blood sausage).

Poulet Boucané. "Buccaneer's chicken" is smoked slowly over burnt sugarcane (a centuries-old warning signal that pirates were coming) in a closed, chimney-topped barbecue. *Boucanage* is also

a French preservation technique, "drying" seasoned meats and poultry on a wood fire (in this case using sugarcane husks). Roughly similar to Jamaica's jerk, it mingles smokiness, sweetness, and spiciness; the marinade typically is a variant of the combustible sauce chien, though milder versions might combine vinegar, lime, garlic, and clove.

'Ti Punch. The primary ingredient in this aperitif is 100-proof rum, occasionally fruit-infused, muddled with lime and simple cane syrup. Novices can request the lighter (weight) *ti-bete*. Another concoction worth sampling is the classic *planteur* (rum with fruit juices and spices); finish dinner with a *rhum vieux* (aged, cognac-quality rum) like Reimonenq's Ste. Rose, or *shrubb*, an orange-and-spice-tinged rum-based liqueur.

Tripe. Another old-fashioned method of economizing was the use of internal organs, offal, which eventually became appropriated by haute cuisine. Tripe (small intestines) is particularly popular. The classic dish is *bébélé*, a stew of tripe, green bananas, tubers (usually breaded as croquettes or *domblés*), and gourds such as *giraumon* (similar to pumpkin).

—Jordan Simon

10

Updated by
Eileen
Robinson
Smith

Sail the waters around the Isles of Guadeloupe and you'll observe nuances in the ocean's color palette as you glide through the gin-clear sea. Things look better from the bow of a sailboat, from the storybook islands of Les Saintes to towns that are not as postcard pretty. This Caribbean coastline is dramatic with white and golden beaches, rocky promontories, and rugged cliffs that span the horizon.

Although Guadeloupe is thought of as one island, it is an archipelago, and each island has its own personality. "The mainland" consists of the two largest islands in the Guadeloupe archipelago: Basse-Terre and Grande-Terre, which look something like a butterfly. The outer islands—Les Saintes, Marie-Galante, and La Désirade—are acknowledged as wonderfully unique, unspoiled travel destinations. Tourism officials are now wisely marketing their country as a plural, Les Îles de Guadeloupe. See which one is your place in the sun. *Vive les vacances!*

It's no wonder that in 1493 Christopher Columbus welcomed the sight of this emerald paradise, where fresh, sweet water flows in cascades. And it's understandable why France annexed it in 1674 and why the British schemed to wrench it from them. In 1749 Guadeloupe mirrored what was happening in the motherland. It, too, was an island divided between royalists and revolutionaries.

The resident British sided with the royalists, so Victor Hugues was sent to banish the Brits. While here, he sent to the guillotine more than 300 planters loyal-to-the-royals and freed the slaves, thus all but destroying the plantocracy. An old saying of the French Caribbean refers to *les grands seigneurs de la Martinique et les bonnes gens de la Guadeloupe* (the lords of Martinique and the bourgeoisie of Guadeloupe), and that still rings true. You'll find more aristocratic descendants of the original French planters on Martinique (known as *békés*) and also more "expensive" people both living and vacationing there. That mass beheading is one of the prime reasons. Napoléon—who ultimately ousted the royals—also ousted Hugues and reestablished slavery. It wasn't until 1848 that an Alsatian, Victor Schoelcher, abolished it for good.

Guadeloupe became one of France's *départements d'outremer* in 1946, meaning that it's a dependent of France. It was designated a region in 1983, making it a part of France, albeit a distant part. This brought many benefits to the islanders, from their fine highway systems to the French social services and educational system, as well as a high standard of living. Certain tensions still exist, though the anticolonial resentment harbored by the older generations is dying out. Guadeloupe's young people realize the importance of tourism to the island's future, and you'll find them welcoming, smiling, and practicing the English and tourism skills they learn in school. Some *français* is indispensable, though you may receive a bewildering response in Creole.

Guadeloupe has more than a bit of France, but the culture of this tropical paradise is more Afro-influenced. Savor the earthier pleasures here, exemplified by the wonderful potpourri of whole spices whose heady aromas flood the outdoor markets.

PLANNING

GETTING HERE AND AROUND

AIR TRAVEL

Nonstop service is available on American Airlines from Miami; on Norwegian from Baltimore (BWI), Boston, and New York–JFK (service is seasonal); and on Seaborne Airlines from San Juan, the latter three times weekly. Seaborne codeshares with American Airlines, Delta, United, and JetBlue. Air Canada flies weekly nonstops between Montreal and Pointe-à-Pitre. Air Antilles Express has service to Martinique; St. Martin; Cayenne, French Guiana; St. Lucia; and Santo Domingo, Dominican Republic.

Air Caraïbes connects the island to St. Maarten; Martinique; Haiti; St. Barth; French Guiana, St. Lucia; Santo Domingo, Dominican Republic; Havana, Cuba; and Paris.

Air France's daily flights between Miami and Guadeloupe stop in Haiti before landing in Pointe-à-Pitre.

LIAT mainly services the English-speaking Caribbean islands, including Antigua, Barbados, and St. Lucia, where U.S. and Canadian travelers can get to Guadeloupe with fewer stopovers. LIAT codeshares with Air Caraïbes.

Contacts Air Antilles Express. ☎ 0890/64–86–48 ⊕ www.airantilles.com. **Air Canada.** ☎ 888/247–2262, 0590/21–12–77 ⊕ www.aircanada.com. **Air Caraïbes.** ☎ 0820/83–58–35 ⊕ www.aircaraibes.com. **Air France.** ☎ 0590/21–13–03, 0820/82–08–20, 800/237–27–47 in the U.S. ⊕ www.airfrance.com. **American Airlines.** ⊕ www.aa.com. **LIAT.** ☎ 0590/21–13–93, 888/844–5428 in Guadaloupe ⊕ www.liatairline.com. **Norwegian.** ☎ 800/357–4159 ⊕ norwegian. com/us. **Seaborne Airlines.** ☎ 866/359–8784 ⊕ www.seaborneairlines.com.

10

Taxi fare to Pointe-à-Pitre is about €30, to Gosier resorts about €35, to Ste-Anne as much as €60, and to St-François nearly €70. Cabs meet all flights at the airport if you decide not to rent a car.

Contacts Aéroport International Pôle Caraïbes (PTP). ⊠ *Morne Mamiel, Les Abymes* ☎ *0590/21–71–71, 0590/21–14–00* ⊕ *www.guadeloupe. aeroport.fr.*

CAR TRAVEL

If you're based in Gosier or at a large resort, you'll probably need a car only for a day or two of sightseeing. That may be enough, since roundabouts, mountain roads, and fast, aggressive drivers are stressful. Your valid driver's license will suffice for up to 20 days. You can get a rental car from the airport or your hotel. Count on spending between €48 and €80 a day for a small car with standard shift; automatics are considerably more expensive and must be reserved in advance. Note that some companies, including Europcar, charge a €25 drop-off fee for the airport, even if you pick the car up there. Allow at least 30 to 60 minutes to drop off your car at the end of your stay. The chances of your getting lost on the way to the airport and to where you need to leave the car (at a car rental box near the airport, where you then wait for a shuttle to bring you and your luggage back to the airport) are such that you should probably allow a full hour. Conscientiously follow every sign that has a picture of a plane. An alternative is to return it in Gosier and put that €25 drop-off fee saved toward a €35 stress-free, taxi ride. Return your vehicle with the same amount of gas or you'll be charged an exorbitant rate.

Car Rental Contacts Avis. ☎ *0590/21–13–54, 800/331–1212* ⊕ *www.avis. fr.* **Budget.** ☎ *0590/21–46–57* ⊕ *www.budget-antilles.com.* **Captheo.** ✛ *From the ferry dock, turn left, walk a couple of blocks. This is on the right, seaside of the street, near the pharmacy* ☎ *0590/81–49–82, 0690/63–58–13.* **Europcar.** ☎ *0590/21–13–52, 0690/35–29–52* ⊕ *www.europcar-guadeloupe.com.* **Hertz.** ☎ *0590/21–13–46, 0590/89–28–05* ⊕ *www.hertzantilles.com.* **Jumbo Car.** ☎ *0820/22–02–30, 0590/91–91–66* ⊕ *www.jumbocar.com.* **MTA Sarl Location.** ⊠ *Rue Commandant Mortenol, Grand-Bourg* ☎ *0690/91–64–63, 0590/97–18–02* ⊕ *voiture-mariegalante.com.* **Sixt.** ☎ *0590/21–13–44* ⊕ *www.sixt.com.*

FERRY TRAVEL

Ferry schedules and fares often change, so phone ahead to confirm. You normally travel to the outlying islands in the archipelago in the morning, returning in the afternoon. Day-trips are generally much cheaper than regular round-trips. Comatrile and Babou One are based

---

DRIVING TIPS

Guadeloupeans are fast and often impatient drivers and they tailgate. Driving around Grande-Terre is relatively easy for there is a well-maintained system of highways. Basse-Terre requires more skill to navigate the hairpin bends in the mountains and around the eastern shore; at night the roads are unlighted and treacherous. Roundabouts (*rond-pointes*) are everywhere. Use your turn signal and proceed cautiously. If you're lost, don't ask people standing on the side of the road; they are waiting for a lift and may jump in. Try to find a gas station. *Je suis perdu!* (I am lost!) is a good phrase to know.

in St-François, L'Express des Iles in Point-à-Pitre, and C.T.M. Deher in Trois-Rivières; both Comatrile and Express des Isles also operate ferries between Terre-de-Haut and Marie-Galante.

International service is offered by Jeans and L'Express des Isles, connecting Pointe-à-Pitre, Guadeloupe, with Martinique and Dominica.

Contacts BABOU One. ⊠ *Marina de St-François, St-François* ☎ *0690/26–60–69, 0590/47–50–31, 0690/63–46–39* ⊕ *www.babouone.fr.* **Comatrile.** ⊠ *Marina de St-François, St-François* ☎ *0690/50–05–09 port, 0590/22–26–31* ⊕ *www.comatrile.com.* **C.T.M. Deher.** ☎ *0590/99–50–68, 0590/92–06–39* ⊕ *www.ctmdeher.com.* **Jeans.** ☎ *0825/01–01–25* ⊕ *www.jeansforfreedom.com.* **L'Express des Isles.** ☎ *0825/35–90–00* ⊕ *www.express-des-iles.com.*

TAXI TRAVEL

Taxis are metered and fairly pricey. Fares jump by 40% between 7 pm and 7 am and on Sunday and holidays.

Contacts CDL Taxi. ☎ *0590/20–74–74.* **Christian Taxi.** ☎ *0690/55–88–17.* **Earl Ruddy Taxi.** ☎ *0690/47–47–74.* **Jean Luc Renault Taxi of St-François.** ☎ *0690/57–59–40.*

HEALTH AND SAFETY

Dengue, chikungunya, and zika have all been reported throughout the Caribbean. We recommend that you protect yourself from these mosquito-borne illnesses by keeping your skin covered and/or wearing mosquito repellent. The mosquitoes that transmit these viruses are as active by day as they are by night.

HOTELS AND RESORTS

Guadeloupe is actually an archipelago of large and small islands. Grande-Terre has the big package hotels that are concentrated primarily in four or five communities on the south coast, whereas wilder Basse-Terre has more locally owned hotels. More distant and much quieter are the Iles des Saintes, Marie-Galante, and La Désirade, in that order. On each of these smaller islands tourism is only a part of the economy and development is light, and any of them will give you a sense of what the Caribbean used to be.

10

Relais and Gites: These small inns offer a more personal—and authentic—kind of Caribbean experience.

Resorts: You can certainly opt for a big, splashy resort with all the amenities. Many of the island's large chain hotels cater to French package groups and are relatively bare-bones, though an increasing number of them are being renovated to the degree that they will appeal more to Americans as well.

Villas: Private villas are another option—particularly for families—but the language barrier is often a deterrent for Americans. Best to go through one of the rental agencies recommended here.

Hotel reviews have been shortened. For full information, visit Fodors.com.

WHAT IT COSTS IN EUROS				
	$	**$$**	**$$$**	**$$$$**
RESTAURANTS	under €12	€12–€20	€21–€30	over €30
HOTELS	under €275	€275–€375	€376–€475	over €475

Restaurant prices are the average cost of a main course at dinner or, if dinner is not served, at lunch. Hotel prices are the lowest cost of a standard double room in high season.

VISITOR INFORMATION

Contacts Comité du Tourisme des Iles de Guadeloupe. ⊠ *5 sq. de la Banque, Pointe-à-Pitre* ☎ *0590/82–09–30* ⊕ *www.lesilesdeguadeloupe. com.* **Guadeloupe Islands Tourist Board.** ⊠ *825 3rd Ave., 29th fl., New York* ☎ *212/745–0950, 212/838–7855 Fax number* **Office de Tourisme de Désirade.** ⊠ *La Capitainerie-Beausejour, waterfront at ferry dock, La Désirade* ☎ *0590/85–00–86.* **Office du Tourisme de Marie-Galante.** ⊠ *Rue du Fort, BP 15, Grand-Bourg* ☎ *0590/97–56–51* ⊕ *www.ot-mariegalante.com.* **Office du Tourisme de St-François.** ⊠ *Av. de l'Europe, St-François* ☎ *0590/68–66–81* ⊕ *www.destination-stfrancois.com.* **Office du Tourisme de Terre de Haut.** ⊠ *Ferry Dock, Jean Calot St., PB 10, Terre-de-Haut* ☎ *0590/94–30–61* ⊕ *www. terredehauttourisme.com.*

EXPLORING

To see each "wing" of the butterfly, you'll need to budget at least one day. They are connected by a bridge, and Grande-Terre has pretty villages along its south coast and the spectacular Pointe des Châteaux. You can see the main sights in Pointe-à-Pitre in a half day. Touring the rugged, mountainous Basse-Terre is a challenge. If time is a problem, head straight to the west coast; you could easily spend a day traveling its length, stopping for sightseeing, lunch, and a swim. You can make day trips to the islands, but an overnight or more works best. Leave your heavy luggage in the baggage room of your "mainland" hotel and take a small bag on the ferry.

GRANDE-TERRE

POINTE-À-PITRE

Although not the capital, this is the island's largest city, a commercial and industrial hub in the southwest of Grande-Terre. The Isles of Guadeloupe have 450,000 inhabitants, most of whom live in the cities. Pointe-à-Pitre is bustling, noisy, and hot—a place of honking horns and traffic jams and cars on sidewalks for want of a parking place. By day its pulse is fast, but at night, when its streets are almost deserted, you may not want to be there.

The heart of the old city is Place de la Victoire; surrounded by wooden buildings with balconies and shutters (including the tourism office) and by sidewalk cafés, it was named in honor of Victor Hugues's 1794

DID YOU KNOW?

There are numerous hiking trails that climb La Soufrière volcano, and some of them can be pretty treacherous. Go with a guide and you can safely take in breathtaking sights, such as the views from Piton Dolomieu.

victory over the British. During the French Revolution Hugues ordered the guillotine set up here so that the public could witness the bloody end of 300 recalcitrant royalists, mainly the prosperous plantation owners.

Even more colorful is the bustling marketplace, between rues St-John Perse, Frébault, Schoelcher, and Peynier. It's a cacophonous place, where shoppers bargain for spices, herbs (and herbal remedies), and a bright assortment of papayas, breadfruits, christophenes, and tomatoes.

WORTH NOTING

Cathédrale de St-Pierre et St-Paul. If you like churches, then make a pilgrimage to the imposing Cathédrale de St-Pierre et St-Paul, built in 1807. Although it has been battered by hurricanes over the years, it has fine stained-glass windows and creole-style balconies. ⊠ *Rue Alexandre Isaac at rue de l'Eglise.*

Musée Schoelcher. Established in a Colonial-style building, Musée Schoelcher celebrates Victor Schoelcher, an abolitionist from Alsace who fought against slavery in the French West Indies in the 19th century. The first museum in Guadeloupe, it was inaugurated in 1887, following a substantial donation in 1883 by "himself." New are 17 ethnographic objects that are part of a collection assembled by the abolitionist during his travels in the Caribbean, Egypt, and Africa, between 1830 and 1847. Presently, the museum contains many of his personal effects, and exhibits trace his life and work. ⊠ *24 rue Peynier, Pointe-à-Pitre* ☎ *0590/82–08–04* ⊠ *€2* ⊙ *Weekdays 9–5.*

Musée St-John Perse. Those with a strong interest in French literature and culture (not your average sightseer) will want to see the Musée St-John Perse, which is dedicated to the poet Alexis Léger, Guadeloupe's most famous son. Better known as Saint-John Perse, he was the winner of the Nobel Prize for literature in 1960. Some of his finest poems are inspired by the history and landscape—particularly the sea—of his beloved Guadeloupe. This literary museum, in a restored colonial house, contains a collection of his poetry and some of his personal belongings. Before you go, look for his birthplace at 54 rue Achille René-Boisneuf. ⊠ *9 rue Nozières, Pointe-à-Pitre* ☎ *0590/90–01–92,* ⊠ *€2.50* ⊙ *Weekdays 9–5, Sat. 8:30–12:30.*

ELSEWHERE ON GRANDE-TERRE

TOP ATTRACTIONS

Ft. Fleur d'Épée. The main attraction in Bas-du-Fort is this fortress, built between 1759 and 1763. It hunkers down on a hillside behind a deep moat. The fort was the scene of hard-fought battles between the French and the English in 1794. You can explore its well-preserved dungeons and battlements and take in a sweeping view of Iles des Saintes and Marie-Galante. The free guided tour here explores the fort's history and architecture and helps explain the living conditions of the soldiers who lived here. Included on the tour is an exploration of its underground galleries, now decorated with graffiti. If a bilingual person is on duty, she will explain it all in English. Call ahead, and to make certain of that day's hours. Registered as a historic monument since 1979, the fort also provides superb views for walkers. ⊠ *Bas du Fort* ☎ *0590/90–94–61* ⊠ *Free* ⊙ *Daily 9–5.*

Gosier. Gosier was still a tiny village in the 1950s, a simple stopping place between Pointe-à-Pitre and Ste-Anne. However, it grew rapidly in the 1960s, when the beauty of the southern coastline began to bring tourists in ever-increasing numbers. Today Gosier is one of Guadeloupe's premier tourist areas while at the same time serving as a chic suburb of Pointe-à-Pitre. People sit at sidewalk cafés reading *Le Monde* as others flip-flop their way to the beach. This resort town has several hotels, nightclubs, shops, a casino, rental car agencies, and a long stretch of sand.

Pointe des Châteaux. A National Grand Site, the island's easternmost point offers a breathtaking view of the Atlantic crashing against huge rocks, carving them into shapes resembling pyramids. A rocky arm reaching out to the ocean, it is a spectacular display of sea versus land. A 9-ton crucifix can be seen for miles out at sea and was erected for the centennial of the Catholic diocese in 1946. There are spectacular views of Guadeloupe's southern and eastern coasts and the island of La Désirade. The beach has few facilities now that vendors have been relocated to Petit Anse Kahouanne, about a mile up the road, so bring your own food and drink. The Village Artisanal is open every day, and in high season taxis run every hour. ⊠ *St-François.*

WORTH NOTING

FAMILY **Aquarium de la Guadeloupe.** Unique in the Antilles, this aquarium in the marina near Pointe-à-Pitre is a good place to spend an hour. Its motto is "Visit the sea." The well-planned facility has an assortment of tropical fish, crabs, lobsters, moray eels, coffer fish, and some live coral. It's also a turtle rescue center, and the shark tank is spectacular. A restaurant serves kid-friendly fare, snacks, salads, pastas, etc. A small shop stocks marine toys and souvenirs. The aquarium also offers twice-daily half-day ecotours via small boats that travel through the mangroves, reefs, and a lagoon, with a biologist guide and a diving instructor on board. Snorkeling gear is included, and kids are more than welcome. ⊠ *Pl. Créole, off Rte. N4, Le Gosier* 🕾 *0590/90–92–38, 0690/90–92–38, 0690/57–60–69 Seatours* ⊕ *www.aquariumdelaguadeloupe.com* 🖅 *€11.50; ecotour €59* ⊙ *Daily 9–6:30; ecotours daily at 8:30 and 1.*

10

Le Moule. On the Atlantic coast, and once the capital city of Guadeloupe, this port city of 24,000 has had more than its share of troubles: it was bombarded by the British in 1794 and 1809 and by a hurricane in 1928. An important tourist center in past decades, it's experiencing a comeback. A large East Indian population, which originally came to cut cane, lives here. Canopies of flamboyant trees hang over the narrow streets, where colorful vegetable and fish markets do a brisk business. The town hall, with graceful balustrades, and a small 19th-century neoclassical church are on the main square. Le Moule's beach, protected by a reef, is perfect for windsurfing. ⊠ *Le Moule.*

Morne-à-l'Eau. This agricultural town of about 16,000 people has an amphitheater-shape cemetery, with black-and-white-checkerboard tombs, elaborate epitaphs, and multicolor (plastic) flowers. On All Saints' Day (November 1), it's the scene of a moving (and photogenic) candlelight service.

Musée Camélia Costumes et Traditions. This museum is a labor of love by its creators, and seeing the dress of black, white, and *métisseé* (mixed-race, or "maroon") societies is a fascinating way to visualize the island's tumultuous history and fascinating heritage. Items that you will remember: madras headdresses; baptism outfits; embroidered maternity dresses; colonial pith helmets and other various chapeaux, as well as the doll collection. Make sure to go out back and visit the replica of a Guadeloupean *case* circa 1920. A film now depicts life of yesteryear. The small museum is privately owned; the founder, Camelia Bausivoir, is a retired English teacher, and she can act as your guide. This represents a collection accrued over decades, and Bausivoir sewed many of the costumes. Call before you go for directions and to make sure that a school group is not there. ⊠ *1 Perinette, Le Gosier* ☎ *0590/83–21–70, 0690/41–51–90* 🖃 *€9* ⊗ *Tues.–Sun. 9–1 and 3–5.*

NEED A BREAK? If you don't want to take time for a two-hour French lunch, watch for gas stations such as **Shell Boutique, Total Boutique,** and **Esso Tigermart,** which sell food. The VITO station on the left going into St-François has good pizza as well as tables and chairs. A Total "fillin' station" might have barbecue ribs, chicken, and turkey.

Port Louis. This fishing village of about 7,000 people is best known for Le Soufleur Plage. It was once one of the island's prettiest beaches, but it has become a little shabby. Yet the road construction is finally coming to an end, and it is looking better. Although the beach is crowded on weekends, it's blissfully quiet during the week. The sand is fringed by flamboyant trees, and there are also spectacular views of Basse-Terre. Near the dock, Chez Henri is a good restaurant, friendly and hip.

Ste-Anne. In the 18th century this town, 8 miles (13 km) east of Gosier, was a sugar-exporting center. Sand has replaced sugar as the town's most valuable asset. La Caravelle and the other beaches are among the best in Guadeloupe. On its main drag, which parallels the waterfront, is a lively group of inexpensive eateries, shops, and artisan stalls. On a more spiritual note, Ste-Anne has a lovely cemetery with stark-white tombs. ⊠ *Ste-Anne.*

St-François. This was once a simple little village, primarily involved with fishing and harvesting tomatoes. The fish and tomatoes are still here, as are the old creole houses and the lively market with recommendable food stalls in the *centre ville*, but increasingly, the St-François marina district is overtaking Gosier as Guadeloupe's most fashionable tourist resort area. Its avenue de l'Europe runs between the marina and the fairways and water obstacles of the municipal golf course, which was designed by Robert Trent Jones Sr. On the marina side is a string of shops (including a huge supermarket), hotels, bars, and restaurants. The Bwa Chik Hotel & Golf, an eco-chic study in recyclable materials, is a favorite with golfers. Other attractions include an array of beaches, a lagoon, and the St-François casino. St-François was designated as a Station Balnéaire (nautical resort) by the French government. With its 220-slip marina, it's a sailing mecca and a departure point for catamaran day sails to the out islands, which are in close proximity. ⊠ *St-François.*

NEED A
BREAK?

There's no wagering at **Hyper Casino**, a *supermarché* on l'avenue de l'Europe at the St-François Marina, but there are esoteric cheeses and baked goods such as pie-size, tropical-fruit tarts. Other supermarkets with good deli or bakery departments are those in the Leader Price and Carrefour chains.

BASSE-TERRE

Basse-Terre (which translates as "low land") is by far the highest and wildest of the two wings of the Guadeloupe butterfly, with the peak of the Soufrière volcano topping off at nearly 4,811 feet. Basse-Terre, where you can find the island's national park, is also an ecotourist's treasure, with lush, equatorial plant life and adventurous opportunities for hikers and mountain bikers on the old *traces*, routes that porters once took across the mountains. You can still find numerous fishing villages and banana plantations stretching as far as the eye can see. The northwest coast, between Bouillante and Grande-Anse, is magnificent; the road twists and turns up steep hills smothered in vegetation and then drops down and skirts deep-blue bays and colorful seaside towns. Constantly changing light, towering clouds, and frequent rainbows only add to the beauty. In fact, Basse-Terre is gaining in popularity each year, and is especially appreciated by young, sporty couples.

BASSE-TERRE

Because Pointe-à-Pitre is so much bigger, few people suspect that this little town of 15,000 is the capital and administrative center of Guadeloupe. But if you have any doubts, walk up the hill to the state-of-the-art Théâtre Nationale, where some of France's finest theater and opera companies perform.

FAMILY **Jardin Botanique.** This exquisite 10-acre park is filled with parrots and flamingoes. A circuitous walking trail takes you by ponds with floating lily pads, cactus gardens, and every kind of tropical flower and plant, including orchids galore. Amid the exotic ferns and gnarled, ancient trees are little wooden bridges and a gazebo. A panoramic restaurant with a surprisingly sophisticated lunch menu plus a snack bar are housed in terraced gingerbread buildings, one overlooking the park's waterfall, the other the mountains. The garden has a children's park and nature-oriented playthings in the shop. A local juice and a snack is included with admission. This excursion is delightful and serene, ideal on an overcast day. ⊠ *Deshaies, Basse-Terre* ☎ *0590/28–43–02* ⊕ *www. jardin-botanique.com* ☎ *€15.90* ☾ *Daily 9–5:30.*

VIEUX-HABITANTS

This was the island's first colony, established in 1635. Beaches, a restored coffee plantation, and the oldest church on the island (1666) make this village worth a stop.

Domaine de Vanibel. Guadeloupean coffee is considered some of the best in the world. Joel Nelson will tell you all about it if you take one of his tours around the grounds of his estate. Dress comfortably as you will be going into the bush, picking vanilla and coffee beans from the trees. His enthusiasm and passion for what he grows and produces makes

10

what could be a ho-hum walk through the woods a pleasurable learning experience. After some 30 minutes or more you will be brought back to the stone cottage that is the Habitation Sucrerie for a coffee tasting and fresh tropical fruits. You might want to buy a bag or two of Mr. Nelson's coffee. And the precious vanilla beans and vanilla powder are also for sale. Also, there are simple gites for two to four persons on the estate. ⊠ *Cousinière Caféière, Vieux-Habitants* ☏ *0590 /98–40–79, 0690/50–63–39* ⊕ *www.vanibel.fr* ⊡ *€7* ⊘ *Mon.–Sat. 8–noon and 2–5; guided tours Mon.–Sat. 2:30 and 3:30 (Jan.–Apr.), 3 pm (May–Dec.).*

Musée du Café/Café Chaulet. From the riverfront Musée du Café/Café Chaulet, dedicated to the art of coffee making, the tantalizing aroma of freshly ground beans reaches the highway. Plaques and photos tell of the island's coffee history. You will learn that coffee was once Guadeloupe's principal crop, and that Chaulets have been planter and exporters since 1900. The shop sells excellent arabica coffee, rum punches, Schrubb (an orange liqueur), hot sauces, sachets of spices, bay-rum lotion, marmalades, and jewelry made from natural materials. Cocoa beans are also grown here. The "resident" chocolate maker, a young French woman, also crafts bonbons and festive holiday candies with lots of dark chocolate and tropical fruit from the island. You will even see the coffee cars—emblazoned Volkswagen Beetles. The Chaulet family respects traditional procedures while bowing to modernity. Their latest product is coffee capsules. And you can now buy online including their "wallpaper," which includes cool vintage posters. ⊠ *The Bouchu, Vieux-Habitants* ☏ *0590/98–54–96* ⊕ *www.cafe-chaulet.com* ⊡ *Museum €6; shop free* ⊘ *Daily 9–5.*

STE-ROSE

In addition to a sulfur bath, there are two good beaches (Amandiers and Clugny) and several interesting small museums in Ste-Rose.

Domaine de Séverin Distillery. At this historic rum distillery, a new "Petit Train" crosses the plantation at 9:30, 10:30, and 11:30 am and again at 2 and 3 pm. (Hours are abbreviated in the low season, as is the train schedule.) The train passes by crayfish ponds (they farm the jumbo ouassous variety), golden fields of sugarcane, the distillery's working waterwheel, and the Big House, the former mansion of the Marsolle family, which has owned the habitation since 1928. The impressive great house, white-pillared with verandas on two stories, is now a museum open for touring. The estate is so picturesque and atmospheric—even a white gazebo with a red roof—that it was recently a film site for the Franco-British series *Murder in Paradise*. A combination tasting room and gift shop sells rum, rum punches (liqueurs), spices, and hot sauces. The simple, open-air dining room here has a good menu and sometimes offers jumbo crayfish. ⊠ *Ste-Rose* ☏ *0590/28–91–86* ⊕ *www. severinrhum.com* ⊡ *€7 visit and rum tasting, €11 complete tour and train ride* ⊘ *Daily 8:30–5:30 for the distillery and La Cave.*

ELSEWHERE ON BASSE-TERRE
TOP ATTRACTIONS

Cascade aux Ecrevisses. Within the Parc National de la Guadeloupe, Crayfish Falls is one of the island's loveliest (and most popular) spots. There's a marked trail (walk carefully—the rocks can be slippery) leading to this splendid waterfall, which dashes down into the Corossol River—a good place for a dip. Come early, though; otherwise you definitely won't have it to yourself. ⊠ *St-Claude* ⊕ *www.guadeloupe-parcnational.com.*

Chutes du Carbet. You can reach three of the Carbet Falls (one drops from 65 feet, the second from 360 feet, the third from 410 feet) via a long, steep path from the village of Habituée. On the way up you pass the Grand Étang (Great Pond), a volcanic lake surrounded by interesting plant life. For those who are fans of *The Walking Dead*, there's also the curiously named Étang Zombi, a pond believed to house evil spirits. If there have been heavy rains, though, don't even think about going here. ⊠ *St-Claude.*

Ilet de Pigeon. This tiny, rocky island a few hundred yards off the coast is the site of the Jacques Cousteau Underwater Park, the island's best scuba and snorkeling site. Although the reefs here are good, they don't rank among the top Caribbean dive spots. Several companies conduct diving trips to the reserve, and it's on the itinerary of some sailing and snorkeling trips. ⊠ *Bouillante.*

Parc National de la Guadeloupe. This 74,100-acre park has been recognized by UNESCO as a Biosphere Reserve. Before going, pick up a *Guide to the National Park* from the tourist office; it rates the hiking trails according to difficulty, and most are quite difficult indeed. Most mountain trails are in the southern half. The park is bisected by the route de la Traversée, a 16-mile (26-km) paved road lined with masses of tree ferns, shrubs, flowers, tall trees, and green plantains. It's the ideal point of entry. Wear rubber-sole shoes and take along a swimsuit, a sweater, water, and perhaps food for a picnic. Try to get an early start to stay ahead of the hordes of cruise-ship passengers making a day of it. Check on the weather; if Basse-Terre has had a lot of rain, give it up. In the past, after intense rainfall, rock slides have closed the road for months. ⊠ *Habitation Beausoleil-Montéran, BP-93, St-Claude* ☎ *0590/80–86–00* ⊕ *www.guadeloupe-parcnational. com* ☒ *Free* ⊙ *Weekdays 8–5:30.*

WORTH NOTING

Bouillante. The name means "boiling," and so it's no surprise that hot springs were discovered here. However, the biggest attraction is scuba diving on nearby Pigeon Island, which is accessed by boat from Plage de Malendure. There's a small information kiosk on the beach at Plage de Malendure that can help you with diving and snorkeling arrangements. ⊠ *Bouillante.*

Les Mamelles. Two mountains—Mamelle de Petit-Bourg, at 2,350 feet, and Mamelle de Pigeon, at 2,500 feet—rise in the Parc National de la Guadeloupe. *Mamelle* means "breast," and when you see the mountains, you'll understand why they got their name. Trails ranging from

10

easy to arduous lace up into the surrounding mountains. There's a glorious view from the lookout point 1,969 feet up Mamelle de Pigeon. If you're a climber, plan to spend several hours exploring this area. If there have been heavy rainfalls, cancel your plans. ⊠ *St-Claude* ⊕ *www. guadeloupe-parcnational.com.*

ILES DES SAINTES

The eight-island archipelago of Iles des Saintes, often referred to as Les Saintes, dots the waters off the southern coast of Guadeloupe. The islands are Terre-de-Haut, Terre-de-Bas, Ilet à Cabrit, Grand Ilet, La Redonde, La Coche, Le Pâté, and Les Augustins. Columbus discovered them on November 4, 1493, and christened them Los Santos (Les Saintes in French) for All Saints' Day.

> ### DRAINAGE DITCHES
>
> Whether you're driving a car or walking on an unlighted street at night, be aware that there are drainage ditches on the side of the road meant to catch the runoff after a rain. Because parking is at a premium, you will see cars straddling the ditches. Don't do it.

Only Terre-de-Haut and Terre-de-Bas are inhabited, with a combined population of little more than 3,000. Many of the Saintois are fair-haired, blue-eyed descendants of Breton and Norman sailors. Unless they are in the tourism industry, they tend to be taciturn and standoffish. Fishing is still their main source of income, and they take pride in their work. The shores are lined with their boats and *filets bleus* (blue nets dotted with orange buoys).

TERRE-DE-HAUT

With 5 square miles (13 square km) and a population of about 1,500, Terre-de-Haut is the largest and most developed of Les Saintes. Its "big city" is Bourg, with one main street lined with bistros, cafés, and shops. Clutching the hillside are trim white houses with bright red or blue doors, balconies, and gingerbread frills.

Terre-de-Haut's ragged coastline is scalloped with lovely coves and beaches, including the semi-nude beach at Anse Crawen. The beautiful bay, complete with a "sugarloaf" mountain, has been called a mini Rio. There are precious few vehicles or taxis on-island, so you'll often find yourself walking, despite the hilly terrain. Or you can add to the din and rent a motorbike. Take your time on these rutted roads, as around any bend there might be a herd of goats chomping on a fallen palm frond. Two traffic lights have brought a small amount of order to the motorbike hordes. When aggressively soliciting you, the scooter agencies will not tell you that it is prohibited to scoot in town from 9 to noon and from 2 to 4.

This island makes a great day-trip, but you can really get a feel for Les Saintes if you stay overnight. It has a bit of the feel of St. Barth but at a fraction of the price. Note: most shops and restaurants close for two hours in the afternoon. ■ TIP➔ A wonderful introduction to the island as well as a travel keepsake is the coffee-table book Carnet de Route-Les Saintes that's on sale in most of the island's shops.

Fort Napoléon. Also known as Louis Castle, this fort was built in 1777 by order of King Louis XVI, and was first known as a military tower. However, it was never used for military purposes, although it did serve as a penitentiary in wartime. The museum here is notable for its exhaustive exhibit of the greatest sea battles ever fought. You can also visit the well-preserved barracks and prison cells, or admire the botanical gardens, which specialize in cacti. ■ TIP→ **This is a hill climb, and if you decide to walk, allow 30 minutes from the village, wear comfortable footwear, and bring water. You will be rewarded with outstanding views of the bay and neighboring islands.** ⊠ *Terre-de-Haut* ☎ *0690/50–73–43* ☜ *€5* ☼ *Daily 9–12:30.*

MARIE-GALANTE

Columbus sighted this 60-square-mile (155-square-km) island on November 3, 1493, named it after his flagship, the *Maria Galanda,* and sailed on. It's dotted with ruined 19th-century sugar mills, and sugar is still its major product. Honey and 59% rum are its other favored harvests. You should make it a point to see one of the distilleries. With its rolling hills of green cane still worked by oxen and men with broad-brim straw hats, it's like traveling back in time to when all of Guadeloupe was still a giant farm.

Although it's only an hour by high-speed ferry from Pointe-à-Pitre, for the most part, the country folk here are still sweet and shy, and crime is a rarity. That said, driving can be stressful thanks to young men in dark cars, rudely intimidating tourist-drivers. You can see swarms of yellow butterflies, and maybe a marriage carriage festooned with flowers, pulled by two white oxen. A daughter of the sea, Marie-Galante has some of the archipelago's most gorgeous, uncrowded beaches. Take time to explore the dramatic coast. You can find soaring cliffs—such as the Gueule Grand Gouffre (Mouth of the Giant Chasm) and Les Galeries (where the sea has sculpted a natural arcade)—and enormous sun-dappled grottoes, such as Le Trou à Diable, whose underground river can be explored with a guide. Port Louis, the island's "second city," is the new hip spot. The ferry dock is in Port Louis, and it's also on the charts for yachts and regattas. After sunset, the no-see-ums and mosquitoes can be a real irritation, so always be armed with repellent. At different times of year, you might experience a lot of nature trying to enter your hotel.

TOP ATTRACTIONS

Fodor'sChoice **Domaine de Bellevue.** If time allows just one distillery here, choose the
★ modern Domaine de Bellevue, whose rum has taken home the gold during official French competitions. Free tastings are just one inviting element. There are award-winning, pure rums (50%–59%) and also excellent tropical liqueurs (punches). Bellevue is the top rum exporter of Guadeloupe/Marie-Galante with the only eco-positive distillery in the world. Down from one of only two restored windmills (c.1821) on-island is a boutique offering everything made from natural materials, such as calabash gourds, as well as coffee-table books. ⊠ *Section Bellevue, Capesterre-de-Marie-Galante* ☎ *0590/97–26–50* ☜ *Free* ☼ *Daily 9:30–1.*

10

Kreol West Indies. This fascinating museum, in a renovated bungalow, houses information and graphics on Guadeloupe's earliest inhabitants, as well as some pirate artifacts. Rooms are furnished with antiques and collectibles that depict island life during various eras, up through the 1950s. Devoted to Creole culture, the museum also doubles as an art gallery, with attractive contemporary paintings by island artists.

> **COMPETITIONS DES BOEUFS TIRANTS**
>
> The annual ox-pulling competitions on Marie-Galante go on for two weeks in November. Oxen were used for the sugar mills and still power the agriculture. Where else will you see this in your lifetime?

This labor of love displays furnishings and descriptives owned by a French "culture lover" Vincent Nicaudie. The gift shop carries quality Marie-Galante logoized T-shirts and caps, beachwear, and island food products. Also, this is a Wi-Fi hot spot. ⊠ *Plage de Grand Bourg, rue Beaurenon prolongee, Grand-Bourg* ✛ *100 meters after exiting the town, continue in the direction of Capesterre and it is right on the road, on the right* ☎ *0590/97–21–56* ⊕ *www.kreolwestindies.com* ⊠ *Free* ☉ *Daily 9:30–noon and 2–6:30.*

WORTH NOTING

Château Murat. A mile from town, the Château Murat is a 19th-century sugar plantation and rum distillery housing exhibits on the history of rum making and sugarcane production that goes back three centuries. This former habitation was once the grandest sugar plantation in Guadeloupe. Various hurricanes left the chateau in ruins, with just remnants of the kitchen, etc., still standing. From the rubble rose the ecomuseum which celebrates island crafts, and there is a garden for medicinal local plants. ⊠ *Rte. de Capesterre, Grand-Bourg* ☎ *0590/97–48–68* ⊠ *Free* ☉ *Weekdays 9–1 and 2:30–5:30, weekends 9–1.*

Distillerie Poisson "Rhum du Père Labat". The Poisson Distillery produces rum (nearly 200,000 liters a year) that is considered some of the finest in the Caribbean, and its atelier turns out lovely pottery. Tastings are available, but watch out—those samples are quite strong, especially considering that it's open only in the morning! ⊠ *Section Poisson, Grand-Bourg* ⊠ *Free* ☉ *Mon.–Sat. 7–noon.*

LA DÉSIRADE

Desirable is the operative word here. This small, safe, somewhat remote island is an absolute find for those who prefer a road less traveled, who want their beaches long and white, and who don't mind that accommodations are simple if the price is right. The Désirade populace (all 1,700 of them) welcome tourism, and these dear hearts have a warm, old-fashioned sense of community.

According to legend, the "desired land" was so named by the crew of Christopher Columbus, whose tongues were dry for want of fresh water when they spied the island; alas, it was the season for drought. The 8-square-mile (21-square-km) island, 5 miles (8 km) east of St-François, is a chalky plateau, with an arid climate, perennial sunshine,

Looking out over Marie-Galante

cacti, and iguanas. You may even see two male iguanas locked in a prehistoric-looking battle. Rent a four-wheel drive to climb the zigzag road that leads to the Grande Montagne. Make a photo stop at the diminutive white chapel, which offers a panorama of the sea below. Afraid that you might zig instead of zag down the precipice? Then take a fun, informative van tour that you join near the tourist office at the harbor near the ferry dock. The ruins of the original settlement—a leper colony—are on the tour.

Only one road runs around the perimeter of the island, and if you're interested in visiting one of the many gorgeous beaches shaded by coconut palms and sea grape trees, you can do that on a scooter. Driving is safer here than most anywhere.

BEACHES

Guadeloupe is an archipelago of five paradises surrounded by both the Caribbean and the Atlantic. Its beaches run the spectrum from white to black. There are idyllic beaches, long stretches of unspoiled beach shaded by coconut palms, with soft, warm sand. Hotel beaches are generally narrow, although well maintained. Some hotels allow nonguests who patronize their restaurants to use their beach facilities. The popular public beaches tend to be cluttered with campers-turned-cafés and cars parked in impromptu lots on the sand. Sunday is the big day, but these same (free) beaches are often quiet during the week.

On the southern coast of Grande-Terre, from Ste-Anne to Pointe des Châteaux, you can find stretches of soft white sand and some sparsely visited areas. The Atlantic waters on the northeast coast are too rough for swimming. Along the western shore of Basse-Terre signposts indicate small beaches. The sand starts turning gray in Malendure; it becomes volcanic black farther south. There's only one official nude beach, Pointe Tarare, but topless bathing is common.

GRANDE-TERRE

L'Autre Bord. The waves on this Atlantic beach give the long expanse of sand a wild look. The beach is protected by an extensive coral reef, which makes it safe for children. Farther out, the waves draw surfers and windsurfers. From its location right in the town of Moule, you can stroll along a seaside promenade fringed by flamboyant trees (also known as flame trees). Many shade trees offer protection; the swaying coconut palms are more for photo composition. Sidewalk cafés provide sustenance. **Amenities:** food and drink; parking (no fee); toilets. **Best for:** surfing; swimming; walking; windsurfing. ⊠ *Le Moule.*

Plage Caravelle. Just southwest of Ste-Anne is one of Grande-Terre's longest and prettiest stretches of sand, the occasional dilapidated shack notwithstanding. Protected by reefs, it's also a fine snorkeling spot. Club Med occupies one end of this beach, and nonguests can enjoy its beach and water sports, as well as lunch and drinks, by buying a day pass. You can also have lunch on the terrace of La Toubana Hotel & Spa, then descend the stairs to the beach or enjoy lunch at its beach restaurant, wildly popular on Sunday. **Amenities:** food and drink; parking (no fee); toilets; water sports. **Best for:** partiers; snorkeling; sunset; swimming; walking; windsurfing. ⊠ *Rte. N4, southwest of Ste-Anne, Ste-Anne.*

Plage de la Chapelle à Anse-Bertrand. If you want a delightful day-trip to the northern tip of Grande-Terre, aim for this spot, one of the loveliest white-sand beaches, whose gentle mid-afternoon waves are popular with families. It's shaded by coco palms, there are the ruins of a chapel to explore, and the sea kayaking's excellent. When the tide rolls in, it's equally popular with surfers. Several little terrace restaurants are at the far end of the beach, but you might want to bring your own mat or beach towel, because no one rents chaise longues. The town has remained relatively undeveloped. **Amenities:** food and drink; showers; toilets. **Best for:** solitude; sunrise; sunset; surfing; swimming; walking; windsurfing. ⊠ *4 miles (6½ km) south of La Pointe de la Grand Vigie.*

Plage du Helleux. Except on Sunday, this long stretch of wild beach—framed by dramatic cliffs—is often completely deserted in the morning or early afternoon. By 4 pm, though, you might find 70 or so young surfers. Many locals take their young children here, but use caution with your own, because the current can be strong. The beach has no facilities of its own, but you can get lunch and drinks at the Hotel Eden Palm. To get here, follow the signs to Hotel Eden Palm and pass the hotel; the beach is down the dirt road to the right. **Amenities:** none. **Best for:** partiers; solitude; surfing; swimming; walking. ⊠ *Rte. N4, Lieu-dit le Helleux, Ste-Anne.*

Pointe Tarare. This secluded strip just before the tip of Pointe des Châteaux is the island's only nude beach. (Technically, this is not allowed by French law.) Small bar-cafés are in the parking area, but it's still best to bring some water, snacks, and beach chairs, because there's no place to rent them. What you do have is one of the coast's most dramatic landscapes; looming above are rugged cliffs topped by a huge crucifix. When approaching St-François Marina, go in the direction of Pointe des Châteaux at the roundabout and drive for about 10 minutes. **Amenities:** food and drink; parking (no fee); toilets. **Best for:** partiers; solitude; sunset; swimming; walking. ⊠ *Rte. N4, southeast of St-François.*

BASSE-TERRE

Plage de la Grande-Anse. One of Guadeloupe's widest beaches has soft beige sand sheltered by palms. To the west it's a round verdant mountain. It has a large parking area and some food stands, but no other facilities. The beach can be overrun on Sundays, not to mention littered, due to the food carts. Right after the parking lot, you can see signage for the creole restaurant Le Karacoli; if you have lunch there (it's not cheap), you can *sieste* on the chaise longues. At the far end of the beach, which is more virgin territory, is Tainos Cottages, which has a restaurant. **Amenities:** food and drink; parking (no fee). **Best for:** partiers; solitude; swimming; walking. ⊠ *Rte. N6, north of Deshaies, Deshaies.*

Plage de Malendure. Across from Pigeon Island and the Jacques Cousteau Underwater Park, this long, gray, volcanic beach on the Caribbean's calm waters has restrooms, a few beach shacks offering cold drinks and snacks, and a huge parking lot. There might be some litter, but the beach is cleaned regularly. Don't come here for solitude, as the beach is a launch point for many dive boats. The snorkeling's good. Le Rocher de Malendure, a fine seafood restaurant, is perched on a cliff over the bay. Food carts work the parking lot. **Amenities:** food and drink; parking (no fee); toilets. **Best for:** partiers; snorkeling; swimming. ⊠ *Rte. N6, Bouillante.*

ILES DES SAINTES

10

FAMILY **Pompierre Bay.** This beach is particularly popular with families with small children, as there's a gradual slope, no drop-off, and a long stretch of shallow water. The calm water also makes for good snorkeling. The isles of Les Saintes offer outstanding snorkeling and scuba diving. On the other end of the island, the conditions are not as good as at Pain de Sucre, but the shouldered sandy bay is larger and there are a lot of fish. Saintois women may be at the entrance selling snacks and drinks. The curve of the beach is called the Bridge of Stone, and you can walk it—carefully—taking a dip in the crater that fills with water from the Atlantic. Morning sun is best; then return to Salako for some grilled fresh fish and a cold one. **Amenities:** food and drink. **Best for:** snorkeling; sunrise; swimming; walking. ⊠ *Terre-de-Haut ✛ Go to the seamen's church near the main plaza, and then head in the direction of Marigot. Continue until you see Le Salako Snack Bar and, voilà! you'll spy a palm-fringed, half-moon bay with some 2,600 feet of tawny sand.*

LA DÉSIRADE

Le Soufleur Plage. To reach one of La Désirade's longest and best beaches from the ferry dock, face town and follow the main road to the right. It's about 15 minutes by car or motor scooter (about €20 a day). White sand, calm waters, and snacks and cold drinks from the beach restaurant await, but there are no chaises, so BYO beach towel or mat. **Amenities:** food and drink; toilets. **Best for:** snorkeling; solitude; sunset; swimming; walking. ⊠ *Rd. 207, La Désirade.*

MARIE-GALANTE

Anse de Vieux Fort. This gorgeous Marie-Galante beach stretches alongside crystal-clear waters that border a large body of freshwater that is ideal for canoeing. It's a surprising contrast from the nearby mangrove swamp you can discover on the hiking trails. The beaches in this area are wide because of the erosion of the sand dunes. It's known as a beach for lovers because of the solitude. Bring your own everything. You can pair a visit to Château Murat with your beach day. **Amenities:** none. **Best for:** snorkeling; solitude; sunset; swimming; walking. ⊠ *Rte. D205.*

Plage de Petite-Anse. This long, golden beach on Marie-Galante is punctuated with sea grape trees. It's idyllic during the week, but on weekends the crowds of locals and urban refugees from the main island arrive. Le Touloulou's great creole seafood restaurant provides the only facilities. The golden sands are ideal for shelling. **Amenities:** food and drink; parking (no fee); toilets. **Best for:** partiers; snorkeling; sunset; swimming; walking. ⊠ *Rte. D203* ✛ *6½ miles (10 km) north of Grand-Bourg.*

WHERE TO EAT

Creole cooking is the result of a fusion of influences: African, European, Indian, and Caribbean. It's colorful, spicy, and made up primarily of local seafood and vegetables (including squashlike christophenes), root vegetables, and plantains, always with a healthy dose of pepper sauce. Favorite appetizers include *accras* (salted codfish fritters), *boudin* (highly seasoned blood sausage), and *crabes farcis* (stuffed land crabs). *Langouste* (lobster), *lambi* (conch), *chatrou* (octopus), and *ouassous* (crayfish) are considered delicacies. *Souchy* (Tahitian-style ceviche), raw fish that is "cooked" when marinated in lime juice or similar marinades, is best at seafront restaurants. *Moules et frites* (mussels in broth served with fries) can be found at cafés, both in the Marina in St-François and Bas du Fort Marina. Many of the best restaurants are in Jarry, a commercial area near Pointe-à-Pitre. All restaurants and bars are smoke-free, as decreed by French law.

Diverse culinary options range from pizza and crepes to Indian cuisine. For a quick and inexpensive meal, visit a *boulangerie,* where you can buy luscious French pastries and simple baguette sandwiches. Look for the recommendable chain Baguet. Good news: while menu prices may seem high, prices include tax and service, but a small extra tip in cash is expected, just as in France. In most restaurants in Guadeloupe (as throughout the Caribbean), lobster is the most expensive item on the menu.

What to Wear: Dining is casual at lunch, but beach attire is not appropriate except at the most laid-back beachside eateries. Dinner is slightly more formal. Long pants, collared shirts, and skirts or dresses are appreciated, although not required. Guadeloupean ladies like to "dress," particularly on weekends, so don't arrive in flip-flops—they'll be in heels.

GRANDE-TERRE

$$$
ECLECTIC

✕**Café Wango.** At this alfresco hot spot, Asian wok dishes, sushi, skewers, fish carpaccios, and tartares dominate the menu, and there are no fewer than nine better-than-average salads. There are also pricey pastas and daily specials like a classic sirloin in a Roquefort-poivre sauce, but the attractive prix-fixe menus are the best choices. Kids are crazy for the ice cream and beg parents for *un coupe*. So many flavors, so little time. Facing the marina's boat slips, the modern furnishings are charcoal gray and burnt orange juxtaposed with flamingo pink walls and napkins. The seats are often filled with a fun, discerning crowd of mainly French expats; parked nearby there may be a couple of Harleys, flying tiny American flags. $ *Average main: €21* ⊠ *St-François Marina, Marines 1, St-François* ☎ *0590/83–50–41* ⊕ *www.cafewango. com* ☉ *Closed June 17–July 6.*

$$$$
ECLECTIC
Fodor'sChoice
★

✕**Iguane Café.** Iguanas are indeed the theme here, and you can still spy them in unexpected places—but their numbers have diminished and the room now has a clean, contemporary appeal, just like the china and glassware. The salon seating for cocktails has a homey feel, with basket-weave rattan furniture and hot-pink accent pillows. Unquestionably original cuisine with Asian, Indian, Creole, and African influences is chef Sylvain Serouart's trademark. Two amuse-bouches will arrive, and there is usually a wonderful foie-gras appetizer—with a vintage-rum crème brûlée and a papaya compôte. Follow with a lobster ravioli dashed with lime, tinted with saffron. The menu is always evolving. Desserts, like a cacao ice-orange-cake, are contemporary marvels. This is a pricey place, but the tasting menu ensures the widest range of tastes. $ *Average main: €35* ⊠ *Rte. de La Pointe des Châteaux, ½ mile (¾ km) from airport, St-François* ☎ *0590/88–61–37* ⊕ *www.iguane-cafe.com* ☉ *Closed Tues. No lunch Mon.–Sat.*

$$$
INDIAN

✕**La Porte des Indes.** Dining here is truly a departure: the open-air pergola, the blue gates, the pungent aromas, and the bust of Ganesha. Within the paisley-covered menu you can find authentic Indian dishes alongside such adaptations as boneless curried chicken with crème fraîche, cashews, and raisins. Vegetarians are catered to, with eggplant puree one of the better options. Children may fill up on the addictive cheese-stuffed naan and may be too stuffed for *kulfi*, Indian ice cream that's topped here with ginger confit. The welcome here is always warm and the service dignified. The Indian chef-owner, Karious Arthur, has a culinary degree from Paris and worked for years in France. Consistently good, the restaurant is always packed on weekends, so be sure to make a reservation. $ *Average main: €30* ⊠ *Desvarieux, St-François*

10

☎ *0590/21–30–87* ⊙ *Closed mid-Sept.–mid-Oct. and Mon. No lunch Tues.–Sat. No dinner Sun.*

$$$$ ✕ **La Toubana Restaurant** (*Le Gran Bleu*). Delicious Caribbean-accented
FRENCH French cuisine draws diners to this open-air restaurant, where a specialty is fresh lobster, plucked from the petite lagoon that beautifies the deck. Foie gras is also a star. Though open, the dining room has deep leather chairs, and, on occasion, a piano player and live music (local music is the norm on Thursday night). You can listen whether you just have a drink at the bar or sit down for dinner. Lunch patrons dine on the terrace near the infinity pool. With your feet dangling in the water and an exotic cocktail in hand, you can watch the sea churn below. $ *Average main: €35* ✉ *La Toubana Hotel & Spa, B. P. 63-Fonds Thezan, Ste-Anne* ☎ *0590/88–25–57.*

$$$ ✕ **Le Mabouya dans la Bouteille.** This fine-dining restaurant in St-François
FRENCH FUSION offers consistently good Franco-fusion cuisine. The French couple who owned a Parisian restaurant for eight years before setting up shop here don't always extend the same hospitality to English-speaking tourists as French patrons, but that and the impractical, silky, maroon napkins aside, this open-air venue is cozy and inviting with displays of vintage corkscrews, etc. (The wine cave doubles as a bottle shop.) More good news: you can now make reservations online. $ *Average main: €27* ✉ *17 Saline Est, St-François* ✛ *5-min walk from marina* ☎ *0590/21–31–14* ⊕ *www.lemabouya.fr* ⊙ *Closed Tues. No lunch* ⌲ *Reservations essential.*

$$$ ✕ **Restaurant la Vieille Tour.** An historic sugar mill is the backdrop for the
FRENCH artistic creations here, which pair refined French preparations with local produce. The lunch menu is a mix of classic restaurant food and lighter dishes. A prix-fixe menu including a main course, a starter or dessert, a glass of wine, and coffee is available. At dinner a more classically French menu with Caribbean influences offers both meat and seafood. Desserts are dazzling, with the pastry chef turning out towers, sauces, and glacés. On Friday and Saturday nights, there's piano music in the lounge. Hotel guests also eat breakfast here. $ *Average main: €26* ✉ *Auberge de la Vieille Tour, rte. 1, Montauban 97, Le Gosier* ☎ *0590/84–23–23* ⌲ *Reservations essential.*

$$$ ✕ **Zawag.** At this secret hideaway you'll see the churning sea below
SEAFOOD and hear the waves crashing against the coral rock upon which it sits.
Fodor's Choice The interior architecture is all hardwood with matching furniture and
★ white linen napkins at dinnertime. Primarily a grill, the simplicity is reflected in the food offerings. Kids are particularly fascinated when the lobster net is dipped into the tank and the thrashing begins. The catch of the day is fresh from the waters below, often accompanied by creole or tropical-fruit sauces. Creole dishes and sides that were gently contemporized by a French chef are offered as nightly specials. Presentations are beautifully exotic. And what's a Zawag? Why, that's a tropical fish that swims in the water that guests see through the open shutters. $ *Average main: €23* ✉ *La Créole Beach Hotel & Spa, Pointe de la Verdure, Le Gosier* ☎ *0590/90–46–46* ⊙ *Closed Sun. and Sept.* ⌲ *Reservations essential.*

BASSE-TERRE

$$$ ✕**Le Rocher de Malendure.** Guests may at first be attracted to the gor-
SEAFOOD geous views of dive boats going to Pigeon Island, but they return again
and again for food. After climbing the worn yellow stairs, diners take
a seat on the open multilevel deck for a delicious meal with those gor-
geous panoramas. Fish is fresh off the boat and your best bet here, so
don't hesitate to try the sushi *antillaise* or grilled crayfish; or better yet
have these jumbos in a rich cream-and-rum-laced sauce—a two-napkin
affair as the shells are left on. Select your lobster from a pool. Both serv-
ers and managers are friendly and efficient for such a busy place; one
or more will be English-speaking. Make a reservation if you want the
best view. $ *Average main: €25* ⊠ *Bord de Mer, Malendure de Pigeon,
Bouillante* ☎ *0590/98–70–84* ⊕ *le-rocher-de-malendure.com* ⊗ *Closed
Sept.–early Oct.*

$$$ ✕**Restaurant La Savane.** Even if there's a downpour, the overhanging gin-
FRENCH gerbread roof over your terrace table will keep you dry as the food and
music keep your spirits high. The family-owned restaurant overlooking
crystalline Deshaies Bay is a dream fulfilled, and much of its success
is directly related to the varied international experiences of the family
members. Emilia, the matriarch who is Portuguese and lived in Angola
for years, brings the African decor and name. Patriarch Vincent, who
is French and was a candy maker in Switzerland, is the chef and pastry
chef. Daughter Tatiana is the welcoming English-speaking server. Chef
Vincent prides himself on using the freshest fish and produce; lobster
must be ordered in advance as he orders them only as needed. Some
diners feel that Savane is expensive, but quality ingredients coupled
with creativity make for happy forks. $ *Average main: €22* ⊠ *Blvd.
des Poissonniers, Deshaies* ☎ *0690/75–70–57* ⊕ *www.restaurant-la-
savane-deshaies.com* ⊗ *Closed Wed. No lunch in low season. No lunch
Mon.–Thurs. in high season* ⌂ *Reservations essential.*

ILES DES SAINTES

$$ ✕**Couleurs du Monde.** This fun, colorful waterfront café offers free Wi-Fi,
CAFÉ books and newspapers to read, teas and coffees, wine, and icy rum
cocktails, all of which encourage lounging. Appetizers include sushi
and smoked-fish plates, while the catch of the day with an exotic sauce
is usually a good choice. After sunset there are aperitifs, and although
reservations are requested for dinner, the friendly, accommodating staff
also takes walk-ins. Finish off with the house-made punch *du monde*.
This is one of the few island restaurants that does not close between
lunch and dinner. To get here from the main dock, take a left to the main
street and walk two blocks. It's across from the kayak-rental company.
$ *Average main: €18* ⊠ *Le Mouillage, Terre-de-Haut* ☎ *0590/92–70–
98* ⊗ *Closed Thurs. and Sept. and Oct.*

$$$ ✕**Restaurant Les Petits Saints.** Chef Xavier Simon is remarkably inven-
ECLECTIC tive with the fresh local produce and seafood, with grilled lobster
the signature dish of his restaurant in Terre-de-Haut. But the menu
isn't limited to fish; meat, vegan, and gluten-free offerings will also be
found on small but ever-changing menu. Much effort has gone into

10

the well-chosen wine list, which includes a full range of aged rums from Guadeloupe. For the finale, desserts dazzle. Contemporary dinnerware brought from France complements the menu and presentation. Service is on the veranda, where the night sounds of the tropics vie with jazz and French music. $ *Average main: €24 ⊠ Hotel Restaurant les Petits Saints, La Savane, Terre-de-Haut ☎ 0590/99–50–99 ⊕ www. petitssaints.com ⊗ Closed Sun. and Mon. and mid-May–Oct. No lunch ⚏ Reservations essential.*

$$$ ✕ **Ti Kaz La.** This small, convivial waterfront restaurant has a lot to rec-
FRENCH   ommend. The talented chef-owner, Philippe Dade, has created a place that's artsy and fun, with contemporary, original works on the wall, hanging plants, and hip music. But you will also like the food: fresh grilled fish—plus authentic *pomme frites*—makes an ideal meal out on the beach terrace. *Le choucroute de la mer,* a Caribbean-accented version of the Alsatian specialty, is also a great choice: fish, scallops, and mussels in a white wine sauce. Desserts are also divine, and one (a mango soufflé) must be ordered in advance. There are two well-priced, three-course, prix-fix menus to help keep prices in check. $ *Average main: €24 ⊠ 10 rue Benoit Cassin, Terre-de-Haut ☎ 0590/99–57–63, 0690/65–52–28 ⊕ www.tikazla.com ⊗ Closed Wed.*

MARIE-GALANTE

$$ ✕ **Chez Henri.** This hip place on the water, flanked by the town pier, is
CARIBBEAN   named for its passionate chef-owner, Henri Vergerolle, an island character who spent much of his life in France but returned to open this restaurant and cultural center. Begin with a rum and fresh-squeezed juice. Smoked fish can be a component of a salad or an appetizer; the creole omelet is also very original. Everything is fresh here, but the limited menu might have only three main courses available (you can always choose the fish of the day). But just kick back and listen to African blues and view the latest art or sculpture exhibits. You might have the good luck to be here when there's a live music concert. $ *Average main: €17 ⊠ 8 rue des Caraibes, St-Louis ☎ 0590/97–04–57 ⊕ www.chezhenri.net ⊗ Closed Mon. No lunch Tues.–Thurs. from Sept.–early Oct.*

$$ ✕ **Le Touloulou Le Restaurant.** On the curve of Plage de Petite-Anse, this
SEAFOOD   casual hotel restaurant has tables in the sand, stylish Euro decor, and the
Fodor'sChoice   freshest, most delicious seafood. Chef José Viator does wonders with fish
★   carpaccio; *ouassous* (jumbo crayfish) in coconut sauce; *bébélé* (a flavorful creole dish with tripe and dumplings); and fricassee of conch or octopus with breadfruit. Set menus are the best value at both lunch and dinner. On weekends, the Creole Brunch from 11 to 4 is particularly celebratory; on weekend nights there's entertainment or dancing. Pergola's, the circular bar, has some of the island's best rum cocktails. $ *Average main: €18 ⊠ Plage de Petite-Anse, Capesterre-de-Marie-Galante ☎ 0590/97–32–63 ⊕ www.letouloulou.com ⊗ Closed mid-Sept.–mid-Oct. No dinner Sun.*

$$$ ✕ **Manman'dlo the Siren.** You may hear that one of the best tables on
FRENCH FUSION   the island is found at the small *hôtel de charme* La Rose du Brésil.
Fodor'sChoice   The rumor is true. First, order a fresh-squeezed lime daiquiri. You will
★   likely want two. The pièce de résistance is the plate of grilled spiny lobster, shrimp, and scallops. Any dish is accompanied by a stew of

local vegetables, and desserts are inspired by the island's tropical fruits. $ *Average main: €28* ✉ *La Rose du Brésil, rte. du litoral, Capesterre-de-Marie-Galante* ☎ *0590/97–47–39* ⊕ *www.larosedubresil.com* ⊙ *Closed Mon. and Tues.* ✍ *Reservations essential.*

WHERE TO STAY

Most of the island's resort hotels are on Grande-Terre: Gosier, St-François, Ste-Anne, and Bas-du-Fort are the major resort areas. With each passing year, the hotels here improve. The Swedish-owned Langley Resort Fort Royal has breathed new life into the north of Basse-Terre, the closest area of that island to Pointe-à-Pitre and Grande-Terre. In general, more tourists are discovering this area and loving the small hotels and unspoiled nature.

Often, hotel rates include a generous buffet breakfast; ask whether this is included in your rate quote. (It usually is.) Many smaller properties do not accept American Express. As dictated by French law, all public spaces in hotels are no-smoking, but hotel rooms are considered private, and properties can choose to offer smoking rooms.

PRIVATE VILLAS AND RENTALS

French Caribbean International. Since 1994, this agency has been a leading resource for lodging bookings on Guadeloupe and its offshore islands of Marie-Galante and Les Saintes, not to mention information on just about everything you need to know about the French islands. You can book both hotels and private villas through the popular website. The company has a global reputation for honesty, exceptional service, and professionalism. ☎ *805/967–9850 in the U.S.* ⊕ *www.frenchcaribbean.com.*

Prestige Villa Rental. This online agency offers luxury villa rental services throughout the French Caribbean, but has good choices on Guadeloupe. The website is in excellent English, offering photos of every room and detailed descriptions. Rental properties range from deluxe to over-the-top, many handpicked for special celebratory occasions. The company's concierge service can provision villas, arrange private chefs and housekeepers, or provide almost any other service from in-villa spa services to tours. The agency's young bilingual owner, who grew up on Guadeloupe, writes an impressive blog giving tips on "doing" the French islands. ☎ *917/720–3120 in U.S.* ⊕ *www.prestigevillarental.com.*

10

GRANDE-TERRE

$

HOTEL

🏨 **Auberge de la Vieille Tour.** At this island classic built around a historic sugar mill, everyone loves the initial welcome: a cool drink and citrus-scented towels dispensed by ladies in white eyelet uniforms. **Pros:** most rooms have great views; breakfast is a highlight; restaurant is one of the better ones on-island. **Cons:** exteriors of some sections are unattractive 1960s-style; it's an uphill climb back from the beach and pool; pool area still needs work. $ *Rooms from: €268* ✉ *Rte. de Montauban, Le*

Gosier ☎ *0590/84–23–23* ⊕ *www.auberge-vieille-tour.fr* ↗ *70 rooms, 32 deluxe rooms, 1 suite* ⍾◯⍾ *Breakfast.*

$ 🍽 **Bwa Chik Hotel & Golf.** This eco-chic, boutique hotel at the marina
HOTEL is the buzz in St-François for its unique decor that combines recycled wood and driftwood with ultra-contemporary Euro furnishings. **Pros:** ideal location, making a car unnecessary; welcoming staff; live jazz nights in season. **Cons:** small pool; no elevators or bellmen; standard rooms could be larger. $ *Rooms from: €146* ⊠ *Av. d'l Europe, St-François* ☎ *0590/88–60–60* ⊕ *www.bwachik.com* ↗ *43 rooms, 11 duplexes* ⍾◯⍾ *Breakfast.*

$$ 🍽 **Club Med La Caravelle.** Facing the island's best white-sand beaches, La
RESORT Caravelle is one of the original clubs in the Caribbean, yet all the facili-
FAMILY ties—including the seafront restaurant and its deck—have a smashing,
Fodor'sChoice contemporary look. **Pros:** large, fun resort; good service; exceptional
★ boutique for shoppers. **Cons:** Club Med experience and kid-friendly atmosphere are not for everyone; older standard rooms are small; Wi-Fi is extra. $ *Rooms from: €333* ⊠ *Quartier Caravelle, Ste-Anne* ☎ *0590/85–49–50, 800/258–2633* ⊕ *www.clubmed.us* ↗ *260 rooms, 37 suites* ⍾◯⍾ *All-inclusive.*

$ 🍽 **Hotel Amaudo.** This *hôtel de charme* is a small mom-and-pop opera-
B&B/INN tion, who in this case are quite sophisticated French managers that will provide any concierge service you might imagine. **Pros:** a moderate price tag for unobstructed sea views; safe environment, with a mechanized security gate; well-maintained and renovated when needed. **Cons:** car needed because of the remote location; no bar, restaurant, or activities; could be too quiet and peaceful. $ *Rooms from: €154* ⊠ *Anse à la Barque, St-François* ☎ *0590/88–87–00* ⊕ *www.amaudo.fr* ↗ *9 rooms, 1 suite* ⍾◯⍾ *Breakfast.*

$$ 🍽 **Hôtel La Cocoteraie.** This boutique hotel's lobby, overlooking a glori-
HOTEL ous pool and with basket-weave rattan furnishings, is a study in refine-
ment. **Pros:** by a calm lagoon; sophisticated clientele; excellent location in St-François. **Cons:** some aspects dated and in need of renovation; some ongoing maintenance issues; not as fun as it used to be. $ *Rooms from: €289* ⊠ *Av. de l'Europe, St-François* ☎ *0590/88–79–81* ⊕ *www. dghotels.com* ↗ *52 suites* ⍾◯⍾ *Breakfast.*

$ 🍽 **La Créole Beach Hotel & Spa.** The magic at this 10-acre complex with
RESORT a contemporary, colorful lobby, cosmopolitan bar, and dual pools lies
Fodor'sChoice in the fun atmosphere the staff are able to create as they unite the dis-
★ parate, mostly French clientele. **Pros:** excellent management and long-term staff; lovely tropical gardens; good food, both at the buffet and the restaurant. **Cons:** some rooms far from the lobby; beach is nice but small; Wi-Fi costs extra. $ *Rooms from: €230* ⊠ *Pointe de la Verdure, Le Gosier* ☎ *0590/90–46–46* ⊕ *www.creolebeach.com* ↗ *276 rooms, 16 junior suites, 6 suites, 13 apartments* ⍾◯⍾ *No meals.*

$$$ 🍽 **La Toubana Hôtel & Spa.** Few hotels on Guadeloupe command such
RESORT a panoramic view of the sea—spanning four islands, no less, and
Fodor'sChoice all the suites offer full sea views, some breathtaking. **Pros:** a special
★ boutique experience with sophisticated style; glass-enclosed cocktail lounge–library has remarkable views; praise-worthy restaurant con-tinues to evolve. **Cons:** the little beach is down the hill, via a very

La Toubana Hôtel & Spa

steep paved path; bedrooms and TVs are small by American standards; some bungalows need renovation. $ *Rooms from: €384* ⊠ *Ste-Anne* ☏ *0590/88–25–57* ⊕ *www.toubana.com* ⤳ *32 bungalows, 12 suites, 3 villas* ⏉❍⏉ *Breakfast.*

$ ⏉☷⏉ **Le Neem Bungalows.** This small resort keeps growing and getting bet-
RENTAL ter, offering a seven-person hot tub and saltwater swimming pool in
FAMILY addition to a petite restaurant; the chef/owner Joel Kichenin even offers creole cooking lessons. **Pros:** good beach just across the street; owners are caring, and one speaks fluent English; two bungalows have kitch-enettes. **Cons:** original bungalows are packed in with no views; some noise from the adjacent accommodations; no full-service hotel ameni-ties. $ *Rooms from: €130* ⊠ *La Coulee rte. de la Pointe des Chateaux, St-François* ☏ *0590/88–69–37, 0690/99–69–37 mobile phone* ⊕ *www. leneem.com* ⤳ *3 bungalows, 5 suites* ⏉❍⏉ *Breakfast.*

BASSE-TERRE

$ ⏉☷⏉ **Caraïb'Bay Hotel.** This complex of colorful duplex bungalows may
B&B/INN not impress you at first, but its service and customer satisfaction have
FAMILY earned it many kudos. **Pros:** homey feel with multilingual library; mod-erate prices, especially with weekly offers; innovative bar and good food. **Cons:** not directly on the beach; not luxuriius; room decor dated. $ *Rooms from: €150* ⊠ *410 Allée du Coeur, Deshaies* ☏ *0590/28–41–71, 0690/35–38–39* ⊕ *www.hotels-guadeloupe.org* ⤳ *12 bungalows, 4 villas* ⏉❍⏉ *Breakfast.*

$ ⏉☷⏉ **Habitation Du Comté.** A decidedly special place, this was the great
B&B/INN house for the owner of a sugarcane plantation, but the stalwart,

hurricane-proof mansion wasn't built eons ago, but rather in 1948. **Pros:** good blackout shutters; blissfully quiet; in-room Wi-Fi is strong and free. **Cons:** may be too quiet for some travelers; isolated location means you need a car; no resort-style amenities. $ *Rooms from: €140* ✉ *Comté de Lohéac, Ste-Rose* ☎ *0590/21–78–81* ⊕ *www.hotelducomte. com* ⇆ *7 double rooms, 1 2-bedroom, 2-bath bungalow* ❍ *Breakfast.*

$ ☷ **Habitation Getz.** This former coffee plantation offers unique accom-
RENTAL modations in its great house or in unique tree houses—ideal for a family
FAMILY that wants to play Swiss Family Robinson. **Pros:** an impressive labor of love; tree houses are unique in Guadeloupe; a good, reasonably priced dinner is offered on Wednesday and Sunday. **Cons:** tree houses are accessed only by a swinging ladder; isolated location means you need a car; towels and linens not changed daily. $ *Rooms from: €100* ✉ *Rte. de Gery, Vieux-Habitants* ☎ *0590/24–46–86, 0690/58–70–20* ⊕ *www. chambrescabanesguadeloupe.com* ⇆ *2 rooms, 3 tree houses* ❍ *Breakfast.*

$ ☷ **L'Habitation Tabanon.** This rental complex is in a small market town
RENTAL in the heart of Basse-Terre, the mountainous, wild side of Guadeloupe,
FAMILY where ecosports and scuba diving are the main draws. **Pros:** a hip place to call home for a week; manager is accommodating and acts as a con-cierge to guests; these well-equipped units are exceptional for Basse-Terre. **Cons:** you will need a car; there are no tourist amenities nearby; no resort services or amenities. $ *Rooms from: €94* ✉ *Moulin de Taba-non, 5 Chemin de Tabanon, Petit-Bourg* ☎ *0690/35–06–11, 0690/40–98–95* ⊕ *www.habitation-tabanon.com* ⇆ *5 apartments* ❍ *No meals.*

$$ ☷ **Langley Resort Fort Royal.** This well-priced, friendly, and fun resort
RESORT offers both simple beachfront bungalows and regular rooms in a mostly
FAMILY all-inclusive environment geared toward less fussy travelers. **Pros:** free Wi-Fi; food and service surprisingly good; bedding and mattresses in main building are comfortable. **Cons:** high-volume, mostly all-inclusive resort that is rare in Guadeloupe; bungalows are small and can be noisy; restaurant gets crowded. $ *Rooms from: €280* ✉ *Bas Vent, Deshaies* ☎ *0590/68–76–70* ⊕ *www.fortroyal.eu* ☉ *Closed Sept. and Oct.* ⇆ *126 rooms, 7 suites, 82 bungalows* ❍ *All-inclusive.*

$ ☷ **Le Jardin Malanga.** This inviting hillside inn is on a former coffee
B&B/INN plantation, where trees laden with fruit are like the temptations of the Garden of Eden. **Pros:** a romantic hideaway with history and character; good food in the restaurant (half board is a good option); breakfast included. **Cons:** no TV or Internet in the bungalows; beds and pil-lows in bungalows more comfortable than those in the colonial house; isolated location not near a beach. $ *Rooms from: €233* ✉ *60 rte. de l'Hermitage, Hermitage, Trois-Rivières* ☎ *0590/92–67–57* ⊕ *www. jardinmalanga.com* ⇆ *9 rooms, 1 suite* ❍ *Breakfast.*

$$ ☷ **Tainos Cottages.** The globe-trotting Frenchman who designed these
B&B/INN seven Indonesian teak cottages resembling Guadeloupean *cases* from
FAMILY the 1920s that overlook a long unspoiled beach, Plage de Grande-Anse, has passed on, and his son has now taken charge of this small paradise. **Pros:** from the smallest to the largest, the cottages are spacious; a dis-count is available for online bookings; family-owned, it is informal with caring service and English spoken. **Cons:** the mosquito netting's there for a reason—bring repellent; bungalows could use some updating; the

Le Jardin Malanga

rustic experience is not for everyone. $ *Rooms from: €300* ✉ *Plage de Grande-Anse, Deshaies* ☎ *0590/28–44–42* ⊕ *www.tainos-cottages.com* 🕙 *Closed late Aug.–late Oct.* ⤳ *7 bungalows* †⊙| *Breakfast.*

$ 🏠 **Tendacayou Ecolodge & Spa.** The result of a remarkable 10-year saga, this quirky and inventive rain-forest resort consists of both tree houses and ground-level bungalows as well as a wonderful restaurant, Le Poisson Rouge, and a moderately priced spa. **Pros:** boardwalks rather than scary ladders access the tree houses; ample homemade breakfast; a boutique jammed with wonderfully exotic treasures from around the world. **Cons:** no air-conditioning, and open-air sleeping is not for everyone; isolated location, with no beach, phones, TVs, or in-room Wi-Fi; prices are expensive for what you get. $ *Rooms from: €260* ✉ *Matouba La Hauf, Deshaies* ☎ *0590/28–42–72* ⊕ *www.tendacayou.com* ⤳ *7 1-bedroom bungalows, 2 3-bedroom bungalows* †⊙| *Breakfast.*

B&B/INN

ILES DES SAINTES

$ 🏠 **Hotel Bois Joli.** The newest seafront section of Bois Joli, which was completed in 2014 and sits apart from the main hotel, houses Terre-de-Haut's best guest rooms (other than those in some luxurious private villas). **Pros:** fairly close to some of the better beaches; the attractive pool is traversed by a diminutive bridge; the hotel is organized, clean, and well-serviced. **Cons:** you'll need a car or scooter to get around; no bellmen and no elevators in the new section; English is lacking throughout (a manager or two is bilingual). $ *Rooms from: €195* ✉ *Terre-de-Haut* ☎ *0590/99–50–38, 0590/99–55–05* ⊕ *www.hotelboisjoli.fr* ⤳ *22 rooms, 8 bungalows* †⊙| *Breakfast.*

HOTEL
FAMILY

10

$ B&B/INN **Hotel Restaurant Les Petits Saints.** This charismatic landmark inn, which draws mainly couples and families, was bought by a French couple who discovered the property while on vacation from their home in California. **Pros:** reminiscent of the island guesthouses of the 1970s; village just down the hill; free Wi-Fi mainly in lobby/restaurant. **Cons:** not luxurious by any means; breakfast and check-out are both early. *[$] Rooms from: €150 ✉ La Savane, Terre-de-Haut ☎ 0590/99–50–99 🌐 www.petitssaints.com ⏲ Closed Sept. 🛏 3 bungalows, 3 suites, 2 studios, 2 rooms 🍴 No meals.*

$ RENTAL **Les Hauts de Grand Anse.** No neighbors and no noise other than the sound of the sea is what guests can expect at this property on pristine Grand Anse and Anse Rodrigue beaches. **Pros:** gorgeous beaches; nearly new and well maintained; incredible sea views. **Cons:** no resort services; no landline telephone; distance to town may necessitate an electric car or scooter. *[$] Rooms from: €58 ✉ Rte.de l'Anse Rodrigue, Terre-de-Haut ☎ 0683/05–63–67, 0690/46–29–19 🌐 www.grandbaie.com 🛏 4 apartments 🍴 No meals.*

$ HOTEL **Lô Bleu Hôtel.** This small, cheerful beachfront hotel is painted sunset orange with marine-blue trim; dramatic nightlights illuminate the beach area, which is furnished with chaises. **Pros:** right on the bay; large front rooms with sea view and balconies; family-friendly, with baby monitors and some bunk beds. **Cons:** no grounds or resort amenities; no restaurant; the front desk does not always speak English. *[$] Rooms from: €122 ✉ Fond de Curé, Terre-de-Haut ☎ 0590/92–40–00, 0690/63–80–36 🌐 www.lobleuhotel.com 🛏 9 rooms, 1 suite 🍴 No meals.*

$ RENTAL **Paradis Saintois.** You'll feel like the king of the hill as you rock yourself to sleep in your hammock on the terrace of your apartment while gazing down on the Caribbean below. **Pros:** lots of fun; super managers; discounts for longer stays. **Cons:** no phones or TVs in some rooms; a hike up the hill from town; no hotel services. *[$] Rooms from: €87 ✉ 211 rte. des Pres Cassin, Terre-de-Haut ☎ 0590/99–56–16 🌐 www.paradissaintois.com 🛏 5 apartments, 3 studios, 1 room 🍴 No meals ☞ 3-night minimum.*

$ RENTAL FAMILY **Residence Anse Caraibe.** This small, quiet apartment complex is perched on a hill right in the village, a five-minute walk from the ferry dock. **Pros:** English-speaking, helpful manager; not all apartments have private terraces; Wi-Fi in all units. **Cons:** no phones or cable TV; up a steep hill; no cushy creature comforts. *[$] Rooms from: €58 ✉ Emmanuel Laurent St., Terre-de-Haut ☎ 0690/46–29–19, 0683/05–63–67 🌐 www.grandbaie.com 🛏 4 studio apartments, 1 2-bedroom apartment, 1 3-bedroom apartment 🍴 No meals.*

$ RENTAL FAMILY **Résidence Grand Baie.** This luxe hilltop, four-unit apartment building offers privacy and a seafront location, 15 minutes from the village. **Pros:** everything feels new; outstanding water views ; quiet and private. **Cons:** not in town, so transportation is a necessity; no hotel or resort services; strictly self-catering. *[$] Rooms from: €68 ✉ Rte. du Figuier, Terre-de-Haut ☎ 0690/46–29–19, 0690/57–68–13 🌐 www.grandbaie.com 🛏 4 units 🍴 No meals.*

MARIE-GALANTE

Accommodations here run the gamut from inexpensive, locally owned beachfront bungalows to complexes with international owners. Bwa Chik Hotel in St-François offers a package that includes ferry tickets.

$

HOTEL

⌂ **Hotel Cap Reva.** One of the largest properties on Marie-Galante faces one of the island's best beaches, offering acres of tropical landscaping surrounding a cheery yellow, hilltop hotel. **Pros:** friendly staff and manager; nice poolside snack bar; WI-Fi is free but only in public areas. **Cons:** hotel needs some upgrades; not all receptionists speak English and the desk is deserted by night; restaurant isn't great. $ *Rooms from:* €185 ⌧ *Plage de la Feuillere, Capesterre-de-Marie-Galante* ☎ *0590/97–20–01* ⊕ *www.capreva.fr* ↪ *22 studios, 12 duplexes* ⎮⊙⎮ *Breakfast.*

$

B&B/INN

⌂ **La Rose du Bresil.** At this pretty, diminutive boutique hotel, all the renovated suites have impressive kitchens, though proximity to a good in-hotel restaurant and others may not be an incentive for cooking. **Pros:** flat-screen, satellite TV; free Wi-Fi in rooms; quality mattresses are replaced regularly. **Cons:** no sea views; no resort amenities. $ *Rooms from: €78* ⌧ *Rte. du Litoral, Capesterre-de-Marie-Galante* ☎ *0590/97–47–39* ⊕ *www.larosedubresil.com* ↪ *7 rooms, two 2-bedroom suites; 1 3-bedroom suite* ⎮⊙⎮ *No meals.*

$

HOTEL

⌂ **Le Soleil Levant Hotel and Resort.** Low prices, gorgeous hilltop views, and nice dual pools keep this simple, family-owned complex filled. **Pros:** family-friendly; good air-conditioning; free, reliable Wi-Fi in rooms. **Cons:** you'll need a car; hotel rooms are not large and get some noisy; staff not accustomed to American guests. $ *Rooms from: €55* ⌧ *Section Marie-Louise, 42 rue de la Marine, Les Hauteurs de Capesterre, Capesterre-de-Marie-Galante* ☎ *0590/97–31–55* ⊕ *www.hotel-soleil-levant.fr* ↪ *8 rooms, 3 apartments, 10 bungalows* ⎮⊙⎮ *No meals.*

$

RENTAL

⌂ **Le Touloulou.** Le Touloulou offers four simple stucco one-bedroom bungalows, two of which have kitchenettes, as well as a two-bedroom bungalow, also with a kitchenette. **Pros:** beachfront location at a budget price; adjacent restaurant and fun bar; genial, bilingual chef-owner. **Cons:** simple, no-frills place; lacks the usual resort amenities; can be loud on weekends. $ *Rooms from: €65* ⌧ *Plage de Petite-Anse, Capesterre-de-Marie-Galante* ☎ *0590/97–32–63, 0690/48–76–77* ⊕ *www.letouloulou.com* ↪ *5 bungalows* ⎮⊙⎮ *No meals* ☞ *A bungalow with a kitchenette is just 5 euros more—way to go.*

$

RENTAL

⌂ **Le Village de Canada.** The decades-old complex offers studios, bungalows, and apartments, some with sea views; there's a pool but no beach, though one is close by. **Pros:** private terraces; moderate prices, especially on a weekly basis; good central location, being equidistant between Grand Bourg and St. Louis. **Cons:** not on the beach; furnishings, TVs, and bedding are dated; a car is a must since there is no restaurant. $ *Rooms from: €77* ⌧ *Section Canada, St-Louis* ☎ *0590/97–86–11* ⊕ *www.villagedecanada.com* ↪ *5 studios, 3 villas, 2 apartments* ⎮⊙⎮ *No meals.*

10

NIGHTLIFE

Guadeloupeans maintain that the beguine began here, and for sure, the beguine and mazurkas were heavily influenced by the European quadrille and orchestrated melodies. Their merging is the origin of West Indian music, and it gave birth to zouk (music with an African-influenced Caribbean rhythm) at the beginning of the 1980s. Still the rage here, it has spread not only to France but to other European countries. Many resorts have dinner dancing or offer regularly scheduled entertainment by steel bands and folkloric groups.

BARS AND NIGHTCLUBS

Bar de la Vieille Tour. The atmospheric piano bar with its planters' chairs and whirring fan blades is as memorable as Rick's Café in *Casablanca*. The terrace tables give you the best views of the Caribbean through the multicolored bougainvillea. Accras (salt-fish fritters), peanuts, and olives usually arrive with your cocktail, which will be as tasty as it is pretty. A bar menu offers a selection of tapas, and the rum carte is extensive, some available by the flight. On Friday and Saturday evenings there's live piano music, and in high season, there's often more live music, like a jazz trio. ⊠ *Rte. de Montauban, Le Gosier* ☎ *0590/84–23–23* ⊕ *auberge-vielle-tour.fr.*

Club Med By Night. Club Med sells night passes that include all cocktails, dinner with wine, and a show in the theater, followed by admission to the disco. Go on Friday for the gala dinner and the most creative show, or on a Tuesday, another special night. A night pass is a good option for single women, who will feel comfortable and safe at the disco, where there are plenty of fun staffers (G.O.s) willing to be dance partners. ⊠ *Quartier Caravelle, Ste-Anne* ☎ *0590/85–49–50* ⊗ *Closed Sept.–early Nov.*

Eden Palm Theater Spectacles. The jazzed-up Eden Palm Theater for years was the stage for Cuban-influenced Caribbean musical reviews on Saturday nights. Now, though it still has a supper club ambience, it's just a fun DJ and dancing on Saturday nights following dinner service. Dinner is a multicourse, Franco-Caribbean affair and may include an alcoholic beverage. The wine carte encompasses bottles from around the world, with some fine bottles. ⊠ *Hotel Eden Palm, Ste-Anne* ☎ *0590/88–48–48* ⊕ *www.edenpalm.com.*

La Rhumerie Bar & Lounge. Something is always happening at La Créole Beach Hotel. The entertainment is often bands playing beguine and zouk, or piano with bass, all of which are very danceable and add to the hotel's conviviality. The tom-tom drummers accompanied by a bevy of native dancers are exciting. A steel band also plays, usually on Monday and Wednesday nights. The busy bar specializes in quality rums from various Caribbean islands, and serves creole tapas including traditional accras. ⊠ *La Créole Beach Hotel & Spa, Pointe de la Verdure, Le Gosier* ☎ *0590/90–46–46.*

CASINOS

Both of the island's casinos are on Grande-Terre and have American-style roulette, blackjack, and stud poker. The legal age for gambling is 21, and French law dictates that everyone show a passport or a local driver's license. Jacket and tie aren't required, but "proper attire" means no shorts, T-shirts, jeans, flip-flops, or sneakers.

Casino de St-François. The small Casino de St-François has a contemporary élan that makes you want to dress up and come on out. There's a dramatic water installation, leather furniture, and an appealing restaurant, Le Joker, open for both lunch and dinner. It has a bar, a piano, and a stage for performers, which also doubles as a disco on Friday and Saturday. The casino opens every day at 10 am. The lighting, installed by Martinique's MPA architectural firm, makes it a handsome showplace, and there are more than 91 slots, as well as American roulette and gaming tables for baccarat, blackjack, craps, and more. ⊠ *Lieu-dit-Saint-Marthe, St-François* ✚ *In front of the golf course, opposite the Centre Commercial* ☎ *0590/88–41–31* ⊕ *www.casinosaintfrancois.com.*

SHOPPING

The island has a lot of desirable French products, from designer fashions for women and men and sensual lingerie to French china and liqueurs. As for local handicrafts, you can find attractive wood carvings, madras table linens, island dolls dressed in madras, woven straw baskets and hats, and *salakos*—fishermen's hats made of split bamboo, some covered in madras—which make great wall decorations. Of course, the favorite Guadeloupean souvenir is rum. Look for *rhum vieux*, the top of the line. Be aware that the only liquor bottles allowed on planes have to be bought in the duty-free shops at the airport. Usually the shops have to deliver purchases to the aircraft. For foodies, the market ladies sell aromatic fresh spices, crisscrossed with cinnamon sticks, in little baskets lined with madras.

GRAND-TERRE

AREAS AND MALLS

Bas-du-Fort's two shopping areas are the Cora Shopping Center and the marina, where there are 20 or so shops and some restaurants, many right on the water. This marina has an active social scene.

Bustling Point-à-Pitre has obtained the prestigious French label of *Ville d'Art et d'Histoire* (town of art and history). You can browse in the street stalls around the harbor quay and at the two markets (the best is the Marché de Frébault). The town's main shopping streets with lots of French merchandise, from pâté to sexy lingerie, are rue Schoelcher, rue de Nozières, and the busy rue Frébault. At the St-John Perse Cruise Terminal, there's an attractive mall with about two dozen shops.

In St-François there are more than a dozen shops surrounding the marina, some selling French lingerie, swimsuits, and fashions. The supermarket has particularly good prices on French wines and cheeses,

10

and if you pick up a fresh baguette, you'll have a picnic. (Then you can go get lost at a secluded beach.) Don't forget some island chocolates or individual fruit and custard tarts.

Destreland. Grande-Terre's largest, most modern shopping mall, Destreland has more than 180 boutiques, restaurants, and stores. This commercial center is a few minutes from the airport, which is a shopping destination in its own right. ⊠ *Les Abymes* ⊕ *www.destreland.com.*

ART

Kreol West Indies Guadeloupe. Housed in a white stucco bungalow with lavender and aqua trim, this is Grand-Terre's first real art gallery and museum shop. This genuinely unique concept melds an historic exhibition with colonial furnishings, such as planters chairs, with hundreds of high-level sculptures and contemporary paintings. A colorful shop, it also specializes in beach bags from recycled materials and island artifacts. ⊠ *Pointe-des-Châteaux Rd., St-François* ✛ *200 yards after the Pointe-des-Châteaux speed bumps* ☏ *0590/24–41–92* ⊕ *www. kreolwestindies.com* ☜ *€2.*

CLOTHING

Boutique Le Gall. The line of fashionable resortwear for women and children sold here is designed by French painter Jean Claude Le Gall. Pieces have hand-painted figures like turtles and dolphins on high-quality cotton knits. There are several other branches of this French favorite across the island, at the Bas-du-Fort Marina and even on Les Saintes. A gift from this store is considered prestigious back in mainland France. ⊠ *La Marina–La Coursive, St-François* ☏ *0590/55–46–95.*

Dody. Across from the market, Dody is the place to go if you want white eyelet lace (blouses, skirts, dresses, even bustiers). A single item can cost up to €300. Madras clothing is both traditional and contemporary, and it looks especially cute in children's clothing. A line of colorful, Carnival-inspired, tropical dresses is a knockout. And for men there are creole suits and cool, madras shirts, and a line of Bebe Creole. Many styles have reduced prices, and there are special-occasion "costumes"—wedding, communion, and confirmation dresses all in white eyelet. Those who love designer ensembles based in Guadeloupean tradition can now shop online. ⊠ *Spice Market Sq., 31 rue Frébault, Pointe-à-Pitre* ☏ *0590/82–18–73* ⊕ *www.dodyshop.com.*

CRAFTS

Centre Artisanat. The Centre Artisanat offers a wide selection of local crafts, including art composed of shells, wood, and stone. One of the outlets sells authentic Panama hats. It is located under a tent across from the waterfront as you first drive into the village. ⊠ *Ste-Anne.*

Madras Bijoux. Bijoux is the French word for jewelry and Madras Bijoux specializes in replicas of authentic creole jewelry, like the multistrand gold bead necklaces. The shop also creates custom designs and does repairs. ⊠ *115 rue Nozières, Pointe-à-Pitre* ☏ *0590/82–88–03.*

BASSE-TERRE

FOOD

Cap Creole."Invite the sea to your table" is Cap Creole's motto. This shop just across from the sea sells smoked fish par excellence. Since 1996 it has been taking the catch of the local fishermen—tuna, marlin, mahimahi, thazard—smoking it, and vacuum packing it. More recently, they have added other products, notably *boudin* (sausage) of fish, conch, and crab in 1-kilo packets. And there are a lot more local gourmet products. This is great stuff if you're in a self-catering villa and want to have appetizers before going out to dinner, or if you want to pack a picnic for a secluded beach. ⊠ *Bouillante* ☎ *0590/95–45–66* ⊕ *www.capcreole.com.*

LES SAINTES

ART

Pascal Foy. Artist Pascal Foy produces stunning homages to traditional creole architecture: paintings of houses that incorporate collage make marvelous wall hangings. As his fame has grown, his media attention has expanded, so prices have risen. You are more likely to find a family member manning the shop nowadays. ⊠ *Rte. à Pompierres, Terre-de-Haut* ☎ *0690/43–13–09.*

CLOTHING

Maogany Boutique. At this shop, which resembles a yacht, the best of the offerings are batiks and clothing in luminescent seashell and blue shades. Ladies love pareus (wraparound fabric for skirts) in the colors of the sea, from pale green to deep turquoise, as well as the jewelry. For men and ladies, there are authentic Panama hats—tropical fedoras in classic white *and* tropical colors. There are also several lines of women's clothing by French designers (like Nathalie Joubert), tunics, crocheted tops, and tiered long skirts. Many items are quite expensive but cool . . . and lightweight. And here the silkscreen is the real deal. ⊠ *26 rue Jean Calot, Terre-de-Haut* ☎ *0590/99–50–12, 0690/74–19–00* ⊕ *www.maogany.com* ⊙ *Closed Mon.*

Tata Somba. This boutique is owned by a French woman with characteristic good taste. Ladies will find French and Italian fashions here, cool, lightweight skirts and dresses, stylish shade hats for the island's strong sun, jewelry, sandals, accessories, and hip clothes for little girls. ⊠ *Terre-de-Haut* ☎ *0590/99–51–65, 0690/64–48–13.*

COSMETICS AND PERFUME

L'Atelier du Savon. L'Atelier du Savon makes all of its soaps from vegetable products, with scents including marine spice and mandarin orange. Beautifully packaged gift baskets include bath salts and aromatic oils. You never know when the sign "Closed today, we are making soap" will go up. ⊠ *Impasse du Mouillage, Terre-de-Haut* ⟷ *Near the pharmacy on rue Jean Calot* ☎ *0590/99–56–24.*

10

MARIE-GALANTE

COSMETICS AND PERFUME

La Suite. This classy boutique is something that you might expect to find in St. Barth or St. Martin, not on the out-island of Marie-Galante. It is a mélange of cosmetics, perfumes, beachwear, vintage island cards and art, sea-grass baskets, and coffee-table books on the island's history and culture. Products are all natural from Guadeloupe and St. Martin— glamorous cosmetics to essential oils such as bug spray and baby-bug off (which you will need on this island). And then there are some stylin' accessories like French sunglasses, flip-flops with wedges and utilitarian ones with recycled rubber from Kenya, beads and original jewelry by island designers like Nathalie Julan. And if you are lucky you may come on a day when an evening soiree is planned, something literary, with a guitarist and flutist performing or a beauty makeover. ⊠ *38 rue du Dr Marcel Etzol, Grand-Bourg* ☎ *0590/97–06–90.*

SPORTS AND THE OUTDOORS

BOATING AND SAILING

Generally speaking, most of the towns and cities of Guadeloupe are not beautiful; however, the craggy coastline and the waters of variegated blues and greens are gorgeous. If you plan to sail these waters, you should be aware that the winds and currents tend to be strong. There are excellent, well-equipped marinas in Pointe-à-Pitre, Bas-du-Fort, Deshaies, St-François, and Gourbeyre. You can rent a yacht (bareboat or crewed) from several companies. To make a bareboat charter, companies will evaluate your navigational and seamanship skills. If you do not pass, you must hire a skipper or be left on dry land.

Antilles Sail. Antilles Sail is a charter operation specializing in catamarans from 40 to 62 feet, which can accommodate eight guests. A new, exciting addition to their fleet is a 45-foot Neel trimaran. For those who don't qualify to captain their own ship, or for those who want to just relax and be pampered, a skipper and crew can be hired. Provisioning and meal service can be arranged, and VIP, dive, and other packages are available. The fleet also contains monohulls from 35 to 55 feet, which are used mainly for bareboating. Antilles Sail can also arrange flights and land stays. ⊠ *Bas-du-Fort Marina, Quai No. 9, Boutique des Moulins, Bas du Fort* ☎ *0590/90–16–81* ⊕ *www.antilles-sail.com.*

DIVING

The main diving area at the **Cousteau Underwater Park,** just off Basse-Terre near Pigeon Island, offers routine dives to 60 feet. The numerous glass-bottom boats and other craft make the site feel like a marine parking lot; however, the underwater sights are spectacular. Guides and instructors are certified under the French CMAS (some also have PADI, but none have NAUI). Most operators offer two-hour dives three times per day for about €50 to €55 per dive; three-dive packages are €120 to €145. Hotels and dive operators usually rent snorkeling gear.

FAMILY **Les Heures Saines.** Les Heures Saines is the premier operator for dives in the Cousteau Underwater Park. Trips to Les Saintes offer one or two dives for average and advanced divers, with plenty of time for lunch and sightseeing. Wreck, night, and nitrox diving are also available. Despite this operator's popularity, it has kept its prices moderate, with many packages available. The instructors, young and fun types from the Metropole, many of them English speakers, are excellent with children. The company also offers winter whale- and dolphin-watching trips with marine biologists as guides aboard a 60-foot catamaran. Inquire also about going canyoning and/or hiking with Les Heures Saines. ⊠ *Le Rocher de Malendure, Plage de Malendure, Bouillante* ☎ *0590/98–86–63* ⊕ *www.heures-saines.gp* 🗠 *From €55.*

FAMILY **Pisquettes Club de Plongée Des Saintes.** With more than 15 years of experience, dive master Cedric Phalipon of Pisquettes Club de Plongée Des Saintes knows all the best sites. He gives excellent lessons, and in English, too. Equipment is replaced frequently and is of a high caliber. Small tanks are available for kids, who are taken buddy-diving. PADI divers are welcomed. Les Saintes is known for its underwater hills, caves, canyons, and wall dives. Divers can see sponges of varied colors and gorgeous underwater trees that sway. Sec Pate is a famous underwater mountain, off the island's coast, in open seas. ⊠ *Le Mouillage, Terre-de-Haut* ⊕ *From the main ferry dock, leaving it behind you, turn left and walk up Main St. Pisquettes is just past the kayak rental shop on the right* ☎ *0590/99–88–80* ⊕ *www.pisquettes.com.*

Plaisir Plongee Karokera (PPK). Plaisir Plongee Karokera (PPK) has a good reputation and is well established among those who dive off Pigeon Island. One dive boat departs three times daily, charging by the dive at rates are generally less than its competition. A second dive boat goes to Les Saintes, with two dives, one at a wreck, the other at a reef, lunch included. Snorkel gear can also be rented for a reasonable price. English-speaking dive masters are PADI-certified. Show your Fodor's guide and ask for a discount. ⊠ *Plage de Malendure, Bouillante* ☎ *0590/98–82–43* ⊕ *www.ppk-plongee-guadeloupe.com* 🗠 *From €35.*

FISHING

Not far offshore from Pigeon-Bouillante, in Basse-Terre, is a bounty of big-game fish such as bonito, dolphinfish, captain fish, barracuda, kingfish, and tuna. You can also thrill to the challenge of the big billfish such as marlin and swordfish. Anglers have been known to come back with as many as three blue marlins in a single day. For Ernest Hemingway wannabes, this is it. To reap this harvest, you'll need to charter one of the high-tech sportfishing machines with flying bridges, competent skippers, and mates. The price is $430 to $600 a day, with lunch and drinks included. The boats can accommodate up to six passengers.

Captain Tony. Like father, like son: Tony Burel has officially taken over the sportfishing boat that he and his dad, Michel, worked for years. It's outfitted to go into combat with the big-game fish, and he has hauled

10

many a billfish aboard. It has the latest generation of electronics and is considered the most commodious sport fisherman on the island. This Burel has 10 fishing years to his credit, five as a guide. Not only does he know where to find blue marlin but yellow-fin tuna, wahoo—"what you like." This reliable big-fishing charter outfit, which charges by the person instead of by the full-boat charter, also allows nonfishers to come at a lower rate and can usually pick anglers up at their hotel for an additional fee. The skipper will be happy to take your picture with your catch of the day. And if you are not into jigging or chumming, check the website for snorkeling adventures and other excursions. ⊠ *Les Galbas, Ste-Anne* ☎ *0690/55–21–35* ⊕ *captaintonyb.com* ✉ *From €160.*

EN ROUTE If you're driving from Ste-Anne to the St-François Marina area, follow signs first to St-François, then look for signs to the marina and Pointe des Châteaux, not St-François centre ville. That is the old town, and although it's a nice detour to see the market, it's also a circuitous route to the marina.

GOLF

Golf Municipal St-François. Golf Municipal St-François is a par-72 course that was designed by Robert Trent Jones in 1978, with later alterations that made it more challenging, though many feel that the putting surfaces could use improvement. The course has an English-speaking pro and electric carts for rent. It's best to reserve tee times a day or two in advance. There are no caddies. Clubs can be rented for a nominal fee. Guests at Bwa Chik Hotel & Golf get a 10% discount. Le Birdy restaurant serves lunch daily and dinner Wednesday and Friday through Sunday, and tapas are offered at the bar. ⊠ *Av. d'l Europe, St-François* ☎ *0590/88–41–87* ✉ *€45 for 9 holes, €65 for 18 holes* 🏌 *18 holes, 6755 yards, par 71.*

HIKING

Fodor's Choice ★ With hundreds of trails and countless rivers and waterfalls, the **Parc National de la Guadeloupe** on Basse-Terre is the main draw for hikers. Some of the trails should be attempted only with an experienced guide. All tend to be muddy, so wear a good pair of boots. Know that even the young and fit can find these outings arduous; the unfit may find them painful. Start off slowly, with a shorter hike, and then go for the gusto. All water sports—even canoeing and kayaking—are forbidden in the center of the park. Scientists are studying the impact of these activities on the park's ecosystem.

Vert Intense. Vert Intense organizes hikes in the national park and to the volcano. You move from steaming hot springs to an icy waterfall in the same hike. Guides are patient and safety-conscious, and can bring you to heights that you never thought you could reach, including the top of Le Soufrière. The volcano hike, the cheapest excursion, must be booked four days in advance. When you are under the fumaroles you can smell the sulfur (like rotten eggs) and you, your hair and clothes will smell like sulfur until you take a shower. A mixed-adventure package spanning three days costs considerably more. The two-day bivouac and other adventures can be extreme, so before you decide to play Indiana Jones, know what is expected. The French-speaking guides, who also know some English and Spanish, can take you to other tropical forests and rivers for canyoning (climbing and scrambling on outcrops, usually along and above the water). If you are just one or two people, the company can team you up with a group. Vert Intense now has a guesthouse, les Bananes Vertes (The Green Bananas), where you can combine a stay with trekking and other activities. ⊠ *Rte. de la Soufrière, St-Claude* ☎ *0590/99–34–73, 0690/55–40–47* ⊕ *www.vert-intense.com* ⊟ *From €30.*

HORSEBACK RIDING

Le Haras de Saint-François. A 50-horse stable, Le Haras de Saint-François has English lessons and Western trail rides for two or three hours. The latter will take you to the beach, where you can go bareback into the sea. ⊠ *Chemin de la Princesse, St-François* ☎ *0690/39–90–00* ⊟ *From €50.*

KAYAKING

Centre Éconautique. Centre Éconautique, aka Clear Blue Caraïbes, has mastered the art of underwater exploration without ever getting your hair wet. Rent a glass-bottom kayak, which allows you to see the myriad colors of one of the world's most beautiful bays here. Paddleboards and clear-bottom, dinghylike inflatables also enable you to play in the water. The tours, which last either two hours or a half day, will let you be privy to the marine beauty of the coral reefs and sea life. Trips to the nearby Isle de Cabrito for a picnic and snorkeling are also offered. To find Centre Éconautique, take a left from the main dock, go two blocks, and look for its colorful signage on the right. It is across from Couleurs du Monde. ⊠ *Ruelle Lasserre, Mouillage, Terre-de-Haut* ☎ *0690/65–79–81* ⊕ *www.clearbluecaraibes.fr* ⊟ *From €20.*

Centre Nautique. On the beach, Centre Nautique rents sea kayaks and Hobie Cats by the hour, even flyboards and stand-up paddleboards. Staff can arrange fishing, catamaran, kayaking, diving, and motorboat excursions. It also runs water taxis to the Islet du Gosier. A motorized catamaran excursion to the gorgeous Grand Cul de Sac includes lunch and drinks. There are PADI instructors for the dive segment of the operation, and certifications are possible. Jet Ski rentals include a guide, and range from 20-minute rentals to guided five-hour tours including lunch. Nonguests are welcome but must call in advance. ⊠ *La Créole Beach Hotel & Spa, Pointe de la Verdure, Le Gosier* ☎ *0590/90–46–59* ⊟ *From €10.*

10

SEA EXCURSIONS

Cool Caraïbes. Relatively new to the catamaran excursion scene, Cool Caraïbes has acquired a 27-passenger cat (three crew). It plies the turquoise waters to both Les Saintes and Marie-Galante, yet not on the same day. For full-day trips, you must be at the dock by 7 am, returning between 5:30 and 6 pm. Coffee and a simple lunch prepared by the crew are served. It is generally crudités, mahimahi with a creole sauce, rice, and tropical fruit for dessert. And yes, there is rum aboard—planters punch. Once on Les Saintes, you are on your own to explore, or you can opt for a mini-bus tour, which is a good choice, especially if you are not one to hike hills or if you have children in tow. There is snorkeling gear and most guests utilize it and swim off the boat. On Marie-Galante, passengers disembark for a 90-minute mini-van tour, which includes a tasting at a rum distillery and a swim and snorkel at a gorgeous white-sand beach. ⊠ *Marina de Bas-du-Fort, Bas du Fort* ⌖ *If you are facing the marina where all the restaurants are, continue left on that street until you see the boat's dock on the right-hand side, near the l'Aquarium au Gosier* ☎ *0690/70–47–18* ⊕ *www.coolcaraibes.com.*

FAMILY **Evasion Tropicale.** Evasion Tropicale operates daylong, ecotouristic, whale-watching cruises. With the help of the onboard hydrophone and the skipper's and researchers' 20 years of experience, sperm whales are easy to find all year long and humpback whales from December through March. Food and drinks are served, and when you arrive back in port you follow the leader to the small whale museum, "Balen ka Souflé." There's a 10-person minimum for trips on the 51-foot motor sailor, but every passenger must also buy an annual membership in the Association for Study and Census of Turtles, Marine and Mammals of the Caribbean. Contributing to the conservation of marine life is a good way to discover and learn about the underwater world, especially for children. Evasion Tropicale received the biodiversity Conservation Award Special Mention in 2013. ⊠ *Rue des paletuviers, Pigeon, Bouillante* ☎ *0590/92–74–24, 0690/57–19–44* ⊕ *www.evasiontropicale.org* ⌑ *From €65.*

Paradoxe Croisieres. A top-of-the-line catamaran, *Paradoxe* sails to Marie-Galante (anchoring at the idyllic beach Anse Canot) in high season, usually on Thursday, but most days it departs from St. François for Petite-Terre, an uninhabited island that's a nature preserve. This isn't your typical booze cruise. In the morning when it anchors off Petite-Terre, the passengers take guided walking tours, always on the lookout for iguanas. Then it's back to the beach to eat a lunch of grilled fish prepared by the boat's crew. In the afternoon guests can snorkel in the lagoon. The trip to Marie-Galante usually includes a bus tour around the island and a visit to a distillery. The company's marina ticket booth is open 8–noon and 4–7. ⊠ *St-François Marina, St-François* ☎ *0590/88–41–73* ⊕ *paradoxe-croisieres.com* ⌑ *From €80.*

JAMAICA

WELCOME TO JAMAICA

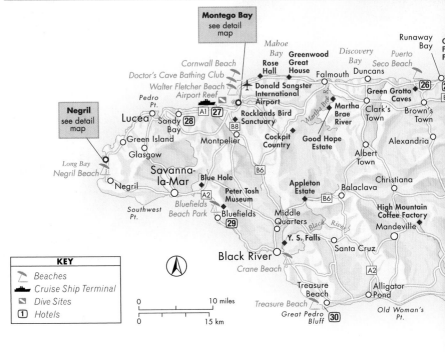

Chances are you will never fully understand Jamaica in all its delightful complexity, but you will probably have a good time trying. You can party in Montego Bay, enjoy the sunset in Negril, or simply relax at one of the island's many all-inclusive resorts. One thing's for sure: along the way you'll discover a rich culture and delicious island cuisine that you'll not soon forget.

OUT OF MANY, ONE PEOPLE

The third-largest island in the Caribbean (after Cuba and Hispaniola), Jamaica is 146 miles (242 km) long and is slightly smaller than the state of Connecticut. It has a population of 2.7 million. With about 800,000 people, the capital, Kingston, is the largest English-speaking city south of Miami (in the Western Hemisphere, at least). The highest point is Blue Mountain Peak at 7,402 feet.

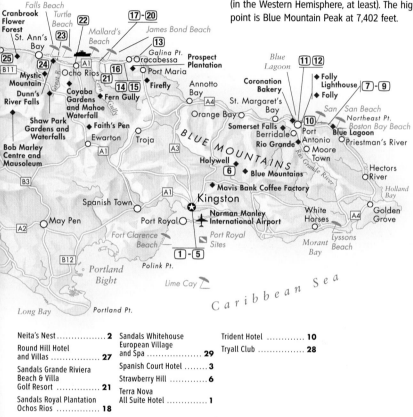

TOP REASONS TO VISIT JAMAICA

1 All-Inclusive Resorts: Come to where they were invented.

2 Great Golf: Golfers will be delighted by the many wonderful courses.

3 Fun for the Kids: Every conceivable activity, great beaches, and many child-friendly resorts appeal to families.

4 Negril Beach: It's simply one of the Caribbean's best.

5 Unique Culture: Jamaica has rich cultural traditions—particularly local music, art, and cuisine.

NEED TO KNOW

AT A GLANCE

Capital: Kingston

Population: 2,784,000

Currency: Jamaican dollar; pegged to U.S. dollar

Money: ATMs common; credit cards and U.S. dollars widely accepted

Language: English

Country Code: ☎ 1 876

Emergencies: ☎ 119

Driving: On the left

Electricity: 110v/50 cycles; plugs are U.S. standard two- and three-prong

Time: One hour earlier than New York during daylight savings; same time as New York otherwise

Documents: A valid passport and a return or ongoing ticket

Major Mobile Companies: Digicel, LIME

WEBSITES

Jamaica Tourist Board: ⊕ www.visitjamaica.com

Come to Jamaica: ⊕ www.cometojamaica.com

GETTING AROUND

✈ **Air Travel:** Donald Sangster International Airport in Montego Bay is the largest, followed by Norman Manley International Airport in Kingston.

🚌 **Bus Travel:** Knutsford Express between major cities is comfortable and reliable.

🚗 **Car Travel:** Driving in Jamaica can be frustrating, and most should not drive here. Conditions are trying; driving is on the left.

⛴ **Ferry Travel:** Paradise Express Ferry is expected to link resort districts in Montego Bay, Ocho Rios, and Negril.

PLAN YOUR BUDGET

	HOTEL ROOM	MEAL	ATTRACTIONS
Low Budget	$275	$15	Rose Hall Great House, $16
Mid Budget	$375	$30	Dunn's River Falls, $20
High Budget	$475	$50	Blue Mountain Bike Tour, $108

WAYS TO SAVE

Eat Local. There's nothing more local (or cheaper) than trying some delicious jerk from a roadside stand.

Ask for complimentary resort transfers. Many resorts will offer complimentary transfers to and from the airport and the resort, if asked.

Bus it between cities. The affordable, air-conditioned Knutsford Express connects Montego Bay, Kingston, Ocho Rios, and Negril.

Avoid cruise ship crowds. Avoid major sights on days with lots of ships to ensure maximum value of your entrance fee.

Hassle Factor	Medium. Flights to Montego Bay and Kingston are frequent; other destinations on the island may take a few extra hours by road.
3 days	Relax poolside or beachside at your resort in Montego Bay or Negril. Take a day-trip to explore the island.
1 week	Split your time between the beach and the mountains, half your time in Montego Bay or Negril, the other half in the Blue Mountains.
2 weeks	Hop across the island to explore its many beach and mountain towns. Start in Montego Bay and visit Cockpit Country. Continue east to Ocho Rios and then to the Blue Mountains. Explore the South Coast and come back nearly full circle to Negril.

WHEN TO GO

High Season: Mid-December through mid-April is the most fashionable and most expensive time to visit, when the weather is typically sunny and warm. Good hotels are often booked far in advance, and you're guaranteed the most entertainment at resorts and the most people with whom to enjoy it.

Low Season: From August to late October, temperatures can grow oppressively hot and the weather muggy, with high risks of tropical storms. Many upscale hotels close during these months for annual renovations. Those remaining open offer deep discounts.

Value Season: From late April to July and again November to mid-December, hotel prices drop 20% to 50% from high season prices. There are chances of scattered showers, but expect sun-kissed days and fewer crowds.

BIG EVENTS

January: Enjoy some smooth sounds and the island breeze at the Jamaica Jazz & Blues Festival in Montego Bay.

June: Choose from over 30 events at Jamaica's biggest music festival of the year—Ocho Rios International Jazz Festival. ⊕ www.ochoriosjazz.com

October: Reel in a prized catch at the annual Port Antonio International Marlin Tournament. ⊕ www. offshoreworldchampionship.com

March–May: The largest island-wide festival is Carnival, which is held in Kingston, Ocho Rios, and Montego Bay every March and April and in Negril every May.

READ THIS

■ *Live and Let Die,* Ian Fleming. Jamaica is the setting for this popular James Bond novel.

■ *The White Witch of Rosehall,* H. G. de Lisser. Chilling story of a haunted great house.

■ *Becka's Buckra Baby,* Thomas MacDermot. The book that established modern Caribbean literature.

WATCH THIS

■ *Cool Runnings.* Feel-good Disney move about Jamaica's first Olympic-ready bobsled team.

■ *Cocktail.* A young Tom Cruise becomes a bartender.

■ *Dr. No.* The first James Bond flick was set in Jamaica.

EAT THIS

■ *Jerk chicken*: rubbed with a spicy sauce and cooked over pimento wood.

■ *Ackee and saltfish*: cod sautéed with ackee, onions, tomatoes, and spices.

■ *Jamaican patties*: yellowish, savory-filled half-moon pastry.

■ *Gizzada*: sweet pastry with spiced coconut filling.

■ *Blue Mountain coffee*: Rich coffee from Jamaica's interior.

■ *Red Stripe*: the national beer.

EATING WELL IN JAMAICA

The multicultural values embodied in Jamaica's national motto, "Out of Many, One People," serve equally well to describe its melting-pot cuisine: a savvy, savory fusion of African, Asian, Arawak-Taíno, and European influences, ingredients, techniques, and traditions.

Even the humble patty blends African peppers, Chinese soy sauce, and Cornish pasties. Sizzling Scotch bonnet peppers are indigenous, as are pimento—from which allspice is produced (Jamaica produces 80% of the world's supply), and the liberally used native ginger is stronger in Jamaica than elsewhere. Aspiring Anthony Bourdains should try beachfront or roadside vans, kiosks, and shacks dishing out darkly bubbling grub from cow foot to curried goat. They offer authentic fare such as succulent slow-cooked jerk with heaping helpings of rice 'n' peas (beans) and provisions (tubers such as yam and cassava).

JERK

Arguably Jamaica's most famous export after reggae and Olympic-caliber runners, jerk (usually chicken or pork but now including goat, fish, and even conch) is marinated for hours in a fiery blend of peppers, pimento, scallion, and thyme, then cooked over an outdoor pit lined with pimento wood. Low, slow heating retains the natural juices while infusing the meat with the flavor of the wood and spices and ensures that the meat lasts in the tropical heat.

The Culinary Jerk Trail spans the island from Negril through Mo'Bay and Ocho Rios to Kingston and Port Antonio. The attraction features 10 of the hottest jerk spots, where diners can interact with chefs and learn the origins behind jerk cooking. For more information, go to ⊕ *www.visitjamaica.com/jerk*.

ACKEE AND SALTFISH
The British brought salt cod with them as a cheap, long-lasting foodstuff for sailors and slaves alike. Ackee, a red tree fruit introduced to Jamaica from western Africa via Britain, is actually poisonous in its natural state. Once the pear-shape fruit's tough, toxic, ruddy membrane is removed, however, the boiled, yellowish, pulpy arils surprisingly resemble scrambled eggs in taste and texture.

EXOTICA (TO SOME)
Goat figures in incendiary curries, as well as in "mannish water," a lusty soup, believed to be an aphrodisiac, that's traditionally served on wedding nights, wakes, and other festive occasions. The soup includes the head, brains, and other organs slow-cooked with various seasonings and tubers. Oxtail is a culinary constant from Italy to Indonesia. Jamaicans serve it stewed, braised, or in soup; inventive chefs might toss it with pasta in rum-cream sauce or use it to stuff quesadillas.

SEAFOOD ESCOVEITCH
Freshly caught fish—including snapper, tuna, wahoo, grouper, and marlin—is often served as *escoveitch*,

aka *escoveech* (fried to a golden crisp then topped with pickled hot peppers, onions, chayote, carrots, and pimento). Despite the linguistic and gastronomic similarity to ceviche and *escabeche*, escoveitch is rarely served cold, though it is usually marinated in vinegar and lime juice before it is cooked.

PROVISIONS
Farmers traditionally cultivated carb-rich crops that could furnish energy for islanders' hardscrabble heavy labor without requiring refrigeration. Pumpkins, coconuts, plantains, breadfruit, sweet potatoes, cassava, yams, and other "provisions" (root and gourd vegetables as well as some fruits) became staples, sometimes replacing expensive imported ingredients (chayote was used in mock-apple crumble). Most homeowners still have kitchen gardens; the Olympic sprinter Usain Bolt credits yams from his native Trelawny Parish for his speed. Today lots of sophisticated chefs here are returning to the "grow what you eat" locavore ethos.

REGGAE

The feel-good beat and impassioned lyrics of reggae resonate with listeners across the globe, and experiencing reggae in the country of its birth is special way to enjoy the music.

Widely considered to be Jamaica's seminal music form, reggae was born out of other genres, including ska and rocksteady, and is relatively young compared with other Jamaican musical styles. In fact, the history of Jamaican music is as long as the history of the island itself. Reggae's origins are firmly rooted in traditions of African music, and its lyrics are inspired by Jamaicans' fervid resistance to colonialism and imperialism. Reggae can be distinguished from earlier music forms by its comparatively faster beat, its experimental tendencies, and a more prominent role for the guitar. Reggae is also more "ragged"—both in sound and in concept. That is, it's both more earthy and down to earth, or folkloric. Lyrically, reggae is rife with social themes, primarily those that explore the plight of the working classes.

REGGAE "RIDDIM"

Pioneering reggae musicians, such as drummer Sly Dunbar and bassist Robbie Shakespeare, shaped the genre by distilling what they viewed as the best elements of ska and rocksteady. Reggae is not complex in terms of chord structure or rhythmic variation. There may be only one to three chords in a typical reggae song, and the danceable feel is propelled most commonly by a rhythm—or "riddim"—called the "drop beat" or "one drop." The drummer's bass drum emphasizes the third beat in a four-beat cycle, creating an anchor that the guitar and bass play on top of. For a more propulsive feel, the drummer may equally emphasize all four beats in each measure. Layered on top of this repetitive, solid foundation are socially conscious lyrics, which often preach resistance to the establishment or beseech listeners to love one another.

REGGAE AND RASTA

Reggae is a musical genre of, by, and for the people, and the influence of Rastafarianism has expanded its folk appeal. Rasta became pervasive in Jamaica in the 1950s, when resistance to colonialism peaked. Rasta, combining spiritual, political, and social concerns, had its origins in the crowning of Haile Selassie I as the emperor of Ethiopia in 1930. Selassie, the only black man to head an independent African nation at the time, became a vital figure and symbol of freedom for Africans in the diaspora. Greatly inspired by Selassie, Jamaicans integrated his empowering messages into many aspects of their culture. Musically, the Rasta influence is felt in reggae in two ways. The lyrics often advocate the idea of returning to Africa, and minor chords and a simple "riddim" structure characterize the songs. In the words of music historian Lloyd Bradley, Rastas were the "underclass of the underclass," and by 1959 more than one in every 25 Jamaicans identified with Rastafarianism. One of them was Bob Marley.

BOB MARLEY

Bob Marley is reggae's oracle, a visionary who introduced the world to the music of Jamaica and the struggles of its people. A stirring performer with a preternatural talent for connecting with audiences, Marley revealed the oppression of his countrymen and their indomitable spirit through his songs of hope, freedom, and redemption. His legacy extends far beyond reggae, influencing generations of artists across multiple genres.

Born in February 1945, Robert Nesta Marley left his home in rural St. Ann's Parish, Jamaica, at 14 to pursue a music career in Kingston. In 1963 Marley joined with singers Peter Tosh and Bunny Livingston to form the group the Wailers, and they began recording singles with a renowned local producer. After a series of stops and starts and a strengthened devotion to the teachings of the Rastafari faith, Bob Marley and the Wailers released *Catch a Fire* in 1973. It was their first release outside of Jamaica, and nearly instantly it became an international success. Marley's global popularity and acclaim grew with albums like *Burnin'* and *Natty Dread*. Regarded by many of his countrymen as a prophet, Marley, whose songs of freedom and revolution reverberated throughout Jamaica, was perceived as a threat in some corridors.

(*left*) Bob Marley; (*upper right*) performing on steel drums; (*lower right*) Jimmy Cliff

The Bob Marley Museum, Kingston

In December 1976, he was wounded in an assassination attempt. Marley left Jamaica for more than a year and in 1977 released his biggest record thus far, *Exodus*, which included the hits "Jammin" and "One Love/People Get Ready." By 1980, Marley was poised to reach even greater heights with an extensive U.S. tour, but while jogging in New York he suddenly collapsed. He died in May 1981, of cancer, at age 36. Marley's spirit and music endure, and his greatest hits collection, *Legend*, is the top-selling reggae album of all time.

THE REGGAE EXPERIENCE IN JAMAICA

Zion Bus Line Tour to Nine Mile. Marley fans won't want to miss this bus pilgrimage to the reggae icon's birthplace and final resting place. The guided tour takes you through the mountains to the small town of Nine Mile. The half-day tour includes a visit to Marley's house, a stop at Mount Zion (a rock where Marley meditated), and the opportunity to view Marley's mausoleum. The tour leaves from Ocho Rios.

Reggae Sumfest in Montego Bay. This weeklong reggae festival is held each July. In addition to featuring musical lineups of the most popular reggae, dance hall, R&B, and hip-hop acts, the Sumfest offers traditional Jamaican food and local crafts. Local favorite Tarrus Riley, as well as international performers, like LL Cool J and Mary J. Blige, have attended.

Bob Marley Museum in Kingston. (☏ *876/630–1588*). If the Zion Bus Tour only whets your appetite for Marley, visit the Bob Marley Museum for a glimpse at another chapter of his life. Housed inside the former headquarters of Marley's label, Tuff Gong Records, it is also the site of the failed attempt on Marley's life that inspired his song "Ambush."

Live Music. Bourbon Beach ☏ *876/957–4432* in Negril features bands on Monday, Thursday, and Saturday nights. Also in Negril is **Rick's Cafe** ☏ *876/957–0380*, which features an in-house band nightly, and **Alfred's Ocean Palace** ☏ *876/957–4669*, where you can dance on the beach to live reggae.

Updated by
Richard Sitler

Jamaicans define enthusiasm. Whether the topic is track and field or politics, the spirit of this island comes out in every interaction. Although the country is well known for its tropical beauty, reggae music, and cuisine, you may find that your interactions with local residents are what you truly remember.

The island is rich in beauty, but a quick look around reveals widespread poverty and a disparity between the lives of resort guests and resort employees that is often staggering. Where vacationers opt to stay in Jamaica depends on factors ranging from vacation length to personal interests. With its direct air connections to many U.S. cities, Montego Bay (or Mo'Bay) is favored by Americans taking short trips; many properties are just minutes from the airport. Other parts of Jamaica can be reached from Montego Bay in 60 to 90 minutes, while eastern areas may be more accessible from the other major airport—in the capital, Kingston.

Some of the island's earliest residents were the Arawak Indians, who arrived from South America around AD 650 and named the island Xaymaca, or "land of wood and water." Centuries later, the Arawaks welcomed Christopher Columbus on his second voyage to the New World. Later, when the Spanish arrived, the peaceful inhabitants were executed or taken as slaves.

The Spanish maintained control of the island until 1655, when the English arrived. Soon, slavery increased as sugar became a booming industry. In 1834 slavery was abolished, but the sugar as well as banana industries continued. Jamaica's plantation owners looked for another source of labor. From 1838 to 1917, more than 30,000 Indians immigrated here, followed by about 5,000 Asians as well as Middle Easterners, primarily from what is now Lebanon. (Today although 95% of the population traces its bloodlines to Africa, Jamaica is a stockpot of cultures, including those of other Caribbean islands, Great Britain, the Middle East, India, China, Germany, Portugal, and South America.)

In the early 1900s the boats that took the banana crop off the island began returning with travelers. By 1960 the tourism industry was the most important form of income, and in 1962, Jamaica gained independence. Along with tourism, agriculture and mining contribute to the island's considerable self-sufficiency.

PLANNING

GETTING HERE AND AROUND

AIR TRAVEL

You can fly to Jamaica from Atlanta (Delta, Southwest), Baltimore–Washington (Southwest), Boston (JetBlue, US Airways), Charlotte (US Airways), Chicago (American), Dallas (American), Detroit (US Airways), Fort Lauderdale (Caribbean Airlines, Spirit), Houston (United), Las Vegas (American), Los Angeles (American), Miami (American, Cayman Airways), New York–JFK (American, Caribbean Airlines, JetBlue), New York–Newark (United), Orlando (JetBlue), Philadelphia (US Airways), Phoenix (US Airways), San Diego (American), or Tampa (American, Cayman Airways). Most international flights come into Montego Bay, but some go to Kingston.

Domestic Airline Contacts Island Hopper's Helicopter Tours. ☎ *876/974–1285.* **Tim Air.** ✉ *Sangster International Airport, Montego Bay* ☎ *876/952–2516* ⊕ *www.timair.net.*

Domestic Airports Ian Fleming International Airport (OCJ). ✉ *8 miles (14 km) east of Ocho Rios, Oracabessa* ☎ *876/975–3101, 876/9753–734* ⊕ *www. ifia.aero.* **Negril Aerodrome.** ✉ *Norman Manley Blvd., Negril* ☎ *876/957–5016.* **Port Antonio Ken Jones Aerodrome.** ✉ *North Coast Hwy., Port Antonio* ☎ *876/913–3926, 876/913–3173* ⊕ *www.airportsauthorityjamaica.aero.*

International Airline Contacts American Airlines. ☎ *800/433–7300 for reservations* ⊕ *www.aa.com.* **Caribbean Airlines.** ☎ *800/920–4225 for reservations* ⊕ *www.caribbean-airlines.com.* **Cayman Airways.** ✉ *91 Owen Roberts Dr.* ☎ *800/422–9626* ⊕ *www.caymanairways.com.* **Delta Airlines.** ☎ *800/221–1212* ⊕ *www.delta.com.* **JetBlue.** ☎ *800/538–2583 for reservations* ⊕ *www. jetblue.com.* **Spirit Airlines.** ☎ *877/211–1546* ⊕ *www.spirit.com.* **Southwest Airlines.** ☎ *800/435–9792 for reservations* ⊕ *www.southwest.com.* **United Airlines.** ☎ *800/864–8331 for reservations* ⊕ *www.united.com.*

International Airports Donald Sangster International Airport (MBJ). ☎ *876/952–3124* ⊕ *www.mbjairport.com.* **Norman Manley International Airport (KIN).** ☎ *876/924–8452* ⊕ *www.nmia.aero.*

CAR TRAVEL

Driving in Jamaica can be an extremely frustrating endeavor. You must constantly be on guard—for enormous potholes, people and animals darting out into the street, and aggressive drivers. Local drivers are quick to pass other cars—and sometimes two cars will pass simultaneously. Gas stations are open daily, and some now accept credit cards, though you shouldn't count on it. Driving in Jamaica is on the left, British-style.

11

CAR RENTALS To rent a car, you must be at least 23 years old, have a valid driver's license (from any country), and have a valid credit or debit card. You may be required to post a security deposit of several hundred dollars before taking possession of your car; ask about it when you make the reservation. Rates average $70 to $120 a day after the addition of the compulsory insurance, which you must usually purchase even if your credit card offers it.

Car-Rental Contacts Avis. ⊠ *Donald Sangster International Airport* ☎ *876/952–0762, 876/979–1060* ⊕ *www.avis.com.jm.* **Budget.** ⊠ *Donald Sangster International Airport* ☎ *877/825–2953* ⊕ *www.budgetjamaica.com.* **Fiesta Car Rentals.** ⊠ *14 Waterloo Rd., Kingston* ☎ *876/926–0133 in Kingston, 800/934–3782, 876/929–3801* ⊕ *www.fiestacarrentals.com.* **Hertz.** ☎ *876/979–0438* ⊕ *www.hertz.com.* **Island Car Rentals.** ⊠ *17 Antiqua Ave., Kingston* ☎ *876/924–8075 in Kingston, 876/952–7225 in Montego Bay, 876/929–5875 for reservations, 866/978–5335 toll-free number for U.S.A. only* ⊕ *www.islandcarrentals.com.*

TAXI TRAVEL

Some but not all of Jamaica's taxis are metered. If you accept a driver's offer of his services as a tour guide, be sure to agree on a price before the vehicle is put into gear. (Note that a one-day tour should run about $150 to $200, in U.S. dollars, depending on distance traveled.) All licensed taxis display red Public Passenger Vehicle (PPV) plates. Your hotel concierge can call a taxi for you, or you can flag one down on the street. Rates are per car, not per passenger, and 25% is added to the rate between midnight and 5 am. Licensed minivans are also available and bear the red PPV plates. JUTA is the largest taxi franchise, with offices in most resort areas.

Taxi Contacts JCAL Tours. ☎ *876/952–7574, 876/952–8277* ⊕ *www.jcaltours.com.* **JUTA Montego Bay.** ☎ *876/952–0813* ⊕ *www.jutatoursltd.com.* **Pat's Car Rental and Taxi.** ⊠ *5 Lewis St., Westmoreland* ☎ *876/918–0431, 876/955–3335 cell, 917/829–6532 international number* ⊕ *www.patscarrentaljamaica.com.*

HEALTH AND SAFETY

Dengue, chikungunya, and zika have all been reported throughout the Caribbean. We recommend that you protect yourself from these mosquito-borne illnesses by keeping your skin covered and/or wearing mosquito repellent. The mosquitoes that transmit these viruses are as active by day as they are by night.

HOTELS AND RESORTS

Resorts: Jamaica is the birthplace of the Caribbean all-inclusive resort, which is still the most popular vacation option here. Montego Bay has the largest concentration of resorts on the island; Negril, known as the Capital of Casual, is a more relaxed haven on the west coast. Both offer a mix of large and small resorts, plus good nightlife. Runaway Bay and Ocho Rios are more than an hour east of Mo'Bay. Port Antonio, a sleepy, laid-back haven, has a few resorts and a quiet atmosphere and is usually accessed by a short flight or long drive from Kingston. The South Coast has a few small resorts, uncrowded beaches, and only one large resort.

Villas and Rentals: The island also has some high-end villas for rent, many near Runaway Bay.

Hotel reviews have been shortened. For full information, visit Fodors.com.

WHAT IT COSTS IN U.S. DOLLARS				
	$	$$	$$$	$$$$
RESTAURANTS	under $12	$12–$20	$21–$30	over $30
HOTELS	under $275	$275–$375	$376–$475	over $475

Restaurant prices are the average cost of a main course at dinner or, if dinner is not served, at lunch. Hotel prices are the lowest cost of a standard double room in high season.

VISITOR INFORMATION

Contacts Jamaica Tourist Board. ☎ 305/665–0557 in Miami, 876/929–9200 in Kingston, 876/952–4425 in Montego Bay ⊕ www.visitjamaica.com.

EXPLORING

Touring Jamaica can be both thrilling and frustrating. Rugged (albeit beautiful) terrain and winding (often potholed) roads make for slow going. *Always* check conditions before you set off by car, but especially in the rainy season, June through October, when roads can be washed out. Two-lane primary roads that loop around and across the island are not particularly well marked. Numbered addresses are seldom used outside major townships, locals drive aggressively, and people and animals have a knack for appearing out of nowhere. That said, Jamaica's scenery shouldn't be missed. To be safe and avoid frustration, stick to guided tours and licensed taxis.

If you're staying in Kingston or Port Antonio, set aside at least one day for the capital and another for a guided excursion to the Blue Mountains. There's at least three days of activity along Mo'Bay's boundaries, but also consider a day trip to Negril or Ocho Rios. If you're based in Ocho Rios, be sure to visit Dunn's River Falls; you may also want to stop by Bob Marley's birthplace, Nine Mile, or Firefly, the restored home of Noël Coward. If Negril is your hub, take in the South Coast, including Y.S. Falls and the Black River.

MONTEGO BAY

As home of the north-shore airport and a busy cruise pier west of town, Jamaica's second-largest city is the first taste most visitors have of the island. Travelers from around the world come and go year-round, drawn to the bustling community's all-inclusive resorts and great beaches. Montego Bay's relative proximity to resort towns like Ocho Rios and Negril also make the town a popular choice. Adventures and one-of-a-kind experiences, not to mention interesting colonial sights, await in surrounding areas.

TOP ATTRACTIONS

Greenwood Great House. Unlike Rose Hall, this historic great house has no spooky legend to titillate, but it's much better than Rose Hall at evoking life on a sugar plantation. The Barrett family, from whom the English poet Elizabeth Barrett Browning descended, once owned all the land from Rose Hall to Falmouth; on their vast holdings they built this and several other great houses. (The poet's father, Edward Moulton Barrett, "the Tyrant of Wimpole Street," was born at nearby Cinnamon Hill, later the estate of country singer Johnny Cash.) Highlights of Greenwood include oil paintings of the Barretts, china made for the family by Wedgwood, a library filled with rare books from as early as 1697, fine antique furniture, and a collection of exotic musical instruments. There's a pub on-site as well. It's 15 miles (24 km) east of Montego Bay. ⊠ *435 Belgrade Ave., Montego Bay* ☎ *876/631–4701* ⊕ *www.greenwoodgreathouse.com* ☎ *$20* ◷ *Daily 9–6; last tour at 5.*

Fodor's Choice
★

Rose Hall. In the 1700s it may well have been one of the greatest great houses in the West Indies. Today it's popular less for its architecture than for the legend surrounding its second mistress, Annie Palmer. As the story goes, she was born in 1802 in England, but when she was 10, her family moved to Haiti. Soon after, her parents died of yellow fever. Adopted by a Haitian voodoo priestess, Annie became skilled in the practice of witchcraft. She moved to Jamaica, married, and became mistress of Rose Hall, an enormous plantation spanning 6,600 acres with more than 2,000 slaves. You can take a spooky nighttime tour of the property—recommended if you're up for a scare—and then have a drink at the White Witch pub, in the great house's cellar. The house is 15 miles (24 km) east of Montego Bay. ⊠ *North Coast Hwy., St. James* ☎ *876/953–2323* ⊕ *www.rosehall.com* ☎ *$20* ◷ *Daily 9:15–5:15; night tours, daily 6:30–9:15 pm.*

WORTH NOTING

Martha Brae River. This gentle waterway about 25 miles (40 km) southeast of Montego Bay takes its name from an Arawak woman who killed herself because she refused to reveal the whereabouts of a local gold mine. According to legend, she agreed to take her Spanish inquisitors there and, on reaching the river, used magic to change its course, drowning herself and the greedy Spaniards with her. Her *duppy* (ghost) is said to guard the mine's entrance. Rafting on this river is a very popular activity—many operators are on hand to take you for a glide downstream. ⊠ *Trelawny.*

Rocklands Bird Sanctuary. A great place to spot birds, this sanctuary is south of Montego Bay. The station was the home of the late Lisa Salmon, one of Jamaica's first amateur ornithologists. Here you can sit quietly and feed a variety of birds—including the doctor bird (also known as the streamer-tail hummingbird), recognizable by its long tail—from your hand. ⊠ *Rock Pleasant District, Anchovy, Montego Bay* ☎ *876/952–2009* ☎ *$15* ◷ *Daily 10–5.*

FALMOUTH

Fodor's Choice ★ **Good Hope Estate.** About a 20-minute drive inland from Falmouth, this estate on more than 2,000 acres provides a sense of Jamaica's rich history as a sugar-estate island, incredible views of the Martha Brae River, and loads of fun. An adventure park offers zip-lining, river tubing, a great house tour, access to a colonial village, an aviary, swimming pool, challenge course for adults, and kids' play area with its own challenge course. Guests may get a taste of Jamaica at the Appleton Estate Jamaica Rum Tavern and Jablum Cafe or enjoy spicy goodness from the Walkerswood Jerk Hut. Adventure park passes entitle visitors to all estate activities. ⊠ *Falmouth* ☎ *876/881–6869, 876/469–3444* ⊕ *www.chukka.com* ✉ *$55.*

RUNAWAY BAY

WORTH NOTING

Green Grotto Caves. A good choice for rainy days, these caves offer 45-minute guided tours that include a look at a subterranean lake. The cave has a long history as a hiding place for everyone from fearsome pirates to runaway slaves to the Spanish governor (he was on the run from the British at the time). It's a good destination if you want to see one of Jamaica's caves without going too far off the beaten path. You'll feel like a spelunker, since you must wear a hard hat throughout the tour. ⊠ *North Coast Hwy., 2 miles (3 km) east of Discovery Bay, Runaway Bay* ☎ *876/973–2841* ⊕ *www.greengrottocavesja.com* ✉ *$20* ⊙ *Daily 9–4.*

OCHO RIOS

Although Ocho Rios isn't near eight rivers, as its name would seem to indicate, it does have a seemingly endless series of cascades that sparkle from limestone rocks along the coast. (The name Ocho Rios came about because the English misunderstood the Spanish *las chorreras*— "the waterfalls.") The town itself isn't very attractive and can be traffic-clogged, but the area has several worthwhile attractions, including the very popular Dunn's River Falls. A few steps from the main road in Ocho Rios are some of the Caribbean's most charming inns and ocean-front restaurants. Lying on the sand of what seems to be your own cove or swinging gently in a hammock while sipping a tropical drink, you'll soon forget the traffic that's just a stroll away. The original "defenders" stationed at the Old Fort, built in 1777, spent much of their time sacking and plundering as far afield as St. Augustine, Florida, and sharing their booty with the local plantation owners who financed their missions. In Discovery Bay, 15 miles (24 km) west, where Columbus landed, there's a small museum with such artifacts as ships' bells and cannons and iron pots used for boiling sugarcane. Don't miss a drive through Fern Gully, south of Ocho Rios via the A3 highway.

TOP ATTRACTIONS

Bob Marley Centre and Mausoleum. The reggae legend was born and is buried at Nine Mile, in the parish of St. Ann, and today his former home is a shrine to his music and values. Tucked behind a tall fence, the site is marked with green and gold flags. Tours are led by Rastafarians, who take visitors through the house and point out the single bed that Marley wrote about in "Is This Love." Visitors also step inside the mausoleum where the singer is interred with his guitar, and there is a restaurant and gift shop. It is best to take a guided excursion from one of the resorts. If you're driving here yourself, be ready for some bad roads, and the hustlers outside the center are some of Jamaica's most aggressive. ⊠ *Nine Mile, Calderwood Post Office, St. Ann's Bay* ✢ *South of Browns Town* ☎ *876/843–0498, 305/665–5379 U.S. number* 🖃 *$19* ⊘ *Daily 9–5.*

Coyaba Gardens and Mahoe Waterfalls. *Coyaba* is a word from the Arawaks, the original inhabitants of Jamaica, meaning paradise. Learn about Jamaican heritage and history at the museum, and then discover what makes Jamaica a natural paradise through a guided 45-minute tour through the lush 3-acre garden and also see the beautiful waterfalls and stunning views. The complex includes a crafts and gift shop and a snack bar, and Mahoe Falls is a good spot for a quiet picnic or swim. ⊠ *Shaw Park Estate, Shaw Park Ridge Rd., Ocho Rios* ☎ *876/974–6235* ⊕ *www.coyabagardens.com* 🖃 *$10* ⊘ *Daily 8–5.*

Fodor's Choice ★

Dunn's River Falls. A popular natural attraction that is an eye-catching sight: 600 feet of cold, clear mountain water splashing over a series of stone steps to the Caribbean Sea. The best way to enjoy the falls is to climb the slippery steps in a swimsuit (there are changing rooms at the entrance), as you take the hand of the person ahead of you. The entrance, which looks like one for an amusement park, is usually crowded, especially when cruise ships are in port, but it is well organized. It's easy to make arrangements and get trusted guides who will offer bits of local lore while showing you where to step. After the climb, you exit through a crowded market, another reminder that this is one of Jamaica's top tourist attractions. If you can, try to visit on a day when no cruise ships are in port. ■ TIP➜ **Always climb with a licensed guide at Dunn's River Falls. Freelance guides might be a little cheaper, but the experienced guides can tell you just where to plant each footstep—helping you prevent a fall.** Ask for a guide at the Dunn's River Falls ticket window. Official licensed guides are inside the Dunn's River Falls property, not outside the gate. They should be able to show you credentials if asked. If you arrange the tour through a resort or cruise ship, the guides provided will be licensed. ⊠ *Off Rte. A1, between St. Ann's Bay and Ocho Rios, Ocho Rios* ☎ *876/974–2857* ⊕ *www.dunnsriverfallsja.com* 🖃 *$20* ⊘ *Daily 8:30–5; last entry at 4 pm.*

Fern Gully. Don't miss this natural canopy of vegetation, which sunlight barely penetrates. (Jamaica has the world's largest number of fern species—more than 570.) The winding road through the gully has been resurfaced, making for a smoother drive, and most tours of the area include a drive through this natural wonder. But to really experience it, stop and take a walk. The 3-mile (5-km) stretch of damp, fern-shaded

Climbing Dunn's River Falls, Ocho Rios

forest includes many walking paths as well as numerous crafts vendors. ⊠ *Rte. A3, south of Ocho Rios.*

Mystic Mountain. This attraction covers 100 acres of mountainside rain forest near Dunn's River Falls. Visitors board the Rainforest Sky Explorer, a chairlift that soars through and over the pristine rain forest to the apex of Mystic Mountain. On top, there is a restaurant with spectacular views of Ocho Rios, arts-and-crafts shops, and the attraction's signature tours, the Rainforest Bobsled Jamaica ride and the Rainforest Zipline Canopy ride. Custom-designed bobsleds, inspired by Jamaica's Olympic bobsled team, run downhill on steel rails with speed controlled by the driver, using simple push-pull levers. Couples can run their bobsleds in tandem. The zip-line tours streak through lush rain forest under the care of an expert guide who points out items of interest. The entire facility was built using environmentally friendly techniques and materials in order to leave the native rain forest undisturbed. ⊠ *North Coast Hwy., Ocho Rios* ☎ *876/974–3990* ⊕ *www.rainforestbobsledjamaica. com* ☞ *$47–$137* ⊙ *Daily 9–5; activities 9–3:30.*

WORTH NOTING

Faith's Pen. To combine a cultural experience with lunch, stop by these stalls with names like Johnny Cool No. 1 and Shut's Night and Day, which offer local specialties. For just a few dollars, buy jerk chicken, curried goat, roasted fish, or mannish water (a goat's-head soup and reported aphrodisiac). Faith's Pen, one of several similar roadside places offering jerk, is 12 miles (19½ km) south of Ocho Rios. ⊠ *Rte. A1, about 4 miles (6½ km) south of Rte. A3.*

Firefly. About 20 miles (32 km) east of Ocho Rios, Noël Coward's vacation home is now a national monument managed by Chris Blackwell's Island Outpost company. Although the setting is Eden-like, the house is surprisingly spartan. Coward decamped uphill from his original home at Blue Harbour to escape the jet-setters who came to visit. He wrote *High Spirits, Quadrille,* and other plays here, and his simple grave is next to a small stage where his works are occasionally performed. Recordings of Coward singing about "mad dogs and Englishmen" echo over the lawns. Tours include a walk through the house and grounds. The view from the house's hilltop perch, which was a lookout for Captain Morgan, is one of the best on the North Coast. Firefly is also a perfect place to host weddings, picnics, photo shoots, stage shows, retreats, full-moon parties, and sunset cocktails. Contact Island Outpost (www. islandoutpost.com) for more information. ⊠ *St. Mary* ☎ *876/420–5544* ⊕ *www.firefly-jamaica.com* ⊒ *$10* ⊗ *Daily 9–4.*

FAMILY **Prospect Plantation.** Prospect Plantation has been an attraction since the start of tourism in Jamaica when such visitors as Winston Churchill and Charlie Chaplain planted trees here. There are many activities that are both fun and educational, from camel safaris to Segway tours. Learn about Jamaica's agriculture heritage while enjoying the flora and fauna and excellent views. The 900-acre property provides room for such exciting activities as the new Wet N' Dirty dune buggy adventure tour. ⊠ *Rte. A1, 4 miles (3 km) east of Ocho Rios, St. Mary* ☎ *876/994–1058* ⊕ *www.prospectoutbackadventures.com* ⊒ *From $38.50.*

Shaw Park Gardens and Waterfalls. Perched above Ocho Rios and originally used for growing sugarcane and later oranges, this estate became the original site of the exclusive Shaw Park Hotel (today relocated to the beach). The owner's daughter, appropriately named Flora, worked to create the lush gardens, which now fill the 25-acre site with flame flowers, birds of paradise, and orchids. There is also a waterfall on the property that is worth seeing. ⊠ *Shaw Park Rd., Ocho Rios* ☎ *876/974–2723, 876/893–5899* ⊒ *$10* ⊗ *Daily 8–5.*

PORT ANTONIO

Port Antonio is one of Jamaica's quietest getaways, primarily preferred by long-staying Europeans. Even with improvement of the North Coast Highway from Ocho Rios, tourism remains slow here. However, in 2013, Trident Castle reopened as part of the Geejam chain, which is expected to boost area tourism.

Port Antonio has also long been a center for some of the Caribbean's finest deep-sea fishing. Dolphin (the delectable fish, not the lovable mammal) is the likely catch here, along with tuna, kingfish, and wahoo. In October the weeklong International Marlin Tournament attracts anglers from around the world. By the time they've all had their fill of beer, it's the fish stories—rather than the fish—that carry the day.

TOP ATTRACTIONS

Blue Lagoon. Steeped in lore, Blue Lagoon is one of Port Antonio's best-known attractions. The azure waters of this spring-fed lagoon are a contrast to the warmer waters of the ocean. How deep is it? According to legend it's bottomless, but it's been measured at 180 feet. There is no fee to access the lagoon, but there are unofficial guides who offer their services and try to make you believe that there is an entry fee. Also numerous vendors have set up at the entry hawking their wares and creating a noisy juxtaposition to the peaceful natural scenery of the lagoon. ⊠ *Port Antonio* ✛ *9 miles (13 km) east of Port Antonio, 1 mile (1½ km) east of San San Beach.*

Boston Beach. A short drive east of Port Antonio is this destination for lovers of jerk pork. The recipe's origins go back to the Arawak, the island's original inhabitants, but modern jerk was perfected by the Maroons. Eating almost nothing but wild hog preserved over smoking coals enabled these former slaves to survive years of fierce guerrilla warfare with the English. Jerk resurfaced in the 1930s, and the spicy barbecue drew diners from around the island. Today a handful of jerk stands, known as the Boston Jerk Centre, offers fiery flavors cooled by *festival* (like a Southern hush puppy) and Red Stripe beer. ⊠ *Rte. A4, east of Port Antonio, Port Antonio.*

Coronation Bakery. Grab some hard-dough bread (originally brought to Jamaica by the Chinese), an unleavened bun called *bulla*, or spicy patties. The bakery's been open for more than seven decades. ⊠ *18 West St., Port Antonio* ☎ *876/993–2710.*

WORTH NOTING

Folly. A favorite photo stop, this structure, little more than ruins, was home to a Tiffany heiress. Built in 1905 and spanning 60 rooms, the house didn't last long because seawater, rather than freshwater, was used in the cement. The ruins have been featured in music videos. In July, the Portland Jerk Festival is held here. The property is down a rough road, and it is surrounded by a huge chain-link fence. However the gate to the fence is wide open. The site is out of the way, and it is probably best not to go there alone. ⊠ *Folly Point, Port Antonio.*

Folly Lighthouse. Since 1888, this red-and-white-stripe masonry lighthouse has stood watch at the tip of Folly Point. Administered by the Jamaica National Heritage Trust, the lighthouse is an often-photographed site near Port Antonio's East Harbour. The lighthouse is down a very rough road that looks abandoned. It is not advisable to go alone. ⊠ *Folly Point, Port Antonio* ⊕ *www.jnht.com/site_folly_point_lighthouse.*

Rio Grande. Jamaica's river-rafting operations began here, on an 8-mile-long (13-km-long), swift, green waterway from Berrydale to Rafter's Rest. (Beyond that, the Rio Grande flows into the Caribbean Sea at St. Margaret's Bay.) The trip of about three hours is made on bamboo rafts pushed along by a guide who is likely to be quite a character. You can pack a picnic lunch to enjoy on the raft or on the riverbank; wherever you lunch, a Red Stripe vendor is likely to appear. A restaurant, a bar, and several souvenir shops can be found at Rafter's Rest. ⊠ *Rte. A4, 5 miles (8 km) west of Port Antonio, Port Antonio.*

Somerset Falls. On the Daniels River, these falls are in a veritable botanical garden. A concrete walk to the falls takes you past the ruins of a Spanish aqueduct and Genesis Falls before reaching Hidden Falls. At

Hidden Falls, you board a boat and travel beneath the tumbling water; more daring travelers can swim in a whirlpool or jump off the falls into a pool of water. The bar and restaurant specializing in local seafood here is a great place to catch your breath. ⊠ *Rte. A4, 13 miles (21 km) west of Port Antonio, Port Antonio* ☎ *876/421–6045* 🖃 *$12* ⊙ *Daily 9–5.*

KINGSTON

Few travelers—particularly Americans—take the time to visit Kingston, although organized day trips make the city accessible from Ocho Rios and Montego Bay. That's understandable, as Kingston can be a tough city to love. It's big and has a bad reputation, with gang-controlled neighborhoods that erupt into violence. However, New Kingston is a vibrant and exciting business district with many places to enjoy. If you yearn to know more about the heart and soul of Jamaica, Kingston is worth a visit. This government and business center is also a cultural capital, home to numerous dance troupes, theaters, and museums. It's also home to the University of the West Indies, one of the Caribbean's largest universities. In many ways, Kingston reflects the true Jamaica—a wonderful cultural mix—more than the sunny havens of the North Coast. As one Jamaican put it, "You don't really know Jamaica until you know Kingston."

The Blue Mountains are a magnificent backdrop for the city, with fabulous homes in the foothills. Views get grander as roads wind up into one of the island's least developed yet most beautiful regions.

TOP ATTRACTIONS

Bob Marley Museum. At the height of his career, Bob Marley purchased a house on Kingston's Hope Road and added a recording studio—painted Rastafarian red, yellow, and green. It now houses this museum, the capital's best-known tourist site. The guided tour takes you through rooms wallpapered with magazine and newspaper articles that chronicle his rise to stardom. There's a 20-minute biographical film on Marley's career. You can also see the bullet holes in the walls from a politically motivated assassination attempt in 1976. ⊠ *56 Hope Rd., Kingston* ☎ *876/978–2991* ⊕ *http://bobmarleymuseum.org/* 🖃 *$20* ⊙ *Mon.–Sat. 9:30–5; last tour at 4.*

Devon House. Built in 1881 as the mansion of the island's first black millionaire, George Stiebel, who made his fortune from gold mining in South America, this National Heritage Site was bought and restored by the Jamaican government in the 1960s. Visit the two-story mansion, furnished with Venetian-crystal chandeliers and period reproductions, on a guided tour. On the grounds there are restaurants, crafts shops, a bakery, and a wine bar. Probably the biggest draw is the Devon House I-Scream shop, where lines of locals form, especially on Sunday, to get a dip of their favorite ice cream, often rum raisin. ⊠ *26 Hope Rd., Kingston* ☎ *876/929–6602* ⊕ *www.devonhousejamaica.com* 🖃 *$10 to tour the house; free admission for the grounds and the shops.*

Hope Royal Botanic Gardens. The largest botanical garden in the Caribbean, originally called the Hope Estate, was founded in the 1600s by an English army officer. Today it's often referred to as Hope Gardens, and the 2,000 acres feature areas devoted to orchids, cacti, and palm trees. The gardens are also home to the Hope Zoo Kingston. ⊠ *Old Hope Rd., Kingston* ☎ *876/927–1257, 876/970–3505* ⊙ *Daily 6–6.*

FAMILY **Hope Zoo Kingston.** Lucas, a regal male lion, is the zoo's most popular sight, but there are many interesting animals, including a colorful array of parrots and other tropical birds. Current exhibits also include zebras, crocodiles, monkeys, and deer. ⊠ *Hope Gardens, Kingston 6, Kingston* ☎ *876/927–1085* 🖾 *J$1,500.*

Jamaica Defence Force Museum. This museum is dedicated to Jamaica's military history. Exhibits include plans of the forts built around Kingston in the 18th century, as well as information, weapons, medals, and uniforms of the West Indies Regiment and the Jamaica Infantry Militia. ⊠ *S. Camp Rd., north of Kingston's National Heroes Park at Arnold Rd., Kingston* ☎ *876/818–4725, 876/920–0186* ⊕ *www.jdfmil.org* 🖾 *J$100* ⊙ *Wed.–Sun. 10–4.*

WORTH NOTING

Bank of Jamaica Money Museum. You don't have to be a numismatist to enjoy the exhibits at this museum, which offers a fascinating look at Jamaica's history through its monetary system. It includes everything from glass beads used as currency by the Taíno Indians to Spanish gold pieces to currency of the present day. Ultraviolet lights enable the viewing of detailed features of historic bank notes. There's also a parallel exhibit on the general history of currency through world history. ⊠ *Duke St., at Nethersole Pl., Kingston* ☎ *876/922–0750* ⊕ *www.boj. org.jm* ⊙ *Weekdays 10–4.*

Emancipation Park. Seven acres of lush greenery make a popular respite from New Kingston's concrete jungle. Locals come to jog, play table tennis, see concerts, and relax. Clowns entertain children, and photographers take romantic pictures of couples by the fountain. At the south entrance, Redemption Song is a pair of monumental statues of slaves, a reminder of the island's colonial past. ⊠ *Knutsford Blvd., at Oxford Rd., Kingston* ☎ *876/926–6312* ⊕ *www.emancipationpark.org. jm* 🖾 *Free.*

Institute of Jamaica. Dating to 1879, this museum covers early Arawak residents to modern times. Collections span art, literature, and natural history, with exhibits from Jamaican furniture to Marcus Garvey. ⊠ *10– 16 East St., Kingston* ☎ *876/922–0620* ⊕ *www.instituteofjamaica.org. jm* 🖾 *J$400* ⊙ *Mon.–Thurs. 9–4:30, Fri. 9–3:30.*

National Gallery of Jamaica. The artists represented may not be household names, but their paintings are sensitive and moving. You can find works by such Jamaican masters as painter John Dunkley and sculptor Edna Manley, and visitors are introduced to the work of contemporary Jamaican artists through events such as the National Biennial and the National Visual Arts Competition and Exhibition, staged each July and August, respectively. Guided tours (J$3,000 for groups of up to 25) must be booked in advance. ⊠ *12 Ocean Blvd., near waterfront, Kingston* ☎ *876/922–1561* ⊕ *www.natgalja.org.jm/ioj_wp* 🖾 *J$400; free last Sun. of month* ⊙ *Tues.–Thurs. 10–4:30, Fri. 10–4, Sat. 10–3, last Sun. of month 10–3.*

National Stadium of Jamaica. Constructed in 1962, this 35,000-seat arena (nicknamed "the Office") hosts national and international soccer matches. It's the home of Jamaica's national team, dubbed the Reggae Boyz, which made strong showings in world competitions several years ago. One of the statues in front of the main entrance honors not a soccer star, but music legend Bob Marley, paying homage to an iconic moment in Jamaican history. During the 1970s, Jamaica was torn by political unrest when the ruling Jamaican Labor Party met a strong challenge by the People's National Party. Armed gangs representing the parties battled in the streets. On April 22, 1978, while Bob Marley and the Wailers were performing the song "Jammin'" at the packed stadium, he called for the leaders of both parties to join him on stage and made a spirited plea for peace and unity. For the night, at least, civility and harmony prevailed. ⊠ *Independence Park, Arthur Wint Dr., Kingston* ☎ *876/968–5280.*

Spanish Town. Originally called Santiago de la Vega (St. James of the Plains), this was the island's capital when it was ruled by Spain. The town, declared a national monument by the Jamaica National Heritage Trust, has a number of historic structures, including the Jamaican People's Museum of Crafts and Technology (in the Old King's House stables) and St. James Cathedral, the oldest Anglican cathedral in the Western Hemisphere. Other historic sites include the Old Barracks Building, built in 1791 to house military personnel. Although in disrepair, its facade of brick and native stone is still imposing. The Phillippo Baptist Church honors a local hero, the Reverend James Mursell Phillippo, a missionary who led the fight for emancipation of Jamaica's slaves. His grave is in the church's graveyard. The Iron Bridge at Spanish Town was built in 1801 of prefabricated cast-iron sections imported from England. The bridge, said to be the oldest such bridge in the Western Hemisphere, has recently been restored and carries pedestrians across the Rio Cobre. ⊠ *Rte. A1, 13 miles (20 km) west of Kingston, Spanish Town.*

Trenchtown Culture Yard. This restored tenement building where Bob Marley spent much of his youth is now a protected National Heritage Site. Marley wrote frequently about life in the "government yard," and the area is credited with being the birthplace of reggae, and it is where the Wailers were formed. They recorded *Catch a Fire* here. The project was developed by the Trenchtown Development Association, a group dedicated to breathing new life into what had been one of Kingston's worst slums. There is a museum of Marley and Wailer memorabilia and a souvenir shop. ⊠ *6–10 1st St., Kingston* ☎ *876/376–0891* ⊕ *www.trenchtowncultureyard.com* ⊠ *$10* ☉ *Daily 6-6.*

BLUE MOUNTAINS

Fodor's Choice
★   Best known as the source of Blue Mountain coffee, these mountains rising out of the lush jungle north of Kingston are a favorite destination with adventure travelers, as well as hikers, birders, and anyone looking to see what lies beyond the beach. You can find guided tours to the mountains from the Ocho Rios and Port Antonio areas, as well as from

Kingston. ■TIP→ Unless you're traveling with a local, don't try to go on your own; the roads wind and dip without warning, and hand-lettered signs blow away, leaving you without a clue as to which way to go. It's best to hire a taxi (look for red PPV license plates to identify a licensed cab) or book a guided tour.

WORTH NOTING

Holywell. In this nature preserve, part of the Blue and John Crow Mountains National Park, nature trails wind through rugged terrain and offer the chance to spot reclusive creatures, including the streamertail hummingbird (known as the doctor bird) and the rare swallowtail butterfly. Rustic camping facilities are available, including showers and shelters. It's about 15 miles (25 km) north of Kingston on a very slow and winding road. ✉ *Rte. B1, northwest of Newcastle, Kingston* ☎ *876/960–2849, 876/960–2848* ⊕ *www.blueandjohncrowmountains. org, www.jcdt.org.jm* ✐ *$5* ☉ *Tues.–Sun. 9–5.*

Mavis Bank Coffee Factory. High in the misty Blue Mountains you can visit the source of some of the best coffee in the world. In this rarefied air where time seems to have stood still, you can tour the factory that was built in 1923 and witness coffee processing from planting to distribution. The tour takes about an hour and includes a sample. ✉ *Gordon Town Rd., Mavis Bank* ☎ *876/977–8005, 876/977–8527* ⊕ *www. jablumcoffee.com* ✐ *$8* ☉ *Weekdays 9–3 (with a break noon–1).*

SOUTH COAST

TOP ATTRACTIONS

Appleton Estate. One of the Caribbean's premier rum distillers, Appleton Estate offers guided tours illustrating the history of rum making in the region. The tour begins with a lively discussion of the days when sugarcane was crushed by donkey power, then proceeds to a behind-the-scenes look at the modern facility. Upon being fully educated about rum you can partake of the samples that flow freely. Furthermore, every visitor receives a complimentary miniature bottle of Appleton. Reservations are not required for the tour, but they also offer tours with lunch. To include lunch with your tour, you must reserve 24 hours in advance. ✉ *Hwy. B6, Siloah* ☎ *876/963–9217* ⊕ *www.appletonrumtour.com* ✐ *$25 without lunch; $40 with lunch* ☉ *Mon.–Sat. 9–3:30.*

WORTH NOTING

High Mountain Coffee Factory. Coffee beans grown on nearby plantations are brought here for processing. Not offering tours currently, but you can stop by the gift shop for a sample taste and purchase their many fine coffee products. The factory is around 5 miles (8 km) east of Mandeville. ✉ *Winston Jones Hwy., Mandeville* ☎ *876/963–4211* ⊕ *www. jamaicastandardproducts.com* ☉ *Mon.–Thurs. 8–5, Fri. 8–4:30.*

Peter Tosh Mausoleum. In the small community of Belmont, this simple white-concrete building contains the grave of reggae great Peter Tosh (born Winston Hubert McIntosh), who was murdered in Jamaica in 1987. Together with Bob Marley and Bunny Wailer, Tosh formed the seminal reggae group the Wailers in 1967. In contrast to the Marley memorials in Kingston and Nine Mile, Tosh's burial place is quiet and uncrowded. ⊠ *Rte. A2, Belmont* 🖃 *Donation suggested* ⊗ *Daily 9–5.*

11

FAMILY **Y.S. Falls.** A quiet alternative to Dunn's River Falls in Ocho Rios, these falls are part of a cattle and horse farm and are reached via a tractor and trailer. There is actually a series of seven falls on the property that cascade into natural pools. An exhilarating zip-line zooms over the cascading falls. Companies in Negril offer excursions for those not staying on the South Coast. ⊠ *North of A2, just past town of Middle Quarters* ☎ *876/997–6360* 🖃 *Entry $15; zip-line canopy $42; tubing $6* ⊗ *Tues.–Sun. 9:30–4:30; last admission 3:30.*

NEGRIL

Negril stretches along the coast south from horseshoe-shape Bloody Bay (named when it was a whale-processing center) along the calm waters of Long Bay to the lighthouse. Nearby, divers spiral downward off 50-foot-high cliffs into the deep green depths as the sun turns into a ball of fire and sets the clouds ablaze with color. Sunset is also the time when Norman Manley Boulevard and West End Road, which intersect, come to life with busy waterside restaurants and reggae stage shows.

TOP ATTRACTIONS

Blue Hole Mineral Spring. At this mineral spring about 20 minutes from Negril, near the community of Little Bay, you can jump 22 feet off a cliff or climb down a ladder to swim in the hole's icy water. Mud around the water's edge is said to be good for your skin, and the water itself is reputed to have therapeutic properties. For those who cannot jump or climb, water is pumped into a swimming pool at the surface. A bar, grill, cabanas, and a volleyball court add to the attractions. Take a chartered taxi from Negril, or call to organize a pickup. ⊠ *Brighton, Westmoreland* ✛ *Near Roaring River* ☎ *876/860–8805, 876/651–7867* 🖃 *$10* ⊗ *Daily 10–6.*

FAMILY **Kool Runnings Adventure Park.** Billing itself as the place where "Jamaica comes to play," this park has 10 waterslides and a ¼-mile (½-km) lazy-river float ride, as well as a go-kart track and kayaking. An adventure zone features outdoor laser combat games and Jamboo rafting (on floating bamboo). There is also bungee jumping, a "kool kanoe" adventure, a wave pool, and paintball. Admission varies by age and area, and the All for One Plan covers both the water park and fun zone. ⊠ *Norman Manley Blvd., Negril* ☎ *876/957–5400* ⊕ *www.koolrunnings.com* 🖃 *$33; All for One Plan $79* ⊗ *Labor Day (May)–early Sept., daily 11–5:30.*

BEACHES

Although hotel beaches are generally private and restricted to guests above the high-water mark, other beaches are public and open to all kinds of vendors, who can sometimes get aggressive. At resort areas, even if the beach area is considered private, the area below the high-water mark is always public, so vendors will roam longer beaches looking for business. In most cases, a simple "no thanks" will do.

MONTEGO BAY

FAMILY **Doctor's Cave Bathing Club.** Located along Montego Bay's touristy Hip Strip, this famous beach first gained notoriety for waters said to have healing powers. It's a popular beach with a perpetual spring-break feel. The clubhouse has changing rooms, showers, a gift shop, and restaurant. You can rent beach chairs, pool floats, and umbrellas. Its location within the Montego Bay Marine Park—with protected coral reefs and plenty of marine life—makes it good for snorkeling and glass-bottom boat rides. Chairs, umbrellas, and pool floats are available to rent for $6 per item for the day. **Amenities:** food and drink; lifeguards; parking (fee); showers; toilets; water sports. **Best for:** partiers; snorkeling; sunset; swimming. ⊠ *Gloucester Ave., Montego Bay* ☎ *876/952–2566* ⊕ *www.doctorscavebathingclub.com* ⊠ *$6* ☉ *Daily 8:30–5.*

FAMILY **Walter Fletcher Beach.** Although not as pretty as Doctor's Cave Beach, this strand is home to Aquasol Theme Park, which offers a large beach (with lifeguards and security personnel) and for an additional cost, glass-bottom boats, snorkeling, go-kart racing, a skating rink at night, and a bar and restaurant. Near the center of town, the beach has unusually fine swimming; the calm waters make it good for children. **Amenities:** food and drink; lifeguards; parking (no fee); showers; toilets; water sports. **Best for:** partiers; snorkeling; sunset; swimming. ⊠ *Gloucester Ave., Montego Bay* ☎ *876/979–9447* ⊠ *$5* ☉ *Daily 9–6.*

RUNAWAY BAY

FAMILY **Puerto Seco Beach.** This public beach looks out on Discovery Bay, the location where, according to tradition, Christopher Columbus first came ashore on this island. The explorer sailed in search of freshwater but found none, naming the stretch of sand Puerto Seco, or "dry port." Today the beach is anything but dry; concession stands sell Red Stripe beer and local food, including jerk and patties, to a primarily local beach crowd. **Amenities:** food and drink; lifeguards; parking (no fee); showers; toilets. **Best for:** snorkeling; swimming. ⊠ *Discovery Bay, 5 miles (8 km) west of Runaway Bay, Runaway Bay.*

OCHO RIOS

Dunn's River Falls Beach. You'll find a crowd (especially if there's a cruise ship in town) at the small beach at the foot of the falls, one of Jamaica's most-visited landmarks. Although tiny—especially considering the crowds—the beach has a great view. Look up for a spectacular vista of the cascading water, the roar from which drowns out the sea as you approach. All-day access to the beach is included in the falls' entrance fee. **Amenities:** lifeguards; parking (no fee); toilets. **Best for:** swimming. ⊠ *Rte. A1, between St. Ann's Bay and Ocho Rios, Ocho Rios* ☎ *876/974–4767* ⊕ *www.dunnsriverfallsja.com* ⊠ *$20* ☉ *Daily 8:30–5; last entry at 4.*

11

PORT ANTONIO

Boston Bay Beach. Considered the birthplace of jerk-style cooking, Boston Bay is the beach that some locals visit just to buy dinner. You can get peppery jerk pork at any of the shacks spewing scented smoke along the small beach, perfect for an after-lunch dip, though these waters are occasionally rough and much more popular for surfing. **Amenities:** food and drink; parking (no fee); toilets; showers. **Best for:** snorkeling; sunrise; surfing; windsurfing. ⊠ *11 miles (18 km) east of Port Antonio, Port Antonio.*

FAMILY **Frenchman's Cove.** This beautiful, petite, somewhat secluded beach is protected by two outcroppings, creating calm waters good for families. A small stream trickles into the cove. You'll find a bar and restaurant serving fried chicken right on the beach. If this stretch of sand looks familiar, it might be because you've seen it in the movies: *Club Paradise, Treasure Island* (the 1990 TV-movie version), and *The Mighty Quinn.* **Amenities:** food and drink; lifeguards; parking (no fee); showers; toilets. **Best for:** partiers; sunrise; swimming. ⊠ *Rte. A4, 5 miles (8 km) east of Port Antonio, Port Antonio* ☎ *876/993–7270* 💲 *$8 for those not staying at Frenchman's Cove Resort.*

SOUTH COAST

If you're looking for something off the main tourist routes, head for Jamaica's largely undeveloped South Coast. Because the population in this region is sparse, these isolated beaches are some of the island's safest, with hustlers practically nonexistent. You should, however, use common sense; never leave valuables unattended on the beach.

Bluefields Beach Park. On the South Coast road to Negril, this relatively narrow stretch of sand and rock near the small community of Bluefields is typically crowded only on weekends and local holidays. The swimming here is good, although the sea is sometimes rough. **Amenities:** food and drink; lifeguards; parking (fee); showers; toilets. **Best for:** sunset; swimming. ⊠ *Bluefields.*

FAMILY **Treasure Beach.** The most atmospheric beach in the southwest is in the community of Treasure Beach. Here there are several long stretches of sand and many small coves. With more rocks and darker sand, the beach isn't as pretty as those to the west or north, but it's a bit of the "real" Jamaica. Both locals and visitors use the beach, though you're as likely to find it deserted, beyond a friendly beach dog. Treasure Beach attracts a bohemian crowd, and you won't find as many hustlers as in North Coast resort towns. **Amenities:** food and drink; parking (no fee). **Best for:** solitude; sunset; walking. ⊠ *Treasure Beach.*

NEGRIL

Fodor's Choice ★ **Negril Beach.** Stretching for 7 miles (11 km)—from Bloody Bay in the north along Long Bay to the cliffs on the southern edge of town—this long, white-sand beach is probably Jamaica's finest. Some stretches remain undeveloped, but these are increasingly few. Along the main stretch, the sand is public to the high-water mark, and visitors and vendors parade from end to end. The walk is sprinkled with good beach bars and open-air restaurants, some of which charge a small fee to use their beach facilities. Bloody Bay is lined with large all-inclusive resorts; these sections are mostly private. Jamaica's best-known nude beach, at Hedonism II, is always among the busiest; only resort guests or day-pass holders may sun here. **Amenities:** food and drink; lifeguards; parking (no fee); toilets; showers; water sports. **Best for:** partiers; sunset; swimming; walking. ✉ *Norman Manley Blvd., Negril.*

WHERE TO EAT

Probably the most famous Jamaican dish is jerk pork—the ultimate island barbecue. The pork (purists cook a whole pig) is covered with a paste of Scotch bonnet peppers, pimento berries (also known as allspice), and other herbs, and cooked slowly over a coal fire. Many aficionados believe the best jerk comes from Boston Beach, near Port Antonio. Jerk chicken and fish are also seen on many menus. The ever-so-traditional rice and peas is similar to the *moros y cristianos* of Spanish-speaking islands: white rice cooked with red kidney beans, coconut milk, scallions, and seasonings.

There are fine restaurants in all the resort areas, many in Kingston and in the resorts themselves. Many restaurants outside the hotels in Mo'Bay and Ocho Rios will provide complimentary transportation.

What to Wear: Dinner dress is usually casual chic (or just plain casual at many local hangouts, especially in Negril). There are a few exceptions in Kingston and at the top resorts; some require semiformal wear (no shorts; collared shirts for men) in the evening during high season. People tend to dress up for dinner; men might be more comfortable in nice slacks, women in a sundress.

MONTEGO BAY

$$
BARBECUE
🍴 **Biggs BBQ Restaurant & Bar.** On the Hip Strip, this authentic barbecue joint, opened by a chef who got his start cooking barbecue in St. Louis, Missouri, features pulled pork, corn bread, mac-and-cheese, baked beans, and, of course, good ol' Memphis-style ribs—a taste of Americana in paradise. Diners have the option of sitting outside for amazing views of the Montego Bay coastline or inside around wooden tables draped in checkered fabric. Drinks like the must-try Bluegrass Lemonade, a heady mix of house-made lemonade and "bluebeery" vodka, are served in traditional jars, and meals are served in half-pound and one-pound portions. [$] *Average main: $15* ✉ *Gloucester Ave., Montego Bay* ☎ *876/952–9488* 🌐 *www.biggsbbqmobay.com.*

$$$$
SEAFOOD
🍴 **Marguerites Seafood By the Sea.** At this romantic seaside restaurant, lobster, shrimp, and fish are the specialties, as is the Caesar salad. You can have your lobster grilled or drenched with linguine, or order the summer surf and turf. Dine on the patio-style terrace or at the water's edge. Walk-in guests can often be accommodated, but reservations are recommended. [$] *Average main: $38* ✉ *Gloucester Ave., Montego Bay* ☎ *876/952–4777* 🌐 *www.margaritavillecaribbean.com* 🕓 *No lunch.*

$$$ CARIBBEAN 🍴 **Pier 1.** After tropical drinks at the deck bar, you'll be ready to dig into the international variations on fresh seafood; the best are the grilled lobster and any preparation of island snapper. Peppered Jamaican shrimp, jerk conch with papaya sauce, and grilled mahimahi are other stand-out choices. Occasional party cruises leave from the marina here, and on Friday night the restaurant is mobbed by locals who come to dance at the weekly Pier Pressure party. [$] *Average main: $22* ✉ *Off Howard Cooke Blvd., Montego Bay* ☎ *876/952–2452, 876/286–7208* 🌐 *www.pieronejamaica.com.*

$$ JAMAICAN Fodor's Choice ★ 🍴 **Pork Pit.** Pork Pit is an authentic Jamaican restaurant. The main offering is fiery jerk (pork, chicken, and shrimp) that is spiced to local tastes, not watered down for tourists. You can get food to go or eat at picnic tables. [$] *Average main: $12* ✉ *27 Gloucester Ave., Montego Bay* ☎ *876/940–3008* ✍ *Reservations not accepted.*

$ JAMAICAN 🍴 **Scotchies.** Many call this open-air jerk eatery the best in Jamaica, but the Scotchies Too branch in Ocho Rios makes it a tough call. Both serve genuine jerk—chicken, pork, fish, sausage, and more—with fiery sauce and delectable side dishes including festival (bread similar to a hush puppy) and rice and peas. This restaurant is a favorite with Montego Bay residents and tourists; you're likely to see a slap-the-table game of dominoes. [$] *Average main: $10* ✉ *North Coast Hwy., across from Holiday Inn SunSpree, 10 miles (16 km) east of Montego Bay, Montego Bay* ☎ *876/794–9457.*

$$$$ INTERNATIONAL 🍴 **Seagrape Terrace.** Named for the trees that line the beach at the Half Moon resorts, this beachside restaurant is open to the public. At lunchtime, a superb buffet and à la carte menu are available. Standout buffet options include roast meats and freshly baked breads. At dinner there's a good selection of seafood, steaks, and ribs, including the herb-roasted Angus beef tenderloin, red wine–braised short ribs, and grilled yellowfin tuna. [$] *Average main: $38* ✉ *Half Moon, North Coast Hwy., 7 miles (11 km) east of Montego Bay, Montego Bay* ☎ *876/953–2211* 🌐 *www.halfmoon.com* ✍ *Reservations essential.*

$$$$ ECLECTIC 🍴 **Sugar Mill.** The former Running Gut Sugar Estate near the Half Moon Resort Golf Course is the setting for the Sugar Mill, where Caribbean dishes with an Asian twist are prepared by one of the top Jamaican chefs. Dine alfresco on a terrace by a 17th-century water, enjoying dishes such as coconut and saffron–poached snapper fillet, pork tenderloin infused with island spices, and tea-smoked duck breast. A well-stocked wine cellar makes the experience complete. The dress code at this romantic and historic setting is "casual elegant." [$] *Average main: $40* ✉ *Half Moon, North Coast Rd., 7 miles (11 km) east of Montego Bay, Montego Bay* ☎ *876/953–2211 ext. 43 for reservations, 800/438–7241* 🌐 *http://halfmoon.rockresorts.com* ⏲ *No lunch* ✍ *Reservations essential.*

OCHO RIOS

$$$ ECLECTIC 🍴 **Almond Tree.** Named for the massive almond tree growing through the roof, this Ocho Rios restaurant has been serving dishes "Back A Yard" (the way things are done back home) for nearly 40 years. For many, the evening starts with a drink at the terrace bar overlooking the

Fresh shrimp offered at a colorful roadside stand

sea. Dinner can be enjoyed on the terrace or in the dining room. There are nightly "yardie specials" and items from the grill including prime fillet mignon, curried goat, tips of chicken Ali Baba, and oxtail with beans. Seafood offerings include Caribbean shrimp, grilled sea trout, and lobster. Pasta, salads, and sandwiches are also on the menu. Lemon or strawberry cheesecake or chocolate truffle torte are dessert possibilities. Reservations recommended on weekends. [$] *Average main: $25* ✉ *Hibiscus Lodge Hotel, 83–85 Main St., Ocho Rios* ☎ *876/974–2676* 🌐 *www.hibiscusjamaica.com.*

$$$ ECLECTIC Fodor's Choice ★ 🍴 **Evita's Italian Restaurant.** Set in an 1860s gingerbread house fronted by an old convertible roadster, Evita's—an island institution and the self-proclaimed "Best Little Pasta House in Jamaica"—is a chic, charming restaurant. Its renowned pasta is a spicy mashup of the best of Italian and Jamaican cuisine. The friendly staff, and sometimes the proprietor herself (the effervescent Eva Myers, who still busily oversees everything to ensure perfection), will guide you through the many inventive choices, which include lasagna Rastafari, jerk spaghetti, and One-Love Penne. Make time for dessert and enjoy the view from the veranda. [$] *Average main: $28* ✉ *Eden Bower Rd., Ocho Rios* ☎ *876/974–2333* 🌐 *www.evitasjamaica.com.*

$ JAMAICAN 🍴 **Ocho Rios Jerk Centre.** This canopied, open-air eatery is a great place for fiery jerk pork, chicken, or seafood such as fish and conch. Frosty Red Stripe beer and cocktails such as the special Jerk Center Cooler—a colorful mix featuring rum and vodka—are perfect complements to the island fare. Milder barbecued meats, also sold by weight (typically, a quarter- or half-pound makes a good serving), turn up on the daily chalkboard menu posted on the wall. It's busy at lunch, especially when passengers from cruise ships swamp the place. $ *Average main: $8* ⊠ *Da Costa Dr., Ocho Rios* ☎ *876/974–2549.*

$ ╳ **Roadster.** This simple, rustic eatery across from Jamaica Inn serves good Jamaican food at unbeatable prices. You can eat under a tree or inside the restaurant, which is run by German-turned-Jamaican-resident Marion Rose and her Jamaican husband. The menu has local favorites such as fried chicken and oxtail. Go early or call ahead with your order, because there's a limited amount of food prepared each day. $ *Average main: $8* ⊠ *Hibiscus Dr., Ocho Rios* ☎ *876/974–2910, 876/402–1602* ▭ *No credit cards.*

JAMAICAN

$ ╳ **Scotchies Too.** The Ocho Rios branch of the longtime Montego Bay favorite has been lauded by international chefs for its excellent jerk. The plates of jerk chicken, sausage, fish, pork, and ribs at this open-air restaurant are all accompanied by festival, bammy, and some fire-breathing hot sauce. Be sure to step over to the kitchen to watch the preparation of the jerk over the pits. $ *Average main: $10* ⊠ *Drax Hall, North Coast Hwy., Ocho Rios* ☎ *876/794–9457.*

JAMAICAN

$$$ ╳ **Toscanini.** At Harmony Hall, this longtime favorite offers seating in the dining room and on the garden veranda. The menu features classic Italian dishes and Jamaican fusion cuisine, all made with fresh, local produce and fresh local fish. Look for marinated marlin, caught in local waters, and tuna, which customers come from Kingston to enjoy. Huge juicy South Coast prawns also draw customers. Desserts such as tiramisu, chocolate profiteroles, and a wicked affogato round off the meal beautifully. Call for a complimentary shuttle in Ocho Rios. $ *Average main: $25* ⊠ *Harmony Hall, North Coast Hwy., Ocho Rios* ✛ *4 miles (6½ km) east of Ocho Rios on the A3 Hwy.* ☎ *876/975–4785* ⊕ *www. harmonyhall.com.*

INTERNATIONAL
Fodor'sChoice
★

PORT ANTONIO

$ ╳ **Boston Jerk Centre.** Actually a collection of about half a dozen open-air stands, this is a culinary landmark thanks to its popular jerk pits. Stroll up to the open pits, fired by pimento logs and topped with a piece of corrugated roofing metal, locally known as zinc, and order meat by the quarter-, half-, or full pound; chicken, pork, goat, and fish are top options. Side dishes are few but generally include festival and rice and peas. $ *Average main: $10* ⊠ *Boston Beach, Rte. A4, east of Port Antonio, Port Antonio* ▭ *No credit cards.*

JAMAICAN
Fodor'sChoice
★

$$$ ╳ **Mille Fleurs.** Enjoy European, Jamaican, and Carribean cuisine while watching the sunset on a terrace surrounded by tropical vegetation. Dishes made with local ingredients change daily, perhaps ackee-fruit soufflé or plantain fritters with black-bean dip. Lobster medallions in a creamy passion sauce is a favorite. Innovative vegetarian options, such as ratatouille with feta and herb crumble, are always on the menu, and Meatless Mondays are a weekly feature. Meal plans available for those staying at Hotel Mockingbird Hill. $ *Average main: $29* ⊠ *Hotel Mockingbird Hill, Port Antonio* ☎ *876/993–7267* ⊕ *www. hotelmockingbirdhill.com.*

JAMAICAN

$ JAMAICAN 🍴 **Woody's Low Bridge Place Fast Food Restaurant & Bar.** Positive vibes and burgers are featured at this roadside eatery. Charles "Woody" Cousins and wife Cherry serve up simple fare from a whitewashed shack whose walls bear Cherry's handwritten affirmations. Besides quintessential American fare from fries to hot dogs, you can order veggie or plantain burgers or a traditional Jamaican dinner made to order. A full range of beverages includes homemade ginger beer and blended drinks. [$] *Average main: $8* ✉ *Drapers Main Rd., Port Antonio* ☎ *876/993–7888* 💳 *No credit cards.*

KINGSTON

$$ JAMAICAN 🍴 **Gloria's.** The unassuming setting belies the excellent food served at this restaurant, frequented by Kingston residents who happily drive to Port Royal for its seafood. Fresh fish is served up steamed, fried, escoveitched, or in brown stew. Garlic or curry lobster and shrimp are other delicious offerings. Sit on the upper deck to catch the cooling sea breeze. [$] *Average main: $12* ✉ *15 Foreshore Rd., Port Royal* ☎ *876/967–8220* 🌐 *http://gloriasseafood.com.*

$ JAMAICAN 🍴 **Hot Pot.** Jamaicans love the Hot Pot for breakfast, lunch, and dinner. Fricassee chicken is the specialty, along with other local dishes like mackerel rundown (salted mackerel cooked with coconut milk and spices) and ackee and salted cod. The restaurant's freshly squeezed juices are excellent—tamarind, sorrel, coconut water, soursop, and cucumber. [$] *Average main: $5* ✉ *2 Altamont Terr., Kingston* ☎ *876/968–8009.*

$$ JAMAICAN Fodor's Choice ★ 🍴 **Redbones Blues Cafe.** At this hip restaurant and bar, there's a lively music-and-arts scene, and the family owners take their social and environmental responsibilities seriously. Not only is the food some of the best in Kingston, but much of the produce is grown on the owners' farm in the hills above the city. The pork is raised at a children's home in Mandeville that has its own farm, and the waiters attended a children's home in Kingston. Choose from delicious dishes such as lamb chops or jerked chicken kebabs, served with a Caribbean fruit salsa. Redbones comes alive at night, with movie nights, literary evenings, music, and other events. There is also a gallery with revolving exhibitions. [$] *Average main: $20* ✉ *1 Argyle Rd., Kingston* ☎ *876/978–8262, 876/978–6091* 🌐 *www.redbonesbluescafe.com* 🕒 *Closed Sun. No lunch Sat.*

BLUE MOUNTAINS

$ CAFÉ 🍴 **Cafe Blue.** Perched on a hillside more than 3,000 feet up in Irish Town, Cafe Blue could be one of the most stunning places to enjoy a cup of coffee in the region where it's produced. It's a hip hideaway for Kingstonians and is popular with Strawberry Hill guests. On offer are many different styles of Blue Mountain, from espresso to latte, as well as a selection of freshly baked cakes. Other café branches are in the Shoppes at Rosehall and Fairview in Montego Bay and the Sovereign Centre in Kingston. [$] *Average main: $10* ✉ *Irish Town* ☎ *876/944–8918* 🌐 *www.jamaicacafeblue.com.*

$$$$ JAMAICAN Fodor's Choice ★ 🍴 **Strawberry Hill.** A favorite with Kingstonians for its elegant Sunday brunch, Strawberry Hill has a stunning location; the open-air terrace has spectacular views of the city and countryside. The restaurant serves a prix-fixe menu with constantly changing dishes for lunch and dinner. Entrées include curried shrimp, coconut-crusted snapper, and Jamaican favorites such as curried goat and jerk chicken. The greens, the milk, and much of the other ingredients come from the Island Outpost farm in the parish of Trelawny and from local farmers. The bar area, a good place for cocktails or after-dinner drinks, features a piano and a fireplace that's usually ablaze in the cool evenings of the Blue Mountains. [$] *Average main: $38* ✉ *Strawberry Hill, New Castle Rd., Irish Town* ☎ *876/944–8400* 🌐 *www.islandoutpost.com* ✍ *Reservations essential.*

SOUTH COAST

$ JAMAICAN 🍴 **Billy's Grassy Park.** In the Middle Quarters strip along the South Coast Highway, this side-of-the-road stop serves fiery Jamaican food, including scorching peppered shrimp caught just behind the kitchen. Billy cooks favorites such as fried fish, curried goat, and chicken over a wood fire. Also on the menu is peanut porridge, a popular, hearty Jamaican breakfast. [$] *Average main: $8* ✉ *A2, about 30 mins east of Whitehouse, Middle Quarters* ☎ *876/366–4182* 💳 *No credit cards.*

$$ ECLECTIC Fodor's Choice ★ 🍴 **Jack Sprat Restaurant.** It's no surprise that this restaurant shares its home resort's bohemian style (it's the beachside dining spot at Jakes). From the casual outdoor tables to the late-night dance-hall rhythm, it's a place to come and chill out. Jerk crab, conch, fish, and lobster join favorites like pizzas and jerk chicken on the menu, all followed by Devon House ice cream. Tables are either shaded by trees or in the open-sided dining porch. [$] *Average main: $15* ✉ *Jakes, Calabash Bay, Treasure Beach* ☎ *876/965–3000* 🌐 *www.jakeshotel.com.*

$$ JAMAICAN 🍴 **Little Ochie.** This casual beachside eatery, a favorite with locals and travelers, is known for its genuine Jamaican dishes like "fish tea" (a spicy bouillon), escoveitch fish, peppered shrimp, jerk chicken, seapuss (octopus), and lobster. Most of the seafood is brought in by fishermen just yards away. For those staying in Treasure Beach, a popular way to reach Little Ochie is by boat. Each year in the second week of July, the place comes alive with the Little Ochie Seafood Fest, a veritable paradise for seafood lovers featuring several stalls serving fresh seafood with all the trimmings, plus music and all-day entertainment. [$] *Average main: $17* ✉ *About 7 miles (11 km) south of A2, Alligator Pond* ☎ *876/852–6430, 876/508–3578* 🌐 *www.littleochie.com.*

$ SEAFOOD Fodor's Choice ★ 🍴 **Pelican Bar.** One of the funkiest places to down a cold Red Stripe, this whimsical structure sits on stilts ½ mile (1 km) offshore between Treasure Beach and Black River, atop a small sandbar, and reachable only by boat. It has become a local legend and a mandatory stop for many visitors to the South Coast. The place serves platters of lobster and other fresh seafood for lunch and dinner. Floyde Forbes (who runs the bar) and local hotels can arrange boat transportation, but the short rides can be pricey. [$] *Average main: $10* ✉ *St. Elizabeth* ☎ *876/354–4218* 💳 *No credit cards.*

NEGRIL

$$ INTERNATIONAL 🍴 **Annie's Restaurant.** For a special occasion or a night of romantic indulgence, book the private dining cave overlooking the sea at this casual but upscale small restaurant at Moon Dance Cliffs. You'll be set up with an intimate table in the small cavern underneath the main dining area, where waitstaff will pamper you with flowers, candles, champagne, and your own music system. The restaurant's main menu is also first-class, with appetizers such as creamy pumpkin soup, cracked conch, and grilled tomatoes topped with goat cheese. The filet mignon is melt-in-your-mouth tender, and the shrimp is also a great option. There's a good mix of seafood, international, local, and vegetarian dishes. [$] *Average main: $20* ✉ *Moon Dance Cliffs, West End Rd., Negril* ☎ *876/957–0872, 815/308–7604* 🌐 *www.moondanceresorts.com/cliffs.*

$$$ INTERNATIONAL 🍴 **Bongos Restaurant.** A grand piano and a well-stocked premium bar add to the upscale feeling at this restaurant, with stylish indoor seating and patio tables. The cuisine is a fusion of the foods from the many cultures that have settled in the Caribbean—from Africa, Spain, the Netherlands, France, Portugal, Denmark, Great Britain, and, later, India and China. The resulting melting pot of flavors makes for mouthwatering contemporary cuisine. The seafood paella for two is a good bet, as is the Lime 'n' Thyme grilled chicken breast with ackee, callaloo, and a mango broad-bean sauce. Alternatively, opt for the vegetarian choice such as the ackee, vegetable, and mixed-bean stew with a cilantro-tomato sauce. [$] *Average main: $25* ✉ *Sandy Haven Resort, Norman Manley Blvd., Negril* ☎ *876/957–3200* 🌐 *www.sandyhavenresort.com* 🕑 *No lunch.*

$$$$ JAMAICAN 🍴 **The Caves Restaurant.** With a reservation, nonguests can savor authentic Jamaican cuisine with a twist at this gorgeous boutique resort on Negril's West End. The price ($100 per person) covers a three-course dinner, welcome drink, and bottle of wine, or you can book a private, romantic, candlelit five-course dinner in a sea-front cave ($300 per couple). When the hotel bar, the Sands, is open (Wednesday and Saturday, 4–7), you can join in cliff-jumping, a popular West End pastime, and enjoy exotic cocktails and fare from the smoky jerk grill, and on Thursdays it offers dining under the stars ($100 per person) to a mento band (traditional reggae). The Blackwell Rum Bar, in a private cave, is open Wednesday–Saturday, 5–10. Much of the produce comes from the hotel's organic farm in the parish of Trelawny. [$] *Average main: $100* ✉ *The Caves, West End Rd., Negril* ☎ *876/957–0270, 876/618–1081* 🌐 *www.islandoutpost.com* 🕑 *No lunch* ✍ *Reservations essential.*

$$ SEAFOOD 🍴 **Cosmo's Seafood Restaurant and Bar.** Owner Cosmo Brown has made this seaside, open-air bistro a pleasant place to spend the afternoon—and maybe stay on for dinner. Fish is the main attraction, and the conch soup—a house specialty—is a meal in itself. You can also find lobster (grilled, thermidor, or curried), fish-and-chips, and the catch of the morning. After lunch, customers often drop cover-ups to take a dip before coffee and dessert and return to lounge in chairs scattered under almond and seagrape trees (there's an entrance fee of J$400 for the beach if you want to use the facilities and J$150 to rent a lounge chair). This is where many Jamaicans chill out when they come to Negril.

$ *Average main: $14* ✉ *Norman Manley Blvd., Negril* ☎ *876/957–4330, 876/957–4784.*

$$ ✕ **The Hungry Lion.** This small but intimate restaurant with stylish decor
ECLECTIC has long been a West End favorite. An eclectic crowd comes to enjoy excellent vegetarian fare and seafood, though Jamaican jerk-chicken kebabs are also available. With the Thai tofu—in a coconut-curry-and-lemongrass sauce—you may be tempted to lick the plate. Other favorites include "shepherd's pie" (a spicy lentil stew topped with mashed potatoes) and Killer Shrimp, marinated and grilled in herbs and coconut milk. There is also a good selection of fresh juices. The good-health accent is set to the tune of world music, jazz and blues, and roots reggae. $ *Average main: $17* ✉ *West End Rd., Negril* ☎ *876/957–4486* ⊗ *No lunch.*

$$$ ✕ **Ivan's Restaurant.** Upscale Caribbean cuisine, stunning cliff-side din-
CARIBBEAN ing, and romance make this one of the best places to eat on Negril's
Fodor's Choice West End. Watch the spectacular sunset while enjoying a cocktail by
★ the simple thatched bar and eatery, decorated with funky art. Dinner opens with a delicious complimentary conch soup. Beautifully presented appetizers include the Calypso Trio—three of the most requested dishes: chicken, sweet pepper, tomato, and pineapple skewer; jerk shrimp; and a Caribbean crab cake with Ivan dip. Don't miss entrées like grilled lobster with garlic butter and mashed potatoes and the seafood linguine: shrimp, lobster, and snapper in a creamy white-wine sauce. For the flambéed banana or pineapple dessert, overproof rum is set on fire for you to blow out and pour over ice cream. Frozen cheesecakes like chocolate mocha, key-lime pie, and peanut butter swirl are also available. You can dress up or dine in casual wear. $ *Average main: $25* ✉ *Catcha Falling Star, West End Rd., Negril* ☎ *876/957–0390, 876/967–0045* ⊕ *www.catchajamaica.com* ⊗ *No lunch.*

$ ✕ **Just Natural.** This low-key eatery with the motto "come and relax"
VEGETARIAN serves vegetarian and seafood dishes as well as fresh fruit and vegetable juices, but it's the surroundings—an enchanting garden on Negril's West End—that make it stand out. Tables and chairs are mismatched, some of them made from recycled materials. They're scattered in the garden, surrounded by orange trees, pretty flowers, and lush vegetation, so that each dining area is private. All food is made to order and well priced. A small soup and dessert are included with dinner. $ *Average main: $8* ✉ *Hylton Ave., ½ mile (1 km) after the lighthouse, Negril* ☎ *876/957–0235, 876/354–4287* ▭ *No credit cards.*

$$ ✕ **Kuyaba on the Beach.** Open all day and right on the beach, this charm-
JAMAICAN ing thatch-roof restaurant is one of the top spots for dinner on Negril's
Fodor's Choice 7-mile (11-km) strip of sand. The menu specializes in Jamaican cuisine
★ with an international twist, with meals covering sea, breeze, and land. There are a few good vegetarian options like the veggie stewed peas and the rasta pasta. All food is cooked to order, so come prepared for a long languorous meal. During the day you can lounge on beach chairs. The restaurant will bring you here for free if you're staying in Negril. $ *Average main: $20* ✉ *Norman Manley Blvd., Negril* ☎ *876/957–4318* ⊕ *www.kuyaba.com.*

$$ **✕ LTU Pub.** This thatched bar and eatery is one of the prettiest on the
INTERNATIONAL West End. Right on the cliffs and practically next door to Rick's Cafe,
it has dazzling views during the day and at sunset and steps down to
the water. At night, you can dine under the stars. Expats and long-term
visitors hang out here to enjoy the laid-back vibe that put Negril on
the map. Appetizer highlights include chicken-and-cheese quesadillas
and coconut shrimp. Entrées feature beef tenderloin in red-wine sauce,
chicken Lola, and snapper stuffed with callaloo. There are lots of pasta
choices, too. Dinners come with a delicious pumpkin soup. $ *Average
main: $15* ⊠ *West End Rd., Negril* ☎ *876/957–0382.*

$$ **✕ Norma's at Seasplash.** Named for the late Norma Shirley, known as the
INTERNATIONAL Julia Child of Jamaica, Norma's at Seasplash is now helmed by a student
of the late chef. Dishes such as braised oxtail with butter beans in a rich
Jamaican sauce and smoked pork chops marinated in ginger make use
of recipes that made Norma famous island-wide. $ *Average main: $16*
⊠ *Sea Splash Hotel, Norman Manley Blvd., Negril* ☎ *876/957–4041*
⊕ *http://seasplash.com.*

$$ **✕ Rockhouse Restaurant.** This restaurant is a must for dinner at least once.
CARIBBEAN The open-air dining area has huge comfy bamboo sofas where you can
Fodor'sChoice relax for an aperitif or after-dinner drink; tables are arranged near the
★ cliff for sensational seaside dining. For special occasions, private tables
for groups can be set up in a cabana, on an intimate terrace, or on a
lower deck. The menu features both traditional Jamaican cooking and
Rockhouse's interpretation of "new Jamaican cuisine," inspired by the
many cultures that have come to the island. Staff are friendly and atten-
tive. Much of the food is organically grown right across the road. $ *Av-
erage main: $17* ⊠ *Rockhouse, West End Rd., Negril* ☎ *876/957–4373*
⊕ *www.rockhousehotel.com.*

$ **✕ Shark's Restaurant.** Unassuming, but nicely decorated, Shark's is a reli-
JAMAICAN able place to sample local cooking in a friendly and laid-back atmo-
sphere. The thatched roadside restaurant has just three tables. Juliet,
who owns and runs the tiny place, also cooks. All the food is delicious,
including chicken fricassee, curried goat, panfried snapper, and grilled
lobster with lashings of garlic butter. $ *Average main: $8* ⊠ *West End
Rd., Negril* ✛ *Across from Tensing Pen resort* ☎ *876/428–8411* ▭ *No
credit cards.*

WHERE TO STAY

Jamaica is the birthplace of the Caribbean all-inclusive resort, a con-
cept that started in Ocho Rios and later spread throughout the island,
so that now most hotel rates are all-inclusive. Package prices usually
include airport transfers, accommodations, three meals a day, snacks,
all bar drinks (often including premium liquors) and soft drinks, a full
menu of sports options (including scuba diving and golf at high-end
resorts), nightly entertainment, and all gratuities and taxes. At most all-
inclusives, the only surcharges are for such luxuries as spa and beauty
treatments, telephone calls, tours, vow-renewal ceremonies, and wed-
dings (often included at high-end establishments).

The all-inclusive market is especially strong with couples. To maintain a romantic atmosphere (no Marco Polo games in the pool), some resorts have minimum age requirements from 12 to 18. Other properties court families with supervised kids' programs, family-friendly entertainment, and in-room amenities for young travelers.

PRIVATE VILLAS

Ocho Rios is filled with private villas, especially in the Discovery Bay area. In Jamaica, most luxury villas come with a full staff, including a housekeeper, cook, butler, gardener, and often a security guard. Many can arrange for a driver for airport transfers, daily touring, or a prearranged number of days of sightseeing.

Demand for larger, more luxurious properties has increased. Numerous villas have five or more bedrooms in different parts of a building—or in different buildings altogether for extra privacy.

Most villas come with linens, and you can often arrange for the kitchen to be stocked with groceries upon your arrival. Air-conditioning, even in the most luxurious villas, is typically limited to bedrooms.

A four-night minimum is average for many villas though this can vary by season and property. Gratuities, usually split among the staff, are typically 10%–15%. Several private companies specialize in finding vacationers rentals at the right size and price.

RENTAL CONTACTS

Jamaica Association of Villas and Apartments. Since 1967, this company, based in Ocho Rios, has handled villas, cottages, apartments, and condos across the island. ☎ *876/452–1268* 🌐 *www.javavillas.org.*

Jamaica Villas by Linda Smith. More than 90 fully staffed villas are available. ✉ *8029 Riverside Dr., Cabin John* ☎ *301/229–4300* 🌐 *www.jamaicavillas.com.*

Luxury Retreats International. This outfit offers numerous luxury villa rentals in Negril, Montego Bay, Ocho Rios (including Discovery Bay), and Port Antonio. ✉ *5530 St. Patrick St., Suite 2210, Montréal* ☎ *877/993–0100* 🌐 *www.luxuryretreats.com/search/caribbean/jamaica.*

MONTEGO BAY

Mo'Bay has miles of hotels, villas, apartments, and duty-free shops. Although without much in the way of must-see culture, at least for the average visitor, it presents a comfortable island backdrop for the many conventions it hosts. And it has the added advantage of being the closest resort area to the Donald Sangster International Airport.

$$ RESORT FAMILY 🏨 **Coyaba Beach Resort and Club.** Privately owned, this intimate property is relaxing, welcoming, and just 10 minutes east of Montego Bay airport. **Pros:** quiet atmosphere of an inn; excellent restaurants; good-size private beach. **Cons:** directly on North Coast Highway; fairly small pool; climb to third-floor rooms can be difficult without elevator. [$] *Rooms from: $369* ✉ *Montego Bay* ☎ *876/953–9150, 877/232–3224*

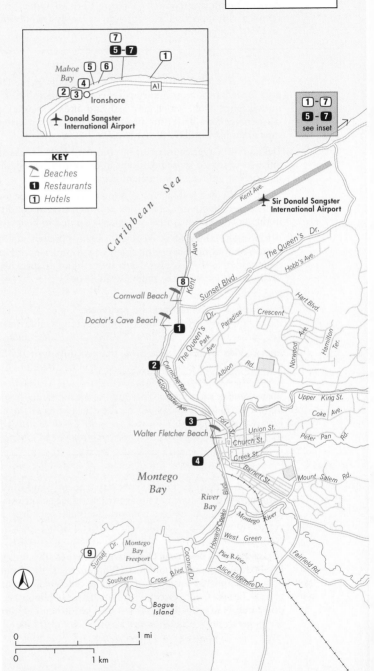

Montego Bay

toll-free 🌐 *www.coyabaresortjamaica.com* 🛏 *50 rooms* 🍴 *Some meals* ☞ *Nanny service available.*

$$$$ HOTEL FAMILY 🏨 **Half Moon, a RockResort.** With its many room categories, massive villas (three to seven bedrooms), shopping village, hospital, school, dolphin attraction, golf course, and equestrian center, this seems more like a town than a mere resort. **Pros:** huge beach; many room categories, including villas; numerous on-site activities. **Cons:** spread out; some accommodations are a long walk from public areas. [$] *Rooms from: $499* ✉ *Rose Hall, Montego Bay* ☎ *876/953–2211* 🌐 *www.halfmoon.com* 🛏 *45 rooms, 152 suites, 33 villas* 🍴 *Some meals.*

$$$$ RESORT FAMILY 🏨 **Hilton Rose Hall Resort and Spa.** Popular with romantic couples, conference groups, and families, Hilton Rose Hall has had many upgrades and enhancements recently that make it a top choice in Montego Bay. **Pros:** family-friendly dining and pool; easy access to golf. **Cons:** kid-filled pool can be noisy; some activities are across the highway. [$] *Rooms from: $489* ✉ *Rose Hall Main Rd., St. James* ✈ *15 miles (24 km) east of Montego Bay* ☎ *876/953–2650* 🌐 *www.rosehallresort.com* 🛏 *488 rooms, 14 suites* 🍴 *All-inclusive.*

$$$ RESORT FAMILY 🏨 **Holiday Inn SunSpree Resort Montego Bay.** Family fun is tops here, but many couples and singles are also drawn to the not-crazy prices and good location, 6 miles (10 km) east of the airport. **Pros:** good family atmosphere; easy access to shopping; free self-serve laundry. **Cons:** numerous children mean some areas can be noisy; only nonmotorized water sports included in rates; directly beside North Coast Highway. [$] *Rooms from: $408* ✉ *North Coast Hwy., 10 miles (16 km) east of Montego Bay, Montego Bay* ☎ *876/953–2485* 🌐 *www.caribbeanhi.com/jamaica* 🛏 *524 rooms, 27 suites* 🍴 *All-inclusive.*

$$ RESORT FAMILY 🏨 **Iberostar Rose Hall Beach.** An extensive array of dining options (including three à la carte restaurants that require reservations) and activities are offered at this all-inclusive resort just 20 minutes east of the airport. **Pros:** numerous on-site activities, including lively shows and entertainment nightly; easy access to airport and Montego Bay; complimentary minibar. **Cons:** high-rise setup can mean elevator wait; fee for motorized water sports and scuba diving; can be noisy; does not have the amenities of its sister Iberostar properties. [$] *Rooms from: $324* ✉ *North Coast Hwy., 8 miles (13 km) east of Montego Bay, Montego Bay* ☎ *876/680–0000* 🌐 *www.iberostar.com* 🛏 *366 rooms* 🍴 *All-inclusive.*

$$$$ RESORT 🏨 **Riu Palace Montego Bay.** This adult-only resort with well-appointed rooms is trendy and sophisticated. **Pros:** on the beach and near activities; free Wi-Fi; double-glass, noise-canceling doors and hydro-massage tubs in every room. **Cons:** parking lot at resort entrance takes away from aesthetics; contemporary design overpowers the expected island flavor; small gym. [$] *Rooms from: $518* ✉ *Blue Mahoe Bay, Ironshore, Montego Bay* ☎ *800/810–9822* 🌐 *www.riu.com* 🛏 *238 rooms* 🍴 *All-inclusive.*

$$$$ HOTEL Fodor's Choice ★ 🏨 **Round Hill Hotel and Villas.** A favorite of celebrities and other wealthy people thanks to its private, elegant villas, this peaceful resort west of Mo'Bay also has stylish hotel rooms in the Pineapple House. **Pros:** personal service; spa; stylish rooms; quiet; bathrooms have deep tubs and large walk-in showers. **Cons:** somewhat remote; expensive; some villas

do not have pools. $ *Rooms from: $819* ✉ *North Coast Hwy., 8 miles (13 km) west of Montego Bay, Montego Bay* ☎ *876/956–7050* ⊕ *www. roundhill.com* ⤳ *36 rooms, 27 villas* |⊙| *Some meals.*

$$
RESORT

Sandals Carlyle. If you can forgo a private beach at your doorstep (there's a public one across the street, and an hourly shuttle that takes you to other Sandals properties), you can stay here for much less than at the other Sandals resorts. **Pros:** moderate price; complimentary shuttle to sister properties; convenient location, very close to airport. **Cons:** no private beach; small pool; limited on-site dining. $ *Rooms from: $275* ✉ *Kent Ave., Montego Bay* ☎ *876/952–4140* ⊕ *www.sandals.com* ⤳ *52 rooms and suites* |⊙| *All-inclusive.*

$$$$
RESORT

Sandals Royal Caribbean Resort & Private Island. Four miles (6 km) east of the airport, this elegant resort has Jamaican-style buildings around attractive gardens. **Pros:** lots of room categories; offshore dining; complimentary shuttles to airport and other Sandals resorts. **Cons:** too quiet for some; smaller beach than Sandals Montego Bay. $ *Rooms from: $505* ✉ *North Coast Hwy., 6 miles (9 km) east of Montego Bay, Montego Bay* ☎ *876/953–2231* ⊕ *www.sandals.com* ⤳ *197 rooms and suites* |⊙| *All-inclusive.*

$$$
RESORT
FAMILY

Sunset Beach Resort. Often packed with charter groups, this expansive resort can be a good value if you don't mind mass tourism. **Pros:** excellent beaches; good restaurants; numerous on-site activities; expansive water activities. **Cons:** can be crowded; high-rise setup means lines for the elevator; too far to walk to other Montego Bay attractions. $ *Rooms from: $440* ✉ *Freeport, Montego Bay* ☎ *876/979–8800* ⊕ *www.sunsetresortsjamaica.com/sunset-beach-resort-montego-bay* ⤳ *430 rooms, 16 suites* |⊙| *All-inclusive.*

$$$$
RESORT

Tryall Club. The sumptuous villas—each with a private pool—and pampering staff lend a home-away-from-home feel to this golfers' haven west of Mo'Bay. **Pros:** excellent golf; villa experience with convenience of a resort; complimentary kids' club plus a nanny service. **Cons:** non-members pay $20 a day for temporary membership to Tryall Club; shared public facilities; somewhat formal atmosphere. $ *Rooms from: $550* ✉ *North Coast Hwy., 15 miles (24 km) west of Montego Bay, Sandy Bay* ☎ *876/956–5660, 800/238–5290 in U.S.* ⊕ *www.tryallclub. com* ⤳ *86 villas* |⊙| *No meals.*

RUNAWAY BAY

The smallest of the resort areas, Runaway Bay, 50 miles (80 km) east of Montego Bay and about 12 miles (19 km) west of Ocho Rios, has a handful of modern hotels, a few all-inclusive resorts, and an 18-hole golf course.

$$$
RESORT

Jewel Paradise Cove Beach Resort & Spa. The full-service Radiant Spa featuring locally sourced natural products, where one can get treatment complete with the relaxing ocean breeze, is the centerpiece of this resort, which focuses on fitness, health, and well-being. **Pros:** free Wi-Fi; complimentary greens fees at Runaway Bay Golf Club; excellent fitness facilities; superb spa with many treatment options ; wellness classes taught by professionals. **Cons:** spa treatments cost extra.

$ *Rooms from: $469* ⊠ *Paradise Cove Dr., Runaway Bay* ☎ *876/972–7400* ⊕ *www.jewelresorts.com* ⤳ *225 rooms* ⊙∣ *All-inclusive.*

$$$
RESORT
FAMILY

Jewel Runaway Bay Beach & Golf Resort. Geared to active adults and families, this all-inclusive has plenty of space to roam, but still feels intimate. **Pros:** extensive sports and water sports; complimentary airport shuttle and greens fees; no superfluous rules or restrictions; excellent children's programs. **Cons:** small property; low-rise layout blocks easy beach access. $ *Rooms from: $399* ⊠ *North Coast Hwy., Runaway Bay* ☎ *876/973–6099* ⊕ *www.jewelresortsrunawaybay.com* ⤳ *266 rooms, 20 suites* ⊙∣ *All meals.*

OCHO RIOS.

Rivers, waterfalls, fern-shaded roads, and tropical lushness fill this fertile North Coast region, halfway between Port Antonio and Mo'Bay. It's a favorite with honeymooners as well as Jamaicans who like to escape crowded Kingston for the weekend. Resorts, hotels, and villas are all a short drive from the frenetic, traffic-clogged downtown, which has a crafts market, boutiques, duty-free shops, restaurants, and several scenic attractions. Ocho Rios is 67 miles (111 km) east of Montego Bay, just under two hours by car.

$$$$
RESORT
FAMILY

Beaches Ocho Rios Resort and Golf Club. The company that specializes in the all-inclusive resort brings its brand of luxury, attention to detail, and attentive staff to this family-oriented property. **Pros:** excellent children's program; numerous dining options; great spa; compact enclosed property. **Cons:** no room service without butler service; restaurants not always open; charge for Wi-Fi. $ *Rooms from: $608* ⊠ *North Coast Hwy., St. Ann's Bay* ☎ *876/975–7777* ⊕ *www.beaches.com* ⤳ *223 rooms, 90 suites* ⊙∣ *All-inclusive* ☞ *2-night minimum.*

$
B&B/INN
Fodor's Choice
★

The Blue House. This stylish boutique B&B is a nice alternative to North Coast all-inclusives. **Pros:** homey; great for single travelers; pool; authentic Jamaica experience; owners very involved in community outreach and charity. **Cons:** not many rooms, so you need to book early for the busy season; not on the beach; far from amenities. $ *Rooms from: $240* ⊠ *Marcliff, White River Estate, Ocho Rios* ☎ *876/994–1367* ⊕ *www.thebluehousejamaica.com* ⤳ *5 rooms* ⊙∣ *Breakfast.*

$
RESORT

ClubHotel Riu Ocho Rios. This sprawling resort, built in two U-shape wings each overlooking a pool, is one of the largest in Jamaica. **Pros:** lots of places to eat; large rooms; expansive beach. **Cons:** long walk to beach; some public areas feel cramped; all-inclusive package is limited. $ *Rooms from: $178* ⊠ *North Coast Hwy., Mammee Bay* ☎ *876/972–2200* ⊕ *www.riu.com* ⤳ *478 rooms, 386 junior suites* ⊙∣ *All-inclusive.*

$$$$
RESORT

Couples Sans Souci Resort and Spa. This classy all-inclusive encourages you to check your cares at the entrance and indulge in soul-nurturing pampering. **Pros:** excellent spa; expansive all-inclusive package; private Au Naturel Beach & Pool; free weddings. **Cons:** some rooms are very isolated and a long walk from public areas; beaches are not as good as others. $ *Rooms from: $950* ⊠ *North Coast Hwy., 2 miles (3 km) east of Ocho Rios, Ocho Rios* ☎ *876/994–1206* ⊕ *www.couples.com* ⤳ *150 suites* ⊙∣ *All-inclusive.*

NUDE BEACHES

It is perhaps ironic that Jamaica, one of the more conservative, religious islands in the Caribbean, has many opportunities for naturists.

TAKING IT OFF

In most places in Jamaica, letting it all hang out comes at a premium of up to 20% above the regular rates. Clothing-optional beaches are found at Hedonism II, Breezes Grand Resort and Spa Negril, Couples Negril, Couples Tower Isle, Couples Sans Souci, and Sunset Beach Resort.

KEEPING IT ON

If you'd rather enjoy the beach in your swimsuit, remember that most of Jamaica's resorts cater to the traditional beachgoer (and all public beaches require swimsuits by law). "Clothing-optional" means you're free to keep your swimsuit (or as much of it) on as you like. Only beaches deemed "nude" actually have a dress code that requires a birthday suit.

$$$$
RESORT
Couples Tower Isle. This all-inclusive has beautiful contemporary decor. **Pros:** some free weddings; excellent beach facilities; reciprocal deal with Couples Sans Souci on Monday, Wednesday, and Friday. **Cons:** far from Montego Bay airport. ⓢ *Rooms from: $950* ⊠ *Tower Isle, Rte. A3, 5 miles (8 km) east of Ocho Rios, St. Mary* ☎ 876/975–4271 ⊕ *www. couples.com* ⇨ *280 rooms, 14 suites* ⊙ *All-inclusive.*

$
RENTAL
Glory Be. When owner Karen Schleifer's aunt Marion Simmons first set eyes on this property, she exclaimed, "Glory be," and that's what the house, frequented by a fashionable 1950s and '60s art and literary crowd, became known as. **Pros:** private; pool; great location on the cliffs; close to Reggae Beach. **Cons:** no natural-sand beach on property; 4 miles (6½ km) from Ocho Rios town center. ⓢ *Rooms from: $150* ⊠ *Tower Isle, Ocho Rios* ☎ 876/975–4213 ⇨ *3 cottages* ⊙ *No meals.*

$$$$
RENTAL
Fodor'sChoice
★
Goldeneye. Whether you're a fan of James Bond or luxury getaways, this exclusive address 20 minutes east of Ocho Rios holds special appeal. **Pros:** spacious; plenty of privacy. **Cons:** remote location; limited dining options; may be too quiet for some. ⓢ *Rooms from: $840* ⊠ *North Coast Hwy., Oracabessa* ☎ 876/622–9007 ⊕ *www.goldeneye. com* ⇨ *1 5-bedroom villa, 20 villas/cottages* ⊙ *No meals.*

$$
RESORT
Fodor'sChoice
★
Hermosa Cove Villa Resort & Suites. Secluded in a walled-in complex, contemporary one- and two-story villas are artfully decorated and set in verdant, lush grounds. **Pros:** quiet, stylish, and comfortable suites and villas; safe and secure. **Cons:** small beach; limited menu at restaurant; isolated; walled-in. ⓢ *Rooms from: $295* ⊠ *Hermosa Cove, Hermosa St., Ocho Rios* ☎ 876/974–3699 ⊕ *www.hermosacove.com* ⇨ *9 cottages* ⊙ *Breakfast.*

$$$$
HOTEL
Fodor'sChoice
★
Jamaica Inn. The Jamaica Inn exemplifies the elegance, luxury, and exquisite service of Jamaica's tourism heyday with attention to details such as fresh flower bouquets in the rooms. **Pros:** elegant accommodations with old-world charm; exceptional service; luxurious spa; fine private dining available; private beach; seems secluded but is centrally located. **Cons:** no in-room TV. ⓢ *Rooms from: $529* ⊠ *North Coast Hwy., 2 miles (3 km)*

east of Ocho Rios, Ocho Rios ☎ *876/974–2514* ⊕ *www.jamaicainn.com* ↩ *48 suites, 4 two-bedroom cottages* ❖❖ *Some meals.*

$$$
RESORT

🏨 **Jewel Dunn's River Beach Resort & Spa.** From the waterfall in the main pool, inspired by the famous Dunn's River Falls, to the bag of jewels placed on your pillow, this upscale resort for adults is intimate and friendly with a classy casual feel. **Pros:** more intimate than most all-inclusives; 9-hole golf course; high-quality service and amenities. **Cons:** crowded beach. $ *Rooms from: $429* ✉ *Mammee Bay, Ocho Rios* ☎ *876/972–7400* ⊕ *www.jewelresorts.com* ↩ *250 rooms, 16 suites* ❖❖ *All-inclusive.*

$$$
RESORT

🏨 **Sandals Grande Riviera Beach & Villa Golf Resort.** This sprawling resort began years ago as two separate properties, and today it continues to have a split personality. **Pros:** airport shuttle; lots of privacy; numerous swimming options; romantic dining options. **Cons:** villas a long way from the beach; some rooms removed from public areas; long wait for the shuttle. $ *Rooms from: $471* ✉ *Main St., Ocho Rios* ☎ *876/974–5691* ⊕ *www.sandals.com* ↩ *260 rooms, 268 villas* ❖❖ *All-inclusive.*

$$$$
RESORT
Fodor's Choice
★

🏨 **Sandals Royal Plantation Ocho Rios.** During its heyday, guests at what was then called Plantation Inn included British royals, Winston Churchill, and authors Noël Coward and Ian Fleming. **Pros:** expansive; stylish accommodations; good dining; room service available. **Cons:** guest rooms and beach are on different levels; small pool and beach. $ *Rooms from: $655* ✉ *Main St., Ocho Rios* ☎ *876/974–5601* ⊕ *www. sandals.com* ↩ *74 suites, 1 villa* ❖❖ *All-inclusive.*

PORT ANTONIO

For an alternative to the hectic tourist scene in the bustling resort towns of Montego Bay and Ocho Rios, head to this quiet community on Jamaica's east end, 133 miles (220 km) east of Montego Bay. Don't look for mixology classes or limbo dances here. The fun is usually found outdoors, followed by a fine evening meal. The area's must-do activities include rafting Jamaica's own Rio Grande, taking an ecohike, and having lunch or a drink at the Jamaica Palace.

$
HOTEL

🏨 **Demontevin Lodge Hotel.** On Titchfield Hill, this fine example of elegant 19th-century Victorian architecture has period decor and furnishings. **Pros:** a taste of old Jamaica; central location; friendly. **Cons:** limited amenities beyond a modest restaurant; some rooms share a bathroom; in need of sprucing up as the property has become more like a museum. $ *Rooms from: $40* ✉ *21 Fort George St., Port Antonio* ☎ *876/993–2604, 876/715–5987* ↩ *13 rooms* ❖❖ *Some meals.*

$
RESORT

🏨 **Frenchman's Cove Resort.** This resort has a pristine location and decor that feels like a time capsule, but a far cry from when Queen Elizabeth II stayed in Villa 18. **Pros:** excellent beach; privacy; large accommodations; kitchens in villas; Continental breakfast included. **Cons:** dated decor; long walk to public areas and beach; some rooms don't have TV; seems very remote. $ *Rooms from: $148* ✉ *Rte. A4, 5 miles (8 km) east of Port Antonio, Port Antonio* ☎ *876/993–7270* ⊕ *www. frenchmanscove.com* ↩ *10 rooms, 2 suites, 16 villas* ❖❖ *Breakfast.*

$$$$ HOTEL Fodor's Choice ★ **Geejam.** Located 10 minutes east of Port Antonio, this stylish rockers' getaway (Gwen Stefani recorded an album here, and it's a favorite of Grace Jones) was once a music producer's hideaway. **Pros:** five-night stay includes ground transfer from Kingston airport; complimentary transportation to nearby beaches; personalized service; Apple TV in all rooms. **Cons:** remote location; limited on-site amenities; may be too quiet for some. [$] *Rooms from: $595* ✉ *North Coast Hwy., Port Antonio* ☎ *876/993–7000* 🌐 *www.geejam.com* 🛏 *1 3-bed villa, 1 suite, 3 cabins* 🍴 *Breakfast.*

$ RESORT FAMILY **Goblin Hill Villas at San San.** Hummingbirds flit about this property, consisting of one- and two-story villas with the conveniences of a hotel. **Pros:** full maid service; roomy; family-friendly. **Cons:** no restaurant; not right on the beach; remote. [$] *Rooms from: $225* ✉ *Rte. A4, 3 miles (5 km) east of Port Antonio, Port Antonio* ☎ *876/925–8108* 🌐 *www.goblinhill.com* 🛏 *28 villas* 🍴 *No meals.*

$$$ HOTEL Fodor's Choice ★ **Hotel Mockingbird Hill.** This eco-friendly boutique hotel is a delight for those who are environmentally conscious and socially aware, with luxury bound to please anyone. **Pros:** numerous ecotourism options; environmentally conscious; carbon offsetting; excellent (but limited) dining. **Cons:** somewhat remote; not directly on the beach; some might some of the furnishings to be a bit spartan. [$] *Rooms from: $408* ✉ *North Coast Hwy., Point Ann, Port Antonio* ☎ *876/993–7267* 🌐 *www.hotelmockingbirdhill.com* 🛏 *10 rooms* 🍴 *Some meals.*

$$$$ HOTEL **Trident Hotel.** What was once a stiff, formal, and traditional hotel has been remade into a stylish contemporary resort, part of the Geejam collection. **Pros:** stylish; movie-screening room; full-service spa; nanny service; private beach. **Cons:** few rooms can make it hard to book at busy times. [$] *Rooms from: $600* ✉ *North Coast Hwy., Point Ann, Port Antonio* ☎ *876/993–2602* 🌐 *www.geejam.com, www.tridentportantonio.com* 🛏 *14 suites* 🍴 *Breakfast* ☞ *5-night minimum Dec. 20–26 and Easter, 7-night minimum Dec. 26–Jan. 3.*

KINGSTON

Visited by few vacationers but a frequent destination for business travelers and visitors with a deep interest in Jamaican heritage and culture, the sprawling city of Kingston is home to some of the island's finest business hotels. Skirting the city are the Blue Mountains, a completely different world from the urban frenzy of the capital city.

$$ HOTEL **The Courtleigh Hotel & Suites.** Aimed at businesspeople, this hotel is in the city's financial district, in the heart of New Kingston and less than a half-hour from Norman Manley International Airport. **Pros:** large rooms; lively nightlife; good business facilities. **Cons:** limited dining options; noisy location; most rooms lack balconies. [$] *Rooms from: $263* ✉ *85 Knutsford Blvd., Kingston* ☎ *876/929–9000* 🌐 *www.courtleigh.com* 🛏 *128 rooms, 36 suites* 🍴 *Breakfast.*

$ HOTEL **Knutsford Court Hotel.** This modest business-district hotel combines business services with a garden-style atmosphere. **Pros:** good value; business amenities; friendly staff. **Cons:** limited leisure amenities; small pool area; no free Wi-Fi. [$] *Rooms from: $168* ✉ *16 Chelsea Ave.,*

Kingston ☎ *876/929–1000* 🌐 *www.knutsfordcourt.com* 🛏 *143 rooms, 18 suites, 5 town houses* 🍴 *Breakfast.*

$ B&B/INN 🏨 **Neita's Nest.** This B&B is for those who want to avoid a corporate hotel and the bustle of the city. **Pros:** inexpensive; intimate experience in a Jamaican family's house; quiet location; free Wi-Fi. **Cons:** far from restaurants and attractions; no amenities within walking distance. [$] *Rooms from: $160* ✉ *Bridgemount, Stony Hill* ☎ *876/469–3005* 🌐 *www.neitasnest.com* 💳 *No credit cards* 🛏 *3 rooms* 🍴 *Breakfast.*

$ HOTEL Fodor's Choice ★ 🏨 **Spanish Court Hotel.** The go-to hotel in Kingston, providing service to business travelers, wedding parties, and tourists, Spanish Court is a calm oasis in New Kingston. **Pros:** great city-center location; 24-hour business center; reasonable prices; energy-conserving features. **Cons:** limited dining options. [$] *Rooms from: $189* ✉ *1 St. Lucia Ave., Kingston* ☎ *876/926–0000* 🌐 *www.spanishcourthotel.com* 🛏 *122 rooms* 🍴 *Breakfast.*

$ HOTEL 🏨 **Terra Nova All Suite Hotel.** This graceful former colonial mansion has refurbished rooms and elegant touches to please the discerning traveler. **Pros:** elegant; great open-air dining; near shops and restaurants. **Cons:** fills up quickly on weekends. [$] *Rooms from: $189* ✉ *17 Waterloo Rd., Kingston* ☎ *876/926–2211* 🌐 *www.terranovajamaica.com* 🛏 *49 suites* 🍴 *Breakfast.*

BLUE MOUNTAINS

$$ HOTEL Fodor's Choice ★ 🏨 **Strawberry Hill.** A 45-minute drive from Kingston—but worlds apart in terms of atmosphere—this exclusive resort was developed by Chris Blackwell, former head of Island Records (the label of Bob Marley, among many others). **Pros:** stylish accommodations with breathtaking mountain views; cool retreat from the heat; great for hiking or exploring nearby coffee plantations. **Cons:** remote location a distance from beaches. [$] *Rooms from: $355* ✉ *New Castle Rd., Irish Town* ☎ *876/944–8400, 800/232–4972* 🌐 *www.islandoutpost.com* 🛏 *12 cottages* 🍴 *Breakfast.*

SOUTH COAST

In the 1970s Negril was Jamaica's most relaxed place to hang out. Today that distinction is held by the South Coast, a long stretch of coastline ranging from Whitehouse to Treasure Beach. Here local residents wave to cars, and travelers spend their days exploring local communities and their nights in local restaurants. The best way to reach the South Coast is from Montego Bay, driving overland, or via Savanna-la-Mar from Negril. Both methods take around 90 minutes to two hours, depending on your final destination.

$ HOTEL Fodor's Choice ★ 🏨 **Jakes.** Seaside charm combines with art to create a chic place that oozes personality. **Pros:** unique accommodations; South Coast friendliness; personalized service. **Cons:** can feel cramped when occasional rainy periods keep you inside; long drive from Montego Bay and Kingston airports. [$] *Rooms from: $135* ✉ *Calabash Bay, Treasure Beach* ☎ *876/965–3000* 🌐 *www.jakeshotel.com* 🛏 *50 rooms, including villas* 🍴 *No meals.*

$$$$ **Sandals Whitehouse European Village and Spa.** The first major resort
RESORT   on the South Coast, this property is one of the most upscale properties in the Sandals chain. **Pros:** great private beach; lots of restaurants;
extensive all-inclusive package includes airport shuttle; stylish rooms
at all levels. **Cons:** some travelers won't like Disney-ish re-creation of
Euro styles; far from independent restaurants and attractions; long
drive from airports. $ *Rooms from: $585* ⊠ *Whitehouse, Westmore-*
land ☎ *876/640–3000* ⊕ *www.sandals.com* ⟿ *360 rooms and suites*
❅ *All-inclusive.*

NEGRIL

Some 50 miles (80 km) west of Mo'Bay, the so-called Capital of Casual
was once a hippie hangout, favored for its inexpensive mom-and-pop
hotels and laid-back atmosphere. Today there's still a little bohemian
flair, but the town is one of the biggest tourist draws on the island, with
several large all-inclusives along Bloody Bay, northeast of town. The
main strip of Negril Beach and the cliffs are still favored by vacationers
who like to get out and explore.

$$$$ **Beaches Negril Resort and Spa.** This family-friendly all-inclusive has
RESORT   something for everyone: a prime Negril Beach location, upscale din-
FAMILY   ing for adults, and multiple attractions for kids and teens. **Pros:** great
beach; extensive water park; friendly staff; lots of activities for kids of
all ages. **Cons:** on major road; children's programs canceled if too few
are enrolled; some activities have a surcharge. $ *Rooms from: $658*
⊠ *Norman Manley Blvd., Negril* ☎ *876/957–9270* ⊕ *www.beaches.com*
⟿ *181 rooms and suites* ❅ *All-inclusive.*

$ **Catcha Falling Star.** Surely one of the prettiest properties on the West
HOTEL   End cliffs, this place proclaims "to rekindle the romance." **Pros:** rooms
Fodor's Choice   for different budgets; romantic; every room is individual. **Cons:** no
★   beach; the cheapest gatehouse cottage may get noise from the street.
$ *Rooms from: $135* ⊠ *West End Rd., Negril* ☎ *876/957–0390*
⊕ *www.catchajamaica.com* ⟿ *7 suites, 11 cottages* ❅ *No meals.*

$$$$ **The Caves.** At this boutique resort, the thatched-roof cottages are
RESORT   individually designed and furnished, most with balconies overlooking
Fodor's Choice   the deep water off Negril's West End honeycombed cliffs. **Pros:** intimate
★   spa on cliff top; quiet and friendly; unobtrusive but excellent service.
Cons: limited on-site dining options; a couple of rooms have no sea
views; no beach; really expensive. $ *Rooms from: $690* ⊠ *1 Love Dr.,*
Negril ☎ *876/957–0270, 876/618–1081* ⊕ *www.islandoutpost.com/*
the_caves ⟿ *13 villas and cottages* ❅ *Breakfast.*

$ **Charela Inn.** This quiet, family-run hotel is on one of the nicest parts
HOTEL   of Negril Beach. **Pros:** friendly owners and staff; great dining; good
beach location; good value for families. **Cons:** some guest rooms are
small; facilities are not luxurious. $ *Rooms from: $210* ⊠ *Norman*
Manley Blvd., Negril ☎ *876/957–4648, 876/957–4277* ⊕ *www.charela.*
com ⟿ *50 rooms* ❅ *Some meals.*

$ **ClubHotel Riu Negril.** At the far north end of Negril on Bloody Bay, this
RESORT   massive resort has a sandy beachfront. **Pros:** economical all-inclusive;
FAMILY   families find plenty of children; good on-site dining. **Cons:** pools and

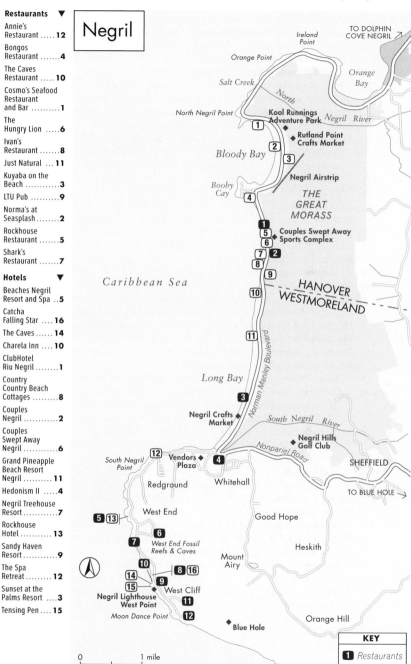

Negril

TO DOLPHIN
COVE NEGRIL

Ireland
Point

Orange Point

Orange
Bay

Salt Creek

North

Negril River

North Negril Point

Kool Runnings
Adventure Park

Rutland Point
Crafts Market

Bloody Bay

Negril Airstrip

*Booby
Cay*

**THE
GREAT
MORASS**

Couples Swept Away
Sports Complex

Caribbean Sea

HANOVER
WESTMORELAND

Long Bay

Norman Manley Boulevard

Negril Crafts
Market

South Negril River

Negril Hills
Golf Club

Nonpariel Road

SHEFFIELD

South Negril
Point

Vendors
Plaza

Redground

Whitehall

TO BLUE HOLE

West End

Good Hope

West End Fossil
Reefs & Caves

Heskith

Mount
Airy

West Cliff

Negril Lighthouse
West Point

Moon Dance Point

Blue Hole

Orange Hill

| 0 | | 1 mile |
| 0 | | 1 km |

KEY

▮ *Restaurants*

▯ *Hotels*

public areas can be overcrowded with families; many rooms a long walk from public areas; long walk from attractions of Negril Beach. $ *Rooms from: $171* ✉ *Norman Manley Blvd., Negril* ☎ *876/957–5700, 876/940–8020* ⊕ *www.riu.com* ⟿ *400 rooms* ⦿ *All-inclusive.*

$
B&B/INN

Country Country Beach Cottages. Owned by Kevin and Joanne Robertson, who also own Montego Bay's Coyaba, this small hotel carries the home-away-from-home feel of its North Coast cousin but with Negril charm. **Pros:** charming guest rooms; oversize accommodations; good Negril Beach location. **Cons:** may be too small for some; nearby Margaritaville makes some rooms noisy at night. $ *Rooms from: $205* ✉ *Norman Manley Blvd., Negril* ☎ *876/957–4273* ⊕ *www.countrynegril.com* ⟿ *18 cottages, 2 apartments* ⦿ *Breakfast.*

$$$$
RESORT

Couples Negril. This couples-only resort emphasizes romance and relaxation and is a more laid-back alternative to the nearby Sandals Negril. **Pros:** free weddings with stays of six nights or more; complimentary airport shuttle; good stretch of beach. **Cons:** long walk along the beach to action outside the resort. $ *Rooms from: $975* ✉ *Norman Manley Blvd., Negril* ☎ *876/957–5960* ⊕ *www.couples.com* ⟿ *234 rooms, 18 suites* ⦿ *All-inclusive.*

$$$$
RESORT

Couples Swept Away Negril. For sports-minded couples, this all-suites resort is known for its expansive sports offerings, top-notch facilities (Jamaica's best and among the Caribbean's best), and healthy cuisine. **Pros:** excellent fitness and sports facilities; complimentary airport shuttle; great spa. **Cons:** the healthy angle's not for everyone; some facilities are across the road; expensive. $ *Rooms from: $1000* ✉ *Norman Manley Blvd., Negril* ☎ *876/957–4061* ⊕ *www.couples.com* ⟿ *312 suites* ⦿ *All-inclusive* ☞ *3-night minimum.*

$
RESORT

Grand Pineapple Beach Resort Negril. This low-rise resort, dubbed "the cutest little resort in Negril," epitomizes the relaxed and funky style that Negril is known for. **Pros:** nice pool on the garden side with snacks available; good value; lovely beach; helpful staff; nice spa. **Cons:** some rooms don't have balconies; nearby bars can be noisy; limit of three to a room. $ *Rooms from: $205* ✉ *Norman Manley Blvd., Negril* ☎ *876/957–4408* ⊕ *www.grandpineapple.com* ⟿ *65 rooms* ⦿ *All-inclusive.*

$$$
RESORT

Hedonism II. The go-to resort for the uninhibited that promises a perpetual spring break for adults. **Pros:** good beaches; more economical than some adult all-inclusives; numerous activities. **Cons:** bacchanalian atmosphere not for everyone; nude beach and pool frequently overcrowded; basic rooms. $ *Rooms from: $466* ✉ *Norman Manley Blvd., Rutland Point, Negril* ☎ *876/957–5200* ⊕ *www.hedonism.com* ⟿ *268 rooms, 12 suites* ⦿ *All-inclusive.*

$
RESORT

Negril Tree House Resort. This established hotel offers great value on the beach. **Pros:** great beach; friendly staff; many nearby restaurants. **Cons:** basic rooms; limited menu at restaurant. $ *Rooms from: $165* ✉ *Norman Manley Blvd., Negril* ☎ *876/957–4287* ⊕ *www.negril-treehouse.com* ⟿ *53 rooms, 13 suites* ⦿ *Breakfast.*

$
HOTEL
Fodor'sChoice
★

Rockhouse Hotel. A sign reads "Spa Zone—Keep the Vibes Calm," not a tall order at this beautiful boutique hotel that attracts discerning travelers, honeymooners, and celebrities. **Pros:** unique accommodations in a beautiful setting; natural, tropical style that is ecologically aware; great dining

The Rockhouse Hotel in Negril has thatched villas on cliffs overlooking the sea.

options. **Cons:** no beach; may be too quiet for some. [$] *Rooms from: $180* ✉ *West End Rd., Negril* ☎ *876/957–4373* 🌐 *www.rockhousehotel.com* 🛏 *9 rooms, 20 villas, 5 studios* 🍴 *No meals.*

$$ HOTEL 🏨 **Sandy Haven Resort.** This small boutique hotel, opened in 2012, is a good value, particularly since it's on a lovely stretch of Negril's famed beach. **Pros:** good value; lovely beach location; good restaurant. **Cons:** beach is not private; limited on-site lunch options. [$] *Rooms from: $315* ✉ *Norman Manley Blvd., Negril* ☎ *876/957–3200, 800/583–8365 toll-free in U.S.* 🌐 *www.sandyhavenresort.com* 🛏 *17 rooms, 18 suites* 🍴 *Breakfast.*

$$ HOTEL 🏨 **The Spa Retreat.** This boutique resort on the cliffs features seven seaside cottages and five rooftop cottages with sea views as well as five similar garden cottages. **Pros:** large groups and wedding parties can rent the whole property; shuttle to beach; on-site restaurant; lovely yoga deck. **Cons:** no natural beach; sea's sometimes too rough for swimming; no relaxation area in spa section. [$] *Rooms from: $325* ✉ *West End Rd., Negril* ☎ *876/957–4329, 855/843–7725* 🌐 *www.thespajamaica.com* 🛏 *17 cottages, one suite* 🍴 *Some meals.*

$$$ RESORT 🏨 **Sunset at the Palms Resort.** A sister of the Sunset Resorts in Montego Bay and Ocho Rios—but far different in scale and atmosphere—this relaxed all-inclusive is a favorite with ecotourists thanks to its emphasis on environmental sustainability. **Pros:** environmentally conscious; beautiful grounds. **Cons:** beach is across street; ecotheme not for everyone; expensive; not within walking distance of many Negril Beach attractions and restaurants. [$] *Rooms from: $422* ✉ *Norman Manley Blvd., Negril* ☎ *876/957–5350* 🌐 *www.sunsetatthepalms.com* 🛏 *85 rooms* 🍴 *All-inclusive.*

$

B&B/INN

Fodor's Choice

★

⛺ Tensing Pen. At this rustic but elegant resort, the cottages are made of stone and wood with thatch roofs; some are on stilts, and they all have big beds. **Pros:** unique accommodations; great snorkeling; spa; spacious rooms. **Cons:** not on beach; barking dogs and other noise sometimes interrupts the quiet. $ *Rooms from: $160* ⊠ *West End Rd., Negril* ☎ *876/957-0387* ⊕ *www.tensingpen.com* ⤳ *21 rooms* ⦙◎⦙ *Breakfast.*

NIGHTLIFE

For the most part, the liveliest late-night happenings that tourists take part in are in the major resort hotels and on the beach in Negril. Some all-inclusives offer a dinner-and-entertainment pass for $50–$100; call ahead and bring a photo ID. *Daily Gleaner,* the *Jamaica Observer,* and the *Star* (online and at newsstands) list who's playing when and where. In Negril, cars with loudspeakers sometimes drive the streets in the afternoon announcing that evening's hot spot.

MONTEGO BAY

ANNUAL EVENTS

Fodor's Choice

★

Jamaica Jazz & Blues. Held in a stadium 25 minutes east of Montego Bay on the last Thursday–Saturday of January, the music festival attracts followers from around the world. Previous headliners include Mary J. Blige, Michael Bolton, Celine Dion, Kenny Rogers, and Alicia Keys. Tickets usually go on sale online in late November or early December. ⊠ *Greenfield Stadium, Trelawny* ⊕ *www.jamaicajazzandblues.com.*

Fodor's Choice

★

Reggae Sumfest. Those who know and love reggae should visit Montego Bay between mid-July and August for this weeklong concert, which attracts big names. Tickets are sold for each night's performances or by multievent passes. ⊠ *Montego Bay* ☎ *876/953-8360, 888/336-3806* ⊕ *www.reggaesumfest.com.*

BARS AND CLUBS

Blue Beat. This lounge moves to a jazz groove on Friday nights and features techno and house music on others. It closes around 10:30 most nights but goes until the wee hours on Friday and Saturday. ⊠ *Gloucester Ave., Montego Bay* ☎ *876/952-4777.*

Club Ville. After 10, the Margaritaville restaurant turns into a hip and happening nightspot. DJs play reggae, house, and R&B along with occasional live performances. Thursday night is Ladies Night and is especially popular among locals. ⊠ *Margaritaville, Gloucester Ave., Montego Bay* ☎ *876/952-4777* ⊕ *www.margaritavillecaribbean.com.*

CASINOS

Mosino Gaming Lounge. The newest gaming lounge to open in Montego Bay, this has become a favorite for gamers and nongamers alike. It houses a full restaurant and sports bar serving tasty apps and entrées. Visitors may try their luck at any of the 214 machines available here, including an assortment of virtual tables and slot machines. ⊠ *Montego Bay* ☎ *876/620-9202.*

Treasure Hunt Gaming Lounge. One of the newer additions to Montego Bay's gaming scene, this lounge is in Ironshore's Whitter Village shopping complex. Guests can try their luck at slot machines or roulette tables or have a drink from the well-stocked bar. ⊠ *Whitter Village, Ocho Rios.*

OCHO RIOS

ANNUAL EVENTS

Jamaican Epicurean Escape. This two-day festival showcases Jamaica's best culinary offerings. Restaurants from around the island set up food stations with dishes that are hard to resist. There are also chefs' demonstrations, cultural craft booths, and other events and entertainment, such as traditional drumming. ⊠ *Grizzly's Plantation Cove, St. Ann's Bay* ☏ 876/815–8500 ⊕ *www.jamaicaepicureanescape.com.*

Jamaica Ocho Rios International Jazz Festival. The biggest event in Ocho Rios, June's jazz festival has been running since 1991, when it was one day. Now nine days, it draws top names. ⊠ *Ocho Rios* ☏ 876/927–3544 ⊕ *www.ochoriosjazz.com.*

Fodor'sChoice ★ **Rebel Salute.** Over the years, this has grown to be one of Jamaica's biggest reggae festivals. As a family-oriented, roots-reggae event, no meat or alcohol is served at the two-day celebration, held in January. ⊠ *Richmond Estate, St. Ann's Bay.*

BARS AND CLUBS

Club Ville. After 10, Margaritaville transforms into this club, with a mix of the hottest tunes of the moment, along with occasional live performances from local entertainers. ⊠ *Margaritaville, Island Village, Ocho Rios* ☏ 876/675–8800 ⊕ *www.margaritavillecaribbean.com.*

KINGSTON

As the cultural hub, Kingston has Jamaica's largest selection of nightlife. Unlike the more tourist-oriented resort communities, nightlife here is aimed at locals, and varies from live music to DJs. Because of Kingston's high crime rate, check with your concierge or a local who knows the scene before heading out.

BARS AND CLUBS

Friday nights in Kingston bring on the Friday Night Jam, a street party that begins when office doors close and entrepreneurial chefs roll out oil drums transformed into jerk pits. Street corners sizzle with spicy fare, music blares, and the city launches into weekend mode.

The *Daily Gleaner,* the *Jamaica Observer,* and the *Star* have listings of who's playing when and where. Also look out for roadside posters.

Redbones Blues Cafe. You can't beat the sophisticated jazz, world music, and other low-key performances on Thursdays at this café and performance space. On Friday, it's rock, reggae, or alternative fusion, and once a month sees house music—this is one of the few venues for electronic music in Kingston. The Redbones Gallery rotates art shows once or twice a month, showcasing paintings, photography, sculptures, and sometimes even furniture. Films are screened once a week in the movie garden, usually Tuesday or Saturday. And the last Wednesday of the month brings an evening of poetry or fiction. Some events have a cover. ✉ *1 Argyle Rd., Kingston* ☎ *876/978–8262, 876/978–6091* ⊕ *www. redbonesbluescafe.com.*

Usain Bolt's Tracks and Records. For fans of sprint superstar Usain Bolt, no trip to Kingston would be complete without a visit to his club, a combination casual restaurant and sports bar that's designed to look like a stadium. There are (of course) large-screen TVs. Upstairs, on the mezzanine, you can see the running shoes Bolt wore on many of his record-breaking runs as well as signed outfits from medal-winning events. A gift shop sells Bolt gear. When not breaking records or out-running competitors, the big man himself regularly shows up at the bar. ✉ *The Marketplace, Constant Spring Rd., Kingston* ☎ *876/906–3903* ⊕ *www.tracksandrecords.com.*

NEGRIL

BARS AND CLUBS

Alfred's Ocean Palace. You can find some of Negril's best live music at this bar, which stages reggae band performances right on the beach on Sunday, Tuesday, and Friday nights. ✉ *Norman Manley Blvd., Negril* ☎ *876/957–4669* ⊕ *www.alfreds.com.*

Bourbon Beach. This beach bar is popular for its live reggae music on Monday, Thursday, and Saturday nights. ✉ *Norman Manley Blvd., Negril* ☎ *876/957–4432, 876/374–4982* ⊕ *www.bbnegril.com.*

Hedonism II. The sexy, always-packed disco here is a wild night out. Non-guest passes ($100 for couples and single men, $50 for single women) include meals, drinks, and use of the facilities from 6 pm to 2 am. (Bring a photo ID, and call a for reservation.) ✉ *Norman Manley Blvd., Negril* ☎ *876/957–5200* ⊕ *www.hedonism.com.*

The Jungle. This hot night spot has two raised bars and a circular dance floor. ✉ *Norman Manley Blvd., Negril* ☎ *876/957–4005.*

Rick's Cafe. Sunset brings the crowds for live reggae. ✉ *West End Rd., Negril* ☎ *876/957–0380.*

SHOPPING

Shopping is not really one of Jamaica's high points, though you will certainly find things to buy. Good choices include Jamaican crafts, which range from artwork to batik fabrics to baskets. Wood carvings are a top purchase; the finest are made from the Jamaican national tree, lignum vitae, or tree of life, a dense, blond wood that requires a talented carver to transform it into dolphins, heads, or fish. Bargaining is expected with crafts vendors. Naturally, Jamaican rum is another top souvenir, as is Tia Maria, the Jamaican-made coffee liqueur. Coffee (both Blue Mountain and the less expensive High Mountain) is sold at nearly every gift shop, but the cheapest prices are often found at local grocery stores, where you can buy coffee beans or ground coffee.

CLOSE UP

Jamaica's 2nd International Champ

Reggae legend Bob Marley used to be Jamaica's only international icon. But these days, the fastest man in the world, Usain Bolt, has also reached global icon status and is hero-worshipped on the island. Bolt holds the current Olympic record for the 100-meter and 200-meter, successfully defending his own titles, and was part of the Jamaican team to win the 4x100-meter relay. He now holds six Olympic gold medals for sprinting and is a five-time world champion. As well as being one of the world's most marketable athletes, he is a goodwill ambassador for Jamaica and undertakes charitable works for children. Bolt grew up in the parish of Trelawny and now lives in Kingston, where he owns the sports bar Tracks and Records. His winning track shoes and outfits are on display there. Bolt is not the only Jamaican sporting star, as fellow athletes Asafa Powell and Yohan Blake are also champion male runners, while Shelly-Ann Fraser-Pryce won the Olympic 100 meters for the second consecutive time. Visitors can tour the training ground in Kingston used by these stars and the many other champion Jamaican runners who dominate international sports.

Unless you have an extremely early flight, you'll find plenty of shopping at the Sangster International Airport, which has a large shopping mall. Fine handmade cigars are available there and at the island's many cigar stores. You can buy Cuban cigars almost anywhere, though they can't be taken back legally into the United States. As a rule, only rum distilleries, such as Appleton's and Sangster's, have better deals than the airport stores. Best of all, if you buy your rum at the airport, you don't have to tote all those heavy, breakable bottles. (Note that if you purchase rum—or other liquids, such as duty-free perfumes—outside the airport, you'll need to place them in your checked luggage when returning home. If you purchase liquids inside the secured area of the airport, you may board with them, but, after clearing U.S. Customs on landing, you will need to place them in your checked bag if continuing on another flight.)

MONTEGO BAY

ART

Gallery of West Indian Art. This is the place to find Jamaican, Cuban, and Haitian paintings. A corner of the gallery is devoted to beautifully carved and painted birds and animals. ⊠ *11 Fairfield Rd., Montego Bay* ☎ *876/952–4547* ⊕ *www.galleryofwestindianart.com.*

HANDICRAFTS

In Montego Bay, the largest crafts market can be found on Fort Street and **Market Street.** Both have a bunch of stalls selling pretty much the same thing. Be prepared to haggle and to be given the hard sell; if you're in the right mood, though, it can be a fun peek into Jamaican commerce away from the resorts.

SHOPPING CENTERS

Half Moon Shopping Village. The bright yellow buildings at Half Moon hotel contain some of the finest and most expensive wares money can buy, as well as more affordable boutiques, a post office, bank, and restaurants. ⊠ *Half Moon, North Coast Hwy., 7 miles (11 km) east of Montego Bay, Montego Bay* ☏ *876/953–2211* ⊕ *www.halfmoon.com.*

Holiday Shopping Centre. Directly across the street from the Holiday Inn SunSpree Resort, this casual shopping area has jewelry, clothing, and crafts stores. ⊠ *Holiday Inn SunSpree Resort, North Coast Hwy., 10 miles (16 km) east of Montego Bay, Montego Bay.*

The Shoppes at Rose Hall. This upscale, open-air shopping center was designed to resemble an old-fashioned main street. Five minutes from the Hilton Rose Hall, it sells jewelry, cosmetics, and designer clothing. Some hotels offer shuttles. ⊠ *Rose Hall, North Coast Hwy., 7 miles (11 km) east of Montego Bay, St. James.*

OCHO RIOS

Ocho Rios has several malls that draw day-trippers from the cruise ships. The best are **Soni's Plaza** and the **Taj Mahal,** two malls on the main street with stores selling jewelry, cigars, and clothing. Another popular mall on the main street is **Ocean Village.** On the North Coast Highway slightly east of Ochos Rios are **Pineapple Place** and **Coconut Grove.**

HANDICRAFTS

Harmony Hall. Eight minutes east of town, a restored 19th-century minister's house now carries original works of art. On sale are late owner Annabella Proudlock's wooden boxes, their covers decorated with reproductions of Jamaican paintings; magnificently displayed larger reproductions of paintings, lithographs, and signed prints of Jamaican scenes; and hand-carved wooden combs. Harmony Hall is also well known for its shows of local artists. It's closed Mondays. ⊠ *Rte. A3, Ocho Rios* ☏ *876/974–2870* ⊕ *www.harmonyhall.com.*

Wassi Art Handcrafted Caribbean Home Accessories. You'll find ceramics and other arts and crafts, all of which are made in Jamaica. ⊠ *Bonham Spring, Ocho Rios* ☏ *876/974–5044* ⊕ *www.wassiart.com.*

MARKETS

Musgrave Market. This traditional market, unlike those in Ocho Rios and Montego Bay, is primarily aimed at locals. Although you can find some crafts here, look for luscious fruits and vegetables, household goods, and clothing in these stalls. ⊠ *West St., Port Antonio.*

Ocho Rios Crafts Market. This largest market has stalls selling everything from straw hats to wooden figurines to T-shirts. Vendors can be aggressive, and haggling is expected. Your best chance of getting a good price is to come on a day when there's no cruise ship in port. ⊠ *Main St., Ocho Rios.*

Pineapple Craft Market. This small, casual market on the outskirts of Ocho Rios has everything from carved figurines to coffee-bean necklaces. ⊠ *Main St., Ocho Rios.*

PORT ANTONIO

HANDICRAFTS

Carriacou Gallery. The work of Hotel Mockingbird Hill owner Barbara Walker and other local artists is showcased. Art classes are also offered. ⊠ *Hotel Mockingbird Hill, off Rte. A4, 6 miles (9½ km) east of Port Antonio, Port Antonio* ☎ *876/993–7267.*

KINGSTON

MARKETS

Kingston Crafts Market. A large assortment of Jamaican handicrafts, including paintings, sculptures, and inexpensive jewelry, can be found in the market's stalls. Although pickpockets have been a problem in the past, it's much safer now. Some bargaining is tolerated, but don't expect many concessions. ⊠ *Harbour St. and Ocean Blvd., Kingston.*

SHOPPING CENTERS

Shops at Devon House. This cluster of mostly upscale shops sells clothing, crafts, and other items. The location, at the historic Devon House, makes it a pleasant spot to spend a morning or afternoon. Don't miss the famous Devon House ice cream and the Brick Oven pastry shop. ⊠ *26 Hope Rd., Kingston* ☎ *876/929–6602.*

SPECIALTY ITEMS

Starfish Oils. Find aromatherapy products, such as fragrant oils, scented candles, and soaps here. Lemongrass, which grows locally, goes in one of the most popular oils, and Blue Mountain coffee is a favorite ingredient in both soap and candles. Another Starfish Oils shop is in Manor Park Plaza, and its products are sold in shops throughout the island. ⊠ *Devon House, Kingston* ☎ *876/901–7113* ⊕ *www.starfishoils.com.*

Tuff Gong Record Shop. Housed in a studio that's part of the Bob Marley group of companies, this shop carries an impressive collection featuring the legend himself and other reggae greats. Marley and Tuff Gong merchandise is also on sale. The building itself is a tourist attraction, since the studio's international clients include Maxi Priest, Steele Pulse, and Sinéad O'Connor. ⊠ *220 Marcus Garvey Dr., Kingston* ☎ *876/923–9380* ⊕ *www.tuffgong.com.*

NEGRIL

MARKETS

Craft Market by Beach Park. This market on the beach side of the bridge at Negril's town center roundabout sells arts and crafts aplenty. ⊠ *Norman Manley Blvd., Negril.*

Rutland Point. With Negril's laid-back atmosphere, it's no surprise that most shopping involves straw hats, woven baskets, and T-shirts, all plentiful at this crafts market on the northern edge of town. The atmosphere is less aggressive here than at similar establishments in Montego Bay and Ocho Rios. ⊠ *Norman Manley Blvd., Negril.*

SHOPPING CENTERS

The Boardwalk Village. Set right on the beach in Negril, this is a nice place to spend half a day perusing souvenir stores and clothing boutiques, and perhaps also having lunch at the restaurant. ⊠ *Norman Manley Blvd., Negril* ⊕ *www.theboardwalkvillagenegril.com.*

Time Square. The mall is known for its luxury goods and souvenirs, including cigars and jewelry. ⊠ *Norman Manley Blvd., Negril* ☎ *876/957–9263* ⊕ *www.timesquareplaza.com.*

SPORTS AND THE OUTDOORS

The tourist board licenses all recreational activity operators and outfitters, which should assure you of fair business practices as long as you deal with companies that display its decals.

BIRD-WATCHING

Jamaica is a major bird-watching destination, thanks to its various natural habitats. The island is home to more than 200 species, some seen only seasonally or in particular parts of the island. Many bird-watchers flock here for the chance to see the vervain hummingbird (the world's second-smallest bird, larger only than Cuba's bee hummingbird) and the Jamaican tody (which nests underground).

PORT ANTONIO

Jamaica Explorations. Hotel Mockingbird Hill is the starting point for guided bird tours in the Reach Falls area ($130) and the Blue Mountains ($330). Transportation is included. In addition to the conventional Reach Falls tour, a more adventurous option includes hiking up the river and swimming across pools and mini-falls. ⊠ *Hotel Mockingbird Hill, Port Antonio* ☎ *876/993–7267* ⊕ *www.jamaicaexplorations.com.*

KINGSTON AND THE BLUE MOUNTAINS

Arrowhead Birding Tours. This company runs birding tours across the island, including one-day outings ($130), customized trips, and eight-day trips in November, February, and March. ⊠ *Kingston* ☎ *876/260–9006* ⊕ *www.arrowheadbirding.com.*

Birdlife Jamaica. This nonprofit organizes bird-watching trips into the Blue Mountains and nearby John Crow Mountains, as well as other parts of the island. ⊠ *University of the West Indies Mona, Dept. of Life Sciences, Mona Rd., Kingston* ☎ *876/260–9006.*

Sun Venture Tours. This outfit offers 25 different special-interest tours for nature lovers, including bird-watching, across the island. ⊠ *30 Balmoral Ave., Kingston* ☎ *876/960–6685, 876/408–6973 after office hrs and weekends* ⊕ *www.sunventuretours.com.*

DIVING AND SNORKELING

Jamaica isn't a major dive destination, but you can find a few rich underwater regions with a wide array of marine life, especially off the North Coast, which is on the edge of the Cayman Trench. Mo'Bay,

11

known for its wall dives, has **Airport Reef** at its southwestern edge. The site has coral caves, tunnels, and canyons. The first marine park in Jamaica, the **Montego Bay Marine Park,** was established to protect the natural resources of the bay; it's easy to see the treasures that lie beneath the surface.

Thanks to a marine area protected since 1966, the Ocho Rios region is also a popular diving destination. Through the years, the protected area grew into the **Ocho Rios Marine Park,** stretching from Mammee Bay and Drax Hall in the west to Frankfort Point in the east. Top dive sites in the area include **Jack's Hall,** a 40-foot dive dotted with all types of coral; **Top of the Mountain,** a 60-foot dive near Dunn's River Falls with many coral heads and gorgonians; and the **Wreck of the *Katryn*,** a 50-foot dive to a deliberately sunk 140-foot former minesweeper.

With its murkier waters, the southern side of the island isn't as popular for diving. However, **Port Royal,** near Kingston's airport, is filled with sunken ships that are home to many varieties of tropical fish; a special permit is required to dive some sites here.

A one-tank dive costs $45–$80. Most large resorts have dive shops, and the all-inclusives sometimes include scuba diving. To dive, you need a certification card, though it's possible to get a taste of scuba and do a shallow dive—usually from shore—after a one-day resort course, which almost every resort with a dive shop offers.

MONTEGO BAY

Jamaica Scuba Divers. With serious scuba facilities for dedicated divers and beginners, this PADI and NAUI outfit offers nitrox diving and instruction as well as instruction in underwater photography, night diving, and open-water diving. Operations are based at Travellers Beach Resort in Negril. Pickup can be arranged from most hotels and other locations along the North Coast. ☎ *876/381–1113* ⊕ *www.scuba-jamaica.com.*

PORT ANTONIO

Wall diving is especially popular in the Port Antonio area. For intermediate and advanced divers, a top spot is **Trident Wall,** lined with stunning black coral. Other favorites include **Alligator Hill,** a moderate to difficult dive known for its tubes and sponges. A beginner site, **Alligator West** is prized for its calm waters.

Lady G'Diver. The only dive operator in Port Antonio runs trips to interesting sites almost every day. Two-tank dive trips depart at around 11 am. Call two or three days in advance. ✉ *Errol Flynn Marina, Ken Wright Dr., Port Antonio* ☎ *876/995–0246* ⊕ *www.ladygdiver.com.*

FISHING

MONTEGO BAY

No Problem Sport Fishing. Charter fishing excursions are available aboard the *E-Zee.* Half- and full-day excursions take anglers in search of big catch. Plan on $600 for a half-day charter and $1,200 for a full day on the seas. A discount is available if paying by cash. Fees include drinks and equipment. ⊠ *The Yacht Club, Montego Bay* ☎ *876/381–3229* ⊕ *www. montego-bay-jamaica.com/ajal/noproblem* ⊠ *3-hr charter $450.*

FALMOUTH

Glistening Waters Marina. Offering deep-sea fishing and other charter trips from Glistening Waters (20 minutes east of Montego Bay), this marina also runs night tours of the lagoon, which is iridescent due to microscopic dinoflagellates that glow when they move. ⊠ *North Coast Hwy., Falmouth* ☎ *876/954–3229* ⊕ *www.glisteningwaters.com.*

GOLF

MONTEGO BAY

Cinnamon Hill Gold Course. On 400 lush acres on the Rose Hall estate, this course, designed by Robert von Hagge and Rick Baril, takes you to the water's edge and up into the hilly jungles. Rates include greens fees, cart, caddy, and tax, and Nike clubs are available for rent. ⊠ *Rose Hall, North Coast Hwy., St. James* ☎ *876/953–2984* ⊕ *www. cinnamonhilljamaica.com* ⊠ *$169 in winter, $49 replay* ⅂ *18 holes, 6828 yards, par 72.*

Half Moon Golf Course. Swaying palms, abundant bunkering, and large greens greet you on this flat Robert Trent Jones Sr.–designed course, home of the Jamaica Open. The course was renovated in 2005 by Jones protégé Roger Rulewich to better position the hazards for today's longer hitters. The Half Moon Golf Academy offers one-day sessions, multiday retreats, and hour-long private sessions. ⊠ *Half Moon, North Coast Hwy., 7 miles (11 km) east of Montego Bay, Montego Bay* ☎ *876/953– 2211* ⊕ *www.halfmoongolf.com* ⊠ *Nonguests $181 for 18 holes, $118 for 9 holes* ⅂ *18 holes, 7141 yards, par 72.*

White Witch Golf Course. One of the nicest courses in Montego Bay, if not Jamaica, is the White Witch course, named for Annie Palmer, the wicked 19th-century plantation mistress, whose great house looms above the course. The course was designed by Robert von Hagge and Rick Baril. Annie's Revenge is one of five tournaments hosted at the course that occupies mountainous terrain high above the sea and features bold, attractive bunkering and panoramic views. Legend has it that Annie still haunts the area, but not your golf game. Rental clubs are available for $65. Prebooking is recommended. ⊠ *Rose Hall Main Rd., Rose Hall, St. James* ☎ *876/632–7444* ⊕ *www.whitewitchgolf.com* ⊠ *$169* ⅂ *18 holes, 6758 yards, par 71.*

Fodor's Choice ★   **Tryall Club Golf Course.** At an exclusive country club 15 miles (24 km) west of Montego Bay, this championship course on the site of a 19th-century sugar plantation blends first-class golf with traces of history. The ambience is peaceful; no one is hurried and playing with a caddy is the norm. The layout takes in the Caribbean coast—the 4th-hole green hugs the sea—before heading up into the hills for expansive vistas. Designed by Ralph Plummer, the course has hosted events such as the Johnnie Walker World Championship. ⊠ *Tryall Club, North Coast Hwy., Sandy Bay* ☎ *876/956–5601* ⊕ *www.tryallclub.com* ⊠ *$150 for 18 holes ($105 guests), $115 for 9 holes ($75 guests)* ⅂ *18 holes, 6836 yards, par 71.*

NEGRIL

Negril Hills Golf Club. Inland from Jamaica's longest stretch of private beach, this course is 1½ hours west of Montego Bay. High points are the lush tropical foliage, picturesque water hazards, elevated tees, gently rolling fairways, tropical mountain vistas, and hard-sloping greens. The 6,333-yard course is walkable but plays longer due to elevated putting surfaces. ⊠ *Negril* ☎ *876/957–4638* ⊕ *www.negrilhillsgolfclub. com* ⊴ *$60* ⌕ *18 holes, 6333 yards, par 72.*

GUIDED TOURS

Because most vacationers avoid renting cars for safety and cost reasons, guided tours with hotel pickup are popular options for exploring. Jamaica's size and slow interior roads mean that you can't expect to see the entire island on one trip; even full-day tours concentrate on one part of the island. Most tours are similar in both content and price. From Montego Bay, tours often include one of the area's plantation houses. Several Negril-based companies offer tours to Y.S. Falls on the South Coast. Tours from Ocho Rios might include top attractions such as Dunn's River Falls or Kingston. In almost all cases, you arrange the tour through your resort.

MONTEGO BAY

Croydon Plantation Tour. Tour the birthplace of the Jamaican hero Sam Sharpe, who led the rebellion that helped put an end to slavery on the island. The tour ($70), run on Tuesday, Thursday, and Friday, visits the plantation, an hour and a half from Montego Bay, where pineapples, sugarcane, and citrus fruits are grown in the foothills of the Catadupa mountains. Pickup is available from hotels around Montego Bay and the Grand Palladium Resort in Hanover. ☎ *876/979–8267* ⊕ *www. croydonplantation.com.*

Glamour Destination Management. One of the island's large tour operators, this company offers a wide selection of guided visits to Rose Hall and Greenwood Great House. ⊠ *1225 Providence Dr., Montego Bay* ☎ *876/953–3810* ⊕ *www.glamourtoursdmc.com.*

Island Routes Caribbean Adventures. Run by Sandals, this company provides a host of luxury group and private guided tours (with certified partners) to guests and nonguests. Guests can book via the website or at an Island Routes tour desk at participating resorts. ⊠ *Queens Dr., Montego Bay* ☎ *888/768–8370 in U.S. and Canada, 888/429–5478 in Jamaica* ⊕ *www.islandroutes.com.*

John's Hall Adventure Tours. This company offers several tours, but the most popular is the City and Culture Tour, which takes visitors to the historic sites of Montego Bay, including churches and a school where guests can interact with the children. The tour then goes to John's Hall Plantation, a working farm around 15 minutes from Montego Bay where a huge variety of fruit is grown. Lunch is included. The City and Culture Tour runs on Monday, Wednesday, Friday and Saturday. ⊠ *26 Hobbs Ave., Montego Bay* ☎ *876/971–6958, 876/952–7218, 876/971–6938.*

JUTA. The island's largest tour operator offers a great house tour and a rafting tour, as well as tours to other parts of the island like Black River, Negril, and Ocho Rios. ☎ *876/952–0813* ⊕ *www.jutatoursltd.com.*

OCHO RIOS

Chukka Caribbean Zion Bus Tour. A country-style bus painted in bright colors travels inland to the village of Nine Mile and the simple house where Bob Marley was born and is now buried. The five-hour tour ($104, including lunch at a jerk stand) is for those 18 and older. ⊠ *Ocho Rios* ☎ *876/619–1441 Digicel in Jamaica, 876/656–8026 Lime in Jamaica, 877/424–8552 in U.S.* ⊕ *http://chukka.com* 💲*$104.*

Jamaica Tours Limited. This operator offers several tours with stops that include gardens and Dunn's River Falls. ☎ *876/974–6447* ⊕ *www. jamaicatoursltd.com.*

PORT ANTONIO

Tours in Port Antonio. Joanna Hart leads an in-depth cultural and historical tour of the Port Antonio area, incorporating the history of the Maroons. ⊠ *Port Antonio* ☎ *876/859–3758* ⊕ *www.toursinportantonio.com.*

KINGSTON

Numerous operators offer tours of the Kingston area, as well as excursions into the Blue Mountains. Professional tour operators provide a valuable service, as neither destination is particularly suited to exploration without a guide. In Kingston, certain areas can be dangerous; an organized tour provides a measure of security. Think twice before roaming in the Blue Mountains, as roads are narrow or in poor condition and signs are few and far between.

Typical city tours include a city overview with stops at Devon House, the Bob Marley Museum, and Port Royal. Niche operators such as Olde Jamaica Tours provide theme tours, including a tour of churches and museums and one that visits the athletic grounds where Usain Bolt and other sprinters have trained.

Jessa Tours, Ltd. Tours visit the Bob Marley Museum, National Gallery, craft market, and other heritage sites. ⊠ *19 Herb McKenley Dr., Kingston* ☎ *876/978–2259* ⊕ *www.jessatours.com.*

Olde Jamaica Tours. This company runs heritage and cultural tours— churches, great houses, and the like—as well as visits to a cricket field and the training ground where Usain Bolt and others have developed their sporting prowess. Though island-wide trips are offered, the focus is on Kingston. ⊠ *5 Cowper Dr., Kingston* ☎ *876/371–3613, 876/328– 1385* ⊕ *www.oldejamaicatours.com.*

Sun Island Executive Tours & Services Ltd. This company offers tours to places of interest around Jamaica and can work with you to design an itinerary. ⊠ *8 Bower Bank Ave., Kingston* ☎ *876/931–8826.*

SOUTH COAST

Countrystyle Community Experiences Tours. Combining your choice of accommodation—whether homestay or hotel—with your interests, these tour packages match you with residents to showcase rural community lifestyles, helping you enjoy Jamaican culture, heritage, cuisine, and music. Additional experiences such as the Jamaica Roots

Experience, Jamaica Taste Experience, and Jamaica Nature Experience are offered in Kingston and Montego Bay. ⊠ *62 Ward Ave., Mandeville* ☎ *876/507–6326, 876/488–7207* ⊕ *www.jamaica-no-problem.com/ community-tours.html.*

Jakes Biking Tour. Jakes offers various area bike tours. In one three-hour tour ($60), a guide leads the way to the gorgeous stretch of sand at Fort Charles or Great Bay, and since Treasure Beach is flat, almost all fitness levels can participate. Jakes also runs hiking tours. ⊠ *Treasure Beach* ☎ *876/965–3000* ⊕ *www.jakeshotel.com.*

NEGRIL

In addition to tours from Montego Bay that give day-trippers a chance to experience Negril, there are several tours available to those who are staying here, including trips to the waterfalls.

The North Coast is known for Dunn's River Falls, and the South Coast for Y.S. Falls (both accessible from Negril on a day tour), but the Negril area is home to some impressive waterfalls of its own. A top activity for travelers tired of the beach, Mayfield Falls is tucked into the Dolphin Head Mountains near Glenbrook. These falls have been the stuff of legend since the 1700s, when locals swore a mermaid lived in these mineral-rich pools. Today the "mermaids" are tourists from Negril and Montego Bay who come to enjoy the waterfalls and underwater caves. Fifty-two varieties of fern are found here, as well as many types of tropical flowers. A visit here includes a guided hike up the river with a stop at a bar and grill along the way. Several operators offer tours, usually with transportation from nearby hotels and lunch included.

Rhodes Hall Eco Tours. Just 15 minutes from Negril, this former sugar plantation offers ecotours in a nature reserve with a crocodile lake and bird sanctuary. Other adventures include horseback riding, snorkeling and scuba diving, glass-bottom boating, and bathing in Rhodes Hall's Magic Blue Mud Mineral Spring Bath. Help arranging transportation from Negril area hotels is provided. ⊠ *Green Island* ☎ *876/957–6422* ⊕ *www.rhodesresort.com* 🏷 *from $25.*

Tropical Tours. One tour takes in the lighthouse and shopping, another Rick's Cafe. Tours leave from Club Riu at 2 for the former, at 4 for the latter. ⊠ *Norman Manley Blvd., Negril* ☎ *876/957–4110 in Negril* ⊕ *www.tropicaltours-ja.com.*

HORSEBACK RIDING

MONTEGO BAY

Braco Stables. These stables are in the Braco area near Duncans in Trelawny, between Montego Bay and Ocho Rios. Two daily estate rides ($70) include complimentary refreshments served poolside at the Braco great house. Experienced riders can also opt for a mountain ride ($100) for a more rugged two-hour tour. ⊠ *Braco, Duncans* ☎ *876/954–0185* ⊕ *www.bracostables.com, www.bracotours.com.*

OCHO RIOS

With its combination of hills and beaches, Ocho Rios is a natural for horseback excursions. Most are guided tours taken at a slow pace and perfect for those with no previous equestrian experience. Many travelers opt to wear long pants for horseback rides, especially those away from the beach.

Fodor's Choice ★ **Chukka Caribbean Adventures.** The two-hour ride-and-swim tour ($159) travels along Papillion Cove (where the 1973 movie *Papillion* was filmed) as well as to locations used in *Return to Treasure Island* (1985) and *Passion and Paradise* (1988). The trail continues along the coastline to Chukka Beach and a bareback ride in the sea. Chukka has a location west of Montego Bay and handles other activities and tours, too. ⊠ *Ocho Rios* ☎ *876/619–1441 Digicel in Jamaica, 876/656–8026 Lime in Jamaica, 877/424–8552 in U.S.* ⊕ *chukka.com* ☞ *$159.*

Hooves. This stable offers several guided tours, including a popular 2½-hour beach ride ($95 from Boscobel, $85 from Ocho Rios, $90 from Runaway Bay—including transportation) suitable for adults and children taller than 3 feet. The trip begins with a visit to the Seville Great House estate before making its way to the beach for a ride. Hooves is home to many rescue horses that have been rehabilitated. ⊠ *Windsor Rd., St. Ann's Bay* ☎ *876/972–0905* ⊕ *www.hooves-jamaica.com.*

Prospect Plantation. The plantation offers horseback rides for ages eight and older, including use of helmets; reservations are required. For the adventurous, there are also guided camel rides. ⊠ *Rte. A1, about 3 miles (5 km) east of Ocho Rios* ☎ *876/974–5335* ☞ *$54.*

SOUTH COAST

Paradise Park. This working farm has been owned and operated by the same family for more than 100 years. Visitors can take horseback rides to explore the farm's fields and pastures and the beaches on the property. Afterward you can take a dip in Sweet River and have a picnic if you bring your own food. Reservations must be made at least 24 hours in advance. ⊠ *Rte. A2, 1 mile (2 km) west of Ferris Cross* ☎ *876/955–2675* ☞ *From $45.*

RIVER BOATING AND RAFTING

Fodor's Choice ★ Jamaica's many rivers mean a multitude of freshwater experiences, from mild to wild. The island's first tourist activity off the beaches was relaxing rafting trips aboard bamboo rafts poled by local boatmen, which originated on the **Rio Grande.** Jamaicans had long used rafts to transport bananas downriver. Decades ago actor and local resident Errol Flynn saw the rafts and thought they'd make a good tourist attraction. Today the slow rides are a favorite with romantic travelers and anyone looking to get off the beach for a few hours. The popularity of the Rio Grande's trips spawned similar trips down the **Martha Brae River,** about 25 miles (38 km) from Mo'Bay. Near Ocho Rios, the **Great River** has lazy river rafting as well as energetic kayaking.

Rafting on the Rio Grande, near Port Antonio

MONTEGO BAY

Jamaica Tours Limited. This big tour company conducts raft trips down the Martha Brae, approximately 25 miles (38 km) east of Mo'Bay; the excursion can include lunch if requested. Price depends on number of people and pickup location. Hotel tour desks can book it. ✉ *Providence Dr., Montego Bay* ☎ *876/953–3700* ⊕ *www.jamaicatoursltd.com.*

River Raft Ltd. This company leads 1½-hour trips down the Martha Brae River, about 25 miles (38 km) from most Mo'Bay hotels. ☎ *876/940–7018, 876/952–0889, 876/952–0889* ⊕ *www.jamaicarafting.com* 🎫 *$60.*

SOUTH COAST

FAMILY **South Coast Safaris Ltd.** On slow boat cruises up the river, keep an eye peeled for crocodiles basking on the banks and swimming in the water—the captain has pet names for some of them. The cruise also passes through a thick mangrove area with egrets and other birds. Back at the landing stage there is a crocodile nursery where you can see young crocs being raised for release. ✉ *1 Crane St., Black River* ☎ *876/965–2513* ⊕ *www.jamaica-southcoast.com* 🎫 *$20.*

SAILING

MONTEGO BAY

Dreamer Catamaran Cruises. Four catamarans, from 53 to 65 feet, take cruises ($83) that include a snorkel stop and visit to Margaritaville. Foot massages for women are followed by dance instruction for all. Children are allowed on only the morning and sunset cruises. Now offering a Montego Bay–to–Negril tour. ⊠ *Cornwall Beach, Gloucester Ave., Montego Bay* ☎ *876/979–0101* ⊕ *www.dreamercatamarans. com* ✉ *$83.*

OCHO RIOS

Five Star Watersports. Several sailing and partying options are available through this company's Cool Runnings catamaran cruises: romantic dinner sails, the Wet and Wild Cruise, and a popular trip to Dunn's River Falls. Boats run only on Sundays with a minimum number of bookings; check when making reservations. ⊠ *121 Main St., Ocho Rios* ☎ *876/974–2446, 876/974–4593* ⊕ *www.fivestarwatersports.com.*

PORT ANTONIO

Errol Flynn Marina. This official national port of entry has 24-hour customs and immigration services. The 32-berth marina, reached via a deepwater channel, includes 24-hour security, an Internet center, swimming pool, laundry, and 100-ton boat lift—the only area facility that can handle vessels of 600 feet. Scuba diving and other water-sports attractions are also here. ⊠ *Ken Wright Dr., Port Antonio* ☎ *876/715–6044* ⊕ *www.errolflynnmarina.com.*

MARTINIQUE

WELCOME TO MARTINIQUE

PARIS IN THE TROPICS

The largest of the Windward Islands, Martinique is 425 square miles (1,101 square km). The southern part of the island is all rolling hills and sugarcane fields; it's also where you'll find the best beaches and most development. In the north are craggy cliffs, lush vegetation, and one of the Caribbean's largest volcanoes, Mont Pelée.

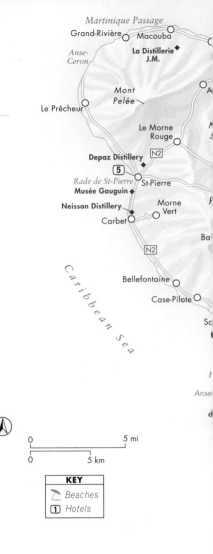

KEY

⟩ Beaches

① Hotels

Joie de vivre is the credo in this French enclave, which is often characterized as a Caribbean suburb of Paris. Exotic fruit grows on the volcanoes' forested flanks amid a profusion of wild orchids and hibiscus. The sheer lushness of it all inspired the tropical paintings of onetime resident Paul Gauguin.

Basse-Pointe
D21
N3
Ajoupa-Bouillon
N1
Le Lorrain
Marigot

ATLANTIC OCEAN

Morne
Jakob
N1
Ste-Marie
6
St. James Distillery
& Rum Museum
D1
D2
Havre
de la
Trinité
Anse
Tartane
Caravelle
Peninsula
Presqu'île du Caravelle
Tartane
La Trinité
7
Pointe
Caracoli
Baie du Galion

Pitons du
Carbet
N4
Gros-Morne
N3
Balata
St-Joseph
N4
Le Robert
N1
Havre du Robert
Pte. Larose
Le Plein Soleil
8
9
4
1 2
N1
Lamentin
Le François
Schoelcher
3
Fort-de-
Baie des France
Flamands
Lamentin
International
Airport
Habitation Clément
Mt. Vauclin
N6
Baie de
Fort-de-France
Pointe
du Bout
N5
Ducos
Le Vauclin
nse-à-l'Ane
Anse-Mitan
15 Les Trois-Îlets
14
13
Pointe
du Bout
12
D7
Mt. Bigot
Rivière-
Salée
D7 N5
Forêt de
Montravail
Anse-d'Arlets
Le
Diamant
11
D7
D17
D18
Rivière-
Pilote
N6
Ste-Luce
D18A
Le Marin
D37
Anse Corps
de Garde
N5
Pointe du
Marin
Cap
Chevalier
Diamant
Beach
Pte. Figuier
10 D9
Ste-Anne
Baie des Anglais
Diamond Rock
Cul-de-Sac
du Marin
Les Salines
La Savane
(Petrified
Forest)
Anse-Trabaud
Grande Anse
Pte. d'Enfer
Pte. des Salines

TOP REASONS TO VISIT MARTINIQUE

1 **The Romance:** A magical sensuality infuses everything; it will awaken dormant desires and fuel existing fires.

2 **Beautiful Beaches:** A full roster of beautiful beaches will let you enjoy sun and sand.

3 **The French Connection:** Excellent French food, not to mention French music

and fashion, make the island a paradise for those in search of the finer things.

4 **Range of Accommodations:** Hospitable, stylish small hotels abound; big resorts, too. Or play expat in a private, luxe villa.

5 **Inviting Waters:** The sea, Caribbean; the ocean, Atlantic—experience the water in a kayak or on a sailboat. Even a ferry works.

NEED TO KNOW

DOMINICA

Atlantic
Ocean

MARTINIQUE

Fort-de-France

Caribbean
Sea

SAINT LUCIA

AT A GLANCE

Capital: Fort-de-France

Population: 403,700

Currency: Euro

Money: ATMs common; few places accept U.S. dollars, so plan on exchanging them for euros.

Language: French, Creole

Country Code: 596

Emergencies: 17

Driving: On the right

Electricity: 220v/50 cycles; plugs are European standard with two round prongs

Time: Same as New York during daylight savings time; one hour ahead otherwise

Documents: Up to 90 days with valid passport

Mobile Phones: GSM (900 and 1800 bands)

Major Mobile Companies: Digicel, Orange

WEBSITES

Martinique Promotion Bureau: 🌐 www.martinique.org

GETTING AROUND

✈ **Air Travel:** Martinique Aimé Césaire Airport is the sole airport.

🚌 **Bus Travel:** Take buses within Fort-de-France; shared minivans go to points outside the capital.

🚗 **Car Travel:** Renting a car will allow you to explore more. Just be prepared for a manual shift, steep mountainous (albeit well-paved and well-marked) roads, and heavy traffic.

⛴ **Ferry Travel:** Ferries connect Fort-de-France to Pointe du Bout, Anse-Mitan, and Anse-l'Ane and are the best way to go into the capital; ferries also travel to St. Lucia, Dominica, and Guadeloupe.

PLAN YOUR BUDGET

	HOTEL ROOM	MEAL	ATTRACTIONS
Low Budget	$200	$12	Fort St. Louise, free
Mid Budget	$300	$25	Botanical park, $18
High Budget	$475	$50	Half-day kite-surfing, $140

WAYS TO SAVE

Shop and eat at open-air markets. Sample local fruits, veggies, spices, and more at "The Big Market" in Fort-de-France and eat at local vendors.

Rent a villa. Unlike other islands where you might want to rent a condo or time-share, multibedroom villas are affordable alternatives to resorts on Martinique.

Take the ferry. The cheapest and best option to travel between the capital and the resort district of Pointe du Bout is via ferryboat.

Look for concessions. Seniors, under 26s, and kids get discounts at attractions.

PLAN YOUR TIME

Hassle Factor	Medium. Many flights to Martinique require a transfer in Miami or another island in the Caribbean.
3 days	Relax poolside or beachside at your resort. Rent a car for a day to check out greater Martinique, not missing Fort-de-France or St. Pierre.
1 week	Explore Martinique in more detail, basing yourself in Pointe du Bout. Rent a car and spend two days exploring either the country's southern half or northern half.
2 weeks	Explore Martinique, coast to coast from Diamond Rock and the Petrified Forest in the South to Caravelle Nature Preserve in the north. Take the ferry to one of Martinique's neighboring islands—Dominica or St. Lucia—for a few days.

WHEN TO GO

High Season: Mid-December through mid-April is the most fashionable and most expensive time to visit, when the weather is typically sunny and warm. Good hotels are often booked far in advance, and you're guaranteed the most entertainment at resorts and the most people with whom to enjoy it.

Low Season: From August to late October, temperatures can grow oppressively hot and the weather muggy, with high risk of tropical storms. Some upscale hotels close during these months for annual renovations. Those remaining open offer discounts.

Value Season: From late April to July and again November to mid-December, hotel prices drop 20% to 50% from high-season prices. There are chances of scattered showers, but expect sun-kissed days, too, and fewer crowds.

BIG EVENTS

February–March: Martinique's Carnival begins in February. Interestingly enough, it keeps going until the day after Ash Wednesday. ⊕ www.martinique.org/carnival-festivities

April–May: Topping the list of the island's food festivals is the weeklong Sainte-Marie Culinary Week.

June: Celebrate the musical traditions of Martinique at Fête de la Musique with free concerts and parties.

December: In odd-numbered years, the Martinique Jazz Festival draws a wide range of international talent.

READ THIS

■ *Lost Body,* Aimé Césaire. Works by Martinique's renowned poet.

■ *Poetics of Relation,* Edouard Glissant. Thought-provoking body of work from the exalted French writer.

■ *The Rose of Martinique,* Andrea Stuart. Biography of Joséphine Bonaparte, who was born here.

WATCH THIS

■ *Thomas Crown Affair.* The romantic thriller starring Pierce Brosnan and Rene Russo was filmed in Martinique.

■ *Volcano!* Silent film from the 1920s.

■ *To Have and Have Not.* Film based on the Ernest Hemingway novel.

EAT THIS

■ *Ecrivesses*: freshwater crayfish, usually served with their heads on.

■ *Moules et frites*: mussels and French fries.

■ *Boudin Creole*: a dark and spicy blood sausage.

■ *Crabe Farci*: spicy crab and stuffing.

■ *Blaff*: marinated fish or poached seafood.

■ *Féroce d'avocat*: cassava fritters of spicy avocado and cod.

Updated by
Eileen
Robinson
Smith

Numerous scattered ruins and other historical monuments reflect the richness of Martinique's sugarcane plantation past, *rhum,* and the legacy of slavery. Called the Rum Capital of the World, it is widely considered the best gourmet island in the Caribbean. It stirs the passions with its distinctive brand of culinary offerings. If you believe in magic, Martinique has it, along with a sensuality that fosters romance. It has become known as the island of *revenants,* those who always return. *Et pourquoi non?*

Martinique is simply one of the most enchanting destinations in the western hemisphere. Francophiles adore this island for its food, rum, *musique,* and élan, and the availability of the finest French products, from Chanel fashions to Limoges china. It is endowed with lots of tropical beauty, including white-sand beaches and rain forests. The volcano Mont Pelée looms over the harbor town of St-Pierre, known as the Pompeii of the Caribbean. Its largest city, Fort-de-France, comes with lots of charm as well as some great restaurants and clubs. Martinicans will be glad you came, and you will be greeted with warm smiles and politesse.

Christopher Columbus first sighted this gorgeous island in 1502, when it was inhabited by the fierce Caraïbes, who had terrorized the peace-loving Arawaks. The Arawaks called their home Madinina (the Isle of Flowers), and for good reason. Exotic wild orchids, frangipani, anthurium, jade vines, flamingo flowers, and hundreds of vivid varieties of hibiscus still thrive here.

The island reflects its rich cultural history. In colonial days Martinique was the administrative, social, and cultural center of the French Antilles; this rich, aristocratic island was famous for its beautiful women. The island even gave birth to an empress, Napoléon's Joséphine. It saw the full flowering of a society ruled by planters, with servants and soirées, wine cellars, and lots of snobbery.

12

Martinique's economy still depends on *les bananes* (bananas), *l'ananas* (pineapples), cane sugar, rum, and fishing. It's also the largest remaining stronghold of the *békés*—the descendants of the original French planters—and they are still the privileged class on any of the French-Caribbean islands. Numbering around 4,000, many control Martinique's most profitable businesses, from banana plantations and rum distilleries to car dealerships. The elite dress in designer outfits straight off the Paris runways. In general, the islanders have style. In the airport waiting room you can almost always tell the Martiniquaises by their fashionable clothes.

Of the island's 400,000 inhabitants, 100,000 live in Fort-de-France and its environs. It has 34 separate municipalities. Though the actual number of French residents from the Metropole (France) does not exceed 15% of the total population, Martinique is a part of France, an overseas *département* to be exact; and French is the official language, though the vast majority of the residents also speak Creole.

Thousands are employed in government jobs offering more paid holidays than most Americans can imagine. Martinicans work hard and enjoy their time off, celebrating everything from *le fin de la semaine* (the weekend) to Indian feast days, sailboat races, and Carnival. Their joie de vivre is infectious. Once you experience it, you'll be back.

PLANNING

GETTING HERE AND AROUND
AIR TRAVEL

There are now nonstop flights from the United States on American Airlines, flying out of Miami every day except Wednesday. Service by Seaborne Airlines offers service three times a week from San Juan. Most travelers are able to connect in San Juan or in Miami and to Air France, as well, which departs Miami three times a week with a stop in a neighboring island. Norwegian Airlines offers seasonal nonstop service to Fort-de-France out of New York, Boston, Baltimore/Washington, D.C., with some of the lowest fares to the Caribbean.

Contacts **Air Antilles Express.** ☎ 0890/64–86–48, 0596/42–18–07 ⊕ www.airantilles.com. **Air Canada.** ☎ 888/247–2262 ⊕ www.aircanada.com. **Air Caraïbes.** ☎ 0820/83–58–35, 0590/82–47–47 in Guadeloupe, reservations ⊕ www.aircaraibes.com; www.aircaraibes-usa.com. **Air France.** ☎ 0892/68–29–72, 0596/55–34–72, 800/237–2747 in U.S., 0596/82–61–61 ⊕ www.airfrance.com. **American Airlines.** ☎ 800/433–7300 ⊕ www.aa.com. **LIAT.** ☎ 0596/42–16–11, ⊕ www.liatairline.com. **Norwegian.** ☎ 800/357–41–59 ⊕ www.norwegian.com. **Seaborne Airlines.** ☎ 866/359–8784 in U.S. ⊕ www.seaborneairlines.com.

AIRPORT Contacts **Martinique Aimé Césaire Airport (FDF).** ☎ 0596/42–16–00 ⊕ www.martinique.aeroport.fr.

BUS TRAVEL

Locals take *collectifs* (white vans holding up to 10 passengers) that cost just a few euros and depart from Pointe Simon, on the waterfront in Fort-de-France, to all parts of the island. Don't be shy; the difference can be €3 versus, say, €60 for a taxi to reach the same destination. Drivers don't usually speak English, and there's no air-conditioning.

Bus Mozaik. The air-conditioned buses of this private company stop within the city; they service Lamentin, Fort-de-France suburbs such as Schoelcher, and as far into the interior of the island as St. Joseph. Buses leave from Pointe Simon, on the waterfront, where the public buses and shared-taxis (white vans) congregate. Fares start at €1.25 one-way; €2.30 for round-trip, if tickets are purchased at a Moziak Kiosk. If bought on the bus, those same rates would be €1.80 and €2.50. For schedules, visit the website. ⊕ *www.aquelleheure.fr/bus.htm.*

CAR TRAVEL

The main highways, about 175 miles (280 km) of well-paved and well-marked roads, are excellent, but only in a few areas are they lighted at night. Many hotels are on roads that are barely passable, so get wherever you're going by nightfall or you could lose your way. Then tell a stranger, *"Je suis perdu!"* ("I am lost!"). It elicits sympathy. If they say, *"Suivez-moi!"*—that's "Follow me!"—stay glued to their bumper. Finally, drive defensively; although Martinicans are polite and lovely people, they drive with aggressive abandon.

Martinique, especially Fort-de-France and environs, is plagued with heavy traffic; if you must drive into Fort-de-France, do it on a weekend. Absolutely avoid the Lamentin Airport area and Fort-de-France during weekday rush hours, roughly 7 to 10 am and 4 to 7:30 pm, and on Sunday night going in the direction of Fort-de-France. That's when everyone comes off the beaches and heads back to the city. Even smaller towns such as La Trinité have rush hours. Watch, too, for *dos d'ânes* (literally, donkey backs), speed bumps that are hard to spot—particularly at night. Gas is costly, at about triple U.S. prices. Diesel is somewhat cheaper, but if you rent an economy car for a full week, you should budget a sufficient amount for fuel.

Be aware that the French gendarmes set up roadblocks, often on Sunday, to stop speeders and drunk drivers, and just to check papers. Now they even have video cameras on the highways. Visitors are not absolved from speeding tickets, because you can be tracked down through the rental car's license plate.

Renting a Car: It's worth the hassle to rent a car—if only for a day or two—so that you can explore more of this beautiful island. Just be prepared for a manual shift, steep mountainous roads, and heavy traffic. Prices are expensive, "in season" about €80 per day or €450 per week (unlimited mileage) for a manual shift, perhaps more for an automatic, which must be ordered in advance (and not all agencies have them). You may save money by waiting to book your car rental on the island for a reduced weekly rate from a local agency. Some of the latter, though, make up their own rules, and they will not be in your favor. There's an extra charge (about $20) if you drop the car off at the airport after having rented it somewhere else on the island. A valid U.S. driver's license or International Driver's Permit is needed to rent a car for up to 20 days. ■TIP→ **Often, the airline you fly in with will have a discount coupon for a rental car, right on the ticket, or in their in-flight magazine. Also, local publications have ads with discounts that can be as much as 40% off (in low season). You can find these at the Tourism Information counter in the airport.**

Contacts Avis. ☎ 0596/42–11–00 ⊕ www.avis-antilles.fr. **Budget.** ✉ Martinique Aimé Césaire Airport, Le Lamentin ☎ 0596/42–04–04 ⊕ www.budget-martinique. com. **Europcar.** ☎ 0596/42–42–42 ⊕ www.europcar-martinique.com. **Hertz.** ✉ Martinique Aime Cesare Airport, Le Lamentin ☎ 0596/51–01–01, 0810/32–31–13 ⊕ www.hertzantilles.com, www.hertzantilles.com/location_voiture_martinique. **JumboCar.** ✉ Martinique Aimé Césaire Aéroport, Le Lamentin ☎ 0596/42–17–01, 0820/22–02–30 ⊕ www.jumbocar.com. **Sixt.** ✉ Martinique Aimé Césaire Airport, Le Lamentin ☎ 0596/60–14–16 ⊕ www.sixt.fr.

FERRY TRAVEL

Weather permitting, *vedettes* (ferries) operate daily between Quai d'Esnambuc in Fort-de-France and the marinas in Pointe du Bout, Anse-Mitan, and Anse-à-l'Ane and are the best way to go into the capital. Any of these trips takes about 20 minutes. Ferries depart every 30 minutes on weekdays; less often in the low season and weekends. Round-trip tickets cost €6.50.

Compagnie Maritime West Indies. Compagnie Maritime West Indies provides rapid sea shuttle service from neighboring St. Lucia. Boats (capacity 15 persons) usually depart daily at 11 am and 4 pm from Castries, St. Lucia, to Le Marin. Fares are approximately €89 round-trip for adults and €69 round-trip for children under 12. It departs from Le Marin at 8 am and from St. Lucia at 11 am. ■TIP→ **A number of airlines fly into St. Lucia, so making arrangements to land there and take Compagnie can be a good way to get to Martinique (especially if you are staying at Club Med or another resort in the south or chartering a sailboat from the marina in Le Marin).** ☎ 0696/21–77–76, 0596/74–93–38 in Martinique, 0758/452–8757 in St. Lucia.

Jeans for Freedom. This branch of the L'Express des Îles company goes between Pointe-à-Pitre, Guadeloupe, and St-Pierre, Martinique; it also makes a brief stop in Dominica; the price is now up to €79. In Guadeloupe, service is also available between Pointe-à-Pitre and Marie-Galante or Les Saintes for €23. Jeans also runs specials like a day-trip out of Fort-de-France to St. Lucia and Antigua. ✉ Pl. du Marche, rue Victor Hugo, St-Pierre ☎ 0825/01–01–25, 0596/78–11–50 ⊕ www. jeansforfreedom.com.

L'Express des Îles. Connecting Martinique with Dominica, St. Lucia, and Guadeloupe, the ferry company also serves Guadeloupe's "out-islands," Marie-Galante and Les Saintes—from Point-A-Pitre, Guadeloupe (one-way €26, round-trip €43). Each one-way trip is €79, but round-trip tickets are just €119. The crossings generally take between three and four hours; if it is raining and the waters are choppy, it can be a rough passage. However, the newest ferry is much larger and stabilized and gives a smooth ride. French films (sometimes R-rated) on flat screens help pass the time. Most of these services are daily, with extra departures on weekends and holidays or for special events—the ferries can often get crowded then. Boats depart from the Terminal Inter Îles–Quai Ouest in Fort-de-France; head there for to-go options that are better than what the boats' snack bars carry; the ferry doesn't always get its food delivery, so it pays to bring some snacks aboard. There are discounted fares for babies, youths, seniors, and families. Note that the ferry charges for luggage that exceeds its weight limits. If traveling from Martinique to Dominica, Guadeloupe, or St. Lucia, a passenger is allowed three pieces of luggage that weigh no more than 25 kg (55 pounds) each; if traveling from Guadeloupe to its out-islands, Les Saintes and Marie-Galante, you're allowed one less bag. In either direction, you're also allowed to carry on one piece of baggage that weighs 10 kg (22 pounds) or less. Be aware that this ferry company also follows airline rules for what you're allowed to pack inside checked and carry-on baggage; check the website for more information. If traveling on a weekend or a French holiday, it is best to reserve and buy tickets online or at the terminal's ticket booth, in advance. ⊠ *Terminal Inter Isles Quai Ouest, Fort-de-France* ☎ *0825/35–90–00, 0590/91–98–53 in Guadeloupe* ⊕ *www.express-des-iles.com.*

TAXI TRAVEL

Taxis, which are metered, are expensive, though you can try bargaining by offering to pay a flat rate to your destination or offering them an hourly rate—try for €40, but you may have to compromise at €50. Taxis generally charge substantially more at night and on Sunday.

Contacts J. Peloponese Taxis. ☎ *0696/25–61–02.* **M. Martial Mercedes Taxis.** ☎ *0596/64–20–24, 0696/45–69–07 mobile.* **Taxi de Place.** ⊠ *Rue Victoire sévre, Fort-de-France* ☎ *0696/31–91–05.*

HEALTH AND SAFETY

In Fort-de-France, an increased police presence and video cameras have helped lower the crime rate. However, you should exercise the same safety precautions you would in any large city. It's best to go downtown at night only as part of a group, preferably of Martinicans. Never leave jewelry, money, or designer sunglasses unattended on the beach or in your car. Keep your laptop under wraps, even in your hotel room, and put valuables in hotel safes.

Dengue, chikungunya, and zika have all been reported throughout the Caribbean. We recommend that you protect yourself from these mosquito-borne illnesses by keeping your skin covered and/or wearing mosquito repellent. The mosquitoes that transmit these viruses are as active by day as they are by night.

HOTELS AND RESORTS

At Martinique, you can stay in tiny inns called *relais créoles,* boutique hotels, and private villas as well as splashy tourist resorts and restored plantation houses. Several hotels are clustered in Pointe du Bout on Les Trois-Ilets Peninsula, which is connected to Fort-de-France by ferry. Other clusters are in Ste-Luce, and Le François has become known for its boutique properties. Hotels and relais can be found all over the island. Because Martinique is the largest of the Windward Islands, this can mean a substantial drive to your hotel after a long flight or ferry trip. You may want to stay closer to the airport on your first night—for instance, at the Hotel Galleria, a no-nonsense hotel within a shopping mall just 10 minutes from the airport, or at a hotel in Fort-de-France. Brand new in the city is the Simon Hotel, part of the Pointe Simon project that includes luxury apartments. If you need to make a last-minute hotel reservation, head for the Tourism Information counter in the airport arrival hall (☏ 0596/42–18–05); it is open between 8 am and 9 pm every day except Sunday, when it's open from 2 pm to 9 pm.

Large Resorts: There are only a few deluxe properties on the island. Those that lack megastar ratings offer an equally appealing mixture of charisma, hospitality, and French style. Larger hotels often have the busy, slightly frenetic feel that the French seem to like.

Relais Créoles: Small, individually owned inns are still available on Martinique, though they may be far removed from the resorts.

Villas: Groups and large families can save money by renting a villa, but the language barrier can be problematic, and often you will need a car.

Hotel reviews have been shortened. For full information, visit Fodors.com.

WHAT IT COSTS IN EUROS				
	$	$$	$$$	$$$$
RESTAURANTS	under €12	€12–€20	€21–€30	over €30
HOTELS	under €275	€275–€375	€376–€475	over €475

Restaurant prices are the average cost of a main course at dinner or, if dinner is not served, at lunch. Hotel prices are the lowest cost of a standard double room in high season.

VISITOR INFORMATION

Contacts Comité Martiniquais du Tourisme. ⊠ *Immeuble Beaupre, Pointe de Jaham, Schoelcher* ☏ *0596/61–61–77* ⊕ *www.martiniquetourisme.com.* **Martinique Promotion Bureau.** ⊠ *825 3rd Ave., 29th fl., New York* ☏ *212/838–6887 in New York* ⊕ *www.martinique.org.* **Office du Tourisme de Fort-de-France.** ⊠ *76 rue Lazare Carnot, Fort-de-France* ☏ *0596/60–27–73* ⊕ *www.tourismefdf.com.*

EXPLORING

The northern part of the island will appeal to nature lovers, hikers, and mountain climbers. The drive from Fort-de-France to St-Pierre is particularly impressive, as is the one across the island, via Morne Rouge, from the Caribbean to the Atlantic. This is Martinique's wild side—a place of waterfalls, rain forest, and mountains. The highlight is Mont Pelée. The south is the more developed half of the island, where the resorts and restaurants are located, as well as the beaches.

FORT-DE-FRANCE

With its historic fort and superb location beneath the towering Pitons du Carbet on the Baie des Flamands, Martinique's capital—home to about one-quarter of the island's 400,000 inhabitants—should be a grand place. It wasn't for decades, but it's now coming up fast. The bay has received the designation One of the Most Beautiful Bays in the World. An ambitious redevelopment project, still ongoing, hopes to make it one of the most attractive cities in the Caribbean.

There is a small Office of Tourism de Fort-de-France at 76 rue Lazare Carnot. It has some brochures in English and helpful, English-speaking staffers. They can organize English-language tours with advance notice. Walking tours are scheduled for Wednesday and Friday at 9 am. They take in a number of historic sites in about an hour and 45 minutes and cost €12. Another Point d'Information Touristique is near the cathedral, at the junction of rues Antoine Siger and Victor Schoelcher. Also, Kiosk number 1 in La Savane is another location for the helpful tourism people; one can now arrange a tour to Fort Louis at that kiosk.

The Stewards Urbains, easily recognized by their red caps and uniforms, are able to answer most visitor questions about the city and give directions. These young gals and *garçons* are multilingual and knowledgeable. When a large cruise ship is in port, they are out in force, positioned in heavily trafficked tourist zones and at the front entrance of Lafayette's department store.

The most pleasant districts of Fort-de-France—Didier, Bellevue, and Schoelcher—are up on the hillside, and you need a car (or a taxi) to reach them. But if you try to drive here, you may find yourself trapped in gridlock in the narrow streets downtown. Parking is difficult, and it's best to try for one of the garages or—as a second choice—outdoor public parking areas. Come armed with some euro coins for this purpose. A taxi or ferry from Pointe du Bout may be a better alternative. Even if your hotel isn't there, you can drive to the marina and park nearby.

There are some fine shops with Parisian wares (at Parisian prices), including French lingerie, St. Laurent clothes, Cacharel perfume, and sexy stiletto heels. Near the harbor is a lively indoor marketplace (*grand marché*), where produce and spices are sold.

A playground on the Malecón, which now has a half-mile wooden boardwalk, has swings, trampolines, benches, and grounds for playing *pétanque*. The urban beach between the Malecón and the fort, La Française, is covered with white sand that was brought in.

TOP ATTRACTIONS

La Savane. The heart of Fort-de-France, La Savane is a 12½-acre park filled with trees, fountains, and benches. A massive revitalization made it the focal point of the city again, with entertainment, shopping, and a pedestrian mall. Attractive wooden stands have been constructed along the edge of the park that house a tourism information office, public restrooms, arts-and-crafts vendors, a crepe stand, an ice-cream stand, and numerous other eateries. Although homeless people frequent the park, they generally do not bother anyone.

12

The Hotel L'Imperatrice, directly across from the park, has become a real gathering place—particularly for its café, which opens to the sidewalk. The hotel also has one of the best kiosks in the Savane for lunch and snacks. The newer Fort Savane, a residence (apartments) for the business and leisure market, is also right across from its namesake park. The Simon Hotel is a short stroll away.

Diagonally across from La Savane, you can catch the ferries for the 20-minute run across the bay to Pointe du Bout and the beaches at Anse-Mitan and Anse-à-l'Ane. It's relatively cheap as well as stress-free—much safer, more pleasant, and faster than by car.

The most imposing historic site in Fort-de-France is **Ft. St-Louis**, which runs along the east side of La Savane. Now a military installation, it's again open to the public. However, you have to arrange a guided tour in advance at the tourism kiosk. ⊠ *Fort-de-France.*

WORTH NOTING

Fort St. Louis. Fort Saint Louis (Lou-ee), an imposing stone fortress that has guarded the island's principal port city for some 375 years, was closed to the public after 9/11, when it was reinstated as an active naval base by the French Navy. The fort officially reopened to the public on July 20, 2014, though it was shuttered in late 2015 for major renovations.

On a hilltop, originally carved out from a rocky promontory jutting out into the Bay of Fort-de-France, at its highest point it towers nearly 200 feet over the city, affording visitors panoramic views of the surrounding seaside urban landscape. A view-experience and photo op, with a spyglass one could see any threatening warships coming for miles in advance . . . location, location.

Guided tours are available in English, French, Spanish, and Italian. Walking shoes are recommended. Visitors must first check in at the Fort-de-France Office de Tourisme information kiosk 1, at the northwest corner of La Savane, at the intersection of rue de la Liberté and boulevard Alfassa. ⊠ *Bd. Chevalier, Sainte-Marthe, Fort-de-France* ☎ *0596/75–41–44* ⊕ *www.tourismefdf.com* 🖃 €8 ⊗ *Tues.–Sat. 9–4.*

Musée d'Archéologie Précolombienne et de Préhistoire. A hidden treasure with an unassuming entrance, it is just down the street from the hotel l'Imperatrice. A multistory archaeological museum, it houses some 2,000 artifacts that go way back to the era when Indians were the indigenous inhabitants. If luck is with you, an English-speaking guide will make it all come alive. Young boys take to this museum, "digging" the early peashooters, poison darts, hammocks that took a year to make, and the shaman's headdress. Women are fascinated by the jewelry fashioned from natural materials, boar tusks, and exotic bird feathers. A good time to sample this dose of prehistory is on a typically hot city day, for the air-conditioning is frigid. ⊠ *9 rue de Liberté, Fort-de-France* ☎ *0596/71–57–05* 🖃 €4.

Musée d'Histoire et d'Ethnographie. This museum is best undertaken at the beginning of your vacation, so you can better understand the history, background, and people of the island. Housed in an elaborate, former military residence (circa 1888) with balconies and fretwork, the museum displays some of the garish gold jewelry that prostitutes wore after emancipation as well as the sorts of rooms that a proper, middle-class Martinican would have lived in. Oil paintings, engravings, and old historical documents also help sketch out the island's culture. ⊠ *10 bd. Général de Gaulle, Fort-de-France* ☎ *0596/72–81–87* ⊠ *€4* ⊙ *Mon. and Wed.–Fri. 8:30–5, Tues. 2–5, Sat. 8–noon.*

Rue Victor Schoelcher. Stores sell Paris fashions and French perfume, china, crystal, and liqueurs, as well as local handicrafts along this street running through the center of the capital's primary shopping district, a six-block area bounded by rue de la République, rue de la Liberté, rue Victor Severe, and rue Victor Hugo. ⊠ *Fort-de-France.*

Schoelcher. Pronounced shell- *share,* this upscale suburb of Fort-de-France is home to the University of the French West Indies and Guyana, as well as Martinique's largest convention center, Palais de Congres de Madiana. Schoelcher was named after abolitionist Victor Schoelcher, who is credited with ending slavery on the island. ⊠ *Schoelcher.*

St-Louis Cathedral. This Romanesque cathedral with lovely stained-glass windows was built in 1878, the sixth church on this site (the others were destroyed by fires, hurricanes, and earthquakes). Classified as a historical monument, it has a marble altar, an impressive organ, and carved wooden pulpits. ⊠ *Rue Victor Schoelcher, Schoelcher* ☎ *0596/60–59–00* ⊙ *Daily 6:30 am–11:30 am. Church services Sun. 7:30–10:30 am; Tues., Wed., and Fri. 6:45 am; Sat. 6:30 pm.*

SOUTH OF FORT-DE-FRANCE

LE FRANÇOIS

With some 16,000 inhabitants, this is the main city on the Atlantic coast. Many of the old wooden buildings remain and are juxtaposed with concrete structures. The classic West Indian cemetery, with its black-and-white tiles, is still here, and a marina is at the end of town. Two of Martinique's best hotels are in this area (Cap Est and Hotel Plein Soleil), as well as some of the island's most upscale residences and most visited distillery/museum, Habitation Clément. Le François is also noted for its snorkeling. Offshore are the privately owned Ilets de l'Impératrice. The islands received that name because, according to legend, this is where Empress Joséphine came to bathe in the shallow basins known as *les fonds blanc* because of their white-sand bottoms. Group boat tours leave from the harbor and include lunch and drinks and one can even buy a package that includes an overnight stay on the remote and romantic, Isle de Oscar. Prices vary. You can also haggle with a fisherman to take you out for a while on his boat. There's a fine bay 6 miles (10 km) farther along the coast where you can swim and go kayaking. The town itself is rather lackluster but authentic, and you'll find a number of different shops and supermarkets, owned by truly lovely, helpful residents.

TOP ATTRACTIONS

Fodor's Choice ★ **Habitation Clément.** Get a glimpse into Martinique's colonial past. Visitors are given a multilingual audio headset, which explains tour highlights. Signage further describes the rum-making process and other

12

aspects of plantation life. The Palm Grove, with an avenue of palms and park benches, is delightful. It was all built with the wealth generated by its rum distillery, and its 18th-century splendor has been lovingly preserved. The plantation's creole house illustrates the adaption to life in the tropics up through the 20th century. An early French typewriter, a crank-up telephone, and decades-old photos of the Cléments and Hayots (béké families), are juxtaposed with modern Afro-Caribbean art. Enjoy the free tastings at the bar of the retail shop. Consider the Canne Bleu, Grappe Blanche, or one of the aged rums, some bottled as early as 1952. ■TIP→ **Children get a discount, but so do parents with children! Also, allow 1½–2 hours to see everything. The ticket office closes at 5.** ⊠ *Domaine de l'Acajou, Le François* ☎ *0596/54–62–07* ⊕ *www.habitation-clement.fr* ⊡ *€12* ☉ *Daily 9–6.*

LES TROIS-ÎLETS

Named after the three rocky islands nearby, this lovely little village (population 3,000) has unusual brick-and-wood buildings roofed with antique tiles. It's known for its pottery, straw, and woodwork, but above all as the birthplace of Napoléon's empress, Joséphine. In the square, where there's also a market and a fine *mairie* (town hall), you can visit the simple church where she was baptized Marie-Joseph Tascher de la Pagerie. The Martinicans have always been enormously proud of Joséphine, even though her husband reintroduced slavery on the island and most historians consider her to have been rather shallow.

ELSEWHERE SOUTH OF FORT-DE-FRANCE

TOP ATTRACTIONS

Diamond Rock. This volcanic mound, 1 mile (1½ km) offshore from the small, friendly village of Le Diamant, is one of the island's best diving spots. In 1804, during the squabbles over possession of the island between the French and the English, the latter commandeered the rock, armed it with cannons, and proceeded to use it as a strategic battery. The British held the rock for nearly a year and a half, attacking any French ships that came along. The French got wind that the British were getting cabin fever on their isolated island and arranged for barrels of rum to float up on the rock. The French easily overpowered the inebriated sailors, ending one of the most curious engagements in naval history. ⊠ *Le Diamant.*

Le Marin. The yachting capital of Martinique, Le Marin is also known for its colorful August carnival and its Jesuit church, circa 1766. From Le Marin a narrow road leads to picturesque Cap Chevalier, about 1 mile (1½ km) from town. Most of the buildings are white and very European. The marina, a hub for charter boats, is often buzzing with charter sailboats departing and celebrities on impressive yachts pulling in. There are waterfront restaurants and clubs that are a magnet for the younger crowd as well as for sailors and tourists at large. ⊠ *Le Marin* ⊕ *www.marin-martinique.fr/agenda.*

Pointe du Bout. This tourist area has a marina and several resort hotels, among them the deluxe Hotel Bakoua and the newly renovated Hôtel La Pagerie. The ferry to Fort-de-France leaves from here. The Village Creole complex with its "residences" for tourists, its cluster of boutiques,

Diamond Rock is one of the island's top dive sites.

ice-cream parlors, and rental-car agencies, forms the hub from which various restaurants and hotels radiate. It's a pretty quiet place in the low season. The beach at Anse-Mitan, which is a little west of Pointe du Bout proper, is one of the best on the island. There are also several small restaurants and inexpensive guesthouses there. The abandoned public housing, a dreadful eyesore, has been demolished. Similarly, the skeleton of the former Kalenda hotel is now being emptied of its asbestos, and the demolition starts in April after the season. ⊠ *Les Trois-Îlets.*

WORTH NOTING

Forêt de Montravail. A few miles north of Ste-Luce, this tropical rain forest is ideal for a short hike. Look for the interesting group of Carib rock drawings. ⊠ *Le Diamant.*

NEED A BREAK?

Le Grand Trianon Boulangerie. If you need a fast French lunch break in Le François, try this bakery, which is in town, near the Carrefour Supermarket. Crisp baguettes and luscious pastries and ice cream are sold, as are prix-fixe lunches with sandwiches or salads. French ladies love to "do lunch" here. ⊠ *Centre Cial Ancienne Usine, Le François* ☏ *0596/77–46–01.*

Le Vauclin. The return of the fishermen at noon is the big event in this important fishing port on the Atlantic. There's also the 18th-century Chapel of the Holy Virgin. Nearby is the highest point in the south, Mont Vauclin (1,654 feet). A hike to the top rewards you with one of the best views on the island. The Hotel Cap Macabou has added activity and tourism to this quiet town. Brand new is Le Village de la Pointe, a self-catering cottage complex, and an even less expensive option. ⊠ *Le Vauclin.*

12

Ste-Anne. A long, nearly white-sand beach and a Catholic church are the highlights of this town on the island's southern tip. A bevy of small, inexpensive cafés offer seafood and creole dishes, pizza parlors, produce markets, and barbecue joints—it's a fun and lively place. To the south of Ste-Anne is Pointe des Salines, the southernmost tip of the island and site of one of Martinique's best beaches. ⊠ *Ste-Anne.*

Ste-Luce. This quaint fishing village has a sleepy main street with tourist shops and markets, and you can see some cool types taking a Pernod. Many young, single people live in this town. From the sidewalk cafés there are panoramic sea views of St. Lucia. Nearby are excellent beaches, nearly white, and several resorts, including three from the Karibea Hotel chain. To the east is Pointe Figuier, an excellent spot for scuba diving. On the way, the Trois-Rivières Distillery is just off the highway, and Club Med is nearby, on its own peninsula. ⊠ *Ste-Luce.*

NORTH OF FORT-DE-FRANCE

BALATA

This quiet little town has two sights worth visiting. Built in 1923 to commemorate those Martinicans who fought and died in World War I, **Balata Church** is an exact replica of Paris's Sacré-Coeur Basilica. The gardens, **Jardin de Balata,** are lovely.

Jardin de Balata (*Balata Gardens*). The Jardin de Balata has thousands of varieties of tropical flowers and plants; its owner is a dedicated horticulturist. There are shaded benches from which to take in the mountain views and a plantation-style house furnished with period furniture. An aerial path gives visitors an astounding, bird's-eye view of the gardens and surrounding hills, from wooden walkways suspended 50 feet in the air. There is no restaurant, though beverages are for sale. This worthy site shows why Martinique is called the Island of Flowers. It's 15 minutes from Fort-de-France, in the direction of St-Pierre. You can order anthuriums and other tropical flowers to be delivered to the airport from the mesmerizing flower boutique here. ■ TIP➡ The gardens close at 6, but the ticket office will not admit anyone after 4:30. Children get a discount. ⊠ *Km. 10, rte. de Balata, Balata* ☎ *0596/64–48–73* ⊕ *www. jardindebalata.fr* ⊠ *€12.80* ☉ *Daily 9–6.*

ST-PIERRE

The rise and fall of St-Pierre is one of the most remarkable stories in the Caribbean and one of its worst disasters. Martinique's modern history began here in 1635. By the turn of the 20th century St-Pierre was a flourishing city of 30,000, known as the Paris of the West Indies. As many as 30 ships at a time stood at anchor. By 1902 it was the most modern town in the Caribbean, with electricity, phones, and a tram. On May 8, 1902, two thunderous explosions rent the air. As the nearby volcano erupted, Mont Pelée split in half, belching forth a cloud of burning ash, poisonous gas, and lava that raced down the mountain at 250 mph. At 3,600°F, it instantly vaporized everything in its path; 30,000 people were killed in two minutes.

The **Cyparis Express,** a small tourist train, will take you around to the main sights with running narrative (in French) for an hour Monday through Saturday, starting at 11 am, with reservations (☎ *0596/55–50–92, 0696/81–88–70*) for €12.

An Office du Tourisme is on the *moderne* seafront promenade. Stroll the main streets and check the blackboards at the sidewalk cafés before deciding where to lunch. At night some places have live music. Like stage sets for a dramatic opera, there are the ruins of the island's first church (built in 1640), the imposing theater, and the toppled statues. This city, situated on its naturally beautiful harbor and with its narrow, winding streets, has the feel of a European seaside hill town. With every footstep, you touch a page of history. Although many of the historic buildings need work, stark modernism has not invaded this burg.

TOP ATTRACTIONS

Fodor'sChoice ★

Depaz Distillery. An excursion to Depaz Distillery is one of the best things to do on the island. Established in 1651, it sits at the foot of the volcano. After a devastating eruption in 1902, the fields of blue cane were replanted, and in time, the rum-making began all over again. A self-guided tour includes the workers' gingerbread cottages. The tasting room sells its rums, including golden and aged rum, and liqueurs made from orange, ginger, and basil, among other flavors, that can enhance your cooking. Unfortunately, the plantation's great house, or château, is still closed to the public. Allow time and make a reservation for Depaz's restaurant, **Le Moulin a Canne** (☎ *0596/69–80–44*). Open only for lunch—even on Sunday when the distillery is closed, it has the views, the service, and flavorful creole specialties as well as some French classics on the menu, plus—you guessed it—Depaz rum to wash it down. It's "on the house." ■TIP→ **Shutters are drawn at the tasting room and the staff leaves at exactly 5 pm (or 4 on Saturday), so plan to be there at least an hour before.** ⊠ *Mont Pelée Plantation, St-Pierre* ☎ *0596/78–13–14* ⊕ *www.depazrhum.com* ⊠ *Distillery free* ☉ *Weekdays 10–5, Sat. 9–4.*

FAMILY

Musée Vulcanologique Frank Perret. For those interested in Mont Pelée's eruption of 1902, the Musée Vulcanologique Frank Perret is a must. It was established in 1933 by Frank Perret, a noted American volcanologist. Small but fascinating and insightful, the museum houses photographs of the old town before and after the eruption, documents, and a number of relics—some gruesome—excavated from the ashy ruins, including molten glass, melted iron, the church bell, and contorted clocks stopped at 8 am. The 30-minute film is a good way to begin. An English-speaking guide is often available and may tell you that the next lava flow is expected within 50 years. (No wonder the price of real estate in St. Pierre is among the lowest on the island.) The museum requires a renovation, and some signage has become difficult to read. ⊠ *Rue Victor Hugo (D10) at rue du Theatre, St-Pierre* ☎ *0596/78–15–16* ⊠ *€5* ☉ *Daily 9–5.*

STE-MARIE

The winding, hilly route to this town of some 20,000 offers breathtaking views of the rugged Atlantic coastline. Ste-Marie is the commercial capital of the island's north. Look for a picturesque mid-19th-century

12

church here. Most come to the area to visit the St. James Distillery and its Musée du Rhum, but the north is also filled with immense natural beauty.

Nearby in Marigot, Habitation La Grange, originally the great house on a grand banana plantation that was converted into a deluxe, historical hotel in the '90s, changed hands. The present owner, an architect, is currently involved in a major restoration, and it is slated to reopen as a boutique property in spring 2015.

St. James Distillery & Rum Museum. The Musée du Rhum, operated by the St. James Rum Distillery, is housed in a graceful, galleried creole house. Interestingly, the distillery was founded in 1765 in Ste-Pierre by a priest who was also an alchemist. It was relocated to Ste-Marie after the 1902 eruption of Mont Pelée. Guided tours can take in the plantation and the displays of the tools of the trade, the art gallery, and include a visit and tasting at the distillery. You can opt to take a little red train tour for €5 that traverses the cane fields and runs between here and the nearby banana museum, while a guide narrates; it runs on many Tuesday and Thursday mornings and Saturday afternoons. ■ TIP➔ **The museum and distillery are closed during the cane harvest, and weekend hours sometimes change; tours may not happen during December. It's a good idea to call ahead.** ✉ *Plan d l'union, St. James Distillery, Ste-Marie* ☎ *0596/69–30–02* ⊡ *Free* ☉ *Daily 9–5.*

ELSEWHERE NORTH OF FORT-DE-FRANCE

TOP ATTRACTIONS

Fodor'sChoice **La Distillerie J.M.** J.M. offers the most innovative and contemporary
★ exhibits in addition to tastings. Long considered to be among the top echelon of Martinique rums, it does not have the same name recognition as some of the other popular labels, like Clément, for example. That is partly because J.M.'s best *rhum vieux* is considerably more expensive than your average bottle. The 10-year-old vintages (44.8 proof) truly rival France's fine cognacs, and a tasting is among the complimentary offerings that are available. Displays allow you to inhale the various aromas of the products, from vanilla and orange to almonds and exotic fruits. Some of the visuals are very high-tech visuals. It is said that J.M. rum is made special by the pure mountain water of Macouba, where the outstanding rain forest is among the only sightseeing options. ■ TIP➔ **Plan to couple a visit to this destination distillery with one to Carbet and St. Pierre, then the Depaz Distillery, in time to take lunch at their fine restaurant. Then proceed to J.M. It is best to either have a either a designated driver, or hire an English-speaking driver for a half or full day.** ✉ *Macouba* ☎ *0596/78–92–55* ⊕ *www.rhum-jm.com* ⊡ *Free* ☉ *Daily 9–5.*

Le Morne Rouge. This town sits on the southern slopes of the volcano that destroyed it in 1902. Today it's a popular resort spot and offers hikers some fantastic mountain scenery. From Le Morne Rouge you can start the climb up the 4,600-foot **Mont Pelée.** But don't try scaling this volcano without a guide unless you want to get buried alive under pumice stones. Instead, drive up to L'Auberge de la Montagne Pelée. (Ask for a room with a view.) From the parking lot it's 1 mile (1½ km)

Le Morne Rouge

up a well-marked trail to the summit. Bring a hooded sweatshirt because there's often a mist that makes the air damp and chilly. From the summit follow the route de la Trace (Route N3), which winds south of Le Morne Rouge to St-Pierre. It's steep and winding, but that didn't stop the *porteuses* (female porters) of old: balancing a tray, these women would carry up to 100 pounds of provisions on their heads for the 15-hour trek to the Atlantic coast. ⊠ *Le Morne-Rouge.*

WORTH NOTING

Ajoupa-Bouillon. Near pineapple fields and filled with flowers, this 17th-century village is the jumping-off point for several sights. The Saut Babin, a 40-foot waterfall, is a half-hour walk from Ajoupa-Bouillon. The Gorges de la Falaise is a river gorge where you can swim. ⊠ *Ajoupa-Bouillon.*

Basse-Pointe. On the route to this village on the Atlantic coast at the island's northern end you pass many banana and pineapple plantations. Just south of Basse-Pointe is a **Hindu temple**, which was built by descendants of the East Indians who settled in this area in the 19th century. The view of Mont Pelée from the temple is memorable. ⊠ *Basse-Pointe.*

Bellefontaine. This colorful fishing village has pastel houses on the hillsides and beautifully painted *gommiers* (fishing boats) bobbing in the water. Look for the restaurant built in the shape of a boat. ⊠ *Bellefontaine.*

Le Prêcheur. This quaint village, the last on the northern Caribbean coast, is surrounded by volcanic hot springs. It was the childhood home of Françoise d'Aubigné, who later became the Marquise de

12

Maintenon and the second wife of Louis XIV. At her request, the Sun King donated the handsome bronze bell that still hangs outside the church. The Tomb of the Carib Indians commemorates a sadder event. It's a formation of limestone cliffs, from which the last of the Caraïbes are said to have flung themselves to avoid capture by the marquise's forebears. ⊠ *Le Prêcheur.*

Neisson Distillery. The producers of one of the best rums on the island, Neisson is a small, family-run operation. Its rum is distilled from pure sugarcane juice rather than molasses. The distillery is open for tours and tastings, and the shop sells *rhum extra-vieux* (vintage rum) that truly rivals cognac. Neisson is one of the distilleries that consistently brings home the gold (and the silver) from rum competitions in France. A passion for history and tradition characterizes the distillery, as does the design of its bottles. Proud of its independence, at a time when most distilleries are absorbed by large groups, the distillery is now run by the daughter and grandson of Hildevert Pamphille Neisson, who founded the distillery in 1931. ⊠ *Domaine Thieubeurt-Bourg, Carbet* ☎ *0596/78–03–70* ⊕ *www.neisson.com* ✉ *Free* ☉ *Weekdays 8:30–5, Sat. 8–noon.*

Presqu'île du Caravelle. Much of the Caravelle Peninsula, which juts 8 miles (13 km) into the Atlantic Ocean, is under the protection of the Regional Nature Reserve and offers places for trekking, swimming, and sailing. This is also the site of Anse-Spoutourne, an open-air sports and leisure center operated by the reserve. The town of Tartane has a popular surfing beach with brisk Atlantic breezes. Hotel La Caravelle is one of the better places to stay in this area. ⊠ *Tartane.*

DID YOU KNOW? One man survived the eruption of Mont Pelée. His name was Cyparis, and he was a prisoner in an underground cell in the town's jail, locked up for public drunkenness. Later, he went on the road with the Barnum & Bailey Circus as a sideshow attraction. Le Petit Train, that gives tours of the town, is named after him, "Cyparis Express."

BEACHES

Take to the beach in Martinique and experience the white sandbars known as Josephine's Baths, where Napoléon's Joséphine would bathe. All of Martinique's beaches are open to the public, but hotels charge a fee for nonguests to use chaise longues, changing rooms, and other facilities. There are no official nudist beaches, but topless bathing is prevalent, as is the case on most French islands. Unless you're an expert swimmer, steer clear of the Atlantic waters, except in the area of Cap Chevalier (Cape Knight) and the Presqu'île du Caravelle (Caravelle Peninsula). The white-sand beaches are south of Fort-de-France; to the north, the sand turns darker, and there are even beaches with silvery-black volcanic sand. Some of the most pleasant strips of sand are around Ste-Anne, Ste-Luce, and Havre du Robert. Some 15 minutes from Le François harbor, the white sandbars that form Josephine's Baths stand in the middle of the sea.

SOUTH OF FORT-DE-FRANCE

Anse Corps de Garde. On the southern Caribbean coast, this is one of the island's best long stretches of white sand. The public beach has picnic tables, restrooms, sea grape trees (which offer some shade), and crowds on weekends, when you'll also usually find plenty of wandering food vendors and the litter that follows them. During the week, the beach is much less busy, usually just with a few tourists and some local kids after school. The water is calm, with just enough wave action to remind you that it's the sea. There are no beach-chair rentals. From Fort-de-France, exit to the right before you get to the town of Ste-Luce. You first see signs for the Karibea Hotels and then one for Corps de Garde, which is on the right. At the stop sign take a left. **Amenities:** food and drink; toilets. **Best for:** partiers; swimming; walking. ⊠ *Ste-Luce.*

Anse-Mitan. There are often yachts moored offshore in these calm waters. This long stretch of beach can be particularly fun on Sunday. Small, family-owned seaside restaurants are half-hidden among palm trees and are footsteps from the lapping waves. Nearly all offer grilled lobster and some form of music on weekends, perhaps a zouk band. Inexpensive waterfront hotels line the clean, golden beach, which has excellent snorkeling just offshore. Chaise longues are available for rent from hotels, and there are also usually vendors on weekends. The abandoned public housing visible from the beach has finally been razed. When you get to Pointe du Bout, take a left at the yellow office of Budget Rent-A-Car, then the next left up a hill, and park near the little white church. **Amenities:** food and drink. **Best for:** partiers; snorkeling; swimming; walking. ⊠ *Pointe du Bout, Les Trois-Îlets.*

Anse Tartane. This patch of sand is on the wild side of the Presqu'île du Caravelle. Ungroomed and in a fairly natural state, it's what the French call a *sauvage* beach. The only people you are likely to see are brave surfers who ride the high waves or some local families. Bliss, the surf school here, has taught many kids. Résidence Oceane looks down on all of this action; it doesn't have a restaurant, but you can get a drink. **Amenities:** parking; toilets (at surf school); water sports. **Best for:** partiers; surfing; walking. ⊠ *Tartane, La Trinité* ⊹ *Turn right before you get to La Trinité, and follow the rte. de Château past the Caravelle hotel. Instead of following the signs to Résidence Oceane, veer left and go downhill when you see the ocean. The road runs right beside the beach. There are several bays and pointes here, but if you keep heading to the right, you can reach the surf school.*

Diamant Beach. The island's longest beach has a splendid view of Diamond Rock, but the Atlantic waters are rough, with lots of wave action—it's not known as a surfers' beach, though. Diamant is often deserted, especially midweek, which is more reason to be careful if you do go swimming. The sand is black here, and it is an experience to snorkel above it. Happily, it's a great place for picnicking and beachcombing; there are shade trees aplenty, and parking is abundant and free. The hospitable, family-run Diamant les Bains hotel is a good lunch spot; if you eat lunch there, the management may let you wash off in the pool overlooking the beach. From Les Trois-Îlets, go in the direction of

The town of St-Pierre is beneath the 4,600-foot Mont Pelée.

Rivière Salée, taking the secondary road to the east, toward Le Diamant. A coastal route, it leads to the beach. **Amenities:** food and drink; parking. **Best for:** solitude; snorkeling; walking. ⊠ *Le Diamant.*

FAMILY **Les Salines.** A short drive south of Ste-Anne brings you to a mile-long (1½-km-long) cove lined with soft white sand and coconut palms. The beach is awash with families and children during holidays and on weekends, but quiet during the week. The far end—away from the makeshift souvenir shops—is most appealing. The calm waters are safe for swimming, even for the kids. You can snorkel, but it's not that memorable. Food vendors roam the sand, and there are also pizza stands and simple seafood restaurants. From Le Marin, take the coastal road toward Ste-Anne. You will see signs for Les Salines. If you see the sign for Pointe du Marin, you have gone too far. **Amenities:** food and drink; parking; showers; toilets. **Best for:** partiers; swimming; walking. ⊠ *Ste-Anne.*

FAMILY **Pointe du Bout.** The beaches here are small, man-made, and lined with resorts. Each little strip is associated with its resident hotel, and security guards and closed gates make access difficult. However, if you take a left across from the main pedestrian entrance to the marina—after the taxi stand—then go left again, you will reach the beach for Hotel Bakoua, which has especially nice facilities and several options for lunch and drinks. If things are quiet—particularly during the week—one of the beach boys may rent you a chaise; otherwise, just plop your beach towel down, face forward, and enjoy the delightful view of the Fort-de-France skyline. The water is dead calm and quite shallow, but it eventually drops off if you swim out a bit. **Amenities:** food and drink; showers. **Best for:** snorkeling; sunset; swimming. ⊠ *Pointe du Bout, Les Trois-Îlets.*

Pointe du Marin. Stretching north from Ste-Anne, this is a good wind-surfing and waterskiing spot. It's also a popular family beach, with restaurants, campsites, and clean facilities available for a small fee. Club Med is on the northern edge, and you can purchase a day pass. From Le Marin, take the coastal road to Ste-Anne. Make a right before town, toward Domaine de Belfond. You can see signs for Pointe du Marin. **Amenities:** food and drink; toilets. **Best for:** swimming; walking; windsurfing. ⊠ *Ste-Anne.*

WHERE TO EAT

Martinique cuisine, a fusion of African and French, is certainly more international and sophisticated than that of its immediate island neighbors. The influx of young chefs, who favor a contemporary and lighter approach, has brought exciting innovations to the table. This haute-nouvelle creole cuisine emphasizes local products, predominantly starchy tubers such as plantains, white yams, yuca, and island sweet potatoes, as well as vegetables such as breadfruit, christophene (also known as chayote), and taro leaves. Many creole dishes have been Frenchified, transformed into mousselines, terrines, and gratins topped with creamy sauces. And then there's the bountiful harvest of the sea—*lambi* (conch), *langouste* (clawless local lobsters), and dozens of species of fish predominate, but you can also find *écrevisses* (freshwater crayfish, which are as luscious as jumbo prawns).

Some local creole specialties are *accras* (cod or vegetable fritters), which are the signature appetizer of Martinique, *crabes farcis* (stuffed land crab), and *feroce* (avocado stuffed with saltfish and farina). You can perk up fish and any other dish with a hit of hot *chien* (dog) sauce. Not to worry—it's made from onions, shallots, hot peppers, oil, and vinegar. To cool your jets, have a 'ti punch—four parts white rum and one part sugarcane syrup.

In Fort-de-France's city market, ladies serve up well-priced creole prix-fixe meals that can include accras, fricassee of octopus and conch, chicken in coconut milk, or grilled whole fish.

As for euro sticker shock, the consolation is that although menu prices may seem steep, they include tax and service. Prix-fixe menus, sometimes with wine, can help keep costs in line.

What to Wear. For dinner, casual resort wear is appropriate. Generally, men wear collared shirts. Women typically wear light cotton sundresses, short or long. At dinnertime, beach attire is too casual for most restaurants. Both the French (expats) ladies and the Martiniquais often "dress." They have an admirable French style, and almost always wear high heels.

SOUTH OF FORT-DE-FRANCE

$$$
FRENCH FUSION

✕ **Atomic Food.** Those who loved chef Damien Pelé's restaurant Fleur de Sel are getting a sense of the differences between it and this new spot (named after the eponymous song by David Guetta) that has opened in the same location, a 19th-century maison bourgeoise just past the village of Trois Ilets. The menu includes many vegetarian options, the ingredients are organic, and the dishes are wildly colorful with extravagant presentations. A new dining terrace has been added in the garden, and manning a bar made from recycled wood and local bamboo is a flamboyant barman, Antoine, a true mixologist. Tapas are served from 5 pm. As there is a Latin ambience, start the party with a cucumber mojito! Ⓢ *Average main: €24 ⊠ 27 av. de l'Impératrice Josephine, Les Trois-Îlets ☎ 0596/68–42–11 ⊙ Closed Sun. Aug.–Oct. No lunch Mar.–Dec.*

$
BAKERY

✕ **Coup d'Coeur.** If perusing the Poterie Village, look no farther for a lunch spot or a tea break. This *patisserie–salon de thé* is on the right, as you first enter the village. In fact, you might make this your daytime go-to restaurant if you are staying in Trois Ilets. When you open the front door, the aromas of fresh-baked goods will have you pressing your finger against the glass display case, euros clutched in your left hand, just like a little kid. Lunch can be a quiche (many varieties), pizza, or creative sandwich, and if you clean your plate then you can be rewarded with a Viennoiserie. Only French butter is used and all products are made in an artisanal manner. Table seating but not waiter service as such. Ⓢ *Average main: €10 ⊠ Village de la Poterie, Les Trois-Îlets ☎ 0596/69–70–32 ⊙ No dinner.*

$$$
SEAFOOD

✕ **La Baraqu' Obama.** If you're looking for a seafront restaurant that specialized in conch and lobster, Obama's is recommended. During lunchtime the alfresco terrace fills up mainly with French tourists supping on grilled lobster with either saltfish or black pudding or veggies, and a dessert. Aromas are drool-worthy with hints of lemon and melted butter. Main courses come with *frites* or rice, and some vegetables and greenery dressed with vinaigrette. There's plenty of Red Desperado (a local beer) and French rosé to wash it all down. The kitchen is across the street, as is the ice cream shop (with excellent tropical fruit flavors) and the Special Bar. Owner Patrick Henry put it together for his son who rocks it on weekends, with salsa on Friday nights. A 4-foot poster of Obama is the major work of art. Ⓢ *Average main: €24 ⊠ Bord de Mer, bd. Kennedy, Ste-Luce ☎ 0696/80–78–75.*

$$$$
FRENCH

✕ **Le Bélem.** This special-occasion restaurant for the well-heeled offers innovative cuisine served in a contemporary, romantic setting, with a bevy of servers who try hard to please, but some diners feel that the menu is too limited. However, a new chef, Jordan Delamotte, has arrived from Paris and seems passionate about reinventing the Franco-Caribbean menu using local ingredients on his ever-changing menu. But you can usually find some preparation of red snapper and an exquisite chocolate soufflé. Start with a cocktail in the super-chic bar lined with old black-and-white photographs of the island; a simple 'ti punch gets an elaborate presentation. ■TIP→ **Although less glamorous, lunch at Campeche, the hotel's beach restaurant, is still a treat, and provides a more affordable alternative.** Ⓢ *Average main: €32 ⊠ Cap Est Lagoon*

12

Resort & Spa, Quartier Cap Est, Le François ☎ *0596/54–80–80* ⊘ *Closed some nights in low season. No lunch* ⌒ *Reservations essential.*

$$
FRENCH FUSION

✕ **Le Pitaya.** This is one hotel restaurant that is not only surprisingly good but affordable. The menu changes nightly, but many items do find their way back regularly. The most economical choice is usually the menu du jour, a modestly priced prix fixe of three courses. A favorite appetizer is the salmon gravlax; among the main courses, shrimp and scallops never disappoint. Desserts range from an upside-down banana tart to a classic chocolate fondant. Lobster is always available—as a grilled half lobster with an assortment of sauces. Relatively small, but open-air and overlooking the dramatically lit pool, it is best for outside guests to reserve. $ *Average main: €20* ✉ *Hotel La Pagerie, rue Chacha, Pointe du Bout, Les Trois-Îlets* ☎ *0596/66–61–54* ⊕ *www. hotel-lapagerie.com* ⌒ *Reservations essential.*

$$$$
FRENCH FUSION
Fodor'sChoice
★

✕ **Le Plein Soleil Restaurant.** Perennially popular with the chic set, Le Plein Soleil's restaurant has a smashing contemporary, creole look. But it's the inventive, beautifully executed menu that cements its well-deserved reputation. It continues to draw applause for the use of the latest techniques from France coupled with remarkable twists on local products. Take a long and leisurely lunch on the terrace, which has a hilltop sea view; by night the mood is romantic, the service fine, the music heady. Soups are like a mixed-media collage. A velouté can be the canvas for a ravioli made of foie gras or pineapple. For the evening's three-course prix-fixe dinner, a thick tuna steak often appears as a main course, but you'll always have a choice of five main courses, two of which are fresh lobster and a steak. Desserts are equally memorable. $ *Average main: €45* ✉ *Hôtel Le Plein Soleil, Pointe Thalèmont, Le François* ☎ *0596/38–07–77* ⊕ *hotelpleinsoleil.fr* ⊘ *No lunch Mon.–Thurs. No dinner Sun.* ⌒ *Reservations essential.*

$$$$
FRENCH FUSION
Fodor'sChoice
★

✕ **Le Zandoli.** Although "le zandoli" is the creole term for the lowly gecko, there's nothing humble about the culinary presentation or the wildly colorful dining room here, which are as slick as anything you might encounter in Paris. The executive chef has worked in Michelin-starred restaurants in France and brings Southeast Asian techniques from his stint in Jakarta. At the start of the meal, an amuse-bouche or two will whet your appetite. The three-course, prix-fixe menu is continually evolving, affected by seasonal market finds and influenced by five continents—one common main is the fillet of beef with chanterelle mushrooms. ■TIP➔ **One can opt for just two courses for a lower price.** You may want to arrive for your dinner reservation early so that you can sit at the bar, which looks like an avant-garde movie set, and have a fanciful, fresh juice cocktail with tiny accoutrements. And in any given month there may be a reception and art exhibition, fashion show or a gala party. $ *Average main: €42* ✉ *La Suite Villa, rte. du Fort d'Alet, Anse Mitan, Les Trois-Îlets* ☎ *0596/59–88–00, 0696/73–73–23* ⊕ *www.la-suite-villa.com* ⊘ *No lunch* ⌒ *Reservations essential.*

$$$
MODERN FRENCH

✕ **Restaurant Le Golf.** You may not expect a golf course to house a great restaurant, but once you're at this terraced, alfresco location, you will find yourself wowed as you look out on acres of rolling greens and the turquoise blue of the Caribbean beyond. The real accomplishment,

CLOSE UP

Dining in Martinique

Dining in Martinique is a delightful culinary experience, but as with driving here, it is best to get some directions before you head out. First of all, as in France, *entrées* are appetizers; the main courses will usually be labeled as follows: *poissons* (fish); *viandes* (meat); or *principal plats* (main dishes). The appetizers are almost as expensive as the mains—and if the appetizer is foie gras, you'll pay just as much as for a main course.

Entrecôte is a sirloin steak, usually cut thin. A filet mignon is a rarity, but you will see *filet mignon du porc,* which is pork tenderloin. *Ecrivesses* (known also as *ouassous* or *z'habitants*) are incredible freshwater crayfish, usually served with their heads on. Similarly, if a fish dish does not specify fillet, it will be served whole—bones, stones, and eyeballs.

Every respectable restaurant has an admirable wine *carte*, and the offerings will be almost completely French, with few half bottles. Wines by the glass are often swill and best avoided.

Finally, don't ever embarrass yourself by asking for a doggie bag, unless you're willing to risk being considered gauche.

however, is on the plates. This chef can elevate a torchon de foie gras or red snapper fillet to fine art. And the food is usually light enough to allow room for one of the rich and satisfying desserts. Theme nights, concerts, and musical entertainment are worth experiencing. Frederic Vasson, the main entertainer here, has opened L'Annex in Marin at the new port. [$] *Average main: €25* ✉ *Golf de Trois-Îlets, Quartier la Pagerie, Les Trois-Îlets* ☎ *0596/48–20–84* 🕒 *No dinner Sun. and Mon.*

FORT-DE-FRANCE AND POINTS NORTH

$$ SEAFOOD 🍴 **Chez Les Pecheurs.** At the sign of the billfish, you'll find the kind of beach restaurant you search for but seldom find, a "feet-in-the-sand" spot opened by a real fisherman. Come for the fisherman's platter, *literally* the catch of the day (which could be *loup de mer*, flying fish, marlin, even sea bass or tuna) with a flavorful red sauce, ripe tomatoes, perfect red beans and rice, and lentil salad (though not all the fish these days is fresh, and the cutlery may be plastic). Grilled crayfish is usually available Thursday through Saturday. Bottles of Neisson rum are plunked in front of a table of the convivial groups of diners here. Don't be surprised if you are told to share a table. Service, mostly pleasant, slows when 30 people sit down. However, not all customers are leaving happy now. Fridays are the big nights, when local bands play and everyone dances on the sand. [$] *Average main: €19* ✉ *Le Bord de Mer, Carbet* ☎ *0596/76–98–39, 0696/23–95–59* 🕒 *No dinner Sun.*

$$$ FRENCH 🍴 **La Cave à Vins.** After you ring the bell, someone will peek out (as in a speakeasy), and the front door of this landmark restaurant will open on a small shop selling French food items, chocolates, and fine wine. Behind the sales floor are two dining rooms, the first modern and whimsical, the second with murals of the French countryside and an

impressive, domed skylight that compensates somewhat for the lack of windows. Meals begin with an amuse-bouche, such as coriander sorbet. One signature dish is duck breast Rossini (with foie gras) finished with a sauce of morels. Contemporary desserts complement such richness; mango pie topped with vanilla ice cream is Martinique's answer to our apple pie. The menu is the same for lunch and dinner, with not much in the way of light fare. It is likely the proprietress, Madame Clementine, will serve you well; it all makes for a most gracious experience. $ Average main: €30 ⊠ 124 rue Victor-Hugo, Fort-de-France ☎ 0596/70–33–02 ⊘ Closed Aug. No dinner Sun. and Mon.

$$
BISTRO
✕ **Le Foyaal Bar & Brasserie.** This versatile brasserie on Fort-de-France's main drag offers a large open dining space and seating on a covered terrace with a view of the sea, though traffic, noise, and dust make eating inside a safer bet. For a light lunch you could have a savory crepe and a small salad, smoked marlin, fried Camembert, or a perfect burger. If you want to go with something more substantial, and creative, there's local octopus or duck in a citrusy sauce. Some waiters speak English, and most are fun and helpful. ■TIP→ Foyaal serves from 7 am into the late night, 1:30 am, even on Sundays when most of the town is closed up. Try sitting at the bar; it's fun and for a lot of French expats, this is their "Cheers." Upstairs at Le Césaire is a more refined (and expensive) dining experience. $ Average main: €20 ⊠ Bord de Mer, 38 rue de Ernest Proges, Fort-de-France ☎ 0596/63–00–38.

$$
SEAFOOD
✕ **Le Petibonum.** This marriage of French island funkiness and South Beach gloss is one-of-a-kind in Martinique. So is charismatic owner Guy Ferdinand, a tall Martinican with curly, blond-streaked hair, who has made this a destination restaurant in the north coast's tiny town of Carbet. Smack on the beach, it's an ideal stopover if you're visiting nearby St-Pierre. So remember to wear your swimsuit, kick off your shoes, and order a perfect mojito. You can lounge on coral rubber chaises, shaded by umbrellas, and be sprayed intermittently with a gentle, cool mist. The appetizers—blue marlin tartare or fried flying fish right from the Carbet shore—are delicious, as are main courses such as the signature jumbo crayfish in a vanilla sauce. There's lobster on Friday nights, when local bands play. It's a scene. On the first Saturday of every month, a big beach party brings in DJs and no cover. $ Average main: €18 ⊠ Le Coin, Le Bord de Mer, Carbet ☎ 0596/78–04–34 ⊕ www.petibonum.com.

$$$$
FRENCH
✕ **Restaurant La Table de Mamy Nounou.** Although the name may sound like a local eatery, it's actually quite an upscale setting serving cuisine raffinée. Sip an aperitif while listening to the mesmerizing music and admiring the view from the lounge decorated with African art (there's free Wi-Fi, too). Chef Jean-Paul Mahler has been the recipient of a number of culinary awards, and his à la carte menu has become increasingly inventive over the years. After your amuse-bouche, dig into luxurious dishes such as foie gras or roasted monkfish. Finish with a mirabelle and vanilla parfait. Lunch is served outdoors on the terrace and has a simpler, less pricey menu, including some salads, even one with smoked chicken. $ Average main: €35 ⊠ L'Anse L'Etang, Tartane ☎ 0596/58–07–32 ⊕ hotel-la-caravelle-martinique.com ⊘ Closed Tues. and June and Sept. ⚑ Reservations essential.

WHERE TO STAY

Larger hotels usually include a big buffet breakfast of eggs, fresh fruit, cheese, yogurt, croissants, baguettes, jam, and café au lait. Smaller relais (inns) often have open-air, terrace kitchenettes. There are only a few hotels that still have rooms in which smoking is allowed. Most hotels do not have elevators, and many are built on hillsides, so if you have issues with stairs or with climbing paths, be sure to ask about that.

PRIVATE VILLAS AND CONDOS

If you're staying a week or longer, you can often save money by renting a villa or apartment with a kitchen for preparing your own meals. The more upscale rentals come with French-speaking maids and cooks. Don't forget to add the cost of a car rental to your vacation budget.

RENTAL CONTACTS

French Caribbean International. French Caribbean International, a highly professional English-speaking reservation service started in 1994 by Gerard Hill, can help you with both villa rentals and hotel rooms in Martinique; it covers all of the French West Indies and has an office in Santa Barbara, California. ⊠ *Santa Barbara* ☎ *805/967–9850 U.S. office* ⊕ *www.frenchcaribbean.com.*

PrestigeVillas. This online agency, which was started by a real go-getter from Guadeloupe, rents luxury villas throughout the French Caribbean. The useful website has photos of every room and detailed descriptions in English. Rental properties range from deluxe to over-the-top, including some that have been handpicked for celebratory occasions. Their concierge service can provision villas or arrange private chefs and housekeepers, orchestrate tours and shopping excursions, and set up in-house spa services. The owner writes an impressive blog with tips on "doing" the French islands. ⊠ *Santa Barbara* ☎ *917/267–7491 in U.S., 336/851–853–01* ⊕ *www.prestigevillarental.com.*

SOUTH OF FORT-DE-FRANCE

$$
RESORT
Fodor'sChoice
★
🛏 **Cap Est Lagoon Resort & Spa.** At Martinique's most exclusive resort, the caring staff strives to make sure that guests, housed in a series of contemporary villas decorated with Southeast Asian influences and (mostly) with views of the crystalline lagoon and private plunge pools, leave satisfied. **Pros:** large central infinity pool; really special lounge bar with a large selection of local rum; a genteel, aristocratic ambience. **Cons:** somewhat isolated; beach is not that big; not so much to do for longer stays. 💲 *Rooms from: €375* ⊠ *Quartier Cap Est, Le François* ☎ *0596/54–80–80, 800/735–2478* ⊕ *www.capest.com* ⇆ *52 suites in 18 villas* ❍ *Breakfast.*

$$$
RESORT
Fodor'sChoice
★
🛏 **Club Med Buccaneer's Creek.** One of the French chain's most upscale, sophisticated resorts offers a lot of fun, good food, and a huge, seaside pool with sensual Indonesian beds to an international mix of singles, couples, and families (though there is no kids' club). **Pros:** on one of the island's best beaches; even waterskiing is included; enjoyable,

professional entertainment in lounge before dinner. **Cons:** no small catamarans or windsurfing; no in-room Wi-Fi; rooms feel dated. $ *Rooms from: €368* ⊠ *Pointe Marin, Ste-Anne* ☎ *0596/76–72–72* ⊕ *www. clubmed.us* ⌁ *280 rooms, 12 suites* ⦿ *All-inclusive.*

$
RENTAL
▦ **Domaine de la Palmeraie.** Unique in Martinique, this complex of six villas is contemporary yet Caribbean, secluded amid acres of zenlike gardens yet a short drive to Diamant's beach and town, which is more of a slice of real island life than a tourist destination. **Pros:** private enclave and owner speaks English; whimsical children's rooms; desks and strong Wi-Fi. **Cons:** some might prefer to be closer to Trois-Îlets or other tourist areas; a rental car is almost a necessity; no air-conditioning in second-floor bedrooms except in the spacious Villa Papaye. $ *Rooms from: €165* ⊠ *Quartier Thoraille, Le Diamant* ☎ *0696/98–97–17* ⊕ *www. domainedelapalmeraie.com* ⌁ *6 villas* ⦿ *No meals.*

$
RESORT
▦ **Hotel Bakoua.** Wrought-iron gates open to this lovely hotel, a throwback to gracious estate living, where you can cocoon yourself in colonial-era style. **Pros:** vintage Caribbean charisma; you don't necessarily need a car; the breakfast buffet with omelet and crepe stations is memorable. **Cons:** some rooms are outdated and renovations have been long promised; facades are not all pretty; can be busy and loud on weekends. $ *Rooms from: €230* ⊠ *Pointe du Bout, Les Trois-Îlets* ☎ *0596/66–02–02* ⊕ *www.hotel-bakoua.fr/en* ⌁ *132 rooms, 6 suites* ⦿ *No meals.*

$
HOTEL
▦ **Hôtel La Pagerie.** For many years the keystone hotel in Pointe du Bout cried out for a metamorphosis, and a major renovation has finally raised it back to a level that U.S. travelers will want to experience. **Pros:** spacious, renovated guest rooms with new bedding; the helpful management and staff that warmly welcomes you; free Wi-Fi. **Cons:** service, while friendly, not always up to four-star standards; among guest complaints are no sea vistas (but pool views); in-room furnishings are not high-end. $ *Rooms from: €215* ⊠ *Rue Chacha, Pointe de Bout, Les Trois-Îlets* ☎ *0596/66–05–30* ⊕ *hotel-lapagerie.com* ⌁ *96 rooms* ⦿ *No meals.*

$
B&B/INN
Fodor's Choice
★
▦ **Hotel Plein Soleil.** Long one of our favorites, this heavenly hideaway is now a modern, Martinique landmark, with accommodations in creole *cases* (cottages)—painted red, purple, and subtle earth tones—with contemporary bathrooms, and terraces that maximize the glorious sea views. **Pros:** owner is on-site and accessible; sophisticated and artistic ambience is unique in Martinique; deluxe breakfast, albeit at an additional cost. **Cons:** rough road (particularly in rainy season) to somewhat remote, hilltop location; smallest rooms have small bathrooms; Wi-Fi is free but seldom works within guest accommodations. $ *Rooms from: €200* ⊠ *Pointe Thalèmont, Le François* ☎ *0596/38–07–77* ⊕ *www.hotelpleinsoleil.fr* ⊘ *Closed Sept.–mid-Oct.* ⌁ *12 rooms, 4 suites* ⦿ *No meals.*

$$
HOTEL
Fodor's Choice
★
▦ **La Suite Villa.** This hilltop boutique hotel gives Les Trois-Îlets some art-infused glamour and manages to maximize the Caribbean views from every room—even the bathrooms. **Pros:** inimitable, whimsical style with a profusion of Caribbean colors; entertaining and artistic owners; upbeat social scene. **Cons:** no elevator in three-story great house; no beach (nearest one is a half-mile away); pool is petite with

12

few chaises. $\boxed{\$}$ *Rooms from: €300 ⊠ Rte. du Fort d'Alet, Anse Mitan, Les Trois-Îlets ☎ 0596/59–88–00 ⊕ www.la-suite-villa.com ⮑ 6 suites, 9 villas* ⦿ *No meals.*

$\$$ ⦿ **Résidence Le Village Créole.** The "village" is comprised of very reaRENTAL sonably priced apartments surrounding a courtyard that houses some FAMILY 20 shops and 10 restaurants/bars. **Pros:** a lot of square footage for the euro; caring, English-speaking management; plump pillows from the U.S.; new double-paned glass. **Cons:** apartments are sparsely furnished; check-out during high season is early, at 10 am; reception office not always staffed. $\boxed{\$}$ *Rooms from: €126 ⊠ Village Créole, Pointe du Bout, Les Trois-Îlets ☎ 0596/66–03–19 ⊕ www.villagecreole.com ⮑ 23 apartments* ⦿ *No meals.*

FORT-DE-FRANCE AND POINTS NORTH

$\$$ ⦿ **Engoulevent.** This small B&B in a suburban house (about 10 minutes B&B/INN from Fort-de-France) has deluxe suites with contemporary decor, as well as Wi-Fi and other attractive amenities and high-end touches. **Pros:** rooms are attractive, particularly rooms 2 and 5; unique on the island. **Cons:** not all the benefits of a hotel; really need a car here; charming manager does not speak English—owners do. $\boxed{\$}$ *Rooms from: €135 ⊠ 22 rte. de l'Union Didier, Fort-de-France ☎ 0596/64–96–00 ⊗ Closed Aug. ⮑ 5 suites* ⦿ *Breakfast.*

$\$$ ⦿ **Fort Savane.** Not to be confused with the military installation (Fort RENTAL Louis) up the hill, this accommodation bills itself as a residence for both business travelers and tourists, but it doesn't have the full range of hotel amenities. **Pros:** personalized concierge service can even obtain a bottle of champagne after midnight; cordial, English-speaking receptionists; excellent location across from the Savane. **Cons:** cheapest rooms are small and some interior rooms are claustrophobic; no restaurant or bar on-site; reception desk is not manned after 8 pm or on weekends (guests must enter with a code). $\boxed{\$}$ *Rooms from: €110 ⊠ 5 rue de la Liberté, Le François ☎ 0596/80–75–75 ⊕ www.fortsavane.fr ⮑ 4 rooms, 8 studios, 2 suites* ⦿ *No meals.*

$\$$ ⦿ **Hotel La Caravelle.** The energetic Mahler family—especially patriarch HOTEL Jean Paul, who worked for decades in luxury hotels worldwide—has brought a sense of style and their own African artwork to this little hotel with a renovation in 2016. **Pros:** caring service; very good restaurant; free Wi-Fi in lounge. **Cons:** no pool; you'll need a car; no in-room Wi-Fi. $\boxed{\$}$ *Rooms from: €84 ⊠ Anse L'Etang, Tartane ☎ 0596/58–07–32 ⊕ www.hotel-la-caravelle-martinique.com ⮑ 14 studios, 1 apartment* ⦿ *No meals.*

$\$$ ⦿ **Hôtel L'Impératrice.** Right across from La Savane stands this hotel, HOTEL which has been owned by the same caring, Martinican family since the 1950s; like the park, it's another landmark that's been revived in recent years. **Pros:** personalized service; taxes and the breakfast buffet are included in the rates; some English is spoken. **Cons:** the small standard rooms in back are quiet but otherwise not desirable; narrow hallways; some maintenance worries, mainly broken air-conditioning units. $\boxed{\$}$ *Rooms from: €99 ⊠ 15 rue de la Libert, Fort-de-France ☎ 0596/63–06–82 ⊕ www.limperatricehotel.fr ⮑ 22 rooms* ⦿ *Breakfast.*

$ HOTEL **Hotel Villa Saint Pierre.** Simple, modern decor typifies this modest bay-front property that is somewhere between a boutique hotel and a French business hotel. **Pros:** caring managers; downtown location. **Cons:** little English spoken; not on a good beach; price is somewhat high for the relatively small rooms. [$] *Rooms from: €135* ✉ *108 rue Bouillé, St-Pierre* ☎ *0596/78–68–45* 🌐 *www.hotel-villastpierre.fr* ⏲ *Closed Sept. and some days in June* 🛏 *9 rooms* 🍴 *Breakfast.*

$ HOTEL **Le Domaine Saint Aubin.** Rooms at this private estate perched on a verdant hilltop offer breathtaking views overlooking the Atlantic are divided between a 19th-century creole plantation house and newer, free-standing cottages. **Pros:** daydream yourself into a more gracious era; hip owners make scintillating company; wheelchair-accessible rooms (and the pool has a chair lift). **Cons:** somewhat remote location requires a car; original rooms have character but are not stylin'; meals limited to breakfast and dinner, which cost extra. [$] *Rooms from: €159* ✉ *Petite Rivière Salée, off Rte. 1, La Trinité* ☎ *0596/69–34–77, 0696/41–88–23* 🌐 *www.domaine-saint-aubin.com* 🛏 *30 rooms, 6 2-bedroom apartments* 🍴 *No meals.*

$ HOTEL **L'Hôtel la Batelière.** The best full-service hotel in Fort-de-France nevertheless gets mixed reviews from most travelers because the hotel (and especially the standard rooms) need a major renovation. **Pros:** lovely pool deck overlooking a small, man-made beach; good and ample breakfast buffet with sea views; safe suburban location with free parking and a public bus nearby. **Cons:** hotel needs a thorough renovation; not all of the front desk or other staffers speak fluent English; draws large meetings and business groups. [$] *Rooms from: €100* ✉ *20 rue des Alizés, Schoelcher* ☎ *0596/61–49–49* 🌐 *www.hotel-bateliere-martinique.com* 🛏 *190 rooms, 3 suites* 🍴 *Breakfast.*

NIGHTLIFE AND PERFORMING ARTS

There are lively discos and nightclubs in Martinique, but a good deal of the fun is to be had by befriending Martinicans and French residents and other expats and hoping they will invite you clubbing or to their private parties. For art openings and other cultural events, check with the Fondation Clément (🌐 *www.fondation-clement.org*), which runs the Habitation Clément, to see what's coming up. In addition to its art exhibits, the foundation throws some of the best parties on the island, which are a chance to toast and clink rum glasses with some of Martinique's leading citizens and culture mavens.

Most leading hotels offer nightly entertainment in season, including the marvelous **Grands Ballets de Martinique,** one of the finest folkloric dance troupes in the Caribbean. Consisting of a bevy of musicians and dancers dressed in traditional costume, the ballet revives the Martinique of yesteryear through dance rhythms such as the beguine and the mazurka. They usually appear on Tuesday at the Hotel Carayou & Spa in Les Trois-Îlets in a dinner performance coupled with an authentic creole buffet. Call first to be sure of the time and to make reservations (or have your hotel make them). You can sometimes catch a performance elsewhere.

BARS AND CAFÉS

Calebasse Café. A diverse, mostly older, crowd gravitates to Calebasse Café, where jazz is the norm, but there may be soul or R&B, reggae, salsa, and there's often a talented local singer. Concerts may be combined with art exhibitions. Funky and hip, the interior is a bit rough but convivial and artsy. If you don't make a reservation on Saturday night, you won't have a seat. The food here isn't wonderful, but if you have the conch tart and the grilled lobster, you'll leave satisfied and avoid the cover charge. Friday and Saturday nights are banging, but call before you go on other nights. Doors open at 6 pm, but the music doesn't start till later in the evening. ■TIP➔ **If an event is destined to be a big draw, a white tent is erected outside.** ✉ *19 bd. Allègre, Le Marin* ☎ *0696/20–68–49, 0596/74–91–93* ☾ *Closed Mon. Low season: closed Tues., Thurs., and Sun.*

L' Bar 'Oc. This sophisticated lounge is the ground floor of a lovely, white home that has some history. The tile floors put it in another era, and thus the name of its former restaurant, Le Belle Epoque, which for decades was a gastronomic favorite on the island. The same owner, Martine, a charming, charismatic Frenchwoman came out of retirement to open instead what is primarily a cocktail lounge with world music and some food served. The house is her home (upstairs) and the neighborhood, Didier, is an upscale suburb of Fort-de-France, but close, not far from the Hotel Bateliere. It attracts the after-work crowd who live in the neighborhood, those staying at The Bat' and the small B&B Engoulevent close by and those savvy, older tourists who hear tell of it. ✉ *97 rte. de Didier, Fort-de-France* ☎ *0596/48–52–52.*

La Marine. La Marine is a busy bar and restaurant with live entertainment, mainly a local band on Saturday nights. Open daily, expats and boaters hang here for the reasonably priced, good pizza and old-world Italian and French classics. As one expat puts it, "It will probably be here for life!" There's nothing contemporary about this place—on quiet nights you can hear the wind in the riggings and check out the boat action on the docks. ✉ *Marina Pointe du Bout, Les Trois-Îlets* ☎ *0596/66–02–32.*

Le Kano Bar Lounge Restaurant. At this trendy, beachfront bar and lounge/restaurant, creole-influenced tapas and brochettes as well as creative Caribbean cocktails are happily consumed while relaxing Caribbean music plays in the background; a full menu is available, too. Spacious with several open rooms leading to the beach, the contemporary Euro furniture is inviting. Guests enjoy some the best Martinican dark (aged) rum. In season, a DJ cranks until 3 am on Friday and Saturday nights. The beach party on Sunday afternoons rocks. Kano is across the street from the Casino des Trois-Îlets, and the ample parking there makes it easy to visit both. ✉ *31 rue des bougainvilliers, facing the casino across the street, Fort-de-France* ☎ *0569/78–40–33.*

Lili's Beach Bar. At this thatch-roof beach bar, on any given night DJs might be spinning local and international sounds, making this a good alternative to clubbing downtown—and you might never know that there was a business hotel and casino right above. Lili's attracts a mainly young crowd, and now, predominantly, a local one as well as guests from L'Hôtel La Batelière. Food is less expensive than at the hotel's restaurant, but don't be in a hurry, especially on the weekends. The bar puts out strong (and pricey) tropical cocktails. With free parking and tight security because of the casino, it is a safe haven for tourists and one sexy party place. ⊠ *L'Hôtel La Batelière, Schoelcher* ☎ *0596/42–89–02.*

CASINOS

To enter a casino, French law requires everyone to show a passport; the legal gambling age is now 21.

Casino Batelière Plazza. On the outskirts of Fort-de-France, the Casino Batelière Plaza was built in a striking nouveau-plantation-house style, all yellow and white. By day it is depressing with locals playing the slot machines and video poker; a few cartons of tropical juice (usually empty) sit on a table with tiny

> **GOOD TO KNOW**
>
> You may see billboards that say "Casino" or even "Geante Casino," with directionals. Do not follow them if you are looking for a gambling casino. *Casino* is the name of a supermarket chain. *Geante* means a mega-supermarket.

plastic glasses. Slots open at 10 am, but table games don't start until after 8 pm. There's always a bar open, and you can often catch live entertainment on weekends after 8. It's open Sunday night, when most places are shut tight. Restaurant Le Club Seven, which serves Franco-creole food, offers themed parties on weekends. A new concert hall is impressive as well. ⊠ *Rue des Alizés, Schoelcher* ☎ *0596/61–73–23* ⊕ *www.casinobatelIereplazza.com.*

Casino Trois-Îlets. The interior of this small casino was designed in a French Quarter style and houses slot machines, blackjack, U.S. roulette, stud poker, and craps (Friday and Saturday). The casino is open daily from 10 am to 3 am, but the gaming tables don't start cranking until 9. On weekends in high season, a DJ spins Caribbean, creole, and international beats, and there's a dance floor. The restaurant serves up a marriage of refined creole and international fare, with fresh local produce; however, the tables are right in the middle of the floor, which is not conducive to fine dining. ■TIP➔ **There is often a cover charge when there is an event.** ⊠ *Rte. de Pointe du Bout, near rte. de Trois-Îlets, Les Trois-Îlets* ☎ *596/66–00–30.*

DANCE CLUBS

Your hotel or the tourist office can put you in touch with the current popular places. It's also wise to check on opening and closing times and cover charges. Several free tourist publications that can be found at hotels tell of the latest happenings at the clubs. For the most part, the discos draw a mixed crowd of Martinicans and tourists, and although a younger crowd is the norm, people of all ages go dancing here.

Jet Set. This hot ticket has salsa going on and live bands that play mainly Caribbean music. It has an inviting ambience and decor and is known for having a courteous crowd. Tourists can feel welcome and will not be hassled. Drinks are less expensive than at many of the clubs. The best is its convenient, easy-to-find location right across from the Savane. Guests at l'Imperatrice or the new Fort Savane can walk to it for it's on the same street. If you're having trouble finding it, look up—it is not on the ground floor. ✉ *Rue de la Liberté at rue Perrinon, Fort-de-France* ⊕ *www.aux-antilles.fr/martinique/sortir/info-jet-set-1019.htm.*

Le Negresco. This is a prime example of a French Antilles urban disco. You will hear zouk, salsa, and kompas. It's hot, it rocks, there are lots of glam outfits, and on busy nights when people are feeling their dances and waving their arms in the air, well, you just have to be there. The weekend is when it really cranks up. On most nights you can expect a cover charge, especially when there's live entertainment. This club, which plays a fair share of Caribbean music, appeals to an older crowd (30s–40s). It generally opens at 9 pm, although that can change due to after-work parties or if they've decided to close. Security is tight; there's a free parking lot just across the street. ✉ *10 rue Commerce, Fort-de-France* ☎ *0596/70–07–03.*

Le Paparazzi Club. You may see Paparazzi advertised as a private club, but anyone looking cool is seldom refused entrée. You may hear that this disco is frequented by kids—the 18- to 25-year-olds—while others categorize it as for those 30-plus. Marc Martial, an English-speaking taxi driver with a late-model Mercedes, says that it is one of the clubs that he takes his American clients to when doing a nocturnal bar crawl. ✉ *8 rue Joseph Compete, Fort-de-France* ☎ *0696/54–05–30, 0696/00–47–81.*

MUSIC CLUBS AND LOUNGES

Jazz musicians, like their music, tend to be informal and independent. Zouk mixes Caribbean rhythm with creole lyrics. Jacob Devarieux is the leading exponent of this style, and he occasionally performs on the island. Otherwise, you're likely to hear one of his followers.

Hotel Cap Macabou, in Vauclin, has "dancing dinners" and theme nights, most often on Friday and Saturday. On Sunday, there's usually a midday buffet with dancing to a band—you can even bring your bathing suit. Check the site for holiday parties.

Club Med Buccaneer's Creek. At Club Med Buccaneer's Creek, you can buy a night pass that will give you all the food, drinks, and entertainment you can handle from 7 pm until the disco closes at 2 am. While this is a hefty price, it includes an extensive buffet dinner with wine, a show in the theater, and drinks and dancing afterward. Friday is the best night to come since both the food and shows are most elaborate. Entertainment changes based on a two-week cycle. Following the show, it's on to dancing at the disco if you can hang. Single women will feel comfortable here and will find willing and very able dance partners. ✉ *Pointe du Marin, Ste-Anne* ☎ *0596/76–83–36.*

Hotel Bakoua. The entertainment here ranges from piano concerts to singers to jazz combos on up to full swimsuit fashion shows or splashy

Traditional madras costumes in Martinique

variety shows, often with special effects. The quality of the entertainment is known island-wide. You can also go to Le Gommier and order a tropical cocktail there. There's a litany of island rums, from white to amber and rhum vieux. It's usually best to call the hotel first to learn what's on the schedule, since events taper off during the low season. ⊠ *Les Trois-Îlets* ☎ *0596/66–02–02.*

Hotel Cap Macabou. Hotel Cap Macabou in Vauclin has "dancing dinners" and theme nights, most often on Friday and Saturday. On Sunday, there's usually a midday buffet with dancing to a band—you can even bring your bathing suit. There are often salsa soirees with Latin music, as well as holiday parties in season, which are quite celebratory. ⊠ *Petit Macabou, Le Vauclin* ☎ *0596/74–24–24* ⊕ *www.capmacabou.com.*

Infinity. Infinity is the latest tenant on the first- and second-story of the building previously occupied by a Mexican restaurant. On the ground floor is a gourmet food boutique, and on the second a sophisticated bar with tables, some on a small terrace. Called a concept bar and an art gallery, there is to be live entertainment during peak season and weekends. The concept is that one chooses from the menu of chichi cocktails (not inexpensive) and then orders some foodstuffs from the shop below. ⊠ *Village Creole, Pointe du Bout, Les Trois-Îlets* ☎ *0596/38–71–68.*

La Villa Créole. This restaurant's Martinican owner, Guy Bruere-Dawson, has been singing and strumming the guitar since the 1980s—in five languages, everything from François Cabrel to Elton John, some Italian and creole ballads, even original ditties. Other singers perform, too, on Friday and Saturday nights, when there might be other entertainment. To see the show, you must order dinner; grilled lobster from the tank is often the best option. There's ample parking and even a small dance floor. The crowd tends to be mature; customer service and satisfaction are high. ✉ *18 rue des Anthuriums, Anse Mitan, Les Trois-Îlets* ☎ *0596/66–05–53* ⊕ *la-villa-creole.biz* ⊗ *Closed Sun. and Mon.*

SHOPPING

12

French fragrances; designer clothes, scarves, and sunglasses; fine china and crystal; leather goods; wine (inexpensive at supermarkets); and liquor are all good buys in duty-free Fort-de-France. Purchases are further sweetened by the 20% discount on luxury items when paid for with certain credit cards. Among the items produced on the island, look for *bijoux creole* (local jewelry, such as hoop earrings and heavy bead necklaces); white, dark, and aged rum; and handcrafted straw goods, pottery, and tapestries.

AREAS AND MALLS

The striking 215,000-square-foot Cour Perrinon Mall in Fort-de-France, bordered by rue Perrinon, houses a Carrefour supermarket, a bookstore, perfume shops, designer boutiques, a French bakery, and a café–brasserie. The area around the cathedral in Fort-de-France has a number of small shops that carry luxury goods. Of particular note are the shops on rue Victor Hugo, rue Moreau de Jones, rue Antoine Siger, and rue Lamartine. Ongoing efforts to be more inviting to the North American market—with particular emphasis on offering English-language classes to staff—have dozens of shops participating. The **Galleries Lafayette** department store on rue Schoelcher in downtown Fort-de-France sells everything from perfume to pâté. On the outskirts of Fort-de-France, the **Centre Commercial de Cluny, Centre Commercial de Dillon, Centre Commercial de Bellevue,** and **Centre Commercial la Rond Point** are among the major shopping malls.

You can find more than 100 thriving businesses—from shops and department stores to restaurants, pizzerias, fast-food outlets, a superb supermarket, and the simple Galleria Hotel (the closest hotel to the airport)—at **La Galleria** in Lamentin. In Pointe du Bout there are a number of appealing tourist shops and boutiques, both in and around **Village Créole**, which alone has more than 20, plus some 10 restaurants–bars, an ice-cream shop, free Wi-Fi, and the Residence Village Creole, with small and family-size furnished apartments, available by the night, the week, or longer, for moderate prices. Village Creole often has live entertainment at night in the courtyard.

ART GALLERIES

Antan Lontan. For years Antan Lontan focused on creating sculptures, busts, statuettes, and artistic lamps that portray Creole women and the story of the Martiniquaise culture. Now his focus has shifted to selling his collection of some 3,000 vintage photos and postcards of Martinique and the Antilles dating from the 1800s through the 1950s. ✉ *Centre*

Commercial, La Veranda, rue du Professeur Raymond Garcin, Fort-de-France ☎ *0596/65–52–72* ⊕ *www.antanlontan-antilles.com.*

Art et Nature. Art et Nature carries unique wood paintings, daubed with 20 to 30 shades of earth and sand. They depict simple Martinican scenes. This dedicated French artist has moved his location from Distillerie Trois Rivières to Le Potterie. ■ TIP→ The small-size artwork makes good take-home gifts. If you want more, his website is set up to take PayPal. ⊠ *Village de la Poterie, Les Trois-Îlets* ☎ *0596/62–59–19* ⊕ *www.artetnaturemartinique.com.*

Galerie de Sophen. Across from the Village Créole, this gallery combines Sophie and Henry, both in name and content. On sale are the originals and limited prints of a French couple who live aboard their sailboat and paint the beauty of the sea and the island, from exotic birds to banana trucks. ⊠ *Pointe du Bout, Les Trois-Îlets* ☎ *0596/66–13–64.*

CLOTHING

Coté Plage Sarl. Stop in here for French sailor jerseys in creative colors, youthful straw purses in bold hues, fun teenage jewelry, and ladies' bathing suits. ⊠ *Village Créole, Pointe du Bout, Les Trois-Îlets* ☎ *0596/66–13–00.*

fashion bay. The newly painted walls of this marina boutique are as fresh as the fashions on the racks. They carry name brands from France and Italy and "hot" teeny, weeny bikinis and big-girl shoes from Rio, like: Bogdanoff; Valerie; Best Montain (Parisian); Pako Litto and Replay (Italian); Anti Flirt and Brigitte Bardot (France); Au Soleil de St. Tropez; Galibelle Shoes, and Brazilian designer high heels; and exclusive in Martinique, bikinis and bracelets from *www.hipanema.com.* French, English, and Italian are spoken, and the sales staff is fun. ⊠ *Marina Pointe du Bout, Pointe du Bout, Les Trois-Îlets* ☎ *0596/66–13–81.*

La Chamade. So you wanna look French? *Femmes,* this urban boutique is a good start, although the chic doesn't come cheap here. You will recognize some well-known brands like Saint-Hillaire, Escada, and Blue Label, and the sexy French shoes are nearly irresistible. The shop does have some good *soldes* (sales), though—and make sure you check the second level. ⊠ *25 rue Schoelcher, Fort-de-France* ☎ *0596/73–28–78.*

La Petite Boutique. La Petite Boutique offers a unique children's collection, including jewelry, madras dollies, and teeny underwear. There are also contemporary mini-styles from Hip Up and Funky Family. ⊠ *Village Créole, Pointe du Bout, Les Trois-Îlets* ☎ *0596/38–00–65.*

Lynx Optique. Lynx Optique has the latest designer sunglasses from such major brands as Chanel, Gucci, Dior, Cartier, and Versace. (French designer brands are less expensive here.) And if you need a pair of prescription lenses or a repair, they can take care of that, too. The staff are professional, polite, and English is spoken. There are several locations throughout the island, this being the most centrally located. ⊠ *20 rue Lamartine, Fort-de-France* ☎ *0596/71–38–48* ⊕ *www.lynx-optique.com.*

Mounia Boutique. Owned by a former Yves St. Laurent model, Mounia carries the top French designers for women and men, including Yves St. Laurent as well as her very own Mounia collection. It will have you opening your wallet wide. Hope for a *solde*. ⌧ *26 rue Perrinon, near old House of Justice, Fort-de-France* ☎ *0596/73–77–27* ☽ *Closed Sun.*

12

GIFTS

Artisanat & Poterie des Trois-Îlets. This complex lets you watch the creation of Arawak- and Carib-style pots, vases, and jars. On the site of an old Jesuit compound, this group of shops is now a major tourist attraction in the area. There are shops with interesting gifts, jewelry, and clothing, especially pareos (wraparound skirts). Several appealing restaurants (particularly the bakery) also make it a good stopover for lunch. ⌧ *Rte. des Trois-Îlets, Les Trois-Îlets* ☎ *0596/68–03–44.*

Bois Nature. This place is all about mood and mystique and eco-sensitivity. Gift items at Bois Nature begin with scented soap, massage oil, aromatherapy sprays, and perfumes. Then there are wind chimes, mosquito netting, shell mobiles, and sun hats made of coconut fiber. The interior decor accessories are unique and worth carrying home on the plane, but they can also ship things home for you. The big stuff includes natural wood-frame mirrors and furniture à la Louis XV. ⌧ *Parking Centre, Commercial place d'armes, Le Lamentin* ☎ *0596/65–77–65* ⊕ *www.boisnature.fr.*

Caz' Art. This is one of those artsy souvenir shops that is so chockablock full that you are fascinated, amazed at every turn. Now there are many small items that would fit in luggage, such as colorful, metallic sculptures. Some of the most fanciful items are home accessories. Luc Ferrari, a designer (and importer) of art deco, showcases his wares here. ⌧ *Village de la Poterie, Les Trois-Îlets* ⊹ *When you first drive in the village, you pass the bakery (pâtissiere) and then this shop is next, also on the right.* ☎ *0596/68–53–56.*

JEWELRY

Pascal Rogatis Jewelry. Authentic creole-style jewelry, popularized after the abolition of slavery and seen in many museums, is for sale here at the number-one jewelry store in Martinique. Most creations are in 18-karat gold, but 9-karat is an option. ⌧ *47 rue Isambert, Fort-de-France* ☎ *0596/71–36–78* ⊕ *www.bijouterie-pascal-derogatis.fr.*

PERFUME

L'Atelier du Parfum Tropical. The trained staff here can formulate your very own eau du parfum from more than 50 available fragrances. The ingredients are natural and from the island. The store also sells soaps and body oils that include a natural bronzer with oil of roucou and a coconut oil base. One purse-size spray that everyone should carry is an anti-mosquito oil with eucalyptus and citronella. Many of the spray atomizers (nonaerosol) are less than 3 ounces and can be carried aboard your homebound plane. ✉ *Village Creole, Pointe du Bout, Les Trois-Îlets* ☎ *0696/80–80–04, 0596/62–22–90* ⊕ *www.parfums-des-iles-martinique.com.*

SPORTS AND THE OUTDOORS

BOATING AND SAILING

You can rent Hobie Cats, Sunfish, and Sailfish by the hour from most hotel beach shacks. As for larger craft, bareboat charters (that is, ones with no crew) can be had for $1,900 to $7,000 a week, depending on the season and the size of the craft. The Windward Islands are a joy for experienced sailors, but the channels between islands are often windy and have high waves. You must have a sailing license or be able to prove your nautical prowess, though you can always hire a skipper and crew. Before setting out, you can get itinerary suggestions; the safe ports in Martinique are many. If you charter for a week, you can go south to St. Lucia or Grenada or north to Dominica, Guadeloupe, and Les Saintes. One-way sailing to St. Martin or Antigua is a popular choice.

■**TIP**➜ Don't even consider striking out on the rough Atlantic side of the island unless you're an experienced sailor. The Caribbean side is much calmer—more like a vast lagoon.

Punch Croisières. A local, French-owned charter company, Punch Croisières has a fleet of 17 sailboats, 14 of which are catamarans from 40 to 47 feet; they go out bareboat or crewed, and you can take a boat to a neighboring island. They are comfortably equipped to go down to the Grenadines or just over to Guadeloupe. This company has been here since 1995 while other charter operations, from the Moorings to Windward Islands Cruising, have pulled out. The staff is really accommodating and English is spoken. Rentals from one week to 11 months are available. ✉ *Marina, Bd. Allègre, Port de Plaisance, Le Marin* ☎ *0596/74–89–18* ⊕ *www.punch-croisieres.com.*

CANOPY TOURS

Mangofil. This professionally run zip-line park is overseen by the proprietors of a similar park in France. All of the platforms, ladders, and stations were installed by members of a special union in France that specializes in such work. Safety is key here, but there's also a lot of fun; there are upgraded food offerings and a picnic area. For kids age 18 months and up, there's also a huge safety net for them to frolic and "dance" among the trees, with toys galore to bounce around with. Here happy hour on the weekends refers to discounted prices for their mini-golf. And mini-golf is open until 11 pm on Fridays, Saturdays, and Sundays. ■**TIP**➜ It's just a small add-on if a "Big Mango" (adult) comes with a little Parcabout (kid). ✉ *Forêt Rateau, rte. de Trois-Îlets, near Le Potterie, Les Trois-Îlets* ☎ *0596/68–08–08* ⊕ *www.mangofil.eu* 🎟 *From €25* ⊘ *Closed Mon. and Tues.*

CANYONING

Bureau de la Randonnée et du Canyoning. Since 1995, the professionals at this company have been leading hikes that take in the island's gorges, canyons, and volcanic landscape. The tours also include some canyoning, which involves climbing up, down, in, and around rocky areas, which are usually near falls or along a stream. For this adrenaline rush, you must be fit and able to hike in the forest for hours. If you are not sure about that, book just the half-day trip, not the full day. These tropical adventures can take you to the Presqu'île du Caravelle, through canals, to Mont Pelée, even to the borders of the craters. Price depends on the destination and the duration. ⊠ *Jolimont, Morne Vert* ☎ *0596/55–04–79, 0696/24–32–25 canyoning, 0696/35–91–28 hiking* ⊕ *www.bureau-rando-martinique.com.*

DAY SAILS

Kata Mambo. The catamaran *Kata Mambo* offers two full-day excursions now. You can sail north to historic St-Pierre and snorkel in clear, Atlantic waters, or you can have a sail coupled with a 4x4 adventure through sugarcane and banana plantations in the south of the island. The full-day trips include rum drinks and a good, multicourse creole lunch. The boat pulls into its slip at the marina at 5 pm. This is a fun day, and you're likely to meet some dolphins. Also, someone in the crew will speak English. This operation has been in the biz since the early 1990s; that longevity attests to its professionalism. ⊠ *Pointe du Bout Marina, Les Trois-Îlets* ☎ *0696/25–23–16, 0596/66–11–83* ⊕ *www.kata-mambo.com* ⊠ *From €80.*

La Belle Kréole. One of the most popular excursion boats takes you to *les fonds blancs,* also known as Empress Joséphine's baths. (These are natural, shallow pools with white-sand bottoms.) You can experience the unique Martinican custom of "baptism by rum" (tilt your head back while standing in waist-deep water, and one of the crew pours rum into your mouth). The cost of the day-trip depends in part on what you choose to have for lunch, which is taken on the remote Isle de Thierry. There's planter's punch and dancing to Martinican music. Yes, it is touristy—you're basically on a booze cruise that lasts from 9 to 5, with lots of loud music—but it's equally popular with locals and families. A two-hour excursion directly to the baths is also available on a smaller boat with capacity for nine guests. ⊠ *Baie du Simon, Slip 36, Le François* ☎ *0596/54–95–57, 0696/25–82–71* ⊕ *www.baignoiredejosephine.com* ⊠ *From €50.*

Fodor's Choice ★ **Les Ballades du Delphis.** This civilized full-day tour uses one of three commodious catamarans, with two departure points: François Bay and Anse Spoutourne (Tartane). The sail from François takes in the famous *fonds blancs* and then the Baie du Robert and l'Îlet Chancel to see sea iguanas and ruins. The Tartane route heads to Treasure Bay, one of the most appealing nature preserves on the island. You'll be served planter's punch, accras (fritters), and a creole-style lunch with fish or chicken. A new offering is a day cruise with an overnight at the guesthouse on islet Oscar, a magical setting, with meals included. All of these cruises

Kayaking is a popular activity on Martinique.

can be idyllic travel memories, especially when you are sailing from islet to islet, between coral reefs and swimming in shallow pools with white-sand bottoms. The boats are available for private party charters or a romantic couple sail. These comfortable catamarans have a capacity for 23 guests and are even wheelchair accessible. ⊠ *La Marina du François, Baie du Simon, Le François* ☎ *0696/90–90–36* ⊕ *www. catadelphis.com* 🖰 *From €80.*

DIVING AND SNORKELING

Martinique's underwater world is decorated with multicolor coral, crustaceans, turtles, and sea horses. Expect to pay €50 to €55 for a single dive; a package of three dives is around €120.

Okeanos Club. This landmark dive operation has a morning trip close to shore; in the afternoon the boats go farther into open water. Lessons (including those for kids 8 to 12) with a PADI-certified instructor can be conducted in English. It's always a fun experience. The dive shop looks out to Diamant Rock, which has wonderful underwater caves and is one of the preferred dives on the island. Okeanos Club goes to 12 different sites, many with catchy names like Little Turtle, and the Gardens of St. Luce, an underwater spot chock-full of colorful sponges. Trips are geared to the level of the clients, from rank beginners to certified divers. Guests from all hotels are welcome, and Okeanos provides pickup from some of them. ⊠ *Pierre & Vacances, Pavilion-Pointe Philippeau rte. de Gros Raisin, Ste-Luce* ☎ *0696/71–94–41* ⊕ *www.okeanos-martinique. com* 🖰 *From €55.*

12

GOLF

Golf de l'Impératrice Josephine (*Martinique Golf and Country Club*). Although it's named in honor of Empress Joséphine Napoléon, this Robert Trent Jones Sr. course is completely American in design, with an English-speaking pro, a pro shop, a bar, and an especially good restaurant. The best hole on the course may just be the par-five 15th. Sandwiched between two good par-3s, the 15th plays to an island fairway and then to a green situated by the shore. Try not to be mesmerized by the turquoise waters. (You can finish your visit here with foie gras torchon or a full meal at Restaurant Le Golf.) The club offers special greens fees to cruise-ship passengers. Club trolleys (called "chariots") are €6 for 18 holes, €4 for 9. There are no caddies. ⊠ *Quartier la Pagerie, Les Trois-Îlets* ☎ *0596/61–05–24* ⌂ *€15 for 9 holes, €22.50 for 18; €25 for cart, 9 holes; €40 for cart, 18 holes* ⌘ *18 holes, 6640 yards, par 71.*

GUIDED TOURS

Your hotel front desk can help arrange a personalized island tour with an English-speaking driver. It's also possible to hire a taxi for the day or half day; there are set rates for certain itineraries, and if you share the ride with others, the per-person price will be whittled down. The Office du Tourisme de Fort-de-France also arranges tours, from walking tours of the city to bus excursions, and can find you English-speaking guides, too.

HIKING

Parc Naturel Régional de la Martinique. Two-thirds of Martinique is designated as protected land. Trails, all 31 of them, are well marked and maintained. At the beginning of each, a notice is posted advising on the level of difficulty, the duration of a hike, and any interesting facts. The Parc Naturel Régional de la Martinique organizes inexpensive guided excursions year-round. If there have been heavy rains, though, give it up. The tangle of ferns, bamboo trees, and vines is dramatic, but during rainy season, the wet, muddy trails will temper your enthusiasm. ⊠ *9 bd. Général de Gaulle, Fort-de-France* ☎ *0596/64–45–64 communications department.*

HORSEBACK RIDING

FAMILY **Ranch Jack.** Ranch Jack has a large stable of some 30 horses. Its trail rides (English-style) cross some beautiful country for 90 minutes to two hours; half-day excursions (inquire about transfers from nearby hotels) go through the fields and forests to the beach. Short rides ranging from an hour are also available. The company has a wonderful program to introduce kids ages three to seven to horses. Online comments reflect riders' satisfaction with the professionalism of the stable and the beautiful acreage they traverse. ⊠ *Morne habitué, Les Trois-Îlets* ☎ *0596/68–37–69, 0696/92–26–58* ✉ *ranch.jack@wanadoo.fr* ⌂ *From €31.*

KAYAKING

It can be great fun to skim the shallow bay while paddling to bird and iguana reserves. Rent colorful fiberglass kayaks to explore the crystal-line Havre du Robert, with its clear, shallow pools (called *fonds blanc*), petite beaches, and islets, such as Iguana Island.

Les Kayaks du Robert. You'll receive one of the island's warmest welcomes at Les Kayaks du Robert. After a memorable paddle through shallow lagoons and mangrove swamps chasing colorful fish, you can enjoy a complimentary glass of juice or planter's punch. An English-speaking guide is available with advance reservation, and reservations are necessary if you are taking a lunch package. If you're going without a guide, ask how to get to various small islets, especially Iguana Island. A waterproof box for your belongings is complimentary; masks and fins are available, and it's a joy to snorkel in the *fonds blancs*. ✉ *Pointe Savane, Le Robert* ☎ *0596/65–33–89* 📧 *From €15.*

PUERTO RICO

WELCOME TO PUERTO RICO

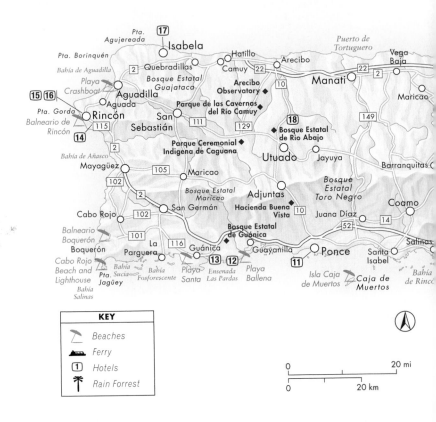

Pta. Agujereada   **17**   Isabela   Hatillo   Arecibo   *Puerto de Tortuguero*   Vega Baja

Pta. Borinquén   **2**   Quebradillas   Camuy   **22**

Bahía de Aguadilla   *Bosque Estatal Guajataca*   Arecibo Observatory ◆   **10**   Manatí   **22**   **2**

Playa Crashboat   Aguadilla   Parque de las Cavernas del Río Camuy   Maricao

15 **16**   Aguada

Pta. Gorda   Rincón   San Sebastián   **111**   **129**   **18**   Bosque Estatal de Río Abajo   **149**

Balneario de Rincón   **115**

14

Bahía de Añasco   **2**   Parque Ceremonial Indígena de Caguana ◆   Utuado   Jayuya   Barranquitas

Mayagüez   **105**   Maricao   *Bosque Estatal Toro Negro*

102

2   *Bosque Estatal Maricao*   Adjuntas   Coamo

Cabo Rojo   **102**   San Germán   Hacienda Buena Vista ◆   **10**   Juana Díaz   **14**

Balneario Boquerón   **101**   La   **116**   Guánica   *Bosque Estatal de Guánica*   **52**   Salinas

Boquerón   Parguera   Guayanilla   **11**   Ponce   Santa Isabel

Cabo Rojo Beach and Lighthouse   *Bahía Sucia*   Pta. Jagüey   *Bahía Fosforescente*   Playa Santa   *Ensenada Las Pardas*   Playa Ballena   *Isla Caja de Muertos*   *Caja de Muertos*   *Bahía de Rincó*

Bahía Salinas   **13** **12**

KEY

🏖 *Beaches*
🚢 *Ferry*
1 *Hotels*
🌴 *Rain Forrest*

| 0 | | 20 mi |
| 0 | | 20 km |

Mother Spain is always a presence here—on a sun-dappled cobblestone street, in the shade of a colonial cathedral or fort. Yet multifaceted Puerto Rico pulses with New World energy. The rhythms of the streets are of Afro-Latin salsa and bomba. And the U.S. flag flaps in the salty breezes wherever you go.

SPANISH AMERICAN

Puerto Rico is 110 miles (177 km) long and 35 miles (56 km) wide. With a population of almost 4 million, it's among the biggest of the Caribbean islands. The first Spanish governor was Juan Ponce de León in 1508; he founded Old San Juan in 1521. The United States won the island in the Spanish-American War in 1898 and made it a commonwealth in 1952.

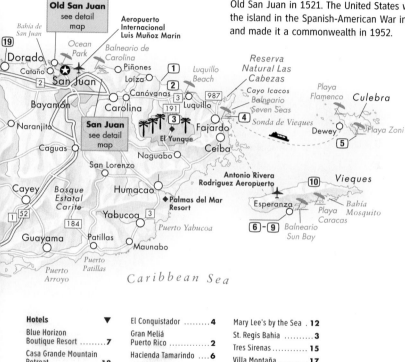

13

PUERTO RICO

TOP REASONS TO VISIT PUERTO RICO

1 The Nightlife: Happening clubs, discos, and bars make San Juan one of the Caribbean's nightlife capitals, rivaling even Miami.

2 The Food: Great restaurants run the gamut from elegant places in San Juan to simple spots serving delicious comida criolla (creole food).

3 The Beaches: Both developed and wild, beaches here suit the needs of surfers, sunbathers, and families.

4 The Nature: Nature abounds, from the underground Río Camuy to El Yunque, the only Caribbean national forest.

5 The Unexpected: Puerto Mosquito—kayak after dark on the astounding bioluminescent bay on Vieques.

NEED TO KNOW

San Juan

Caribbean Sea

AT A GLANCE

Capital: San Juan

Population: 3,474,182

Currency: U.S. dollar

Money: ATMs common; credit cards widely accepted.

Language: Spanish, English

Country Code: ☎ "1" or "001" like the mainland U.S.

Emergencies: ☎ 911

Driving: On the right

Electricity: 120v/60 cycles; plugs are U.S. standard two- and three-prong

Time: Same as New York during daylight savings time; one hour ahead otherwise

Documents: Enter Puerto Rico as you would domestically in the U.S.; no passport required for U.S. citizens

Major Mobile Companies: AT&T, Claro, Sprint, T-Mobile US

WEBSITES

Puerto Rico Travel: ⊕ www.puertorico.com

Puerto Rico Tourism Company: ⊕ www.seepuertorico.com

GETTING AROUND

✈ **Air Travel:** Luis Muñoz Marín airport in San Juan is the largest. Others include: Isla Grande, Aguadilla, Ponce, Vieques, and Culebra.

🚌 **Bus Travel:** Buses operate throughout San Juan. Outside of San Juan, travel by *públicos*, which are usually shared 17-passenger vans.

🚗 **Car Travel:** Renting a car is a good idea if you want to see Puerto Rico beyond San Juan, but in the city you may be happier with buses and taxis.

⛴ **Ferry Travel:** Passenger ferries run from Fajardo, a 90-minute drive from San Juan, to Culebra and Vieques.

PLAN YOUR BUDGET

	HOTEL ROOM	MEAL	ATTRACTIONS
Low Budget	$200	$12	San Juan National Historic Site, $5
Mid Budget	$300	$30	Play at Teatro Tapia, $30
High Budget	$475	$50	Zip-line tour, $85

WAYS TO SAVE

Eat local cuisine. As a general rule, restaurants serving Puerto Rican cuisine tend to be the most affordable on the island.

Visit on weekdays. Since so many Americans come here for quick weekend getaways, weekday prices at hotels tend to be much cheaper.

Take the ferry. A cheaper alternative to flying to Vieques or Culebra is to take the ferry from Fajardo.

Scour the web. Most tour outfitters in Puerto Rico have websites than offer online discounts.

WHEN TO GO

High Season: From mid-December through mid-April, the weather is typically sunny and warm. Good hotels are often booked far in advance, everything is open, and prices are highest.

Low Season: From August to late October, temperatures can grow oppressively hot and the weather muggy, with high risks of tropical storms. Many upscale hotels offer deep discounts.

Value Season: From late April to July and again November to mid-December, hotel prices drop 20% to 50% from high-season prices. There are chances of scattered showers, but expect sun-kissed days and fewer crowds.

BIG EVENTS

January: The annual Fiestas de la Calle San Sebastián feature four nights of live music as well as food festivals and cabezudos parades. ⊕ www.seepuertorico.com/en/what-to-do/events

March: The annual Heineken JazzFest attracts some 15,000 aficionados to San Juan for four days of outdoor concerts. ⊕ www.prheinekenjazz.com

April: Puerto Rico's largest culinary event, Saborea Puerto Rico, is a three-day extravaganza held at Escambrón Beach in San Juan. ⊕ www.saboreapuertorico.com

May: During Puerto Rico Restaurant Week, dozens of restaurants offer a three-course prix-fixe menu. ⊕ www.puertoricorestaurantweek.com

READ THIS

■ *La Carreta,* René Marqués. A family emigrates from Puerto Rico to the U.S.

■ *The Puerto Ricans,* Olga Jiménez de Wagenheim and Kal Wagenheim. An anthology of important writings about Puerto Rico.

■ *The Rum Diary,* Hunter S. Thompson. The gonzo journalist moves to San Juan.

WATCH THIS

■ *Amistad.* Puerto Rico served as the set for this Spielberg drama.

■ *Captain Ron.* This Disney flick was filmed in Puerto Rico.

■ *Contact.* Arecibo Observatory in Puerto Rico is the blockbuster.

EAT THIS

■ *Lechón*: seasoned, spit-roasted whole pig

■ *Empanadillas*: turnovers filled with beef, crabmeat, conch, or lobster

■ *Pasteles*: stuffed, mashed root vegetable wrapped in a plantain leaf

■ *Mofongo*: plantains mashed with garlic, olive oil, and salt

■ *Amarillos*: fried ripe, yellow plantain slices

■ *Bacalaítos*: deep-fried salt cod fritters

EATING AND DRINKING WELL IN PUERTO RICO

More chefs and restaurateurs are fusing international ingredients with traditional dishes. However, even the most avant-garde chefs use local produce as an homage to classic *comida criolla*.

Standard meats like chicken, pork, and lamb are given an added zest by sauces made from such tropical fruits as tamarind, mango, or guava. Puerto Rican cooking uses a lot of local vegetables: plantains are cooked a hundred different ways, and yams and other root vegetables are served baked, fried, stuffed, boiled, and mashed. Rice and beans are accompaniments to almost every dish. *Sofrito*—a garlic, onion, sweet pepper, cilantro, oregano, and tomato puree—is used as a base for practically everything. *Arroz con pollo* (chicken with rice), *pernil* (roasted pork shoulder), *sancocho* (beef, chicken, or pork feet and tuber soup), and *bistec encebollado* (steak and onions) are all typical plates. Also look for fritters served along highways and beaches. You may find *empanadillas* (stuffed fried turnovers), *sorullitos* (cheese-stuffed corn sticks), and *bacalaítos* (codfish fritters).

Cocina Criolla: *Cocina or comida criolla* (creole cooking), the local Puerto Rican food, is an aggregate of Caribbean cuisines, sharing basic ingredients common to Cuban, Dominican, and even Brazilian culinary traditions. Conventional wisdom says that the secret of the cocina criolla depends on the use of sofrito, *achiote* (the inedible fruit of a small Caribbean shrub whose seeds are sometimes ground as a spice or simmered in oil to release their color), lard, and the *caldero* (cooking pot).

Coffee: Cultivated at high altitudes in cool, moist air and mineral-rich soil, the island's coffee beans (called cherries) are black and aromatic. The dominant bean is the *arabica*, known as the richest and most flavorful among the coffee varieties. A lengthy ripening process acts as a sort of "prebrew," imbuing the bean with a rich flavor and a slightly sweet aftertaste. Look for local brands: Yaucono Selecto, Rioja, Yaucono, Hacienda San Pedro, Café Rico, Crema, Adjuntas, Coqui, and Alto Grande Super Premium. Alto Grande, guaranteed to have been grown at high altitudes, has gained the most fame off the island.

Fruits and Vegetables: Tropical fruits often wind up at the table in the form of delicious juices. A local favorite is pineapple juice from crops grown in the north of the island. Coconut, mango, acerola (Caribbean cherry), papaya, lime, and tamarind are other local favorites. Puerto Rico is home to terrific lesser-known fruits; these include the *caimito* (also called a star apple), *quenepa* (a Spanish lime with a yellow sweet-tart pulp surrounded by a tight, thin skin), and *zapote* (a plum-size fruit that tastes like peach, avocado, and vanilla). The Plaza del Mercado in Río Piedras is a good place to look for the unusual.

Local Seafood: The freshest seafood is to be found on the northern and western coasts, where seaside shacks and kiosks serve up red snapper, grouper, conch, crab, and spiny lobster in traditional

recipes. Fried fish is also popular, served with *mojo isleño*, a sauce made with olives, onions, pimientos, capers, tomatoes, and vinegar.

Plantains and Mofongo: *Plátanos*, or plantains, are related to bananas but are larger and starchier. They are served mostly as side dishes and may be eaten green or ripe. They can be fried, baked, boiled, or roasted and served either whole or in slices. Of all the delicious plantain preparations, one of the tastiest is also the simplest—*mofongo*. Fried green plantains are mashed with a wooden *pilón*, mixed with garlic, pork fat, and other flavorings. When it's stuffed with chicken, beef, or some other meat, *mofongo* becomes one of Puerto Rico's signature entrées.

Rice: Rice is omnipresent, and most often it's served with *habichuelas* (beans). Rice stuck to the pot, known as *pegao*, is the most highly prized, full of all the ingredients that have sunk to the bottom.

Rum: Although rum was first exported in 1897, it took a bit longer for it to become the massive industry it is today. The Bacardí family set up shop near San Juan in 1959, after fleeing Cuba. The company's product, lighter-bodied than those produced by most other distilleries, gained favor around the world. Today Puerto Rico produces more than 35 million gallons of rum a year.

13

Updated
by Paulina
Salach and
Julie Schwietert
Collazo

Sunrise and sunset are both worth waiting for when you're in Puerto Rico. The pinks and yellows that hang in the early-morning sky are just as compelling as the sinewy reds and purples that blend into the twilight. It's easy to compare them, as Puerto Rico is small enough to have breakfast in Fajardo, looking eastward over the boats headed to Vieques and Culebra, and lobster dinner in Rincón as the sun is sinking into the inky-blue water.

Known as the Island of Enchantment, Puerto Rico conjures a powerful spell. Here traffic actually leads you to a "Road to Paradise," whether you're looking for a pleasurable, sunny escape from the confines of urbanity or a rich supply of stimulation to quench your cultural and entertainment thirst. On the island you have the best of both worlds, natural and urban thrills alike, and although city life is frenetic enough to make you forget you're surrounded by azure waters and warm sand, traveling a few miles inland or down the coast can easily make you forget you're surrounded by development.

Puerto Rico was populated primarily by Taíno Indians when Columbus landed in 1493. In 1508 Ponce de León established a settlement and became the first governor; in 1521 he founded what is known as Old San Juan. For centuries, while Africans worked on the coastal sugarcane fields, the French, Dutch, and English tried unsuccessfully to wrest the island from Spain. In 1898, as a result of the Spanish-American War, Spain ceded the island to the United States. In 1917 Puerto Ricans became U.S. citizens, and in 1952 Puerto Rico became a semiautonomous commonwealth.

Since the 1950s, Puerto Rico has developed exponentially, as witnessed in the urban sprawl, burgeoning traffic, and growing population (estimated at nearly 4 million); yet *en la isla* (on the island) a strong Latin sense of community and family prevails. Puertorriqueños are fiercely proud of their unique blend of heritages.

Music is another source of Puerto Rican pride. Like wildflowers, *vellon-eras* (jukeboxes) pop up almost everywhere, and when one is playing, somebody will be either singing or dancing along—or both. Cars often vibrate with *reggaetón,* an aggressive beat with lyrics that express social malaise. Salsa, a fusion of West African percussion, jazz, and other Latin beats, is the trademark dance. Although it may look difficult to master, it's all achieved by just loosening your hips. You may choose to let your inhibitions go by doing some clubbing *a la vida loca* made famous by pop star Ricky Martin. Nightlife options are on par with any cosmopolitan city—and then some.

13

By day you can drink in the culture of the Old World; one of the richest visual experiences in Puerto Rico is Old San Juan. Originally built as a fortress by the Spaniards in the early 1500s, the Old City has myriad attractions that include restored 16th-century buildings and 200-year-old houses with balustraded balconies of filigreed wrought iron that overlook narrow cobblestone streets. Spanish traditions are also apparent in the countryside festivals celebrated in honor of small-town patron saints. For quiet relaxation or experiences off the beaten track, visit coffee plantations, colonial towns, or outlying islets where nightlife is virtually nonexistent.

And you don't come to a Caribbean island without taking in some of the glorious sunshine and natural wonders. In the coastal areas the sun mildly toasts your body, and you're immediately healed by soft waves and cool breezes. In the misty mountains, you can wonder at the flickering night flies and the star-studded sky while the *coquís* (tiny local frogs) chirp their legendary sweet lullaby. On a moonless night, watch the warm ocean turn into luminescent aqua-blue speckles on your skin. Then there are the island's many acres of golf courses, numerous tennis courts, rain forests, and dozens of beaches that offer every imaginable water sport.

PLANNING

GETTING HERE AND AROUND
AIR TRAVEL

San Juan's busy Aeropuerto Internacional Luis Muñoz Marín (SJU) receives flights from all major American carriers, and there are dozens of daily flights to Puerto Rico from the United States. Nonstop options include American Airlines from Chicago, Dallas, Miami, and New York–JFK; Delta from Atlanta and New York–JFK; JetBlue from Boston, Chicago, Fort Lauderdale, Hartford, Newark, New York–JFK, Orlando, and Tampa; Southwest from Atlanta, Baltimore, Fort Lauderdale, Houston, Orlando, and Tampa; Spirit Airlines from Fort Lauderdale; United from Chicago, Houston, Newark, Philadelphia, and Washington, D.C.–Dulles; and US Airways from Charlotte, Chicago, Philadelphia, and Washington, D.C.–Dulles.

SJU is a major regional hub; many travelers make connections here to other islands in the Caribbean. Sometimes known as Isla Grande, San Juan's other airport, the Aeropuerto Fernando L. Ribas Dominicci

(SIG), is in Miramar near the Convention Center. It handles mainly short hops to Vieques and other nearby islands, though both airports offer flights to Culebra, Vieques, and other destinations on Puerto Rico and throughout the Caribbean. Air Flamenco and Vieques Air Link offer daily flights from SJU and SIG to Vieques and Culebra. Cape Air flies from SJU to Vieques and Culebra.

International Airline Contacts American Airlines. ☎ *800/433-7300* ⊕ *www. aa.com.* **Delta Airlines.** ☎ *800/221-1212 U.S. reservations, 800/241-4141 international reservations* ⊕ *www.delta.com.* **JetBlue.** ☎ *800/538-2583* ⊕ *www. jetblue.com.* **Spirit Airlines.** ☎ *801/401-2222* ⊕ *www.spirit.com.* **United Airlines.** ☎ *800/864-8331* ⊕ *www.united.com.*

Regional Airline Contacts Air Flamenco. ☎ *787/724-1818* ⊕ *www. airflamenco.net.* **Cape Air.** ☎ *800/227-3247* ⊕ *www.capeair.com.* **Vieques Air Link.** ☎ *787/741-8331, 888/901-9247* ⊕ *www.viequesairlink.com.*

Airports Aeropuerto Internacional Luis Muñoz Marín (*SJU*). ☎ *787/253-2329* ⊕ *www.aeropuertosju.com.* **Aeropuerto Fernando L. Ribas Dominicci** (*SIG*). ✉ *Calle Lindbergh, San Juan* ☎ *787/729-8715 ext. 3331.*

BOAT AND FERRY TRAVEL

Part of the Department of Transportation, the Autoridad de Transporte Marítimo (Maritime Transport Authority) runs passenger and cargo ferries from Fajardo, about a 90-minute drive from San Juan, to Culebra and Vieques. There are a limited number of seats on the ferries, so get to the terminal in plenty of time.

Contact Autoridad de Transporte Marítimo. ✉ *Carr De Maternillo, Fajardo* ☎ *787/494-0934* ⊕ *www.dtop.gov.pr.*

CAR TRAVEL

In San Juan it's often more trouble than it's worth to rent a car. Elsewhere a car is probably a necessity. A valid driver's license from your country of origin can be used in Puerto Rico for three months. Rates start as low as $25 a day. Several well-marked multilane highways link population centers. Driving distances are posted in kilometers, but speed limits are posted in miles per hour. Road signs are in Spanish.

International Agencies Avis. ✉ *San Juan International Airport, Terminal Bldg., Carolina* ☎ *787/253-5926* ⊕ *www.avis.com.* **Hertz.** ✉ *Luis Muñoz Marín International Airport, Salvador Caro Ave., Carolina* ☎ *787/791-0840* ⊕ *www.hertz.com.* **National.** ✉ *Luis Muñoz Marín International Airport, Carolina* ⊹ *Salvador Caro Ave.* ☎ *787/791-1805* ⊕ *www.nationalcar.com.* **Thrifty.** ✉ *Marginal Los Angeles #10030, Carolina* ☎ *787/253-2525* ⊕ *www.thriftypr.com.*

Local Agencies Charlie Car Rental. ☎ *787/728-2418* ⊕ *www.charliecars. com.* **Vias.** ✉ *Hotel Villa del Sol, 4 Rosa St., Isla Verde* ☎ *787/791-4120* ⊕ *www. viascarrental.com.*

TAXI TRAVEL

The Puerto Rico Tourism Company has instituted a well-organized taxi program. White taxis with the "taxi turistico" logo run from the airport or the cruise-ship piers to Isla Verde, Condado/Ocean Park, and Old San Juan, with fixed "zone" rates ranging from $10 to $24. If you take a cab going somewhere outside the fixed zones, insist on setting the meter. City tours start at $36 per hour. In other towns down cabs on the street, but it's easier to have your hot you. ■TIP➔ Make sure the driver is clear on whether charge a flat rate or use a meter to determine the fare.

Contacts **Major Cab Company.** ☎ 787/723–2460. **Metro Taxi.** ☎ *787/725–2870* ⊕ *www.metrotaxipr.com.*

HEALTH AND SAFETY

Dengue, chikungunya, and zika have all been reported in the Caribbean. We recommend that you protect yourself from these mosquito-borne illnesses by keeping your skin covered and/or wearing mosquito repellent. The mosquitoes that transmit these viruses are as active by day as they are by night.

HOTELS AND RESORTS

If you want easy access to shopping, dining, and nightlife, then you should stay in San Juan, which also has decent—though by no means the island's best—beaches. Most other large, deluxe resorts are along the northeast coast, but there are a few along the southern coast. Rincón, in the west, has a concentration of resorts and great surfing. Other small inns and hotels are in the interior, including a few around El Yunque. Look to Vieques and Culebra if you want to find excellent beaches and little development. Many larger resorts in Puerto Rico charge resort fees, which are uncommon elsewhere in the Caribbean.

Big Hotels: San Juan's beaches are lined with large-scale hotels that include happening restaurants and splashy casinos. Most are spread out along Condado and Isla Verde beaches.

Paradores: Small inns (many offering home-style comida criolla cooking) are spread around the island, though they are rarely on the beach.

Upscale Beach Resorts: All over the island—but particularly along the north coast—large tourist resorts offer all the amenities along with a hefty dose of isolation. Just be prepared for expensive food and few off-resort restaurants nearby.

Hotel reviews have been shortened. For full information, visit Fodors.com.

WHAT IT COSTS IN U.S. DOLLARS				
	$	$$	$$$	$$$$
RESTAURANTS	under $12	$12–$20	$21–$30	over $30
HOTELS	under $275	$275–$375	$376–$475	over $475

Restaurant prices are the average cost of a main course at dinner or, if dinner is not served, at lunch. Hotel prices are the lowest cost of a standard double room in high season.

VISITOR INFORMATION

Contact **Puerto Rico Tourism Company.** ✉ *Ochoa Bldg., Calle Tanca and Calle Comercio, across from Pier 1, Old San Juan* ☎ *787/721–2400* ⊕ *www.seepuertorico.com.*

PLORING

OLD SAN JUAN

Old San Juan, the original city founded in 1521, contains carefully pre-served examples of 16th- and 17th-century Spanish colonial architecture. More than 400 buildings have been beautifully restored. Graceful wrought-iron and wooden balconies with lush hanging plants extend over narrow streets paved with *adoquines* (blue-gray stones originally used as ballast on Spanish ships). The Old City is partially enclosed by walls that date from 1633 and once completely surrounded it. Designated a U.S. National Historic Zone in 1950, Old San Juan is chockablock with shops, open-air cafés, homes, tree-shaded squares, monuments, and people. You can get an overview on a morning's stroll, which includes some steep climbs. However, if you plan to immerse yourself in history or to shop, you'll need a couple of days.

TOP ATTRACTIONS

FAMILY
Fodor'sChoice
★

Castillo San Cristóbal. This huge stone fortress, built between 1634 and 1790, guarded the city from land attacks from the east. The largest Spanish fortification in the New World, San Cristóbal was known in the 17th and 18th centuries as the Gibraltar of the West Indies. Five freestanding structures divided by dry moats are connected by tunnels. You're free to explore the gun turrets (with cannon in situ), officers' quarters, re-created 18th-century barracks, and gloomy passageways. Along with El Morro, San Cristóbal is a National Historic Site administered by the U.S. Park Service; it's a World Heritage Site as well. Rangers conduct tours in Spanish and English. ⊠ *Calle Norzagaray at Av. Muñoz Rivera, Old San Juan* ☎ 787/729–6777 ⊕ *www.nps.gov/saju* ≋ *$5 includes admission to El Morro* ☉ *Daily 9–6.*

FAMILY
Fodor'sChoice
★

Castillo San Felipe del Morro (*El Morro*). At the northwestern tip of the Old City, El Morro ("the promontory") was built by the Spaniards between 1539 and 1786. Rising 140 feet above the sea, the massive six-level fortress was built to protect the port and has a commanding view of the harbor. It is a labyrinth of cannon batteries, ramps, barracks, turrets, towers, and tunnels, which you're free to wander. The cannon emplacement walls and the dank secret passageways are a wonder of engineering. A small but enlightening museum displays ancient Spanish guns and other armaments, military uniforms, and blueprints for Spanish forts in the Americas, although Castillo San Cristóbal has more extensive and impressive exhibits. There's also a gift shop. The fort is a National Historic Site administered by the U.S. Park Service and is a World Heritage Site as well. Various tours and a video are available in English. ⊠ *Calle del Morro, Old San Juan* ☎ 787/729–6960 ⊕ *www.nps.gov/saju* ≋ *$5 includes admission to Castillo San Cristóbal* ☉ *Daily 9–6.*

La Fortaleza. Sitting atop the fortified city walls overlooking the harbor, La Fortaleza was built between 1533 and 1540 as a fortress, but it proved insufficient, mainly because it was built inside the bay. It was attacked numerous times and occupied twice, by the British in 1598 and

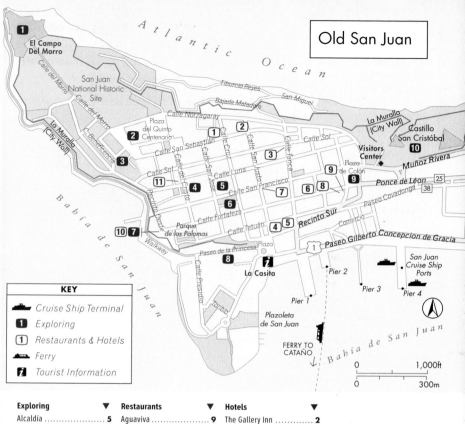

Old San Juan

KEY

- 🚢 Cruise Ship Terminal
- **1** Exploring
- ① Restaurants & Hotels
- ⛴ Ferry
- 🛈 Tourist Information

the Dutch in 1625. When the city's other fortifications were finished, this became the governor's palace. Changes made over the past four centuries have resulted in the current eclectic yet eye-pleasing collection of marble and mahogany, medieval towers, and stained-glass galleries. Still the official residence of the island's governor, it is the western hemisphere's oldest executive mansion in continual use. Guided tours of the gardens and exterior are conducted several times a day in English and Spanish. Call ahead, as the schedule changes daily. Proper attire is required: no sleeveless shirts or very short shorts. Tours begin near the main gate in a yellow building called the Real Audiencia, housing the Oficina Estatal de Preservación Histórica. ✉ *Western end of Calle Fortaleza, Old San Juan* ☎ 787/721–7000 ⊕ *www.fortaleza.gobierno.pr* ✉ *Free* ⊙ *Weekdays 9–4:30.*

Paseo de la Princesa. Built in the mid-19th century to honor the Spanish princess of Asturias, this street has a broad pedestrian walkway and is spruced up with flowers, trees, benches, and street lamps. Unfurling westward from Plaza del Inmigrante along the base of the fortified city walls, it leads to the Fuente Raíces, a striking fountain depicting the various ethnic groups of Puerto Rico. Take a seat and watch the boats zip across the water. Beyond the fountain is the beginning of Paseo del Morro, a well-paved shoreline path that hugs Old San Juan's walls and leads past the city gate at Calle San Juan and continues to the tip of the headland, beneath El Morro. ✉ *Paseo de la Princesa, Old San Juan.*

WORTH NOTING

Alcaldía. San Juan's city hall was built between 1602 and 1789. In 1841, extensive alterations made it resemble Madrid's city hall, with arcades, towers, balconies, and an inner courtyard. Renovations have refreshed the facade and some interior rooms, but the architecture remains true to its colonial style. Only the patios are open to public viewings. A municipal tourist information center and an art gallery with rotating exhibits are in the lobby. Call ahead to schedule a free tour. ✉ *153 Calle San Francisco, Plaza de Armas, Old San Juan* ☎ 787/480–2910 ⊕ *www. sanjuanciudadpatria.com* ✉ *Free* ⊙ *Weekdays 8–4.*

Casa Blanca. The original structure here was a wooden house built in 1521 as a home for Ponce de León; he died in Cuba without ever living here. His descendants occupied the house's sturdier replacement, a lovely colonial mansion with tile floors and beamed ceilings, for more than 250 years. It was the home of the U.S. Army commander in Puerto Rico from the end of the Spanish-American War in 1898 to 1966. Several rooms decorated with colonial-era furnishings are open to the public. A guide will show you around, and then you can explore on your own. Don't miss the stairway descending from one of the bedrooms. (Despite local lore, this leads to a small room and not to a tunnel to nearby El Morro.) The lush garden, complete with watchtower, is a quiet place to unwind. ✉ *1 Calle San Sebastián, Old San Juan* ☎ *787/725–1454* ✉ *Free* ⊙ *Wed.–Sun. 10–2.*

Catedral de San Juan Bautista. The Catholic shrine of Puerto Rico had humble beginnings in the early 1520s as a thatch-roof, wooden structure. After a hurricane destroyed the church, it was rebuilt in 1540, when it was given a graceful circular staircase and vaulted Gothic ceilings. Most of the work on the present cathedral, however, was done in the 19th century. The remains of Ponce de León are behind a marble tomb in the wall near the transept, on the north side. The trompe l'oeil work on the inside of the dome is breathtaking. Unfortunately, many of the other frescoes suffer from water damage. ✉ *151 Calle Cristo, Old San Juan* ☎ *787/722–0861* 🎟 *$1 donation suggested* ☉ *Mon.–Sat. 9–5, Sun. 9–1.*

Museo de las Américas. On the second floor of the imposing former military barracks, Cuartel de Ballajá, this museum houses four permanent exhibits: Folk Arts, African Heritage, the Indian in America, and Conquest and Colonization. You'll also find a number of temporary exhibitions of works by regional and international artists. A wide range of handicrafts is available in the gift shop. ✉ *Calle Norzagaray and Calle del Morro, Old San Juan* ☎ *787/724–5052* ⊕ *www.museolasamericas. org* 🎟 *$6* ☉ *Tues.–Fri. 9–noon and 1–4, Sat 10–5, Sun. noon–5.*

Plaza de Armas. The Old City's original main square was once used as military drilling grounds. Bordered by Calles San Francisco, Rafael Cordero, San José, and Cruz, it has a fountain with 19th-century statues representing the four seasons as well as a bandstand, a small café, and kiosk selling snacks and fruit frappés. The Alcaldía commands the north side. This is a popular, bustling meeting place, often filled with artists sketching caricatures, pedestrians in line at the food stands, and hundreds of pigeons waiting for handouts. ✉ *Calle San José, Old San Juan.*

Plaza de Colón. The Americas' tallest statue of Christopher Columbus stands atop a soaring column and fountain in this bustling Old San Juan square, kitty-corner to Castillo San Cristóbal. Once called St. James Square, it was renamed in 1893 to honor the 400th anniversary of Columbus's arrival in Puerto Rico. Bronze plaques on the statue's base relate episodes in his life. Local artisans often line the plaza, so it's a good place for souvenirs. Cool off with a fresh fruit frappé or smoothie at the kiosk. ✉ *Old San Juan.*

GREATER SAN JUAN

Taxis, buses, *públicos* (shared vans), or a rental car are needed to reach the "new" San Juan. Avenidas Muñoz Rivera, Ponce de León, and Fernández Juncos are the main thoroughfares that cross Puerta de Tierra, east of Old San Juan, to the business and tourist districts of Santurce, Condado, Ocean Park, and Isla Verde. Dos Hermanos Bridge connects Puerta de Tierra with Miramar, Condado, and Isla Grande. Isla Grande Airport, from which you can take short hops, is on the bay side of the bridge. On the other side, the Condado Lagoon is bordered by Avenida Ashford, which goes past the high-rise Condado hotels, and Avenida Baldorioty de Castro Expreso, which barrels east to the airport and beyond. Due south of the lagoon is Miramar, a residential area with fashionable turn-of-the-20th-century homes and a few hotels and great restaurants. Isla Verde, with its glittering beachfront hotels, casinos, discos, and public beach, is to the east, near the airport.

Hear your footsteps echo throughout Castillo San Felipe's vast network of tunnels, designed to amplify the sounds of approaching enemies.

TOP ATTRACTIONS

Museo de Arte Contemporáneo de Puerto Rico. This Georgian-style structure, once a public school, displays a dynamic range of works by established and up-and-coming Latin American artists. Many works have strong political messages, including pointed commentaries on Puerto Rico's status as a commonwealth. Only part of the permanent collection's more than 900 works is on display at a time, but it might be anything from ceramics to videos. ⊠ *1220 Av. Ponce de León, at Av. R.H. Todd, Santurce* 🕾 *787/977–4030* ⊕ *www.mac-pr.org* ✉ *$5* ⊘ *Tues.–Fri. 10–4, Sat. 11–5.*

Fodor'sChoice ★ **Museo de Arte de Puerto Rico.** One of the Caribbean's biggest museums, this beautiful neoclassical building was once the San Juan Municipal Hospital. The collection of Puerto Rican art starts with the colonial era, when most art was commissioned for churches. Works by José Campeche, the island's first great painter, include his masterpiece, *Immaculate Conception*, finished in 1794. Also well represented is Francisco Oller y Cestero, who was the first to move beyond religious subjects to paint local scenes. Another room has works by artists inspired by Oller. The original building, built in the 1920s, proved too small to house the collection; a newer east wing is dominated by a five-story stained-glass window by local artist Eric Tabales. The museum also has a beautiful garden with native flora and a 400-seat theater with a remarkable hand-crocheted lace curtain. ⊠ *299 Av. José de Diego, Santurce* 🕾 *787/977–6277* ⊕ *www.mapr.org* ✉ *$6; free Wed. 2–8* ⊘ *Tues. and Thurs.–Sat. 10–5, Wed. 10–8, Sun. 11–6.*

WORTH NOTING

El Capitolio. The white-marble Capitol, a fine example of Italian Renaissance style, dates from 1929. The grand rotunda, which can be seen from all over San Juan, was completed in the late 1990s. Fronted by eight Corinthian columns, it's a dignified home for the commonwealth's constitution. Although the Senate and House of Representatives have offices in the more modern buildings on either side, the Capitol is where the legislators meet. Guided tours, which last about an hour and include the rotunda, are by appointment only. ⊠ *Av. Constitución, Puerta de Tierra* ☎ *787/724–2030, 787/721–5200 guided tours* ⌕ *Free* ☉ *Weekdays 8:30–4:30.*

Museo de Historia, Antropología y Arte. The Universidad de Puerto Rico's small Museum of History, Anthropology and Art offers rotating exhibitions in three areas. Its archaeological and historical collection covers the Native American influence on the island and the Caribbean, the colonial era, and the history of slavery. There's also a small collection of Egyptian antiquities. Art holdings include a range of Puerto Rican popular, graphic, folk, and fine art; the museum's prize exhibit is the painting *El Velorio (The Wake)*, by the 19th-century artist Francisco Oller. If you're looking to see something in particular, call before you go, as only a small portion of the collection is on display at a time. Guided tours in English are available; call for reservations. ⊠ *Universidad de Puerto Rico, Av. Ponce de León, San Juan* ☎ *787/763–3939* ⌕ *Free* ☉ *Mon., Tues., Thurs., and Fri. 9–4; Wed. 9–8:30; Sun. 11:30–4:30.*

SAN JUAN ENVIRONS

WORTH NOTING

Casa Bacardí Visitor Center. Exiled from Cuba, the Bacardí family built a small rum distillery here in the 1950s. Today it's the world's largest, able to produce 100,000 gallons of spirits a day and 21 million cases a year. A basic tour of the visitor center includes one free drink, or you can opt for a mixology class or rum tasting. If you don't want to drive, you can take a ferry from Pier 2 for 50¢ and then a *público* (public van service) from the ferry pier to the factory for about $3 per person. ⊠ *Bay View Industrial Park, Rte. 165, Km 2.6, at Rte. 888, Cataño* ☎ *787/788–8400* ⊕ *www.visitcasabacardi.com* ⌕ *Tour $12; mixology class or rum tasting $45* ☉ *Mon.–Sat. 9–4:30, Sun. 10–4:30; last tour at 4:15.*

EASTERN PUERTO RICO

EL YUNQUE

Fodor's Choice ★ The more than 100 billion gallons of precipitation that El Yunque receives annually spawns rushing streams and cascades, outsize impatiens and ferns, and 240 tree species. In the evening millions of inch-long coquís (tree frogs) begin their calls. El Yunque is also home to the *cotorra*, Puerto Rico's endangered green parrot, as well as 67 other types of birds.

El Yunque is the only tropical rain forest in the U.S. National Forest System, spanning 28,000 acres, reaching an elevation of more than 3,500 feet, and receiving an estimated 200–240 inches of rain each year. The forest's 13 hiking trails are extremely well maintained; many are easy to navigate and less than 1 mile (1½ km) long. It's about 73°F year-round, but expect rain nearly every day. Post-shower times bring the best bird-watching. For easy parking and fewer crowds, arrive early in the day, although the park rarely gets crowded by U.S. National Park standards.

Carve out some time to stop at the cathedral-like **El Portal Visitor Center** (⊠ *Rte. 191, Km 4.3, off Rte. 3* ☎ *787/888–1880* ⊕ *www.fs.usda.gov/ elyunque* 🖃 *$4* ⊙ *Daily 9–4:30*). Enter via an elevated walkway that transports visitors across the forest canopy, 60 feet above the ground. Signs identify and explain the birds, animals, and other treasures seen among the treetops. Below the walkway, there's a ground-level nature trail with stunning views of the lower forest and coastal plain. Inside the center, interactive exhibits explain the El Yunque National Forest's history, topography, flora, and fauna. The facility also has a well-stocked bookstore and gift shop.

The 13 official trails throughout El Yunque are well marked, and easy for both beginners and children. The trails on the north side of El Yunque, the park's main tourist hub, tend toward folks with minimal or no hiking experience. There are several short trails (about ½ mile [.8 km]) that are completely paved. On the south side, expect fewer people and moderate to challenging hikes. These trails, as well as the marked trails found lower in the forest, are not maintained. Regardless of where you go, you'll be immersed in the sounds, smells, and scenic landscape of the park. For avid outdoor adventurers, it's possible to hike between the north and south sides of El Yunque. If you prefer to see the sights from a car, as many people do, simply follow Route 191 as it winds into the mountains, and stop at several observation points along the way.

TOUR OPERATORS

Many companies in San Juan offer excursions to El Yunque. A National Forest Service ranger leads one-hour English and Spanish tours from the **Palo Colorado Information Center** along the Caimitillo and Baño de Oro trails (⊙ *11 am–1 pm $5, seniors, and kids 5–12,* 🖃 *$3*). Tours are first-come, first-served.

Acampa Nature Adventure Tours. Book a half-day excursion with Acampa Nature Adventure Tours and choose from a moderate hike at lower elevations of the forest to more challenging treks to the El Yunque peak at 3,500 feet. Rates start at $89, with an eight-person minimum, and include round-trip transportation to and from your hotel, park fees, and lunch. ⊠ *1221 Av. Piñero, San Juan* ☎ *787/706–0695* ⊕ *www. acampapr.com.*

Eco Action Tours. Eco Action Tours will pick you up at your hotel and take you to the rain forest, where small groups will hike, swim in the falls, and learn about the flora and fauna. Half-day rates are reasonable, starting at $58 (not including entry free). Full-day tours are $68 and can be combined with a stop at Luquillo Beach. ☎ *787/791–7509* ⊕ *www.ecoactiontours.com.*

FAJARDO

Founded in 1772, Fajardo was once known as a port where pirates stocked up on supplies. It later developed into a fishing community and an area where sugarcane flourished. (There are still cane fields on the city's fringes.) Today it's a hub for the yachts that use its marinas, the divers who head to its good offshore sites, and the day-trippers who travel by catamaran, ferry, or plane to the offshore islands of Culebra and Vieques. With the most significant docking facilities on the island's eastern side, Fajardo is often congested and difficult to navigate.

Reserva Natural Las Cabezas de San Juan. The 316-acre reserve on a headland north of Fajardo is owned by the nonprofit Conservation Trust of Puerto Rico. You ride in open-air trolleys and wander down boardwalks through seven ecosystems, including lagoons, mangrove swamps, and dry-forest areas. Green iguanas skitter across paths, and guides identify other endangered species. A half-hour hike down a wooden walkway brings you to the mangrove-lined **Laguna Grande,** where bioluminescent microorganisms glow at night. The restored **Fajardo Lighthouse** is the final stop on the tour; its Spanish-colonial tower has been in operation since 1882, making it Puerto Rico's second-oldest lighthouse. The first floor houses ecological displays, and a winding staircase leads to an observation deck. The only way to see the reserve is on a guided tour; reservations are required and can be made through the trust website. ⊠ *Rte. 987, Km 6, Fajardo* ☎ *787/722–5882* ⊕ *www.paralanaturaleza. org* ⊒ *$10.*

VIEQUES AND CULEBRA

VIEQUES

This island off Puerto Rico's east coast is famed for its Playa Sun Bay, a gorgeous stretch of sand with picnic facilities and shade trees. In 2003 the U.S. Navy withdrew its military operations and turned over two-thirds of Vieques to the local government. It's being transformed into the Vieques National Wildlife Refuge. Vieques has two communities— Isabel Segunda, where the ferries dock, and the smaller Esperanza. Both have restaurants and hotels with surprising sophistication.

Fodor's Choice
★

Puerto Mosquito Bioluminescent Bay. East of Esperanza, Puerto Mosquito is one of the world's best spots for a glow-in-the-dark experience with undersea dinoflagellates—microorganisms that light up when the water around them is agitated. Local operators offer kayak trips or excursions on nonpolluting boats to see the bay's light show. Look behind your boat at the twinkling wake. Even the fish that swim through and jump from the water bear an eerie glow. The high concentration of dinoflagellates sets the bay apart from other spots (including in Puerto Rico) that are home to these microorganisms. The bay is at its best when there's little or no moonlight; rainy nights are beautiful, too, because raindrops hitting the water produce ricochets that shimmer like diamonds. Note that licensed operators are prohibited from leading tours on the day before, during, and after a full moon. ⊠ *Unpaved roads off Rte. 997.*

CULEBRA

Culebra is known around the world for its curvaceous coastline. Playa Flamenco, the tiny island's most famous stretch of sand, is considered one of the best beaches in the world. If Playa Flamenco gets too crowded, as it often does around Easter and Christmas, you can find many other nearly deserted beaches. There's archaeological evidence that Taíno and Carib peoples lived on Culebra long before the late-15th-century arrival of the Spanish, who didn't bother laying claim to it until 1886. Its dearth of freshwater made it an unattractive location for a settlement. Although the island now has modern conveniences, its pace seems little changed from a century ago. There's only one town, Dewey, named after U.S. Admiral George Dewey. When the sun goes down, Culebra winds down as well. But during the day it's a delightful place to stake out a spot on Playa Flamenco or Playa Zoni and read, swim, or search for shells. So what causes stress on the island? Nada.

13

SOUTHERN PUERTO RICO

Bosque Estatal de Guánica (*Guánica State Forest*). This 9,900-acre United Nations Biosphere Reserve is a great place for hiking. An outstanding example of a tropical dry coastal forest, it has some 700 species of plants, from the prickly-pear cactus to the gumbo limbo tree, and offers superb bird-watching; its more than 100 species include the pearly-eyed thrasher, lizard cuckoo, and nightjar.

The popular **Ballena Trail,** which begins at the ranger station on Route 334, is an easy 1¼-mile (2-km) walk that follows a partially paved road past a mahogany plantation to a dry plain covered with stunted cactus. A sign reading "Guayacán centenario" leads you to an extraordinary guayacán tree with a 6-foot-wide trunk. The moderately difficult, 3½-mile (5½-km) **Fuerte Trail** leads to an old fort built by the Spanish Armada. It was destroyed in the Spanish American War in 1898, but you can see ruins of the old observatory tower.

In addition to using the main entrance on Route 334, you can enter on Route 333, which skirts the forest's southwestern quadrant, or try the less explored western section, off Route 325. ⊠ *Rte. 334, Guánica* ☎ *787/821–5706* 🏷 *Free* ☼ *Daily 8:30–4:30.*

PONCE

The island's second-largest urban area, Ponce shines in 19th-century style with pink-marble-bordered sidewalks, painted trolleys, and horse-drawn carriages. Stroll around the main square, the Plaza de las Delicias, with its perfectly pruned India-laurel fig trees, graceful fountains, gardens, and park benches. View the Catedral de Nuestra Señora de la Guadalupe (Our Lady of Guadalupe Cathedral), perhaps even attend the 6 am Mass, and walk down Calles Isabel and Cristina to see turn-of-the-20th-century wooden houses with wrought-iron balconies.

TOP ATTRACTIONS

Fodor's Choice ★ **Castillo Serrallés.** This lovely Spanish-style villa—so massive that townspeople dubbed it a castle—was built in the 1930s for Ponce's wealthiest family, the makers of Don Q rum. Guided tours provide a glimpse into the lifestyle of a sugar baron, and a permanent exhibit explains the area's sugarcane and rum industries. The dining room, with original hand-carved furnishings, and the extensive garden, with sculptured bushes and a shimmering reflection pool, are highlights. A large cross looming over the house is an observatory; from the top, you can see the Caribbean. ⌧ *17 El Vigía, El Vigía* ☎*787/259–1774* ⊕*www. museocastilloserralles.com* ✉ *$12.80 adults, $5.50 kids, with Japanese garden, cross observatory, and butterfly sanctuary* ☉ *Wed.–Sun. 9:30–5:30.*

FAMILY **Hacienda Buena Vista.** Built by Salvador de Vives in 1838, this was one of the area's largest coffee plantations. It's a technological marvel—water from the nearby Río Canas was funneled into narrow brick channels that could be diverted to perform any number of tasks, including turning the waterwheel. (Seeing the two-story wheel slowly begin to turn is fascinating, especially for kids.) Nearby is the two-story manor house, with a kitchen dominated by a massive hearth and furniture that hints at life on a coffee plantation nearly 150 years ago. In 1987 the plantation was restored by the Puerto Rican Conservation Trust, which leads several tours each day (at least one in English) by reservation only (call several days ahead or reserve online). A gift shop sells coffee beans and other souvenirs. Allow an hour to drive the winding road from Ponce. ⌧ *Rte. 123, Km 17.3, Sector Corral Viejo* ☎*787/284–7020 weekdays* ⊕ *www.paralanaturaleza.org* ✉ *$10* ☉ *Wed.–Sun. Call or visit online for schedule of available tours and times.*

Fodor's Choice ★

Fodor's Choice ★ **Museo de Arte de Ponce.** Designed by Edward Durrell Stone, who also designed the original Museum of Modern Art in New York City and the Kennedy Center in Washington, D.C., Ponce's art museum is easily identified by the hexagonal galleries on the second story. The museum has one of the best art collections in Puerto Rico, which is why residents of San Juan frequently make the trip. The 4,500-piece collection includes works by famous Puerto Rican artists such as Francisco Oller, represented by a lovely landscape called *Hacienda Aurora*. European works include paintings by Peter Paul Rubens and Thomas Gainsborough as well as pre-Raphaelite paintings, particularly the mesmerizing *Flaming June*, by Frederick Leighton, which has become the museum's unofficial symbol. The museum also offers special exhibits, three sculpture gardens, and a café. ⌧ *2325 Blvd. Luis A. Ferre Aguayo, Sector Santa María* ☎ *787/840–1510* ⊕ *www.museoarteponce.org* ✉ *$6* ☉ *Mon. and Wed.–Sat. 10–5, Sun. noon–5.*

FAMILY **Parque de Bombas.** After El Morro in Old San Juan, this distinctive red-and-black-stripe building may be the second-most-photographed structure in Puerto Rico. Built in 1882 as a pavilion for an agricultural and industrial fair, it was converted the following year into a firehouse. In 1990, it took on a new life, this time, as a small museum tracing the history—and glorious feats—of Ponce's fire brigade. Kids love the antique fire truck on the lower level. Short tours in English and Spanish are given on the hour starting at 10; if the trolley is running, you can sign up for free tours of the historic downtown here, too. Helpful tourism officials staff a small information desk inside. ⌧ *Plaza de las Delicias, Ponce* ☎ *787/284–3338* ⊕ *www.visitponce.com* ✉ *Free* ☉ *Daily 9–5:30.*

Fodor's Choice ★

Today it's a museum, but for more than 100 years Parque de Bombas served as Ponce's main firehouse.

WORTH NOTING

Centro Ceremonial Indígena de Tibes (*Tibes Indian Ceremonial Center*). This archaeological site, discovered after flooding from a tropical storm in 1975, is the island's most important. Dating from AD 300–700, it includes nine playing fields used for a ritual ball game that some think was similar to soccer. The fields are bordered by smooth stones, some of which are engraved with petroglyphs that might have ceremonial or astronomical significance. In the eye-catching *Plaza de Estrella* (Plaza of the Star), stones are arranged in a pattern resembling a rising sun, perhaps used to chart the seasons. A village with thatched huts has been reconstructed. Visit the small museum before taking a walking tour of the site. ✉ *Rte. 503, Km 2.5, Barrio Tibes* ☎ *787/840–2255, 787/840–5685* 💲 *$3* ⊘ *Tues.–Sun. 9–3* ☞ *Call ahead to confirm current "last entry" time for the day you intend to visit.*

Museo de la Historia de Ponce. Housed in two adjoining neoclassical mansions, this museum includes 10 rooms with exhibits covering the city's residents, from Taíno Indians to Spanish settlers to the mix of the present. Guided tours in English and Spanish give an overview of the city's history. Though descriptions are mostly in Spanish, displays of clothing from different eras are interesting. ✉ *53 Calle Isabel, at Calle Mayor, Ponce* ☎ *787/844–7071* 💲 *Free* ⊘ *Tues.–Sun. 9–4.*

SAN GERMÁN

Around San Germán's (population 39,000) two main squares—Plazuela Santo Domingo and Plaza Francisco Mariano Quiñones (named for an abolitionist)—are buildings done in every conceivable style of architecture found on the island, including mission, Victorian, creole, and Spanish colonial. The city's tourist office offers a free, guided trolley tour. Students and professors from the Inter-American University often fill the center's bars and cafés.

Capilla de Porta Coeli (*Heaven's Gate Chapel*). One of the oldest religious buildings in the Americas, this mission-style chapel overlooks the long, rectangular Plazuela de Santo Domingo. It's not a grand building, but its position at the top of a stone stairway gives it a noble air. Queen Isabel Segunda decreed that the Dominicans should build a church and monastery in San Germán, so a rudimentary building was erected in 1609, replaced in 1692 by the structure seen today. (Sadly, most of the monastery was demolished in 1866, leaving only a vestige of its facade.) The chapel functions as a museum of religious art, displaying painted wooden statuary by Latin American and Spanish artists. ⊠ *East end of Plazuela Santo Domingo, San Germán* ☎ *787/892–5845* ☐ *$3* ⊘ *Weekdays 9–noon and 1–4:30.*

CENTRAL PUERTO RICO

Fodor'sChoice **Arecibo Observatory.** Hidden among pine-covered hills, this observatory
★ is home to the world's largest radar-radio telescope. Operated by the National Astronomy and Ionosphere Center of Cornell University, the 20-acre dish lies in a 563-foot-deep sinkhole in the karst landscape. If the 600-ton platform hovering eerily over the dish looks familiar, it may come from the movie *Contact*. You can walk around the viewing platform and explore two levels of interactive exhibits on planetary systems, meteors, and weather phenomena in the visitor center. There's also a gift shop. Note that the trail leading to the observatory is extremely steep. Those with difficulty walking or a medical condition can ask at the gate about a courtesy shuttle. ⊠ *Rte. 625, Km 3, Arecibo* ☎ *787/878–2612* ⊕ *www.naic.edu* ☐ *$10* ⊘ *Mid-Jan.–May and Aug.–mid-Dec., Wed.–Sun. 9–4; June, July, and mid-Dec.–mid-Jan., daily 9–4.*

Parque de las Cavernas del Río Camuy. The 268-acre Parque de las Cavernas del Río Camuy contains one of the world's largest cave networks. A tram takes you down a trail shaded by bamboo and banana trees to Cueva Clara, where the stalactites and stalagmites turn the entrance into a toothy grin. Hour-long guided tours in English and Spanish lead you on foot through the 180-foot-high cave, which is teeming with wildlife. You're likely to see blue-eyed river crabs and long-legged tarantulas. More elusive are the more than 100,000 bats that make their home in the cave. They don't come out until dark, but you can feel the heat they generate at the cave's entrance (not to mention smell their presence). The visit ends with a tram ride to Tres Pueblos sinkhole, where you can see the third-longest underground river in the world passing from one cave to another. Tours are first-come, first-served; plan to arrive early on weekends, when local families join the crowds. Tours are sometimes canceled if it's raining, as the steep walkways can get slippery. There's a picnic area, cafeteria, and gift shop. ⊠ *Rte. 129, Km 18.9, Camuy* ☎ *787/898–3100* ☐ *$10* ⊘ *Wed.–Sun. 8–4; last tour at 3:45.*

WESTERN PUERTO RICO

MAYAGÜEZ

With a population of slightly more than 100,000, this is the largest city on Puerto Rico's west coast. Although bypassed by the mania for restoration that has spruced up Ponce and Old San Juan, Mayagüez is graced by some lovely turn-of-the-20th-century architecture, such as the landmark art deco Teatro Yagüez and the Plaza de Colón.

FAMILY **Zoológico de Puerto Rico.** Puerto Rico's only zoo is just north of downtown. Its 45-foot-tall aviary lets you walk through a rain-forest environment as tropical birds fly overhead. There's also a butterfly park where you can let brilliant blue morphos land on you, and an arthropodarium where you can get up close and personal with spiders and their kin. Video monitors in the floor show the bugs that normally get trampled underfoot. The older section of the 45-acre park has undergone an extensive renovation, with most cages replaced by fairly natural-looking environments. A popular resident is Mundi, a female elephant who arrived as a baby more than two decades ago. There are also plenty of lions, tigers, and even bears. ✉ *Rte. 108, north of Rte. 65, Mayagüez* ☎ *787/834–8110* ⊕ *www.parquesnacionalespr.com* 🎟 *$13; parking $3* ⊘ *Wed.–Sun. 8:30–4.*

RINCÓN

Jutting into the ocean along the rugged western coast, Rincón, meaning "corner" in Spanish, may have gotten its name because it's tucked into a bend of the coastline. Some, however, trace the name to Gonzalo Rincón, a 16th-century landowner who let poor families live on his land. Whatever the truth, the name suits the town, which is like a little world unto itself.

Though now home to resorts, including the luxurious Horned Dorset Primavera—Puerto Rico's only Relais & Chateaux property—Rincón remains laid-back. The town is still a mecca for wave-seekers, particularly surfers from the East Coast of the United States, who often prefer the relatively quick flight to Aguadilla's airport instead of the long haul to the Pacific. One of Rincón's greatest attractions is the diving and snorkeling at nearby Desecheo Island, but the town caters to all sorts of travelers, from budget-conscious surfers to families to honeymooners seeking romance.

BEACHES

In Puerto Rico the Foundation for Environmental Education, a non-profit agency, designates Blue Flag beaches. They have to meet 27 criteria, focusing on water quality, the presence of a trained staff, and the availability of facilities such as water fountains and restrooms. Surprisingly, two such beaches are in San Juan: Balneario El Escambrón, in Puerta de Tierra, and Balneario de Carolina, in Isla Verde. The government maintains 13 *balnearios* (public beaches), which are gated and equipped with dressing rooms, lifeguards, parking, and, in some cases, picnic tables, playgrounds, and camping facilities.

SAN JUAN

The city's beaches can get crowded, especially on weekends. There's free access to all of them, but parking can be an issue in the peak sun hours—arriving early or in the late afternoon is a safer bet.

FAMILY **Balneario de Carolina.** When people talk about a "beautiful Isla Verde beach," this is it. East of Isla Verde, this Blue Flag beach is so close to the airport that leaves rustle when planes take off. Thanks to an offshore reef, the surf is not as strong as other nearby beaches, so it's good for families. There's plenty of room to spread out underneath the palm and almond trees, and there are picnic tables and barbecue grills. Though there's a charge for parking, there's not always someone to take the money. On weekends, the beach is crowded; get here early to nab parking. **Amenities:** lifeguards; parking (fee); showers; toilets. **Best for:** swimming; walking. ⊠ *Av. Los Gobernadores, Carolina* ☎ *787/791–2410* ⊠ *$3 parking* ⊗ *Tues.–Sun. 8–5.*

FAMILY **Balneario El Escambrón.** In Puerta de Tierra, this government-run beach has a patch of honey-colored sand shaded by coconut palms. An offshore reef generally makes surf gentle, so it's favored by families. Nearby restaurants make picnicking easy. **Amenities:** food and drink; lifeguards, parking (fee); showers; toilets. **Best for:** swimming; walking. ⊠ *Av. Muñoz Rivera, Puerta de Tierra* ⊠ *$5 parking* ⊗ *Daily 8–5:30.*

EASTERN PUERTO RICO

FAMILY **Balneario Seven Seas.** One of Puerto Rico's prized Blue Flag beaches, this long stretch of powdery sand near the Reserva Natural Las Cabezas de San Juan has calm, clear waters that are perfect for swimming. There are plenty of picnic tables, as well as restaurants just outside the gates. **Amenities:** food and drink; parking (fee); showers; toilets. **Best for:** swimming. ⊠ *Rte. 195, Km. 4.8, Las Croabas* ☎ *787/863–8180* ⊠ *$5 parking* ⊗ *Apr.–Aug., daily 8:30–6; Sept.–Mar., Wed.–Sun. 8:30–5.*

FAMILY **Luquillo Beach** (*Balneario La Monserrate*). Signs refer to this gentle beach off Route 3 as Balneario La Monserrate, but everyone simply calls it Luquillo Beach. Lined with colorful lifeguard stations and shaded by soaring palm trees, it's a magnet for families and has picnic areas and 60-plus kiosks serving fritters and drinks—a local hangout. Lounge chairs and umbrellas are available to rent, as are kayaks and Jet Skis. Its most distinctive facility is the Mar Sin Barreras (Sea Without Barriers), a low-sloped ramp into the water that allows wheelchair users to take a dip. On busy days, the beach can be crowded and littered with a party atmosphere. **Amenities:** food and drink; lifeguards, parking (fee); showers; toilets; water sports. **Best for:** partiers; swimming; walking. ⊠ *Off Rte. 3, Luquillo* ☎ *787/889–5871* ⊠ *$4 per car* ⊗ *Wed.–Sun. 8:30–5.*

VIEQUES AND CULEBRA

VIEQUES

Balneario Sun Bay. Just east of Esperanza, this mile-long stretch of sand skirts a perfect crescent-shaped bay. Dotted with picnic tables, this beach gets packed on holidays and weekends. On weekdays, when crowds are thin, you might see wild horses grazing among the palm trees. Parking is $2, but often there is no one at the gate to take your money. **Amenities:** food and drink; parking (fee); showers; toilets. **Best for:** snorkeling; swimming; walking. ⊠ *Rte. 997, Esperanza* 🕾 *787/741–8198* ⊕ *www. parquesnacionalespr.com* 🖃 *$2 parking* ☉ *Wed.–Sun. 8:30–5.*

Playa Caracas (*Red Beach*). One of the first stretches of sand east of Esperanza, this well-maintained beach boasts covered cabañas for lounging. Less rustic than other nearby beaches, it is sheltered from waves. **Amenities:** parking (free), toilets. **Best for:** snorkeling; swimming; walking. ⊠ *Off Rte. 997.*

CULEBRA

FAMILY

Fodor'sChoice

★

Playa Flamenco. Consistently ranked one of the most beautiful beaches in the world, this beach has snow-white sands, turquoise waters, and lush hills rising on all sides. During the week, it's pleasantly uncrowded; on weekends it fills up with day-trippers from the mainland. With kiosks selling simple dishes and vendors for lounge-chair and umbrella rentals, it's easy to make a day of it. There's great snorkeling past the old dock. Tanks on the northern end of the beach are a reminder that the area was once a military base. **Amenities:** food and drink; parking (free); showers; toilets. **Best for:** snorkeling; swimming; walking. ⊠ *Rte. 251, west of the airport* 🕾 *787/742–0700.*

SOUTHERN PUERTO RICO

Isla Caja de Muertos (*Coffin Island*). Named for its shape, this island, which stretches for 2 miles (3 km) and is 5 miles (8 km)off the coast, has the best beaches near Ponce and some of the best snorkeling in southern Puerto Rico. Due to hawksbill turtle nesting (May–December), the island is protected by the Reserva Natural Caja de Muertos, but you can still swim, snorkel, and dive here. A 30-minute hike across the island leads to a small lighthouse dating to 1887. Scheduled boats leave La Guancha Friday–Sunday at 8:30 am, daily in high season. You must pack in what you need (drinks and food) and pack out your garbage. **Amenities:** toilets. **Best for:** snorkeling; swimming; walking. ⊠ *Boats leave from La Guancha, at the end of Rte. 14, Ponce.*

WESTERN PUERTO RICO

Balneario de Rincón. Families enjoy the tranquil waters, playground, and shelters for seaside picnics. The beach is within walking distance to the center of town. **Amenities:** parking (free); showers; toilets. **Best for:** sunset; swimming. ⊠ *Calle Cambija, Rincón.*

Playa Crashboat. Here you'll find the colorful fishing boats pictured on postcards. Named for rescue boats used when nearby Ramey Air Force

Base was in operation, the beach has soft, sugary sand and water as smooth as glass. A food stand serves the catch of the day with cold beer. Right before you cross the bridge leading to the beach, a lookout point on your left makes a great photo op. **Amenities:** food and drink; parking (free); showers; toilets. **Best for:** partiers; snorkeling; swimming. ⊠ *End of Rte. 458, off Rte. 107, Aguadilla.*

WHERE TO EAT

In cosmopolitan San Juan, European, Asian, Middle Eastern, and chic fusion eateries vie for attention with family-owned restaurants specializing in seafood or *comida criolla* (creole cooking). Many of the most innovative chefs here have restaurants in the city's large hotels, but don't be shy about venturing into stand-alone establishments—traditionally concentrated in Condado and Old San Juan. The historic center is also home to new restaurants and cafés offering artisanal cuisine—crop-to-cup coffee, rustic homemade pizzas, and creative vegetarian food—at affordable prices. But as the San Juan metro area develops, great restaurants are popping up in other parts of the city, including Santurce, Miramar, and Ocean Park. Throughout the island, there's a radiant pride in what the local land can provide, and enthusiastic restaurateurs are redefining what Puerto Rican food is, bite by tasty bite.

What to Wear: Dress codes vary greatly, though a restaurant's prices are a fairly good indicator of its formality. For less expensive places, anything but beachwear is fine. Ritzier eateries will expect collared shirts for men (jacket and tie requirements are rare) and chic attire for women. When in doubt, do as the Puerto Ricans often do and dress up.

SAN JUAN

OLD SAN JUAN

$$$$
SEAFOOD

× **Aguaviva.** The name means "jellyfish," which explains why this ultra-modern place has dim blue lighting and jellyfish-shape lamps floating overhead. Eating here is like being submerged in the sea. The extensive, ever-changing menu by Chef Hector Crespo features inventive ceviches, including truffle tuna tartare with cucumber and green apple. For something more filling, try the lobster yuca gnocchi or orzo paella, with generous seafood, chicken, chorizo, and a saffron beurre blanc—oh so tasty and enough for two. Another splurge, the gravity-defying *torres del mar* (towers of the sea) comes hot or cold and includes oysters, mussels, shrimp—you name it. The oysters Rockefeller alone are worth the trip. $ *Average main: $31* ⊠ *364 Calle Fortaleza, Old San Juan* ☎ *787/722–0665* ⊕ *www.oofrestaurants.com* ☉ *No lunch.*

$
BURGER

× **Bistro Burger.** After exploring El Morro, head to Bistro Burger on Calle San Sebastián for what locals consider the best burgers in town. Choose from the house burgers, all named after local artists, or build your own burger with homemade ingredients. The Daphne Elvira is a great choice, made with chorizo and pork, Manchego cheese, red onion, and *acerola* (Caribbean cherry) ketchup on fresh foccacia bread. Don't leave without trying the *ropa vieja* egg rolls made with tender, stewed beef.

The kitchen is open late on weekends, making Bistro Burger the perfect place to grab a bite after bar-hopping on Calle San Sebastián. $ *Average main: $9* ⊠ *157 Calle San Sebastián, Old San Juan* ☎ 787/664–3626.

$ **✕ Café Cuatro Sombras.** If you want to try locally grown, single-origin, shade-grown coffee, this micro-roastery and café is the place to do it. Owners Pablo Muñoz and Mariana Suárez grow their beans in the mountains of Yauco on a hacienda that has been in the Muñoz family since 1846. The wood planks lining the banquette are from coffee storage pallets, and red accents recall perfectly ripe coffee beans. *Cuatro sombras* (four shades) refers to the four types of trees traditionally used in Puerto Rico to provide shade for coffee plants. And although it's the delicious, medium-bodied brew that steals the show, there's also a small but tasty menu of pastries and sandwiches. $ *Average main: $7* ⊠ *259 Calle Recinto Sur, Old San Juan* ☎ 787/724–9955 ⊕ *www.cuatrosombras.com* ⊗ *No dinner.*

CAFÉ
Fodor's Choice
★

$ **✕ Casa Cortés ChocoBar.** The Cortés family has been making bean-to-bar chocolate for more than 85 years. In 2013 they opened Puerto Rico's first "choco bar" to share their passion. The walls in this vivid, modern space are decorated with ads from the '50s, original chocolate bar molds, a time line of chocolate, and two flat screens showing the chocolate-making process. From pastries to tapas, breakfast dishes to panini sandwiches, the chef integrates chocolate into every bite without overpowering. Ripe plantain *mofonguitos* are filled with chocolate and bacon bits. The panfried jumbo shrimp with a chocolate lemon sauce is delicious. Bonbons, chocolate bars, and even chocolate soaps are available for sale. Locals from all over the metro area flock here for weekend brunch; arrive early to avoid a long wait. On Thursday, Saturday, and Sunday an upstairs gallery offers a glimpse of the family's private contemporary Caribbean art collection. $ *Average main: $10* ⊠ *210 Calle San Francisco, Old San Juan* ☎ 787/722–0499 ⊕ *www.casacortespr.com* ⊗ *Closed Mon.*

CONTEMPORARY

$$$ **✕ Dragonfly.** Dark and sexy, this popular Latin-Asian restaurant, all done up in Chinese red, feels more like a fashionable after-hours lounge than a restaurant. The romantic ambience, created partly through tightly packed tables and low lighting, is a big draw. Small plates, meant to be shared, come in generous portions. Don't miss the Peking duck nachos, pork and sweet plantain dumplings, and inventive cocktails that complement the food. $ *Average main: $21* ⊠ *364 Calle Fortaleza, Old San Juan* ☎ 787/977–3886 ⊕ *www.oofrestaurants.com* ⊗ *No lunch* ⚐ *Reservations not accepted.*

ASIAN

$$ **✕ La Fonda del Jibarito.** The menus are handwritten and the tables wobble, but Sanjuaneros have favored this casual, no-frills, family-run restaurant—tucked away on a quiet cobbled street—for years. The *bistec encebollado*, goat fricassee, and shredded beef stew are among the specialties on the menu of typical Puerto Rican comida criolla dishes. The tiny back porch is filled with plants, and the dining room is filled with fanciful depictions of life on the street outside. Troubadours serenade patrons, which include plenty of cruise-ship passengers when ships are in dock. $ *Average main: $14* ⊠ *280 Calle Sol, Old San Juan* ☎ 787/725–8375.

PUERTO RICAN

13

$$$$ ECLECTIC Fodor's Choice ★ 🍴 **Marmalade.** Peter Schintler, the U.S.-born owner-chef of Old San Juan's hippest—and finest—restaurant, apprenticed with Raymond Blanc and Gordon Ramsay. Here he's created a class act famous for its ultra-chic lounge bar. The restaurant's sensual and minimalist orange-and-white decor features high-back chairs and cushioned banquettes. The menu uses many sustainable and nonmodified ingredients prepared California-French fashion, resulting in complex flavors and strong aromas. The yellowtail is served with lemongrass and compressed watermelon while the pork cheeks are served with a peach-poblano marmalade. For dessert, indulge in the Millionaires ice cream, topped with honeycomb and shaved truffles. You can build your own four- to six-course tasting menu, with or without pairings from the *Wine Spectator* Award of Excellence wine list, or order à la carte. The restaurant is accommodating to vegetarians, vegans, and those with dietary restrictions. [$] *Average main: $32* ✉ *317 Calle Fortaleza, Old San Juan* ☎ *787/724–3969* 🌐 *www.marmaladepr.com* ⏲ *No lunch* ✍ *Reservations essential.*

$$$ VEGETARIAN Fodor's Choice ★ 🍴 **Verde Mesa.** With punched-tin ceilings, mason-jar light fixtures, and eclectic decor inspired by Versailles' *Petit Trianon*, this pescatarian restaurant focuses on pleasing the senses. Executive Chef Gabriel Hernandez sources most of the organic produce from local farms, creating a menu that changes seasonally. Flavor combinations are anything but accidental. Start with a garlicky hummus of red lentils. The signature Verde Mesa rice is a mixture of in-season vegetables and chickpeas, and there are also quite a few expertly prepared seafood dishes. You might find tuna, salmon, and scallops on the menu, depending on what's fresh that day. Swordfish is sometimes served as a refreshing ceviche dish that will melt in your mouth. Scallops might be served on a bed of stewed white beans with pineapple, sunflowers, and salsa verde. The restaurant has a small, yet impressive wine selection to pair with your meal. Reservations are not accepted, so arrive early if going for dinner. [$] *Average main: $22* ✉ *107 Calle Tetuán, at Calle San José, Old San Juan* ☎ *787/390–4662* 🌐 *www.verdemesa.com* ⏲ *Closed Sun. and Mon.* ✍ *Reservations not accepted.*

$ CAFÉ 🍴 **Waffle-era Tea Room.** The only tearoom in Puerto Rico is hugely popular, and its relocation to a larger space (with reservations) made locals very happy. You can choose from nearly 30 loose teas, including white and fruity blends as well as black, or a carefully crafted cocktail menu, but you may be more curious about the coffee setup, which looks like a mad scientist's experiment. It's a siphon fire-brewing system, a painstaking process popular in Japan. Food consists of house-made sweet or savory waffles or smaller "wafflitos" (the crème brûlée wafflito is decadent) and a tapas menu with signature ham-hugged dates stuffed with Gorgonzola and cherry tomatoes, wrapped in fire-torched, brandy-infused prosciutto. A "waffle-izza" has fresh tomato sauce and blow-torch-melted mozzarella. [$] *Average main: $9* ✉ *252 Calle San José, Old San Juan* ☎ *787/721–1512* 🌐 *www.waffle-era.com* ⏲ *No dinner.*

GREATER SAN JUAN

$$$ PUERTO RICAN Fodor's Choice ★ 🍴 **Jose Enrique.** Since 2007, Chef Jose Enrique's eponymous restaurant has been the preferred choice of locals, and he is the first Puerto Rican chef to receive the prestigious James Beard award nomination, for three consecutive years. His elevated Puerto Rican cuisine is served in a casual

setting. The menu, on an eraser board, changes all the time, but crab fitters are a staple, as is the whole fried yellowtail snapper served over a root mash with avocado and papaya salsa. The no-reservation policy means you'll wait for a table. Put your name on the list and wander around La Placita, where you can sip cheap drinks and mingle with locals. $ *Average main: $30* ⊠ *176 Calle Duffaut, La Placita de Santurce, Santurce* ☎ *787/725–3518* ⊕ *www.joseenriquepr.com* ⊗ *Closed Sun. and Mon. No lunch Sat.* ⋈ *Reservations not accepted.*

$$
CAFÉ

✕ **Kasalta.** Those who think coffee can never be too strong should make a beeline to Kasalta and its amazing pitch-black brew. Display cases are full of luscious pastries, including the *quesito* (cream cheese–filled puff pastry), and sandwiches include the *medianoche,* made famous when President Obama ordered one while campaigning. For dinner, dive into a fish dish or paella, or do like the locals and make a meal out of savory Spanish tapas. Quality is occasionally uneven, and some staff members are curt with tourists. $ *Average main: $16* ⊠ *1966 Calle McLeary, Ocean Park* ☎ *787/727–7340* ⊕ *www.kasalta.com.*

$$$$
ECLECTIC
Fodor's Choice
★

✕ **1919.** Michelin-starred, Puerto Rico–born Chef Juan José Cuevas successfully operates this fine-dining restaurant in San Juan's most striking hotel, once home to the Vanderbilt family. The main dining room is set on the Atlantic Ocean; elegant and sophisticated, it is large yet intimate, with tables spread out to allow for privacy and comfort. Brazilian-tigerwood tables, dark wood floors, and three striking chandeliers with drooping pearl shells are reminiscent of the Gatsby era. The international cuisine—prix fixe or à la carte—changes seasonally and focuses on local ingredients. You might find a sashimi trio of hamachi, scallops, and tuna; roasted local honey duck breast; or cochinillo ravioli with burrata and caramelized eggplant on the menu. For pairings, choose from more than 200 wines or take advantage of the Champagne table service. $ *Average main: $36* ⊠ *Vanderbilt Hotel, 1055 Av. Ashford, Condado* ☎ *787/724–1919* ⊕ *www.1919restaurant.com* ⊗ *Closed Sun. and Mon. No lunch.*

$$$
CARIBBEAN

✕ **Pamela's.** If you dream of dining right on the beach, head to this Ocean Park favorite. If you prefer air-conditioning, opt for the elegant glassed-in solarium, with black cobblestone floors and slow-turning ceiling fans. The menu—a contemporary, creative mix of Caribbean spices and other tropical ingredients with an accent on fresh seafood—has red snapper, blackened salmon with a Caribbean vegetable medley, and a bouillabaisse-like seafood sofrito with shrimp, mussels, clams, and calamari. $ *Average main: $30* ⊠ *Numero Uno Guest House, 1 Calle Santa Ana, Ocean Park* ☎ *787/726–5010* ⊕ *www.numero1guesthouse.com.*

$$$$
ECLECTIC
Fodor's Choice
★

✕ **Pikayo.** Celebrity chef and Puerto Rico native Wilo Benet's flagship restaurant makes the most of its elegant surroundings at the Condado Plaza Hilton. Works from local artists line the walls, and the atmosphere is formal but never hushed. The menu offers a twist on traditional Puerto Rican classics as well as more international flavors. Choose from the thoughtfully crafted tasting menu or order à la carte. Of the large selection of starters, the pork-belly sliders, spicy tuna on crispy rice (known as *pegao*), and foie gras with ripe plantains and black-truffle honey are particularly good. Main course options include succulent petit duck *magret* with cremini mushrooms and a raspberry vinegar *gastrique* and North Atlantic swordfish in a pigeon pea escabeche with a ripe plantain emulsion. Don't be surprised if Benet stops by to make sure everything is to your liking. $ *Average main: $37* ⊠ *Condado Plaza Hilton, 999 Av. Ashford, Condado* ☎ *787/721–6194* ⊕ *www.wilobenet.com/pikayo* ⊘ *No lunch*.

EASTERN PUERTO RICO

$$$$
FRENCH

✕ **Chez Daniel.** When the stars are out, it would be hard to find a more romantic setting than this eatery in a marina. Dozens of gleaming white boats are anchored so close that you could practically hit them with a baguette. The dining room has a chummy atmosphere, probably because many patrons seem to know each other. For alone time, ask for a table on one of the private terraces. Chef Daniel Vasse's Frenchcountry-style dishes are some of the island's best. The Marseille-style bouillabaisse is full of fresh fish and bursts with the flavor of a white garlic sauce. Something less French? Choose steak or fish simply prepared on the grill, and pair it with a bottle from the extensive wine cellar. Sunday brunch ($45 including one brunch cocktail), with its seemingly endless seafood bar, draws people from all over the island. $ *Average main: $33* ⊠ *Palmas del Mar, Anchor's Village Marina, Rte. 906, Km 86.4, Humacao* ☎ *787/850–3838* ⊕ *www.chezdanielpr.com* ⊘ *Closed Mon. and Tues. No lunch* ⟐ *Reservations essential*.

$$$
CARIBBEAN

✕ **Pasión por el Fogón.** At this beloved Fajardo restaurant, Chef Myrta Pérez Toledo transforms traditional dishes into something special. Succulent cuts of meat and fish are presented in unexpected ways. A perfectly cooked flank steak, rolled into a cylinder standing on one end, has a slightly sweet tamarind sauce that brings out the meat's earthy flavors. If you're a seafood lover, start with the lime-infused red-snapper ceviche and move on to lobster medallions broiled in butter. For dessert, order the Caribbean Sun, an ice cream sundae that blends caramel, cinnamon, and chocolate toppings. $ *Average main: $28* ⊠ *Rte. 987, Km 2.3, Fajardo* ☎ *787/863–3502* ⊕ *www.pasionporelfogon.net* ⊘ *No lunch weekdays* ⟐ *Reservations essential*.

VIEQUES AND CULEBRA

VIEQUES

$$
PUERTO RICAN
Fodor'sChoice
★

✕ **Conuco.** A mix of locals and tourists frequent Conuco, soft-spoken Puerto Rico native Rebecca Betancourt's homage to local food with an upscale twist. Barnlike open windows look out onto one of Isabel Segunda's main streets, and within, the airy room is simple but cozy, enhanced by bright yellow walls, sea foam chairs, and ceiling fans. A back patio offers alfresco dining. Start with sangria rum punch, then move onto *any* of the menu's many selections; they're all that wonderful. Piping-hot arepas are piled high with pepper and octopus salad, while small *tostones rellenos* (fried plantains) are shaped into cups filled with a citrusy ceviche. *Sorullitos* (cheesy corn fritters) and *bacalaítos* (cod fritters) are reimagined with modern flair. The only thing trumping the flavors of a juicy *churrasco* (skirt steak) and overflowing seafood mofongo is the wow-factor of Betancourt's presentations. [$] *Average main: $15* ✉ *110 Luis Muñoz Rivera, Isabel Segunda* ☎ *787/741–2500* 🌐 *www.restauranteconuco.com* 🕘 *Closed Sun. and Mon. No lunch.*

$$$ ECLECTIC Fodor's Choice ★ 🍴 **El Quenepo.** This elegant yet unpretentious spot brings fine dining and a touch of class to the Esperanza waterfront. Six stable doors on a powder-blue building open to ocean views. The menu, which changes yearly, features local herbs and fruits such as quenepas and breadfruit in artfully prepared dishes that owners Scott and Kate Cole call "fun, funky island food." Scott is the chef, known for seafood specials highlighting the daily catch; Kate is the consummate hostess. Start with the popular grilled Caesar salad followed by sensational mofongo stuffed with shrimp and lobster in sweet-and-spicy criollo sauce. There's a large wine list, and the sangria is delicious. Lucky walk-ins can grab a seat at the more casual high bar tables, but for a true experience, make a reservation. [$] *Average main: $25* ✉ *148 Calle Flamboyán, Esperanza* ☎ *787/741–1215* 🌐 *www.elquenepovieques.com* 🕘 *Closed Sun. No lunch* ✍ *Reservations essential.*

CULEBRA

$$ CARIBBEAN 🍴 **Mamacita's.** Pull your dinghy up to the dock and watch the resident iguanas plod past at this simple open-air, tin-roofed restaurant on a rough-plank deck beside the Dewey canal. Painted pink, purple, and green, the space is littered with palm tree trunks. Tarpon cruise past, and the to-and-fro of boaters adds to the show at Culebra's favorite watering hole and gringo hangout. Mamacita's down-home menu changes nightly. It's heavy on burgers and sandwiches but includes an excellent mahimahi. Open times vary by season. [$] *Average main: $12* ✉ *66 Calle Castelar, Dewey* ☎ *787/742–0090* 🌐 *www.mamacitasguesthouse.com.*

$$$ ECLECTIC 🍴 **Susie's.** *Sanjuanera* owner-chef Susie Hebert learned her culinary skills at San Juan's swank Caribe Hilton and Ritz-Carlton before settling on Culebra and opening her casual and unpretentious fine-dining restaurant, a soothing zen space filled with banquettes, pillows, and couches. A huge courtyard is perfect for dining under the stars. The Caesar salad excels. Follow it with garam masala crusted grouper fillet. Feeling carnivorous? The filet mignon with horseradish, garlic, Dijon aioli is divine. Susie's is open seasonally, so call ahead. [$] *Average main: $21* ✉ *Rte. 250, Las Delicias, Dewey* ☎ *787/742–1141* 🌐 *www.susiesculebra.com* 🕘 *Closed Wed. and Thurs. No lunch* ✍ *Reservations essential.*

THE NORTHERN COAST AND CENTRAL PUERTO RICO

$$$ ITALIAN Fodor's Choice ★ 🍴 **Grappa.** Dorado's most charming restaurant—and perhaps the most appealing one on the northern coast—Grappa is spectacular, both in design and on the plate. Specializing in Italian fare, the kitchen staff make pasta by hand and serve it with fruits of the sea or delicious, tender beef. The setting is romantic and intimate, and with a small dining room, reservations are essential. Service excels. [$] *Average main: $22* ✉ *247 Calle Mendéz Vigo, Dorado* ☎ *787/796–2674* 🕘 *Closed Mon. and Tues.* ✍ *Reservations essential.*

$$$$
ECLECTIC
Fodor'sChoice
★

✕**Hacienda Luz de Luna.** This is one restaurant where you can't show up unannounced, nor would you ever recognize it from a sign outside, simply because there isn't one. That's the intrigue of this "underground restaurant" where guests are invited to dine at the home of renowned-chef Ventura Vivoni Rivera. In 2008, he had a dream to cook for strangers in the historic

DID YOU KNOW?

The seafood shacks of Joyuda are so well known for fresh fish that locals flock there from as far away as Ponce and San Juan. In Boquerón people line up at pushcarts where vendors sell oysters on the half shell.

hacienda built in 1887. Three weekends per month, Ventura prepares a 10-course meal for a maximum of 35 guests, served during two daily seatings (at 1 and 6 pm). Hosted by the chef's father, Edric, the evening begins with a tour of property, starting at the orchard where lemons grow the size of coconuts. Sprawling 374 acres is the family's farm and small factory where soap, jam, candy, and coffee are produced. Each unique menu (emailed to guests in advance) is never repeated, but might include coffee-crusted pork with mango puree or grilled fish with crunchy rice. This dining experience generally takes up to five hours and costs $75; be sure to reserve well in advance. $ *Average main: $75* ✉ *Carretera 135, Km. 73.3, Barrio Yahuecas, Adjuntas, Adjuntas* ☎ *787/829–9096* ⊕ *www.restaurartevidaventura.com* ▭ *No credit cards* ⚲ *Reservations essential.*

SOUTHERN PUERTO RICO

$$
SEAFOOD

✕**El Ancla.** Families favor this laid-back restaurant at water's edge. Generous and affordable plates of fish, crab, and other fresh seafood come with *tostones* (fried plantains), french fries, and garlic bread. Try the shrimp in garlic sauce, salmon fillet with capers, or delectable mofongo stuffed with seafood, and finish with a fantastic flan. The piña coladas—with or without rum—are exceptional. The area needs improvement, but the views are worth it. $ *Average main: $20* ✉ *805 Av. Hostos Final, Ponce* ☎ *787/840–2450* ⊕ *www.restauranteelancla.com.*

$$
ECLECTIC

✕**Lola.** In the heart of downtown, this trendy bistro has an eclectic menu to match the decor. Grab a seat in a red velvet booth and start with the sampler of mahimahi nuggets, bruschetta, fried plantains, and egg rolls. The menu ranges from tuna steak to filet mignon to three-cheese risotto. Be sure to ask about the daily specials, which are always worth trying. This is a great place to admire work by local artists and sip on a Lola Martini (grapefruit, cranberry, champagne, lime, and rum). $ *Average main: $18* ✉ *Ramada Inn, Calle Reina and Calle Union, Ponce* ☎ *787/813–5033* ⊕ *www.lolacuisine.com.*

WESTERN PUERTO RICO

$$$
ECLECTIC

✕**The Eclipse.** Beautiful beachfront dining, farm-to-table ingredients, and fantastic service are worth a drive from San Juan. The setting is rustic yet elegant, and the view is ideal. Executive Chef Jeremie Cruz flawlessly executes dishes full of local flavors. Wonderful sweet and savory brunch selections range from coconut brioche french toast with caramelized bananas and nuts to pizza frittatas. Lunch brings delicious classic Neapolitan pizzas baked in a handmade brick oven. The catch of the day (from Isabela) ceviche is perfectly marinated. On top of the varied dinner menu, Chef Jeremie creates a three-course menu daily that highlights the freshest products he can find. Wine pairings are optional and suggested, given the spectacular wine list. $ *Average main: $28* ⊠ *Villa Montaña, Carretera 4466, Km 1.9, Isabela* ☎ *787/872–9554* ⊕ *www.villamontana.com.*

$$
PUERTO RICAN

✕ **Rincón Tropical.** Don't be scared off by the cheap plastic tables and chairs. They are almost always full of locals enjoying the fresh seafood. The kitchen keeps it simple, preparing dishes with a light touch. Highlights include dorado a la criolla, mahimahi with peppers and onions in a tomato sauce, as well as fried red snapper with rice and beans and shrimp mofongo. Fried plantains make a nice accompaniment to almost anything. Weekdays bring an affordable lunch special. $ *Average main: $15* ⊠ *Rte. 115, Km 12, Rincón* ☎ *787/823–2017* ⊕ *www.rinconpr. com/rincontropical.*

WHERE TO STAY

In San Juan, the best beaches are in Isla Verde, though Condado is more centrally located. Old San Juan offers easy access to dining and nightlife. Outside San Juan, particularly on the east coast, you can find self-contained luxury resorts that cover hundreds of acres. Around the island, government-sponsored *paradores* are rural inns, others offer no-frills apartments, and some are large hotels close to either an attraction or beach.

PRIVATE VILLAS AND CONDOS

In the west, southwest, and south—as well as on the islands of Vieques and Culebra—smaller inns and condominiums for short-term rentals are the norm. Villa and apartment rentals are increasingly popular.

Island West Properties. Around for years, this office has cornered the market for renting villas in Rincón by the day, week, or month. ⊠ *Rte. 413, Km 0.7, Rincón* ☎ *787/823–2323* ⊕ *www.island-west.com.*

Rainbow Realty. A list of rental properties is available from this gay-friendly company. ⊠ *278 Calle Flamboyán, Esperanza* ☎ *787/741–4312* ⊕ *www.viequesrainbowrealty.com.*

SAN JUAN

OLD SAN JUAN

$
B&B/INN

🛏 **The Gallery Inn.** No two rooms in this 200-year-old mansion are alike, but all have four-poster beds, handwoven tapestries, and quirky antiques in every nook and cranny. **Pros:** one-of-a-kind lodging; ocean views; wonderful classical music concerts. **Cons:** several narrow, winding staircases; an uphill walk from rest of Old San Juan; sometimes raucous pet macaws and cockatoos. $ *Rooms from: $160* ⊠ *204–206 Calle*

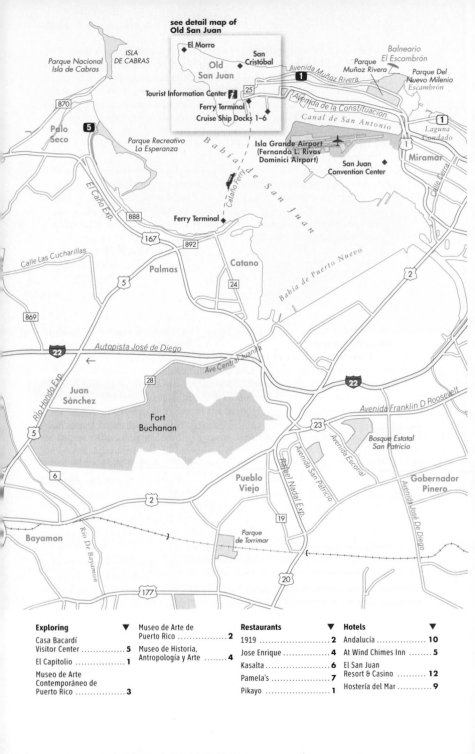

see detail map of
Old San Juan

El Morro

San
Cristóbal

Old
San Juan

Tourist Information Center

Ferry Terminal
Cruise Ship Docks 1–6

Parque Nacional
Isla de Cabras

ISLA
DE CABRAS

Palo
Seco

870

5

Parque Recreativo
La Esperanza

El Caño Exp.

888

167

892

Calle Las Cucharillas

Palmas

5

869

22

Autopista José de Diego

Rio Hondo Exp.

Juan
Sánchez

28

Fort
Buchanan

5

6

2

Bayamon

Rio De Bayamón

177

Ave Central Juanita

Avenida Muñoz Rivera

Parque
Muñoz Rivera

Balneario
El Escambrón

Parque Del
Nuevo Milenio
Escambrón

Avenida de la Constitución

Canal de San Antonio

25

Isla Grande Airport
(Fernando L. Rivas
Dominici Airport)

San Juan
Convention Center

Laguna
Condado

1

Miramar

Calle Cerra

Bahía de San Juan

Cataño Ferry

Ferry Terminal

Catano

24

Bahía de Puerto Nuevo

2

22

Avenida Franklin D Roosevelt

23

Bosque Estatal
San Patricio

Avenida San Patricio

Avenida Escorial

Gobernador
Pinero

Avenida José De Diego

Pueblo
Viejo

Rafael Nadal Exp.

19

Parque
de Torrimar

20

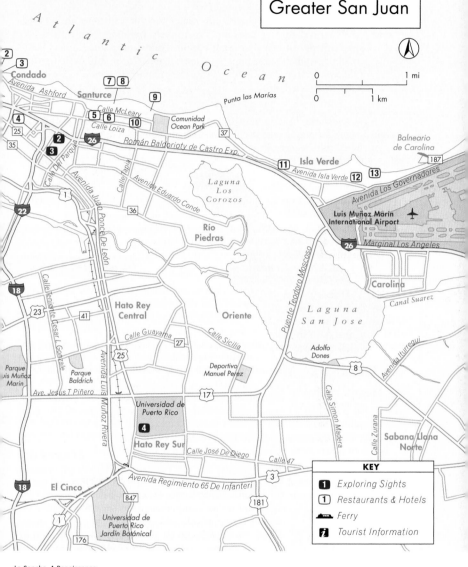

Greater San Juan

Atlantic Ocean

Condado
Avenida Ashford
Santurce
Calle McLeary
Punta las Marías
Calle Loiza
Comunidad
Ocean Park
Román Baldorioty de Castro Exp.
Isla Verde
Avenida Isla Verde
Balneario
de Carolina
Calle Del Parque
Avenida Juan Ponce De León
Calle Tapia
Avenida Eduardo Conde
Laguna
Los
Corozos
Luis Muñoz Marín
International Airport
Marginal Los Angeles
Río
Piedras
Calle Teniente César L González
Hato Rey
Central
Oriente
Laguna
San Jose
Carolina
Canal Suarez
Parque
Luis Muñoz
Marin
Parque
Baldrich
Ave. Jesús T Piñero
Calle Guayama
Avenida Luis Muñoz Rivera
Calle Sicilia
Deportivo
Manuel Perez
Adolfo
Dones
Calle Simon Madera
Avenida Iturregui
Sabana Llana
Norte
Universidad de
Puerto Rico
Hato Rey Sur
Calle José De Diego
Calle 47
Calle Zurana
El Cinco
Avenida Regimiento 65 De Infanteri
Universidad de
Puerto Rico
Jardín Botánical
Puente Teodoro Moscoso
Avenida Los Governadores

KEY

1	Exploring Sights
1	Restaurants & Hotels
Ferry	
i	Tourist Information

0 ___ 1 mi
0 ___ 1 km

Norzagaray, Old San Juan ☎ *787/722–1808* 🌐 *www.thegalleryinn.com* 🛏 *20 rooms, 5 suites* 🍴 *Breakfast.*

$$ HOTEL Fodor's Choice ★ 🏨 **Hotel El Convento.** There's no longer anything austere about this 350-year-old former convent. **Pros:** lovely building; atmosphere to spare; plenty of nearby dining options. **Cons:** near some noisy bars; small pool; small bathrooms. [$] *Rooms from: $285* ✉ *100 Calle Cristo, Old San Juan* ☎ *787/723–9020* 🌐 *www.elconvento.com* 🛏 *52 rooms, 6 suites* 🍴 *No meals.*

GREATER SAN JUAN

$ B&B/INN 🏨 **Andalucía.** In a Spanish-style house, this friendly little inn evokes its namesake region with such details as hand-painted tiles and ceramic pots filled with greenery. **Pros:** terrific value; helpful hosts; gorgeous courtyard. **Cons:** not right on the beach; some rooms smaller than others. [$] *Rooms from: $99* ✉ *2011 Calle McLeary, Ocean Park* ☎ *787/309–3373* 🌐 *www.andalucia-puertorico.com* 🛏 *11 rooms* 🍴 *No meals.*

$ B&B/INN 🏨 **At Wind Chimes Inn.** Hidden behind a whitewashed wall covered with bougainvillea, this Spanish-style villa feels like an exclusive retreat. **Pros:** charming architecture; on the edge of Condado; on-site bar (opens at 5); use of Acacia Seaside Inn facilities. **Cons:** busy street; old-fashioned rooms; only a few rooms have closets. [$] *Rooms from: $109* ✉ *1750 Av. McLeary, Condado* ☎ *787/727–4153, 800/946–3244* 🌐 *www.atwindchimesinn.com* 🛏 *21 rooms, 1 suite* 🍴 *No meals.*

$$$ RESORT FAMILY 🏨 **El San Juan Resort & Casino.** Much of the classical appeal remains; the lobby's intricately carved mahogany walls and ceiling date to 1955. **Pros:** beautiful pool; great dining options in and near hotel; fantastic beach. **Cons:** noise in lobby from bars and casino; parking lot a long walk from hotel entrance; small bathrooms. [$] *Rooms from: $450* ✉ *6063 Av. Isla Verde, Isla Verde* ☎ *787/791–1000* 🌐 *www.elsanjuanhotel.com* 🛏 *386 rooms, 22 suites* 🍴 *No meals.*

$ B&B/INN 🏨 **Hostería del Mar.** Decorated in bright blues and whites, the rooms at this casual beachfront inn have an Asian feel, with influences from Bali, Malaysia, and India. **Pros:** plasma TVs; right on the beach; good on-site dining. **Cons:** long walk to other restaurants; no pool; Wi-Fi in lobby only; needs a face-lift. [$] *Rooms from: $139* ✉ *1 Calle Tapia, Ocean Park* ☎ *787/727–3302* 🌐 *www.hosteriadelmarpr.com* 🛏 *23 rooms, 2 suites* 🍴 *No meals.*

$$ RESORT Fodor's Choice ★ 🏨 **La Concha—A Renaissance Resort.** Every detail feels tropical and sexy, from the undulating ceiling in the sprawling lobby to Perla, the signature shell-shape restaurant and architectural marvel. **Pros:** stunning architecture; numerous on-site social activities; beautiful guest rooms. **Cons:** noisy bar/lobby, particularly when there's live music; beach can be narrow at high tide. [$] *Rooms from: $299* ✉ *1077 Av. Ashford, Condado* ☎ *787/721–7500* 🌐 *www.laconcharesort.com* 🛏 *257 rooms, 226 suites* 🍴 *No meals.*

$ HOTEL 🏨 **Numero Uno Guest House.** It's common to hear guests trading stories about how often they've returned to this relaxing retreat. **Pros:** friendly atmosphere; great restaurant; on the beach. **Cons:** a long walk to other restaurants; small pool. [$] *Rooms from: $150* ✉ *1 Calle Santa Ana, Ocean Park* ☎ *787/726–5010, 866/726–5010* 🌐 *www.numero1guesthouse.com* 🛏 *11 rooms* 🍴 *Breakfast.*

Hotel El Convento

$$$$ RESORT FAMILY 🏨 **The Ritz-Carlton, San Juan.** Elegant marble floors and fountains don't undermine the beach getaway feel. **Pros:** good service; excellent restaurant options; spruced-up guest rooms; modern spa and fitness center. **Cons:** not much within walking distance; expensive. [$] *Rooms from: $629* ✉ *6961 Av. de los Gobernadores, Isla Verde* ☎ *787/253–1700, 800/241–3333* 🌐 *www.ritzcarlton.com/sanjuan* 🛏 *416 rooms, 11 suites* 🍴 *No meals.*

$ HOTEL 🏨 **San Juan Water Beach Club Hotel.** Water is everywhere at this boutique hotel, from droplets in the reception area to a deluge running down the elevators' glass walls. **Pros:** fun atmosphere; interesting design; great nightlife; on the beach; great food. **Cons:** dark hallways; small pool. [$] *Rooms from: $219* ✉ *2 Calle Tartak, Isla Verde* ☎ *787/728–3666, 888/265–6699* 🌐 *www.waterbeachhotel.com* 🛏 *80 rooms, 4 suites* 🍴 *No meals.*

NORTHERN COAST

$$$$ RESORT Fodor's Choice ★ 🏨 **Dorado Beach, A Ritz-Carlton Reserve.** Following a $342-million renovation, this resort's big draws include a restaurant from Fodor's Tastemaker Chef José Andrés and an incredible setting along 3 miles (5 km) of Puerto Rican coastline. **Pros:** all rooms are beachfront; golf, tennis, and water activities; excellent spa and gourmet dining. **Cons:** daily resort fee of $95. [$] *Rooms from: $1,399* ✉ *100 Dorado Beach Dr., Dorado* ☎ *787/626–1100* 🌐 *www.ritzcarlton.com* 🛏 *100 rooms, 14 suites, 1 villa* 🍴 *No meals.*

El San Juan Resort & Casino

EASTERN PUERTO RICO

$$$$ RESORT **[hotel] El Conquistador, A Waldorf Astoria Resort & Spa.** Perched on a bluff overlooking the ocean, this sprawling complex on the northern tip of the island is one of its most popular destination resorts. **Pros:** bright, spacious rooms; unbeatable views of nearby islands; good dining options. **Cons:** must take boat to reach beach; long waits at funicular running between levels; self-parking far from hotel entrance; hidden fees like parking ($16/day) and kids club ($70/day). [$] *Rooms from: $400* ✉ *1000 Av. El Conquistador, Fajardo* ☎ *787/863–1000, 888/543–1282* 🌐 *www.elconresort.com* 🛏 *750 rooms, 15 suites, 234 villas* 🍴 *Breakfast.*

$$ RESORT **[hotel] Gran Meliá Puerto Rico Golf Resort.** This massive resort, on a stretch of pristine coastline, has an open-air lobby with elegant floral displays that resemble a Japanese garden, while the swimming pool's columns recall ancient Greece. **Pros:** beautiful setting; lovely pool area; short walk to beach. **Cons:** scarce parking; blank and uninviting facade. [$] *Rooms from: $319* ✉ *200 Coco Beach Blvd., Río Grande* ☎ *787/809–1770, 877/476–3542* 🌐 *www.gran-melia-puerto-rico.com* 🛏 *544 suites, 6 villas* 🍴 *Some meals.*

$$$$ RESORT Fodor's Choice ★ **[hotel] St. Regis Bahia Beach Resort.** Between El Yunque National Forest and the Río Espíritu Santo, this luxurious, environmentally aware property has raised the bar for lodgings in Puerto Rico. **Pros:** privacy; impeccable service; luxurious amenities. **Cons:** isolated location; slim off-property restaurant selection; very, very expensive. [$] *Rooms from: $800* ✉ *Rte. 187, Km 4.2, Río Grande* ☎ *787/809–8000* 🌐 *www.stregisbahiabeach.com* 🛏 *139 rooms, 35 suites* 🍴 *No meals.*

$$ RESORT FAMILY **Wyndham Grand Rio Mar Beach Resort & Spa.** This sprawling 500-acre resort, fresh off a top-to-bottom renovation, offers a host of outdoor activities, including championship golf and tennis and hiking excursions in the nearby rain forest. **Pros:** expansive beachfront; good restaurants; casino; plenty of outdoor activities. **Cons:** dark and depressing parking garage; occasionally long lines at check-in; far from off-site restaurants. *Rooms from: $305 ✉ 6000 Río Mar Blvd., Río Grande ☎ 787/888–6000 www.wyndhamriomar.com 400 rooms, 40 suites No meals.*

VIEQUES AND CULEBRA

VIEQUES

$ HOTEL **Blue Horizon Boutique Resort.** The six Mediterranean-style villas here were the tiny island's first taste of luxury, and it's still a lovely place, to a large extent because of its perch across sprawling lawns that overlook a breathtaking sea. **Pros:** eye-popping view; private accommodations; spacious grounds; free Wi-Fi in public areas. **Cons:** inconsistent service; no elevator. *Rooms from: $250 ✉ Rte. 996, Km 4.2, Esperanza ☎ 787/741–3318 www.bluehorizonboutiqueresort.com 10 rooms, 1 suite Breakfast.*

$ HOTEL Fodor's Choice ★ **Hacienda Tamarindo.** The centuries-old tamarind tree rising more than three stories through the center of the main building gives this plantation-style house and former dance hall its name. **Pros:** beautiful views; nicely designed rooms; excellent breakfasts. **Cons:** drive to beaches; small parking lot; no full-service restaurant; no elevator. *Rooms from: $199 ✉ Rte. 997, Km 4.5, Esperanza ☎ 787/741–8525 www.haciendatamarindo.com 16 rooms, 1 penthouse suite, 1 villa Breakfast.*

$ HOTEL **Hix Island House.** Constructed entirely of concrete and set in a tropical forest, the four buildings of this hotel echo the gray granite boulders strewn around Vieques and blend seamlessly with the environment. **Pros:** acclaimed architecture; secluded setting; friendly staff. **Cons:** the lack of windows means bugs (especially pesky mosquitoes) get in; damp linens and clothing after tropical showers; no elevator; no TVs or phones, no Wi-Fi in rooms (a pro for some). *Rooms from: $225 ✉ Rte. 995, Km 1.5 ☎ 787/435–4590 www.hixislandhouse.com 19 rooms Breakfast.*

$ B&B/INN **Malecón House.** Posh boutique spots like this seaside escape in Esperanza are raising the bar on Vieques lodging. **Pros:** affordable waterfront property; tasty breakfasts; welcoming hosts. **Cons:** in-town location not for those seeking seclusion. *Rooms from: $180 ✉ 105 Calle Flamboyán, Esperanza ☎ 787/741–0663 www.maleconhouse.com 13 rooms Breakfast.*

$$$$ RESORT Fodor's Choice ★ **W Retreat & Spa.** Hovering over two gorgeous beaches, this über-hip resort is the island's hot spot for urbane fashionistas, yet manages to still be family-friendly. **Pros:** sensational decor; full-service spa; free transfers to/from airport. **Cons:** high prices even in low season; expensive resort fee, applied daily. *Rooms from: $885 ✉ Rte. 200, Km 3.2, Isabel Segunda ☎ 787/741–4100 www.wvieques.com 156 rooms, 20 suites No meals.*

CULEBRA

$ ⬚ **Club Seabourne.** The most sophisticated place in Culebra, this clus-
HOTEL   ter of slate-blue plantation-style cottages paints a pretty picture on a
Fodor'sChoice   hilltop overlooking Fulladoza Bay. **Pros:** lovely cottages; lush gardens;
★   pool; airport or ferry transfers included. **Cons:** some steps to negotiate; no elevator; spotty Internet and cell phone reception. $ *Rooms
from: $249* ⊠ *Rte. 252, northwest of town* ☎ *787/742–3169* ⊕ *www.
clubseabourne.com* ↩ *3 rooms, 8 deluxe villas, 2 family villas* ⦿| *Break-
fast* ☞ *The on-site restaurant serves dinner but not lunch.*

SOUTHERN PUERTO RICO

$ ⬚ **Copamarina Beach Resort and Spa.** The most beautiful resort on the
RESORT   southern coast is set on 16 palm-shaded acres facing the Caribbean.
Fodor'sChoice   **Pros:** tropical decor; plenty of activities; great dining options; 10-min-
★   ute boat ride to Gilligan's Island. **Cons:** somewhat distant from other
attractions; 20% resort fee. $ *Rooms from: $190* ⊠ *Rte. 333, Km 6.5,
Guánica* ☎ *787/821–0505, 800/468–4553* ⊕ *www.copamarina.com*
↩ *104 rooms, 2 villas* ⦿| *Some meals.*

$ ⬚ **Hotel Meliá.** In the heart of the city, this family-owned hotel has
HOTEL   been a local landmark for more than 120 years; in fact, it claims to
be the island's oldest hotel. **Pros:** great location on the main square;
walking distance to downtown sites; good dining options nearby; budget-friendly. **Cons:** somewhat dated decor; front rooms can be noisy;
Internet service is often spotty. $ *Rooms from: $145* ⊠ *75 Calle Cristina, Ponce* ☎ *787/842–0460* ⊕ *www.meliacenturyhotel.com* ↩ *68
rooms, 10 suites* ⦿| *No meals.*

$ ⬚ **Mary Lee's by the Sea.** This meandering cluster of apartments sits
RENTAL   on quiet grounds full of brightly colored flowers. **Pros:** home away
from home; warm and friendly owner; near pristine beaches and forests. **Cons:** weekly maid service unless requested daily; no nightlife; no
pool; rooms a bit dated. $ *Rooms from: $130* ⊠ *Rte. 333, Km 6.7,
Guánica* ☎ *787/821–3600* ⊕ *www.maryleesbythesea.com* ↩ *10 apart-
ments* ⦿| *No meals.*

CENTRAL PUERTO RICO

$ ⬚ **Casa Grande Mountain Retreat.** This is as close as you can get to sleep-
HOTEL   ing in a tree house. **Pros:** unspoiled setting with spectacular views;
accessible for people with disabilities; outdoor activities. **Cons:** no air-
conditioning; long drive to other sights/restaurants; pool closes at 6.
$ *Rooms from: $131* ⊠ *Rte. 612, Km 0.3, Utuado* ☎ *787/894–3939*
⊕ *www.hotelcasagrande.com* ↩ *20 rooms* ⦿| *No meals.*

WESTERN PUERTO RICO

$ ⬚ **The Lazy Parrot.** Painted in eye-popping tropical hues, this moun-
HOTEL   tainside hotel doesn't take itself too seriously. **Pros:** economy rooms
available; tropical setting; microwaves in rooms; pool. **Cons:** not on
the beach; stairs to climb; some may consider the whimsical style tacky.

Tres Sirenas

$ *Rooms from: $155* ✉ *Rte. 413, Km 4.1, Rincón* ☎ *787/823–5654, 800/294–1752* ⊕ *www.lazyparrot.com* 🍴 *22 rooms* ¶◎¶ *No meals.*

$ 🏠 **Lemontree Oceanfront Cottages.** Right on the beach, this pair of lemon-
HOTEL yellow buildings holds six apartments with names like Mango, Cocoa, Banana, and Piña. **Pros:** far from the crowds; on-call massage therapist; spacious balconies. **Cons:** very narrow beach; it's a drive to shops and restaurants; no elevator. $ *Rooms from: $155* ✉ *Rte. 429, Km 4.1, Rincón* ☎ *787/823–6452* ⊕ *www.lemontreepr.com* 🍴 *6 apartments* ¶◎¶ *No meals.*

$ 🏠 **Tres Sirenas.** Waves gently lap against the shore at this boutique inn
B&B/INN named Three Mermaids for the owners' daughters. **Pros:** in-room mas-
Fodor'sChoice sage; spotless; tastefully decorated; discounted rates May–October.
★ **Cons:** usually booked; Wi-Fi occasionally drops. $ *Rooms from: $230* ✉ *26 Seabeach Dr., Rincón* ☎ *787/823–0558* ⊕ *www.tressirenas.com* 🍴 *2 rooms, 1 studio, 2 apartments* ¶◎¶ *Breakfast.*

$ 🏠 **Villa Montaña.** This cluster of villas, on a deserted stretch of beach
RESORT between Isabela and Aguadilla, feels like a little town. **Pros:** bikes
Fodor'sChoice and playground; secluded beach; great food. **Cons:** a bit pricey; far
★ from off-site restaurants; airplane noise; some dated rooms. $ *Rooms from: $255* ✉ *Rte. 4466, Km 1.9, Isabela* ☎ *787/872–9554* ⊕ *www.villamontana.com* 🍴 *74 rooms, 52 villas* ¶◎¶ *No meals.*

NIGHTLIFE AND PERFORMING ARTS

Qué Pasa, the official visitor's guide, has listings of events in San Juan and out on the island. The local blog ⊕ *puertoricodaytrips.com* is another great source for event listings.

NIGHTLIFE

Wherever you go, dress to impress. Puerto Ricans have flair, and both men and women love getting dressed up to go out. Bars are usually casual, but if you have on jeans, sneakers, and a T-shirt, you may be refused entry at swankier nightclubs and discos.

In Old San Juan, Calle San Sebastián is lined with bars and restaurants. Evenings begin with dinner and stretch into the wee hours (often until 3 or 4) at bars at the more upscale, SoFo (south of Fortaleza) end. An eclectic crowd heads to the Plaza del Mercado in Santurce after work to hang out in the plaza or enjoy drinks and food in one of the small establishments skirting the farmers' market. Condado and Ocean Park have their share of nightlife, too. Most are restaurant-and-bar environments.

Just east of San Juan along Route 187, funky Piñones has a collection of open-air seaside eateries that are popular with locals. On weekend evenings many places have merengue combos, Brazilian jazz trios, or reggae bands. In Ponce, people embrace the Spanish tradition of the *paseo,* an evening stroll around the Plaza de las Delicias, and the boardwalk at La Guancha is also a lively scene. Live bands often play on weekends. Elsewhere *en la isla,* nighttime activities center on the hotels and resorts.

OLD SAN JUAN AND GREATER SAN JUAN

BARS AND MUSIC CLUBS

Fodor'sChoice ★ **La Factoría.** La Factoría, the former Hijos de Borinquen, is hands-down the best mixology bar in San Juan. There's no sign on the door, so look for the terra-cotta building on the corner of San Sebastián and San José. Artisanal cocktails are crafted with the highest-quality ingredients. Many bitters are homemade as is the ginger beer, which is used in their popular Get Lucky Mule. You can order one of the specialty cocktails listed on the chalkboard (the Spiced Old Fashioned is fantastic) or chat with one of the bartenders who will create the perfect drink based on your preferences. Whether its sweet, spicy, bitter, or something completely out of the box, these drinks will blow your mind. Behind the bar, there is a secret wooden door that leads to VINO Wine Bar, which has a great speakeasy feel. Tasty tapas are available and can be enjoyed in the adjacent room. The bars stays open until the sun comes, up and there is a DJ on weekends in the back room. ⊠ *148 Calle San Sebastián, Old San Juan* ☏ *787/594–5698.*

The Mezzanine at St. Germain. On top of St. Germain Bistro & Café, and in the former headquarters of the Nationalist Party, The Mezzanine is a contemporary take on the 1920s speakeasy. The chic space is conducive for sipping old-fashioneds or our favorite, the Peridot, made with gin and muddled basil and orange—very refreshing after walking the hills of Old San Juan. Tapas are served all day. Choose from the Brie and prosciutto *montaditos* with wild mushroom oil, the sweet and tangy meatballs, or the Greek-style ceviche. The Mezzanine also hosts one of the best happy hours in town, Tuesday through Friday from 4 to 8. Enjoy select tapas and cocktails for half off. You can't beat that in San Juan! Their boozy brunch is very popular on weekends. ⊠ *156 Calle Sol, 2nd fl., Old San Juan* ☎ *787/724–4657* ⊕ *www.themezzaninepr. com* ⊘ *Closed Mon.*

Mist. On the roof of the San Juan Water Beach Club Hotel, this sexy spot offers some of Isla Verde's best ocean views. On the weekends there's a DJ, and locals pack in to relax at the bar or on the white leather beds reserved for bottle service. The eclectic menu by Chef Raul Correa focuses on locally sourced ingredients. Don't miss the creative cocktails and delicious pizzas with homemade cheese. ⊠ *San Juan Water Beach Club Hotel, 2 Calle Tartak, Isla Verde* ☎ *787/725–4664* ⊕ *www. waterbeachhotel.com.*

Nuyorican Café. Something interesting happens nearly every night (it's closed Monday and Tuesday) at this hipper-than-hip, no-frills, wood-paneled performance space. It might be an early evening play, poetry reading, or talent show or, later on, a band playing Latin jazz, Cuban *son*, Puerto Rican salsa, or rock. On Wednesday nights, the owner plays the conga drums with the house salsa band, Comborican. During breaks the youthful, creative crowd chats in an alley outside. There is usually a $5 cover. ⊠ *312 Calle San Fransico, entrance on Callejón de la Capilla, Old San Juan* ☎ *787/977–1276* ⊕ *www.nuyoricancafepr.com.*

CASINOS

By law, all casinos must be in hotels, and most of them are in San Juan. The government keeps a close eye on them. Dress for the larger casinos is on the formal side, and the atmosphere is refined, particularly in the Isla Verde resorts. Casinos set their own hours but are generally open from noon to 4 am. In addition to slot machines, typical games include blackjack, roulette, craps, Caribbean stud (a five-card poker game), and *pai gow* poker (a combination of American poker and the Chinese game pai gow). Hotels with casinos have live entertainment most weekends, as well as restaurants and bars. The minimum age to gamble (and to drink) is 18.

The Casino at The Ritz-Carlton, San Juan. With its golden columns, turquoise and bronze walls, and muted lighting, the Ritz casino, the largest in San Juan, stays refined by day or night. There's lots of activity, yet everything is hushed. ⊠ *6991 Av. de los Gobernadores, Isla Verde* ☎ *787/253–1700* ⊕ *www.ritzcarlton.com/sanjuan.*

The El San Juan Casino. Neither the clangs of the slots nor the sounds of the salsa band disrupt the semblance of Old World. The polish continues in the adjacent lobby, with its huge chandeliers and mahogany paneling. ⊠ *6063 Av. Isla Verde, Isla Verde* ☎ *787/791–1000.*

San Juan Marriott Resort & Stellaris Casino. The crowd is casual and the decor tropical and bubbly at this spacious gaming room. Right outside, there's a huge bar, where Latin musicians perform Wednesday through Sunday, and an adjacent café. ⊠ *1309 Av. Ashford, Condado* ☎ *787/722–7000.*

DANCE CLUBS

Brava. Dress to impress at this chic hotel dance club, where a long line of young people (21+) waits to get in Thursday–Saturday. Each of the two levels has its own DJ and dance floor. ✉ *El San Juan Resort & Casino, 6063 Av. Isla Verde, Isla Verde* ☎ *787/791–2781* ⊕ *www.bravapr.com.*

PERFORMING ARTS

Orquesta Sinfónica de Puerto Rico (*Puerto Rico Symphony Orchestra*). Under the direction of conductor Maximiano Valdés, this 80-member orchestra performs a 52-week season that includes classical music, operas, ballets, and popular music. The orchestra plays mostly at Centro de Bellas Artes Luis A. Ferré but also gives outdoor concerts at museums and universities around the island as well as doing educational outreach in island schools. Pablo Casals helped create the group in 1956. ✉ *San Juan* ☎ *787/918–1107* ⊕ *www.cba.gobierno.pr.*

Teatro Tapia. Named for Puerto Rican playwright Alejandro Tapia y Rivera, this is the oldest theater in Puerto Rico. It hosts traveling and locally produced theatrical and musical productions. Matinee performances for families are also held, especially around the holidays. ✉ *Plaza Colón, Calle Fortaleza, Old San Juan* ☎ *787/480–5004.*

SHOPPING

San Juan has the island's best range of stores (many closed on Sunday), but it isn't a free port, so you won't find bargains on electronics and perfumes. You can, however, find excellent prices on china, crystal, clothing, and jewelry. When shopping for local crafts, you'll find tacky along with treasures; in many cases you can watch the artisans at work. Popular items include *santos* (small carved figures of saints or religious scenes), hand-rolled cigars, handmade *mundillo* lace from Moca, *vejigantes* (colorful masks used during Carnival and local festivals) from Loíza and Ponce, and fancy men's shirts called guayaberas.

Old San Juan—especially Calles Fortaleza and Cristo—has T-shirt emporiums, crafts stores, bookshops, art galleries, jewelry boutiques, and even shops that specialize in made-to-order Panama hats. Calle Cristo has factory outlets, including Coach and Dooney & Bourke.

With many stores selling luxury items and designer fashions, the shopping spirit in the San Juan neighborhood of Condado is reminiscent of Miami. Avenida Ashford, the heart of San Juan's fashion district, has plenty of high-end clothing stores.

SAN JUAN

ART

Galería Botello. This influential gallery displays art by the late Angel Botello, who was hailed as the Caribbean Gauguin as far back as 1943. (His works also hang in the Museo de Arte de Puerto Rico.) His paintings often feature the bright colors of the tropics and usually depict island scenes. Also on display here are works by other prominent local artists, Puerto Rican santos, and sculptures by Botello. ⊠ *208 Calle Cristo, Old San Juan* ☎ *787/723–9987* ⊕ *www.botello.com.*

Galería Petrus. Among those who have displayed their works at Galería Petrus are Dafne Elvira, whose surreal oils and acrylics tease and seduce (witness a woman emerging from a banana peel); Marta Pérez, another surrealist, whose bewitching paintings examine such themes as how life on a coffee plantation might have been; and Elizam Escobar, a former political prisoner whose oil paintings convey the horrors human beings must endure. Exhibitions change frequently and focus on local artists. ⊠ *726 Calle Hoare, Miramar* ☎ *787/289–0505* ⊕ *www.petrusgallery.com.*

CIGARS

Cigar House. The Cigar House has an eclectic selection of local and imported cigars from Nicaragua, Honduras, and the Dominican Republic. At the lounge and bar, you can enjoy your purchase with a glass of your favorite spirit. ⊠ *257 Calle Fortaleza, Old San Juan* ☎ *787/723–5223* ⊕ *www.thecigarhousepr.com.*

CLOTHING

Cappalli. Noted local designer Lisa Cappalli sells her feminine, sensuous designs in this elegant boutique, which specializes in ready-to-wear and custom fashions including a small collection of whimsical, lacy wedding gowns. ⊠ *206 Calle O'Donnell, Old San Juan* ☎ *787/289–6565.*

Nativa. The window displays are almost as daring as the clothes at this shop catering to trendy young ladies looking for party dresses, jumpers, accessories, and shoes. ⊠ *55 Calle Cervantes, Condado* ☎ *787/724–1396* ☉ *Closed Sun.*

Nono Maldonado. Known for high-end, elegant men's and women's clothes, particularly in linen, Nono Maldonado worked for many years as the fashion editor of *Esquire* and presents a periodic couture collection. This second-floor store also serves as the designer's studio. ⊠ *1112 Av. Ashford, 2nd fl., Condado* ☎ *787/721–0456* ⊕ *www.nonomaldonado.com.*

Otto. Otto Bauzá stocks international lines of casual and formal wear for younger men. His shop is closed Sunday and Monday. ⊠ *69 Av. Condado, Condado* ☎ *787/722–4609.*

GIFTS

Eclectika. This boutique carries a variety of items, mostly from Indonesia, from bedspreads to beaded and wooden jewelry, furnishings to hand fans. Everything is reasonably priced. ⊠ *204 Calle O'Donnell, Plaza Colón, Old San Juan* ☎ *787/721–7236.*

Haitian Gallery. The shop carries Haitian masks, statues, paintings, and wooden works of art. The second floor houses a large selection of paintings from the Caribbean. ⊠ *367 Calle Fortaleza, Old San Juan* ☎ *787/725–0986* ⊕ *www.haitiangallerypr.com.*

Spicy Caribbee. Kitchen items, cookbooks, jams, spices, and sauces from around the Caribbean are on offer. ⊠ *154 Calle Cristo, Old San Juan* ☎ *888/725–7259* ⊕ *www.spicycaribbee.com.*

13

JEWELRY

Bared & Sons. The store carries Rolex, Cartier, Bulgari, and Brietling watches and a large selection of fine jewelry. Look for the massive clock face on the corner. ⊠ *206 San Justo, Old San Juan* ☎ *787/724–4811.*

Catalá Joyeros. Family-run since the 1930s, the store is known for its large selection of pearls and precious stones, and for its jewelry design. ⊠ *Plaza de Armas, 152 Calle Rafael Cordero, Old San Juan* ☎ *787/722–3231* ⊕ *www.catalajoyeros.com.*

SOUVENIRS

Mi Pequeño San Juan. You might find a reproduction of your hotel at this shop, which specializes in tiny ceramic versions of San Juan doorways. The works are created by hand in the shop, which also carries fine art prints. ⊠ *152 Calle Fortaleza, Old San Juan* ☎ *787/721–5040* ⊕ *www. mipequenosanjuan.com.*

SPORTS AND THE OUTDOORS

BOATING AND SAILING

East Island Excursions. This outfit operates 45- to 65-foot catamarans, two of the which are powered to cut down on travel time to outlying islands. Trips may include offshore snorkeling, stops at isolated beaches, and a lunch buffet. An evening excursion to Vieques to see the bioluminescent bay includes dinner at a local restaurant. All of the plush craft are outfitted with swimming decks, freshwater showers, and full-service bars. ⊠ *Marina Puerto del Rey, Rte. 3, Km 51.4, Fajardo* ☎ *787/860–3434, 877/937–4386* ⊕ *www.eastislandpr.com.*

DIVING AND SNORKELING

The diving is excellent off Puerto Rico's south, east, and west coasts, as well as its nearby islands. Particularly striking are dramatic walls created by a continental shelf off the south coast near La Parguera and Guánica. There's also some fantastic diving near Fajardo and around Vieques and Culebra, two small islands off the east coast. It's best to choose specific locations with the help of a guide or outfitter. Escorted half-day dives range from $65 to $120 for one or two tanks, including all equipment; in general, double those prices for night dives. Packages that include lunch and other extras are more. Snorkeling excursions, which include transportation, equipment rental, and sometimes lunch, start at $50. Equipment rents for about $5 to $10.

Aquatic Adventures. Captain Taz Hamrick takes guests out on snorkeling and PADI-certified scuba trips, as well as charters to the surrounding keys. ⊠ *372 Sector Fulladoza, Dewey* ☎ *515/290–2310, 787/209–3494* ⊕ *www.diveculebra.com.*

Culebra Divers. Run by Monika and Walter Rieder, the island's premier dive shop caters to those new to scuba as well as those adept at underwater navigation. The company's 25-foot cabin cruisers travel to more than 50 local sites to see spotted eagle rays, octopus, moray eels, and turtles. You can also rent a mask and snorkel to explore on your own. ✉ *4 Calle Pedro Marquez, Dewey* ☎ *787/742–0803* ⊕ *www. culebradivers.com.*

Sea Ventures Dive Center. Here you can get diving certification, arrange dive trips to 20 offshore sites, including Culebra and Vieques, and organize boating and sailing excursions. ✉ *Marina Puerto del Rey, Rte. 3, Km 51.2, Fajardo* ☎ *787/863–3483, 800/739–3483* ⊕ *www. divepuertorico.com.*

GOLF

Aficionados may know that Puerto Rico is the birthplace of golf legend Chi Chi Rodríguez—and that he had to hone his craft somewhere. There are nearly 20 courses, including many championship links. Call ahead for tee times, as hours vary and several hotel courses give preference to guests. Greens fees are $20–$165.

The **Puerto Rican Golf Association** (✉ *264 Av. Matadero, Suite 11, San Juan* ☎ *787/793–3444* ⊕ *www.prga.org*) is a good source for information on courses and tournaments.

Arthur Hills Golf Course at El Conquistador, A Waldorf Astoria Resort. Named for its designer, the 18-hole course is famous for its mountainous terrain with elevation changes of more than 200 feet—rare in the Caribbean. From the highest spot, on the 15th hole, you have great views of the surrounding mountains and rain forest. The trade winds make every shot challenging—if the gorgeous views, strategic bunkering, and many water hazards haven't already distracted you. You are also likely to spot the harmless and generally timid iguana that populate the area. ✉ *El Conquistador Resort, 1000 Av. El Conquistador, Fajardo* ☎ *787/863–6784* ⊕ *www.elconresort.com* ▱ *Up to $210* ⚑ *18 holes, 6746 yards, par 72.*

Fodor's Choice ★ **Golf Links at Royal Isabela.** Mixing luxurious service, ecological sensitivity, and an incomparable setting along dramatic bluffs at Puerto Rico's northwest edge, this 18-hole course, which opened in 2011, is already considered among the Caribbean's best. Designed and developed by Stanley and Charlie Pasarell with assistance from course architect David Pfaff, it can play to as much as 7,667 yards and a par of 72 or 73 depending upon how you play the Fork in the Road 6th. The course doesn't have one signature moment; it has many, from the 6th to the island green at 9 to the carry over the sea at 12, to name a few. Carts are available, though walking is encouraged and caddies are mandatory. ✉ *396 Ave. Noel Estrada, Isabela* ☎ *787/609–5888* ⊕ *www. royalisabela.com* ▱ *$250 ($125 guests); caddie $90 for 2 players* ⚑ *18 holes, 7667 yards, par 73.*

TPC Dorado Beach. Four 18-hole regulation courses blend Caribbean luxury and great golf at this icon with a storied tradition and were purchased by TPC in 2015. Designed by Robert Trent Jones Sr., the famous East and West courses (East was renovated by Robert Trent Jones, Jr. in 2011; West is closed for renovation) are in a secluded seaside sanctuary along 2 miles (3 km) of northeasterly shore within the former

Rockefeller estate. Two Plantation Courses—the Sugarcane (more challenging) and Pineapple (easier)—complete the offerings. ⊠ *5000 Plantation Dr., Dorado* ☎ *787/262–1010* ⊕ *www.doradobeachclubs.com* 🖃 *East $282, Plantation Courses $170* 🏌. *East Course: 18 holes, 7200 yards, par 72; West Course: 18 holes, 6360 yards, par 72; Sugarcane: 18 holes, 7119 yards, par 72; Pineapple: 18 holes, 6196 yards, par 72.*

HORSEBACK RIDING

Horseback riding is a well-established family pastime in Puerto Rico, with *cabalgatas* (group day rides) frequently organized on weekends through mountain towns.

Carabalí Rainforest Park. A family-run operation, this hacienda is a good place to jump in the saddle and ride one of Puerto Rico's Paso Fino horses. Hour-long rides take you around the 600-acre ranch, while two-hour treks take you to a river where you and your horse can take a dip. If you prefer something more high-tech, rent a four-wheeler for an excursion through the foothills of El Yunque. ⊠ *Rd. 3, Km. 31.6, Luquillo* ☎ *787/889–4954* ⊕ *www.carabalirainforestpark.com.*

SURFING

The best surfing beaches are along the northwestern coast from Isabela south to Rincón, which gained notoriety by hosting the World Surfing Championship in 1968. Today the town draws surfers from around the globe, especially in winter, when the waves are at their best.

East of the city, in Piñones, the Caballo has deep- to shallow-water shelf waves that require a big-wave board known as a gun. Playa La Pared, near Balneario de Luquillo, is a surfer haunt with medium-range waves. Numerous local competitions are held here throughout the year.

Desecheo Surf & Dive Shop. This shop rents boogie boards and a variety of short and long surfboards as well as snorkeling equipment; sets up surfing lessons, and sells swimwear, sandals, sunglasses, and surf gear. ⊠ *Rte. 413, Km 2.5, Maria's Beach, Rincón* ☎ *787/823–0390* ⊕ *www.desecheosurfshop.com.*

Mar Azul. One of the best surf shops on the entire island has Rincon's best selection of performance surfboards and stand-up paddleboards to buy or rent. Inquire about surfing and paddleboard lessons. ⊠ *Rte. 413, Km 4.4, Rincón* ☎ *787/823–5692* ⊕ *www.puertoricosurfinginfo.com.*

14

ST. BARTHÉLEMY

Visit Fodors.com for advice, updates, and bookings

WELCOME TO ST. BARTHÉLEMY

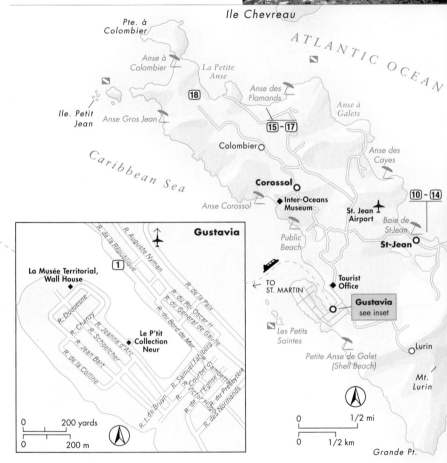

Gustavia

La Musée Territorial, Wall House ◆

Le P'tit Collection Neur ◆

R. de la République
R. Auguste Nyman
R. de la Paix
R. du Roi Oscar II
R. du Général de Gaulle
R. du Bord de Mer
R. Duquesne
R. Chanzy
R. Jeanne d'Arc
R. Schoelcher
R. Jean Bart
R. de la Colline
R. J. de Bruyn
R. Samuel Fahlberg
R. Courbet Gambett
R. Victor Hugo
R. de l'Eglise du Presbytère
R. des Normands

0   200 yards
0   200 m

Ile Chevreau

ATLANTIC OCEAN

Pte. à Colombier

Anse à Colombier

La Petite Anse

Anse des Flamands

18

Anse à Galets

Ile. Petit Jean

Anse Gros Jean

15 - 17

Anse des Cayes

Colombier ○

Caribbean Sea

Corossol ○

◆ Inter-Oceans Museum

Anse Corossol

St. Jean Airport

10 - 14

Baie de St-Jean

Public Beach

St-Jean ○

TO ST. MARTIN →

Tourist Office ◆

Gustavia see inset

Les Petits Saintes

Petite Anse de Galet (Shell Beach)

○ Lurin

Mt. Lurin

0   1/2 mi
0   1/2 km

Grande Pt.

Chic travelers put aside their cell phones long enough to enjoy the lovely beaches— long, surf-pounded strands; idyllic crescents crowned by cliffs or forests; glass-smooth lagoons perfect for windsurfing. Nothing on St. Barth comes cheap. But on a hotel's awning-shaded terrace St. Barth's civilized ways seem worth every penny.

LA RIVIERA DES CARAÏBES

Just 8 square miles (21 square km), St. Barth is a hilly island with many sheltered bays. Development is tightly controlled, so you will find no high-rise resorts to spoil your views. The French, who had controlled the island since the late 17th century, gave it to Sweden in 1784 but reclaimed it in 1877.

TOP REASONS TO VISIT ST. BARTHÉLEMY

1 The Scene: The island is active, sexy, hedonistic, and hip, and the human scenery is as beautiful as the sparkling-blue sea vistas.

2 Super Style: St. Barth continues to change and evolve, becoming ever more chic.

3 Great Dining: New restaurants tempt gourmets and gourmands.

4 Shopping Galore: If you're a shopper, you'll find bliss stalking the latest in French clothes and accessories with prices up to 30% less than in the states.

5 Getting Out on the Water: Windsurfing, kitesurfing, and other water sports make going to the beach more than just a lounging experience.

NEED TO KNOW

AT A GLANCE

Capital: Gustavia

Population: 8,400

Currency: Euro

Money: ATMs are common and dispense only euros; U.S. dollars are accepted in most places as are credit cards.

Language: French

Country Code: 590

Emergencies: 18

Driving: On the right

Electricity: 230v/60 cycles; plugs are European standard with two round prongs

Time: Same as New York during daylight savings time; one hour ahead otherwise

Documents: Up to 90 days with valid passport

Mobile Phones: GSM (900 and 1800 bands)

Major Mobile Companies: Digicel, Orange, CHIPPIE, Dauphin Telecom

WEBSITES

St. Barths Online: ⊕ www. st-barths.com

GETTING AROUND

✈ **Air Travel:** Fly into St. Maarten's Queen Juliana International Airport, and connect to a 10-minute flight to the landing strip at Gustaf III Airport.

🚌 **Bus Travel:** There are no bus services on St. Barth.

🚗 **Car Travel:** Almost everyone will want to rent a car in St. Barth to avoid the high taxi prices. Sometimes you can rent directly from your hotel or villa property manager.

⛴ **Ferry Travel:** Three companies provide passenger ferry service between St. Maarten/St-Martin and Gustavia.

PLAN YOUR BUDGET

	HOTEL ROOM	MEAL	ATTRACTIONS
Low Budget	€300	€20	Flamands Beach, free
Mid Budget	€750	€40	Jet Ski rental, €140/hr
High Budget	€1200	€75	Full-day private catamaran, €1,080

WAYS TO SAVE

Picnic. Good food requires deep pockets on St. Barth. The easiest way to save is to get supplies at a market and picnic on the beach.

Rent a villa or cottage. There are some reasonable villas and cottages for rent by the week, even during high season.

Explore the island by scooter. Several companies rent motorbikes, scooters, and mopeds. Scooter and motorbike rental places are mostly along rue de France in Gustavia and around the airport in St-Jean.

Hit the beach. St. Barth's dozen-plus beaches are all free and open to the public.

PLAN YOUR TIME

Hassle Factor	Medium. Flights to St. Maarten are frequent and connections to St. Barth run almost every hour until dusk.
3 days	Relax poolside or beachside at your resort and take in the scene—active, sexy, hedonistic, and hip. Rent a car and explore this tiny island, allotting time in Gustavia to shop and eat.
1 week	Enjoy your resort and explore the island, with ample time to sample each of the 14 major beaches in a single week. Hike the trail down to Colombier and snorkel in the turquoise sea. Get out on the water to windsurf, kitesurf, snorkel or just take in the sunset on an evening cruise.
2 weeks	Explore St. Barth coast to coast, both above and under the sea. Take time to visit some of the other neighboring islands, including St. Maarten and Anguilla (both connected by direct 10- to 15-minute flights) or Saba (connected by two 10-minute flights).

WHEN TO GO

High Season: Mid-December through mid-April is the most fashionable (on an island where fashion is everything) and most expensive time to visit. Good hotels are often booked far in advance, and you're guaranteed the most entertainment at resorts.

Low Season: From August to late October, temperatures can grow oppressively hot and the weather muggy, with a high risk of tropical storms. Many upscale hotels close during these months for annual renovations. Those remaining open offer some discounts.

Value Season: From late April to July and again November to mid-December, hotel prices drop 20% to 30% from high-season prices. There are chances of scattered showers, but expect sun-kissed daytime temperatures and fewer crowds.

BIG EVENTS

January: The St. Barth Music Festival showcases a wide variety of musical and dance performances usually held the second and third weeks of the month. ⊕ www.stbartsmusicfestival.org

April: St. Barth Festival of Caribbean Cinema celebrates Caribbean-made documentaries and feature films. ⊕ www.stbarthff.org

August: The St. Barth Summer Sessions features 30 top musicians from around the world over 10 days. ⊕ www.stbarthsummersessions.com

October: The Taste of St. Barth is an international gourmet food festival that brings renowned chefs to the island.

READ THIS

■ *The Insiders' Guide to Becoming a Yacht Stewardess: Confessions from My Years Afloat with the Rich and Famous,* Julie Perry. A fascinating how-to.

■ *The Messenger,* Daniel Silva. Part of this award-winning novel takes place on the island.

■ *St. Barts Breakdown: A Mick Sever Mystery,* Don Bruns. The meeting of a music journalist and music legend proves lethal.

WATCH THIS

■ *Salt.* Scenes from this Angelina Jolie spy thriller were filmed on the island.

■ *Arthur.* The wedding scene between characters Arthur and Susan was filmed in St. Barth, in both the original and the 2011 reboot.

EAT THIS

■ *Féroce d'avocat*: patties of spicy avocado and cod.

■ *Tacos la langouste*: lobster tacos.

■ *Giraumon soup*: thick pumpkin squash soup.

■ *'Ti punch*: a rum, lime, and sugar mixture, similar to a Brazilian caipirinha.

■ *Tartare de poisson pays*: local fish tartare.

■ *Cheeseburger at Le Select*: a St. Barth tradition since 1978.

Updated by
Elise Meyer

St. Barthélemy blends the respective essences of the Caribbean, France, and *Architectural Digest* in perfect proportions. A sophisticated but unstudied approach to relaxation and respite prevails: you can spend the day on a beach, try on the latest French fashions, catch a gallery exhibition, and watch the sunset while nibbling tapas over Gustavia Harbor, then choose from nearly 100 excellent restaurants for an elegant or easy evening meal. You can putter around the island, scuba dive, windsurf on a quiet cove, or just admire the lovely views.

A mere 8 square miles (21 square km), St. Barth is a hilly island, with many sheltered inlets and picturesque, quiet beaches. The town of Gustavia wraps itself around a modern harbor lined with everything from size-matters megayachts to rustic fishing boats to sailboats of all descriptions. Red-roof villas dot the hillsides, and glass-front shops line the streets. Beach surf runs the gamut from kiddie-pool calm to serious-surfer dangerous, beaches from deserted to packed. The cuisine is tops in the Caribbean, and almost everything is tidy, stylish, and up-to-date. French *savoir vivre* prevails.

Christopher Columbus came to the island—called "Ouanalao" by its native Caribs—in 1493; he named it for his brother Bartolomé. The first French colonists arrived in 1648, drawn by its location on the West Indian Trade Route, but they were wiped out by the Caribs, who dominated the area. Another small group from Normandy and Brittany arrived in 1694. This time the settlers prospered—with the help of French buccaneers, who took advantage of the island's strategic location and protected harbor. In 1784 the French traded the island to King Gustav III of Sweden in exchange for port rights in Göteborg. The king dubbed the capital Gustavia, laid out and paved streets, built three forts, and turned the community into a prosperous free port. The island thrived as a shipping and commercial center until the 19th century, when earthquakes, fires, and hurricanes brought financial ruin. Many residents fled for newer lands of opportunity, and Oscar II of Sweden returned the island to France. After briefly considering selling it to America, the French took possession of St. Barthélemy again on August 10, 1877.

Today the island is a free port, and in 2007 it became a Collectivity, a French-administered overseas territory. Arid, hilly, and rocky, St. Barth was unsuited to sugar production and thus never developed an extensive slave base. Some of the residents are descendants of the tough Norman and Breton settlers of three centuries ago, but you are more likely to encounter attractive French twenty- and thirtysomethings from Normandy and Provence, who are friendly, English speaking, and here for the sunny lifestyle.

14

PLANNING

GETTING HERE AND AROUND

AIR TRAVEL

There are no direct flights to St. Barth. Most North Americans fly first into St. Maarten's Queen Juliana International Airport, from which the island is 10 minutes by air. Winair, which celebrated its 50th anniversary of service to St. Barth in 2013, has regularly scheduled flights from St. Maarten. Through Winair's affiliation with major airlines, you can check your luggage all the way from your home airport to St. Barth under certain circumstances. Tradewind Aviation has regularly scheduled service from San Juan and also does V.I.P charters. Anguilla Air Services and St. Barth Commuter have scheduled flights and also do charters. Leave ample time between your scheduled flight and your connection in St. Maarten: 90 minutes is the minimum recommended (and be aware that luggage frequently doesn't make the trip; your hotel or villa-rental company may be able to send someone to retrieve it). It's a good idea to pack a change of clothes, required medicines, and a bathing suit in your carry-on—or better yet, pack very light and don't check baggage at all.

Airports Gustaf III Airport (SBH). ⊠ *St. Jean Rd., St-Jean* ☎ *0590/27–75–81.*

Airlines St. Barth Commuter. ☎ *0590/27–54–54* ⊕ *www.stbarthcommuter. com.* **Tradewind Aviation.** ☎ *203/267–3305* ⊕ *www.tradewindaviation.com.* **Trans Anguilla Airways.** ☎ *264/498–5922* ⊕ *www.transanguilla.com.* **Winair.** ☎ *0590/27–61–01, 866/466–0410* ⊕ *www.fly-winair.com.*

BOAT AND FERRY TRAVEL

St. Barth can be reached via ferry service from St. Maarten/St. Martin to Quai de la République in Gustavia. Voyager offers several daily round-trips for about $110 per person from either Marigot or Oyster Pond. Great Bay Express has two or three round-trips a day from Bobby's Marina in Philipsburg for €90 if reserved in advance, €95 for same-day tickets, and €56 for a same-day round-trip. Private boat charters are also available, but they are very expensive; Master Ski Pilou offers transfers from St. Maarten.

Contacts Great Bay Express. ✉ *Quai Gustavia, Gustavia* ☎ *599/542-0032* ⊕ *www.greatbayferry.com.* **Master Ski Pilou.** ☎ *0590/27-91-79* ⊕ *www.masterski-pilou.com.* **Voyager.** ☎ *0590/87-10-68* ⊕ *www.voy12.com.*

BACKUP FERRY

Even if you are flying to St. Barth, it's a good idea to keep the numbers and schedules for the three ferry companies handy in case your flight is delayed. If you are planning to spend time in St. Maarten before traveling on to St. Barth, the ferry is half the cost and somewhat more reliable than a flight, and you can leave from Marigot, Oyster Pond, or Philipsburg. Check at the St. Barth Tourist Information counter at Princess Juliana Airport for specifics.

14

CAR TRAVEL

Roads are sometimes unmarked, so get a map and look for signs, nailed to posts at all crossroads, pointing to a destination. Roads are narrow and sometimes very steep, but have been improved; even so, check the brakes and gears of your rental car before you drive away. Maximum speed is 30 mph (50 kph). Driving is on the right, as in the United States and Europe. Parking is an additional challenge. There are two gas stations on the island, one near the airport and one in Lorient. They aren't open after 5 pm or on Sunday, and pumps at the station near the airport accept chip-and-pin credit cards (almost all U.S. credit cards now have the required chip). Considering the short distances, a full tank should last most of a week.

Car Rentals: You must have a valid driver's license and be 25 or older to rent, and in high season there may be a three-day minimum. During peak periods, such as Christmas week and February, arrange for your car rental ahead of time. Rental agencies operate out of Gustaf III Airport, and some will bring cars to your hotel. Alternately, when you make your hotel reservation, ask if the hotel has its own cars available to rent; some hotels provide 24-hour emergency road service—something most rental companies don't. A tiny but powerful Smart car is a blast to buzz around in, and also a lot easier to park than larger cars. Expect to pay at least $55 per day. For a green alternative, consider rental of an electric car. They're available for about $85 per day.

Contacts Avis. ☎ *0590/27-66-30* ⊕ *www.avis-sbh.com.* **Budget.** ☎ *0590/27-66-30* ⊕ *www.st-barths.com/budget.* **Cool Rental.** ☎ *0590/27-52-58* ⊕ *www.cool-rental.com.* **Europcar.** ☎ *0590/29-41-86* ⊕ *www.europcar-stbarth.com.* **Gumbs.** ☎ *0590/27-75-32* ⊕ *www.gumbs-car-rental.com.* **Gust Smart of St-Barth.** ☎ *0690/41-66-72.* **Hertz.** ☎ *0590/52-34-03* ⊕ *www.hertzstbarth.com.* **Turbé.** ☎ *0590/27-71-42* ⊕ *www.turbe-car-rental.com.*

MOPED, SCOOTER, AND BIKE TRAVEL

Several companies rent motorbikes, scooters, mopeds, ATVs, and mountain bikes. Motorbikes go for about $30 per day and require a $100 deposit. ATV rental starts at $40 per day. Helmets are required. Scooter and motorbike rental places are mostly along rue de France in Gustavia and around the airport in St-Jean.

Contacts Barthloc Rental. ✉ *Rue de France, Gustavia* ☎ *0590/27–52–81*
⊕ *www.barthloc.com.* **Chez Béranger.** ✉ *21 rue du général de Gaulle, Gustavia*
☎ *0590/27–89–00* ⊕ *www.beranger-rental.com.* **Fun Motors.** ✉ *Les Galeries du
Commerce, St-Jean* ☎ *0590/27–54–83* ⊕ *www.funmotorsjpf.com.*

TAXI TRAVEL

Taxis are expensive and not particularly easy to arrange, especially
in the evening. There's a taxi station at the airport and another at the
ferry dock in Gustavia; from elsewhere you must contact a dispatcher
in Gustavia or St-Jean. Fares are regulated by the Collectivity, and drivers accept both dollars and euros. If you go out to dinner by taxi, let
the restaurant know if you will need a taxi at the end of the meal, and
they will call one for you. Limo-style private car-and-driver service is
available 24/7 through Taxi Prestige.

Contacts Taxi Association. ☎ *0590/27-66-31.* **Taxi Prestige.** ☎ *0590/27-70-
57* ⊕ *www.stbarts-limousine.com.*

HEALTH AND SAFETY

There's relatively little crime on St. Barth. Visitors can travel anywhere
on the island with confidence. Most hotel rooms have safes for your
valuables. As anywhere, don't tempt loss by leaving cameras, laptops,
or jewelry out in plain sight in your hotel room or villa or in your car.
Don't walk barefoot at night. There are venomous centipedes that can
inflict a remarkably painful sting. If you ask residents, they will tell
you that they drink only bottled water, although most cook or make
coffee with tap water.

Dengue, chikungunya, and zika have all been reported throughout
the Caribbean. We recommend that you protect yourself from these
mosquito-borne illnesses by keeping your skin covered and/or wearing
mosquito repellent. The mosquitoes that transmit these viruses are as
active by day as they are by night.

HOTELS AND RESORTS

Small luxury hotels: The largest hotel on the island has about 70 rooms,
but the majority are stratospherically expensive.

Villas: About half the accommodations on St. Barth are in private villas.

Hotel reviews have been shortened. For full information, visit Fodors.com.

WHAT IT COSTS IN EUROS			
$	$$	$$$	$$$$
RESTAURANTS under €12	€12–€20	€21–€30	over €30
HOTELS under €275	€275–€375	€376–€475	over €475

Restaurant prices are the average cost of a main course at dinner or, if dinner is
not served, at lunch. Hotel prices are the lowest cost of a standard double room in
high season.

VISITOR INFORMATION

Contact Office du Tourisme. ✉ *Quai Général de Gaulle, Gustavia* ☎ *0590/27-
87-27* ⊕ *www.saintbarth-tourisme.com.*

EXPLORING

With practice, negotiating St. Barth's narrow, steep roads soon becomes fun. Infrastructure upgrades and small, responsive rental cars have improved driving. Free maps are everywhere, and roads are smooth and well marked. The tourist office has annotated maps with walking tours that highlight sights of interest.

GUSTAVIA

You can easily explore all of Gustavia during a two-hour stroll. Some shops close from noon to 3 or 4, so plan lunch accordingly, but stores stay open past 7 in the evening. Parking in Gustavia is a challenge, especially during vacation times. A good spot to park is rue de la République, alongside the catamarans, yachts, and sailboats.

FAMILY **Le Musée Territorial, Wall House.** On the far side of the harbor known as La Pointe, the charming Municipal Museum has watercolors, portraits, photographs, traditional costumes, and historic documents detailing the island's history as well as displays of the island's flowers, plants, and marine life. There are also changing contemporary art exhibitions. ⊠ *La Pointe, Gustavia* ☎ *0590/29–71–55* 💷 *€2* 🕙 *Mon., Tues., Thurs., and Fri. 8:30–1 and 2:30–5; Wed and Sat. 9–1.*

Le P'tit Collectionneur. Encouraged by family and friends, André Berry opened this private museum to showcase his lifelong passion for collecting fascinating objects such as 18th-century English pipes and the first phonograph to come to the island. He will happily show you his treasures. ⊠ *La Pointe, Gustavia* 💷 *€2* 🕙 *Mon.–Sat. 10–noon and 4–6.*

ANSE DE TOINY

Over the hills beyond Grand Cul de Sac is this much-photographed coastline. Stone fences crisscross the steep slopes of Morne Vitet, one of many small mountains on St. Barth, along a rocky shore that resembles the rugged coast of Normandy. Nicknamed the "washing machine" because of its turbulent surf, it is not recommended even to expert swimmers because of the strong undertow. ■ TIP➜ **There is a tough but scenic hike around the point. Take the road past Le Toiny hotel to the top to the start of the trail.**

COROSSOL

Traces of the island's French provincial origins are evident in this two-street fishing village with a little rocky beach.

LORIENT

Site of the first French settlement, Lorient is one of the island's two parishes; a restored church, a school, and a post office mark the spot. Note the gaily decorated graves in the cemetery.

ST-JEAN

There is a monument at the crest of the hill that divides St-Jean from Gustavia. Called *The Arawak,* it symbolizes the soul of St. Barth. A warrior, one of the earliest inhabitants of the area (AD 800–1,800), holds a lance in his right hand and stands on a rock shaped like the island; in his left hand he holds a conch shell, which sounds the cry of nature; perched beside him are a pelican (which symbolizes the air and survival by fishing) and an iguana (which represents the earth). The half-mile-long crescent of sand at St-Jean is the island's favorite beach. A popular activity is watching and photographing the hair-raising airplane landings (but it is extremely dangerous to stand at the beach end of the runway). Some of the best shopping on the island is here as are several restaurants.

BEACHES

There is a beach in St. Barth to suit every taste. Wild surf, complete privacy in nature, a dreamy white-sand strand, and a spot at a chic beach club close to shopping and restaurants—they're all within a 20-minute drive.

There are many *anses* (coves) and nearly 20 *plages* (beaches) scattered around the island, each with a distinct personality; all are open to the public, even if they front a tony resort. Because of the number of beaches, even in high season you can find a nearly empty one, despite St. Barth's tiny size. That's not to say that all beaches are equally good or even equally suitable for swimming, but each has something to offer. Unless you are having lunch at a beachfront restaurant with lounging areas set aside for patrons, you should bring an umbrella, beach mat, and water (all of which are easily obtainable all over the island). Topless sunbathing is common, but nudism is supposedly forbidden—although both Grande Saline and Gouverneur are de facto nude beaches, albeit less than in the past. Shade is scarce.

Anse à Colombier. The beach here is the island's least accessible, thus the most private; to reach it you must take either a rocky footpath from Petite Anse or brave the 30-minute climb down (and back up) a steep, cactus-bordered trail from the top of the mountain behind the beach. Appropriate footgear is a must, and on the beach, the only shade is a rock cave. But this is a good place to snorkel. Boaters favor this cove for its calm anchorage. **Amenities:** none. **Best for:** snorkeling; swimming. ⊠ *Colombier.*

Anse de Grand Cul de Sac. The shallow, reef-protected beach is nice for small children, fly-fishermen, kayakers, and windsurfers—and for the amusing pelicanlike frigate birds that dive-bomb the water fishing for their lunch. There is a good dive shop. You needn't do your own fishing; you can have a wonderful lunch at one of the excellent restaurants, and use their lounge chairs for the afternoon. **Amenities:** food and drink; parking (no fee); toilets; water sports. **Best for:** swimming; walking. ⊠ *Grand Cul de Sac.*

FAMILY
Fodor's Choice
★
Anse de Grande Saline. With its peaceful seclusion and sandy ocean bottom, this is just about everyone's favorite beach and is great for swimming, too. Without any major development, it's an ideal Caribbean strand, though there can be a bit of wind at times. In spite of the prohibition, young and old alike go nude. The beach is a 10-minute walk up a rocky dune trail, so wear sneakers or water shoes, and bring a blanket, umbrella, and beach towels. There are several good lunch restaurants near the parking area, but the beach itself is just sand, sea, and sky. The big salt ponds here are no longer in use, and the place looks a little desolate on approach, but don't despair. **Amenities:** parking (no fee). **Best for:** nudists; swimming; walking. ⊠ *Grande Saline.*

> **PICKING THE RIGHT BEACH**
>
> For long stretches of talcum-soft pale sand choose La Saline, Gouverneur, or Flamands. For seclusion in nature, pick the tawny grains of Corossol. But the most remarkable beach on the island, Shell Beach, is right in Gustavia and hardly has sand at all! Millions of tiny pink shells wash ashore in drifts, thanks to an unusual confluence of ocean currents, sea-life beds, and hurricane action.

14

FAMILY
Anse de Lorient. This beach is popular with families and surfers, who like its waves and central location. Be aware of the level of the tide, which can come in very quickly. Hikers and avid surfers like the walk over the hill to Pointe Milou in the late afternoon, when the waves roll in. **Amenities:** parking (no fee). **Best for:** snorkeling; surfing; swimming. ⊠ *Lorient.*

Anse des Flamands. This is the most beautiful of the hotel beaches—a roomy strip of silken sand. Come here for lunch and then spend the afternoon sunning, enjoying long beach walks, and swimming in the turquoise water. From the beach, you can take a brisk hike along a paved sidewalk to the top of the now-extinct volcano believed to have given birth to St. Barth. **Amenities:** food and drink; toilets. **Best for:** snorkeling; swimming; walking. ⊠ *Anse des Flamands.*

FAMILY
Anse du Gouverneur. Because it's so secluded, this beach is a popular place for nude sunbathing. Truly beautiful, it has blissful swimming and views of St. Kitts, Saba, and St. Eustatius. Venture here at the end of the day and watch the sun set behind the hills. The road here from Gustavia also offers spectacular vistas. Legend has it that pirates' treasure is buried in the vicinity. There are no restaurants, toilets, or other services here, so plan accordingly. **Amenities:** parking (no fee). **Best for:** nudists; sunset; swimming; walking. ⊠ *Le Gouverneur.*

FAMILY
Baie de St-Jean. Like a mini–Côte d'Azur—beachside bistros, terrific shopping, bungalow hotels, bronzed bodies, windsurfing, and day-trippers who tend to arrive on BIG yachts—the reef-protected strip is divided by Eden Rock promontory. Except when the hotels are filled, you can rent chaises and umbrellas at La Plage restaurant or Eden Rock, where you can lounge for hours over lunch. **Amenities:** food and drink; toilets. **Best for:** partiers; walking. ⊠ *St-Jean.*

WHERE TO EAT

Dining on St. Barth compares favorably to almost anywhere in the world. Varied and exquisite cuisine, a French flair in the decor, sensational wine, and attentive service make for a wonderful epicurean experience in almost any of the more than 80 restaurants. On most menus, freshly caught local seafood mingles on the plate with top-quality provisions that arrive regularly from Paris. Interesting selections on the Cartes de Vins are no surprise, but don't miss the sophisticated cocktails whipped up by island bartenders. They are worlds away from cliché Caribbean rum punches with paper umbrellas. The signature drink of St. Barth is called "'ti punch," a rum concoction similar to a Brazilian caipirinha. It's also fun to sit at a bar and ask the attractive bartender for his or her own signature cocktail.

Most restaurants offer a chalkboard of daily specials, usually a good bet. But even the pickiest eaters will find something on every menu. Some level of compliance will be paid to dietary restrictions, especially if explained in French; just be aware that French people generally let the chef work his or her magic. Vegetarians will find many options on every menu. Expect meals to be costly, but you can dine superbly and somewhat economically if you limit pricey cocktails, watch wine selections, share appetizers or desserts, and pick up snacks and picnics from one of the well-stocked markets. Or you can follow the locals to small *crêperies,* cafés, sandwich shops, and pizzerias in the main shopping areas. Lunch is usually less costly than dinner. *Ti creux* means "snack" or "small bite."

Lavish publications feature restaurant menus and contacts. Ask at your hotel or look on the racks at the airport. Reservations are strongly recommended and, in high season, essential. Lots of restaurants now accept reservations on their website or by email. Check social media. Except during the Christmas–New Year's season it's not usually necessary to book far in advance. A day's—or even a few hours'—notice is usually sufficient. At the end of the meal, as in France, you must request the bill. Until you do, you can feel free to linger at the table and enjoy the complimentary vanilla rum that's likely to appear.

Check restaurant bills carefully. A *service compris* (service charge) is always added by law, but you should leave the server 5% to 10% extra in cash. You'll usually come out ahead if you charge restaurant meals on a credit card in euros instead of paying with American currency, as your credit card might offer a better exchange rate than the restaurant (unless your credit card charges a conversion surcharge). Many restaurants serve locally caught *langouste* (lobster); priced by weight, it's usually the most expensive item on a menu and, depending on its size and the restaurant, will range in price from $40 to $60. *In menu prices below, it has been left out of the range.*

What to Wear: A bathing suit and gauzy top or shift is acceptable at beachside lunch spots, but not really in Gustavia. Jackets are never required and are rarely worn by men, but most people do dress fashionably for dinner. St. Barth is for fashionistas; women wear whatever is hip, current, and sexy. You can't go wrong in a tank dress or a sexy top with white jeans, high sandals, and flashy accessories. The sky is the limit for high fashion at nightclubs and lounges in high season, when you might (correctly) think everyone in sight is a model. Leave some space in your suitcase; you can buy the perfect outfit here on the island. Nice shorts (not beachy ones) at the dinner table may label a man *américain,* but many locals have adopted the habit, and nobody cares much. Wear them with a pastel shirt to really fit in (never tucked in). Pack a light sweater or shawl for the occasional breezy night.

ANSE DE TOINY

$$$$
MODERN FRENCH

✕ **Le Toiny.** Hôtel Le Toiny's dramatic, redesigned, cliff-side dining porch showcases nature and gastronomy in equal parts. Less stuffy than in the past, the food is notable for its innovation and extraordinary presentation, and the warm but consummately professional service sets a high standard. There are starters like shrimp tempura and avocado bruschetta to share, then luxurious first courses like black truffle pasta, seared foie gras, black cod, and other interesting grilled fish and meat entreés complimented by exotic ingredients. For lunch (reservations mandatory) you can dine and relax at the hotel's new private beach club. $ *Average main: €47* ⊠ *Hôtel Le Toiny, Anse de Toiny* ☎ *0590/29–88–88* ⊕ *www.letoiny.com* ☉ *Closed Sept.–mid-Oct.* ⚑ *Reservations essential.*

14

FLAMANDS

$$$$
MODERN FRENCH
Fodor's Choice
★

✕ **La Case de L'Isle.** You can't top the view or the service at this waterfront restaurant at the renowned Cheval Blanc St-Barth Isle de France, and at night there is no more romantic spot on the island. Lighter versions of traditional French fare are served. At lunch you can have your toes in the sand or sit on the porch while enjoying a composed salad, a fish tartare, or club sandwich. For dinner, choose from tender Moroccan-style lamb, or Asian-inspired steamed fish with dumplings. Light, fruity desserts satisfy the chic crowd. Occasional fashion shows featuring the lovely beachwear from the on-site boutique are a fun diversion. $ *Average main: €45* ⊠ *Cheval Blanc St-Barth Isle de France, Flamands Beach, Anse des Flamands* ☎ *0590/27–61–81* ⊕ *www.isle-de-france. com* ⚑ *Reservations essential.*

$$$
FRENCH FUSION

✕ **La Langouste.** This small but friendly beachside restaurant in the pool courtyard of Hôtel Baie des Anges lives up to its name by serving fresh-grilled local lobster—and lobster thermidor—at prices that are somewhat gentler than at most other island venues. Try starters like local squash *gratin*, beef *carpaccio*, scallop-and-leek samosas, a warm goat cheese salad, or one of the five soups, including classic Caribbean fish soup and lobster bisque. The well-prepared fish and pasta dishes are great main options, and there are always choices for meat fans as well. Classic French desserts like Floating Island with vanilla sauce, crepes suzette, and a fruit tart are worth the calories. $ *Average main: €26* ⊠ *Hôtel Baie des Anges, Anse des Flamands* ☎ *0590/27–63–61* ⊕ *www. hotel-baie-des-anges.com* ☉ *Closed late Aug.–mid-Oct.* ⚑ *Reservations essential.*

Le Toiny, Anse de Toiny

GRAND CUL DE SAC

$$$$
ECLECTIC
FAMILY

✕ **Bartolomeo.** Locavores will like the refined cuisine at this pretty restaurant in the gardens of the Guanahani hotel. Influenced by Provence and Italy, beautifully presented dishes use some organic and local products. Try the ravioli or seafood risotto followed by beef tenderloin, organic chicken breast, or suckling veal. Look for desserts utilizing chocolate or Caribbean fruit. On Thursday, when the restaurant is closed, Le Guanahani hosts a fun beach lobster BBQ with music. ■ TIP➔ **Long pants are required.** $ *Average main: €43* ✉ *Hotel Guanahani, Grand Cul de Sac* 📞 *0590/27–66–60* 🕙 *Closed Thurs. No lunch* ⚲ *Reservations essential.*

$$
CARIBBEAN

✕ **La Gloriette.** Everyone has a great time eating a beachside lunch at shady picnic tables under coccoloba trees. Those who remember the original creole restaurant here will be happy to know that the *accras* (salt-cod fritters with spicy sauce) are as good as ever. There are huge, fresh salads and many daily specials on the blackboard. Grilled fish is super-fresh, and the sushi-style tatakis are light and delicious. At dinner there are good pizzas for dining in or taking back to your villa. Artisanal, island-flavored rums are offered after the meal and available at the tiny shop. $ *Average main: €19* ✉ *Plage de Grand Cul de Sac, Grand Cul de Sac* 📞 *0590/29–85–71* 🕙 *Closed Wed.*

GRANDE SALINE

$$$$
MODERN FRENCH
FAMILY
Fodor's Choice
★

✕ **L' Esprit.** Renowned chef Jean-Claude Dufour (formerly of Eden Rock) brings innovative dishes to a romantic terrace close to Saline Beach. The menu has lots of variety, from light French dishes with a Provençal twist to interesting salads (like soba noodles with shrimp and lime), roasted pigeon with foie gras, steak, and tasty vegetarian options. The chocolate cake is a pleasing dessert, but the memory of the sweet service will last longer. $ *Average main: €38* ⊠ *Anse de Grande Saline, Grande Saline* ☎ *0590/52–46–10* ⊘ *No lunch Wed. and Sun.*

$$$
INTERNATIONAL
Fodor's Choice
★

✕ **Le Tamarin.** A leisurely lunch here en route to Grande Saline beach is a St. Barth *must,* but this spot is also tops for dinner or an after-beach snack, too. A beautiful tropical garden with a truly wondrous tamarind tree shades the lounge chairs surrounding the palapa of the restaurant and gives it its name. There is even a lovely small boutique if you want to shop between courses. The lunch menu features sandwiches, sashimi, burgers, and simple grills. Dinner brings heartier plates including duck breast and veal roast. Don't miss the beautifully presented, enormous profiteroles for dessert. The service is attentive and friendly, and the wine list is excellent. $ *Average main: €30* ⊠ *Grande Saline* ☎ *0590/29– 27–74* ⊕ *www.tamarinstbarth.com* ⊘ *Closed Tues.*

$$$$
STEAKHOUSE

✕ **Meat and Potatoes.** If you think that St. Barth is sometimes too "girly," you will love this restaurant at the end of the road to Saline Beach. The white interior is lined with banquettes heaped with red, black, and gray pillows. A half-dozen cuts of steak, from tenderloins to T-bones, can be paired with 15 sauces, at least a dozen starchy sides (including the Provençal *pommes ratte,* potato wedges cooked in duck fat, fresh rosemary, and sea salt), and some vegetables for good measure—all à la carte. People love the Burger Party on Thursdays. For the red-meat averse, there is fresh fish and a vegetarian menu. The wine list is full of complementary bottles, heavy on Bordeaux's best. $ *Average main: €35* ⊠ *Grande Saline* ☎ *0590/51–15–98* ⊘ *No lunch.*

$$$$
INTERNATIONAL
Fodor's Choice
★

✕ **On the Rocks.** Settle into your table perched high above St-Jean beach at the gleaming, wood-framed terrace restaurant at the Eden Rock Hotel to enjoy a sophisticated world-class meal. Chef Eric Desbordes, formerly of Le Bristol in Paris, and executive superchef Jean Georges Vongerichten pair up for a supreme culinary experience. Linger over a creative cocktail while you decide on your dinner, helped by the charming and well-informed waitstaff. For a splurge go for the artichoke ravioli with seared foie gras or gossamer tuna sashimi. The black cod is extraordinary, and the veal "filet mignon" is a blast of taste. Fabulous desserts are edible works of art, gorgeously plated, some garnished with gold leaf. $ *Average main: €63* ⊠ *St-Jean* ☎ *0590/29–79–99* ⊕ *www. edenrockhotel.com* ⊘ *Closed Sept. and Oct.*

$$$$
FRENCH
FAMILY

✕ **Restaurant La Santa Fé.** Perched at the top of the Lurin hills on the way to Gouverneur Beach, this relaxed and scenic restaurant serves panoramic views with both lunch and dinner. The chef comes from Provence and trained at some its best restaurants before moving to the Caribbean. Salads and light lunch offerings are great before the beach, but come for dinner—especially if you are a fan of authentic French cuisine—for delicious osso buco, roasted French Bresse chicken, and

14

sea scallop tart with fresh vegetables. $ *Average main: €34* ⊠ *Rte. de Lurin, Lurin* ☎ *0590/27–61–04* ⊙ *Closed Wed. and Sept.–mid-Oct.*

GUSTAVIA

$$$$
MODERN FRENCH

✕ **Bagatelle St Barth.** The sophisticated St-Tropez–inspired eatery, right on the harbor, is a scene-y place to watch big boats and enjoy pizzas (try the truffle one) and simple favorites like duck breast, steak, and local fish. You can book a table on the terrace, and cocktails are special and strong. Fans of sister establishments in New York's Meatpacking District and Los Angeles will recognize the friendly service, lively atmosphere, and great music provided by resident DJs. Come late—the party and champagne get going after 11. $ *Average main: €34* ⊠ *Rue Samuel Fahlberg, Gustavia* ☎ *0590/27–51–51* ⊕ *www.bistrotbagatelle. com* ⊙ *Closed Sun. No lunch* ⚹ *Reservations essential.*

$$$$
LATIN AMERICAN
Fodor's Choice
★

✕ **Bonito.** Decorated like a chic beach house, Bonito features big white canvas couches for lounging, in the center; tables around the sides; an open kitchen; and three bar areas—all on a hill above Gustavia Harbor. The young Venezuelan owners go to great lengths to see that guests are having as much fun as they are. The specialty is ceviche, in combos in many varieties that are prettily arrayed on poured-glass platters. Traditionalists might like the grilled octopus or foie gras. Carnivores love the rack of lamb. The dessert menu has primarily French pastry classics, but the restaurant is also famous for its *tres leches* cake. $ *Average main: €41* ⊠ *Rue Lubin Brin, Gustavia* ☎ *0590/27–96–96* ⊕ *www. ilovebonito.com* ⊙ *Closed Wed. and late Aug.–early Nov. No lunch* ⚹ *Reservations essential.*

$$$
ECLECTIC

✕ **Dõ Brazil.** In addition to lunch and dinner, this restaurant on Shell Beach has live music for sundown cocktail hour Thursday–Saturday as well as top DJs spinning the latest club mixes for evening events. Tasty fare includes duck spring rolls, carpaccios, Caesar salad, burgers, wok noodles and vegetables, and grilled fresh fish for lunch. The extensive cocktail menu is tempting, but your bar bill can quickly exceed the price of dinner. There is also a children's menu. $ *Average main: €26* ⊠ *Shell Beach, Gustavia* ☎ *0590/29–06–66* ⊕ *www.dobrazil.com* ⊙ *Closed Sept. and Oct.*

$$$
ASIAN

✕ **Eddy's.** By local standards, dinner in the pretty, open-air, tropical garden here is reasonably priced. The cooking is French-creole-Asian. Fish specialties, especially the sushi tuna sampler, are fresh and delicious, and there are always plenty of daily specials. Just remember some mosquito repellent for your ankles. $ *Average main: €24* ⊠ *12 rue Samuel Fahlberg, Gustavia* ☎ *0590/27–54–17* ⊙ *Closed Sun. and Sept. and Oct. No lunch* ⚹ *Reservations not accepted.*

$$$$
MEDITERRANEAN

✕ **La Guérite.** This stylish restaurant, a sister of a well-beloved Cannes hot spot, has taken the place formerly occupied by the Wall House restaurant at the far side of Gustavia Harbor. The room is beautiful, overlooking the yachts; the service helpful and friendly; and the food is fresh, tasty, healthy, and well prepared, with a touch of Greek influence. For starters, try flavorful grilled peppers or the restaurant's clever play on the local *accras* (codfish fritters) made here with zucchini. For mains, try excellent charcoal-roasted whole *loup de mer* or tender gnocchi.

Desserts show the sophisticated influence of modernist cuisine. $ *Average main: €33* ⊠ *La Pointe, Gustavia* ☎ *0590/88–44–42* ⊕ *www. laguerite-sbh.com* ☉ *No lunch Sun.* ⌨ *Reservations essential.*

$$$
CARIBBEAN

✕ **Le Palace.** Tucked into a tropical garden, this popular restaurant, also known as Pipiri Palace, is famous for its barbecued ribs, beef fillet, and rack of lamb. Lunch features a well-priced prix-fixe menu. For dinner, fish-market specialties like curried red snapper cooked in a banana leaf and grilled tuna are good, as is grilled duck. The blackboard's daily specials are usually a great choice, and the island's best tarte tatin is made with salted caramel. $ *Average main: €30* ⊠ *Rue du Général de Gaulle, Gustavia* ☎ *0590/27–53–20* ☉ *Closed Sun. and mid-June–July.*

$$
BRASSERIE
FAMILY

✕ **Le Repaire.** Overlooking the harbor, this friendly classic French brasserie is busy from its early-morning opening to its late-night closing. The flexible hours are great if you arrive on the island mid-afternoon and need a substantial snack. Grab a cappuccino, pull a captain's chair up to the street-side rail, and watch the pretty people go by. The menu ranges from cheeseburgers, served only at lunch, along with the island's best fries, to simply grilled fish and meat, pastas, risottos, mixed salads, and wonderful ice cream sundaes. $ *Average main: €19* ⊠ *Rue de la République, Gustavia* ☎ *0590/27–72–48* ☉ *Closed Sun.*

$$$
FRENCH

✕ **Les Bananiers.** Ask the locals where to eat, and they will surely recommend this casual spot in Colombier, adjacent to a wonderful bakery. The food is classic French, the service is warm, the prices are gentle, and you can eat in or take out. Choose from dishes like classic fish soup, grilled duck breast, escargots in garlic butter, thin-crust pizza, and fresh fish. Order early in the day for takeout pizza. $ *Average main: €23* ⊠ *Rte. de Colombier, Colombier* ☎ *0590/27–93–48.*

$$$$
ITALIAN
Fodor'sChoice
★

✕ **L'Isola.** The chic sister of Santa Monica, California's Via Veneto packs in happy guests for classic Italian dishes, dozens of house-made pasta dishes, prime meats, and a huge, well-chosen wine list. Restaurateur Fabrizio Bianconi wants it to feel like a big Italian party, and with all the celebrating in this pretty and romantic room, it sounds like he succeeded. Favorite dishes include a hearty veal chop in a sage-butter sauce and several different (all heavenly) risottos. $ *Average main: €38* ⊠ *33 rue du Roi Oscar II, Gustavia* ☎ *0590/51–00–05* ⊕ *www.lisolastbarth. com* ☉ *Closed Sept. and Oct. No lunch* ⌨ *Reservations essential.*

$
PIZZA

✕ **L'Isoletta.** This casual Roman-style pizzeria run by the popular L'Isola restaurant is a lively, chic lounge-style gastropub serving delicious thin-crust pizzas by the slice or the meter. There are even dessert pizzas, and excellent *tiramisu*. Lasagnas and focaccia sandwiches are also available to eat in or take out. It's open from lunch until 11 pm. $ *Average main: €10* ⊠ *Rue du Roi Oscar II, Gustavia* ☎ *0590/52–02–02* ⌨ *Reservations not accepted.*

$$$$
CARIBBEAN

✕ **Maya's.** New Englander Randy Gurley and his wife, Maya (a French-born chef), provide returning guests with a warm welcome and a very pleasant, albeit expensive, dinner on their cheerful dock decorated with big round tables and crayon-color canvas chairs, all overlooking Gustavia Harbor. A market-inspired menu of good, simply prepared and garnished dishes—like roast quail and Indian-spiced fish—changes daily, assuring the restaurant's ongoing popularity. $ *Average main:*

14

€39 ✉ *Public, Gustavia* ☎ *0590/27–75–73* 🌐 *www.mayas-stbarth.com* 🕑 *Closed Sun. No lunch* ✍ *Reservations essential.*

$$$$ JAPANESE FUSION 🍴 **Orega.** This brand new restaurant occupies the central former location of longtime St. Barth mainstay Le Sapotillier. The cuisine is French-Japanese fusion, a tasty combination, and the pretty room is decorated in natural woods, neutral linen, and good art. There are lots of sushi rolls and sashimi options, as well as interesting plays on ingredients from both France and Japan, like the wagyu beef *gyoza* (dumplings) with mushrooms, or toro tuna with Petrossian caviar fit for an oligarch. Main courses include duck confit and Kobe beef. Fusion desserts like green tea crème brûlée, and Japanese lemon tart offer a successful meal-ending treat. [$] *Average main: €41* ✉ *13 rue Samuel Fahlberg, Gustavia* ☎ *0590/52–45–31* 🌐 *www.oregarestaurant.com* 🕑 *Closed Tues.*

POINTE MILOU

$$$$ ECLECTIC Fodor's Choice ★ 🍴 **Le Ti St. Barth Caribbean Tavern.** Chef-owner Carole Gruson captures the island's funky, sexy spirit in her wildly popular hilltop spot. Come to dance to great music with the attractive bar crowd, lounge at a pillow-strewn banquette, or chat on the torch-lighted terrace. By the time your appetizers arrive, you'll be best friends with the next table. Top-quality fish and meats are cooked on the traditional charcoal barbecue. Big spenders love the Angus beef fillet Rossini with truffles, but there are lighter options like wok shrimp with Chinese noodles, and seared tuna with caviar. Provocatively named desserts, such as Nymph Thighs (airy lemon cake with vanilla custard), Daddy's Balls (passion-fruit sorbet and ice cream), and Sweet Thai Massage (kiwi, pineapple, mango, and lychee salad) end the meal on a fun note. By then someone is sure to be dancing on the tables. There's an extensive wine list. The famously raucous full-moon parties, cabarets, and Monday Plastic Boots ladies' nights are all legendary. [$] *Average main: €53* ✉ *Pointe Milou* ☎ *0590/27–97–71* 🌐 *www.caroleplaces.com* ✍ *Reservations essential.*

ST-JEAN

$$$$ INTERNATIONAL 🍴 **La Plage.** Dining in St. Barth–style is spot-on at this eatery in Le Tom Beach Hôtel, a prime place to watch people and the action on St. Jean Beach. Passion-fruit martinis are a must, as are the fresh-caught grilled spiny lobsters and roasted beet "carpaccio." There are beach lounges for daytime and music all day long. Check the local papers for special events and parties. [$] *Average main: €36* ✉ *Le Tom Beach Hôtel, Plage de St-Jean, St-Jean* ☎ *0590/52–81–33* 🌐 *www.tombeach.com.*

$$$$ ECLECTIC Fodor's Choice ★ 🍴 **The Sand Bar.** At this Eden Rock hotel eatery, lunch on the terrace with the beautiful blue water sparkling beyond is incomparable. Star chef Jean Georges Vongerichten's cuisine is tailored to the setting—all the things you'd be tempted to eat at the beach. Delicious light salads, soups, and carpaccio are highlights, but there are also heartier salads with fish and chicken, simple grilled fish and meat entrées, and delicious wood-oven pizzas, such as fontina and truffle. Beautiful desserts include chocolate and lemon tart, and there's brunch on Sundays. With the

Eden Rock's world-class people-watching, you never know who'll be checking out a menu next to you. $ *Average main: €41* ✉ *Eden Rock, Baie de St-Jean, St-Jean* ☎ *0590/29–79–99* ⊕ *www.edenrockhotel.com* ⚓ *Reservations essential.*

WHERE TO STAY

There's no denying that hotel rooms and villas on St. Barth carry high prices. You're paying primarily for the privilege of staying on the island, and even at $800 a night the bedrooms tend to be small. Still, if you're flexible—in terms of timing and in your choice of lodgings—you can enjoy a holiday in St. Barth and still afford to send the kids to college.

The most expensive season falls during the holidays (mid-December to early January), when hotels are booked far in advance, may require a 10- or 14-day stay, and can be double the high-season rates. A 5% government tourism tax on room prices (excluding breakfast) is in effect; be sure to ask if it is included in your room rate or added on.

When it comes to booking a hotel on St. Barth, the reservation manager can be your best ally. Rooms within a property can vary greatly. It's well worth the price of a phone call or the time invested in emails to make a personal connection, which can lead to a room that meets your needs or preferences. Details of accessibility, views, recent redecorating, meal options, and special package rates are topics open for discussion. Quoted hotel rates are per room, not per person, and include service charges and often airport transfers. Bargain rates found on Internet booking sites can sometimes yield unpleasant surprises in terms of the actual room you get. Consider contacting the hotel and mentioning the rate you found. Often they will match it, and you'll end up with a better room.

PRIVATE VILLAS AND CONDOS

On St. Barth the term *villa* describes anything from a small cottage to a luxurious, modern estate. Today almost half of St. Barth's accommodations are in villas, a great option, especially if traveling with friends or family. Even more advantageous to Americans, villa rates are usually quoted in dollars, thus bypassing unfavorable euro fluctuations. Most villas have a small private swimming pool and maid service daily except Sunday. They are well furnished with linens, kitchen utensils, and such electronic playthings as smart-phone docks, CD and DVD players, satellite TV, and broadband Internet. Weekly in-season rates range from $1,400 to "oh-my-gosh." Most villa-rental companies are based in the United States and have extensive websites that allow you to see pictures or panoramic videos of the place you're renting; their local offices oversee maintenance and housekeeping and provide concierge services. Just be aware that there are few beachfront villas, so if you have your heart set on "toes in the sand" and a cute waiter delivering your Kir Royale, stick with the hotels or villas operated by hotel properties.

CLOSE UP

St. Barth's Spas

Visitors to St. Barth can enjoy more than the comforts of home by taking advantage of the myriad wellness, spa, and beauty treatments available on the island. Major hotels—the Cheval Blanc St-Barth Isle de France, Guanahani, and Christopher—have beautiful, comprehensive, on-site spas. Others, including the Le Village St. Barth Hotel, Le Sereno, and Hôtel Le Toiny, have added spa cottages, where treatments and services can be arranged on-site. Depending on availability, all island visitors can book services at these. There is a new wellness retreat here, with metabolic and detox programs available. In addition, scores of independent therapists will come to your hotel room or villa and provide any therapeutic discipline you can think of, including yoga, Thai massage, shiatsu, reflexology, and even manicures, pedicures, and hairdressing. You can get recommendations at the tourist office in Gustavia.

RECOMMENDED COMPANIES

Eden Rock Villa Rental. Eden Rock Villa Rental manages 80 super-luxe villas and cottages. Provided with each are butlers, chefs, and concierge services, giving you the privacy of a villa but the service of a luxury hotel. ☎ *0590/27–14–94* 🌐 *www.edenrockvillarental.com.*

Marla. This local St. Barth villa-rental company represents more than 100 villas, many of which are not listed with other companies. ✉ *18, Rue du Roi Oscar II, Gustavia* ☎ *0590/27–62–02* 🌐 *www.marlavillas.com.*

St. Barth Properties, Inc. Owned by American Peg Walsh, a regular on St. Barth since 1986, this company represents more than 120 properties. The excellent website offers virtual tours of most of the villas and even details on availability. ✉ *Gustavia* ☎ *508/528–7727, 800/421–3396* 🌐 *www.stbarth.com.*

Wimco. Based in Rhode Island, Wimco oversees bookings for more than 230 properties, at $2,000–$10,000 a week for two- and three-bedroom villas and from $7,000 for larger villas. The website, which occasionally lists last-minute specials, has interactive floor plans, and a catalog is available by mail. The company can arrange for babysitters, massages, chefs, and other in-villa services as well as private air charters. ☎ *800/932–3222* 🌐 *www.wimco.com.*

ANSE DE TOINY

$$$$ HOTEL Fodor's Choice ★

🏨 **Hôtel Le Toiny.** Privacy, serenity, and personalized service please international sophisticates, who gravitate to this remote hotel since you never have to leave if you don't want to. **Pros:** extremely private; flawless service; environmental awareness. **Cons:** isolated (at least half an hour's drive from town); must take a hotel shuttle to reach the beach. [$] *Rooms from: €1,545* ✉ *Anse de Toiny* ☎ *0590/27–88–88* 🌐 *www.letoiny.com* ⏲ *Closed Sept.–late Oct.* 🛏 *14 1-bedroom villas, 1 3-bedroom villa* 🍴 *Breakfast.*

Hotel Guanahani and Spa, Grand Cul de Sac

COLOMBIER

$ B&B/INN **Le P'tit Morne.** Each of the modestly furnished but clean and freshly decorated, painted mountainside studios has a private balcony with panoramic views of the coastline. **Pros:** reasonable rates; great area for hiking. **Cons:** rooms are basic; remote location; not on the beach. *Rooms from: €204 Colombier 0590/52–95–50 www.timorne.com/fr 14 rooms Breakfast.*

FLAMANDS

$$$$ RESORT Fodor's Choice ★ **Cheval Blanc St-Barth Isle de France.** Nestled along a pristine white-sand beach, in tropical gardens, or on a hillside, the spacious rooms, suites, and villas of this intimate, casual, and refined resort are private and luxurious. **Pros:** prime beach location; terrific management; great spa; excellent restaurant. **Cons:** car needed to get around; one day you'll have to leave this paradise. *Rooms from: €935 B.P. 612 Baie des Flamands, Anse des Flamands 0590/27–61–81 www.chevalblanc.com Closed Sept.–mid-Oct. 40 rooms, suites, villas, and bungalows Breakfast.*

$$ HOTEL FAMILY **Hôtel Baie des Anges.** Everyone is treated like family at this casual retreat with 10 clean, spacious units, 2 of which are completely renovated, modern two-bedroom oceanfront suites, one with a Jacuzzi. **Pros:** on St. Barth's longest beach; family-friendly; excellent value. **Cons:** a bit remote from town, necessitating a car. *Rooms from: €300 Anse des Flamands 0590/27–63–61 www.hotel-baie-des-anges.com Closed Sept. 10 rooms No meals.*

$$$$ ⊞ **Hotel Taïwana.** This classic island retreat delights young international
RESORT guests who appreciate spiffy updates in spacious rooms and suites
FAMILY around a charming atrium garden. **Pros:** busy social scene; great beach
Fodor'sChoice access. **Cons:** may be too scene-y for some; every room is different, so
★ choose carefully; the courtyard room has no view. $ *Rooms from: €895*
⊠ *Baie De Flamands, Anse des Flamands* ☎ *0590/29–80–08* ⊕ *www.
hoteltaiwana.com* ↘ *7 rooms, 15 suites* ⏐⊙⏐ *Breakfast.*

GRAND CUL DE SAC

$$$$ ⊞ **Hotel Guanahani and Spa.** St. Barth's largest full-service resort has
RESORT lovely rooms and suites (14 have private pools) and impeccable service,
FAMILY not to mention one of the island's only children's programs (actually
Fodor'sChoice more of a nursery). **Pros:** fantastic spa; beachside sports; family-
★ friendly. **Cons:** lots of walking around property; steep walk to beach.
$ *Rooms from: €995* ⊠ *Grand Cul de Sac* ☎ *0590/52–90–00* ⊕ *www.
leguanahani.com* ⊙ *Closed Sept.* ↘ *36 suites, 31 rooms* ⏐⊙⏐ *Breakfast.*

$$$ ⊞ **Hotel Les Ondines Sur La Plage.** Right on the beach, this reasonably
RENTAL priced, intimate gem comprises modern, comfortable apartments with
FAMILY room to spread out. **Pros:** close to restaurants and water sports; nice
pool; airport transfers included. **Cons:** not a resort; narrow beach; you'll
need a car. $ *Rooms from: €450* ⊠ *Grand Cul de Sac* ☎ *0590/27–69–64*
⊕ *www.st-barths.com/les-ondines* ⊙ *Closed Sept.–mid-Oct.* ↘ *7 rooms,
suites, and villas* ⏐⊙⏐ *Breakfast.*

$$$$ ⊞ **Le Sereno.** Those seeking a restorative, sensuous escape discover nir-
RESORT vana at the quietly elegant, aptly named Le Sereno, set on a beachy cove
Fodor'sChoice of turquoise sea, between the island's highest mountain and the foamy
★ waves. **Pros:** beach location; super-chic comfort; friendly atmosphere.
Cons: no air-conditioning in bathrooms; construction in process nearby.
$ *Rooms from: €870* ⊠ *B.P. 19 Grand-Cul-de-Sac, Grand Cul de Sac*
☎ *0590/29–83–00* ⊕ *www.lesereno.com* ⊙ *Closed late Aug.–mid-Oct.*
↘ *37 suites and villas* ⏐⊙⏐ *Some meals.*

GRANDE SALINE

$ ⊞ **Salines Garden Cottages.** Budget-conscious beach lovers who don't
RENTAL require a lot of coddling need look no further than these petite garden
FAMILY cottages, a short stroll from St. Barth's best beach. **Pros:** only property
walkable to Salines Beach; quiet; good restaurants nearby. **Cons:** far
from town; not very private; strict cancellation policy. $ *Rooms from:
€180* ⊠ *Grande Saline* ☎ *0590/51–04–44* ⊕ *www.salinesgarden.com*
⊙ *Closed mid-Aug.–mid-Oct.* ↘ *5 cottages* ⏐⊙⏐ *Breakfast.*

GUSTAVIA

$ ⊞ **Sunset Hotel.** Ten simple, utilitarian rooms (one can accommodate three
HOTEL people) sit across from Gustavia's harbor and offer an economical and
handy, if not luxurious, option for those who want to stay in town. **Pros:**
reasonable rates; in town. **Cons:** no elevator; not resortlike in any way.
$ *Rooms from: €110* ⊠ *Rue de la République, Gustavia* ☎ *0590/27–
77–21* ⊕ *www.saint-barths.com/sunset-hotel* ↘ *10 rooms* ⏐⊙⏐ *No meals.*

Eden Rock, St-Jean

LORIENT

$ RENTAL FAMILY 🏨 **Les Mouettes.** This guesthouse offers clean, simply furnished, and economical bungalows with kitchenettes that open directly onto the beach but are also very close to the road. **Pros:** on the beach; family-friendly. **Cons:** basic rooms without TVs; strict prepayment and cancellation policies; no pool. [$] *Rooms from: €207* ✉ *Lorient* ☎ *0590/27–77–91* 🌐 *www.lesmouetteshotel.com* 💳 *No credit cards* 🛏 *7 bungalows* 🍴 *No meals.*

$ B&B/INN 🏨 **Normandie Hotel.** There's nothing in this price range that compares to these small but stylish and immaculate rooms. **Pros:** friendly management; pleasant atmosphere; good value. **Cons:** tiny rooms; small bathrooms. [$] *Rooms from: €210* ✉ *Lorient* ☎ *0590/27–61–66* 🌐 *normandiehotelstbarts.com* 🛏 *8 rooms* 🍴 *Breakfast.*

POINTE MILOU

$$$$ RESORT FAMILY 🏨 **Christopher.** This longtime favorite of European families delivers a high standard of professionalism and courteous service. **Pros:** comfortable elegance; family-friendly; reasonable price. **Cons:** on the water but not on a beach; three-night minimum. [$] *Rooms from: €510* ✉ *Pointe Milou* ☎ *0590/27–63–63* 🌐 *www.hotelchristopher.com* 🕒 *Closed Sept.–mid-Oct.* 🛏 *42 rooms* 🍴 *Breakfast.*

ST-JEAN

$$$$
RESORT
FAMILY
Fodor's Choice
★

Eden Rock. Even on an island known for gourmet cuisine and luxury hotels, this icon stands out—thanks to two top-tier Jean-Georges Vongerichten eateries, spacious rooms (redecorated in 2015), stunning bay views, and cosseting service. **Pros:** chic clientele; beach setting; stylish facilities; walk to shopping and restaurants. **Cons:** some suites near street are noisy. $ *Rooms from: €1,500* ⊠ *Baie de St-Jean, St-Jean* ☎ *0590/29–79–99, 877/563–7015 in U.S.* ⊕ *www.edenrockhotel.com* ⊗ *Closed Sept 1.–mid-Oct.* ⚑ *33 rooms, 2 villas* ⦿ *Breakfast.*

$$$
HOTEL
FAMILY
Fodor's Choice
★

Emeraude Plage. Right on the beach of Baie de St-Jean, this petite resort consists of small but immaculate bungalows and villas with modern, fully equipped outdoor kitchens on small private patios. **Pros:** beachfront and in-town location; good value; cool kitchens on each porch. **Cons:** smallish rooms. $ *Rooms from: €445* ⊠ *Baie de St-Jean, St-Jean* ☎ *0590/27–64–78* ⊕ *www.emeraudeplage.com* ⊗ *Closed Sept.–mid-Oct.* ⚑ *28 bungalows* ⦿ *No meals.*

$
HOTEL
FAMILY
Fodor's Choice
★

Le Village St. Barth Hotel. For two generations the Charneau family has offered friendly hotel service, villa advantages, and reasonable rates, making guests feel like a part of the family. **Pros:** convenient location; wonderful management; friendly clientele; on-site spa and gym. **Cons:** steep walk to hotel, many steps; rooms close to street can be noisy. $ *Rooms from: €270* ⊠ *Colline de St-Jean, St-Jean* ☎ *0590/27–61–39, 800/651–8366* ⊕ *www.levillagestbarth.com* ⚑ *5 rooms, 20 cottages, 1 3-bedroom villa, 2 2-bedroom villas* ⦿ *Breakfast.*

$$$
RENTAL
FAMILY

Les Îlets de la Plage. On the far side of the airport and the far corner of Baie de St-Jean, these well-priced, island-style one-, two-, and three-bedroom bungalows (four on the beach, seven up a small hill) have small kitchens, open-air sitting areas, and comfortable bathrooms. **Pros:** beach location; apartment conveniences; front porches. **Cons:** TVs by request and with limited French programming; air-conditioning only in bedrooms; next to airport. $ *Rooms from: €465* ⊠ *Plage de St-Jean, St-Jean* ☎ *0590/27–88–57* ⊕ *www.lesilets.com* ⊗ *Closed Sept. and Oct.* ⚑ *11 bungalows* ⦿ *Breakfast.*

$$
HOTEL

Le Tom Beach Hôtel. This chic but casual boutique hotel on busy St-Jean beach is fun for social types; the nonstop house party often spills onto the terraces and lasts into the wee hours. **Pros:** party central at beach, restaurant, and pool; in town. **Cons:** trendy social scene is not for everybody, especially light sleepers. $ *Rooms from: €320* ⊠ *Plage de St-Jean, St-Jean* ☎ *0590/52–81–20* ⊕ *www.tombeach.com* ⚑ *12 rooms* ⦿ *Breakfast.*

NIGHTLIFE

Most of the nightlife in St. Barth is centered on Gustavia, though there are a few places to go outside of town. "In" clubs change from season to season, so you might ask around for the hot spot of the moment, but none really get going until about midnight. Theme parties are the current trend. Check the daily *St. Barth News* or *Le Journal de Saint-Barth* for details. A late (10 pm or later) reservation at one of the club–restaurants will eventually become a front-row seat at a party. *Saint-Barth Collector Guest Book* contains current information about sports, spas, nightlife, and the arts.

GUSTAVIA

Bar de l'Oubli. Where young locals gather for drinks is a great breakfast option, too (cash only). ⊠ *Rue du Roi Oscar II, Gustavia* ☎ *0590/27–70–06* ⊕ *www.bardeloubli.com.*

Le Repaire. This restaurant lures a crowd for cocktail hour and its pool table. ⊠ *Rue de la République, Gustavia* ☎ *0590/27–72–48.*

Le Sélect. Quite possibly the inspiration for Jimmy Buffett's "Cheeseburger in Paradise," St. Barth's original hangout has been around since 1949. The Facebook page has vintage photos. In the boisterous garden, the barefoot boating set gathers for a cold Carib beer at lower-than-usual prices while listening to a local band or DJ. ⊠ *Rue du Centenaire, Gustavia* ☎ *0590/27–86–87.*

ST-JEAN

Le Nikki Beach. This place rocks on weekends at lunch—especially Sundays—when the scantily clad young and beautiful lounge on the white canvas banquettes. Check out crazy theme nights on Facebook or in the local papers. ⊠ *St-Jean* ☎ *0590/27–64–64* ⊕ *www.nikkibeach.com.*

SHOPPING

Fodor's Choice
★

St. Barth is a duty-free port, and its sophisticated visitors find shopping in its 200-plus boutiques a delight, especially for beachwear, accessories, jewelry, and casual wear. It's no overstatement to say that shopping for fashionable clothing, jewels, and designer accessories is better in St. Barth than anywhere else in the Caribbean. New shops open all the time, so there's always something to discover. Some stores close from noon to 3, but they are open until 7 pm. Many are closed on Sunday. A popular afternoon pastime is strolling the two major shopping areas in Gustavia and St-Jean. While high fashion is as pricey here as everywhere, French brands sell for up to 30% less than in the U.S.

In Gustavia, boutiques pack the three major shopping streets. Quai de la République, which is right on the harbor, rivals New York's Madison Avenue or Paris's avenue Montaigne for high-end designer retail, including shops for **Louis Vuitton, Bulgari, Cartier, Chopard, Erès,** and **Hermès.** These shops often carry items that are not available in the United States. The elegant Carré d'Or plaza and the adjacent **Coeur Vendome** are great fun to explore. Shops are also clustered in **La Savane Commercial Center** (across from the airport), **La Villa Créole** (in St-Jean), and **Espace Neptune** (on the road to Lorient). It's worth working your way from one end to the other at these shopping complexes—just to see or, perhaps, be seen. Boutiques in all three areas carry the latest in French and Italian sportswear, charming children's togs, and some haute couture. Bargains may be tough to come by, but you might be able to snag that *Birkin* that has a long waiting list stateside, and in any case, you'll have a lot of fun hunting around.

For locally made art and handicrafts, the tourist office can provide information and arrange visits to studios of island artists, including Christian Bretoneiche, Robert Danet, Nathalie Daniel, Patricia Guyot, Rose Lemen, Aline de Lurin, and Marion Vinot. Gustavia, La Villa Créole, and the larger hotels have a few good gallery/craft boutiques.

GUSTAVIA

BOOKS

La Case Aux Livres. This full-service bookstore and newsstand has hundreds of English titles for adults and kids. Its blog lists author appearances. ⊠ *9 rue de la République, Gustavia* ☎ *0590/27–15–88* ⊕ *www.lacaseauxlivres.com.*

CLOTHING

Be Shorts. Beautiful tailored cotton shirts in fun prints and stripes for men and women, and colorful Bermuda shorts to coordinate, are popular in St-Tropez and St. Barth. ⊠ *Le Carré d'Or, Gustavia* ☎ *0590/27–54–33.*

Boutique Lacoste. This store has a huge selection of the once-again-chic alligator-logo wear for men, women, and kids ⊠ *Rue du Bord de Mer, Gustavia* ☎ *0590/27–66–90.*

Calypso. This well-known retailer carries sophisticated, sexy resort wear and accessories by Balenciaga, Chloe, and D Squared, among others. ⊠ *Le Carré d'Or, Gustavia* ☎ *0590/27–69–74* ⊕ *www.calypsostbarth.com/boutiques/st-barth.*

Hermès. This independently owned franchise (closed September and October) has prices slightly below those in the States. ⊠ *Rue de la République, Gustavia* ☎ *0590/27–66–15.*

Kokon. This boutique offers a nicely edited mix of designs for on-island or off, including the bo'em, Lotty B. Mustique, and Day Birger lines, and cute shoes to go with them by Heidi Klum for Birkenstock. ⊠ *Rue Samuel Fahlberg, Gustavia* ☎ *0590/29–74–48.*

Linen. This shop offers tailored linen shirts for men in a rainbow of soft colors and soft slip-on driving mocs in classic styles. ⊠ *Rue Lafayette, Gustavia* ☎ *0590/27–54–26* ⊕ *www.linensbh.com.*

Lolita Jaca. This store has trendy, tailored sportswear and floaty silk charmeuse and cotton gauze tunics perfect for the beach. ⊠ *Le Carré d'Or, Gustavia* ☎ *0590/27–59–98* ⊕ *www.lolitajaca.com.*

Mademoiselle Hortense. Charming tops and dresses for the young and young at heart in pretty Liberty prints are made on the island. Great crafty bracelets and necklaces to accent your new styles are also here. ⊠ *Rue de la République, Gustavia* ☎ *0590/27–13–29.*

Marina St. Barth. The trendy, sexy resort wear here, worn by the young and the beautiful, ranges from floaty beachwear to Havaianas. Lines include Ondade and Façonnable, and there are unusual ponchos by Lotus London, high-fashion T-shirts by Eleven Paris, and elegant silk tunics by Jodé. ⊠ *Rue du Roi Oscar II, Gustavia* ☎ *0590/29–37–30* ⊕ *www.marina-stbarth.com.*

Shops on rue de France, Gustavia

Pati de St Barth. This is the largest of the three shops that stock the chic, locally made T-shirts, totes, and beach wraps that have practically become the logo of St. Barth. The newest styles have hand-done graffiti-style lettering. The shop also has some handicrafts and other giftable items and great sandals. ✉ *Rue du Bord de Mer, Gustavia* ☎ *0590/29–78–04* ⊕ *www.pati-de-stbarth.com.*

Poupette St. Barth. All the brilliant color-crinkle silk, chiffon batik, and embroidered peasant skirts and tops are designed by the owner. There also are great belts and beaded bracelets. An outpost is at Hotel Taïwana. ✉ *Rue de la République, Gustavia* ☎ *0590/27–55–78* ⊕ *www. poupettestbarth.com.*

Saint-Barth Stock Exchange. On the far side of Gustavia Harbor, the island's consignment and discount shop is a blast to explore. ✉ *La Pointe, Gustavia* ☎ *0590/27–68–12.*

Vanita Rosa. This store showcases beautiful lace and linen sundresses, peasant tops, accessories galore, and very cool designer vintage. ✉ *Rue du Roi Oscar II, Gustavia* ☎ *0590/52–43–25* ⊕ *www.vanitarosa.com.*

Victoire. Classic, well-made sportswear in luxurious fabrics and great colors has a French twist on preppy that plays as well in Nantucket and Greenwich as it does on St. Barth. A small sidewalk café has Wi-Fi and terrific *macarons*. ✉ *Rue du Général de Gaulle, Gustavia* ☎ *0590/29–84–60* ⊕ *www.victoire-paris.com.*

FOODSTUFFS

A.M.C. This supermarket is a bit older than Marché U in St-Jean but can supply nearly anything you might need. It's closed Sunday. ⊠ *Quai de la République, Gustavia.*

HOME FURNISHINGS

French Indies Design. This beautiful shop on the far side of Gustavia Harbor is the brainchild of Karine Bruneel, a St. Barth–based architect and interior designer. There are lovely items to accent your home (or yacht) including furniture, textiles, glassware, and unusual decorative baskets, candles, and pottery. ⊠ *Maison Suédoise, Gustavia* ☎ *0590/29–66–38* ⊕ *www.frenchindiesdesign.fr.*

JEWELRY

Bijoux de la Mer. South Sea pearls in wonderful hues are strung in clusters on leather to wrap around the neck or arms. ⊠ *Rue de la République, Gustavia* ☎ *0590/52–37–68* ⊕ *bijouxdelamersbh.com.*

Carat. Carat has Chaumet and a large selection of Breitling watches, plus rarities by Richard Mille, Tourbillon, Panerai, and Breguet. ⊠ *Rue de la République, Gustavia* ☎ *0590/27–67–22* ⊕ *www.caratsaintbarth.com.*

Donna del Sol. This designer carries beautiful handmade gold chains, Tahitian pearl pieces, and baubles in multicolor diamonds. Have something special in mind? She'll design and produce custom items. ⊠ *Rue Auguste Nyman, Gustavia* ☎ *0590/27–90–53* ⊕ *www.donnadelsol.com.*

Fabienne Miot. Unusual and artistic jewelry features rare stones and cultured pearls, watches, and jewelry. ⊠ *Rue de la République, Gustavia* ☎ *0590/27–73–13* ⊕ *www.fabiennemiot.com.*

Kalinas Perles. Beautiful freshwater pearls are knotted onto the classic St. Barth–style leather thongs by artist Jeremy Albaledejo, who also showcases other artisans' works. ⊠ *23 rue du Général de Gaulle, Gustavia* ☎ *0690/65–93–00* ⊕ *www.kalinasperles.com.*

LEATHER GOODS AND ACCESSORIES

Human Steps. This popular boutique stocks a well-edited selection of chic shoes and leather accessories from names like YSL, Prada, Balenciaga, Miu Miu, and Jimmy Choo. ⊠ *39 rue de la République, Gustavia* ☎ *0590/27–93–79* ⊕ *www.human-steps.fr.*

Longchamp. Fans of the popular travel bags, handbags, and leather goods will find a good selection at about 20% off stateside prices. ⊠ *Rue de France, Gustavia* ☎ *0590/51–96–60.*

LIQUOR AND TOBACCO

Couleurs des Iles 120% Lino. This shop has many rare varieties of smokables, Panama hats, and good souvenir T-shirts, too. Head to the back for the stash of rare Puro Vintage. ⊠ *Rue du Général de Gaulle, Gustavia* ☎ *0590/27–79–20.*

La Cave du Port Franc. This store has a huge selection of wine, especially from France. ⊠ *Rue de la République, Gustavia* ☎ *0590/27–65–27* ⊕ *www.lacaveduportfranc.com.*

M'Bolo. Sample infused rums, including lemongrass, ginger, and the island favorite, vanilla, and bring some home in beautiful handblown bottles. Laguiole knives and local spices are sold, too. ⊠ *Rue du Général de Gaulle, Gustavia* ☎ *0590/27–90–54.*

LORIENT

COSMETICS

Ligne St. Barth. Superb skin-care products are made on-site from local tropical plants. Call to request a visit from a beautician or therapist to your villa or yacht. ⊠ *Rte. de Saline, Lorient* ☎ *0590/27–82–63* ⊕ *www. lignestbarth.com.*

FOODSTUFFS

JoJo Supermarché. This well-stocked counterpart to Gustavia's supermarket gets daily deliveries of bread and produce. JoJoBurger, next door, is the local surfers' spot for a (very good) quick burger. ⊠ *Lorient* ☎ *0590/27–63–53.*

ST-JEAN

CLOTHING

Bamboo St. Barth. Beach fashions like cotton tunics, cocktails-on-the-yacht dresses, and sexy Australian swimsuits by Nicole Olivier and Seafolly can be paired with sassy sandals and costume jewelry. ⊠ *Pelican Beach, St-Jean* ☎ *0690/52–08–82.*

Black Swan. This shop has an unparalleled selection of bathing suits. ⊠ *La Villa Créole, St-Jean* ☎ *0590/52–48–30* ⊕ *www.blackswanstbarth.com.*

Cabane St. Barth. Stocked with stenciled cotton, gauzy beach tops, great straw fedoras, and caftans (for all ages), this shop is open nonstop every day. ⊠ *Pelican Beach, St-Jean* ☎ *0590/51–21–02.*

Filles des Iles. In addition to high-quality, flattering French attire and sophisticated swimwear that even women of a certain age can wear, the shop stocks delicious artisanal fragrances and chic accessories, like bejeweled sandals. ⊠ *8 Villa Créole, St-Jean* ☎ *0590/29–04–08.*

Iléna. Incredible beachwear and lingerie by Chantal Thomas, Sarda, and others includes Swarovski crystal–encrusted bikinis for the young and gorgeous. ⊠ *La Villa Créole, St-Jean* ☎ *0590/29–84–05.*

KIWI St. Tropez. This popular resortwear boutique for women, men, and kids has a branch in Gustavia, too. ⊠ *3 Villa Créole, St-Jean* ☎ *0590/27–57–08* ⊕ *www.kiwi.fr.*

Lili Belle. The nice selection comprises wearable and current styles. ⊠ *Pelican Beach, St-Jean* ☎ *0590/87–46–14.*

Morgan. This shop has a line of popular casual wear in the trendy vein. ⊠ *La Villa Créole, St-Jean* ☎ *0590/27–57–22.*

SUD SUD.ETC. This store stocks everything for the beach: inflatables, mats, bags, and beachy shell jewelry, as well as bikinis and gauzy cover-ups. ⊠ *La Villa Creole, St-Jean.*

14

FOODSTUFFS

Marché U. This modern, fully stocked supermarket across from the airport has a wide selection of French cheeses, pâtés, cured meats, produce, fresh bread, wine, and liquor. There is also a good selection of prepared foods and organic items. It's closed Sunday afternoon. ⊠ *Face à l'aéroport, St-Jean* ☎ *0590/27–68–16.*

Maya's to Go. This is the place to go for prepared picnics, meals, salads, and rotisserie chickens from the kitchen of the popular restaurant in Gustavia. It's closed Monday. ⊠ *Les Galeries du Commerce, St-Jean* ☎ *0590/29–83–70* ⊕ *www.mayastogo.com* ☼ *Closed Mon.*

SPORTS AND THE OUTDOORS

BOATING AND SAILING

St. Barth is a popular yachting and sailing center, thanks to its location midway between Antigua and St. Thomas.

Gustavia's harbor, 13 to 16 feet deep, has mooring and docking facilities for 40 yachts. There are also good anchorages at Public, Corossol, and Colombier. You can charter sailing and motorboats in Gustavia Harbor for as little as a half day, staffed or bareboat. Ask at the Gustavia tourist office or your hotel for a list of recommended charter companies.

Carib Waterplay. On St. Jean beach for over 30 years, this outfit lets you try windsurfing, kayaking, and stand-up paddling; rents waterbikes; and gives kids' windsurf lessons. You can rent beach chairs for the day here. ⊠ *St-Jean* ☎ *0690/61–80–81* ⊕ *www.caribwaterplay.com.*

Jicky Marine Service. This company offers private full-day outings on motorboats, Zodiacs, and 42- or 46-foot catamarans to the uninhabited Île Fourchue for swimming, snorkeling, cocktails, or lunch as well as weekly half- and full-day group cruises and twice-weekly group sunset catamaran cruises. Private fishing charters are also offered, as is private transport from St. Martin. An unskippered motorboat rental runs about €290 a day. A one-hour group Jet Ski tour of the island is also offered, as are private tours. ⊠ *26 rue Jeanne D'Arc, Gustavia* ☎ *0590/27–70–34* ⊕ *www.jickymarine.com.*

Top Loc Boat Rental. Charter a catamaran or a powerboat for a day of fun on the water. Rental for a half-day on the catamaran including an open bar is €580. Half-day skippered rental of an eight-person powerboat is €850. ⊠ *Airport Office, St-Jean* ☎ *0590/29–02–02* ⊕ *www.top-loc.com.*

DIVING AND SNORKELING

Several dive shops arrange scuba excursions. Depending on weather conditions, you may dive at **Pain de Sucre, Coco Island,** or toward nearby **Saba.** There's also an underwater shipwreck, plus sharks, rays, sea tortoises, coral, and the usual varieties of colorful fish. The waters on the island's leeward side are the calmest. For the uncertified, there's a shallow reef right off the beach at Anse de Cayes, which you can explore with mask and fins, and a hike down to the beach at Corossol brings you to a very popular snorkeling spot.

Big Blue. This is the only dive operator in St. Barth that offers underwater scooters to divers. The company offers snuba and snorkeling, too. ⊠ *Public Beach, Gustavia* ☏ *0690/38–11–24* ⊕ *www.stbarthbigblue. net.*

La Bulle Diving Center. PADI certification, day and night dives, and snorkeling trips with friendly and watchful supervision make this a popular outfit. A beginners' package (€210) includes instruction and two dives. ⊠ *La Pointe, Gustavia* ☏ *0690/77–76–55* ⊕ *www.labullesbh.com.*

Ouanalao Dive. Three organized dives a day, a good dive shop, snorkeling tours, and instruction are offered at the Grand Cul-de Sac beach location. A two-tank dive is €140. ⊠ *Grand Cul de Sac* ☏ *0690/63–74–34* ⊕ *www.ouanalaodive.com.*

FAMILY **Plongée Caraïbe.** This company is recommended for its up-to-the-minute equipment, dive boat, and scuba discovery program. They offer nitrox diving and certification. It also runs two-hour group snorkeling trips on the *Blue Cat Catamaran* (€60), or you can enjoy a private charter from €490. ⊠ *Quai de la République, Gustavia* ☏ *0590/27–55–94* ⊕ *www. plongee-caraibes.com.*

Réserve Naturelle de Saint-Barthélemy. Most of the waters surrounding St. Barth are protected in the island's nature reserve, which provides information from its Gustavia office. The diving here isn't nearly as rich as in more dive-centered destinations like Saba and St. Eustatius, but the options aren't bad either. ⊠ *Gustavia* ☏ *0590/27–88–18* ⊕ *www. reservenaturellestbarth.com.*

Splash. This company offers PADI and CMAS (Confédération Mondiale des Activités Subaquatiques—World Underwater Federation) diver training at all levels. All instructors speak French, Russian, and English. Although the boat normally leaves daily at 9, 11:30, 2, and in the evening for a night dive, times are adjusted to suit preferences. Seabob scuba scooters run €150 per hour. ⊠ *Gustavia* ☏ *0590/56–90–24.*

FISHING

Most fishing is done in the waters north of Lorient, Flamands, and Corossol. Popular catches are tuna, marlin, wahoo, and barracuda. The annual St. Barth Open Fishing Tournament, organized by Océan Must, is in mid-July.

Océan Must Marina. This outfitter arranges deep-sea fishing expeditions as well as bareboat and staffed boat charters. ⊠ *La Pointe, Gustavia* ☏ *0590/27–62–25* ⊕ *www.oceanmust.com.*

GUIDED TOURS

You can arrange island tours by minibus or car at hotel desks or through taxi operators in Gustavia or at the airport. The tourist office runs a variety of tours for about €46 for a half day for up to eight people. You can also download up-to-the-minute walking and driving tour itineraries from the office's website.

JC Taxi. Since 1986, native-born Jean-Claude has been providing safe and comfortable transportation in a 10-passenger minivan. Island tours and night driving are available. ⊠ *Gustavia* ☎ *0690/49–02–97.*

St. Barth Jetski. This company leads tours of the island by water on a Jet Ski or Flyboard, St. Barth's newest water-play craze. ⊠ *Quai du Yacht Club, Rue Jeanne d'Arc, Gustavia* ☎ *0690/49–54–72* ⊕ *www. jetskirentalstbarts.com.*

St. Barth Mobilité. This company offers transportation, tours, and guided help for those with limited mobility. ☎ *0690/77–66–73* ⊕ *www. stbarthmobilite.com.*

ST. KITTS AND NEVIS

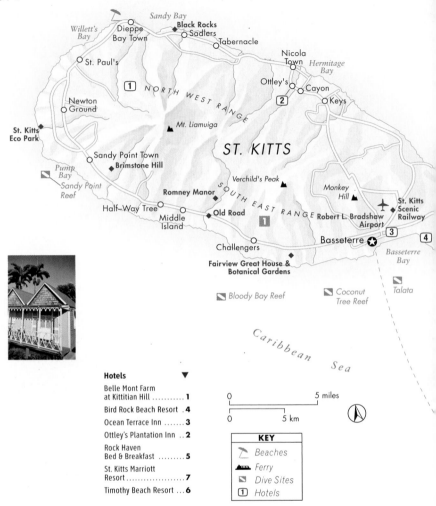

Hotels ▼

Belle Mont Farm
at Kittitian Hill **1**

Bird Rock Beach Resort . **4**

Ocean Terrace Inn **3**

Ottley's Plantation Inn .. **2**

Rock Haven
Bed & Breakfast **5**

St. Kitts Marriott
Resort **7**

Timothy Beach Resort ... **6**

| 0 | | 5 miles |
| 0 | | 5 km |

KEY

⚓ Beaches
🚢 Ferry
◼ Dive Sites
① Hotels

TOP REASONS TO VISIT ST. KITTS AND NEVIS

1 History: Both St. Kitts and Nevis are steeped in history; Brimstone Hill Fortress is a man-made UNESCO World Heritage Site.

2 Luxury: Luxurious, restored plantation inns can be found on both islands.

3 Landscape: Both islands have extinct volcanoes and luxuriant rain forests ideal for hikes, as well as fine diving and snorkeling sites.

4 Unspoiled: You'll find less development—particularly on Nevis—and more cordial and courteous islanders than on more touristy islands.

5 Water Activities: Both islands feature aquatic activities aplenty, with fine sailing, deep-sea fishing, diving (especially off St. Kitts), and windsurfing (especially around Nevis).

WELCOME TO ST. KITTS AND NEVIS

THE MOTHER COLONY AND HER SISTER

St. Kitts, a 65-square-mile (168-square-km) island, is 2 miles (3 km) from smaller Nevis, about 40 square miles (121 square km). The two former British colonies are joined in a sometimes strained independence. St. Kitts is often called "The Mother Colony," because it was the first permanent English settlement in the Caribbean.

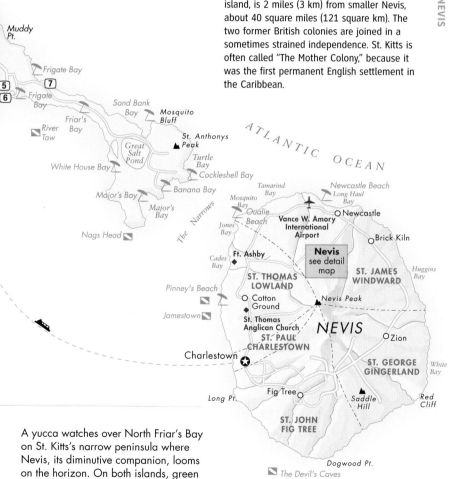

A yucca watches over North Friar's Bay on St. Kitts's narrow peninsula where Nevis, its diminutive companion, looms on the horizon. On both islands, green fields of sugarcane run to the sea, once-magnificent plantation houses are now luxurious inns, and lovely stretches of uncrowded beach stretch before you.

NEED TO KNOW

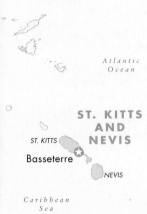

AT A GLANCE

Capital: Basseterre

Population: 54,190

Currency: Eastern Caribbean dollar; pegged to the U.S. dollar

Money: Few ATMs; credit cards accepted at resorts, cash elsewhere. U.S. dollars commonly accepted

Language: English

Country Code: ☎ 1 869

Emergencies: ☎ 911

Driving: On the left

Electricity: 230v/60 cycles; plugs are UK standard three-prong

Time: Same as New York during daylight savings time; one hour ahead otherwise

Documents: Up to 90 days with valid passport

Major Mobile Companies: Digicel, LIME, Orange, CHIPPIE

WEBSITES

St. Kitts and Nevis Hotel and Tourism Association: ⊕ www.stkittsnevishta.org.

GETTING AROUND

✈ **Air Travel:** St. Kitts has some nonstop flights from the U.S.; only intra-Caribbean flights land in Nevis.

🚌 **Bus Travel:** Buses serve St. Kitts, leaving from Basseterre. In Nevis, buses loop around on the main ring road with no set schedule.

🚗 **Car Travel:** In St. Kitts, you can get by without a car in the Frigate Bay-Basseterre area, but elsewhere you'll need to rent a car. In Nevis it's often easier to just take taxis and guided tours.

⚓ **Ferry Travel:** Ferries link St. Kitts and Nevis in 30 to 45 minutes.

PLAN YOUR BUDGET

	HOTEL ROOM	MEAL	ATTRACTIONS
Low Budget	$225	$12	Alexander Hamilton Museum, $5
Mid Budget	$425	$25	Brimstone Hill, $10
High Budget	$550	$40	St. Kitts Scenic Railway, $89

WAYS TO SAVE

Eat local. Local eateries are far cheaper (and better) than ones catering specifically to the hordes of tourists.

Stay at a cozy inn. St. Kitts's and Nevis's high-priced resorts get a lot of attention, but several local inns and lodges have retained their historic roots and a far lower price tag.

Rent a car on-island. Car rental prices from local retailers and hotels are often cheaper than those from larger agencies secured on the Web (though cars may be a bit more worn).

Go hiking. The nature trails on both St. Kitts and Nevis are exhilarating and dirt cheap.

Hassle Factor	Medium. Flights to St. Kitts are frequent; Nevis requires a 30- to 45-minute ferry from St. Kitts.
3 days	Relax for a day poolside or beachside at your quiet Nevis resort. Take a day to hop over to explore St. Kitt's two can't miss sights: the St. Kitts Scenic Railway and Brimstone Hill.
1 week	Split your time between St. Kitts and Nevis. On St. Kitts, enjoy the beaches and rent a car to do some island exploration. On Nevis, hit Pinney's Beach and then check out the historic plantations dotting the island's interior.
2 weeks	Explore the waters surrounding these islands with dives and sunset sails. Take a short trip over to neighboring Antigua and Montserrat (connected by short flights) for more island adventures.

WHEN TO GO

High Season: Mid-December through mid-April is the most fashionable and most expensive time to visit, when the weather is typically sunny and warm. Good hotels are often booked far in advance, and you're guaranteed the most entertainment at resorts and the most people with whom to enjoy it.

Low Season: From August to late October, temperatures can grow oppressively hot and the weather muggy, with high risks of tropical storms. Some hotels close during these months for annual renovations. Those remaining open offer deep discounts.

Value Season: From late April to July and again November to mid-December, hotel prices drop 20% to 50% from high-season prices. There are chances of scattered showers, but expect sun-kissed daytime temperatures, too, and fewer crowds.

BIG EVENTS

December–January: Carnival on St. Kitts is celebrated during the 10 days right after Christmas.

April: Spectators flock to the annual Nevis–St. Kitts Cross Channel Swim to watch championship swimmers compete. ⊕ www.neviscycleclub.com

June–July: The St. Kitts Music Festival is the biggest event on the island and draws international singing stars. ⊕ www.stkittsmusicfestival.com

June–July: Nevis Culturama is the island's summer carnival.

READ THIS

■ *Quitting America: The Departure of a Black Man from his Native Land,* Randall Robinson. A U.S. Army officer emigrates.

■ *Cambridge,* Caryl Phillips. The lives of unlikely individuals intersect during Nevis's slave period.

■ *Caribbean Chemistry: Tales from St. Kitts,* Christopher Vanier. A memoir of growing up on St. Kitts.

WATCH THIS

■ *Missing in Action 2: The Beginning.* Prequel filmed in St. Kitts.

■ *The Hurricane.* About Rubin "Hurricane" Carter, co-produced by St. Kitts native Rudy Langlais.

■ *Sugar Hill.* Another Langlais film set in Harlem.

EAT THIS

■ *Stewed saltfish*: a hash with tomatoes and onions.

■ *Spicy plantains*: plantains fried with hot sauce, onions, and ginger.

■ *Pelau*: rice layered with pig tail, meat, and vegetables.

■ *Breadfruit*: sliced wedges seasoned and cooked in chicken broth.

■ *Coconut droppers*: boiled dumplings made from shredded coconut and flour.

Updated by
Jordan Simon

These idyllic sister islands, 2 miles (3 km) apart at their closest point, offer visitors a relatively authentic island experience. Both have luxuriant mountain rain forests; uncrowded beaches; historic ruins; towering, long-dormant volcanoes; charming if slightly dilapidated Georgian capitals in Basseterre (St. Kitts) and Charlestown (Nevis); intact cultural heritage; friendly if shy people; and restored 18th-century sugar plantation inns run by elegant, if sometimes eccentric, expatriate owners.

The islands' history follows the usual Caribbean route: Amerindian settlements, Columbus's voyages, fierce colonial battles between the British and French, a boom in sugar production second only to that of Barbados. St. Kitts became known as the mother colony of the West Indies: English settlers sailed from there to Antigua, Barbuda, Tortola, and Montserrat, and the French dispatched colonists to Martinique, Guadeloupe, St. Martin, and St. Barth.

St. Kitts and Nevis, in addition to Anguilla, achieved self-government as an associated state of Great Britain in 1967. Anguillians soon made their displeasure known, separating immediately, whereas St. Kitts and Nevis waited until 1983 to become an independent nation. The two islands, despite their superficial similarities, have taken increasingly different routes regarding tourism. Nevis received an economic boost from the Four Seasons, which helped establish it as an upscale destination. St. Kitts, however, had yet to define its identity at a time when most islands have found their tourism niche but is now making up for lost time and notoriety with several high-profile high-end projects, including Kittitian Hill and Christophe Harbour, with a Park Hyatt. A fierce sibling rivalry has ensued.

Though its comparative lack of development is a lure, the Kittitian government is casting its economic net in several directions. Golf, eco-tourism, and scuba diving are being aggressively promoted. And the government hopes the number of available rooms will increase roughly 30% by 2017 to more than 2,000, according to the "build it and they will come" philosophy. But is St. Kitts ready to absorb all this? The island offers a surprisingly diverse vacation experience while retaining its essential Caribbean flavor. Divers have yet to discover all its underwater attractions, and nature lovers will be pleasantly surprised by the hiking. There's now every kind of accommodation, as well as gourmet dining, golf, and gaming.

Meanwhile, Nevis seems determined to stay even more unspoiled (there are still no traffic lights). Its natural attractions and activities certainly rival those of St. Kitts, from mountain biking and ecohiking to windsurfing and deep-sea fishing, though lying in a hammock and dining on romantic candlelit patios remain cherished pursuits. Pinney's Beach, despite occasional hurricane erosion, remains a classic Caribbean strand. Its historic heritage, from the Caribbean's first hotel to Alexander Hamilton's childhood home, is just as pronounced, including equally sybaritic plantation inns that seem torn from the pages of a romance novel.

Perhaps it's a warning sign that many guests call the catamaran trip to Nevis the high point of their stay on St. Kitts—and many Kittitians build retirement and second homes on Nevis. The sister islands' relationship remains outwardly cordial if slightly contentious. Nevis papers sometimes run blistering editorials advocating independence, though one plebiscite has already failed. St. Kitts and Nevis may separate someday, but for now their battles are confined to ad campaigns and political debates. Fortunately, well-heeled and barefoot travelers alike can still happily enjoy the many energetic and easygoing enticements of both blissful retreats.

15

PLANNING

GETTING HERE AND AROUND
AIR TRAVEL
Many travelers connect in Antigua, San Juan, St. Maarten, or St. Thomas. To Nevis, it's almost always cheaper to fly into St. Kitts and then take a regularly scheduled ferry, but check the schedules or book a transfer from your resort (if available) in advance. St. Kitts unveiled the YU Lounge, available not just to private jet passengers but any commercial travelers willing to pay for a restful, hassle-free executive retreat that eliminates the need to go through Customs and Immigration (and offering its own approved security screening).

There are nonstop flights to St. Kitts from Atlanta (Delta), as well as Charlotte, Miami, and New York–JFK (American). There are no nonstops from the United States to Nevis.

Airline Contacts American. ☎ 869/465–2273, 869/469–8995. **LIAT.** ☎ 869/465–1330, 869/469–5238 on Nevis ⊕ www.liatairline.com. **Seaborne.** ☎ 866/359–8784 ⊕ www.seaborneairlines.com. **United.** ☎ 800/864–8331 ⊕ www.united.com. **Winair.** ☎ 869/469–5302 ⊕ www.fly-winair.sx.

Airport Contacts **Robert L. Bradshaw International Airport** (*SKB*). ☎ *869/465–8013.* **Vance W. Amory International Airport** (*NEV*). ☎ *869/469–9343.*

CAR TRAVEL

Driving Tips: One well-kept main road circumnavigates St. Kitts and is usually clearly marked, making it difficult to get lost, though the northeast can get a bit bumpy and the access roads to the plantation inns are notoriously rough.

The roads on Nevis are generally smooth, at least on the most traveled north, west, and south sides of the island. The east coast has some potholes, and pigs, goats, and sheep still insist on the right-of-way all around the island. Drivers on both islands tend to travel at a fast clip and pass on curves, so drive defensively. Driving is on the left, British-style, though you will probably be given an American-style car.

Renting a Car: You can get by without a car if you are staying in the Frigate Bay–Basseterre area, but elsewhere you'll need to rent a car. On Nevis it's often easier to just take taxis and guided tours. On St. Kitts, present your valid driver's license and $24 at the police station traffic department on Cayon Street in Basseterre or fire station in Frigate Bay to get a temporary driving permit (on Nevis the car-rental agency will help you obtain the $24 local license at the police station). The license is valid for three months on both islands. On either island, car rentals start at about $45 per day for a compact; expect to pay a few extra bucks for air-conditioning. Most agencies offer substantial multiday discounts.

Contacts in St. Kitts Avis. ✉ *South Independence Sq., Basseterre* ☎ *869/465–6507, 954/284–5331 for U.S. reservations* ⊕ *www.avisstkitts.com.* **Delisle Walwyn.** ✉ *Liverpool Row, Basseterre* ☎ *869/465–8449.* **TDC/Thrifty Rentals.** ✉ *West Independence Sq., Central St., Basseterre* ☎ *869/465–2991, 869/465–2511* ⊕ *www.tdclimited.com/dept_content.asp?did=8.*

Contacts in Nevis Funky Monkey Tours and Rentals. ☎ *869/665–6045, 869/665–6245* ⊕ *www.funkymonkeytours.com.* **Nevis Car Rentals.** ☎ *869/469–9837.* **Striker's Car Rental.** ✉ *Hermitage Rd., Gingerland* ☎ *869/469–2654* ⊕ *www.strikerscarrentals.com.* **TDC/Thrifty Rentals.** ✉ *Bay Rd., Charlestown* ☎ *869/469–5430* ⊕ *www.tdclimited.com/dept_content.asp?did=8.*

FERRY TRAVEL

There are several ferry services between St. Kitts and Nevis, all with schedules that are subject to abrupt change. Most companies make two or three daily trips. All the ferries take about 30 to 45 minutes and cost $8–$10. An additional EC$1 tax for port security is paid separately on departure.

Contacts Ferry Schedule. ⊕ *www.thestkittsnevisobserver.com.*

TAXI TRAVEL

Taxi rates are government regulated and posted at the airport, the dock, and in the free tourist guide. Be sure to clarify whether the fare is in EC or U.S. dollars. There are fixed rates to and from all the hotels and to and from major points of interest.

Airport Transfers: On St. Kitts the fares from the airport range from EC\$32 to Frigate Bay to EC\$72 for the farthest point. From the airport on Nevis it's EC\$27 to Nisbet Plantation, EC\$54 to the Four Seasons, and EC\$67 to Montpelier. There is a 50% surcharge between 10 pm and 6 am.

Contacts St. Kitts Taxi Association. ☎ 869/465-8487, 869/465-4253, 869/465-7818 after-hrs. **Nevis Taxi Service.** ☎ 869/469-5631, 869/469-9790 for the airport,, 869/469-5515 after dark.

HOTELS AND RESTAURANTS

St. Kitts has a wide variety of places to stay—beautifully restored plantation inns, full-service affordable hotels, simple beachfront cottages, comfortable condos, and all-inclusive resorts. One large resort—the Marriott—is more midrange than upscale and attracts large groups and package tourists. Choose St. Kitts if you want a wider choice of activities and accommodations (you can always do Nevis as a day trip). Nevis is a small island with no large resorts, and most accommodations are upscale—primarily plantation inns and the luxurious Four Seasons. It's much quieter than St. Kitts, so choose it if you want to get away from the hectic island scene and simply relax in low-key comfort and surprisingly high style.

Four Seasons Resort Nevis: Really in a class by itself, the Four Seasons is the only sizable, lavish, high-end property on either island until the 125-room Park Hyatt opens on Banana Bay (the first phase will debut in late 2016) as part of the massive upscale Christophe Harbour development. If you can afford it, the resort is certainly one of the Caribbean's finest; recent post-hurricane renovations improved on near-perfection.

Plantation Inns: St. Kitts and Nevis feature renovated, historic plantation houses that have been turned into upscale inns. On Nevis, the inns are the most distinctive form of lodging. They are usually managed by hands-on owner-operators and offer fine cuisine and convivial hospitality; though not usually on a beach, most of these inns have beach clubs with free private shuttle service.

Hotel reviews have been shortened. For full information, visit Fodors.com.

WHAT IT COSTS IN U.S. DOLLARS			
$	$$	$$$	$$$$
RESTAURANTS under $12	$12–$20	$21–$30	over $30
HOTELS under $275	$275–$375	$376–$475	over $475

Restaurant prices are the average cost of a main course at dinner or, if dinner is not served, at lunch. Hotel prices are the lowest cost of a standard double room in high season.

HEALTH AND SAFETY

Dengue, chikungunya, and zika have all been reported throughout the Caribbean. We recommend that you protect yourself from these mosquito-borne illnesses by keeping your skin covered and/or wearing mosquito repellent. The mosquitoes that transmit these viruses are as active by day as they are by night.

15

VISITOR INFORMATION

Contacts Nevis Tourism Authority. ⊠ *Elm House, Park La., Lower Froyle, Alton, Hampshire* ☎ *01420/520810* ⊕ *www.nevisisland.com.* **St. Kitts Tourism Authority.** ☎ *212/535–1234 Permanent Mission to the UN in New York City, 800/582–6208, 866/556–3847 for Nevis alone, 914/949–2164 Tourism Authority in Tarrytown, NY* ⊕ *www.stkittstourism.kn.* **St. Kitts and Nevis Hotel and Tourism Association.** ☎ *869/465–5304* ⊕ *www.stkittsnevishta.org.*

ST. KITTS

EXPLORING

You can explore Basseterre, the capital city, in a half hour or so, and should allow four hours for an island tour. Main Road traces the northwestern perimeter of the island through seas of sugarcane and past breadfruit trees and stone walls. Villages with tiny pastel-color houses of stone and weathered wood are scattered across the island, and the drive back to Basseterre around the island's other side passes through several of them. The most spectacular stretch of scenery is on Dr. Kennedy Simmonds Highway, which goes to the tip of the Southeast Peninsula. This modern road twists and turns through the undeveloped grassy hills that rise between the calm Caribbean and the windswept Atlantic, passing the shimmering pink Great Salt Pond, a volcanic crater, and seductive beaches. Major developments are underway, including the Kittitian Hill and Christophe Harbour megadevelopments. The 6-furlong Belmont Park racetrack and state-of-the-art stables opened in 2009 but, despite the exciting equine environment that lured as many as 9,000 spectators, has closed indefinitely, its planned entertainment complex, with an upscale restaurant as well as polo grounds, go-karts, a retail complex, and bird and butterfly parks, on hold.

BASSETERRE

On the south coast, St. Kitts's walkable capital is graced with tall palms and flagstone sidewalks; although many of the buildings appear rundown, there are interesting shops, excellent art galleries, and some beautifully maintained houses. Duty-free shops and boutiques line the streets and courtyards radiating from the octagonal **Circus**, built in the style of London's famous Piccadilly Circus.

WORTH NOTING

Independence Square. There are lovely gardens and a fountain on the site of a former slave market at Independence Square. The square is surrounded on three sides by 18th-century Georgian buildings. ⊠ *Off Bank St., Basseterre.*

National Museum. In the restored former Treasury Building, the National Museum presents an eclectic collection of artifacts reflecting the history and culture of the island. ⊠ *Bay Rd., Basseterre* ☎ *869/465–5584* 🖂 *$3* 🕑 *Weekdays 9:15–5, Sat. 9:15–1.*

Port Zante. Port Zante is an ambitious, ever-growing 27-acre cruiseship pier and marina in an area that has been reclaimed from the sea.

The domed welcome center is an imposing neoclassical hodgepodge, with columns and stone arches, shops, walkways, fountains, and West Indian–style buildings housing luxury shops, galleries, restaurants, and a small casino. A second pier, 1,434 feet long, has a draft that accommodates even leviathan cruise ships. The selection of shops and restaurants (Twist serves global fusion cuisine and rocks with DJs several nights of the week) is expanding as well. ☒ *Waterfront, behind Circus, Basseterre* ⊕ *www.portzantemarina.com.*

St. George's Anglican Church. This handsome stone building has a crenellated tower originally built by the French in 1670 that is called Nôtre-Dame. The British burned it down in 1706 and rebuilt it four years later, naming it after the patron saint of England. Since then it has suffered a fire, an earthquake, and hurricanes and was once again rebuilt in 1869. ☒ *Cayon St., Basseterre.*

ELSEWHERE ON ST. KITTS

TOP ATTRACTIONS

15

Brimstone Hill. This 38-acre fortress, a UNESCO World Heritage Site, is part of a national park dedicated by Queen Elizabeth in 1985. After routing the French in 1690, the English erected a battery here; by 1736 the fortress held 49 guns, earning it the moniker Gibraltar of the West Indies. In 1782, 8,000 French troops laid siege to the stronghold, which was defended by 350 militia and 600 regular troops of the Royal Scots and East Yorkshires. When the English finally surrendered, they were allowed to march from the fort in full formation out of respect for their bravery (the English afforded the French the same honor when they surrendered the fort a mere year later). A hurricane severely damaged the fortress in 1834, and in 1852 it was evacuated and dismantled. The beautiful stones were carted away to build houses.

The citadel has been partially reconstructed and its guns remounted. It's a steep walk up the hill from the parking lot. A seven-minute orientation film recounts the fort's history and restoration. You can see remains of the officers' quarters, redoubts, barracks, ordnance store, and cemetery. Its museum collections were depleted by hurricanes, but some pre-Columbian artifacts, objects pertaining to the African heritage of the island's slaves (such as masks and ceremonial tools), weaponry, uniforms, photographs, and old newspapers remain. The spectacular view includes Montserrat and Nevis to the southeast; Saba and St. Eustatius to the northwest; and St. Barth and St. Maarten to the north. Nature trails snake through the tangle of surrounding hardwood forest and savanna (a fine spot to catch the green vervet monkeys—inexplicably brought by the French and now outnumbering the residents—skittering about). ☒ *Main Rd., Brimstone Hill* ☎ *869/465–2609* ⊕ *www. brimstonehillfortress.org* 🎫 *$10* ⊙ *Daily 9:30–5:30.*

FAMILY **St. Kitts Eco Park.** Created in collaboration with the Taiwanese government, St. Kitts Eco Park essentially functions as an agro-tourism demonstration farm, with soaring, light-filled glass and fiber-reinforced concrete structures that are powered by state-of-the-art solar trackers. Antique cannons and old-fashioned gas lamps lead to the handsome Victorian plantation-style visitors center, divided into Kittitian and

Taiwanese sections, each selling local foodstuffs and specialty items (ceramics for St. Kitts, tea and technology for Taiwan). You can stroll through the greenhouse, viewing orchids in the working nursery, then scale the watchtower for scintillating views of the farm and Caribbean, with Saba and Statia in the distance. Kids will love challenging the map mazes (plantings shaped like the partner nations), while parents can wander the orchards and desert garden or savor bush tea in the herb gazebo. The property provides environmental edutainment while delivering on its so-called 4G promise: greenhouse, green beauty, green energy, green landscape. ⊠ *Sir Gillies Estate, Sandy Point* ☎ *869/465-8755* ⊕ *www.ecopark.kn* ⊠ *$8* ⊙ *Mon.–Sat. 9–4.*

St. Kitts Scenic Railway. The old narrow-gauge train that had transported sugarcane to the central sugar factory since 1912 is all that remains of the island's once-thriving sugar industry. Two-story cars bedecked in bright Kittitian colors circle the island in just under four hours (a Rail and Sail option takes guests going or on the return via catamaran). Each passenger gets a comfortable, downstairs air-conditioned seat fronting vaulted picture windows and an upstairs open-air observation spot. The conductor's running discourse embraces not only the history of sugar cultivation but also the railway's construction, local folklore, island geography, even other agricultural mainstays from papayas to pigs. You can drink in complimentary tropical beverages (including luscious guava daiquiris) along with the sweeping rain-forest and ocean vistas, accompanied by an a cappella choir's renditions of hymns, spirituals, and predictable standards like "I've Been Workin' on the Railroad." ⊠ *Needsmust Estate* ☎ *869/465-7263* ⊕ *www.stkittsscenicrailway.com* ⊠ *$99* ⊙ *Departures vary according to cruise-ship schedules (call ahead, but at least once daily Dec.–Apr., usually 8:30 am).*

WORTH NOTING

Black Rocks. This series of lava deposits was spat into the sea ages ago when the island's volcano erupted. It has since been molded into fanciful shapes by centuries of pounding surf. ⊠ *Atlantic coast, outside town of Sadlers, Sandy Bay, Sand Bank Bay.*

Fairview Great House & Botanical Gardens. Parts of this French colonial great house set on more than 2 lush tropical acres date back to 1701, with an impeccably restored interior in period fashion. Each room is painted in different colors from pomegranate to lemon. Furnishings include a 16-seat mahogany dinner table set with china and silver; docents relate fascinating factoids (chaises were broadened to accommodate petticoats—or "can-can skirts," in local parlance). Cross the cobblestone courtyard to the original kitchen, replete with volcanic stone and brick oven, and bathing room (heated rocks warmed spring water in the tub). The fieldstone cellar now contains the gift shop, offering local pottery, art, and honey harvested on-site at the apiary. You can wander meticulously maintained gardens with interpretive signage, filled with chattering birds and monkeys. The Nirvana restaurant offers pan-Asian food; dips in the pool are a bonus. ⊠ *Artist's Level Hill, Boyd's* ☎ *869/465-3141* ⊕ *www.nirvanafairview.com and www.fairviewstkitts.com* ⊠ *$10* ⊙ *Daily 9–5 (last entrance 4:30).*

Cannons at Brimstone Hill, a UNESCO World Heritage Site on St. Kitts

Old Road. This site marks the first permanent English settlement in the West Indies, founded in 1624 by Thomas Warner. Take the side road toward the interior to find some Carib petroglyphs, testimony of even earlier habitation. The largest depicts a female figure on black volcanic rock, presumably a fertility goddess. Less than a mile east of Old Road along Main Road is **Bloody Point,** where French and British soldiers joined forces in 1629 to repel a mass Carib attack; reputedly so many Caribs were massacred that the stream ran red for three days. ✛ *Main Rd. west of Challengers.*

Romney Manor. The ruins of this somewhat restored house (reputedly once the property of Thomas Jefferson) and surrounding replicas of chattel-house cottages are set in 6 acres of glorious gardens, with exotic flowers, an old bell tower, and an enormous, gnarled 350-year-old saman tree (sometimes called a rain tree). Inside, at **Caribelle Batik,** you can watch artisans hand-printing fabrics by the 2,500-year-old Indonesian wax-and-dye process known as batik. You can also stroll to the 17th-century ruins of Wingfield Manor, site of the first land grant in the British West Indies, and home to a zip-lining outfit. A new bar offers splendid panoramic vistas of the rain forest. Look for signs indicating a turnoff for Romney Manor near Old Road. ⊠ *Old Road Town* ☎ *869/465–6253* ⊕ *www.caribellebatikstkitts.com* ✉ *Free* ☺ *Daily 9–5.*

BEACHES

Beaches on St. Kitts are free and open to the public (even those occupied by hotels). The best beaches, with powdery white sand, are in the Frigate Bay area or on the lower peninsula. The Atlantic waters are rougher, and many black-sand beaches northwest of Frigate Bay double as garbage dumps.

Banana/Cockleshell Bays. These twin connected eyebrows of glittering champagne-color sand—stretching nearly 2 miles (3 km) total at the southeastern tip of the island—feature majestic views of Nevis and are backed by lush vegetation and coconut palms. The first-rate restaurant-bar Spice Mill (next to Rasta-hue Lion Rock Beach Bar—order the knockout Lion Punch) and Reggae Beach Bar & Grill bracket either end of Cockleshell. At this writing, plans for a 125-room mixed-use Park Hyatt (with additional residential condos and villas) are back on schedule for opening by late 2016. The water is generally placid, ideal for swimming. The downside is irregular maintenance, with seaweed (particularly after rough weather) and occasional litter, especially on Banana Bay. Follow Simmonds Highway to the end and bear right, ignoring the turnoff for Turtle Beach. **Amenities:** food and drink; parking. **Best for:** partiers; snorkeling; swimming; walking. ⊠ *Banana Bay.*

Friar's Bay. Locals consider Friar's Bay, on the Caribbean (southern) side, the island's finest beach. It's a long, tawny scimitar where the water always seems warmer and clearer. The upscale Carambola Beach Club has co-opted roughly one third of the strand. Still, several happening bars, including Jam Rock (great grouper and jerk), ShipWreck and Sunset, serve terrific, inexpensive, local food and cheap, frosty drinks. Chair rentals cost around $3, though if you order lunch, you can negotiate a freebie. Friar's is the first major beach along Southeast Peninsula Drive (aka Simmonds Highway), approximately a mile (1½ km) southeast of Frigate Bay. **Amenities:** food and drink. **Best for:** snorkeling; swimming; walking. ⊠ *South Friar's Bay.*

Frigate Bay. The Caribbean side offers talcum-powder-fine beige sand framed by coconut palms and sea grapes, and the Atlantic side (a 15-minute stroll)—sometimes called North Frigate Bay—is a favorite with horseback riders. South Frigate Bay is bookended by the Timothy Beach Club's Sunset Café and the popular, pulsating Buddies Beach Hut. In between are several other lively beach spots, including Cathy's (fabulous jerk ribs), Chinchilla's, Vibes, and Mr. X Shiggidy Shack. Most charge $3 to $5 to rent a chair, though they'll often waive the fee if you ask politely and buy lunch. Locals bar-hop late into Friday and Saturday nights. Waters are generally calm for swimming; the rockier eastern end offers fine snorkeling. The incomparably scenic Atlantic side is—regrettably—dominated by the Marriott (plentiful dining options), attracting occasional pesky vendors. The surf is choppier and the undertow stronger here. On cruise-ship days, groups stampede both sides. **Amenities:** food and drink; water sports. **Best for:** partying; snorkeling; swimming; walking. ⊠ *Frigate Bay* ✛ *Less than 3 miles (5 km) from downtown Basseterre.*

Sand Bank Bay. A dirt road, nearly impassable after heavy rains, leads to a long mocha crescent on the Atlantic. The shallow coves are protected here, making it ideal for families, and it's usually deserted. Brisk breezes lure the occasional windsurfer, but avoid the rocky far left area because of fierce sudden swells and currents. This exceptionally pretty beach lacks shade; Christophe Harbour has constructed several villas and a beach club (whose upscale Pavilion restaurant is open to the public only for dinner). As you drive southeast along Simmonds Highway, approximately 10 miles (16 km) from Basseterre, look for an unmarked dirt turnoff to the left of the Great Salt Pond. **Amenities:** none. **Best for:** solitude; swimming; windsurfing. ⊠ *Sand Bank Bay.*

White House Bay. The beach is rocky, but the snorkeling, taking in several reefs surrounding a sunken tugboat, as well as a recently discovered 18th-century British troop ship, is superb. It's usually deserted, though the calm water (and stunning scenery) makes it a favorite anchorage of yachties. There is little shade, but also little seaweed. Christophe Harbour's sexy beach bar (open from late afternoon), Salt Plage, anchors one end. A dirt road skirts a hill to the right off Simmonds Highway approximately 2 miles (3 km) after Friar's. **Amenities:** food and drink. **Best for:** snorkeling; solitude. ⊠ *White House Bay.*

WHERE TO EAT

St. Kitts restaurants range from funky beachfront bistros to elegant plantation dining rooms (most with prix-fixe menus); most fare is tinged with the flavors of the Caribbean. Many restaurants offer West Indian specialties such as curried mutton, pepper pot (a stew of vegetables, tubers, and meats), and Arawak chicken (seasoned and served with rice and almonds on breadfruit leaf).

What to Wear. Throughout the island, dress is casual at lunch (but no bathing suits). Dinner, although not necessarily formal, definitely calls for long pants and sundresses.

$$$$
ECLECTIC
✕ **Carambola Beach Club.** This ultrastylish restaurant unfurls sensuously down South Friar's Bay, like something out of St. Tropez. More casual lunches take full advantage of the beachfront setting, with white tents and hedonistic beach beds. But nighttime is truly spectacular, as outdoor fiber-optic fountains enhance the visual flair of the vast, sleek-but-not-slick interior replete with eat-in wine cellar and tile-and-layered-wood sushi bar. Starters include the original maki rolls. Seafood such as breaded grouper in orange beurre blanc is masterfully executed; nothing at Carambola is overcooked. The sole letdown is the wine list. Although it's the island's largest, it lacks imagination; however, the by-the-glass selections are at least reasonably priced, and there are a few prizes. $ *Average main: US$31* ⊠ *South Friar's Bay* 📞 *869/465–9090* ⊕ *www.carambolabeachclub.com* ⊗ *No dinner Mon. and Tues.* ⚎ *Reservations essential* ☞ *Lunch is offered only on cruise-ship days; call ahead to confirm hrs of operation.*

$
CARIBBEAN
✕ **El Fredo's.** This humble wood shack across from the waterfront dishes out some of the finest local fare on St. Kitts. No surprise you'll find politicians and expats grabbing a quick lunch (it's a terrific place to

Royal Palm

eavesdrop on local gossip) alongside local workers shyly flirting with the waitresses. With just a few genre paintings for atmosphere, the decor is basic. The draw is the traditional stewed oxtail, curry goat, or swordfish creole served with heaping helpings of fungi (cornmeal), rice and peas, and dumplings. Join the locals for bounteous dishes that they swear will cure—or at least absorb—any hangover. $ *Average main: US$10* ✉ *Newtown Bay Rd. at Sanddown Rd., Basseterre* ☎ *869/764–9228* 🖦 *No credit cards* ⏱ *Closed Sun. No dinner.*

$$$
SEAFOOD

✕ **Fisherman's Wharf.** Part of the Ocean Terrace Inn, this extremely casual waterfront eatery, completely reinvented in late 2013, is decorated in contemporary nautical style, with sail rigging, walls splashed with aqua waves, illuminated water features, a mauve plexiglass marine display case, and a stylish open kitchen whose mosaic-work gleams like fish scales. Try the excellent conch chowder, followed by fresh grilled lobster or other shipshape seafood, and finish off your meal with a slice of the memorable banana cheesecake. The place is generally hopping, especially on weekend nights between karaoke and live bands jamming atop the split-level, breeze-swept bar. $ *Average main: US$24* ✉ *Ocean Terrace Inn, Wigley Ave., Basseterre* ☎ *869/465–2754* ⊕ *www.oceanterraceinn.com, www.fishermanswharfstkitts.com* ⏱ *Closed Sun. No lunch.*

$$$$
CARIBBEAN
Fodor's Choice
★

✕ **The Kitchen.** This stunner in the so-called great house—the soaring stone-steel-and-wood space of Belle Mont Farm at Kittitian Hill—is the ultimate in farm-to-table cuisine. The Kitchen offers a series of sustainable seasonal treats, sourced mostly from the farm itself and other local suppliers who practice ethical farming, fishing, and animal husbandry.

Begin your evening with handcrafted ultra-fresh cocktails in the Mill Bar, in a handsome faux sugar mill. Then repair to the main dining room or terrace overlooking the Caribbean to savor the multicourse repast. Executive Chef Christophe Letard's parade of dishes tease and titillate the taste buds, with daring counterpoints of color, flavor, and texture. Desserts can be sublime. Champagne Sunday brunch is already an island mover-and-shaker tradition. The all-organic wine list was curated by Isabelle Legeron, MW, France's only female master of wine, who cofounded London's RAW Natural Wine Fair. $ *Average main: US$75* ⊠ *Belle Mont Farm at Kittian Hill, Frigate Bay* ☎ *869/465–7388* ⊕ *www.bellemontfarm.com* ⌂ *Reservations essential.*

$$$$
FRENCH
✕ **La Belle Vie.** This *très sympa* nod to St. Kitts's French heritage is aptly titled "the good life." The cozy antiques-strewn lobby–bar leads to the semi-enclosed garden dining patio. Everything brims with brio from the brioches baked on-site to Brel and Aznavour on the sound track (accompanied by tree frogs). Nantes-born Fabien Richard deftly executes bistro fare at fair prices. You could feast on appetizers alone, but opt for the bargain three-course prix-fixe. Even the old-fashioned veggie dishes are a delight. Save room for dessert. A few minor complaints include: mosquitoes on still nights, limited wine selection, and the occasional overcooked if tasty entrée. $ *Average main: US$34* ⊠ *19 Golf View, Frigate Bay* ☎ *869/465–5216, 869/764–6035* ⊕ *www.labellevieskitts. com* ⊙ *Closed Sun. No lunch* ⌂ *Reservations essential.*

$$$
ECLECTIC
✕ **Marshall's.** The pool area of Horizons Villa Resort is transformed into a stylish eatery thanks to smashing ocean views, potted plants, serenading tree frogs, and elegant candlelit tables. Jamaican chef Verral Marshall fuses ultrafresh local ingredients with global influences. Most dishes are regrettably orthodox (rack of lamb in port reduction) if artfully plated, and the execution is uneven. But the housemade sorbets are very good. $ *Average main: US$30* ⊠ *Horizons Villa Resort, Frigate Bay* ☎ *869/466–8245* ⊕ *www.marshallsdining.com* ⊙ *No lunch* ⌂ *Reservations essential.*

$$$$
ECLECTIC
Fodor's Choice
★
✕ **The Pavilion.** Imagine a semi-alfresco cathedral constructed of raw limestone coral overlooking a palm-fringed sandy crescent: that's The Pavilion, the ritzy Christophe Harbour beach club open to nonmembers for dinner only. The soaring interior blends colonial and contemporary with aplomb: a curved exhibition kitchen, streamlined bar stools, and abstract pendant lamps contrast with "found" sculptural sea fans and driftwood, antique settees, and 19th-century black-and-white photos of Kittitian scenes. Executive Chef Damien Heaney similarly blends tradition and innovation. Even such "traditional" fare as conch fritters is goosed with pickled ginger and passion-fruit coulis and artfully presented with swirls of jerk mayo. Heaney's dishes provide textbook examples of how to juxtapose textures, flavors, even colors. Wednesday night's Chef's Appreciation prix fixe is a fine buy. The wine list features some surprising bargains, especially among whites, and you can finish your meal in style with one of a dozen aged rums. $ *Average main: US$35* ⊠ *Christophe Harbour, Sand Bank Bay* ☎ *869/465–8304* ⊕ *www.christopheharbour.com* ⊙ *No dinner Sun. and Mon. No lunch unless member* ⌂ *Reservations essential.*

$$$

ECLECTIC

✕**Reggae Beach Bar & Grill.** Treats at this popular daytime watering hole include honey-mustard ribs, coconut shrimp, grilled lobster, decadent banana bread pudding with rum sauce, and an array of tempting tropical libations. Business cards and pennants from around the world plaster the bar, and the open-air space is decorated with nautical accoutrements, from fishnets and turtle shells to painted wooden crustaceans. You can snorkel here, spot hawksbill turtles and the occasional monkey, visit the enormous house pig Wilbur, laze in a palm-shaded hammock, or rent a kayak, Hobie Cat, or snorkeling gear. Beach chairs and Wi-Fi are free. Locals come Friday nights for bonfire dinners and Sunday afternoons for dancing to live bands. $ *Average main: US$21* ⊠ *S.E. Peninsula Rd., Cockleshell Beach* ☎ *869/762–5050* ⊕ *www.reggaebeachbar. com* ⊗ *No dinner.*

$$$$

ECLECTIC

Fodor'sChoice

★

✕**Royal Palm.** A 65-foot, spring-fed pool bisects this elegant restaurant at Ottley's Plantation Inn into a semi-enclosed lounge with sea views and a breezy alfresco stone patio. Delectable dishes (prix fixe menus are also available) blend indigenous ingredients with Asian, Mediterranean, and Latin touches. Desserts are simple yet sinful indulgences such as coconut-cream cheesecake. The combination of superb food, artful presentation, romantic setting, and warm bonhomie is unbeatable. $ *Average main: US$39* ⊠ *Ottley's Plantation Inn, Ottley's Village* ☎ *869/465–7234* ⊕ *www.ottleys.com* ⚲ *Reservations essential* ⌁ *Prix-fixe $66.*

$$$$

ECLECTIC

✕**Serendipity.** This stylish restaurant occupies an old creole home whose charming enclosed patio offers lovely views of Basseterre and the bay. The interior lounge is even more conducive to romantic dining, with cushy sofas, patterned hardwood floors, porcelain lamps, and African carvings. The ambitious menu of starters and main courses reflects co-owner-chef Alexander James's peripatetic postings, including crispy fried Brie, spring rolls with plum dipping sauce, mahimahi with a cheese-and-basil crust, or teriyaki-glazed tiger shrimp. The wine list is well considered; vegetarians will be delighted by the many creative options; and very affordable lunches feature gargantuan tapas-style selections. $ *Average main: US$33* ⊠ *3 Wigley Ave., Basseterre* ☎ *869/465–9999* ⊕ *www.serendipitystkitts.net* ⊗ *Closed Sun. No lunch weekends* ⚲ *Reservations essential.*

$$$$

ECLECTIC

Fodor'sChoice

★

✕**Spice Mill.** This beachfront beauty references the Caribbean's multi-ethnic cuisine, a melting pot of African, French, English, Iberian, Asian, and Dutch influences. But the kitchen also stays home in proper locavore fashion, as does the bar, sourcing as much local produce as possible from Kittitian farmers and fishermen (who might troop through the restaurant with 30 just-caught snapper). Spice Mill merrily marries those gastronomic traditions, juxtaposing colors, tastes, and textures right from the dips served with scrumptious homemade breads. Panko-crusted crab cakes and seafood risotto are popular offerings. The culinary globe-trotting approach also dictates the decor—a mix of regional (coconut-wood-top bar, Carib canoe, and crayfish baskets from Dominica) and cosmopolitan (white beach beds, cushioned couches) elements, making even the bar (open daily and serving light snacks) a barefoot-chic hangout. Lunch is considerably cheaper and more island-flavored. $ *Average main: US$35* ✉ *Cockleshell Beach* ☎ *869/465–6455, 869/765–6706* 🌐 *www.spicemillrestaurant.com* 🕒 *No dinner Thurs.* ✍ *Reservations essential.*

$$ SEAFOOD 🍴 **Sprat Net.** This simple cluster of picnic tables—sheltered by a brilliant-turquoise corrugated-tin roof and decorated with driftwood, life preservers, photos of coastal scenes, and fishnets—sits on a sliver of sand. Nonetheless, it's an island hot spot. There's nothing fancy on the menu: just grilled fish, lobster, ribs, and chicken served with mountains of coleslaw and peas and rice. But the fish is amazingly fresh: the fishermen–owners heap their catches on a center table from which you choose your own dinner, then watch it grilled to your specification before dining family-style on paper plates. An adjacent hut serves up the final food group: pizza, Wednesday–Sunday. Sprat Net offers old-style Caribbean flavor, with the cheapest drinks and best bands on weekends. No wonder cars line up along the road, creating an impromptu jump-up. $ *Average main: US$15* ✉ *Main Rd., Old Road Town* ☎ *869/466–7535* 💳 *No credit cards* 🕒 *Closed Sept. No lunch.*

15

WHERE TO STAY

St. Kitts has an appealing variety of places to stay—beautifully restored plantation inns (where a meal plan including afternoon tea in addition to breakfast and dinner is the norm), full-service, affordable hotels, simple beachfront cottages, and all-inclusive resorts. There are also several guesthouses and self-serve condos. Increasing development has been touted (or threatened) for years. The ritzy 125-unit Park Hyatt plans to debut its first Caribbean property on Banana Bay, in partnership with the grand Christophe Harbour development that will sprawl across the Southeast Peninsula, offering spectacular villas, beach clubs, celebrity restaurants, a megayacht marina, a Tom Fazio–designed golf course, and other boutique hotels. Several upscale villa compounds are being developed, such as the culture-oriented, eco-centric Kittitian Hills (architect Bill Bensley designed some of Thailand's most remarkable resorts), which will include an "edible" golf course (greens will intersect with farmland), spa, cosmopolitan retail village, farm-to-table restaurants, and a variety of sustainable lodgings in vernacular style, most with fabulous views. The first phase of spectacular hillside cottages opened in 2014; the resort is scheduled for completion in late 2016. Another deluxe condo complex, the sparkling 185-unit Ocean's Edge on the Atlantic side of Frigate Bay, opened its first two beachfront blocks in late 2012.

$$$$ RESORT Fodor's Choice ★ 🏨 **Belle Mont Farm at Kittitian Hill.** Spectacularly perched atop a hill with sweeping views, Belle Mont Farm is the opening salvo in the eco-centric Kittitian Hill development. **Pros:** eco-friendly; luxurious; technologically state-of-the-art. **Cons:** pricey; still-water design features attract mosquitoes; beach club a bumpy ride away. $ *Rooms from: US$651* ✉ *St. Paul's* ☎ *855/846–3951 reservations, 869/465–7388* 🌐 *www.bellemontfarm.com* 🛏 *84 cottages, 10 villas, 1 farmhouse* 🍽 *Breakfast.*

$ RESORT 🏨 **Bird Rock Beach Resort.** This basic scuba-set resort crowns a bluff above Basseterre, delivering amazing views of the town, sea, and

Ottley's Plantation Inn

mountains from every vantage point. **Pros:** exuberant clientele; great diving; excellent value; superb views; bike and kayak rental; complimentary Frigate Bay shuttle. **Cons:** small man-made beach; insufficient parking; difficult for physically challenged to maneuver; several rooms leased long-term to students; poor lighting; dilapidated decor; spotty Wi-Fi. [$] *Rooms from: US$90* ✉ *2 miles (3 km) east of Basseterre, Basseterre* ☎ *869/465–8914, 877/244–6285* 🌐 *www.birdrockbeach.com* 🛏 *30 rooms, 16 studios* 🍴 *Some meals.*

$ HOTEL 🏨 **Ocean Terrace Inn.**"OTI," as locals call it, is a rarity: a smart, intimate, "boutique-y" business hotel that also appeals to vacationers. **Pros:** excellent service; fine facilities for a small hotel; good restaurants; walking distance to Basseterre attractions and restaurants. **Cons:** must drive to beaches; sprawling layout; difficult for physically challenged to navigate. [$] *Rooms from: US$264* ✉ *Wigley Ave., Basseterre* ☎ *869/465–2754, 800/524–0512* 🌐 *www.oceanterraceinn.com* 🛏 *50 rooms* 🍴 *Some meals.*

$$ HOTEL Fodor's Choice ★ 🏨 **Ottley's Plantation Inn.** You're treated like a beloved relative rather than a commercial guest at this quintessential Caribbean hotel, formerly a sugar plantation, at the foot of Mt. Liamuiga. **Pros:** posh yet unpretentious luxury; wonderfully helpful staff and owners; gorgeous gardens; excellent dining. **Cons:** no beach; bumpy access road; rates do not include 22% room tax and service. [$] *Rooms from: US$285* ✉ *Southwest of Nicola Town, Ottley's Village* ☎ *869/465–7234, 800/772–3039* 🌐 *www.ottleys.com* 🛏 *24 rooms* 🍴 *Some meals.*

$ B&B/INN 🏨 **Rock Haven Bed & Breakfast.** This restful, cozy bed-and-breakfast, a two-minute drive from Frigate Bay beaches (airport transfers are included), provides true local warmth, courtesy of Judith and Keith Blake. **Pros:** genuine island hospitality; immaculately maintained; delicious breakfasts. **Cons:** long walk to beach; car recommended to get around. [$] *Rooms from: US$199* ✉ *Frigate Bay* ☎ *869/465–5503* 🌐 *www.rock-haven.com* 🛏 *2 rooms* 🍴 *Breakfast.*

$ RESORT 🏨 **St. Kitts Marriott Resort.** This big, bustling beachfront resort offers something for everyone from families to conventioneers, golfers to gamblers. **Pros:** great range of activities; good bars; recently refurbished rooms; plentiful on-site duty-free shopping; enormous main pool. **Cons:** impersonal service; occasional time-share pitches; surprise extra charges; mostly mediocre food; not enough units feature ocean views. [$] *Rooms from: US$229* ✉ *858 Frigate Bay Rd., Frigate Bay* ☎ *869/466–1200, 800/223–6388* 🌐 *www.stkittsmarriott.com* 🛏 *320 rooms, 73 suites* 🍴 *No meals.*

$ RENTAL 🏨 **Timothy Beach Resort.** The only St. Kitts resort sitting directly on a Caribbean beach (until the Park Hyatt opens) is incomparably located and restful, a great budget find thanks to smiling service and simple but sizable apartments. **Pros:** complimentary Wi-Fi; close to the beach action; pleasant on-site restaurant and bar; plentiful deals. **Cons:** occasionally worn decor; can hear boisterous beach bar music weekend nights; no view from most bedrooms. [$] *Rooms from: US$160* ✉ *1 South Frigate Bay Beach, Frigate Bay* ☎ *869/465–8597, 845/201–0047, 888/229–2747* 🌐 *www.timothybeach.com* 🛏 *60 apartments* 🍴 *No meals.*

15

NIGHTLIFE

Most nightlife revolves around the hotels, which host folkloric shows and calypso and steel bands of the usual limbo-rum-and-reggae variety. The growing Frigate Bay "strip" of beach bars, including Mr. X Shiggidy Shack, Patsy's, Monkey Bar, Inon's, Buddies Beach Hut, Chinchilla, and Vibes, is the place to party hearty on weekend nights.

Look for such hard-driving local exponents of soca music as Nu-Vybes, Grand Masters, Small Axe, and Royalton 5; and "heavy dance-hall" reggae group House of Judah. The Marriott's large, glitzy casino has table games and slots.

BARS AND CLUBS

Circus Grill. A favorite happy-hour watering hole is the Circus Grill, a second-floor eatery whose veranda offers views of the harbor and the activity on the Circus. ✉ *Bay Rd., Basseterre* ☎ *869/465–0143.*

Keys Lounge. This low-key, classy hangout has jazz-salsa duos, cushy sofas, high-back straw chairs, chess-set tables, and a superlative selection of aged rums. If it's packed, try the hotel's Lobby Bar for tapas on tap or 'tinis with 'tude. ✉ *St. Kitts Marriott Resort, Frigate Bay* ☎ *869/466–1200.*

Mr. X's Shiggidy Shack. Mr. X's Shiggidy Shack is known for its sizzling Thursday-night bonfire parties, replete with fire-eaters, and raucous karaoke Saturdays. For locals it's a must-stop on the Friday-night liming circuit of Frigate Bay bars. ✉ *Frigate Bay* ☎ *869/762–3983, 869/465–0673.*

Fodor's Choice   **Salt Plage.** This happening beachfront nightspot merges with the hand-
★   somely recycled, rusting ruins of a former salt storage chattel house (the
lavatories are particularly creative, incorporating old depth meters and
a reclaimed engine room). Turquoise tables and white chairs dot the
multitiered bleached-wood deck, all optimally placed for sunset viewing. DJs and live bands are on tap most nights; boaters often anchor
at the dock, joining in the fun. The menu and drinks list conjure a
Cannes in the Caribbean feel. Savory light bites (priced between $10
and $20) include fish tacos, ceviches, and lobster kebabs. There's bottle
service (but of course!), and a small but savvy wine selection to help further loosen inhibitions. ⊠ *White House Bay* ☏ *869/466–7221* ⊕ *www.
christopheharbour.com.*

SHOPPING

St. Kitts has limited shopping, but several duty-free shops offer good
deals on jewelry, perfume, china, and crystal. Numerous galleries sell
excellent paintings and sculptures. The batik fabrics, scarves, caftans,
and wall hangings of Caribelle Batik are well known. British expat Kate
Spencer is an artist who has lived on the island for years, reproducing
its vibrant colors on everything from silk pareus (beach wraps) and
scarves to note cards. Other good island buys include crafts, jams, and
herbal teas. Don't forget to pick up some CSR (Cane Spirit Rothschild),
which is distilled from fresh wild sugarcane right on St. Kitts. The Brin-
ley Gold Company has made a splash among spirits connoisseurs with
its coffee, mango, coconut, lime, and vanilla rums (there is a tasting
room at Port Zante).

AREAS AND MALLS

Most shopping plazas are in downtown Basseterre, on the streets radiating from the Circus.

All Kind of Tings. All Kind of Tings, a peppermint-pink edifice on Liverpool Row at College Street Ghaut, functions as a de facto vendors'
market, where several booths sell local crafts and cheap T-shirts. Its
courtyard frequently hosts folkloric dances, fashion shows, poetry read-
ings, and steel-pan concerts. ⊠ *Liverpool Row, Basseterre.*

Pelican Mall. This shopping arcade, designed to look like a traditional
Caribbean street, has more than 20 stores (purveying mostly resort
wear, souvenirs, and liquor), a restaurant, tourism offices, and a bandstand near the cruise-ship pier. ⊠ *Bay Rd., Basseterre.*

Port Zante Mall. Directly behind Pelican Mall, on the waterfront, is Port
Zante, the deepwater cruise-ship pier where a much-delayed upscale
shopping–dining complex is becoming a 30-shop area (including the
usual ubiquitous large jewelry concerns like Abbott's, Diamonds International, and Kay Jewelers); the Amina Market here is a fine source for
cheap local crafts. If you're looking for inexpensive, islandy T-shirts and
souvenirs, check out the series of vendors' huts behind Pelican Mall to
the right of Port Zante as you face the sea. ⊠ *Cruise Ship Pier, Basseterre*
⊕ *www.portzante.com.*

Shoreline Plaza. Shoreline Plaza is next to the Treasury Building, right on Basseterre's waterfront. The shops mainly sell locally made souvenirs and handicrafts, as well as T-shirts. ⊠ *Basseterre.*

TDC Mall. TDC Mall is just off the Circus in downtown, with a few boutiques, selling mostly island wear. ⊠ *Bank St., Basseterre.*

ART

Spencer Cameron Art Gallery. Spencer Cameron Art Gallery has historical reproductions of Caribbean island charts and prints, in addition to owner Rosey Cameron's popular Carnevale clown prints and a wide selection of exceptional artwork by Caribbean artists. It also showcases the work of Glass Island (exquisite Italianate art glass from frames to plates in sinuous shapes and seductive colors) and various local craftspeople, including the marvelous pottery of Carla Astaphan. The gallery will mail anywhere. ⊠ *10 N. Independence Sq., Basseterre* ☎ *869/465–1617, 869/664–4157.*

HANDICRAFTS

Caribelle Batik. Caribelle Batik sells gloriously colored batik wraps, kimonos, caftans, T-shirts, dresses, wall hangings, and the like; you can watch the process in back. ⊠ *Romney Manor, Old Road Town* ☎ *869/465–6253* ⊕ *www.caribellebatikstkitts.com.*

Crafthouse. The Crafthouse is one of the best sources for local dolls, wood carvings, and straw work. ⊠ *Southwell Industrial Site, Bay Rd., Basseterre* ☎ *869/465–7754.*

Palms Court Gardens. Talk about multitasking: this little oasis offers a restaurant, an infinity pool and hot tub with bay views, miniature botanical gardens, and the Shell Works atelier and gift shop, where artisans fashion graceful napkin holders, candlesticks, stemware, wall hangings, and jewelry from coral, sea fans, mother-of-pearl, and other marine materials. There's a $2 admission, which is refunded with a purchase. ⊠ *Corner of Wilkin and Wigley Sts., Basseterre* ☎ *869/465–6060* ⊕ *www.palmscourtgardens.com.*

SPORTS AND THE OUTDOORS

BOATING AND FISHING

Most operators are on the Caribbean side of Frigate Bay, known for its gentle currents. Turtle Bay offers stronger winds and stunning views of Nevis. Though not noted for big-game fishing, several steep offshore drop-offs do lure wahoo, barracuda, shark, tuna, yellowtail snapper, and mackerel. Rates are occasionally negotiable; figure approximately $400 for a four-hour excursion with refreshments.

Leeward Island Charters. The knowledgeable Todd Leypoldt of Leeward Island Charters takes you out on his charter boats, *Spirit of St. Kitts*, *Caona*, and *Eagle*. He's also available for snorkeling charters, beach picnics, and sunset-moonlight cruises. ⊠ *Basseterre* ☎ *869/465–7474* ⊕ *www.leewardislandschartersstkitts.com.*

Mr. X's Watersports. Found within Mr. X's Shiggidy Shack this shop rents small craft, including motorboats (waterskiing and Jet Skiing are available). Paddleboats and sailboats can be rented by the hour. Deep-sea fishing charters, snorkeling tours, water taxis, sunset cruises, and private charters with captain and crew are available. Mr. X and his cohorts are usually hanging out at the adjacent open-air Monkey Bar. ⊠ *Frigate Bay* ☏ *869/465–0673.*

Reggae Beach Bar & Grill. This establishment rents kayaks and snorkeling equipment from the restaurant, offers sailing lessons, and can also arrange fishing trips, as well as water taxis to Nevis. ⊠ *S.E. Peninsula Rd., Cockleshell Beach* ☏ *869/762–5050* ⊕ *www.reggaebeachbar.com.*

DIVING AND SNORKELING

Though unheralded as a dive destination, St. Kitts has more than a dozen excellent sites, protected by several new marine parks. The surrounding waters feature shoals, hot vents, shallows, canyons, steep walls, and caverns at depths from 40 to nearly 200 feet. The St. Kitts Maritime Archaeological Project, which surveys, records, researches, and preserves the island's underwater treasures, has charted several hundred wrecks of galleons, frigates, and freighters dating back to the 17th century. **Bloody Bay Reef** is noted for its network of underwater grottoes daubed with purple anemones, sienna bristle worms, and canary-yellow sea fans that seem to wave you in. **Coconut Tree Reef,** one of the largest in the area, includes sea fans, sponges, and anemones, as well as the Rocks, three enormous boulders with impressive multilevel diving. The only drift-dive site, **Nags Head,** has strong currents, but experienced divers might spot gliding rays, lobsters, turtles, and reef sharks. Since it sank in 50 feet of water in the early 1980s, the *River Taw* makes a splendid site for less experienced divers. **Sandy Point Reef** has been designated a National Marine Park and includes Paradise Reef, with swim-through 90-foot sloping canyons, and Anchors Away, where anchors have been encrusted with coral formations. The 1985 wreck of the *Talata* lies in 70 feet of water; barracudas, rays, groupers, and grunts dart through its hull.

Dive St. Kitts. This PADI–NAUI facility offers competitive prices, computers to maximize time below, a wide range of courses from refresher to rescue, and friendly, laid-back dive masters. The Bird Rock location features superb shore diving (unlimited when you book packages): common sightings 20 to 30 feet out include octopuses, nurse sharks, manta and spotted eagle rays, sea horses, even barracudas George and Georgianna. It also offers kayak and snorkeling tours. ⊠ *2 miles (3 km) east of Basseterre, Frigate Bay* ☏ *869/465–1189, 869/465–8914* ⊕ *www.divestkitts.com.*

Kenneth's Dive Center. Kenneth Samuel, the owner of this PADI company, takes small groups of divers with C cards to nearby reefs on his two custom-built catamarans. Rates average $70 for single-tank dives, $105 for double-tank dives; add $10 for equipment. Night dives, including lights, are $80–$100, and snorkeling trips (four-person minimum) are $40, drinks included. After nearly 30 years' experience, former fisherman Samuel is considered an old pro (Jean-Michel Cousteau requested his guidance upon his first visit in the 1990s) and strives to keep groups small and prices reasonable. ⊠ *Bay Rd., Basseterre* ☏ *869/465–2670* ⊕ *www.kennethdivecenter.com.*

Pro-Divers. Owned by Auston Macleod, a PADI-certified dive master–instructor, this outfitter offers resort and certification courses running $125–$600, including specialty options from deep diving to digital underwater photography. Dive computers are included gratis. He offers introductory scuba courses Sunday through Thursday at 10 am and Friday and Saturday at 2:30 pm at the Marriott for guests only (the $20 fee is refunded if you purchase dives). He also takes groups to snorkeling sites accessible only by boat via his custom-built 38-foot catamaran, *Kuriala.* ✉ *Fisherman's Wharf, Ocean Terrace Inn, Basseterre* ☎ *869/660–3483* ⊕ *www.prodiversstkitts.com.*

GOLF

St. Kitts hopes to market itself as a golf destination with the remodeling of the Royal St. Kitts Golf Course and two upcoming resort and villa developments that include 18-hole courses, one called Irie Fields, an edible layout with sweeping water views at Kittitian Hill, and the other designed by Tom Fazio (which promises to be one of the Caribbean's most spectacular, with huge elevation drops, ruins, extraordinary sweeping vistas, and carries over ravines: "Scottsdale meets Pebble Beach").

Royal St. Kitts Golf Club. This 18-hole links-style championship course underwent a complete redesign by Thomas McBroom to maximize Caribbean and Atlantic views and increase the challenge (there are 12 lakes and 83 bunkers). Holes 15 through 17 (the latter patterned after Pebble Beach No. 18) skirt the Atlantic in their entirety, lending new meaning to the term sand trap. The sudden gusts, wide but twisting fairways, and extremely hilly terrain demand pinpoint accuracy and finesse, yet holes such as 18 require pure power. The development includes practice bunkers, a putting green, a short-game chipping area, and the fairly high-tech Royal Golf Academy. Twilight and super-twilight discounts are offered. ✉ *St. Kitts Marriott Resort, 858 Zenway Blvd., Frigate Bay* ☎ *869/466–2700, 866/785–4653* ⊕ *www.royalstkittsgolfclub.com* 🖃 *$150 for Marriott guests in high season, $165 for nonguests* ⚲ *18 holes, 6900 yards, par 71.*

GUIDED TOURS

The taxi driver who picks you up will probably offer to act as your guide to the island. Each driver is knowledgeable and does a three-hour tour of Nevis for $75 or a four-hour tour of St. Kitts for $80. He can also make a lunch reservation at one of the plantation restaurants, and you can incorporate this into your tour.

Kantours. On St. Kitts, Kantours offers comprehensive general island tours on both St. Kitts and Nevis, as well as a variety of specialty excursions, including ATV expeditions and Snuba adventures. ✉ *Liverpool Row, Basseterre* ☎ *869/465–2098, 869/465–3141 in St. Kitts,, 869/469–0136 in Nevis* ⊕ *www.kantours.com.*

Tropical Tours. The friendly guides at Tropical Tours can run you around St. Kitts (from $27 per person), arrange kayaking and snorkeling, deep-sea fishing (from $145 per person), and take you to the volcano or rain forest for $52 per person and up. ✉ *22 Cayon St., Basseterre* ☎ *869/465–4167, 869/465–4039* ⊕ *www.tropicaltoursstkitts-nevis.com.*

15

HIKING

Trails in the central mountains vary from easy to don't-try-it-by-yourself. Monkey Hill and Verchild's Peak aren't difficult, although the Verchild's climb will take the better part of a day. Don't attempt Mt. Liamuiga without a guide. You'll start at Belmont Estate—at the west end of the island—on horseback, and then proceed on foot to the lip of the crater, at 2,600 feet. You can go down into the crater—1,000 feet deep and 1 mile (1½ km) wide, with a small freshwater lake—clinging to vines and roots and scaling rocks, even trees. Expect to get muddy. There are several fine operators (each hotel recommends its favorite); tour rates generally range from $50 for a rain-forest walk to $95 for a volcano expedition and usually include round-trip transportation from your hotel and picnic lunch.

Duke of Earl's Adventures. Owner Earl "The Duke of Earl" Vanlow is as entertaining as his nickname suggests—and his prices are slightly cheaper ($50 for a rain-forest tour includes refreshments, $75 volcano expeditions add lunch; hotel pickup and drop-off is complimentary). He genuinely loves his island and conveys that enthusiasm, encouraging hikers to swing on vines or sample unusual-looking fruits during his rain-forest trip. He also conducts a thorough volcano tour to the crater's rim and a drive-through ecosafari tour ($55 with lunch). ☎ *869/465–1899, 869/663–0994.*

Greg's Safaris. Greg Pereira of Greg's Safaris, whose family has lived on St. Kitts since the early 19th century, takes groups on half-day trips into the rain forest and on full-day hikes up the volcano and through the grounds of a private 18th-century great house. The rain-forest trips include visits to sacred Carib sites, abandoned sugar mills, and an excursion down a 100-foot coastal canyon containing a wealth of Amerindian petroglyphs. The Off the Beaten Track 4x4 Plantation Tour provides a thorough explanation of the role sugar and rum played in the Caribbean economy and colonial wars. He and his staff relate fascinating historical, folkloric, and botanical information. ☎ *869/465–4121* ⊕ *www.gregsafaris.com.*

HORSEBACK RIDING

Wild North Frigate Bay and desolate Conaree Beach are great for riding, as is the rain forest.

Trinity Stables. Guides from Trinity Stables offer beach rides ($50) and trips into the rain forest ($60), both including hotel pickup. The latter is intriguing, as guides discuss plants' medicinal properties along the way (such as sugarcane to stanch bleeding) and pick oranges right off a tree to squeeze fresh juice. Otherwise, the staffers are cordial but shy; this isn't a place for beginners' instruction. ⊠ *Palmetto Point* ☎ *869/465–3226, 869/726–3098.*

SEA EXCURSIONS

In addition to the usual snorkeling, sunset, and party cruises (ranging in price from $40 to $100), most companies offer whale-watching excursions during the winter migrating season, January through April. And on land, turtle-watches during nesting season are becoming popular.

Blue Water Safaris. Blue Water Safaris offers half-day snorkeling trips or beach barbecues on deserted cays, as well as sunset and moonlight cruises on its 65-foot catamarans *Irie Lime* and *Swaliga,* and the smaller *Falcon.* Prices include refreshments and/or meals. It also runs kayaking tours. Boats depart from Port Zante. ⊠ *Princess St., Basseterre* ☎ *869/466–4933* ⊕ *www.bluewatersafaris.com* ⚓ *From $50.*

Leeward Island Charters. This reliable outfit offers day and overnight charters on two catamarans—the 67-foot *Eagle* and 78-foot *Spirit of St. Kitts,* as well as the 47-foot *Caona.* Day sails are from 9:30 to 4:30 and include a barbecue, an open bar, and use of snorkeling equipment. The Nevis trip stops at Pinney's Beach for a barbecue and at Shooting Bay, a tiny cove in the bullying shadow of a sheer cliff, where petrels and frigate birds inspect your snorkeling skills. The crews are mellow, affable, and knowledgeable about island life. ⊠ *586 Fort St., Basseterre* ☎ *869/465–7474* ⊕ *www.leewardislandscharters.com.*

ZIP-LINING

FAMILY **Sky Safari Tours.** On these popular tours, would-be Tarzans and Janes whisk through the "Valley of the Giants" (so dubbed for the towering trees) at speeds up to 50 mph (80 kph) along five cable lines; the longest (nicknamed "The Boss") stretches 1,350 feet through towering turpentine and mahogany trees draped thickly with bromeliads, suspended 250 feet above the ground. Following the Canadian-based company's mantra of "faster, higher, safer," it uses a specially designed trolley with secure harnesses attached. Many of the routes afford unobstructed views of Brimstone Hill and the sea beyond. The outfit emphasizes environmental and historic aspects. Guides provide nature interpretation and commentary, and the office incorporates Wingfield Estate's old sugar plantation, distillery, and church ruins, which visitors can explore. Admission is usually $65–$85, depending on the tour chosen. It's open daily 9–6, with the first and last tours departing at 10 and 3. ⊠ *Wingfield Estate, Wingfield Estate* ☎ *869/466–4259, 869/465–4347* ⊕ *www.skysafaristkitts.com.*

NEVIS

EXPLORING

Nevis's Main Road makes a 21-mile (32-km) circuit through the five parishes; various offshoots of the road wind into the mountains. You can tour Charlestown, the capital, in a half hour or so, but you'll need three to four hours to explore the entire island.

CHARLESTOWN

About 1,200 of Nevis's 10,000 inhabitants live in the capital. If you arrive by ferry, as most people do, you'll walk smack onto Main Street from the pier. It's easy to imagine how tiny Charlestown, founded in 1660, must have looked in its heyday. The weathered buildings still have fanciful galleries, elaborate gingerbread fretwork, wooden shutters, and hanging plants. The stone building with the clock tower (1825, but mostly rebuilt after a devastating 1873 fire) houses the courthouse and second-floor library (a cool respite on sultry days). The little park next to the library is Memorial Square, dedicated to the fallen of World Wars I and II. Down the street from the square, archaeologists have discovered the remains of a Jewish cemetery and synagogue (Nevis reputedly had the Caribbean's second-oldest congregation), but there's little to see.

Alexander Hamilton Birthplace. The Alexander Hamilton Birthplace, which contains the Hamilton Museum, sits on the waterfront. This bougainvillea-draped Georgian-style house is a reconstruction of what is believed to have been the American patriot's original home, built in 1680 and likely destroyed during a mid-19th-century earthquake. Born here in 1755, Hamilton moved to St. Croix when he was about 12. He moved to the American colonies to continue his education at 17; he became George Washington's Secretary of the Treasury and died in a duel with political rival Aaron Burr in 1804. The Nevis House of Assembly occupies the second floor; the museum downstairs contains Hamilton memorabilia, documents pertaining to the island's history, and displays on island geology, politics, architecture, culture, and cuisine. The gift shop is a wonderful source for historic maps, crafts, and books on Nevis. ✉ *Low St., Charlestown* ☎ *869/469–5786* ⊕ *www.nevisheritage.org, www.nevis-nhcs.org* 🖘 *$5, with admission to Museum of Nevisian History $7* ☽ *Weekdays 9–4, Sat. 9–noon.*

ELSEWHERE ON NEVIS

TOP ATTRACTIONS

Botanical Gardens of Nevis. In addition to terraced gardens and arbors, this remarkable 7.8-acre site in the glowering shadow of Mt. Nevis has natural lagoons, streams, and waterfalls, superlative bronze mermaids, Buddhas, egrets and herons, and extravagant fountains. You can find a proper rose garden, sections devoted to orchids and bromeliads, cacti, and flowering trees and shrubs—even a bamboo garden. The entrance to the Rain Forest Conservatory—which attempts to include every conceivable Caribbean ecosystem and then some—duplicates an imposing Mayan temple. A splendid re-creation of a plantation-style great house contains the appealing Oasis in the Gardens Thai restaurant with sweeping sea views (and wonderfully inventive variations on classic cocktails utilizing local ingredients), and the upscale World Art & Antiques Gallery selling artworks, textiles, jewelry, and Indonesian teak furnishings sourced during the owners' world travels. ✉ *Montpelier Estate* ☎ *869/469–3509* ⊕ *www.botanicalgardennevis.com* 🖘 *$13; $8 children 6–12* ☽ *Mon.–Sat. 9–4.*

Museum of Nevis History. Purportedly this is the western hemisphere's largest collection of Lord Horatio Nelson memorabilia, including letters, documents, paintings, and even furniture from his flagship. Nelson was based in Antigua but came on military patrol to Nevis, where he met and eventually married Frances Nisbet, who lived on a 64-acre plantation here. Half the space is devoted to often-provocative displays on island life, from leading families to vernacular architecture to the adaptation of traditional African customs, from cuisine to Carnival. The shop is an excellent source for gifts, from homemade soaps to historical guides. ✉ *Bath Rd., Charlestown* ☎ *869/469–0408* ⊕ *www.*

Mt. Nevis rising behind the Botanical Gardens of Nevis

nevis-nhcs.org, www.nevisheritage.org ✉ *$5, with Hamilton Museum $7* ⏱ *Weekdays 8:30–4, Sat. 10–1.*

WORTH NOTING

Bath Springs. The Caribbean's first hotel, the Bath Hotel, built by businessman John Huggins in 1778, was so popular in the 19th century that visitors, including such dignitaries as Samuel Taylor Coleridge and Prince William Henry, traveled two months by ship to "take the waters" in the property's hot thermal springs. It suffered extensive hurricane and earthquake damage over the years and long languished in disrepair. Local volunteers have cleaned up the spring and built a stone pool and steps to enter the waters; now residents and visitors enjoy the springs, which range from 104°F to 108°F, though signs still caution that you bathe at your own risk, especially if you have heart problems. The development houses the Nevis Island Administration offices; there's still talk of adding massage huts, changing rooms, a restaurant, and a cultural/history center on the original hotel property. ✉ *Charlestown* ✛ *Follow Main St. south from Charlestown.*

Eden Brown Estate. This government-owned mansion, built around 1740, is known as Nevis's haunted house, or haunted ruins. In 1822 a Miss Julia Huggins was to marry a fellow named Maynard. However, come wedding day, the groom and his best man killed each other in a duel. The bride-to-be became a recluse, and the mansion was closed down. Local residents claim they can feel the presence of "someone" whenever they go near the eerie old house with its shroud of weeds and wildflowers. Though memorable more for the story than the hike or ruins, it's always open, and it's free. ⊠ *East Coast Rd., between Lime Kiln and Mannings, Eden Brown Bay.*

Ft. Ashby. Overgrown with tropical vegetation, this site overlooks the place where the settlement of Jamestown fell into the sea after a tidal wave hit the coast in 1680. Needless to say, this is a favorite scuba-diving site. ⊠ *Main Rd., 1½ miles (2½ km) southwest of Hurricane Hill, Asbby Fort.*

Fothergills Nevisian Heritage Village. On the grounds of a former sugar plantation–cotton ginnery, this ambitious, ever-expanding project traces the evolution of Nevisian social history, from the Caribs to the present, through vernacular dwellings that re-create living conditions over the centuries. The Carib chief's thatched hut includes actual relics such as weapons, calabash bowls, clay pots, and cassava squeezers. Wattle-and-daub structures reproduce slave quarters; implements on display include coal pots and sea fans (used as sieves). A post-emancipation gingerbread chattel house holds patchwork quilts and flour-bag dresses. There's a typical sharecropper's garden explaining herbal medicinal folklore and blacksmith's shop. Docents are quite earnest and go on at great (mostly fascinating) length. ⊠ *Gingerland* ☎ *869/469–5521, 869/469–2033* ☜ *$3* ☺ *Mon.–Sat. 9–4; sometimes closes early, call ahead.*

Mansa's Farm. Anyone who wants a real sense of island daily life and subsistence should call Mervin "Mansa" Tyson. He'll take you past his fruit trees and herb gardens through rows of tomatoes, cucumbers, string beans, eggplant, zucchini, sweet pepper, melons, and more. Discussing the needs for at least partial organic growing practices, he passionately explains how he adapted traditional folk pesticides and describes the medicinal properties of various plants, cultivated and wild. He'll prepare a lunch using his produce, including delectable refreshing fruit drinks at his Mansa's Last Stand grocery across from the beach. Weekend barbecues are a highlight. All in all, this agritourism foray redefines food for thought. ⊠ *Cades Bay* ☎ *869/469–8520* ☜ *Varies* ☺ *Call for appointment.*

St. John's Figtree Church. Among the records of this church built in 1680 is a tattered, prominently displayed marriage certificate that reads "Horatio Nelson, Esquire, to Frances Nisbet, Widow, on March 11, 1787."⊠ *Church Ground* ✣ *Located about 10 mins south of Charlestown on the main road.*

St. Thomas Anglican Church. The island's oldest church was built in 1643 and has been altered many times over the years. The gravestones in the old churchyard have stories to tell, and the church itself contains memorials to Nevis's early settlers. ⊠ *Main Rd. just south of Cotton Ground, Jessup.*

BEACHES

All beaches on Nevis are free to the public (the plantation inns cordon off "private" areas on Pinney's Beach for guests), but there are no changing facilities, so wear a swimsuit under your clothes.

Newcastle Beach. This broad swath of soft ecru sand shaded by coconut palms is near Nisbet Plantation, on the channel between St. Kitts and Nevis. It's popular with snorkelers, but beware stony sections and occasional strong currents that kick up seaweed and roil the sandy bottom. **Amenities:** food and drink. **Best for:** snorkeling. ⊠ *Newcastle.*

Oualie Beach. South of Mosquito Bay and north of Cades and Jones Bays, this beige-sand beach lined with palms and sea grapes is where the folks at Oualie Beach Hotel can mix you a drink and fix you up with water-sports equipment. There's excellent snorkeling amid calm water and fantastic sunset views with St. Kitts silhouetted in the background. Several beach chairs and hammocks (free with lunch, $3 rental without) line the sand and the grassy "lawn" behind it. Oualie is at the island's northwest tip, approximately 3 miles (5 km) west of the airport. **Amenities:** food and drink; water sports. **Best for:** snorkeling; sunset. ⊠ *Oualie Beach.*

Pinney's Beach. The island's showpiece has soft golden sand on the calm Caribbean, lined with a magnificent grove of palm trees. The Four Seasons Resort is here, as are the plantation inns' beach clubs and casual beach bars such as Sunshine's, Chevy's, and the Lime (which morphs into the island's disco Friday nights). Beach chairs are gratis when you purchase a drink or lunch. Regrettably, the waters can be murky and filled with kelp if the weather has been inclement anywhere within a hundred miles, depending on the currents. **Amenities:** food and drink; water sports. **Best for:** swimming; walking. ⊠ *Pinney's Beach.*

15

WHERE TO EAT

Dinner options range from intimate meals at plantation guesthouses (where the menu is often prix fixe) to casual eateries. Seafood is ubiquitous, and many places specialize in West Indian fare. The island tried to raise its profile as a fine-dining destination by holding NICHE (Nevis International Culinary Heritage Exposition), a gastronomic festival with guest chefs and winemakers offering cooking seminars and tastings during the second half of October; the event has been tabled the past couple of years.

What to Wear: Dress is casual at lunch, although beach attire is unacceptable. Dress pants and sundresses are appropriate for dinner.

$$$ ✕ **Bananas.** Peripatetic English owner Gillian Smith has held jobs with
ECLECTIC Disney and Relais & Châteaux, and everything about Bananas borrows from her wildly diverse experiences. Even the setting is delightfully deceptive: the classic stone, brick, and wood plantation great house nestled amid extravagant gardens was painstakingly built by Gillian herself in 2006. Her fun, shabby-chic sensibility informs every aspect of the restaurant and adjacent art gallery in a faux chattel house. The colonial look (pith helmets, steamer trunks, beamed ceiling, chandeliers dangling from a corrugated tin roof) contrasts with Turkish kilims and Moroccan lamps. The food is equally eclectic and globe-trotting, running from bourbon-glazed guava ribs to baked gnocchi. Despite the improvisational ambience, there's no monkeying around with quality at Bananas.

$ *Average main: US$29* ✉ *Hamilton's Estate* ☎ *869/469–1891* ⊕ *www. bananasrestaurantnevis.com* ⊗ *Closed Sun.* ⌂ *Reservations essential.*

$$$$
ECLECTIC
Fodor'sChoice
★

✕**Coconut Grove.** This thatch-palm roof, rough-timber structure sports a sensuous South Seas look, best appreciated on the deck as the sun fireballs across the Caribbean. The service is warm, the champagne is properly chilled, and the splendid Pacific Rim–Mediterranean fusion fare seems designed to complement the admirable, 8,000-bottle wine cellar rather than the other way around. Chef Steve Smith, a CIA grad and registered dietitian, has introduced heart-healthier options such as curry-scented pumpkin soup and whole-wheat-flour–and–black-bean brownies. Nonetheless, the menu also includes such indulgences as foie gras steeped in aged rum and candied cherries or baked Camembert. Happy hour, 11 pm–midnight, often ushers in impromptu dancing, continuing the "Bali high" theme. The downstairs "Coco Beach" has an infinity pool for use, sensational St. Kitts views, affordable, creative, lighter daytime fare when open for lunch (call ahead), and live music many evenings. $ *Average main: US$36* ✉ *Nelson's Spring, Pinney's Beach* ☎ *869/469–1020* ⊕ *www.coconutgroverestaurantnevis.com* ⊗ *Closed Aug.–Oct.* ⌂ *Reservations essential.*

$$$$
STEAKHOUSE
Fodor'sChoice
★

✕**Coral Grill.** Coral Grill is the Four Seasons' stunning, less formal steakhouse, formerly the clubby Dining Room. The imposing space is light and bright. The graceful patio, beamed cathedral ceilings, flagstone hearth, and parquet floors remain from the restaurant's previous incarnation; yet an open contemporary lounge that wouldn't be out of place in Santa Monica bisects the vast interior. The grilled items shine here, from Wagyu steak to gossamer lobster tails. Or opt for the decadent foie gras burger. Meats are served with a choice of sauces. The streamlined but comprehensive wine list features some surprisingly fair prices. The hotel can arrange a unique interactive dive-and-dine experience, plunging you into the deep to pluck lobster and other marine creatures that the chefs will cook for you later. $ *Average main: US$43* ✉ *Four Seasons Nevis, Pinney's Beach* ☎ *869/469–1111, 869/469–6238* ⊕ *www. fourseasons.com/nevis* ⊗ *No lunch* ⌂ *Reservations essential.*

$$
SEAFOOD
FAMILY

✕**Double Deuce.** Mark Roberts, the former chef at Montpelier, decided to chuck the "five-star lifestyle" and now co-owns this jammed, jamming bar just off Pinney's, which lures locals with fine, fairly priced fare and creative cocktails. The overgrown shack is plastered with sailing and fishing pictures, Balinese masks, fishnets, license plates, and wind chimes. Behind the cool mauve bar is a gleaming modern kitchen where Mark (and fun-loving firebrand partner Lyndeta) prepare sublime seafood he often catches himself (try the ginger garlic shrimp), as well as organic beef burgers, velvety pumpkin soup, inventive pastas, lip-smacking ribs, and some British pub standards. Stop by for free Wi-Fi and proper espresso, a game of pool, riotous karaoke on Thursdays, or Sunday bingo. $ *Average main: US$18* ✉ *Pinney's Beach* ☎ *869/469–2222* ⊕ *www.doubledeucenevis.com* ▭ *No credit cards* ⊗ *Closed Mon.* ⌂ *Reservations essential.*

$$$
ECLECTIC
Fodor'sChoice
★

✕**Hermitage Plantation Inn.** After cocktails in the inn's antiques-filled parlor (the knockout rum punches are legendary), dinner is served on the veranda. Many ingredients are harvested from the inn's herb garden, fruit trees, piggery, and livestock collection; the scrumptious cured meats, baked goods, preserves, and ice creams are homemade. Sumptuous dishes are prepared by long-time expat maestro Janice Ryan. A traditional wood-burning oven yields savory items as well, including what may be the best thin-crust pizzas within hundreds of miles. Wednesday night pig roasts are an island must; Friday night pizza and Caribbean *cicchetti* (small side dishes) are quite popular. The ever-growing wine list is exceptionally priced. $ *Average main: US$30* ✉ *Gingerland* ☎ *869/469–3477* ⊕ *www.hermitagenevis.com* ⚓ *Reservations essential.*

$$$$
CARIBBEAN

✕ **Mango.** This sophisticated beach bar at the Four Seasons is a perennial hot spot, thanks to a gorgeous outdoor deck overlooking the illuminated water, sizzling music, fab drinks (as well as an extensive rum bar with more than 100 selections), hip decor, and a farm- and sea-to-table menu showcasing local ingredients, many grown by the staff. You can savor artfully presented, robustly flavored Caribbean classics with inventive accents such as barbecue pork-and-plantain empanadas, lobster fritters, or mango-Myers's rum barbecued baby back ribs. The kitchen also delights with updated twists, such as chilled corn-and-coconut soup. Half the menu is gluten-free. $ *Average main: US$39* ✉ *Four Seasons Resort, Pinney's Beach* ☎ *869/469–1111, 869/469–6238* ☾ *No lunch.*

$$$$
ECLECTIC

✕ **Mount Nevis Hotel & Beach Club.** Mount Nevis's sublime open-air dining room by the pool offers a splendid view of St. Kitts. Before dinner, savor cocktails in the distinctive lounge, accented by sisal rugs, mosaic tiles, towering bamboo stalks, and a cool mostly blue color scheme. Chef Eric Vasson deftly blends local ingredients, many grown in the organic garden, with a cornucopia of Caribbean-Continental cuisines. Sterling starters on the ever-changing menu might include some preparation of poke; main courses include a variety of steak, lamb, and fish. Finish with tropical variations on classics such as coconut flan. $ *Average main: US$31* ✉ *Shaws Rd., Mount Nevis* ☎ *869/469–9373* ⊕ *www.mountnevishotel.com* ⚓ *Reservations essential.*

$$$$
ECLECTIC

✕ **Nisbet Great House.** The blissfully air-conditioned great house is an oasis of polished hardwood floors, mahogany and cherry wood furnishings, equestrian bronzes, antique hurricane lamps, wicker furnishings, and works by famed Nevisian artist Eva Wilkin. Tables on the veranda look down the palm-tree-lined fairway to the sea. The four-course menu combines Continental, Pacific Rim, and Caribbean cuisines with local ingredients. The more mature clientele dictates less complex options from house-cured gravlax to filet mignon. But Executive Chef Antonio Piani might sneak in conch-breadfuit-and-dumpling soup or a stuffed lobster. Enjoy an impressively cosmopolitan selection of cocktails or coffee with soft live music in the front bar. Witty, dapper maître d' Patterson Fleming (his cravat collection, more than 1,000 augmented by guests over the years, is enviable!) ensures a smooth, swank experience. $ *Average main: US$65* ✉ *Nisbet Plantation and Beach Club, Newcastle* ☎ *869/469–9325* ⊕ *www.nisbetplantation.com* ⚓ *Reservations essential.*

$$$$
ECLECTIC
Fodor's Choice
★

✕ **Restaurant 750.** The Hoffman family presides over a scintillating evening, starting with canapés and cocktails in Montpelier's civilized plantation great room. Dinner is served on the breezy west veranda, overlooking the lights of Charlestown and St. Kitts. Executive Chef

15

Cristian Bassi Andreasi uses the inn's organic herb gardens and fruit trees to full advantage. The changing three-course menu usually includes her signature pan-seared sea scallops with green asparagus cream; the dark chocolate tart with caramelized banana is divine. The exemplary wine list is perfectly matched to the cuisine. Finish with one of the infused rums. $ *Average main: US$60* ⊠ *Montpelier Plantation & Beach, Montpelier Estate* ☎ *869/469–3462* ⊕ *www.montpeliernevis. com* ⊘ *Closed late Aug.–early Oct.* ⌲ *Reservations essential.*

$$$ ╳ **The Rocks at Golden Rock.** This glam eatery's tiered setting may be a
ECLECTIC   genuine artistic and engineering masterpiece. Glass panels and ceilings display the night sky while reflecting patio lights. A series of cascading waterfalls, pools, and fountains filigree the surrounding landscaped jungle with liquid silver. Strategically placed boulders resemble hulking Henry Moore sculpture. Playfully contrasting classic and modern, a stone gazebo recalls an upside-down plantation-era copper boiler. Contemporary and colonial artworks from Mali and Afghanistan grace the interior. Sadly, the kitchen doesn't quite match the setting's splendor or creativity. But the atmosphere more than compensates, and solid choices include jerk pork or pan-roasted snapper. $ *Average main: US$28* ⊠ *Gingerland* ☎ *869/469–3346* ⊕ *www.goldenrocknevis.com* ⌲ *Reservations essential.*

$$ ╳ **Sunshine's.** Everything about this shack overlooking (and spilling
CARIBBEAN   onto) the beach is larger than life, including the Rasta man Llewelyn "Sunshine" Caines himself. Flags and license plates from around the world reflect the international patrons (including an occasional movie or sports star wandering down from the Four Seasons). Picnic tables are splashed with bright sunrise-to-sunset colors; even the palm trees are painted, though "it gone upscaled," as locals say, with VIP cabanas. Fishermen cruise up with their catch—you might savor lobster rolls or snapper creole. Don't miss the lethal house specialty, Killer Bee rum punch. As Sunshine boasts, "One and you're stung, two, you're stunned, three, it's a knockout." $ *Average main: US$18* ⊠ *Pinney's Beach* ☎ *869/469–5817* ⊕ *www.sunshinesnevis.com.*

$$$ ╳ **Yachtsman Grill.** This beachfront eatery features nautical decor (sail-
ECLECTIC   boat models, keels, fishing rods, outboard motors) and seafood to match (pick your own lobster from the tank). Meat lovers are not ignored; there are steaks, BBQ ribs, and lamb chops. There's also a wood-fired pizza oven. The place overflows with good cheer, especially during the joyous happy hours. Oenophiles will appreciate the Cruvinet dispensing several wines by the glass; the convivial owners, Greg and Evelyn, adore Austrian bottlings ("Not Australian, Austrian . . . as in *The Sound of Music*, birthplace of coffeehouses, lederhosen, dirndl dresses, schnitzel, and so on. . . ."). $ *Average main: US$25* ⊠ *Hamilton Beach Villas, Nelson Spring* ☎ *869/469–1382* ⊕ *www.yachtsmangrill.com* ▭ *No credit cards.*

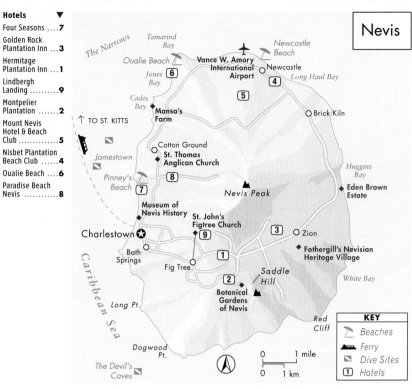

15

WHERE TO STAY

Many lodgings are in restored manor or plantation houses scattered throughout the island's five parishes (counties). The owners often live at these inns, and it's easy to feel as if you've been personally invited down for a visit. Before dinner you may find yourself in the drawing room having a cocktail and conversing with the family, other guests, or visitors who have come for a meal. Meal plans for most inns include breakfast and dinner (plus afternoon tea) and offer a free shuttle service to their "private" stretch of beach. If you require TVs and air-conditioning, you're better off staying at hotels and simply dining with the engaging inn owners. Two major (by Nevisian standards) condo developments, with at least Phase 1 completed by late 2016, will nearly double the island's room inventory. Hamilton Beach Villas & Spa opened its first fully equipped condos on Cotton Ground Beach in 2013; the 10-building project will comprise a total of 79 self-catering units, as well as a spa, gym, pool, and tennis courts when it is completed in 2016. The even more ambitious Tamarind Cove broke ground in 2012, though development had stalled; plans call for six buildings housing 91 units, plus a pool, clubhouse with restaurant and shopping arcade, seafront boardwalk with more retail and dining, and a 120-berth marina. Other small upscale compounds are in various stages of

Four Seasons Resort Nevis

development, including the Paradise Villa development (not to be confused with Paradise Beach), the overhauled Cliffdwellers at Tamarind Bay and the Zenith Beach houses, connected with the delightful Chrishi Beach Club on Cades Bay.

$$$$ RESORT FAMILY Fodor's Choice ★ **Four Seasons Resort Nevis.** This beachfront beauty impeccably combines world-class elegance with West Indian hospitality while scrupulously maintaining and upgrading facilities. **Pros:** luxury without attitude; superlative service; marvelous food; dazzling golf and spa. **Cons:** pricey; sometimes overrun by conventions and incentive groups (off-season mainly); berms added as secondary defense against storm surges impede some beachfront room views. [$] *Rooms from: US$650* ✉ *Pinney's Beach* ☎ *869/469–1111, 869/469–6238, 800/332–3442 in U.S., 800/268–6282 in Canada* 🌐 *www.fourseasons.com/nevis* 🛏 *179 rooms, 17 suites, 61 villas* 🍴 *No meals.*

$$ HOTEL **Golden Rock Plantation Inn.** Acclaimed artists Brice Marden and wife Helen Harrington have imparted a chic, modernist sensibility to this 18th-century estate property while respecting its storied past. **Pros:** eco-friendly; artsy crowd; glorious grounds; free Wi-Fi. **Cons:** no actual beach though there are two beach clubs; lack of air-conditioning can be uncomfortable on still days. [$] *Rooms from: US$290* ✉ *Gingerland* ☎ *869/469–3346* 🌐 *www.goldenrocknevis.com, www.golden-rock.com* ⏲ *Closed mid-Aug.–mid-Oct.* 🛏 *16 rooms, 1 suite* 🍴 *Breakfast.*

$ HOTEL Fodor's Choice ★ **Hermitage Plantation Inn.** A snug 1670 great house—reputedly the Caribbean's oldest surviving wooden building—forms the heart of this breeze-swept hillside hideaway. **Pros:** wonderful sense of history; delightful owners and clientele; delicious food. **Cons:** long drive to beach; hillside setting difficult for physically challenged to negotiate. [$] *Rooms from: US$255* ✉ *Hermitage Rd., Gingerland* ☎ *869/469–3477, 800/682–4025* 🌐 *www.hermitagenevis.com* 🛏 *8 rooms, 8 cottages, 1 house* 🍴 *Some meals.*

$ B&B/INN 🏨 **Lindbergh Landing.** Spencer and Jacqueline "Jackie" Harvey's charming and chill hillside inn abounds in color and personality. **Pros:** affordable; warm hospitality; sensational views. **Cons:** no air-conditioning can be problematic on rare still days; dicey Wi-Fi signal; three-day minimum stay required. [$] *Rooms from: US$150* ✉ *Dr. Penn Heights, Church Ground* ☎ *869/469–3398* 🌐 *www.lindberghlandingnevis.com* 🛏 *2 rooms* 🍴 *No meals.*

$$$ RESORT Fodor's Choice ★ 🏨 **Montpelier Plantation & Beach.** This Nevisian beauty, a Rélais & Châteaux property, epitomizes understated elegance and graciously updated plantation living. **Pros:** impeccable service and attention to detail; lovely cuisine; exquisite gardens; complimentary Wi-Fi. **Cons:** some may find it a little stuffy; no beach on-site. [$] *Rooms from: US$445* ✉ *Montpelier Estate* ☎ *869/469–3462, 800/735–2478* 🌐 *www.montpeliernevis.com* ⏲ *Closed mid-Aug.–mid-Oct.* 🛏 *17 rooms, 2 one-bedroom villas, 1 two-bedroom villa* 🍴 *Breakfast.*

$$ HOTEL FAMILY 🏨 **Mount Nevis Hotel & Beach Club.** The personable, attentive Meguid family blends the intimacy of the plantation inns, contemporary amenities of the Four Seasons, and typical Nevisian warmth in this hilltop aerie. **Pros:** friendly staff; fantastic views; free Wi-Fi; complimentary cell phone (pay for card). **Cons:** lacks beach; long drive to many island activities; occasional plane noise. [$] *Rooms from: US$350* ✉ *Shaws Rd., Mount Nevis* ☎ *869/469–9373, 800/756–3847* 🌐 *www.mountnevishotel.com* 🛏 *32 rooms, 32 suites, 10 villas* 🍴 *Breakfast.*

$$$$ RESORT Fodor's Choice ★ 🏨 **Nisbet Plantation Beach Club.** At this beachfront plantation inn, pale yellow cottages face a regal, palm-lined grass avenue that sweeps to a lovely champagne-hue beach. **Pros:** beautiful setting; plentiful recreational options; free Wi-Fi; complimentary afternoon tea. **Cons:** long drive to most activities on island; airplanes occasionally whoosh by; food is variable. [$] *Rooms from: US$739* ✉ *Newcastle* ☎ *869/469–9325, 800/742–6008* 🌐 *www.nisbetplantation.com* 🛏 *36 rooms* 🍴 *Some meals.*

$ RESORT 🏨 **Oualie Beach Hotel.** These creole-style gingerbread cottages daubed in cotton-candy colors sit just steps from a beach facing St. Kitts and are carefully staggered to ensure sea views from every room. **Pros:** fantastic water-sports operations; affordable (especially with recreational packages); appealing beach; Green Globe–certified; free Wi-Fi. **Cons:** showing some wear; not ideal for less active types. [$] *Rooms from: US$180* ✉ *Oualie Beach* ☎ *869/469–9735* 🌐 *www.oualiebeach.com* 🛏 *32 rooms* 🍴 *Some meals.*

$$$$ RENTAL 🏨 **Paradise Beach Nevis.** This exclusive villa enclave cascades down a lushly landscaped hill to Pinney's Beach. **Pros:** luxurious; well equipped; private and quiet. **Cons:** pricey; few on-site facilities; not the nicest stretch of Pinney's Beach. [$] *Rooms from: US$2780* ✉ *Pinney's Beach* ☎ *869/469–7900* 🌐 *www.paradisebeachnevis.com* 🛏 *2 3-bedroom villas, 5 4-bedroom villas* 🍴 *No meals* ☞ *3-night minimum stay.*

15

Nevis's Day at the Races

One of the Caribbean's most festive, endearingly idiosyncratic events is the Nevis Turf and Jockey Club's Day at the Races, held 9 to 12 times a year on the wild and windswept Indian Castle course. I first experienced the event in the mid-1990s, when I met club president Richard "Lupi" Lupinacci, owner of the Hermitage Plantation Inn. Before even introducing himself, Richard sized me up in the driveway: "You look about the right size for a jockey. How's your seat?" His equally effervescent wife, Maureen, then interceded, "Darling, if you loathe horses, don't worry. In fact, Lupi and I have an agreement about the Jerk and Turkey Club. I get major jewels for every animal he buys."

Since my riding skills were rusty, it was decided that I should be a judge (despite questionable vision,

even with glasses). "If it's really by a nose, someone will disagree with you either way," I was reassured. The next day presented a quintessential Caribbean scene. Although a serious cadre of aficionados (including the German consul) talked turf, the rest of the island seemed more interested in liming and enjoying lively music. Local ladies dished out heavenly barbecued chicken and devilish gossip. Sheep and cattle unconcernedly ambled across the course. But when real horses thundered around the oval, the wooden stands groaned under the weight of cheering crowds, and bookies hand-calculated the payouts.

The irregularly scheduled races continue, albeit now on a properly sodded track, as does the equine hospitality.

—Jordan Simon

NIGHTLIFE

In season it's usually easy to find a local calypso singer or a steel or string band performing at one of the hotels, notably the Four Seasons and Oualie Beach (which also features string musicians on homemade instruments Tuesday evening), as well as at the Pinney's bars. Scan the posters plastered on doorways announcing informal jump-ups. Though Nevis lacks high-tech discos, many restaurants and bars have live bands or DJs on weekends.

FAMILY

Fodor'sChoice

★

Chrishi Beach Club. Though more a daytime hangout (especially Sunday when Nevisians descend on the lovely beach with their families), Chrishi Beach Club remains happening through sunset thanks to vivacious Norwegian expats Hedda and Christian "Chrishi" Wienpahl. You can sprawl on beach waterbeds in the shady "Love Shack + Bar," or on comfy chaises in the "stripper" lounge, replete with pole for shimmying. Enjoy the righteous lounge mix (and mixology), the movie nights, the glorious St. Kitts views, and what Hedda calls "European café-style" food (salads, pizzas, sandwiches like Brie with sun-dried tomatoes and cranberries, and more substantial dishes like butterflied prawns in garlic-parsley sauce). Kids have their own club with fresh-fruit smoothies, DJs spin on Sexy Saturday Nights, frequent film nights are wildly popular, and Hedda's fun funky HWD jewelry line (incorporating leather, coins, found objects) is on sale. Their new Zenith Resort, an adjacent villa development, has some spectacular units. No surprise that the menu boasts it's "The Place to See and Be Seen." ⊠ *Next to Sea Bridge and Mansa's, Cades Bay* ☎ *869/662–3958, 869/662–3959* ⊕ *www.chrishibeachclub.com.*

Water Department Barbecue. The Water Department Barbecue is the informal name for a lively Friday-night jump-up that's run by two fellows (nicknamed he Pump Boys) from the local water department. Friday afternoons the tents go up and the grills are fired. Cars line the streets and the guys dish up fabulous barbecue ribs and chicken—as certain customers lobby to get their water pressure adjusted. It's a classic Caribbean scene. ⊠ *Pump Rd., Charlestown.*

SHOPPING

Nevis is certainly not the place for a shopping spree, but there are some unusual and wonderful surprises, notably the island's pottery, hand-embroidered clothing, and dolls by Jeannie Rigby. Honey is another buzzing biz. Quentin Henderson, the amiable former head of the **Nevis Beekeeping Cooperative,** will even arrange trips by appointment to various hives for demonstrations of beekeeping procedures. Other than a few hotel boutiques and isolated galleries, virtually all shopping is concentrated on or just off Main Street in Charlestown. The lovely old stonework and wood floors of the waterfront Cotton Ginnery Complex make an appropriate setting for stalls of local artisans.

ART

Eva Wilkin Gallery. Nevis has produced one artist of some international repute, the late Dame Eva Wilkin, who for more than 50 years painted island people, flowers, and landscapes in an evocative art naïf style. Her originals are now quite valuable, but prints are available in some local shops. The Eva Wilkin Gallery occupies her former atelier (hours are extremely irregular, so call ahead). If the paintings, drawings, and prints are out of your price range, consider buying the lovely note cards based on her designs; the owners are also promoting promising regional artists. ⊠ *Clay Ghaut Estate, Gingerland* ☎ *869/469–2673.*

CLOTHING

Most hotels have their own boutiques.

Island Fever. The island's classiest shop carries an excellent selection of everything from bathing suits and dresses to straw bags and jewelry. ⊠ *Main St., Charlestown* ☎ *869/469–0867.*

HANDICRAFTS

CraftHouse. This marvelous source for local specialties, from vetiver mats to leather moccasins, also has a smaller branch in the Cotton Ginnery. ⊠ *Pinney's Rd., Charlestown* ☎ *869/469–5505.*

Nevis Handicraft Co-op Society. This shop across from the tourist office offers works by local artisans (clothing, ceramic ware, woven goods) and locally produced honey, hot sauces, and jellies (try the guava and soursop). ⊠ *Main St., Charlestown* ☎ *869/469–1746.*

Newcastle Pottery. This cooperative has continued the age-old tradition of hand-built red-clay pottery fired over burning coconut husks. It's

15

possible to watch the potters and purchase wares at their small New-castle factory. ⊠ *Main Rd., Newcastle* ☎ *869/469–9746.*

LOCAL GIFTS

Philatelic Bureau. St. Kitts and Nevis are famous for their decorative, and sometimes valuable, stamps. Collectors will find real beauties here, including the butterfly, hummingbird, and marine-life series. ⊠ *Cotton Ginnery, opposite the tourist office, Charlestown* ☎ *869/469–0617.*

SPORTS AND THE OUTDOORS

BIKING

Windsurfing Nevis/Wheel World. This shop offers mountain-bike rentals, apparel, and specially tailored tours on Gary Fisher, Trek, Hybrid, and MTB bikes. The tours ($60–$80), led by Winston Crooke, a master windsurfer and competitive bike racer, encompass lush rain forest, majestic ruins, and spectacular views. Costs vary according to itinerary and ability level but are aimed generally at experienced riders. Winston and his team delight in sharing local knowledge, from history to culture. For those just renting (rates from $25 daily, $150 weekly), Winston determines your performance level and suggests appropriate routes. ⊠ *Oualie Beach* ☎ *869/469–9682* ⊕ *www.bikenevis.com.*

DIVING AND SNORKELING

The **Devil's Caves** make up a series of grottoes where divers can navigate tunnels, canyons, and underwater hot springs while viewing lobsters, sea fans, sponges, squirrelfish, and more. The village of **Jamestown,** which washed into the sea around Ft. Ashby, just south of Cades Bay, makes for superior snorkeling and diving. Reef-protected Pinney's Beach offers especially good snorkeling. Single-tank dives are usually $80, two-tank dives $100; packages provide deep discounts.

FAMILY **Scuba Safaris.** This PADI five-star facility and NASDS Examining Station is staffed by experienced dive masters who offer everything from a resort course to full certification to nitrox. Their equipment is always state-of-the-art, including underwater scooters. It also provides a snorkeling learning experience that enables you not only to see but to listen to sea life, including whales and dolphins, as well as an exhilarating underwater scooter safari, night dives, and kids' bubble-makers. ⊠ *Oualie Beach* ☎ *869/469–9518* ⊕ *www.divenevis.com.*

FISHING

Fishing here focuses on kingfish, wahoo, grouper, tuna, and yellowtail snapper, with marlin occasionally spotted. The best areas are Monkey Shoals and around Redonda. Charters cost approximately $450–$500 per half day, $850–$1,000 per full day, and usually include an open bar.

Deep Venture. Run by fisherman–chef Matt Lloyd, Deep Venture does day-fishing charters (he keeps the catch), providing a real insight into both commercial fishing and the Caribbean kitchen. ⊠ *Oualie Beach* ☎ *869/469–5110.*

GOLF

Four Seasons Golf Course. The Robert Trent Jones Jr.–designed Four Seasons Golf Course is beautiful and impeccably maintained. The front 9 holes are fairly flat until hole 8, which climbs uphill after your tee shot. Most of the truly stunning views are along the back 9. The signature hole is the 15th, a 660-yard monster that encompasses a deep ravine; other holes include bridges, steep drops, rolling pitches, extremely tight and unforgiving fairways, sugar-mill ruins, and fierce doglegs. Attentive attendants canvas the course with beverage buggies, handing out chilled, peppermint-scented towels and preordered Cubanos that help test the wind. There are huge kids', twilight, and off-season discounts. ⊠ *Four Seasons Resort Nevis, Pinney's Beach* ☎ *869/469–1111* ⊕ *www.fourseasons.com/nevis* ✍ *$160; rental clubs $50* ⚐ *18 holes, 6766 yards, par 72.*

GUIDED TOURS

TC's Island Tours. TC, a Yorkshire lass who used to drive a double-decker bus in England and has been married to a Nevisian for more than a decade, offers entertaining explorations via TC's Island Tours. ☎ *869/469–2911.*

HIKING

The center of the island is Nevis Peak—also known as Mt. Nevis—which soars 3,232 feet and is flanked by Hurricane Hill on the north and Saddle Hill on the south. If you plan to scale Nevis Peak, a daylong affair, it's highly recommended that you go with a guide. Your hotel can arrange it (and a picnic lunch) for you. The 9-mile (15-km) **Upper Round Road Trail** was constructed in the late 1600s and cleared and restored by the Nevis Historical and Conservation Society. It connects the Golden Rock Plantation Inn, on the east side of the island, with Nisbet Plantation Beach Club, on the northern tip. The trail encompasses numerous vegetation zones, including pristine rain forest, and impressive plantation ruins. The original cobblestones, walls, and ruins are still evident in many places.

Sunrise Tours. Run by Lynell and Earla Liburd (and their son Kervin), Sunrise Tours offers a range of hiking trips, but their most popular is Devil's Copper, a rock configuration full of ghostly legends. Local people gave it its name because at one time the water was hot—a volcanic thermal stream. The area features pristine waterfalls and splendid bird-watching. They also do a Nevis village walk, a Hamilton Estate Walk, a Charlestown tour, an Amerindian walk along the wild southeast Atlantic coast, and trips to the rain forest and Nevis Peak. They love highlighting Nevisian heritage, explaining time-honored cooking techniques, the many uses of dried grasses, and medicinal plants. Hikes range from $25 to $40 per person, and you receive a certificate of achievement. ☎ *869/469–2758* ⊕ *www.nevisnaturetours.com.*

HORSEBACK RIDING

Hermitage Stables. Here you can opt for everything from horseback riding to jaunts in hand-carved mahogany carriages. ⊠ *Hermitage Plantation Inn, Hermitage Rd., Gingerland* ☎ *869/469–3477* ⊕ *www.hermitagenevis.com.*

Nevis Equestrian Centre. The Nevis Equestrian Centre offers leisurely beach rides as well as more demanding canters through the lush hills, starting at $75. Lessons are sometimes available ($30 group, $40 private). ✉ *Clifton Estate, Cotton Ground* ☎ *869/662–9118* ⊕ *www. nevishorseback.com.*

WINDSURFING

Windsurfing Nevis. Waters are generally calm and northeasterly winds steady yet gentle, making Nevis an excellent spot for beginners and intermediates. Windsurfing Nevis offers top-notch instructors (Winston Crooke is one of the best in the islands) and equipment for $30 per hour. Beginners get equipment and two-hour instruction for $60. Groups are kept small (eight maximum), and the equipment is state-of-the-art from Mistral, North, and Tushingham. It also offers kayak rentals and tours along the coast, stopping at otherwise inaccessible beaches. ✉ *Oualie Beach* ☎ *869/469–9682.*

ST. LUCIA

WELCOME TO ST. LUCIA

THE CARIBBEAN'S TWIN PEAKS

St. Lucia, 27 miles (43.5 km) by 14 miles (22.5 km), is a volcanic island covered to a large extent by lush rain forest, much of which is protected as a national park. The most notable geological features are the Pitons, some 2,600-foot-high twin peaks designated a UNESCO World Heritage Site in 2004.

KEY		
⊿	Beaches	
◩	Dive Sites	
⚓	Ferry	
🚢	Cruise Ship Terminal	
①	Hotels	

Explorers, pirates, soldiers, sugar planters, and coal miners have made their mark on this lovely landfall, and the lush tropical peaks known as the Pitons (Gros and Petit) have witnessed them all. Today's visitors come to snorkel and scuba dive in St. Lucia's calm cobalt-blue waters, sun themselves on its multihued beaches, and experience nature at its finest.

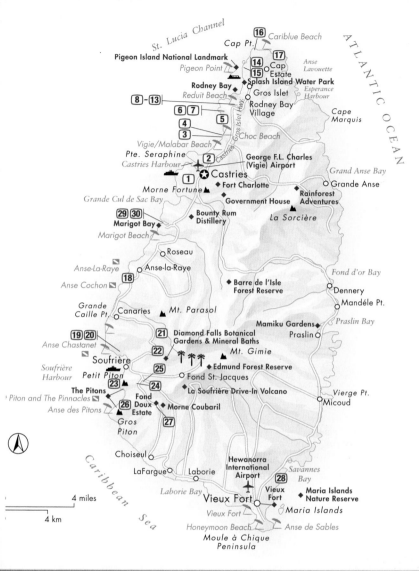

TOP REASONS TO VISIT ST. LUCIA

1 The Beauty: Magnificent, lush scenery makes St. Lucia one of the most beautiful Caribbean islands.

2 The Romance: A popular honeymoon spot, St. Lucia has abundant romantic retreats.

3 Indulgent Accommodations: Sybaritic lodging options include an all-inclusive spa resort, a posh sanctuary sandwiched between

a mountain and the beach, and two resorts with prime locations between the Pitons.

4 The Music: Performers and fans from around the world come for the annual St. Lucia Jazz & Arts Festival.

5 The Welcome: The friendly St. Lucians love sharing their island and their cultural heritage with visitors.

NEED TO KNOW

MARTINIQUE

Atlantic Ocean

Castries

ST. LUCIA

Caribbean Sea

SAINT VINCENT

AT A GLANCE

Capital: Castries

Population: 182,270

Currency: Eastern Caribbean dollar; pegged to the U.S. dollar at EC$2.67/$1

Money: ATMs common but dispense only local currency; major credit cards and U.S. dollars widely accepted

Language: English, Creole patois

Country Code: ☎ 1 758

Emergencies: ☎ 999

Driving: On the left

Electricity: 220v/50 cycles; plugs are U.K. standard, square with three-pins; many hotels also have 110v outlets or lend plug adapters

Time: Same as Eastern time during daylight savings; one hour ahead otherwise

Documents: A valid passport and a return or ongoing ticket.

Major Mobile Companies: Digicel, LIME

GETTING AROUND

✈ **Air Travel:** Flights from the U.S. land at Hewanorra International Airport in Vieux Fort. Intra-Caribbean flights land at George F.L. Charles Airport in Castries.

🚌 **Bus Travel:** Minivans and jitneys offer inexpensive transportation aimed primarily at locals, and these are fine for short trips.

🚗 **Car Travel:** St. Lucia's winding and mountainous roads can make driving a challenge, especially for those not used to driving on the left. Most travelers can get by with taxis or tours.

⛴ **Boat Travel:** Express des Isles ferry service connects St. Lucia with Martinique, Dominica, and Guadeloupe.

PLAN YOUR BUDGET

	HOTEL ROOM	MEAL	ATTRACTIONS
Low Budget	$250	$15	"Drive in" volcano, Mt. Soufrière, $2
Mid Budget	$400	$25	Diamond Falls Botanical Gardens & Mineral Baths, $7
High Budget	$650	$50	Rainforest Sky Ride, $80

WAYS TO SAVE

Stay at a cozy inn. Smaller properties offer more intimate (and far cheaper) than the typical beach resort.

Shop at open-air markets. Buy local fruits, veggies, spices, souvenirs, and more at the public markets in Castries.

Take the public minibus. Especially in the north, a jitney journey that costs a dollar or two is much more expensive by taxi.

Do a full-day tour. Instead of renting a car or taking multiple taxis or mini tours, do an attractions blitz with a full-day island tour.

PLAN YOUR TIME

Hassle Factor	Medium. Flights to St. Lucia are frequent; but once you've arrived, expect a lengthy drive from the airport to the resort areas.
3 days	Base yourself at a resort in Soufrière. Revel in the awe-inspiring beauty of Petit Piton and Gros Piton. Snorkel in surrounding reefs, relax beachside and also visit Mount Soufrière.
1 week	Split your time between the south (in or near Soufrière) and Marigot Bay. Visit all of St. Lucia's natural attractions in the south and relax in picturesque Marigot Bay. Rent a car or hire a taxi to explore the north of the island, checking out the Castries' market and Pigeon Island.
2 weeks	Spend a full week in or near Soufrière to fully appreciate the grandeur of the area. Split your second week between Marigot Bay and Rodney Bay. Don't miss the Gros Islet Jump Up on Friday night.

WHEN TO GO

High Season: Mid-December through mid-April is the most fashionable and most expensive time to visit, when visitors seek relief from the winter chill back home. Luxury hotels are often booked very far in advance; you're guaranteed the most entertainment at resorts and the most people with whom to enjoy it.

Low Season: From August through late October, the weather can be oppressively hot and humid, with a high risk of tropical storms. Substantial rain may occur from August through early November. Some upscale hotels close during September and October; those that remain open offer deep discounts.

Value Season: From late April through July and from November through mid-December, hotel prices drop 20% to 50% (except during the St. Lucia Jazz & Arts Festival and Carnival). Expect scattered showers but many sun-kissed days and fewer crowds.

BIG EVENTS

May: St. Lucia Jazz & Arts Festival is the year's big event and one of the largest musical events in the entire Caribbean. ⊕ www.stluciajazz.org

July: St. Lucia Carnival is celebrated mainly in Castries and Gros Islet. Expect costumes, music, and basic hedonistic fare! ⊕ www.luciancarnival.com

December: The finish of the Atlantic Rally for Cruisers, the world's largest ocean-crossing race, is marked by a week of festivities at Rodney Bay. ⊕ www.worldcruising.com/arc/arcitinerary.aspx

READ THIS

■ *Omeros,* Derek Walcott. Epic work by the St. Lucian Nobel Prize–winning poet and playwright.

■ *Volcano,* Patricia Rice. St. Lucia is the setting for a steamy, drama-filled love story.

■ *Take Me There,* Leslie Esdaile. Another steamy romance novel set on St. Lucia.

WATCH THIS

■ *Doctor Doolittle.* The original 1967 version was filmed in Marigot Bay.

■ *Firepower.* Scenes from this 1979 British thriller, starring Sophia Loren and James Coburn, were filmed in St. Lucia.

EAT THIS

■ *Green figs and saltfish*: breakfast dish of boiled green bananas and saltfish

■ *Crab back*: land crab meat and stuffing, served in the shell

■ *Cassava bread*: unleavened bread made from cassava (manioc) flour with dried fruits often folded in

■ *Christophene au gratin*: chayote, baked with cheese and cream

■ *Piton*: the award-winning local beer

■ *Bounty rum*: golden rum and the islanders' spirit of choice

Updated by
Jane E. Zarem

A verdant, mountainous island located halfway between Martinique and St. Vincent, St. Lucia has evolved into one of the Caribbean's most popular vacation destinations—particularly for honeymooners and other romantics enticed by the island's striking natural beauty, many splendid resorts and appealing inns, and welcoming atmosphere.

The capital city of Castries and nearby villages in the northwest are home to 40% of the 180,000 St. Lucians. This area, Rodney Bay Village (farther north), Marigot Bay (just south of the capital), and Soufrière (southwestern coast) are the destinations of most vacationers. In central and southwestern areas, dense rain forest, jungle-covered mountains, and vast banana plantations dominate the landscape. A tortuous road follows most of the coastline, bisecting small villages, cutting through mountains, and passing fertile valleys. Petit Piton and Gros Piton, unusual twin peaks that anchor the southwestern coast and rise to more than 2,600 feet, are familiar landmarks for sailors and aviators as well as a UNESCO World Heritage Site. Divers are attracted to the reefs in the National Marine Reserve between the Pitons and extending north past Soufrière, the capital during French colonial times. Most of the natural tourist attractions are in this area, along with several fine resorts and inns.

The pirate François Le Clerc, nicknamed Jambe de Bois (Wooden Leg) for obvious reasons, was the first European "settler." In the late 16th century Le Clerc holed up on Pigeon Island, just off St. Lucia's northernmost point, using it as a staging ground for attacking passing ships. Now, Pigeon Island National Landmark is a public park connected by a causeway to the mainland; Sandals Grande St. Lucian Spa & Beach Resort, one of the largest resorts in St. Lucia, and the Landings, a luxury villa community, sprawl along that causeway.

Like most of its Caribbean neighbors, St. Lucia was first inhabited by Arawaks and then the Carib people. British settlers attempted to colonize the island twice in the early 1600s, but it wasn't until 1651, after the French West India Company suppressed the local Caribs, that Europeans gained a foothold. For 150 years, battles between the French and the British over the island were frequent, with a dizzying 14 changes in power before the British finally took possession in 1814. The Europeans established sugar plantations, using slaves from West Africa to work the fields. By 1838, when the slaves were emancipated, more than 90% of the population was of African descent—roughly the same proportion as today.

On February 22, 1979, St. Lucia became an independent state within the British Commonwealth of Nations, with a resident governor-general appointed by the Queen. Still, the island appears to have retained more relics of French influence—notably the island's patois, cuisine, village names, and surnames—than of the British. Most likely, that's because the British contribution primarily involved the English language, the educational and legal systems, and the political structure, whereas the French culture historically had more influence on the arts—culinary, dance, and music.

PLANNING

GETTING HERE AND AROUND
AIR TRAVEL

American Airlines flies nonstop to Hewanorra from Charlotte, Miami, and Philadelphia, with connecting service from other major cities. Delta flies nonstop to Hewanorra from Atlanta and New York–JFK. JetBlue flies nonstop to Hewanorra from Boston and New York–JFK, with connecting service from other cities. United flies weekend nonstops to Hewanorra from New York–Newark and Chicago. LIAT flies to George F.L. Charles Airport from several neighboring islands.

Airline Contacts American Airlines. ☎ 800/744–0006, 758/459–6500 ⊕ www.aa.com. **Delta.** ☎ 758/454–3119, 800/221–1212 ⊕ www.delta.com. **JetBlue.** ☎ 877/766–9614 ⊕ www.jetblue.com. **LIAT.** ☎ 888/844–5428, 758/452–2348 ⊕ www.liat.com. **United.** ☎ 800/864–8331 ⊕ www.united.com.

Airports George F.L. Charles Airport (SLU). ☎ 758/457–6149. **Hewanorra International Airport** (UVF). ☎ 758/457–6160.

Air Transfers St. Lucia Helicopters. ☎ 758/453–6950 ⊕ www.stluciahelicopters.com.

BOAT AND FERRY TRAVEL

When cruise ships are in port in Castries, a water taxi shuttles back and forth between Pointe Seraphine (on the north side of the harbor) and La Place Carenage (on the south side) for $3 per person each way. The L'Express des Iles ferry travels between St. Lucia and Martinique, Dominica, and Guadeloupe. A number of water taxi companies provide service and tours to (and from) locations along the western coast of the island, including Pigeon Island, Rodney Bay, Vigie Marina (Castries), Castries Harbour, Marigot Bay, Anse Cochon, Anse Chastanet, and Soufrière. Tours can be customized or customary, private or with others, and may focus on snorkeling, sightseeing, or simply the sunset. All of the companies offer similar service/tours and will arrange to meet their customers at any coastal location.

Contacts Feel Good Water Taxi & Tours. ⊠ *Bayfront, Soufrière* ☎ *758/721–2174* ⊕ *www.feelgoodwatertaxiandtours.com.* **Israel King Water Taxi & Tours.** ⊠ *Rodney Bay Marina, Rodney Bay* ☎ *758/717–3301.* **L'Express des Iles.** ☎ *758/456–5000* ⊕ *www.express-des-iles.com.* **Solomon Water Taxi & Tours.** ☎ *758/717–4087* ⊕ *www.solomon-saintlucia.com.*

BUS TRAVEL

Privately owned and operated minivans constitute St. Lucia's bus system, an inexpensive and efficient means of transportation used primarily by local people. Buses have green number plates beginning with the letter "M." They are a good way to travel between Castries and the Rodney Bay area; the fare is EC$2.50 (ideally payable in local currency). You can also travel from Castries to Soufrière or Vieux Fort (two-plus hours, EC$10), but those are definitely arduous rides. Wait at a marked stop and hail the passing minivan. Let the conductor or driver know where you need to go, and he'll stop at the appropriate place.

CAR TRAVEL

Roads throughout St. Lucia, except north of Castries, are winding and mountainous, making driving a challenge for timid or apprehensive drivers and exhausting for everyone else. Drive on the left, British-style. Seat belts are required; speed limits are enforced, especially in Castries.

Car-Rental Contacts Avis. ⊠ *Hewanorra International Airport, Vieux Fort* ☎ *758/454–6325, 758/452–2046 George F. L. Charles Airport* ⊕ *www.avisstlucia.com* ⊠ *Bay Gardens Beach Resort, Rodney Bay Village* ☎ *758/453–1356* ⊕ *www.avisstlucia.com.* **Avis.** ⊠ *Bay Gardens Beach Resort, Rodney Bay Village* ☎ *758/453–1356* ⊕ *www.avisstlucia.com* **Cool Breeze Jeep/Car Rental.** ☎ *758/459–7729* ⊕ *www.coolbreezecarrental.com.* **Cost-Less Rent-a-Car.** ⊠ *Harmony Suites, Rodney Bay* ☎ *758/450–3416, 908/818–8506 in the U.S.* ⊕ *www.costless-rentacar.com.* **Courtesy Car Rentals.** ☎ *758/452–8140, 315/519–7684 in the U.S.* ⊕ *www.courtesycarrentals.com.* **Hertz.** ⊠ *Hewanorra International Airport, Vieux Fort* ☎ *758/454–9636* ⊕ *www.hertz.com.*

TAXI TRAVEL

Fully licensed taxis have number plates beginning with "TX." They are unmetered, although fares are flat rate and fairly standard. Sample fares for up to four passengers are: Castries to Rodney Bay, $25; Rodney Bay to Cap Estate, $12; Castries to Cap Estate, $30; Castries to Marigot Bay, $30; Castries to Anse la Raye, $40; Castries to Soufrière, $80–$100; Castries to Vieux Fort, $80; Marigot Bay to Vieux Fort, $70; and Soufrière to Vieux Fort, $75–$80. Always ask the driver to quote the price *before* you get in, and be sure that you both understand whether it's quoted in EC or U.S. dollars. Drivers are generally careful, knowledgeable, and courteous.

HEALTH AND SAFETY

Dengue, chikungunya, and zika have all been reported throughout the Caribbean. We recommend that you protect yourself from these mosquito-borne illnesses by keeping your skin covered and/or wearing mosquito repellent. The mosquitoes that transmit these viruses are as active by day as they are by night.

HOTELS AND RESORTS

Nearly all St. Lucia's resorts and small inns face or are near unspoiled beaches or are hidden away on secluded coves or tucked into forested hillsides in three locations along the calm Caribbean (western) coast. They're in the greater Castries area between Marigot Bay, a few miles south of the city, and Labrelotte Bay in the north; in and around Rodney Bay Village and north to Cap Estate; and in and around Soufrière on the southwest coast near the Pitons. There's only one resort in Vieux Fort, near Hewanorra. The advantage of being in the north is that you have access to a wider range of restaurants and nightlife; in the south, you are close to most of St. Lucia's "natural wonders" but may be limited to your hotel's offerings and a few other restaurants—albeit some of the best—in and around Soufrière.

Beach Resorts: Most people choose to stay in one of St. Lucia's many beach resorts, the majority of which are upscale and fairly pricey. Several are all-inclusive, including three Sandals resorts, two Sunswept resorts (The Body Holiday and Rendezvous), St. James's Club Morgan Bay, and East Winds Inn. Others may offer an all-inclusive option.

Small Inns: If you are looking for something more intimate and perhaps less expensive, a locally owned inn or small hotel is a good option; it may or may not be directly on the beach.

Villas: Luxury villa communities that operate like hotels are a good alternative for families. Several are in the north in the Cap Estate area.

Hotel reviews have been shortened. For full information, visit Fodors.com.

WHAT IT COSTS IN U.S. DOLLARS				
	$	$$	$$$	$$$$
RESTAURANTS	under $12	$12–$20	$21–$30	over $30
HOTELS	under $275	$275–$375	$376–$475	over $475

Restaurant prices are the average cost of a main course at dinner or, if dinner is not served, at lunch. Hotel prices are the lowest cost of a standard double room in high season.

VISITOR INFORMATION

Contacts St. Lucia Tourist Board. ☏ *212/867–2950, 800/456–3984 in U.S.* ⊕ *www.stlucianow.com.* **Soufrière Tourist Information Centre.** ✉ *Maurice Mason St., Soufrière* ☏ *758/459–7419* ⊕ *www.stlucianow.com.*

EXPLORING

Except for a small area in the extreme northeast, one main highway circles all of St. Lucia. The road snakes along the coast, cuts across mountains, makes hairpin turns and sheer drops, and reaches dizzying heights. It takes at least four hours to drive the whole loop. Even

at a leisurely pace with frequent sightseeing stops, and whether you're driving or being driven, the curvy roads make it a tiring drive in a single outing.

Between Castries and Cap Estate, in the far north, the road is mainly flat. The area is built up with businesses, resorts, and residences, so the two-lane road is often clogged with traffic—especially just north of Castries and around Rodney Bay Village but less as you approach Pigeon Island and Cap Estate. Frequent bus service is available on this route.

The West Coast Road between Castries and Soufrière (a 1½-hour journey) has steep hills and sharp turns, but it's well marked and incredibly scenic. South of Castries, the road tunnels through Morne Fortune, skirts the island's largest banana plantation (more than 127 varieties of bananas, called "figs" in this part of the Caribbean, grow on the island), and passes through tiny fishing villages. Just north of Soufrière, the road negotiates the island's fruit basket where most of the mangoes, breadfruit, tomatoes, limes, and oranges are grown. In the mountainous region that forms a backdrop for Soufrière, you will notice 3,118-foot Mt. Gimie (pronounced Jimmy), St. Lucia's highest peak. Approaching Soufrière, you'll have spectacular views of the Pitons; the spume of smoke wafting out of the thickly forested mountainside just east of Soufrière emanates from the so-called "drive-in" volcano.

16

The landscape changes dramatically between the Pitons and Vieux Fort on the island's southeastern tip. Along the South Coast Road traveling southeasterly from Soufrière, the terrain starts as steep mountainside with dense vegetation, progresses to undulating hills, and finally becomes rather flat and comparatively arid. Anyone arriving at Hewanorra International Airport, which is in Vieux Fort, and staying at a resort near Soufrière will travel along this route, a journey of about 45 minutes each way.

From Vieux Fort north to Castries, a 1½-hour drive, the East Coast Road twists through Micoud, Dennery, and other coastal villages. It then winds up, down, and around mountains, crosses Barre de l'Isle Ridge, and slices through the rain forest. Much of the scenery is breathtaking. The Atlantic Ocean pounds against rocky cliffs, and acres and acres of bananas and coconut palms blanket the hillsides. If you arrive at Hewanorra and stay at a resort in Marigot Bay, Castries, Rodney Bay, or Cap Estate, you'll travel along the East Coast Road.

CASTRIES AND THE NORTH

Castries, the capital city, and the area north and just south of it are the island's most developed areas. The roads are mostly flat, straight, and easy to navigate. The beaches are among the island's best. Rodney Bay Village, Rodney Bay Marina, and many resorts, restaurants, and nightspots are north of Castries. Pigeon Island, one of the important historical sites, is at the island's northwestern tip. Picturesque Marigot Bay, about 15 minutes south of Castries, is both a yacht haven and a lovely destination for landlubbers.

Embracing Kwéyòl

English is St. Lucia's official language, but most St. Lucians speak Kwéyòl—a French-based Creole language—and often use it for informal conversations among themselves. Primarily a spoken language, Kwéyòl in its written version doesn't look at all like French; pronounce the words phonetically, though—*entenasyonnal* (international), for example, or the word *Kwéyòl* (Creole) itself—and you indeed sound as if you're speaking French.

Pretty much the same version of the Creole language, or patois, is spoken in the nearby island of Dominica. Otherwise, the St. Lucian Kwéyòl is quite different from that spoken in other Caribbean islands that have a French and African heritage, such as Haiti, Guadeloupe, and Martinique—or elsewhere, such as Mauritius, Madagascar, and the state of Louisiana. The Kwéyòl spoken in St. Lucia and Dominica is mostly unintelligible to people from those other locations—and vice versa.

St. Lucia embraces its Creole heritage by devoting the month of October each year to celebrations that preserve and promote Creole culture, language, and traditions. Events and performances highlight Creole music, food, dance, theater, native costumes, church services, traditional games, folklore, native medicine—a little bit of everything, or *tout bagay*, as you say in Kwéyòl.

Creole Heritage Month culminates at the end of October with all-day events and activities on Jounen Kwéyòl Entenasyonnal, or International Creole Day, which is recognized by all countries that speak a version of Creole.

TOP ATTRACTIONS

Castries. The capital, a busy commercial city of about 65,000 people (one-third of the island's population), wraps around sheltered Castries Bay. Morne Fortune rises sharply to the south, creating a dramatic green backdrop. The charm of Castries lies in its liveliness rather than its architecture, since four fires between 1796 and 1948 destroyed most of the colonial buildings. Freighters (exporting bananas, coconut, cocoa, mace, nutmeg, and citrus fruits) and cruise ships come and go frequently, making Castries Harbour one of the Caribbean's busiest ports. **Pointe Seraphine** is a duty-free shopping complex on the north side of the bay, about a 20-minute walk or 2-minute cab ride from the city center; a launch ferries passengers across the harbor when cruise ships are in port. Pointe Seraphine's attractive Spanish-style architecture houses more than a dozen duty-free shops, a tourist information kiosk, and a taxi stand. **La Place Carenage,** on the south side of the harbor near the pier and markets, is another duty-free shopping complex with a dozen or more shops and a café. **Derek Walcott Square,** a green oasis bordered by Brazil, Laborie, Micoud, and Bourbon streets, honors the hometown poet who won the 1992 Nobel Prize in Literature—one of two Nobel laureates from St. Lucia. The late Sir W. Arthur Lewis won the 1979 Nobel in economics. (Interestingly, both Nobel laureates shared the same birthday, January 23!) Some of the few 19th-century buildings that survived fire, wind, and rain can be seen on Brazil Street, the square's southern border. On the Laborie Street side, there's a huge, 400-year-old samaan (monkeypod) tree with leafy branches that shade a good portion of the square. Directly across Laborie Street from Derek Walcott Square is the Roman Catholic **Cathedral of the Immaculate Conception,** which was built in 1897. Though it's rather somber on the outside, colorful murals by St. Lucian artist Dunstan St. Omer decorate the interior walls. The murals were reworked prior to the visit of Pope John Paul II in 1985. The church has an active parish and is open daily for both public viewing and religious services. ⊠ *Castries.*

FAMILY

Fodor'sChoice

★

Castries Market. Under a brilliant orange roof, this bustling market is at its liveliest on Saturday morning, when farmers bring their produce and spices to town—as they have for more than a century. (It's closed Sunday.) Next door to the produce market is the **Craft Market,** where you can buy pottery, wood carvings, handwoven straw articles, and innumerable souvenirs, trinkets, and gewgaws. At the **Vendors' Arcade,** across Peynier Street from the Craft Market, you'll find still more handicrafts and souvenirs. ⊠ *Jeremie and Peynier Sts., Castries.*

Fodor'sChoice

★

Marigot Bay. This is one of the prettiest natural harbors in the Caribbean. In 1778, British admiral Samuel Barrington sailed into this secluded bay-within-a-bay and, the story goes, covered his ships with palm fronds to hide them from the French. Today this small community, just 4 miles (7 km) south of Castries, is a favorite anchorage for boaters and a peaceful destination for landlubbers, with a luxury resort, several small inns and restaurants, and a marina village with a snack shop, grocery store, and boutiques. A 24-hour ferry (EC$5 round-trip) connects the bay's two shores—a voyage that takes a minute or so each way. ⊠ *Marigot Bay.*

FAMILY

Rainforest Adventures. Ever wish you could get a bird's-eye view of the rain forest? Or at least experience it without hiking up and down miles of mountain trails? Here's your chance. Depending on your athleticism and spirit of adventure, choose a two-hour aerial tram ride, a zip-line experience, or both. Either activity guarantees a magnificent view as you peacefully ride above or actively zip through the canopy of the 3,442-acre Castries Waterworks Rain Forest in Babonneau, 30 minutes east of Rodney Bay. On the tram ride, eight-passenger gondolas glide slowly among the giant trees, twisting vines, and dense thickets of vegetation accented by colorful flowers, as a tour guide explains and shares anecdotes about the various trees, plants, birds, and other wonders of nature found in the area. The zip line, on the other hand, is a thrilling experience in which you're rigged with a harness, helmet, and clamps that attach to cables strategically strung through the forest. Short trails connect 18 platforms, so riders come down to earth briefly and hike to the next station before speeding through the forest canopy to the next stop. There's even a nighttime zip-line tour. ■TIP→ **Bring binoculars and a camera.** ⊠ *Chassin, Babonneau* ☎ *758/458–5151, 866/759–8726 in the U.S.* ⊕ *www.rainforestadventure.com* ☛ *Tram $80, zip line $80, combo $95* ☉ *Tues.–Thurs. and Sun. 9–4, night zip at 6.*

Rodney Bay Village. Hotels, popular restaurants, a huge mall, and the island's only casino surround a natural bay and an 80-acre man-made lagoon named for Admiral George Rodney, who sailed the British navy out of Gros Islet in 1780 to attack and ultimately destroy the French fleet. With 253 slips, Rodney Bay Marina is one of the Caribbean's premier yachting centers; each December, it's the destination of the Atlantic Rally for Cruisers, a transatlantic sailing competition for racing yachts. Yacht charters and sightseeing day trips can be arranged at the marina. Rodney Bay Village is about 15 minutes north of Castries. ⊠ *Rodney Bay.*

FAMILY
Fodor'sChoice
★
Splash Island Water Park. The Eastern Caribbean's first open-water-sports park, installed just off Reduit Beach a dozen or so yards from the sand in front of Bay Gardens Beach Resort, thrills kids and adults alike—but mostly kids. They spend hours on the colorful, inflatable, modular features that include a trampoline, climbing wall, monkey bars, swing, slide, hurdles, double rocker, and water volleyball net. Children must be at least six, and everyone must wear a life vest. A team of lifeguards is on duty when the park is open. ⊠ *Reduit Beach, Reduit Beach Rd., Rodney Bay* ✛ *Facing Bay Gardens Beach Resort* 🕾 *758/457–8532* ⊕ *www.stluciawaterpark.com* 🖃 *$11.50 per hr; $34.50 half-day pass; $57.50 full-day pass* ⊙ *Daily 9–6.*

WORTH NOTING

Bounty Rum Distillery. St. Lucia Distillers, which produces the island's own Bounty and Chairman's Reserve rums, offers 90-minute Rhythm of Rum tours that cover the history of sugar, the background of rum, a detailed description of the distillation process, colorful displays of local architecture, a glimpse at a typical rum shop, Caribbean music, and a chance to sample the company's rums and liqueurs. The distillery is at the Roseau Sugar Factory in the Roseau Valley, on the island's largest banana plantation a few miles south of Castries and not far from Marigot. Reservations for the tour are essential. ⊠ *Roseau Sugar Factory, West Coast Rd., near Marigot Bay, Marigot Bay* 🕾 *758/456–3148* ⊕ *www.saintluciarums.com* 🖃 *$8* ⊙ *Weekdays 9–3.*

Ft. Charlotte. Begun in 1764 by the French as the Citadelle du Morne Fortune, Ft. Charlotte was completed after 20 years of battling and changing hands. Its old barracks and batteries are now government buildings and local educational facilities, but you can drive around and look at the remains of redoubts, a guardroom, stables, and cells. You can also walk up to the Inniskilling Monument, a tribute to the 1796 battle in which the 27th Foot Royal Inniskilling Fusiliers wrested the Morne from the French. At the military cemetery, first used in 1782, faint inscriptions on the tombstones tell the tales of French and English soldiers who died in St. Lucia. Six former governors of the island are also buried here. From this point atop Morne Fortune, you have a beautiful view of Castries Harbour, Martinique farther north, and the Pitons to the south. ⊠ *Morne Fortune.*

Government House. The official residence of the governor-general—and one of the island's few remaining examples of Victorian architecture—is perched high above Castries, halfway up Morne Fortune (Hill of Good Fortune), which forms a backdrop for the capital city. Morne Fortune has also seen more than its share of *bad* luck, including devastating hurricanes and four fires that leveled Castries. Within Government House is **Le Pavillon Royal Museum,** which houses important historical photographs and documents, artifacts, crockery, silverware, medals, and awards; original architectural drawings of the house are displayed on the walls. Note that you must make an appointment to visit. ⊠ *Morne Fortune* ☎ *758/452–2481* ⊠ *Free* ☉ *Tues. and Thurs. 10–noon and 2–4, by appointment only.*

FAMILY **Pigeon Island National Landmark.** Jutting out from the northwest coast, Pigeon Island connects to the mainland via a causeway. Tales are told of the pirate Jambe de Bois (Wooden Leg), who once hid out on this 44-acre hilltop islet—a strategic point during the French and British struggles for control of St. Lucia. Now Pigeon Island is a national park and a venue for concerts, festivals, and family gatherings. There are two small beaches with calm waters for swimming and snorkeling, a restaurant, and picnic areas. Scattered around the grounds are ruins of barracks, batteries, and garrisons that date from 18th-century French and English battles. In the Museum and Interpretative Centre, housed in the restored British officers' mess, a multimedia display explains the island's ecological and historical significance. The site is administered by the St. Lucia National Trust. ⊠ *Pigeon Island* ☎ *758/452–5005* ⊕ *www. slunatrust.org* ⊠ *$7* ☉ *Daily 9–5.*

16

SOUFRIÈRE AND THE WEST COAST

The oldest town in St. Lucia and the island's former colonial capital, Soufrière was founded by the French in 1746 and named for its proximity to the volcano of the same name. The wharf is the center of activity in this sleepy town (population, 9,000), particularly when a cruise ship anchors in pretty Soufrière Bay. French colonial influences are evident in the second-story verandas, gingerbread trim, and other appointments of the wooden buildings that surround the market square. The market building itself is decorated with colorful murals.

The site of much of St. Lucia's renowned natural wonders, Soufrière is the destination of most sightseeing trips. Here you can get up close to the iconic Pitons and visit St. Lucia's "drive-in" volcano, botanical gardens, working plantations, waterfalls, and countless other examples of the natural beauty for which the island is deservedly famous. Note that souvenir vendors station themselves outside some of the popular attractions in and around Soufrière, and they can be persistent. Be polite but firm if you're not interested.

TOP ATTRACTIONS

Fodor'sChoice **Diamond Falls Botanical Gardens & Mineral Baths.** These splendid gardens
★ are part of Soufrière Estate, a 2,000-acre land grant presented by King Louis XIV in 1713 to three Devaux brothers from Normandy in recognition of their services to France. The estate is still owned by their descendants; Joan DuBouley Devaux maintains the gardens. Bushes and shrubs bursting with brilliant flowers grow beneath towering trees and line pathways that lead to a natural gorge. Water bubbling to the surface from underground sulfur springs streams downhill in rivulets to become Diamond Waterfall, deep within the botanical gardens. Through the

centuries, the rocks over which the cascade spills have become encrusted with minerals tinted yellow, green, and purple. Near the falls, mineral baths are fed by the underground springs. King Louis XVI of France provided funds in 1784 for the construction of a building with a dozen large stone baths to fortify his troops against the St. Lucian climate. It's claimed that the future Joséphine Bonaparte bathed here as a young girl while visiting her father's plantation nearby. During the Brigand's War, just after the French Revolution, the bathhouse was destroyed. In 1930 André DuBoulay had the site excavated, and two of the original stone baths were restored for his use. Outside baths were added later. For a small fee, you can slip into your swimsuit and soak for 30 minutes in one of the outside pools; a private bath costs slightly more. ⊠ *Soufrière Estate, Diamond Rd., Soufrière* ☎ *758/459–7155* ⊕ *www. diamondstlucia.com* 🖃 *$7, public bath $6, private bath $7* ⊗ *Mon.–Sat. 10–5, Sun. 10–3.*

Fodor'sChoice
★
The Pitons. Rising precipitously from the cobalt-blue Caribbean just south of Soufrière Bay, these two unusual mountains—named a UNESCO World Heritage Site in 2004—have become the iconic symbol of St. Lucia. Covered with thick tropical vegetation, the massive outcroppings were formed by a volcanic eruption 30 to 40 million years ago. They are not identical twins, since 2,619-foot Petit Piton is taller than 2,461-foot Gros Piton (Gros Piton is broader). It's possible to climb the Pitons, but it's a strenuous trek. Gros Piton is the easier climb and takes about four hours round-trip. Either climb requires permission and a guide ($30); register at the base of Gros Piton. ⊠ *Soufrière.*

WORTH NOTING

Edmund Forest Reserve. Dense tropical rain forest that stretches from one side of St. Lucia to the other, sprawling over 19,000 acres of mountains and valleys, is home to a multitude of exotic flowers, trees, plants, and rare birds—including the brightly feathered Jacquot parrot. The Edmund Forest Reserve, on the island's western side, is most easily accessible from the road to Fond St. Jacques, which is just east of Soufrière. A trek through the verdant landscape, with spectacular views of mountains, valleys, and the sea beyond, can take three or more hours. The ranger station at the reserve entrance is a 30-minute drive from Soufrière and 90 minutes or more from the northern end of St. Lucia. You'll need a four-wheel drive vehicle to drive inland to the trailhead, which can take another hour. The trek itself is a strenuous hike, requiring stamina and sturdy hiking shoes. Your hotel can help you obtain permission from the St. Lucia Forestry Department to access reserve trails and to arrange for a naturalist or forest officer guide—necessary because the vegetation is so dense. ⊠ *Soufrière* ☎ *758/450–2231 Forestry Dept.* 🖃 *Guide for nature trails $10, hiking trails $25, bird-watching $25* ⊗ *Daily by appointment only.*

FAMILY
Fond Doux Estate. One of the earliest French estates established by land grants (1745 and 1763), this plantation still produces cocoa, citrus, bananas, coconut, and vegetables on 135 hilly acres. The restored 1864 plantation house is still in use as well. A 30-minute walking tour begins at the cocoa fermentary, where you can see the drying process. You then follow a trail through the cultivated area, where a guide points

out various fruit- or spice-bearing trees and tropical flowers. Additional trails lead to old military ruins, a religious shrine, and a vantage point for viewing the spectacular Pitons. Cool drinks and a creole buffet lunch are served at the Cocoa Pod restaurant. Souvenirs, including just-made chocolate sticks, are sold at the boutique. ⊠ *Vieux Fort Rd., Château Belair* ☎ *758/459–7545* ⊕ *www.fonddouxestate.com* 🖅 *$30, including lunch; free to resort guests* ⊙ *Daily 11–2.*

FAMILY **La Soufrière Drive-In Volcano.** As you approach the volcano, your nose will pick up the strong scent of sulfur from more than 20 belching pools of murky water, crusty sulfur deposits, and other multicolor minerals baking and steaming on the surface. Despite its name, you don't actually drive all the way in. Rather, you drive within a few hundred feet of the gurgling, steaming mass and then walk behind your guide—whose service is included in the admission price—around a fault in the substratum rock. It's a fascinating, educational half hour, though it can also be pretty stinky on a hot day. ⊠ *Soufrière* ☎ *758/459–7686* ⊕ *www. soufrierefoundation.org* 🖅 *$5* ⊙ *Daily 9–5.*

FAMILY **Morne Coubaril.** On the site of an 18th-century estate, a 250-acre land grant in 1713 by Louis XIV of France, the original plantation house has been rebuilt and a farm workers' village has been re-created. It does a good job of showing what life was like for both the owners (a single family owned the land until 1960) and those who did all the hard labor over the centuries producing cotton, coffee, sugarcane, and cocoa. Cocoa, coconuts, and manioc are still grown on the estate using traditional agricultural methods. On the 30-minute estate tour, guides show how coconuts are opened and roasted for use as oil and animal feed and how cocoa is fermented, dried, crushed by dancing on the beans, and finally formed into chocolate sticks. Manioc roots (also called cassava) are grated, squeezed of excess water, dried, and turned into flour used for baking. The grounds are lovely for walking or hiking, and the views of mountains and Soufrière Bay are spellbinding. More adventurous visitors will enjoy Soufrière Hotwire Rides, an hourlong zip-line excursion with eight stations, taking you by Petit Piton and through the adjacent rain forest. A large, open-air restaurant serves a creole buffet luncheon by reservation only. ⊠ *West Coast Rd., 2 miles (3 km) south of Soufrière, Soufrière* ☎ *758/459–7340, 758/712–5808 reservations* ⊕ *www.mornecoubarilestate.com, www.stluciaziplining.com* 🖅 *$10; with lunch $24; zip line $69; all 3 and transportation $99* ⊙ *Daily 8–5.*

VIEUX FORT AND THE EAST COAST

Although less developed for tourism than the island's north and west, the area around Vieux Fort and points north along the eastern coast are home to some of St. Lucia's unique ecosystems and interesting natural attractions.

WORTH NOTING

Barre de l'Isle Forest Reserve. St. Lucia is divided into eastern and western halves by Barre de l'Isle ridge. A mile-long (1½-km-long) trail cuts through the reserve, and four lookout points provide panoramic views. Visible in the distance are Mt. Gimie, immense green valleys, both the

Caribbean Sea and the Atlantic Ocean, and coastal communities. The trailhead is a half-hour drive from Castries. It takes about an hour to walk the trail—an easy hike—and another hour to climb Mt. LaCombe Ridge. Permission from the St. Lucia Forestry Department is required to access the trail in Barre de l'Isle; a naturalist or forest officer guide ($10) will accompany you. ⊠ *Micoud Hwy., Ravine Poisson ✛ Midway between Castries and Dennery* ☎ *758/468–5648 Forestry Dept.* ⊕ *forestryeeunit.blogspot.com* ✉ *$10 for the guide* ☉ *Daily by appointment only* ☞ *Call weekdays 8:30–4:30.*

Mamiku Gardens. One of St. Lucia's largest and loveliest botanical gardens surrounds the hilltop ruins of the Micoud Estate. Baron Micoud, an 18th-century colonel in the French army and governor-general of St. Lucia, deeded the land to his wife, Madame de Micoud, to avoid confiscation by the British during one of the many times when St. Lucia changed hands. Locals abbreviated her name to "Ma Micoud," which, over time, became Mamiku. (The estate did become a British military outpost in 1796, but shortly thereafter was burned to the ground by slaves during the Brigand's War.) The estate is now primarily a banana plantation, but the gardens themselves—including several secluded or "secret" gardens—are filled with tropical flowers and plants, delicate orchids, and fragrant herbs. ⊠ *Micoud Hwy., just north of Micoud, Praslin* ☎ *758/455–3729* ⊕ *www.mamikugardens.com* ✉ *$8, guided tour $10* ☉ *Daily 9–5* ☞ *Guided tours must be booked at least 3 days in advance.*

Maria Islands Nature Reserve. Two tiny islands in the Atlantic Ocean off St. Lucia's southeastern coast make up the reserve, which has its own interpretive center. The 25-acre Maria Major and the 4-acre Maria Minor are inhabited by two rare species of reptiles: the colorful Zandoli Terre ground lizard and the harmless Kouwes grass snake. They share their home with frigate birds, terns, doves, and other wildlife. There's a small beach for swimming and snorkeling, as well as an undisturbed forest, a vertical cliff covered with cacti, and a coral reef for snorkeling or diving. The St. Lucia National Trust offers tours, including a boat trip to the islands, by appointment only; bring your own picnic lunch, as there are no facilities. ⊠ *Vieux Fort* ☎ *758/454–5014 for tour reservations* ⊕ *www.slunatrust.org* ✉ *$35* ☉ *Aug.–mid-May, Wed.–Sun. 9:30–5 by appointment only.*

Vieux Fort. St. Lucia's second-largest town is also the location of Hewanorra International Airport. From the Moule à Chique Peninsula, the island's southernmost tip, you can see much of St. Lucia to the north and the island of St. Vincent 21 miles (34 km) to the south. This is where the waters of the clear Caribbean Sea blend with those of the deeper blue Atlantic Ocean. ⊠ *Vieux Fort.*

16

BEACHES

The sand on St. Lucia's beaches ranges from warm gold to silvery black, and the island has some of the best off-the-beach snorkeling in the Caribbean—especially along the western coast just north of Soufrière.

St. Lucia's longest, broadest, and most popular beaches are in the north, which is also the flattest part of this mountainous island and the location of most resorts, restaurants, and nightlife. Many of the island's biggest resorts front the beaches from Choc Bay to Rodney Bay and north to Cap Estate. Elsewhere, tiny coves with inviting crescents of sand offer great swimming and snorkeling opportunities. Beaches are all public, but hotels flank many along the northwestern coast. A few secluded stretches of beach on the southwestern coast, south of Marigot Bay and accessible primarily by boat, are popular swimming and snorkeling stops on catamaran day sails or powerboat sightseeing trips. Don't swim along the windward (eastern) coast, as the Atlantic Ocean is too rough—but the views are spectacular. At Coconut Bay Beach Resort, which has a beautiful beach facing the Atlantic at the southernmost tip of the island, the water is rough—but an artificial reef makes it safe for swimming and water sports, especially kitesurfing.

Anse Chastanet. In front of the resort of the same name and Jade Mountain, this palm-studded, dark-sand beach just north of Soufrière has a backdrop of green mountains, brightly painted fishing skiffs bobbing at anchor, calm waters for swimming, and some of the island's best reefs for snorkeling and diving right from shore. Anse Chastanet Resort's gazebos are among the palms; its dive shop, restaurant, and bar are on the beach and open to the public. The mile-long dirt road from Soufrière, though, is a challenge even for taxi drivers, given its usual (and colossal, by design) state of disrepair. **Amenities:** food and drink; parking (no fee); toilets; water sports. **Best for:** snorkeling; sunset; swimming. ⊠ *Anse Chastanet Rd., 1 mile (1½ km) north of Soufrière, Soufrière.*

Anse Cochon. This dark-sand beach in front of Ti Kaye Resort & Spa is accessible by boat or by jeep via Ti Kaye's mile-long, tire-crunching access road. The calm water and adjacent reefs, part of the National Marine Reserve, are superb for swimming, diving, and snorkeling. In fact, most catamaran cruises to Soufrière stop here for day-trippers to take a quick swim on the northbound leg. Moorings are free, and boaters and swimmers can enjoy refreshments at Ti Kaye's beach bar. Snorkeling equipment is available ($11) at the dive shop on the beach. **Amenities:** food and drink; toilets; water sports. **Best for:** snorkeling; swimming. ⊠ *Off West Coast Rd., 3 miles (5 km) south of Anse la Raye, Anse La Raye.*

Anse des Pitons (*Sugar Beach*). The white sand on this crescent beach, snuggled between the Pitons, was imported years ago and spread over the natural black sand. Accessible through the Sugar Beach, a Viceroy Resort, property or by boat, Anse des Pitons offers crystal-clear water for swimming, excellent snorkeling and diving, and breathtaking scenery—you're swimming right between the Pitons, after all. The underwater area here is protected as part of the National Marine Reserve. Neighboring resorts Ladera and Boucan provide shuttle service to the beach. **Amenities:** food and drink; toilets; water sports. **Best for:** snorkeling; sunset; swimming. ⊠ *Val des Pitons, 3 miles (5 km) south of Soufrière, Soufrière.*

Marigot Beach (*Labas Beach*). Calm waters rippled only by passing yachts lap a sliver of sand on the north side of Marigot Bay adjacent to the Marigot Beach Club & Dive Resort, across the bay from Capella at Marigot Bay, and a short walk from Mango Beach Inn. Studded with palm trees, the tiny but extremely picturesque beach is accessible by a ferry (EC$5 round-trip) that operates continually from one side of the bay to the other, with pickup at the Marina Village; you can find refreshments at adjacent restaurants. **Amenities:** food and drink; toilets; water sports. **Best for:** swimming. ⊠ *Marigot Bay.*

FAMILY **Pigeon Point.** This small beach within the national landmark, on the northwestern tip of St. Lucia, has golden sand, a calm sea, and a view that extends from Rodney Bay to Martinique. It's a perfect spot for picnicking, and you can take a break from the sun by visiting the nearby Museum and Interpretive Centre. **Amenities:** food and drink; toilets. **Best for:** snorkeling; solitude; swimming. ⊠ *Pigeon Island National Landmark, Pigeon Island* ⊠ *$7 park admission.*

FAMILY
Fodor's Choice
★
Reduit Beach. Many feel that Reduit (pronounced red-wee) is the island's finest beach. The long stretch of golden sand that frames Rodney Bay is within walking distance of many hotels and restaurants in Rodney Bay Village. Bay Gardens Beach Resort, Royal St. Lucia by Rex Resorts, and St. Lucian by Rex Resorts all face the beachfront; blu St. Lucia, Harmony Suites, and Ginger Lily hotels are across the road. At the Royal's water-sports center, you can rent sports equipment and beach chairs and take windsurfing or waterskiing lessons. Kids (and adults alike) love Splash Island Water Park, an open-water inflatable playground near Bay Gardens Beach Resort with a trampoline, climbing wall, monkey bars, swing, slide, and more. **Amenities:** food and drink; toilets; water sports. **Best for:** snorkeling; sunset; swimming; walking; windsurfing. ⊠ *Rodney Bay.*

Vigie/Malabar Beach. This 2-mile (3-km) stretch of lovely white sand runs parallel to the George F. L. Charles Airport runway in Castries and continues on past the Rendezvous resort, where it becomes Malabar Beach. In the area opposite the airport departure lounge, a few vendors sell refreshments. **Amenities:** food and drink. **Best for:** swimming. ⊠ *Adjacent to George F.L. Charles Airport runway, Castries.*

16

WHERE TO EAT

Bananas, mangoes, passion fruit, plantains, breadfruit, okra, avocados, limes, pumpkins, cucumbers, papaya, yams, christophenes (also called chayote), and coconuts are among the fresh fruits and vegetables that grace St. Lucian menus. The French influence is strong, and most chefs cook with a creole flair. Resort buffets and restaurant fare include standards like steaks, chops, pasta, and pizza—and every menu lists fresh fish along with the ever-popular lobster, which is available in season—August through March.

Soups and stews are traditionally prepared in a coal pot—unique to St. Lucia—a rustic clay casserole on a matching clay stand that holds the hot coals. Chicken and pork dishes and barbecues are also popular here.

As they do throughout the Caribbean, local vendors set up barbecues along the roadside, at street fairs, and at Friday-night "jump-ups" and do a bang-up business selling grilled fish or chicken legs, bakes (fried biscuits), and beer. You can get a full meal for less than $10.

Guests at St. Lucia's all-inclusive resorts take meals at hotel restaurants—which are generally quite good and in some cases exceptional—but it's fun when vacationing to try some of the local restaurants, as well, for lunch when sightseeing or for a special night out.

What to Wear: Dress on St. Lucia is casual but conservative. Shorts are usually fine during the day, but bathing suits and immodest clothing are frowned upon anywhere but at the beach. Nude or topless sunbathing is prohibited. In the evening, the mood is casually elegant; but even the fanciest places generally expect only a collared shirt and long pants for men and a sundress or slacks for women.

CASTRIES AND THE NORTH

$$$ SEAFOOD

🍴 **Buzz Seafood & Grill.** Opposite the Royal St. Lucia by Rex Resorts hotel and Reduit Beach, this dining spot is part of Rodney Bay's "restaurant central." Starting with cool drinks (maybe a Buzz cooler) and warm appetizers (perhaps lobster and crab cakes, stuffed portobello mushroom, or tempura shrimp) at the bar, diners make their way to the dining room or garden for some serious seafood or a good steak, baby back ribs, West Indian pepper-pot stew, spicy Moroccan-style lamb shanks, or simple chicken and chips. The seared yellowfin tuna, potato-crusted red snapper, and seafood creole are big hits, too. There's also a vegetarian menu. Fresh lobster is available in season (September–April). [$] *Average main: US$30* ✉ *Reduit Beach Ave., Rodney Bay* ☎ *758/458–0450* 🌐 *www.buzzstlucia.com* 🕒 *Closed Mon. No lunch* ✍ *Reservations essential.*

$$$$ ECLECTIC Fodor's Choice ★

🍴 **The Cliff at Cap.** High on top of a cliff at the northern tip of St. Lucia, the open-air dining room at Cap Maison welcomes diners to what Executive Chef Craig Jones calls "nouveau" French West Indian cuisine. True, he incorporates local vegetables, fruits, herbs, and spices with the best meats and fresh-caught seafood you'll find on the island; but the technique and presentation—and the service—lean more toward the French. In addition to the mouthwatering à la carte menu, there's a five-course, prix-fixe chef's table (tasting) menu ($89, $134 with course-matching wines) and a vegetarian menu. Lucky Cap Maison guests who choose a meal plan get to dine here daily, but nonguests make up about 40% of the dinner clientele. Day or night, this is one of the loveliest dining venues on St. Lucia. At lunch, the view on a clear day stretches to Martinique; in the evening, twinkling stars and waves crashing far below lend an air of romance. And daily wine tastings ($75–$100) and the Friday night "dine and wine" experience ($150) in Cellar Maison, which boasts more than 2,000 bottles, are quite special. [$] *Average main: US$36* ✉ *Cap Maison, Smuggler's Cove Dr., Cap Estate* ☎ *758/457–8681* 🌐 *www.thecliffatcap.com* ✍ *Reservations essential.*

$$$$
FRENCH
Fodor's Choice ★

🍴 **Coal Pot.** Popular since it opened in 1966, this tiny waterfront restaurant overlooks pretty Vigie Cove. For a light lunch, opt for a bowl of creamy pumpkin soup, Greek salad with chicken or shrimp, or broiled fresh fish. Dinner might start with a divine lobster bisque, followed by fresh seafood accompanied by one (or more) of the chef's fabulous sauces—ginger, coconut-curry, lemon-garlic butter, or wild mushroom. Heartier eaters may prefer duck, lamb, beef, or chicken laced with peppercorns, red wine, onion, or Roquefort sauce. [$] *Average main: US$32* ✉ *Vigie* ☎ *758/452–5566* 🌐 *www.coalpotrestaurant.com* 🕒 *Closed Sun. No lunch Sat.* ✍ *Reservations essential.*

$$$$
FRENCH
Fodor's Choice ★

🍴 **Jacques Waterfront Dining.** Chef-owner Jacky Rioux (aka Froggie Jacques) creates magical dishes in his waterfront restaurant overlooking Rodney Bay. The cooking is decidedly French, as is Rioux, but fresh produce and local spices create a memorable fusion cuisine. You might start with a bowl of Mediterranean fish soup, a grilled portobello mushroom, or tomato-and-basil tart. Main dishes include fresh-caught fish grilled with lime and olive oil, grilled rack of lamb, and breast of chicken stuffed with mushrooms and prosciutto in a Bordeaux wine reduction. The wine list is impressive. Coming by boat? You can tie up at the dinghy dock. [$] *Average main: US$32* ✉ *Reduit Beach Ave., end of road, Rodney Bay* ☎ *758/458–1900* 🌐 *www.jacquesrestaurant.com* ✍ *Reservations essential.*

$$$
CARIBBEAN

🍴 **KoKo Cabana Bistro & Bar.** Poolside at the Coco Palm hotel, this alfresco bistro and bar attracts mostly hotel guests for breakfast but a wider clientele for lunch or dinner—and happy hour. Lunch is a good bet if you're poking around Rodney Bay, need a break from Reduit Beach, or are just looking for a good meal in an attractive spot. The dinner menu focuses on Caribbean favorites such as jerk baby back ribs with guava barbecue sauce, perfectly grilled fish or steak with coconut curry sauce and local vegetables, a huge lamb shank, and always a pasta dish or two. For dessert, try the key lime pie or chocolate cake. A live band entertains most evenings and always at the Friday night Caribbean buffet. [$] *Average main: US$27* ✉ *Coco Palm, Rodney Bay* ☎ *758/456–2866, 877/655–2626 in the U.S.* 🌐 *www.coco-resorts.com* ✍ *Reservations essential.*

$$$$
SEAFOOD

🍴 **The Naked Fisherman Beach Bar & Grill.** The rather sophisticated beachside restaurant at Cap Maison is tucked into a cliff surrounding a crescent of sand at the northern tip of St. Lucia. During the day, match a glass (or bottle) of excellent wine to an arugula and apricot salad, crispy calamari, grilled island catch, Caribbean roti, or perfectly cooked Wagyu beef or fish burger with shoestring fries—sprinkled with parmigiano Reggiano, of course—while staring across the sea as far as Martinique. The atmosphere changes in the evening, when the surf gently laps the sand and candlelit lanterns grace the alfresco dining deck. The dinner menu is a little more substantial but still focuses on excellent seafood—barbecued prawns, grilled fish or lobster in season, chilled seafood platter—along with and "beef and reef" with twice-cooked potato chips. Desserts are mini but rich, which you'll appreciate when negotiating the 92 steps back to the road—and reality. [$] *Average main: US$35* ✉ *Cap Maison, Smugglers Cove Dr., Cap Estate* ✣ *On the* *beach, 92 steps down from (and back up to) the road* ☎ *758/457–8694* 🌐 *nakedfishermanstlucia.com* ⏲ *No dinner Sun.–Tues.*

$$$ CARIBBEAN Fodor's Choice ★ 🍴 **The Pink Plantation House.** A 140-year-old, pretty-in-pink, French Colonial plantation house is the setting for authentic French creole cuisine—the inspiration of local artist Michelle Elliott, whose ceramics and paintings are displayed for sale in a cozy room set up as a gift shop. Diners enjoy grilled fish, steak, rack of lamb, jumbo shrimp, or chicken breast matched with interesting homemade sauces and accompanied by steamed rice, fried plantains, sautéed vegetables, breadfruit/sweet potato balls, local peas, and christophene gratin. Alternatively, you can have a main-course salad or vegetarian dish. You'll really fell like you've been carried back to the 19th century. The three-story house, a labyrinth of rooms filled with antiques, is wrapped in a forest of tropical plants and trees. The service is friendly; the food is good; the atmosphere is, well, historic. **TIP→ Arrange taxi transportation, as it's really hard to find—particularly at night.** [$] *Average main: US$25* ✉ *Chef Harry Dr., Morne Fortune* ☎ *758/452–5422* ⏲ *No dinner Sun.* ✍ *Reservations essential.*

$$$$ ASIAN Fodor's Choice ★ 🍴 **Tao.** For a special evening, head for this Cap Estate restaurant on the premises of the Body Holiday resort. On a second-floor balcony at the edge of Cariblue Beach, you'll enjoy a pleasant breeze and a starry sky while you dine on fusion cuisine—mouthwatering Asian tastes with a Caribbean touch. Appetizers such as Thai-style coconut soup, rice paper vegetable rolls, or Peking duck pancakes can be followed by mahimahi marinated in sake, sesame seed-crusted chicken breast, or East 'n West (grilled strip steak and peppered shrimp). Fine wines accompany the meal, desserts are extravagant, and service is superb. Seating is limited and hotel guests have priority, so reserve early. [$] *Average main: US$35* ✉ *The Body Holiday, Cariblue Beach, Cap Estate* ☎ *758/457–7800* 🌐 *www.thebodyholiday.com* ⏲ *No lunch* ✍ *Reservations essential.*

MARIGOT BAY

$$ CAFÉ FAMILY 🍴 **Bayside Café/Baguet Shop.** Join the yachties and nearby hotel guests for breakfast, lunch, afternoon tea, an evening snack, or just dessert at this café in the Marina Village on Marigot Bay. Open all day every day, Bayside Café offers a full breakfast menu—along with freshly baked croissants and muffins, fruit and vegetable juices, and smoothies—from 7 to noon. From noon until 11 at night, enjoy a quick snack, soup and salad, sandwiches on freshly baked bread or a brioche roll, grilled fish or beef burgers, pizza, pasta, fish skewers, or grilled skirt steak. Iced coffee or tea—or a cup of espresso, cappuccino, or latte—goes well with dessert, perhaps coconut cheesecake or a banana split! Eat in (well, outside on the dock), get it to go, or select something quickly from the grab 'n go counter. [$] *Average main: US$14* ✉ *Marina Village, Marigot Bay* ☎ *758/458–5300* ✍ *Reservations not accepted.*

$$$ SEAFOOD FAMILY 🍴 **Chateau Mygo.** Walk down a garden path to Chateau Mygo (a colloquial corruption of "Marigot"), pick out a table on the deck, and soak up the waterfront atmosphere of what may be the Caribbean's prettiest bay. The tableau is mesmerizing—and that's at lunch, when you can order a sandwich, burger, roti, fish- or chicken-and-chips, salads, or

grilled fish or savory coconut chicken with peas and rice and vegetables. At dinner, chef Shaid Rambally—whose family has owned and operated this popular dockside restaurant since the mid-1970s—draws on three generations of East Indian and creole family recipes. Beautifully grilled fresh tuna, red snapper, kingfish, mahimahi, and local lobster are embellished with flavors such as ginger, mango, papaya, or passion fruit, and then dished up with regional vegetables—perhaps callaloo, okra, dasheen, breadfruit, christophene, or yams. You can also have roast pork, beef, a chicken dish, pizza, or sushi. This is a very casual restaurant with delicious, reasonably priced meals. And oh, that view! $ *Average main: US$22* ⊠ *Marigot Bay* ☎ *758/451–4772* ⊕ *www. chateaumygo.com.*

$$$
SEAFOOD
FAMILY

✕ **Doolittle's.** Named for the protagonist in the original (1967) *Dr. Doolittle* movie, part of which was filmed in Marigot Bay, this indoor-outdoor restaurant at Marigot Beach Club & Dive Resort is on the north side of the bay. You'll have a beautiful waterside view—watch yachts quietly slip by—as you enjoy your meal. The menu includes light meals such as sandwiches, burgers, grilled chicken, and salads at lunchtime, and in the evening, seafood, steak, chicken, and Caribbean specials such as curries and stews. Take the little ferry (complimentary for diners) across the bay to get here. During the day, bring your bathing suit; the beach is just outside. ■ TIP→ **In the evening, it's a great spot for drinks and entertainment.** $ *Average main: US$28* ⊠ *Marigot Beach Club & Dive Resort, Marigot Bay* ☎ *758/451–4974* ⊕ *www. marigotbeachclub.com.*

$$$$
CARIBBEAN
Fodor'sChoice
★

✕ **Rainforest Hideaway.** Enjoy high-end Caribbean tastes and flavors at this romantic and upscale hideaway on the north shore of pretty Marigot Bay. It's definitely worth the 20-minute-or-so drive from Castries. A little ferry (complimentary for diners) whisks you from the mainland to the alfresco restaurant, which is perched on a dock. Fresh local fish—including the ubiquitous (and foreign) lionfish that is the scourge of local waters but tastes delicious—and prime meats are enhanced by fresh herbs grown in the backyard garden, which is also the source of exotic local vegetables and fruits featured in various dishes. Entrées such as cardamom-and-sugarcane-infused duck breast with plum reduction, coconut-crusted sea bass with chipotle and coco relish, and grilled beef tenderloin with yam fries and vegetable gateaux are impressive. The menu is prix-fixe: $48 for two courses; $59 includes dessert. Dinner is accompanied by a blanket of stars overhead and live jazz on Monday, Wednesday, Thursday, and Saturday nights. $ *Average main: US$38* ⊠ *Marigot Bay* ☎ *758/286–0511* ⊕ *www. rainforesthideawaystlucia.com* ☾ *Closed Sun., Tues. June–Sept. No lunch* ☜ *Reservations essential.*

16

SOUFRIÈRE

$$$
INDIAN

✕ **Apsara.** India has had an important influence on the Caribbean islands, from the heritage of their people to the colorful madras plaids and the curry flavors that are a staple of Caribbean cuisine. At night, Anse Chastanet's Trou au Diable restaurant transforms into Apsara, an extraordinarily romantic, candlelit, beachfront dining experience with

Amazing views at Dasheene at Ladera

modern Indian cuisine. The innovative menu, mixing East Indian and Caribbean cooking, produces food that's full of flavor but not too spicy, although you can opt for some hotter dishes. Tangy crab and potato cakes with sweet yogurt or local vegetable samosas might be followed by tamarind-roasted duck breast, pickled goat vindaloo, or tandoori-roasted salmon, lamb, chicken, or lobster. Definitely order the naan, either plain or flavored with almond, coconut, or raisin. For dessert, choose the mango, saffron, or sea moss *kulfi* (Indian-style ice cream) or go all the way with Apsara's Temptation (tandoori-baked pineapple with honey, saffron, and passion-fruit syrup, kulfi, and sun-blushed chili). $\boxed{S}$ *Average main: US$28 ⊠ Anse Chastanet, Old French Rd., Soufrière ☎ 758/459–7354 ⊕ www.ansechastanet.com ☉ Closed Tues. No lunch ⌂ Reservations essential.*

$$$$
CARIBBEAN
✕ **Boucan.** Aah . . . chocolate! Here on the Rabot Estate, a working cocoa plantation, that heavenly flavor is infused into just about every dish—cacao gazpacho or citrus salad with white chocolate dressing for starters. The main course might be red snapper roasted in cacao butter, rib-eye steak "matured and infused" with cacao nibs, cacao- and herb-encrusted pork medallions, or local dorado fillet with a port wine and cacao sauce. You get the picture. Dessert, of course, is the grand chocolate finale: cacao crème brûlée, meringue floating in a sea of chocolate crème anglaise, dark chocolate mousse, even cacao sorbet. Yum. $\boxed{S}$ *Average main: US$32 ⊠ Boucan by Hotel Chocolat, Rabot Estate, West Coast Rd., 3 miles (5 km) south of Soufrière, Soufrière ☎ 758/572–9600 ⊕ www.hotelchocolat.com ⌂ Reservations essential.*

$$$
CARIBBEAN
Fodor's Choice
★

✕**Dasheene at Ladera.** The terrace restaurant at Ladera resort has breathtaking, close-up views of the Pitons and the sea between them, especially beautiful at sunset. The ambience is casual by day and magical at night. Appetizers may include silky sweet-potato-and-coconut soup or Caribbean lamb salad. Typical entrées are "fisherman's catch" with a choice of flavored butters or sauces, shrimp Dasheene (panfried with local herbs), grilled rack of lamb with coconut risotto and curry sauce, or pan-seared fillet of beef marinated in a lime-and-pepper seasoning. Light dishes, pasta dishes, and fresh salads are also served at lunch—along with that million-dollar view. $ *Average main: US$30* ⊠ *Ladera, 2 miles (3 km) south of Soufrière, Soufrière* ☎ *758/459–6623* ⊕ *www. ladera.com* ⌚ *Reservations essential.*

$$
CARIBBEAN

✕**The Hummingbird.** The cheerful restaurant-bar in the Hummingbird Beach Resort specializes in French creole cuisine, starting with fresh seafood or chicken seasoned with local herbs and accompanied by fresh-picked vegetables from the Hummingbird's garden. Sandwiches on homemade bread and salads are also available. At lunch, sit outside by the pool for a magnificent view of the Pitons (you're welcome to take a dip). Wednesday night is Creole night, with live entertainment, dancing, and special dishes. $ *Average main: US$20* ⊠ *Hummingbird Beach Resort, Anse Chastanet Rd., Soufrière* ☎ *758/459–7985* ⊕ *www. hummingbirdbeachresort.com.*

$$$
CARIBBEAN
FAMILY

✕**Jardin Cacao at Fond Doux Estate.** The small, rustic restaurant at Fond Doux Estate—a working plantation—is one of the most popular spots to enjoy a creole lunch when touring the natural sights in and around Soufrière. Help yourself to the buffet, containing stewed chicken, grilled fish, rice and beans, macaroni and cheese, caramelized plantains, figs (green bananas), breadfruit balls, purple yams, salad, and more. Nearly all ingredients are locally sourced. Wash it all down with a rum punch or local fruit juice, and finish with something sweet such as coconut or banana cake. Dinner, by candlelight, is à la carte: a choice of seafood, chicken, beef, and pasta dishes with a local twist—pepper pot, for example. Most people who come for lunch also take a short tour and learn about how the cacao growing on the plantation is turned into delicious chocolate. You can buy chocolate in the gift shop to take home. $ *Average main: US$25* ⊠ *Fond Doux Holiday Plantation, Château Belair* ☎ *758/459–7545* ⊕ *www.fonddouxestate.com* ⌚ *Reservations essential.*

$$$$
CARIBBEAN

✕**Orlando's.** British-born of Jamaican/Barbadian heritage, chef Orlando Sachell is a man on a mission. He opened his restaurant in downtown Soufrière to present his "Share the Love" (or STL) style of cooking, which focuses on Caribbean cuisine. Orlando supports local farmers and fishers by using only locally grown organic produce, local meats, and freshly caught fish in his delicious—and world-class—dishes. Dinner offers a choice of two varying five-course menus—starting with soup (pumpkin is *the* best!) and salad, then a fish dish followed by beef or chicken, and ultimately dessert. Portions are small, but the flavors and richness of the food make it perfectly filling. And if there's something on the menu that doesn't appeal to you or can't eat, Chef Orlando is very accommodating. $ *Average main: US$32* ⊠ *Cemetery Rd., Soufrière*

16

Sandals Grande St. Lucian Spa & Beach Resort

☎ 758/459–5955 ⊕ *www.orlandosrestaurantstl.com* ⊘ *Closed Mon. and Tues.* ⚓ *Reservations essential.*

$$ ✕ **The Still.** When you're visiting Diamond Falls and other Soufrière
CARIBBEAN attractions, this makes a convenient (buffet) lunch spot. Located on
FAMILY a 400-acre working plantation just outside of town, the two dining
rooms here seat up to 400 people, so it's also a popular stop for tour
groups and cruise passengers. The emphasis is on local cuisine, using
vegetables such as christophene, breadfruit, yam, and callaloo along
with grilled fish or chicken; there are also pork and beef dishes. All of
the fruits and vegetables are organically grown on the estate. $ *Average main: US$20* ✉ *The Still Plantation, La Perle Estate, Soufrière*
☎ 758/459–7224 ⊕ *www.thestillplantation.com* ⊘ *No dinner.*

WHERE TO STAY

Most people—particularly honeymooners—stay in grand beach resorts,
most of which are upscale and pricey. Several are all-inclusive, including
three Sandals resorts, two resorts owned or managed by Sunswept (The
Body Holiday and Rendezvous), St. James's Club Morgan Bay, and East
Winds Inn. Smaller and less expensive, St. Lucia's dozens of small inns
and hotels are primarily locally owned and frequently quite charming.
They may or may not be directly on the beach. Luxury villa communi-
ties and independent private villas are other alternatives. Most of the
villa communities are in the north near Cap Estate.

PRIVATE VILLAS AND CONDOS

Luxury villa and condo communities can be an economical option for families, couples vacationing together, and other groups. Villa units are privately owned, but nonowners can rent from property managers for short-term stays, much like reserving hotel accommodations.

Rental villas are staffed with a housekeeper and cook who specializes in local cooking; in some cases, a caretaker lives on the property and a gardener and night watchman are on staff. All properties have telephones, and some have Internet access. Telephones may be barred against outgoing overseas calls; plan to use a phone card, calling card, or your own cell phone. Most villas have TVs, DVDs, and CD players. All private villas have a swimming pool; condos share a community pool. Vehicles are generally not included in the rates, but rental cars can be arranged and delivered to the villa upon request. Linens and basic supplies (such as bath soap, toilet tissue, and dish-washing detergent) are included. Pre-arrival grocery stocking can be arranged.

Units with one to nine bedrooms and the same number of baths run $250 to $3,500 per night, depending on the size of the villa, the amenities, the number of guests, and the season. Rates include utilities and government taxes. Your only additional cost will be for groceries and staff gratuities. A security deposit is required upon booking and refunded after departure less any damages or unpaid miscellaneous charges.

RENTAL CONTACTS

Discover Villas of St. Lucia. ⊠ *Cap Estate* ☎ *758/484–3066, 758/450–0002* ⊕ *www.a1stluciavillas.com.*

Tropical Villas. ⊠ *Cap Estate* ☎ *758/450–8240* ⊕ *www.tropicalvillas.net.*

CASTRIES AND THE NORTH

$ • RESORT • FAMILY • Fodor's Choice ★ **Bay Gardens Beach Resort & Spa.** One of three Bay Gardens properties in Rodney Bay Village, this family-friendly resort has a prime location on beautiful Reduit Beach. **Pros:** on St. Lucia's best beach; Splash Island Water Park; excellent value; complimentary Wi-Fi. **Cons:** very popular, so book ahead in season. $ *Rooms from: US$204* ⊠ *Reduit Beach Ave., Rodney Bay* ☎ *758/457–8006, 877/620–3200 in U.S.* ⊕ *www. baygardensbeachresort.com* ⊃ *36 rooms, 36 suites* ❏ *Some meals.*

$ • HOTEL **Bay Gardens Hotel.** Independent travelers and regional businesspeople swear by this cheerful, well-run boutique hotel in Rodney Bay Village. **Pros:** terrific value; Croton suites are best bet; complimentary Wi-Fi. **Cons:** not beachfront, although there's a beach shuttle; heavy focus on business travelers. $ *Rooms from: US$130* ⊠ *Castries–Gros Islet Hwy., Rodney Bay* ☎ *758/457–8010, 877/620–3200* ⊕ *www.baygardenshotel. com* ⊃ *59 rooms, 28 suites* ❏ *No meals.*

$$ • RESORT • FAMILY **blu St. Lucia.** Singles, couples, families, and business travelers all find this a good base in Rodney Bay Village—right across from Reduit Beach—and a reasonably priced one, too. **Pros:** excellent location; a peaceful refuge close to the Rodney Bay restaurants and action; complimentary Wi-Fi. **Cons:** not beachfront, although pretty close; bathrooms have showers only. $ *Rooms from: US$367* ⊠ *Reduit Beach*

Ave., Rodney Bay ☎ *758/456–9800, 877/502–2022 in U.S.* 🌐 *www.harlequinblu.com* 🛏 *72 rooms* 🍴 *Breakfast.*

$$$$ RESORT Fodor's Choice ★ 🏨 **The Body Holiday.** At this adults-only spa resort on picturesque Cariblue Beach—where daily treatments are included in the rates—you can customize your own "body holiday" online even before you leave home. **Pros:** daily spa treatments included; excellent dining; interesting activities, such as archery, include free instruction; special rates for solo travelers. **Cons:** expensive; no room TVs; small bathrooms; lots of steps to the spa, though you can get a ride. [$] *Rooms from: US$1050* ✉ *Cariblue Beach, Cap Estate* ☎ *758/457–7800, 800/544–2883* 🌐 *www.thebodyholiday.com* 🛏 *152 rooms, 3 suites* 🍴 *All-inclusive.*

$$$$ RESORT Fodor's Choice ★ 🏨 **Calabash Cove Resort & Spa.** The luxurious suites and Balinese-inspired cottages at this inviting boutique resort spill gently down a tropical hillside to a secluded beach on Bonaire Bay, just south of Rodney Bay. **Pros:** stylish, sophisticated, and friendly atmosphere; great food; wedding parties can reserve the entire resort. **Cons:** the long, bone-crunching dirt road at the entrance; steps to the cottages and beach may be difficult for those with physical challenges. [$] *Rooms from: US$868* ✉ *Bonaire Estate, Off Castries–Gros Islet Hwy., south of Rodney Bay, Marisule Estate* ☎ *758/456–3500, 800/917–2683 in U.S.* 🌐 *www.calabashcove.com* 🛏 *17 suites, 9 cottages* 🍴 *Breakfast.*

$$$$ RESORT FAMILY Fodor's Choice ★ 🏨 **Cap Maison.** Prepare to be spoiled by the doting staffers at this intimate villa resort—the luxurious service includes unpacking (if you wish) and a personal butler for any little needs that arise. **Pros:** private and elegant; outstanding service; rooftop plunge pools; cocktails with a view at Cliff Bar or surf side at Rock Maison. **Cons:** air-conditioning in bedrooms only; 92 steps to the beach. [$] *Rooms from: US$716* ✉ *Smuggler's Cove Dr., Cap Estate* ☎ *758/457–8670, 888/765–4985 in U.S.* 🌐 *www.capmaison.com* 🛏 *10 rooms, 39 suites in 22 villas* 🍴 *Some meals.*

$ HOTEL FAMILY 🏨 **Coco Palm.** This popular hotel in Rodney Bay Village overlooks an inviting pool and a separate cozy guesthouse, Kreole Village, at the edge of the property. **Pros:** excellent value; love those swim-up rooms; complimentary Wi-Fi. **Cons:** not directly on the beach; skip the all-inclusive package, as good restaurants are nearby; nightly entertainment can be loud (until 10). [$] *Rooms from: US$132* ✉ *Rodney Bay* ☎ *758/456–2800, 877/655–2626 in U.S.* 🌐 *www.coco-resorts.com* 🛏 *91 rooms, 12 suites* 🍴 *Some meals.*

$$$$ RESORT 🏨 **East Winds Inn.** Guests keep returning to this small all-inclusive resort on a secluded beach halfway between Castries and Rodney Bay, where 7 acres of botanical gardens surround 13 duplex gingerbread-style cottages, three ocean-view rooms, and a suite. **Pros:** lovely beach; excellent dining; peaceful and quiet. **Cons:** not best choice for families, though children welcome; very expensive; six-night minimum. [$] *Rooms from: US$935* ✉ *La Brelotte Bay, Gros Islet* ☎ *758/452–8212* 🌐 *www.eastwinds.com* 🛏 *30 suites* 🍴 *All-inclusive.*

$$$$ RESORT FAMILY 🏨 **The Landings.** On 19 acres along the Pigeon Point Causeway at the northern edge of Rodney Bay, this villa resort surrounds a private, 80-slip harbor where residents can dock their own yachts, literally, at their doorstep. **Pros:** spacious, beautifully appointed units; perfect for yachties, couples, families, even business travelers; personal chef service; kids' club and playground. **Cons:** condo atmosphere; little hike

to beach from some rooms. 🟡 *Rooms from: US$585* ✉ *Pigeon Island Causeway, Gros Islet* ☎ 758/458–7300, 866/252–0689 in U.S. ⊕ *www. landingsstlucia.com* ⤳ *80 units* ⎪◯⎪ *Breakfast.*

$$$$
RESORT

📶 **Rendezvous.** Romance is alive and well at this easygoing, all-inclusive, boutique resort (for couples only) that stretches along the dreamy white sand of Malabar Beach at the end of the George F.L. Charles Airport runway. **Pros:** convenient to Castries and Vigie Airport; romance in the air; popular wedding venue. **Cons:** no room TVs; occasional flyover noise. 🟡 *Rooms from: US$872* ✉ *Malabar Beach, Vigie* ☎ 758/457–7900, 800/544–2883 in U.S. ⊕ *www.theromanticholiday.com* ⤳ *57 rooms, 35 suites, 8 cottages* ⎪◯⎪ *All-inclusive.*

$$$$
RESORT
FAMILY

📶 **Royal St. Lucia by Rex Resorts.** This luxurious all-suites resort on St. Lucia's best beach caters to every whim—for the whole family. **Pros:** great beachfront; family-friendly; convenient to restaurants, clubs, and shops; two suites equipped for disabled guests. **Cons:** don't expect all-day dining—get snacks at the nearby supermarket. 🟡 *Rooms from: US$691* ✉ *Reduit Beach Ave., Rodney Bay* ☎ 758/452–8351, 305/471–6170 ⊕ *www.rexcaribbean.com* ⤳ *96 suites* ⎪◯⎪ *No meals.*

$$$$
RESORT
FAMILY

📶 **St. James's Club Morgan Bay.** Singles, couples, and families enjoy tons of sports and activities at this all-inclusive resort on 22 secluded acres surrounding a stretch of white-sand beach. **Pros:** six restaurants, six bars, four pools, four tennis courts, and more; children's club with organized activities; free waterskiing, sailing, and tennis lessons; great waterside dining evenings at Morgan's Pier. **Cons:** huge resort can be very busy, especially when full; relatively small beach given resort's size; Wi-Fi only in some rooms and for a fee. 🟡 *Rooms from: US$720* ✉ *Choc Bay, Choc* ☎ 758/450–2511, 866/830–1617 ⊕ *www.morganbayresort.com* ⤳ *235 rooms, 100 suites* ⎪◯⎪ *All-inclusive.*

16

$$$$
RESORT

📶 **Sandals Grande St. Lucian Spa & Beach Resort.** Couples—particularly young honeymooners and those getting married here—love this busy, busy, busy resort, the biggest and splashiest of the three St. Lucia Sandals properties. **Pros:** excellent beach, over-the-water hammocks; 12 restaurants, countless activities; free scuba for certified divers; service with a smile. **Cons:** really long ride (at least 90 minutes) to Hewanorra, but transfers are complimentary; beach can be crowded. 🟡 *Rooms from: US$1468* ✉ *Pigeon Island Causeway, Pigeon Island* ☎ 758/455–2000 ⊕ *www.sandals.com* ⤳ *272 rooms, 29 suites* ⎪◯⎪ *All-inclusive.*

$$$$
RESORT

📶 **Sandals Halcyon Beach Resort & Spa.** This is the most intimate and low-key of the three Sandals resorts on St. Lucia; like the others, it's beachfront, all-inclusive, for couples only, and loaded with amenities and activities. **Pros:** all the Sandals amenities in a more intimate setting; lots of dining and activity choices; exchange privileges (including golf) at other Sandals properties. **Cons:** it's Sandals, so it's a theme property that's not for everyone; it's small, so book well in advance. 🟡 *Rooms from: US$1162* ✉ *Choc Bay, Choc* ☎ 758/453–0222, 888/726–3257 ⊕ *www.sandals.com* ⤳ *169 rooms* ⎪◯⎪ *All-inclusive.*

$$$$
RESORT

📶 **Sandals Regency La Toc Golf Resort & Spa.** The second-largest of the three Sandals, this resort distinguishes itself with a 9-hole golf course (for guests only); like the others, though, this Sandals is all-inclusive and for couples only. **Pros:** lots to do; picturesque; on-site golf; complimentary airport

Sandals Halcyon Beach, Kelly's Dockside Seaside Bar & Grill

shuttle. **Cons:** somewhat isolated; expert golfers will prefer the St. Lucia Golf & Country Club. [$] *Rooms from: US$1184* ✉ *La Toc Rd., Castries* ☎ *758/452–3081, 888/726–3257* 🌐 *www.sandals.com* ⛳ *9-hole course on the property* 🛏 *212 rooms, 116 suites* 🍴 *All-inclusive.*

$ RENTAL **Villa Beach Cottages.** Tidy housekeeping cottages with gingerbread-laced facades are steps from the beach at this family-run establishment 3 miles (5 km) north of the airport in Castries. **Pros:** on the beach; beautiful sunsets; peaceful and quiet. **Cons:** close quarters; rent a car, as you'll go out for meals (or groceries). [$] *Rooms from: US$245* ✉ *John Compton Hwy., Choc* ☎ *758/450–2884, 866/542–1991 in U.S.* 🌐 *www.villabeachcottages.com* 🛏 *20 units* 🍴 *No meals.*

$$ RESORT FAMILY **Windjammer Landing Villa Beach Resort.** Mediterranean-style villas—which are as appropriate for a family or group vacation as for a romantic getaway—climb the hillside on one of St. Lucia's prettiest bays. **Pros:** lovely, spacious units; beautiful sunset views; family-friendly; in-unit dining. **Cons:** far from main road, so you'll need a car if you plan to leave the property often. [$] *Rooms from: US$308* ✉ *Trouya Point Rd., La Brellotte Bay, Bois d'Orange* ☎ *758/456–9000, 877/522–0722 in the U.S.* 🌐 *www.windjammer-landing.com* 🛏 *331 units* 🍴 *Some meals.*

MARIGOT BAY

$$$$ RESORT FAMILY Fodor's Choice ★ **Capella Marigot Bay.** Five miles (8 km) south of Castries, this ultra-chic—yet laid-back—villa resort climbs the hillside overlooking what author James Michener called "the most beautiful bay in the Caribbean." **Pros:** personalized service; stunning bay view; oversize villa accommodations; ground-level units good for those with difficulty

negotiating stairs; complimentary hourly treats at the pool. **Cons:** car recommended to explore beyond Marigot Bay; nearby beach is tiny, so head to Anse Cochon (complimentary transfers). [$] *Rooms from: US$550* ✉ *Marigot Bay* ✣ *South side of the bay, overlooking the marina* ☎ *758/458–5300, 877/384–8037 in U.S.* 🌐 *www.capellahotelgroup.com* 🛏 *67 rooms, 57 suites* 🍴 *Breakfast.*

$ RESORT 🏨 **Marigot Beach Club & Dive Resort.** Divers love this place, and everyone loves the location facing the little palm-studded beach at Marigot Bay. **Pros:** great value for divers; beautiful views of Marigot Bay; good casual dining; deeply discounted rates off-season. **Cons:** beach is tiny (though inviting). [$] *Rooms from: US$217* ✉ *Marigot Bay* ☎ *758/451–4974* 🌐 *www.marigotbeachclub.com* 🛏 *35 rooms, 1 two-bedroom apartment* 🍴 *Some meals.*

SOUFRIÈRE AND THE SOUTHWEST COAST

$$$$ RESORT 🏨 **Anse Chastanet Resort.** Spectacular, individually designed rooms—some with fourth walls open to the stunning Pitons view—peek out of the thick rain forest that cascades down a steep hillside to the beach. **Pros:** great location for divers; the open-wall Piton views. **Cons:** no pool; entrance road is annoying even in a 4WD vehicle; steep hillside not conducive to strolling or to guests with walking or cardiac issues; no in-room TVs, phones, or air-conditioning. [$] *Rooms from: US$575* ✉ *Anse Chastanet Rd., Soufrière* ☎ *758/459–7000, 800/223–1108 in U.S.* 🌐 *www.ansechastanet.com* 🛏 *49 rooms* 🍴 *No meals.*

$$$$ HOTEL Fodor's Choice ★ 🏨 **Boucan by Hotel Chocolat.** Anyone who loves chocolate will love this themed boutique hotel just south of Soufrière and within shouting distance of the Pitons. **Pros:** small and sophisticated; chocolate lover's dream; self-guided trail walks throughout the estate; cocoa tours; daily beach shuttle service. **Cons:** no air-conditioning, but naturally breezy; no TV, but a preloaded iPod and free Wi-Fi; no children under 12; car advised; not for anyone allergic to or less than thrilled by chocolate. [$] *Rooms from: US$495* ✉ *Rabot Estate, West Coast Rd., 2 miles (3 km) south of Soufrière, Soufrière* ☎ *758/572–9600* 🌐 *www.thehotelchocolat.com* 🛏 *14 rooms* 🍴 *Breakfast.*

$$ RESORT FAMILY Fodor's Choice ★ 🏨 **Fond Doux Plantation & Resort.** Here at one of Soufrière's most active agricultural plantations, nine historic homes salvaged from all around the island have been rebuilt on the 135-acre estate and refurbished as guest accommodations. **Pros:** an exotic, eco-friendly experience; striking location on an 18th-century plantation; quiet and secluded, "far from the madding crowd". **Cons:** no air-conditioning; no TV; a car is advised, as beach and local sights are a few miles away; not all cottages have a kitchen. [$] *Rooms from: US$300* ✉ *Fond Doux Estate, 4 miles (7 km) south of Soufrière, Soufrière* ☎ *758/459–7545* 🌐 *www.fonddouxestate.com* 🛏 *9 cottages, 6 suites* 🍴 *Some meals.*

$ B&B/INN 🏨 **Hummingbird Beach Resort.** Unpretentious and welcoming, this delightful little inn on Soufrière Harbour has simply furnished rooms—a traditional motif emphasized by four-poster beds and African wood sculptures—in small seaside cabins. **Pros:** local island hospitality; small and quiet; small beach; good food. **Cons:** few resort amenities—but that's part of the charm; most rooms have no air-conditioning.

Jade Mountain

[$] *Rooms from: US$100* ✉ *Anse Chastanet Rd., Soufrière* ☎ *758/459–7985* 🌐 *www.hummingbirdbeachresort.com* 🛏 *9 rooms, 2 with shared bath; 1 suite; 1 cottage* 🍴 *Some meals.*

$$$$ RESORT Fodor's Choice ★ 🏨 **Jade Mountain.** This premium-class, premium-priced, adults-only hotel is an architectural wonder perched on a picturesque mountainside overlooking the Pitons and the Caribbean. **Pros:** amazing accommodations; huge in-room pools; incredible Pitons view from every "sanctuary". **Cons:** sky-high rates; no air-conditioning (except in one "sky suite"); not a good choice for anyone with disabilities. [$] *Rooms from: US$1415* ✉ *Anse Chastanet, Anse Chastanet Rd., Soufrière* ☎ *758/459–4000* 🌐 *www.jademountainstlucia.com* 🛏 *28 rooms* 🍴 *No meals.*

$$$$ B&B/INN Fodor's Choice ★ 🏨 **Ladera.** The elegantly rustic Ladera, perched 1,100 feet above the sea directly between the two Pitons, is one of the most sophisticated small inns in the Caribbean but, at the same time, takes a local, eco-friendly approach to furnishings, food, and service. **Pros:** local flavor and style; breathtaking Pitons vista; private plunge pools; excellent cuisine; complimentary Wi-Fi. **Cons:** expensive; communal infinity pool is small; open fourth walls and steep drops make this the wrong place for people with disabilities; no air-conditioning (but breezy, so no real need); car suggested. [$] *Rooms from: US$995* ✉ *Rabot Estate, Soufrière–Vieux Fort Hwy., 3 miles (5 km) south of town, Soufrière* ☎ *758/459–6600, 866/290–0978 in the U.S.* 🌐 *www.ladera.com* ⏲ *Closed Sept.* 🛏 *32 suites* 🍴 *Some meals.*

$ B&B/INN FAMILY 🏨 **La Haut Plantation.** It's all about the view—the Pitons, of course—and the appeal of staying in an intimate and affordable family-run inn. **Pros:** lovely for weddings and honeymoons but also for families; stunning

Piton views; complimentary fresh fruit daily. **Cons:** no air-conditioning in some rooms; spotty Wi-Fi access; vehicle recommended. $ *Rooms from: US$260* ✉ *West Coast Rd., just north of Soufrière, Soufrière* ☎ *758/459–7008, 866/773–4321 in the U.S.* ⊕ *www.lahaut.com* ↪ *17 rooms* ⏐○⏐ *No meals.*

$$$
RESORT
⚏ **Stonefield Estate Resort.** The 18th-century plantation house and several gingerbread-style cottages that dot this 26-acre family-owned estate, a former lime and cocoa plantation that spills down a tropical hillside, afford eye-popping views of Petit Piton. **Pros:** very private, very quiet, very natural setting; beautiful pool; great sunset views from villa decks; lovely wedding venue. **Cons:** car is recommended; fitness facility could use air-conditioning; no room TVs. $ *Rooms from: US$400* ✉ *West Coast Rd., 1 mile (1½ km) south of Soufrière, Soufrière* ☎ *758/459–7037, 800/420–5731 in U.S.* ⊕ *www.stonefieldresort.com* ↪ *16 villas* ⏐○⏐ *Breakfast.*

$$$$
RESORT
FAMILY
Fodor'sChoice
★
⚏ **Sugar Beach, A Viceroy Resort.** Located in Val des Pitons, the steep valley between the Pitons and the most dramatic 192 acres in St. Lucia, magnificent private villas are tucked into the dense tropical foliage that covers the hillside and reaches down to the sea. **Pros:** exquisite accommodations, scenery, service, and amenities; huge infinity pool; complimentary Wi-Fi and use of iPad during stay; amazing location, beautiful grounds. **Cons:** very expensive; fairly isolated, so a meal plan makes sense; car advised. $ *Rooms from: US$855* ✉ *Val des Pitons, 2 miles (3 km) south of town, Soufrière* ☎ *800/235–4300 in U.S., 758/456–8000* ⊕ *www.viceroyhotelsandresorts.com/sugarbeach* ↪ *11 rooms, 59 villas, 8 bungalows* ⏐○⏐ *Some meals.*

$$$
RESORT
Fodor'sChoice
★
⚏ **Ti Kaye Resort & Spa.** Rustic elegance is not an oxymoron at this upscale cottage community that spills down a hillside above fabulous Anse Cochon beach. **Pros:** great for a wedding, honeymoon, or getaway; garden showers; good restaurant; excellent snorkeling; on-site dive shop. **Cons:** far from anywhere; long, bumpy dirt access road; all those steps to the beach; not for those with physical challenges; no kids under 12. $ *Rooms from: US$420* ✉ *Off the West Coast Rd., halfway between Anse la Raye and Canaries, Anse La Raye* ☎ *758/456–8101* ⊕ *www.tikaye.com* ↪ *33 rooms* ⏐○⏐ *Some meals.*

VIEUX FORT

$$$$
RESORT
FAMILY
⚏ **Coconut Bay Beach Resort & Spa.** The only resort in Vieux Fort, Coconut Bay is a sprawling (85 acres), family-friendly, seaside retreat minutes from Hewanorra International Airport. **Pros:** great for families or couples; excellent kitesurfing; friendly and sociable atmosphere. **Cons:** bathrooms have showers only; rough surf beyond the reef. $ *Rooms from: US$689* ✉ *Eau Piquant, Vieux Fort* ☎ *758/459–6000, 877/352–8898 in U.S.* ⊕ *www.cbayresort.com* ↪ *223 rooms, 27 suites* ⏐○⏐ *All-inclusive.*

16

NIGHTLIFE AND PERFORMING ARTS

NIGHTLIFE

Most resort hotels have entertainment—island music, calypso singers, or steel bands, as well as disco, karaoke, or staff/guest talent shows—every night in high season and a night or two each week in the off-season. Otherwise, Rodney Bay Village is the best bet for nightlife. The many restaurants and bars there attract a crowd nearly every night.

BARS

Doolittle's. The music changes nightly, a mix of calypso, soul, salsa, steel band, reggae, limbo, and other dance music; live band on Saturday nights. ⊠ *Marigot Beach Club & Dive Resort, Marigot Bay* ☎ *758/451–4974* ⊕ *www.marigotbeachclub.com.*

Jambe de Bois. Enjoy live jazz on weekend evenings at this cozy Old English–style pub within the Pigeon Island National Landmark. ⊠ *Pigeon Island National Landmark, Pigeon Island* ☎ *758/450–8166.*

CASINOS

Treasure Bay Casino. St. Lucia's first (and only, so far) casino has more than 250 slot machines, 22 gaming tables (poker, blackjack, roulette, and craps), and a sports bar with 28 screens. ⊠ *Baywalk Mall, Reduit Beach Ave., just off Castries–Gros Islet Hwy., Rodney Bay* ☎ *758/459–2901* ⊕ *www.treasurebaystlucia.com.*

DANCE CLUBS

Most dance clubs with live bands have a cover charge of $10–$20 (EC$25–EC$50), and the music usually starts at 11 pm.

Verve. Considered the "hottest" party spot in Rodney Bay Village; dance to the DJ's "awesome vibes" (and sometimes live bands) every night until 2 am (or later). ⊠ *Reduit Beach Ave., Rodney Bay* ☎ *758/450–1934.*

STREET PARTIES

FAMILY **Anse la Raye Seafood Friday.** For a taste of St. Lucian village life, head for this street festival, held every Friday night beginning at 6:30. The main street in this tiny fishing village—about halfway between Castries and Soufrière—is closed to vehicles, and residents prepare what they know best: fish cakes, grilled or stewed fish, hot bakes (biscuits), roasted corn, boiled crayfish, and lobster (grilled before your eyes). Prices range from a few cents for a fish cake or bake to $10 or $15 for a whole lobster. Walk around, eat, chat with locals, and listen to live music until the wee hours. ⊠ *Main St., off West Coast Rd., Anse La Raye.*

Fodor'sChoice **Gros Islet Jump-Up.** The island's largest street party is a Friday-night
★ ritual. Huge speakers set up on the street blast Caribbean music all night long. Sometimes there are live bands. When you take a break from dancing, you can buy barbecue fish or chicken, rotis, beer, and soda from villagers who set up grills along the roadside. It's the ultimate "lime" experience. ⊠ *Dauphin St., off Castries–Gros Islet Hwy., Gros Islet.*

PERFORMING ARTS

Fodor's Choice ★ **St. Lucia Jazz & Arts Festival.** This 10-day music festival, which has been held in early May for more than 25 years, is one of the premier events in the Caribbean. International jazz greats perform at outdoor venues on Pigeon Island and at hotels, restaurants, and nightspots throughout St. Lucia; free concerts are also held at Derek Walcott Square in downtown Castries. ⊠ *Pigeon Island* ⊕ *www.stluciajazz.org.*

SHOPPING

The island's best-known products are artwork and wood carvings, straw mats, clay pottery, and clothing and household articles made from batik and silk-screened fabrics that are designed and produced in island workshops. You can also take home straw hats and baskets and locally grown cocoa, coffee, spices, sauces, and flavorings.

AREAS AND MALLS

Baywalk Mall, at Rodney Bay Village, is a 60-store complex of boutiques, restaurants, banks, a beauty salon, jewelry and souvenir stores, a large supermarket (great for snacks, picnic items, or a bottle of wine), and the island's first (and only, so far) casino.

Along the harbor in Castries, rambling structures with bright-orange roofs cover several open-air markets that are open from 6 am to 5 pm Monday through Saturday. Saturday morning is the busiest and most colorful time to shop. For more than a century, farmers' wives have gathered at the **Castries Market** to sell produce—which you can enjoy on the island but, alas, can't bring to the United States. You can take spices (such as cocoa sticks or balls, turmeric, cloves, bay leaves, ginger, peppercorns, cinnamon sticks, vanilla beans, nutmeg, and mace), though, as well as locally bottled hot-pepper sauces—all of which cost a fraction of what you'd pay back home. The adjacent **Craft Market** has aisles and aisles of baskets and other handmade straw work, rustic brooms made from palm fronds, wood carvings, leather work, clay pottery, and souvenirs—all at affordable prices. The **Vendors' Arcade,** across the street from the Craft Market, is a maze of stalls and booths where you can find handicrafts among the T-shirts and costume jewelry.

Gablewoods Mall, on the Gros Islet Highway in Choc Bay, a couple miles north of downtown Castries, has about 35 shops that sell groceries, wines and spirits, jewelry, clothing, crafts, books and overseas newspapers, music, souvenirs, household goods, and snacks.

Along with boutiques, restaurants, and other businesses that sell services and supplies, a large supermarket is the focal point of each **J.Q.'s Shopping Mall;** one is at Rodney Bay Village, another is at Vieux Fort.

Marigot Marina Village, in Marigot Bay, has shops and services for boaters and landlubbers alike, including a bank, grocery store, business center, art gallery, assortment of boutiques, a restaurant, and a casual café.

Duty-free shopping areas are at **Pointe Seraphine,** an attractive Spanish-motif complex on Castries Harbour with a dozen shops that are open

16

mainly when a cruise ship is in port, and **La Place Carenage,** an inviting three-story complex on the opposite side of the harbor. You can also find duty-free items at stores in Baywalk Mall and J.Q.'s Rodney Bay Mall, in a few small shops at the arcade at the Royal St. Lucia by Rex Resorts hotel—all in Rodney Bay Village—and, of course, in the departure lounge at Hewanorra International Airport. You must present your passport and airline ticket to purchase items at the duty-free price.

Vieux Fort Plaza, near Hewanorra International Airport in Vieux Fort, is the main shopping center in the southern part of St. Lucia. It has a bank, supermarket, bookstore, toy shop, and clothing stores.

ART

Caribbean Art & Antiques. On offer here are original artwork by local artists, including Llewellyn Xavier and Mervyn Charles, antique maps and prints, and hand-painted silk. ⊠ *Golf Park Rd., Cap Estate* ☎ *758/450–9740.*

Llewellyn Xavier. World-renowned St. Lucian artist Llewellyn Xavier creates modern art, ranging from vigorous oil abstracts that take up half a wall to small objects made from beaten silver and gold. Much of his work has an environmental theme and is created from recycled materials. Xavier's work is owned by major museums in New York and Washington, D.C. Other pieces are sold in gift shops throughout the island. Call to arrange a studio visit. ⊠ *Mount du Cap, Cap Estate* ☎ *758/450–9155* ⊕ *www.llewellynxavier.com.*

CLOTHING AND TEXTILES

The Bagshaws of St. Lucia. Using Sydney Bagshaw's original designs, this shop in La Toc sells clothing and table linens in colorful tropical patterns. The fabrics are silk-screened by hand in an adjacent workroom. You can also find Bagshaw boutiques at Pointe Seraphine and La Place Carenage, as well as a selection of items in gift shops at Hewanorra Airport. Visit the workshop to see how the designs are turned into colorful silk-screened fabrics, which are then fashioned into clothing and household articles. It's open weekdays from 8:30 to 5, Saturday 8:30 to 4, and Sunday 10 to 1—but call ahead if you want a demonstration. Weekend hours may be extended if a cruise ship is in port. ⊠ *La Toc Rd., Castries* ☎ *758/451–9249.*

The Batik Studio. The superb batik sarongs, scarves, and wall panels sold here are designed and created on-site by the shop's proprietor, Joan Alexander Stowe. ⊠ *Hummingbird Beach Resort, Anse Chastanet Rd., Soufrière* ☎ *758/459–7985.*

Caribelle Batik. Craftspeople demonstrate the art of batik and silk-screen printing while seamstresses use the batik fabric to make clothing and wall hangings, which you can buy in the shop. The studio is in an old Victorian mansion, high atop Morne Fortune and a 10-minute drive south of Castries. There's a terrace where you can have a cool drink and a garden full of tropical orchids and lilies. Caribelle Batik creations are also available in gift shops throughout St. Lucia. ⊠ *Howelton*

House, Old Victoria Rd., Morne Fortune ☎ *758/452–3785* ⊕ *www. caribellebatikstlucia.com.*

Sea Island Cotton Shop. High-quality T-shirts, Caribelle Batik clothing and other resort wear, and colorful souvenirs are sold at attractive prices. ✉ *Baywalk Mall, Reduit Beach Ave., off Castries–Gros Islet Hwy., Rodney Bay* ☎ *758/458–4220* ⊕ *www.seaislandstlucia.com.*

HANDICRAFTS

Choiseul Arts & Crafts Centre. A project of the Ministry of Education to encourage skill development and local crafts, this center carries handmade furniture, clay pots, wood carvings, and straw items. Many of St. Lucia's artisans come from the area—on the southwest coast, halfway between Soufrière and Vieux Fort. It's closed Sunday. ✉ *South Coast Hwy., 5 miles (8 km) south of Choiseul Village, La Fargue* ☎ *758/454–3226.*

Eudovic's Art Studio. This workshop, studio, and art gallery has wall plaques, masks, and abstract figures hand-carved from local mahogany, red cedar, and eucalyptus wood by sculptor Vincent Joseph Eudovic. ✉ *West Coast Rd., Goodlands, The Morne, Morne Fortune* ☎ *758/452–2747* ⊕ *www.eudovicart.com.*

Melting Pot West Indian Craft Studio and Shop. Artist and master carver Winston Febrier sells his wood carvings and unique hand-painted masks, which are on display in his small studio perched on the cliff overlooking the village of Anse la Raye. As friendly as he is talented, Winston is a joy to chat with as you pick out a piece of local artwork to take home. He'll even carve something to order—while you wait, if you wish. ✉ *West Coast Rd., just beyond the viewpoint south of Anse la Raye, Anse La Raye* ☎ *758/488–8620.*

Fodor'sChoice
★   **Zaka.** You may get a chance to talk with artist and craftsman Simon Gajhadhar, who fashions totems and masks from driftwood, branches, and other environmentally friendly wood sources—taking advantage of the natural nibs and knots that distinguish each piece. Once the "face" is carved, it is painted in vivid colors to highlight the exaggerated features and provide expression. ✉ *Jalousie Rd., off Soufrière–Vieux Fort Rd., Malgretoute* ☎ *758/457–1504* ⊕ *www.zaka-art.com.*

PERFUME

Caribbean Perfumes. Using exotic flowers, fruits, tropical woods, and spices, Caribbean Perfumes blends eight lovely scents for women and two aftershaves for men. The reasonably priced fragrances, all made in St. Lucia, are available at the perfume and duty-free shops at Baywalk Mall in Rodney Bay and at most gift shops. ✉ *Reduit Beach Ave., Rodney Bay* ☎ *758/453–7249* ⊕ *www.caribbeanperfumes.com.*

SPORTS AND THE OUTDOORS

BIKING

Bike St. Lucia. Small groups of bikers are accompanied on jungle biking tours along 8 miles (13 km) of groomed trails—with naturally occurring challenges (such as rocks and roots) and a few mud holes to challenge purists—that meander through the remnants of the 18th-century Anse Mamin Plantation, part of the 600-acre Anse Chastanet Estate in Soufrière. Stops are made to explore the French colonial ruins, study the beautiful tropical plants and fruit trees, have a picnic lunch, and take a dip in a river swimming hole or at the beach. There's an orientation loop for learning or brushing up on off-road riding skills, and there are beginner, intermediate, and advanced tracks. If you're staying in the north, you can arrange a tour that includes transportation to the Soufrière area. ⊠ *Anse Mamin Plantation, adjacent to Anse Chastanet Resort, Soufrière* ☎ *758/457–1400* ⊕ *www.bikestlucia.com.*

BOATING AND SAILING

Rodney Bay and Marigot Bay are both centers for bareboat and crewed yacht charters. Their marinas offer safe anchorage, shower facilities, restaurants, groceries, and maintenance for yachts sailing the waters of the eastern Caribbean. Charter prices range from $1,900 to nearly $50,000 per week, depending on the season, the type and size of vessel, and whether it's crewed. Some boat charter companies do not operate in August and September due to possible weather issues.

Bateau Mygo. Choose a monohull or catamaran for your half-, full-, or two-day cruise along the west coast, or charter by the week and explore neighboring islands. ⊠ *Chateau Mygo Villas, Marigot Bay* ✛ *Adjacent to the Marina Village* ☎ *758/458–3947* ⊕ *www.sailsaintlucia.com.*

Destination St. Lucia Ltd. *(DSL).* For its bareboat yacht charters, DSL's vessels include two 42-foot catamarans and several monohulls ranging in length from 32 to 50 feet. ⊠ *Rodney Bay Marina, Rodney Bay* ☎ *758/452–8531* ⊕ *www.dsl-yachting.com.*

Moorings Yacht Charters. Bareboat and crewed catamarans and monohulls ranging from Beneteau 39s to Morgan 60s are available for charter. You can also plan a one-way sail through the Grenadines, either picking up or dropping off at the company's facility in Grenada. ⊠ *Rodney Bay Marina, Rodney Bay* ☎ *758/451–4357, 844/505–9186 in U.S.* ⊕ *www. moorings.com.*

DIVING AND SNORKELING

Fodor's Choice
★ On-site dive shops at resorts include the Body Holiday, Sandals Grande, and Rendezvous in the north; Marigot Beach Club and Ti Kaye farther south; and Anse Chastanet and Sugar Beach, a Viceroy Resort, in Soufrière. Nearly all dive operators, regardless of their location, provide transportation from Rodney Bay, Castries, Marigot Bay, or Soufrière. Depending on the season, the particular trip, and whether you have

16

your own gear, prices range from about $40 for a one-tank shore dive to $115 to $140 for a two-tank boat dive, $225 to $360 for a 6-dive package over three days, and $350 to $550 for a 10-dive package over five days—plus a National Marine Reserve permit fee of $6 per day. Dive shops provide instruction for all levels. For beginners, a 30-minute resort course (pool training followed by an open-water dive) runs about $80 to $175, depending on the number of dives included. Snorkelers can rent equipment for $10 to $15 and are generally welcome on dive trips for $50–$55 to $75. All prices generally include taxi/boat transfers, lunch, and equipment.

Anse Chastanet, near the Pitons on the southwestern coast, is the best beach-entry dive site. The underwater reef drops from 20 feet to nearly 140 feet in a stunning coral wall.

A 165-foot freighter, *Lesleen M,* was deliberately sunk in 60 feet of water near **Anse Cochon** to create an artificial reef; divers can explore the ship in its entirety and view huge gorgonians, black coral trees, gigantic barrel sponges, lace corals, schooling fish, angelfish, sea horses, spotted eels, stingrays, nurse sharks, and sea turtles.

Anse la Raye, midway up the west coast, is one of St. Lucia's finest wall and drift dives and a great place for snorkeling.

At the **Pinnacles,** four coral-encrusted stone piers rise to within 10 feet of the surface.

Superman's Flight is a dramatic drift dive along the steep walls beneath the Pitons. At the base of **Petit Piton,** a spectacular wall drops to 200 feet, where you can view an impressive collection of huge barrel sponges and black coral trees; strong currents ensure good visibility.

DIVE OPERATORS

Dive Fair Helen. In operation since 1992 and owned by a St. Lucian environmentalist, this PADI center offers half- and full-day excursions on two custom-built dive boats to wreck, wall, and marine reserve areas, as well as night dives and instruction. ✉ *Marina Village, Marigot Bay* ☎ *758/451–7716* ⊕ *www.divefairhelen.com.*

Fodor's Choice ★ **Dive Saint Lucia.** Operating out of a LEED platinum-certified building at Rodney Bay Marina, St. Lucia's state-of-the-art dive center has a purpose-built training pool, fully equipped classrooms for adult and junior instruction, fully equipped compressors, a PADI 5-star Instructor Development Center (IDC), equipment rental and storage, guided dives, and two specialized dive boats (46-foot Newton)—each with a 30-diver capacity. Facilities are handicap-accessible and include a motorized lift chair. Dive trips include lunch, drinks, and hotel transfers (north of Castries). ✉ *Rodney Bay Marina, Castries-Gros Islet Hwy., Rodney Bay* ☎ *758/451–3483* ⊕ *www.divesaintlucia.com.*

Island Divers. At the edge of the National Marine Park at Soufrière, with two reefs and an offshore wreck accessible from shore, this dive shop at Ti Kaye Resort & Spa offers shore dives, boat dives, PADI certification, equipment rental, and an extensive list of specialty courses. Hotel transfers available. ✉ *Ti Kaye Resort & Spa, off West Coast Rd.,* *between Anse la Raye and Canaries, Anse La Raye* ☎ *758/456–8110* ⊕ *www.tikaye.com/diving.*

Scuba St. Lucia. Daily beach and boat dives and resort and certification courses are available from this PADI 5-star facility located on Anse Chastanet Beach, and so is underwater photography and snorkeling equipment. Transportation from the north of the island can be arranged. ⊠ *Anse Chastanet Resort, Anse Chastanet Rd., Soufrière* ☎ *758/459–7755, 800/223–1108 in U.S.* ⊕ *www.scubastlucia.com.*

FISHING

Among the deep-sea creatures you can find in St. Lucia's waters are dolphin (the fish, also called dorado or mahimahi), barracuda, mackerel, wahoo, kingfish, sailfish, and white and blue marlin. Sportfishing is generally done on a catch-and-release basis, but the captain may permit you to take a fish back to your hotel to be prepared for your dinner. Neither spearfishing nor collecting live fish in coastal waters is permitted. Half- and full-day deep-sea fishing excursions can be arranged at Vigie Marina. A half day of fishing on a scheduled trip runs about $85–$90 per person; a private charter costs $500–$1,200 for up to six or eight people, depending on the size of the boat and the length of time. Beginners are welcome.

16

Captain Mike's. Named for Captain Mike Hackshaw and run by his family, Bruce and Andrew, this operation has a fleet of Bertram powerboats (31 to 46 feet) that accommodate up to eight passengers for half- or full-day sportfishing charters; tackle and cold drinks are supplied. Customized sightseeing or whale/dolphin-watching trips ($50 per person) can also be arranged for four to six people. ⊠ *Vigie Marina, Vigie* ☎ *758/452–7044* ⊕ *www.captmikes.com.*

Hackshaw's Boat Charters. In business since 1953, this company runs charters on *Blue Boy,* a 31-foot Bertram; *Limited Edition,* a 47-foot custom-built Buddy Davis; and *Party Hack,* a 64-foot double-deck power catamaran also used for snorkeling, whale-watching, and party cruises. ⊠ *Vigie Marina, Seraphine Rd., Vigie* ☎ *758/453–0553* ⊕ *www.hackshaws.com.*

GOLF

St. Lucia Golf Resort & Country Club. St. Lucia's only public course is at the island's northern tip and features broad views of both the Atlantic and the Caribbean, as well as many spots adorned with orchids and bromeliads. Wind and the demanding layout present challenges. The Cap Grill serves breakfast and lunch until 7 pm; the Sports Bar is a convivial meeting place all day long. You can arrange lessons at the pro shop and perfect your swing at the 350-yard driving range. Fees include carts, which are required; club and shoe rentals are available. Reservations are essential. Complimentary transportation from your hotel (north of Castries) is available for parties of three or more. ⊠ *Cap Estate* ☎ *758/450–8523* ⊕ *www.stluciagolf.com* ✉ *$120 for 18 holes, $90 for 9 holes* Ⳬ *18 holes, 6685 yards, par 71.*

GUIDED TOURS

Taxi drivers are well informed and can give you a full tour and often an excellent one, thanks to government-sponsored training programs. Full-day island tours cost about $140 for up to four people, depending on the route and whether entrance fees and lunch are included; half-day tours, $100. If you plan your own day, expect to pay the driver $40 per hour plus tip.

Island Routes. This Sandals partner offers dozens of adventure tours, including guided, drive-it-yourself dune buggy safaris of Soufrière's natural sites and attractions (six hours, $175). A longer version includes a cruise down the west coast from Rodney Bay. Drivers must be at least 23, have a valid driver's license, and be able to operate a manual transmission. Other tours include ATV adventures (two hours, $140), a guided historical tour beginning in Marigot Bay (eight hours, $125), and many, many more. ⊠ *Castries* 🕾 *877/768–8370 in U.S., 758/455–2000* ⊕ *www.islandroutes.com.*

Jungle Tours. This company specializes in rain-forest hiking tours in small groups and for all ability levels. You're required only to bring hiking shoes or sneakers and have a willingness to get wet and have fun. The cost is $95 per person and includes lunch, fees, and transportation via an open Land Rover truck. ⊠ *Cas en Bas* 🕾 *758/715–3438* ⊕ *www.jungletoursstlucia.com.*

St. Lucia Helicopters. How about a bird's-eye view of the island? A 10-minute North Island tour ($108 per person) leaves from the hangar in Castries, continues up the west coast to Pigeon Island, then flies along the rugged Atlantic coastline before returning inland over Castries. The 20-minute South Island tour ($176 per person) starts at Pointe Seraphine and follows the western coastline, circling beautiful Marigot Bay, Soufrière, and the majestic Pitons before returning inland over the volcanic hot springs and tropical rain forest. A complete island tour combines the two and lasts 30 minutes ($220 per person). All tours require a minimum of four passengers. ⊠ *George F. L. Charles Airport, Island Flyers Hangar, Vigie* 🕾 *758/453–6950* ⊕ *www.stluciahelicopters.com.*

St. Lucia Heritage Tours. The Heritage Tourism Association of St. Lucia (HERITAS), a volunteer group that represents local sites and institutions, puts together "authentic St. Lucia experiences" that focus on local culture and traditions. Groups are kept small, and the tours can be tailored to your interests. Some of the sites visited include a 19th-century plantation house surrounded by nature trails, a 20-foot waterfall hidden away on private property, and a living museum presenting Creole practices and traditions. Other options include bird-watching, turtle-watching, horseback riding, garden walks, culinary experiences, and rain-forest treks. Prices vary. ⊠ *John Compton Hwy., Castries* 🕾 *758/458–1454* ⊕ *www.heritagetoursstlucia.org.*

HIKING

St. Lucia Forestry Department. Trails under this department's jurisdiction include the Barre de L'Isle Trail (just off the highway, halfway between Castries and Dennery), the Forestiere Trail (20 minutes east of Castries), the Des Cartiers Rain Forest Trail (west of Micoud), the Edmund Rain Forest Trail and Enbas Saut Waterfalls (east of Soufrière), the Millet Bird Sanctuary Trail (east of Marigot Bay), and the Union Nature Trail (north of Castries). Most are two-hour hikes on 2-mile (3-km) loop trails; the bird-watching tour lasts four hours. The Forestry Department provides guides ($2–$30, depending on the hike), who explain the plants and trees that you'll encounter and keep you on the right track. Seasoned hikers climb the Pitons, the two volcanic cones rising 2,461 feet and 2,619 feet from the ocean floor just south of Soufrière. Hiking is recommended only on Gros Piton, which offers a steep but safe trail to the top. The first half of the hike is moderately difficult; reaching the summit is challenging and should be attempted only by those who are physically fit. The view from the top is spectacular. Tourists are also permitted to hike Petit Piton, but the second half of the hike requires a good deal of rock climbing, and you'll need to provide your own safety equipment. Hiking either Piton requires permission and a knowledgeable guide ($45), both arranged through the St. Lucia Forestry Department. ✉ *Stanislaus James Bldg., Waterfront, Castries* ☎ *758/468–5648, 758/450–2231 for Piton permission* ⊕ *malff.com.*

16

HORSEBACK RIDING

Creole horses, a breed native to South America and popular on St. Lucia, are fairly small, fast, sturdy, and even-tempered animals suitable for beginners. Established stables can accommodate all skill levels. They offer countryside trail rides, beach rides with picnic lunches, plantation tours, carriage rides, and lengthy treks. Prices run about $40 for a one-hour guided ride, $60 for two hours, and $70–$90 for a three- or four-hour beach ride with swimming (with the horses) and lunch. Transportation is usually provided between the stables and nearby hotels. Local people sometimes appear on beaches with their steeds and offer 30-minute rides for $10 to $15; ride at your own risk.

FAMILY **Atlantic Shores Riding Stables.** Two-hour trail rides roam along the beach and through the countryside. Beginners are welcome. ✉ *Micoud Hwy., Vieux Fort* ☎ *758/454–8660* ⊕ *www.atlanticridingstables.com.*

FAMILY **Trim's National Riding Stable.** At the island's oldest riding stable there are four riding sessions per day, both beach tours and trail rides, plus riding lessons, party rides, and horse-and-carriage tours to Pigeon Island. ✉ *Cas en Bas* ☎ *758/450–8273* ⊕ *www.trimsridingstlucia.com.*

SEA EXCURSIONS

Fodor'sChoice A day sail or sea cruise from Rodney Bay or Vigie Cove to Soufrière
★ and the Pitons is a wonderful way to see St. Lucia and get to its distinctive natural sites. Prices for a full-day sailing excursion to Soufrière run about $110 per person and include a land tour to the Diamond Falls

Botanical Gardens, lunch, a stop for swimming and snorkeling, and a visit to pretty Marigot Bay. You can even add zip-lining! Half-day cruises to the Pitons, three-hour whale-watching tours, and two-hour sunset cruises along the northwest coast cost $45–$60 per person.

FAMILY   **Captain Mike's Whale/Dolphin Watching Tours.** With 20 species of whales and dolphins living in Caribbean waters, your chances of sighting some are very good on these three-hour trips ($50 per person) aboard *Free Willie*, a 60-foot Defender. ⊠ *Vigie Marina, Ganthers Bay, Castries* ☎ *758/452–7044* ⊕ *www.captmikes.com.*

FAMILY   ***Endless Summer* Cruises.** *Endless Summer*, a 56-foot party catamaran, runs
Fodor's Choice   day trips along the coast to Soufrière—hotel transfers, tour, entrance
★   fees, lunch, and drinks included—for $110 per person. A half-day swimming and snorkeling trip is also available. For romantics, there's a sunset cruise for $60, including dinner and entertainment. ⊠ *Reduit Beach Ave., Rodney Bay* ☎ *758/450–8651* ⊕ *www.stluciaboattours.com.*

Mystic Man Tours. Glass-bottom boat, sailing, catamaran, deep-sea fishing, snorkeling, and/or whale- and dolphin-watching tours are all great family excursions; there's also a sunset cruise. Most trips depart from Soufrière. ⊠ *Maurice Mason St., Soufrière* ⊹ *On the bayfront* ☎ *758/459–7783, 800/401–9804* ⊕ *www.mysticmantours.com.*

FAMILY   **Sea Spray Cruises.** Sail down the west coast from Rodney Bay to Soufrière on *Mango Tango* (a 52-foot catamaran), *Tango Too* (an 80-foot cat'), *Jus Tango* (a 65-foot cat')—or the tall ship *Black Magic*, which is all decked out as a pirate ship. The all-day Tout Bagay (a little bit of everything) tour includes a visit to the sulfur springs, drive-in volcano, and Morne Coubaril Estate. The view of the Pitons from the water is majestic. You'll have lunch and drinks on board, plenty of music, and an opportunity to swim at a remote beach. Tout Bagay operates Monday, Wednesday, and Saturday. Sea Spray operates several other boat tours, including a sunset cruise, on other days. ⊠ *Rodney Bay Marina, Rodney Bay* ☎ *758/458–0123, 321/220–9423 in U.S.*

WINDSURFING AND KITEBOARDING

Reef Kite and Surf Centre. This water-sports center offers equipment rental and lessons from certified instructors. Windsurfing equipment rental is $50 for a half day, $70 full day. Kitesurfing equipment rents for $60 half day, $80 full day. A three-hour beginning windsurfing course costs $100, including equipment; a two-hour "taster" session is $75. For kitesurfing, the three-hour starter costs $200, including equipment and safety gear; the two-hour taster, $90. Kitesurfing is particularly strenuous, so participants must be excellent swimmers and in good health. ⊠ *The Reef Beach Café, Anse de Sables Beach, Micoud Hwy., Vieux Fort* ☎ *758/454–3418.*

ST. MAARTEN/
ST. MARTIN

WELCOME TO ST. MAARTEN/ ST. MARTIN

TWO NATIONS, ONE ISLAND

St. Maarten/St. Martin is home to approximately 77,000 people from more than 100 countries, but governance of the 37-square-mile (96-square-km) island is split between France and the Netherlands. It's the smallest island in the world divided between two ruling powers. The Dutch capital is Philipsburg; the French capital is Marigot.

TOP REASONS TO VISIT ST. MAARTEN/ST. MARTIN

1 Great Food: The island has so many good places to dine that you could eat out for a month and never repeat a restaurant visit.

2 Lots of Shops: Philipsburg is one of the top shopping spots in the Caribbean, and the galleries and boutiques of Marigot and Grand Case bring a touch of France.

3 Beaches Large and Small: Thirty-seven picture-perfect beaches are spread out all over the island.

4 Water Sports Galore: The wide range of land and water sports adventures will satisfy almost any need and give you the perfect excuse to try everything from ATVs to zip-lines.

5 Nightlife Every Night: After-dark entertainment options include shows, lounges, discos, beach bars, and casinos.

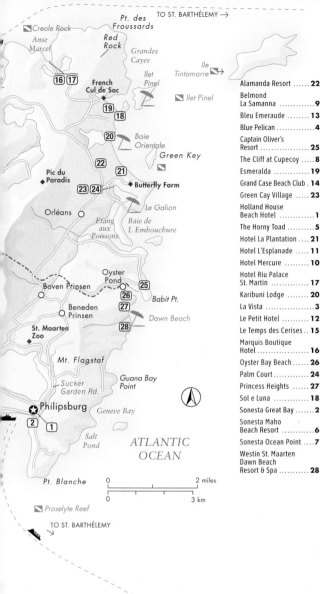

St. Maarten/St. Martin, a half-Dutch, half-French island, is a place where gastronomy flourishes, where most resorts are large rather than small, where casinos draw gamblers, where sporting opportunities are plentiful, and where the sunning, as on the south end of Orient Beach, is sometimes au naturel.

NEED TO KNOW

Atlantic Ocean

Marigot

ST. MARTIN

Philipsburg

ST. MAARTEN

Caribbean Sea

AT A GLANCE

Capital: Phillipsburg (D); Marigot (F)

Population: 77,740

Currency: Netherlands Antilles florin (D); Euro (F)

Money: ATMs are common and dispense dollars or euros, depending on where you are; credit cards and U.S. dollars widely accepted.

Language: Dutch, French, English

Country Code: ☎ 1 721 (D); 1 590 (F)

Emergencies: ☎ 911 (D); 17 (F)

Driving: On the right

Electricity: 110v/60 cycles (D) and 220v/60 cycles (F); plugs are U.S. standard two- and three-prong (D) and European standard with two round prongs (F).

Time: Same as New York during daylight savings time; one hour ahead otherwise

Documents: A valid passport and a return or ongoing ticket.

GETTING AROUND

✈ **Air Travel:** All international flights land at Princess Juliana airport on the Dutch side.

🚌 **Bus Travel:** Cheap minibuses cover most of the island but run with no set schedule (check the destination sign on the dashboard).

🚗 **Car Travel:** Most visitors will want to rent a car. Traffic can be heavy, but for the sake of convenience, there is no substitute.

⛴ **Ferry Travel:** Ferries connect the island to St. Barthelemy (45–80 minutes, from the Dutch or French side); to Anguilla (20 minutes, from the French side); and to Saba (one to two hours, from the Dutch side).

PLAN YOUR BUDGET

	HOTEL ROOM	MEAL	ATTRACTIONS
Low Budget	$200	$12	Ferry to Pinel Island, $12
Mid Budget	$300	$25	Snorkel Trip, $45
High Budget	$475	$50	Two-site dive with Octopus Diving, $105

WAYS TO SAVE

Eat at *lolos*. St. Maarten's open-air roadside barbecues are some of the best and cheapest food on the island.

Rent a condo. Condos appeal to travelers who want many of the same amenities as pricey villas, including kitchens.

Rent a car on-island. Car rental prices from local retailers and hotels may be cheaper than those from larger agencies secured on the Web (though cars may be a bit more worn).

Cross the border. When in doubt, go Dutch . . . side that is. Almost everything is cheaper there.

PLAN YOUR TIME

Hassle Factor	Low. Flights to Princess Juliana International Airport are frequent and the island is easy to navigate.
3 days	Relax poolside or beachside at your resort on either the French or Dutch side. Partake in some water sports; diving, snorkeling, sailing, and windsurfing are all top draws. Spend a day at a beach club and dine and gamble in Cupecoy.
1 week	Relax at your resort but rent a car to explore the island in detail. Check out several of the island's 37 beaches, stroll the boardwalk of Dutch-side Philipsburg, and check out the restaurants and shops of Grand Case. Dine at the *lolos* in Grand Case and spend some time out on the water. Ferry out to Pinel Island.
2 weeks	Explore both the French and Dutch sides of the island in full, take a number of day trips: St. Eustatius for a day to hike (short flight), Anguilla for a day to see the regions' superlative beaches (short ferry), St. Barthélemy to shop and dine (short ferry or flight), and Saba to dive and hike. (short flight).

WHEN TO GO

High Season: Mid-December through mid-April is the most fashionable and most expensive time to visit, when the weather is typically sunny and warm. Good hotels are often booked far in advance, and you're guaranteed the most entertainment at resorts and the most people with whom to enjoy it.

Low Season: From August to late October, temperatures can grow oppressively hot and the weather muggy, with high risks of tropical storms. Some upscale hotels close during these months for annual renovations. Those remaining open may offer discounts.

Value Season: From late April to July and again November to mid-December, hotel prices tend to drop from high-season prices (though all-inclusives tend to stay at same rates year-round, catering to Europeans coming for their summer vacations). There are chances of scattered showers, but expect sun-kissed days, too.

BIG EVENTS

January–February: The French side's Carnival is a pre-Lenten bash of costume parades, music competitions, and feasts. Grand Case hops every Tuesday evening with music and parades mid-January through the end of Carnival.

March: The Dutch side hosts the Heineken Regatta, with as many as 300 sailboats competing from around the world. ⊕ www.heinekenregatta.com

April: Carnival takes place after Easter on the Dutch side with a parade and music competition.

July: On the French side, parades, ceremonies, and celebrations commemorate Bastille Day on July 14; there's more revelry later on Grand Case Day.

READ THIS

■ *A Time to Love,* Barbara Delinsky. A story of self-love.

■ *Gone Bamboo,* Anthony Bourdain. This culinary mystery has more to do with murder than food.

■ *The Making of an Island: St. Martin,* Jean Glasscock. The interesting genesis of this dual-nation island.

WATCH THIS

■ *Speed 2: Cruise Control.* The less-than-acclaimed sequel was filmed around St. Maarten.

■ *Once Around.* 1990s romantic comedy.

EAT THIS

■ *Lolo fare*: barbecued ribs, chicken, fish, and local specialties cooked beachside or roadside over metal drums.

■ *Fresh fish*: try local grouper, conch, mahimahi, and triggerfish, as well as Caribbean spiny lobster.

■ *Goat stew*: thick stew of veggies, goat, and often pig's tail.

■ *French bread and pastry*: bakeries all over the island produce excellent treats.

■ *Accras*: codfish fritters served with a spicy creole sauce.

■ *Johnnycakes*: fried bread served with any meal.

Updated by
Elise Meyer

St. Maarten/St. Martin is unique among Caribbean destinations. The 37-square-mile (96-square-km) island is a seamless place (there are no border gates), but it is governed by two nations—the Netherlands and France—and has residents from more than 100 countries. A call from the Dutch side to the French is an international call, currencies are different, and even the vibe is different. Only the island of Hispaniola, which encompasses Haiti and the Dominican Republic, is in a similar position in the Caribbean.

Happily for Americans, who make up the majority of visitors to St. Maarten/St. Martin, English works in both nations. Dutch St. Maarten might feel particularly comfortable for Americans: the prices are a bit lower (not to mention in U.S. dollars), the big hotels have casinos, and there is more nightlife. Huge cruise ships disgorge masses of shoppers into the Philipsburg shopping area at mid-morning, when roads can quickly become congested. But once you pass the meandering, unmarked border to the French side, you find a hint of the south of France: quiet countryside, fine cuisine, and in Marigot, a walkable harbor area with outdoor cafés, an outdoor market, and some shops to explore.

Almost 4,000 years ago, it was salt and not tourism that drove the little island's economy. Arawak Indians, the island's first known inhabitants, prospered until the warring Caribs invaded, adding the peaceful Arawaks to their list of conquests. Columbus spotted the isle on November 11, 1493, and named it after St. Martin (whose feast day is November 11), but it wasn't populated by Europeans until the 17th century, when it was claimed by the Dutch, French, and Spanish. The Dutch and French finally joined forces to claim the island in 1644, and the Treaty of Concordia partitioned the territory in 1648. According to legend the border was drawn along the line where a French man and a Dutch man, walking along opposite coasts, met.

Both sides of the island offer a touch of European culture along with a lot of laid-back Caribbean ambience. Water sports both serene and extreme abound—diving, snorkeling, sailing, windsurfing, kite surfing, and even hover-boarding. With soft trade winds cooling the subtropical climate, it's easy to while away the day relaxing on one of the 37 beaches, strolling Philipsburg's boardwalk, shopping along Front Street or the harbors of Marigot. Although luck is an important commodity at St. Maarten's 13 casinos, chance plays no part in finding a good meal at the excellent eateries or after-dark fun in the subtle to sizzling nightlife. Heavy development—especially on the Dutch side—has stressed the island's infrastructure, but some of the more dilapidated roads have been improved. A series of large roundabouts, with the beginnings of some decent signage, and attractive monumental sculptures have improved traffic flow (remember, the cars already in the roundabout have right-of-way). At long last, the eyesore of hurricane-wrecked buildings that lined the golf course at Mullet Bay have been demolished and landscaped to parkland, and most welcome is the new bridge that crosses Simpson Bay lagoon, connecting the airport and Cole Bay, and shortening the trip to Marigot.

When cruise ships are in port (and there can be as many as seven at once), shopping areas are crowded and traffic moves at a snail's pace. Instead spend days at your resort or one of the full-service beach clubs, or out on the water, and plan shopping excursions for the early morning or at cocktail hour, after "rush hour" traffic calms down. Still, these are minor inconveniences compared with the feel of the sand between your toes or the breeze through your hair, gourmet food sating your appetite, and being able to crisscross between two nations on one island.

17

PLANNING

GETTING HERE AND AROUND
AIR TRAVEL

More than 20 carriers fly to the island. There are nonstop flights from Atlanta (Delta, seasonal), Charlotte (American), Miami (American), New York–JFK (American, Delta, JetBlue), New York–Newark (United), and Philadelphia (American). There are also some nonstop charter flights (including GWV/Apple Vacations from Boston). You can also connect in San Juan on Air Sunshine, JetBlue, or LIAT. Many smaller Caribbean-based airlines, including Air Caraïbes, Anguilla Air Services, Caribbean Airlines, Copa, Insel, LIAT, St. Barth Commuter, and Winair (Windward Islands Airways), offer service from other islands in the Caribbean.

Airline Contacts Air Caraïbes. ☎ 0590/52–05–10 ⊕ www.aircaraibes.com. **Air Sunshine.** ✉ Airport Rd., Simson Bay Lagoon ☎ 800/434–8900 ⊕ www. airsunshine.com. **American Airlines.** ☎ 721/545–2040, 800/433–7300 ⊕ www. aa.com. **Anguilla Air Services.** ✉ Airport Rd., Simson Bay Lagoon ☎ 264/498–5922 ⊕ www.anguillaairservices.com. **Caribbean Airlines.** ☎ 721/546–7610 ⊕ www.caribbean-airlines.com. **Copa Airlines.** ✉ Airport Rd., Simson Bay Lagoon ☎ 877/389–3606 ⊕ www.copaair.com. **Delta Airlines.** ☎ 721/546–7615 ⊕ www.delta.com. **Insel Air.** ☎ 599/546–7621 ⊕ www.fly-inselair.com. **JetBlue.**

☎ 721/546–7797 ⊕ www.jetblue.com. **LIAT.** ☎ 721/546–7676 ⊕ www.liatairline. com. **St. Barth Commuter.** ☎ 0590/87–80–73 ⊕ www.stbarthcommuter.com. **United Airlines.** ☎ 721/546–7663 ⊕ www.united.com. **Winair.** ☎ 721/545–4237 ⊕ www.fly-winair.sx.

Airports Aéroport de L'Espérance (SFG). ☒ Rte. de l'Espérance, Grand Case ☎ 0590/27–11–00 ⊕ www.aeroport-saintmartin.com. **Princess Juliana International Airport** (SXM). ☎ 721/546–7542, 721/549–0200 airport information booth ⊕ www.sxmairport.com.

BOAT AND FERRY TRAVEL

You can take ferries to St. Barth (45–80 minutes, €55–€90 from the Dutch or French side, though you can pay in dollars); to Anguilla (20 minutes, $25 from the French side); and to Saba (one to two hours, $90–$100 from the Dutch side).

Contacts Aqua Mania Adventures. ☒ Pelican Marina, Simpson Bay ☎ 721/544–2640 ⊕ www.stmaarten-activities.com. **Dawn II.** ☎ 599/416–2299 ⊕ www.sabactransport.com. **Great Bay Express.** ☒ Bobby's Marina Village, Philipsburg ☎ 721/542–0032 Dutch side, 690/88–38–99 French side ⊕ www. greatbayferry.com. **Link Ferries.** ☎ 264/497–2231 in Anguilla, 264/497–3290 in Anguilla ⊕ www.link.ai. **Shauna.** ☎ 264/476–0975 in Anguilla. **Voyager II.** ☎ 0590/87–10–68 ⊕ www.voy12.com.

CAR TRAVEL

It's easy to get around the island by car. Most roads are paved and in generally good condition. However, they can be crowded, especially when the cruise ships are in port; you might experience traffic jams, particularly around Marigot and Philipsburg. Be alert for potholes and speed bumps, as well as the island tradition of stopping in the middle of the road to chat with a friend or yield to someone entering traffic. Few roads are identified by name or number, but most have signs indicating the destination. Driving is on the right. There are gas stations all over the island.

Car Rentals: You can book a car at Juliana International Airport, where all major rental companies have booths, but it is often much cheaper to reserve a car in advance from home. A shuttle to the rental-car lot is provided. Rates are among the best in the Caribbean, as little as $20–$35 per day. You can also rent a car on the French side, but this rarely makes sense for Americans because of the exchange rates.

Car-Rental Contacts Avis. ☒ Airport Rd., Simpson Bay ☎ 721/545–2847, 800/331–1084 ⊕ www.avis-sxm.com. **Dollar/Thrifty Car Rental.** ☒ 102 Airport Rd. ☎ 721/545–2393 ⊕ www.thriftycarrentalsxm.com. **Empress Rent-a-Car.** ☎ 721/520–2391 ⊕ www.empressrentacar.com. **Europcar.** ☒ Airport Rd., Simpson Bay ☎ 721/545–3141 ⊕ www.europcar.com. **Golfe Car Rental.** ☒ Rte. de l'Espérance, Grand Case ☎ 0690/35–04–75 ⊕ www.golfecarrental. com. **Hertz.** ☒ 82 Airport Rd., Simpson Bay ☎ 721/545–4541 ⊕ www.hertz. sxmrentacar.com. **Unity.** ☒ 6 Sister Modesta Rd., Simpson Bay ☎ 721/520–5767 ⊕ www.unitycarrental.com.

SCOOTER TRAVEL

Though traffic can be heavy, speeds are generally slow, so a moped can be a good way to get around. Scooters rent for as low as €30 per day and motorbikes for €37 a day at Eugene Moto, on the French side. The Harley-Davidson dealer, on the Dutch side, rents hogs for $99 a day or $900 per week.

Contacts Eugene Moto. ✉ *Sandy Ground Rd., Sandy Ground* ☎ *0590/87–13–97.* **Harley-Davidson.** ✉ *71 Union Rd., Cole Bay* ☎ *721/544–2704* ⊕ *www. hdsxm.com.*

TAXI TRAVEL

There is a government-sponsored taxi dispatcher at the airport and the harbor. Posted fares are for one or two people. Add $5 for each additional person, half price for kids. The first bag is free; after that it's $1 per bag. It costs about $18 from the airport to Philipsburg or Marigot, and about $30 to Dawn Beach. After 10 pm fares go up 25%, and after midnight 50%. Licensed drivers can be identified by the "taxi" license plate on the Dutch side and the window sticker on the French. You can hail cabs on the street or call the taxi dispatch to have one sent. Fixed fares apply from Juliana International Airport and the Marigot ferry to hotels around the island.

Taxi Contacts Dutch St. Maarten Taxi Association. ☎ *721/543–7815, 9247 24-hour hotline* ⊕ *www.taxistmaarten.com.* **Juliana Airport Taxi Dispatch.** ☎ *721/542–1680* ⊕ *www.sxmairporttaxis.com/.* **Marigot Taxi Dispatch.** ☎ *0590/87–56–54.*

17

HEALTH AND SAFETY

Dengue, chikungunya, and zika have all been reported throughout the Caribbean. We recommend that you protect yourself from these mosquito-borne illnesses by keeping your skin covered and/or wearing mosquito repellent. The mosquitoes that transmit these viruses are as active by day as they are by night.

HOTELS AND RESORTS

The island, though small, is well developed—some say overdeveloped—and offers a wide range of lodging. The larger resorts and time-shares are mostly on the Dutch side; the French side has more intimate properties. Just keep in mind that the popular restaurants around Grand Case, on the French side, are a long drive from most Dutch-side hotels. French-side hotels often charge in euros. Be wary of very low–price alternatives, as some of these can be run-down time-shares, short-term housing for temporary workers, or properties used by very low-end tour companies. Additionally, note locations very close to the airport to avoid unpleasant, noisy surprises. In general, the newer a property, the better.

Resorts and Time-Shares: In general, many of the older properties, especially the time-shares, are suffering from the wear-and-tear of multiple owners, and it is hard to recommend many of them because of great variances from unit to unit. Some have undergone full or partial renovations. Ask for a renovated unit when you reserve. There are several with all-inclusive options, but keep in mind that restaurants at all price points are easily accessible before you lock yourself into a meal plan.

Small Inns: Small guesthouses and inns can be found on both sides of the island. It is worth considering these, especially if you are not the big-resort type. Several are quite modern and attractive, and located beachfront.

Villas and Condos: Both sides of the island have a wide variety of villas and condos for every conceivable budget. Some of the resorts offer villa alternatives, which make for a good compromise, and perhaps better security. In addition, some of the high-end condo developments are offering unsold units as rentals, and some are brand-new and terrific bargains.

Hotel reviews have been shortened. For full information, visit Fodors.com.

WHAT IT COSTS IN U.S. DOLLARS				
	$	**$$**	**$$$**	**$$$$**
RESTAURANTS	under $12	$12–$20	$21–$30	over $30
HOTELS	under $275	$275–$375	$376–$475	over $475

Restaurant prices are the average cost of a main course at dinner or, if dinner is not served, at lunch. Hotel prices are the lowest cost of a standard double room in high season.

VISITOR INFORMATION

Contacts Dutch-side Tourist Information Bureau. ⊠ *Krippa Bldg. Unit 10, Jurancho Yrausquin bd. 6, Philipsburg* ☎ *721/542–2337* ⊕ *www. vacationstmaarten.com.* **French-side Office de Tourisme.** ⊠ *Rte. de Sandy Ground, facing Marina de la Port-Royale, Marigot* ☎ *0590/87–57–21* ⊕ *www. stmartinisland.org/.*

EXPLORING

The best way to explore St. Maarten/St. Martin is by car. Though often congested, especially around Philipsburg and Marigot, the roads are fairly good, though narrow and winding, with some speed bumps, potholes, roundabouts, and an occasional wandering goat herd. Few roads are marked with their names, but destination signs are common. Besides, the island is so small that it's hard to get really lost—at least that is what locals tell you.

If you're spending a few days, get to know the area with a scenic loop around the island. Be sure to pack a towel and some water shoes, a hat, sunglasses, and sunblock. Head up the east shoreline from Philipsburg, and follow the signs to Dawn Beach and Oyster Pond. The road winds past soaring hills, turquoise waters, quaint West Indian houses, and wonderful views of St. Barth. As you cross over to the French side, turn into Le Galion for a stop at the calm sheltered beach, the stables, the butterflies, or the windsurfing school; then keep following the road toward Orient Bay, the St-Tropez of the Caribbean. Continue to Anse Marcel, Grand Case, Marigot, and Sandy Ground. From Marigot, the flat island of Anguilla is visible. Completing the loop brings you past

Cupecoy Beach, through Maho and Simpson Bay, where Saba looms in the horizon, and back over the mountain road into Philipsburg.

DUTCH SIDE

PHILIPSBURG

The capital of Dutch St. Maarten stretches about a mile (1½ km) along an isthmus between Great Bay and the Salt Pond and has five parallel streets. Most of the village's dozens of shops and restaurants are on Front Street, narrow and cobblestone, closest to Great Bay. It's generally congested when cruise ships are in port because of its many duty-free shops and several casinos. Little lanes called *steegjes* connect Front Street with Back Street. Along the beach is a ½-mile-long (1-km-long) boardwalk with restaurants, souvenir shops, and beach concessions where you can rent chairs and umbrellas for about $15, with cold drinks included. There are many Wi-Fi hot spots.

St. Maarten Museum. Hosting rotating cultural exhibits addressing the history, industry, geology, and archaeology of the island, the museum contains artifacts ranging from Arawak pottery shards to objects salvaged from the wreck of the HMS *Proselyte*. An interesting exhibit about hurricanes focuses on Hurricane Luis, which devastated the island in 1995. There is a good reference and video library as well. ⊠ *7 Front St., Philipsburg* ☎ *721/542–4917* ⊕ *www.museumsintmaarten. org* 🖃 *Free* ⊘ *Weekdays 10–4.*

FAMILY **Yoda Guy Movie Exhibit.** This odd-sounding exhibit is actually a nonprofit museum run by Nick Maley, a movie-industry artist who was involved in the creation of Yoda and other icons. You can learn how the artist worked while enjoying the models and memorabilia on display—a must-see for *Star Wars* fans but of interest to most movie buffs. Maley is happy to autograph souvenirs for sale. ⊠ *19a Front St., Philipsburg* ☎ *721/542–4009* ⊕ *www.netdwellers.com/mz/planetp/home.*

ELSEWHERE IN ST. MAARTEN

FAMILY **The Carousel.** After riding this beautiful restored Italian carousel, kids of all ages can enjoy dozens of flavors of homemade Italian gelato or French pastries. There's even an espresso bar with great coffee drinks and a small cocktail bar, and an engaging photo exhibit of famous people eating ice cream. ⊠ *60 Welfare Rd., Cole Bay* ☎ *721/544–3112* ⊕ *www.carouselstmaarten.com* 🖃 *$2* ⊘ *Mon.–Thurs. 2–10:30, Fri.– Sun. 2–11.*

FAMILY **St. Maarten Zoo.** This somewhat run-down little enclave houses scaly, furry, and feathered friends indigenous to the Caribbean and South America, including multihued parrots, iguanas, peacocks, turtles, monkeys, a few snakes, an alligator, and a capybara. You can feed most of the animals with crackers available at the entrance. There is also a small playground. ⊠ *Madame Estate, Arch Rd., Philipsburg* ☎ *721/543–2030* ⊕ *www.stmaartenzoo.com* 🖃 *$10 adults, $5 children* ⊘ *Weekdays 9–5.*

17

Concordia

The smallest island in the world to be shared between two different countries, St. Maarten/St. Martin has existed peacefully in its divided state for more than 360 years. The Treaty of Concordia, which subdivided the island, was signed in 1648 and was really inspired by the two resident colonies of French and Dutch settlers (not to mention their respective governments) joining forces to repel a common enemy, the Spanish, in 1644. Although the French were promised the side of the island facing Anguilla and the Dutch the south side of the island, the boundary itself wasn't firmly established until 1817 and only then after several disputes (16 of them, to be exact).

Visitors to the island will likely not be able to tell that they have passed from the Dutch to the French side unless they notice that the roads on the French side feel a little smoother. In 2003 the population of St. Martin (and St. Barthélemy) voted to secede from Guadeloupe, the administrative capital of the French West Indies. That detachment became official in 2007, and St. Martin is now officially known as the Collectivité de Saint-Martin.

FRENCH SIDE

MARIGOT

It is great fun to spend a few hours exploring the harbor, shopping stalls, open-air cafés, and boutiques of St. Martin's biggest town, especially on Wednesday and Saturday, when the daily open-air crafts markets expand to include fresh fruits and vegetables, spices, and all manner of seafood. The market might remind you of Provence, especially when aromas of delicious cooking waft by. Be sure to climb up to the fort for the panoramic view, stopping at the museum for an overview of the island. Marina Port La Royale is the shopping–lunch spot central to the port, but rue de la République and rue de la Liberté, which border the bay, have some duty-free shops and boutiques. The West Indies Mall offers a deluxe (and air-conditioned) shopping experience. There's less bustle here than in Philipsburg, but the open-air cafés are still tempting places to sit and people-watch. From the harbor front you can catch ferries for Anguilla and St. Barth. Parking can be a real challenge during the business day, and even at night during the high season.

Fort Louis. Though not much remains of the structure itself, Fort Louis, which was completed by the French in 1789, is great fun if you want to climb the 92 steps to the top for the wonderful views of the island and neighboring Anguilla. On Wednesday and Saturday there is a market in the square at the bottom. ⊠ *Marigot*.

FRENCH CUL DE SAC

North of Orient Bay Beach, the French colonial mansion of St. Martin's mayor is nestled in the hills. Little red-roof houses look like open umbrellas tumbling down the green hillside. The area is peaceful and good for hiking. From the beach here, shuttle boats make the five-minute trip to Ilet Pinel, an uninhabited island that's fine for picnicking, snorkeling, sunning, and swimming. There are full-service beach clubs there, so just pack the sunscreen and head over.

GRAND CASE

The Caribbean's own Restaurant Row is the heart of this French-side town, a 10-minute drive from either Orient Bay or Marigot, stretching along a narrow beach overlooking Anguilla. You'll find a first-rate restaurant for every palate, mood, and wallet. At lunchtime, or with kids, head to the casual *lolos* (open-air barbecue stands) and feet-in-the-sand beach bars. Twilight drinks and tapas are fun. At night, stroll the strip and preview the sophisticated offerings on the menus posted outside before you settle in for a long and sumptuous meal (reservations are required for some of the top restaurants). If you still have the energy, there are lounges with music (usually a DJ) that get going after 10 pm.

ORLÉANS

North of Oyster Pond and the Étang aux Poissons (Fish Lake) is the island's oldest settlement, also known as the French Quarter. You can still see a few vibrantly painted West Indian–style homes with the original gingerbread fretwork. There are also large areas of the nature and marine preserve trying to save the island's fragile ecosystem.

PIC DU PARADIS

Fodor'sChoice ★ Between Marigot and Grand Case, Paradise Peak, at 1,492 feet, is the island's highest point. There are two observation areas. From them, the tropical forest unfolds below, and the vistas are breathtaking. The road is quite isolated and steep, best suited to a four-wheel-drive vehicle. There have also been some problems with crime in this area, so it might be best to go hiking with an experienced local guide.

FAMILY Fodor'sChoice ★ **Loterie Farm.** Halfway up the road to Pic du Paradis is a peaceful 150-acre private nature preserve, opened to the public in 1999 by American expat B.J. Welch. There are trail maps, so you can hike on your own or hire a guide. Marked trails traverse native forest with tamarind, gum, mango, and mahogany trees. With luck you can see a greenback monkey. L'Eau Lounge is a lovely tropical garden with a chain of spring-fed pools and Jacuzzi area with lounge chairs, great music, roaming iguanas, and chic tented cabanas with a St. Barth–meets–Wet 'n' Wild atmosphere; groups should consider the VIP private tree house/cabanas complete with champagne and attentive service. A delicious, healthy treetop lunch or dinner can be had at **Hidden Forest Café,** and if you are brave—and over 4 feet 5 inches tall—you can try soaring over trees on one of the longest zip lines in the western hemisphere. There is a mild version, but people love the extreme one. "Treehab," a wild party at the end of every month, brings the island's best DJs; and the Garden Groove Party enlivens every Saturday night in June, July, and August. ✉ *103 rte. de Pic du Paradis, Rambaud* ☎ *0590/87–86–16* ⊕ *www.loteriefarm. com* ✈ *Hiking €5, guide €25, zip line €40–€60* ☼ *Tues.–Sun. 9–3:30.*

ELSEWHERE IN ST. MARTIN

FAMILY Fodor'sChoice ★ **Butterfly Farm.** If you arrive early in the morning when the butterflies first break out of their chrysalis, you can marvel at butterflies and moths from around the world and the host plants with which each evolved. At any given time, some 40 species of butterflies—and as many as 600

17

individual insects—flutter inside the lush screened garden and hatch on the plants housed there. Butterfly art and knickknacks are for sale in the gift shop. In case you want to come back, your ticket, which includes a guided tour, is good for your entire stay. ⊠ *Le Galion Beach Rd., Quartier d'Orléans* ☎ *0590/87–31–21* ⊕ *www.thebutterflyfarm. com* 🖭 *$12* ⊙ *Daily 9–3:30, last tour at 3.*

BEACHES

For such a small island, St. Maarten/St. Martin has a wide array of beaches, from the long expanse of Baie Orientale on the French side to powdery-soft Mullet Bay on the Dutch side.

Warm surf and a gentle breeze can be found at the island's 37 beaches, and every one of them is open to the public. Try several. Each is unique: some bustling and some bare, some refined and some rocky, some good for snorkeling and some for sunning. Whatever your fancy, it's here, including a clothing-optional beach at the south end of beautiful Baie Orientale. And several of the island's gems don't have big hotels lining their shores. Many beaches have chair rental concessions and beach bars. ∎TIP➔ **Petty theft from cars in beach parking lots is an unfortunate fact of life in St. Maarten and St. Martin. Leave nothing in your parked car, not even in the glove compartment or trunk.**

DUTCH SIDE

Several of the best Dutch-side beaches are developed and have large-scale resorts. But others, including Simpson Bay and Cupecoy, have little development. You'll sometimes find vendors or beach bars to rent chairs and umbrellas (but not always).

Cupecoy Beach. Near the Dutch-French border, this picturesque area of sandstone cliffs, white sand, and shoreline caves is a necklace of small beaches that come and go according to the whims of the sea. Even though the western part is more developed, the surf can be rough, and it's a steep walk down to the beach. Break-ins have been reported in cars, so don't leave anything at all in your vehicle. **Amenities:** food and drink. **Best for:** solitude; sunset. ⊠ *Between Baie Longue and Mullet Bay, Cupecoy.*

Dawn Beach. True to its name, this is the place to be at sunrise. On the Atlantic side of Oyster Pond, just south of the French border, it's a first-class beach for sunning and snorkeling, but the winds and rough water mean only strong swimmers should attempt to take a dip. It's not usually crowded, and there are several good restaurants nearby. To find it, follow the signs to the Westin or Mr. Busby's restaurant. **Amenities:** food and drink. **Best for:** snorkeling; sunrise. ⊠ *South of Oyster Pond, Dawn Beach.*

Great Bay. This bustling white-sand beach curves around Philipsburg just behind Front Street, making it easy to find. Here you'll find boutiques, eateries, a pleasant boardwalk, and rental chairs and umbrellas. Busy with cruise-ship passengers, the beach is best west of Captain Hodge

The view from Fort Louis, high above Marigot

Pier or around Antoine Restaurant. **Amenities:** food and drink. **Best for:** swimming; walking. ⊠ *Philipsburg.*

Little Bay. Despite its popularity with snorkelers, divers, kayakers, and boating enthusiasts, Little Bay isn't usually crowded, perhaps due to its gravelly sand. It does boast panoramic views of St. Eustatius, Philipsburg, the cruise-ship terminal, Saba, and St. Kitts. The beach is west of Fort Amsterdam and accessible via the Divi Little Bay Beach Resort. **Amenities:** food and drink; parking; toilets. **Best for:** snorkeling; swimming; walking. ⊠ *Little Bay Rd., Little Bay.*

FAMILY
Fodor's Choice
★
Mullet Bay Beach. Many believe that this mile-long, powdery white-sand beach behind the Mullet Bay Golf Course is the island's best. You can rent umbrellas and chairs here. Swimmers like it because the water is usually calm, but when the swell is up, surfers take over. The calm cove at the south end is good for kids. Listen for the "whispering pebbles" as the waves wash up. There are two beach bars that serve lunch and cold drinks. **Amenities:** food and drink. **Best for:** snorkeling; surfing; swimming. ⊠ *South of Cupecoy, Mullet Bay.*

Simpson Bay Beach. This secluded, half-moon stretch of white sand on the island's Caribbean side is a hidden gem. It's mostly surrounded by private residences, with no big resorts, no Jet Skiers, and no crowds. It's just you, the sand, and the water (along with one funky beach bar to provide some chairs and nourishment). Southeast of the airport, follow the signs to Mary's Boon and the Horny Toad guesthouses. **Amenities:** food and drink; showers; toilets. **Best for:** solitude; swimming; walking. ⊠ *Simpson Bay.*

FRENCH SIDE

Almost all of the French-side beaches, whether busy Baie Orientale or less busy Baie des Pères (Friar's Bay), have beach clubs and restaurants. For about $25 a couple you get two chaises (*transats*) and an umbrella (*parasol*) for the day, not to mention chair-side service for drinks and food. Only some beaches have bathrooms and showers, so if that is your preference, inquire.

Anse Heureuse (*Happy Bay*). Not many people know about this romantic, hidden gem. Happy Bay has powdery sand, gorgeous luxury villas, and stunning views of Anguilla. The snorkeling is also good. To get here, turn left on the rather rutted dead-end road to Baie des Péres (Friar's Bay). The beach itself is a 10- to 15-minute walk from the last beach bar. **Amenities:** food and drink; toilets. **Best for:** snorkeling; solitude; swimming; walking. ⊠ *Happy Bay.*

Baie de Grand Case. Along this skinny stripe of a beach bordering the culinary capital of Grand Case, the old-style gingerbread architecture sometimes peeps out between the bustling restaurants and boutiques. The sea is calm, and there are tons of fun lunch options from bistros to beachside barbecue stands (called *lolos*). Several of the restaurants rent chairs and umbrellas; some include their use for lunch patrons. In between there is a bit of shopping—for beach necessities but also for the same kinds of handicrafts found in the Marigot market. **Amenities:** food and drink; toilets. **Best for:** swimming; walking. ⊠ *Grand Case.*

FAMILY **Baie des Pères** (*Friar's Bay*). This quiet, somewhat rocky cove close to Marigot has beach grills and bars, with chaises and umbrellas, calm waters, and a lovely view of Anguilla. Kali's Beach Bar, open daily for lunch and (weather permitting) dinner, has a Rasta vibe and color scheme. It's the best place to be on the full moon, with music, dancing, and a huge bonfire, but you can get lunch, beach chairs, and umbrellas anytime. Friar's Bay Beach Café is a French bistro on the sand, open from breakfast to sunset. To get to the beach, take National Road 7 from Marigot, go toward Grand Case to the Morne Valois hill, and turn left on the dead-end road at the sign. **Amenities:** food and drink; toilets. **Best for:** partiers; swimming; walking. ⊠ *Anse des Pères.*

Baie Longue (*Long Bay*). Though it extends over the French Lowlands, from the cliff at La Samanna to La Pointe des Canniers, the island's longest beach has no facilities or vendors. It's a great place for a romantic walk, but be warned that car break-ins are a particular problem here. To get here, take National Road 7 south of Marigot. Baie Longue Road is the first entrance to the beach. It's worth a splurge for lunch or a sunset cocktail at the elegant La Samanna. **Amenities:** none. **Best for:** solitude; walking. ⊠ *Baie Longue.*

Fodor'sChoice **Baie Orientale** (*Orient Bay*). Many consider this the island's most beauti-
★ ful beach, but its 2 miles (3 km) of champagne sand, underwater marine reserve, variety of water sports, beach clubs, and hotels also make it one of the most crowded. Lots of "naturists" take advantage of the clothing-optional policy, so don't be shocked. Early-morning nude beach walking is de rigueur for the guests at Club Orient, at the southeastern end of the beach. Plan to spend the day at one of the clubs; each bar has

different color umbrellas, and all boast terrific restaurants and lively bars. You can have an open-air massage, try any sea toy you fancy, and stay until dark. To get here from Marigot, take National Road 7 past Grand Case, past the Aéroport de L'Espérance, and watch for the left turn. **Amenities:** food and drink; parking; toilets; water sports. **Best for:** nudists; partiers; swimming; walking; windsurfing. ⊠ *Baie Orientale.*

Baie Rouge (*Red Bay*). Here you can bask with the millionaires renting the big-ticket villas in the "neighborhood." The gorgeous beach and its salt ponds make up a nature preserve, site of the oldest habitation in the Caribbean. This area is widely thought to have the best snorkeling on the island. You can swim the crystal waters along the point and explore a swim-through cave. The beach is fairly popular with gay men in the mornings and early afternoons. The little restaurant Chez Raymond is open every day, and cocktail hour starts when the conch shell blows, so keep your ears open. There is a sign and a right turn after you leave Baie Nettlé. **Amenities:** food and drink; toilets. **Best for:** snorkeling; swimming; walking. ⊠ *Baie Rouge.*

FAMILY

Fodor's Choice

★

Ilet Pinel. A protected nature reserve, this kid-friendly island is a five-minute ferry ride from French Cul de Sac ($7 per person round-trip). The ferry runs every half hour from mid-morning until 4 pm. The water is clear and shallow, and the shore is sheltered. Snorkelers can swim a trail between both coasts of this pencil-shaped speck in the ocean. You can rent equipment on the island or in the parking lot before you board the ferry for about $12. Two beach clubs offer lunch: Karibuni (closed September) has the freshest fish, great salads, tapas, and drinks—try the frozen mojito and homemade ice cream. Yellow Beach has more of a party vibe with cocktail tables in the water. Chairs and umbrellas can be rented for $25 for two. **Amenities:** food and drink; parking. **Best for:** snorkeling; swimming. ⊠ *Ilet Pinel.*

FAMILY

Le Galion. A coral reef borders this quiet, protected beach, part of the island's nature preserve. The water is calm, clear, and quite shallow, so it's paradise with young kids. It's a full-service place, with chair rentals, a good restaurant, and water-sports operators. Kiteboarders and windsurfers like the trade winds at the far end of the beach. On Sunday there are always groups picnicking and partying. To get here, follow signs to the Butterfly Farm and continue toward the water. **Amenities:** food and drink; parking; toilets; water sports. **Best for:** partiers; small children; swimming; windsurfing. ⊠ *Quartier d'Orléans.*

WHERE TO EAT

Although most people come to St. Maarten/St. Martin for sun and fun, they leave praising the cuisine. On an island that covers only 37 square miles (96 square km), there are more than 400 restaurants. You can sample the best dishes from France, Thailand, Italy, Vietnam, India, Japan, and, of course, the Caribbean.

Many of the best restaurants are in Grand Case (on the French side), but you should not limit your culinary adventures to that village. Great dining thrives throughout the island, from the bistros of Marigot and the hopping upscale restaurants of Cupecoy to the tourist-friendly low-key eateries of Simpson Bay and the many *lolos* (roadside barbecue stands) throughout. Loyalists on both "sides" will cheerfully try to steer you to their favorites, and though it's common to cite high euro prices to deter exploration, quite a few restaurants still offer a one-to-one exchange rate if you use cash. Besides, main-course portions are often large enough to be shared.

During high season, it's essential to make reservations. Usually you can make them the same day. Dutch-side restaurants sometimes include a 15% service charge, so check your bill before tipping. On the French side, service is usually included (worth checking, here, too), but it is customary to leave 5%–10% extra. Don't leave tips on your credit card—it's customary to tip in cash. A taxi is probably the easiest solution to the parking problems in Grand Case, Marigot, and Philipsburg. Grand Case has two lots—each costs $4—at each end of the main boulevard, but they're often packed by 8 pm. Restaurants will be happy to call you a cab to return at the end of the meal.

What to Wear: Although appropriate dining attire ranges from swimsuits to sport jackets, casual dress is usually appropriate. For men, a nice shirt and khakis or jeans will take you anywhere; for women, dressy pants, a skirt, or even fancy shorts are usually acceptable. Jeans are fine in the less formal eateries.

DUTCH SIDE

CUPECOY

$$$$ SEAFOOD

🍴 **Bluefin.** The attractive white interior of this restaurant in the newly renovated Starz Casino complex has a Hamptons vibe. On the menu is the owner's catch of the day, prepared simply with fresh vegetables artistically garnishing the geometric plates. Lobsters from the tank are delectable, and there is plenty for meat lovers, too. Don't miss the traditional French *soupe de poisson* as a starter. [$] *Average main: $35* ✉ *Starz Casino Complex, Cupecoy* ☎ *721/584–2626* 🌐 *www.bluefinsxm.com* ✍ *Reservations essential.*

$$$ MEDITERRANEAN FAMILY

🍴 **Le Bateau Ivre.** In the middle of the plaza in the newish Porto Cupecoy Marina complex, this place is a good choice for an easy lunch thanks to big salads, American-style sandwiches, and varied crepes. Night brings French bistro classics plus seafood specials, frequently accompanied by a singer performing Edith Piaf. You can sit outdoors and admire the yachts or indoors for a more lounge-y feel. [$] *Average main: $26* ✉ *Marina Porto Cupecoy, Maho Reef* ☎ *721/526–2157* ⏲ *Closed Tues.*

$$$$ ECLECTIC FAMILY

🍴 **Mario Bistrot.** Over the harbor of Porto Cupecoy, you can sit next to the yachts (or inside) and enjoy the convivial atmosphere and good cooking that ensures the ongoing popularity of this dinner spot. The cooking is an eclectic mix of Continental and Caribbean with a little Asian flare. The tasty bouillabaisse is tinged with red curry, the tender brisket is prepared like a French beef bourguignonne, and piquant marinated chicken has a tasty pineapple chutney topping. Desserts are lavish and original creations; try the pear-and-macadamia tart with caramel sauce and salty-caramel ice cream. [$] *Average main: $35* ✉ *Porto Cupecoy, 56 Rhine Rd., Cupecoy* ☎ *721/523–2760* 🌐 *www.mariobistrot.com/.*

$$$ ASIAN FUSION 🍴 **Shanghai Brasserie.** The Porto Cupecoy plaza is a great destination for a tasty dinner, and one of the best places to try is this newcomer that serves a mixture of Szechuan and French food in a Tokyo Rose theme room with a touch of art deco. Sit inside or out on the patio and enjoy dumplings, tea-smoked duck, or something from the brasserie side of the extensive menu. [$] *Average main: $23* ✉ *Porto Cupecoy, Cupecoy* ☎ *721/546–4949* 🌐 *www.shanghaibrasserie.com* ✍ *Reservations essential.*

$$$$ ECLECTIC Fodor's Choice ★ 🍴 **Temptation.** Chef Dino Jagtiani trained at the Culinary Institute of America, and his dishes combine spices and ingredients that provide a full-blown blast of taste. Try hot and cold soup (together in one bowl), Middle East–spiced lamb sliders, excellent Angus steaks, or layered eggplant parmigiana. Jagtiani compares dessert to lovemaking ("both intimate, and not to be indulged in lightly"), crafting such creations as a tempura apple pie with cinnamon ice cream and caramel sauce. The extensive wine list features a number of reasonably priced selections. Enjoy the live piano in this sophisticated spot at the newly renovated Starz Casino. [$] *Average main: $36* ✉ *Starz Casino Courtyard, 106 Rhine Rd., Cupecoy* ☎ *721/545–5714* 🌐 *temptation-sxm.com* ⏲ *No lunch* ✍ *Reservations essential.*

$$ THAI FAMILY 🍴 **Thai Savanh'.** In a corner of the Starz Casino, this little restaurant does not look like much, but the authentic and supremely tasty Thai cuisine hits the spot when you're craving something spicy and exotic. From salad rolls and *nems* (spring rolls) to delicious curries, noodle dishes, and skewered satays, the food is satisfying and the portions are generous. [$] *Average main: $18* ✉ *Starz Casino, Rhine Rd., Cupecoy* ☎ *721/ 553–1204* ⏲ *Closed Sun.* 💳 *No credit cards.*

17

MAHO

$$$ ASIAN Fodor's Choice ★ 🍴 **Bamboo.** This hip mainstay on the top level of the Maho central shopping area features red lacquer walls, lounging tables, Indonesian art, a first-rate lounge, and electro-house tunes. You can get terrific sushi and sashimi, both classic Japanese varieties and Americanized ones. Asian hot appetizers and exotic cocktails like the Tranquility (citrus vodka and smoky oolong tea) are good, too. If you're not into sushi, try the roast chicken, steak, or seared salmon. Solo visitors have a great time hanging at the bar, and the place rocks till late night. From 5 to 7 pm sake, beer, and wine are half price, as are tapas and appetizers. [$] *Average main: $25* ✉ *Sonesta Maho Beach Resort & Casino, 1 Rhine Rd., Maho Reef* ☎ *721/545–3622* 🌐 *www.bamboo-sxm.com* ⏲ *Closed Sun.*

OYSTER POND

$$$ ECLECTIC FAMILY Fodor's Choice ★ 🍴 **Big Fish.** Big Fish offers big portions of fresh-caught fish, sushi, and upscale steaks served in a modern, Miami Beach atmosphere. The service is friendly and attentive. Great starters include their signature Hurricane Shrimp (with a closely guarded secret recipe), or crab cakes with a creative cocktail. Try just-caught grouper in lobster sauce, sparkling sushi, a Kobe beef burger, or melting short ribs. Leave room for Bailey's Crème Brûlée for dessert. On Tuesday nights you can bring your own wine with no corkage fee. [$] *Average main: $28* ✉ *14 Emerald Merit Rd., Oyster Pond* ☎ *721/543–6288* 🌐 *www.bigfishsxm.com* ⏲ *Closed late Aug.–mid Sept. No lunch.*

$$ ✕ **Mr. Busby's Beach Bar.** Come for beachside breakfast or lunch, under
ECLECTIC swaying palm trees; all the island favorites are here, including good
johnnycake sandwiches for breakfast. Burgers, ribs, salads, and sand-
wiches are served at lunch. At night it turns into Daniel's with pizza and
Italian specialties. $ *Average main: $13* ✉ *6 Emerald Merit Rd., Oyster
Pond* ☎ *721/543–6088* ⊕ *www.dawnbeachsxm.com.*

PHILIPSBURG

$ ✕ **Au Petit Café.** There are only a small number of tables (both indoor
CAFÉ and out) at this tiny bistro in the quaint shopping arcade just off Front
Street. Stop by for a quick, inexpensive snack or for a freshly ground cup
of coffee. Watching employees make crepes is half the fun; eating them
is the other half. You can also order hearty salads, pizza, and hot or cold
sandwiches on fresh bread to enjoy with the large selection of good teas.
It's open from 8 am to 4:30 pm. $ *Average main: $9* ✉ *120 Old St., Phil-
ipsburg* ☎ *721/552–8788* ⊟ *No credit cards* ⊗ *Closed Sun. No dinner.*

$$$$ ✕ **Ocean Lounge.** An airy modern veranda perched on the Philipsburg
ECLECTIC boardwalk gives a distinct South Beach vibe. You'll want to linger over
FAMILY fresh fish and steaks as you watch tourists pass by on romantic strolls
by night or determined cruise-ship passengers surveying the surrounding
shops by day. Daily three-, four-, and five-course tasting menus are a
pretty good deal. There is also a fun beachfront lounge with a menu of
bar snacks and martinis. It's a bit hard to park here so consider taking
a taxi at night. $ *Average main: $34* ✉ *Holland House Beach Hotel, 43
Front St., Philipsburg* ☎ *721/542–2572* ⊕ *www.hhbh.com.*

$$ ✕ **Taloula Mango's.** Ribs and burgers are the specialty at this casual
ECLECTIC beachfront restaurant, but the jerk chicken and thin-crust pizza, not to
FAMILY mention a few vegetarian options like tasty falafel, are not to be ignored.
On weekdays lunch is accompanied by (warning: loud) live music; every
Friday during happy hour a DJ spins tunes. In case you're wondering,
the restaurant got its name from the owner's golden retriever. $ *Aver-
age main: $17* ✉ *Sint Rose Shopping Mall, off Front St. on boardwalk,
Philipsburg* ☎ *721/542–1645* ⊕ *www.taloulamango.com.*

SIMPSON BAY

$ ✕ **Beirut.** Beruit serves delicious, fresh Middle Eastern specialties such
LEBANESE as falafel, kabobs, and salads, as well as meze such as baba ganoush.
FAMILY The friendly Lebanese owners make everyone feel right at home. There's
a hookah bar in the back in the evenings. $ *Average main: $11* ✉ *29
Airport Rd., Simpson Bay* ☎ *721/545–3612.*

$$$ ✕ **Izi Ristorante Italiano.** The former chef of La Gondola serves up huge,
ITALIAN sharable portions of more than 400 dishes in this popular, cheerful,
FAMILY centrally located space. For something fun, diners are invited to create
their own menu: pick a pasta and sauce, then add your choice of meat,
fish, and veggies. $ *Average main: $23* ✉ *Paradise Mall, 67 Welfare
Rd., Simpson Bay* ☎ *721/544–3079* ⊕ *www.iziristoranteitaliano.com*
⊗ *Closed Tues. May–Nov. No lunch* ⚖ *Reservations essential.*

$$ ✕ **Karakter Beach Lounge.** This funky and charming modern beach bar,
ECLECTIC right behind the airport, serves up fun, great music, relaxation, and a lot
FAMILY of style. The vibe is more like St-Tropez than St. Maarten. Open from
Fodor'sChoice 9 am till 10 pm, the restaurant serves up fresh fruit smoothies, tropical
★ cocktails, fresh fruit salads, healthy sandwiches, and tapas. There is live

music in the evening. A sign near the shower/bathhouse invites you to "come hang out here and shower before you go to the airport"—in case you want to spend every second possible on the sand. $ *Average main: $14 ⊠ 121 Simpson Bay Rd., Simpson Bay* ☎ *721/523–9983* ⊕ *www. karakterstmaarten.com/.*

$$
CARIBBEAN
FAMILY
✕ **Skipjack's.** Right on Simpson Bay, Skipjack's is popular for crowd pleasers such as fried calamari, shrimp cocktail, sandwiches, and a good variety of fresh seafood. The lobster, both from Maine and the spiny Caribbean variety, is a specialty. The restaurant has a friendly attitude that makes it great for families. If you are in a villa or condo and feel like cooking, the fish market here is one of the best. $ *Average main: $18 ⊠ Welfare Rd., Simpson Bay* ☎ *721/ 544–2313* ⊕ *www.skipjacks-sxm.com* ⊟ *No credit cards.*

$$$$
FRENCH
Fodor's Choice
★
✕ **So French.** A sister property to the popular Dutch-side restaurant La Cigale, So French is gaining its own following with charming staff and a constantly changing menu. On a breezy porch with great views of Pelican Bay, diners enjoy such delicious starters such as house-made gravlax, gazpacho, or a delicious slice of foie gras served with a dried-fruit chutney, followed by entrées such as roasted duck breast, pork tenderloin in a caramel sauce, and creole spiced roasted turbot. The melted chocolate dessert, served with salted caramel ice cream, is excellent here. $ *Average main: $33 ⊠ 1 Citrine Rd., Billy Folly, Simpson Bay* ☎ *721/544–1143* ⊕ *www.sxmrestaurantsofrench.com.*

$
VEGETARIAN
FAMILY
Fodor's Choice
★
✕ **Top Carrot.** Open from 7:30 am to 6 pm, this friendly café and juice bar is a popular healthy breakfast and lunch stop. It features fresh and tasty vegetarian entrées, sandwiches, salads, and homemade pastries The fresh fruit and vegetable juices and smoothies are excellent. Favorites include a pastry stuffed with pesto, avocado, red pepper, and feta cheese, and a cauliflower, spinach, and tomato quiche. The house-made granola and yogurt are popular, but folks also drop in just for espresso and the large selection of teas. Many also come for the free Wi-Fi. Adjacent to the restaurant is a gift shop with Asian-inspired items, spiritual books, yoga theme T-shirts, and cotton beach cover-ups. $ *Average main: $9 ⊠ Airport Rd., near Simpson Bay Yacht Club, Simpson Bay* ☎ *721/544–3381* ⊙ *Closed Sun. No dinner.*

$
CAFÉ
✕ **Zee Best.** This friendly bistro serves one of the best breakfasts on the island. There's a huge selection of fresh-baked pastries—try the almond croissants—plus sweet and savory crepes, omelets, quiches, and other treats from the oven. When you sit down, a basket of assorted pastries arrives, and you are charged for the ones you select. Specialties include the St. Martin omelet, filled with ham, cheese, mushrooms, onions, green peppers, and tomatoes. Best of all, breakfast is served until 2. Lunch includes sandwiches, salads, and the chef's famous spaghetti Bolognese. ■ **TIP→ There are also locations near the airport and at Port de Plaisance.** $ *Average main: $8 ⊠ Plaza del Lago, Simpson Bay* ☎ *721/544–2477* ⊕ *www.zeebestrestaurant.com* ⊟ *No credit cards* ⊙ *No dinner.*

17

FRENCH SIDE

BAIE DES PÈRES

$$ BISTRO FAMILY Fodor'sChoice ★ 🍴 **Friar's Bay Beach Café.** There is a sophisticated vibe at this quiet, rather elegant beach club that may make you feel as if you're on a private beach. You can rent lounge chairs and umbrellas and spend the whole day relaxing, drinking, and dining. With decor less funky than some other beach-club restaurants, it is open from breakfast through the spectacular sunset, offering a menu reminiscent of a French bistro. A blackboard lists specials, carpaccios of meat and fish are sparklingly fresh, and the salads are terrific. French standbys include tomato and goat cheese tartlets, and "international" ones add burgers and sandwiches. Sunday evenings have live music until 9. Watch for the red-and-black signs on the road between Grand Case and Marigot, and drive slow because the road is rough. [$] *Average main: €18* ✉ *Friar's Bay Rd., Anse des Pères* ☎ *0590/49–16–87* 💳 *No credit cards* 🕒 *No dinner.*

BAIE NETTLÉ

$$$ ECLECTIC 🍴 **Dreams.** Visit this lively beach club for the day, relaxing and dining on sushi, tapas, great salads, pizza, and French specialties. Visit after dark and it's a restaurant/lounge party, with a DJ and dancing on Saturday night. [$] *Average main: €27* ✉ *Baie Nettlé* ☎ *690/75–91–05* 🌐 *dreams-sxm.com* 🕒 *Closed Sun. night.*

$$$$ FRENCH Fodor'sChoice ★ 🍴 **La Cigale.** On the edge of Baie Nettlé, this restaurant has wonderful views of the lagoon from its dining room and open-air patio, but the charm comes from the devoted attention of adorable owner Olivier, helped by his mother and brother and various cousins, too. The delicious food is edible sculpture: ravioli of lobster with wild mushrooms and foie gras are poached in an intense lobster bisque, and house-smoked gravlax and salmon is garnished with a garlic cream sauce. For dessert, the house-made ginger ice cream with flambéed pineapple is a favorite. New in 2016 is a sister restaurant, So French, in the Pelican Bay area. [$] *Average main: €43* ✉ *101 Laguna Beach, Baie Nettlé* ☎ *0590/87–90–23* 🌐 *www.restaurant-lacigale.com* 🕒 *Closed Sun. and Sept. and Oct. No lunch* ✍ *Reservations essential.*

$$$$ FRENCH FAMILY Fodor'sChoice ★ 🍴 **Le Sand.** A stylish, upscale St. Barth vibe and beachfront location make this a great choice. Relax on the terrace for cocktails and snacks, or park yourself on a lounge chair on the beach with an umbrella for the day and enjoy the service, music, and ambience. The refined food is fresh and nicely presented; the snapper and beef and fish tartares are standouts, but real credit is due to the management and staff, who are friendly and attentive. [$] *Average main: €35* ✉ *Sandy Bay, Baie Nettlé* ☎ *0690/73–14–38.*

$$$ ITALIAN FAMILY Fodor'sChoice ★ 🍴 **Mezza Luna.** Under the shady pergolas at Mezza Luna you can sit with your feet in the sand any time of day and enjoy gorgeous beach views. Everything (including the perfectly cooked pasta) is homemade from first-rate ingredients. In addition to pasta, the extensive menu and chalkboard of daily specials feature updated Italian dishes with a bit of island flair. *Burrata* is paired with prosciutto. Shaved raw artichoke with arugula and Parmesan is refreshing, and Duck Breast O.M.G. deserves the moniker, which could also be applied to the truffle risotto.

House-made tiramisu is the perfect ending. Pizza is available for take-out. $ *Average main: €28* ✉ *501 Nettlé Bay Beach Club, Baie Nettlé* ☎ *690/73–19–18.*

$$$ ✕ **Ma Ti' Beach.** On the road to Marigot, this casual beach bar has
FRENCH   better-than-average food and great views across the turquoise water
FAMILY   to Anguilla. You can always get fresh lobster from the tank, and the traditional French onion soup with a cheesy crust is excellent. If the *moules frites* (fresh mussels) are a special, snap them up. $ *Average main: €23* ✉ *Anse Marigot, across from Mercure resort, Baie Nettlé* ☎ *0590/87–01–30.*

BAIE ORIENTALE

$$$ ✕ **L'Astrolabe.** Chef Maxime Orea gets raves for his modern interpre-
FRENCH   tations of classic French cuisine served around the pool at this cozy,
Fodor'sChoice   relaxed restaurant in the Esmeralda Resort. Corn soup, duck liver "tril-
★   ogy," an amazing roast duck with spiced apple sauce, and deliciously fresh fish dishes are just some of the offerings. There are also lots of vegetarian choices, a three-course prix fixe with a choice of any menu item (a couple with a small supplement), a children's menu, Monday night jazz, and a lobster party with live music every Friday night. $ *Average main: €26* ✉ *Esmeralda Resort, Baie Orientale* ☎ *0590/87–11–20* ⊕ *www.astrolabe-sxm.com* ⊗ *No lunch. No dinner Wed.* ⌕ *Reservations essential.*

$$$ ✕ **La Table d'Antoine.** Settle in here for an evening of attentive, friendly
FRENCH   service and hearty French-country food with a side dish of lively people-
FAMILY   watching. The varied menu features slightly unfamiliar dishes that are worth a try, many with a Provençal touch, like the caramelized onion tart. There are several gluten-free options, and a kid's menu. Desserts are delicious, as is the selection of house-made infused rums. $ *Average main: €25* ✉ *Pl. de la Baie Orientale, Baie Orientale* ☎ *0590/52–97–57* ⊕ *www. latabledantoinesxm.com* ⊗ *Closed Tues. Closed Mon. in low season.*

$$$ ✕ **Palm Beach.** As stylish as its Florida namesake, this beach club sets the
FRENCH FUSION   stage with Balinese art and furniture, big comfy chaises on the beach,
FAMILY   and an active bar. There are three big tree house–like lounges for lunch or to spend the afternoon, plus a spa for beachside massages. Salads, tartares, and Thai-influenced salads and noodle specialties are served in a pavilion shaded by sail-like awnings. The Sunday night beach party is the place to be, and there are monthly daytime beach parties, too. $ *Average main: €21* ✉ *Baie Orientale* ☎ *0690/35–99–06* ⊕ *www. palmbeachsxm.net* ⊗ *No dinner.*

$$$$ ✕ **Waikiki Beach.** Sit at a picnic table or on a lounge bed, and enjoy the
ECLECTIC   essence of Orient Beach with great food and people-watching. It's an all-day beach party. If there's a big cruise-ship group, however, you may just want to head down to the beach. During the Christmas holiday season, top DJs are brought in for partying into the night, and every Sunday there is a bountiful buffet lunch with lively music and a sexy fashion show that draws raves. $ *Average main: €35* ✉ *5 Baie Orientale, Baie Orientale* ☎ *0590/87–43–19* ⊕ *www.waikikibeachsxm.com.*

17

FRENCH CUL DE SAC

$$$ ╳ **Anse Marcel Beach.** Beachside calm with a side order of chic is on the

MODERN FRENCH menu at this lovely and private cove restaurant/beach club, good for

Fodor'sChoice a beach day, a sunset cocktail, and great swimming. You can dine and

★ lounge all day, either in the tented pavilion or on the beach. The food changes according to market availabilities, but there are always salads, tasty mussels, fresh grilled fish and lobster, steaks, and sandwiches; try the smoked salmon and bagel combo if it's offered. The desserts are amazing, especially the crepes. There is safe, private parking for cars and moorings available for boats. Reservations are essential in high season. $ *Average main: €24* ⊠ *Anse Marcel Beach, Anse Marcel* ☎ *0690/26-38-50* ⊕ *www.ansemarcelbeach.com.*

$$$ ╳ **Le Ti Bouchon.** This tiny restaurant, close to Anse Marcel hotels, cap-

FRENCH tures the spirit of Lyon, the capital of French gastronomy, where casual

Fodor'sChoice small restaurants serve hearty traditional cuisine, wine comes by the

★ pitcher, and the patron is very much part of the party. The eight tables are set on the porch of a traditional cottage, and the menu (written on a chalkboard) changes frequently. Chances are you will become fast friends with the owner, Momo, join in conversations with the next table, and linger over your chocolate mousse. Dietary restrictions are handled with grace and accuracy. There are two seatings for dinner. $ *Average main: €30* ⊠ *110 rte. de Cul de Sac, Cul de Sac* ☎ *0690/64-84-64* ⊕ *www.tibouchonrestaurant.com* ⊘ *Closed late July–mid Oct. No lunch* ⌲ *Reservations essential.*

$$$ ╳ **Sol e Luna.** Charming and romantic, Sol e Luna has a modern tropical

FRENCH FUSION style, with waterfall plunge pools and great views over Orient Bay. The menu offers French classics tinged with exotic flavors. Start with the baked goat cheese with basil and dried tomatoes, or a lobster mojito with edamame, mint, and sesame oil. Mains include shell pasta with shellfish, veal tournedos with foie gras, and rare yellowfin tuna with braised endive and bok choi. The restaurant is part of a guesthouse complex with six lovely suites if you love this romantic spot so much that you can't bear to leave. $ *Average main: €27* ⊠ *61 rte. de Mont Vernon, Cul de Sac* ☎ *0590/29-08-56* ⊕ *www.solelunarestaurant.com* ⌲ *Reservations essential.*

GRAND CASE

$$ ╳ **Bacchus.** If you want to lunch with the savviest locals, you have to

FRENCH scrape yourself off the beach and head into an industrial park outside

Fodor'sChoice Grand Case, where Benjamin Laurent, the best wine importer in the

★ Caribbean, has built this lively, deliciously air-conditioned reconstruction of a wine cellar. First-rate starters, salads, and main courses made from top ingredients brought in from France are lovingly prepared. You can also buy gourmet groceries or order from the extensive take-out menu. Smokers hang in the cigar–rum lounge. Naturally, the wines are sublime, and you can get an amazing education along with a great lunch. Enter at the "Hope Estate" sign in the roundabout across from the road that leads to the Grand Case airport. $ *Average main: €20* ⊠ *18–19 Hope Estate, Grand Case Rd., Grand Case* ☎ *0590/87-15-70* ⊕ *www.bacchussxm.com* ⊘ *Closed Sun. No dinner.*

$$ CARIBBEAN FAMILY Fodor's Choice ★ 🍴 **Cynthia's Talk of the Town.** Although St. Martin is known for upscale dining, each town has its barbecue stands, called *lolos*—even Grand Case. Locals flock to the half-dozen stands in the middle of town, on the water side, for a fun, relatively cheap, and iconic St. Martin meal. With plastic utensils and paper plates, Cynthia's couldn't be more informal. The menu includes everything from succulent grilled ribs to stewed conch, fresh snapper, and grilled lobster at the most reasonable prices on the island. All come with several tasty sides, like plantains, curried rice, beans, and coleslaw. Don't miss the johnnycakes. The service is friendly, if a bit slow; sit back with a $1.50 beer and enjoy the experience. On weekends there is often live music. At this writing, a 1:1 euro-dollar exchange rate is offered. **■ TIP→ Come earlier in the day for fresher fare.** [$] *Average main: €14* ✉ *Bd. de Grand Case, Grand Case* ☎ *0590/35–67–84* 💳 *No credit cards* ✍ *Reservations not accepted.*

$$$ FRENCH 🍴 **L'Auberge Gourmande.** With a formal, French-provincial dining room framed by elegant arches, L'Auberge Gourmande is in one of the island's oldest creole houses. The light Provençal cuisine includes roasted rack of lamb with an herb crust over olive mashed potatoes, Dover sole in almond butter, and pork filet mignon stuffed with apricots and walnuts. There are daily specials, vegetarian options, a kids' menu, and a good selection of wines. [$] *Average main: €27* ✉ *89 bd. de Grand Case, Grand Case* ☎ *0590/87–73–37* 🌐 *www.laubergegourmande.com* 🕒 *Closed Sept. No lunch.*

17

$$$ FRENCH 🍴 **Le Cottage.** Inventive French cuisine is prepared with a light touch and presented with flair, and perhaps a bit of humor, here. There are lots of themed "tasting" plates with interesting variations on an ingredient. Alternatively, try a prix-fixe meal. Huge portions of hearty French food are served by a genial staff to a lively community gathered on the street-front porch. The caramel dessert tasting features a perfect soufflé or the house-made salted caramel meringues. Consider the lobster tasting menu or combine almost any three courses from the menu. [$] *Average main: €29* ✉ *97 bd. de Grand Case, Grand Case* ☎ *0590/29–03–30* 🌐 *www.lecottagesxm.com* 🕒 *No lunch* ✍ *Reservations essential.*

$$$$ FRENCH Fodor's Choice ★ 🍴 **Le Pressoir.** This restaurant in a carefully restored West Indian house painted in brilliant reds and blues has charm to spare. The name comes from the historic salt press that sits opposite the restaurant, but the thrill comes from the culinary creations of chef Franc Mear and the hospitality of his beautiful wife, Melanie. If you are indecisive, or just plain smart, try any (or all) of the degustations (tastings) of four soups, four foie gras preparations, or four fruit desserts—all sophisticated preparations with adorable presentations. Foie gras is served in a dollhouse-size terrine with a teensy glass of Sauternes. There is a €15 kids' dinner. [$] *Average main: €35* ✉ *30 bd. de Grand Case, Grand Case* ☎ *0590/87–76–62* 🌐 *www.lepressoirsxm.com* 🕒 *Closed mid-Sept.–mid-Oct. and Sun. in May–Dec. No lunch* ✍ *Reservations essential.*

$$$$ FRENCH FUSION 🍴 **Le Shambala.** Romantic and beachy-chic, this waterfront restaurant has a lavish south-of-France vibe, with prices to match. Come for the sunset and start with an interesting cocktail before moving on to bruschetta, quiche, steak tartare, roast chicken, or simply prepared fish with fresh veggies. Sophisticated desserts—all made in-house—can be

paired with a glass of champagne (more than a dozen types to choose from). $ *Average main: €31* ⊠ *28 bd. de Grand Case, Grand Case* ☎ *0590/29–17–09* ⊕ *www.leshambala.com* ⚐ *Reservations essential.*

$$$$
FRENCH

✕ **Le Tastevin.** In the heart of Grand Case and on everyone's list of favorites, this attractive wood-beam room has been attractively redecorated and modernized. Tasty food served on a breezy porch over a glittering blue sea is enhanced by Joseph, the amiable owner. Salads and simple grills rule for lunch; at dinner, try one of the seasonal specials featuring what's best in the local markets. $ *Average main: €32* ⊠ *86 bd. de Grand Case, Grand Case* ☎ *0590/87–55–45* ⊕ *www.letastevin-restaurant.com* ☉ *Closed mid-Aug.–Sept.* ⚐ *Reservations essential.*

$$
INTERNATIONAL

✕ **Rainbow.** Rainbow's beachfront deck with a front-row seat (or lounge chair) on Grand Case beach is a good bet for breakfast, lunch, or dinner. The eclectic menu is mostly French, but you can choose snacks, sandwiches, burgers, steak, and grilled fish, and lobster, too. It's fun to come here at the end of the day for tapas and dynamite sundowner cocktails. There's a happy hour party every Monday night with all-you-can-eat tapas and a good DJ. $ *Average main: €20* ⊠ *176 bd. de Grand Case, Grand Case* ☎ *590/87–55–80* ⊕ *www.rainbowcafe.fr* ▭ *No credit cards.*

$$$
ITALIAN

✕ **Spiga.** In a beautifully restored creole house, tasty cuisine fuses Italian and Caribbean ingredients and cooking techniques. Follow one of the ample appetizers with an excellent pasta, fresh fish, or meat dish, such as the pesto-crusted rack of lamb. Vegetarian and gluten-free options are noted on the menu. Try the tiramisu or one of the grappas. Ask for a table outside on the porch. $ *Average main: €29* ⊠ *4 rte. de L'Espérance, Grand Case* ☎ *0590/52–47–83* ⊕ *www.spiga-sxm.com* ☉ *Closed mid-Sept.–late Oct. and Tues. in June–mid-Sept. No lunch* ⚐ *Reservations essential.*

MARIGOT

$$$
FRENCH

✕ **Bistro Nu.** It's hard to top the authentic French comfort food and reasonable prices you can find at this intimate restaurant tucked in a Marigot alley. Traditional French dishes like steak au poivre, sweetbreads with mushroom sauce, and sole meunière are served in a friendly, intimate dining room, which is now air-conditioned. The prix-fixe menu is a very good value, as are many of the bottles on the wine list. The place is popular, and the few tables are routinely packed until it closes at midnight. It can be difficult to park here, so take your chances at finding a spot on the street near the soccer stadium—or try a taxi. $ *Average main: €24* ⊠ *Allée de l'Ancienne Geôle, Marigot* ☎ *590/87–97–09* ⊕ *www.bistronu.com* ☉ *Closed Sun.* ⚐ *Reservations essential.*

$$
CARIBBEAN

✕ **Enoch's Place.** Enoch's lolo-style creole cooking is a Marigot must. Specialties include garlic shrimp, fresh lobster, and rice and beans like your St. Martin mother used to make. Try the saltfish and fried johnnycake— a great breakfast option. The food more than makes up for the lack of decor. Come early as some of the best dishes run out. $ *Average main: €13* ⊠ *Marigot Market, Front de Mer, Marigot* ☎ *0590/29–29–88* ▭ *No credit cards* ☉ *Closed Sun. No dinner* ⚐ *Reservations not accepted.*

$$
CONTEMPORARY

✕ **La Source.** Somewhat hidden behind the boutiques in Marina Port La Royale (look near Vilebrequin), this tiny "healthy" restaurant features a French seasonal menu as well as sandwiches, salads, soups, fair-trade coffee and teas, and organic pastries. A bargain lunch includes the special of the day and a drink, and the organic pasta dishes are delicious and inventive. The light choices, which include crab tartare with seaweed and organic-chicken salad, are terrific. $ *Average main: €14* ✉ *Marina Port La Royale, Marigot* ☎ *0590/27–17–27.*

$$ ✕ **Le Marrakech.** Some 20 years ago, the charming owners renovated
MOROCCAN this historic St. Martin *case.* After several other restaurant ventures,
Fodor'sChoice they returned to the cottage to serve up delicious, authentic Moroc-
★ can cuisine in a beautiful and romantic space with an open garden that feels like Morocco. The food is fragrant and delicious, with portions so huge you'll have enough for lunch the next day. The couscous and tagines are authentically spiced and delivered in Moroccan serving pieces by the affable and professional staff. The mixed appetizers (*meze*) are delectable, and the royal couscous is justly popular. Lounge in the tented courtyard after dinner—you may be entertained by a talented belly dancer. The restaurant is on Marigot's main road across from the stadium. $ *Average main: €18* ✉ *169 rue de Hollande, Marigot* ☎ *0590/27–54–48* ⊕ *www.marrakechsxm.wordpress.com* ☯ *Closed Sun. No lunch* ⟋ *Reservations essential.*

$$$ ✕ **Tropicana.** This bustling bistro at the Marina Port La Royale is busy
FRENCH all day long, thanks to a varied menu, (relatively) reasonable prices, and friendly staff. Salads are superb lunch options, especially the salade Niçoise with medallions of crusted goat cheese. Dinner brings some exceptional steak and seafood dishes, and the wine list is quite extensive. Desserts are tasty, including old standbys like crème brûlée. You can dine outside or in. $ *Average main: €21* ✉ *Marina Port La Royale, Marigot* ☎ *0590/87–79–07.*

PIC DU PARADIS

$$ ✕ **Hidden Forest Café.** Schedule your trip to Loterie Farm to take in lunch
CARIBBEAN or dinner in lovely tree-house pavilions with a safari vibe the hip clien-
FAMILY tele can appreciate. The yummy, locally sourced food is inventive and
Fodor'sChoice fresh. Curried-spinach chicken with banana fritters is a popular pick,
★ but there are great choices for vegetarians, too, including cumin lentil balls. Those with stouter appetites dig into the massive black Angus tenderloin. Loterie Farm's other eatery, Treelounge, features great cocktails and tapas, is open Monday through Saturday, and stays open late with frequent live music. $ *Average main: €20* ✉ *Loterie Farm, 103 rte. de Pic du Paradis, Rambaud* ☎ *0590/87–86–16* ⊕ *www.loteriefarm. com* ☯ *Closed Mon.*

QUARTIER D'ORLEANS

$$ ✕ **Yvette's Restaurant.** Follow the locals to Yvette's restaurant, in a private
CARIBBEAN house, for the island's best creole-Cajun cooking. All the St. Maarten
FAMILY favorites are dished up in big portions. This is the place to try pickled conch, stuffed crab backs, conch and dumplings, coconut curry chicken, and curry goat. Fried plantains, rice and peas, and hot johnnycakes come on the side. It's hard to find, so consider scoping it out in the daylight before your visit, or come for lunch. $ *Average main: €19* ✉ *Quartier d'Orléans* ✛ *Located on the side street off the main road of Quartier d'Orléans, across the road from the pharmacy.* ☎ *590/87– 32–03* ☯ *Closed Wed.* ▭ *No credit cards.*

17

CLOSE UP

St. Maarten vs. St. Martin

If this is your first trip to St. Maarten/ St. Martin, you're probably wondering which side will better suit your needs. That's hard to say, because in some ways the difference between the two can seem as subtle as the hazy boundary dividing them. But there are some major distinctions.

St. Maarten, the Dutch side, has the casinos, more nightlife, smaller price tags, and bigger hotels. St. Martin, the French side, has no casinos, less nightlife, and hotels that are smaller and more intimate. Many have kitchenettes, and most include breakfast. There are many good restaurants on the Dutch side, but if fine dining makes your vacation, staying on the French side will minimize time spent driving.

WHERE TO STAY

St. Maarten/St. Martin accommodations range from modern megaresorts such as the Hotel Riu Palace and the Westin St. Maarten to condos, villas, and stylish intimate guesthouses. On the Dutch side many hotels cater to groups, and although that's also true to some extent on the French side, you can find a larger collection of intimate accommodations there. ■ TIP→ Off-season rates (April through the beginning of December) can be as little as half the high-season rates.

TIME-SHARE RENTALS

Time-share properties are scattered around the island, mostly on the Dutch side. There's no reason to buy a share, as these condos are rented out whenever the owners are not in residence. If you stay in one, try to avoid a sales pitch which can last over two hours! Most rent by the night, but there's often substantial savings if you secure a weekly rate. Not all offer daily maid service. As some properties are undergoing renovations at this writing, ask about construction conditions, and in any case, ask for a recently renovated unit.

PRIVATE VILLAS

Villas are a great lodging option, especially for families who don't need to keep the kids occupied, or groups of friends who like hanging out together. Since these are for the most part freestanding houses, their greatest advantage is privacy. Properties are scattered throughout the island, often in gated communities or on secluded roads. Some have bare-bones furnishings, whereas others are over-the-top luxurious, with gyms, theaters, game rooms, and several different pools. There are private chefs, gardeners, maids, and other staffers to care for both the villa and its occupants.

Villas are secured through rental companies. They offer weekly prices that range from reasonable to more than many people make in a year. Check around, as prices for the same property vary from agent to agent. Because of the economy, many villas are now offered by the night rather than the week. Rental companies usually provide airport transfers and concierge service, and for an extra fee will even stock your refrigerator.

RENTAL CONTACTS

Caribbean Real Estate. Romac Southeby's International Realty rents luxury villas, many in gated communities. ⊠ *54 Simpson Bay Rd., Simpson Bay* ☎ *877/537–9282 in the U.S.* ⊕ *www.caribbeanbestrealestate.com.*

French Caribbean International. This company offers rental properties on the French side. ☎ *800/322–2223 in U.S.* ⊕ *www.frenchcaribbean.com.*

HomeAway. This listing service is the world's leading vacation rentals marketplace. To rent a condo, you contact the owner directly. ☎ *512/684–1098* ⊕ *www.homeaway.com.*

Island Hideaways. The island's oldest rental company rents villas on both sides. ☎ *800/832–2302 in U.S.,* ⊕ *www.islandhideaways.com.*

Island Properties. This company's properties are scattered around the island. ⊠ *62 Welfare Rd., Simpson Bay* ☎ *721/544–4580, 866/370–7979 in U.S.* ⊕ *www.remaxislandproperties.com.*

Jennifer's Vacation Villas. You can rents villas on both sides of the island from this company. ⊠ *Plaza Del Lago, Simpson Bay Yacht Club, Simpson Bay* ☎ *631/546–7345 in New York, 721/544–3107 in St. Maarten* ⊕ *www.jennifersvacationvillas.com.*

Pierres Caraïbes. Owned by American Leslie Reed and associated with Sotheby's, this company rents upscale St. Martin villas. First-rate properties are available in all sizes and prices. ⊠ *Plaza Caraïbes, rue Kennedy, Bldg. A, Marigot* ☎ *0590/51–02–85, 213/805–0840 in U.S.* ⊕ *www.stmartinsothebysrealty.com.*

Villas of Distinction. This is one of the oldest villa-rental companies on both the French and Dutch sides. The website can have special deals. ☎ *800/289–0900 in U.S.* ⊕ *www.villasofdistinction.com.*

WIMCO. This outfit has more hotel, villa, apartment, and condo listings in the Caribbean than most other companies. ☎ *401/849-8012 in U.S.* ⊕ *www.wimco.com.*

17

DUTCH SIDE

CUPECOY

$$$
RENTAL

The Cliff at Cupecoy Beach. These luxurious, high-rise condos are rented out when the owners are not in residence; depending on the owner's personal style, they can be downright fabulous. **Pros:** great views; good for families; close to Maho casinos and restaurants; tight security. **Cons:** no hotel services other than concierge. $ *Rooms from: $425* ⊠ *Rhine Rd., Cupecoy* ☎ *866/978–5839, 721/546–6633* ⊕ *www.cliffsxm.com* ↝ *72 apartments* ⊙ *No meals.*

MAHO

$$
RESORT
FAMILY

Sonesta Maho Beach Resort & Casino. The island's largest hotel, which is on Maho Beach and typically caters to big groups, isn't luxurious or fancy, but this family-friendly, full-service resort offers everything right on the premises at reasonable rates, and it's located very close to the airport. **Pros:** huge resort complex; lots of shopping; nonstop activities.

Westin St. Maarten Dawn Beach Resort & Spa

Cons: ongoing renovations; not for a quiet getaway; limited dining choices on all-inclusive plan. *[$] Rooms from: $283 ⊠ 1 Rhine Rd., Box 834, Maho Reef ☎ 721/545–2115, 800/223–0757, 800/766–3782 ⊕ www.sonesta.com/mahobeach ⤳ 537 rooms ⁙ All-inclusive.*

$$$$ ⊡ **Sonesta Ocean Point.** The roomy suites in this sophisticated, luxuri-
RESORT ous enclave are some of the very best accommodations on the island.
Fodor's Choice **Pros:** brand-new comfortable rooms; great design; private dining.
★ **Cons:** access is through the Sonesta Maho complex; proximity to air-
port gives you a lot of chances to watch the dramatic plane landings,
it can be noisy. *[$] Rooms from: $744 ⊠ 14 A Rhine Rd., Maho Reef ☎ 721/545–3100 ⊕ www.sonesta.com/oceanpoint ⤳ 219 rooms and suites; 25 deluxe suites with butler service ⁙ All-inclusive.*

OYSTER POND

$ ⊡ **Oyster Bay Beach Resort.** Jutting out into Oyster Bay, this condo/time-
RESORT share resort sits on Dawn Beach and is convenient to groceries, restau-
FAMILY rants, and the Westin. **Pros:** lots of activities; nightly entertainment;
comfortable accommodations. **Cons:** isolated location; need a car to get
around; older units are plain. *[$] Rooms from: $235 ⊠ 10 Emerald Merit Rd., Oyster Pond ☎ 721/543–6040 ⊕ www.oysterbaybeachresort.com ⤳ 157 units ⁙ No meals.*

$ ⊡ **Princess Heights.** Perched on a hill 900 feet above Oyster Bay, reno-
RENTAL vated, spacious suites offer privacy, luxury, and white-balustrade balconies with a smashing view of St. Barth. **Pros:** away from the crowds;
friendly staff; gorgeous vistas. **Cons:** not on the beach; numerous steps
to climb; not easy to find; need a car to get around. *[$] Rooms from: $218*

✉ *156 Oyster Pond Rd., Oyster Pond* ☎ *855/248–9264, 800/881–1744 in U.S.* ⊕ *www.princessheights.com* ⊲ *51 suites* ⁙ *No meals.*

$ ⊡ **Westin St. Maarten Dawn Beach Resort & Spa.** Straddling the border
RESORT between the Dutch and French sides, the modern Westin sits on one
FAMILY of the island's best beaches. **Pros:** on Dawn Beach; plenty of activities; no smoking. **Cons:** very big; a bit off the beaten track; time-share
salespeople can be bothersome, rooms slated for updating. **$** *Rooms
from: $199* ✉ *144 Oyster Pond Rd., Oyster Pond* ☎ *721/543–6700,
800/228–3000 in U.S.* ⊕ *www.westinstmaarten.com* ⊲ *317 rooms, 15
suites, 99 1-, 2-, and 3-bedroom condos* ⁙ *No meals.*

PELICAN KEY

$$ ⊡ **Blue Pelican.** The 13 modern and chic apartment units hidden in
RENTAL this private enclave in Pelican Key were built by the owners of Hotel
Fodor'sChoice L'Esplanade and Le Petit Hotel, on the French side, and share the French
★ management's vision, graciousness, obsessive attention to detail, and
concern for guest comfort and safety. **Pros:** nicest place in the area;
great pool; excellent management and security. **Cons:** residence, not
a resort; not on the beach; no restaurant; need a car to get around;
seven-night minimum. **$** *Rooms from: $290* ✉ *Billy Folly Rd., Pelican
Key* ☎ *0690/50–60–20* ⊕ *www.bluepelicansxm.com* ⊲ *13 apartments*
⁙ *No meals.*

PHILIPSBURG

$$ ⊡ **Holland House Beach Hotel.** This historic hotel is in an ideal location
HOTEL for shoppers and sun worshippers; it faces the Front Street pedestrian
mall, and to the rear are the boardwalk and a long stretch of Great
Bay Beach. **Pros:** easy access to beach and shops; free Wi-Fi. **Cons:** in
a busy, downtown location; no pool; not very resorty. **$** *Rooms from:
$275* ✉ *43 Front St., Philipsburg* ☎ *721/542–2572* ⊕ *www.hhbh.com*
⊲ *48 rooms, 6 suites* ⁙ *Breakfast.*

$$ ⊡ **Sonesta Great Bay Beach Resort and Casino.** This Philipsburg adults-
RESORT only all-inclusive is well positioned even if it doesn't offer the height
of luxury: away from the docks that are usually crawling with cruise
ships, but only a 10-minute walk from downtown Philipsburg. **Pros:**
unlimited food and bar; nice beach and pool; enough activities to keep
you busy. **Cons:** bare white hallways have hospital-like feel; expensive
Wi-Fi; although beach is beautiful, pollution can be a problem; staff can
be indifferent. **$** *Rooms from: $312* ✉ *19 Little Bay Rd., Philipsburg*
☎ *721/542–2447, 800/223–0757 in U.S.* ⊕ *www.sonesta.com/greatbay*
⊲ *257 rooms* ⁙ *All-inclusive.*

SIMPSON BAY

$ ⊡ **The Horny Toad.** Because of its stupendous view of Simpson Bay and
B&B/INN the simple but comfortable rooms with creative decor, this lovely guest-
Fodor'sChoice house is widely considered the best on this side of the island. **Pros:** tidy
★ rooms; friendly vibe and fantastic owner; beautiful beach is usually
deserted. **Cons:** rooms are very basic; need a car to get around; no kids
under seven; no pool. **$** *Rooms from: $218* ✉ *2 Vlaun Dr., Simpson
Bay* ☎ *721/545–4323, 800/417–9361 in U.S.* ⊕ *www.thtgh.com* ⊲ *8
rooms* ⁙ *No meals.*

17

$ RENTAL **La Vista.** Hibiscus and bougainvillea line brick walkways that connect the wood-frame bungalows and beachfront suites of this intimate and friendly, family-owned time-share resort perched at the foot of Pelican Key. **Pros:** close to restaurants and bars. **Cons:** no-frills furnishings; need a car to get to more swimmable beaches. [$] *Rooms from: $220* ✉ *53 Billy Folly Rd., Simpson Bay* ☎ *721/544–3005, 888/790–5264 in U.S.* 🌐 *www.lavistaresort.com* 🛏 *50 suites, penthouses, and cottages* 🍴 *No meals.*

FRENCH SIDE

ANSE MARCEL

$$$ RESORT FAMILY Fodor's Choice ★ **Hotel Riu Palace St. Martin.** Now under the RIU brand, this family-friendly all-inclusive (including alcoholic beverages) is well located: on a great beachy cove on 18 acres in a quiet part of St. Martin. **Pros:** all-inclusive; activities galore; great beach; huge pool. **Cons:** rooms face garden or marina, not ocean; need a car to get around; lots of families at school-vacation times; beach can be busy; ongoing renovations. [$] *Rooms from: €442* ✉ *BP 581, Anse Marcel* ☎ *0590/87–67–00, 800/333–3333 in U.S.* 🌐 *www.riu.com/en/Paises/saint-martin/saint-martin-island/hotel-riu-palace-st-martin* 🛏 *189 rooms, 63 suites* 🍴 *All-inclusive.*

$$ HOTEL **Marquis Boutique Hotel.** This fun property with a funky St. Barth vibe has spectacular vistas and intimate surroundings, but be warned of the heights and steep walks. **Pros:** romantic; doting staff; amazing views. **Cons:** not on beach; on a steep hill. [$] *Rooms from: €305* ✉ *Pigeon Pea Hill, Anse Marcel* ☎ *0590/29–42–30* 🌐 *www.hotel-marquis.com* 🛏 *17 rooms* 🍴 *Breakfast.*

BAIE LONGUE

$$$$ RESORT FAMILY Fodor's Choice ★ **Belmond La Samanna.** A long stretch of pretty, white-sand beach borders this classic resort, where service is warm and professional. **Pros:** chic decor; great beach; beach cabanas, convenient location; romantic; excellent spa. **Cons:** rather pricey for standard rooms; small pools. [$] *Rooms from: €905* ✉ *Baie Longue* ☎ *0590/87–64–00, 800/854–2252 in U.S.* 🌐 *www.belmond.com/la-samanna-st-martin* 🕑 *Closed Sept. and Oct.* 🛏 *27 rooms, 54 suites* 🍴 *Breakfast.*

BAIE NETTLÉ

$ RESORT FAMILY **Hotel Mercure St. Martin and Marina.** This modern option with an arty vibe by a quiet beach bay is centrally located. **Pros:** good location; pet- and family-friendly; great spa; lots of activities, including for kids. **Cons:** bay-side beach isn't great for swimming; ground-floor rooms are noisy and have no view; no elevators. [$] *Rooms from: €228* ✉ *Baie Nettlé* ☎ *0590/87–54–54* 🌐 *www.mercure.com* 🛏 *170 rooms* 🍴 *Breakfast.*

Belmond La Samanna

BAIE ORIENTALE

$ RESORT FAMILY 🏨 **Alamanda Resort.** One of the few resorts directly on the white-sand beach of Orient Bay, this hotel has a funky feel and spacious, colonial-style suites with terraces that overlook the pool, beach, or ocean. **Pros:** pleasant property; friendly staff; right on Orient Beach. **Cons:** some rooms are noisy; could still use some updating despite renovations. [$] *Rooms from: €272* ✉ *Baie Orientale* ☎ *0590/52–87–40* 🌐 *www.hotelalamanda.com* 🛏 *42 rooms* 🍴 *Breakfast.*

$$ RESORT FAMILY 🏨 **Esmeralda Resort.** Almost all of these traditional Caribbean-style, kitchen-equipped villas, which can be configured to meet guests' needs, have their own pool, and the fun of Orient Beach and the hotel's beach club is a two-minute walk away. **Pros:** beachfront location; private pools; plenty of activities; frequent online promotions. **Cons:** need a car to get around; iffy Wi-Fi service. [$] *Rooms from: €341* ✉ *Baie Orientale* ☎ *0590/87–36–36* 🌐 *www.esmeralda-resort.com* 🕒 *Closed Sept. and Oct.* 🛏 *65 rooms* 🍴 *Breakfast.*

$$$$ RENTAL FAMILY 🏨 **Green Cay Village.** Surrounded by 5 acres of lush greenery high above Baie Orientale, these villas are a great deal for families or other groups looking for privacy and the comforts of home. **Pros:** beautiful setting near Baie Orientale; good for families with teens or older kids. **Cons:** need a car to get around; beach is a five-minute walk; need to be vigilant about locking doors, as there have been reports of crime in the area. [$] *Rooms from: €660* ✉ *Parc de la Baie Orientale, Baie Orientale* ☎ *0590/87–38–63* 🌐 *www.greencay.com* 🛏 *9 villas* 🍴 *Breakfast.*

$ 🏨 **Hotel La Plantation.** Perched high above Baie Orientale, this colonial-style hotel is a charmer. **Pros:** relaxing atmosphere; eye-popping views; lots of area restaurants. **Cons:** small pool; beach is a 10-minute walk away. [$] *Rooms from: €205* ✉ *C5 Parc de La Baie Orientale, Baie Orientale* ☎ *0590/29–58–00* 🌐 *www.la-plantation.com* 🕒 *Closed Sept.–mid-Oct.* 🛏 *51 rooms* 🍴 *Breakfast.*
HOTEL
FAMILY

$ 🏨 **Palm Court.** The romantic beachfront units of this *hôtel de charme* are steps from the fun of Orient Beach yet private, quiet, and stylish. **Pros:** big rooms; romantic decor; nice garden. **Cons:** across from, but not on the beach. [$] *Rooms from: €231* ✉ *Parc de la Baie Orientale, Baie Orientale* ☎ *800/480–8555, 590/87–41–94* 🌐 *palmcourthotel.com* 🕒 *Closed Sept.* 🛏 *24 rooms* 🍴 *Breakfast.*
HOTEL
Fodor's Choice ★

FRENCH CUL DE SAC

$$ 🏨 **Karibuni Lodge.** Lovely in every way, this super-chic yet reasonably priced enclave of spacious suites surrounded by gorgeous tropical gardens offers stunning views of tiny Ilet Pinel. **Pros:** stylish; eco-friendly; lushly comfortable; amazing views. **Cons:** removed from the action; need a car; not a resort; not on the beach. [$] *Rooms from: €313* ✉ *29 Terrasses de Cul de Sac, Cul de Sac* ☎ *0690/64–38–58* 🌐 *www.lekaribuni.com* 🛏 *6 suites* 🍴 *Breakfast.*
B&B/INN
Fodor's Choice ★

GRAND CASE

$$ 🏨 **Bleu Emeraude.** The 11 spacious apartments in this tidy complex sit right on a sliver of Grand Case Beach. **Pros:** modern and updated; walk to restaurants; attractive decor. **Cons:** not resorty. [$] *Rooms from: €360* ✉ *240 bd. de Grand Case, Grand Case* ☎ *0590/87–27–71* 🌐 *www.bleuemeraude.com* 🛏 *4 studios, 6 1-bedroom apartments, 1 2-bedroom apartment* 🍴 *Breakfast.*
RENTAL
FAMILY

$$ 🏨 **Grand Case Beach Club.** This beachfront property on a cove at the east end of Grand Case has a friendly staff and spectacular sunset views. **Pros:** reasonably priced; comfortable rooms; walking distance to restaurants. **Cons:** small beach; dated decor and buildings; need a car to explore. [$] *Rooms from: €366* ✉ *21 rue de la Petite Plage, at north end of bd. de Grand Case, Grand Case* ☎ *0590/87–51–87, 800/344–3016 in U.S.* 🌐 *www.grandcasebeachclub.com* 🛏 *72 apartments* 🍴 *Breakfast.*
RESORT
FAMILY

$$$ 🏨 **Hôtel L'Esplanade.** Fans return again and again to the classy, loft-style suites in this immaculate boutique hotel. **Pros:** attentive management; very clean; updated room decor; family-friendly feel. **Cons:** lots of stairs to climb; not on the beach. [$] *Rooms from: €415* ✉ *Grand Case* ☎ *0590/87–06–55, 866/596–8365 in U.S.* 🌐 *www.lesplanade.com* 🛏 *24 units* 🍴 *No meals.*
HOTEL
FAMILY
Fodor's Choice ★

$$$ 🏨 **Le Petit Hotel.** Surrounded by some of the best restaurants in the Caribbean, this beachfront boutique hotel oozes charm and has the same caring, attentive management as Hotel L'Esplanade. **Pros:** walking distance to everything in Grand Case; friendly staff; clean, updated rooms. **Cons:** many stairs to climb; no pool. [$] *Rooms from: €435* ✉ *248 bd. de Grand Case, Grand Case* ☎ *0590/29–09–65* 🌐 *www.lepetithotel.com* 🛏 *9 rooms, 1 suite* 🍴 *Breakfast.*
HOTEL
FAMILY
Fodor's Choice ★

Palm Court

$$
B&B/INN
Fodor's Choice
★

🍽 **Le Temps des Cerises.** Named for the classic 19th-century French chanson, Le Temps des Cerises is the first hotel representing the fashion house of the same name based in Marseille. **Pros:** chic decor; comfortable rooms; right on the beach. **Cons:** can be a bit noisy. $ *Rooms from: €340* ⊠ *158 bd. de Grand Case, Grand Case* ☎ *590/51–36–27* ⊕ *www. letempsdesceriseshotel.com* ⤷ *9 rooms.*

MONT VERNON

$$
B&B/INN

🍽 **Sol e Luna Guesthouse.** Independent couples who don't want a big resort love the six comfortable suites in this hillside guesthouse overlooking a pretty pool, a salt pond, and on to Orient Bay. **Pros:** spacious suites; good location for exploring; romantic; good on-site restaurant. **Cons:** not a full-service hotel; need a car; quite a few steps to climb around the property. $ *Rooms from: €304* ⊠ *61 Mont Vernon, Anse Marcel* ☎ *590/29–08–56* ⊕ *www.solelunarestaurant.com* ☾ *Closed Sept.* ⤷ *6 suites.*

OYSTER POND

$
HOTEL

🍽 **Captain Oliver's Resort.** This cluster of older pink bungalows is perched high on a hill above a lagoon with lots of lush landscaping and a fine view of the Caribbean and St. Barth. **Pros:** reasonably priced; ferry trips leave from the hotel. **Cons:** not on beach; not fancy or modern; needs updating; must have a car. $ *Rooms from: €123* ⊠ *Oyster Pond* ☎ *0590/87–40–26* ⊕ *www.captainolivers.com* ☾ *Closed Sept. and Oct.* ⤷ *50 suites* 🍴 *Breakfast.*

NIGHTLIFE

St. Maarten has lots of evening and late-night action. To find out what's doing, pick up *St. Maarten Nights* or *St. Maarten Events,* both distributed free in the tourist office and hotels. The glossy *Discover St. Martin/ St. Maarten* magazine, also free, has articles on island history and on the newest shops, discos, and restaurants. Or buy a copy of Thursday's *Daily Herald* newspaper, which lists the week's entertainment.

The island's 13 casinos are only on the Dutch side. All have craps, blackjack, roulette, and slot machines. You must be 18 or older to gamble. Dress is casual (but not bathing suits or skimpy beachwear). Most casinos are in hotels, but there are also some independents.

DUTCH SIDE

CUPECOY

CASINOS

Starz Casino. Completely redecorated in 2015 in a brilliant color scheme with new lighting, this attractive casino, anchored by some of the best restaurants on the Dutch side, is popular with gamblers and non-gamblers alike. It has high-tech video slot machines and gaming tables offering blackjack, roulette, three-card poker, and Caribbean poker. Sports fans will enjoy the Sports Bar surrounded by big-screen TVs. ⊠ *106 Rhine Rd., Cupecoy* ☎ *721/545–4601* ⊕ *www.starzsxm.com.*

MAHO

BARS AND CLUBS

Fodor's Choice
★

Sky Beach. For those who don't want to leave the beach vibe after the sun goes down, this elegant rooftop pulses with techno and house music while guests lounge on beds in cabanas. (In case of rain, there's a tent.) Sand volleyball is fun, and the happening bar serves delicious cocktails. Great views and stargazing come with the territory. In-the-know clubbers come here before Tantra starts to wake up after midnight. It's open every day from 4 pm until 1 am. The website lists special events and parties. ⊠ *Sonesta Maho Beach Resort & Casino, 1 Rhine Rd., Maho Reef* ☎ *721/520–1757* ⊕ *www.theskybeach.com.*

Soprano's Piano Bar. Starting each night at 8, the pianist takes requests for oldies, romantic favorites, or smooth jazz. Come for happy hour (8–9), with a full menu that includes pizza. The bar is open until 3. Special events are posted on the website. ⊠ *Sonesta Maho Beach Resort & Casino, 1 Rhine Rd., Maho Reef* ☎ *721/545–2485* ⊕ *www. sopranossxm.com.*

Sunset Bar and Grill. This popular spot offers a relaxed, anything-goes atmosphere. Enjoy live music Wednesday through Sunday as you watch planes from the airport next door fly directly over your head, while you enjoy a BBC (Bailey's banana colada), the island's favorite tropical drink, or a bucket of Caribs. Bring your camera for stunning photos, but expect a high noise level. ⊠ *Maho Beach, Beacon Hill # 2, Maho Reef* ☎ *721/545–2084* ⊕ *www.sunsetsxm.com.*

Gambling is the most popular indoor activity in St. Maarten.

Tantra Nightclub & Sanctuary. This is definitely the hottest nightclub in the Maho complex. Come late—things don't really get going until after 1 am. On Wednesday nights ladies drink champagne for free, and drinks are $2 for everyone on Fridays. Celebrity DJs spin on Saturdays. Feel free to dress up. There is bottle and table service by reservation. It's closed Monday, Tuesday, and Thursday. ⊠ *Sonesta Maho Beach Resort & Casino, 1 Rhine Rd., Maho Reef* ☎ *721/545–2861* ⊕ *www. tantrasxm.com.*

CASINOS
Casino Royale. This is the largest casino on the island, with some 1,300 square meters of gaming and a full theater with 750 seats for events and shows. There are 21 tables for gaming, including roulette (American and French), craps, blackjack, and poker (three-card, Let It Ride, and Caribbean). The 410 slot machines include a variety of classics and modern video slots. It's open till 4 a.m. ⊠ *Sonesta Maho Beach Resort & Casino, 1 Rhine Rd., Maho Reef* ☎ *721/545–2590* ⊕ *www. playmaho.com.*

OYSTER POND
CASINOS
Westin Casino. This is somewhat more sedate than other island casinos. If you get tired of the slot machines and gaming tables, beautiful Dawn Beach is just outside. ⊠ *Westin St. Maarten Dawn Beach Resort & Spa, 144 Oyster Pond Rd., Oyster Pond* ☎ *721/543–6700* ⊕ *www. westinstmaarten.com.*

PHILIPSBURG
BARS AND CLUBS

Ocean Lounge. Sip a guavaberry colada, and sample tapas with your chair pointed toward the boardwalk at this quintessential people-watching venue. There's free parking for patrons until midnight; enter on Back Street, and look for the Holland House banner. ⊠ *Holland House Beach Hotel, 43 Front St., Philipsburg* ☎ *721/542–2572* ⊕ *www.hhbh.com.*

CASINOS

Beach Plaza Casino. In the heart of the shopping area, this casino has more than 180 slots, a sports book, and multigame machines with touch screens. Because of its location, it is popular with cruise-ship passengers. ⊠ *Front St., Philipsburg* ☎ *721/543–2031* ⊕ *www.atlantisworld.com.*

SIMPSON BAY
BARS AND CLUBS

FAMILY **Buccaneer Beach Bar.** Conveniently located on Kim Sha Beach, this family-friendly bar can provide you a BBC (Bailey's banana colada), a slice of pizza, a sunset, and a nightly fireball show. ⊠ *10 Billy Folly Rd., behind Festiva Atrium Beach Resort, Simpson Bay* ☎ *721/522–9700* ⊕ *www.buccaneerbeachbar.com.*

Le Shore. With special events and parties almost every night, this nighttime hot spot in the middle of Simpson Bay is reminiscent of Miami or Vegas. It's billed as a private club, but if you call for a reservation or just dress nicely, you shouldn't have a problem getting in. ⊠ *111 Welfare Rd., Simpson Bay* ☎ *721/586–4499* ⊕ *www.shoreclubsxm.com.*

Pineapple Pete. You can groove to live music or hit the game room for a couple of rounds of pool. ⊠ *Airport Rd., Simpson Bay* ☎ *721/544–6030* ⊕ *www.pineapplepete.com.*

The Red Piano. This bar has a great pool room, terrific live music, and tasty cocktails every night from 8 until 3. ⊠ *Hollywood Casino, 35 Billy Folly Rd., Simpson Bay* ☎ *721/544–6008* ⊕ *www.theredpianosxm.com.*

CASINOS

Paradise Plaza Casino & Sports Book. Betting on sporting events is the big thing here, which explains the 20 televisions tuned to whatever game happens to be on. There are also 250 slots and multigame machines. ⊠ *69 Welfare Rd., Simpson Bay* ☎ *721/543–4721* ⊕ *www.atlantisworld. com/paradise-plaza-casino-sports-book-simpson-bay.*

FRENCH SIDE

BAIE DES PÈRES
BARS AND CLUBS

Kali's Beach Bar. This happening spot has featured live music late into the night since the late 1980s. On the night of the full moon and on every Friday night, the beach bonfire and late-night party here is the place to be, but it's a great place to hang out all day long on chaises you can rent for the day. Be sure to ask Kali for some tastes of his homemade fruit-infused rum. ⊠ *Anse des Pères* ☎ *690/49–06–81.*

SHOPPING

Shopaholics are drawn to the array of stores, and jewelry in particular is big business on both sides of the island. Duty-free shops can offer substantial savings—about 15% to 30% below U.S. and Canadian prices—on cameras, expensive jewelry, watches, liquor, cigars, and designer clothing, but not always, so make sure you know U.S. prices to know if you're getting a deal, and be prepared to bargain hard. Stick with the big vendors that advertise in the tourist press, and you will be more likely to avoid today's ubiquitous fakes and replicas. On both sides of the island, be alert for idlers. They can snatch unwatched purses.

Prices are in dollars on the Dutch side, in euros on the French side. As for bargains, there are more to be had on the Dutch side; prices on the French side may be higher than those back home, and being in euros doesn't help. Merchandise may not be from the newest collections, especially with regard to clothing; there are items available on the French side that are not available on the Dutch side.

DUTCH SIDE

MAHO

You'll find a moderately good selection of stores in Maho Village, near the Sonesta resort. The glitzy Blue Mall opened in 2013.

AREAS AND MALLS

FAMILY **Blue Mall.** Between Maho and Cupecoy, Blue Mall is a modern shopping space with a growing selection of shops. It's convenient, especially if it's sporting attire or beachwear that you are seeking. Don't expect the range of shops you would find at a mall at home. There is a food court on the top floor with a fun children's playground ($10 per child), which is a boon if want to get the kiddies out of the heat and sun. ⊠ *162 Rhine Rd, Cupecoy* ☎ *721/545–2418.*

CLOTHING

Aqua. Nautical striped beachwear for adults and kids, home goods, including good-quality beach towels, and matching plastic picnic-ware, and fanciful paper goods are sold here and at the shop off Front Street in Philipsburg. Proceeds benefit autism awareness. ⊠ *Maho Center, Maho Reef* ⊕ *www.aquamaritime.hr.*

PHILIPSBURG

Philipsburg's **Front Street** has reinvented itself. Now it's mall-like, with a redbrick walk and streets, palm trees lining the sleek boutiques, jewelry stores, souvenir shops, outdoor restaurants, and the old reliables, such as McDonald's and Burger King. Here and there a school or a church appears to remind visitors there's more to the island than shopping. On Back Street, the **Philipsburg Market Place** is a daily open-air market where you can haggle on handicrafts, souvenirs, and beachwear. **Old Street,** near the end of Front Street, has stores, boutiques, and open-air cafés offering French crepes, rich chocolates, and island mementos.

17

ART GALLERIES

Art Lovers. All of the island's best artists and galleries are represented at this central gallery cooperative in the Porto Cupecoy marina area. Visit here, and you can have an overview of the artists' work, as well as make arrangements to visit their studios and galleries. Pick up "The Art Lovers Map," which details contact and location information, making it very easy to purchase a long-lasting souvenir of your island visit. ⊠ *Porto Cupecoy, Cupecoy* ☎ *690/62–15–76* ⊕ *www.artlovers-sxm.com.*

CANDY

FAMILY **SXM Candy Store.** It's a blast to pop into this tiny shop at the marina end of the Philipsburg boardwalk, where every candy you can imagine is stacked floor to ceiling in colorful array. You can find old-fashioned and hard-to-find European favorites. "The Candy Man" is a friendly and funny feature of the shop. ⊠ *Boardwalk, Philipsburg.*

HANDICRAFTS

Shipwreck Shop. With outlets all over the island, this chain stocks a little of everything: colorful hammocks, handmade jewelry, and lots of the local Guavaberry liqueur. But the main store has the largest selection. ⊠ *42 Front St., Philipsburg* ☎ *721/542–2962, 721/542–6710* ⊕ *www.shipwreckshops.com.*

JEWELRY AND GIFTS

Little Europe. Come here to buy fine jewelry, crystal, and china. There is also a branch in Marigot. ⊠ *80 Front St., Philipsburg* ☎ *721/542–4371* ⊕ *www.littleeurope.com.*

Little Switzerland. The large Caribbean duty-free chain sells watches, fine crystal, china, perfume, and jewelry. There are five locations on the island, one a Tiffany boutique. ⊠ *52 Front St., Philipsburg* ☎ *721/542–3530* ⊕ *www.littleswitzerland.com.*

Oro Diamante. This store carries loose diamonds, jewelry, watches, perfume, and cosmetics. It specializes in natural colored diamonds. ⊠ *62-B Front St., Philipsburg* ☎ *599/543–0342, 800/635–7950 in U.S.* ⊕ *www.oro-diamante.com.*

LEATHER GOODS AND ACCESSORIES

Furla. This is the place for very "in" Italian leather purses. ⊠ *13 Front St., Philipsburg* ☎ *599/542–9958.*

LIQUOR

Guavaberry Emporium. Visitors come for free samples at the small factory where the Sint Maarten Guavaberry Company makes its famous liqueur. The many versions include one made with jalapeño peppers. Check out the hand-painted bottles. The store also sells a gourmet barbecue and hot sauce collection and souvenir hats. ⊠ *8–10 Front St., Philipsburg* ☎ *721/542–2965* ⊕ *www.guavaberry.com.*

FRENCH SIDE

GRAND CASE

ART

Tropismes Gallery. Contemporary Caribbean artists showcased here include Paul Elliot Thuleau, who is a master of capturing the sunshine of the islands, and Nathalie Lepine, whose portraits show a Modigliani influence. This is a serious gallery with some very good artists. It's open 10–1 and 5–9 daily. ⊠ *107 bd. de Grand Case, Grand Case* ☎ *0690/54–62–69* ⊕ *www.tropismesgallery.com.*

CLOTHING

Voila!!! The trendy beach attire, arty accessories, and souvenirs are fun to try on and buy here. Late hours mean you can shop before or after dinner. ⊠ *101 bd. de Grand Case, Grand Case* ☎ *590/29–84–87* ⊕ *www.voilasxm.com.*

MARIGOT

ART

Galerie Camaïeu. This gallery sells both originals and copies of works by Caribbean artists. It's closed Sunday, plus Saturday May–November. ⊠ *8 rue de Kennedy, Marigot* ☎ *0590/87–25–78* ⊕ *www.camaieu-artgallery.com.*

Gingerbread Galerie. This gallery on the town side of the marina specializes in Haitian folk art and sells both expensive paintings and more reasonably priced decorative pieces of folk art. ⊠ *Marina Port La Royale, Marigot* ☎ *0590/87–73–21* ⊕ *www.gingerbread-gallery.com.*

CLOTHING

Some of the best shops are in the modern, air-conditioned West Indies Mall and the Plaza Caraïbes center across from Marina Port La Royale.

120% Lino. This store has nicely made classy shirts and pants made of pure linen in pastel tones. ⊠ *21 Marina Port La Royale, Marigot* ☎ *590/87–25–43* ⊕ *www.120percento.com/negozi/store-stmartin.*

Banana Moon. A terrific selection of bathing suits and other beachwear is sold here. The well-made bathing suit tops and bottoms are sold separately to ensure a good fit. ⊠ *Marina Port La Royale, Marigot* ☎ *0590/87–87–15* ⊕ *www.bananamoon.com.*

Lacoste. The preppy clothier has everything with the alligator logo for men, women, and children. Prices are somewhat lower than in the United States. ⊠ *West Indies Mall, Front de Mer, Marigot* ☎ *590/52–84–84.*

Vilebrequin. This shop on the marina has a vast selection of brightly patterned status swimsuits for men and boys. ⊠ *Marina Port La Royale, Marigot* ☎ *0590/29–13–09.*

JEWELRY AND GIFTS

Art of Time. This reputable shop carries Mikimoto, Pandora, and David Yurman, among many others, as well as high-end designer watches, including Chanel, Baum & Mercier, Technomarine, Bidat, and Chopard. ⊠ *3 rue du Général de Gaulle, Marigot* ☎ *0590/52–24–80* ⊕ *www.artoftimejewelers.com.*

17

Manek's. Two floors house electronics, luggage, perfume, jewelry, Cuban cigars, duty-free liquors, and tobacco products. ⊠ *Rue de la République, Marigot* ☎ *0590/87–54–91.*

LEATHER GOODS AND ACCESSORIES

Longchamp. This is the local outpost for the chic French leather-goods company, with an especially good selection of the Pliage line of foldable, durable, coated-zipper totes with leather handles. ⊠ *11 rue du Général de Gaulle, Marigot* ☎ *0590/87–92–76* ⊕ *www.longchamp.com.*

SPORTS AND THE OUTDOORS

BOATING AND SAILING

The island is surrounded by water, so why not get out and enjoy it? The water and winds are perfect for skimming the surf. It'll cost you around $1,200 to $1,500 per day to rent a 28- to 40-foot powerboat, considerably less for smaller boats or small sailboats. Drinks and sometimes lunch are usually included on crewed day charters, and some tours are eco-oriented.

DUTCH SIDE

Random Wind. This company offers full-day sailing and snorkeling trips on a traditional 54-foot clipper. Charter prices depend on the size of the group and whether lunch is served. The regularly scheduled Paradise Daysail ($109 adults, $85 kids) includes food and drink, snorkeling equipment, and standup paddleboard. Departures, weekdays at 9:45, are from SkipJack's at Simpson Bay. Everyone loves "flying" from the Tarzan swing. ■ TIP→ **You can get the best rates from the website rather than hotels or cruises.** ⊠ *Ric's Place, Simpson Bay* ☎ *721/587–5742* ⊕ *www.randomwind.com.*

Rhino Safari. Take a 2½-hour guided water tour around the island on a 10-foot inflatable watercraft. The boats are stable, easy to pilot, and riding the waves is a blast. The tour includes 45 minutes of snorkeling (equipment provided) at Creole Rock, one of the best spots on the island. Choose from several departures and routes every day. ⊠ *58 Welfare Rd., Simpson Bay* ☎ *721/544–3150* ⊕ *www.rhinorides.com* 🛥 *From $138 for 2 people on 1 boat.*

St. Maarten 12-Metre Challenge. Sailing experience is not necessary as participants compete on 68-foot racing yachts, including Dennis Connor's *Stars and Stripes* (the actual boat that won the America's Cup in Freemantle, Australia, in 1987), *Canada II,* and *True North I.* Everyone is allocated a crew position, either grinding winches, trimming sails, punching the stopwatch, or bartending. The thrill is priceless, but book well in advance; this is the most popular shore excursion in the Caribbean. It is offered up to four times daily and lasts 2½–3 hours. Children over 12 (7 with sailing experience) may participate. ⊠ *Bobby's Marina, Philipsburg* ☎ *721/542–0045* ⊕ *www.12metre.com.*

FRENCH SIDE

MP Yachting. You can rent boats of all sizes, with or without a crew, for short trips and long. ⊠ *Marina Port La Royale, Marigot* ☎ *0690/53–37–40* ⊕ *www.mpyachting.com.*

Sun Evasion. This charter company has locations all over the world. You can take a half- or full-day charter to Tintamarre, St. Barth, or Ilet Pinel on a mono- or multihull powerboat, available with or without a skipper. ■TIP➔ **Book online for a 10% discount.** ⊠ *Rue de Galisbay Port, Marigot* ☎ *0690/35–03–18* ⊕ *www.sun-evasion.com.*

DIVING

Diving in St. Maarten/St. Martin is mediocre at best, but those who want to dive will find a few positives. The water temperature here is rarely below 70°F (21°C) and visibility is often 60 to 100 feet. The island has more than 30 dive sites, from wrecks to rocky labyrinths. Right outside Philipsburg, 55 feet under the water, is the HMS *Proselyte*, once explored by Jacques Cousteau. Although it sank in 1801, the boat's cannons and coral-encrusted anchors are still visible.

Off the north coast, in the protected and mostly current-free Grand Case Bay, is **Creole Rock.** The water here ranges in depth from 10 feet to 25 feet. Other sites off the north coast include **Ilet Pinel,** with its good shallow diving; **Green Key,** with its vibrant barrier reef; and **Tintamarre,** with its sheltered coves and geologic faults. On average, one-tank dives start at $58; two-tank dives are about $100. Certification courses start at about $450.

The Dutch side offers several full-service outfitters and SSI (Scuba Schools International) and/or PADI certification. There are no hyperbaric chambers on the island.

DUTCH SIDE

Dive Safaris. Certified divers who have dived within the last two years can watch professional feeders give reef sharks a little nosh in a half-hour shark-awareness dive. The company also offers a full PADI training program and can tailor dive excursions and sophisticated, sensitive instruction to any level. ⊠ *16 Airport Rd., Simpson Bay* ☎ *721/545–2401* ⊕ *www.divesafarisstmaarten.com.*

Ocean Explorers Dive Center. St. Maarten's oldest dive shop offers different types of certification courses. Serious divers like the six-person maximum policy on trips, but this means you should reserve in advance. ⊠ *113 Welfare Rd., Simpson Bay* ☎ *721/544–5252* ⊕ *www.stmaartendiving.com.*

FRENCH SIDE

Octopus. The well-stocked dive shop offers PADI diving certification courses and all-inclusive dive packages, as well as highly recommended private and group snorkel trips starting at $55, including all necessary equipment. The shop also services regulators. ⊠ *15 bd. de Grand Case, Grand Case* ☎ *914/487–1315, 690/88–53–39 cell phone* ⊕ *www.octopusdiving.com.*

17

FISHING

You can angle for yellowtail snapper, grouper, marlin, tuna, and wahoo on deep-sea excursions. Costs range from $150 per person for a half day to $250 for a full day. Prices usually include bait and tackle, instruction for novices, and refreshments. Ask about licensing and insurance.

DUTCH SIDE

Lee's Deepsea Fishing. When you return from an excursion with this outfit, Lee's Roadside Grill will cook the tuna, wahoo, or mahimahi you catch. Rates start at $800 for a half day trip for six people. ✉ *84 Welfare Rd., Cole Bay* ☎ *721/544–4233* ⊕ *www.leesfish.com.*

Private Yacht Charter. This company leads deep-sea fishing, snorkeling, and catamaran trips, including snacks and drinks. Multiday charters are also available. ✉ *Oyster Pond Great House Marina, 14 Emerald Merit Rd., Oyster Pond* ☎ *721/581–5305* ⊕ *www.privateyachtcharter-sxm.com.*

Rudy's Deep Sea Fishing. One of the more experienced sport-angling outfits runs private charter trips. Half-day excursions for up to four people start at $575, $50 each additional for up to six. Three-quarter- and full-day trips are also available. ■TIP→ **Check the website for great tips on fishing around St. Maarten.** ✉ *14 Airport Rd., Simpson Bay* ☎ *721/545–2177* ⊕ *www.rudysdeepseafishing.com.*

GOLF

DUTCH SIDE

Mullet Bay Golf Course. St. Maarten is not a golf destination. Nevertheless, there have been marked improvements to this golf course, which is again 18 holes (and the island's only choice), though hardly a must-play. Good clubs are available for rent, and you can wear sneakers if you don't have golf shoes with you. ✉ *Airport Rd., north of airport, Mullet Bay* ☎ *721/545–2850* ⌑ *$125* ⚐ *18 holes, 6200 yards, par 70.*

HORSEBACK RIDING

DUTCH SIDE

Lucky Stables. These stables in Cay Bay offer hour-long rides every hour on the hour. For a romantic treat, book a sunset ride with champagne and a bonfire (complete with marshmallows) for $100 per person. All experience levels are welcome, as the horses only walk, but advanced riders can book private rides if they want to trot and canter. ✉ *64 Traybay Dr., Cay Bay* ☎ *721/544–5255* ⊕ *www.seasidenaturepark.com.*

FRENCH SIDE

Bayside Riding Club. This established outfit can accommodate all levels on group beach rides around a nature preserve; 1 to 1½ hours costs €80 (cash only). You actually take the horses into the water, so bring a towel and a plastic bag for your clothes, and leave your valuables behind. It's closed Sunday and Monday. ✉ *Galion Beach Rd., Baie Orientale* ☎ *721/581–0206 on Dutch side, 0690/62–36–18 on French side* ⊕ *www.baysideranch.com.*

KAYAKING

Kayaking is becoming very popular and is almost always offered at the many water-sports operations on both the Dutch and the French sides. Rental starts at about $15 per hour for a single and $19 for a double.

DUTCH SIDE

TriSports. This company organizes leisurely 2½-hour kayaking and snorkeling excursions in addition to its biking and hiking tours; $49 includes all equipment. ⊠ *Airport Rd., 14B, Simpson Bay* ☎ *721/545–4384* ⊕ *www.trisportsxm.com.*

FRENCH SIDE

FAMILY **Wind Adventures.** Near Le Galion Beach, this outfitter offers rentals and instruction in kayaking, kitesurfing, windsurfing, wakeboard, Hobie Cats, and standup paddle surfing as well as ecotours. ⊠ *Baie Orientale* ☎ *0590/29–41–57* ⊕ *www.wind-adventures.com.*

SEA EXCURSIONS

DUTCH SIDE

FAMILY **Aqua Mania Adventures.** You can take day cruises to Prickly Pear Cay, off Anguilla, aboard the *Lambada,* or sunset and dinner cruises on the 65-foot sail catamaran *Tango. The Edge* goes to St. Barth and Saba. There are tours on inflatable boats, scuba and snorkel trips, and motor cruises around the island. The company also operates a floating playground called Playstation 4 Kids. ⊠ *Pelican Marina, Simpson Bay* ☎ *721/544–2640, 721/544–2631* ⊕ *www.stmaarten-activities.com.*

Bluebeard II. The 60-foot, custom-built day-sail catamaran is specially designed for maximum safety and comfort. *Bluebeard II* sails around Anguilla's south and northwest coasts to Prickly Pear Cay, where there's a coral reef for snorkeling and powdery white sands for sunning. Thrill-seekers might prefer the three-hour racing trip aboard a 52-footer built for speed. Private charters are also available. ⊠ *Billy Folly Rd., 10, Simpson Bay* ☎ *721/587–5935* ⊕ *www.bluebeardcharters.com.*

Celine. For low-impact sunset and dinner cruises, try the catamaran *Celine.* There are also full-day sails with breakfast, lunch, and drinks included, private charters, and a pub crawl by boat. ⊠ *SkipJack's Restaurant, Simpson Bay* ☎ *721/526–1170, 721/552–1335* ⊕ *www.sailstmaarten.com.*

FAMILY **Golden Eagle.** The sleek 76-foot catamaran *Golden Eagle* takes day-sailors on eco-friendly excursions to outlying islets and reefs for snorkeling and partying. They can pick you up from your hotel or condo. ⊠ *Bobby's Marina, Jurancho Yrausquin bd., Philipsburg* ☎ *721/543–0068* ⊕ *www.toursxm.com.*

17

SNORKELING

Some of the best snorkeling on the Dutch side can be found around the rocks below Fort Amsterdam off Little Bay Beach, in the west end of Maho Bay, off Pelican Key, and around the reefs off Oyster Pond Beach. On the French side, the area around Baie Orientale—including Caye Verte and Tintamarre—is especially lovely and is officially classified and protected as a regional underwater nature reserve. There is a new eco-snorkel trail at Pinel Island. Sea creatures also congregate around Creole Rock at the point of Baie de Grand Case. The average cost of an afternoon snorkeling trip is $45–$55 per person.

DUTCH SIDE

FAMILY   **Blue Bubbles.** This company offers both boat and shore snorkel excursions as well as Jet Skiing, parasailing, and snuba for beginner divers. ⊠ *153 Front St., Philipsburg* ☎ *721/556–8484* ⊕ *www.bluebubblessxm.com.*

TURKS AND CAICOS ISLANDS

WELCOME TO TURKS AND CAICOS ISLANDS

TO BAHAMAS

Caicos Passage

Three Mary's Cays

Kew

Parrot Cay

Fort George Cay

Spanish Point

Football Fields ◣ Pine Cay

Flamingo Pond

Highas Cay

Juniper Hole

Platico Point

Northwest Point

Little Water Cay

North Caicos

Providenciales

Grace Bay

Caicos Conch Farm

Conch Bar Caves

Cheshire Hall

Middle Caicos

Sapodilla Hill

Juba Point

Southwest Bluff

Providenciales
see detail map

Ocean Hole

Vine Point

Toll Crawl Point

West Caicos

C A I C O S

I S L A N D S

Southwest Reef

◣ Molasses Reef

| 0 | | | 14 miles |
| 0 | | | 21 km |

KEY	
◣	Dive Sites
1	Hotels

C A I C O S   B A N K

Little Ambergris Cay

SEAL CAYS

White Cay

The Turks and Caicos Islands make up the southern extension of the Lucayan archipelago, just north of Hispaniola; only 8 of the 40+ islands are inhabited. Divers and snorkelers can explore one of the world's largest coral reefs. Land-based pursuits don't get much more taxing than teeing off at the Provo Golf and Country Club or sunset-watching from the seaside terrace of a laid-back resort.

GEOGRAPHICAL INFO

Sea creatures far outnumber humans in this archipelago of over 40 islands, where the total population is a mere 32,000. From the tourist hub of Providenciales (aka Provo) to the country's quiet capital of Grand Turk, the entire chain offers miles of undeveloped beaches, crystal-clear water, and laid-back luxury accommodations.

Hotels ▼

Blue Horizon Resort **5**
Castaway, Salt Cay **7**
Hollywood
Beach Suites **3**
Meridian Club **1**
Parrot Cay Resort **2**
Pelican Beach Hotel **4**
South Caicos Ocean &
Beach Resort **6**
Villas of Salt Cay **8**

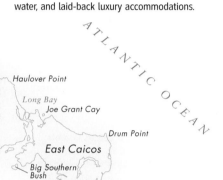

18

TURKS AND CAICOS ISLANDS

Haulover Point

Long Bay
Joe Grant Cay

ATLANTIC OCEAN

Drum Point

East Caicos

Big Southern Bush

Big Cameron Cay

Middle Creek Cay

Sail Rock Island

Horse Cay

Boiling Hole
Cockburn Harbor ◆ **6** *South Caicos*
High Point
Long Cay

Six Hill Cays

Columbus Passage

Black Forest ◤

The Library ◤

Grand Turk
see detail map

Grand Turk Island

◆ *Grand Turk*

Gibb's Cay

Long Cay

TURKS ISLANDS

Fish Cays

Cotton Cay

◆ *Salt Cay*
7 **8**

East Cay

Toney Rock

Big Ambergris Cay

AMBERGRIS CAYS

South Point

Mouchoir Passage

Bush Cay
Shot Cay

Big Sand Cay

TOP REASONS TO VISIT TURKS AND CAICOS

1 Beautiful Beaches: Even on Provo, there are miles of deserted beaches without any beach umbrellas in sight.

2 Excellent Diving: The third-largest coral-reef system in the world is among the world's top dive sites.

3 Easy Island-Hopping: Island-hopping beyond the beaten path will give you a feel for the country as a whole.

4 The Jet Set: Destination spas, penthouse suites, and exclusive villas and resorts make celebrity spotting a possibility; keep your eyes open!

5 Exploring on the Sea: You'll find excellent fishing and boating among the uninhabited coves and cays.

NEED TO KNOW

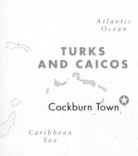

Atlantic Ocean

TURKS AND CAICOS

Cockburn Town ✪

Caribbean Sea

AT A GLANCE

Capital: Cockburn Town

Population: 33,100

Currency: U.S. dollar

Money: ATMs on Provo and Grand Turk; cash more common than credit.

Language: English

Country Code: ☎ 1 649

Emergencies: ☎ 999

Driving: On the left

Electricity: 120v/60 cycle; plugs are U.S. standard two- and three-prong

Time: EST (same as New York); the islands do not recognize Daylight Savings Time as of 2015

Documents: Up to 90 days with valid passport

Mobile Phones: Up to 4G

Major Mobile Companies: Digicel, LIME

WEBSITES

Turks & Caicos Islands Tourist Board: ⊕ www.turksandcaicostourism.com

WhereWhenHow: ⊕ www.WhereWhenHow.com

GETTING AROUND

✈ **Air Travel:** All international flights go to Providenciales (PLS); only small planes serve other islands.

🚌 **Bus Travel:** Reliable bus services do not exist on any island.

🚗 **Car Travel:** You can get by without a car on Provo and some smaller islands, but it's a necessity on North Caicos or Middle Caicos.

⛴ **Ferry Travel:** Scheduled ferries connect Provo with both North Caicos and South Caicos, as well as Grand Turk with Salt Cay.

PLAN YOUR BUDGET

	HOTEL ROOM	MEAL	ATTRACTIONS
Low Budget	$200	$12	Snorkeling at Coral Gardens, Free
Mid Budget	$350	$25	National museum, $7
High Budget	$650	$45	Day Trip to North Caicos, $165

WAYS TO SAVE

Dine at the magic hour. Dinner is more expensive than lunch, so arrive 15 minutes before the switch-over and save.

Stay on smaller islands. Provo is expensive, but on the smaller islands, hotels and villas are basic and comfortable and tend to be a more economical alternative.

Rent a car on Provo. Cars are the best option if you want to explore; a longer round-trip taxi trip can be as expensive as one daily car rental.

Dine in or grab takeout. IGA Gourmet on Provo has a good deli with a wide variety and a full salad bar, or you can get take-out to eat in your condo or hotel room.

Hassle Factor	Medium. Flights to Providenciales from the U.S. are frequent, but smaller islands will require an additional short flight or ferry transfer.
3 days	Relax poolside or beachside on Provo, preferably along beautiful Grace Bay. Rent a car and explore the southern shores and western tip of the island.
1 week	Spend more time on Provo, and then set sail for an outer island getaway—to nearby Pine Cay or Parrot Cay. Take a day trip to lush North Caicos or visit historical Grand Turk.
2 weeks	After fully exploring Provo, relax for a day on a private cay and check out the natural beauty of North and Middle Caicos. Spend several days in Grand Turk and Salt Cay for some rustic, laid-back charm.

WHEN TO GO

High Season: Mid-December through mid-April is the most fashionable albeit the most expensive time to visit, when the weather is typically sunny and warm (though January through March can bring on "Christmas Winds," with swells and chilly water). Popular hotels and villas are often booked a year in advance.

Low Season: From August to late October, temperatures can be oppressively hot and the weather muggy, with higher risks of tropical storms; however, hurricanes are less common. Lodging discounts are more widely available during this season.

Value Season: Great weather and discounted lodging occurs from late April to July and again November to mid-December. There are chances of scattered showers, but expect sun-kissed days and fewer crowds. Both water and air temperatures in the Turks and Caicos are most comfortable April to June.

BIG EVENTS

April: Held on Easter Monday, the Turks and Caicos Kite Flying Competition is geared at both kids and adults, taking place on several different islands.

November: The Caribbean Food and Wine Festival brings in chefs and vintners for a long weekend filled with revelry. The Turks and Caicos Conch Festival is held on the last Saturday in Blue Hills on Provo.

December: The Junkanoo New Year's Eve street party with live bands, parades, and fireworks erupts in Grace Bay.

READ THIS

■ *Tour of the Turks and Caicos Islands,* Olivia Osprey. Inspiring coffee table book.

■ *Water and Light: A Diver's Journey to a Coral Reef,* Stephen Harrigan. A diver's incredible accounts of diving off Grand Turk.

■ *The Birds of the Turks & Caicos,* Richard Ground. A guide to the natural habitats of the TCI.

WATCH THIS

■ *The Right Stuff.* Refers to the United States' tracking station on Grand Turk.

■ *Turks & Caicos (2014).* A thriller set in the Turks and Caicos

EAT THIS

■ *Peas and hominy*: pigeon peas and grits, usually with conch or pig's tail

■ *Boil fish and johnny-cake*: boiled fish alongside sweet, fried bread

■ *Conch salad*: Diced conch, onions, bell peppers, fresh lime, sour orange juice, and hot sauce—ceviche style

■ *Conch stew*: pounded conch in a thick, rich gravy

■ *Fresh lobster*: cooked multiple ways, often caught off Provo or South Caicos

■ *Turk's Head beer*: local brew of choice

Updated
by Laura
Adzich-Brander

With crystal-clear turquoise waters, you may find it difficult to stray far from the beach in the Turks and Caicos. You may find no need for museums, and no desire to see ruins or even to read books. You may simply find yourself hypnotized by the myriad ocean blues. And because the beaches are among the most incredible you will ever see, don't be surprised if you wake up on your last morning to realize that you didn't find a lot of time for anything else.

Although ivory-white, soft, sandy beaches and breathtaking turquoise waters are shared among all the islands, the landscapes are a series of contrasts, from the dry, arid bush and scrub on the flat, coral islands of Salt Cay, Grand Turk, South Caicos, Pine Cay, and Providenciales, to the greener, foliage-rich undulating landscapes of Middle Caicos, North Caicos, and Parrot Cay.

A much-disputed legend has it that Columbus first discovered these islands in 1492. Despite being on the map for longer than most other island groups, the Turks and Caicos Islands (pronounced *kay*-kos) still remain part of the less discovered Caribbean. More than 40 islands—only 8 inhabited—make up this self-governing overseas territory of the United Kingdom that lies just 575 miles (925 km) southeast of Miami on the third-largest coral-reef system in the world.

The political and historical capital of the country is the island of Grand Turk; however, Providenciales is the tourist hub, thanks to the beauty of Grace Bay and its incredible crescent of powder-soft sand. Once home to a population of around 500 people plus a few donkey carts, Provo is now the center of activity, where one may enjoy resorts, spas, restaurants, and water sports. Condo-style hotels or one of the many self-contained villa residences become *home* for the majority of visitors who come to the Turks and Caicos.

The country's colonial past can be seen in the wood-and-stone, Bermudian-style clapboard houses—often wrapped in deep-red bougainvillea—that line the streets on the quiet islands of Grand Turk, Salt Cay, and South Caicos. Donkeys roam free in and around the salt ponds, which are a legacy from a time when residents of these island communities worked hard as both slaves and then laborers to rake salt (then known as "white gold") bound for the United States and Canada. In Salt Cay, the remains of wooden windmills are now home to large osprey nests. In Grand Turk and South Caicos, the crystal-edged tidal ponds are regularly visited by flocks of rose-pink flamingos hungry for the brine shrimp and blue-green algae to be found in the shallow waters.

In all, only 32,000 people live in the Turks and Caicos Islands; less than half are "Turks Islanders," the native population that is mainly descended from Loyalist and Bermudian slaves who settled here beginning in the 1600s. The majority of residents work in tourism, fishing, and offshore finance. Indeed, for residents and visitors alike, life in "TCI" is anything but taxing. But even though most visitors come to do nothing—a specialty in the islands—it does not mean there's nothing to do.

PLANNING

GETTING HERE AND AROUND

AIR TRAVEL

You can fly nonstop from several cities in the U.S.: Atlanta (Delta), Boston (JetBlue), Dallas (American), Charlotte (American), Fort Lauderdale (JetBlue), Miami (American), New York (Delta, JetBlue, United), and Philadelphia (American).

Although carriers and schedules vary seasonally, there are many nonstop and connecting flights to Providenciales from several U.S. cities on American, Delta, JetBlue, and United Airways. There are also flights connecting other parts of the Caribbean: Antigua (British Airways); Cap Haitien, Haiti (Caicos Express, InterCaribbean); Kingston, Jamaica (InterCaribbean); Nassau, Bahamas (Bahamasair); Port au Prince, Haiti (InterCaribbean); Puerto Plata, Dominican Republic (InterCaribbean); Santiago, Dominican Republic (InterCaribbean). Flights directly connecting the Canadian cities of Toronto and Montréal are WestJet and Air Canada. European cities are accessed through London on British Airways.

Airports: The main gateway into the Turks and Caicos Islands is the Providenciales International Airport (PLS). For private planes, Provo Air Center is a full-service FBO (Fixed Base Operator) offering refueling, maintenance, and short-term storage, as well as on-site customs and immigration clearance, a lounge, and concierge services. There are smaller airports on Grand Turk (GDT), North Caicos (NCS), South Caicos (XSC), and Salt Cay (SLX). Other than with Grand Turk, if you are going on to other islands in the chain, you will stop in Provo first for customs, then go from there.

Airline Contacts American Airlines. ⊠ *Providenciales International Airport, Airport Rd.* ✛ *Upstairs in the airport terminal* ☎ *800/433–7300* ⊕ *www.aa.com.* **Caicos Express Airways.** ⊠ *Southern Shores, Leeward Hiwy., Downtown* ✛ *Across from Grace Bay Auto, just past the DoIt Centre as you travel to*

18

the airport ☎ *649/941–5730 main office, 305/677–3116 overseas Vonage,, 649/946–8131 International Airport, 649/946–2178 Grand Turk Airport* ⊕ *www. caicosexpressairways.com.* **Delta.** ✉ *Providenciales International Airport (PLS), Airport Rd., Airport* ☎ *800/221–1212* ⊕ *www.delta.com.* **InterCaribbean Airways.** ✉ *Old Private Airport, Old Airport Rd., Airport* ⊹ *Behind Kischo on Airport Rd. (giant yellow building)* ☎ *649/946–4181 Providenciales, 649/443–3160 Grand Turk* ⊕ *www.intercaribbean.com.* **JetBlue.** ✉ *Providenciales International Airport (PLS), Airport Rd., Airport* ☎ *800/538–2583* ⊕ *www.jetblue.com.* **United Airlines.** ✉ *International Airport (PLS), Airport* ☎ *800/864–8331* ⊕ *www. united.com.*

Airport Contacts Turks & Caicos Islands Airport Authority. ✉ *Providenciales International Airport (PLS), Airport Rd., Airport* ☎ *649/946-4420 general inquiries* ⊕ *www.tciairports.com.*

BOAT AND FERRY TRAVEL

Despite the islands' relative proximity, ferry service is limited in the Turks and Caicos. You can take a ferry from Provo to North Caicos and to South Caicos. There's also a ferry from Grand Turk to Salt Cay; however, the service is often inconsistent due to weather. Air service or private boat charter is your best bet for a visit to Salt Cay.

Contacts Caribbean Cruisin'. ✉ *Walkin Marina, Heaving Down Rock, Leeward Hwy. E, Leeward* ☎ *649/946–5406, 649/231–4191* ⊕ *www.tciferry.com.* **Salt Cay Ferry.** ☎ *649/231–6663* ⊕ *saltcaytours.com.*

CAR TRAVEL

Driving here is on the left side of the road, British-style; when pulling out into traffic, remember to look to your right. Give way to anyone entering a roundabout, as roundabouts are still a relatively new concept in the Turks and Caicos; stop even if you are on what appears to be the primary road. The maximum speed is 40 mph (64 kph), 20 mph (30 kph) through settlements; speed limits, as well as the use of seat belts, are enforced.

If you are staying on Provo, you may find it useful to have a car; it's nice to enjoy a few days of exploring or also to get away from your hotel for dinner. On Grand Turk, you can rent a car, but you probably won't need to. Car- and jeep-rental rates average $39 to $100+ per day on Provo, plus a $15 surcharge per rental as a government tax. Be sure to check if the company you are renting from includes insurance with your rental. Many do not include liability. Reserve well ahead of time during peak season. Most agencies offer free mileage and airport pickup service. Major agencies with offices on Providenciales include Alamo, Avis, Budget, and Hertz. You might also try local Provo agencies such as Grace Bay Car Rentals, Rent a Buggy, Tropical Auto Rentals, and Caicos Wheels. There are a number of local operators on Grand Turk as well as on North Caicos, where they meet the ferries when they arrive at Sandy Point.

Contacts Alamo. ✉ *Providenciales International Airport, Airport* ☎ *649/941–3659* ⊕ *www.alamo.com.* **Avis.** ☎ *649/946–4705, 649/941–7557* ⊕ *www.avis. tc.* **Budget.** ✉ *Town Centre Mall, Downtown* ⊹ *Downtown on your left just before Airport Rd.* ☎ *649/946–4079* ⊕ *www.budget.com.* **Caicos Wheels.**

✉ *Ports of Call Plaza, Grace Bay Rd., Grace Bay* ☎ *954/363–1119 US Vonage, 649/946–8302 local number* ⊕ *www.caicoswheels.com.* **Grace Bay Car Rentals.** ✉ *Grace Bay Plaza, Grace Bay Rd., Grace Bay* ⊹ *Next door to Bella Luna* ☎ *649/941–8500 main hotline, 649/946–4404* ⊕ *www.gracebaycarrentals. com.* **Island Auto Rentals.** ✉ *Grand Turk Cruise Port, Grand Turk Cruise Terminal* ☎ *649/232–0933, 649/231–4214, 649/946–2042.* **Pelican Car Rentals.** ✉ *Pelican Beach Hotel, King's Hwy., Whitby* ☎ *649/331–7620 Donna, 649/946– 7112 Pelican Beach Hotel, 649/241–2076 Susan* ⊕ *www.pelicanbeach.tc.* **Rent a Buggy.** ✉ *1081 Leeward Hwy., right next door to Mac Motors, which is right next door to Central Plaza, Downtown* ☎ *649/946–4158 landline, 649/231–6161 mobile* ⊕ *www.rentabuggy.tc.* **Scooter Bob's.** ⊹ *Located right after the Marina entrance, next door to Turtle Cove Inn* ☎ *649/946–4684* ⊕ *www.scooterbobstci. com.* **Tony's Car Rental.** ✉ *Outside cruise-terminal gates, Grand Turk Cruise Terminal* ☎ *649/231–1806 main line, 649/946–2934 after hours* ✉ *thriller@ tciway.tc* ⊕ *www.tonyscarrental.com.* **Tropical Auto Rentals.** ✉ *Tropicana Plaza, Leeward Hwy., Grace Bay* ⊹ *At the junction of Leeward Hiwy. and Sand Castle Dr.* ☎ *649/946–5300* ⊕ *www.tropicalautorentaltci.com.*

TAXI TRAVEL

Taxis are available at the airports on both Provo and Grand Turk. Many resorts arrange their guests' transfers; ask for assistance if the service is not included. When booking your accommodations, be sure to ask upfront about the arrangements. A trip via taxi between Provo's airport and most major hotels runs between $15 and $23 per person. Taxis (actually large vans) in Providenciales are regulated by the government at a per-person rate, zone determined. On Grand Turk, a trip from the airport to Cockburn Town is about $8. You will also be able to organize a ride from the ferry dock on North Caicos. On the family islands, taxis are not metered, so it's best to discuss the cost for your trip in advance.

HEALTH AND SAFETY

Dengue, chikungunya, and zika have all been reported throughout the Caribbean. We recommend that you protect yourself from these mosquito-borne illnesses by keeping your skin covered and/or wearing mosquito repellent. The mosquitoes that transmit these viruses are as active by day as they are by night.

HOTEL AND RESORTS

The Turks and Caicos can be an expensive destination. Most hotels on Providenciales are pricey, but there are some moderately priced options; most accommodations are condo-style, and not all resorts are family-friendly. You'll find a sprinkling of upscale properties on the outer islands—including the famous Parrot Cay—but the majority of places are smaller inns and private self-contained villas. What you give up in luxury, however, you gain back tenfold in island charm. Though the smaller islands are relatively isolated, their quiet ambience and "beauty by nature" is what makes them so attractive.

Resorts: Most of the resorts on Provo are upscale; most are condo-style, giving the option of preparing some meals in or having a private chef prepare something extra special for you. There are two all-inclusive resorts on Provo—Club Med and Beaches. A few resorts are closed for

18

a short period during the fall for maintenance. Be sure to double check if your heart is set on a particular property.

Small Inns: Most of the more modest inns with fewer amenities are on the outlying islands, with a few such options on Provo. Some are devoted to diving.

Villas and Condos: Villas and condos are plentiful, particularly on Provo, and usually represent good value for families. However, there are also larger villas that are fully staffed for those looking for the ultimate in pampering or wish a more exclusively private venue for their special event. Many of the more popular properties book up to two years in advance, so you need to plan ahead to get what suits you best.

Hotel reviews have been shortened. For full information, visit Fodors.com.

WHAT IT COSTS IN U.S. DOLLARS				
	$	$$	$$$	$$$$
RESTAURANTS	under $12	$12–$20	$21–$30	over $30
HOTELS	under $275	$275–$375	$376–$475	over $475

Restaurant prices are the average cost of a main course at dinner or, if dinner is not served, at lunch. Hotel prices are the lowest cost of a standard double room in high season.

TOURS

⇨ *See also Sports and Outdoors under individual islands*

FAMILY **Big Blue Unlimited.** Big Blue Unlimited's educational ecotours include
Fodor'sChoice three-hour kayak trips and other guided journeys throughout the cays
★ that lie to the northeast of the island, as well as on North, Middle, and South Caicos. Its Coastal Ecology and Wildlife tour is a kayak adventure through red mangroves to bird habitats, rock iguana hideaways, and natural fish nurseries. The North Caicos Mountain Bike Eco Tour gets you on a bike to explore the island, which includes the plantation ruins, inland lakes, and flamingo pond with a stop for lunch featuring local cuisine along the way. Package costs range from $85 to $225 per person. With 18 years of experience, their service is exceptional. ⊠ *Leeward Marina, Marina Rd., Leeward* ✛ *Next door to Blue Haven Resort and Marina* ☎ *649/946–5034 main office number, 649/231–6455 cell number* ⊕ *www.bigblueunlimited.com.*

VISITOR INFORMATION

The tourist offices on Grand Turk and Providenciales are open daily from 9 to 5.

Contacts Turks & Caicos Islands Tourist Board, Grand Turk. ⊠ *Front St., Cockburn Town* ✛ *Across from the Cruise Ship Welcome Centre downtown, across the street and down 4 doors from the National Museum.* ☎ *649/946–2321* ⊕ *www.turksandcaicostourism.com.* **Turks & Caicos Islands Tourist Board, Providenciales.** ⊠ *Stubbs Diamond Plaza, Grace Bay* ☎ *649/946–4970* ⊕ *www.turksandcaicostourism.com.* **Turks & Caicos Reservations.** ☎ *877/774–5486 U.S., 649/941–8988 local* ⊕ *www.turksandcaicosreservations.tc.*

PROVIDENCIALES

The sight of the shallow, crystal-clear turquoise waters of Chalk Sound National Park never fails to dazzle visitors as it comes into view upon their aircraft's approach to the island. With an increasing number of new visitors arriving each year, Provo, as the island is commonly called, is a top Caribbean destination. But don't worry. There's plenty of gorgeous beaches and world-class services to go around. Although you may start to believe that every road leads to a large, luxurious resort, there are plenty of sections of beach where you can escape the din. Most of the modern resorts, exquisite spas, water-sports operators, shops, restaurants, and the island's only golf course are scattered along the north shore, fringed by the exquisite stretch of Grace Bay Beach. And even though almost all of the country's grand condominium resorts are found on Provo, it's still possible to find deserted stretches of ivory-white shoreline, particularly on the more secluded southern shores and western tip of the island.

Although you may be quite content enjoying the beachscape and top-notch amenities on Provo, it's also a great jumping-off point for island-hopping tours by sea or by air, as well as both fishing and diving trips. The well-maintained road network enables you to get around easily and make the most of the main tourism and sightseeing spots. Just beware: driving is on the left-hand side!

EXPLORING

WORTH NOTING

18

FAMILY **Caicos Conch Farm.** More than 3 million conchs are farmed at this commercial operation on the northeast tip of Provo, as well as the breeding stock for five different freshwater fish for future farming. It's a popular tourist attraction, too, with guided tours and a small gift shop selling conch-related souvenirs, jewelry, and freshwater conch pearls. You can even meet Jerry and Sally, the resident conchs that are brought out on demand. ⊠ *Leeward-Going-Through, Leeward* ✛ *The last turnoff to the right before Walkin Marina in Leeward; watch for the sign.* ☎ *649/946–5330* ⊕ *www.caicosconchfarm.net* ⬛ *$12* ⊗ *Weekdays 9–4, Sat. 9–2:30.*

Fodor's Choice **Chalk Sound National Park.** As you drive out to the end of South Dock
★ Road, on your right you will catch glimpses of the beautiful Chalk Sound; the water here is luminescent. The best places to stop for pictures are on Chalk Sound Drive. You can enjoy lunch overlooking the park at Las Brisas Restaurant or drive to the very end of the road and take a walk along the shoreline where there are few homes. No matter how many times you see it, it will always manage to take your breath away. ⊠ *Chalk Sound Rd., Chalk Sound.*

Cheshire Hall. Just east of downtown Provo are the eerie remains of an 18th-century cotton plantation owned by the Loyalist Thomas Stubbs. A trail weaves through the ruins, where guided interpretive tours tell the story of the island's doomed cotton industry and about the plantation itself. A variety of local plants are also identified. Contact the Turks &

Providenciales

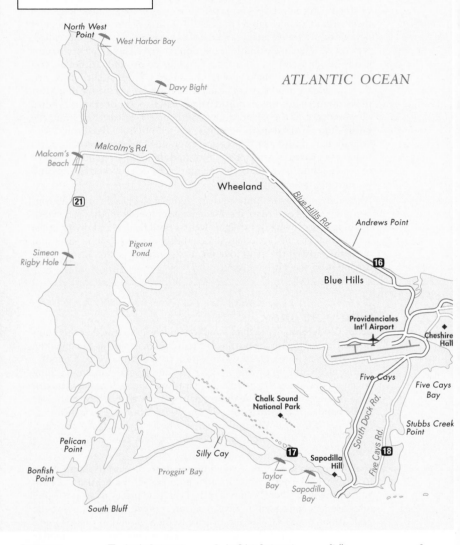

North West Point

West Harbor Bay

Davy Bight

ATLANTIC OCEAN

Malcom's Rd.

Malcom's Beach

Wheeland

21

Blue Hills Rd.

Andrews Point

Simeon Rigby Hole

Pigeon Pond

16

Blue Hills

Providenciales Int'l Airport

Cheshire Hall

Five Cays

Five Cays Bay

Chalk Sound National Park

South Dock Rd.

Stubbs Creek Point

Pelican Point

Silly Cay

17

Sapodilla Hill

18

Five Cays Rd.

Bonfish Point

Proggin' Bay

Taylor Bay

Sapodilla Bay

South Bluff

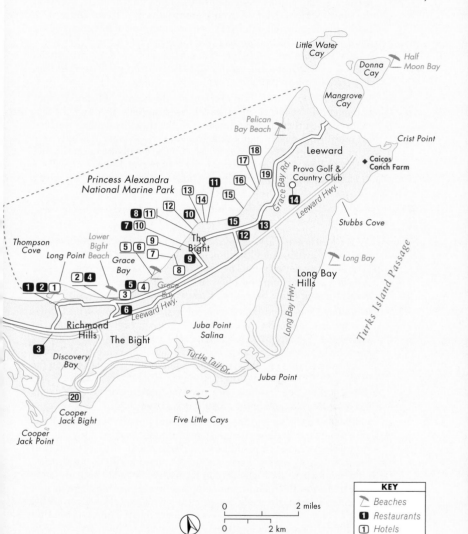

Water Cay

Little Water Cay

Donna Cay

Half Moon Bay

Mangrove Cay

Pelican Bay Beach

Leeward

Crist Point

◆ Caicos Conch Farm

Provo Golf & Country Club

Grace Bay Rd.

Princess Alexandra National Marine Park

Leeward Hwy.

Stubbs Cove

Thompson Cove

Lower Bight Beach

Long Point

Grace Bay

The Bight

Long Bay

Long Bay Hills

Turks Island Passage

Grace Bay

Leeward Hwy.

Richmond Hills

The Bight

Long Bay Hwy.

Juba Point Salina

Turtle Tail Dr.

Juba Point

Discovery Bay

20

Cooper Jack Bight

Five Little Cays

Cooper Jack Point

KEY

◿ Beaches
🬛 Restaurants
① Hotels

0 ——— 2 miles
0 ——— 2 km

Caicos National Trust to visit; there's a nominal fee that goes toward preserving the nation's heritage. If this piques your interest, a visit to the North Caicos Wades Green plantation or the Turks and Caicos National Museum in Grand Turk will provide more of the story. ⊠ *Leeward Hwy., next to the entrance into the National Hospital (Providenciales), Downtown* ☎ *649/941–5710 for Turks and Caicos National Trust* ⊕ *www.tcnationaltrust.org* ⊠ *$10* ⊙ *Weekdays 8:30–4:30, Sat. 9–1 (guided tour required).*

FAMILY   **Sapodilla Hill.** On this hilltop overlooking the beauty of Sapodilla Bay, you might find what is left of several rock carvings. It is thought that sailors carved the names and dates into the rocks while they watched over their ships from a high vantage point, perhaps while the hulls were being cleaned or repairs were being made. The details are uncertain, but they have been dated back to the mid-1700s to mid-1800s. You will see replicas displayed at Provo's International Airport. ⊠ *Off South Dock Rd., west of South Dock, Chalk Sound.*

BEACHES

All the beaches of Turks and Caicos have bright white sand that's soft like baby powder. An added bonus is that no matter how hot the sun gets, your feet never burn. The soft sand extends to the ocean, so there is little fear of stepping on rocks or corals. Even the beach areas with corals for snorkeling have clear, clean sand for water entry.

Fodor'sChoice   **Grace Bay.** The world-famous sweeping stretch of ivory-white, pow-
★   der-soft sand on Provo's north shore is simply breathtaking. Protected within the Princess Alexandra National Park, it's home to migrating starfish, as well as many schools of tiny fishes. The majority of Provo's beachfront resorts are along this shore, and it's the primary reason the Turks and Caicos is a world-class destination. **Amenities:** food and drink; parking (free); water sports. **Best for:** sunset; swimming; walking. ⊠ *Grace Bay Rd., along the north shore, Grace Bay.*

Fodor'sChoice   **Half Moon Bay.** This natural ribbon of sand linking two uninhabited
★   cays is only inches above the sparkling turquoise waters. Only minutes from Provo's eastern tip, Half Moon Bay is one of the most gorgeous beaches in the country. There are small limestone cliffs to explore on either end where rock iguanas sun themselves, as well as small, sandy coves. Most of the island's tour companies run excursions here or simply offer a beach drop-off. As an alternative, rent a kayak from Big Blue Unlimited and venture over independently. **Amenities:** none. **Best for:** solitude; swimming; walking. ⊠ *Between Big Water Cay and Little Water Cay* ⊕ *http://bigblueunlimited.com.*

Lower Bight Beach. Lower Bight Beach blends right into Grace Bay Beach as the western extension of Provo's Princess Alexandra National Park; visitors to the island think the two beaches are one and the same. Unlike its world-famous counterpart, the Bight Beach has off-the-beach snorkeling where the fringing reef comes in to touch the shore. The Provo Sailing Club gives lessons most Saturdays for the residents of the island and also holds the Annual Fools Regatta in June, which everyone can enjoy. Both are held at the far western end in what is known as the

Children's Park. **Amenities:** food and drink; parking (free). **Best for:** snorkeling; swimming; walking. ⊠ *Lower Bight Rd., The Bight* ✛ *The Children's Park is at the junction of Pratt's Rd. and Lower Bight Rd.*

Malcolm's Beach. This is one of the most stunning beaches you'll ever see, but you'll need to tread carefully; the road is a little rough in spots, and there have been reports of break-ins at the parking area. It's best not to keep any valuables in your car or on your person, and never go alone. Bring your own food and drinks because there are no facilities for miles around. **Amenities:** parking (free). **Best for:** solitude; swimming; walking. ⊠ *Malcolm's Beach Rd., Northwest Point* ✛ *On Leeward Hwy., take the Fuller Walkin roundabout toward Blue Hills. Keep to the Millenium Hwy. until after it turns into hard-packed sand. Turn left at the intersection where right indicates the route to Wheeland. Follow the road until the end, which takes about 20 mins. Expect a relatively rough, windy, and isolated road.*

Pelican Beach. Pelican Beach is another gorgeous stretch of beach that blends right into Grace Bay Beach at its eastern extension, also within the protection of the Princess Alexandra National Park. There is little distinction between where one beach ends and the other begins. Because of a cut in the reef, you may find wonderful shells here to enjoy—but remember that you are within the national park, so they must be left behind for others to see long after you have gone home. This end of the bay is slightly quieter than the rest, as there is much less development here. Enjoy. **Amenities:** parking (free). **Best for:** solitude; swimming; walking. ⊠ *Sandpiper Ave., Leeward* ✛ *Travel east along Grace Bay Rd. until you pass the small manned gatehouse. At the big circle take your first left, Sandpiper Ave. At the small roundabout, take a left and follow until the road ends, and park. The beach blends with Grace Bay Beach to the left; on the right, walk around to Pelican Beach. Some acknowlege a small stretch in between as Leeward Beach.*

Sapodilla Bay. One of the best of the many secluded beaches around Provo is this peaceful quarter-mile cove protected by Sapodilla Hill. The soft strand here is lapped by calm waves, while yachts and small boats rock with the gentle motion. During low tide, little sandbar "islands" form—they're great for a beach chair and make the waters easily accessible by young children. **Amenities:** parking (free). **Best for:** sunbathing. ⊠ *End of South Dock Rd., Chalk Sound* ✛ *From Leeward Hwy., take Roundabout 6 at the bottom of the Leeward Hwy. hill toward Five Cays. Follow until almost the end, and at the small police station turn right onto Chalk Sound Rd. The road on the left leads to a small parking area that offers public access to the beach.*

FAMILY **Taylor Bay.** Taylor Bay is shallow for hundreds of feet, making it the perfect place for kids; they become giddy at the fact that they can run free through shallow waters without their parents worrying about them. The beach also offers gorgeous views of the villas that hang over the shoreline on one side of the bay with natural coastline on the other. As it has had many amazing reviews over the years, don't expect to have this one all to yourself. There is even the odd tour that pulls up. **Amenities:** none. **Best for:** sunbathing; wading. ⊠ *Sunset Dr., Chalk Sound* ✛ *From*

18

Leeward Hwy., take the roundabout exit towards Five Cays at the bottom of the Leeward Hwy. hill. Follow the road until almost the end, and at the small police station, take a right onto Chalk Sound Rd. Take a left at Ocean Point Dr., and park next to the tennis courts where there are big boulders blocking a sand path. Follow this path to the beach.

West Harbour Bay. This is about as isolated as it gets on Provo. West Bay has long stretches of beaches to walk and possibly not see another person for hours. Occasionally Captain Bill's Outback Adventure excursion stops here to explore the nearby pirate caves. You might see large red starfish in the water here, or if you walk out to Bonefish Point you may spot small reef sharks and the odd ray hunting in the shallows. Don't leave valuables in your car, as there have been break-ins reported in the past. **Amenities:** none. **Best for:** exploring; solitude; swimming; walking. ✉ *Northwest Point* ✧ *Traveling west on Millenium Hwy. past Blue Hills, take the last left before Provo's landfill site. Continue for 5 miles (8 km) along a relatively rough road until you come to the ocean's edge. Walk along the shoreline to get to the caves. Walk right to Bonefish Point.*

WHERE TO EAT

Whichever Provo restaurant you choose, you'll experience fresh seafood specials, artistic presentations, and a full range of Caribbean of spices. You will also find a range of ethnic restaurants representing many regions around the globe. Very few restaurants close during the slow season as they once did; however, there are a few that do, with exact dates fluctuating annually.

Pick up a free copy of *Where When How's Dining Guide*, which you will find as a free publication island wide; it has menus, websites, and photos of almost all of the well-established restaurants.

THE BIGHT

$$ BAKERY Fodor's Choice ★ 🍴 **Crust Bakery and Cafe.** A fabulous new bakery—that's so much more—has found a home adjacent to the Graceway IGA on Leeward Highway. At Crust Bakery and Cafe you'll find a variety of handcrafted European breads baked daily, including sourdough and baguettes, a variety of sweets, chocolate croissants, and delicious cinnamon buns, as well as great café lattes and espresso. Their hot breakfasts are a hit, or wait until later in the day for a homemade soup, lasagna, burgers, or something with an island twist. Enjoy their selections out front on their canopied terrace, or take away for a picnic lunch in your villa. Crust will also deliver—even to private yachts—and they prepare specialty cakes upon request. [$] *Average main: $12* ✉ *Graceway House, Leeward Hwy., The Bight* ✧ *Adjoining the Graceway IGA* ☎ *649/946–5003* 🌐 *Facebook Crust Bakery and Cafe* ✍ *Reservations not accepted.*

$$ MEXICAN 🍴 **Somewhere Café and Lounge.** Right on Grace Bay Beach overlooking tranquil waters, the Somewhere Café is a pleasant, casual dining option. It's the perfect spot to enjoy midday, as bathing attire is perfectly acceptable, with Coral Gardens snorkeling only a few steps away. There's an adult-only bar/lounge on the upper deck, offering amazing views and full breeze. Much of the menu is made from scratch, with desserts

prepared by residents and delivered daily. You will thoroughly enjoy the chips-and-salsa trio; the guac is to die for. All the regular Mexican dishes are there, plus a super Tex-Mex breakfast. The portions are large. There's live music four nights a week, with a DJ on Sunday afternoons starting at 2:30, making this a very lively spot. $ *Average main: $18* ⊠ *Coral Gardens Resort, Lower Bight Rd., The Bight* ✛ *Right on the beach* ☎ 649/941–8260 ⊕ *www.somewherecafeandlounge.com.*

$$$$

ECLECTIC

✕ **Stelle.** Stelle serves an eclectic cuisine with an Asian influence while incorporating island touches. You will find such mains as Thai-style steamed snapper and lobster linguine Al Ajillo, as well as a grilled rack of lamb with a pomegranate reduction. Complete the evening with a Cuban-style coffee alongside their Bambarra Rum Crème Brûlée. You can choose either indoor dining or outdoor seating overlooking the pool at Gansevoort resort. $ *Average main: $37* ⊠ *Gansevoort Resort, Lower Bight Rd., The Bight* ☎ 649/941–7555 ⊕ *www.gansevoorttc.com.*

CHALK SOUND

$$$

INTERNATIONAL

FAMILY

Fodor's Choice

★

✕ **Las Brisas Restaurant and Bar.** With exquisite views of Chalk Sound, the restaurant terrace and elevated gazebo offer picture-postcard views of the intensely blue waters. This is the only restaurant on Provo that offers an authentic paella (if you order this, give it time—the flavors have to simmer). The menu also includes tapas, so you can enjoy a long lunch, indulging while you gaze at the gorgeous water. Dinner takes a little longer, as everything is made to order; you pick out your fish or meat, decide how you want it prepared, and choose a sauce for it. Try any one of their beef entrées, as they are all wonderful; their seafood creole is also great. If you want to experience Chalk Sound from the water, Las Brisas also has a cruising boat that holds up to 12 people. You can start your evening with a cruise at $50/person and ask for your predinner cocktails and appetizers to be served on board. $ *Average main: $30* ⊠ *Neptune Villas, #533 Chalk Sound Dr., Chalk Sound* ✛ *Take South Dock Rd. and turn right at Chalk Sound Dr. to Neptune Villas on your right.* ☎ 649/331–4328 *villas,* 649/946–5306 *restaurant* ⊕ *www.neptunevillastci.com* ☉ *Closed Tues.*

18

GRACE BAY

$$$$

ECLECTIC

FAMILY

Fodor's Choice

★

✕ **Bay Bistro.** You simply can't eat any closer to the beach than here at Bay Bistro, directly on Grace Bay Beach. You have the option of dining on a covered deck, on an open-air patio, or with your feet in the sand, surrounded by palm trees with the sound of lapping waves. The coffee-rubbed tuna appetizer—with a hint of wasabi—is the best. Their fish-and-chips are quite lovely, and for the carnivore, the beef tenderloin is to die for. Seasonally, lobster is brought to their back door daily by local fishermen. End the evening with homemade ice cream. Their weekend brunches include such favorites as eggs Benedict—one of the few places on island to find it—with mimosas included. Be sure to reserve if you are coming with a large group, as it is quite a popular way to begin a lazy day. Around the time of the full moon, call for the date of their memorable beach barbecue: grilled shrimp, roast suckling pig, side fixings—all enjoyed while sitting around a wonderful bonfire on the beach. $ *Average main: $32* ⊠ *Sibonné Beach Hotel, Princess Dr., right next door to the*

Somerset, Grace Bay ☎ *649/946–5396 main line, 649/432–1025* 🌐 *www.baybistrorestaurant.com* ✍ *Reservations essential.*

$$$$ ITALIAN 🍴 **Caicos Café Bar and Grill.** Here the island dishes come with an Italian twist. Everything is fresh and carefully prepared. The bread is even baked fresh daily at the bakery next door. A favorite of residents is the Mediterranean-style seafood casserole, made with white wine and a light tomato sauce. This restaurant is also a good option for vegetarians. On windy nights, the inland setting offers protection from the breezes, and the large flamboyant tree is quite spectacular, especially when it is in full bloom. (Bug spray at night may be necessary.) [$] *Average main: $32* ✉ *Caicos Café Plaza, Governor's Rd., Grace Bay* ☎ *649/946–5278* ⏲ *Closed Sun.* ☞ *Dress is island chic; no sleeveless tops or short pants for men please.*

$$$$ INTERNATIONAL FAMILY Fodor's Choice ★ 🍴 **Coco Bistro.** With tables exotically set within a mature palm grove, Coco Bistro is one of the most popular restaurants on Provo. Main courses combine continental dishes with a Caribbean flair, and seafood abounds. Be sure to try their Caicos lobster bisque; it's flambé style with cognac and a hint of spicy cream. The roast rack of lamb with an herb crust is also amazing. **TIP→ This is a must-visit, so be sure to make reservations at least one week ahead during nonpeak season, two to three weeks ahead in peak season.** [$] *Average main: $40* ✉ *Governor's Rd., Grace Bay* ✣ *Just down from Sunshine Nursery* ☎ *649/946–5369* 🌐 *www.cocobistro.tc* ⏲ *Closed Mon.* ✍ *Reservations essential.*

$$$$ ECLECTIC 🍴 **Coyaba Restaurant.** Directly behind Grace Bay Club at Caribbean Paradise Inn, this posh little restaurant is in a palm-fringed setting. The nostalgic favorites here are served with tempting twists in conversation-piece crockery. Chef Paul Newman uses his culinary expertise for the frequently changing menu featuring daily specials, which include exquisitely presented dishes such as crispy, whole yellow snapper fried in Thai spices. An ever popular dish is his lobster thermidor in a Dijon-mushroom cream sauce. You may want to try several different appetizers instead of an entrée for dinner; guava-and-tamarind barbecue ribs and coconut-shrimp tempura are two good choices if you go that route. If you enjoy creative menus, this is the place for you. Coyaba keeps the resident expat crowd happy with traditional favorites such as lemon meringue pie, albeit with a tropical twist. Don't skip dessert; Paul makes an excellent chocolate fondant. Be forewarned, if the evening looks like rain, much of the seating is not under cover, making the dining a bit more crowded than usual. Children dine only in the very early evening hours. [$] *Average main: $45* ✉ *Caribbean Paradise Inn, Bonaventure Crescent, Grace Bay* ✣ *Just off Grace Bay Rd. Watch for their sign next to Casablanca Casino.* ☎ *649/946–5186* 🌐 *www.coyabarestaurant.com* ⏲ *Closed Tues. and Sept. and Oct.* ✍ *Reservations essential.*

$$ ECLECTIC 🍴 **Fairways Bar & Grill.** Located at the Provo Golf and Country Club, Fairways is open seven days a week for breakfast and lunch. Hot or cold breakfast is offered during the week, while Sunday brunch features such favorites as waffles and eggs Benedict. Lunches are snack-style bites along with an array of sandwiches and a *very* wide range of burgers. Asian Friday Night kicks off during busy season only, when the Filipino chef creates a number of delicious dishes, including Thai red and green

curries, as well as barbecue pork loin served on bamboo sticks. Golfers will enjoy the view down the fairway and over a green. On other nights there are rugby matches on the big screen and bar food is served. [$] *Average main: $18* ✉ *Governor's Rd., Grace Bay* ✥ *Opposite Opus upstairs in the Golf Club* ☎ *649/946–5833 restaurant, 649/946–5991 pro shop* 🌐 *www.provogolfclub.com.*

$$$$ INTERNATIONAL 🍴 **Grace's Cottage.** This is considered one of the prettiest settings on Provo, and the name says it all. Imagine dining under the stars amidst an English-style garden or at one of the tables artfully set upon the graceful covered veranda skirting the gingerbread cottage. Tangy and exciting entrées include saffron seafood, vegetarian risotto, and the Cornish hen with wild rice. The portions are small, but the quality is high. You might want to end with the delicious chocolate soufflé. A nice touch is the small stool ladies are given so that their purses do not have to sit on the ground. On Tuesday night, live music adds to the good vibes. [$] *Average main: $42* ✉ *Point Grace, off Grace Bay Rd., Grace Bay* ✥ *In between the Sands and Regent Grand* ☎ *649/946–5096* 🌐 *www.pointgrace.com* ✍ *Reservations essential* ☞ *Smart casual attire for dinner.*

$$$$ ECLECTIC 🍴 **Hemingway's Restaurant.** The casual yet gorgeous setting, with a patio and deck offering unobstructed views of Grace Bay, makes this one of the most popular tourist restaurants. At lunch you can't miss with the soft grouper tacos or fish-and-chips. The mango shrimp salad is also excellent. For dinner there is a great kids' menu as well. Order the popular Old Man and the Sea, which features the fresh fish of the day. If you're on a budget, go right before 6 pm, when you can still order the less expensive lunch menu items. Live music a couple of nights a week adds to the ambience. Ask when Brentford Handfield and his son take the stage. [$] *Average main: $35* ✉ *The Sands at Grace Bay, Grace Bay Rd., Grace Bay* ☎ *649/941–8408* 🌐 *www.hemingwaystci.com.*

18

$$$$ ECLECTIC Fodor's Choice ★ 🍴 **Infiniti.** This chic palapa-style, waterfront, open-air restaurant has the most romantic setting along Grace Bay, and for most, in all of the Turks and Caicos Islands. Despite its elite clientele and higher prices, the restaurant offers a memorable dining experience minus any formality or attitude; guests are expected to wear island chic (men, no sleeveless shirts please). Oil lamps create an evening glow, and the murmur of trade winds adds to the Edenic ambience. Mesmerizing ocean views, along with exquisite service, make this an ideal choice when you want the best without a care in the world. The kitchen uses the island's bountiful seafood and fresh produce to craft superb cuisine. They also offer a raw bar, featuring a variety of ceviches: scallops, salmon, and mahimahi. It's a good thing the setting is amazing, as the portions are "elegantly" sized. [$] *Average main: $40* ✉ *Grace Bay Club, Grace Bay Circle Rd., Grace Bay* ☎ *649/946–5050 ext. 1 for the restaraunt* 🌐 *www.gracebayresorts.com* ⏲ *No lunch* ✍ *Reservations essential.*

$$$$ INTERNATIONAL Fodor's Choice ★ 🍴 **The Somerset's Pavillion Restaurant and LunaSea.** Located at the Somerset Resort, dining may be at one of several tables elegantly set overlooking a formal garden courtyard. Indoors, there is a different vibe altogether—cool and chic with high ceilings. It is one of Provo's few indoor, air-conditioned restaurants. The executive chef mixes international styles with a Caribbean, Asian, and European flair. Some of the standouts are

their classic steak-and-lobster combination and the house-made angolotti pasta, which is stuffed with plantains and sweet potatoes and done in a curry coconut cream sauce. A must-try is their conch spring rolls, which took first place in the 2015 Conch Festival competition. End the meal with a salted caramel chocolate flan or their dessert pizza, prepared with Granny Smith apples and mascarpone with maple sugar icing drizzle. Ask for simpler off-the-menu options for the children. Brad, the chef, is also available for in-room chef service at the Somerset. If you're looking for something a little more casual, try the Somerset's poolside dining at LunaSea for stunning views of Grace Bay. [$] *Average main: $40* ✉ *The Somerset, Princess Dr., Grace Bay* ✣ *Tucked next to the Regent Palms* ☎ *649/339–5900 hotel front desk* 🌐 *www.thesomerset.com* 🕒 *Main restaurant closed Thurs.* ☞ *Island chic at the main restaurant.*

TURTLE COVE

$$ DELI 🍴 **Angela's Top o' the Cove New York Style Delicatessen.** Order a coffee, tea, bagel, deli sandwich, salad, or dessert at this island institution (opened in 1992) on Leeward Highway, just south of Turtle Cove. They also have great pizza, which you can order by the slice or by the box. There are tables in air-conditioned comfort, as well as on a shaded patio outside. The location's not close to where most tourists stay, but it's worth the drive. From the deli case you can also buy the fixings for a picnic; the shelves are stocked with a selection of fancier food items, as well as some beer and wine. They have a nice casual breakfast that starts at 6:30 am for early risers. [$] *Average main: $12* ✉ *Leeward Hwy., Turtle Cove* ☎ *649/946–4694* 🌐 *www.provo.net/topothecove* 🕒 *No dinner* ✍ *Reservations not accepted.*

$$$$ ECLECTIC 🍴 **Magnolia Wine Bar and Restaurant.** The hands-on owners here, Gianni and Tracey Caporuscio, make success seem simple. Expect well-prepared, uncomplicated dishes. From their outstanding appetizers, try the panko-crusted shrimp or the roasted beets and fresh mozzarella. One of their must-have entrées and a signature dish is the sesame-encrusted rare seared tuna. Their Banoffee Pie or Vanilla Roasted Strawberries should end every meal. The bar deck's atmosphere is romantic, with only a few tables tucked off to the side. The wine menu offers a handpicked list of specialty wines that can be ordered by the glass. The hilltop setting is a great place to watch the sunset with the best views over Turtle Cove Marina and the north shore. [$] *Average main: $35* ✉ *76 Sunburst Rd., Turtle Cove* ✣ *On the ridge overlooking Turtle Cove, just off Lower Bight Rd. in the old Miramar Hotel* ☎ *649/941–5108* 🌐 *www.magnoliaprovo.com* 🕒 *Closed Mon. No lunch* ✍ *Reservations essential.*

$$$ ECLECTIC FAMILY 🍴 **Tiki Hut.** From a location overlooking the marina, the ever-popular Tiki Hut serves consistently tasty, value-priced meals in a fun atmosphere. Locals take advantage of the Wednesday-night chicken-and-rib special, and the lively bar is a good place to sample local Turk's Head brew. There's a special family-style menu, the best kids' menu on Provo. Don't miss pizzas made with the signature white sauce, or the jerk wings, coated in a secret barbecue sauce and then grilled—they're out of this world. The restaurant can be busy, with long waits for tables. It's part of a little drama on the island; 23 years ago they settled right on the water and then moved to a much larger location at the end of the marina. For you

die-hard fans, they have moved "back to where it all began." However, it is bigger and better than ever. Doug, one of the longtime owners, has upscaled the operation since it last sat here, offering four different seating options: lounge-style closest to the water, a beer garden picnic-table deck for regular fare, undercover A-frame indoor dining, and Bamboo Room poolside dining as an option for private parties. $ *Average main: $25* ⊠ *Turtle Cove Marina, Lower Bight Rd., Turtle Cove* ✛ *At Turtle Cove Inn* ☎ 649/941–5341 ⊕ *www.tikihut.tc.*

ELSEWHERE ON PROVIDENCIALES

$$ ✕ **Bugaloos.** Dinner and lunch is served totally island-style at this fabu-
CARIBBEAN lous spot overlooking the Caicos Banks on the southern shores of Provi-
Fodor's Choice denciales. Local cuisine at its finest and a wide drink menu is served
★ daily with live music every day from 1 to 4, and Tuesday, Saturday, and Sunday evenings from 6 pm until 9, or later. You can even grab the mike most nights to belt out a favorite tune, and dancing to the island beat is most welcome! Enjoy the warm breezes and lively conversation, and check out their small gift shop. Bugaloos makes a perfect stop when exploring Chalk Sound and Silly Creek. $ *Average main: $18* ⊠ *Five Cay's Rd., Five Cay's* ✛ *Take South Dock Rd. toward Chalk Sound, turning left at the service station midway into the Five Cays Settlement. Keep to the left when the road splits into a Y. You will see the restaurant on your left immediately as the ocean comes into view. It's right next door to Sunny's Fish Plant.* ☎ 649/941–3863 ⊕ *www.bugaloostci.com.*

$$$ ✕ **Da Conch Shack.** An institution on Provo for many years, this brightly
CARIBBEAN colored beach shack is justifiably famous for its conch and seafood. The
FAMILY conch is fished fresh out of the shallows and broiled, spiced, cracked, or fried to absolute perfection. This is the freshest conch anywhere on the island, as the staff collect it from their "pens" several times a day as needed. If you don't wish to try this island delicacy, there are a few chicken dishes to choose from, as well as their blackened grouper. They also have Johnny fries, a local tradition of french fries with a black-bean-and-local-pepper sauce. Give them a call to find out when they offer live music from 7 to 10 pm (Hump and Bump Night) or have a DJ on-site. You get to dine with your feet in the sand or on a wooden deck, right on the water's edge. $ *Average main: $25* ⊠ *Blue Hills Rd., Blue Hills* ✛ *Right on the beach and next door to Kalooki's* ☎ 649/946–8877 ⊕ *www.conchshack.tc.*

18

WHERE TO STAY

Most of the resorts on Providenciales are on Grace Bay, but a few are off the beaten track. You will find choices dotted along smaller bays around the island or even off the beach.

PRIVATE VILLA RENTALS

On Provo you can rent a self-catering apartment or a private house. For the best villa selection, make your reservations six months to a year in advance, or you may not get your first choice. Most villas can be rented on multiple villa-rental sites, which act as booking agents, and most have property managers or owners on-island to assist you. Vacation Rentals By Owners (VRBO) is an excellent overview of what is available.

RENTAL CONTACTS

Coldwell Banker TCI. Several agents at Coldwell Banker will assist you in selecting a property island wide. ✉ *La Petite Place, Governor's Rd.* ✥ *Next door to Ports of Call, facing Seven Stars Resort* ☎ *649/946–4969* 🌐 *www.coldwellbankertci.com.*

Prestigious Properties. Prestige offers modest to magnificent condos and villas throughout Providenciales. ✉ *Prestige Place, 229 Governor's Rd., Grace Bay* ✥ *Across from Casablanca* ☎ *649/946–4379* 🌐 *www.prestigiousproperties.com.*

T.C. Safari. Based in Florida, T.C. Safari offers reservation services for numerous properties around Provo. ☎ *649/941–5043 local number with answering service, 904/491–1415 U.S. number* 🌐 *www.tcsafari.com.*

THE BIGHT

$$$ RESORT

🏨 **Beach House Turks and Caicos.** On the quieter, western end of Grace Bay, this intimate all-suites resort has a unique Caribbean air. **Pros:** less populated end of the beach, plus one of the widest stretches; great snorkeling very close by off the beach; more playful vibe. **Cons:** small bathrooms. [$] *Rooms from: $450* ✉ *218 Lower Bight Rd., The Bight* ✥ *Between West Bay Club and Coral Gardens resorts* ☎ *649/946–5800, 855/946–5800* 🌐 *www.beachhousetci.com* 🛏 *21 suites* 🍴 *Breakfast.*

$$$$ RESORT Fodor's Choice ★

🏨 **Gansevoort Turks + Caicos.** South Beach Miami meets island time at this gorgeous resort with modern, chic furnishings and minimalistic vibe. **Pros:** service is excellent; staff is eager to please; gorgeous heated pool and amazing rooms with unprecedented views; great ambience. **Cons:** need transportation for shops and exploring. [$] *Rooms from: $500* ✉ *Lower Bight Rd., The Bight, The Bight* ✥ *In between the Bight Park and the Beach House* ☎ *649/941–7555, 649/946–5134* 🌐 *www.gansevoorttc.com* 🛏 *55 rooms, 34 suites, 4 penthouses* 🍴 *Breakfast.*

GRACE BAY

$$$$ RESORT FAMILY

🏨 **The Alexandra Resort.** This beachfront resort, on a fine stretch of Grace Bay Beach, offers spacious accommodations and amenities that appeal to families, couples, and corporate travelers alike. **Pros:** very prestigious address at a reasonable rate. **Cons:** some rooms do not have king beds. [$] *Rooms from: $575* ✉ *Princess Dr., Grace Bay* ✥ *Right next door to the Palms Resort* ☎ *649/946–5807, 888/695–7591* 🌐 *www.alexandraresort.com* 🛏 *90 suite property* 🍴 *No meals.*

$$$$ RESORT FAMILY Fodor's Choice ★

🏨 **Beaches Turks & Caicos Resort Villages & Spa.** Designed for families who are eager to spend some time together and reconnect and recharge, Beaches is is the largest resort in the Turks and Caicos Islands with much to see and do. **Pros:** great place for families; gorgeous pools; many quality on-site restaurants from which to choose. **Cons:** with an all-inclusive plan you miss out on the island's other great restaurants; excursions such as catamaran trip can get crowded; per person rate schedule. [$] *Rooms from: $770* ✉ *Lower Bight Rd., Grace Bay* ☎ *649/946–8000, 800/232–2437* 🌐 *www.beaches.com* 🛏 *758 rooms and suites* 🍴 *All-inclusive.*

$$$$ RESORT FAMILY

🏨 **Grace Bay Club.** This stylish resort retains a loyal following because of its helpful, attentive staff and unpretentious elegance. **Pros:** gorgeous pool and restaurant lounge areas with outdoor couches, daybeds, and

CLOSE UP

What Is a Potcake?

Feral dogs in the Bahamas and Turks and Caicos Islands are called potcakes. Traditionally, they would be fed from the leftover scraps of food that formed at the bottom of the pot in yesteryears; this is how they got their name. Much is being done these days to control the stray dog population. The TCSPCA and Potcake Place are two agencies working to adopt out the puppies. You can "travel with a cause" by adopting one of these gorgeous pups; they come with all their shots and all the papers required to bring them back home to the United States or Canada. Even if you don't adopt, you can help by volunteering as a carrier—bringing one back to its adoptive family. Customs in the U.S. is actually easier when you are bringing back a potcake! You can also choose to borrow a pup for a couple of hours to take it for a walk, an activity that has become increasingly popular with those who are sad to have had to leave their canines back at home. For more information on how you can help, check out the website for Potcake Place (🌐 *www.potcakeplace.com*).

fire pits; adult-only sections. **Cons:** have to stay in Estates section to use its beautiful pool; expensive. [$] *Rooms from: $700* ✉ *Bonaventure Crescent, Grace Bay* ✣ *Off Governor's Rd.* ☎ *649/946–5050, 800/946–5757* 🌐 *www.gracebayclub.com* 🛏 *82 suites* 🍴 *Breakfast.*

$ RENTAL — 🏨 **The Island Club.** If you're on a budget, you will find that this small condo complex gives you excellent value. **Pros:** you can't get a better deal on Provo; centrally located so you can walk everywhere; laundry facilities on-site. **Cons:** only a few condos in the complex are in the short-term rental pool, so availability is limited; a block from the beach; queen beds in the master bedroom. [$] *Rooms from: $250* ✉ *Grace Bay Rd., Grace Bay* ✣ *Next to Salt Mills* ☎ *649/946–5866* 🌐 *www.islandclubgracebay.com* 🛏 *24 2-bedroom apartments* 🍴 *No meals.*

$ RESORT FAMILY — 🏨 **Ocean Club.** Enormous, locally painted pictures of hibiscus make a striking first impression as you enter the reception area at one of the island's most well-established condominium resorts. **Pros:** family-friendly resort with shuttles between the two shared properties; screened balconies and porches allow a respite from incessant air-conditioning. **Cons:** if you don't have a rental car, you have to take the shuttle to get closer to the "hub". [$] *Rooms from: $229* ✉ *Governor's Rd., Grace Bay* ✣ *Opposite Provo Golf Club* ☎ *649/946–5880, 800/457–8787* 🌐 *www.oceanclubresorts.com* 🛏 *174 suites* 🍴 *No meals.*

$$$$ RESORT FAMILY Fodor's Choice ★ — 🏨 **The Palms.** High on luxury, The Palms has consistently scored in the top 100 hotels in the world. **Pros:** lively; one of the best spas in the Caribbean; wide range of amenities. **Cons:** in the summer, the sunken pool bar area can get a bit hot when the trade winds die; expensive. [$] *Rooms from: $650* ✉ *Princess Dr., Grace Bay* ✣ *Between the Alexandra and the Somerset* ☎ *649/946–8666, 866/630–5890* 🌐 *www.thepalmstc.com* 🛏 *72 suites* 🍴 *Breakfast.*

$$$$ RESORT — 🏨 **Point Grace.** Keeping history in mind, this resort was built with a turn-of-the-20th-century British colonial feel; dark mahogany, granite, marble, and teak create a sense of warmth and comfort within each

of the 33 luxurious one- to four-bedroom suites and penthouses. **Pros:** relaxing environment; beautiful pool. **Cons:** can be extremely quiet (signs around the pool remind you). $ *Rooms from: $515* ✉ *Grace Bay Rd., Grace Bay* ✛ *Next door to the Sands* ☎ *649/946–5096 general number, 888/209–5582 toll-free reservations, 649/941–7743 reservations* ⊕ *www.pointgrace.com* ⊗ *Closed Sept.* ⥱ *23 oceanfront suites, 10 cottage suites* ⦂○⦂ *Breakfast* ☞ *Full meal plan may be arranged.*

$ ⛺ **Royal West Indies Resort.** With a contemporary take on colonial archi-

RESORT tecture and the outdoor feel of a botanical garden, this unpretentious resort on Grace Bay Beach has plenty of garden-view and beachfront studios and suites for moderate self-catering budgets. **Pros:** great bang for your buck; on one of the widest stretches of Grace Bay Beach. **Cons:** Club Med next door can be noisy; staying in a unit at the back of the resort is no different from staying at some of the off-the-beach properties because of the resort configuration. $ *Rooms from: $245* ✉ *Bonaventure Crescent off Governor's Rd., Grace Bay* ✛ *Between Club Med and Grandview* ☎ *649/946–5004, 800/332–4203* ⊕ *www. royalwestindies.com* ⥱ *115 suites* ⦂○⦂ *No meals.*

$ ⛺ **Sands at Grace Bay.** Spacious gardens and winding pools set the tone

RESORT for one of Provo's most popular family-friendly resorts. **Pros:** one of

FAMILY the best places for families; central to shops and numerous restaurants; screened balconies and porches give an escape from incessant air-conditioning. **Cons:** avoid courtyard rooms, which are not worth the price; restaurant is busy. $ *Rooms from: $250* ✉ *Grace Bay Rd., Grace Bay* ☎ *649/941–5199, 877/777–2637* ⊕ *www.thesandstc.com* ⥱ *114 suites* ⦂○⦂ *No meals.*

$$$$ ⛺ **Seven Stars.** Fronting gorgeous Grace Bay Beach, the tallest prop-

RESORT erty on the island also sets a high mark for luxury within its three

FAMILY buildings, a magnificent heated pool, and large in-room bathrooms.

Fodor'sChoice **Pros:** beachside location; lovely inside and out; walking distance to

★ everything in Grace Bay; terrific bar by the beach. **Cons:** some find the giant scale of the resort too big for the rest of the island; higher density than most other resorts. $ *Rooms from: $490* ✉ *Grace Bay Rd., Grace Bay* ☎ *649/941–7777, 866/570–7777* ⊕ *www.sevenstarsgracebay.com* ⥱ *123 suites* ⦂○⦂ *Breakfast.*

$ ⛺ **Sibonné Beach Hotel.** Dwarfed by most of the nearby resorts, the small-

HOTEL est hotel on Grace Bay Beach has snug (by Provo's spacious standards) but pleasant rooms with Bermudan-style balconies and a tiny circular pool that's hardly used because the property is right on the beach. **Pros:** closest property to the beach; the island's best bargain. **Cons:** pool is small and dated; some rooms have a double bed. $ *Rooms from: $125* ✉ *Princess Dr., Grace Bay* ✛ *Right next door to the Somerset resort* ☎ *649/946–5547, 800/528–1905* ⊕ *www.sibonne.com* ⊗ *Closed Sept.* ⥱ *29 rooms, 1 apartment* ⦂○⦂ *No meals.*

$$$$ ⛺ **The Somerset.** This luxury resort has the wow factor, starting with

RESORT the architecture and ending in your luxuriously appointed suite. **Pros:** the most beautiful architecture on Provo; located in middle, so you can walk to snorkel and to shops. **Cons:** the cheapest rooms are not worth the dollar value—they can get noisy. $ *Rooms from: $650* ✉ *Princess*

West Bay Club

Dr., Grace Bay ✛ Between the Palms and Sibonné ☎ *649/339–5900, 888/386–8770* ⊕ *www.thesomerset.com* ⤴ *53 suites* ❍ *Breakfast.*

$$$$
RENTAL
🏨 **The Tuscany.** This self-catering, quiet, upscale resort is the place for mature, independent travelers to unwind without the need for resort amenities. **Pros:** luxurious; all condos have ocean views; beautiful pool. **Cons:** no restaurant or reception, and it's at the far end of the hub; very expensive for a self-catering resort; can feel like no one else is on the property. $ *Rooms from: $550* ✉ *Governor's Rd., Grace Bay ✛ Right across from the golf course* ☎ *649/941–4667, 866/359–6466* ⊕ *www. thetuscanyresort.com* ⤴ *30 condos* ❍ *No meals.*

$$$$
RENTAL
🏨 **Villa Renaissance.** Short-term rentals are available at Villa Renaissance, and guests love the quiet, resident feel of this luxury property modeled after a Tuscan villa. **Pros:** luxury for less; one of the prettiest courtyards in Provo. **Cons:** not a full-service resort. $ *Rooms from: $580* ✉ *Ventura Dr., Grace Bay ✛ In between Regent Grand and the Mansions* ☎ *649/941–4358* ⊕ *www.villarenaissanceturksandcaicos. com* ⤴ *30 units as short-term rental* ❍ *No meals.*

$$$$
RESORT
🏨 **West Bay Club.** A prime location on a pristine stretch of Grace Bay Beach just steps away from the best off-the-beach snorkeling makes this luxury resort a top pick. **Pros:** all rooms have a beach view; amazing luxury for the price. **Cons:** you'll need transportation to go shopping and to get to the main hub. $ *Rooms from: $500* ✉ *242 Lower Bight Rd., The Bight, The Bight ✛ Between the Gansevoort and the Beach House* ☎ *649/946–8550, 855/749–5750* ⊕ *www.thewestbayclub.com* ⤴ *46 suites* ❍ *Breakfast.*

$$$ **Windsong Resort.** On a gorgeous beach lined with several appealing
RESORT resorts, Windsong simply makes you feel at home. **Pros:** pool is unique;
Fodor's Choice huge, gorgeous bathrooms; amazing penthouse rooftop decks. **Cons:**
★ studios have only a refrigerator and microwave; no restaurant on-site.
$ *Rooms from: $390 ⊠ Stubbs Rd., The Bight ⊹ Between Coral Gardens and Beaches Resort ☎ 649/941–7700, 800/946–3766 U.S. toll-free,, 649/333–7700 additional local number ⊕ www.windsongresort.com ⇒ 16 studios, 30 suites ⧐ Breakfast.*

TURTLE COVE

$ **Harbour Club Villas.** Although not on the beach, this small complex of
RENTAL villas is by the marina, making it a good base for scuba diving, bone-
FAMILY fishing, or that quieter-style vacation. **Pros:** centrally located so only a
five-minute drive from Grace Bay; great value; great base for divers;
personable and friendly hosts; immaculately clean. **Cons:** need a car
to get around the island; have to drive to a beach. $ *Rooms from:
$255 ⊠ 36 Turtle Tail Dr., Turtle Cove ⊹ Next to South Side Marina
☎ 649/941–5748, 888/240–0447 ⊕ www.harbourclubvillas.com ⇒ 6
villas ⧐ No meals.*

$ **Turtle Cove Hotel and Residence.** One of the first to be built on the
HOTEL island, this two-story lodging is affordable and comfortable. **Pros:** very
reasonable prices for Provo; nice marina views. **Cons:** older; not on
the beach; requires a car to get groceries or for other shopping excur-
sions; can be a bit noisy with Tiki Hut next door. $ *Rooms from: $129
⊠ Turtle Cove Marina, Lower Bight Rd., Turtle Cove ☎ 649/946–4203
local direct dial, 888/495–6077 U.S. toll-free ⊕ www.turtlecoveinn.com
⇒ 28 rooms, 2 suites ⧐ No meals.*

ELSEWHERE ON PROVIDENCIALES

$$$$ **Amanyara.** Amanyara is nestled in nature with the ultimate zenlike
RESORT atmosphere, and it's *the* place for peace and quiet in a remote setting on
Fodor's Choice a stunning waterfront. **Pros:** wonderful architecture; fabulous restau-
★ rant; the best sunset location on Provo; unprecedented service; the best
full-service secluded beach on Provo; privacy. **Cons:** isolated; far from
restaurants, outside excursion companies, and other beaches. $ *Rooms
from: $1650 ⊠ Northwest Point ⊹ Off Millenium Hwy. ☎ 649/941–
8133 ⊕ www.aman.com ⇒ 36 one-bedroom pavilions, 2 two-bedroom
pool pavilion suites, 20 villas ⧐ No meals ⌖ Special packages are
available with some meal inclusions.*

NIGHTLIFE

Although Provo is not known for its nightlife, there are some live bands
and bars worth checking out. Popular singers such as Brentford Hand-
field, Justice, Corey Forbes, and Quinton Dean perform at numerous
restaurants and barbecue bonfires. Danny Buoy's, where you can always
watch the latest game on big video screens, gets going late at night.
Be sure to see if any ripsaw bands—aka rake-and-scrape—are play-
ing while you're on island; this is one of the quintessential local music
genres: it's popular at local restaurants in Blue Hills. You can also find
karaoke around the island if you enjoy holding the mike.

Best Spas in Provo and Beyond

CLOSE UP

A Turks Island Salt Glow, in which the island's sea salt is mixed with gentle oils to exfoliate, smooth, and moisturize the skin, is just one of the treatments you can enjoy in the island's spas. Being pampered spa-style has become as much a part of a Turks and Caicos vacation as sunning on the beach. Marine-based ingredients fit well with the Grace Bay backdrop at the Thalasso Spa at **Point Grace,** where massages take place in two simple, bleached-white cottages standing on the dune line, which means you have a spectacular view of the sea-blue hues—if you manage to keep your eyes open. The Regent Spa at **The Palms** offers individual treatments, with a water feature by day, a fire feature at night. The signature body scrub uses hand-crushed local conch shells to smooth the skin. The widest choice of Asian-inspired

treatments (and the most unforgettable scenery) can be found at the 6,000-square-foot Como Shambhala Spa at the **Parrot Cay Resort,** which has outdoor whirlpools and a central beech-wood lounge overlooking the shallow turquoise waters and mangroves. Another more than luxurious experience is the spa at Amanyara, situated in total seclusion along the northwest shoreline.

Provo also has a noteworthy day spa that's not in one of the Grace Bay resorts. **Spa Tropique** blends Swedish, therapeutic, and reflexology massage techniques using oils made from natural plants and products produced locally and within the Caribbean region. The Mango Passion Scrub is one of the most popular treatments. ✉ *Ports of Call, Grace Bay Rd., Grace Bay, Providenciales* ☎ *649/331–2400* ⊕ *www.spatropique.com.*

18

Late-night action can be found at Casablanca Casino, where many end the night. And every Sunday, Seven Stars features a beach bonfire and barbecue with live music to be enjoyed while you dine. Reservations are required for this popular event.

Keep abreast of events and specials by checking **TCI eNews** (⊕ *www. tcienews.com*).

BARS AND CLUBS

Danny Buoy's. A popular Irish pub, Danny Buoy's has lots of slot machines, as well as big-screen TVs. It's a great place to watch sports broadcasts from all over. Different nights feature different nightlife; Tuesday and Thursday are karaoke, while Friday and Saturday nights have live music followed by a DJ until 2 am. It's open late every night. Currently, it's a hot spot for a nightcap, with the kitchen closing at midnight. They don't want to send you home hungry, so there's pizza until 2 am. ✉ *Grace Bay Rd., Grace Bay* ✛ *Across from Regent Village* ☎ *649/946–5921* ⊕ *www.dannybuoys.com.*

Blue Haven Resort, The Pool Bar. Bar servers at the Pool Bar are more than happy to keep the drinks flowing by delivering them to your quiet spot on the water's edge, with Mangrove Cay and the mega yachts of the marina as a dramatic backdrop. Three gas fireplace seating areas are absolutely wonderful spots from which to enjoy a breezy evening.

✉ *Blue Haven Resort, Leeward Marina, Leeward* ✛ *Far eastern tip of the island* ☏ *649/946–9900 hotel, front desk* ⊕ *www.bluehaventci.com.*

SHOPS AND SPAS

Handwoven straw baskets and hats, polished conch-shell crafts, paintings, wood carvings, model sailboats, handmade dolls, and metalwork are crafts native to the islands and nearby Haiti. The natural surroundings have inspired local and international artists to paint, sculpt, print, craft, and photograph; most of their creations are on sale in Providenciales.

SHOPPING AREAS

There are several main shopping areas in Provo: Grace Bay has the newer **Saltmills** complex and **La Petite Place** retail plaza, the new **Regent Village**, and the original **Ports of Call** shopping village.

ART AND CRAFTS GALLERIES

Fodor'sChoice ★ **Anna's and Anna's Too.** Anna's sells original artworks, silk-screen paintings, sculptures, and handmade sea-glass jewelry, most made by local artists and artisans. It's a treasure trove of fabulous finds! You won't leave without picking up a little something to take home with you. Her newest edition is Anna's Too, just a couple of doors down. This wonderful shop is filled with fantastic women's wear—all cotton, comfortable, and colorful. Tucked alongside are books and pillows as well as other home decor items. ✉ *Saltmills Plaza, Grace Bay Rd., Grace Bay* ☏ *649/941–8841 Anna's Too, 649/941–8842 Anna's* ⊕ *www.anna.tc* ☾ *Closed Sun.*

ArtProvo. This gallery features a wide selection of designer wall art, but native crafts, jewelry, handblown glass, candles, and other gift items are also available including locally made bath products. Mary, the gallery's owner, has lived in TCI for 35 years and has developed relationships with many local artists and artisans. She features creations by the island's own Jill Segal, Alexis, as well as Dwight Outten. Sandra Knuyt's cigar-smoking female characters are a favorite that will fit into any home. ✉ *Regent Village, Regent St., Grace Bay* ✛ *Turn off Grace Bay Rd. at Caicos Adventures* ☏ *649/941–4545* ⊕ *www.artprovo.tc* ☾ *Closed Sun.*

Making Waves Art Studio. Alex, the owner and resident artist, paints turquoise scenes, often on wood that doesn't require framing. She is happy to discuss the possibility of transforming your thoughts and emotions about one special spot onto canvas as the perfect thing to take home. You'll find artists working on-site. Come and enjoy meeting these beasts in their natural habitats. They don't mind being fed! And bring wine! ✉ *F104, Regent St., Grace Bay* ✛ *Turn onto Regent St. off Grace Bay Rd. opposite Danny Buoy's* ☏ *649/242–9588* ⊕ *www.makingwavesart. com* ☾ *Closed Sun.*

FOOD

After 5 Island Concierge. Sometimes you just need help before or during your trip. After 5 Island Concierge can do anything to ease your holiday worries from grocery delivery and meal reservations to organizing private wine tastings and sorting out bulk wine delivery for that extra-special party or event. They will also help you arrange for a personal chef or catering service so that meals are not a concern during your stay. Virtually any service you can think of can be arranged through this company. Talk to Kristi. ☎ 649/232–3483 ⊕ www.islandconciergetc.com.

Fodor's Choice ★ **Graceway IGA.** With a large fresh-produce section, bakery, gourmet deli, and extensive meat counter, Provo's largest supermarket will have what you're looking for. The most consistently well-stocked store on the island carries known brands from the United Kingdom and North America, as well as a good selection of other international foods, and prepared items such as a great rotisserie chicken and pizza. The IGA also has an excellent selection of wine, beers, and spirits; no alcohol sales on Sundays. Expect prices to be higher than at home. This supermarket is one of the reasons why visitors come back to TCI again and again. They know they will find everything they choose back home—and then some. ⊠ Leeward Hwy., The Bight ✛ Halfway down the island on the main highway ☎ 649/941–5000 ⊕ www.gracewayiga.com.

$mart. The IGA has now opened its third location downtown: $mart. It is another North American–style supermarket but offers more to locals at lower prices. You can cut your travel budget considerably by purchasing Essentials, their reduced items, and lower-priced soft drinks and dairy products, as well as more reasonably priced meats, fruits, and vegetables. This branch also carries alcoholic beverages. ⊠ Town Centre Mall, Downtown ☎ 649/946–5525 ⊕ www.gracewaysupermarket.com.

LIQUOR

Fodor's Choice ★ **Wine Cellar.** Visit this store for its large selection of duty-free spirits, wine, and beer. The Wine Cellar also carries a range of cigars. ⊠ 1025 Leeward Hwy., The Bight ✛ East of Suzie Turn ☎ 649/946–4536 ⊕ www.winecellar.tc.

SPAS

Except for Parrot Cay, Provo is the best destination in the Turks and Caicos if you are looking for a spa vacation. The spas here offer treatments with all the bells and whistles, and most get very good word of mouth. All of Provo's high-end resorts have spas, but if you're staying at a villa, Spa Tropique or Teona Spa will bring their services to you.

Anani Spa at Grace Bay Club. Anani Spa at Grace Bay Club is on the villas side of the complex. There are eight treatment rooms in total, but treatments can also be performed on your terrace if you're staying at Grace Bay Club, or in the spa tent on the oceanfront. Spa packages are available so that you can enjoy a combination of treatments designed to work together. One of their signature treatments is the Exotic Lime and Ginger Salt Glow; you will emerge refreshed and polished! ⊠ Villas at Grace Bay Club, Bonaventure Crescent, Grace Bay ☎ 649/946–5050 ⊕ www.gracebayresorts.com.

Beaches Red Lane Spa. One unique feature about this spa is that it has one hot plunge pool and one cold plunge pool. During special hours, it offers kids' treatments, too. Although Beaches is an all-inclusive resort, spa treatments are an additional charge to guests. The spa services are available only to resort guests. ⊠ Beaches Turks & Caicos Resort

18

Villages & Spa, Lower Bight Rd., Grace Bay ☎ *649/946–8000 resort general number, 4151 extension for spa from within the resort* ⊕ *www. beaches.com* ☞ *Open only to resort guests.*

Fodor'sChoice **Como Shambhala at Parrot Cay.** Asian holistic treatments, yoga with the
★ world's leading teachers in a stunning pavilion, and a signature health-conscious cuisine are all part of the program here. In fact, visiting masters from "off island" are featured throughout the year. The infinity pool, Pilates studio, steam room, sauna, and outdoor Jacuzzi make you feel complete. If you're staying on Provo, you can call for reservations, but you have to pay for a day pass to Parrot Cay. Some consider this to be one of the finest spas in the world. ✉ *Parrot Cay Resort* ☎ *649/946–7788* ⊕ *www.comoshambhala.com.*

Fodor'sChoice **The Palms Resort and Spa.** Widely considered one of the best spas in the
★ Caribbean, the Palms Spa is an oasis of relaxation. In the main facility you will find a pedicure/manicure space, gym, boutique, and yoga and Pilates pavilion, as well as men's and women's steam rooms and saunas. Outdoors, white tented cabanas grace the edge of a beautiful reflection pool, its waters catching images of towering palms and flowering bougainvillea. However, you don't even have to leave your room; massages may be arranged so that you can enjoy the wonderful sea views right from your very own balcony. Guests are encouraged to indulge in one of the locally inspired signature treatments: a mother-of-pearl body exfoliation incorporating the queen conch shell, or the 90-minute Zareeba herbal cleansing and detox. Rest a while and sip herbal tea or replenish with citrus-infused water before or after your treatment. ✉ *The Palms, Princess Dr., Grace Bay* ☎ *649/946–8666 resort general number, 649/946–8667 direct dial, spa line* ⊕ *www.thepalmstc.com.*

Spa Sanay. Located at the Alexandra Resort, Spa Sanay offers facials, massages, body treatments, and nail services. There is also a line of men's-only services, as well as select services where the therapist comes to you. ✉ *Alexandra Resort, Princess Dr., Grace Bay* ✛ *In the resort's Marlin Bldg., ground floor* ☎ *649/432–1092 direct dial* ⊕ *www. spasanay.com.*

Spa Tropique. You pick the place, and this spa comes to you—an ideal option for those in more isolated villas who can't bear to leave their island paradise. The spa can also come to your hotel room. Have your treatment on your balcony or on the beach or by the pool, which will make it seem extra special. The spa also has locations at Ports of Call, both Ocean Clubs, and the Sands Resort. ✉ *Ports of Call, Grace Bay Rd., Grace Bay* ✛ *Upstairs in Ports of Call* ☎ *649/331–2400* ⊕ *www. spatropique.com.*

Fodor'sChoice **Teona Spa.** Although the spa for the Regent Grand and Renaissance,
★ Teona has opened their second location at the Somerset. Both spaces exude a peace-filled ambience, with every detail carefully thought out. Hush as you enter, and relax while you're there. It is the spa choice for many island residents. Take a peek at the spa specials; there is always a combination package put together for special times of the year. Or try one of the spa parties. What better way to spend time with a young one than a Mommy and Me day? And if you wish to have your treatment

in your own space, Teona will come to you. The team also offers wedding packages to include makeup and hair. ⊠ *The Regent Grand Resort, Ventura Dr., Grace Bay ✛ Turn off Grace Bay Rd. at the Goldsmiths into Regent Village* ☎ *649/941–5051 main spa, 649/339–5900 Somerset location* ⊕ *www.teonaspa.com.*

Fodor'sChoice ★ **Thalasso Spa at Point Grace.** Thalasso Spa at Point Grace offers their services from within three whitewashed open-air cabanas set upon the dunes overlooking Grace Bay. They share the European philosophy of the famous Thalgo Spas of France and combine it with the perfect Caribbean ambience for your enjoyment. Treatments combine elements of the ocean, including sea mud, seaweed, and sea salt, with the properties of seawater to pamper you from head to toe. The setting alone, with the salt air and sea breezes, is worth the visit. This is another favorite with residents. ⊠ *Point Grace Resort, Grace Bay Rd., Grace Bay* ☎ *649/946–5096* ⊕ *www.pointgrace.com.*

SPORTS AND THE OUTDOORS

BICYCLING

Most hotels have bicycles available for guests, or you can rent one from an independent company. Stick to the sidewalks on Grace Bay Road; drivers don't pay much attention to bikes. The island thanks you, as you'll create less dust within its arid environment.

Caicos Cyclery. Comfortable beach cruisers are available from Caicos Cyclery from $20 a day, as well as the wider-tired Choppers, mountain bikes, and hybrids. Delivery to a private villa is possible. You can also look forward to a 30% discount with a week's rental. ⊠ *Saltmills Plaza, Grace Bay Rd., Grace Bay ✛ Adjoining Big Al's Island Grill* ☎ *649/941–7544 direct dial* ⊕ *www.caicoscyclery.com.*

BOATING AND SAILING

Provo's calm, reef-protected seas combine with constant easterly trade winds for excellent sailing conditions. Several multihulled vessels offer charters with snorkeling stops, food and beverage service, and sunset vistas. Prices range from $89 per person for group trips (subject to passenger minimums) to upwards of $600 or more for private charters.

Fodor'sChoice ★ **Caicos Dream Tours.** Caicos Dream Tours offers several boating options, including one that has you diving for conch before lunch off a gorgeous beach. You may choose from two different excursions shared with others, starting at $89/person, or decide to charter a private boat for as many as 12 people, beginning at $1,100 for a half day. With seven boats in their fleet, Dream Tours is able to accommodate up to 150 guests at the same time, so wedding parties and conference groups have the option of enjoying a day out together. Maximum capacity on one boat is 40 guests. They also offer a bottom-fishing charter for up to six people for those die-hard fishermen traveling together. Note that Caicos Dream Tours is the only island excursion operator that offers a combo of bottom-fishing and snorkeling on the same charter; this one makes the whole family happy! ⊠ *Alexandra Resort, Princess Dr., Grace Bay* ☎ *649/231–7274* ⊕ *www.caicosdreamtours.com.*

18

FAMILY

Fodor's Choice

★

Island Vibes. Turks and Caicos–born and raised, the boys who own and operate Island Vibes make their excursions stand out. If conditions are right, they'll give you the opportunity to snorkel out over the wall, where the reef drops an amazing 3,000 feet. With a 12-foot curve slide off the roof, a diving board, and spacious bathroom on board with freshwater showers, these fun excursions add just a little more excitement to your day. Join a group for the half-day snorkel at $89/person, or throw yourself into their full-day barbecue adventure that combines an amazing lunch set up under the shade of tall island pines with exploring small cays, snorkeling, conch diving, and just plain beach strolling. There is also the option of a private sunset cruise seven days a week. ✉ *Turtle Cove Marina, Lower Bight Rd., Turtle Cove* ☎ *649/231–8423* ⊕ *www.islandvibestours.com* ✉ *Starting at $89/person.*

FAMILY

Sail Provo. Very popular for private charters, Sail Provo also offers scheduled half-day, full-day, sunset, and dedicated snorkeling trips to those who don't mind sharing with other holidaymakers on 52- and 38-foot sailing catamarans. They also head out on starlit evening cruises to share the marine world's glowworm extravaganza: underwater creatures light up the sea's surface not long after sunset a few days after the full moon each month. Check out their website to peruse the wide variety of excursions they offer with a beach pickup right in front of your Grace Bay resort. ✉ *Blue Haven Marina, Marina Rd., Leeward* ✛ *Far eastern tip of the island* ☎ *649/946–4783 local office, 649/331–3184 local mobile as an alternative* ⊕ *www.sailprovo.com.*

Silver Deep. Silver Deep excursions include several half-day and full-day trip options. You can choose from all types of fishing, a dedicated snorkeling adventure, exploration of North and Middle Caicos, and the most popular: a Native Beach Barbecue. Their most unique opportunity is their night-fishing private charter, just in case your days are too busy with naps and enjoying the beach. Other private charters may be arranged starting at $1,100; your itinerary may be personalized to include a multitude of activities, keeping all members in your group happy. ✉ *Ocean Club West Plaza, Grace Bay Rd., Grace Bay* ✛ *Right across from Caicos Café Plaza* ☎ *649/946–5612, 649/232–5612 mobile* ⊕ *www.silverdeep.com* ✉ *From $99 / person.*

FAMILY

Fodor's Choice

★

Sun Charters. The *Atabeyra*, operated by Sun Charters, is a 70-foot schooner with a big wide belly. It's the residents' choice for special events, as it is by far the most family-friendly adventure. Kids can run around without too many worries about going overboard, and the boom overhead is strong enough for them to sit and survey the seascape—just as a pirate would have done. Although they are primarily known as a private charter service, they also offer an amazing sunset rum punch party and glowworm excursions as their specialty, with a weekly Sail & Snorkel for individuals to join in on. Their newest trip is Night with the Stars, where the Atabeyra sails out at sunset and then throws anchor in a secluded spot; a night sky app and laser discussion will introduce you to a light-pollution-free night sky. The boat is perfect for larger groups who wish to sail together, accommodating 2 to 50 people. ✉ *Blue Haven Resort, Marina Rd., Leeward* ✛ *Operates from* *the resort's VIP dock in front of Fire and Ice Restaurant* ☎ *649/231–0624* ⊕ *www.suncharters.tc.*

Undersea Explorer. For sightseeing below the waves, try the *Undersea Explorer,* a semi-submarine operated by Caicos Tours out of Turtle Cove Marina. It's an ocean adventure that takes you into the underwater world without getting wet! Your one-hour tour of the reef is led by a knowledgeable captain and viewed through large windows below the surface on either side, all in air-conditioned comfort. It's the perfect trip for young and old alike. Your choice: the Mermaid Adventure, which is a theatrical voyage with a "surprise" spotting of Mermaid Bella along the way and a pirate captain making a guest appearance, or the Turtle Reef Adventure, which sticks strictly to the business of exploring the reef as an informative voyage. ⊠ *Turtle Cove Marina, Lower Bight Rd., Turtle Cove* ☎ *649/432–0006 main line* ⊕ *www.caicostours.com* ☒ *$60* ☉ *Closed Sun.*

Water Play Provo. Right on the beach, Water Play Provo has kiteboards, windsurfers, stand-up paddleboards, and kayaks. You can take a lesson, join a guided tour, or rent the equipment for multiple days or by the week. The owner, Jill, also conducts swim lessons in private villa pools; she specializes in infant self-rescue, and she's also an open-water swim coach and an American Red Cross swim instructor. ⊠ *Ocean Club (East), Governor's Rd., Grace Bay* ⊹ *Found on the Tuscany side of Ocean Club on Grace Bay Beach* ☎ *649/231–3122* ⊕ *www.waterplayprovo.com.*

DIVING AND SNORKELING

Fodor's Choice
★

The island's many shallow reefs offer excellent and exciting snorkeling relatively close to shore. Try **Smith's Reef** over Bridge Road east of Turtle Cove, or the Bight Reef in front of Coral Gardens, to explore the reef as it comes in to touch the shoreline. A third option is the patch coral just off Babalua Beach, located between the north shore's Turtle Cove and Thompson Cove; you will need a car to get there.

Scuba diving in the crystalline waters surrounding the islands ranks among the best in the Caribbean. The reef and wall drop-offs thrive with bright, unbroken coral formations and lavish numbers of fish and marine life. Mimicking the idyllic climate, waters are warm all year, averaging 76°F to 78°F in winter and 82°F to 84°F in summer. With minimal rainfall and soil runoff, visibility is usually very good and frequently superb, ranging from 60 feet to more than 150 feet. An extensive system of marine national parks and boat moorings, combined with an eco-conscious mind-set among dive operators, contributes to an uncommonly pristine underwater environment.

Dive operators in Provo regularly visit sites at **Grace Bay** and **Pine Cay** for spur-and-groove coral formations and bustling reef diving. They make the longer journey to the dramatic walls at **North West Point** and **West Caicos** depending on weather conditions. Instruction from the major diving agencies is available for all levels and certifications, including technical diving. An average one-tank dive costs $45; a two-tank dive, $90; they go upwards from there depending on the number of divers aboard,

18

Diving with stingrays

where the dive sites are, and what services are included. There are also two live-aboard dive boats available for charter working out of Provo.

FAMILY
Fodor's Choice
★

Big Blue Unlimited. This ecotour operator got its start offering dive excursions in 1997, but has since widened its scope considerably. Big Blue has several educational kayak ecotours to choose from, as well as the very popular stand-up paddleboard (SUP) safari tours as an alternative, though they don't cover quite as much territory as the kayak tours. Big Blue also has outposts on Middle, North, and South Caicos, with an extensive network of guides, bikes, kayaks, and boats, so they are able to offer a number of interactive ecotourism excursions for those wishing to learn more about what Turks and Caicos has to offer. Private charters up to a maximum of 12 passengers may incorporate a snorkeling adventure to the reef off the outer islands or on the Caicos Banks near French Cay and West Caicos. They are also the only operator offering excursions to the pristine coral reefs surrounding South Caicos. As their latest foray, they are now also recognized for their outstanding kiteboarding and kitesurfing instruction, downwinders, and kite safaris. The Cabrinha Kite and Board gear is used for both instruction and rentals. ⊠ *Leeward Marina, Marina Rd., Leeward* ☎ *649/946–5034* ⊕ *www.bigblueunlimited.com.*

FAMILY
Caicos Adventures. Run by the well-known and friendly Frenchman Fifi Kunz, Caicos Adventures offers daily excursions out of their private marina on the south side of Provo to sites off West Caicos, French Cay, and Southwest Reef. The company runs two dive boats, with groups up to 20 able to dive together. If you are not yet certified, you may enjoy one of their snorkel adventures as an alternative. They also have the

Lady K, a luxury motorboat, available for private charters operating out of Blue Haven Marina on the eastern tip of the island. It's best to book over the phone. ✉ *Regent Village, Grace Bay Rd., Grace Bay* ⟊ *Their private marina is off Venetian Rd. Watch for their sign on the right just after you pass between Flamingo Lake and Turtle Lake.* ☎ 649/941–3346 ⊕ *www.caicosadventures.com.*

Dive Provo. Dive Provo is a PADI five-star operation that runs daily one- and two-tank dives to popular Grace Bay sites, as well as to West Caicos. In addition, they offer the exciting night dive, as well as their unique three-tank Scuba Safari, where they head out to dive sites farther afield, such as Molasses Reef, Sandbore Channel, and Southwest Reef. This excursion includes one tank of nitrox to make it easier on the diver to spend as much time as possible under the water. Note that this is not offered to junior divers. Dive Provo has a full array of dive courses: Discover Scuba, Open Water Certification, Advanced Open Water, and Nitrox Certification. They also offer snorkeling excursions. Check out their packages including accommodation; it's a great way to save money on your next dive holiday. ✉ *Ports of Call, Grace Bay Rd., Grace Bay* ☎ 649/946–5040, 800/234–7768 ⊕ *www.diveprovo.com.*

Fodor's Choice
★

Flamingo Divers. Flamingo Divers is a PADI 5 Star Gold Palm Facility offering high-end service in small groups of up to a maximum of eight divers. Operating out of their south-side location, Mickey and Jayne will take you through amazing sites off Northwest Point, West Caicos, as well as French Cay when the seas permit. With 15 years of experience diving the waters around Provo, they know their territory! ✉ *Venetian Rd.* ⟊ *Drive south on Venetian Rd. Look for the Flamingo Divers sign on the right after passing between Flamingo Lake and Turtle Lake as you approach the ocean's edge.* ☎ 649/946–4193 ⊕ *www. flamingodivers.com.*

Provo Turtle Divers. Provo Turtle Divers, with offices at Ocean Club East and Turtle Cove Landing, has been operating dive trips on Provo since the 1970s. The staff is friendly, knowledgeable, and unpretentious. Their boats operate solely out of Southside Marina off Venetian Road. This location makes their boat trips quicker to the less traveled sites off French Cay, West Caicos, Northwest Point, and Sandbore Channel. Their years of experience make diving with them like spending the day with friends. ✉ *Turtle Cove Landing, Lower Bight Rd., Turtle Cove* ☎ 649/946–4232, 800/833–1341 ⊕ *www.provoturtledivers.com* ⊙ *The shop is closed on Sun. even though the boats still go out.*

FISHING

The islands' fertile waters are great for angling—anything from bottom and reef-fishing (most likely to produce plenty of bites and a large catch) to bonefishing (among the finest in the Caribbean) and deep sea fishing. Every July the Caicos Classic IGFA Billfish Release Tournament attracts anglers from across the islands, as well as internationally, who compete to catch the biggest Atlantic blue marlin, Atlantic sailfish, and white marlin—all indigenous to the waters surrounding TCI. For any fishing activity, you are required to purchase a $15 visitor's fishing license; operators generally furnish all equipment, drinks, and snacks.

18

Diving the Turks and Caicos Islands

Scuba diving was the original water sport that lured visitors to the Turks and Caicos Islands in the 1970s. Aficionados are still drawn by the abundant marine life, including humpback whales in winter, the pristine waters of TCI's warm and calm seas, as well as the intrigue of its wall diving, with continuous vertical faces of hundreds of feet. And the magnificent fringing coral reef that runs the full length of the country's north shore is the third largest in the world!. Diving the Turks and Caicos—especially off Grand Turk, South Caicos, and Salt Cay—remains among the finest in the world.

Off Providenciales, many dive sites are found along the north shore, with boat times of anywhere from 10 to 45 minutes. Dive sites feature spur-and-groove coral formations atop a coral-covered slope. Popular stops such as **Aquarium, Pinnacles,** and

Grouper Hole have large schools of fish, turtles, nurse sharks, and gray reef sharks. From the south side, dive boats go to **French Cay, West Caicos, South West Reef,** and **Northwest Point,** with longer boat access times. Known for typically calm conditions and excellent visibility, the West Caicos Marine National Park is a favorite stop. The area has dramatic walls and marine life, including sharks, eagle rays, and octopus, with large stands of pillar coral and huge barrel sponges.

Off Grand Turk, the 7,000-foot coral wall is actually within swimming distance off the beach. Buoyed sites along the wall have swim-through tunnels, cascading sand chutes, imposing coral pinnacles, dizzying vertical drops, and undercuts where the wall goes beyond the vertical and fades beneath the reef.

While die-hard anglers have a wide range of fishing to choose from, families may look forward to a combination excursion incorporating family-friendly fishing along with a beach barbecue featuring the catch of the day. Prices range from $600 upward, depending on the length of trip and size of boat.

Grand Slam Fishing Charters. For deep-sea fishing trips in search of marlin, sailfish, wahoo, tuna, barracuda, and shark, look up this company. Grand Slam operates three boats: a 45-foot Hatteras, a 42-foot Pursuit, and a 28-foot WorldCat. ⊠ *Turtle Cove Marina, Turtle Cove* ☎ 649/231–4420 ✎ *info@gfishing.com* ⊕ *www.gsfishing.com.*

FAMILY

Fodor'sChoice

★

Silver Deep. Silver Deep has been operating out of Provo for more than 25 years. In the fishing department, they offer the full range: deep-sea, bone-, fly-, night-, and bottom-fishing. Families can choose to participate in a private excursion where fishing, beach time, and snorkeling can all be included to keep every member content. With a large fleet of boats in which they work, there is the perfect fit for all occasions—no matter the charter request or the water conditions on any given day. ⊠ *Ocean Club West Plaza, Governor's Rd., Grace Bay* ✛ *Opposite Caicos Café Plaza* ☎ 649/946–5612, 649/232–5612 ⊕ *www.silverdeep.com.*

GOLF

Fodor's Choice ★ **Provo Golf Club.** Among the Caribbean's top courses, the 18 holes here (par 72) are a combination of lush greens and fairways, rugged limestone outcroppings, and freshwater lakes. Rack rates are $185 for 18 holes, however the avid golfer can save through their twilight specials, a multi-round pass, or a biweekly or monthly pass. The club also offers two hard-court flood-lit tennis courts, which are among the island's best. Nonmembers can play until 5 pm for $20/hour/adult or $15/hour/junior (reservation required), with racket rentals available. Inquire at the pro shop about tennis lessons. ✉ *Governor's Rd., Grace Bay* ☎ *649/946–5991, 877/218–9124* 🌐 *www.provogolfclub.com* 🎟 *$185 for 18 holes, $95 for 9 holes with shared cart* ⛳ *18 holes, 6705 yards, par 72.*

HORSEBACK RIDING

FAMILY **Provo Ponies.** Provo Ponies offers morning and afternoon rides along quiet dirt roads, through short brush trails, and then out onto the beauty of Long Bay Beach, where you and your horse may take a dip in the shallow waters of the Caicos Banks before heading back to the stable. Horses are matched according to your riding ability, with no rider under seven and no double riding allowed. Reservations are required, and there is a 240-pound weight limit. Pickup at your Grace Bay hotel or villa can be arranged for an additional $10 per person, which is great for those who've decided not to hire a rental car. It's closed on Sundays to give the horses their well-deserved rest. ✉ *Dolphin Rd., Long Bay* ✣ *Take Leeward Hwy. east to Long Bay Hills Rd. Turn left onto Lignumvitae and left again onto Dolphin La.* ☎ *649/946–5252, 649/241–6350* 🌐 *www.provoponies.com* 🎟 *A 60-min ride is $96; a 90-min ride is $118, with an additional fee for a private ride* ⏲ *Closed Sun.*

18

PARROT CAY

Once said to be a hideout for Calico Jack Rackham and his fellow pirates Mary Read and Anne Bonny, the 1,000-acre cay, between Fort George Cay and North Caicos, is now the site of a luxury resort.

The only way to reach Parrot Cay is by private boat or the resort's private ferry from its dock in Leeward.

WHERE TO STAY

$$$$ RESORT Fodor's Choice ★ 🏨 **Parrot Cay Resort.** This private paradise, on its own island, pairs tranquility with service ranked at the top in Turks and Caicos. **Pros:** impeccable service; gorgeous, secluded beach; spa is considered one of the best in the world. **Cons:** only two restaurants to choose from island-wide; excursions are expensive. [$] *Rooms from: $550* ✣ *Northeastern tip of Parrot Cay* ☎ *649/946–7788, 855/727–7682* 🌐 *www.comohotels.com/parrotcay* 🛏 *113 rooms* 🍴 *Breakfast.*

Parrot Cay Resort

PINE CAY

15 to 20 minutes by boat from Provo.

Pine Cay's 2½-mile-long (4-km-long) beach is among the most beautiful in the archipelago. The 800-acre private island, which is in the string of small cays between Provo and North Caicos, is home to a secluded resort and almost 40 private residences. The beach alone is reason to stay here: the sand seems a little whiter, the water a little brighter than beaches on the other cays. Nonguests of the Meridian Club can make reservations for lunch. Expect to pay $85 plus taxes for the day, plus a fee for the boat transfer; there are themed buffets on Sunday.

WHERE TO STAY

$$$$
RESORT
Fodor's Choice
★

The Meridian Club, Turks & Caicos. On one of the most beautiful beaches in Turks and Caicos, the Meridian Club is the place to de-stress, with no phones or TVs and no worries. **Pros:** one of the finest beaches in the Caribbean; rates include some of the best food served in TCI, as well as snorkeling trips. **Cons:** no TVs or phones, so you are truly unplugged here; expensive to get back to Provo for shopping or other Provo-based excursions or activities; the simplicity comes at a cost. $ *Rooms from: $895* ⊠ *North Shore* ☎ *649/946–7758, 866/746–3229, 888/286–7993* ⊕ *www.meridianclub.com* ⊗ *Closed Aug.– Oct.* ⇆ *12 beachfront rooms, 1 cottage* ⍩ *All meals.*

NORTH CAICOS

This 41-square-mile (106-square-km) island is the lushest in the Turks and Caicos chain. With an estimated population of only 1,500, the expansive island allows you to get away from it all. Bird lovers can observe the large resident flock of flamingos here, anglers will take delight in the ease of access to shallow creeks and banks plentiful in bonefish, while history buffs can visit the ruins of a Loyalist plantation. Although there's little traffic, almost all the roads are paved, so bicycling is an excellent way to sightsee. Even though it's a quiet place, you can find some small eateries around the settlements and in Whitby, giving you a chance to try local and seafood specialties, sometimes served with homegrown okra or corn. The beaches are in a natural state here, so are often scattered with seaweed and pine needles, as no major resorts rake them daily. Nevertheless, these secluded, less manicured strands of soft sand are breathtaking and offer beachcombing—while those on Provo do not.

North Caicos may be described as rustic, especially in comparison with the much more polished Provo. Accommodations are clean but fairly basic. Locals are consistently friendly, and life always seems to move slowly here.

EXPLORING

WORTH NOTING

Flamingo Pond. The pond is home to approximately 2,000 resident flamingos. These spectacular pink birds come and go during the day, so if you miss them on your drive down the island, be sure to double check at the end of the day. Bring binoculars to get a better look; they feed quite a ways out, and you're not allowed to hike closer. ⊠ *Whitby Hwy.* ✛ *South of Whitby, east of Kew.*

Kew. This settlement includes a small school and church, as well as tropical fruit trees that produce limes, papayas, and the more exotic custard apples. Nearby are the well-preserved ruins—old cauldrons, main house structure, and other outbuildings—of Wade's Green Plantation. Kew's heartbeat is still present, and visiting will give you a better understanding of the daily life of the islanders before development; it's wonderful to see the more traditional lifestyle coexisting with the present day. Contact the National Trust to make arrangements to view the plantation. ⊠ *Kew* ☎ *649/941–5710 National Trust* ⊕ *tcnationaltrust.org.*

Three Mary Cays. Three small rocky cays within swimming distance of Whitby Beach give you some of the best secluded snorkeling in all of the Turks and Caicos. You will often find ospreys nesting there, too. This is a wildlife protection area, so don't feed the fish or touch any of the corals. ✛ *Off Whitby Beach.*

FAMILY **Wades Green.** You wander down the shaded laneway, bordered by walls made from the rocks once found in the fields of this cotton plantation established by Loyalist Wade Stubbs in 1789. The walls of the great house still stand, albeit with foliage now growing on the inside. Giant iron cauldrons, once used to prepare meals for the slaves, rest in the

18

CLOSE UP

Local Souvenirs

What should you bring home after a fabulous vacation in the Turks and Caicos Islands? Here are a few suggestions, some of which are free.

You can bring home up to three conch shells (shells only). If you do not call the U.S. or Canada home, please check your country's import regulations for conch. For some, you will need a formal letter from TCI's DEMA (Department of Environment and Marine Affairs). The Middle Caicos Co-op shop features a local artisan from 11 to 2 daily right next door to Daniel's Cafe in Conch Bar, Middle Caicos, while their local handicrafts along with others from around the islands may also be found at Anna's in Saltmills Plaza, Art Provo in Regent Plaza, Turks & Caicos

National Trust in Town Center Mall, as well as Mama's in Ports of Call—all located right on Provo.

The Conch Farm sells beautiful, affordable jewelry made from conch shells and freshwater pearls.

One of the best souvenirs is the hardcover coffee-table cookbook from the Red Cross. Not only is it gorgeous, featuring recipes from all the great chefs of the Turks and Caicos, but the proceeds help the Red Cross.

If you're a dog lover, then maybe the best free souvenir would be to adopt a potcake puppy. Dogs come with a carrier, papers, and all their shots—and one will remind you year after year of your terrific vacation.

yard. There are also partial remains of the kitchen, the overseer's house, slave quarters, and several storage buildings. A lookout tower provides views for miles. Contact TCI National Trust to arrange a visit. ✉ *Kew* ☎ *649/941–5710 TCI National Trust* ⊕ *tcnationaltrust.org* 💲*$10* ⊗ *By appointment only.*

WHERE TO EAT

$$
AMERICAN
✕ **Last Chance Bar and Grill.** Overlooking the serene waters of Bottle Creek, this little spot makes a great stop for day-trippers going to or from Middle Caicos, as well as for those enjoying the beauty of North Caicos for a day or longer. In addition to making smaller items such as conch fritters and burgers, owner Howard Gibbs provides full meals of fresh-caught grouper and local lobster at reasonable prices. Housed in an old stone constructed home, you'll find true island ambience indoors or on the restaurant's new large wooden terrace that offers spectacular views. 💲 *Average main: $20* ✉ *Bottle Creek* ✛ *Just south of Bottle Creek along the main road, King's Hwy.* ☎ *649/232–4141* ⊕ *www. greatbonefishing.com* ▬ *No credit cards* ⊗ *Closed Sun.* ☞ *Reservations highly recommended to make sure Howard's in.*

$$$
ECLECTIC
Fodor'sChoice
★
✕ **Silver Palms Restaurant.** A real gem, Silver Palms has exquisite food, with local seafood and international cuisine served with delicious home-baked bread and lovely desserts. Dine indoors or out on their screened patio. The service is excellent. 💲 *Average main: $25* ✉ *Whitby* ✛ *Right next door to Ocean Beach Hotel* ☎ *649/946–7113* ⊗ *Closed Sept.–Nov.* ⚘ *Reservations essential.*

WHERE TO STAY

$$ RENTAL **Hollywood Beach Suites.** With 7 miles (11 km) of secluded beach and few others to share it with, this property can only be described as simple and relaxing. **Pros:** secluded and tranquil; updated furnishings; daily light housekeeping. **Cons:** might feel a little too quiet and secluded. *[$] Rooms from: $300 ✉ Hollywood Beach Dr., Whitby ☎ 649/231–1020, 800/551–2256 🌐 www.hollywoodbeachsuites.com 🛏 4 suites 🍴 No meals.*

$ HOTEL **Pelican Beach Hotel.** North Caicos islanders Susan and Clifford Gardiner built this small, palmetto-fringed hotel in the 1980s on this quiet and almost deserted beach in Whitby. **Pros:** the beach may be steps from your room. **Cons:** property is tired; location may be too remote and sleepy for some people; beach is au naturelle—a positive for many. *[$] Rooms from: $150 ✉ Whitby ☎ 649/946–7112 🌐 www.pelicanbeach.tc ⏲ Closed for maintenance Sept. and Oct. Check for dates 🛏 14 rooms, 2 suites 🍴 Some meals ☞ Stay may include breakfast plan.*

MIDDLE CAICOS

At 48 square miles (124 square km) and with fewer than 300 residents, this is the largest and least developed of the inhabited islands within the Turks and Caicos chain. A limestone ridge runs to about 125 feet above sea level, creating dramatic cliffs on the north shore and a cave system farther inland. Middle Caicos has rambling trails along the coast; the **Crossing Place Trail,** maintained by the National Trust, follows the path used by the early settlers to go between the islands. Inland are quiet settlements with friendly residents. This is the real thing.

18

EXPLORING

FAMILY Fodor's Choice ★ **Conch Bar Caves.** These limestone caves make up one of the largest cave systems in the Caribbean, with good examples of stalactites and stalagmites, as well as small—and slightly eerie—underground bodies of water. Archaeologists have discovered Lucayan artifacts in the caves and the surrounding area; these natives to the island would have used the caves to weather out storm season. Currently, the caves are inhabited by five species of bats—some of which are endangered and bring scientists here annually to study them—but they don't bother visitors. Visits can be arranged through TCI's National Trust. Guides provide flashlights and a sense of humor. It's best to wear sturdy shoes, as the ground is rocky and damp in places. If you don't have much time, Indian Cave is a smaller version that's worth exploring. Watch for the sign on your left after leaving the causeway. It's only a few steps off the road, parallel with Blue Horizon Resort. *✉ Conch Bar ✥ Main cave system is just outside of Conch Bar; Indian Cave is near Blue Horizon Resort on main highway ☎ 649/941–5710 TCI National Trust, local direct dial 🌐 tcnationaltrust.org/Conch-Bar-Caves 🎟 $10 adult admission, $2 students, $5 teachers ☞ Must arrange through TCI National Trust.*

WHERE TO EAT

$$$
SEAFOOD
Fodor's Choice
★

× **Mudjin Bar and Grill.** The restaurant at Blue Horizon Resort is a fabulous spot to enjoy lunch, dinner, or as an afternoon respite over a refreshing cocktail. The view overlooking the beautiful Mudjin Harbour and miles of north shore beach just may be the best in Turks and Caicos. Daily lunches concentrate on seafood items such as Lobster Bites, when in season, cracked conch and conch fritters, and fish-and-chips, although there are also burgers, Caesar wraps, and some vegetarian options (rare in these parts). Dinner is by reservation only and features a choice of several daily specials. $ *Average main: $25* ⊠ *Blue Horizon Resort, Mudjin Harbour ✛ Just after the causeway on your left* ☎ *649/946–6141* ⊕ *www.bhresort.com* ☉ *Closed Sept. Closed Sun. Aug.–Nov.* ⌂ *Reservations essential.*

WHERE TO STAY

$
HOTEL
Fodor's Choice
★

▦ **Blue Horizon Resort.** At this property, dramatic cliffs skirt one of the most beautiful beaches in the Turks and Caicos while blue-roofed cottages dot the hillside, all with outstanding views of the coastline and reef beyond. **Pros:** breathtaking views of Mudjin Harbour from the rooms; lack of development makes you feel like you're away from it all. **Cons:** need a car to explore; may be too isolated for some; three-night minimum. $ *Rooms from: $270* ⊠ *Mudjin Harbour ✛ Just after crossing the causeway on your left* ☎ *649/946–6141* ⊕ *www.bhresort. com* ☉ *Closed Sept.* ⇝ *5 cottages, 2 villas* ⁙⊘ *No meals.*

SPORTS AND THE OUTDOORS

CAVE TOURS

Fodor's Choice
★

Cardinal Arthur. Although exploring Middle Caicos on your own can be fun, a guided tour with Cardinal can illuminate the island's secret spots, from caves to where flamingos flock. He has lived on Middle Caicos his entire life, so his stories go back years and years, and his local knowledge of the flora and fauna satiates the appetite of budding naturalists. He is able to tell you the history of every nook and cranny of both Middle and North, as well as drop you off on hidden beaches—some accessible only by skiff. He can arrange almost anything! ⊠ *Conch Bar* ☎ *649/241–0730.*

SOUTH CAICOS

This 8½-square-mile (21-square-km) island was once an important salt producer; today it's the heart of the fishing industry. Nature prevails, with long, white beaches, jagged bluffs, quiet backwater bays, and salt flats. Diving and snorkeling on the pristine wall and reefs are a treat enjoyed by only a few.

In 2008 hurricanes Hanna and Ike gave South Caicos a one-two punch. Although the island has recovered, the few dive operators that were here have disappeared. The only way to dive (other than independently) is through a charter with Big Blue Unlimited out of Providenciales.

The biggest draw for South Caicos is its excellent diving and snorkeling on the wall and reefs (with an average visibility of 100 feet). It's practically the only thing to do on South Caicos other than lie on the lovely beaches, enjoy a mountain bike ride, or go kayaking. Making up the third-largest reef in the world, the coral walls surrounding South Caicos are dramatic, dropping from 50 feet to 6,000 feet in the blink of an eye. Several local fishermen harvest spiny lobsters for consumption in the Turks and Caicos, as well as for export.

EXPLORING

At the northern end of the island are fine white-sand beaches; the south coast is great for scuba diving along the drop-off, and there's excellent snorkeling off the windward (east) coast, where stands of elkhorn and staghorn coral shelter a wide variety of marine life Spiny lobster and queen conch are found on the shallow Caicos Bank to the west and are harvested for export by local processing plants. The bonefishing here is some of the best in the West Indies.

Boiling Hole. Abandoned *salinas* (natural salt pans) make up the center of this island, the largest receiving its water directly from an underground cave system that is connected directly to the ocean through this "boiling" hole. Don't expect anything too dramatic, other than a sense of what the industry once was.

Cockburn Harbour. The best natural harbor in the Caicos chain hosts the Big South Regatta each May. It began as a sailing regatta where all the families with traditional Caicos sloops would come over from Middle and North to race, but sloops are now being replaced with conch boats hosting 85-hp motors for a rip-roaring race. ⊠ *Cockburn Harbour.*

WHERE TO EAT

Restaurant choices on South Caicos are limited and no one consistently takes credit cards, so you most definitely should bring cash. The Dolphin Pub at South Caicos Ocean & Beach Resort is truly the only restaurant that operates with regular hours. There you can find a wide range on the menu including fresh catch and a fully stocked bar. **Darryl's** (on Stubbs Road) is a more casual restaurant, along with the Chicken Shack; expect to pay $10 to $20 for what they have available. Ask around to find out when (or if) these local favorites will be open; if you are staying over on the island, your accommodations will assist you in making "reservations." There are a couple of other dining spots operated directly out of a private residence; advance notice must be given so that the proprietor can prepare in advance.

$$ ✕ **Dolphin Grill at the Ocean & Beach Resort.** Located at South Caicos
ECLECTIC Ocean & Beach Resort, the grill is currently the only restaurant that operates ocean-side. Here you can find a diverse menu that includes burgers, chicken, and freshly caught fish, as well as some exquisite lobster dishes (when in season). At night this turns into a gathering place for visitors and locals alike; it can be quite lively. If you are around for lunch, this is your only sure choice without advance notice.

[$] Average main: $20 ✉ South Caicos Ocean & Beach Resort, Tucker Hill ☎ 649/946–3219 🌐 oceanandbeachresort.com ☞ Open for breakfast upon request.

WHERE TO STAY

$ HOTEL 🏨 **South Caicos Ocean & Beach Resort.** Rustic and basic—though perfectly acceptable—this two-story building has small balconies or patios and views of the never-ending turquoise water off of every room. **Pros:** each room has stunning views of Caicos Bank; it has the only real restaurant on the island. **Cons:** you need cash for everything but your room; not on the beach. *[$] Rooms from: $125 ✉ Tucker Hill ☎ 649/946–3219 direct dial, 877/774–5486 Turks and Caicos Reservations—for reservations only 🌐 southcaicos.oceanandbeachresort.com ➪ 24 rooms, 6 apartments 🍴 No meals.*

GRAND TURK

Just 7 miles (11 km) long and a little more than 1 mile (1½ km) wide, this island, the capital and seat of the Turks and Caicos government, has been a longtime favorite destination for divers eager to explore the 7,000-foot coral-encrusted wall that drops down within yards of the shoreline. This tiny, quiet island is home to white-sand beaches, the National Museum, and a small population of wild horses and donkeys, which leisurely meander past the white-walled courtyards, pretty churches, and bougainvillea-covered colonial inns on their daily commute into town. But things aren't entirely sleepy: a cruise-ship complex at the southern end of the island brings about 600,000 visitors per year. That said, the dock is self-contained and is about 3 miles (5 km) from the tranquil, small hotels of Cockburn Town, Pillory Beach, and the Ridge and far from most of the western-shore dive sites.

EXPLORING

Pristine beaches with vistas of turquoise waters, small local settlements, historic ruins, and native flora and fauna are among the sights on Grand Turk. Fewer than 4,000 people live on this 7½-square-mile (19-square-km) island, and it's easy to find your way around, as there aren't many roads.

COCKBURN TOWN

WORTH NOTING

The buildings in the country's capital and seat of government reflect a 19th-century Bermudian style. Narrow streets are lined with low stone walls and old street lamps. The once-vital *salinas* (natural salt pans, where the sea leaves a film of salt) have been restored, and covered benches along the sluice ways offer shady spots for observing the many wading birds, including flamingos, that frequent the shallows. Be sure to pick up a copy of the TCI Tourist Board's *Heritage Walk* guide to discover Grand Turk's rich architecture.

All in the Family

CLOSE UP

Local islanders, from the taxi driver meeting you to the chef feeding you, are often connected. "Oh, him?" you will hear. "He my cousin!" Development did not come to these islands until much later than most Caribbean nations, and as a result such family connections, as well as crafts, bush medicine, ripsaw music, storytelling, and even recipes, have remained constant. But where do such traditions come from? Researchers come closer and closer to finding out as they put the many pieces together. Many claim that their great-great-grandparents told them their forebears came directly from Africa. For decades their stories were ignored. Indeed, most experts believe the descendants to be of mostly second-generation Bermudian and Caribbean slaves.

In 2005, however, museum researchers continued their search for a slave ship called *Trouvadore,* supposedly lost on the coastline of East Caicos. The ship, which wrecked off East Caicos in 1841, carried a cargo of 193 Africans, captured to be sold into slavery long after slavery was abolished through international treaties; the illegal cargo was bound for Cuba and wrecked while trying to avoid British patrol vessels. All aboard miraculously survived the wreck, and all the Africans were found and freed in the Turks and Caicos Islands. Since there were only a few thousand inhabitants in the islands at the time, these first-generation African survivors were a significant minority (about 7% of the population then).

During one expedition, divers found a wrecked ship of the right time period. If these remains are the *Trouvadore,* many islanders may finally have a physical link to their past to go with their more intangible cultural traditions. So while you're in the islands, look closely at the intricately woven baskets, and listen carefully to the African rhythms in the ripsaw music and the stories you hear. For more information, check out the website ⊕ *www.trouvadore.org.*

18

Her Majesty's Prison. This prison was built out of stone in the 1830s to incarcerate men and women who had committed mostly petty crimes. As time passed, the prison expanded, housing even modern-day drug runners until it closed in the 1990s. Through a self-guided tour, you will see the cells, solitary-confinement area, and exercise yard. The prison is open only when there is a cruise ship at the port. It is worth the stop. ⊠ *Pond St., Cockburn Town* ⊕ *visittci.com* ✉ *$7* ⊙ *Open when a ship is in port.*

FAMILY
Fodor'sChoice
★

Turks and Caicos National Museum. In one of the island's oldest stone buildings, the National Museum houses several interactive exhibits, as well as a super little gift shop with books and local handicrafts. The complete collection of preserved artifacts raised from the noteworthy Molasses Reef Wreck is here. Dating back to the early 1500s, it is the earliest European shipwreck yet excavated in the New World. There is also a natural-history exhibit including artifacts left by the Taíno (or Lucayans), the earliest migrants to settle in the Turks and Caicos Islands. The museum also has a 3-D coral reef exhibit that compliments its presentation on the history of diving. Another gallery is dedicated to

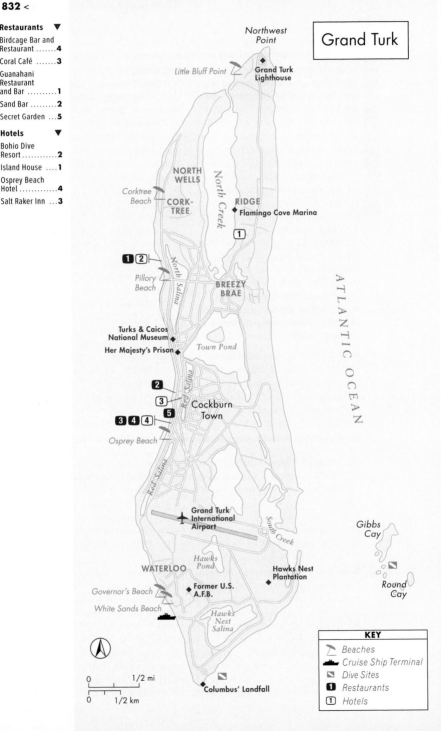

Grand Turk

Northwest
Point

Little Bluff Point

Grand Turk
Lighthouse

NORTH
WELLS

Corktree
Beach

CORK-
TREE

RIDGE

North Creek

Flamingo Cove Marina

① 1

❶ ②

Pillory
Beach

North Salina

BREEZY
BRAE

Turks & Caicos
National Museum

Her Majesty's Prison

Town Pond

❷ 2

③ 3

Salina

Cockburn
Town

❸ 3 ④ 4 ④ 4 ❺ 5

Osprey Beach

Red Salina

Grand Turk
International
Airport

South Creek

ATLANTIC OCEAN

Gibbs
Cay

Hawks
Pond

Round
Cay

WATERLOO

Governor's Beach

White Sands Beach

Former U.S.
A.F.B.

Hawks Nest
Plantation

Hawks
Nest
Salina

Columbus' Landfall

0   1/2 mi
0   1/2 km

KEY

➤ *Beaches*

⚓ *Cruise Ship Terminal*

◣ *Dive Sites*

❶ *Restaurants*

① *Hotels*

Grand Turk's involvement in the Space Race. John Glenn made landfall here after being the first American to orbit Earth. A fascinating display is a collection of "messages in a bottle" that have washed ashore from all over the world. This is the perfect spot to start your walking tour of the historical waterfront. ⊠ *Guinep House, Front St., Cockburn Town* ☎ *649/946–2160, 505/216–1795* ⊕ *www.tcmuseum.org* ✉ *$7 general admission, $5 for cruise passengers and hotel guests, children free* ⊙ *Mon.–Thurs. 9 – 2, Fri. 1– 5, and when a ship is in port.*

BEYOND COCKBURN TOWN

Grand Turk Lighthouse. More than 150 years ago, the main structure of the lighthouse was prefabricated in the United Kingdom and then transported to the island; once erected, it helped prevent ships from wrecking on the northern reefs for more than 100 years, originally designed to burn whale oil as its light source. You can use this landmark as a starting point for a breezy cliff-top walk by following the donkey trails to the deserted eastern beach. Unfortunately, the cruise-ship world has made its mark here, and zip lines block the panoramic view and spoil the location's solitude. If you are stretched for time, you might want to take a pass. ⊠ *Lighthouse Rd., North Ridge* ⊕ *visittci.com.*

BEACHES

Governor's Beach. Directly in front of the official British governor's residence, known as Waterloo, is a long stretch of beach framed by tall casuarina trees that provide plenty of natural shade. To have it all to yourself, go on a day when cruise ships are not in port. There are a couple of picnic tables where you can enjoy a picnic lunch, and there is a decent snorkeling spot just offshore. **Amenities: none. Best for:** swimming; walking. ✛ *20- to 30-min walk north of the Cruise Center.*

18

WHERE TO EAT

Conch in every shape and form, fresh grouper, as well as lobster when it's in season are favorite dishes at the laid-back restaurants found along the historical waterfront. Away from these more touristy areas, smaller and less expensive eateries serve chicken and ribs, curried goat, peas and rice, and other native island specialties. If you are driving around, don't hesitate to stop and try what's offered at roadside stands; the food is most often incredibly tasty! Be prepared for higher prices than in the United States, as almost everything that goes with the catch of the day must be imported.

COCKBURN TOWN

$$$ ✕ **Birdcage Bar and Restaurant.** This restaurant is a little more upscale

CARIBBEAN than most of the other dining spots on the island, with a lovely view of the ocean and tablecloths in the evening. There's also a full bar for those looking for a specialty drink. It's become the place to be on Sunday and Wednesday nights, when a sizzling menu of barbecue ribs, chicken, and lobster combines with live music. The rest of the week offers a slightly different menu without the band. Arrive early to secure waterfront tables, but note that a table around the Osprey's pool is also lovely.

Simple island weddings are also a possibility here. $ *Average main: $24* ⊠ *Osprey Beach Hotel, 1 Duke St., Cockburn Town* ☎ 649/946–2666 ⊕ *www.ospreybeachhotel.com/dining.*

$$
CAFÉ
Fodor's Choice
★

✕**Coral Cafe.** The Coral Cafe is a wonderful little gem hidden away in the annex of the Osprey Beach Hotel. An amazing array of coffees are served up by a barista along with freshly baked bread, scones, or a delicious croissant; there's even a gluten-free option. There are great breakfasts, including fresh bagels with lox and cream cheese. For lunch, you'll find wraps, salads, and sandwiches. The staff is warm and welcoming. $ *Average main: $12* ⊠ *Corner of Duke St. and Roberts Alley, Cockburn Town* ☎ 649/245–0648 ⊘ *No dinner* ⊟ *No credit cards.*

$$
ECLECTIC

✕**Sand Bar.** Run by two Canadian sisters, this popular beachside bar is very good value and the perfect spot to enjoy island time. No shoes or shirt required. The menu includes fresh-caught fish, lobster, and conch, as well as typical North American fare—burgers, quesadillas, and chicken and ribs—served island-style with peas and rice. The covered wooden deck juts out over the beach offering shade during the day; it's also a great place to enjoy a casual dinner while watching the sun set. The atmosphere is relaxed and the service friendly, and locals often meet here to socialize. If you're just over for a day, be sure to get there before 2:30, as they stop service for a couple of hours midday to gear up for the evening crowd. If you're staying the night, drop by for some late-evening conversation. $ *Average main: $14* ⊠ *Duke St., Cockburn Town* ☎ 649/243–2666 ⊘ *Closed Sat.*

$$
SEAFOOD

✕**Secret Garden.** Tucked away amidst tall tamarind and neem trees in a pretty courtyard garden behind the historical Salt Raker Inn, the Secret Garden serves simply prepared, local dishes such as grilled grouper and snapper, conch, and lobster. Many evenings feature live music—guaranteed on Fridays. Locals love this place. Be sure to try their grits if you're around for breakfast. Note that there is free Wi-Fi in the restaurant. $ *Average main: $17* ⊠ *Salt Raker Inn, Duke St., Cockburn Town* ☎ 649/946–2260, 649/243–5522 ⊕ *www. saltrakerinn.com* ⊘ *Closed Mon.*

ELSEWHERE ON GRAND TURK

$$$
INTERNATIONAL

✕**Guanahani Restaurant and Bar.** Off the town's main drag, this restaurant sits on a stunning but quiet stretch of beach just north of Cockburn Town. The food goes beyond the usual Grand Turk fare and is some of the island's best. The menu changes daily, based partly on the fresh catch-of-the-day, with a wonderful barbecue on Saturday nights including live music beachside; enjoy your choice of several mains, salads, and desserts. Dine inside by candlelight or out under starry skies. A special tapas menu is available at lunch in addition to the regular fare. $ *Average main: $30* ⊠ *Bohio Dive Resort & Spa, Pillory Beach* ☎ 649/946–2135 ⊕ *www.bohioresort.com.*

Cockburn Town, Grand Turk

WHERE TO STAY

COCKBURN TOWN

$ HOTEL Fodor's Choice ★ **Osprey Beach Hotel.** You cannot get any closer to the water's edge than this two-story oceanfront hotel adorned with artistic touches, including evocative island watercolors painted by Nashville artist, Tupper Saussay. **Pros:** within walking distance of several waterfront restaurants, all dive operators and excursions. **Cons:** three-night minimum; rocky beachfront; very thin walls so privacy can be an issue; courtyard suites lack atmosphere. [$] *Rooms from: $165* ✉ *1 Duke St., Cockburn Town* ☎ *649/946–2666* 🌐 *www.ospreybeachhotel.com* ⇨ *11 rooms, 16 suites plus Atrium balcony or courtyard accommodations* 🍴 *No meals.*

$ B&B/INN **Salt Raker Inn.** An unpretentious inn filled with island character and charm, this 19th-century house was built by shipwright Jonathan Glass in the 1850s, complete with its quirky nautical features. **Pros:** ambience and character; an easy walk to everything on the historical waterfront. **Cons:** the lack of no-smoking rooms; older bathrooms. [$] *Rooms from: $115* ✉ *Duke St., Cockburn Town* ☎ *649/946–2260* 🌐 *www.hotelsaltraker.com* ⇨ *10 rooms, 3 suites* 🍴 *No meals.*

ELSEWHERE ON GRAND TURK

$ RESORT **Bohio Dive Resort.** Divers are drawn to this basic yet comfortable hotel, whose on-site dive shop means there's no wait for some of the world's best diving. **Pros:** Guanahani is a great restaurant; on a gorgeous beach; steps away from awesome snorkeling. **Cons:** three-night minimum doesn't allow for quick getaways from Provo. [$] *Rooms from:*

*$190 ⊠ Pillory Beach ☎ 649/946–2135 ⊕ www.bohioresort.com ↴ 12
rooms, 4 suites ⏐◯⏐ No meals.*

$ 🛏 **Island House.** Years of experience helped Colin Brooker create this
RENTAL   comfortable, peaceful boutique hotel that overlooks North Creek and
FAMILY   Westside Beach. **Pros:** full condo units feel like a home away from
Fodor'sChoice   home. **Cons:** not on the beach; you need a car to get around. $ *Rooms*
★   *from: $165 ⊠ Lighthouse Rd., North Ridge ☎ 649/232–1439 ⊕ www.
islandhouse.tc ↴ 4 suites ⏐◯⏐ No meals ↻ 3-night minimum.*

NIGHTLIFE

Grand Turk is a quiet place where you come to relax and unwind,
perhaps do a bit of diving. Most of the nightlife consists of little more
than happy hour at sunset. Most restaurants turn into gathering places
where you can talk with new friends you've made that day, or enjoy
live music such as traditional rake-and-scrape. The Bohio encourages
dancing! Once you get yourself settled, ask around to find out the
where and when.

SHOPPING

Shopping in Grand Turk is hard to come by—choices are slim. Let's
just say that no true shopaholic would want to come here for vacation.
You can get the usual T-shirts and dive trinkets at all the dive shops, but
there are only a few options for more interesting shopping opportunities: The Grand Turk Inn's boutique, the National Museum's gift shop,
The Gallery-Grand Turk. When a ship is in port, the shops at the pier
are open, increasing your options dramatically.

SPORTS AND THE OUTDOORS

BICYCLING

Out of all the islands in Turks and Caicos, Grand Turk is the perfect
island for biking: it's small enough that it is possible to tour it all that
way. The island's mostly flat terrain isn't very taxing, and most roads
have hard surfaces. Take water with you: there are few places to stop for
refreshments. Most hotels have bicycles available, but you can also rent
them for $20 a day from Grand Turk Diving across from the Osprey
with a $200 deposit.

DIVING AND SNORKELING

With the wall just yards off shore, diving doesn't get any better than in
Grand Turk. Divers may explore undersea cathedrals, coral gardens,
and countless tunnels, or watch an octopus dance down a sandy slope.
But take note: you must present your valid certification before you're
allowed to dive. As its name suggests, the **Black Forest** offers staggering
black-coral formations as well as the occasional black-tip shark. In the
Library you can study fish galore, including large numbers of yellowtail
snapper. The Columbus Passage separates South Caicos from Grand
Turk, each side of the 22-mile-wide (35-km-wide) channel dropping
7,000 feet. From January through March, humpback whales migrate
through en route to their winter breeding grounds. **Gibb's Cay,** a small

cay a couple of miles off Grand Turk, is where you can swim with stingrays, making for a great excursion.

Blue Water Divers. In operation on Grand Turk since 1983, Blue Water Divers is the only PADI Green Star Award recipient-star dive center on the island, priding themselves on their personalized service and small group diving. The owner, Mitch, may not go diving very often anymore, but he may put some of your underwater experiences to music in the evenings when he plays at the Osprey Beach Hotel or Salt Raker Inn! In addition, Blue Water Divers offers Gibbs Cay snorkel and Salt Cay trips. ⊠ *Osprey Beach Hotel, The Atrium, 1 Duke St., Cockburn Town* ☎ *649/946–2432* ⊕ *www.grandturkscuba.com.*

Crystal Seas Adventures. Proprietor Tim Dunn, who is an actual descendent of the original owners of Salt Cay's historic White House, knows the waters around Grand Turk and Salt Cay as well as anybody. His company offers a variety of excursions: swimming with stingrays at Gibbs Cay, excursions to secluded cays, snorkel trips, plus whale-watching from January through March. Crystal Seas Adventures will cater to Salt Cay visitors as well. ⊠ *Grand Turk Cruise Terminal* ⚓ *Next door to the Cruise Terminal* ☎ *649/243–9843* ⊕ *www.crystalseasadventures.com.*

Grand Turk Diving. This company offers full-service dives, as well as trips to nearby Gibbs Cay and Salt Cay. GT Diving also offers shore diving when you purchase at least two days of package diving; however, it is a lengthy swim so few do it more than once. In addition, they offer bicycles for hire at $20 for a 24-hour period. ⊠ *Duke St., Cockburn Town* ⚓ *Across from the Osprey Beach Hotel* ☎ *649/946–1559* ⊕ *www.gtdiving.com.*

Oasis Divers. Oasis Divers provides excellent personalized service, with full gear handling and dive site briefing included. They also supply nitrox for those who are specifically trained. In addition, Oasis Divers offers a variety of other tours, including their land-based one on Segways, as well as whale-watching when the animals migrate past. ⊠ *Duke St., Cockburn Town* ☎ *649/946–1128 direct dial, 800/892–3995 toll-free* ⊕ *www.oasisdivers.com.*

GUIDED TOURS

Fodor's Choice
★

Mountain Air Helicopters TCI Ltd. Next door to the Grand Turk Cruise Terminal, Mountain Air offers tours that include a 15-minute fly over the island of Grand Turk and neighboring Gibbs Cay. En route you will see the coral reef, ship wrecks, historical sites, as well as sharks, rays, and turtles from the air. They also provide custom tours incorporating any of the other islands in the chain, including Provo. The helicopter is an EC-130 that can carry up to four passengers in air-conditioned comfort. ⊠ *Grand Turk Cruise Terminal* ⚓ *Next door to Grand Turk Cruise Terminal* ☎ *649/343–6327* ⊕ *www.gthelitours.com* 💲 *From $120/person with a minimum of 3 persons.*

KAYAKING

Oasis Divers offers glass-bottom kayak and ecosafari tours. Check out their website for the options available, as something the whole family can enjoy.

SALT CAY

Fewer than 100 people live on this 2½-square-mile (6-square-km) dot of land, their unassuming lifestyle set against a backdrop of whitewashed cottages, stone ruins, and weathered wooden windmills standing sentry in the abandoned salinas. Bordered by beaches where weathered green and blue sea glass and pretty shells often wash ashore, Salt Cay lives up to its reference as "the island that time forgot." Beneath the waves, 10 dive sites are minutes from the shore, while humpback whales pass by on their way south to their breeding grounds from January through March.

EXPLORING

Salt sheds and salinas are silent reminders of the days when the island was a leading producer of salt, for a period of time the largest harvester of salt in the world. Now the ponds attract abundant birdlife, both migratory and resident.

What little development there is on Salt Cay is found in its main community, Balfour Town. It's home to the majority of accommodation, a few small shops, as well as the main dock and the Coral Reef Bar & Grill, where folks hang out to watch the sun set and enjoy a beverage. As a visitor, you can cover the entire island on foot if you are so inclined, while others may consider zipping around by motorized golf cart. Renting a sea kayak to explore the coastline is a great option in order to see the island from a different view.

White House. This grand stone and plaster house, which once belonged to a wealthy salt merchant, is testimony to Salt Cay's heyday. Still owned by the descendants of the original family, it's sometimes open for tours when Tim Dunn, one of the successors, is on island. He's pleased to share the house, where you will see some of the original furnishings, books, and a medicine cabinet that dates back to around 1835. ✉ *Victoria St., Balfour Town* ☎ *649/243–9843* 🎫 *Free* 🕒 *By appointment only.*

WHERE TO EAT

$$ CARIBBEAN 🍴 **Pat's Place.** Island native Patricia Ann Simmons can give you a lesson in the medicinal qualities of her garden plants and periwinkle flowers, as well as provide excellent native cuisine for a very reasonable price in her comforting Salt Cay home. Home cooking doesn't get any closer to home than this. Try her conch fritters, cracked conch, or chicken-and-chips for lunch and the steamed grouper or red snapper with peas and rice for dinner. As with most places in Salt Cay, you must place your order by 2 pm and tell them what time you want to eat dinner. Pat cooks only upon request with reservation. Beer and wine are offered with the evening meal, and payment is by cash only. [$] *Average main: $15* ✉ *South District* ☎ *649/946–6919* 💳 *No credit cards* ✍ *Reservations essential.*

$$$ ECLECTIC Fodor's Choice ★ 🍴 **Porter's Island Thyme Bistro.** Owner Porter Williams and his wife, Haidee, have been traveling back and forth to Salt Cay for more than 20 years. Their love of the island resulted in the creation of Porter's Island Thyme in December of 1999, now fondly thought of as *the* gathering spot. The bistro, a block from the dock and overlooking the salina, has evolved over the years; today, it offers great cuisine, blending an Asian influence with local and international ingredients. Breakfast is amazing—eggs Benedict, Belgian waffles, and breakfast burritos. On the lunch and dinner menus, you'll find a variety of seafood and meat selections. There are also activity nights—Texas Hold'em, karaoke, or Nintendo Wii bowling—and a nightly selection of tapas during happy hour, including Wednesday Wing Night, Friday-night pizza, or the amazing Lobster Mania on Thursday (in season). There's also a small shop with gifts and tourist information. Reservations for dinner are essential and must be made by 3 pm. [$] *Average main: $26* ✉ *Dickenson Square, Balfour Town* ☎ *649/946–6977* 🌐 *www.islandthyme.tc* 🕒 *Closed Sun. and June–Nov.* ✍ *Reservations essential.*

WHERE TO STAY

$$ RENTAL Fodor's Choice ★ 🏨 **Castaway, Salt Cay.** Their slogan says it all: "solitude, romantic sunsets, sugar sand beaches." **Pros:** on a spectacular beach; truly a getaway-from-it-all; perfect for relaxing. **Cons:** it's a dark, secluded road into town at night. [$] *Rooms from: $299* ✉ *North Beach* ☎ *649/946–6977 direct dial (most consistently answered during season), 772/713–9502 U.S. number* 🌐 *www.castawayonsaltcay.com* 🕒 *Closed June–Nov.* 🛏 *4 suites* 🍴 *No meals.*

$ RENTAL 🏨 **Villas of Salt Cay.** One of the most convenient places to stay in Salt Cay, these centrally located, beachfront villas are in the middle of everything, offering simple accommodation at an affordable price. **Pros:** bedrooms are set up for extra privacy; on Victoria Street within walking distance of everything; on a private stretch of beach. **Cons:** no rooms have air-conditioning; cabanas only have small kitchenettes; shared pool. [$] *Rooms from: $175* ✉ *Victoria St., Balfour Town* ☎ *649/241–1009* ✉ *scdivers@tciway.tc* 🌐 *www.villasofsaltcay.tc* 🕒 *Closed Sept.* 🛏 *1 2-bedroom villa, 1 2-bedroom cottage, 3 cabanas* 🍴 *No meals.*

SPORTS AND THE OUTDOORS

DIVING AND SNORKELING

There are 10 excellent dive sites off shore from Salt Cay, or as an alternative, scuba divers can explore the wreck of the *Endymion,* a British 44-gun warship that went down in 1790. Coral-encrusted cannons and anchors can still be seen, a 45-minute boat ride away.

Fodor's Choice ★ **Salt Cay Divers.** Salt Cay Divers conducts daily dive trips and rents out all necessary equipment, with night diving upon request. Snorkeling equipment ($25/day) is also available for your own independent adventure, or you can arrange a guided snorkel trip. Stay above water and explore the coastline in one of their kayaks ($35/half day). In season, SC Divers also offers whale-watching excursions. With limited flight and ferry service for access to the island, note that they can even help get you to Salt Cay from Grand Turk through their private charter service. ⊠ *Balfour Town* ☎ *649/241–1009* ⊕ *www.saltcaydivers.tc.*

KAYAKING

If you fancy exploring the coastline of Salt Cay, renting sea kayaks from Salt Cay Divers (⊕ *www.saltcaydivers.tc*) is another option for visitors to this tiny island.

WHALE-WATCHING

During the winter months (January through March), Salt Cay is a center for whale-watching, when some 2,500 humpback whales migrate past close to shore. Whale-watching trips can most easily be organized through your inn or guesthouse; out of Salt Cay you can choose from Salt Cay Divers or Crystal Seas Adventures, who will come over from Grand Turk for the excursion.

UNITED STATES
VIRGIN ISLANDS

WELCOME TO THE UNITED STATES VIRGIN ISLANDS

ATLANTIC

Big Hans
Lollick

Inner
Brass

Picara Pt.

Santa
Maria

Botany
Bay

Stumpy
Bay

Dorothea

Magens
Bay

Lovelund Bay

Thatch
Cay

Fortuna

Brewers
Bay

David Pt.

St. Thomas
see detail
map

Cyril E. King
International
Airport

Hassel
Island

Charlotte
Amalie

ST. THOMAS

Pillsbury
Sound

Red
Hook

Nadir

Water
Island

Frenchman
Bay

Bovoni
Bay

Long Pt.

Great
St. James
Island

Little St. James
Island

TO
← PUERTO RICO

this area not to scale
see above

Cane
Bay

Davis
Bay

Hams Bay

Frederiksted

Henry E. Rohlsen
International
Airport

Krause Pt.

West End
Salt Pond

Long Pt.
Bay

Long Pt.

Sandy
Pt.

AMERICA'S CARIBBEAN

About 1,000 miles (1,600 km) from the southern tip of Florida, the U.S. Virgin Islands were acquired from Denmark in 1917. St. Croix, at 84 square miles (218 square km), is the largest of the islands; St. John, at 20 square miles (52 square km), is the smallest. Together, they have a population of around 110,000, half of whom live on St. Thomas.

A perfect combination of the familiar and the exotic, the U.S. Virgin Islands are a little bit of home set in an azure sea. With hundreds of idyllic coves and splendid beaches, chances are that on one of the three islands you'll find your ideal Caribbean vacation spot.

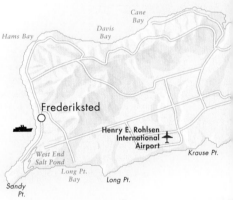

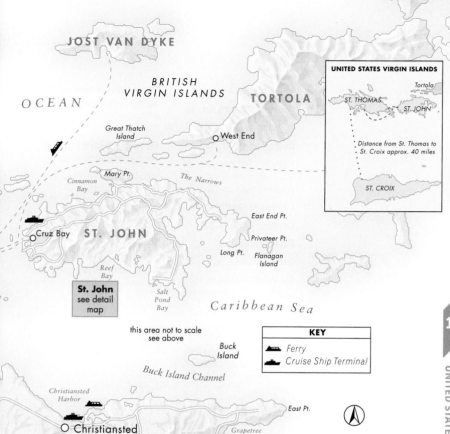

TOP REASONS TO VISIT THE UNITED STATES VIRGIN ISLANDS

1 Incomparable Sailing: St. Thomas is one of the Caribbean's major sailing centers.

2 Great Hiking: Two-thirds of St. John is a national park that's crisscrossed by excellent hiking trails.

3 Beaches: Though Magens Bay on St. Thomas and Trunk Bay on St. John are two of the most perfect beaches you'll ever find, St.

Croix's West End beaches are fetching in their own way.

4 Shopping: Shopping on both St. Thomas and St. Croix is stellar.

5 Deep-Sea Fishing: St. Thomas is one of the best places to catch Atlantic blue marlin between the months of June and October.

NEED TO KNOW

AT A GLANCE

Capital: Charlotte Amalie

Population: 110,000

Currency: U.S. dollar

Money: ATMs are common and cash is more widely accepted than credit.

Language: English

Country Code: 1 340

Emergencies: 911

Driving: On the left

Electricity: 110v/60 cycle; plugs are U.S. standard two- and three-prong.

Time: Same as New York during daylight savings time; one hour ahead otherwise

Documents: Enter USVI as you would domestically

Mobile Phones: GSM (850 and 1900 bands)

Major Mobile Companies: AT&T, Choice Wireless, Sprint, T-Mobile US

WEBSITES

USVI Division of Tourism: ⊕ *www.visitusvi.com*

Charlotte Amalie

UNTIED STATES VIRGIN ISLANDS

GETTING AROUND

✈ **Air Travel:** Cyril E. King Airport is on St. Thomas; Henry Rohlsen Airport is on St. Croix.

🚌 **Bus Travel:** On St. Thomas, large buses are comfortable but slow. Modern Vitran buses run on St. John.

🚗 **Car Travel:** You will need a rental car on St. Croix or if you are staying in a private villa in St. Thomas or St. John.

⛴ **Ferry Travel:** Ferries frequently go between St. Thomas and St. John and between St. Thomas, St. John, and Tortola. There's less frequent service to Virgin Gorda and Jost Van Dyke.

PLAN YOUR BUDGET

	HOTEL ROOM	MEAL	ATTRACTIONS
Low Budget	$200	$15	Annaberg Plantation, Free
Mid Budget	$300	$25	Sunset sail, $35
High Budget	$475	$50	Half-day trip to Buck Island, $70

WAYS TO SAVE

Shop frugally. Groceries on the USVI are expensive, so it pays to stock up on the basics at warehouse-style stores like Cost-U-Less or in local farmer' markets.

Go green. St. John has a couple of great camping spots, like the ecotents at Condordia Eco-Resort. On St. Croix, Mount Victory Camp offers a remarkable quietude with screened-in tent-cottages.

Take public transportation. Bus and jitney fares on all islands are no more than $1 or $2.

Look online. The USVI tourism board includes a dedicated section to money-saving packages and promotions.

PLAN YOUR TIME

Hassle Factor	Low. Flights to St. Thomas are frequent, and the islands are easy to navigate.
3 days	Land in St. Thomas and immediately head to pristine St. John to relax at your resort. Be sure to hike the Reef Bay trail and snorkel in the surrounding waters.
1 week	Split your time between St. John and the rugged coast of St. Croix. On St. John, snorkel at Trunk Bay and check out the food scene at Cruz Bay. On St. Croix, stroll around Christiansted, dive "the Wall," and take a boat trip to Buck Island.
2 weeks	Split your time evenly between St. John, St. Croix, and St. Thomas while allotting two days to visit the BVI on day trips. On St. Thomas, shop along Charlotte Amalie's Main Street and swim at Magens Bay. Take the day ferries to visit Anegada and Tortola.

WHEN TO GO

High Season: Mid-December through mid-April is the most fashionable and most expensive time to visit, when the weather is typically sunny and warm. Good hotels are often booked far in advance, and you're guaranteed the most entertainment at resorts and the most people with whom to enjoy it.

Low Season: From August to late October, temperatures can grow oppressively hot and the weather muggy, with high risks of tropical storms. Many upscale hotels offer deep discounts.

Value Season: From late April to July and again November to mid-December, hotel prices drop 20% to 50% from high-season prices. There are chances of scattered showers, but expect sun-kissed days, too, and fewer crowds.

BIG EVENTS

March–April: Expect to see plenty of Mocko Jumbies, St. Thomas's otherworldly stilt walkers, during Carnival, which takes place after Easter.

June–July: St. John celebrates Carnival in summer with plenty of street celebrations and a huge parade on the 4th of July.

July: Emancipation Day, on July 3, celebrates the date slavery was abolished in the Danish West Indies in 1848.

December–January: The Crucian Christmas Festival is a nearly monthlong celebration coinciding with the island's Christmas Carnival, ending January 6 with a huge parade.

READ THIS

■ *In a Pirate's Arms,* Mary Kingsley. Romance novel set in 1800s St. Thomas.

■ *Afoot on St. Croix,* Rebecca M. Hale. Dark mystery in tropical paradise.

■ *The Cat Letters: A Tale of Longing, Adventure and True Love,* Lexis De Rothschild. A lovesick woman writes letters to her cat from St. Thomas.

WATCH THIS

■ *Trading Places.* Some scenes in the 1980s comedy were filmed in the USVI.

■ *The Twilight Saga: Breaking Dawn—Part 1.* Concluding scenes were filmed in the USVI.

■ *Shawshank Redemption.* Scenes from the epic were filmed in the USVI.

EAT THIS

■ *Caribbean pate:* a triangular fried pastry stuffed with spicy ground beef, conch, or salted fish

■ *Dundersloe:* the Virgin Islands version of peanut brittle

■ *Fish and fungi:* simmered fish with okra-studded cornmeal polenta

■ *Goat water:* mutton stew, chockful of veggies

■ *Potato stuffing:* a mix of mashed white potatoes, tomato sauce, and seasonings

■ *Mauby:* a somewhat bitter, root beer–like drink made from the bark of the mauby tree.

Updated
by Carol
Buchanan
and Carol M.
Bareuther

The U.S. Virgin Islands—St. Thomas, St. John, and St. Croix—may fly the American flag, but "America's Paradise" is in reality a mix of the foreign and familiar that offers something for everyone to enjoy. The history, beautiful beaches, myriad activities, good food, and no-passport-required status make the Virgin Islands an inviting beach destination for many Americans.

With three islands to choose from, you're likely to find your piece of paradise. Check into a beachfront condo on the East End of St. Thomas; then eat burgers and watch football at a beachfront bar and grill. Or stay at an 18th-century plantation great house on St. Croix, go horseback riding at sunrise, and then dine that night on local seafood classics. Rent a tent or a cottage in the pristine national park on St. John; then take a hike, kayak off the coast, read a book, or just listen to the sounds of the forest. Or dive deep into "island time" and learn the art of limin' (hanging out, Caribbean-style) on all three islands.

History books give credit to Christopher Columbus for discovering the New World. In reality, the Virgin Islands, like the rest of the isles in the Caribbean chain, were populated as long ago as 2000 BC by nomadic waves of seagoing settlers as they migrated north from South America and eastward from Central America and the Yucatán Peninsula.

Columbus met the descendants of these original inhabitants during his second voyage to the New World, in 1493. He anchored in Salt River, a natural bay west of what is now Christiansted, St. Croix, and sent his men ashore in search of fresh water. Hostile arrows rather than welcoming embraces made for a quick retreat, but Columbus did have time to name the island Santa Cruz (Holy Cross) before sailing north. He eventually claimed St. John, St. Thomas, and what are now the British Virgin Islands for Spain and at the same time named this shapely silhouette of 60-some islands Las Once Mil Vírgenes, for the 11,000 legendary virgin followers of St. Ursula. Columbus believed the islands barren of the costly spices he sought, so he sailed off, leaving more than a century's gap in time before the next Europeans arrived.

Pioneers, planters, and pirates from throughout Europe ushered in the era of colonization. Great Britain and the Netherlands both claimed St. Croix in 1625. This peaceful coexistence ended abruptly when the Dutch governor killed his English counterpart, thus launching years of battles for possession that would see seven flags fly over this southern-most Virgin isle. Meanwhile, St. Thomas's sheltered harbor proved a magnet for pirates such as Blackbeard and Bluebeard. The Danes first colonized the island in 1666, naming their main settlement Taphus for its many beer halls. In 1691 the town received the more respectable name of Charlotte Amalie in honor of Danish king Christian V's wife. It wasn't until 1718 that a small group of Dutch planters raised their country's flag on St. John. As on the other Virgin Islands, a plantation economy soon developed.

Plantations depended on slave labor, and the Virgin Islands played a key role in the triangular route that connected the Caribbean, Africa, and Europe in the trade of sugar, rum, and human cargo. By the early 1800s a sharp decline in cane prices because of competing beet sugar and an increasing number of slave revolts motivated Governor-General Peter von Scholten to abolish slavery in the Danish colonies on July 3, 1848. This holiday is now celebrated as Emancipation Day.

After emancipation, the island's economy slumped. Islanders owed their existence to subsistence farming and fishing. Meanwhile, during the American Civil War the Union began negotiations with Denmark for the purchase of the Virgin Islands in order to establish a naval base. However, the sale didn't happen until World War I, when President Theodore Roosevelt paid the Danes $25 million for the three largest islands; an elaborate Transfer Day ceremony was held on the grounds of St. Thomas's Legislature building on March 31, 1917. A decade later, Virgin Islanders were granted U.S. citizenship. Today the U.S. Virgin Islands is an unincorporated territory, meaning that citizens govern themselves and vote for their own governors, but cannot vote for president or congressional representation.

Nowadays, Virgin Islanders hail from more than 60 nations. The Danish influence is still strong in architecture and street names. Americana is everywhere, too, most notably in recognizable fast-food chains, familiar TV shows, and name-brand hotels. Between this diversity and the wealth that tourism brings, Virgin Islanders struggle to preserve their culture. Their rich, spicy West Indian–African heritage comes to full bloom at Carnival time, when celebrating and playing *mas* (with abandon) take precedence over everything else.

There's evidence, too, of growing pains. Traffic jams are common, a clandestine drug trade fuels crime, and there are few beaches left that aren't fronted by a high-rise hotel. Despite fairly heavy development, wildlife has found refuge here. The brown pelican is on the endangered list worldwide but is a common sight here. The endangered native boa tree is protected, as is the hawksbill turtle, whose females lumber onto the beaches to lay eggs.

PLANNING

GETTING HERE AND AROUND

AIR TRAVEL

Fly nonstop to St. Thomas from Atlanta (Delta), Boston (American, seasonal; JetBlue via San Juan, seasonal), Charlotte (American), Chicago (United), Fort Lauderdale (Spirit), Miami (American), New York–JFK (American), New York–Newark (United), Philadelphia (American), or Washington, D.C.–Dulles (United). Fly nonstop to St. Croix from Miami (American). In the winter, American flies nonstop from Charlotte, N.C.

If you can't fly nonstop, then you can connect in San Juan on Seaborne Airlines or Cape Air. You can also take a seaplane between St. Thomas and St. Croix. The only option for St. John is a ferry from either Red Hook or Charlotte Amalie in St. Thomas. Both Caneel Bay and the Westin have private ferries.

Airline Contacts American Airlines. ☎ *800/474–4884* ⊕ *www.aa.com.*
Cape Air. ☎ *800/CAPE–AIR (227–3247)* ⊕ *www.capeair.com.* **Delta Airlines.**
☎ *800/221–1212* ⊕ *www.delta.com.* **JetBlue.** ☎ *800/538–2583* ⊕ *www.jetblue.*
com. **Seaborne Airlines.** ☎ *787/949–7800* ⊕ *www.seaborneairlines.com.* **Spirit**
Airlines. ☎ *800/772–7117* ⊕ *www.spiritair.com.* **United Airlines.** ☎ *800/241–*
6522, 340/774–9190 in St. Thomas ⊕ *www.united.com.*

Airports Cyril E. King Airport (*STT*). ⊠ *Rte. 30, Lindbergh Bay* ☎ *340/774–*
5100. **Henry Rohlsen Airport** (*STX*). ⊠ *Airport Rd., off Rte 66, Anguilla*
☎ *340/778–1012.*

BOAT AND FERRY TRAVEL

There's frequent service between St. Thomas and St. John and their neighbors, the BVI. Check with the ferry companies for the current schedules. These schedules are also printed in the free *St. Thomas + St. John This Week* magazine and on the website of the **Virgin Islands Vacation Guide & Community** (⊕ *www.vinow.com*).

There's frequent daily service from both Red Hook and Charlotte Amalie to Cruz Bay, St. John. About every hour there's a car ferry, which locals call the barge. You should arrive at least 15 minutes before departure.

Ferry Contacts Inter-Island Boat Service. ☎ *340/776–6597 in St. John.*
Native Son. ☎ *340/774–8685 in St. Thomas* ⊕ *www.nativesonferry.com.*
Smith's Ferry. ☎ *340/775–7292 in St. Thomas* ⊕ *www.smithsferry.com.*
Speedy's. ☎ *284/495–5235 in Tortola* ⊕ *www.speedysbvi.com.*

CAR TRAVEL

Driving is on the left, British-style. The law requires that *everyone* wear a seat belt. Traffic can be bad during rush hour on all three islands.

Car Rentals in St. Thomas: Avis, Budget, and Hertz all have counters at Cyril E. King Airport, but there are some other offices as well; in addition, there are local companies.

Car Rentals in St. John: All the car-rental companies in St. John are locally owned. Most companies are just a short walk from the ferry dock. Those a bit farther away will pick you up.

Car Rentals in St. Croix: There are both local and national companies on St. Croix; if your company doesn't have an airport location, you'll be picked up or a car will be delivered to you.

St. Thomas Car Rental Contacts Avis. ⊠ *Cyril E. King Airport, 70 Lindbergh Bay, 4 miles west of Charlotte Amalie, Lindbergh Bay* ☎ *340/774–1468,* ⊕ *www.avis.com.* **Budget.** ⊠ *Cyril E. King Airport, 70 Lindbergh Bay, 4 miles west of Charlotte Amalie, Lindbergh Bay* ☎ *340/776–5774* ⊕ *www. budgetstt.com.* **Dependable Car Rental.** ⊠ *Estate Contant, 12 Lindbergh Bay, 1½ miles (3 km) east of Cyril E. King Airport off Rte. 308, turning north at the Medical Arts Bldg., Lindbergh Bay* ☎ *340/774–2253, 800/522–3076* ⊕ *www.dependablecar.com.* **Discount Car Rental.** ⊠ *Cyril E. King Airport, 70 Lindbergh Bay, 4 miles west of Charlotte Amalie; car rental is located adjacent to the entrance road of the airport, 1 min from the terminal* ☎ *340/776–4858, 877/478–2833* ⊕ *www.discountcar.vi.* **Hertz.** ⊠ *Cyril E King Airport, Airport Rd., 8100 Lindbergh Bay, 4 miles west of Charlotte Amalie, Lindbergh Bay* ☎ *340/774–1879* ⊕ *www.hertz.com.*

St. John Car Rental Contacts Best. ⊠ *Near library, Cruz Bay* ☎ *340/693–8177* ⊕ *www.bestcarrentalvi.com.* **Cool Breeze.** ⊠ *1 block east of the passenger ferry dock, Cruz Bay* ☎ *340/776–6588* ⊕ *www.coolbreezecarrental.com.* **Courtesy.** ⊠ *Near St. Ursula's Church, Cruz Bay* ☎ *340/776–6650* ⊕ *www. courtesycarrental.com.* **Denzil Clyne.** ⊠ *North Shore Rd., across from creek, Cruz Bay* ☎ *340/776–6715.* **O'Connor Car Rental.** ⊠ *Rte. 104, near the roundabout, Cruz Bay* ☎ *340/776–6343* ⊕ *www.oconnorcarrental.com.* **St. John Car Rental.** ⊠ *Bay St., near Wharfside Village, Cruz Bay* ☎ *340/776–6103* ⊕ *www. stjohncarrental.com.* **Spencer's Jeep.** ⊠ *Boulon Center Rd., near creek, Cruz Bay* ☎ *340/693–8784, 888/776–6628.*

St. Croix Car Rental Contacts Avis. ⊠ *Henry E. Rohlsen Airport* ☎ *340/778– 9355, 800/354–2847* ⊕ *www.avis.com.* **Budget.** ⊠ *Henry E. Rohlsen Airport* ☎ *340/778–9636, 888/264–8894.* **Hertz.** ⊠ *Henry E. Rohlsen Airport* ☎ *340/778–1402, 888/248–4261* ⊕ *www.rentacarstcroix.com.* **Judi of Croix.** ☎ *340/773–2123, 877/903–2123* ⊕ *www.judiofcroix.com.* **Olympic.** ⊠ *Rte. 70, Christiansted* ☎ *340/718–3000, 888/878–4227* ⊕ *www.olympicstcroix.com.*

TAXI TRAVEL

USVI taxis don't have meters; fares are per person, set by a schedule, and drivers usually take multiple fares, especially from the airport, ferry docks, and cruise-ship terminals. Many taxis are open safari vans, but some are air-conditioned vans.

St. Thomas East End Taxi. ⊠ *Urman Victor Fredericks Marine Terminal, 6117 Red Hook Quarters, off Rte. 38 in Red Hook* ☎ *340/775–6974* ⊕ *eastendtaxi. cbt.cc.* **Islander Taxi Services.** ⊠ *Fortress Storage, Bldg. K, Ste. 2025, at the intersection of Rtes. 313 and 38, Charlotte Amalie* ☎ *340/774–4077* ⊕ *www. islandertaxiservice.com.* **Virgin Islands Taxi Association.** ⊠ *68A Estate Contant, Charlotte Amalie* ☎ *340/774–4550, 340/774–7457* ⊕ *vitaxiassociation.com.*

19

St. John Paradise Taxi. ✉ *Waterfront, Cruz Bay* ☎ *340/714–7913.*

St. Croix Antilles Taxi Service. ☎ *340/773–5020.* **St. Croix Taxi Association.** ✉ *Henry E. Rohlsen Airport* ☎ *340/778–1088* ⊕ *www.stcroixtaxi.com.*

HEALTH AND SAFETY

Dengue, chikungunya, and zika have all been reported in the Caribbean. We recommend that you protect yourself from these mosquito-borne illnesses by keeping your skin covered and/or wearing mosquito repellant. The mosquitoes that transmit these viruses are as active by day as they are at night.

HOTELS AND RESORTS

St. Thomas is the most developed of the Virgin Islands; choose it if you want extensive shopping opportunities and a multitude of activities and restaurants. St. John, the least developed of the three, has a distinct following; it's the best choice if you want a small-island feel and easy access to great hiking. However, most villas there aren't directly on the beach. St. Croix is a sleeper. The diversity of the accommodations means that you can stay in everything from a simple inn to a luxury resort, but none of the beaches is as breathtaking as those on St. Thomas and St. John.

Resorts: Whether you are looking for a luxury retreat or a moderately priced vacation spot, there's going to be something for you in the USVI. St. Thomas has the most options. St. John has only two large resorts, both upscale; others are small, but it has two unique eco-oriented camping options. St. Croix's resorts are more midsize.

Small Inns: Particularly on St. Croix, you'll find a wide range of attractive and accommodating small inns; if you can live without being directly on the beach, these friendly, homey places are a good option. St. Thomas also has a few small inns in the historic district of Charlotte Amalie.

Villas: Villas are plentiful on all three islands, but they are especially popular on St. John, where they represent the majority of the available lodging. They're always a good bet for families who can do without a busy resort environment.

Hotel reviews have been shortened. For full information, visit Fodors.com.

WHAT IT COSTS IN U.S. DOLLARS			
$	**$$**	**$$$**	**$$$$**
RESTAURANTS under $12	$12–$20	$21–$30	over $30
HOTELS under $275	$275–$375	$376–$475	over $475

Restaurant prices are the average cost of a main course at dinner or, if dinner is not served, at lunch. Hotel prices are the lowest cost of a standard double room in high season.

VISITOR INFORMATION

Contacts USVI Department of Tourism. ☎ *340/774–8784, 800/372–8784* ⊕ *www.visitusvi.com.*

ST. THOMAS

Updated by
Carol M.
Bareuther

If you fly to the 32-square-mile (83-square-km) island of St. Thomas, you land at its western end; if you arrive by cruise ship, you come into one of the world's most beautiful harbors. Either way, one of your first sights is the town of Charlotte Amalie. From the harbor you see an idyllic-looking village that spreads into the lower hills. If you were expecting a quiet hamlet with its inhabitants hanging out under palm trees, you've missed that era by about 300 years. Although other islands in the USVI developed plantation economies, St. Thomas cultivated its harbor, and it became a thriving seaport soon after it was settled by the Danish in the 1600s.

HOP ON THE BUS

On St. Thomas the island's large buses make public transportation a very comfortable—though slow—way to get from east and west to Charlotte Amalie and back (service to the north is limited). Buses run about every 30 minutes from stops that are clearly marked with "Vitran" signs. Fares are $1 between outlying areas and town and 75¢ in town. There are also safari taxis (open-air seats with a roof built on the back of a pickup truck) or "dollar buses" that run the same routes for $1 a ride.

The success of the naturally perfect harbor was enhanced by the fact that the Danes—who ruled St. Thomas with only a couple of short interruptions from 1666 to 1917—avoided involvement in some 100 years' worth of European wars. Denmark was the only European country with colonies in the Caribbean to stay neutral during the War of the Spanish Succession in the early 1700s. Thus, products of the Dutch, English, and French islands—sugar, cotton, and indigo—were traded through Charlotte Amalie, along with the regular shipments of slaves. When the Spanish wars ended, trade fell off, but by the end of the 1700s Europe was at war again, Denmark again remained neutral, and St. Thomas continued to prosper. Even into the 1800s, while the economies of St. Croix and St. John foundered with the market for sugarcane, St. Thomas's economy remained vigorous. This prosperity led to the development of shipyards, a well-organized banking system, and a large merchant class. In 1845 Charlotte Amalie had 101 large importing houses owned by the English, French, Germans, Haitians, Spaniards, Americans, Sephardim, and Danes.

Charlotte Amalie is still one of the world's most active cruise-ship ports. On almost any day at least one and sometimes as many as eight cruise ships are tied to the docks or anchored outside the harbor. Gently rocking in the shadows of these giant floating hotels are just about every other kind of vessel imaginable: sleek sailing catamarans that will take you on a sunset cruise complete with rum punch and a Jimmy Buffett sound track, private megayachts for billionaires, and barnacle-bottom sloops—with laundry draped over the lifelines—that are home to world-cruising gypsies. Huge container ships pull up in Sub Base, west of the harbor, bringing in everything from breakfast cereals to tires. Anchored right along the waterfront are down-island barges that ply the waters

19

Fort Christian (1672–80) is the oldest surviving structure in St. Thomas.

between the Greater Antilles and the Leeward Islands, transporting goods such as refrigerators, VCRs, and disposable diapers.

The waterfront road through Charlotte Amalie was once part of the harbor. Before it was filled in to build the highway, the beach came right up to the back door of the warehouses that now line the thoroughfare. Two hundred years ago those warehouses were filled with indigo, tobacco, and cotton. Today the stone buildings house silk, crystal, and diamonds. Exotic fragrances are still traded, but by island beauty queens in air-conditioned perfume palaces instead of through open market stalls. The pirates of old used St. Thomas as a base from which to raid merchant ships of every nation, though they were particularly fond of the gold- and silver-laden treasure ships heading to Spain. Pirates are still around, but today's versions use St. Thomas as a drop-off for their contraband: illegal immigrants and drugs.

EXPLORING

To explore outside Charlotte Amalie, rent a car or hire a taxi. Your rental car should come with a good map; if not, pick up the pocket-size "St. Thomas–St. John Road Map" at a tourist information center. Roads are marked with route numbers, but they're confusing and seem to switch numbers suddenly. Roads are also identified by signs bearing the St. Thomas–St. John Hotel and Tourism Association's mascot, Tommy the Starfish. More than 100 of these color-coded signs line the island's main routes. Orange signs trace the route from the airport to Red Hook, green signs identify the road from town to Magens Bay,

Tommy's face on a yellow background points from Mafolie to Crown Bay through the north side, red signs lead from Smith Bay to Four Corners via Skyline Drive, and blue signs mark the route from the cruise-ship dock at Havensight to Red Hook. These color-coded routes are not marked on most visitor maps, however. Allow yourself a day to explore, especially if you want to stop to take pictures or to enjoy a light bite or refreshing swim. Most gas stations are on the island's more populated eastern end, so fill up before heading to the north side. And remember to drive on the left!

CHARLOTTE AMALIE

Look beyond the pricey shops, T-shirt vendors, and bustling crowds for a glimpse of the island's history. The city served as the capital of Denmark's outpost in the Caribbean until 1917, an aspect of the island often lost in the glitz of the shopping district.

Emancipation Gardens, right next to the fort, is a good place to start a walking tour. Tackle the hilly part of town first: head north up Government Hill to the historic buildings that house government offices and have incredible views. Several regal churches line the route that runs west back to the town proper and the old-time market. Virtually all the alleyways that intersect Main Street lead to eateries serving frosty drinks, sandwiches, and West Indian fare. There are public restrooms in this area, too. Allow an hour for a quick view of the sights.

A note about the street names: In deference to the island's heritage, the streets downtown are labeled by their Danish names. Locals will use both the Danish name and the English name (such as Dronningens Gade and Norre Gade for Main Street), but most people refer to things by their location ("a block toward the waterfront off Main Street" or "next to the Little Switzerland Shop"). You may find it more useful if you ask for directions by shop names or landmarks.

TOP ATTRACTIONS

FAMILY **Fort Christian.** St. Thomas's oldest standing structure, this remarkable building was built between 1672 and 1680 and now has U.S. National Landmark status. Over the years, it was used as a jail, governor's residence, town hall, courthouse, and church. In 2005, a multimillion-dollar renovation project started to stabilize the structure and halt centuries of deterioration. This project is still ongoing, but you can see historic features from the outside like the four renovated faces of the famous 19th-century clock tower. ✉ *Waterfront Hwy., east of shopping district, Charlotte Amalie* ☎ *340/774–5541* ⊕ *stthomashistoricaltrust.org.*

Hassel Island. East of Water Island in Charlotte Amalie harbor, Hassel Island is part of the Virgin Islands National Park. On it are the ruins of a British military garrison (built during a brief British occupation of the USVI during the 1800s) and the remains of a marine railway (where ships were hoisted into dry dock for repairs). Daily guided kayak tours to the island are available from VI Ecotours. The St. Thomas Historical Trust leads three-hour walking tours throughout the year. ✉ *Charlotte Amalie harbor, Charlotte Amalie* ☎ *340/776–6201 Virgin Islands National Park main office* ⊕ *www.nps.gov/viis.*

19

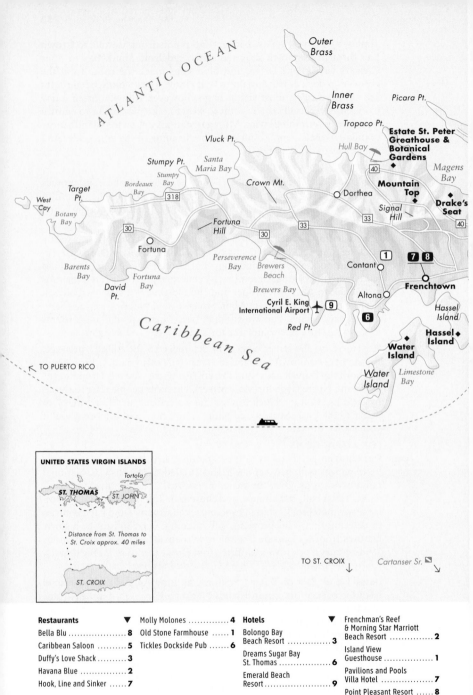

ATLANTIC OCEAN

Outer
Brass

Inner
Brass

Picara Pt.

Tropaco Pt.

**Estate St. Peter
Greathouse &
Botanical
Gardens**

Hull Bay

Magens
Bay

Vluck Pt.

Santa
Maria Bay

Stumpy Pt.

Stumpy
Bay

Bordeaux
Bay

Target
Pt.

West
Cay

Botany
Bay

Crown Mt.

Dorthea

**Mountain
Top**

Signal
Hill

**Drake's
Seat**

40

318

30

Fortuna

Fortuna
Hill

30

33

33

40

Barents
Bay

David
Pt.

Fortuna
Bay

Perseverence
Bay

Brewers
Beach

Brewers Bay

Contant

1

7 8

Frenchtown

Altona

Hassel
Island

6

**Hassel
Island**

**Cyril E. King
International Airport**

9

Red Pt.

**Water
Island**

Caribbean Sea

Water
Island

Limestone
Bay

TO PUERTO RICO

TO ST. CROIX

Cartanser Sr.

UNITED STATES VIRGIN ISLANDS

Tortola

ST. THOMAS

ST. JOHN

Distance from St. Thomas to
St. Croix approx. 40 miles

ST. CROIX

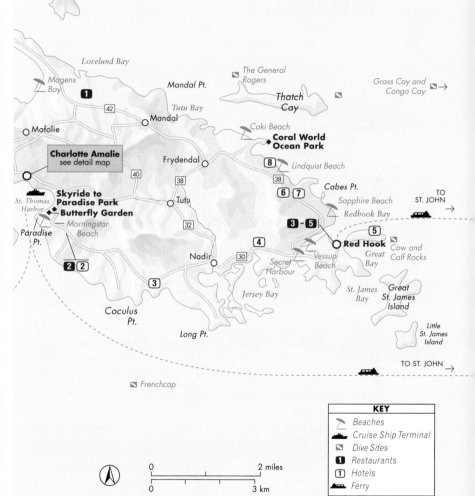

St. Thomas

Hans
Lollick

Lovelund Bay

Magens
Bay

1

Mafolie

Mandal Pt.

Tutu Bay

Mandal

42

Charlotte Amalie
see detail map

40

St. Thomas
Harbor

Skyride to
Paradise Park
Butterfly Garden

Paradise
Pt.

Morningstar
Beach

38

Frydendal

Tutu

32

38

The General
Rogers

Thatch
Cay

Grass Cay and
Congo Cay →

Coki Beach

Coral World
Ocean Park

8   Lindquist Beach

38

Cabes Pt.

6 **7**

Sapphire Beach

Redhook Bay

3 - **5**

TO
ST. JOHN

2 **2**

3

Nadir

30

4

Secret
Harbour

Vessup
Beach

Red Hook

5

Cow and
Calf Rocks

Great
Bay

St. James
Bay

Great
St. James
Island

Coculus
Pt.

Jersey Bay

Long Pt.

Little
St. James
Island

TO ST. JOHN →

Frenchcap

0 _____ 2 miles

0 _____ 3 km

KEY

Beaches
Cruise Ship Terminal
Dive Sites
1 Restaurants
1 Hotels
Ferry

99 Steps. This staircase "street," built by the Danes in the 1700s, leads to the residential area above Charlotte Amalie and to Blackbeard's Castle, a U.S. national historic landmark. If you count the stairs as you go up, you'll discover, as thousands have before you, that there are more than the name implies. ⊠ *Look for steps heading north from Government Hill, Charlotte Amalie.*

Pissarro Building. Housing several shops and an art gallery, this was the birthplace and childhood home of the acclaimed 19th-century impressionist painter Camille Pissarro, who lived for most of his adult life in France. The art gallery on the second floor contains three original pages from Pissarro's sketchbook and two pastels by Pissarro's grandson, Claude. ⊠ *14 Dronningens Gade (Main St.), between Raadets Gade and Trompeter Gade, Charlotte Amalie.*

FAMILY **Roosevelt Park.** The former Coconut Park was renamed in honor of Franklin D. Roosevelt in 1945. It's a great place to put your feet up and people-watch. Five granite pedestals represent the five branches of the military, bronze urns commemorate special events and can be lighted, and inscribed bronze plaques pay tribute to the territory's veterans who died defending the United States. There's also a children's playground. ⊠ *Intersection of Norre Gade and Rte. 35, adjacent to the Memorial Moravian Church, Charlotte Amalie* ☎ *340/774–5541* ⊕ *www.stthomashistoricaltrust.org.*

Seven Arches Museum and Gallery. This restored 18th-century home is a striking example of classic Danish–West Indian architecture. There seem to be arches everywhere—seven to be exact—all supporting a "welcoming arms" staircase that leads to the second floor and the flower-framed front doorway. The Danish kitchen is a highlight: it's housed in a separate building away from the main house, as were all cooking facilities in the early days (for fire prevention). Inside the house you can see mahogany furnishings and gas lamps and colorful abstract canvases painted by the museum's curator, a local artist. ⊠ *Government Hill, 3 buildings east of Government House, 18A–B Dronningens Gade, Charlotte Amalie* ☎ *340/774–9295* ⊕ *www.sevenarchesmuseum.com* ✉ *$5 donation* ⊗ *By appointment only.*

WORTH NOTING

All Saints Episcopal Church. Built in 1848 from stone quarried on the island, the church has thick, arched window frames lined with the yellow brick that came to the islands as ballast aboard ships. Merchants left the brick on the waterfront when they filled their boats with molasses, sugar, mahogany, and rum for the return voyage. The church was built in celebration of the end of slavery in the USVI. ⊠ *13 Commandant Gade, near the Emancipation Garden U.S. Post Office, Charlotte Amalie* ☎ *340/774–0217* ⊗ *Mon.–Sat. 9–3.*

Educators Park. A peaceful place amid the town's hustle and bustle, the park has memorials for three famous Virgin Islanders: educator Edith Williams, J. Antonio Jarvis (a founder of the *Daily News*), and educator and author Rothschild Francis. The last gave many speeches here. ⊠ *Main St., across from Emancipation Garden post office, Charlotte Amalie.*

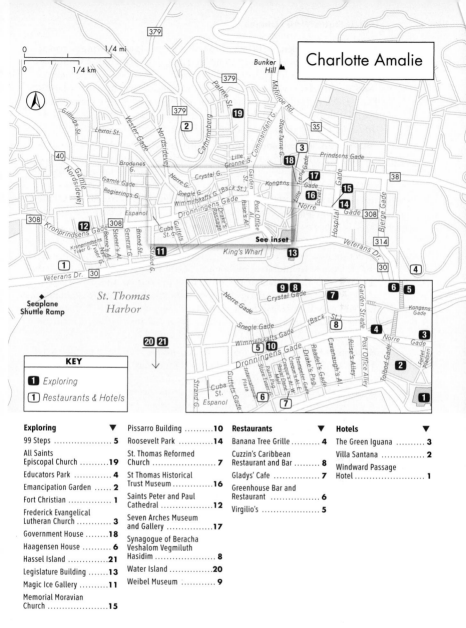

Charlotte Amalie

KEY

🔲 Exploring

⬜ Restaurants & Hotels

Emancipation Garden. A bronze bust of a freed slave blowing a conch shell commemorates slavery's end in 1848—the garden was built to mark emancipation's 150th anniversary in 1998. The gazebo here is used for official ceremonies. Two other monuments show the island's Danish-American connection—a bust of Denmark's King Christian and a scaled-down model of the U.S. Liberty Bell. ⊠ *Between Tolbod Gade and Fort Christian, next to Vendor's Plaza, Charlotte Amalie.*

Frederick Evangelical Lutheran Church. This historic church has a massive mahogany altar, and its pews—each with its own door—were once rented to families of the congregation. Lutheranism is the state religion of Denmark, and when the territory was without a minister, the governor—who had his own elevated pew—filled in. ⊠ *7 Norre Gade, across from Emancipation Garden and the Grand Hotel, Charlotte Amalie* 📞 *340/776–1315* ⊕ *www.felc1666.org* ⊗ *Mon.–Sat. 9–4.*

Government House. Built in 1867, this neoclassical white brick-and-wood structure houses the offices of the governor of the Virgin Islands. Inside, the staircases are of native mahogany, as are the plaques, hand-lettered in gold with the names of the governors appointed and, since 1970, elected. Brochures detailing the history of the building are available, but you may have to ask for them. ⊠ *Government Hill, 21–22 Kongens Gade, across from the Emancipation Garden post office, Charlotte Amalie* 📞 *340/774–0001* 🎫 *Free* ⊗ *Weekdays 8–5.*

Haagensen House. This lovingly restored house was built in the early 1800s by Danish entrepreneur Hans Haagensen. It's surrounded by an equally impressive cookhouse, outbuildings, and terraced gardens. A lower-level banquet hall showcases antique prints and photographs. A guided tour includes this property, plus other restored 19th-century houses, a rum factory, amber museum, and finally, the lookout tour at Blackbeard's Castle. ⊠ *Government Hill, 29-30 Kongens Gade, behind Hotel 1829, Charlotte Amalie* 📞 *340/776–1234* 🎫 *Tours $12.50* ⊗ *Nov.–Apr., Tues.–Thurs. 9–2.*

Legislature Building. Its bland exterior conceals the vociferous political wrangling of the Virgin Islands Senate. Constructed originally by the Danish as a police barracks, the building was later used to billet U.S. Marines, and much later it housed a public school. You're welcome to sit in on sessions in the upstairs chambers. ⊠ *Waterfront Hwy. (aka Rte. 30), across from Fort Christian, Charlotte Amalie* 📞 *340/774–0880* ⊕ *www.legvi.org* ⊗ *Daily 8–5.*

Magic Ice Gallery. This is one cool gallery! Life-size ice carvings feature sea life, a pirate ship, a chapel, a bar (a complimentary drink is included in the tour), a slide you can ride down, and much more. Insulated ponchos with hoods and mittens are provided, but you don't get to keep them. ⊠ *Charlotte Amalie Waterfront, 21 Dronningens Gade* ✛ *Next to the Pizza Hut on the Waterfront* 📞 *340/422–6000* ⊕ *www.magicice. vi* 🎫 *$22* ⊗ *Daily 10–5; Fri. 5–8 pm Happy Hour.*

Memorial Moravian Church. Built in 1884, this church was named to commemorate the 150th anniversary of the Moravian Church in the Virgin Islands. ⊠ *17 Norre Gade, next to Roosevelt Park, Charlotte Amalie* 📞 *340/776–0066* ⊕ *www.memorialmoravianvi.org* ⊗ *Weekdays 8–5.*

St. Thomas Historical Trust Museum. Tours of the museum take 30 minutes and include a wealth of pirate artifacts, as well as West Indian antique furniture, old-time postcards, and historic books. The Trust office, also located at the museum, is where you can book reservations for the one-hour historic Charlotte Amalie walking tour and three-hour Hassel Island tour, both of which have to be scheduled by appointment. ⊠ *West end of Roosevelt Park, Charlotte Amalie* ☎ *340/774–5541* ⊕ *www. stthomashistoricaltrust.org* ☉ *Wed. 10–2.*

St. Thomas Reformed Church. This church has an austere loveliness that's amazing considering all it's been through. Founded in 1744, it's been rebuilt twice after fires and hurricanes. The unembellished cream-color hall is quite peaceful. The only other color is the forest green of the shutters and the carpet. Call ahead if you wish to visit at a particular time, as the doors are sometimes locked. Services are held at 9 am each Sunday. ⊠ *5 Crystal Gade at Nye Gade, 1½ blocks north of Main St., Charlotte Amalie* ☎ *340/776–8255* ⊕ *www.stthomasreformedchurch. org* ☉ *Weekdays 9–5.*

Saints Peter and Paul Cathedral. This building was consecrated as a parish church in 1848, and serves as the seat of the territory's Roman Catholic diocese. The ceiling and walls are covered with a 11 murals depicting biblical scenes; they were painted in 1899 by two Belgian artists, Father Leo Servais and Brother Ildephonsus. The marble altar and walls were added in the 1960s. A $2 million restoration project completed in 2015 includes over a dozen statues of handcrafted saints representing the many nationalities of the congregants who worship here. ⊠ *22-AB Kronprindsens Gade, 1 block west of Market Sq., Charlotte Amalie* ☎ *340/774–0201* ⊕ *cathedralvi.com* ☉ *Mon.–Sat. 8–5.*

Synagogue of Beracha Veshalom Vegmiluth Hasidim. The synagogue's Hebrew name translates as the Congregation of Blessing, Peace, and Loving Deeds. The small building's white pillars contrast with rough stone walls, as does the rich mahogany of the pews and altar. The sand on the floor symbolizes the exodus from Egypt. Since the synagogue first opened its doors in 1833, it has held a weekly service, making it the oldest synagogue building in continuous use under the American flag and the second-oldest (after the one on Curaçao) in the western hemisphere. Guided tours can be arranged. Brochures detailing the key structures and history are also available. Next door the Weibel Museum showcases Jewish history on St. Thomas. ⊠ *Synagogue Hill, 15 Crystal Gade, Charlotte Amalie* ✧ *From Main St., walk up Raadet's Gade (H. Stern is on the corner) to the top of the hill, turn left and synagogue is the 2nd bldg. on right* ☎ *340/774–4312* ⊕ *www.synagogue.vi* ☉ *Weekdays 9–4.*

Weibel Museum. In this museum next to the Synagogue of Beracha Veshalom, 300 years of Jewish history on St. Thomas are showcased. The small gift shop sells a commemorative silver coin celebrating the anniversary of the Hebrew congregation's establishment on the island in 1796. There are also tropically inspired items, such as menorahs painted to resemble palm trees. ⊠ *Synagogue Hill, 15 Crystal Gade, Charlotte Amalie* ✧ *From Main St., walk up Raadet's Gade (H. Stern is on the*

19

Coral World Ocean Park offers interactive sea-life encounters.

corner) to the top of the hill, turn left and it's the 2nd bldg. on right ☎ *340/774–4312* ⊕ *synagogue.vi* ✉ *Free* ⊙ *Weekdays 9–4.*

EAST END

Although the eastern end has many major resorts and spectacular beaches, don't be surprised if a cow or a herd of goats crosses your path as you drive through the relatively flat, dry terrain.

TOP ATTRACTIONS

FAMILY

Fodor'sChoice

★

Coral World Ocean Park. This interactive aquarium and water-sports center lets you experience a variety of sea life and other animals. There's a new 2-acre dolphin habitat under construction, as well as several outdoor pools where you can pet baby sharks, feed stingrays, touch starfish, and view endangered sea turtles. During the Sea Trek Helmet Dive, you walk along an underwater trail wearing a helmet that provides a continuous supply of air. You can also try "snuba," a cross between snorkeling and scuba diving. Swim with a sea lion and have a chance at playing ball or getting a big, wet, whiskered kiss. You can also buy a cup of nectar and let the cheerful lorikeets perch on your hand and drink. The park also has an offshore underwater observatory, an 80,000-gallon coral reef exhibit (one of the largest in the world), and a nature trail with native ducks and tortoises. Daily feedings take place at most exhibits. ⊠ *Coki Point north of Rte. 38, 6450 Estate Smith Bay, Frydendal* ☎ *340/775–1555* ⊕ *www.coralworldvi.com* ✉ *$19 general admission; combination tickets from $41* ⊙ *Daily 9–4. Off-season (May–Oct.) hrs may vary, so call to confirm.*

WORTH NOTING

Red Hook. The IGY American Yacht Harbor marina here has fishing and sailing charter boats, a dive shop, and powerboat-rental agencies. There are also several bars and restaurants, including Molly Molone's, Fish Tails, Duffy's Love Shack, and the Caribbean Saloon. Ferries depart from Red Hook en route to St. John and the British Virgin Islands. ✉ *Red Hook, Intersection of Rtes. 38 and 32.*

SOUTH SHORE

TOP ATTRACTIONS

FAMILY **Skyride to Paradise Point.** Fly skyward in a seven-minute gondola ride to Paradise Point, an overlook with breathtaking views of Charlotte Amalie and the harbor. You'll find several shops, a bar, a restaurant, and a wedding gazebo. A ¼-mile (½-km) hiking trail leads to spectacular views of St. Croix. Wear sturdy shoes, as the trail is steep and rocky. You can also skip the $21 gondola ride and taxi to the top for $7 per person from the Havensight Dock. ✉ *Rte. 30, across from Havensight Mall, Havensight* ☏ *340/774–9809* ⊕ *www.ridetheview.com* 🎫 *$21* ⊙ *Thurs.–Tues. 9–5, Wed. 9–9.*

WORTH NOTING

FAMILY **Butterfly Garden.** Step into this 10,000-square-foot mesh enclosure and watch hundreds of colorful, exotic butterflies flutter all around you. A 25-minute tour takes you through their life cycle. Outside the enclosure, you can wander a garden of native plants designed to attract local butterflies and hummingbirds. The butterflies are most active in the morning. If you're a photographer, you'll probably prefer the afternoon, when the butterflies move more slowly and are more easily captured in pictures. ✉ *Havensight Mall, 9016 Havensight Mall, adjacent to West Indian Company cruise-ship dock, Havensight* ☏ *340/715–3366* ⊕ *www.butterflygardenvi.com* 🎫 *$12* ⊙ *Nov.–Apr. 8:30–4 on days a cruise ship is at the Havensight Dock. Off-season (May–Oct.) hrs may vary, so call to confirm.*

Frenchtown. Popular for its bars and restaurants, Frenchtown is also the home of descendants of immigrants from St. Barthélemy (St. Barth). You can watch them pull up their brightly painted boats and display their equally colorful catch of the day along the waterfront. If you chat with them, you can hear speech patterns slightly different from those of other St. Thomians. Get a feel for the residential district of Frenchtown by walking west to some of the town's winding streets, where tiny wooden houses have been passed down from generation to generation. ✉ *Turn south off Waterfront Hwy. (Rte. 30) at post office, Frenchtown.*

French Heritage Museum. Next to Joseph Aubain Ballpark, the museum houses fishing nets, accordions, tambourines, mahogany furniture, photographs, and other artifacts illustrating the lives of the French descendants during the 18th through 20th centuries. Admission is free, but donations are accepted. ✉ *Rue de St. Anne and rue de St. Barthélemy, next to Joseph Aubain Ballpark, Frenchtown* ☏ *340/714–2583* ⊕ *www.frenchheritagemuseum.com* 🎫 *Free* ⊙ *Weekdays 10–1.*

19

FAMILY   **Water Island.** This island, the fourth-largest of the U.S. Virgin Islands,
Fodor'sChoice   floats about a ¼ mile (½ km) out in Charlotte Amalie harbor. A ferry
★   between Crown Bay Marina and the island operates several times daily
Monday through Saturday 6:30–6 and Sunday and holidays 8–5 at a cost
of $10 round-trip. From the ferry dock, it's a hike of less than a half-mile
to Honeymoon Beach (though you have to go up a big hill), where Brad
Pitt and Cate Blanchett filmed a scene of the movie *The Curious Case
of Benjamin Button.* Get lunch from a food truck that pulls up daily.
Monday night is Movie Night at Honeymoon Beach, a fun activity for
the whole family after a day on the beach. ⊠ *Charlotte Amalie harbor,
Charlotte Amalie* ☎ *340/690–4159 for ferry information.*

WEST END

WORTH NOTING

Drake's Seat. Sir Francis Drake was supposed to have kept watch over his
fleet, looking for enemy ships from this vantage point. The panorama
is especially breathtaking (and romantic) at dusk, and if you arrive late
in the day, you can miss the hordes of day-trippers on taxi tours who
stop here to take pictures. ⊠ *Rte. 40, located ¼ mile (½ km) west of
the intersection of Rtes. 40 and 35, Mafolie.*

Estate St. Peter Greathouse and Botanical Gardens. This unusual spot is
perched on a mountainside 1,000 feet above sea level, with views of
more than 20 islands and islets. You can wander through a gallery displaying local art, sip a complimentary rum punch while looking out at
the view, or follow a nature trail that leads you past nearly 70 varieties
of tropical plants, including 17 varieties of orchids. ⊠ *Rte. 40, directly
across from Tree Limin' Extreme Zipline, Estate St. Peter* ☎ *340/774–
4999* ⊕ *www.greathousevi.com* ☑ *$8* ☉ *Daily 9–5.*

FAMILY   **Mountain Top.** Head out to the observation deck—more than 1,500 feet
above sea level—to get a bird's-eye view that stretches from Puerto Rico's
out-island of Culebra in the west all the way to the British Virgin Islands
in the east. There's also a restaurant, restrooms, and duty-free shops that
sell everything from Caribbean art to nautical antiques, ship models,
and touristy T-shirts. Kids will like talking to the parrots—and hearing
them answer back. ⊠ *Head north off Rte. 33, look for signs, Estate St.
Peter* ☎ *340/774–2400* ⊕ *www.mountaintopvi.com* ☑ *Free* ☉ *Daily 8–5.*

BEACHES

All 44 St. Thomas beaches are open to the public, although you can
reach some of them only by walking through a resort. Hotel guests
frequently have access to lounge chairs and floats that are off-limits to
nonguests; for this reason you may feel more comfortable at one of the
beaches not associated with a resort, such as Magens Bay or Lindquist
Beach (which both charge an entrance fee to cover beach maintenance)
or Coki Beach, the latter abutting Coral World Ocean Park and offering the island's best off-the-beach snorkeling. Remember to remove all
your valuables from the car and keep them out of sight when you go
swimming. Break-ins are possible on all three of the U.S. Virgin Islands;
most locals recommend leaving your windows down and leaving absolutely nothing in your car.

EAST END

FAMILY
Fodor's Choice
★
Coki Beach. Funky beach huts selling local foods such as pâtés (fried turnovers with a spicy ground-beef filling), quaint vendor kiosks, and a brigade of hair braiders and taxi men make this beach overlooking picturesque Thatch Cay feel like a carnival. But this is the best place on the island to snorkel and scuba dive. Fish, including grunts, snappers, and wrasses, are like an effervescent cloud you can wave your hand through. **Amenities:** food and drink; lifeguards; parking; restrooms; showers; water sports. **Best for:** partiers; snorkeling. ⊠ *Rte. 388, next to Coral World Ocean Park, Estate Smith Bay.*

Fodor's Choice
★
Lindquist Beach. The newest of the Virgin Islands' public beaches has a serene sense of wilderness that isn't found on the more crowded beaches. A lifeguard is on duty between 8 am and 5 pm. Picnic tables are available. Try snorkeling over the offshore reef. **Amenities:** lifeguards; parking; showers; toilets. **Best for:** snorkeling; solitude. ⊠ *Rte. 38, at end of a bumpy road past the paved parking lot* ⌂ *$4 per person; $2 per vehicle to park.*

FAMILY
Sapphire Beach. A steady breeze makes this beach a boardsailor's paradise. The swimming is great, as is the snorkeling, especially at the reef near Pettyklip Point. Beach volleyball is big on the weekends. Sapphire Beach Resort and Marina has a snack shop, a bar, and water-sports rentals. **Amenities:** parking; restrooms. **Best for:** snorkeling; swimming; windsurfing. ⊠ *Rte. 38, ½ mile (1 km) north of Red Hook, Sapphire Bay.*

Secret Harbour. Placid waters make it easy to stroke your way out to a swim platform offshore from the Secret Harbour Beach Resort & Villas. Nearby reefs give snorkelers a natural show. There's a bar and restaurant, as well as a dive shop. **Amenities:** food and drink; parking; restrooms; water sports. **Best for:** snorkeling; sunset; swimming. ⊠ *Rte. 322, take first right off Rte. 322, Red Hook.*

Vessup Beach. This wild, undeveloped beach is lined with sea grape trees and century plants. It's close to Red Hook harbor, so you can watch the ferries depart. The calm waters are excellent for swimming. It's popular with locals on weekends. **Amenities:** parking; water sports. **Best for:** swimming. ⊠ *Off Rte. 322, Nazareth.*

SOUTH SHORE

Brewers Beach. Watch jets land at the Cyril E. King Airport as you dip into the usually calm seas. Rocks at either end of the shoreline, patches of grass poking randomly through the sand, and shady tamarind trees 30 feet from the water give this beach a wild, natural feel. Civilization has arrived, in the form of one or two mobile food vans parked on the nearby road. Buy a fried-chicken leg and johnnycake or burgers and chips to munch on at the picnic tables. **Amenities:** food and drink; lifeguards; parking; restrooms. **Best for:** sunset; swimming. ⊠ *Rte. 30, west of University of the Virgin Islands.*

FAMILY
Fodor's Choice
★
Magens Bay. Deeded to the island as a public park, this heart-shape stretch of white sand is considered one of the most beautiful in the world. The bottom of the bay is flat and sandy, so this is a place for sunning and swimming rather than snorkeling. On weekends and holidays the sounds of music from groups partying under the sheds fill the air.

19

There's a bar, snack shack, and beachwear boutique; and bathhouses with restrooms, changing rooms, and saltwater showers are close by. Sunfish, kayaks, and paddleboards are the most popular rentals at the watersports kiosk. East of the beach is Famous Delite (formerly Udder Delite), a one-room shop that serves a Virgin Islands tradition—a milk shake with a splash of Cruzan rum. (Kids can enjoy virgin versions, which have a touch of soursop, mango, or banana flavoring). If you arrive between 8 am and 5 pm, you pay an entrance fee of $4 per person, $2 per vehicle; it's free for children under 12. **Amenities:** food and drink; lifeguards; parking (fee); restrooms; showers; water sports. **Best for:** partiers; swimming; walking. ⊠ *Magens Bay, Rte. 35, at end of road on north side of island* ☎ *340/777–6300* ⊕ *www.magensbayauthority.com.*

Morningstar Beach. At this ¼-mile-long (½-km-long) beach at the Frenchman's Reef and Morning Star Marriott Beach Resort, amenities include beachside bar service. A concession rents floating mats, snorkeling equipment, sailboards, and Jet Skis. Swimming is excellent; there are good-size rolling waves year-round, but do watch the undertow. If you're feeling lazy, rent a lounge chair with umbrella and order a libation from one of two full-service beach bars. At 7 am and again at 5 pm, you can catch the cruise ships gliding majestically out to sea from the Charlotte Amalie harbor. **Amenities:** food and drink; parking; restrooms; water sports. **Best for:** partiers; surfing; swimming. ⊠ *Rte. 315* ⊹ *2 miles (3 km) southeast of Charlotte Amalie, past Havensight Mall and cruise-ship dock.*

WHERE TO EAT

The beauty of St. Thomas and its sister islands has attracted a cadre of professionally trained chefs who know their way around fresh fish and local fruits. You can dine on terrific cheap local dishes such as goat water (a spicy stew) and fungi (a cornmeal side dish that's similar to polenta) as well as imports that include hot pastrami sandwiches and raspberries in crème fraîche.

Restaurants are spread all over, although fewer are found on the west and northwest parts of the island. Most restaurants out of town are easily accessible by taxi and have ample parking. If you dine in Charlotte Amalie, take a taxi. Parking close to restaurants can be difficult to find, and walking around after dark isn't always safe.

If your accommodations have a kitchen and you plan to cook, there's good variety in St. Thomas's mainland-style supermarkets. Just be prepared for grocery prices that are about 20% to 30% higher than those in the United States. As for drinking, a beer in a bar that's not part of a hotel will cost between $5 and $6 and a piña colada $8 or more.

What to Wear: Dining on St. Thomas is informal. Few restaurants require a jacket and tie. Still, at dinner in the snazzier places shorts and T-shirts are inappropriate; men would do well to wear slacks and a shirt with buttons. Dress codes on St. Thomas rarely require women to wear skirts, but you can never go wrong with something flowing.

CHARLOTTE AMALIE

$$$$
ECLECTIC
Fodor's Choice
★

✗ **Banana Tree Grille.** The eagle's-eye view of the Charlotte Amalie harbor from this breeze-cooled restaurant is as fantastic as the food. Linen tablecloths, china, and silver place settings combine with subdued lighting to make an elegant space. To start, try plump escargots in an arugula-garlic pesto sauce or crispy calamari dipped in tangy lemon aioli. The signature dish here—and worthy of its fame—is a grass-fed pasture-raised filet mignon topped with plump shrimp and served with velvety béarnaise sauce and fresh asparagus. Arrive before 6 pm to watch the cruise ships depart from the harbor while you enjoy a drink at the bar. $ *Average main: $42* ⊠ *Bluebeard's Castle, Bluebeard's Hill, 1331 Estate Taamburg, Charlotte Amalie* ☎ *340/776–4050* ⊕ *www.bananatreegrille.com* ☾ *Closed Mon. No lunch* ⚑ *Reservations essential.*

$$
CARIBBEAN

✗ **Cuzzin's Caribbean Restaurant and Bar.** In a 19th-century livery stable on Back Street, this restaurant is hard to find but well worth it if you want to sample bona fide Virgin Islands cuisine. For lunch, order tender slivers of conch stewed in a rich onion-and-butter sauce, shrimp creole, or savory stewed chicken. At dinner the island-style mutton, served in thick gravy and seasoned with locally grown herbs, offers a tasty treat that's deliciously different. Side dishes include peas and rice, boiled green bananas, fried plantains, and potato stuffing. $ *Average main: $15* ⊠ *7 Wimmelskafts Gade, also called Back St., Charlotte Amalie* ☎ *340/777–4711* ⊕ *cuzzinsvi.com* ☾ *Closed Sun.*

$$
CARIBBEAN
Fodor's Choice
★

✗ **Gladys' Cafe.** Even if the local specialties—conch in butter sauce, jerk pork, panfried yellowtail snapper—didn't make this a recommended café, it would be worth coming for Gladys's smile. Her cozy alleyway restaurant is rich in atmosphere with its mahogany bar and native stone walls, making dining a double delight. While you're here, pick up a $5 or $10 bottle of her special hot sauce. There are mustard-, oil and vinegar–, and tomato-based versions; the tomato-based sauce is the hottest. $ *Average main: $14* ⊠ *Waterfront, 28A Dronningens Gade, west side of Royal Dane Mall, Charlotte Amalie* ☎ *340/774–6604* ⊕ *www.gladyscafe.com* ☾ *No dinner* ⚑ *Only Amex credit cards accepted.*

$$
AMERICAN
FAMILY

✗ **Greenhouse Bar and Restaurant.** Fun-lovers come to this waterfront restaurant to eat, listen to music, and play games, both video and pool. Even the most finicky eater should find something to please on the eight-page menu that offers burgers, salads, and pizza served all day long, along with peel-and-eat shrimp, Caribbean lobster tail, Alaskan king crab, and Black Angus filet mignon for dinner. This is generally a family-friendly place, though the Two-for-Tuesdays happy hour and Friday-night live reggae music that starts thumping at 10 pm draw an occasionally rambunctious young-adult crowd. $ *Average main: $18* ⊠ *Waterfront Hwy. at Storetvaer Gade, Charlotte Amalie* ☎ *340/774–7998* ⊕ *www.thegreenhouserestaurant.com.*

$$$$
ITALIAN

✗ **Virgilio's.** For the island's best northern Italian cuisine, don't miss this intimate, elegant hideaway that's on a quiet side street. Eclectic art covers the two-story brick walls, and the sound of opera sets the stage for a memorable meal. Come here for more than 40 homemade pastas topped with superb sauces—capellini with fresh tomatoes and

19

CLOSE UP

Where to Shop for Groceries

High food prices in Virgin Islands supermarkets are enough to dull anyone's appetite. According to a report by the U.S. Virgin Islands Department of Labor, food is significantly more expensive than on the mainland.

Although you'll never match the prices back home, you can shop around for the best deals. If you're traveling with a group, it pays to stock up on the basics at warehouse-style stores like Pricesmart (membership required) and Cost-U-Less. Even the nonbulk food items here are sold at lower prices than in the supermarkets or convenience stores. Good buys include beverages, meats, produce, and spirits.

After this, head to supermarkets such as Plaza Extra, Pueblo, and Food Center. Although the prices aren't as good as at the big-box stores, the selection is better.

Finally, if you want to splurge on top-quality meats, exotic produce and spices, and imported cheeses and spirits, finish off your shopping at high-end shops such as Moe's Fresh Market or Gourmet Gallery.

The Fruit Bowl is the place for fresh produce. The prices and selection are unbeatable.

For really fresh tropical fruits, vegetables, and seasoning herbs, visit the farmers' markets in Smith Bay (daily), at Market Square (daily), at Yacht Haven Grande (first and third Sunday of the month), and in Estate Bordeaux (second and fourth Sunday of every month).

garlic or peasant-style spaghetti in a rich tomato sauce with mushrooms and prosciutto. House specialties include osso buco and tiramisu, which are expertly crafted by chef Ernesto Garrigos, who has prepared these two dishes on the Discovery Channel's *Great Chefs of the World* series. $ *Average main: $36* ⊠ *18 Dronningens Gade, Charlotte Amalie* ☎ *340/776–4920* ⊕ *www.virgiliosvi.com* ⊙ *Closed Sun.* ⌂ *Reservations essential.*

EAST END

$$$ ✕**Caribbean Saloon.** Sports on wide-screen TVs and live music on week-
AMERICAN   ends are two added attractions at this hip sports bar that's in the center of the action in Red Hook. The menu ranges from finger-licking barbecue ribs to more sophisticated fare, such as the signature filet mignon wrapped in bacon and smothered in melted Gorgonzola cheese. There's always a catch of the day; the fishing fleet is only steps away. A late-night menu is available from 10 pm until 4 am. $ *Average main: $28* ⊠ *American Yacht Harbor, Bldg. B, Rte. 32, Red Hook* ☎ *340/775–7060* ⊕ *www.caribbeansaloon.com.*

$$ ✕**Duffy's Love Shack.** If the floating bubbles don't attract you to this
ECLECTIC   zany eatery, the lime-green shutters, loud rock music, and fun-loving waitstaff just might. It's billed as the "ultimate tropical drink shack," and the bartenders shake up such exotic concoctions as the Love Shack Volcano—a 50-ounce flaming extravaganza. The menu has a selection of burgers, tacos, burritos, and salads. Try the grilled fish tacos or Caribbean Pu-Pu platter that includes conch fritters, coconut shrimp,

and Puerto Rican–style *piononos* (sweet plantains stuffed with savory meat or cheese and deep fried). [$] *Average main: $15* ✉ *Red Hook Shopping Center, Rte. 32 and 6500 Red Hook Plaza, located in the parking lot, Red Hook* ☎ *340/779–2080* 🌐 *www.duffysloveshack.com.*

$$$ IRISH FAMILY 🍴 **Molly Molones.** This dockside eatery has a devoted following among local boaters, who swear by the traditional American and Irish fare. Opt for eggs Benedict or rashers of Irish sausages and eggs for breakfast, or fork into fish-and-chips, cottage pie, or corned beef and cabbage for lunch or dinner. Beware: the resident iguanas will beg for table scraps—bring your camera. [$] *Average main: $24* ✉ *American Yacht Harbor, Bldg. D, Rte. 32, Red Hook* ☎ *340/775–1270* 🌐 *www.mollymolonesusvi.com/.*

$$$$ ECLECTIC Fodor's Choice ★ 🍴 **Old Stone Farmhouse.** Dine in the splendor of a beautifully restored plantation house. Come early and sidle up to the beautiful mahogany bar, where you can choose from an extensive wine list. Then start with a first course of spicy Crab cakes or zesty PEI mussels, move on to a butter-soft Hereford beef fillet, braised short ribs with sweet and savory sides of yams, broccolini and mushrooms or a peppercorn crusted locally caught tuna steak, and finish with a thick, rich pineapple crème brûlée. Exotic meats such as camel and kangaroo are available on the special Butcher's Block entrée selections. Personalized attention makes dining here a delight. [$] *Average main: $36* ✉ *Rte. 42, 1 mile (1½ km) west of entrance to Mahogany Run Golf Course, Lovenlund* ☎ *340/777–6277* 🌐 *oldstonefarmhouse.com* ⏲ *Closed Mon.* ✍ *Reservations essential.*

SOUTH SHORE

$$$$ ECLECTIC Fodor's Choice ★ 🍴 **Havana Blue.** The cuisine here is described as Latin America meets Pacific Rim, but however you describe it, the dining experience is outstanding. A glowing wall of water meets you as you enter this beachfront eatery, and then you're seated at a table laid with linen and silver that's illuminated in a soft blue light radiating from above. Be sure to sample the mango mojito, made with fresh mango, crushed mint, and limes. Entrées include mojito-glazed fork tender skirt steak, chile-blackened ahi tuna, and sofrito-marinated chicken breast. Hand-rolled cigars and aged rums finish the night off in true Latin style. For something really special, request an exclusive table for two set on Morning Star Beach—you get a seven-course tasting menu, champagne, and your own personal waiter, all for $375 for two. [$] *Average main: $36* ✉ *Marriott Morningstar Beach Resort, Rte. 315, 2nd fl., above front desk, Estate Bakkero* ☎ *340/715–2583* 🌐 *www.havanabluerestaurant.com* ⏲ *No lunch* ✍ *Reservations essential.*

WEST END

$$$ AUSTRIAN 🍴 **Bella Blu.** In a quaint building in Frenchtown, this place has an ever-changing display of local art on the walls and delicious specials to match. The Austrian-inspired menu includes five varieties of schnitzel and boasts a Caribbean flair with fresh-fish dishes such as house-specialty snapper Provençal. Lunchtime attracts a business crowd that breaks bread and brokers deals at the same time. Fork into omelets, pancakes, or waffles during Saturday's jazz brunch from 10 am to 3

pm. $ *Average main: $27* ✉ *Frenchtown Mall, 24-A Honduras St., across from the ballpark, Frenchtown* ☎ *340/774–4349* ⊕ *www. bellabludining.com* ☉ *Closed Sun.* ⌔ *Reservations essential.*

$$$ ✕ **Hook, Line and Sinker.** Anchored on the breezy Frenchtown water-
SEAFOOD   front and close to the pastel-painted boats of the local fishing fleet, this
FAMILY   harbor-view eatery serves high-quality fish dishes. The almond-crusted
            yellowtail snapper is a house specialty. Spicy jerk-seasoned swordfish
            and grilled tuna topped with a yummy mango-rum sauce are also good
            bets. This is one of the few independent restaurants serving Sunday
            brunch. $ *Average main: $24* ✉ *Frenchtown Mall, 2 Honduras St., at
            the head of the Frenchtown Marina docks, Frenchtown* ☎ *340/776–
            9708* ⊕ *www.hooklineandsinkervi.com.*

$$ ✕ **Tickles Dockside Pub.** Nautical types as well as the local working crowd
AMERICAN   come here for casual fare with homey appeal: chicken-fried steak, meat
FAMILY   loaf with mashed potatoes, and baby back ribs. Hearty breakfasts fea-
            ture eggs and pancakes, and lunch is a full array of burgers, salads,
            sandwiches, and soups. From November through April, the adjacent
            marina is full of enormous yachts, which make for some great eye
            candy while you dine. $ *Average main: $17* ✉ *Crown Bay Marina,
            8168 Crown Bay Marina, Ste. 308, off Rte. 304, Contant* ☎ *340/777–
            8792* ⊕ *ticklesdocksidepub.com.*

WHERE TO STAY

Of the USVI, St. Thomas has the most rooms and the greatest number and variety of resorts. You can let yourself be pampered at a luxuri-ous resort—albeit at a price of $400 to more than $600 per night, not including meals. For much less, there are fine hotels (often with rooms that have a kitchen and a living area) in lovely settings throughout the island. There are also guesthouses and inns with great views and great service at about half the cost of what you'll pay at the beachfront pleasure palaces. Many of these are east and north of Charlotte Amalie or overlooking hills—ideal if you plan to get out and mingle with the locals. There are also inexpensive lodgings (most right in town) that are perfect if you just want a clean room to return to after a day of exploring or beach bumming.

East End condominium complexes are popular with families. Although condos are pricey (winter rates average $350 per night for a two-bed-room unit, which usually sleeps six), they have full kitchens, and you can definitely save money by cooking for yourself—especially if you bring some of your own nonperishable foodstuffs. (Virtually everything on St. Thomas is imported, and restaurants and shops pass shipping costs on to you.) Though you may spend some time laboring in the kitchen, many condos ease your burden with daily maid service and on-site restaurants; a few also have resort amenities, including pools and tennis courts. The East End is convenient to St. John, and it's a hub for the boating crowd, with some good restaurants. *The prices below reflect rates in high season, which runs from December 15 to April 15. Rates are 25% to 50% lower the rest of the year.*

PRIVATE VILLAS AND CONDOMINIUMS

St. Thomas has a wide range of private villas. Most will require that you book for seven nights during high season, five in low season. A minimum stay of up to two weeks is often required during the Christmas season. The agents who represent villa owners usually have websites and brochures that show photos of the properties they represent. Private owners make their villas available on ⊕ *www.vrbo.com*, so this is a great site for island villas and condos in all price ranges. Some villas are suitable for travelers with disabilities, but be sure to ask specific questions about your own needs.

RENTAL CONTACTS

Calypso Realty. ☎ *340/774–1620, 800/747–4858* ⊕ *www.calypsorealty.com.*

McLaughlin-Anderson Luxury Caribbean Villas. Handling rental villas throughout the U.S. Virgin Islands, British Virgin Islands, and Grenada, McLaughlin-Anderson has a good selection of complexes in St. Thomas's East End. ☎ *340/776–0635, 800/537–6246* ⊕ *www. mclaughlinanderson.com.*

CHARLOTTE AMALIE

Accommodations in and near town mean that you're close to the airport, shopping, and a number of restaurants. The downside is that this is the most crowded and noisy area of the island. Crime can also be a problem. Don't go for a stroll at night in the heart of town. Use common sense and take the same precautions you would in any major city. Properties along the hillsides are less likely to have crime problems, and they also get a steady breeze from the cool trade winds. This is especially important if you're visiting in summer and early fall.

$

HOTEL

🖬 **The Green Iguana.** Atop Blackbeard's Hill, this value-priced small hotel offers the perfect mix of gorgeous harbor views, proximity to shopping (five-minute walk), and secluded privacy provided by the surrounding showy trees and bushy hibiscus. **Pros:** personalized service; near the center of town; laundry on premises. **Cons:** need a car to get around; town may be noisy at night depending on seasonal events. $ *Rooms from: $150* ⊠ *1002 Blackbeard's Hill, Charlotte Amalie* ☎ *340/776–7654, 855/473–4733* ⊕ *www.thegreeniguana.com* ⥱ *9 rooms* ⦿*No meals.*

$

HOTEL

Fodor's Choice

★

🖬 **Villa Santana.** Built by exiled General Antonio López Santa Anna of Mexico, this 1857 landmark provides a panoramic view of the harbor and plenty of West Indian charm, which will make you feel as if you're living in a charming slice of Virgin Islands history. **Pros:** historic charm; plenty of privacy. **Cons:** not on a beach; no restaurant; need a car to get around. $ *Rooms from: $170* ⊠ *2602 Bjerge Gade, 2D Denmark Hill, Charlotte Amalie* ☎ *340/776–1311* ⊕ *www.villasantana.com* ⥱ *6 rooms* ⦿*No meals.*

$

HOTEL

🖬 **Windward Passage Hotel.** Business travelers, tourists on their way to the British Virgin Islands, and laid-back vacationers who want the convenience of being able to walk to duty-free shopping, sights, and restaurants stay at this harbor-front hotel. **Pros:** walking distance to Charlotte Amalie; nice harbor views; across from BVI ferry terminal. **Cons:** basic rooms; on a busy street; no water sports, but dive shop is on property. $ *Rooms from: $220* ⊠ *Waterfront Hwy., Charlotte*

19

The Ritz-Carlton St. Thomas

Amalie ☎ *340/774–5200, 800/524–7389* 🌐 *www.windwardpassage.com* 🛏 *140 rooms, 11 suites* 🍴 *No meals.*

EAST END

You can find most of the large, luxurious beachfront resorts on St. Thomas's East End. The downside is that these properties are about a 30-minute drive from town and a 45-minute drive from the airport (substantially longer during peak hours). On the upside, they tend to be self-contained, plus there are a number of good restaurants, shops, and water-sports operators in the area. Once you've settled in, you don't need a car to get around.

$$$$ RESORT FAMILY 🏨 **Dreams Sugar Bay St. Thomas.** This family-friendly, all-inclusive resort is unmistakable for its terra-cotta high-rise accommodations surrounded by palm trees and lush greenery. **Pros:** gorgeous pool area; full-service spa; on-site casino. **Cons:** some steps to climb; lawn by pool teems with iguanas; limited dining options. [$] *Rooms from: $750* ✉ *6500 Estate Smith Bay, Estate Smith Bay* ☎ *340/777–7100, 800/927–7100* 🌐 *www.dreamsresorts.com* 🛏 *297 guest rooms and suites* 🍴 *All-inclusive.*

$$ RENTAL 🏨 **Pavilions and Pools Villa Hotel.** Perfect for couples craving privacy, the villas here have full kitchens, lots of space, and sunken garden showers. **Pros:** intimate atmosphere; friendly host; private pools. **Cons:** on a busy road; long walk to beach; rooms could use a bit of refurbishment. [$] *Rooms from: $300* ✉ *6400 Estate Smith Bay, off Rte. 38, Estate Smith Bay* ☎ *340/775–6110, 800/524–2001* 🌐 *www.pavilionsandpools.com* 🛏 *25 1-bedroom villas* 🍴 *Breakfast.*

$$
RESORT
🏨 **Point Pleasant Resort.** Hilltop suites give you an eagle's-eye view of the East End and beyond, and those in a building adjacent to the reception area offer incredible sea views. **Pros:** lush setting; convenient kitchens; pleasant pools. **Cons:** steep climb from beach; need a car to get around; some rooms need refurbishing. $ *Rooms from: $320* ✉ *6600 Estate Smith Bay, off Rte. 38, Estate Smith Bay* ☎ *340/775–7200, 888/619–4010* ⊕ *www.pointpleasantresort.com* 🛏 *128 suites* ⏐⊘ *No meals.*

$$$$
RESORT
FAMILY
🏨 **Ritz-Carlton, St. Thomas.** Everything sparkles at the island's most luxurious resort, from the in-room furnishings and amenities to the infinity pool, white-sand, eco-friendly Blue Flag–designated beach, and turquoise sea beyond. **Pros:** gorgeous views; great water-sports facilities; beautiful beach; airport shuttle. **Cons:** service can sometimes be spotty for such an upscale (and pricey) hotel; food and drink can lack flair and are expensive ($19 hamburger, $12 piña colada); half-hour or more drive to town and airport. $ *Rooms from: $680* ✉ *6900 Estate Great Bay, off Rte. 317, Estate Great Bay* ☎ *340/775–3333, 800/241–3333* ⊕ *www.ritzcarlton.com* 🛏 *255 rooms, 20 suites, 2 villas, 81 condos* ⏐⊘ *No meals.*

$$$
RENTAL
🏨 **Secret Harbour Beach Resort.** There's not a bad view from these low-rise studios and one- and two-bedroom condos, which are either beachfront or perched on a hill overlooking an inviting cove. **Pros:** beautiful beach and great snorkeling; good restaurant; secluded location. **Cons:** car needed to get around; condo owners are territorial about beach chairs. $ *Rooms from: $420* ✉ *Rte. 317, Nazareth* ☎ *340/775–6550, 800/524–2250* ⊕ *www.secretharbourvi.com* 🛏 *73 suites* ⏐⊘ *No meals.*

SOUTH SHORE

The South Shore of St. Thomas connects town to the East End of the island via a beautiful road that rambles along the hillside with frequent peeks between the hills for a view of the ocean and, on a clear day, of St. Croix some 40 miles (64 km) to the south. The resorts here are on their own beaches. They offer several opportunities for water sports, as well as land-based activities, fine dining, and evening entertainment.

$$$
RESORT
🏨 **Bolongo Bay Beach Resort.** All the rooms at this family-run resort tucked along a 1,000-foot-long palm-lined beach have balconies with ocean views; down the beach are nine condos with full kitchens. **Pros:** family-run property; on the beach; water sports abound. **Cons:** a bit run-down; on a busy road; need a car to get around. $ *Rooms from: $385* ✉ *Rte. 30, Bolongo* ☎ *340/775–1800, 800/524–4746* ⊕ *www.bolongobay.com* 🛏 *71 rooms, 9 condos* ⏐⊘ *No meals.*

$$$
RESORT
FAMILY
🏨 **Frenchman's Reef & Morning Star Marriott Beach Resort.** Set majestically on a promontory overlooking the east side of Charlotte Amalie's harbor, Frenchman's Reef is a high-rise, full-service super-hotel; Morning Star is the even more upscale boutique property that's closer to the fine white-sand beach. **Pros:** beachfront location; good dining options; plenty of activities. **Cons:** musty smell on lower levels; long walk between resorts; a crowded-cruise-ship feel. $ *Rooms from: $475* ✉ *Rte. 315, Estate Bakkero* ☎ *340/776–8500, 800/233–6388* ⊕ *www.marriott.com* 🛏 *479 rooms, 27 suites, 220 2- and 3-bedroom time-share units* ⏐⊘ *No meals.*

19

WEST END

A few properties are in the hills overlooking Charlotte Amalie to the west or near French Town, which is otherwise primarily residential.

$ | **Emerald Beach Resort.** You get beachfront ambience at this reasonably
HOTEL | priced mini resort tucked beneath the palm trees, but the trade-off is that it's directly across from a noisy airport runway. **Pros:** beachfront location; good value; great Sunday brunch. **Cons:** airport noise until 10 pm; on a busy road; limited water sports. $ *Rooms from: $260* ☒ *8070 Lindberg Bay, Lindbergh Bay* ☎ *340/777–8800, 800/780–7234* ⊕ *www.emeraldbeach.com* ⇆ *90 rooms* ⦿ *Breakfast.*

$ | **Island View Guesthouse.** Perched 545 feet up the face of Crown Moun-
B&B/INN | tain, this small, homey inn has hands-on owners who can book tours or offer tips about the best sightseeing spots. **Pros:** spectacular views; friendly atmosphere; good value. **Cons:** small pool; need a car to get around. $ *Rooms from: $150* ☒ *Rte. 332, Contant* ☎ *340/774–4270, 800/524–2023* ⊕ *www.islandviewstthomas.com* ⇆ *12 rooms, 10 with bath* ⦿ *Breakfast.*

NIGHTLIFE AND PERFORMING ARTS

On any given night, especially in season, you can find steel-pan bands, rock and roll, piano music, jazz, broken-bottle dancing (actual dancing atop broken glass), disco, and karaoke. Pick up a free copy of the bright yellow *St. Thomas–St. John This Week* magazine (⊕ *www. virginislandsthisweek.com*) when you arrive (it can be found at the airport, in stores, and in hotel lobbies). The back pages list who's playing where. The Friday edition of the *Daily News* carries complete listings for the upcoming weekend.

NIGHTLIFE

CHARLOTTE AMALIE

Greenhouse Bar and Restaurant. Once this popular eatery puts away the salt-and-pepper shakers after 10 pm, it becomes a rock-and-roll club with a DJ or live reggae bands bringing the weary to their feet six nights a week. ☒ *Waterfront Hwy., at Storetvaer Gade, Charlotte Amalie* ☎ *340/774–7998* ⊕ *www.thegreenhouserestaurant.com.*

EAST END

Duffy's Love Shack. At this island favorite, funky cocktails, a loud sound system, and dancing under the stars are the big draws for locals and visitors alike. ☒ *Red Hook Plaza, Rte. 32, Red Hook* ☎ *340/779–2080* ⊕ *www.duffysloveshack.com.*

SOUTH SHORE

Epernay Bistro & Wine Bar. Sometimes you need nothing more than small tables for easy chatting and wine and champagne by the glass. You can also mix and mingle with island celebrities here. The action at this intimate restaurant and nightspot runs from 4 pm until the wee hours Monday through Saturday. ☒ *Frenchtown Mall, 24-A Honduras St., Frenchtown* ☎ *340/774–5348* ⊕ *www.epernaystthomas.com.*

FAMILY | **Iggies Beach Bar.** Bolongo Bay's beachside bar offers karaoke on Saturday nights, so you can sing along to the sounds of the surf or the latest hits here. There's live music nightly, and you can dance inside or kick up your heels under the stars. On Wednesday it's Carnival Night, complete with steel-pan music, a limbo show, and a West Indian buffet. ⊠ *Bolongo Bay Beach Club & Villas, Rte. 30, Bolongo* ☎ *340/775–1800* ⊕ *www.iggiesbeachbar.com.*

PERFORMING ARTS

SOUTH SHORE

FAMILY

Fodor'sChoice

★

Pistarkle Theater. This theater in the Tillett Gardens complex is air-conditioned and has more than 100 seats; it hosts a half-dozen productions annually, plus a children's summer drama camp. ⊠ *Tillett Gardens, Rte. 38, across from Tutu Park Shopping Mall, Tutu* ☎ *340/775–7877* ⊕ *pistarckletheater.com.*

FAMILY

Fodor'sChoice

★

Reichhold Center for the Arts. St. Thomas's major performing arts center has an amphitheater, and its more expensive seats are covered by a roof. Throughout the year there's an entertaining mix of local plays, dance exhibitions, and music of all types. ⊠ *Rte. 30, across from Brewers Beach, Estate Lindberg Bay* ☎ *340/693–1559* ⊕ *www.reichholdcenter.com.*

SHOPPING

Fodor'sChoice

★

St. Thomas lives up to its billing as a duty-free shopping destination. Even if shopping isn't your idea of how to spend a vacation, you still may want to slip in on a quiet day (check the cruise-ship listings—Monday and Sunday are usually the least crowded) to browse. Among the best buys are liquor, linens, china, crystal (most stores will ship), and jewelry. The amount of jewelry available makes this one of the few items for which comparison shopping is worth the effort. Local crafts include shell jewelry, carved calabash bowls, straw brooms, woven baskets, and dolls. Spice mixes, hot sauces, and tropical jams and jellies are other native products.

On St. Thomas stores on Main Street in Charlotte Amalie are open weekdays and Saturday 9 to 5. The hours of the shops in the Havensight Mall (next to the cruise-ship dock) and the Crown Bay Commercial Center (next to the Crown Bay cruise-ship dock) are the same, though occasionally some stay open until 9 on Friday, depending on how many cruise ships are anchored nearby. You may also find some shops open on Sunday if cruise ships are in port. Hotel shops are usually open evenings as well.

There's no sales tax in the USVI, and you can take advantage of the $1,200 duty-free allowance per family member (remember to save your receipts). Although you can find the occasional salesclerk who will make a deal, bartering isn't the norm.

CHARLOTTE AMALIE

The prime shopping area in **Charlotte Amalie** is between Post Office and Market squares; it consists of two parallel streets that run east–west (Waterfront Highway and Main Street) and the alleyways that connect them. Particularly attractive are the historic **A.H. Riise Alley, Drake's Passage, Royal Dane Mall, Palm Passage,** and pastel-painted **International Plaza.**

19

Vendors Plaza, on the waterfront side of Emancipation Gardens in Charlotte Amalie, is a central location for vendors selling handmade earrings, necklaces, and bracelets; straw baskets and handbags; T-shirts; fabrics; African artifacts; and local fruits. Look for the many brightly colored umbrellas.

ART

Camille Pissarro Art Gallery. This second-floor gallery, at the birthplace of St. Thomas's famous artist, offers a fine collection of original paintings and prints by local and regional artists. ✉ *14 Main St., Charlotte Amalie* ☎ *340/774–4621.*

Gallery St. Thomas. The gallery in this charming space has a nice collection of fine art and collectibles, including paintings, wood sculptures, glass, and jewelry that are from or inspired by the Virgin Islands. ✉ *Palm Passage, 5143 Palm Passage, Ste. A-13, Charlotte Amalie* ☎ *340/777–6363* 🌐 *gallerystthomas.com.*

CAMERAS AND ELECTRONICS

Boolchand's. This store sells brand-name cameras, audio and video equipment, and binoculars. ✉ *Havensight Mall, Bldg. II, Ste. C, Rte. 30, Havensight* ☎ *340/776–0302* 🌐 *www.boolchand.com* ⏲ *Closed Sun. (if no cruise ship is in port).*

Royal Caribbean. Find a wide selection of cameras, camcorders, stereos, watches, and clocks at this store. There are also branches at Yacht Haven Grande and the Crown Bay Center. ✉ *33 Main St., Charlotte Amalie* ☎ *340/776–4110* 🌐 *www.royalcaribbeanvi.com* ✉ *Havensight Mall, Bldg. I, Rte. 30, Havensight* ☎ *340/776–8890* 🌐 *royalcaribbeanvi.com.*

CHINA AND CRYSTAL

Little Switzerland. This popular Caribbean chain carries crystal from Baccarat, Waterford, and Orrefors; and china from Kosta Boda, Rosenthal, and Wedgwood. There's also an assortment of Swarovski cut-crystal animals, gemstone globes, and many other affordable collectibles. It also does a booming mail-order business. A branch located at the Crown Bay Center is open when a cruise ship is in port. ✉ *5 Dronningens Gade, across from Emancipation Garden, Charlotte Amalie* ☎ *340/776–2010* 🌐 *www.littleswitzerland.com.*

CLOTHING

FAMILY **Fresh Produce Sportswear.** This clothing store doesn't sell lime-green mangoes, peachy-pink guavas, or sunny-yellow bananas, but you will find these fun, casual colors on its clothing for children and adults. This is one of 30 stores nationwide to stock all of the California-created, tropical-feel line of women's separates. The dresses, shirts, slacks, and skirts are in small to plus sizes, and bags and hats and other accessories are also available. ✉ *Riise's Alley, 5189 Dronningens Gade, across from the Rolex store, Charlotte Amalie* ☎ *340/774–0807* 🌐 *www.freshproduceclothes.com.*

FAMILY **Local Color.** This St. Thomas chain has clothes for men, women, and children among its brand names, which include Jams World, Fresh Produce, and Urban Safari. You can also find St. John artist Sloop Jones's colorful, hand-painted island designs on cool dresses, T-shirts, and sweaters.

The tropically oriented accessories include big-brimmed straw hats, bold-color bags, and casual jewelry. ✉ *Waterfront Hwy., at Raadets Gade, Charlotte Amalie* ☎ *340/776–5860* ⊕ *www.localcolorvi.com.*

Fodor's Choice ★ **The Belgian Chocolate Factory.** Whet your appetite while watching these handcrafted chocolates being made behind the glass in the store's kitchen. Milk, dark and white chocolate come in over 50 varieties with fillings like pralines, marshmallow, fruits, and caramel. Gift boxes make these sweets an easy souvenir or present for friends back home. ✉ *5093 Dronningens Gade, Ste. 3, Charlotte Amalie* ⊕ *Located in the A.H. Riise Mall in Hibiscus Alley* ☎ *340/777–5247* ⊕ *www. thebelgianchocolatefactory.com.*

HANDICRAFTS

Native Arts and Crafts Cooperative. This crafts market is made up of a group of more than 40 local artists—including schoolchildren, senior citizens, and people with disabilities—who create the handcrafted items for sale here: African-style jewelry, quilts, calabash bowls, dolls, soaps, carved-wood figures, woven baskets, straw brooms, note cards, and cookbooks. ✉ *48B Tolbod Gade, across from Emancipation Garden, Charlotte Amalie* ☎ *340/777–1153.*

JEWELRY

Fodor's Choice ★ **Cardow Jewelers.** You can get gold in several lengths, widths, sizes, and styles, along with jewelry made of diamonds, emeralds, and other precious gems from this small chain's main store. You're guaranteed 40% to 60% savings off U.S. retail prices, or your money will be refunded within 30 days of purchase. There's also a line of classy commemorative Virgin Islands watches made on-site. Branches located at the Cyril E. King Airport and Crown Bay Center. ✉ *5195 Dronningens Gate, across from Emancipation Garden, Charlotte Amalie* ☎ *340/776–1140* ⊕ *www.cardow.com.*

Diamonds International. At this large chain with several outlets on St. Thomas, just choose a diamond, emerald, or tanzanite gem and a mounting, and you can have your dream ring set in an hour. Famous for having the largest inventory of diamonds on the island, this shop welcomes trade-ins, has a U.S. service center, and includes diamond earrings with every purchase. Branches located at Frenchman's Reef & Morningstar Marriott Resort, Crown Bay Center, and Havensight Mall. ✉ *31 Main St., Charlotte Amalie* ☎ *340/774–3707* ⊕ *www.diamondsinternational. com* ✉ *3A Main St., Charlotte Amalie* ☎ *340/774–1516* ⊕ *www. diamondsinternational.com.*

H. Stern Jewelers. The World Collection of jewels set in modern, fashionable designs and an exclusive sapphire watch have earned this Brazilian jeweler a stellar reputation. ✉ *5332 Dronningens Gade, Charlotte Amalie* ☎ *340/776–1146* ⊕ *www.hstern.net.*

Jewels. This jewelry store sells name-brand jewelry and watches in abundance. Designer jewelry lines include David Yurman, Bulgari, Chopard, and Penny Preville. The selection of watches includes Jaeger le Coultre, Tag Heuer, Breitling, Movado, and Gucci. Branches at Havensight Mall, Crown Bay Center, and the Ritz-Carlton, St.

19

Thomas. ✉ *Main St., at Riise's Alley, Charlotte Amalie* ☎ *248/809–5560* ⊕ *www.jewelsonline.com.*

Rolex Watches at A. H. Riise. A.H. Riise is the official Rolex retailer of the Virgin Islands, and this shop offers one of the largest selections of these fine timepieces in the Caribbean. An After Sales Service Center helps you keep your Rolex ticking for a lifetime. ✉ *37 Main St., at Riise's Alley, Charlotte Amalie* ☎ *340/777–6789* ⊕ *www.ahriise.com.*

LEATHER GOODS

Coach. This designer leather store has a full line of fine leather handbags, belts, gloves, and more for women, plus briefcases and wallets for men. Accessories for both sexes include organizers, travel bags, and cell-phone cases. ✉ *Yacht Haven Grande, 5328 Yacht Haven Grande, Ste. 104, Charlotte Amalie* ☎ *340/776–1930* ⊕ *www.coach.com.*

LINENS

Fabric in Motion. Fine Italian linens share space with Liberty London's silky cottons, colorful batiks, cotton prints, ribbons, and accessories in this small shop. ✉ *7 Store Tvaer Gade, Charlotte Amalie* ☎ *340/774–2006.*

Mr. Tablecloth. This store has prices to please, and the friendly staff here will help you choose from the floor-to-ceiling selection of linens, which include Tuscan lace tablecloths and Irish linen pillowcases. ✉ *6–7 Main St., Charlotte Amalie* ☎ *340/774–4343* ⊕ *mrtablecloth-vi.com.*

LIQUOR AND TOBACCO

A.H. Riise Liquors and Tobacco. This giant duty-free liquor outlet carries a large selection of tobacco (including imported cigars), as well as cordials, wines, and rare vintage Armagnacs, cognacs, ports, and Madeiras. It also stocks fruits in brandy and barware from England. Enjoy rum samples at the tasting bar. The prices are among the best in St. Thomas. ✉ *37 Main St., at Riise's Alley, Charlotte Amalie* ☎ *340/777–2222* ⊕ *www.ahriise.com.*

EAST END

Red Hook has **American Yacht Harbor,** a waterfront shopping area with a dive shop, a tackle store, clothing and jewelry boutiques, a bar, and a few restaurants.

ART

The Color of Joy Art & Framing. This gallery offers locally made arts and crafts, including pottery, batik, hand-painted linen-and-cotton clothing, glass plates and ornaments, and watercolors by owner Corinne Van Rensselaer. There are also original prints by many local artists. Framing is available. ✉ *Rte. 322, about 100 yards west of Ritz-Carlton, Red Hook* ☎ *340/775–4020* ⊕ *www.thecolorofjoyvi.com.*

FOODSTUFFS

Food Center. This supermarket sells fresh produce, meats, and seafood. There's also an on-site bakery and deli with hot and cold prepared foods, which are the big draw here, especially for those renting villas, condos, or charter boats in the East End area. ✉ *Rte. 32, 1 mile (2 km) west of Red Hook, Estate Frydenhoj* ☎ *340/777–8806* ⊕ *www.foodcentervi.com.*

Made in St. Thomas

Date-palm brooms, frangipani-scented perfume, sun-scorched hot sauces, aromatic mango candles: these are just a few of the handicrafts made in St. Thomas.

Justin Todman, aka the Broom Man, keeps the art of broom making alive. It's a skill he learned at the age of six from his father. From the fronds of the date palm, Todman cuts, strips, and dries the leaves. Then he weaves them into distinctively shaped brooms with birch-berry wood for handles. There are feather brooms, cane brooms, multicolor-yarn brooms, tiny brooms to fit into a child's hand, and tall, long-handled brooms to reach cobwebs on the ceiling. Some customers buy Todman's brooms— sold at the **Native Arts and Crafts Cooperative**—not for cleaning but rather for celebrating their nuptials. It's an old African custom for the bride and groom to jump over a horizontally laid broom to start their new life.

Gail Garrison puts the essence of local flowers, fruits, and leaves into perfumes, powders, and body splashes. Her Island Fragrances line includes frangipani-, white ginger–, and jasmine-scented perfumes; aromatic mango, lime, and coconut body splashes; and bay rum after-shave for men. Garrison compounds, mixes, and bottles the products herself in second-floor offices on Charlotte Amalie's Main Street.

Jerome's, Blind Betty's, and Virgin Fire are brands of hot sauces made in St. Thomas and St. John. Gladys Isles, owner of Gladys' Cafe, makes and sells her own special recipe hot sauce that isn't for the faint-hearted.

Jason Budsan traps the aromas of the islands, such as ripe mango and night jasmine, into sumptuous candles he sells at his **Tillett Gardens** workshop.

19

Moe's Fresh Market. This gourmet market near the ferry to St. John has the best deli cheeses, prepared-to-order subs, and selection of organic foods, coffees, and wines on the island. ⌂ *Rte. 32, 6502 Smith Bay Road, Red Hook* ☎ *340/693–0254* ⊕ *moesvi.com.*

JEWELRY

Jewels. Designer jewelry available in this major chain includes David Yurman, Bulgari, Chopard, and Penny Preville. The selection of watches is also extensive. ⌂ *Ritz-Carlton St. Thomas, Rte. 322, Nazareth* ☎ *248/809–5560* ⊕ *www.jewelsonline.com.*

SOUTH SIDE

West of Charlotte Amalie, the pink-stucco **Nisky Center,** on Harwood Highway about ½ mile (1 km) east of the airport, is more of a home-town shopping center than a tourist area, but there's a bank, clothing store, and a few other stores.

At the Crown Bay cruise-ship pier, the **Crown Bay Center,** off the Harwood Highway in Sub Base about ½ mile (1 km), has quite a few shops that are branches of Main Street retailers.

Havensight Mall, next to the cruise-ship dock, may not be as charm-ing as downtown Charlotte Amalie, but it does have more than 60 shops. It also has a bank, a pharmacy, a gourmet grocery, and smaller branches of many downtown stores. The shops at **Port of $ale,** adjoining Havensight Mall (its buildings are pink instead of brown), sell discount goods. Next door to Port of $ale is the **Yacht Haven Grande** complex, a stunning megayacht marina with beautiful, safe walkways and many upscale shops.

East of Charlotte Amalie on Route 38, **Tillett Gardens** (⊕ *www.tillett gardens.com*) is an oasis of artistic endeavor. The late Jim and Rhoda Tillett converted this Danish farm into an artists' retreat in 1959. Today you can watch artisans produce candles, soaps, pottery, and other handicrafts. Something special is often happening in the gardens as well, including concerts and an arts-and-crafts fair, held in November and May.

Tutu Park Shopping Mall, across from Tillett Gardens, is the island's only enclosed mall. More than 50 stores and a food court are anchored by Kmart and the Plaza Extra grocery store. Archaeologists have discovered evidence that Arawak Indians once lived near the grounds.

ART
Mango Tango. This gallery sells and displays works by popular local artists—originals, prints, and note cards. There's a one-person or multiple-person show at least one weekend a month. ⊠ *4003 Raphune Hill, off Rt. 38, Raphune Hill, above the Paint Depot, ½ mile (1 km) east of Charlotte Amalie, Raphune* ☎ *340/777–3060.*

CAMERAS AND ELECTRONICS
Boolchand's. This store sells brand-name cameras, audio and video equipment, and binoculars. ⊠ *Havensight Mall, Rte. 30, Bldg. II, Ste. C, Havensight* ☎ *340/776–0302* ⊕ *www.boolchand.com.*

CHINA AND CRYSTAL
Scandinavian Center. Find the best of Scandinavia here, including Royal Copenhagen, Georg Jensen, Kosta Boda, and Orrefors. Owners Søren and Grace Blak make regular buying trips to northern Europe and are a great source of information on crystal. Online ordering is available if you want to add to your collection once home. A branch at the Crown Bay Center is open only when a cruise ship is in port. ⊠ *Havensight Mall, Bldg. III, Rte. 30, Havensight* ⊹ *It's the last store closest to cruise ship dock* ☎ *340/777–8620, 877/454–8377* ⊕ *www.scandinaviancenter.com.*

FOODSTUFFS
Fodor's Choice   **Fruit Bowl.** This grocery store is the best place on the island to go for fresh ★   fruits and vegetables. There are many ethnic, vegetarian, and health-food items as well as a fresh meat area, seafood department, and salad bar. ⊠ *Wheatley Center, Intersection of Rtes. 38 and 313, Charlotte Amalie* ☎ *340/774–8565* ⊕ *www.thefruitbowlvi.com.*

Gourmet Gallery. This is where visiting megayacht owners (or their staff) go to buy their caviar. There's also an excellent and reasonably priced wine selection, as well as specialty ingredients for everything from tacos to curries to chow mein. A full-service deli offers imported meats, cheeses, and in-store prepared foods that are perfect for a picnic. There's another branch at Havensight Mall, Building VI. ⊠ *Crown Bay Marina, Rte. 304, Contant* ☎ *340/776–8555* ⊕ *gourmetgallery.net.*

HANDICRAFTS

Caribbean Marketplace. This is a great place to buy handicrafts from the Caribbean and elsewhere. Also look for Sunny Caribee spices, teas from Tortola, and coffee from Trinidad. ✉ *Havensight Mall, Rte. 30, next to Deli Deck, Havensight* ☎ *340/776–5400.*

JEWELRY

H. Stern Jewelers. This Brazilian jeweler is known for the modern settings and designs of its offerings. The jewelry vault design center is located on Main Street, Charlotte Amalie. ✉ *5332 Dronningens Gade, Havensight* ☎ *340/776–1146* ⊕ *www.hstern.net.*

Jewels. Head here for name-brand jewelry and designer watches in abundance. Locations also at Havensight Mall, Crown Bay Center, and the Ritz-Carlton, St. Thomas. ✉ *38 Dronningens Gade (Main St.), Charlotte Amalie* ☎ *248/809–5560* ⊕ *www.jewelsonline.com.*

LIQUOR AND TOBACCO

Al Cohen's Discount Liquor. This warehouse of a store holds an extremely large wine and liquor selection. ✉ *Rte. 30, across from the main entrance to Havensight Mall, Havensight* ☎ *340/774–3690.*

Tobacco Discounters. This duty-free outlet carries a full line of discounted brand-name cigarettes, cigars, and tobacco accessories. ✉ *9100 Port of $ale Mall, Rte. 30, next to Havensight Mall, Havensight* ☎ *340/774–2256.*

MUSIC

Music Shoppe II. This is a good place to buy CDs of the latest Caribbean releases—steel pan, reggae, and calypso, plus contemporary tunes in a broad range of genres. ✉ *Havensight Mall, Bldg. III, Rte. 30, Ste. D, Havensight* ☎ *340/774–1900* ⊕ *musicshoppe2.com.*

TOYS

FAMILY **Kmart.** This giant discount chain store has five aisles of toys for boys and girls: Barbie dolls, hula hoops, computer games, dollhouses, talking teddies, and more. ✉ *Tutu Park Shopping Mall, Rte. 38, Tutu* ☎ *340/714–5839* ⊕ *www.kmart.com* ✉ *Lockhart Gardens, Rte. 38, Charlotte Amalie* ☎ *340/774–4046* ⊕ *www.kmart.com.*

19

SPORTS AND THE OUTDOORS

AIR TOURS

Caribbean Buzz Helicopters. Near to the UVI field, Caribbean Buzz Helicopters offers a minimum 30-minute tour that includes St. Thomas, St. John, the west end of Tortola, Jost Van Dyke, and all the cays in between. It's a nice ride if you can afford the splurge (tours are from $600 for up to three people), but in truth, you can see most of the aerial sights from Paradise Point or Mountain Top, and there's no place you can't reach easily by car or boat. ✉ *Jet Port, 8202 Lindbergh Bay, Charlotte Amalie* ☎ *340/775–7335* ⊕ *www.caribbean-buzz.com.*

BOATING AND SAILING

Calm seas, crystal waters, and nearby islands (perfect for picnicking, snorkeling, and exploring) make St. Thomas a favorite jumping-off spot for day- or weeklong sails or powerboat adventures. With more than

100 vessels from which to choose, St. Thomas is the charter-boat center of the U.S. Virgin Islands. You can go through a broker to book a sailing vessel with a crew or contact a charter company directly. Crewed charters start at approximately $3,400 per person per week, and bareboat charters can start at $2,000 per person for a 50- to 55-foot sailboat (not including provisioning), which can comfortably accommodate up to six people. If you want to rent your own boat, hire a captain. Most local captains are excellent tour guides.

Single-day charters are also a possibility. You can hire smaller boats for the day, including the services of a captain if you wish to have someone take you on a guided snorkeling trip around the islands.

Island Yachts. The sailboats from Island Yachts are available for charter with or without crews. ⊠ *6100 Red Hook Quarter, 18B, Red Hook* ☎ *340/775–6666, 800/524–2019* ⊕ *www.iyc.vi.*

Fodor'sChoice ★ **Magic Moments.** *Luxury* is the word at Magic Moments, where crews aboard the 45-foot *Sea Ray* and 52-foot *Sunseeker* offer pampered island-hopping snorkeling cruises for $475 to $700 per person (children ages 2–10 are half price). Nice touches include a wine-and-lobster lunch and icy-cold eucalyptus-infused washcloths for freshening up. ⊠ *American Yacht Harbor, 6501 Red Hook Plaza, Ste. 201, Docks B and C, Red Hook* ☎ *340/775–5066* ⊕ *www.yachtmagicmoments.com.*

Nauti Nymph. A large selection of 28- to 35-foot powerboats and power catamarans are available from this company. Rates, which vary from $620 to $1,085 a day, include snorkeling gear, water skis, and outriggers, but not fuel. Half-day rates available. You can hire a captain for $140 more per day. ⊠ *American Yacht Harbor Marina, 6501 Red Hook Plaza, Ste. #201, Dock B & C, Red Hook* ☎ *540/775–5066, 800/734–7345* ⊕ *www.nautinymph.com.*

Stewart Yacht Charters. Run by longtime sailor Ellen Stewart, this company is skilled at matching clients with yachts and crews for weeklong charter holidays. ⊠ *6501 Red Hook Plaza, Ste. 20, Red Hook* ☎ *340/775–1358, 800/432–6118* ⊕ *www.stewartyachtcharters.com.*

VIP Yacht Charters. 48 to 59 feet, including a selection of stable trawlers, are available for bareboat charter. Professional captains available on request, for an extra charge. ⊠ *Compass Point Marina, 6300 Estate Frydenhoj, south of Rte. 32, Ste. 27, Estate Frydenhoj* ☎ *340/774–9224, 866/847–9224* ⊕ *www.vipyachts.com.*

DIVING AND SNORKELING

Popular dive sites include such wrecks as the *Cartanser Sr.,* a beautifully encrusted World War II cargo ship sitting in 35 feet of water, and the *General Rogers,* a Coast Guard cutter resting at 65 feet. Here you can find a gigantic resident barracuda. Reef dives offer hidden caves and archways at **Cow and Calf Rocks,** coral-covered pinnacles at **Frenchcap,** and tunnels where you can explore undersea from the Caribbean to the Atlantic at **Thatch Cay, Grass Cay,** and **Congo Cay.** Many resorts and charter yachts offer dive packages. A one-tank dive starts at $110; two-tank dives are $130 and up. Call the USVI Department of Tourism to obtain a free eight-page guide to Virgin Islands dive sites. There are plenty of snorkeling possibilities, too.

Admiralty Dive Center. Boat dives, rental equipment, and a retail store are available from this dive center. You can also get multiple-tank packages if you want to dive over several days. ⊠ *Windward Passage Hotel, Waterfront Hwy. (Rte. 30), Charlotte Amalie* ☎ *340/777–9802, 888/900–3483* ⊕ *www.admiraltydive.com.*

Blue Island Divers. This full-service dive shop offers both day and night dives to wrecks and reefs and specializes in custom dive charters. ⊠ *Crown Bay Marina, Rte. 304, Contant* ☎ *340/774–2001* ⊕ *www. blueislanddivers.com.*

B.O.S.S. Underwater Adventure. As an alternative to traditional diving, try an underwater motor scooter called BOSS, or Breathing Observation Submersible Scooter. A 3½-hour tour, including snorkel equipment, rum punch, and towels, is $140 per person. ⊠ *Crown Bay Marina, Rte. 304, Charlotte Amalie* ☎ *340/777–3549* ⊕ *www.bossusvi.com.*

FAMILY **Coki Dive Center.** Snorkeling and dive tours in the fish-filled reefs off Coki Beach are available from this PADI Five Star outfit, as are classes, including one on underwater photography. It's run by the avid diver Peter Jackson. ⊠ *Rte. 388, at Coki Point, Frydendal* ☎ *340/775–4220* ⊕ *www.cokidive.com.*

FAMILY **Snuba of St. Thomas.** In snuba, a snorkeling and scuba-diving hybrid, a 20-foot air hose connects you to the surface. The cost is $74. Children must be eight or older to participate. ⊠ *Rte. 388, at Coki Point, Estate Smith Bay* ☎ *340/693–8063* ⊕ *www.visnuba.com.*

St. Thomas Diving Club. This PADI Five Star center offers boat dives to the reefs around Buck Island and nearby offshore wrecks, as well as multiday dive packages. ⊠ *Bolongo Bay Beach Resort, Rte. 30, Bolongo* ☎ *340/776–2381* ⊕ *www.stthomasdivingclub.com.*

FISHING

Fishing here is synonymous with blue marlin angling—especially from June through October. Four 1,000-pound-plus blues, including three world records, have been caught on the famous North Drop, about 20 miles (32 km) north of St. Thomas. A day charter for marlin with up to six anglers costs $1,800 for the day. If you're not into marlin fishing, try hooking sailfish in winter, dolphinfish (the fish that's also known as mahimahi, not the mammal) in spring, and wahoo in fall. Inshore trips for four hours start at $600. To find the trip that will best suit you, walk down the docks at either American Yacht Harbor or Sapphire Beach Marina in the late afternoon and chat with the captains and crews.

Abigail III. Captain Red Bailey's *Abigail III* specializes in marlin fishing. It operates out of the Sapphire Condominium Resort's marina. ⊠ *Estate Smith Bay, Rte. 38, ¼ mile (½ km) northwest of Red Hook, Sapphire Bay* ☎ *340/775–6024* ⊕ *www.visportfish.com.*

FAMILY
Fodor's Choice
★
Double Header Sportfishing. This company offers trips out to the North Drop on its 40-foot sportfisher and half-day reef and bay trips aboard its two speedy 35-foot center consoles. ⊠ *Sapphire Bay Marina, Rte. 38, Sapphire Bay* ☎ *340/777–7317* ⊕ *www.doubleheadersportfishing.net.*

19

Marlin Prince. Captain Eddie Morrison, one of the most experienced charter operators in St. Thomas, specializes in fly-fishing for blue marlin from his 45-foot Viking boat. ⊠ *American Yacht Harbor, 6100 Red Hook Quarters #2, slip A-16, Red Hook* ☎ *340/693–5929* ⊕ *www. marlinprince.com.*

GOLF

Fodor's Choice ★ **Mahogany Run Golf Course.** The Mahogany Run Golf Course is the only course in St. Thomas, and it attracts golfers who are drawn by its spectacular view of the British Virgin Islands and the challenging three-hole Devil's Triangle of holes 13–15. This Tom and George Fazio–designed course is not particularly long, but in addition to the scenery, you will experience lots of natural flora and fauna. There's a fully stocked pro shop, snack bar, and open-air clubhouse. Walking is not permitted and the course enforces a dress code. It's open daily, and there are frequently informal weekend tournaments. ⊠ *Rte. 42, Lovenlund* ☎ *340/777–6006, 800/253–7103* ⊕ *www.mahoganyrungolf.com* ✉ *$165 for 18 holes; $115 for 9 holes during peak winter season* ⅄ *18 holes, 6022 yards, par 70.*

GUIDED TOURS

FAMILY **VI Taxi Association Tropical Paradise St. Thomas Island Tour.** Aimed at cruise-ship passengers, this two-hour tour for two people is done in an open-air safari bus or enclosed van. Most vehicles can accommodate wheelchairs. The $29 tour includes stops at Drake's Seat and Mountain Top. Other tours include a three-hour trip to Coki Beach with a shopping stop in downtown Charlotte Amalie for $35 per person, a three-hour trip to the Coral World Ocean Park for $45 per person, and a five-hour beach tour to St. John for $75 per person. For $35 to $40 for two, you can hire a taxi for a customized three-hour drive around the island. Make sure to see Mountain Top, as the view is wonderful. ☎ *340/774–4550* ⊕ *http://vitaxiassociation.com/tours.html.*

SEA EXCURSIONS

Landlubbers and seafarers alike can experience wind in their hair and salt spray in the air while exploring the waters surrounding St. Thomas. Several businesses can book you on a snorkel-and-sail to a deserted cay for a half day that starts at $95 per person or a full day (at least $130 per person). An excursion over to the British Virgin Islands starts at $150 per person, not including $20 per person customs fees. A luxury daylong motor-yacht cruise complete with lunch is $475 or more per person.

FAMILY Fodor's Choice ★ **Adventure Center.** For a soup-to-nuts choice of sea tours including a stand-up paddleboard safari, full- and half-day sails, sunset cruises, fishing trips, powerboat rentals and kayak tours, contact the Adventure Center. ⊠ *Frenchman's Reef & Morning Star Marriott Beach Resort, Rte. 315, Estate Bakkero* ☎ *340/774–2992, 866/868–7784* ⊕ *www. adventurecenters.net.*

SEA KAYAKING

The best way to experience the mangroves of any island is on the water, ideally by kayak. These boats are very stable and come in both single and double sizes. You don't need any experience, just a little stamina to paddle and guide your boat, making for a slow-paced and relaxing soft-adventure voyage.

FAMILY
Fodor's Choice
★

Virgin Islands Ecotours. Fish dart, birds sing, and iguanas lounge on the limbs of dense mangrove trees deep within a marine sanctuary on St. Thomas's southeast shore. With Virgin Islands Ecotours you can learn about the islands' natural history in a guided kayak-snorkel tour to Patricia Cay or via an inflatable boat tour to Cas Cay for snorkeling and hiking. Both are 2½ hours long. VI Ecotours also offers three- and five-hour guided kayak tours to St. Thomas's Mangrove Lagoon, Hassel Island, Henley Cay, and St. John's Caneel Bay. All trips include free snorkel instruction with snacks on three-hour trips and lunch on five-hour trips. The historic Hassel Island tour includes a visit to some of the historic forts and military structures on the island, a short hike to a breathtaking vista, and a swim off a deserted beach. ⊠ *Mangrove Lagoon, Rte. 32, 2 miles (3 km) east of the intersection of Rtes. 32 and 30, Nadir* ☎ *340/779–2155, 877/845–2925* ⊕ *www.viecotours. com* 🎫 *From $69 to $139 per person.*

WINDSURFING

Expect some spills, anticipate the thrills, and try your luck clipping through the seas. Most beachfront resorts rent Windsurfers and offer one-hour lessons for about $120.

Adventure Watersports. PASA (Professional Air Sports Association)-certified instructor Jon Moore offers beginner and intermediate-advanced kitesurfing lessons in the wonderfully windy East End Marine Reserve at Cas Cay. A three-hour beginner lesson costs $385 for one student or $475 for two. Gear, board, and kite provided. ⊠ *East End Marine Reserve, Cas Cay, Rte. 38, Estate Frydenhoj* ☎ *340/998–6240* ✉ *info@ adventurewatersportsvi.com* ⊕ *adventurewatersportsvi.com.*

FAMILY

Tree Limin' Extreme. Ride through rain forest and then break into clearings with views that stretch to the British Virgin Islands. Six zip lines mean wait times are low, even on busy cruise ship days. Two sky bridges and a really cool "yo-yo" zip (yes, it makes you feel like the old-time kids toy) sets this apart from standard zip-line tours. ⊠ *7406 St. Peter, Estate St. Peter* ✛ *Across from the St. Peter Mountain Greathouse & Botanical Gardens* ☎ *340/777–9477* ⊕ *ziplinestthomas.com* 🎫 *$109.*

19

ST. JOHN

Updated
by Carol
Buchanan

St. John's heart is Virgin Islands National Park, a treasure that takes up a full two-thirds of St. John's 20 square miles (53 square km). The park helps keep the island's interior in its pristine and undisturbed state, but if you go at midday, you'll probably have to share your stretch of beach with others, particularly at Trunk Bay.

The island is booming (its population of 5,000 is joined by more than 800,000 visitors each year), and it can get crowded at the ever-popular Trunk Bay Beach during the busy winter season; parking woes plague the island's main town of Cruz Bay, but you won't find traffic jams or pollution. It's easy to escape from the fray, however: just head off on a hike or go early or late to the beach. The sun won't be as strong, and you may have that perfect crescent of white sand all to yourself.

St. John doesn't have a major agrarian past like her sister island, St. Croix, but if you're hiking in the dry season, you can probably stumble upon the stone ruins of old plantations. The less adventuresome can visit the repaired ruins at the park's Annaberg Plantation and Caneel Bay Resort.

In 1675 Jorgen Iverson claimed the unsettled island for Denmark. By 1733 there were more than 1,000 slaves working more than 100 plantations. In that year the island was hit by a drought, hurricanes, and a plague of insects that destroyed the summer crops. With famine a real threat and the planters keeping them under tight rein, the slaves revolted on November 23, 1733. They captured the fort at Coral Bay, took control of the island, and held it for six months. During this period, about 20% of the island's total population was killed, the tragedy affecting both black and white residents in equal percentages. The rebellion was eventually put down with the help of French troops from Martinique. Slavery continued until 1848, when slaves in St. Croix marched on Frederiksted to demand their freedom from the Danish government. This time it was granted. After emancipation, St. John fell into decline, with its inhabitants eking out a living on small farms. Life continued in much the same way until the national park opened in 1956 and tourism became an industry.

Of the three U.S. Virgin Islands, St. John has the strongest sense of community, which is primarily rooted in a desire to protect the island's natural beauty. Despite the growth, there are still many pockets of tranquility. Here you can truly escape the pressures of modern life for a day, a week—perhaps forever.

EXPLORING

St. John is an easy place to explore. One road runs along the northern shore, another across the center of the mountains. There are a few roads that branch off here and there, but it's hard to get lost. Pick up a map at the visitor center before you start out and you'll have no problems. Few residents remember the route numbers, so have your map in hand if you stop to ask for directions. Bring along a swimsuit for stops at some of the most beautiful beaches in the world. You can spend all day or just a couple of hours exploring, but be advised that the roads are narrow and wind up and down steep hills, so don't expect to get anywhere in a hurry. There are lunch spots at Cinnamon Bay and in Coral Bay, or you can do what the locals do—find a secluded spot for a picnic. The grocery stores in Cruz Bay sell Styrofoam coolers just for this purpose.

If you plan to do a lot of touring, renting a car will be cheaper and will give you much more freedom than relying on taxis; on St. John taxis are shared safari vans, and drivers are reluctant to go anywhere until they have a full load of passengers. Although you may be tempted by an open-air Suzuki or jeep, a conventional car will let you lock up your valuables. You can get just about everywhere on the paved roads without four-wheel drive unless it rains. Then four-wheel drive will help you get up the wet, hilly roads. You may be able to share a van or open-air

Sugar mill ruins at Annaberg Plantation

vehicle (called a safari bus) with other passengers on a tour of scenic mountain trails, secret coves, and eerie bush-covered ruins.

CRUZ BAY

St. John's main town may be compact (it consists of only several blocks), but it's definitely a hub: the ferries from St. Thomas and the British Virgin Islands pull in here, and it's where you can get a taxi or rent a car to travel around the island. There are plenty of shops, a number of watering holes and restaurants, and a grassy square with benches where you can sit back and take everything in. Look for the current edition of the handy, amusing "St. John Map," featuring Max the Mongoose.

TOP ATTRACTIONS

Fodor'sChoice
★
Virgin Islands National Park. There are more than 20 trails on the north and south shores, with guided hikes along the most popular routes. A full-day trip to Reef Bay is a must; it's an easy hike through lush and dry forest, past the ruins of an old plantation, and to a sugar factory adjacent to the beach. It can be a bit arduous for young kids, however. The park runs a $40 guided tour to Reef Bay that includes a safari bus ride to the trailhead and a boat ride back to the Visitors Center. The schedule changes from season to season; call for times and to make reservations, which are essential. To pick up a useful guide to St. John's hiking trails, see various large maps of the island, and find out about current Park Service programs, including guided walks and cultural demonstrations, stop by the park visitor center at the western tip of the park in Cruz Bay on North Shore Road. ⊠ *North Shore Rd., near creek, Cruz Bay* ☎ *340/776–6201* ⊕ *www.nps.gov/viis.*

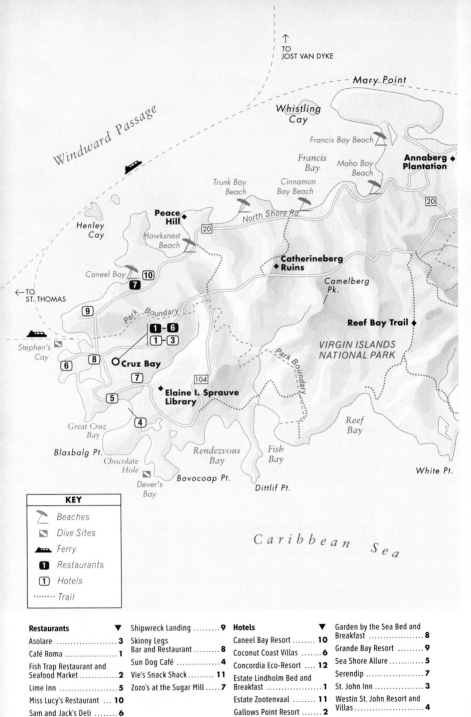

↑
TO
JOST VAN DYKE

Windward Passage

Mary Point

Whistling Cay

Francis Bay Beach

Francis Bay

Maho Bay Beach

Annaberg ◆ Plantation

Cinnamon Bay Beach

Trunk Bay Beach

North Shore Rd.

20

Henley Cay

Peace Hill ◆

20

Hawksnest Beach

Catherineberg ◆ Ruins

Camelberg Pk.

Caneel Bay

10

7

← TO ST. THOMAS

9

Park Boundary

Reef Bay Trail ◆

VIRGIN ISLANDS NATIONAL PARK

Stephen's Cay

1 - 6

1 - 3

Park Boundary

6

8

○ **Cruz Bay**

7

5

104

◆ Elaine I. Sprauve Library

4

Great Cruz Bay

Reef Bay

Blasbalg Pt.

Chocolate Hole

Rendezvous Bay

Fish Bay

White Pt.

Dever's Bay

Bovocoap Pt.

Dittlif Pt.

Caribbean Sea

KEY

Beaches
Dive Sites
Ferry
1 Restaurants
① Hotels
······· Trail

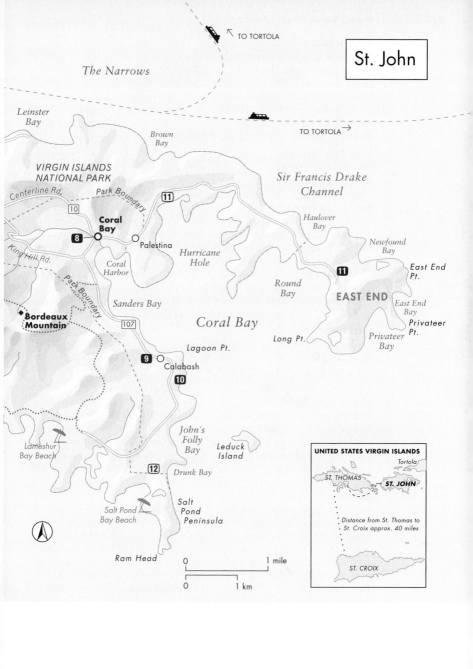

WORTH NOTING

Elaine Ione Sprauve Library. On the hill just above Cruz Bay is the Enighed Estate great house, built in 1757. *Enighed* is Danish for "concord" (unity or peace). The house and its outbuildings (a sugar factory and horse-driven mill) were destroyed by fire and hurricanes, and the house sat in ruins until 1982. The library offers Internet access for $2 an hour. ⊠ *Rte. 104, make a right past St. Ursula's Church, Cruz Bay* ☎ *340/776–6359* ✍ *Free* ⊙ *Weekdays 9–5.*

NORTH SHORE
TOP ATTRACTIONS

Fodor'sChoice   **Annaberg Plantation.** In the 18th century, sugar plantations dotted the
★   steep hills of this island. Slaves and free Danes and Dutchmen toiled to harvest the cane that was used to create sugar, molasses, and rum for export. Built in the 1780s, the partially restored plantation at Leinster Bay was once an important sugar mill. Although there are no official visiting hours, the National Park Service has regular tours, and some well-informed taxi drivers will show you around. Occasionally you may see a living-history demonstration—someone making johnnycakes or weaving baskets. For information on tours and cultural events, contact the V.I. National Park Visitors Center. ⊠ *Leinster Bay Rd., Annaberg* ☎ *340/776–6201* ⊕ *www.nps.gov/viis* ✍ *Free* ⊙ *Daily dawn–dusk.*

WORTH NOTING

Peace Hill. It's worth stopping here, just past the Hawksnest Bay over-look, for great views of St. John, St. Thomas, and the BVI. On the flat promontory is an old sugar mill. ⊠ *Off Rte. 20, Estate Denis Bay.*

MID ISLAND
TOP ATTRACTIONS

Fodor'sChoice   **Reef Bay Trail.** This is one of the most interesting hikes on St. John, but
★   unless you're a rugged individualist who wants a physical challenge (and that describes a lot of people who stay on St. John), you can probably get the most out of the trip if you join a hike led by a park service ranger. A ranger can identify the trees and plants on the hike down, fill you in on the history of the Reef Bay Plantation, and tell you about the petroglyphs on the rocks at the bottom of the trail. A side trail takes you to the plantation's great house, a gutted but mostly intact structure with vestiges of its former beauty. Take the safari bus from the park's visitor center. A boat takes you from the beach at Reef Bay back to the visitor center, saving you the uphill climb. It's a good idea to make reservations for this trip, especially during the winter season. They can be made at the Friends of the Park store, in Mongoose Junction. ⊠ *Rte. 10, Reef Bay* ☎ *340/779–8700 for reservations* ⊕ *www.nps.gov/viis* ✍ *$40 includes a safari bus ride to the trailhead, a guided tour, and a boat ride back to the visitor center* ⊙ *Tours at 9:30 am; days change seasonally.*

WORTH NOTING

Catherineberg Ruins. At this fine example of an 18th-century sugar and rum factory, there's a storage vault beneath the windmill. Across the road, look for the round mill, which was later used to hold water. In the 1733 slave revolt Catherineberg served as headquarters for the Amina warriors, a tribe of Africans captured into slavery. ⊠ *Catherineberg Rd., off Rte. 10.*

CLOSE UP

St. John Archaeology

Archaeologists continue to unravel St. John's past through excavations at Trunk Bay and Cinnamon Bay, both prime tourist destinations within Virgin Islands National Park.

Work began back in the early 1990s, when the park wanted to build new bathhouses at the popular Trunk Bay. In preparation for that project, the archaeologists began to dig, turning up artifacts and the remains of structures that date to AD 900. The site was once a village occupied by the Taíno, a group that lived in the area until AD 1500. A similar but slightly more recent village was discovered at Cinnamon Bay.

By the time the Taíno got to Cinnamon Bay, roughly a century later, their society had developed to include chiefs, commoners, workers, and slaves. The location of the national park's busy Cinnamon Bay campground was once a Taíno temple that belonged to a king or chief. When archaeologists began digging in 1998, they uncovered several dozen *zemis,* which are small clay gods used in ceremonial activities, as well as beads, pots, and many other artifacts.

Near the end of the Cinnamon Bay dig archaeologists turned up another less ancient but still surprising discovery. A burned layer indicated that a plantation slave village had also stood near Cinnamon Bay campground; it was torched during the 1733 revolt because its slave inhabitants had been loyal to the planters. Since the 1970s, bones from slaves buried in the area have been uncovered at the water's edge by beach erosion.

CORAL BAY AND ENVIRONS

Coral Bay. This laid-back community at the island's dry eastern end is named for its shape rather than for its underwater life—the word *coral* comes from *krawl,* Dutch for "corral." Coral Bay is growing fast, but it's still a small, neighborly place. You'll probably need a four-wheel-drive vehicle if you plan to stay at this end of the island, as some of the rental houses are up unpaved roads that wind around the mountain. If you come just for lunch, a regular car will be fine. ⊠ *Coral Bay.*

19

BEACHES

St. John is blessed with many beaches, and all of them fall into the good, great, and don't-tell-anyone-else-about-this-place categories. Some are more developed than others—and many are crowded on weekends, holidays, and in high season—but by and large they're still pristine. Beaches along the southern and eastern shores are quiet and isolated. Break-ins occur on all the U.S. Virgin Islands; most locals recommend leaving your windows down and leaving absolutely nothing in your car, rather than locking it up and risking a broken window.

NORTH SHORE

Cinnamon Bay Beach. This long, sandy beach faces beautiful cays and abuts the national park campground. You can rent water-sports equipment here—a good thing, because there's excellent snorkeling off the point to the right; look for the big angelfish and large schools of purple triggerfish. Afternoons on Cinnamon Bay can be windy—a boon for windsurfers but an annoyance for sunbathers—so arrive early to beat the gusts. The Cinnamon Bay hiking trail begins across the road from the beach parking lot; ruins mark the trailhead. There are actually two paths here: a level nature trail (signs along it identify the flora) that loops through the woods and passes an old Danish cemetery, and a steep trail that starts where the road bends past the ruins and heads straight up to Route 10. Restrooms are on the main path from the commissary to the beach and scattered around the campground. **Amenities:** food and drink; parking; showers; toilets; water sports. **Best for:** snorkeling; swimming; walking; windsurfing. ⊠ *North Shore Rd., Rte. 20, about 4 miles (6 km) east of Cruz Bay, Cinnamon Bay* ⊕ *www.nps.gov/viis.*

Francis Bay Beach. Because there's little shade, this beach gets toasty warm in the afternoon when the sun comes around to the west, but the rest of the day it's a delightful stretch of white sand. The only facilities are a few picnic tables tucked among the trees and a portable restroom, but folks come here to watch the birds that live in the swampy area behind the beach. The park offers bird-watching hikes here on Friday morning; sign up at the visitor center in Cruz Bay. To get here, turn left at the Annaberg intersection. **Amenities:** parking; toilets. **Best for:** snorkeling; swimming; walking. ⊠ *North Shore Rd., Rte. 20, ¼ mile (½ km) from Annaberg intersection, Francis Bay* ⊕ *www.nps.gov/viis.*

Hawksnest Beach. Sea grapes and waving palm trees line this narrow beach, and there are restrooms, cooking grills, and a covered shed for picnicking. A patchy reef just offshore means snorkeling is an easy swim away, but the best underwater views are reserved for ambitious snorkelers who head farther to the east along the bay's fringes. Watch out for boat traffic—a channel guides dinghies to the beach, but the occasional boater strays into the swim area. It's the closest drivable beach to Cruz Bay, so it's often crowded with locals and visitors. **Amenities:** parking; toilets. **Best for:** snorkeling; swimming. ⊠ *North Shore Rd., Rte. 20, about 2 miles (3 km) east of Cruz Bay, Estate Hawksnest* ⊕ *www.nps.gov/viis.*

Maho Bay Beach. Maho Bay Beach is a gorgeous strip of sand that sits right along the North Shore Road. It's a popular place, particularly on weekends, when locals come out in droves to party at the picnic tables at the south end of the beach. Snorkeling along the rocky edges is good, but the center is mostly sea grass. If you're lucky, you'll cross paths with turtles. **Amenities:** parking; toilets. **Best for:** snorkeling; swimming. ⊠ *North Shore Rd., Rte. 20, Estate Maho Bay* ⊕ *www.nps.gov/viis.*

Fodor'sChoice **Trunk Bay Beach.** St. John's most photographed beach is also the preferred
★ spot for beginning snorkelers because of its underwater trail. (Cruise-ship passengers interested in snorkeling for a day flock here, so if you're looking for seclusion, arrive early or later in the day.) Crowded or not, this stunning beach is one of the island's most beautiful. There are changing rooms with showers, bathrooms, a snack bar, picnic tables, a gift shop, phones, lockers, and snorkeling-equipment rentals. The parking lot often overflows, but you can park along the road as long as the

tires are off the pavement. **Amenities:** food and drink; lifeguards; parking; toilets; water sports. **Best for:** snorkeling; swimming; windsurfing. ✉ *North Shore Rd., Rte. 20, about 2½ miles (4 km) east of Cruz Bay, Estate Trunk Bay* 🌐 *www.nps.gov/viis* 🎫 *$5.*

CORAL BAY AND ENVIRONS

Lameshur Bay Beach. This sea grape–fringed beach is toward the end of a partially paved road on the southeast coast. The reward for your long drive is good snorkeling and a chance to spy on some pelicans. The beach has a couple of picnic tables, rusting barbecue grills, and a portable restroom. The ruins of the old plantation are a five-minute walk down the road past the beach. The area has good hiking trails, including a trek (more than a mile) up Bordeaux Mountain before an easy walk to Yawzi Point. **Amenities:** parking; toilets. **Best for:** snorkeling; swimming; walking. ✉ *Off Rte. 107, about 1½ miles (2½ km) from Salt Pond, Lameshur Bay* 🌐 *www.nps.gov/viis.*

Salt Pond Bay Beach. If you're adventurous, this rocky beach on the scenic southeastern coast—next to rugged Drunk Bay—is worth exploring. It's a short hike down a hill from the parking lot, and the only facilities are an outhouse and a few picnic tables scattered about. Tide pools are filled with all sorts of marine creatures, and the snorkeling is good, particularly along the bay's edges. A short walk takes you to a pond where salt crystals collect around the edges. Hike farther uphill past cactus gardens to Ram Head for see-forever views. Leave nothing valuable in your car, as thefts are common. **Amenities:** parking; toilets. **Best for:** snorkeling; swimming; walking. ✉ *Rte. 107, about 3 miles (5 km) south of Coral Bay, Concordia* 🌐 *www.nps.gov/viis.*

WHERE TO EAT

The cuisine on St. John seems to get better every year, with chefs vying to see who can come up with the most imaginative dishes, whether you're at one of the elegant establishments at Caneel Bay Resort (where men may be required to wear a jacket at dinner) or a casual joint near Cruz Bay. For quick lunches, try the West Indian food stands in Cruz Bay Park and across from the post office. The cooks prepare fried chicken legs, pâtés (meat- and fish-filled pastries), and callaloo.

Some restaurants close for vacation in September and even October. If you have your heart set on a special place, call ahead to make sure it's open during these months.

CRUZ BAY AND ENVIRONS

$$$$ ASIAN

🍴 **Asolare.** Contemporary Asian cuisine dominates the menu at this elegant open-air eatery in an old St. John house. Come early and relax over drinks while you enjoy the sunset lighting up the harbor. Start with the sesame-crusted goat cheese salad, then move on to entrées such as apple-wood-smoked tenderloin with wasabi or pan-roasted cod with a red curry sauce. If you still have room for dessert, try the mimosa-poached pears with honey. [$] *Average main: $36* ✉ *Rte. 20 on Caneel Hill, Cruz Bay* ☎ *340/779–4747* 🌐 *www.asolarestjohn.com* 🕒 *No lunch.*

$$$ ITALIAN FAMILY 🍴 **Café Roma.** This second-floor restaurant in the heart of Cruz Bay is *the* place for traditional Italian cuisine: lasagna, spaghetti and meatballs, and seafood manicotti. Small pizzas are available at the table, but larger ones are for takeout or at the bar. Tiramisu is a dessert specialty. This casual place can get crowded in winter, so show up early. [$] *Average main: $27* ✉ *Vesta Gade, Cruz Bay* ☎ *340/776–6524* 🌐 *www.stjohn-caferoma.com* ⏲ *No lunch.*

$$$$ AMERICAN FAMILY 🍴 **Fish Trap Restaurant and Seafood Market.** The main dining room here is open to the breezes and it buzzes with a mix of locals and visitors, but the back room has air-conditioning. Start with a tasty appetizer such as conch fritters or fish chowder (a creamy combination of snapper, white wine, paprika, and spices). You can always find steak and chicken dishes, as well as the interesting fish of the day. [$] *Average main: $33* ✉ *Bay and Strand Sts., next to Our Lady of Mount Carmel Church, Cruz Bay* ☎ *340/693–9994* 🌐 *www.thefishtrap.com* ⏲ *Closed Mon. No lunch.*

$$$ ECLECTIC 🍴 **Lime Inn.** The vacationers and mainland transplants who call St. John home like to flock to this alfresco spot for the congenial hospitality and good food, including all-you-can-eat shrimp on Wednesday night. Fresh lobster is the specialty, and the menu also includes shrimp-and-steak dishes and rotating chicken and pasta specials. [$] *Average main: $30* ✉ *Lemon Tree Mall, King St., Cruz Bay* ☎ *340/776–6425* 🌐 *www.limeinn.com* ⏲ *Closed Sun.*

$ DELI Fodor's Choice ★ 🍴 **Sam and Jack's Deli.** The sandwiches are scrumptious, but this deli also dishes up wonderful to-go meals that just need heating. If the truffle–wild mushroom ravioli is on the menu, don't hesitate to order it—it's a winner. There are a few seats inside, but most folks opt to eat at the tables in front of the deli. [$] *Average main: $12* ✉ *Marketplace Shopping Center, Rte. 104, Cruz Bay* ☎ *340/714–3354* 🌐 *www.samandjacksdeli.com.*

NORTH SHORE

$$ ECLECTIC Fodor's Choice ★ 🍴 **Sun Dog Café.** There's an unusual assortment of dishes at this charming alfresco restaurant, which you'll find tucked into a courtyard in the upper reaches of the Mongoose Junction shopping center. Kudos to the white pizza with artichoke hearts, roasted garlic, mozzarella cheese, and capers. The Jamaican jerk chicken salad and the black-bean quesadilla are also good choices. [$] *Average main: $19* ✉ *Mongoose Junction Shopping Center, North Shore Rd., Cruz Bay* ☎ *340/693–8340* 🌐 *www.sundogcafe.com.*

$$$$ ITALIAN Fodor's Choice ★ 🍴 **Zozo's at the Sugar Mill.** Creative takes on old standards coupled with lovely presentations draw crowds to this restaurant at Caneel Bay Resort. Start with crispy fried calamari served with a pesto mayonnaise. The chef dresses up roasted mahimahi with a pistachio crust and serves it with grilled polenta and a sweet pepper chutney. The slow-simmered osso buco comes with prosciutto-wrapped asparagus and saffron risotto. The sunset views will take your breath away. [$] *Average main: $43* ✉ *Caneel Bay Resort, Rte. 20, Estate Caneel Bay* ☎ *340/693–9200* 🌐 *www.zozos.net* ⏲ *No lunch.*

CORAL BAY AND ENVIRONS

$$$ ✕ **Miss Lucy's Restaurant.** Sitting seaside at remote Friis Bay, Miss Lucy's
CARIBBEAN dishes up Caribbean food with a contemporary flair. Dishes such as
tender conch fritters, a spicy West Indian stew called *callaloo*, and fried
fish make up most of the menu, but you also find a generous paella filled
with seafood, sausage, and chicken on the menu. Sunday brunches are
legendary, and if you're around when the moon is full, stop by for the
monthly full-moon party. The handful of small tables near the water
is the nicest, but if they're taken or the mosquitoes are swarming, the
indoor tables do nicely. $ *Average main: $25* ✉ *Rte. 107, Friis Bay*
☎ *340/693–5244* ☾ *Closed Mon. No dinner Sun.*

$$$ ✕ **Shipwreck Landing.** A favorite with locals and visitors, this alfresco res-
AMERICAN taurant serves up tasty food in a casual setting. Opt for the tables closest
to the road for the best breezes and water views. The menu includes
lots of seafood, but the chicken and beef dishes ensure that everyone's
satisfied. If it's a day when the chef has prepared homemade soup, try
at least a cup. For lunch, the grilled mahimahi sandwich is always a
good bet. $ *Average main: $30* ✉ *Rte. 107, Coral Bay* ☎ *340/693–5640*
⊕ *www.shipwrecklandingstjohn.com.*

$ ✕ **Skinny Legs Bar and Restaurant.** Sailors who live aboard boats anchored
AMERICAN offshore and an eclectic coterie of residents and visitors gather for lunch
and dinner at this funky spot in the middle of a boatyard and shopping
complex. It's a great place for burgers, fish sandwiches, and whatever
sports are on the satellite TV. $ *Average main: $11* ✉ *Rte. 10, Coral*
Bay ☎ *340/779–4982* ⊕ *www.skinnylegs.com.*

$ ✕ **Vie's Snack Shack.** Stop by Vie's when you're out exploring the island.
CARIBBEAN Although it's just a shack by the side of the road, Vie's serves up some
great cooking. The garlic chicken legs are crisp and tasty, and the conch
fritters are really something to write home about. Plump and filled with
fresh herbs, a plateful will keep you going for the rest of the afternoon.
Save room for a wedge of coconut pie—called a tart in this neck of the
woods. $ *Average main: $12* ✉ *Rte. 10, Estate Hansen Bay* ☎ *340/693–*
5033 ▭ *No credit cards* ☾ *Closed Sun. and Mon. No dinner.*

19

WHERE TO STAY

St. John doesn't have many beachfront hotels, but that's a small price
to pay for all the pristine sand. However, the island's two excellent
resorts—Caneel Bay Resort and the Westin St. John Resort and Villas—are on the beach. Sandy, white beaches string out along the north
coast, which is popular with sunbathers and snorkelers and is where you
can find the Caneel Bay Resort and Cinnamon and Maho Bay campgrounds. Most villas are in the residential south-shore area, a 15-minute
drive from the north-shore beaches. If you head east, you come to the
laid-back community of Coral Bay, where there are growing numbers
of villas and cottages. Bands sometimes play at a couple of Coral Bay's
nightspots, so if you're renting a villa in the hills above the village, you
may hear music later than you'd like. A stay outside Coral Bay will be
peaceful and quiet.

If you're looking for West Indian village charm, there are a few inns in Cruz Bay. Keep in mind that when bands play at any of the town's bars (some of which stay open until the wee hours), the noise can be a problem. Your choice of accommodations also includes condominiums and cottages near town; two campgrounds, one at the edge of a beautiful beach (bring bug repellent); ecoresorts; and luxurious villas, often with a pool or a hot tub (sometimes both) and a stunning view.

If your lodging comes with a fully equipped kitchen, you'll be happy to know that St. John's handful of grocery stores sell everything you're likely to need—though the prices will take your breath away. If you're on a budget, consider bringing some staples (pasta, canned goods, paper products) from home. Hotel rates throughout the island are fairly expensive, but they do include endless privacy and access to most water sports.

Many of the island's condos are just minutes from the hustle and bustle of Cruz Bay, but you can find more scattered around the island. St. John also has a handful of camping spots ranging from the basic Cinnamon Bay Campground to the more comfortable Maho Bay Camps. They appeal to those who don't mind bringing their own beach towels from home or busing their own tables at dinner. If you want your piña colada delivered beachside by a smiling waiter, you'd be better off elsewhere—and ready to pay for the privilege.

PRIVATE CONDOS AND VILLAS

Here and there between Cruz Bay and Coral Bay are about 500 private villas and condos (prices range from $ to $$$$). With pools or hot tubs, full kitchens, and living areas, these lodgings provide a fully functional home away from home. They're perfect for couples and extended groups of family or friends. You need a car, since most lodgings are in the hills and very few are at the beach. Villa managers usually pick you up at the dock, arrange for your rental car, and answer questions on arrival as well as during your stay. Prices drop in the summer season, which is generally after April 15. Some companies begin off-season pricing a week or two later, so be sure to ask.

If you want to be close to Cruz Bay's restaurants and boutiques, a villa in the Chocolate Hole and Great Cruz Bay areas will put you a few minutes away. The Coral Bay area has a growing number of villas, but you'll be about 20 minutes from Cruz Bay. Beaches lie out along the North Shore, so you won't be more than 15 minutes from the water no matter where you stay.

RENTAL CONTACTS

Carefree Get-Aways. This company manages vacation villas on the island's southern and western edges. ☎ *340/779–4070, 888/643–6002* ⊕ *www.carefreegetaways.com.*

Caribbean Villas & Resorts. Caribbean Villas handles condo rentals for Cruz Views and Gallow's Point Resort, as well as for many private villas. ☎ *340/776–6152, 800/338–0987* ⊕ *www.caribbeanvilla.com.*

Caribe Havens. Specializing in the budget market, Caribe Havens has properties scattered around the island. ⊠ *Box 455, Cruz Bay* ☎ *340/776–6518* ⊕ *www.caribehavens.com.*

Catered to Vacation Homes. Specializing in luxury villas, this company has listings mainly in the middle of the island and on the western edge. ⊠ *Marketplace Ste. 206, 5206 Enighed, Cruz Bay* ☎ *340/776–6641, 800/424–6641* ⊕ *www.cateredto.com.*

Island Getaways. Options from Island Getaways are mainly villas in the Rendezvous, Chocolate Hole, and Coral Bay areas. ☎ *340/693–7676, 888/693–7676* ⊕ *www.islandgetawaysinc.com.*

On-Line Vacations. On-Line Vacations books villas for most management companies and is based on St. John. ☎ *340/776–6036, 888/842–6632* ⊕ *www.onlinevacations.com.*

Private Homes for Private Vacations. This company handles villa rentals across the island. ⊠ *7605 Mamey Peak Rd., Coral Bay* ☎ *340/776– 6876* ⊕ *www.privatehomesvi.com.*

Seaview Vacation Homes. As the name implies, this company's specialty is houses with views of the ocean: they are in the Chocolate Hole, Great Cruz Bay, and Fish Bay areas. ☎ *340/776–6805, 888/625–2963* ⊕ *www. seaviewhomes.com.*

Star Villas. Star has cozy villas just outside Cruz Bay. ☎ *340/776–6704* ⊕ *www.starvillas.com.*

St. John Properties. This firm handles villas mainly in the Cruz Bay area but has a couple mid-island properties as well. ⊠ *Cruz Bay* ☎ *800/283– 1746, 340/693–8485* ⊕ *www.stjohnproperties.com.*

St. John Ultimate Villas. ☎ *340/776–4703, 888/851–7588* ⊕ *www. stjohnultimatevillas.com.*

Vacation Vistas. This company's villas are mainly in the Chocolate Hole, Great Cruz Bay, and Rendezvous areas. ☎ *340/776–6462* ⊕ *www. vacationvistas.com.*

Windspree. Windspree's stock is mainly in and around Coral Bay. ⊠ *7924 Emmaus, Coral Bay* ☎ *340/693–5423, 888/742–0357* ⊕ *www. windspree.com.*

CRUZ BAY AND ENVIRONS

$ **Coconut Coast Villas.** This small condominium complex with stu-
RENTAL dio, two-, and three-bedroom apartments is a 10-minute walk from Cruz Bay, but is insulated from the town's noise in a sleepy suburban neighborhood. **Pros:** good snorkeling; full kitchens; walk to Cruz Bay. **Cons:** small beach; some uphill walks; nearby utility plant can be noisy. $ *Rooms from: $169* ⊠ *Near pond, Turner Bay, Cruz Bay* ☎ *340/693–9100, 800/858–7989* ⊕ *www.coconutcoast.com* ↝ *9 units* ⏐◯⏐ *No meals.*

$$ **Estate Lindholm Bed and Breakfast.** Built among old stone ruins on
B&B/INN a lushly planted hill overlooking Cruz Bay, Estate Lindholm has an enchanting setting. **Pros:** lush landscaping; gracious host; pleasant decor. **Cons:** can be noisy; some uphill walks; on a busy road. $ *Rooms from: $365* ⊠ *Rte. 20, at Caneel Hill, Cruz Bay* ☎ *340/776–6121, 800/322–6335* ⊕ *www.estatelindholm.com* ↝ *14 rooms* ⏐◯⏐ *Breakfast.*

19

Caneel Bay Resort

$$$$ RENTAL 🏨 **Gallows Point Resort.** You're a short walk from restaurants and shops at this waterfront location just outside Cruz Bay, but once you step into your condo, the hustle and bustle are left behind. **Pros:** walk to shopping; excellent restaurant; comfortably furnished rooms. **Cons:** some rooms can be noisy; mediocre beach; insufficient parking. [$] *Rooms from: $495* ✉ *Bay St., Cruz Bay* ☎ *340/776–6434, 800/323–7229* 🌐 *www.gallowspointresort.com* 🛏 *60 units* 🍴 *No meals.*

$ B&B/INN 🏨 **Garden by the Sea Bed and Breakfast.** Located in a middle-class residential neighborhood, this cozy bed-and-breakfast is an easy walk from Cruz Bay. **Pros:** homey atmosphere; great breakfasts; breathtaking view from deck; near a bird-filled salt pond. **Cons:** noise from nearby power substation; some uphill walks; basic amenities. [$] *Rooms from: $225* ✉ *Near pond, Enighed* ☎ *340/779–4731* 🌐 *www.gardenbythesea.com* 💳 *No credit cards* 🛏 *3 rooms* 🍴 *Breakfast.*

$$$ RENTAL 🏨 **Grande Bay Resort.** Located just a few minutes' walk from Cruz Bay's restaurants and shops, this modern condominium complex puts you close to the town's hustle and bustle. **Pros:** close to restaurants and shops; modern decor; walking distance to the ferry. **Cons:** need car or taxi to reach island attractions and the best beaches; beach across the street is minimal. [$] *Rooms from: $405* ✉ *Bay St., Cruz Bay* ☎ *340/693–4668* 🌐 *www.grandebayresortusvi.com* 🛏 *64 condos* 🍴 *No meals.*

$$$$ RENTAL 🏨 **Sea Shore Allure.** Located at the water's edge in a residential neighborhood, Sea Shore Allure combines attractive and modern decor with an easy, and safe, walk to Cruz Bay's restaurants and shops. **Pros:** lovely decor; waterfront location; close to town. **Cons:** need car or taxi to get to beach; road passes through modest but safe local neighborhood. [$] *Rooms*

from: $510 ✉ Pond Mouth Rd., Turner Bay, Cruz Bay ☎ 340/779–2880, 855/779–2880 ⊕ www.seashoreallure.com ⇆ 8 units ⦿ No meals.

$ | **Serendip.** This complex offers modern apartments on lush grounds
RENTAL | with lovely views and makes a great pick for a budget stay in a residential locale. **Pros:** comfortable accommodations; good views; nice neighborhood. **Cons:** no beach; need car to get around; nearby construction. $ *Rooms from: $225 ✉ Off Rte. 104, Enighed ☎ 340/776–6646, 888/800–6445 ⊕ www.serendipstjohn.com ⇆ 10 apartments ⦿ No meals.*

$ | **St. John Inn.** A stay here gives you a bit of style at what passes for
B&B/INN | budget prices in St. John. **Pros:** walk to restaurants and shops; convivial atmosphere; pretty pool. **Cons:** need a car to get around; noisy location; insufficient parking. $ *Rooms from: $200 ✉ Off Rte. 104, Cruz Bay ☎ 340/693–8688, 800/666–7688 ⊕ www.stjohninn.com ⇆ 12 units ⦿ Breakfast.*

$$$$ | **Westin St. John Resort and Villas.** The island's largest resort provides a
RESORT | nice beachfront location and enough activities to keep you busy. **Pros:**
FAMILY | entertaining children's programs; pretty pool area; many activities. **Cons:** mediocre beach; long walk to some parts of the resort; need car to get around. $ *Rooms from: $800 ✉ Rte. 104, Estate Chocolate Hole and Great Cruz Bay ☎ 340/693–8000, 888/627–7206 ⊕ www. westinresortstjohn.com ⇆ 96 rooms, 200 villas ⦿ No meals.*

NORTH SHORE

$$$ | **Caneel Bay Resort.** If you dream of spending your days on gorgeous
RESORT | beaches, paddling kayaks to and fro, and enjoying languorous dinners
Fodor'sChoice | with your feet in the sand, there's no finer laid-back-luxury resort on
★ | St. John. **Pros:** seven lovely beaches; gorgeous rooms; lots of amenities. **Cons:** staff can be chilly; isolated location; pricey; no TVs or phones (just a warning for tech-junkies). $ *Rooms from: $459 ✉ Rte. 20, Estate Caneel Bay ☎ 340/776–6111, 855/226–3358 ⊕ www.caneelbay. com ⇆ 166 rooms ⦿ Breakfast.*

CORAL BAY AND ENVIRONS

$ | **Concordia Eco-Resort.** This off-the-beaten-path resort is on the remote
RENTAL | Salt Pond peninsula. **Pros:** good views; eco-friendly environment; beach
Fodor'sChoice | nearby. **Cons:** need car to get around; lots of stairs. $ *Rooms from:*
★ | *$195 ✉ Off Rte. 107, Concordia ☎ 340/693–5855, 800/392–9004 ⊕ www.concordiaeco-resort.com ⇆ 17 studios, 25 tents ⦿ No meals.*

$$ | **Estate Zootenvaal.** Comfortable and casual, this small cottage colony
RENTAL | gives you the perfect place to relax. **Pros:** quiet beach; private; near restaurants. **Cons:** some traffic noise; no air-conditioning in some units. $ *Rooms from: $290 ✉ Rte. 10, Hurricane Hole, Estate Zootenvaal ☎ 340/776–6321 ⊕ www.estatezootenvaal.com ⇆ 4 units ⦿ No meals.*

19

Yoga is a morning ritual at Concordia Eco-Resort.

NIGHTLIFE

St. John isn't the place to go for glitter and all-night partying. Still, after-hours Cruz Bay can be a lively little town in which to dine, drink, dance, chat, or flirt. Notices posted on the bulletin board outside the Connections telephone center—up the street from the ferry dock in Cruz Bay—or listings in *Tradewinds* (⊕ *www.stjohntradewindsnews.com*) will keep you apprised of special events, comedy nights, movies, and the like.

CRUZ BAY

Tap Room. A rotating selection of distinctive brews makes the Tap Room popular with locals and visitors. ⊠ *Mongoose Junction Shopping Center, Cruz Bay* ☎ *340/715–7775* ⊕ *www.stjohnbrewers.com.*

Woody's. Folks like to gather here, where the sidewalk tables provide a close-up view of Cruz Bay action. ⊠ *Near First Bank, Cruz Bay* ☎ *340/779–4625* ⊕ *www.woodysseafood.com.*

CORAL BAY AND ENVIRONS

Shipwreck Landing. Live rock, bluegrass, and more are on tap several nights a week at this restaurant. ⊠ *Rte. 107, Coral Bay* ☎ *340/693–5640.*

Skinny Legs Bar and Restaurant. Landlubbers and old salts listen to music and swap stories at this popular casual restaurant and bar on the far side of the island. ⊠ *Rte. 10, Coral Bay* ☎ *340/779–4982* ⊕ *www. skinnylegs.com.*

FREE PARKING Cruz Bay's parking problem is maddening. Your best bet is to rent a car from a company that allows you to park in its lot. Make sure you ask before you sign on the dotted line if you plan to spend time in Cruz Bay.

SHOPPING

CRUZ BAY

Luxury goods and handicrafts can be found on St. John. Most shops carry a little of this and a bit of that, so it pays to poke around. The Cruz Bay shopping district runs from **Wharfside Village,** just around the corner from the ferry dock, to **Mongoose Junction,** an inviting shopping center on North Shore Road. (The name of this upscale shopping mall, by the way, is a holdover from a time when those furry island creatures gathered at a nearby garbage bin.) Out on Route 104, stop in at the **Marketplace** to explore its gift and crafts shops. On St. John, store hours run from 9 or 10 to 5 or 6. Wharfside Village and Mongoose Junction shops in Cruz Bay are often open into the evening.

ART

Fodor'sChoice ★ **Bajo el Sol.** This gallery sells works by owner Livy Hitchcock, plus pieces from a roster of the island's best artists. You can also shop for oils, pastels, watercolors, and turned-wood pieces. ⊠ *Mongoose Junction Shopping Center, North Shore Rd., Cruz Bay* ☎ *340/693–7070* ⊕ *www.bajoelsolgallery.com.*

Caravan Gallery. Caravan sells affordable jewelry, unique gifts, and artifacts that its owner, Radha Speer, has traveled the world to find. The more you look, the more you see—Caribbean larimar jewelry, unusual sterling pieces, and tribal art cover the walls and tables, making this a great place to browse. ⊠ *Mongoose Junction Shopping Center, North Shore Rd., Cruz Bay* ☎ *340/779–4566* ⊕ *www.caravangallery.com.*

Coconut Coast Studios. This waterside shop, a five-minute walk from the center of Cruz Bay, showcases the work of Elaine Estern. She specializes in undersea scenes. ⊠ *Frank Bay, Cruz Bay* ☎ *340/776–6944* ⊕ *www.coconutcoaststudios.com.*

BOOKS

National Park Headquarters Bookstore. The bookshop at Virgin Islands National Park Headquarters sells several good histories of St. John, including *St. John Backtime: Eyewitness Accounts From 1718 to 1956,* by Ruth Hull Low and Rafael Lito Valls, and, for intrepid explorers, longtime resident Pam Gaffin's *St. John Feet, Fins and Four-Wheel Drive,* a "complete guide to all of the island's beaches, trails, and roads." ⊠ *Rte. 20, Cruz Bay* ☎ *340/776–6201* ⊕ *www.nps.gov/viis.*

CLOTHING

Big Planet Adventure Outfitters. You knew when you arrived that someplace on St. John would cater to the outdoor enthusiasts who hike up and down the island's trails. This store sells flip-flops and Reef footwear, along with colorful and durable cotton clothing and accessories by Billabong. The store also sells children's clothes. ⊠ *Mongoose Junction Shopping Center, North Shore Rd., Cruz Bay* ☎ *340/776–6638* ⊕ *www.big-planet.com.*

Bougainvillea Boutique. This store is your destination if you want to look as if you've stepped out of the pages of the resort-wear spread in an upscale travel magazine. Owner Susan Stair carries very chic men's and women's clothes, straw hats, leather handbags, and fine gifts.

19

✉ *Mongoose Junction Shopping Center, North Shore Rd., Cruz Bay* ☎ *340/693–7190* ⊕ *www.shoppingstjohn.com.*

FOOD

If you're renting a villa, condo, or cottage and doing your own cooking, there are several good places to shop for food; just be aware that prices are much higher than those at home.

Starfish Market. The island's largest store usually has the best selection of meat, fish, and produce. ✉ *The Marketplace, Rte. 104, Cruz Bay* ☎ *340/779–4949* ⊕ *www.starfishmarket.com.*

GIFTS

Fodor'sChoice

★

Bamboula. This multicultural boutique carries unusual housewares, rugs, bedspreads, accessories, and men's and women's clothes and shoes that owner Jo Sterling has found on her world travels. ✉ *Mongoose Junction Shopping Center, North Shore Rd., Cruz Bay* ☎ *340/693–8699* ⊕ *www. bamboulastjohn.com.*

Best of Both Worlds. Pricey metal sculptures and attractive artworks hang from the walls of this gallery; the nicest are small glass decorations shaped like mermaids and sea horses. ✉ *Mongoose Junction Shopping Center, North Shore Rd., Cruz Bay* ☎ *340/693–7005* ⊕ *www. thebestofstjohn.com.*

Donald Schnell Studio. You'll find distinctive clay pieces, unusual hand-blown glass, wind chimes, kaleidoscopes, fanciful fountains, and pottery bowls here. Your purchases can be shipped worldwide. ✉ *Amore Center, Rte. 104, near roundabout, Cruz Bay* ☎ *340/776–6420* ⊕ *donaldschnell.com/studio.*

Fabric Mill. There's a good selection of women's clothing in tropical brights, as well as lingerie, sandals, and batik wraps here. Or take home several yards of colorful batik fabric to make your own dress. ✉ *Mongoose Junction Shopping Center, North Shore Rd., Cruz Bay* ☎ *340/776–6194* ⊕ *www.fabricmillstj.com.*

Gallows Point Gift and Gourmet. The store at Gallows Point Resort has a bit of this and a bit of that. Shop for Caribbean books and CDs, picture frames decorated with shells, and T-shirts with tropical motifs. Residents and visitors also drop by for a cup of coffee. ✉ *Gallows Point Resort, Bay St., Cruz Bay* ☎ *340/693–7730* ⊕ *www.gallows pointgg.com.*

Nest and Company. This small shop carries perfect take-home gifts in colors that reflect the sea. Shop here for soaps in tropical scents, dinnerware, and much more. ✉ *Mongoose Junction Shopping Center, North Shore Rd., Cruz Bay* ☎ *340/715–2552* ⊕ *www.nestvi.net.*

Pink Papaya. Head to this shop and art gallery for the work of long-time Virgin Islands resident Lisa Etre. There's also huge collection of one-of-a-kind gifts, including bright tableware, trays, and tropical jewelry. ✉ *Lemon Tree Mall, King St., Cruz Bay* ☎ *340/693–8535* ⊕ *www. pinkpapaya.com.*

JEWELRY

Free Bird Creations. This is your on-island destination for special hand-crafted jewelry—earrings, bracelets, pendants, chains—as well as a good selection of water-resistant watches. ⊠ *Dockside Mall, next to ferry dock, Cruz Bay* ☎ *340/693–8625* ⊕ *www.freebirdcreations.com.*

Little Switzerland. A branch of the St. Thomas store, Little Switzerland carries diamonds and other jewels in attractive yellow- and white-gold settings, as well as strings of creamy pearls, watches, and other designer jewelry. ⊠ *Mongoose Junction Shopping Center, North Shore Rd., Cruz Bay* ☎ *340/776–6007* ⊕ *www.littleswitzerland.com.*

R&I PATTON goldsmithing. This store is owned by Rudy and Irene Patton, who design most of the lovely silver and gold jewelry on display. The rest comes from various designer friends. Sea fans (those large, lacy plants that sway with the ocean's currents) in filigreed silver, starfish and hibiscus pendants in silver or gold, and gold sand-dollar-shape charms and earrings are choice selections. ⊠ *Mongoose Junction Shopping Center, North Shore Rd., Cruz Bay* ☎ *340/776–6548* ⊕ *www.pattongold.com.*

CORAL BAY AND ENVIRONS

CLOTHING

Sloop Jones. This store's worth the trip all the way out to the island's East End to shop for made-on-the-premises clothing and pillows, in fabrics splashed with tropical colors. The clothes are made from cotton, gauze, and modal, and are supremely comfortable. Sloop also holds painting workshops. ⊠ *Off Rte. 10, East End* ☎ *340/779–4001* ⊕ *www.sloopjones.com.*

FOOD

Love City Mini Mart. The store may not look like much from the road, but it's one of the very few places to shop in Coral Bay and has a surprising selection. ⊠ *Off Rte. 107, Coral Bay* ☎ *340/693–5790.*

GIFTS

Mumbo Jumbo. With what may be the best prices in St. John, Mumbo Jumbo carries tropical clothing, stuffed sea creatures, and other gifty items in a cozy little shop. ⊠ *Skinny Legs Shopping Complex, Rte. 10, Coral Bay* ☎ *340/779–4277.*

19

SPORTS AND THE OUTDOORS

BOATING AND SAILING

If you're staying at a hotel or campground, your activities desk will usually be able to help you arrange a sailing excursion aboard a nearby boat. Most day sails leaving Cruz Bay head out along St. John's north coast. Those that depart from Coral Bay might drop anchor at some remote cay off the island's East End or even in the nearby British Virgin Islands. Your trip usually includes lunch, beverages, and at least one snorkeling stop. Keep in mind that inclement weather could interfere with your plans, though most boats will still go out if rain isn't too heavy.

Ocean Runner. For a speedier trip to the cays and remote beaches off St. John, you can rent a powerboat with a captain from Ocean Runner. The company rents two-engine boats for $580 to $710 per day. Gas and oil will run you $100 to $300 a day extra, depending on how far you're going. ✉ *Wharfside Village, Waterfront, Cruz Bay* 🕾 *340/693–8809* ⊕ *www.oceanrunnerusvi.com.*

St. John Concierge Service. The capable staff can find a charter sail or powerboat that fits your style and budget. The company also books fishing and scuba trips. ✉ *Henry Samuel St., across from post office, Cruz Bay* 🕾 *340/514–5262* ⊕ *www.stjohnconciergeservice.com.*

DIVING AND SNORKELING

Although just about every beach has nice snorkeling—Trunk Bay, Cinnamon Bay, and Waterlemon Cay at Leinster Bay get the most praise— you need a boat to head out to the more remote snorkeling locations and the best scuba spots. Sign on with any of the island's water-sports operators to get to spots farther from St. John. If you use the one at your hotel, just stroll down to the dock to hop aboard. Their boats will take you to hot spots between St. John and St. Thomas, including the tunnels at **Thatch Cay,** the ledges at **Congo Cay,** and the wreck of the *General Rogers.* Dive off St. John at **Stephens Cay,** a short boat ride out of Cruz Bay, where fish swim around the reefs as you float downward. At **Devers Bay,** on St. John's south shore, fish dart about in colorful schools. **Carval Rock,** shaped like an old-time ship, has gorgeous rock formations, coral gardens, and lots of fish. It can be too rough here in winter, though. Count on paying $75 for a one-tank dive and $90 for a two-tank dive. Rates include equipment and a tour. If you've never dived before, try an introductory course, called a resort course. Or if certification is in your vacation plans, the island's dive shops can help you get your card.

Cruz Bay Watersports. Cruz Bay Watersports offers regular reef, wreck, and night dives and USVI and BVI snorkel tours. The company holds both PADI Five Star and NAUI-Dream-Resort status. ✉ *Lumberyard Shopping Complex, Boulon Center Rd., Cruz Bay* 🕾 *340/776–6234* ⊕ *www.cruzbaywatersports.com* ✉ *Westin St. John, Rte. 104, Estate Chocolate Hole and Great Cruz Bay* 🕾 *340/776–6234.*

Low Key Watersports. Low Key Watersports offers two-tank dives and specialty courses. It's a PADI Five Star training facility. ✉ *1 Bay St., Cruz Bay* 🕾 *340/693–8999* ⊕ *www.divelowkey.com.*

FISHING

Well-kept charter boats—approved by the U.S. Coast Guard—head out to the north and south drops or troll along the inshore reefs, depending on the season and what's biting. The captains usually provide bait, drinks, and lunch, but you need to bring your own hat and sunscreen. Fishing charters run about $1,100 for the full-day trip.

FAMILY **Offshore Adventures.** An excellent choice for fishing charters, Captain Rob Richards is patient with beginners—especially kids—but also enjoys going out with more experienced anglers. He runs the 40-foot center console *Mixed Bag I* and 32-foot *Mixed Bag II.* Although he's based in St. John, he will pick up parties in St. Thomas. ✉ *Westin St.*

John, 3008 Chocolate Hole Rd., Estate Chocolate Hole and Great Cruz Bay ☎ 340/513–0389 ⊕ www.sportfishingstjohn.com.

GUIDED TOURS

In St. John, taxi drivers provide tours of the island, making stops at various sites, including Trunk Bay and Annaberg Plantation. Prices run around $15 a person. The taxi drivers congregate near the ferry in Cruz Bay. The dispatcher will find you a driver for your tour.

V.I. National Park Visitors Center. Along with providing trail maps and brochures about Virgin Islands National Park, the park service gives several guided tours, both on- and offshore. Some are offered only during particular times of the year, and some require reservations. ⊠ *Cruz Bay ☎ 340/776–6201 ⊕ www.nps.gov/viis.*

HIKING

Virgin Islands National Park has more than 20 trails from which to choose. Guided trips with the park service are a popular way to explore and are highly recommended, but you can also set out on your own. To find a hike that suits your ability, stop by the park's visitor center in Cruz Bay and pick up the free trail guide; it details points of interest, trail lengths, and estimated hiking times, as well as any dangers you might encounter. Although the park staff recommends long pants to protect against thorns and insects, most people hike in shorts because it can get very hot. Wear sturdy shoes or hiking boots even if you're hiking to the beach. Don't forget to bring water and insect repellent.

HORSEBACK RIDING

Carolina Corral. Clip-clop along the island's byways for a slower-pace tour of St. John. Carolina Corral offers horseback trips and wagon rides down scenic roads with owner Dana Barlett. She has a way with horses and calms even the most novice riders. ⊠ *Off Rte. 10, Coral Bay ☎ 340/693–5778 ⊕ www.carolinacorral.com ☜ $75 for 1-hr ride.*

SEA KAYAKING

Poke around the clear bays here and explore undersea life from a sea kayak. Rates run about $70 for a full day in a double kayak. Tours start at $65 for a half day.

Arawak Expeditions. This company uses traditional and sit-on-top kayaks for exploring the waters around St. John on guided tours. ⊠ *Mongoose Juction Shopping Center, North Shore Rd., Cruz Bay ☎ 340/693–8312, 800/238–8687 ⊕ www.arawakexp.com ☜ From $75 per person.*

Crabby's Watersports. Explore Coral Bay Harbor and Hurricane Hole on the eastern end of the island in a sea kayak or on a stand-up paddleboard from Crabby's Watersports. Crabby's also rents snorkel gear, beach chairs, umbrellas, coolers, and floats. ⊠ *Rte. 107, next to Cocoloba shopping center, Coral Bay ☎ 340/714–2415 ⊕ www.crabbyswatersports.com.*

Hidden Reef EcoTours. Coral reefs, mangroves, and lush sea-grass beds filled with marine life are what you can see on Hidden Reef's two- and three-hour, full-day and full-moon kayak tours through Coral Reef National Monument and its environs. ⊠ *Rte. 10, East End ☎ 340/513–9613, 877/529–2575 ⊕ www.kayaksj.com.*

19

WINDSURFING

Cinnamon Bay Watersports. Steady breezes and expert instruction make learning to windsurf a snap. Try Cinnamon Bay Campground, where rentals are $40 to $100 per hour. Lessons are available right at the waterfront; just look for the Windsurfers on the beach. The cost for a one-hour lesson starts at $60, plus the cost of the board rental. You can also rent kayaks, stand-up paddleboards, bodyboards, small sailboats, and surfboards. ⊠ *Rte. 20, Cinnamon Bay* ☎ *340/693–5902, 340/626–4769* ⊕ *www.windnsurfingadventures.com.*

ST. CROIX

Updated by Carol Buchanan

History is a big draw in St. Croix: planes are filled with Danish visitors who come mainly to explore the island's colonial history. Of course, like the rest of us, they also make sure to spend some time sunning at the island's powdery beaches, getting pampered at the hotels, and dining at interesting restaurants.

Until 1917 Denmark owned St. Croix and her sister Virgin Islands, a fact reflected in street names in the main towns of Christiansted and Frederiksted as well as the surnames of many island residents. In the 18th and 19th centuries, some of those early Danish settlers, as well as other Europeans, owned plantations, all of them worked by African slaves and white indentured servants lured to St. Croix to pay off their debt to society. Some of the plantation ruins—such as the Christiansted National Historic Site, Whim Plantation, the ruins at St. George Village Botanical Garden, and those at Estate Mount Washington and Judith's Fancy—are open for easy exploration. Others are on private land, but a drive around the island reveals the ruins of 100 plantations here and there on St. Croix's 84 square miles (218 square km). Their windmills, great houses, and factories are all that's left of the 224 plantations that once grew sugarcane, tobacco, and other crops at the island's height.

The downturn began in 1801, when the British occupied the island. The end of the slave trade in 1803, an additional British occupation (from 1807 to 1815), droughts, the development of the sugar-beet industry in Europe, political upheaval, and an economic depression all sent the island into a downward spiral.

St. Croix never recovered. The end of slavery in 1848, followed by labor riots, fires, hurricanes, and an earthquake during the last half of the 19th century, brought what was left of the island's economy to its knees. In the 1920s, the start of prohibition in the United States ended the island's rum industry, further crippling the economy. The situation remained dire—so bad that President Herbert Hoover called the territory an "effective poorhouse" during a 1931 visit—until the rise of tourism in the late 1950s and 1960s. With tourism came economic improvements coupled with an influx of residents from other Caribbean islands and the mainland. For years Hovensa Oil Refinery was an economic stimulus until it shuttered its doors in 2012. Currently the economy is struggling and a number of businesses have closed.

Today suburban subdivisions fill the fields where sugarcane once waved in the tropical breeze. Condominium complexes line the beaches along the north coast outside Christiansted. Large houses dot the rolling hillsides. Modern strip malls and shopping centers sit along major roads, and it's as easy to find a McDonald's as it is Caribbean fare.

Although St. Croix sits definitely in the 21st century, with only a little effort you can easily step back into the island's past.

EXPLORING

Although there are things to see and do in St. Croix's two towns, Christiansted and Frederiksted (both named after Danish kings), there are lots of interesting spots in between them and to the east of Christiansted. Just be sure you have a map in hand (pick one up at rental-car agencies, or stop by the tourist office for an excellent one that's free). Many secondary roads remain unmarked; if you get confused, ask for help. Locals are always ready to point you in the right direction.

St. Croix Visitor Center. Friendly advice as well as useful maps and brochures are available from the visitor center. ⊠ *Strand Street Pier, Strand St., Frederiksted* ☎ *340/773–0495* ⊕ *www.visitusvi.com* ⊙ *Weekdays 8–5.*

CHRISTIANSTED

In the 1700s and 1800s Christiansted was a trading center for sugar, rum, and molasses. Today law offices, tourist shops, and restaurants occupy many of the same buildings, which start at the harbor and go up the gently sloped hillsides.

Your best bet to see the historic sights in this Danish-style town is in the morning, when it's still cool. Break for lunch at an open-air restaurant before spending as much time as you like exploring the shopping opportunities. You can't get lost, since all streets lead back downhill to the water.

19

TOP ATTRACTIONS

FAMILY
Fodor's Choice
★

Fort Christiansvaern. The large yellow fortress dominates the waterfront. Because it's so easy to spot, it makes a good place to begin a walking tour. In 1749 the Danish built the fort to protect the harbor, but the structure was repeatedly damaged by hurricane-force winds and had to be partially rebuilt in 1771. It's now a national historic site, the best preserved of the few remaining Danish-built forts in the Virgin Islands. The park's visitor center is here. Rangers are on hand to answer questions. ■ TIP→ **Your paid admission also includes the Steeple Building.** ⊠ *Hospital St., Christiansted* ☎ *340/773–1460* ⊕ *www.nps.gov/chri* 🎫 *$3* ⊙ *Weekdays 8–4:30, weekends 9–4:30.*

Government House. One of the town's most elegant structures was built as a home for a Danish merchant in 1747. Today it houses offices. If you're here weekdays from 8 to 4:30, slip into the peaceful inner courtyard to admire the still pools and gardens. A sweeping staircase leads you to a second-story ballroom, still used for official government functions. ⊠ *King St., Christiansted* ☎ *340/773–1404.*

St. Croix

↑
TO
ST. THOMAS

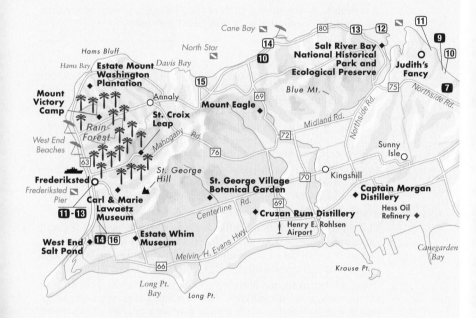

Cane Bay
North Star
Hams Bluff
Hams Bay
Davis Bay
Estate Mount Washington Plantation
Mount Victory Camp
Annaly
Rain Forest
St. Croix Leap
West End Beaches
Mahogany Rd.
Frederiksted
Frederiksted Pier
11 - 13
Carl & Marie Lawaetz Museum
St. George Hill
West End Salt Pond
14 16
Estate Whim Museum
Long Pt. Bay
Long Pt.
66
Melvin H. Evans Hwy.
Centerline Rd.
Mount Eagle
15
69
Blue Mt.
Salt River Bay National Historical Park and Ecological Preserve
80
13
12
14
10
Judith's Fancy
11
9
10
75
Northside Rd.
7
76
72
Midland Rd.
Northside Rd.
Sunny Isle
70
Kingshill
Captain Morgan Distillery
Hess Oil Refinery
St. George Village Botanical Garden
Cruzan Rum Distillery
Henry E. Rohlsen Airport
69
Canegarden Bay
Krause Pt.

KEY

- ⚓ Beaches
- 🔲 Dive Sites
- 🚢 Cruise Ship Terminal
- 🌴 Rain Forest
- **1** Restaurants
- 1 Hotels

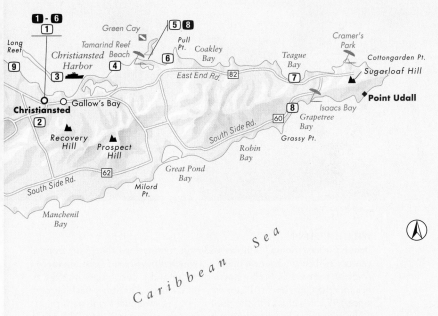

Buck Island *Buck Island*

Buck Island Reef National Monument

1 - 6
1

Green Cay

Long Reef

9

Tamarind Reef Beach

Christiansted Harbor

3

4

5 8

Pull Pt.

6

Coakley Bay

East End Rd. 82

Teague Bay

7

Cramer's Park

Cottongarden Pt.

Sugarloaf Hill

Point Udall

Christiansted

Gallow's Bay

2

Recovery Hill

Prospect Hill

South Side Rd.

62

South Side Rd.

Milord Pt.

Great Pond Bay

Robin Bay

60

8

Isaacs Bay

Grapetree Bay

Grassy Pt.

Manchenil Bay

C a r i b b e a n   S e a

0 ——————— 1 miles

0 ——————— 1 km

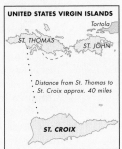

UNITED STATES VIRGIN ISLANDS

Tortola

ST. THOMAS

ST. JOHN

Distance from St. Thomas to St. Croix approx. 40 miles

ST. CROIX

Fort Christiansvaern is a National Historic Site.

WORTH NOTING

Danish Customs House. Built in 1830 on foundations that date from a century earlier, the historic building, which is near Fort Christiansvaern, originally served as both a customshouse and a post office. In 1926 it became the Christiansted Library, and it's been a national park facility since 1972. It's closed to the public, but the sweeping front steps make a nice place to take a break. ✉ *King St., Christiansted* ☎ *340/773–1460* ⊕ *www.nps.gov/chri.*

D. Hamilton Jackson Park. When you're tired of sightseeing, stop at this shady park on the street side of Fort Christiansvaern for a rest. It's named for a famed labor leader, judge, and journalist who started the first newspaper not under the thumb of the Danish crown (his birthday, November 1, is a territorial holiday celebrated with much fanfare in St. Croix). ⚠ **There are no facilities.** ✉ *Between Fort Christiansvaern and Danish Customs House, Christiansted.*

Scale House. Constructed in 1856, this was once the spot where goods passing through the port were weighed and inspected. The park staffers here have on offer a good selection of books about St. Croix history and its flora and fauna. ✉ *King St., Christiansted* ☎ *340/773–1460* ⊕ *www.nps.gov/chri.*

Steeple Building. The first Danish Lutheran church on the island when it was built in 1753, the Steeple Building is now used as a museum. It's worth the short walk to see the archaeological artifacts and exhibits on plantation life, the architectural development of Christiansted, the island's native inhabitants, and Alexander Hamilton, who grew up in St.

Croix. Hours are irregular, so ask at the visitor center. Your paid admission includes Fort Christiansvaern, too. ⊠ *Church St., Christiansted* ☎ *340/773–1460* ⌷ *$3.*

EAST END

An easy drive along flat, well-marked roads to St. Croix's eastern end takes you through some choice real estate. Ruins of old sugar estates dot the landscape. You can make the entire loop on the road that circles the island in about an hour, a good way to end the day. If you want to spend a full day exploring, you can find some nice beaches and easy walks with places to stop for lunch.

WORTH NOTING

Buck Island Reef National Monument. Buck Island has pristine beaches that are just right for sunbathing, but there's also some shade for those who don't want to fry. The snorkeling trail set in the reef allows close-up study of coral formations and tropical fish. Overly warm seawater temperatures have led to a condition called coral bleaching that has killed some of the coral. The reefs are starting to recover, but how long it will take is anyone's guess. There's an easy hiking trail to the island's highest point, where you can be rewarded for your efforts by spectacular views of St. John. Charter-boat trips leave daily from the Christiansted waterfront or from Green Cay Marina, about 2 miles (3 km) east of Christiansted. Check with your hotel for recommendations. ⊠ *Off North Shore of St. Croix* ☎ *340/773–1460* ⊕ *www.nps.gov/buis.*

Point Udall. This rocky promontory, the easternmost point in the United States, is about a half-hour drive from Christiansted. A paved road takes you to an overlook with glorious views. More adventurous folks can hike down to the pristine beach below. On the way back, look for the Castle Aura, an enormous Moorish-style mansion. It was built by Nadia Farber, the former Contessa de Navarro, who's an extravagant local character. ■TIP➔ Point Udall is sometimes a popular spot for thieves, so don't leave anything valuable in your car, and keep it locked. ⊠ *Rte. 82, Whim.*

MID ISLAND

A drive through the countryside between these two towns takes you past ruins of old plantations, many bearing whimsical names (Morningstar, Solitude, Upper Love). The traffic moves quickly—by island standards—on the main roads, but you can pause and poke around if you head down some side lanes. It's easy to find your way west, but driving from north to south requires good navigation. Don't leave your hotel without a map. Allow an entire day for this trip, so you'll have enough time for a swim at a north shore beach. Although you can find lots of casual eateries on the main roads, pick up a picnic lunch if you plan to head off the beaten path.

TOP ATTRACTIONS

FAMILY

Fodor'sChoice

★

Estate Whim Museum. The restored estate, with a windmill, cook house, and other buildings, gives a sense of what life was like on St. Croix's sugar plantations in the 1800s. The oval-shape great house has high ceilings and antique furniture and utensils. Notice its fresh, airy atmosphere—the waterless stone moat around the great house was used

19

Turtles on St. Croix

Green, leatherback, and hawksbill turtles crawl ashore during their annual April-to-November nesting season to lay their eggs. They return from their life at sea every two to seven years to the beach where they were born. Since turtles can live for up to 100 years, they may return many times to nest in St. Croix.

The leatherbacks like Sandy Point National Wildlife Refuge and other spots on St. Croix's western end, but the hawksbills prefer Buck Island and the East End. Green turtles are also found primarily on the East End.

All are endangered species that face numerous predators, some natural, some the result of the human presence. Particularly in the Frederiksted area, dogs and cats prey on the nests and eat the hatchlings.

Occasionally a dog will attack a turtle about to lay its eggs, and cats train their kittens to hunt at turtle nests, creating successive generations of turtle-egg hunters. In addition, turtles have often been hit by fast-moving boats that leave large slices in their shells if they don't kill them outright.

The leatherbacks are the subject of a project by the Earthwatch conservation group. Each summer, teams arrive at Sandy Point National Wildlife Refuge to ensure that poachers, both natural and human, don't attack the turtles as they crawl up the beach. The teams also relocate nests that are laid in areas prone to erosion. When the eggs hatch, teams stand by to make sure the turtles make it safely to the sea, and scientists tag them so they can monitor their return to St. Croix.

---

not for defense but for gathering cooling air. If you have kids, the grounds are the perfect place for them to run around, perhaps while you browse in the museum gift shop. It's just outside of Frederiksted. ⊠ *Rte. 70, Whim* ☎ *340/772–0598* ⊕ *www.stcroixlandmarks.com* 🎟 *$10* ⊙ *Wed.–Sat. 10–3 and cruise-ship days.*

Fodor's Choice **St. George Village Botanical Garden.** At this 17-acre estate, fragrant flora
★ grows amid the ruins of a 19th-century sugarcane plantation. There are miniature versions of each ecosystem on St. Croix, from a semi-arid cactus grove to a verdant rain forest. The small museum is also well worth a visit. ⊠ *Rte. 70, turn north at sign, Estate Saint George* ☎ *340/692–2874* ⊕ *www.sgvbg.org* 🎟 *$8* ⊙ *Daily 9–5.*

WORTH NOTING

Captain Morgan Distillery. The base for Captain Morgan brand rum is made from molasses at this distillery. The tour includes exhibits on island and rum history, a movie about the process, and a tram tour of the distillery. In keeping with the company's responsible-drinking policy, the drink samples at the end of the tour are limited to two. ⊠ *Melvin Evans Hwy. and Rte. 663, Annaberg and Shannon Grove* ☎ *340/713–5654* ⊕ *www.captainmorganvisitorscenter.com* 🎟 *$10* ⊙ *Weekdays 9–5.*

Cruzan Rum Distillery. A tour of the company's factory, which was established in 1760, culminates in a tasting of its products, all sold here at good prices. It's worth a stop to look at the distillery's charming old buildings even if you're not a rum connoisseur. ⊠ *West Airport Rd., Diamond* ☏ *340/692–2280* ⊕ *www.cruzanrum.com* ✆ *$8* ⊙ *Weekdays 9–4.*

FREDERIKSTED AND ENVIRONS

St. Croix's second-largest town, Frederiksted, was founded in 1751. Just as Christiansted is famed for its Danish buildings, Frederiksted is known for its Victorian architecture. A stroll around its historic sights will take you no more than an hour. Allow a little more time if you want to duck into the few small shops. One long cruise-ship pier juts into the sparkling sea. It's the perfect place to start a tour of this quaint city.

WORTH NOTING

Caribbean Museum Center for the Arts. Sitting across from the waterfront in a historic building, this small museum hosts an always-changing roster of exhibits. Many are cutting-edge multimedia efforts that you might be surprised to find in such an out-of-the-way location. The openings are popular events. ⊠ *10 Strand St., Frederiksted* ☏ *340/772–2622* ⊕ *www. cmcarts.org* ✆ *Free* ⊙ *Thurs.–Sat. (and any cruise-ship day) 10–5.*

Estate Mount Washington Plantation. Several years ago, while surveying the property, the owners discovered the ruins of a sugar plantation beneath the rain-forest brush. The grounds have since been cleared and opened to the public. You can take a self-guided walking tour of the mill, the rum factory, and other ruins. ⊠ *Rte. 63, Estate Mount Washington and Washington Hill* ⊙ *Daily dawn–dusk.*

FAMILY **Fort Frederik.** On July 3, 1848, 8,000 slaves marched on this fort to demand their freedom. Danish governor Peter von Scholten, fearing they would burn the town to the ground, stood up in his carriage parked in front of the fort and granted their wish. The fort, completed in 1760, houses an art gallery and a number of interesting historical exhibits, including some focusing on the 1848 Emancipation and the 1917 transfer of the Virgin Islands from Denmark to the United States. It's within earshot of the Frederiksted Visitor Center. ⊠ *Waterfront, Frederiksted* ☏ *340/772–2021* ✆ *$3* ⊙ *Weekdays (and any cruise-ship day) 9–4.*

Frederiksted Visitor Center. Head here for brochures from numerous St. Croix businesses, as well as a few exhibits about the island. ⊠ *Pier Strand Street, Frederiksted* ☏ *340/773–0495* ⊙ *Weekdays 8–5.*

West End Salt Pond. A bird-watcher's delight, this salt pond attracts a large number of winged creatures, including flamingos. ⊠ *Veteran's Shore Dr., Hesselberg.*

NORTH SHORE

WORTH NOTING

Judith's Fancy. In this upscale neighborhood are the ruins of an old great house and tower of the same name, both remnants of a circa-1750 Danish sugar plantation. The "Judith" comes from the first name of a woman buried on the property. From the guardhouse at the neighborhood entrance, follow Hamilton Drive past some of St. Croix's loveliest houses. At the end of Hamilton Drive the road overlooks Salt River

19

Bay, where Christopher Columbus anchored in 1493. On the way back, make a detour left off Hamilton Drive onto Caribe Road for a close look at the ruins. The million-dollar villas are something to behold, too. ⊠ *Turn north onto Rte. 751, off Rte. 75, Estate Judith's Fancy.*

Mount Eagle. At 1,165 feet, this is St. Croix's highest peak. Leaving Cane Bay and passing North Star Beach, follow the coastal road that dips briefly into a forest; then turn left on Route 69. Just after you make the turn, the pavement is marked with the words "The Beast" and a set of giant paw prints. The hill you're about to climb is the famous Beast of the St. Croix Half Ironman Triathlon, an annual event during which participants must cycle up this intimidating slope. ⊠ *Rte. 69, Estate Fountain.*

Salt River Bay National Historical Park and Ecological Preserve. This joint national and local park commemorates the area where Christopher Columbus's men skirmished with the Carib Indians in 1493 on his second visit to the New World. The peninsula on the bay's east side is named for the event: Cabo de las Flechas (Cape of the Arrows). Although the park is still developing, it has several sights with cultural significance. A ball court, used by the Caribs in religious ceremonies, was discovered at the spot where the taxis park. Take a short hike up the dirt road to the ruins of an old earthen fort for great views of Salt River Bay. The area also encompasses a coastal estuary with the region's largest remaining mangrove forest, a submarine canyon, and several endangered species, including the hawksbill turtle and the roseate tern. A visitor center, open in winter only, sits just uphill to the west. The water at the beach can be on the rough side, but it's a nice place for sunning. ⊠ *Rte. 75 to Rte. 80, Estate Salt River* ☎ *340/773–1460* ⊕ *www. nps.gov/sari* ☉ *Call for seasonal hrs.*

BEACHES

St. Croix's beaches aren't as spectacular as those on St. John or St. Thomas. But that's not to say you won't find some good places to spread out for a day on the water. The best beach is on nearby Buck Island, a national monument where a marked snorkeling trail leads you through an extensive coral reef while a soft, sandy beach beckons a few yards away. Other great beaches are the unnamed West End beaches both south and north of Frederiksted. You can park yourself at any of the handful of restaurants north of Frederiksted. Some rent loungers, and you can get food and drinks right on the beach. Remember to remove all your valuables from the car and keep them out of sight when you go swimming. Break-ins happen on all three of the U.S. Virgin Islands, and most locals recommend leaving your windows down and leaving nothing in your car.

EAST END

Fodor's Choice   **Buck Island.** Part of Buck Island Reef National Monument, this is a
★   must-see for anyone in St. Croix. The beach is beautiful, but its finest treasures are those you can see when you plop off the boat and adjust your mask, snorkel, and fins to swim over colorful coral and darting fish. Don't know how to snorkel? No problem—the boat crew will

have you outfitted and in the water in no time. Take care not to step on those black-pointed spiny sea urchins or touch the mustard-color fire coral, which can cause a nasty burn. Most charter-boat trips start with a snorkel over the lovely reef before a stop at the island's beach. An easy 20-minute hike leads uphill to an overlook for a bird's-eye view of the reef below. You'll find restrooms at the beach. **Amenities:** toilets. **Best for:** snorkeling; swimming. ⊠ *5 miles (8 km) north of St. Croix* ☎ *340/773–1460* ⊕ *www.nps.gov/buis.*

NORTH SHORE

Cane Bay. On the island's breezy North Shore, Cane Bay does not always have gentle waters, but there are seldom many people around, and the scuba diving and snorkeling are wondrous. You can see elkhorn and brain corals, and less than 200 yards out is the drop-off called Cane Bay Wall. Cane Bay can be an all-day destination: you can rent kayaks and snorkeling and scuba gear at water-sports shops across the road, and a couple of casual restaurants beckon when the sun gets too hot. **Amenities:** food and drink; water sports. **Best for:** solitude; snorkeling; swimming. ⊠ *Rte. 80, about 4 miles (6 km) west of Salt River, Cane Bay.*

FREDERIKSTED

West End beaches. There are several unnamed beaches along the coast road north of Frederiksted, but it's best if you don't stray too far from civilization. For safety's sake, most vacationers plop down their towel near one of the casual restaurants spread out along Route 63. The beach at the Rainbow Beach Club, a five-minute drive outside Frederiksted, has a bar, a casual restaurant, water sports, and volleyball. If you want to be close to the cruise-ship pier, just stroll on over to the adjacent sandy beach in front of Fort Frederik. On the way south out of Frederiksted, the stretch near Sandcastle on the Beach hotel is also lovely. **Amenities:** food and drink; water sports. **Best for:** snorkeling, swimming, walking. ⊠ *Rte. 63, north and south of Frederiksted, Frederiksted.*

19

WHERE TO EAT

Seven flags have flown over St. Croix, and each has left its legacy in the island's cuisine. Fresh local seafood is plentiful and always good; wahoo, mahimahi, and conch are most popular. Island chefs often add Caribbean twists to familiar dishes. For a true island experience, stop at a local restaurant for goat stew, curried chicken, or fried pork chops. Regardless of where you eat, your meal will be an informal affair. As is the case everywhere in the Caribbean, prices are higher than you'd pay on the mainland. Some restaurants may close for a week or two in September or October, so if you're traveling during these months, it's best to call ahead.

CHRISTIANSTED

$$$ ✕ **Angry Nates.** Serving breakfast, lunch, and dinner, Angry Nates has
ECLECTIC something for everyone on its extensive menu. Dinner can be as fancy as tilapia and garlic shrimp with mushrooms, white wine, and garlic butter, or as basic as a burger or chicken sandwich. If your taste buds run to hot, try the shrimp *pistolette*—a hallowed-out baguette filled with shrimp and laced with really hot sauce. $ *Average main: $25*

Some of St. Croix's best beaches are on the West End of the island around Frederiksted.

✉ *King Cross St., at the Boardwalk, Christiansted* ☎ *340/692–6283* 🌐 *www.angrynates.com.*

$ ECLECTIC 🍴 **Avocado Pitt.** Locals gather at this Christiansted waterfront spot for the breakfast and lunch specials, as well as for a bit of gossip. Breakfast runs to stick-to-the-ribs dishes like oatmeal and pancakes. Lunches include such basics as a crispy chicken-breast sandwich. The yellowfin tuna sandwich is made from fresh fish and gives a new taste to a standard lunchtime favorite. [$] *Average main: $12* ✉ *King Christian Hotel, 59 Kings Wharf, Christiansted* ☎ *340/773–9843* ⏲ *No dinner.*

$$ FRENCH 🍴 **Café Christine.** At this favorite with the professionals who work in downtown Christiansted, the presentations are as dazzling as the food. The small menu changes daily, but look for dishes such as shrimp-and-asparagus salad drizzled with a lovely vinaigrette or a vegetarian plate with quiche, salad, and lentils. Desserts are perfection. If the pear pie topped with chocolate is on the menu, don't hesitate. This tiny restaurant has tables in both the air-conditioned dining room and on the outside porch that overlooks historic buildings. [$] *Average main: $14* ✉ *Apothecary Hall Courtyard, 6 Company St., Christiansted* ☎ *340/713–1500* 💳 *No credit cards* ⏲ *Closed weekends and July–mid-Nov. No dinner.*

$ CARIBBEAN 🍴 **Harvey's.** The dining room is plain, even dowdy, and plastic lace tablecloths constitute the sole attempt at decor. But who cares?—the food is delicious. Daily specials, such as mouthwatering goat stew and tender conch in butter, served with big helpings of rice and vegetables, are listed on the blackboard. Genial owner Sarah Harvey takes great pride in her kitchen, bustling out from behind the stove to chat and urge you to eat up. [$] *Average main: $11* ✉ *11B Company St., Christiansted* ☎ *340/773–3433* ⏲ *Closed Sun. No dinner.*

$$$
ECLECTIC
FAMILY
Fodor's Choice
★

✕ **Rum Runners.** The view is as stellar as the food at this highly popular local standby. Sitting right on the Christiansted boardwalk, Rum Runners serves a little bit of everything, including a to-die-for salad of crispy romaine lettuce and tender grilled lobster drizzled with lemongrass vinaigrette. Heartier fare includes baby-back ribs cooked with the restaurant's special spice blend and Guinness stout. $ *Average main: $25* ⊠ *Hotel Caravelle, 44A Queen Cross St., Christiansted* ☎ *340/773–6585* ⊕ *www.rumrunnersstcroix.com.*

$$$
ECLECTIC

✕ **Savant.** Savant is one of those small but special spots that locals love. The cuisine is a fusion of Mexican, Thai, and Caribbean—an unusual combination that works surprisingly well. You can find anything from fresh fish to Thai curry with chicken to stuffed fillet with portobello mushrooms and goat cheese. With 20 tables crammed into the indoor dining room and small courtyard, this little place can get crowded. Call early for reservations. $ *Average main: $27* ⊠ *4C Hospital St., Christiansted* ☎ *340/713–8666* ⊕ *www.savantstx.com* ☾ *Closed Sun. No lunch.*

WEST OF CHRISTIANSTED

$$$
ECLECTIC
FAMILY

✕ **Gayle'z Breezez.** This aptly named restaurant, *the* place on the island for Sunday brunch, is poolside at the Club St. Croix condominiums. Visitors and locals are drawn by its reasonable prices and good food. Locals also gather for lunch, when the menu includes everything from burgers to blackened prime rib with a horseradish sauce. For dessert, try the amaretto cheesecake with either chocolate or fruit topping. $ *Average main: $25* ⊠ *Club St. Croix, 3280 Golden Rock, off Rte. 752, Estate Golden Rock* ☎ *340/718–7077.*

$$$
ITALIAN

✕ **Salud Bistro.** This eatery's imaginative menu takes its cue from the fresh flavors of the Mediterranean. Start with the savory cheese plate served with homemade bread and crostini before moving on to fresh fish or grilled duck in a hibiscus confit. $ *Average main: $27* ⊠ *Princess Plaza, Rte. 75, La Grande Princesse* ☎ *340/718–7900* ⊕ *www.saludbistro.com* ☾ *Closed Sun. No lunch.*

EAST END

$$$
ECLECTIC

✕ **The Deep End.** A favorite with locals and vacationers, this poolside restaurant serves up terrific burgers, steak, and seafood, as well as delicious pasta dishes and popular salads. To get here from Christiansted, take Route 82 and turn left at the sign for Green Cay Marina. $ *Average main: $23* ⊠ *Tamarind Reef Hotel, Rte. 82, Annas Hope* ☎ *340/718–7071.*

NORTH SHORE

$$
AMERICAN

✕ **Off the Wall.** Divers fresh from a plunge at the North Shore's popular Cane Bay Wall gather at this breezy spot on the beach. If you want to sit a spell before you order, a hammock beckons. Deli sandwiches, served with potato chips, make up most of the menu. Pizza and salads are also available. $ *Average main: $14* ⊠ *Rte. 80, Cane Bay* ☎ *340/718–4771* ⊕ *www.otwstx.com.*

19

FREDERIKSTED

$$$ ECLECTIC

🍴 **Beach Side Café.** Sunday brunch is big, but locals and visitors also flock to this oceanfront bistro at Sandcastle on the Beach resort for lunch and dinner. Both menus include burgers and salads, but at dinner the crispy half duck with berry sauce shines. For lunch, the hummus plate is a good bet. [$] *Average main: $29* ✉ *Sandcastle on the Beach, 127 Smithfield, Frederiksted* ☎ *340/772–1266* 🌐 *www.beachsidecafestx.com* ⏲ *Closed Tues. and Wed.*

$$$ AMERICAN Fodor's Choice ★

🍴 **Blue Moon.** This terrific little bistro, which has a loyal local following, offers a changing menu that draws on Cajun and Caribbean flavors. Try the spicy gumbo with andouille sausage or crab cakes with a spicy aioli for your appetizer. The pasta verde with vegetables makes a good entrée, and they serve delicious and decadent desserts. There's live jazz on Wednesday and Friday. [$] *Average main: $23* ✉ *7 Strand St., Frederiksted* ☎ *340/772–2222* 🌐 *www.thebluemoonstcroix.com* ⏲ *Closed Sun. and Mon.*

$ ECLECTIC

🍴 **Polly's at the Pier.** With an emphasis on fresh ingredients, this very casual spot right on the waterfront serves delicious fare. The gourmet grilled-cheese sandwich comes with your choice of three cheeses as well as delicious additions like basil, fresh Bosc pears, and avocado. Salads are a specialty, and many are made with local Bibb lettuce and organic mixed greens. [$] *Average main: $11* ✉ *3 Strand St., Frederiksted* ☎ *340/719–9434* ⏲ *No dinner.*

$ DELI FAMILY

🍴 **Turtles Deli.** You can eat outside at this tiny spot just as you enter downtown Frederiksted. Lunches are as basic as a corned beef on rye or as imaginative as the Raven (turkey breast with bacon, tomato, and melted cheddar cheese on French bread). Also good is the Beast, named after the grueling hill that challenges bikers in the annual triathlon. It's piled high with hot roast beef, raw onion, and melted Swiss cheese with horseradish and mayonnaise. Early risers stop by for cinnamon buns and espresso. Turtles After Dark, upstairs, is open 5 to 10 pm. [$] *Average main: $12* ✉ *38 Strand St., at Prince Passage, Frederiksted* ☎ *340/772–3676* 🌐 *www.turtlesdeli.com* 💳 *No credit cards* ⏲ *Closed Sun.*

WHERE TO STAY

If you sleep in either the Christiansted or Frederiksted area, you'll be closest to shopping, restaurants, and nightlife. Most of the island's other hotels will put you just steps from the beach. St. Croix has several small but special properties that offer personalized service. If you like all the comforts of home, you may prefer to stay in a condominium or villa. Room rates on St. Croix are competitive with those on other islands, and if you travel off-season, you can find substantially reduced prices. Many properties offer money-saving honeymoon and dive packages. Whether you stay in a hotel, a condominium, or a villa, you'll enjoy up-to-date amenities. Most properties have room TVs, but at some bed-and-breakfasts there might be only one, in the common room.

Although a stay right in historic Christiansted may mean putting up with a little urban noise, you probably won't have trouble sleeping.

Christiansted rolls up the sidewalks fairly early, and humming air conditioners drown out any noise. Solitude is guaranteed at hotels and inns outside Christiansted and those on the outskirts of sleepy Frederiksted.

PRIVATE CONDOMINIUMS AND VILLAS

Most of the villas in St. Croix are in the center or on the East End. Renting a villa gives you the convenience of home as well as top-notch amenities. Many have pools, hot tubs, and deluxe furnishings. Most companies meet you at the airport, arrange for a rental car, and provide helpful information about the island.

If you want to be close to the island's restaurants and shopping, look for a condominium or villa in the hills above Christiansted or on either side of the town. An East End location gets you out of Christiansted's hustle and bustle, but you're still only 15 minutes from town. North Shore locations are lovely, with gorgeous sea views and lots of peace and quiet.

RENTAL CONTACTS

Vacation St. Croix. ⊠ *400 La Grande Princess, Christiansted* ☏ *340/718–0361, 877/788–0361* ⊕ *www.vacationstcroix.com.*

CHRISTIANSTED

$ | **Hotel Caravelle.** A stay at the Caravelle, which is near the harbor,
HOTEL | puts you at the waterfront end of a pleasant shopping arcade and steps from shops and restaurants. **Pros:** good restaurant; convenient location; parking. **Cons:** no beach; busy neighborhood. $ *Rooms from: $150* ⊠ *44A Queen Cross St., Christiansted* ☏ *340/773–0687, 800/524–0410* ⊕ *www.hotelcaravelle.com* ⊅ *43 rooms, 1 suite* ⦿*No meals.*

$ | **Hotel on the Cay.** Hop on the free ferry to reach this peaceful lodging
RESORT | in the middle of Christiansted Harbor. **Pros:** quiet; convenient location; lovely beach. **Cons:** accessible only by ferry; no parking available. $ *Rooms from: $149* ⊠ *Protestant Cay, Christiansted* ☏ *340/773–2035, 855/654–0301* ⊕ *www.hotelonthecay.com* ⊅ *54 rooms* ⦿*No meals.*

WEST OF CHRISTIANSTED

$ | **Carringtons Inn.** Local flavor, personalized service, and individual style
B&B/INN | make this intimate inn a welcome respite from the realm of cookie-
Fodor'sChoice | cutter resorts, with its location in a former private home that offers a
★ | lovely pool and unbeatable ocean views. **Pros:** feels like a private home; welcoming host; tasteful rooms; great breakfasts. **Cons:** no beach; need car to get around. $ *Rooms from: $150* ⊠ *56 Estate Hermon Hill, Christiansted* ☏ *340/713–0508, 877/658–0508* ⊕ *www.carringtonsinn. com* ⊅ *5 rooms* ⦿*Breakfast.*

$ | **Club St. Croix.** Sitting beachfront just outside Christiansted, this mod-
RENTAL | ern condominium complex faces a lovely sandy beach. **Pros:** beachfront
FAMILY | location; good restaurant; full kitchens. **Cons:** need car to get around; sketchy neighborhood. $ *Rooms from: $195* ⊠ *Rte. 752, Estate Golden Rock* ☏ *340/718–9150, 800/524–2025* ⊕ *www.antillesresorts.com* ⊅ *53 apartments* ⦿*No meals.*

$ | **Colony Cove.** In a string of condominium complexes, Colony Cove lets
RENTAL | you experience comfortable beachfront living. **Pros:** beachfront loca-
FAMILY | tion; comfortable units; good views. **Cons:** sketchy neighborhood; need car to get around. $ *Rooms from: $235* ⊠ *Rte. 752, Estate Golden*

19

Rock ☎ *340/718–1965, 800/524–2025* 🌐 *www.antillesresorts.com* 🛏 *62 apartments* 🍴 *No meals.*

$ RESORT 🏨 **The Palms at Pelican Cove.** A 10-minute drive from Christiansted's interesting shopping and restaurants, this resort, with its mixed-bag of guests, has a gorgeous strand of white sand at its doorstep. **Pros:** nice beach; good dining options; friendly staff. **Cons:** need car to get out and about; neighborhood not the best. [$] *Rooms from: $254* ✉ *Off Rte. 752, La Grande Princesse* ☎ *340/718–8920, 800/548–4460* 🌐 *www.palmspelicancove.com* 🛏 *41 rooms* 🍴 *No meals.*

EAST END

$$ RESORT FAMILY 🏨 **The Buccaneer.** Aimed at travelers who want everything at their fingertips, this resort has sandy beaches, swimming pools, and extensive sports facilities. **Pros:** beachfront location; numerous activities; nice golf course. **Cons:** pricey rates; insular environment; need car to get around. [$] *Rooms from: $299* ✉ *Rte. 82, Box 25200, Shoys* ☎ *340/712–2100, 800/255–3881* 🌐 *www.thebuccaneer.com* 🛏 *138 rooms, 1 villa* 🍴 *Breakfast.*

$ RESORT FAMILY 🏨 **Chenay Bay Beach Resort.** The seaside setting and complimentary tennis and water-sports equipment make this resort a real find, particularly for families with active kids. **Pros:** beachfront location; pretty grounds; friendly staff. **Cons:** need car to get around; lacks pizzazz. [$] *Rooms from: $194* ✉ *Rte. 82, Christiansted* ☎ *340/718–2918,* 🌐 *www.chenaybay.com* 🛏 *50 rooms* 🍴 *No meals.*

$$$ RESORT 🏨 **Divi Carina Bay Resort.** An oceanfront location, the island's only casino, and plenty of activities make this resort a good bet. **Pros:** spacious beach; good restaurant; on-site casino. **Cons:** need car to get around; many stairs to climb; staff can seem chilly. [$] *Rooms from: $418* ✉ *25 Rte. 60, Estate Turner Hole* ☎ *340/773–9700, 877/773–9700* 🌐 *www.divicarina.com* 🛏 *174 rooms, 2 suites, 20 villas* 🍴 *All-inclusive.*

$ HOTEL 🏨 **Tamarind Reef Resort.** Spread out along a sandy beach, these low-slung buildings offer casual comfort. **Pros:** good snorkeling; tasty restaurant; rooms have kitchenettes. **Cons:** need car to get around; motel-style rooms. [$] *Rooms from: $200* ✉ *5001 Tamarind Reef, off Rte. 82, Annas Hope* ☎ *340/718–4455, 800/619–0014* 🌐 *www.tamarindreefresort.com* 🛏 *39 rooms* 🍴 *No meals.*

$$ RENTAL 🏨 **Villa Madeleine.** If you like privacy and your own private pool, you'll like Villa Madeleine. **Pros:** pleasant decor; full kitchens; private pools. **Cons:** lower units sometimes lack views; need car to get around; no beachfront. [$] *Rooms from: $285* ✉ *Off Rte. 82, Teague's Bay* ☎ *340/718–0361, 877/788–0361* 🌐 *www.vacationstcroix.com* 🛏 *43 villas* 🍴 *No meals.*

FREDERIKSTED

$ RESORT 🏨 **Sandcastle on the Beach.** Right on a gorgeous stretch of white beach, Sandcastle has a tropical charm that harks back to a simpler time in the Caribbean; its nearness to Frederiksted's interesting dining scene is also a plus. **Pros:** lovely beach; close to restaurants; gay-friendly. **Cons:** neighborhood sketchy at night; need car to get around; no children's activities. [$] *Rooms from: $149* ✉ *127 Smithfield, Frederiksted* ☎ *340/772–1205, 800/524–2018* 🌐 *www.sandcastleonthebeach.com* 🛏 *9 rooms, 10 suites, 3 villas* 🍴 *No meals.*

NORTH SHORE

$ B&B/INN **Arawak Bay: The Inn at Salt River.** With stellar views of St. Croix's North Shore and an affable host, this small inn allows you to settle into island life at a price that doesn't break the bank. **Pros:** 20 minutes from Christiansted; good prices. **Cons:** no beach nearby; can be some road noise. [$] *Rooms from: $140* ✉ *Rte. 80, Estate Salt River* ☎ *340/772–1684* 🌐 *www.arawakbaysaltriver.co.vi* 🛏 *12 rooms* 🍴 *Breakfast.*

$$ RESORT **Renaissance St. Croix Carambola Beach Resort and Spa.** We like this resort's stellar beachfront setting and peaceful ambience. **Pros:** lovely beach; relaxing atmosphere; close to golf. **Cons:** isolated location; need car to get around. [$] *Rooms from: $329* ✉ *Rte. 80, Estate Fountain* ☎ *340/778–3800, 888/503–8760* 🌐 *www.carambolabeachresort.com* 🛏 *150 rooms* 🍴 *No meals.*

$ B&B/INN **Villa Margarita.** This quiet retreat provides a particularly good base if you want to admire the dramatic views of the windswept coast. **Pros:** friendly host; great views; snorkeling nearby. **Cons:** isolated location; need car to get around; limited amenities. [$] *Rooms from: $145* ✉ *Off Rte. 80, Estate Salt River* ☎ *340/692–1408* 🌐 *www.villamargarita.com* 🛏 *3 units* 🍴 *No meals.*

$ HOTEL **Waves at Cane Bay.** St Croix's famed Cane Bay Wall is just offshore from this hotel, giving it an enviable location. **Pros:** great diving; restaurants nearby; beaches nearby. **Cons:** need car to get around; on main road; bland decor. [$] *Rooms from: $120* ✉ *Rte. 80, Cane Bay* ☎ *340/718–1815* 🌐 *www.thewavescanebay.com* 🛏 *10 rooms* 🍴 *No meals.*

NIGHTLIFE AND PERFORMING ARTS

Christiansted has a lively and eminently casual club scene near the waterfront. Frederiksted has a couple of restaurants and clubs offering weekend entertainment. To find out what's happening in St. Croix's ever-changing nightlife and eclectic arts scene, check out the local newspapers—*V.I. Daily News* (🌐 *virginislandsdailynews.com*) and *St. Croix Avis*.

CHRISTIANSTED

Fort Christian Brew Pub. Locals and visitors come here to listen to live music several nights a week. ✉ *Boardwalk at end of Kings Alley, Christiansted* ☎ *340/713–9820* 🌐 *www.fortchristianbrewpub.com.*

Hotel on the Cay. This off-shore resort hosts a West Indian buffet on Tuesday night in the winter season, when you can watch a broken-bottle dancer (a dancer who braves a carpet of shattered glass) and mocko jumbie (stilt-dancing) characters. ✉ *Protestant Cay, Christiansted* ☎ *340/773–2035* 🌐 *www.hotelonthecay.com.*

EAST END

Divi Carina Bay Resort. Although you can gamble at the island's only casino, it's really the music that draws big crowds to this resort. ✉ *25 Rte. 60, Estate Turner Hole* ☎ *340/773–7529* 🌐 *www.divicarina.com.*

MID ISLAND

Whim Plantation Museum. The museum outside Frederiksted hosts classical music concerts in winter. ⊠ *Rte. 70, Whim* 🕾 *340/772–0598* ⊕ *www.stcroixlandmarks.com.*

FREDERIKSTED

Fodor'sChoice
★
Blue Moon. Blue Moon is a popular waterfront restaurant in Frederiksted, and it's the place to be for live jazz on Wednesday and Friday. It's one of the few nightlife options at this end of the island. ⊠ *7 Strand St., Frederiksted* 🕾 *340/772-2222* ⊕ *www.bluemoonstcroix.com.*

Fodor'sChoice
★
Sunset Jazz. This outdoor event is a hot ticket in Frederiksted, drawing crowds of visitors and locals at 5:30 pm on the third Friday of every month to watch the sun go down and listen to good music. ⊠ *Waterfront, Frederiksted* 🕾 *340/690–1741.*

SHOPPING

Although the shopping on St. Croix isn't as varied or extensive as that on St. Thomas, the island does have several small stores with unusual merchandise. St. Croix shop hours are usually Monday through Saturday 9 to 5, but there are some shops in Christiansted open in the evening. Stores are often closed on Sunday.

CHRISTIANSTED

In Christiansted the best shopping areas are the **Pan Am Pavilion** and **Caravelle Arcade**, off Strand Street, and along **King** and **Company streets.** These streets give way to arcades filled with boutiques. **Gallows Bay** has a blossoming shopping area in a quiet neighborhood.

BOOKS

Undercover Books. This well-stocked independent bookseller sells Caribbean-themed books as well as the latest good reads. The store is in the Gallows Bay shopping area. ⊠ *5030 Anchor Way, across from post office, Gallows Bay* 🕾 *340/719–1567* ⊕ *www.undercoverbooksvi.com.*

CLOTHING

From the Gecko. This store sells the most stylish clothes on St. Croix. ⊠ *55 Company St., Christiansted* 🕾 *340/778–9433* ⊕ *www.fromthegecko.com.*

Hot Heads. This small store sells hats, hats, and more hats, which are often perched on top of cotton shifts, comfortable shirts, and trendy tropical wear. If you forgot your bathing suit, this store has a good selection. ⊠ *1244 Queen Cross St., Christiansted* 🕾 *340/773–7888.*

Island Tribe. Colorful batik dresses, shirts, shifts, and scarves in soft rayon and cotton round out your tropical wardrobe. Sizes range from small to 4X. The clothing, and an interesting array of jewelry, comes from Bali. ⊠ *57 Company St., Christiansted* 🕾 *340/719–0936.*

GIFTS

The Blue Mutt. Shop for a good cause at this small store that benefits the St. Croix Animal Welfare Center. The shelves are filled with local art, T-shirts, cards, soaps, candles, dog accessories, and much more. ⊠ *5 Company St., Christiansted* 🕾 *340/690–4624.*

Cache of the Day. This tiny store sells whatever its sea theme has tossed up. Mermaid dolls recline on shelves next to dishtowels printed with shapes of the sea. There are stuffed animals and jewelry that make perfect gifts. ⊠ *55 Company St., Christiansted* ☎ *340/773–3648.*

Many Hands. This shop sells pottery in bright colors, paintings of St. Croix and the Caribbean, prints, and maps. They are all made by local artists, and they all make for perfect take-home gifts. ■TIP➡ **The owners ship all over the world.** ⊠ *21 Pan Am Pavilion, Strand St., Christiansted* ☎ *340/773–1990.*

Mitchell-Larsen Studio. This glass gallery offers an interesting amalgam of carefully crafted glass plates, suncatchers, and more. The pieces, all made on-site by a St. Croix glassmaker, are often whimsically adorned with tropical fish, flora, and fauna. ⊠ *58 Company St., Christiansted* ☎ *340/719–1000* ⊕ *www.mitchelllarsenstudio.com.*

Fodor's Choice
★
Royal Poinciana. The attractive Royal Poinciana is filled with island seasonings and hot sauces, West Indian crafts, bath gels, and herbal teas. Shop here for tablecloths and paper goods in bright tropical colors. ⊠ *1113 Strand St., Christiansted* ☎ *340/773–9892.*

HOUSEWARES
Designworks. This store and gallery carries furniture as well as one of the largest selections of local art, along with Caribbean-inspired bric-a-brac in all price ranges. If a mahogany armoire or four-poster bed catches your fancy, the staff can have it shipped from its mainland warehouse to your home at no charge. ⊠ *6 Company St., Christiansted* ☎ *340/713–8102* ⊕ *www.islandlivingstore.com.*

JEWELRY
Crucian Gold. St. Croix native Brian Bishop's trademark piece is the Turk's Head ring (a knot of interwoven gold strands). His son, Nathan Bishop, is now creating contemporary sterling and gold pendants, rings, and earrings. ⊠ *1112 Strand St., Christiansted* ☎ *340/773–5241* ⊕ *www.cruciangold.com.*

Gold Worker. This shop specializes in handcrafted jewelry in silver and gold that will remind you of the Caribbean. Hummingbirds dangle from silver chains and sand dollars adorn gold necklaces. The sugar mills in silver and gold speak of St. Croix's past. ⊠ *3 Company St., Christiansted* ☎ *340/514–6042.*

ib designs. This small shop showcases the handcrafted jewelry of local craftsman Whealan Massicott. Whether in silver or gold, the designs are simply elegant. ⊠ *Company St. at Queen Cross St., Christiansted* ☎ *340/773–4322* ⊕ *www.islandboydesigns.com.*

Nelthropp and Low. The jewelers at Nelthropp and Low can create one-of-a-kind pieces to your design. The shop specializes in gold jewelry but also carries diamonds, emeralds, rubies, and sapphires. ⊠ *1102 Strand St., Christiansted* ☎ *340/773–0365,* ⊕ *www.nelthropp-low.com.*

19

Sonya's. This store is owned and operated by Sonya Hough, who invented the popular hook bracelet. She has added interesting decoration to these bracelets: the swirling symbol used in weather forecasts to indicate hurricanes. ⊠ *1 Company St., Christiansted* ☎ *340/778–8605* ⊕ *www.sonyaltd.com.*

LIQUOR AND TOBACCO

Baci Duty Free. The walk-in humidor here has a good selection of Arturo Fuente, Partagas, and Macanudo cigars. Baci also carries high-end liquor, sleek Swiss-made watches, and fine jewelry. ⊠ *1235 Queen Cross St., Christiansted* ☎ *340/773–5040* ⊕ *www.bacidutyfree.com.*

WEST OF CHRISTIANSED

FOOD

Pueblo. This market is similar to those stores back on the mainland. ⊠ *Golden Rock Shopping Center, Rte. 75, Christiansted* ☎ *340/718–0118.*

EAST END

FOOD

Seaside Market and Deli. Although it's on the smallish side, this market has good-quality deli items. ⊠ *Rte. 82, Mount Welcome Estate* ☎ *340/719–9393.*

MID ISLAND

FOOD

Cost-U-Less. This warehouse-type store is great for visitors because it doesn't charge a membership fee. It's in the busy Sunny Isle area. ⊠ *Rte. 70, Peter's Rest* ☎ *340/719–4442* ⊕ *www.costuless.com.*

Plaza Extra. This supermarket chain has a good selection of Middle Eastern foods, in addition to the usual grocery-store items. ⊠ *Queen Mary Hwy., Rte. 70, Mount Pleasant* ☎ *340/719–1870* ⊕ *www.plazaextra.com* ⊠ *Rte. 70, Sion Farm* ☎ *340/778–6240* ⊕ *www.plazaextra.com.*

Pueblo. This stateside-style market has another branch west of Christiansted. ⊠ *Villa La Reine Shopping Center, Rte. 75, La Reine* ☎ *340/778–1272.*

LIQUOR AND TOBACCO

Kmart. The U.S. discount chain has two branches on St. Croix, both of which carry a huge line of deep-discounted, duty-free liquor, among many other items. ⊠ *Sunshine Mall, Rte. 70, Frederiksted* ☎ *340/692–5848* ⊠ *Sunny Isle Shopping Center, Rte. 70, Sunny Isle* ☎ *340/719–9190.*

FREDERIKSTED

The best shopping in Frederiksted is along **Strand Street** and in the side streets and alleyways that connect it with **King Street.** Most stores close on Sunday, except when a cruise ship is in port. Keep in mind that Frederiksted has a reputation for muggings, so it's best to stick to populated areas of Strand and King streets, where there are few—if any—problems.

SPORTS AND THE OUTDOORS

BOAT TOURS

Almost everyone takes a day trip to Buck Island aboard a charter boat. Most leave from the Christiansted waterfront or from Green Cay Marina and stop for a snorkel at the island's eastern end before dropping anchor off a gorgeous sandy beach for a swim, a hike, and lunch. Sailboats can often stop right at the beach; a larger boat might have to anchor a bit farther offshore. A full-day sail runs about $100, with lunch included on most trips. A half-day sail costs about $68.

Big Beard's Adventure Tours. From catamarans that depart from the Christiansted waterfront, you'll head to Buck Island for snorkeling before dropping anchor at a private beach for a barbecue lunch. ⊠ *Queen Cross St. Waterfront, Christiansted* ☎ *340/773–4482* ⊕ *www.bigbeards.com.*

Buck Island Charters. These charters are on two trimarans, *Teroro II* and *Dragonfly,* which leave Green Cay Marina for full- or half-day sails. Bring your own lunch. ⊠ *Green Cay Marina, Annas Hope* ☎ *340/718–3161* ⊕ *www.gotostcroix.com.*

Caribbean Sea Adventures. With their crafts leaving from the Christiansted waterfront, Caribbean Sea Adventures has both half- and full-day trips to Buck Island. ⊠ *Christiansted Boardwalk, Christiansted* ☎ *340/773–2628* ⊕ *www.caribbeanseaadventures.com.*

DIVING AND SNORKELING

At **Buck Island,** a short boat ride from Christiansted or Green Cay Marina, the reef is so nice that it's been named a national monument. You can dive right off the beach at **Cane Bay,** which has a spectacular drop-off called the Cane Bay Wall. Dive operators also do boat trips along the wall, usually leaving from Salt River or Christiansted. **Frederiksted Pier** is home to a colony of sea horses, creatures seldom seen in the waters of the Virgin Islands. At **Green Cay,** just outside Green Cay Marina in the East End, you can see colorful fish swimming around the reefs and rocks. Two exceptional North Shore sites are **North Star** and **Salt River,** which you can reach only by boat. At Salt River you can float downward through a canyon filled with colorful fish and coral.

The island's dive shops take you out for one- or two-tank dives. Plan to pay about $65 for a one-tank dive and $100 for a two-tank dive, including equipment and an underwater tour. All companies offer certification and introductory courses called resort dives for novices.

Which dive outfit you pick usually depends on where you're staying. Your hotel may have one on-site. If so, you're just a short stroll away from the dock. If not, other companies are close by. Where the dive boat goes on a particular day depends on the weather, but in any case, all St. Croix dive sites are special. All shops are affiliated with PADI, the Professional Association of Diving Instructors.

Cane Bay Dive Shop. This is the place to go if you want to do a beach dive or boat dive along the North Shore. The famed Cane Bay Wall is 200 yards from the PADI Five Star facility. This company also has shops at Pan Am Pavilion in Christiansted, on Strand Street in Frederiksted, and

19

at the Divi Carina Bay Resort. ⊠ *Rte. 80, Cane Bay* ☎ *340/718–9913, 800/338–3843* ⊕ *www.canebayscuba.com.*

Dive Experience. Handy for those staying in Christiansted, Dive Experience runs trips to the North Shore walls and reefs, in addition to offering the usual certification and introductory classes. It's a PADI Five Star facility. ⊠ *Boardwalk and Kings Alley, Christiansted* ☎ *340/773–3307, 800/235–9047* ⊕ *www.divexp.com.*

N2 the Blue. N2 takes divers right off the beach near the Frederiksted Pier, on night dives off the Frederiksted Pier, or on boat trips to the Salt River Wall. ⊠ *202 Custom House St., Frederiksted* ☎ *340/772–3483,* ⊕ *www.n2theblue.com.*

St. Croix Ultimate Bluewater Adventures. This company can take you to your choice of more than 75 sites; it also offers a variety of packages that include hotel stays, stylish and comfortable island wear, and dive gear available at the dive shop. ⊠ *Queen Cross St., Christiansted* ☎ *340/773–5994, 877/567–1367* ⊕ *www.stcroixscuba.com.*

FISHING

Since the early 1980s, some 20 world records—many for blue marlin—have been set in these waters. Sailfish, skipjack, bonito, tuna (allison, blackfin, and yellowfin), and wahoo are abundant. A charter runs about $500 for a half-day (for up to six people), with most boats going out for four-, six-, or eight-hour trips.

Captain Festus. Captain Festus takes you to spots all around St. Croix on his 55-foot boat *Sea Hunter* and 35-foot *Triton.* ⊠ *Kings Wharf, Christiansted* ☎ *340/277–1751.*

Gone Ketchin'. Captain Grizz, a true old salt, heads these trips. ⊠ *Salt River Marina, Rte. 80, Estate Salt River* ☎ *340/713–1175* ⊕ *www. goneketchin.com.*

GOLF

Fodor's Choice **Buccaneer Golf Course.** This 18-hole course is close to Christiansted and
★ features views of the Caribbean from 13 of its holes. Golf lessons and club rentals are available. ⊠ *Rte. 82, Shoys* ☎ *340/712–2144* ⊕ *www. thebuccaneer.com* ⊠ *$95 for 18 holes; $65 for 9 holes; additional $25 for cart rental.* ⅃. *18 holes, 5688 yards, par 70.*

Carambola Golf Club. Golfers should enjoy the exotic beauty of this difficult course in the rain forest designed by Robert Trent Jones Sr. because they might not enjoy their score. An extra sleeve of balls might also be required. The long water holes never return splash balls and the jungle rough seldom does. Most fairways are forgiving with ample landing area, but the length of many holes makes it challenging. ⊠ *Rte. 69, Estate River* ☎ *340/778–5638* ⊕ *www.golfcarambola.com* ⊠ *$125* ⅃. *18 holes, 5727 yards, par 72.*

The Links at Divi St. Croix. This attractive minigolf course is just across from the Divi Carina Bay Resort. ⊠ *Rte. 60, Estate Turner Hole* ☎ *340/773–9700* ⊕ *www.divicarina.com* ⊠ *$8.*

Reef Golf Course. If you want to enjoy panoramic Caribbean views without paying high costs, the public, 9-hole Reef Golf course on the island's East End is the place to go. The course design is basic, but the views

Seaside horseback riding on the shores of St. Croix

from the hillside are spectacular. Trees on this course very seldom enter into play, and sand traps are absent. The seventh hole with its highly elevated tee is the most interesting. ⊠ *Rte. 82, Teague's Bay* ☎ *340/773–8844* ⌨ *$40* ⚑ *9 holes, 2395 yards, par 35.*

GUIDED TOURS

Sweeny's St. Croix Safari Tours. These van tours of St. Croix depart from Christiansted and last about five hours. Costs run from $70 per person, including admission fees to attractions. ⊠ *Christiansted* ☎ *340/773–6700* ⊕ *www.gotostcroix.com.*

19

HIKING

Ay-Ay Eco Hike and Tours. Ras Lumumba Corriette takes hikers up hill and down dale in some of St. Croix's most remote places, including the rain forest and Mount Victory. Some hikes include stops at old ruins. The cost is $60 per person for a three- or four-hour hike. There's a three-person minimum. ☎ *340/772–4079* ⊕ *www.chantvi.org.*

HORSEBACK RIDING

Paul and Jill's Equestrian Stables. From Sprat Hall, just north of Frederiksted, co-owner Jill Hurd will take you through the rain forest, across the pastures, along the beaches, and through valleys—explaining the flora, fauna, and ruins on the way. A 1½-hour ride costs $100. ⊠ *Rte. 58, Frederiksted* ☎ *340/772–2880, 340/332–0417* ⊕ *www. paulandjills.com.*

KAYAKING

Caribbean Adventure Tours. These kayak tours take you on trips through Salt River Bay National Historical Park and Ecological Preserve, one of the island's most pristine areas. All tours cost $50. ✉ *Salt River Marina, Rte. 80, Estate Salt River* ☎ *340/778–1522* ⊕ *www.stcroixkayak.com.*

Virgin Kayak Tours. Virgin runs guided kayak trips on the Salt River and rents kayaks so you can tour around the Cane Bay area by yourself. Tours start at $50, and kayak rentals are $50 for the entire day. ✉ *Rte. 80, Salt River Marina, Estate Salt River* ☎ *340/718–0071* ⊕ *www. virginkayaktours.com.*

WATER SPORTS

St. Croix Watersports. St. Croix Watersports rents WaveRunners, stand-up paddleboards, kayaks, windsurfers, and snorkel gear. The half-hour guided WaveRunner tour allows you to zip around Christiansted's harbor in style for $79. ✉ *Hotel on Cay, Protestant Cay, Christiansted* ☎ *340/773–7060* ⊕ *www.stcroixwatersports.com.*

INDEX

PHOTO CREDITS

Front cover: Westend61 GmbH / Alamy. [Description: Tourists on the beach near Sainte-Anne, Guadeloupe, Caribbean]. Back cover, from left to right: BlueOrange Studio/Shutterstock; Blacqbook/Shutterstock; Raffles Hotels and Resorts. Spine: Natchapon L./Shutterstock. 1, Timothy O'Keefe / age fotostock. 2, Alvaro Leiva / age fotostock. Chapter 1 Experience the Caribbean: 10–11, Christian Goupi / age fotostock. 28 (left), Leslie78 l Dreamstime.com. 28 (top center), Hoffmann / Shutterstock. 28 (bottom right), Peter Guttman. 28 (bottom center), Michael DeFreitas / age fotostock. 28 (top right), Durden-Images/iStockphoto. 29 (top left), The Dominican Republic Ministry of Tourism. 29 (center), Alvaro Leiva / age fotostock. 29 (right), Franz Marc Frei / age fotostock. 29 (bottom left), Eqroy8 l Dreamstime.com. 30, Fyletto l Dreamstime.com. 31, BlueOrange Studio / Shutterstock. 32, Kmiragaya l Dreamstime.com. 33, Diana DeLucia. Chapter 2 Anguilla: 49, Chris Caldicott / age fotostock. 50 (bottom), aturkus/Flickr. 50 (top), Philip Coblentz/Digital Vision. 54, Ku. 56, Rick Strange / age fotostock. 68, Straw Hat. 70, The Leading Hotels of the World. Chapter 3 Antigua and Barbuda: 81, Philip Coblentz/Medioimages. 82 (top and bottom), Philip Coblentz/Digital Vision. 86, Geoff Howes/Antigua & Barbuda Tourist Office. 88, Alvaro Leiva / age fotostock. 92, Steve Geer/iStockphoto. 101, nik wheeler / Alamy. Chapter 4 Aruba: 115, Henry George Beeker / Alamy. 116 (bottom), Philip Coblentz/Medioimages. 116 (top), Aruba Tourism Authority. 120, Famke Backx/iStockphoto. 137, Amsterdam Manor Beach Resort Aruba. 148, Aruba Tourism Authority. Chapter 5 Barbados: 151, John Miller / age fotostock. 152, Doug Scott/age fotostock. 156, Barbados Tourism Authority/Andrew Hulsmeier. 165, Walter Bibikow / age fotostock. 170, St. Nicholas Abbey. 184, Fairmont Hotels & Resorts. 186, Coral Reef Club. 189, Roy Riley / Alamy. Chapter 6 British Virgin Islands: 199, Alvaro Leiva / age fotostock. 200 (bottom), Joel Blit/Shutterstock. 200 (top), lidian neeleman/iStockphoto. 204, Ramunas Bruzas/Shutterstock. 213, Walter Bibikow / age fotostock. 221, Charles Krallman/Surfsong Villa Resort. 223, Alvaro Leiva / age fotostock. 228, FB-Fischer/imagebroker.net/photolibrary.com. 238, Bitter End Yacht Club International, LLC. 241, Andre Jenny / Alamy. 246, Paul Zizka/ Shutterstock. Chapter 7 Cayman Islands: 249, Peter Heiss/iStockphoto. 250 (top and bottom), Cayman Islands Department of Tourism. 251, Kevin Panizza/istockphoto. 254, Cayman Islands Department of Tourism. 263, Cayman Islands Department of Tourism. 282, Don McDougall/Cayman Islands Department of Tourism. 294, Corbis. 299, DurdenImages/iStockphoto. Chapter 8 Curaçao: 311, Philip Coblentz/Digital Vision. 312 (bottom), Fotoconcept Inc./ age fotostock. 312 (top), Curaçao Tourism. 316, Curaçao Tourism. 319, Walter Bibikow / age fotostock. 323, Curacao Tourist Board. 326, Walter Bibikow / age fotostock. Chapter 9 Dominican Republic: 347, Doug Scott/age fotostock. 348 (bottom), Doug Scott/age fotostock. 348 (top), Guy Thouvenin/age fotostock. 352, Valio84sl l Dreamstime.com. 353 (top), Wikipedia. 353 (bottom), unforth/Flickr. 354, Anguilla Tourist Board. 355, The Dominican Republic Ministry of Tourism. 363, Harry Pujols/Flickr. 369, The Dominican Republic Ministry of Tourism. 393, tedmurphy/Flickr. 398, Peninsula House. Chapter 10 Guadeloupe: 415, Bruno Morandi/ age fotostock. 416, Bruno Morandi/age fotostock. 420, Susanne Kischnick / Alamy. 421 (left), wikipedia.org. 421 (right), Photocuisine / Alamy. 422, Holger W./shutterstock. 427, TristanDeschamps/ F1 Online/age fotostock. 437, Philippe Michel / age fotostock. 447, La Toubana Hotel and Spa. 449, Philippe Giraud. Chapter 11 Jamaica: 461, Ronn Ballantyne / Alamy. 462 (bottom), Torrance Lewis/ Jamaica Tourist Board/Fotoseeker.com. 462 (top), Julian Love/Jamaica Tourist Board/Fotoseeker.com. 466, Brian Nejedly. 467 (left), LarenKates/Flickr. 467 (right), Jamaica Inn. 468, Pictorial Press Ltd / Alamy. 469 (top), Lisafx l Dreamstime.com. 469 (bottom), Philippe Jimenez/wikipedia.org, 470, Courtesy of the Bob Marley Museum, 471, Jamaica Tourist Board. 478, Franz Marc Frei / age fotostock. 490, Torrance Lewis/Jamaica Tourist Board/Fotoseeker.com. 509, Nick Hanna / Alamy. 523, Sergio Pitamitz / age fotostock. Chapter 12 Martinique: 525, P. Narayan / age fotostock. 526, Philip Coblentz/ Medioimages. 527, Maison de la France/LEJEUNE Nicole. 530, Luc Olivier for the Martinique Tourist Board. 540, GARDEL Bertrand / age fotostock. 544, Walter Bibikow / age fotostock. 547, Luc Olivier for the Martinique Tourist Board. 560, Frameme/wikipedia.org. 566, Luc Olivier for the Martinique Tourist Board. Chapter 13 Puerto Rico: 569, Danita Delimont/AWL Images. 570 (bottom), John Rodriguez/iStockphoto. 570 (top), Morales/age fotostock. 574, David R. Frazier Photolibrary, Inc. / Alamy. 575 (left), Steve Manson/ iStockphoto. 575 (right), Christian Sumner/iStockphoto. 576, Lori Froeb/ Shutterstock. 582, Katja Kreder / age fotostock. 585, Tomás Fano/Flickr. 591, Franz Marc Frei / age fotostock. 607, Hotel El Convento. 608, Thomas Hart Shelby. 611, Tres Sirenas Beach Inn. Chapter 14 St. Barthélemy: 619, Fred Friberg / age fotostock. 620 (bottom), SuperStock / age fotostock. 620 (top), Philip Coblentz/Digital Vision. 624, Hotel Carl Gustaf. 626, Christian Wheatley/iStockphoto. 634, Restaurant Le Gaiac. 641, Hotel Guanahani and Spa. 643, Eden Rock – St Barths. 647, Tibor Bognar / age fotostock. Chapter 15 St. Kitts and Nevis: 653, Peter Phipp/age fotostock. 654, Doug Scott/age fotostock. 655, Peter Phipp/age fotostock. 658, Lidian Neeleman/iStockphoto. 665, Roger Brisbane,